Comparing, Designing, and Deploying VPNs

Mark Lewis, CCIE No. 6280

Cisco Press

800 East 96th Street
Indianapolis, Indiana 46240 USA

Comparing, Designing, and Deploying VPNs

Mark Lewis

Copyright © 2006 Cisco Systems, Inc.

Cisco Press logo is a trademark of Cisco Systems, Inc.

Published by:
Cisco Press
800 East 96th Street
Indianapolis, IN 46240 USA

Printed in the United States of America 1 2 3 4 5 6 7 8 9 0

First Printing   April 2006

Library of Congress Cataloging-in-Publication Number: 2003114910

ISBN: 1-58705-179-6

Trademark Acknowledgments

Corporate and Government Sales

Cisco Press offers excellent discounts on this book when ordered in quantity for bulk purchases or special sales.

For more information, please contact **U.S. Corporate and Government Sales,** 1-800-382-3419 or corpsales@pearsontechgroup.com.

For sales outside the U.S., please contact **International Sales,** international@pearsoned.com.

Warning and Disclaimer

Feedback Information

At Cisco Press, our goal is to create in-depth technical books of the highest quality and value. Each book is crafted with care and precision, undergoing rigorous development that involves the unique expertise of members from the professional technical community.

Readers' feedback is a natural continuation of this process. If you have any comments regarding how we could improve the quality of this book, or otherwise alter it to better suit your needs, you can contact us through email at feedback@ciscopress.com. Please make sure to include the book title and ISBN in your message.

We greatly appreciate your assistance.

Publisher	John Wait
Editor-in-Chief	John Kane
Cisco Representative	Anthony Wolfenden
Cisco Press Program Manager	Jeff Brady
Production Manager	Patrick Kanouse
Senior Development Editor	Christopher Cleveland
Copy Editor and Indexer	Keith Cline
Technical Editors	Henry Benjamin, Lei Chen, Mark Newcomb, Ajay Simha
Book and Cover Designer	Louisa Adair
Composition	Interactive Composition Corporation

CISCO SYSTEMS

Corporate Headquarters
Cisco Systems, Inc.
170 West Tasman Drive
San Jose, CA 95134-1706
USA
www.cisco.com
Tel: 408 526-4000
      800 553-NETS (6387)
Fax: 408 526-4100

European Headquarters
Cisco Systems International BV
Haarlerbergpark
Haarlerbergweg 13-19
1101 CH Amsterdam
The Netherlands
www-europe.cisco.com
Tel: 31 0 20 357 1000
Fax: 31 0 20 357 1100

Americas Headquarters
Cisco Systems, Inc.
170 West Tasman Drive
San Jose, CA 95134-1706
USA
www.cisco.com
Tel: 408 526-7660
Fax: 408 527-0883

Asia Pacific Headquarters
Cisco Systems, Inc.
Capital Tower
168 Robinson Road
#22-01 to #29-01
Singapore 068912
www.cisco.com
Tel: +65 6317 7777
Fax: +65 6317 7799

Cisco Systems has more than 200 offices in the following countries and regions. Addresses, phone numbers, and fax numbers are listed on the
Cisco.com Web site at www.cisco.com/go/offices.

Argentina • Australia • Austria • Belgium • Brazil • Bulgaria • Canada • Chile • China PRC • Colombia • Costa Rica • Croatia • Czech Republic
Denmark • Dubai, UAE • Finland • France • Germany • Greece • Hong Kong SAR • Hungary • India • Indonesia • Ireland • Israel • Italy
Japan • Korea • Luxembourg • Malaysia • Mexico • The Netherlands • New Zealand • Norway • Peru • Philippines • Poland • Portugal
Puerto Rico • Romania • Russia • Saudi Arabia • Scotland • Singapore • Slovakia • Slovenia • South Africa • Spain • Sweden
Switzerland • Taiwan • Thailand • Turkey • Ukraine • United Kingdom • United States • Venezuela • Vietnam • Zimbabwe

About the Author

Mark Lewis, CCIE No. 6280, is technical director of MJL Network Solutions (www.mjlnet.com), a leading provider of internetworking solutions that focuses on helping enterprise and service provider customers to implement leading-edge technologies. Mark specializes in next-generation network technologies and has extensive experience designing, deploying, and migrating large-scale IP/MPLS networks. He is an active participant in the IETF, a member of the IEEE, and a certified Cisco Systems instructor. Mark is also the author of *Troubleshooting Virtual Private Networks,* published by Cisco Press.

Mark can be contacted at mark@mjlnet.com.

About the Technical Reviewers

Henry Benjamin, CCIE No. 4695, holds three CCIE certifications (Routing and Switching, ISP Dial, and Communications and Services). He has more than 10 years experience with Cisco networks and recently worked for Cisco in the internal IT department helping to design and implement networks throughout Australia and Asia. Henry was a key member of the CCIE global team, where he was responsible for writing new laboratory examinations and questions for the CCIE exams. Henry is an independent consultant with a large security firm in Australia. Henry is the author of *CCIE Security Exam Certification Guide* and *CCNP Practical Studies: Routing,* both published by Cisco Press.

Lei Chen, CCIE No. 6399, received a master of science degree in computer science from DePaul University in 2000. He joined the Cisco NSITE system testing group in 2000, and then went on to support Cisco high-tier customers as part of the Cisco TAC VPN team in 2002. He has first-hand experience in troubleshooting, designing, and deploying IPsec VPNs.

Mark Newcomb, CCNP, CCDP, is a retired network security engineer. Mark has more than 20 years experience in the networking industry, focusing on the financial and medical industries. Mark is a frequent contributor and reviewer for Cisco Press books.

Ajay Simha, CCIE No. 2970, joined the Cisco TAC in 1996. He then went on to support tier 1 and 2 ISPs as part of the Cisco ISP Expert team. He worked as an MPLS deployment engineer from October 1999 to November 2003. Currently, he is a senior network consulting engineer in Advanced Services at Cisco working on Metro Ethernet and MPLS design and deployment. Ajay is the coauthor of the Cisco Press title *Traffic Engineering with MPLS.*

Acknowledgments

I'd like to thank a number of people who helped me to complete this book. I'd like to thank Michelle, Chris, John, and Patrick at Cisco Press, who helped to get this project started in the first place and then provided indispensable help and encouragement along the way.

And I'd also like to thank the technical reviewers—Mark Newcomb, Henry Benjamin, Ajay Simha, and Lei Chen—who all provided useful comments and suggestions.

This Book Is Safari Enabled

The Safari® Enabled icon on the cover of your favorite technology book means the book is available through Safari Bookshelf. When you buy this book, you get free access to the online edition for 45 days.

Safari Bookshelf is an electronic reference library that lets you easily search thousands of technical books, find code samples, download chapters, and access technical information whenever and wherever you need it.

To gain 45-day Safari Enabled access to this book

- Go to http://www.ciscopress.com/safarienabled

- Complete the brief registration form

- Enter the coupon code GBCR-98XD-CWIL-XSD7-VQQE

If you have difficulty registering on Safari Bookshelf or accessing the online edition, please e-mail customer-service@safaribooksonline.com.

Contents at a Glance

Table of Contents

Icons Used in This Book

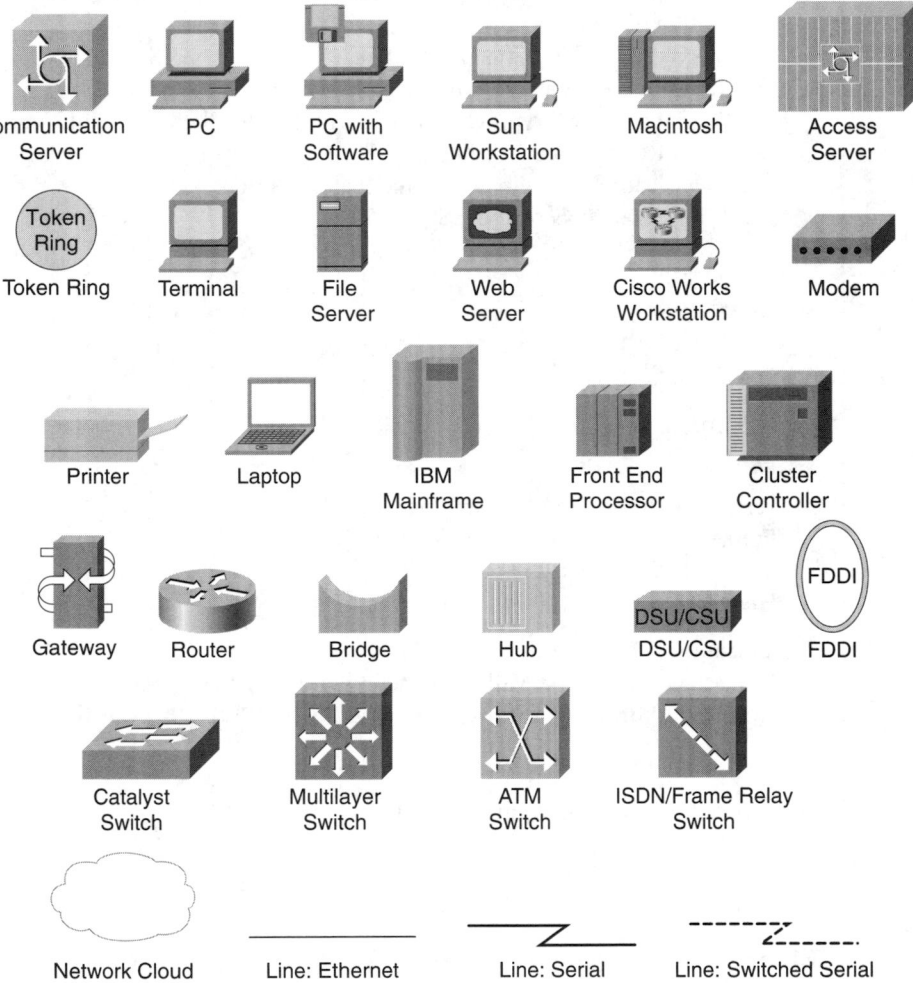

Communication Server | PC | PC with Software | Sun Workstation | Macintosh | Access Server

Token Ring | Terminal | File Server | Web Server | Cisco Works Workstation | Modem

Printer | Laptop | IBM Mainframe | Front End Processor | Cluster Controller

Gateway | Router | Bridge | Hub | DSU/CSU | FDDI

Catalyst Switch | Multilayer Switch | ATM Switch | ISDN/Frame Relay Switch

Network Cloud | Line: Ethernet | Line: Serial | Line: Switched Serial

Command Syntax Conventions

The conventions used to present command syntax in this book are the same conventions used in the Cisco IOS Command Reference. The Command Reference describes these conventions as follows:

- **Boldface** indicates commands and keywords that are entered literally as shown. In actual configuration examples and output (not general command syntax), boldface indicates commands that are manually input by the user (such as a **show** command).

- *Italics* indicate arguments for which you supply actual values.

- Vertical bars | separate alternative, mutually exclusive elements.

- Square brackets [ ] indicate optional elements.

- Braces { } indicate a required choice.

- Braces within brackets [{ }] indicate a required choice within an optional element.

Introduction

As the number and sophistication of virtual private network (VPN) technologies has grown, the complexity of choice, design, and deployment has also increased.

It is now possible to implement site-to-site VPNs, remote access VPNs, LAN-to-LAN VPNs, trusted VPNs, secure VPNs, L1VPNs, L2VPNs, L3VPNs, VPWS VPNs, VPLS VPNs, IPLS VPNs, network-based VPNs, C(P)E-based VPNs, multiservice VPNs, provider-provisioned VPNs, customer-provisioned VPNs, Internet VPNs, intranet VPNs, extranet VPNs, point-to-point VPNs, multipoint-to-multipoint VPNs, overlay VPNs, peer (-to-peer) VPNs, connection-oriented VPNs, connectionless VPNs, and clientless VPNs.

And then there are L2TPv3-based VPNs, AToM-based VPNs, MPLS Layer 3 VPNs, L2F VPNs, L2TPv2 VPNs, PPTP VPNs, and SSL VPNs.

No wonder VPNs can be confusing!

This book shows you how to navigate the spaghetti soup of VPN terminology and acronyms and how to differentiate and select the appropriate VPN type.

But, the ability to differentiate and select the appropriate VPN type is not enough! After you have decided which VPN type is appropriate, the next steps are its design and deployment.

Thankfully, this book also steers you through the design and deployment phases and shows you how each individual VPN technology works in detail, what its capabilities are, how it can be configured, and what the advanced design and implementation considerations are.

Motivation for the Book

Although existing material describes the various VPN technologies, it became obvious to me that a requirement exists for a single book that not only clarifies the differences between the various VPN types and technologies but also describes those various VPN technologies in detail. Hopefully, this book fulfills that requirement and clears up a lot of the confusion that has hitherto existed with regard to VPNs.

Who Should Read This Book?

In this book, you will find in-depth coverage of site-to-site VPN technologies such as L2TPv3, AToM, MPLS Layer 3 (RFC2547bis) VPNs, IPsec, VPLS, and IPLS. You will also find detailed examinations of remote access VPN technologies, including L2TPv2/3, IPsec, and SSL. In addition, you will find information about how to integrate remote access VPN technologies with site-to-site VPNs.

So, who will find this breadth and depth of VPN technology coverage useful? It will be very useful to network architects, network implementation engineers, network support staff, and IT manager/CIOs involved with selecting, designing, deploying, and supporting VPNs. It will also be helpful to people preparing for networking tests such as the Security and Service Provider CCIE exams.

How This Book Is Organized

This book is organized such that it can either be dipped into for information on a specific VPN type or it can be read from cover to cover.

If you are in the process of comparing and evaluating different VPN types with a view to their deployment in your network, or are preparing for a networking exam that includes coverage of VPN technologies, you may want to read Chapter 1 (which gives a high-level comparison), followed by one or more of the following chapters that deal with specific VPN technologies.

If, on the other hand, you are looking to improve and deepen your knowledge of VPN technologies in general, you might want to read the book cover to cover.

The book is arranged as follows:

- **Chapter 1, "What Is a VPN?"**—Chapter 1 poses (and answers) the deceptively simple question "What is a VPN?" In this chapter, you will find a high-level discussion and comparison of the various VPN types and technologies, which will clarify what the various VPN terms mean and how the technologies work. By the end of this chapter, the previously confused will be a lot more clear about what a VPN really is.

- **Chapter 2, "Designing and Deploying L2TPv3-Based Layer 2 VPNs (L2VPN)"**—L2TP has evolved from a tunneling protocol for PPP to become, in its latest incarnation (L2TPv3), a universal transport mechanism for a host of protocols such as Ethernet, Frame Relay, ATM (cell-relay and AAL5), HDLC, and PPP. This chapter discusses in-depth L2TPv3's advantages and disadvantages, how it operates, and how L2TPv3-based Layer 2 VPNs can be designed and deployed.

- **Chapter 3, "Designing and Implementing AToM-Based Layer 2 VPNs (L2VPN)"**—Any Transport over MPLS (AToM) provides a similar transport mechanism to L2TPv3, but over MPLS rather than IP. It, too, can transport protocols including Ethernet, Frame Relay, and ATM, and as such can be used to consolidate service provider networks and build Layer 2 VPNs. AToM's underlying technology, configuration, verification, and advanced design considerations are examined in this chapter.

- **Chapter 4, "Designing MPLS Layer 3 Site-to-Site VPNs"**—MPLS Layer 3 VPNs provide a highly scalable VPN architecture that provides any-to-any connectivity and can support real-time applications such as voice and video. This chapter provides a detailed discussion of the principles of its operation, its configuration, the provision of complex topologies, and Internet access.

- **Chapter 5, "Advanced MPLS Layer 3 VPN Deployment Considerations"**—Building on the foundation of Chapter 4, this chapter describes how MPLS Layer 3 VPNs can be extended to support carrier customers, interprovider and inter-autonomous system VPNs, QoS, and customer IPv6 VPNs.

- **Chapter 6, "Deploying Site-to-Site IPsec VPNs"**—IPsec remains a popular choice for implementing site-to-site VPNs. In this chapter, you can find a description of the algorithms and mechanisms that underlie IPsec, together with an in-depth discussion of the fundamentals of IPsec site-to-site VPN configuration using preshared key, encrypted nonce, and digital certificate authentication. Also included is detailed information about issues with IPsec and NAT (and how to get around them).

- **Chapter 7, "Scaling and Optimizing IPsec VPNs"**—This chapter builds on the discussion of the fundamentals of site-to-site IPsec VPNs in Chapter 6 by describing their scaling and optimization. Specific topics covered include Tunnel Endpoint Discovery (TED), Dynamic Multipoint VPN (DMVPN), scaling IPsec VPNs using digital signature authentication, quality of service (QoS), and avoiding the performance degradation caused by IPsec packet fragmentation.

- **Chapter 8, "Designing and Implementing L2TPv2 and L2TPv3 Remote Access VPNs"**— L2TP can be used to implement industry-standard remote access VPNs. This chapter provides comprehensive information about designing and deploying L2TP voluntary tunnel mode/ client-initiated and compulsory tunnel mode/NAS-initiated remote access VPNs. Methods of securing L2TP remote access VPNs using IPsec as well as the integration of L2TP remote access VPNs with MPLS Layer 3 VPNs are also discussed.

- **Chapter 9, "Designing and Deploying IPsec Remote Access and Teleworker VPNs"**— IPsec can not only be used to provision site-to-site VPNs, but can also be used to implement remote access VPNs. A thorough description of their design and deployment is included in this chapter. The chapter describes configuration as well as special considerations, including the integration of IPsec remote access VPNs with MPLS Layer 3 VPNs, provisioning high availability, and allowing or disallowing split tunneling.

- **Chapter 10, "Designing and Building SSL Remote Access VPNs (WebVPN)"**—Although SSL is a relative newcomer as a VPN technology, it can provide significant advantages, especially if remote access users need to access the corporate network from insecure locations such as Internet cafés and airport kiosks.

  In this chapter, you will find detailed information on designing and deploying both clientless remote access SSL VPNs, and SSL remote access VPNs using the Cisco SSL VPN Client. Also included is an examination of the Cisco Secure Desktop, which enables users to greatly improve the security of SSL VPN connections from insecure locations.

- **Appendix A, "VPLS and IPLS Layer 2 VPNs"**—This appendix describes two VPN technologies that provide multipoint Ethernet connectivity for customer sites. VPLS provides multipoint, multiprotocol connectivity, but does involve a relatively high degree of complexity; whereas IPLS provides multipoint, IP-only connectivity with a lower degree of complexity.

- **Appendix B, "Answers to Review Questions"**—You will find the answers to the review questions at the end of each chapter here.

Understanding VPN Technology

CHAPTER 1

What Is a Virtual Private Network?

A virtual private network (VPN) allows the provisioning of private network services for an organization or organizations over a public or shared infrastructure such as the Internet or service provider backbone network. The shared service provider backbone network is known as the *VPN backbone* and is used to transport traffic for multiple VPNs, as well as possibly non-VPN traffic.

VPNs provisioned using technologies such as Frame Relay and Asynchronous Transfer Mode (ATM) virtual circuits (VC) have been available for a long time, but over the past few years IP and IP/Multiprotocol Label Switching (MPLS)-based VPNs have become more and more popular.

This book focuses on describing the deployment of IP- and IP/MPLS-based VPNs.

The large number of terms used to categorize and describe the functionality of VPNs has led to a great deal of confusion about what exactly VPNs are and what they can do. The sections that follow cover VPN devices, protocols, technologies, as well as VPN categories and models.

VPN Devices

Before describing the various VPN technologies and models, it is useful to first describe the various customer and provider network devices that are relevant to the discussion.

Devices in the customer network fall into one of two categories:

- **Customer (C) devices**—C devices are simply devices such as routers and switches located within the customer network. These devices do not have direct connectivity to the service provider network. C devices are not aware of the VPN.

- **Customer Edge (CE) devices**—CE devices, as the name suggests, are located at the edge of the customer network and connect to the provider network (via Provider Edge [PE] devices).

    In CE-based VPNs, CE devices are aware of the VPN. In PE-based VPNs, CE devices are unaware of the VPN.

    CE devices are either categorized as Customer Edge routers (CE-r), or Customer Edge switches (CE-s).

In a site-to-site VPN, devices in the service provider network also fall into one of two categories:

- **Service Provider (P) devices**—P devices are devices such as routers and switches within the provider network that do not directly connect to customer networks. P devices are unaware of customer VPNs.

- **Service Provider Edge (PE) devices**—PE devices connect directly to customer networks via CE devices. PE devices are aware of the VPN in PE-based VPNs, but are unaware of the VPN in CE-based VPNs.

  There are three types of PE device:

  — Provider Edge routers (PE-r)

  — Provider Edge switches (PE-s)

  — Provider Edge devices that are capable of both routing and switching (PE-rs)

Figure 1-1 illustrates customer and provider network devices.

Figure 1-1 *Customer and Provider Network Devices*

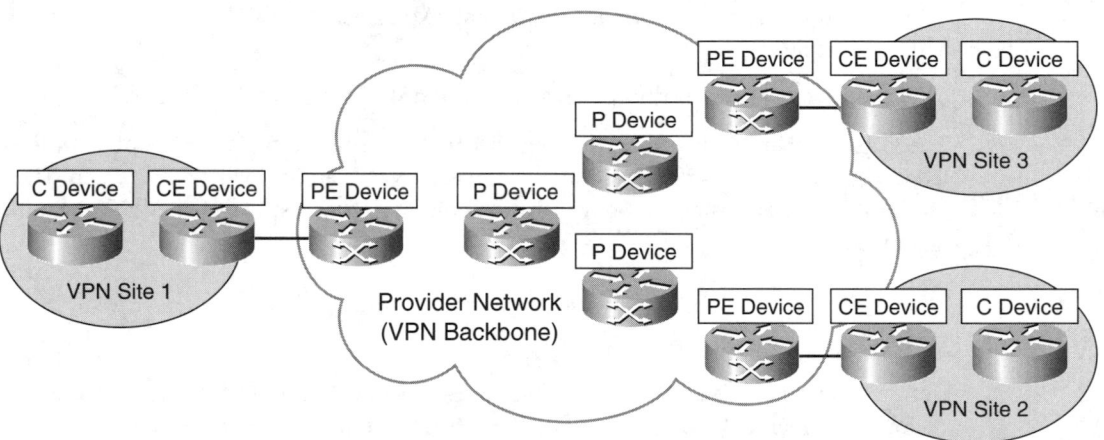

In Layer 2 VPNs, such as a Virtual Private LAN Service (VPLS), an additional level of hierarchy can be introduced into the network to improve scalability (VPLS then becomes Hierarchical VPLS [H-VPLS]). In this case, the functionality of the PE device is divided between a User-facing PE (U-PE) devices and Network-facing PE (N-PE) devices.

Note that alternative (and dated) equivalent terms for the U-PE and N-PE are PE-CLE and PE-POP, respectively. In addition, where a Layer 2 PE-U device is installed in a multitenant building, this may be referred to as an MTU-s. Figure 1-2 illustrates U-PE and N-PE devices.

Figure 1-2   *User-Facing and Network-Facing PE Devices*

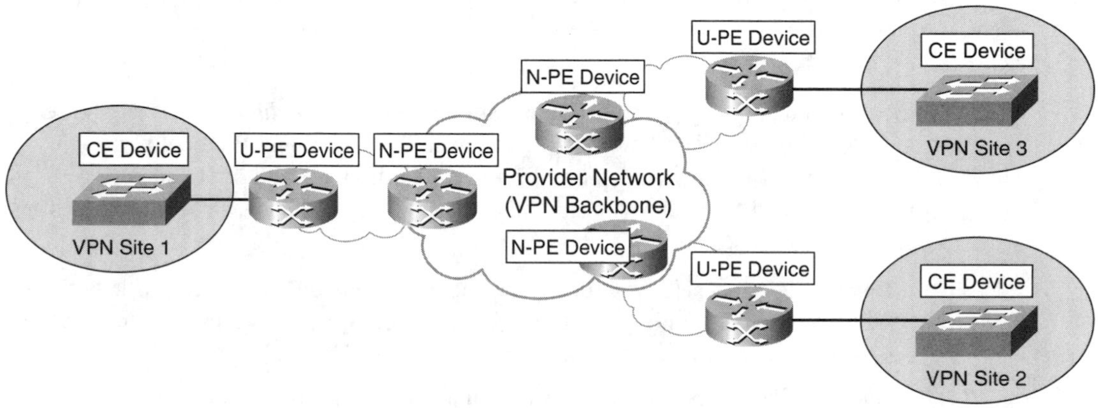

Other device types used in VPNs include Network Access Servers (NAS) and VPN gateways/concentrators. A NAS is a device that interfaces between an access network (such as a Public Switched Telephone Network [PSTN]) and a packet-switched network (such as an IP backbone). In a remote access VPN, a NAS can serve as a tunnel endpoint.

Note that depending upon the remote access VPN protocol in use, the NAS may variously be called a Layer Two Forwarding (L2F) Protocol NAS, a Layer Two Tunneling Protocol (L2TP) Access Concentrator (LAC), or a Point-to-Point Tunneling Protocol (PPTP) Access Concentrator (PAC).

See Figure 1-5 for an illustration of the role performed by a NAS.

A VPN gateway/concentrator acts as the endpoint of a VPN tunnel, especially in a remote access VPN or CE-based site-to-site VPN. See Figure 1-5 later in the chapter for an illustration of the role performed by a VPN gateway/concentrator.

Depending on the remote access VPN protocol in use, the VPN gateway/concentrator may, for example, be called an L2F Home Gateway, an L2TP Network Server (LNS), or a PPTP Network Server (PNS).

VPN Technologies and Protocols

A number of technologies and protocols are used to enable site-to-site and remote access VPNs. These protocols and technologies are described in the sections that follow.

Technologies and Protocols Used to Enable Site-to-Site VPNs

In site-to-site VPNs (discussed later in this chapter), customer user data traffic is either tunneled between CE devices or between PE devices.

NOTE	Site-to-site VPNs are also occasionally referred to as *LAN-to-LAN VPNs*.

Protocols and technologies used to enable site-to-site VPNs *include* IP Security (IPsec), Generic Routing Encapsulation (GRE), the Layer Two Tunneling Protocol version 3 (L2TPv3), Draft Martini pseudowires (emulated circuits), IEEE 802.1Q tunneling (Q-in-Q), and MPLS Label Switched Paths (LSP). These protocols and technologies are described as follows:

- **IPsec**—IPsec consists of a suite of protocols designed to protect IP traffic between security gateways or hosts as it transits an intervening network. IPsec tunnels are often used to build a site-to-site between CE devices (CE-based VPNs).

- **GRE**—GRE can be used to construct tunnels and transport multiprotocol traffic between CE devices in a VPN. GRE has little or no inherent security, but GRE tunnels can be protected using IPsec.

- **Draft Martini (Any Transport over MPLS [AToM])**—Draft Martini transport allows point-to-point transport of protocols such as Frame Relay, ATM, Ethernet, Ethernet VLAN (802.1Q), High-Level Data Link Control (HDLC), and PPP traffic over MPLS.

- **L2TPv3**—L2TPv3 allows the point-to-point transport of protocols such as Frame Relay, ATM, Ethernet, Ethernet VLAN, HDLC, and PPP traffic over an IP or other backbone.

- **IEEE 802.1Q tunneling (Q-in-Q)**—802.1Q tunneling allows a service provider to tunnel tagged Ethernet (802.1Q) customer traffic over a shared backbone. Customer 802.1Q traffic is tunneled over the shared provider backbone by prepending another 802.1Q tag.

- **MPLS LSPs**—An LSP is a path via Label Switch Routers (LSR) in an MPLS network. Packets are switched based on labels prepended to the packet. LSPs may be signaled using the Tag Distribution Protocol (TDP), the Label Distribution Protocol (LDP), or the Resource Reservation Protocol (RSVP).

Technologies and Protocols Used to Enable Remote Access VPNs

Protocols used to enable remote access VPNs (discussed later in this chapter) include the following:

- **The Layer Two Forwarding (L2F) Protocol**—L2F is a Cisco proprietary protocol that is designed to allow the tunneling of PPP (or Serial Line Interface Protocol [SLIP]) frames between a NAS and a VPN gateway device located at a central site. Remote access users connect to the NAS, and the PPP frames from the remote access user are then tunneled over the intervening network to the VPN (home) gateway.

VPN Devices 9

- **The Point-to-Point Tunneling Protocol (PPTP)**—PPTP is a protocol that was developed by a consortium of vendors, including Microsoft, 3Com, and Ascend Communications. Like L2F, PPTP allows the tunneling of remote access client PPP frames between a NAS and a VPN gateway/concentrator. PPTP also allows a tunnel to be set up directly from a remote access client to a VPN gateway/concentrator.

  PPP encapsulated packets carried over PPTP tunnels are often protected using Microsoft Point-to-Point Encryption (MPPE).

- **The Layer 2 Tunneling Protocol versions 2 and 3 (L2TPv2/L2TPv3)**—L2TP is an Internet Engineering Task Force (IETF) standard and combines the best features of L2F and PPTP. In a remote access environment, L2TP allows either tunneling of remote access client PPP frames via a NAS to a VPN gateway/concentrator or tunneling of PPP frames directly from the remote access client to the VPN gateway/concentrator.

  L2TP has limited intrinsic security, and so L2TP tunnels are often protected using IPsec.

- **IPsec**—As well as enabling site-to-site VPNs, IPsec can also be used to securely tunnel data traffic between remote access or mobile users and a VPN gateway/concentrator.

- **The Secure Sockets Layer (SSL)**—SSL is a security protocol that was originally developed by Netscape Communications (SSL versions 1, 2, and 3), and it provides secure remote access for mobile users or home users. Functionality may be limited (when compared with L2F, PPTP, L2TPv2, or IPsec) if *clientless* SSL remote access VPNs are deployed.

  Note that Transport Layer Security (TLS), an IETF standard, is similar to SSLv3.

  In spite of the limited functionality provided by clientless SSL VPNs, one advantage of this type of remote access VPN is that no special client software is required because SSL is included in pretty much every web browser. Therefore, if a remote user has a web browser, the user has SSL client software.

  Because no special client software is required other than a web browser, SSL VPNs are sometimes referred to as *web VPNs* or *clientless VPNs*.

  More functionality may be added to SSL VPNs by installing specific SSL VPN client software on remote access client devices.

Modeling and Characterizing VPNs

A plethora of methods are used to model and characterize VPNs. The purpose of this section is to introduce and explain each of these models and characterizations.

As you read this section, you may ask yourself how it is that we have ended up with so many terms to describe VPNs. The answer is a desire to accurately describe the characteristics of a VPN protocol or technology but also a simple lack of coordination among protocol designers and engineers (this is getting much better), and on top of that a certain amount of "help" from our marketing colleagues ("How can I differentiate our products?").

As you read this section, be sure to refer to Figure 1-3. Figure 1-3 clarifies the relationship of the VPN models to each other; it also describes the VPN (tunneling) protocols and technologies associated with the various models.

The bottom level of the hierarchy in Figure 1-3 describes protocols or mechanisms used to tunnel VPN traffic between CE or PE devices.

Figure 1-3   *Virtual Private Networks*

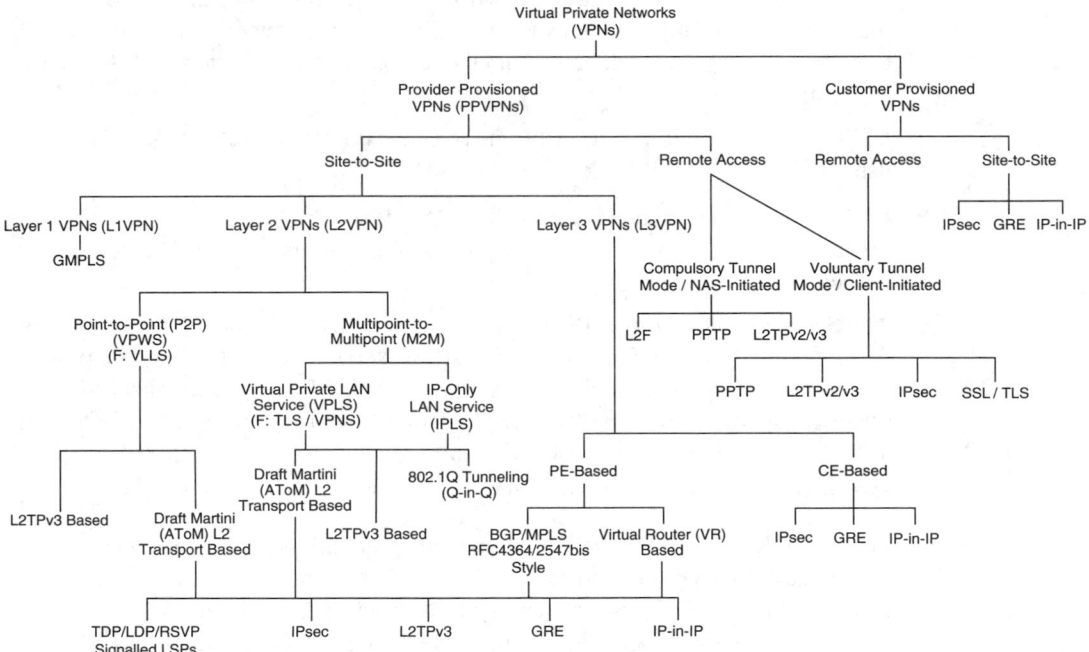

Note that in Figure 1-3, F: denotes a former name for a particular technology.

Service Provider and Customer Provisioned VPNs

VPNs can be either one of the following:

- **Service provider provisioned**—VPNs that are configured and managed by a service provider or providers
- **Customer provisioned**—VPNs that are configured and managed by the (service provider) customer itself

Note that the customer of the service provider may be either an enterprise or another service provider, in which case, the service provider that offers the VPN service is known as a *carrier of carriers*, and the service offered to the customer service provider is known as a *carrier's carrier* VPN service.

Additionally, a VPN service might be offered over the backbone networks of multiple cooperating autonomous systems and/or service providers. In this case, the VPN service is known as an *inter-AS* or *interprovider* VPN service.

Examples of provider provisioned VPNs are as follows:

- Virtual Private Wire Service (VPWS) VPNs
- Virtual Private LAN Service (VPLS) VPNs
- IP-Only Private LAN Service (IPLS) VPNs
- BGP/MPLS (RFC4364/2547bis) VPNs (BGP/MPLS VPNs are also known as MPLS Layer 3 VPNs.)
- Virtual Router (VR)-based VPNs
- IPsec VPNs

Examples of customer provisioned VPNs are as follows:

- GRE VPNs
- IPsec VPNs

Site-to-Site and Remote Access VPNs

VPNs, whether provider or customer provisioned, fall into one of two broad categories:

- Site to site
- Remote access

Site-to-site VPNs allow connectivity between an organization's (or organizations') geographically dispersed sites (such as a head office and branch offices).

Figure 1-4 illustrates a typical site-to-site VPN.

There are two types of site-to-site VPN:

- **Intranet VPNs**—Allow connectivity between sites of a single organization
- **Extranet VPNs**—Allow connectivity between organizations such as business partners or a business and its customers

Remote access VPNs (also called *access VPNs*) allow mobile or home-based users to access an organization's resources remotely.

Figure 1-5 illustrates typical remote access VPNs.

Figure 1-4 *Typical Site-to-Site VPN*

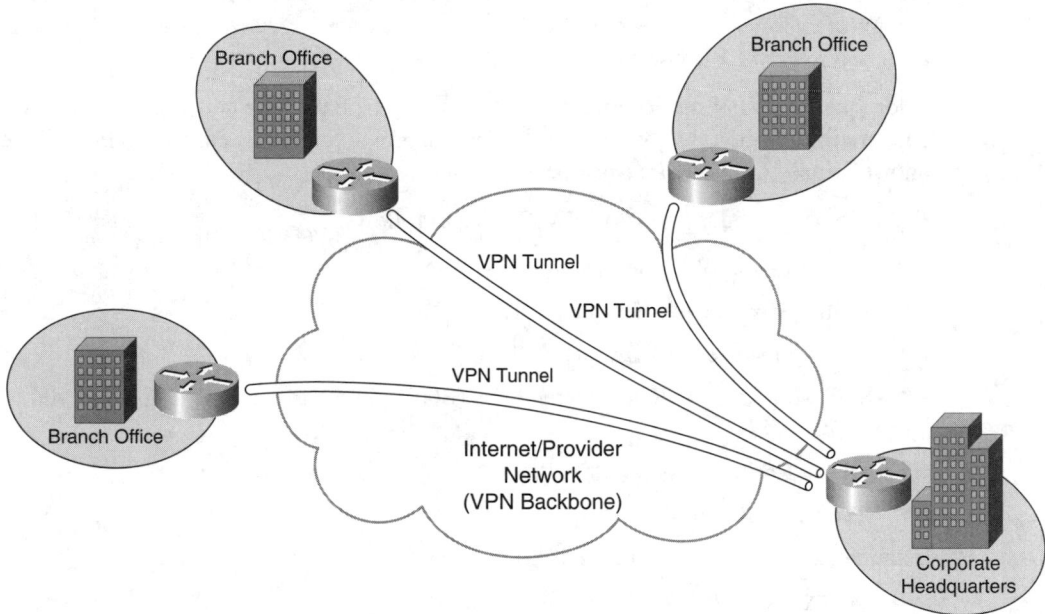

Figure 1-5 *Remote Access VPNs*

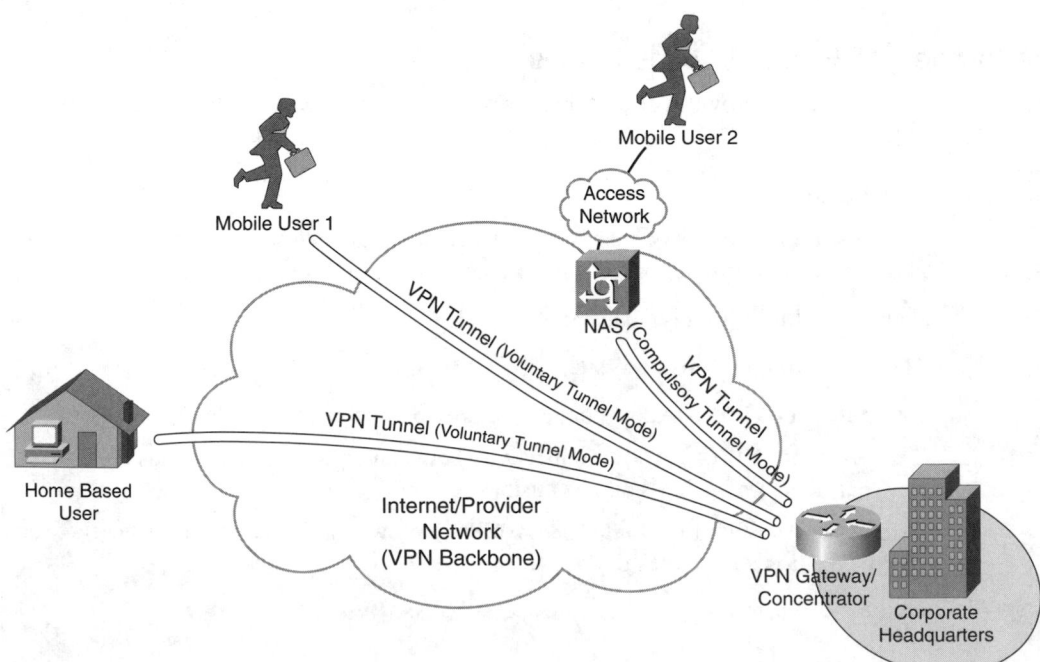

Service Provider Provisioned Site-to-Site VPNs

Service provider provisioned site-to-site VPNs (PPVPN) fall into one of three categories: Layer 1 VPNs, Layer 2 VPNs, and Layer 3 VPNs. Layer 2 and Layer 3 site-to-site VPN types are described in the sections that follow.

NOTE   Layer 1 VPNs are used to transport Layer 1 services over an intervening shared network controlled and managed by Generalized Multiprotocol Label Switching (GMPLS).

At the time of this writing, the development of L1VPNs is in its relative infancy, and so L1VPNs are not discussed further in this book.

Layer 2 VPNs

Layer 2 site-to-site VPNs (L2VPN) can be provisioned between switches, hosts, and routers and allow data link layer connectivity between separate sites. Communication between customer switches, hosts, and routers is based on Layer 2 addressing, and PE devices perform forwarding of customer data traffic based on incoming link and Layer 2 header information (such as MAC address, Frame Relay Data Link Connection Identifier [DLCI], and so on).

There are two categories of provider provisioned L2VPN:

- **Point-to-point (P2P) circuit-based VPNs**—P2P-based VPNs are also known as *Virtual Private Wire Service (VPWS) VPNs* and are constructed using, for example, Draft Martini (MPLS) or L2TPv3 pseudowires (emulated circuits).

    It is worth noting that VPWS was formerly known as Virtual Leased Line Service (VLL service or VLLS).

- **Multipoint-to-multipoint (M2M) VPNs**—M2M VPNs come in two varieties:
    - Virtual Private LAN Service (VPLS) VPNs
    - IP-Only LAN Service (IPLS) VPNs

Layer 3 VPNs

Layer 3 site-to-site VPNs (L3VPN) interconnect hosts and routers at separate customer sites. These customer hosts and routers communicate based on Layer 3 (network layer) addressing, and PE devices forward customer traffic based on incoming link, and on addresses contained in the (outer) IP header.

There are two overall types of L3VPN:

- **PE-based VPNs**—In a PE-based L3VPN, PE devices participate in customer network routing and forward traffic based on customer network addressing. Customer traffic is (usually) forwarded between PE devices over VPN tunnels that may take the form of (MPLS) LSPs, IPsec tunnels, L2TPv3 tunnels, or GRE tunnels, for example. In this case, CE devices are not aware that they are participating in a VPN.

  PE-based VPNs are also sometimes referred to as *Network-based VPNs*.

  PE-based L3VPNs can be further classified as follows:

  — **RFC4364/2547bis style**—In this type of PE-based L3VPN, the PE devices maintain separate routing and forwarding tables for each VPN. Customer routes are advertised between PE devices using Multiprotocol Border Gateway Protocol (MP-BGP), and customer address space and routes are disambiguated using BGP attributes.

  — **Virtual Router (VR) based**—In this type of PE-based L3VPN, completely separate logical routers are maintained on the PE devices for each VPN. Each logical router maintains its own entirely separate routing protocol instances.

  Figure 1-6 illustrates a typical PE-based VPN.

Figure 1-6 *Typical PE-Based Site-to-Site VPN*

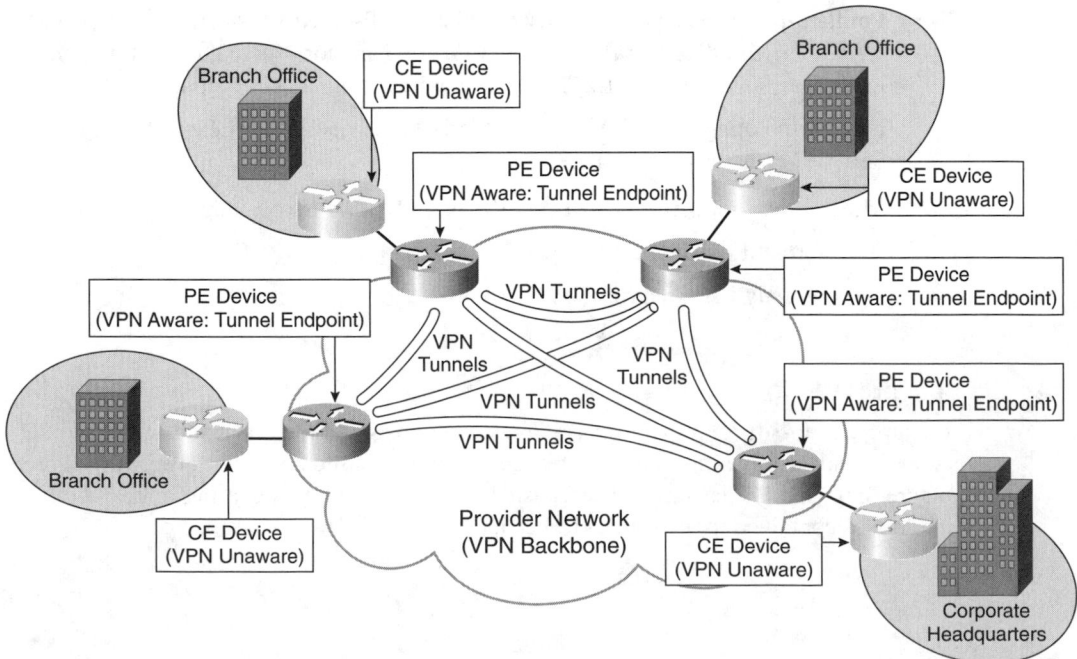

- **CE-based VPNs**—In a CE-based L3VPN, PE devices do not participate in (and are unaware of) customer network routing and forward customer traffic based on globally unique addressing. In this case, tunnels are configured between CE devices using protocols such as GRE and IPsec.

  CE-based VPNs are also sometimes referred to as *CPE-based VPNs*.

  Figure 1-7 illustrates a typical CE-based site-to-site VPN.

Figure 1-7 *Typical CE-Based Site-to-Site VPN*

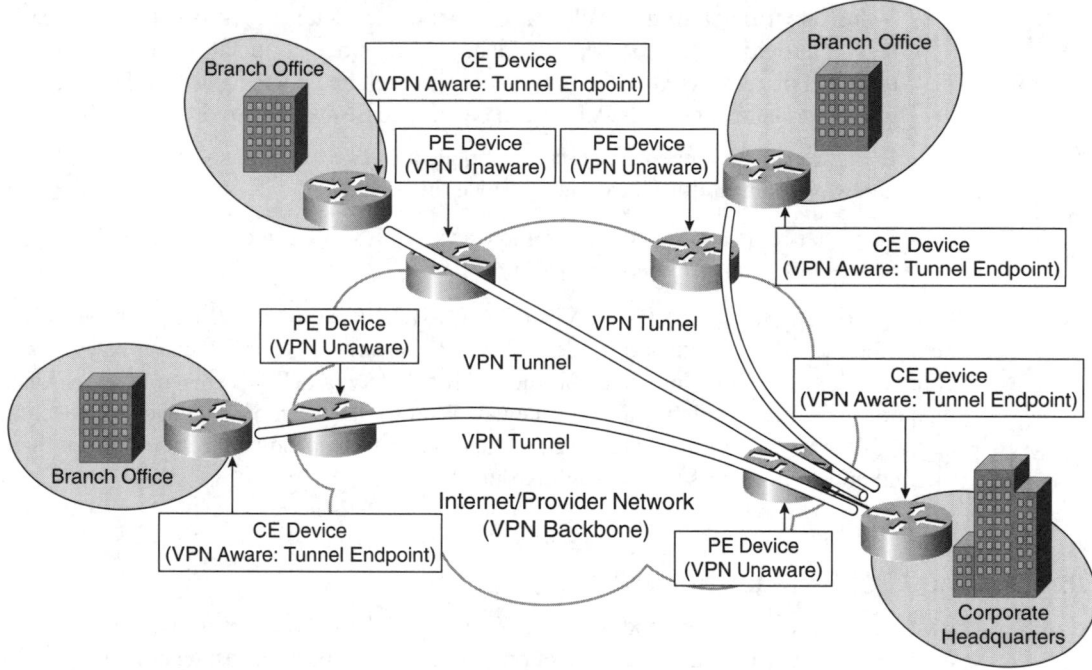

Customer Provisioned Site-to-Site VPNs

Customer provisioned site-to-site VPNs are configured on CE devices such as routers and firewalls. In this case, tunnels are configured between CE devices in the VPN, and customer data traffic is sent over these tunnels. Protocols used to encapsulate user data traffic as it is sent over the tunnels between VPN sites include GRE and IPsec.

Service Provider and Customer Provisioned Remote Access VPNs

Remote access VPNs can be configured in either compulsory tunnel mode or voluntary tunnel mode. These two modes of operation are described as follows:

- **Compulsory tunnel mode**—Compulsory tunnel mode remote access VPNs are service provider provisioned. In this mode of operation, the remote access client connects to a NAS that then tunnels client data traffic to and from a VPN gateway. Compulsory tunnel mode remote access VPNs are provider provisioned. Examples of protocols used to provision compulsory tunnel mode remote access are L2F, PPTP, and L2TP.

In Figure 1-5, mobile user 2 is connected via a compulsory mode tunnel to the VPN gateway/concentrator.

Compulsory tunnel mode remote access VPNs are sometimes referred to as *NAS-initiated remote access VPNs*.

- **Voluntary tunnel mode**—Voluntary tunnel mode remote access VPNs are either service provider or customer provisioned. In this mode of operation, data traffic is tunneled directly between the remote access client and a VPN gateway. Voluntary tunnel mode remote access VPNs can be either customer or provider provisioned.

  In Figure 1-5, the home-based user and mobile user 1 are both connected to the VPN gateway/concentrator via voluntary mode tunnels.

  Note that voluntary tunnel mode remote access VPNs are sometimes referred to as *client-initiated remote access VPNs*.

One type of remote access VPN is a Virtual Private Dialup Network (VPDN). This term can be used to describe remote access VPNs (L2F, PPTP, and L2TP) in which remote users connect over a PSTN or Integrated Services Digital Network (ISDN) to a *dial* NAS. User data traffic is then tunneled to a VPN gateway. With so many remote users now connecting over cable, Digital Subscriber Line (DSL), and other high-speed connections, rather than via dial connections, this term is slightly outdated.

Other Methods of Categorizing VPNs

Yes, there are yet more methods of categorizing VPNs! VPNs can be further categorized depending on whether they are connection oriented or connectionless, whether they are overlay or peer to peer, and whether they are secure or trusted.

Overlay and Peer-to-Peer VPNs

A VPN can be categorized as either an overlay or peer VPN depending on whether PE devices are aware of customer network addressing, and route customer traffic based on customer network address space.

Overlay and peer VPNs are summarized as follows:

- **Overlay VPNs**—In an overlay network, a VC or tunnel connects CE devices. No routing information is exchanged with the service provider, and PE devices are unaware of customer network address space and do not route customer traffic based on customer network addressing.

Examples of overlay VPNs include those built using Frame Relay or ATM virtual circuits, as well as those built using GRE or IPsec tunnels.

- **Peer VPNs**—In a peer VPN, PE devices are aware of customer network addressing and route customer data traffic according to customer network addressing. In peer VPNs, routes are exchanged between CE devices and PE devices.

  Older types of peer VPN often involve PE devices partitioning customer data traffic by simply using access control lists (ACL). A more modern example of peer VPNs is BGP/MPLS (RFC4364/2547bis) VPNs.

Connection-Oriented and Connectionless VPNs

VPNs can be either connection oriented or connectionless depending on whether VCs or tunnels are provisioned to carry VPN traffic.

Connection-oriented and connectionless VPNs are described as follows:

- **Connection-oriented VPNs**—In connection-oriented VPNs, VCs or tunnels are set up to carry VPN traffic.

  Examples of connection-oriented VPNs are those provisioned using Frame Relay or ATM VCs, as well as those provisioned using L2TP or IPsec tunnels.

- **Connectionless VPNs**—In connectionless VPNs, neither VCs nor tunnels are set up to carry VPN traffic.

  PE-based VPNs that rely on the partitioning of customer data traffic by using ACLs configured on PE devices are connectionless VPNs.

Trusted and Secure VPNs

VPNs can be described as being either *trusted* or *secure*. Whether a VPN is trusted or secure depends on whether customer data traffic is authenticated and encrypted as it passes between VPN peers (sites in an site-to-site VPN, or a remote access client and a VPN gateway/concentrator in a remote access VPN).

Trusted and secure VPNs are described as follows:

- **Trusted VPNs**—Provisioned by a service provider, and although customer traffic is not encrypted over the service provider backbone, customers trust the service provider to ensure that data traffic is kept secure in transit between the customer's sites.

  Examples of trusted VPNs are Frame Relay, ATM, and BGP/MPLS (RFC4364/2547bis) VPNs.

- **Secure VPNs**—Customer data traffic data is authenticated and encrypted over the service provider backbone or Internet between VPN peers.

  Examples of secure VPNs are IPsec VPNs, SSL VPNs, PPTP VPNs secured with MPPE, and L2TP VPNs secured using IPsec.

And Finally. . .

And finally, here are two or three sundry VPN classifications:

- **Transport/Application Layer VPNs**—SSL sits on top of TCP in the protocol stack, and SSL VPNs are therefore sometimes referred to as either *Transport* or *Application Layer VPNs*.

- **Internet VPNs**—Designed to run over the public Internet.

- **Multiservice VPNs**—Provide a framework for converged services, including voice, video, and data.

Deploying Site-to-Site and Remote Access VPNs: A Comparison

So now you know the VPN protocols and technologies, and how they are categorized, but how do they compare? Included in this section are comparisons of site-to-site as well as remote access VPN technologies.

Before comparing the various VPN technologies, however, it is worth noting that these VPN technologies are often complementary. For example, although it might seem that BGP/MPLS (RFC4364/2547bis) VPNs and IPsec VPNs are competing provider provisioned site-to-site VPN technologies, IPsec tunnels can, in fact, be used to tunnel VPN traffic between PE routers in an BGP/MPLS (RFC4364/2547bis) VPN backbone. IPsec and L2TP can additionally be used to provide off-net (remote access) for mobile or home-based users to a BGP/MPLS (RFC4364/2547bis) VPN.

Similarly, although it appears GRE and IPsec are competing customer provisioned site-to-site VPN technologies, in fact, hybrid GRE/IPsec VPNs are commonly deployed. Hybrid GRE/IPsec VPNs are often deployed because GRE has little or no inherent security, whereas IPsec can provide strong security. On the other hand, IPsec cannot transport multiprotocol, whereas GRE can. So, by deploying a GRE over IPsec site-to-site VPN, you combine multiprotocol with strong security—the best of both worlds!

Site-to-Site VPN Deployment

Figure 1-3 shows a number options for provider provisioned, as well as customer provisioned, site-to-site VPNs.

Provider provisioned site-to-site VPNs can be either L2VPNs or L3VPNs, as follows:

- **L2VPNs**—VPWS, VPLS, and IPLS
- **L3VPNs**—BGP/MPLS (RFC4364/2547bis), VR, IPsec, GRE, and IP-in-IP

Customer provisioned site-to-site VPNs can be deployed using the following protocols:

- IPsec
- GRE
- IP-in-IP

When comparing both provider and customer provisioned site-to-site VPNs, it is important to consider a number of factors. Some of the most important technical considerations for service providers and customers when deploying site-to-site VPNs are as follows:

- **Point-to-point or multipoint**—Is point-to-point or multipoint (any-to-any) connectivity inherent?

- **Provisioning topologies**—How easy is it to deploy a full range of topologies such as full mesh, hub and spoke, partial mesh.

- **Scalability**—How easy is it to deploy a VPN with a large number of sites?

- **Geographic reach**—Is geographic reach limited to a service provider backbone, or can it be extended across the Internet?

- **Security**—Is traffic authenticated and encrypted? Is traffic crossing the VPN vulnerable to replay attacks? Is traffic resistant to insertion attacks (where malicious data is inserted into the protocol stream)?

- **Inherent multicast support**—Can multicast traffic be natively supported across the VPN?

- **Inherent multiprotocol support**—Can multiprotocol traffic (including legacy protocols such as IPX) be transported?

- **Quality of service (QoS) support**—How does this technology differentiate levels of service for voice, video, and data applications?

Table 1-1 shows how these considerations apply to the various site-to-site VPN technologies.

Remote Access VPN Deployment

When deploying remote access VPNs, it is also important to have an understanding of how the various technologies compare. For this reason, a technical comparison of the various remote access VPN technologies is included in this section.

Compulsory tunnel mode/NAS-initiated remote access VPNs can be deployed using the following protocols:

- L2F
- PPTP
- L2TPv2/L2TPv3

Voluntary/client-initiated remote access VPNs can be deployed using the following protocols:

- PPTP
- L2TPv2/L2TPv3
- IPsec
- SSL/TLS

Table 1-1 *Technical Considerations for Site-to-Site VPN Technologies*

	Provider Provisioned VPNs						Customer Provisioned VPNs	
	L2VPNs			L3VPNs				
	VPWS	VPLS	IPLS	BGP/MPLS (RFC4364/ 2547bis)	IPsec	GRE	IPsec	GRE
Point-to-point(P2P)/ multipoint (MP)	P2P	MP	MP	MP	P2P	P2P	P2P	P2P
Provisioning topologies (full mesh, hub and spoke, partial mesh)	Must build topologies by provisioning P2P pseudowires	Inherently fully meshed (any-to-any connectivity)	Inherently fully meshed (any-to-any connectivity)	Inherently fully meshed (any-to-any connectivity); can provision other topologies simply by controlling VPN route distribution	Must build topologies by provisioning P2P tunnels	Must build topologies by provisioning P2P tunnels	Must build topologies by provisioning P2P tunnels	Must build topologies by provisioning P2P tunnels
Scalability	Good	Good (in the metro area)	Good (in the metro area)	Excellent	Good (more scalable using DMVPN[2])	Good	Good (more scalable using DMVPN[2])	Good
Geographic Reach	Draft Martini deployments (normally[1]) limited to MPLS backbone / L2TPv3 can transit any IP-enabled backbone network	Deployments using Draft Martini (normally[1]) limited to MPLS backbone	Deployments using Draft Martini (normally[1]) limited to MPLS backbone	Normally[1] limited to MPLS backbone networks	Deployments can transit IP-enabled backbone network (including Internet)	Deployments can transit IP-enabled backbone network (including Internet)	Deployments can transit IP-enabled backbone network (including Internet)	Deployments can transit IP-enabled backbone network (including Internet)

continues

Security	Draft Martini deployments: good (comparable to FR/ATM networks); L2TPv3 deployments: good (tunnel authentication/64-bit cookie enables resistance to blind insertion attacks/excellent protection with IPsec [per RFC3193])	Deployments using Draft Martini: good (comparable to FR/ATM networks); deployments using L2TPv3: good (tunnel authenti-cation/64-bit cookie enables resistance to blind insertion attacks/excellent protection with IPsec [perRFC3193])	Good (comparable to Frame Relay/ATM networks)	Excellent (depending on IPsec transforms deployed)	Poor	Excellent (depending on IPsec transforms deployed)	Poor
Inherent multicast support	Yes	Yes	No (enable with Multicast VPNs [MVPNs] or GRE tunnels between CEs)	No (enable with GRE/IPsec)	Yes	No (enable with GRE/IPsec)[6]	Yes
Inherent multiprotocol support	Yes	No (IP only)	No (requires mesh of CE-CE GRE tunnels)	No (enable with GRE/IPsec or Virtual Tunnel Interface [VTI])	Yes	No (enable with GRE/IPsec or Virtual Tunnel Interface [VTI])	Yes
QoS Support	Draft Martini (MPLS backbone): traffic differentiation dependent on EXP[3] bits (E-LSPs) or labels (L-LSPs) / hard QoS guarantees with TE[4] and fast reroute; L2TPv3 - ToS[5] bits marked	Using Draft Martini (MPLS backbone): traffic differentiation dependent on EXP bits (E-LSPs) or labels (L-LSPs) / hard QoS guarantees with TE and fast reroute; L2TPv3- ToS bits marked	MPLS backbone: traffic differentiation dependent on EXP bits (E-LSPs) or labels (L-LSPs) / hard QoS guarantees with TE and fast reroute	ToS bits copied to outer IP header (specified in RFC2401)	Can copy ToS bits to outer IP header	ToS bits copied to outer IP header (specified in RFC2401)	Can copy ToS bits to outer IP header

[1] Draft Martini pseudowires / BGP/MPLS (RFC4364/2547bis) deployments can be extended over an IP backbone using IPsec/GRE/L2TPv3

[2] Dynamic Multipoint VPN

[3] Experimental bits (in an MPLS shim-header)

[4] MPLS traffic engineering

[5] Type of Service bits (in an IP header)

[6] Work to enable secure multicast is ongoing in the IETF Multicast Security (msec) working group

Some of the most important technical considerations for service providers and customers when deploying remote access VPNs are as follows:

- **Functionality**—How much functionality is provided to remote users? Is it comparable to local users at the central site?

- **Security**—Is traffic (origin/integrity) authenticated and encrypted? Is traffic crossing the VPN vulnerable to replay or insertion attacks? Are remote user devices secure/protected?

- **Scalability**—How easy is it to support a large number of remote access VPN users?

- **Inherent multiprotocol support**—Can multiprotocol traffic be transported?

- **Inherent multicast support**—Can multicast traffic be natively supported across the VPN?

Table 1-2 shows how these considerations apply to the various remote access VPN technologies. Note that other important considerations, such as manageability and high availability, do not relate directly to the protocols and technologies themselves, but instead to particular vendor implementations and so are not described in this chapter.

Summary

This chapter introduced, explained, and compared VPN devices, protocols, technologies, and models.

VPNs may be service provider or customer provisioned and fall into one of two broad categories:

- Site-to-site VPNs connect the geographically dispersed sites of an organization or organizations.

- Remote access VPNs connect mobile or home-based users to an organization's resources at a central site.

Review Questions

1 What type of connectivity is provided by site-to-site and remote access VPNs?

2 What protocols and technologies are commonly used to enable site-to-site VPNs?

3 What protocols are commonly used to enable remote access VPNs?

4 What are the two main categories of provider provisioned Layer 2 VPNs?

5 Name the two overall types of Layer 3 VPN.

Table 1-2   *Technical Considerations for Remote Access VPN Technologies*

	Compulsory Tunnel Mode/NAS Initiated			Voluntary Tunnel Mode/Client Initiated			
	L2F	PPTP	L2TPv2/3	PPTP	L2TPv2/3	IPsec	SSL/TLS
Functionality	Comparable to local users	Comparable to local users	Comparable to local users	Comparable to local users	Comparable to local users	Comparable to local users	Limited functionality (clientless SSL VPNs)/ comparable to local users (using specific SSL VPN client software)
Security	Limited: tunnel authentication only (can be secured using IPsec)	Reasonable[1] (with MS-CHAPv2 and MPPE and 128-bit keys)	Limited: tunnel authentication and hidden AVPs[2] (can be secured with IPsec per RFC3193)	Reasonable[1] (with MS-CHAPv2 and MPPE and 128-bit keys)	Limited: tunnel authentication and hidden AVPs (can be secured with IPsec per RFC3193)	Excellent (depending on transform set)	Excellent (depending on SSL version and selected cipher suite)
Scalability	Very good	Very good	Very good	Very good	Very good	Very good (with hardware acceleration)	Good (with hardware acceleration)
Inherent multiprotocol support	Yes	Yes	Yes	Yes	Yes	No	No
Inherent multicast support	Yes	Yes	Yes	Yes	Yes	No	No

[1]PPTP security has been called into question—See http://www.schneier.com/paper-pptpv2.html and http://ciac.llnl.gov/ciac/bulletins/i-087.shtml

[2]Attribute-value pairs—Protocol constructs that allow great protocol extensibility

PART II

Site-to-Site VPNs

CHAPTER 2

Designing and Deploying L2TPv3-Based Layer 2 VPNs

Layer 2 VPNs (L2VPN) can be used to provide site-to-site Layer 2 connectivity. As discussed in Chapter 1, "What Is a Virtual Private Network?" L2VPNs can be built using technologies and protocols such as the Layer Two Tunneling Protocol version 3 (L2TPv3, RFC3931) and Any Transport over MPLS (AToM) and can fall into three categories:

- **Virtual Private Wire Service (VPWS)** — This type of L2VPN provides point-to-point MAN or WAN transport for Layer 2 protocols and connections such as Ethernet, High-Level Data Link Control (HDLC), PPP, Frame Relay, and ATM.

- **Virtual Private LAN Service (VPLS)** — A VPLS provides multipoint Ethernet connectivity.

- **IP-only Private LAN Service (IPLS)** — This is a newer type of L2VPN, and it provides multipoint IP-only connectivity.

A common question asked about L2VPNs (including L2TPv3-based L2VPNs) is why they might be preferred over Layer 3 site-to-site VPNs and when their deployment might be suitable.

L2TPv3 pseudowire (emulated circuit)-based L2VPNs are typically deployed by service providers in order to consolidate legacy and newer IP network infrastructure and offer newer Ethernet-based WAN connectivity to their customers. Figure 2-1 illustrates an L2TPv3-based L2VPN. Figure 2-1 shows L2TPv3 sessions over an IP backbone network between service Provider Edge (PE) routers: London.PE, Birmingham.PE, and Amsterdam.PE. The L2TPv3 sessions in Figure 2-1 are transporting the following Layer 2 protocol connections:

- An Ethernet connection between Customer Edge (CE) routers mjlnet.London.PE and mjlnet.Birmingham.CE

- A Frame Relay connection between CE routers cisco.Birmingham.CE and cisco.Amsterdam.CE

- A PPP connection between CE routers vectorit.London.CE and vectorit.Amsterdam.CE

Figure 2-1   *L2TPv3-Based L2VPN*

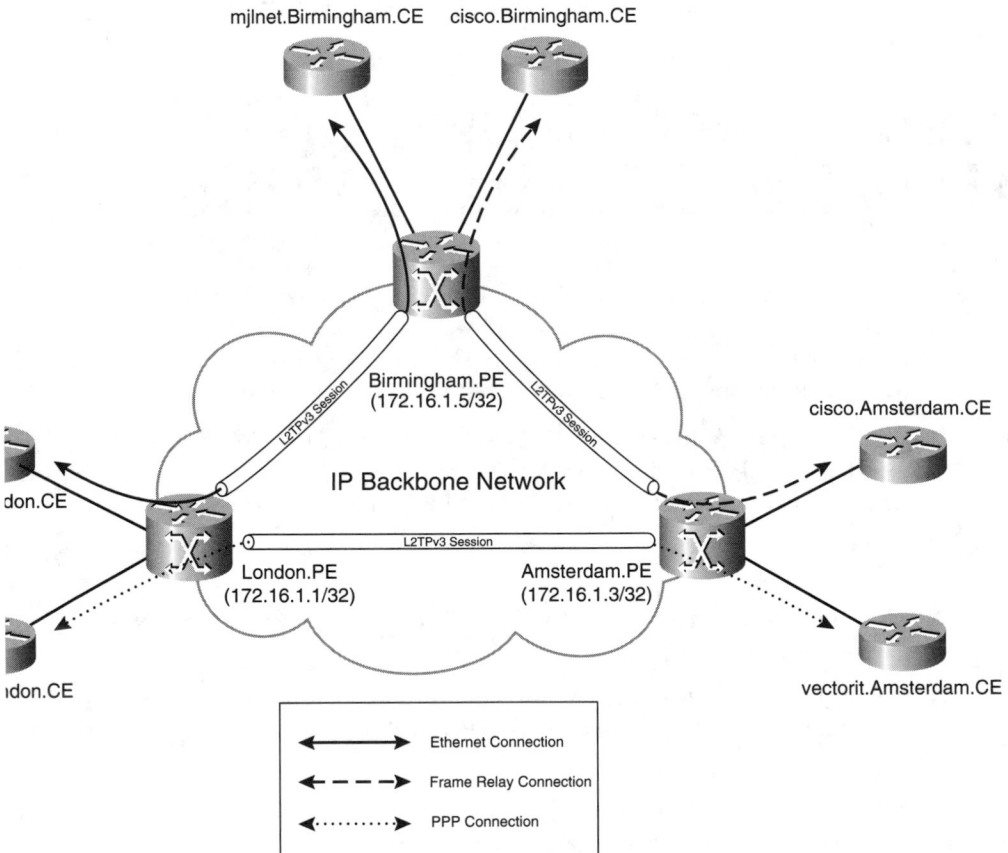

Benefits and Drawbacks of L2TPv3-Based L2VPNs

For service providers, some of the main benefits and drawbacks of deploying L2TPv3-based L2VPNs are as follows:

- L2TPv3 requires only an IP-enabled backbone. It does not require that the service provider backbone network be MPLS enabled.

- L2TPv3 pseudowires enable service providers to consolidate legacy networks with newer IP-enabled networks.

For example by moving customer ATM and Frame Relay circuits from legacy networks to L2TPv3 pseudowires over an IP-enabled backbone, the service provider can decommission those legacy networks and, therefore, substantially reduce capital and operational expenditure (the service provider now only has to maintain a single network infrastructure, rather than multiple network infrastructures).

- Even after it decommissions legacy networks, a service provider can maintain revenues derived from legacy services, while developing newer services such as Ethernet MAN/WAN service offerings.

For enterprises, on the other hand, the main advantages and disadvantages of deploying L2TPv3-based L2VPNs are as follows:

- When using L2TPv3 pseudowires to connect sites, an enterprise can have complete control of routing. L2TPv3 pseudowires transport Layer 2 protocols, and so enterprise CE devices such as routers can maintain routing protocol adjacencies and exchange routing information over a service provider network. CE devices do not exchange routing information with service provider devices.

  In contrast, if an enterprise chooses to connect sites using an MPLS Layer 3 VPN (L3VPN), CE devices exchange routing information with PE devices, and PE routers participate in the enterprise's routing.

- L2TPv3 pseudowires can transport non-IP protocols such as IPX and AppleTalk—this is again because L2TPv3 transports Layer 2 protocols such as Ethernet, PPP, HDLC, ATM, and Frame Relay, and as such, L2TP Control Connection Endpoints (LCCEs) are completely unaware of Layer 3 protocols that might be transported by those Layer 2 protocols. Other VPN types such as MPLS L3VPNs do not have this capability natively.

  So, L2TPv3 pseudowires are one solution for connecting sites requiring non-IP connectivity.

- L2TPv3 can be used to help migrate networks to IP version 6 (IPv6) using the Cisco L2TPv3 IPv6 demultiplex capability. An enterprise or service provider can use this capability to transparently connect islands of IPv6 over an IPv4 network, while not interrupting regular IPv4 routing.

You should now have a pretty good understanding of the benefits and drawbacks of L2TPv3-based L2VPNs. The sections that follow cover L2TPv3 pseudowire operation, pseudowire configuration, and pseudowire design and deployment considerations.

L2TPv3 Pseudowire Operation

L2TPv3 is, as previously described, a tunneling protocol that can be used for transporting Layer 2 protocols. It can operate in a number of different configurations (one of which is discussed in this chapter) and tunnel a number of different Layer 2 protocols and connections over a packet-switched network (PSN). This chapter assumes that the PSN over which L2TPv3 tunnels Layer 2 protocols is an IP network.

L2TPv3 can transport a number of Layer 2 protocols and connection types, including the following:

- Ethernet
- Ethernet VLAN (802.1Q)
- Frame Relay
- HDLC and HDLC-like protocols
- PPP
- ATM (both ATM Adaption Layer 5 [AAL5] and cell relay)

To understand L2TPv3 pseudowires, it is essential to have a firm grasp of the following:

- L2TPv3 deployment models
- L2TPv3 message types
- The L2TPv3 control connection

L2TPv3 deployment models, message types, and the control connection are examined in the following three sections.

L2TPv3 Deployment Models

There are three basic deployment models for L2TPv3:

- L2TP Access Concentrator (LAC)-to-L2TP Network Server (LNS)
- LAC-to-LAC
- LNS-to-LNS

A LAC functions as a cross-connect between data links and L2TP sessions (emulated Layer 2 connections), whereas an LNS terminates L2TP sessions and processes the encapsulated Layer 3 protocol packets on virtual interfaces.

The LAC-to-LAC model is used to configure the L2TPv3 pseudowire-based VPNs discussed in this chapter. The LAC-to-LNS and LNS-to-LNS models are discussed further in Chapter 8, "Designing and Implementing L2TPv2 and L2TPv3 Remote Access VPNs."

Figure 2-1 illustrates the LAC-to-LAC deployment model.

NOTE   A *pseudowire* is an emulated circuit that crosses a PSN. One pseudowire corresponds to one L2TPv3 session.

L2TPv3 Message Types

L2TPv3 uses two types of message:

- **Control connection messages**—Used for signaling between LCCEs
- **Session data (channel) messages**—Used to transport Layer 2 protocols and connections

Figure 2-2 shows the format of control channel and session data (channel) messages.

Figure 2-2   *Control Channel and Data Channel Messages*

Control Channel Message:

IP Header
Control Message Header
Control Message AVPs

Data Channel Message:

IP Header
Data Channel Message (Session) Header
Optional Layer-2 Specific Sublayer
Payload

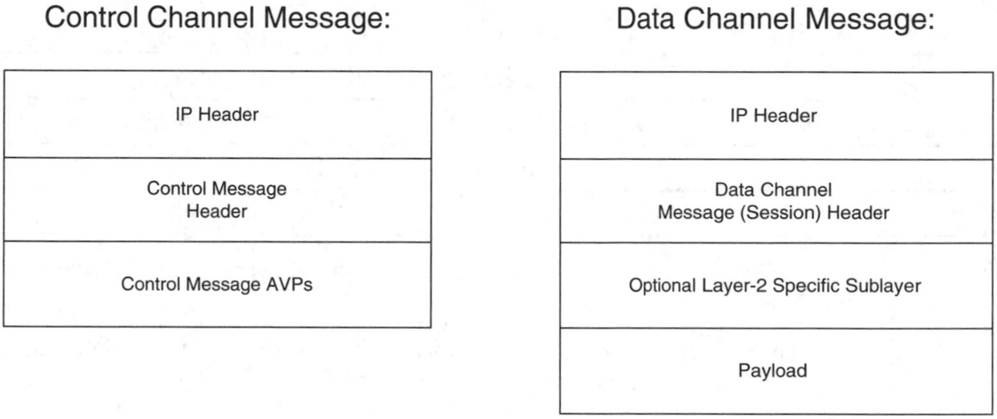

As shown in Figure 2-2, the control channel message consists of the following:

- The IP packet header. The protocol ID contained in the header is 115 (L2TPv3).

Note   L2TPv3 control and data channel messages can be carried either directly over IP (protocol ID 115) or over IP/UDP (UDP port 1701). On Cisco routers, L2TPv3 control and data messages are carried directly over IP in a LAC-to-LAC deployment.

- The control message header.
- Control message attribute-value pairs (AVP). AVPs are used to specify a variable (the attribute) and the value associated with that variable.

    AVPs perform a number of functions, *including* the following:

    — General functions such as control channel message authentication and integrity

    — Communicating error and result codes and messages

— Communicating control connection management information such as host names, router IDs, supported pseudowires types, control connection IDs, session IDs, required Layer 2–specific sublayers, connection speeds, and any data-sequencing requirements

— Communicating circuit status and error information

Figure 2-3 shows the control connection message header format.

Figure 2-3　*L2TPv3 Control Connection Message Header (over IP) Format*

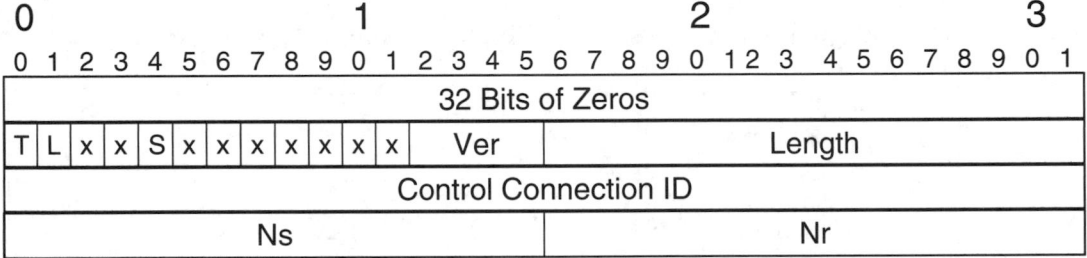

The fields of the control connection message header shown in Figure 2-3 have the following functions:

- The first field consists of 32 bits that must all be set to 0. This field identifies this message as a control message.

- The T, L, and S flags:

  — The T bit must be set to 1 and identifies this as a control connection message (along with the 32 bits of 0s).

  — The L bit must be set to 1 and indicates that the Length field is present in the message.

  — The S bit must be set to 1 and indicates that the Next Sent (Ns) and Next Received (Nr) fields are present in the control channel message.

- The Version (Ver) field must contain the value 3 to indicate that this is an L2TPv3 control channel message.

- The Length field specifies the length of the control channel message beginning with the Flags field.

- The Control Connection ID uniquely identifies the control channel (more than one control channel may be established on a particular LCCE).

- The Next Sent (Ns) field indicates the sequence number of this message.

- The Next Received (Nr) field indicates the sequence number of the next control channel message expected from the peer LCCE.

The data channel message shown in Figure 2-2 consists of the following:

- The IP header (protocol ID 115)

- The Data Channel Message (Session) header

- An optional Layer 2–specific sublayer
- The payload, which carries the Layer 2 protocol frames, cell(s), or Service Data Unit (SDU) received by an LCCE on an attachment circuit (from a CE device).

Figure 2-4 depicts the L2TPv3 Data Channel (Session) Message header.

Figure 2-4   *L2TPv3 Session Header (over IP)*

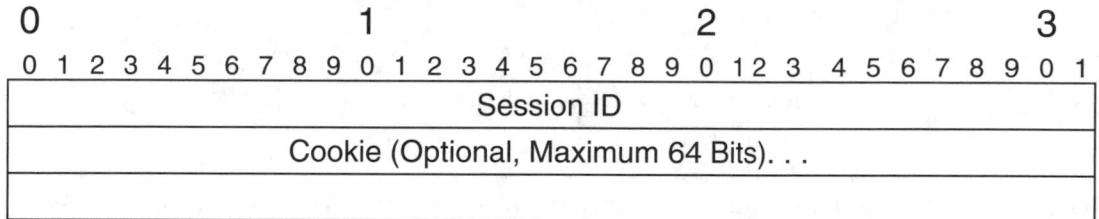

The fields in the L2TPv3 data channel message are as follows:

- Session ID, which uniquely identifies this L2TPv3 session.
- Cookie, which is optional, and can be used in combination with the Session ID to ensure that a data channel message is correctly associated with the appropriate local attachment circuit, as well as offering a certain level of protection against blind-insertion attacks.

  Blind-insertion attacks involve an attacker attempting to insert malicious packets into an L2TPv3 data channel message stream (without being able to directly sniff the data channel). The cookie helps to protect against these insertion attacks because an attacker will find it difficult to guess the cookie (assuming that the cookie is randomly chosen).

  The cookie, if present, can be either 32 or 64 bits in length.

Figure 2-5 shows the optional Layer 2–specific sublayer shown in the data channel message (refer to Figure 2-2 for the overall data channel message format).

Figure 2-5   *Optional Default Layer 2–Specific Sublayer*

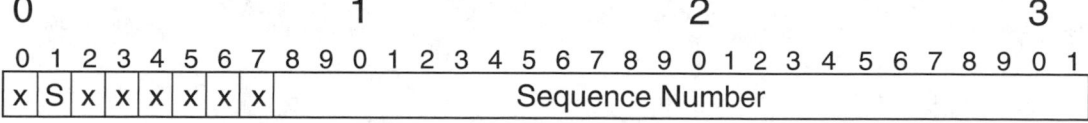

The S flag in the default Layer 2 specific sublayer is set to 1 if sequencing of data channel messages is enabled. In this case, a non-0 sequence number will be contained in the Sequence Number field.

The L2TPv3 Control Connection

Control connection messages are used for the following functions:

- Setting up the control connection itself
- Dynamically establishing L2TPv3 sessions
- Providing a keepalive mechanism for the control connection and sessions
- Signaling circuit status changes
- Tearing down L2TP sessions, as well as the control connection itself

These various functions are explained in this section.

NOTE   A LAC that participates in a control connection can also be referred to as an *L2TP Control Connection Endpoint* (LCCE).

The acronyms PE router, LAC, and LCCE are used interchangeably in this chapter. The one exception is the discussion later in this chapter of static L2TPv3 sessions without a control connection between PE routers/LACs. In this case, the terms *PE router* and *LAC* may be used, but the term *LCCE* is not used simply because without a control connection being established, a PE router/LAC cannot be considered the endpoint of a control connection.

L2TPv3 Control Connection Setup

Figure 2-6 illustrates control connection setup.

Figure 2-6   *Control Connection Setup*

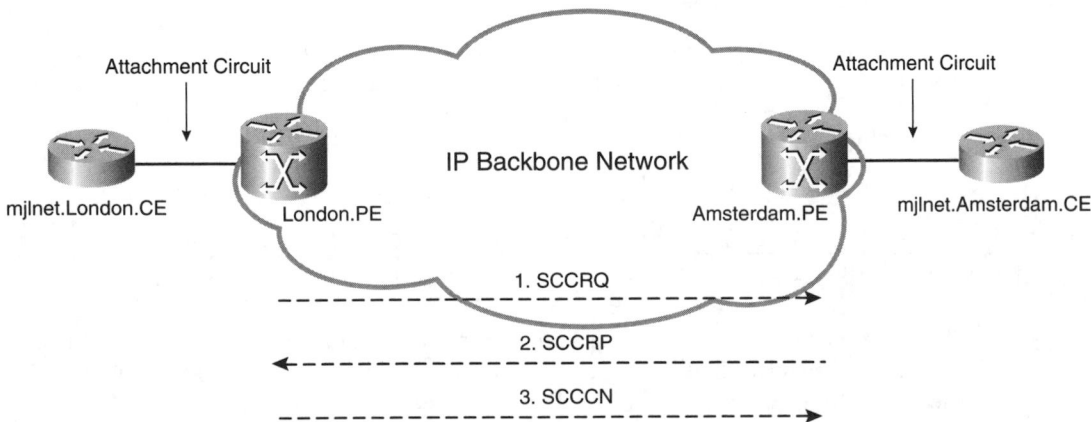

As you can see in Figure 2-6, control connection setup consists of the exchange of three messages between LCCEs:

Step 1   One LCCE (London.PE, in Figure 2-1) sends a Start-Control-Connection-Request (SCCRQ) message to its peer.

The SCCRQ is used to indicate that the sender wants to establish a control connection with the peer LCCE. In addition, the SCCRQ is used to specify information such as the types of pseudowire (Ethernet, Frame Relay, and so on) that the sender can support.

Table 2-1 summarizes the pseudowire types that are supported with L2TPv3 on Cisco routers at the time of this writing.

Table 2-1   *Supported Pseudowire Types for L2TPv3*

Pseudowire (PW) Type	Description
0x0001	Frame Relay DLCI
0x0002	ATM AAL5 SDU VCC transport
0x0003	ATM transparent cell transport (port mode)
0x0004	Ethernet VLAN
0x0005	Ethernet
0x0006	HDLC
0x0007	PPP
0x0009	ATM cell transport VCC mode
0x000A	ATM cell transport VPC mode
0x000B	IP Layer 2 Transport

The SCCRQ, as well as other control channel messages, carry authentication information if authentication is configured.

Step 2   If the SCCRQ is acceptable, the peer LCCE (Amsterdam.PE) responds with a Start-Control-Connection-Reply (SCCRP) message.

The SCCRP indicates that the sender accepts the control connection setup request (in the form of the SCCRQ). The SCCRP also includes information regarding the types of pseudowire that the sender supports.

Step 3   The LCCE that sent the SCCRQ (London.PE) now responds to the SCCRP with a Start-Control-Connection-Connected (SCCCN) message indicating completion of control channel setup.

That is the theory of control channel setup. Example 2-1 shows L2TPv3 control connection establishment in practice.

Example 2-1 *L2TPv3 Control Connection Setup Between Two Cisco LCCEs*

```
Amsterdam.PE#debug vpdn l2x-events
L2X protocol events debugging is on
Amsterdam.PE#
00:16:46: L2TP: I SCCRQ from London.PE tnl 23658  (line 1)
00:16:46: Tnl47781 L2TP: Message digest match performed, passed.

00:16:46: Tnl47781 L2TP: Control connection authentication skipped/passed.
00:16:46: Tnl47781 L2TP: New tunnel created for remote London.PE, address 172.16.1.1
00:16:46: Tnl47781 L2TP: O SCCRP  to London.PE tnlid 23658 (line 2)
00:16:46: Tnl47781 L2TP: Control channel retransmit delay set to 1 seconds
00:16:46: Tnl47781 L2TP: Tunnel state change from idle to wait-ctl-reply
00:16:46: Tnl47781 L2TP: Tunnel state change from wait-ctl-reply to established
00:16:46: Tnl47781 L2TP: I SCCCN  from London.PE tnlid 23658 (line 3)
00:16:46: Tnl47781 L2TP: Control channel retransmit delay set to 1 seconds
00:16:46: Tnl47781 L2TP: SM State established (line 4)

Amsterdam.PE#
```

In highlighted line 1, Amsterdam.PE receives a SCCRQ from London.PE. The SCCRQ is acceptable, and Amsterdam.PE responds with an SCCRP in highlighted line 2. Highlighted line 3 shows that an SCCCN has been received from London.PE. Finally, the control channel state changes to established (highlighted line 4).

L2TPv3 Control Connection Teardown

If an LCCE wants to tear down a control connection, it can signal this to its peer LCCE using a Stop-Control-Connection-Notification (StopCCN) message (see Figure 2-7).

An LCCE can choose to tear down a control channel for a number of reasons, including if an administrator uses the **clear l2tun** command to manually request control channel teardown.

Figure 2-7 *Control Connection Teardown*

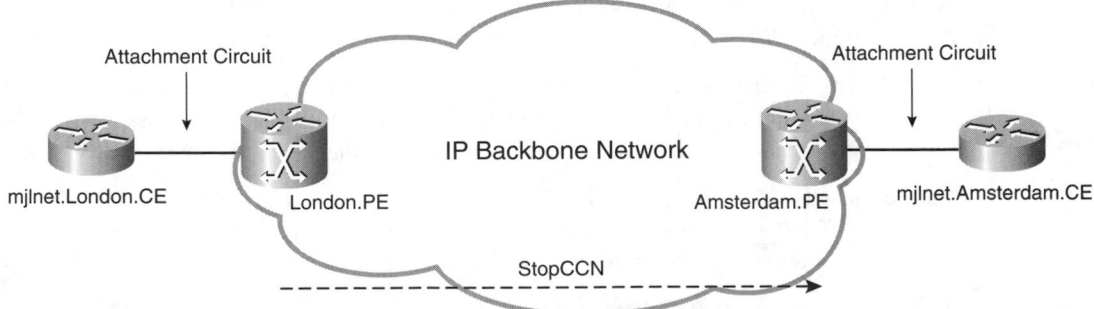

Example 2-2 shows control connection teardown.

Example 2-2 *Control Connection Teardown*

```
Amsterdam.PE#debug vpdn l2x-events
L2X protocol events debugging is on
Amsterdam.PE#
03:39:51: Tnl28072 L2TP: Perform early message digest validation for StopCCN
03:39:51: Tnl28072 L2TP: No message digest AVP, skip validation.
03:39:51: Tnl28072 L2TP: Control connection authentication skipped/passed.
03:39:51: Tnl28072 L2TP: I StopCCN from London.PE tnl 64207 (line 1)
03:39:51: Tnl28072 L2TP: Shutdown tunnel
03:39:51: Tnl28072 L2TP: Tunnel state change from established to idle (line 2)

Amsterdam.PE#
```

Amsterdam.PE receives a StopCCN message from London.PE in highlighted line 1. In highlighted line 2, the tunnel (control channel) state changes from established to idle. The control channel has been torn down. That is control channel setup and teardown. But how about L2TPv3 session setup and teardown?

L2TPv3 Session Setup

After a control connection has been set up (see Figure 2-6), dynamic session (pseudowire) establishment can begin, as shown in Figure 2-8.

Figure 2-8 *L2TPv3 Session (Pseudowire) Setup*

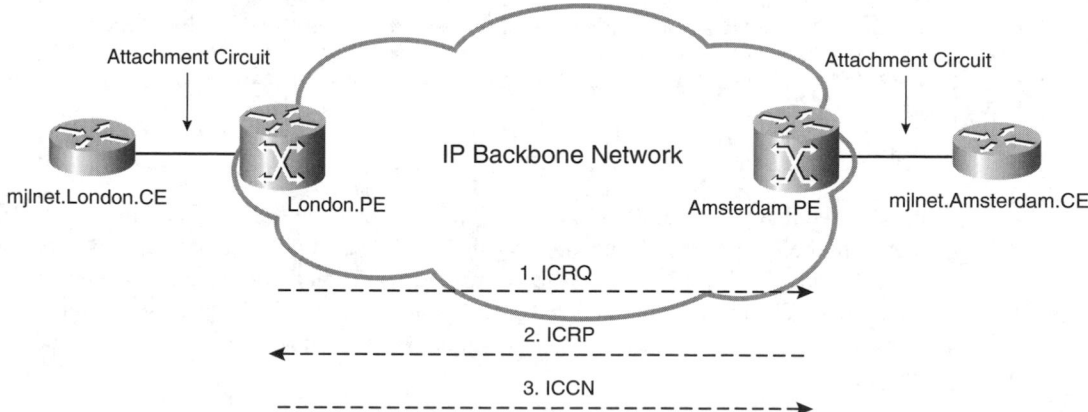

L2TPv3 session setup consists of the exchange of three messages:

Step 1   The LAC that wants to set up a session (London.PE, in this example) sends an Incoming-Call-Request (ICRQ) message to its peer LAC (Amsterdam.PE, in this example).

The ICRQ can include information such as pseudowire type, required Layer 2–specific sublayer, and circuit status.

Step 2   If the peer LAC (Amsterdam.PE) accepts the ICRQ, it responds with an Incoming-Call-Response (ICRP) message.

The ICRP can contain information such as required Layer 2–specific sublayer and circuit status.

Step 3   Finally, the LAC that wants to set up the session (London.PE) sends an Incoming-Call-Connected (ICCN) message to its peer LAC (Amsterdam.PE) to complete session setup.

Example 2-3 shows L2TPv3 session setup.

Example 2-3   *L2TPv3 Session Setup Between Two LACs*

```
London.PE#debug vpdn l2x-events
L2X protocol events debugging is on
London.PE#
00:16:46: Tnl/Sn11744/5823 L2TP: O ICRQ to Amsterdam.PE 34855/0 (line 1)
00:16:46: Tnl/Sn11744/5823 L2TP: Session state change from wait-for-tunnel to
  wait-reply
00:16:46: Tnl11744 L2TP: Perform early message digest validation for ICRP (line 2)
00:16:46: Tnl11744 L2TP: Message digest match performed, passed.

00:16:46: Tnl11744 L2TP: Control connection authentication skipped/passed.
00:16:46: Tnl/Sn11744/5823 L2TP: O ICCN to Amsterdam.PE 34855/64191 (line 3)
00:16:46: Tnl11744 L2TP: Control channel retransmit delay set to 1 seconds
00:16:46: Tnl/Sn11744/5823 L2TP: Session state change from wait-reply to established
  (line 4)

London.PE#
```

In highlighted line 1, London.PE sends an ICRQ message to Amsterdam.PE. Amsterdam.PE replies with the ICRP message shown in highlighted line 2. Highlighted line 3 shows that London.PE now send an ICCN message to Amsterdam.PE. In highlighted line 4, you can see that the L2TPv3 session has now become established. After the L2TPv3 session has been established, data traffic can be transported between the attachment circuits over the pseudowire.

L2TPv3 Session Teardown

An LCCE can dynamically request that a session be torn down by sending a Call-Disconnect-Notify (CDN) message (see Figure 2-9).

An LCCE can choose to tear down a session for a range of reasons. One reason is if an LCCE receives an ICRQ message containing a virtual circuit (VC) ID that is not configured on the local LCCE (VC IDs are used to associate local and remote attachment circuits with a pseudowire).

Figure 2-9   *L2TPv3 Session (Pseudowire) Teardown*

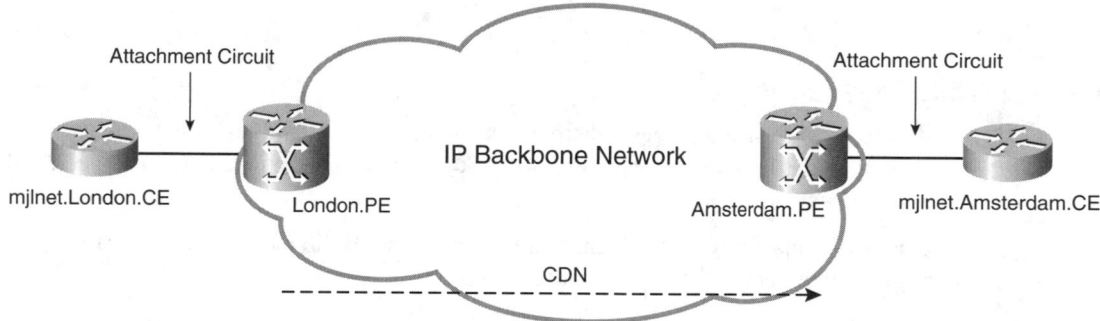

Example 2-4 shows the transmission of a CDN message when an ICRQ is received that contains a VC ID that it does not recognize.

Example 2-4   *Transmission of a CDN Message*

```
London.PE#debug vpdn l2x-events
L2X protocol events debugging is on
London.PE#
02:53:53: Tnl56029 L2TP: Perform early message digest validation for ICRQ
02:53:53: Tnl56029 L2TP: No message digest AVP, skip validation.
02:53:53: Tnl56029 L2TP: Control connection authentication skipped/passed.
02:53:53: Tnl56029 L2TP: I ICRQ from Amsterdam.PE tnl 21530 (line 1)
02:53:53: Tnl/Sn56029/9629 L2TP: Session state change from idle to wait-connect
02:53:53: Tnl/Sn56029/9629 L2TP: Accepted ICRQ, new session created (line 2)
02:53:53: Tnl/Sn56029/9629 L2TP: Xconnect VC ID 1002 not provisioned (line 3)
02:53:53: Tnl/Sn56029/9629 L2TP: O CDN to Amsterdam.PE 21530/8987 (line 4)
02:53:53: Tnl56029 L2TP: Control channel retransmit delay set to 1 seconds
02:53:53: Tnl/Sn56029/9629 L2TP: Destroying session (line 5)
02:53:53: Tnl/Sn56029/9629 L2TP: Session state change from wait-connect to idle
 (line 6)

London.PE#
```

Highlighted line 1 shows that London.PE has received an ICRQ from its peer, Amsterdam.PE. In line 2, London.PE apparently accepts the ICRQ and creates a new session. But, in highlighted line 3, London.PE reports that the VC ID (1002) contained in the ICRQ is not provisioned on the local LCCE (London.PE). Because London.PE does not recognize the VC ID, it sends a CDN message to tear down the session (see highlighted line 4).

Then, in highlighted lines 5 and 6, London.PE reports that it is destroying the session, and the session state changes to idle. The session has been torn down.

Okay, that is control channel and session setup and teardown. There are, however, another couple of messages that you need to know to complete your understanding of the control channel (as far as the LAC-to-LAC model is concerned)—the Hello and the Set-Link-Info (SLI) messages.

Hello and SLI Messages

In the absence of any messages (whether control messages or data session messages) from its peer, a LAC sends a Hello message to check that it still has connectivity to its peer, and that its peer is still alive.

The period of inactivity that will cause a LAC to send a Hello message to its peer is configurable but defaults to 60 seconds.

Figure 2-10 illustrates the transmission of a Hello message.

Figure 2-10 *Transmission of a Hello Message*

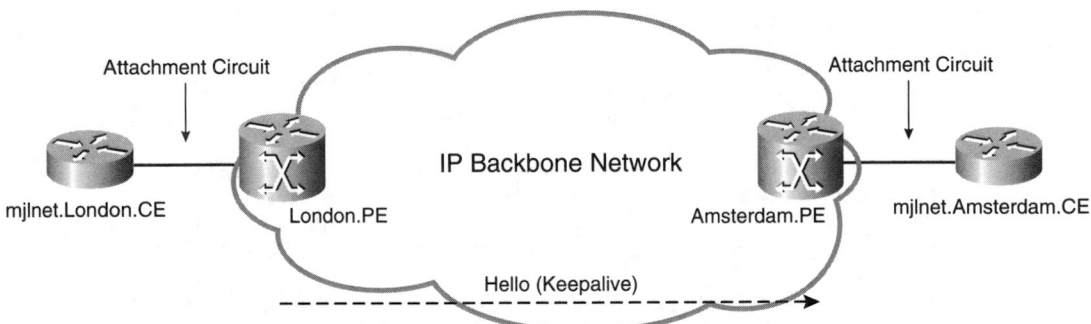

Example 2-5 shows the transmission of a Hello message.

Example 2-5 *Transmission of a Hello Message*

```
London.PE#debug vpdn l2x-events
L2X protocol events debugging is on
London.PE#
00:17:46: Tnl11744 L2TP: O Hello  to Amsterdam.PE tnlid 34855 (line 1)
00:17:46: Tnl11744 L2TP: Control channel retransmit delay set to 1 seconds
00:17:46: Tnl11744 L2TP: Perform early message digest validation for ACK (line 2)
00:17:46: Tnl11744 L2TP: Message digest match performed, passed.

00:17:46: Tnl11744 L2TP: Control connection authentication skipped/passed.
London.PE#
```

Highlighted line 1 shows the transmission of a Hello message to Amsterdam.PE. Then, in highlighted line 2, an acknowledgment (ACK) is received from Amsterdam.PE (it's alive!).

Another function of the control channel is to signal circuit status changes using the SLI message as illustrated in Figure 2-11.

Figure 2-11 *Signaling Circuit Status Changes Using the SLI Message*

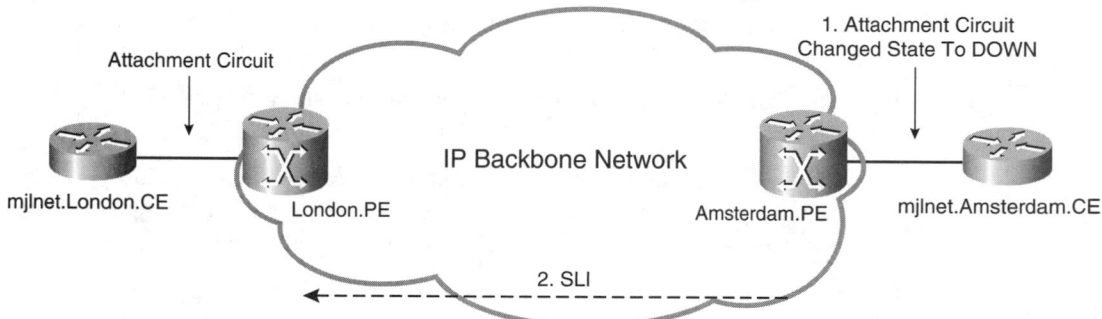

In Figure 2-11, the attachment circuit between Amsterdam.PE and mjlnet.Amsterdam.CE has changed state to down, and so Amsterdam signals this to London.PE using the SLI message.

NOTE   For detailed, step-by-step, information on debugging and troubleshooting L2TPv3-based VPNs, refer to *Troubleshooting Virtual Private Networks* by Mark Lewis (Cisco Press).

Configuring and Verifying L2TPv3 Pseudowires

As previously mentioned, you configure L2TPv3-based pseudowires in two ways:

- Using dynamic L2TPv3 session setup
- Using static L2TPv3 session setup

As described earlier in this chapter, dynamic L2TPv3 session setup requires the exchange of control channel messages, whereas static L2TPv3 session setup does not *require* the exchange of any control channel messages.

The advantages and disadvantages of dynamic and static L2TPv3 session configuration are as follows:

- Dynamic sessions require a control channel (setup consisting of three messages [see Figure 2-6]), as well as the exchange of three additional control channel messages per session (see Figure 2-8).

  With static sessions, there is no session or (potentially) control channel setup traffic overhead (no ICRQ, ICRP, ICCN, and potentially no SCCRQ, SCCRP, and SCCN messages).

Note, however, that the bandwidth overhead on the network for control connection and session setup messages is generally relatively negligible even with a large number of sessions.

- Session IDs and (any) cookies are negotiated during dynamic session establishment. Cookie values assigned during dynamic session establishment are randomly chosen.

    If you configure static L2TPv3 sessions, you must manually provision local and remote session IDs and cookies.

    Manual allocation of cookies may be undesirable because random cookie values can help prevent blind-insertion attacks (where an attacker attempts to inject malicious packets into an L2TPv3 session packet stream).

    Random cookie values (particularly 64-bit cookie values) help to prevent blind-insertion attacks because an attacker will typically have more trouble guessing a randomly generated cookie value than guessing a nonrandom cookie value allocated to a session by an administrator.

- Configuration and management of more than a small number of static L2TPv3 sessions may be impractical.

- Path maximum transmission unit (MTU) Discovery (PMTUD) for L2TPv3 pseudowires is not supported for static sessions.

Now that you understand some of the advantages and disadvantages of dynamic and static L2TPv3 sessions, it is time to move on to configuration.

Deploying L2TPv3 Pseudowires with Dynamic Session Setup

This section covers the configuration of dynamic L2TPv3 session setup.

Figure 2-12 shows a reference network used throughout this section.

Figure 2-12 *Reference Network*

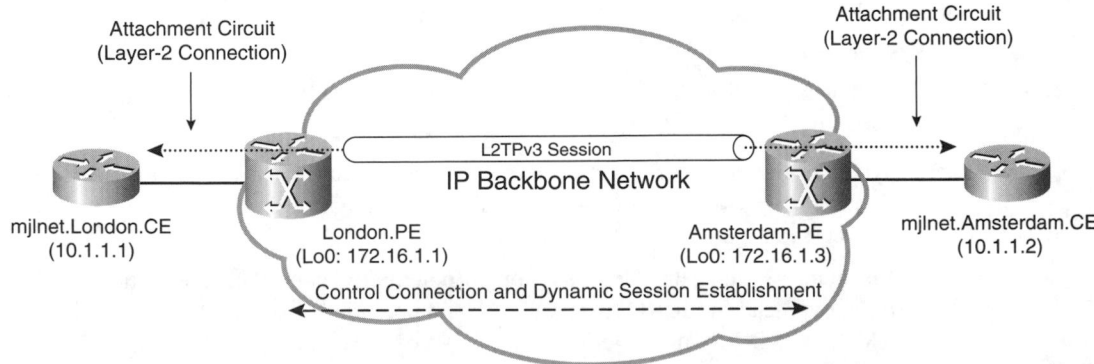

Configuration of L2TPv3 pseudowires with dynamic session establishment consists of the following steps:

Step 1   Configure Cisco Express Forwarding (CEF).

Step 2   Configure a loopback interface to use as the pseudowire endpoint.

Step 3   Configure an L2TP class (optional).

Step 4   Configure a pseudowire class.

Step 5   Bind attachment circuits to pseudowires.

These steps must be specified on both LACs between which pseudowires are configured.

Step 1: Configure CEF

The first step when deploying L2TPv3 pseudowires is to configure CEF. CEF can be configured using the global configuration mode **ip cef** or **ip cef distributed** commands.

If you do not configure CEF, L2TPv3 pseudowires will not function.

Step 2: Configure a Loopback Interface to Use as the Pseudowire Endpoint

You should now configure a loopback interface to use as the endpoint of L2TPv3 pseudowires. Configuring a loopback interface for this purpose is a good idea because loopback interfaces do not go down (unlike physical interfaces).

Example 2-6 shows the configuration of a loopback interface to use as the pseudowire endpoint.

Example 2-6   *Configuration of a Loopback Interface to Use as the Pseudowire Endpoint*

```
!
interface Loopback0
 ip address 172.16.1.1 255.255.255.255
!
```

Be sure that the IP address that you configure on the loopback interface that you use as the pseudowire endpoint is reachable from the peer LAC (by advertising it in the backbone network interior gateway protocol [IGP] or via other means, as appropriate).

If the IP address on the loopback interface is not reachable from the peer LAC, L2TPv3 pseudowires will not function.

Step 3: Configure an L2TPv3 Class (Optional)

Although it is optional, recommended practice advises that you should configure an L2TPv3 class. The L2TPv3 class enables you to configure a number of control channel parameters such as authentication, keepalive (Hello) intervals, receive window size, retransmission parameters, and timeouts.

In early specifications of the L2TPv3 protocol, a Challenge Handshake Authentication Protocol (CHAP)-like mechanism was used for L2TPv3 control channel authentication. This authentication mechanism is borrowed from L2TPv2 (RFC2661).

Example 2-7 shows the configuration of an L2TPv3 class with CHAP-like authentication.

Example 2-7 *Configuration of an L2TPv3 Class with CHAP-Like Authentication*

```
!
l2tp-class mjlnet.Class.To.Amsterdam
 authentication
 password 7 02050D480809
!
```

The **l2tp-class** *l2tp-class-name* command configures the L2TPv3 class name (in Example 2-7, **mjlnet.Class.To.Amsterdam**).

The **authentication** command then enables L2TPv3 control channel authentication.

Finally, the **password [0 | 7]** *password* command is used to configure the shared password. This password must be configured identically on peer LCCEs or control channel setup will fail.

In RFC 3931 (L2TPv3), a new authentication mechanism was introduced (it makes use of different AVPs than CHAP-like authentication). This new mechanism can be referred to as *digest secret authentication*.

Example 2-8 shows the configuration of digest secret authentication.

Example 2-8 *Configuration of Digest Secret Authentication*

```
!
l2tp-class mjlnet.PW.To.Amsterdam
 digest secret mjlnet hash sha
!
```

The **digest [secret [0 | 7]** *password*] [**hash {md5 | sha}**] command is used in Example 2-8 to configure digest secret authentication, configure a password, and specify the hash algorithm (Message Digest 5 [MD5] or Secret Hash Algorithm [SHA-1]). The password and hash algorithm must be consistent between peer LCCEs or again control channel establishment will fail.

You might be wondering which type of authentication you should configure, the CHAP-like authentication shown in Example 2-7 or the digest secret authentication shown in Example 2-8. The answer is, it depends (of course!).

Digest secret authentication was first introduced in Cisco IOS Software Release 12.0(29)S, and so if one or both of your LCCEs are running a version prior to 12.0(29)S, you will have to stick with the older CHAP-like authentication. If both the LCCEs are running 12.0(29), you can use digest secret authentication. Digest secret authentication is more secure than the older CHAP-like authentication.

Before finishing this section, it is worth mentioning the **digest check** command, which is used to configure integrity checking for control channel messages. This command was also introduced in Cisco IOS Software Release 12.0(29)S. You can configure this command only if digest secret authentication is also enabled.

Step 4: Configure a Pseudowire Class

A pseudowire class is used to configure the pseudowire encapsulation and pseudowire endpoint address (the loopback interface configured in Step 2).

Example 2-9 shows the configuration of a pseudowire class.

Example 2-9 *Configuration of a Pseudowire Class*

```
!
pseudowire-class mjlnet.PW.To.Amsterdam
 encapsulation l2tpv3
 protocol l2tpv3 mjlnet.Class.To.Amsterdam
 ip local interface Loopback0
!
```

The **pseudowire-class** [*pw-class-name*] command is used to configure the pseudowire class name. Next, the **encapsulation l2tpv3** command is used to specify the pseudowire encapsulation type. The control channel protocol is configured, and the L2TPv3 class (configured in Step 3) is linked to the pseudowire class using the **protocol {l2tpv3 | none}** [*l2tpv3-class-name*] command. Then the **ip local interface** *interface-name* command is used to specify the interface to be used as the pseudowire endpoint (see Step 2). Another (optional) command that can be configured within the pseudowire class is **sequencing**. This command is used to specify that sequencing should be used on the pseudowire (see Figure 2-5).

Step 5: Bind Attachment Circuits to Pseudowires

The **xconnect** command is used to bind attachment circuits to L2TPv3 pseudowires.

As discussed earlier in this chapter, Cisco routers support the following L2TPv3 pseudowires (at the time of this writing):

- Ethernet port
- Ethernet VLAN (802.1Q)
- HDLC

- PPP
- Frame Relay (DLCI-to-DLCI and trunks)
- ATM (AAL5 and cell relay)
- IP Layer 2 transport

The following sections discuss binding attachment circuits to each of these pseudowire types (with the exception of IP Layer 2 transport), as well as design and deployment considerations for each pseudowire type. IP Layer 2 transport is covered toward the end of the chapter.

Transporting Ethernet Traffic over L2TPv3 Pseudowires

One of the most popular types of traffic over L2TPv3 pseudowires is Ethernet. Ethernet traffic can be transported over L2TPv3 in two forms:

- Ethernet port (raw Ethernet frames)
- Ethernet VLAN (tagged Ethernet [802.1Q] frames)

The following two sections describe the operation, configuration, and verification of Ethernet traffic transport over L2TPv3 pseudowires.

It is worth noting that when transporting Ethernet traffic in point-to-point (VPWS) Ethernet port or Ethernet VLAN mode, the peer LCCEs are completely transparent to Ethernet hosts at either end of the pseudowire and do *not* maintain a MAC address table.

Ethernet Port Transport with L2TPv3 Pseudowires   When using Ethernet port transport, *raw* Ethernet frames are transported over the point-to-point L2TPv3 pseudowire between LCCEs. Before examining the transport of Ethernet frames over an L2TPv3 pseudowire, however, it is a good idea to first take a look at Ethernet frames themselves.

Figure 2-13 depicts the two commonly used Ethernet frames formats, Ethernet II and IEEE 802.3. The lengths of the various Ethernet frame fields, in bytes, are shown in brackets in the figure.

The fields of the Ethernet II/802.3 frames have the following functions:

- **Preamble (including the Start-of-Frame [SOF] delimiter)**—This is an 8-byte pattern of alternating 1s and 0s, with the two final bits set to 1. This preamble and SOF is used to inform hosts on an Ethernet segment that a frame is on the way.
- **Destination Address**—This is the 6-byte destination MAC address.
- **Source Address**—The 6-byte source MAC address.
- **Type (Ethernet II)**—This is a 2-byte field that specifies the higher-layer protocol. 802.3 replaces the Type field with a Length field, which indicates the length of the Data field.

- **Data (including any padding)**—This is a variable-length field that contains data to be sent to a higher-layer protocol.
- **Frame Check Sequence (FCS)**—A 2-byte cyclic redundancy check (CRC) that is used for error detection.

Figure 2-13 *Ethernet II And IEEE 8023 Frame Formats*

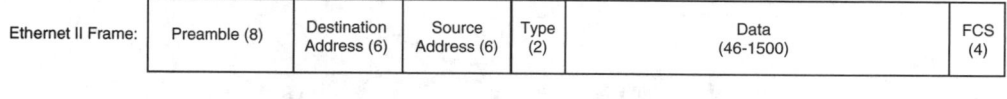
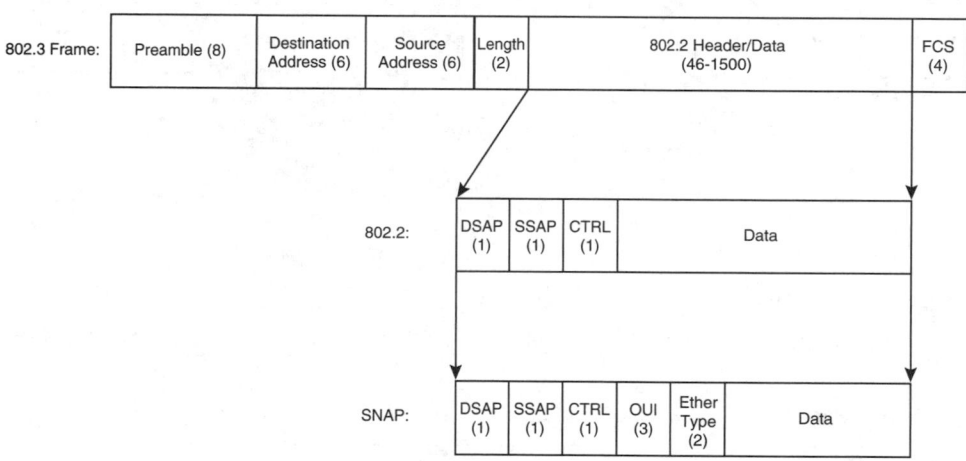

In an 802.3 frame, an 802.2 Logical Link Control (LLC) header usually follows the Length field. The fields of the 802.2 header are as follows:

- **Destination Service Access Point (DSAP)**—A 1-byte field that indicates a service access point (SAP [memory buffer]) on the receiving host.
- **Source Service Access Point (SSAP)**—A 1-byte field that indicates a SAP on the sending host.
- **Control (CTRL)**—A 1-byte field that contains command, response, and sequence number information.

The Subnetwork Access Point (SNAP) header enables proprietary protocols to be carried in the 802.2 LLC frame. If you are using SNAP, the 802.2 DSAP and SSAP are set to 0xAA, and the Control field is set to 0x03. The SNAP header has two additional fields:

- **Organizational Unique Identifier (OUI)**—This 3-byte field is a vendor code.
- **Ether Type**—This 2-byte field indicates the Ether Type.

When an ingress PE receives an Ethernet frame on an attachment circuit, it removes the preamble and FCS, inserts the frame into an L2TPv3 packet, and transmits it to the egress LCCE.

Figure 2-14 shows the transmission of an Ethernet frame over an L2TPv3 pseudowire.

Figure 2-14 *Transmission of an Ethernet Frame over an L2TPv3 Pseudowire*

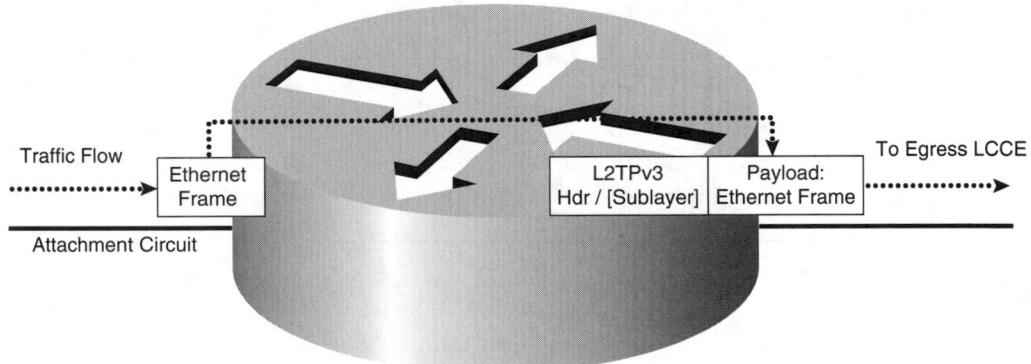

Example 2-10 shows the configuration of Ethernet port transport over an L2TPv3 pseudowire.

Example 2-10 *Configuration of Ethernet Port Transport over an L2TPv3 Pseudowire*

```
!
! On London.PE (line 1)
!
l2tp-class mjlnet.Class.To.Amsterdam
 digest secret mjlnet hash sha
!
pseudowire-class mjlnet.PW.To.Amsterdam
 encapsulation l2tpv3
 protocol l2tpv3 mjlnet.Class.To.Amsterdam
 ip local interface Loopback0
!
interface FastEthernet0/0
 xconnect 172.16.1.3 1001 pw-class mjlnet.PW.To.Amsterdam (line 2)
!
```

```
!
! On Amsterdam.PE (line 3)
!
l2tp-class mjlnet.Class.To.London
 digest secret mjlnet hash sha
!
pseudowire-class mjlnet.PW.To.London
 encapsulation l2tpv3
```

Example 2-10 *Configuration of Ethernet Port Transport over an L2TPv3 Pseudowire (Continued)*

```
 protocol l2tpv3 mjlnet.Class.To.London
 ip local interface Loopback0
 !
 !
 interface FastEthernet0/0
  xconnect 172.16.1.1 1001 pw-class mjlnet.PW.To.London (line 4)
```

Configuration of London.PE is shown beginning in highlighted line 1, and configuration of Amsterdam.PE is shown beginning in highlighted line 3. As you can see, excluding the configuration of the L2TPv3 class and pseudowire class, the only command to configure is **xconnect** *peer-ip-address vcid* **pw-class** *name*.

The **xconnect** command is configured directly under the Ethernet interface (highlighted lines 2 and 4) and is used to bind the interface to an L2TPv3 pseudowire to the specified peer (IP address), with the specified VC ID, and using the configured pseudowire class. The VC ID must be identical on peer LCCEs for a particular pseudowire; otherwise, pseudowire setup will fail.

An Ethernet port L2TPv3 pseudowire can be verified using the **show l2tun session** command, as shown in Example 2-11.

Example 2-11 *Verifying an Ethernet Port L2TPv3 Pseudowire Using the* **show l2tun session** *Command*

```
London.PE#show l2tun session all
 Session Information Total tunnels 1 sessions 1
 Tunnel control packets dropped due to failed digest 0

Session id 63438 is up, tunnel id 52193
Call serial number is 1812600007
Remote tunnel name is Amsterdam.PE
  Internet address is 172.16.1.3
  Session is L2TP signaled (line 1)
  Session state is established, time since change 00:00:45
    0 Packets sent, 0 received
    0 Bytes sent, 0 received
    Receive packets dropped:
      out-of-order:            0
      total:                   0
    Send packets dropped:
      exceeded session MTU:    0
      total:                   0
  Session vcid is 1002
  Session Layer 2 circuit, type is Ethernet, name is FastEthernet0/0 (line 2)
  Circuit state is UP (line 3)
    Remote session id is 18582, remote tunnel id 33034
  DF bit off, ToS reflect disabled, ToS value 0, TTL value 255
  No session cookie information available
  FS cached header information:
    encap size = 24 bytes
    00000000 00000000 00000000 00000000
    00000000 00000000
  Sequencing is off
```

Highlighted line 1 shows that the session (pseudowire) is L2TPv3 signaled, and highlighted lines 2 and 3 show that the pseudowire type is Ethernet port (**Ethernet**) and that the pseudowire state is **UP** (active).

Ethernet VLAN Transport with L2TPv3 Pseudowires

The second method of transporting Ethernet traffic over an L2TPv3 pseudowire is to use Ethernet VLAN transport. When using Ethernet VLAN transport, attachment circuits use an 802.1Q encapsulation, and 802.1Q frames are transported over the L2TPv3 pseudowire.

Figure 2-15 shows the IEEE 802.1Q frame format. Lengths of frame fields, in bytes, are shown in brackets.

Figure 2-15 *IEEE 8021Q Frame Formats*

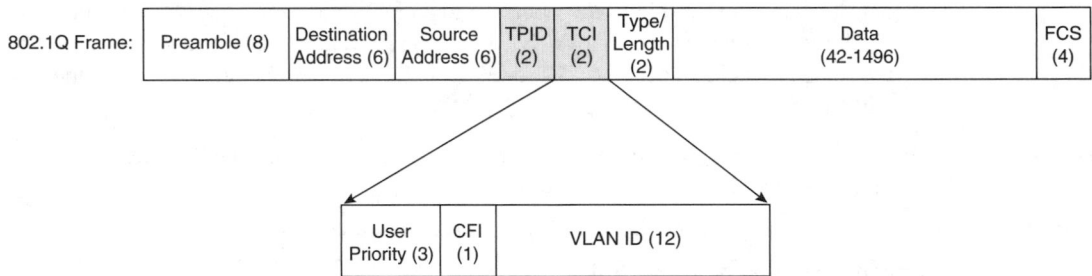

All of the fields in Figure 2-15 have already been described with the exception of the Tag Protocol ID (TPID) and Tag Control Information (TCI) fields:

- **TPID**—This 2-byte field has a fixed value of 0x8100. The purpose of this field is to inform a device that this frame is a tagged (802.1Q) frame.

- **TCI**—This 2-byte field breaks down into three subfields:

  - **User Priority**—A 3-bit field that indicates the priority (QoS) setting for the frame. The operation of this field is defined by IEEE 802.1p.

  - **Canonical Format Indicator (CFI)**—A 1-bit field that when set to 0 indicates that information in the frame is carried in a canonical (Ethernet) format. If set to 1, information is carried in a noncanonical (Token Ring) format.

  - **VLAN ID**—A 12-bit field used to indicate the VLAN.

It is possible for an egress PE router to rewrite the VLAN ID field of 802.1Q frames that it receives over the pseudowire from the ingress PE router. So, for example, frames with a VLAN ID of 100 might be transported over the pseudowire from the ingress PE router, and the egress PE router might be configured to rewrite the VLAN ID to 200 before forwarding them on its local attachment circuit.

Example 2-12 shows the configuration of Ethernet VLAN transport over an L2TPv3 pseudowire.

Example 2-12 *Configuration of Ethernet VLAN Transport over an L2TPv3 Pseudowire*

```
!
! On London.PE (line 1)
!
l2tp-class mjlnet.Class.To.Amsterdam
 digest secret mjlnet hash sha
!
pseudowire-class mjlnet.PW.To.Amsterdam
 encapsulation l2tpv3
 protocol l2tpv3 mjlnet.Class.To.Amsterdam
 ip local interface Loopback0
!
!
!
!
interface FastEthernet0/0
 no ip address
 no ip directed-broadcast
!
interface FastEthernet0/0.1 (line 2)
 encapsulation dot1Q 200 (line 3)
 xconnect 172.16.1.3 1002 pw-class mjlnet.PW.To.Amsterdam (line 4)
!
!
```

```
!
! On Amsterdam.PE (line 5)
!
l2tp-class mjlnet.Class.To.London
 digest secret mjlnet hash sha
!
!
pseudowire-class mjlnet.PW.To.London
 encapsulation l2tpv3
 protocol l2tpv3 mjlnet.Class.To.London
 ip local interface Loopback0
!
!
!
interface FastEthernet0/0
 no ip address
 no ip directed-broadcast
!
interface FastEthernet0/0.1 (line 6)
 encapsulation dot1Q 200 (line 7)
 xconnect 172.16.1.1 1002 pw-class mjlnet.PW.To.London (line 8)
!
```

Highlighted lines 2 to 4 show the relevant configuration for Ethernet VLAN transport on London.PE.

In highlighted line 2, interface Fast Ethernet 0/0.1 is created, and in highlighted line 3, IEEE 802.1Q encapsulation is enabled for VLAN 200 using the **encapsulation dot1Q** *vlan-id* command.

Next, in highlighted line 4, the **xconnect** *peer-ip-address vcid* **pw-class** *name* command is used to bind the interface to a pseudowire to the specified peer (172.16.1.3, Amsterdam.PE), with the specified VC ID (1002), and using the specified pseudowire class (mjlnet.PW.To. Amsterdam).

Highlighted lines 6 to 8 show the corresponding configuration for Amsterdam.PE. In highlighted line 6, interface Fast Ethernet 0/0.1 is created. Then in highlighted lines 7 and 8, IEEE 802.1Q encapsulation for VLAN 200 is configured, and the **xconnect** command is used to bind the interface to a pseudowire to London.PE (172.16.1.1), with VC ID 1002, and using pseudowire class mjlnet.PW.To.London.

Notice that the VLAN ID specified using the **encapsulation dot1q** *vlan-id* command is the same at both ends of the pseudowire (VLAN ID 200, see highlighted lines 3 and 7), and so no VLAN ID rewrite by the egress LCCE is necessary in this example.

As shown in Example 2-13, verification of an Ethernet VLAN pseudowire is again achieved via the **show l2tun session** command.

Example 2-13 *Verification of an Ethernet VLAN Pseudowire Using the* **show l2tun session** *Command*

```
London.PE#show l2tun session all
 Session Information Total tunnels 1 sessions 1
 Tunnel control packets dropped due to failed digest 0

Session id 20476 is up, tunnel id 22418
Call serial number is 3243000000
Remote tunnel name is Amsterdam.PE
  Internet address is 172.16.1.3
  Session is L2TP signaled (line 1)
  Session state is established, time since change 00:02:26
    0 Packets sent, 0 received
    0 Bytes sent, 0 received
    Receive packets dropped:
      out-of-order:             0
      total:                    0
    Send packets dropped:
      exceeded session MTU:     0
      total:                    0
  Session vcid is 1002
  Session Layer 2 circuit, type is Ethernet Vlan, name is FastEthernet0/0.1:200 (line 2)
  Circuit state is UP (line 3)
    Remote session id is 31207, remote tunnel id 28218
  DF bit off, ToS reflect disabled, ToS value 0, TTL value 255
  No session cookie information available
  FS cached header information:
    encap size = 24 bytes
    00000000 00000000 00000000 00000000
    00000000 00000000
  Sequencing is off
```

As you can see in highlighted line 1, the pseudowire is L2TPv3 signaled. Highlighted line 2 and 3 show that the pseudowire type is Ethernet VLAN, and that the pseudowire is in an UP state.

Transporting HDLC, PPP, and X.25 over L2TPv3 Pseudowires

Another encapsulation type that is supported for transport over L2TPv3 pseudowires is HDLC, including HDLC-like protocols such as the PPP and X.25).

HDLC Traffic Transport over L2TPv3

Figure 2-16 shows a Cisco HDLC frame. Note that field lengths (in bytes) are shown in brackets in Figure 2-16.

Figure 2-16 *Cisco HDLC Frame*

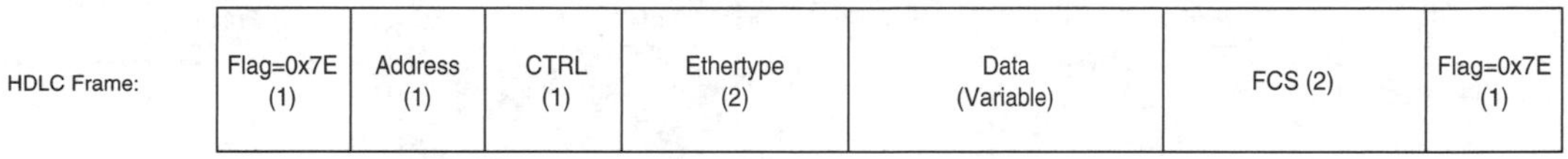

HDLC Frame:

Flag=0x7E (1)	Address (1)	CTRL (1)	Ethertype (2)	Data (Variable)	FCS (2)	Flag=0x7E (1)

The fields of the Cisco HDLC frame are as follows:

- **Flag**—This 1-byte field contains a value of 0x7E and indicates the start of the HDLC frame.
- **Address**—This 1-byte field can contain the following values:
  - Unicast frame, 0x0F
  - Broadcast frame, 0x80
  - Padded frame, 0x40
  - Compressed frame, 0x20
- **Control (CTRL)**—This 1-byte field has a value of 0 and is not checked on reception.
- **Ethertype**—This 2-byte field contains a standard Ethernet protocol type. This field is not contained within the standard (ISO/IEC 13239) HDLC frame.
- **Data (Information)**—This variable-length field carries higher-layer protocol information.
- **Frame Check Sequence (FCS)**—This 2- or 4-byte field carries error checking information.
- **Flags**—This 1-byte field carries a value of 0x7E, and indicates the end of the HDLC frame.

As illustrated in Figure 2-17, when an ingress LCCE receives an HDLC frame on an attachment circuit, it encapsulates the frame in an L2TPv3 packet and transmits that packet to the egress LCCE.

Although the ingress LCCE encapsulates each HDLC frame in an L2TPv3 packet, certain parts of the HDLC frame are not sent. The Flags fields, together with the FCS (see Figure 2-16) are discarded by the ingress LCCE, and any bit stuffing is undone prior to the encapsulation of an HDLC frame in L2TPv3.

The egress LCCE removes each HDLC frame from the L2TPv3 packets received from the ingress LCCE and reconstitutes the Flags fields and FCS before sending each HDLC frame on the attachment circuit.

Figure 2-17 *Ingress LCCE Encapsulates Each HDLC Frame in a Separate L2TPv3 Packet and Transmits It to the Egress LCCE*

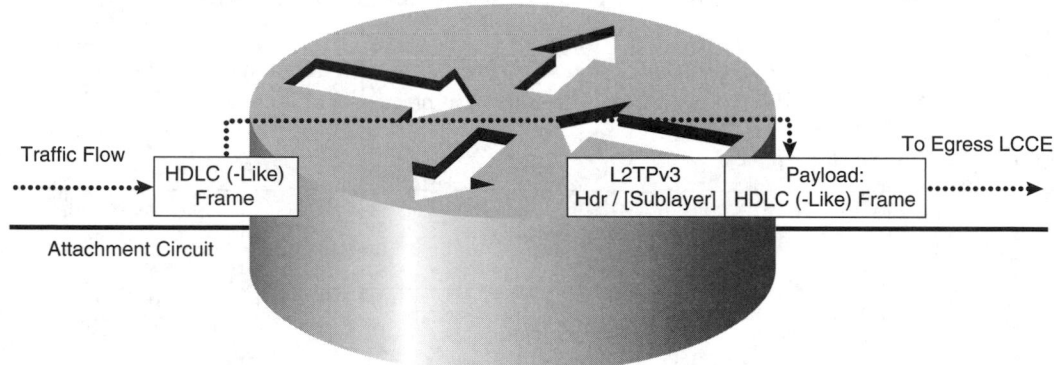

Example 2-14 shows the configuration of HDLC (or HDLC-like) traffic transport over an L2TPv3 pseudowire.

Example 2-14 *Configuration of HDLC Traffic Transport over an L2TPv3 Pseudowire*

```
!
! On London.PE (line 1)
!
l2tp-class mjlnet.Class.To.Amsterdam
 digest secret mjlnet hash sha
!
pseudowire-class mjlnet.PW.To.Amsterdam
 encapsulation l2tpv3
 protocol l2tpv3 mjlnet.Class.To.Amsterdam
 ip local interface Loopback0
!
interface Serial4/0
 no ip address
 no ip directed-broadcast
 no cdp enable
 xconnect 172.16.1.3 1001 pw-class mjlnet.PW.To.Amsterdam (line 2)
!

!
! On Amsterdam.PE (line 3)
!
l2tp-class mjlnet.Class.To.London
 digest secret mjlnet hash sha
!
!
pseudowire-class mjlnet.PW.To.London
 encapsulation l2tpv3
 protocol l2tpv3 mjlnet.Class.To.London
 ip local interface Loopback0
```

Example 2-14 *Configuration of HDLC Traffic Transport over an L2TPv3 Pseudowire (Continued)*

```
!
!
interface Serial4/1
 no ip address
 no ip directed-broadcast
 no cdp enable
 xconnect 172.16.1.1 1001 pw-class mjlnet.PW.To.London (line 4)
!
```

The configuration for HDLC traffic transport is simple.

The relevant configuration for London.PE is shown in highlighted line 2, and the relevant configuration for Amsterdam.PE is shown in highlighted line 4.

As you can see, the only required command (apart from the standard L2TP class and pseudowire class configuration) is **xconnect** *peer-ip-address vcid* **pw-class** *name*. This command binds the serial interface to an L2TPv3 pseudowire with the specified VC ID, to the specified peer, using the specified pseudowire class.

As shown in Example 2-15, you can use the **show l2tun session** command to verify HDLC L2TPv3 pseudowires.

Example 2-15 *Verifying HDLC L2TPv3 Pseudowires Using the **show l2tun session** Command*

```
London.PE#show l2tun session all
 Session Information Total tunnels 1 sessions 1
 Tunnel control packets dropped due to failed digest 0

Session id 9303 is up, tunnel id 56029
Call serial number is 3616600000
Remote tunnel name is Amsterdam.PE
  Internet address is 172.16.1.3
  Session is L2TP signaled (line 1)
  Session state is established, time since change 03:20:04
    1396 Packets sent, 1401 received
    95030 Bytes sent, 86705 received
    Receive packets dropped:
      out-of-order:           0
      total:                  0
    Send packets dropped:
      exceeded session MTU:   0
      total:                  0
  Session vcid is 1001
  Session Layer 2 circuit, type is HDLC, name is Serial4/0 (line 2)
  Circuit state is UP (line 3)
    Remote session id is 8661, remote tunnel id 21530
  DF bit off, ToS reflect disabled, ToS value 0, TTL value 255
  No session cookie information available
  FS cached header information:
    encap size = 24 bytes
    00000000 00000000 00000000 00000000
    00000000 00000000
  Sequencing is off
```

Highlighted line 1 shows that the session (pseudowire) is L2TPv3 signaled, and highlighted line 2 and 3 show that the pseudowire type is HDLC and the pseudowire is in an UP (active) state.

PPP Traffic Transport over L2TPv3

Figure 2-18 shows a PPP frame (PPP in HDLC-like framing). You may like to compare the PPP frame in Figures 2-18 with the Cisco HDLC frame in Figure 2-16.

Figure 2-18 *PPP Frame (PPP in HDLC-Like Framing)*

PPP Frame:

Flag=0x7E (1)	Address (1)	CTRL (1)	Protocol (1 or 2)	Information (Variable)	Padding (Variable)	FCS (2 or 4)	Flag=0x7E (1)

PPP in HDLC-like framing can be described as follows:

- **Flag**—Has a value of 0x7E and indicates the start of the frame.

- **Address**—This 1-byte field contains the All-Stations address (0xFF).

- **Control (CTRL)**—This 1-byte field contains the value 0x03 (Unnumbered Information with Poll/Final bit set to 0).

- **Protocol**—A 1- or 2-byte field that identifies the datagram/protocol (such as the Link Control Protocol [LCP], CHAP) contained in the Information field.

- **Information**—This variable-length field (0 or more) contains the datagram for the protocol identified in the Protocol field.

- **Padding**—An optional field that is used to pad the Information field up to the Maximum Receive Unit (MRU).

- **Frame Check Sequence (FCS)**—A 2-byte field containing a checksum used for error detection.

- **Flag**—This 1-byte field contains the value 0x7E. This field is used to indicate the end of the frame.

One important fact to understand about PPP transport over L2TPv3 pseudowires is that the LCCEs do not participate in PPP negotiation. Instead, CE devices at the either end of the attachment circuits negotiate PPP between themselves.

Figure 2-19 illustrates PPP negotiation when transporting PPP over an L2TPv3 pseudowire. In Figure 2-19, PPP negotiation takes place between mjlnet.London.CE and mjlnet.Amsterdam.CE. London.PE and Amsterdam.PE do not participate in PPP negotiation.

Encapsulation of PPP frames by the ingress LCCE and decapsulation by the egress LCCE are as described in the section "HDLC Traffic Transport over L2TPv3" on page 53 (see also Figure 2-17).

Figure 2-19 *PPP Negotiation When Transporting PPP over an L2TPv3 Pseudowire*

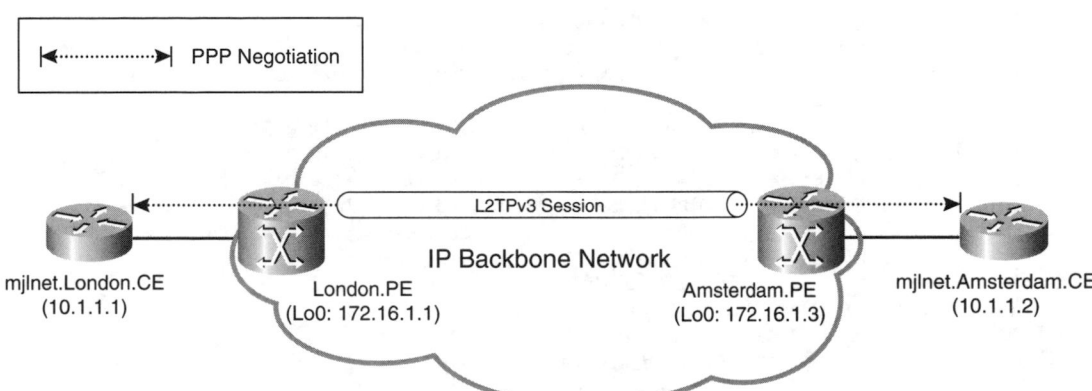

The configuration and verification of PPP traffic transport over L2TPv3 are exactly as described for HDLC traffic transport in the section titled "HDLC Traffic Transport over L2TPv3" on page 53.

NOTE   Configuring a PPP pseudowire (rather than an HDLC pseudowire) to transport PPP traffic is also a possibility.

The configuration of a PPP pseudowire is as shown in Example 2-14, with the one exception that the **encapsulation ppp** command must be configured on the attachment circuits (interfaces serial 4/0 and 4/1 on London.PE and Amsterdam.PE respectively in Example 2-14).

Example 2-16 shows PPP negotiation between peers over the HDLC L2TPv3 pseudowire.

Example 2-16 *PPP Negotiation Between Peers over the HDLC L2TPv3 Pseudowire*

```
mjlnet.London.CE#debug ppp negotiation
PPP protocol negotiation debugging is on
mjlnet.London.CE#
00:18:12: %LINK-3-UPDOWN: Interface Serial0, changed state to up (line 1)
00:18:12: Se0 PPP: Treating connection as a dedicated line
00:18:12: Se0 PPP: Phase is ESTABLISHING, Active Open (line 2)
00:18:12: Se0 LCP: O CONFREQ [Closed] id 32 len 15
00:18:12: Se0 LCP:    AuthProto CHAP (0x0305C22305)
00:18:12: Se0 LCP:    MagicNumber 0x001CE60C (0x0506001CE60C)
00:18:12: Se0 LCP: I CONFREQ [REQsent] id 52 len 15
00:18:12: Se0 LCP:    AuthProto CHAP (0x0305C22305)
00:18:12: Se0 LCP:    MagicNumber 0x078A1107 (0x0506078A1107)
00:18:12: Se0 LCP: O CONFACK [REQsent] id 52 len 15
00:18:12: Se0 LCP:    AuthProto CHAP (0x0305C22305)
00:18:12: Se0 LCP:    MagicNumber 0x078A1107 (0x0506078A1107)
```

continues

Example 2-16 *PPP Negotiation Between Peers over the HDLC L2TPv3 Pseudowire (Continued)*

```
00:18:12: Se0 LCP: I CONFACK [ACKsent] id 32 len 15
00:18:12: Se0 LCP:    AuthProto CHAP (0x0305C22305)
00:18:12: Se0 LCP:    MagicNumber 0x001CE60C (0x0506001CE60C)
00:18:12: Se0 LCP: State is Open
00:18:12: Se0 PPP: Phase is AUTHENTICATING, by both (line 3)
00:18:12: Se0 CHAP: O CHALLENGE id 18 len 39 from "mjlnet.London.CE" (line 4)
00:18:12: Se0 CHAP: I CHALLENGE id 7 len 36 from "mjlnet.Amsterdam.CE" (line 5)
00:18:12: Se0 CHAP: O RESPONSE id 7 len 39 from "mjlnet.London.CE" (line 6)
00:18:12: Se0 CHAP: I RESPONSE id 18 len 36 from "mjlnet.Amsterdam.CE" (line 7)
00:18:12: Se0 CHAP: O SUCCESS id 18 len 4 (line 8)
00:18:12: Se0 CHAP: I SUCCESS id 7 len 4 (line 9)
00:18:12: Se0 PPP: Phase is UP (line 10)
00:18:12: Se0 IPCP: O CONFREQ [Closed] id 5 len 10
00:18:12: Se0 IPCP:    Address 10.1.1.1 (0x0306C0A80101)
00:18:12: Se0 CDPCP: O CONFREQ [Closed] id 5 len 4
00:18:12: Se0 IPCP: I CONFREQ [REQsent] id 5 len 10
00:18:12: Se0 IPCP:    Address 10.1.1.2 (0x0306C0A80102)
00:18:12: Se0 IPCP: O CONFACK [REQsent] id 5 len 10
00:18:12: Se0 IPCP:    Address 10.1.1.2 (0x0306C0A80102)
00:18:12: Se0 CDPCP: I CONFREQ [REQsent] id 5 len 4
00:18:12: Se0 CDPCP: O CONFACK [REQsent] id 5 len 4
00:18:12: Se0 IPCP: I CONFACK [ACKsent] id 5 len 10
00:18:12: Se0 IPCP:    Address 10.1.1.1 (0x0306C0A80101)
00:18:12: Se0 IPCP: State is Open
00:18:12: Se0 CDPCP: I CONFACK [ACKsent] id 5 len 4
00:18:12: Se0 CDPCP: State is Open
00:18:12: Se0 IPCP: Install route to 10.1.1.2
00:18:13: %LINEPROTO-5-UPDOWN: Line protocol on Interface Serial0, changed state to
    up (line 11)

mjlnet.London.CE#
```

In highlighted line 1, interface serial 0 changes state to UP on mjlnet.London.CE. The PPP phase changes to ESTABLISHING in highlighted line 2. LCP negotiation then takes place; and in highlighted line 3, the PPP phase changes to AUTHENTICATING—PPP authentication is about to begin. CHAP authentication now takes place (see highlighted lines 4 to 9).

Normally, PPP authentication is not required for (virtual) leased lines, but in Example 2-16, the CHAP CHALLENGE and RESPONSE messages clearly show that PPP negotiation takes place between mjlnet.London.CE and mjlnet.Amsterdam.CE (and does not involve the LCCEs). In highlighted line 10, the PPP phase changes to UP, and Network Control Protocol (NCP) negotiation (including IP Control Protocol [IPCP] negotiation) begins. When NCP negotiation is complete, the line protocol on interface serial 0 changes state to UP (highlighted line 11).

X.25 Traffic Transport over L2TPv3   If you are familiar with X.25, you will probably not be surprised to learn that an HDLC L2TPv3 pseudowire can also be used to transport X.25 traffic.

X.25 is an ITU standard and operates at Layers 1, 2, and 3 of the OSI model, with X.21, X.21bis, EIA/TIA-232/449/530, or G.703 commonly used at Layer 1, Link Access Procedure Balanced (LAPB) used at Layer 2, and the Packet Layer Protocol (PLP) used at Layer 3.

X.25 has, to a great extent, been replaced by Frame Relay and other packet/cell-switched technologies. But if you do have an island or two of X.25 remaining in your network, you can transport it over your IP backbone using L2TPv3 pseudowires.

HDLC L2TPv3 pseudowires can be used to transport LAPB frames, and this frame format is illustrated in Figure 2-20.

As a side note, if you compare the LAPB frame shown in Figure 2-20 with the Cisco HDLC frame shown in Figure 2-16, it should be pretty evident that the LAPB frame format is a variant of the HDLC frame format.

Figure 2-20 *LAPB Frame*

LAPB Frame:

Flag=0x7E (1)	Address (1)	CTRL (1 or 2)	Information (Variable)	FCS (2)	Flag=0x7E (1)

The LAPB frame fields can be described as follows:

- **Flag**—A 1-byte field contains the value 0x7E. This field indicates the start of the frame.

- **Address**—This 1-byte field indicates DTE/DCE Command/Response.

- **Control**—This 1- or 2-byte field indicates one of three LAPB frame types (Unnumbered, Supervisory, or Information).

- **Information**—This variable-length field contains the PLP packet.

- **Frame Check Sequence (FCS)**—A 2-byte checksum.

- **Flag**—This 1-byte field contains the value 0x7E. It indicates the end of the frame.

It is worth noting that the LCCEs do not participate in X.25—they are neither X.25 (LAPB) DCEs nor DTEs but simply forward LAPB frames over the pseudowire between attachment circuits.

Configuration and verification of X.25 traffic transport over L2TPv3 is again exactly as described in the section, "HDLC Traffic Transport over L2TPv3."

Example 2-17 shows the output of the **debug x25 all** command when ping (ICMP Echo [Echo/Echo Reply]) is sent over the L2TPv3 pseudowire.

Example 2-17 *Output of the* **debug x25 all** *Command When ping Is Sent over the L2TPv3 Pseudowire*

```
mjlnet.London.CE#debug x25 all
X.25 packet debugging is on

mjlnet.London.CE#ping 10.1.1.2
Type escape sequence to abort.
Sending 5, 100-byte ICMP Echos to 10.1.1.2, timeout is 2 seconds:
!!!!!
Success rate is 100 percent (5/5), round-trip min/avg/max = 140/146/168 ms
mjlnet.London.CE#
00:16:23: Serial0: X.25 O D1 Data (103) 8 lci 1024 PS 2 PR 2 (line 1)
00:16:23: Serial0: X.25 I D1 RR (3) 8 lci 1024 PR 3 (line 2)
00:16:23: Serial0: X.25 I D1 Data (103) 8 lci 1024 PS 2 PR 3 (line 3)
00:16:23: Serial0: X.25 O D1 Data (103) 8 lci 1024 PS 3 PR 3
00:16:23: Serial0: X.25 I D1 Data (103) 8 lci 1024 PS 3 PR 4
00:16:23: Serial0: X.25 O D1 Data (103) 8 lci 1024 PS 4 PR 4
00:16:24: Serial0: X.25 I D1 Data (103) 8 lci 1024 PS 4 PR 5
00:16:24: Serial0: X.25 O D1 Data (103) 8 lci 1024 PS 5 PR 5
00:16:24: Serial0: X.25 I D1 Data (103) 8 lci 1024 PS 5 PR 6
00:16:24: Serial0: X.25 O D1 Data (103) 8 lci 1024 PS 6 PR 6
00:16:24: Serial0: X.25 I D1 Data (103) 8 lci 1024 PS 6 PR 7
mjlnet.London.CE#
```

Highlighted line 1 shows an outbound (**O**) data packet. The modulo of the VC is shown (**8**), together with the Logical Channel Identifier (LCI [the VC number], **1024**). This packet contains an ICMP Echo. The packet send (PS) and packet receive (PR) sequence numbers are also shown (2 and 2, respectively).

In highlighted line 2, you can see an inbound (**I**) Receiver Ready (**RR**) message. This serves as an acknowledgment of a frame, and indicates that the peer is ready to receive the next frame in the sequence.

Finally, in highlighted line 3, you can see an inbound data packet. This contains an ICMP Echo Reply.

Deploying Frame-Relay L2TPv3 Pseudowires

So, now to Frame Relay. Frame Relay can be transported over L2TPv3 in two ways:

- **Using Frame Relay DLCI-to-DLCI permanent virtual circuit (PVC) pseudowires**—When you are using this method, LCCEs participate in the Local Management Interface (LMI) and perform Frame Relay switching.

- **Using Frame Relay PVC trunk connections**—When you are using this method, LCCEs do not participate in LMI and transparently forward Frame Relay frames.

Before discussing these two methods of transporting Frame Relay over L2TPv3 pseudowires, it is a good idea to take a brief look at the basics of Frame Relay operation and frame formats.

Frame Relay Operation and Frame Formats

Frame Relay is a packet-switching technology that provides Layer 2 connectivity over a WAN.

As illustrated in Figure 2-21, the Frame Relay frame can range from 2 to 4 bytes in length.

Figure 2-21 *Frame Relay Frame*

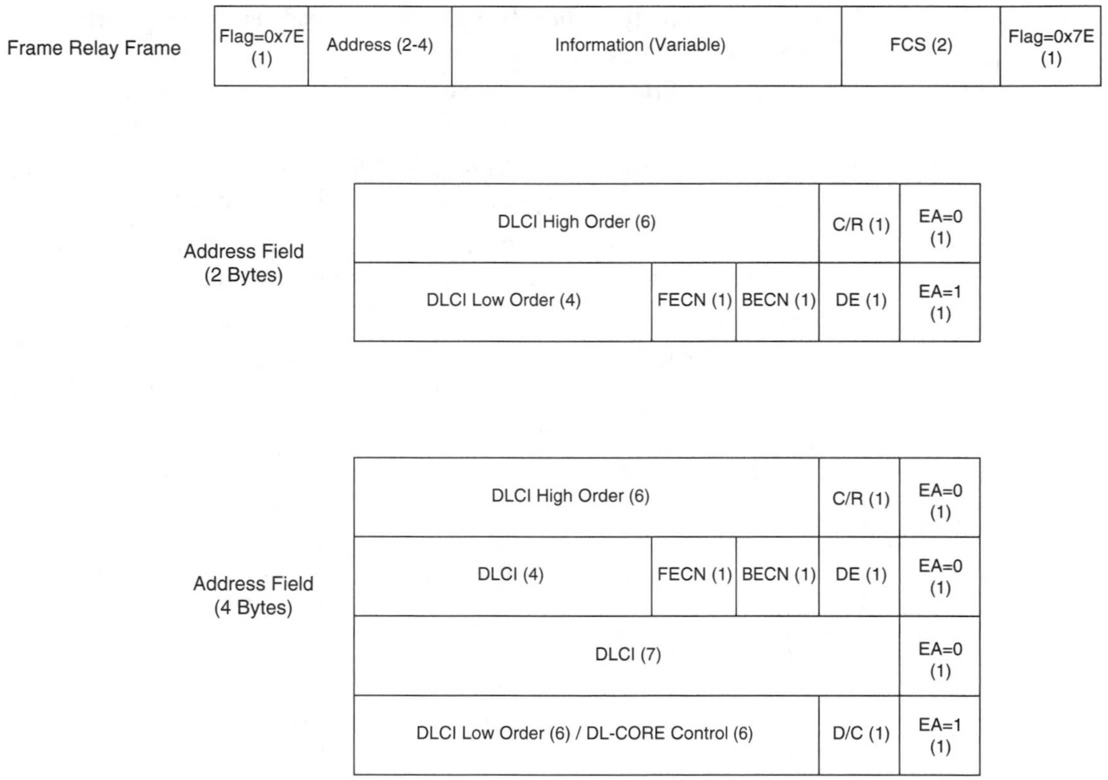

Frame Relay Frame	Flag=0x7E (1)	Address (2-4)	Information (Variable)	FCS (2)	Flag=0x7E (1)

Address Field (2 Bytes)

DLCI High Order (6)		C/R (1)	EA=0 (1)
DLCI Low Order (4)	FECN (1) BECN (1)	DE (1)	EA=1 (1)

Address Field (4 Bytes)

DLCI High Order (6)		C/R (1)	EA=0 (1)
DLCI (4)	FECN (1) BECN (1)	DE (1)	EA=0 (1)
DLCI (7)			EA=0 (1)
DLCI Low Order (6) / DL-CORE Control (6)		D/C (1)	EA=1 (1)

At the top of Figure 2-21, you can see the Frame Relay frame format, comprising five fields:

- **Flag**—This 1-byte has a fixed value of 0x7E and indicates the beginning of the Frame Relay frame.

- **Address**—This can be 2, 3, or 4 bytes in length (ITU Q.922), depending on whether extended addressing is used.

- **Information**—This variable-length field carries higher-layer protocol information.

- **FCS**—This 2-byte frame check sequence is used for error control.

- **Flag**—This 1-byte flag indicates the end of the Frame Relay frame. Its value is fixed (0x7E).

As mentioned, the Address field can be 2, 3, or 4 bytes, and L2TPv3 pseudowires support the transport of Frame Relay frames with Address fields of 2 or 4 bytes in length (per Frame Relay Forum [FRF] specifications).

The formats of the 2- and 4-byte Address fields are also shown in Figure 2-21. The Address field comprises the following:

- **Data Link Connection Identifier (DLCI)**—This uniquely identifies the Frame Relay connection on the local link.

- **Command/Response (C/R)**—This may be used by higher-layer protocols or services.

- **Forward Explicit Congestion Notification (FECN)**—When set to 1, this bit is used to indicate to the receiver that congestion was experienced in the network.

- **Backward Explicit Congestion Notification (BECN)**—When set to 1, this bit is used to indicate to the sender that congestion was experienced in the network.

- **Discard Eligibility (DE)**—When set to 1, this bit indicates that if congestion is experienced in the network, this frame is eligible to be dropped.

- **Extended Address (EA)**—If set to 1, this bit setting allows extended addressing to be used (the Address field can be extended to 2, 3, or 4 bytes).

- **Data/Control (D/C)**—Indicates the existence of the DLCI or DL-core data or control field.

Now on to the main theme of this section—how to transport Frame Relay traffic over L2TPv3 pseudowires. As previously mentioned, there are two ways to transport Frame Relay over L2TPv3:

- Using DLCI-to-DLCI switching

- Using Frame Relay trunks

The sections that follow examine these methods in more detail.

Frame Relay Traffic Transport over L2TPv3 Using DLCI-to-DLCI Switching

Figure 2-22 illustrates Frame Relay transport over L2TPv3 using DLCI-to-DLCI connections. In Figure 2-22, the ingress LCCE receives Frame Relay frames on the attachment circuit, and places each of those frames in the payload of a separate L2TPv3 packet before forwarding them to the egress LCCE. The egress LCCE performs the same process in reverse—it removes each Frame Relay frame from the payload of the L2TPv3 packet and forwards it on its attachment circuit.

It is important to note that before the ingress LCCE places a Frame Relay frame into an L2TPv3 packet, it removes the Flags fields and the FCS (see Figure 2-21), as well as undoing any bit stuffing.

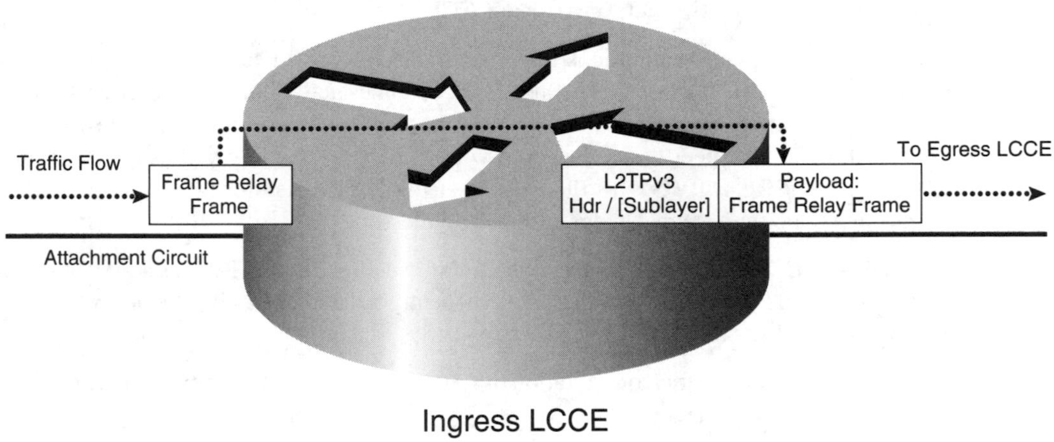

Figure 2-22 *Frame Relay Transport over L2TPv3 Using DLCI-to-DLCI Switching*

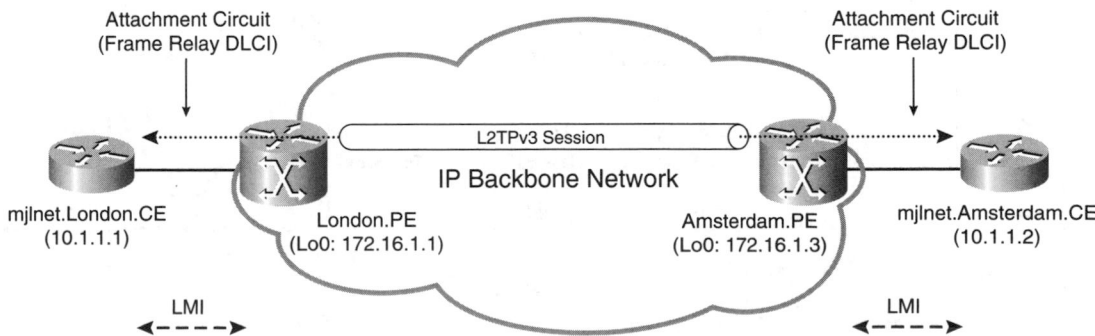

Ingress LCCE

Another important thing to note about the encapsulation of a Frame Relay frame in L2TPv3 is the default sublayer. There is no service-specific sublayer for Frame Relay, and the default sublayer is only used if sequencing is configured. If sequencing is not configured, no sublayer is sent with the L2TPv3 packet.

The rest of the encapsulation is standard and consists of the IP header specified protocol 115 (L2TPv3), the L2TPv3 session header, and the payload containing the Frame Relay frame itself.

If you are transporting Frame Relay traffic using a DLCI-to-DLCI connection with L2TPv3, the Local Management Interface (LMI) is terminated on the local LCCE, as illustrated in Figure 2-23.

Figure 2-23 *LMI Is Terminated on the Local LCCE*

As shown in Figure 2-23, the LMI functions between London.CE and London.LCCE, as well as Amsterdam.CE and Amsterdam.LCCE.

Before finishing this section, it is important to discuss circuit status signaling. When a Frame Relay PVC is created (and the circuit becomes active) on an LCCE, an ICRQ message is sent to the peer LCCE signaling creation of a corresponding L2TPv3 session (pseudowire). The peer LCCE responds with an ICRP (assuming that its local attachment circuit Frame Relay PVC is also active). When the L2TPv3 session is established, an LCCE can signal a circuit status change using a SLI message.

Finally, an LCCE can tear down a Frame Relay pseudowire (L2TPv3 session) using a CDN message (see Figure 2-9) if a PVC is permanently deleted or has been inactive for an extended period of time.

Example 2-18 shows the configuration of Frame Relay traffic transport over L2TPv3 using DLCI-to-DLCI connections.

Example 2-18 *Configuration of Frame Relay Traffic Transport over L2TPv3 Using DLCI-to-DLCI Connections*

```
!
! On London.PE (line 1)
!
frame-relay switching (line 2)
!
l2tp-class mjlnet.Class.To.Amsterdam
 digest secret mjlnet hash sha
!
pseudowire-class mjlnet.PW.To.Amsterdam
 encapsulation l2tpv3
 protocol l2tpv3 mjlnet.Class.To.Amsterdam
 ip local interface Loopback0
!
!
interface Serial4/2
 encapsulation frame-relay (line 3)
 frame-relay intf-type dce (line 4)
!
!
connect Amsterdam.PVC Serial4/2 100 l2transport (line 5)
 xconnect 172.16.1.3 2001 pw-class mjlnet.PW.To.Amsterdam (line 6)
!
!
```
```
!
! On Amsterdam.PE (line 7)
!
frame-relay switching (line 8)
!
l2tp-class mjlnet.Class.To.London
 digest secret mjlnet hash sha
!
```

Example 2-18 *Configuration of Frame Relay Traffic Transport over L2TPv3 Using DLCI-to-DLCI Connections (Continued)*

```
pseudowire-class mjlnet.PW.To.London
 encapsulation l2tpv3
 protocol l2tpv3 mjlnet.Class.To.London
 ip local interface Loopback0
!
!
interface Serial3/2
 encapsulation frame-relay (line 9)
 frame-relay intf-type dce (line 10)
!
connect London.PVC Serial3/2 200 l2transport (line 11)
 xconnect 172.16.1.1 2001 pw-class mjlnet.PW.To.London (line 12)
!
!
```

Highlighted lines 1 to 6 show the configuration of a Frame Relay DLCI-to-DLCI switching L2TPv3 pseudowire on London.PE. In highlighted line 2, the **frame-relay switching** command is used to configure the switching of Frame Relay PVCs. The **encapsulation frame-relay** command in highlighted line 3 is then used to configure Frame Relay encapsulation on interface serial 4/2 (the local attachment circuit). Next, the **frame-relay interface-type [dce | dte | nni]** command is used to configure the Frame Relay interface type, which in this example is DCE.

Highlighted line 5 shows the **connection** *name* **serial** *interface-number dlci* **l2transport** command. This command is used to configure a connection name for the Frame Relay DLCI-to-DLCI switching L2TPv3 pseudowire and specify the corresponding serial interface number and DLCI.

The **xconnect** *peer-ip-address vcid* **pw-class** *name* command is then used to bind the serial interface and DLCI to an L2TPv3 pseudowire with the specified VC ID, to the specified peer, using the specified pseudowire class.

Highlighted lines 7 to 12 show the configuration of the other end of the Frame Relay DLCI-to-DLCI switching L2TPv3 pseudowire on Amsterdam.PE.

You can verify Frame Relay DLCI-to-DLCI switching L2TPv3 pseudowires using the **show l2tun session** command (see Example 2-19).

Example 2-19 *Verifying Frame Relay DLCI-to-DLCI Switching L2TPv3 Pseudowires Using the* **show l2tun session** *Command*

```
London.PE#show l2tun session all
 Session Information Total tunnels 1 sessions 1
 Tunnel control packets dropped due to failed digest 0

 Session id 9305 is up, tunnel id 7047
 Call serial number is 2591400001
```

continues

Example 2-19 *Verifying Frame Relay DLCI-to-DLCI Switching L2TPv3 Pseudowires Using the* **show**
l2tun session *Command (Continued)*

```
Remote tunnel name is Amsterdam.PE
  Internet address is 172.16.1.3
  Session is L2TP signaled (line 1)
  Session state is established, time since change 02:46:42
    8 Packets sent, 5 received
    2552 Bytes sent, 150 received
    Receive packets dropped:
      out-of-order:          0
      total:                 0
    Send packets dropped:
      exceeded session MTU:  0
      total:                 0
  Session vcid is 2001
  Session Layer 2 circuit, type is Frame Relay, name is Serial4/2:100 (line 2)
  Circuit state is UP (line 3)
    Remote session id is 35698, remote tunnel id 30881
  DF bit off, ToS reflect disabled, ToS value 0, TTL value 255
  No session cookie information available
  FS cached header information:
    encap size = 24 bytes
    00000000 00000000 00000000 00000000
    00000000 00000000
  Sequencing is off
```

Highlighted line 1 shows that the pseudowire is L2TPv3 signaled. In highlighted line 2, you
can see that the pseudowire is a Frame Relay DLCI-to-DLCI switching pseudowire and that
interface serial 4/2 and DLCI 100 is bound to this pseudowire. Highlighted line 3 shows
that the pseudowire is in an UP (active) state.

Frame Relay Traffic Transport over L2TPv3 Using Frame Relay Trunks   The
second method of transporting Frame Relay traffic over L2TPv3 is to use a Frame Relay
trunk. In this case, the LMI is not terminated at the local LCCE but is instead active between
the CE devices connected to each LCCE (see Figure 2-24).

The configuration of a Frame Relay trunk does not involve any special configuration. In
fact, the configuration is *identical* to that for an HDLC pseudowire (see Example 2-14 on
page 54).

If you are wondering why an HDLC pseudowire can be used for the transport of Frame
Relay traffic, you might remember that an HDLC pseudowire can transport HDLC and
HDLC-like frames—Frame Relay frames fall into the "HDLC-like" category.

Implementing ATM Pseudowires

ATM is a widely deployed method of provisioning WAN connectivity. Service providers
can use L2TPv3 pseudowires to converge their legacy ATM networks with their IP
networks.

Figure 2-24 *LMI Is Not Terminated at the Local LCCE*

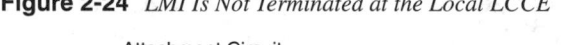

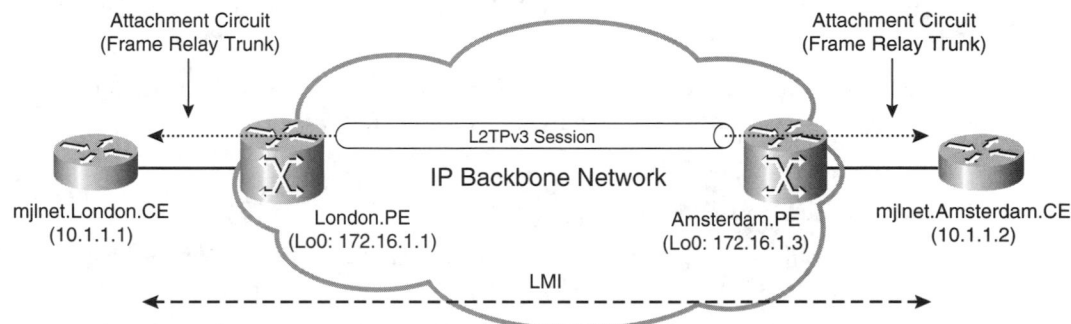

Before discussing the transport of ATM traffic over an L2TPv3 pseudowire, it is a good idea to take a brief look at how ATM operates.

ATM Operation, Cell, PDU, and SDU Formats   The basic operation of ATM is best understood by first examining the ATM reference model shown in Figure 2-25.

Figure 2-25 *ATM Protocol Reference Model*

Higher Layers		
AAL Layer	1. Convergence Sublayer (CS) 2. Segmentation and Reassembly (SAR) Sublayer	
ATM Layer		
Physical Layer	1. Transmission Convergence (TC) Sublayer 2. Physical Medium Dependent (PMD) Sublayer	

As you can see from looking at Figure 2-25, ATM operates at the physical (PHY) layer, the ATM layer, the ATM Adaption Layer (AAL), and higher layers.

The physical layer is split into two sublayers:

- The Physical Medium Dependent (PMD) sublayer

- The Transmission Convergence (TC) sublayer.

The PMD sublayer describes how ATM cells will be transmitted and received over a particular physical transmission medium.

The TC sublayer is responsible for breaking ATM cells into a bit stream for transmission by the PMD sublayer, as well as receiving a bit stream from the PMD sublayer and forming this bit stream back into ATM cells. The TC sublayer is also responsible for generation and verification of the Header Error Control (HEC) field in the ATM cell header (described later in this section), in addition to mapping ATM cells into an appropriate physical layer frame format.

The layer above the PHY layer in the ATM protocol reference model is the ATM layer. This layer performs a plethora of functions, *including* the following:

- Construction of ATM cells
- Generic Flow Control (GFC)
- ATM cell switching using the Virtual Path Identifier (VPI) and Virtual Channel Identifier (VCI) fields in the ATM cell header
- Distinguishing between different ATM cell types based on the Payload Type (PT) field of the ATM cell header
- Processing ATM cells appropriately based on the Cell Loss Priority (CLP) bit in the ATM cell header
- Supporting ATM quality of service (QoS)

Figure 2-26 illustrates the ATM cell and header formats.

Figure 2-26 *ATM Cell and Header Formats*

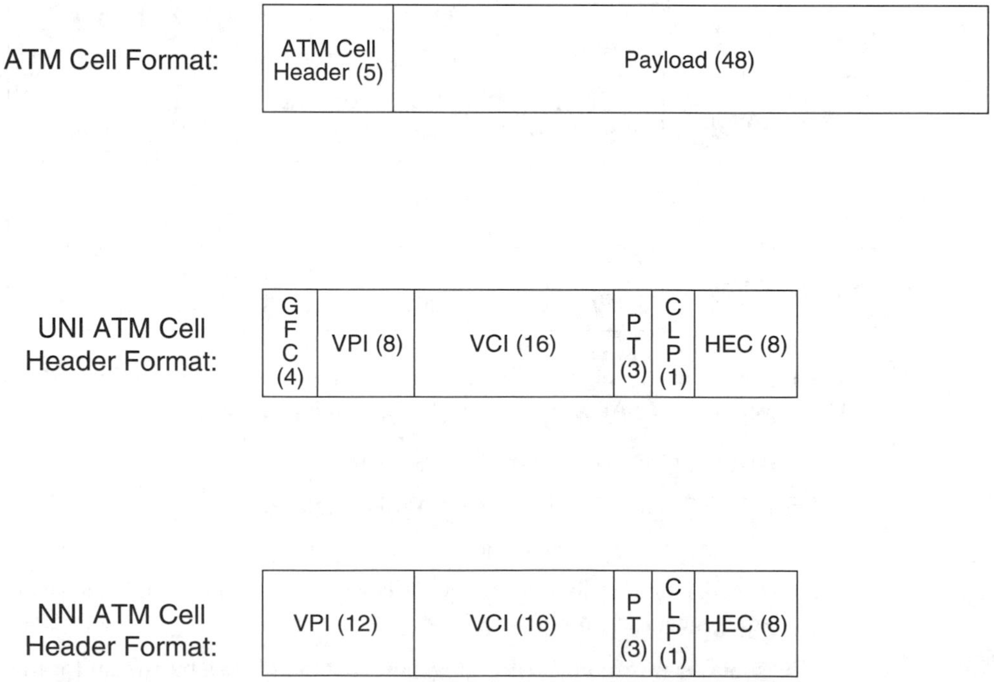

Figure 2-26 shows that the ATM cell consists of a 5-byte header and a 48-byte payload—a total size of 53 bytes.

Below the ATM cell, you can see the User-to-Network Interface (UNI) ATM cell header, and the Network-to-Network Interface (NNI) ATM cell header. The length of each field of the UNI and NNI cell headers in bits is shown in brackets in Figure 2-26.

The UNI defines an interface between user equipment, such as a router with an ATM interface, and an ATM network. The NNI, on the other hand, defines an interface between ATM switches in an ATM network.

The UNI ATM cell header consists of six fields:

- **Generic Flow Control (GFC)**—This field provides functions such as multiplexing (allowing multiple stations to share an interface).

- **Virtual Path Identifier (VPI)**—This field identifies a specific ATM virtual path on a physical circuit.

- **Virtual Channel Identifier (VCI)**—This field identifies a particular ATM virtual channel on a physical circuit.

- **Payload Type (PT)**—This field specifies whether the ATM cell carries user data; operation, administration, and maintenance (OAM) information; or resource management (RM) information.

The PT field can also be used to indicate that the cell experienced congestion (Explicit Forward Congestion Indication [EFCI]) as it passed through a network, as well as indicate the final cell in an AAL5 Protocol Data Unit (PDU) (AAL indicate=1).

The precise PT bit settings are as follows:

000 — user data cell; EFCI=0; AAL indicate=0

001 — user data cell; EFCI=0; AAL indicate=1

010 — user data cell; EFCI=1; AAL indicate=0

011 — user data cell; EFCI=1; AAL indicate=1

100 — OAM F5 segment cell

101 — OAM F5 end-to-end cell

110 — Resource Management (RM) cell

111 — (Reserved for future use)

- **Cell Loss Priority (CLP)**—This bit indicates the cell's discard priority. When the network is congested, cells with this bit set to 1 are discarded first.

- **Header Error Control (HEC)**—This field contains a cyclic redundancy check (CRC) of the fields in the ATM cell header.

In Figure 2-25, you can see that above the ATM layer is the ATM AAL. The AAL layer passes data between services and protocols at higher layers and the ATM layer. There are five AALs named, appropriately enough, AAL1, AAL2, AAL3/4, and AAL5. L2TPv3 can support the transport of AAL5 CPCS-SDUs. The AAL layer can be broken into two sublayers:

- The Segmentation And Reassembly (SAR) sublayer
- The Convergence Sublayer (CS)

The SAR sublayer is responsible for reassembling AAL SAR PDUs (which are contained in the payload of ATM cells) into CPCS-PDUs. The CS can itself is subdivided into two further sublayers: the Common Part Convergence Sublayer (CPCS) and the Service Specific Convergence Sublayer (SSCS). The CPCS is responsible for extracting the payload of CPCS-PDUs (which contain AAL Service Data Units [AAL SDUs]).

The optional SSCS performs services specific to certain protocols or functions (such as Frame Relay network interworking) residing at higher layers. If required by higher-layer protocols or functions, the payload of the CPCS-PDUs is passed to the SSCS by the CPCS, and the SSCS extracts AAL SDUs. If the SSCS is not required by higher-layer protocols or functions, the CPCS passes AAL SDUs directly to higher layers.

Figure 2-27 illustrates the relationships between ATM cells, SAR PDUs, AAL5 CPCS-PDUs, and AAL5 SDUs. It also illustrates that SAR PDUs are extracted from the payloads of ATM cells. SAR PDUs are then reconstructed into a CPCS-PDU. An AAL5 SDU is then extracted from the payload of a CPCS-PDU.

As shown in Figure 2-27, the AAL5 CPCS PDU is composed of the following fields:

- **CPCS Payload**—This field contains the AAL5 SDU.
- **PAD**—This variable-length field ensures that the overall length CPCS-PDU is a multiple of 48 bytes. Because the CPCS-PDU is a multiple of 48 bytes, it can be segmented exactly into ATM cell payloads (which are 48 bytes long).
- **CPCS UU**—The CPCS User-to-User field is used to pass information between AAL users.
- **Common Part Indicator (CPI)**—This field ensures that the CPCS-PDU trailer aligns with a 64-bit boundary.
- **Length**—This specifies the overall length of the CPCS-PDU.
- **CRC**—The CRC field contains a checksum value, and allows the receiver of a CPCS-PDU to detect errors.

Figure 2-27 *ATM Cells, SAR-PDUs, AAL5 CPCS-PDU, and AAL5 SDU*

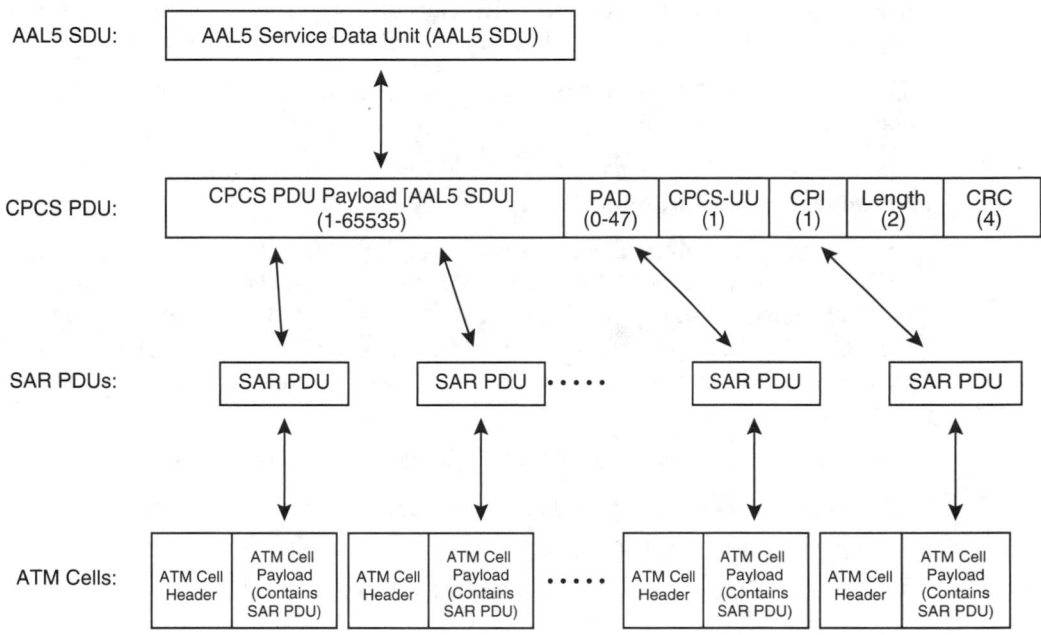

Operations, Administration, and Management (OAM)   OAM ATM cells are used to support monitoring and diagnostic functions in an ATM network.

Figure 2-28 shows the format of OAM cells.

Figure 2-28 *Format of OAM Cells*

G F C	VPI	VCI	P T	C L P	HEC	OAM Type (4 bits)	OAM Function Type (4 bits)	Function Specific (45 Octets)	Rsvd (6 bits)	CRC (10 bits)

There are two types of ATM OAM cells: F4 OAM cells and F5 OAM cells. F4 OAM cells are used in conjunction with ATM virtual path (VP) flows, and F5 OAM cells are used in conjunction with VC flows. Both F4 and F5 OAM cell flows may be either end-to-end (between ATM endpoints such as routers) or limited to a particular segment.

The overall OAM cell format is identical for both F4 and F5 OAM cells (see Figure 2-28). The method of identifying a particular ATM cell as an OAM cell differs, however, depending on whether the OAM cell is an F4 or F5 OAM cell.

If an OAM cell is an F4 OAM cell, it is identified as such by specifying the values 3 or 4 in the VCI field of the ATM cell header. Remember that because F4 OAM cells are used in conjunction with VPs, the VCI field is not used to switch cells in this case.

The value 3 in the VCI field of the ATM cell header is used to specify that this is an F4 OAM cell limited to a particular segment.

The value 4 in the VCI field of the ATM cell header, on the other hand, is used to identify an end-to-end F4 OAM cell.

F5 OAM cells are identified in a different manner to F4 OAM cells because F5 OAM cells are used in conjunction with VCs. Remember that for VCs, both the VPI *and* VCI are used to switch cells, and so the VCI cannot be used to identify F5 OAM cells. Instead of using the VCI field, therefore, certain values of the PT field in the ATM cell header identify F5 OAM cells limited to a particular segment and F5 OAM cells used between ATM endpoints.

The PT field values used to identify F5 OAM cells are as follows:

- **100**—F5 OAM cells limited to a particular segment
- **101**—End-to-end F5 OAM cells

The specific fields of the OAM cell (see Figure 2-28) are as follows:

- **OAM Cell Type**—This describes the function of the OAM cell, which can be one of the following:
  - Fault management
  - Performance management
  - Activation and deactivation
  - System management
- **OAM Function Type**—This field describes the *specific* function of the OAM cell, as follows:
  - **Fault management**—Alarm Indication Signal (AIS), Remote Defect Indication (RDI), continuity check, and loopback testing
  - **Performance management**—Forward monitoring and backward reporting
  - **Activation and deactivation**—Performance monitoring and continuity check
  - **System management**—Not yet defined
- **Function Specific fields**—Information regarding the OAM cell function can be contained within these fields.
- **Reserved**—This field is reserved for future use.
- **CRC**—This a cyclic redundancy check on the OAM cell.

As previously mentioned, the two options for the transport of ATM over L2TPv3 are ATM cell relay and AAL5 CPCS-SDU.

When you are using cell relay, OAM cells are transparently forwarded over the pseudowire. When you are using AAL5 CPCS-SDU transport, on the other hand, there are two methods of handling OAM cells: either the cells can be transparently forwarded over the pseudowire, or OAM can be locally terminated on the PE routers. When OAM is locally terminated, a PE router can signal defects to its peer PE router using SLI messages.

If you want to configure transparent forwarding of OAM cells with AAL5 CPCS-SDU transport, the attachment circuit VPI/VCIs at both ends of the pseudowire must match. If they do not match, you must locally terminate OAM on the PE routers. In addition, local termination is also necessary if the PE routers in use do not support transparent forwarding of OAM cells with AAL5 CPCS-SDU transport.

The two commands that are relevant if you want to configure OAM local termination (OAM local emulation) are as follows:

- **oam-ac emulation-enable** [*ais-rate*]—Enables F5 OAM local termination, and enables you to specify a rate at which AIS cells are sent (the default is one every second).

- **oam-pvc manage** [*frequency*]—Optionally used to generate loopback cells on the attachment circuit to verify connectivity on the VC. The optional *frequency* parameter can be used to specify the interval between loopback cells (the default is one every 10 seconds).

Both the **oam-ac emulation-enable** and the **oam-pvc manage** commands can be configured in either ATM VC configuration mode or VC class configuration mode. If the **oam-ac emulation-enable** command is configured on one PE router, it must also be configured on the peer PE router (for the same pseudowire)—if it is not, the pseudowire will not become active.

Transporting ATM Traffic over L2TPv3   Now that you know the basics of the operation of ATM, it is time to examine how ATM traffic is transported over L2TPv3 pseudowires.

L2TPv3 can now support two basic options with regard to the transport of ATM traffic:

- ATM cell relay
- AAL5 CPCS-SDU

The encapsulation shown in Figure 2-29 is used when transporting ATM traffic over L2TPv3 pseudowires.

Figure 2-29 *Encapsulation When Transporting ATM Traffic over L2TPv3*

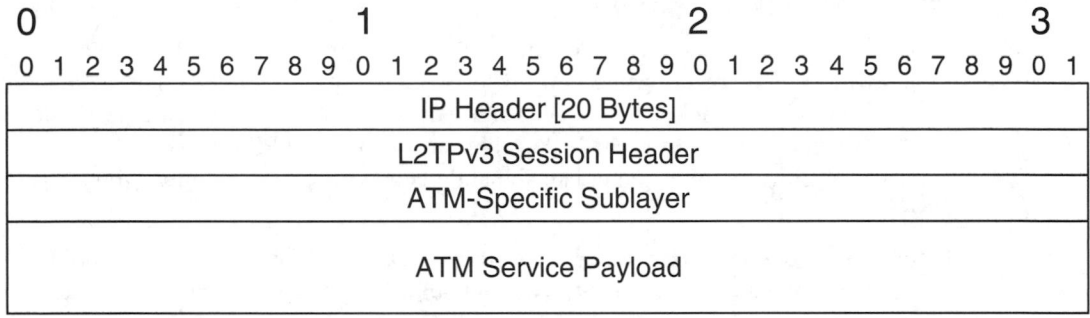

In Figure 2-29, you can see that the first element of the L2TPv3 pseudowire packet used to transport ATM traffic is the IP header. As previously discussed, this IP header specifies IP protocol 115 (L2TPv3). Next comes the L2TPv3 session header, as described earlier in this chapter (see Figure 2-4). Following the L2TPv3 session header is the ATM-specific sublayer.

The ATM service payload contains an ATM cell or cells (if ATM cell relay is being used), or an AAL5 CPCS-PDU (if AAL5 CPCS-SDU transport is being used). The ATM-specific sublayer shown in Figure 2-29 is detailed in Figure 2-30.

Figure 2-30 *ATM-Specific Sublayer*

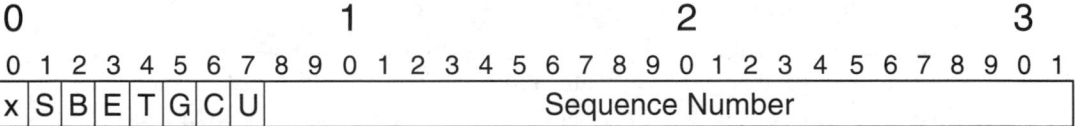

The ATM-specific sublayer is optional when using ATM cell relay mode and mandatory for AAL5 SDU mode.

The S bit is set to 1 when there is a valid sequence number (a non-0 value) contained in the Sequence Number field.

The B and E bits can collectively be set to a non-0 value if an AAL5 SDU received on the attachment circuit needs to be fragmented for it to be sent over the L2TPv3 pseudowire. Specific B and E bit settings are defined as follows:

- **00**—The complete unfragmented payload is carried in this L2TPv3 packet.
- **01**—This L2TPv3 packet carries the first fragment.
- **10**—This L2TPv3 packet carries the last fragment.
- **11**—This L2TPv3 packet carries an intermediate fragment.

The Transport Type (T) bit is used to indicate whether the ATM service payload contains an ATM admin cell or an AAL5 payload. If the T bit is set to 1, the ATM service payload contains an ATM admin cell (carried as described in the section "Configuring ATM VCC Cell Relay L2TPv3 Pseudowires" on page 79); and if the T bit is set to 0, the ATM service payload contains an AAL5 payload.

Next is the G bit. This bit is set to 1 by the ingress LCCE when the EFCI bit of either the final cell comprising an incoming AAL5 CPCS-PDU or a single cell to be transported is set to 1 (see Figure 2-26 on page 68). The egress LCCE sets the EFCI bit on all cells corresponding to an AAL5 CPCS-PDU to the value specified in the G bit (either 1 or 0) as it transmits them on the egress ATM attachment circuit.

The ingress LCCE sets the C bit to 1 if the CLP bit of any of the cells (see Figure 2-26 on page 68) corresponding to an AAL5 CPCS-PDU has their CLP bit set to 1, or if, when transporting single ATM cells, the CLP bit of a single cell is set to 1. The egress LCCE sets the CLP bit of all cells that correspond to AAL5 CPCS-PDU to the value contained in the C bit of the ATM-specific sublayer.

The final bit in the ATM-specific sublayer is the U bit. This bit is the Command/Response (C/R) bit and is set by the ingress LCCE when transporting FRF 8.1 Frame Relay/ATM PVC service interworking traffic to value of the least significant bit of the AAL5 CPCS User-to-User Indication (UU) bit (see Figure 2-27 on page 71), which may contain the Frame Relay C/R bit. The egress LCCE copies the U bit to the least significant bit of the UU field of the AAL5 CPCS-PDU before transmitting it on the attachment circuit.

As already mentioned, there are two ways to transport ATM traffic over an L2TPv3 pseudowire—ATM cell relay and AAL5 SDU transport. These two methods of ATM traffic transport are examined in the following two sections.

ATM Cell Relay (Cell Mode)   The first method of forwarding ATM traffic over an L2TPv3 pseudowire is to use cell relay. In this case, the ingress LCCE/PE encapsulates one or more ATM cells in L2TPv3 before forwarding the L2TPv3 packet to the egress LCCE/PE.

ATM cell relay can be preformed in three ways:

- **ATM Virtual Channel Connection (VCC) mode cell relay**—In VCC mode, one or more VCCs is mapped to an L2TPv3 pseudowire. Normally, only one VCC is mapped to a single L2TPv3 pseudowire—this ensures that QoS or other requirements are met.

- **ATM Virtual Path Connection (VPC) mode cell relay**—In this mode, one or more VPCs are mapped to an L2TPv3 pseudowire. Usually, a single VPC is mapped to a L2TPv3 pseudowire.

- **ATM port mode cell relay**—In this case, a port is mapped to an L2TPv3 pseudowire. The ingress LCCE sends all ATM cells received on this port over the pseudowire, with the exception of idle or unassigned ATM cells, which the ingress LCCE discards.

When performing cell relay, an LCCE can either encapsulate and transmit a single ATM cell per L2TPv3 packet or encapsulate and transmit more than one ATM cell per L2TPv3 packet. The encapsulation and transmission of a single ATM cell per L2TPv3 packet is referred to in this chapter as *single cell relay*, and the encapsulation and transmission of more than one ATM cell per L2TPv3 is called *cell concatenation* or *cell packing*.

Single ATM Cell Relay   As previously described, the encapsulation and transmission of a single ATM cell per L2TPv3 packet can be referred to as *single ATM cell relay*.

In Figure 2-31, the ingress LCCE receives a single ATM cell on an attachment circuit and then encapsulates that single ATM cell in an L2TPv3 packet and transmits it to the egress LCCE.

Figure 2-31 *Single ATM Cell Relay*

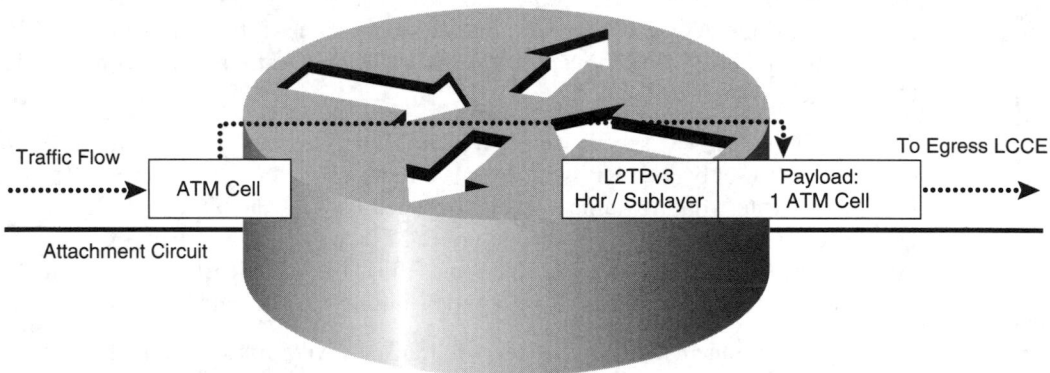

It is worth noting the complete ATM cell received on the attachment circuit is not encapsulated and transmitted in an L2TPv3 packet—more on this later.

The egress LCCE performs the process shown in Figure 2-31, just in reverse—it receives the L2TPv3 packet containing the ATM cell, decapsulates it, reconstructs the complete ATM cell, and transmits it on the attachment circuit.

Figure 2-32 shows encapsulation of a single ATM cell in an L2TPv3 packet. The IP header and L2TPv3 session header have previously been described. The ATM-specific sublayer has also been previously described, but it is worth emphasizing that it is optional when using ATM cell relay.

Following the ATM-specific sublayer are the VPI, VCI, PTI, and C (CLP) fields. These fields are copied directly from the ATM cell header of the ATM cell received by the ingress LCCE on the attachment circuit (see Figure 2-26 on page 68).

The ATM cell Payload field contains the payload of the ATM cell received by the ingress LCCE.

Figure 2-32 *Encapsulation of a Single ATM Cell in an L2TPv3 Packet (over IP)*

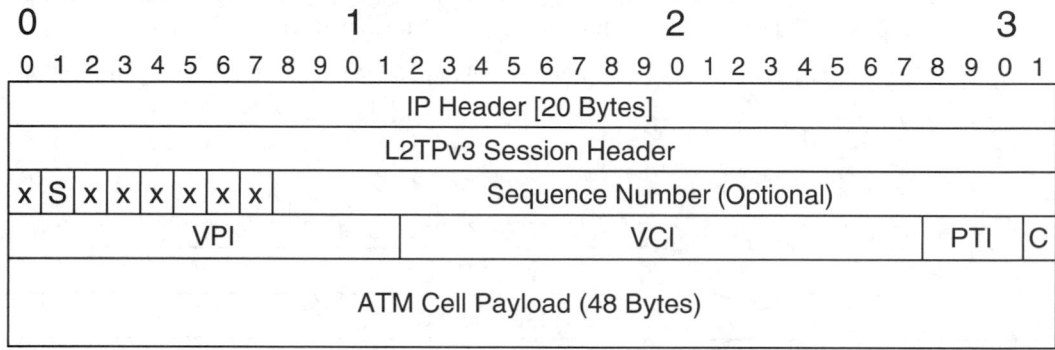

You'll notice that HEC field is not carried in L2TPv3 packets sent by the ingress LCCE. This field is reconstructed by the egress LCCE before transmitting the cells on its attachment circuit.

The advantage of single ATM cell relay is that each ATM cell is transmitted on the L2TPv3 pseudowire as soon as it is received on the attachment circuit—no delay occurs between the reception of each ATM cell and its transmission on the pseudowire (with the exception of the time required for the encapsulation of the cell in L2TPv3).

The disadvantage of single ATM cell relay is the packet (and bandwidth) overhead required for encapsulation of each and every ATM cell in a separate L2TPv3 packet.

ATM Cell Relay with Cell Packing   The alternative to single ATM cell relay is ATM cell relay with cell packing. In this case, the ingress LCCE packs a configured number of ATM cells into each L2TPv3 packet before transmission to the egress LCCE.

Figure 2-33 illustrates ATM cell relay with cell packing.

Figure 2-33 *ATM Cell Relay with Cell Packing*

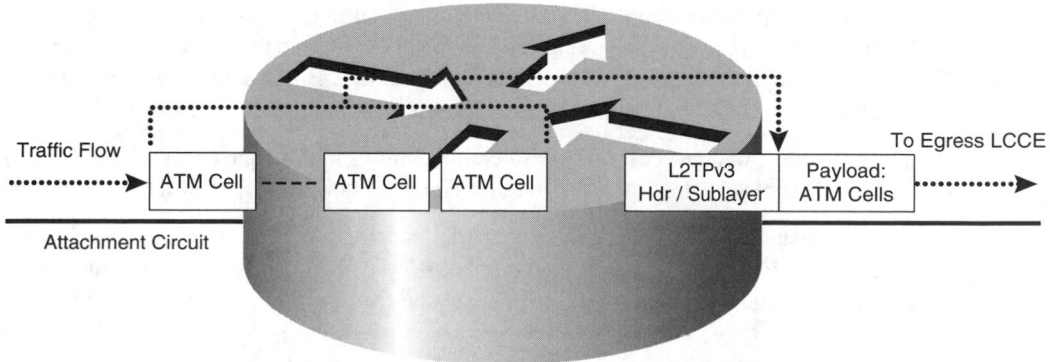

The egress LCCE again performs the process shown in Figure 2-31 in reverse—it receives the L2TPv3 packet containing the packed ATM cells, decapsulates them, reconstructs the complete ATM cells, and transmits them on the attachment circuit.

Figure 2-34 illustrates the L2TPv3 encapsulation for ATM cell relay with cell packing.

Figure 2-34 *L2TPv3 Encapsulation for ATM Cell Relay with Cell Packing*

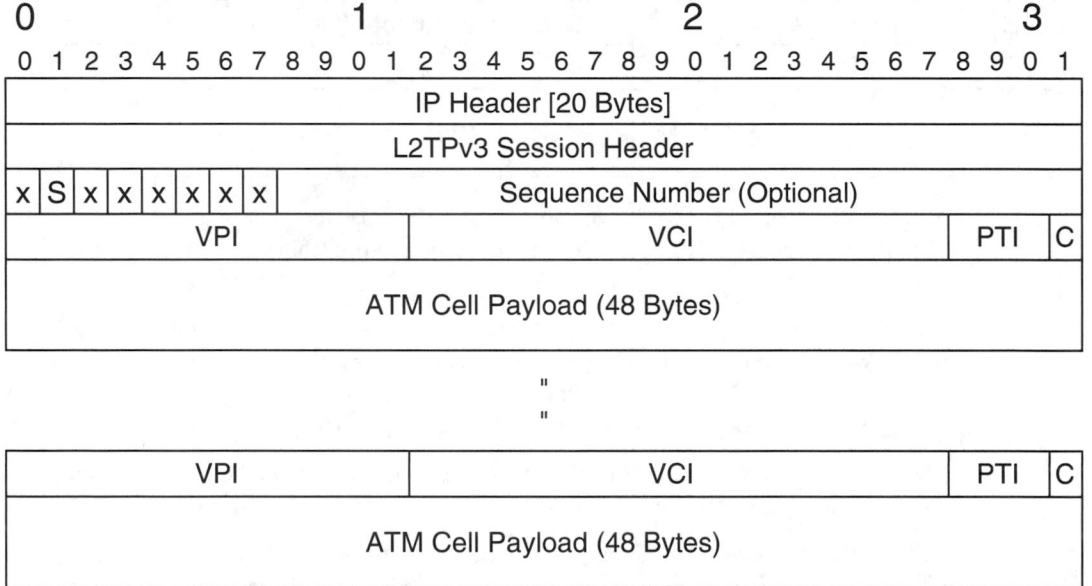

All the fields of the L2TPv3 encapsulation shown in Figure 2-34 have been previously described. The only difference between Figure 2-34 and Figure 2-32 is, of course, the number of ATM cells carried in the L2TPv3 packet payload.

An LCCE can signal the maximum number of ATM cells packed into a single L2TPv3 packet that it can support using an ICRQ or ICRP message during L2TPv3 session setup or using an SLI message after session setup if it wants to signal a change in the maximum number of ATM cells it can support. In effect, an LCCE tells its peer LCCE, "Don't send me any more than x ATM cells in an L2TPv3 packet, because x is the maximum that I can support."

The advantage of ATM cell relay with cell packing is that the packet (and bandwidth) overhead required is less than that required on a per cell basis than single ATM cell relay.

The disadvantage of ATM cell relay with cell packing is that there is a delay while the ingress LCCE buffers the configured number ATM cells (or waits for a configured timeout) before packing them into an L2TPv3 packet and transmitting it to the egress LCCE.

Deploying L2TPv3 Pseudowires for ATM Cell Relay   Now it is time to put the theory into practice. As previously described, ATM cell relay can operate in three different modes with L2TPv3:

- ATM VCC mode cell relay
- ATM VPC mode cell relay
- ATM port mode cell relay

The configuration of these three modes is described in the following sections.

Configuring ATM VCC Cell Relay L2TPv3 Pseudowires   Example 2-20 shows the configuration of an ATM VCC mode single cell relay L2TPv3 pseudowire.

Example 2-20 *Configuration of ATM VCC Mode Single Cell Relay with L2TPv3*

```
!
! On London.PE (line 1)
!
l2tp-class mjlnet.Class.To.Amsterdam
 digest secret mjlnet hash sha
!
pseudowire-class mjlnet.PW.To.Amsterdam
 encapsulation l2tpv3
 protocol l2tpv3 mjlnet.Class.To.Amsterdam
 ip local interface Loopback0
!
!
interface ATM1/0
 no atm enable-ilmi-trap
 no atm ilmi-keepalive
 pvc 6/100 l2transport (line 2)
  encapsulation aal0 (line 3)
  xconnect 172.16.1.3 1003 pw-class mjlnet.PW.To.London (line 4)
  !
 !
```
```
!
! On Amsterdam.PE (line 5)
!
l2tp-class mjlnet.Class.To.London
 digest secret mjlnet hash sha
!
pseudowire-class mjlnet.PW.To.London
 encapsulation l2tpv3
 protocol l2tpv3 mjlnet.Class.To.London
 ip local interface Loopback0
!
!
interface ATM1/0
 no atm enable-ilmi-trap
 no atm ilmi-keepalive
```

continues

Example 2-20 *Configuration of ATM VCC Mode Single Cell Relay with L2TPv3 (Continued)*

```
 pvc 6/100 l2transport (line 6)
  encapsulation aal0 (line 7)
  xconnect 172.16.1.1 1003 pw-class mjlnet.PW.To.London (line 8)
 !
```

Highlighted lines 2 to 4 show the configuration of an ATM VCC cell relay pseudowire on London.PE. In highlighted line 2, the **pvc** *vpi/vci* **l2transport** command configures the VPI and VCI for a PVC and identifies the PVC as being switched (to a pseudowire [L2TPv3 session]). The **encapsulation aal0** command, shown in highlighted line 3, is then used to specify ATM Adaption Layer 0 encapsulation (cell relay).

Finally, the **xconnect** *peer-ip-address vcid* **pw-class** *pseudowire-class* command (highlighted line 4) is used to specify that the PVC should be switched to the pseudowire with VC ID 1003, to peer LCCE/PE 172.16.1.3 (Amsterdam.PE), using pseudowire class mjlnet.PW.To.Amsterdam.

The corresponding configuration on Amsterdam.PE is similar (see highlighted lines 6 to 8). The only difference between the configuration of London.PE and Amsterdam.PE is the peer IP address and pseudowire class name configured using the **xconnect** command in highlighted line 8. The peer IP address (172.16.1.1) is London.PE, and the pseudowire class name corresponds to a locally configured pseudowire class (mjlnet.PW.To.London).

After the L2TPv3 pseudowire has been configured, you can verify the status of the corresponding L2TPv3 session using the **show l2tun session** command (see Example 2-21).

Example 2-21 *Verifying Session Status for the ATM VCC Cell Relay Mode L2TPv3 Pseudowire Using the* **show l2tun session** *Command*

```
London.PE#show l2tun session all
  Session Information Total tunnels 1 sessions 1
  Tunnel control packets dropped due to failed digest 0

 Session id 5155 is up, tunnel id 33080 (line 1)
 Call serial number is 135100001
 Remote tunnel name is Amsterdam.PE
   Internet address is 172.16.1.3
   Session is L2TP signaled (line 2)
   Session state is established, time since change 00:02:04
     15 Packets sent, 15 received
     780 Bytes sent, 780 received
     Receive packets dropped:
       out-of-order:           0
       total:                  0
     Send packets dropped:
       exceeded session MTU:   0
       total:                  0
```

Example 2-21 *Verifying Session Status for the ATM VCC Cell Relay Mode L2TPv3 Pseudowire Using the* **show l2tun session** *Command (Continued)*

```
Session vcid is 1003 (line 3)
Session Layer 2 circuit, type is ATM VCC CELL, name is ATM1/0:6/100 (line 4)
Circuit state is UP
  Remote session id is 13915, remote tunnel id 10630
DF bit off, ToS reflect disabled, ToS value 0, TTL value 255
No session cookie information available
FS cached header information:
  encap size = 24 bytes
  00000000 00000000 00000000 00000000
  00000000 00000000
Sequencing is off
London.PE#
```

If you take a look at highlighted line 1, you can see that the session (pseudowire) is in an up (active) state, and in highlighted line 2 you can see that session is L2TPv3 signaled.

The session VC ID is shown in highlighted line 3 (1003), and the session type (ATM VCC cell relay) is shown in highlighted line 4.

Configuring ATM VPC Cell Relay L2TPv3 Pseudowires   The configuration of ATM VPC cell relay L2TPv3 pseudowires is similar to that for VCC cell relay L2TPv3 pseudowires—there are just one or two relatively minor differences.

Example 2-22 shows the configuration of an ATM VPC single cell relay L2TPv3 pseudowire.

Example 2-22 *Configuration of an ATM VPC Mode Single Cell Relay L2TPv3 Pseudowire*

```
!
! On London.PE (line 1)
!
l2tp-class mjlnet.Class.To.Amsterdam
 digest secret mjlnet hash sha
!
pseudowire-class mjlnet.PW.To.Amsterdam
 encapsulation l2tpv3
 protocol l2tpv3 mjlnet.Class.To.Amsterdam
 ip local interface Loopback0
!
!
interface ATM1/0
 no ip address
 no ip directed-broadcast
 atm pvp 6 l2transport (line 2)
  xconnect 172.16.1.3 1013 pw-class mjlnet.PW.To.Amsterdam (line 3)
 no atm enable-ilmi-trap
 no atm ilmi-keepalive
!
```

continues

Example 2-22 *Configuration of an ATM VPC Mode Single Cell Relay L2TPv3 Pseudowire (Continued)*

```
!
! On Amsterdam.PE (line 4)
!
l2tp-class mjlnet.Class.To.London
 digest secret mjlnet hash sha
!
pseudowire-class mjlnet.PW.To.London
 encapsulation l2tpv3
 protocol l2tpv3 mjlnet.Class.To.London
 ip local interface Loopback0
!
!
interface ATM1/0
 no ip address
 no ip directed-broadcast
 atm pvp 6 l2transport (line 5)
  xconnect 172.16.1.1 1013 pw-class mjlnet.PW.To.London (line 6)
 no atm enable-ilmi-trap
 no atm ilmi-keepalive
!
```

If you examine the configuration shown in Example 2-22 and compare it with the configuration for ATM VCC cell relay shown in Example 2-20, you'll see that the configurations are remarkably similar.

The significant difference between the two configurations is the replacement of the **pvc** *vpi/vci* **l2transport** and **encapsulation aal0** commands (highlighted lines 2, 3, 6, and 7 in Example 2-20) with the **atm pvp** *pvi* **l2transport** command (highlighted lines 2 and 5 in Example 2-22).

The **atm pvp** *vpi* **l2transport** command is used to bind a PVP to a pseudowire.

The **xconnect** *peer-ip-address vcid* **pw-class** *pseudowire-class* command (highlighted lines 3 and 6) configures the VC so that it is switched to the pseudowire with the specified VC ID (1013), to the specified peer LCCE (172.16.1.3 [Amsterdam.PE] and 172.16.1.1 [London.PE]), with the specified pseudowire class (mjlnet.PW.To.Amsterdam and mjlnet.PW.To.London).

So, a pretty straightforward configuration. As shown in Example 2-23, you can verify an ATM PVP using the **show atm vp** *vpi* command.

Example 2-23 *Verifying an ATM PVP Using the* **show atm vp vpi** *Command*

```
Amsterdam.PE#show atm vp 6
ATM1/0 VPI: 6, Cell Relay, PeakRate: 149760, CesRate: 0, DataVCs: 0, CesVCs: 0, (line 1)
Status: ACTIVE (line 2)

   VCD    VCI Type    InPkts  OutPkts  AAL/Encap    Status
     2      3 PVC          0        0  F4 OAM       ACTIVE
     3      4 PVC          0        0  F4 OAM       ACTIVE
```

Example 2-23 *Verifying an ATM PVP Using the* **show atm vp vpi** *Command (Continued)*

```
TotalInPkts: 0, TotalOutPkts: 0, TotalInFast: 0, TotalOutFast: 0, TotalBroadcast
s: 0
Amsterdam.PE#
```

The first highlighted line in Example 2-23 shows that the PVP with VPI 6 is bound to an ATM PVP cell relay pseudowire, and the second highlighted line shows that the PVP is active.

If you look below that, you can see a couple of active VCs. If you are a *particularly* inquisitive type then you might be interested to notice the VCIs and cell types (see the VCI and AAL/Encap columns)—the VCIs are 3 and 4, and the AAL/Encap is F4 OAM. Remember that F4 OAM uses these two VCIs (segment and end-to-end F4 OAM).

You can also verify the ATM VPC cell relay L2TPv3 pseudowire using the **show l2tun session** command (see Example 2-24).

Example 2-24 *Verifying the ATM VPC Cell Relay L2TPv3 Pseudowire Using the* **show l2tun session** *Command*

```
London.PE#show l2tun session all
 Session Information Total tunnels 1 sessions 1 (line 1)
 Tunnel control packets dropped due to failed digest 0

 Session id 23709 is up, tunnel id 52241
 Call serial number is 3217100029
 Remote tunnel name is Amsterdam.PE
   Internet address is 172.16.1.3
 Session is L2TP signaled (line 2)
   Session state is established, time since change 00:04:28
     0 Packets sent, 0 received
     0 Bytes sent, 0 received
     Receive packets dropped:
       out-of-order:            0
       total:                   0
     Send packets dropped:
       exceeded session MTU:    0
       total:                   0
   Session vcid is 1003
   Session Layer 2 circuit, type is ATM VPC CELL, name is ATM1/0:6 (line 3)
   Circuit state is UP (line 4)
     Remote session id is 48356, remote tunnel id 59240
   DF bit off, ToS reflect disabled, ToS value 0, TTL value 255
   No session cookie information available
   FS cached header information:
     encap size = 24 bytes
     00000000 00000000 00000000 00000000
     00000000 00000000
   Sequencing is off
London.PE#
```

Highlighted lines 1 and 2 show that 1 tunnel (control connection) and 1 session are active, and that the pseudowire is L2TPv3 signaled.

Then, in highlighted line 3 and 4, you can see this is an ATM VPC cell relay L2TPv3 pseudowire, and the pseudowire is in an UP (active) state.

Configuring ATM Port Mode Cell Relay L2TPv3 Pseudowires   The final ATM cell relay pseudowire mode is port mode cell relay. In this mode, all ATM cells received on an interface are forwarded over the L2TPv3 pseudowire, with the exception of unassigned or idle cells.

Example 2-25 shows the configuration of an ATM port mode cell relay L2TPv3 pseudowire.

Example 2-25 *Configuration of ATM Port Mode Cell Relay L2TPv3 Pseudowire*

```
!
! On London.PE (line 1)
!
l2tp-class mjlnet.To.Amsterdam
 digest secret mjlnet hash sha
!
pseudowire-class mjlnet.PW.To.Amsterdam
 encapsulation l2tpv3
 protocol l2tpv3 mjlnet.Class.To.Amsterdam
 ip local interface Loopback0
!
!
interface ATM1/0
 no ip address
 no ip directed-broadcast
 atm mcpt-timers 300 600 900
 no atm enable-ilmi-trap
 no atm ilmi-keepalive
 xconnect 172.16.1.3 1003 pw-class mjlnet.PW.To.Amsterdam (line 2)
 !
```

```
!
! On Amsterdam.PE (line 3)
!
!
l2tp-class mjlnet.Class.To.London
 digest secret mjlnet hash sha
!
pseudowire-class mjlnet.PW.To.London
 encapsulation l2tpv3
 protocol l2tpv3 mjlnet.Class.To.London
 ip local interface Loopback0
!
!
interface ATM1/0
 no ip address
 no ip directed-broadcast
 no atm enable-ilmi-trap
 no atm ilmi-keepalive
 xconnect 172.16.1.1 1003 pw-class PW.01.mjlnet.To.London (line 4)
 !
```

The first thing that you'll notice about the configuration of ATM port mode cell relay is its relative simplicity. There is no need to configure the **pvc** *vpi/vci* **l2transport** or **atm pvp** *pvi* **l2transport** commands. In fact, the only command that you need to configure on the ATM interface is **xconnect** *peer-ip-address vcid* **pw-class** *pseudowire-class*, as shown in highlighted lines 2 and 4.

Once again, you can verify the pseudowire using the **show l2tun session** command (see Example 2-26).

Example 2-26 *Verifying the ATM Port Mode Cell Relay L2TPv3 Pseudowire Using the* **show l2tun session** *Command*

```
London.PE#show l2tun session all
 Session Information Total tunnels 1 sessions 1
 Tunnel control packets dropped due to failed digest 0

Session id 23720 is up, tunnel id 52241
Call serial number is 3217100035
Remote tunnel name is Amsterdam.PE
  Internet address is 172.16.1.3
  Session is L2TP signaled (line 1)
  Session state is established, time since change 00:01:21
    0 Packets sent, 0 received
    0 Bytes sent, 0 received
    Receive packets dropped:
      out-of-order:           0
      total:                  0
    Send packets dropped:
      exceeded session MTU:   0
      total:                  0
  Session vcid is 1003 (line 2)
  Session Layer 2 circuit, type is ATM CELL, name is ATM1/0: (line 3)
  Circuit state is UP
    Remote session id is 48367, remote tunnel id 59240
  DF bit off, ToS reflect disabled, ToS value 0, TTL value 255
  No session cookie information available
  FS cached header information:
    encap size = 24 bytes
    00000000 00000000 00000000 00000000
    00000000 00000000
  Sequencing is off
London.PE#
```

Highlighted lines 1 and 2 shows that the pseudowire is L2TPv3 signaled, and that the VC ID associated with the pseudowire is 1003. Finally, highlighted line 3 shows that the pseudowire is ATM port mode cell relay (**ATM CELL**).

Configuring ATM VCC or VPC Cell Relay with Cell Packing   Earlier in chapter, cell packing (cell concatenation) was discussed. You will recall that when using cell packing, the ingress LCCE packs more than one cell into each L2TPv3 packet before forwarding them to the egress LCCE.

Example 2-27 shows the configuration of an ATM VCC cell relay L2TPv3 pseudowire with cell packing. You might like to compare this with the configuration of a single cell ATM VCC cell relay L2TPv3 pseudowire shown in Example 2-20 on page 79.

Example 2-27 *Configuration of Cell Packing with an L2TPv3 Pseudowire*

```
!
! On London.PE (line 1)
!
l2tp-class mjlnet.Class.To.Amsterdam
 digest secret mjlnet hash sha
!
pseudowire-class mjlnet.PW.To.Amsterdam
 encapsulation l2tpv3
 protocol l2tpv3 mjlnet.PW.To.Amsterdam
 ip local interface Loopback0
!
!
interface ATM1/0
 no ip address
 no ip directed-broadcast
 atm mcpt-timers 30 60 90 (line 2)
 no atm enable-ilmi-trap
 no atm ilmi-keepalive
 pvc 6/100 l2transport (line 3)
  encapsulation aal0
  cell-packing 15 mcpt-timer 2 (line 4)
  xconnect 172.16.1.3 1003 pw-class mjlnet.PW.To.Amsterdam
 !
!
```
```
!
! On Amsterdam.PE (line 5)
!
l2tp-class mjlnet.Class.To.London
 digest secret mjlnet hash sha
!
pseudowire-class mjlnet.PW.To.London
 encapsulation l2tpv3
 protocol l2tpv3 mjlnet.Class.To.London
 ip local interface Loopback0
!
!
interface ATM1/0
 no ip address
 no ip directed-broadcast
 atm mcpt-timers 30 60 90 (line 6)
 no atm enable-ilmi-trap
 no atm ilmi-keepalive
 pvc 6/100 l2transport (line 7)
  encapsulation aal0
  cell-packing 15 mcpt-timer 2 (line 8)
  xconnect 172.16.1.1 1003 pw-class mjlnet.PW.To.London
 !
!
```

Highlighted lines 2, 4, 6, and 8 show the relevant cell-packing configuration on London.PE and Amsterdam.PE. When cell packing is used, the ingress LCCE packs a configured maximum number of ATM cells into an L2TPv3 packet as long as that maximum number of cells is received before a maximum cell packing timeout has expired. If the timeout expires before the maximum number of cells is received by the ingress LCCE, the cells that have been received are packed into an L2TPv3 packet and sent to the egress LCCE.

The **atm mcpt-timers** [*timeout-value-1 timeout-value-2 timeout-value-3*] command enables you to specify three maximum cell-packing timeouts. In Example 2-27, highlighted lines 2 and 6, timeouts of 30, 60, and 90 microseconds are configured on London.PE and Amsterdam.PE.

In highlighted lines 4 and 8, the **cell-packing** [*cells*] [**mcpt-timer** *timer*] command is used to enable cell packing. The *cells* parameter is used to specify the maximum number of cells that can be packed into a single packet. The *timer* parameter is used to specify one of the three timeouts configured using the **atm mcpt-timers** command. In this example, a maximum of 15 cells is specified, together with a timeout of 60 microseconds (the second of the timeouts configured using the **atm mcpt-timers** command).

The number of cells that you can configure using the **cell-packing** command can range between 2 and the MTU on the ingress LCCE divided by 52. The default number of cells, if you do not specify one, is the outgoing interface MTU divided by 52.

After cell-packing has been configured, you can check the status of cell packing using the **show atm cell-packing** command (see Example 2-28).

Example 2-28 *Checking the Status of Cell Packing Using the* **show atm cell-packing** *Command*

```
London.PE#show atm cell-packing
                             average              average
           circuit       local nbr of cells   peer nbr of cells    MCPT
           type          MNCP  rcvd in one pkt MNCP sent in one pkt (us)
ATM1/0    vc   6/100      15       3            15      1           60 (line 1)
London.PE#
```

Example 2-28 shows that cell packing is configured for an ATM VCC cell relay pseudowire with the associated local attachment circuit VPI/VCI of 6/100 (circuit type).

The output also shows the maximum number of cells packed on the local and remote LCCEs (**local MNCP** and **peer MNCP**, respectively), the average number of cells that the local LCCE has received and sent in one L2TPv3 packet, and the maximum cell packing timeout. So that is the configuration of an ATM VCC cell relay L2TPv3 pseudowire with cell packing.

The configuration of an ATM VPC cell relay L2TPv3 pseudowire with cell packing is almost identical, as shown in Example 2-29. You might also like to compare the configuration shown in Example 2-29 with the configuration of a single cell ATM VPC cell relay L2TPv3 pseudowire in Example 2-22 on page 81.

Example 2-29 *Configuration of Cell Packing with an L2TPv3 Pseudowire*

```
 !
 ! On London.PE (line 1)
 !
 l2tp-class mjlnet.To.Amsterdam
  digest secret mjlnet hash sha
 !
 pseudowire-class mjlnet.PW.To.Amsterdam
  encapsulation l2tpv3
  protocol l2tpv3 mjlnet.Class.To.Amsterdam
  ip local interface Loopback0
 !
 !
 interface ATM1/0
  no ip address
  no ip directed-broadcast
  atm mcpt-timers 30 60 90 (line 2)
  no atm enable-ilmi-trap
  no atm ilmi-keepalive
  atm pvp 6 l2transport (line 3)
   cell-packing 15 mcpt-timer 2 (line 4)
   xconnect 172.16.1.3 1003 pw-class mjlnet.PW.To.Amsterdam
   !
 !

 !
 ! On Amsterdam.PE (line 5)
 !
 l2tp-class mjlnet.Class.To.London
  digest secret mjlnet hash sha
 !
 pseudowire-class mjlnet.PW.To.London
  encapsulation l2tpv3
  protocol l2tpv3 mjlnet.Class.To.London
  ip local interface Loopback0
 !
 !
 interface ATM1/0
  no ip address
  no ip directed-broadcast
  atm mcpt-timers 30 60 90 (line 6)
  no atm enable-ilmi-trap
  no atm ilmi-keepalive
  atm pvp 6 l2transport (line 7)
   cell-packing 15 mcpt-timer 2 (line 8)
   xconnect 172.16.1.1 1003 pw-class mjlnet.PW.To.London
   !
 !
```

Implementing AAL5 SDU Mode L2TPv3 Pseudowires   As discussed, a second method of transporting ATM traffic can be used with AAL5 traffic. It is possible to map an AAL5 VC to an L2TPv3 session.

In AAL5 SDU mode, the ingress LCCE reassembles AAL5 SDUs, and then inserts those AAL5 SDUs into L2TPv3 packets, as shown in Figure 2-35. Note that the AAL5 trailer and padding bytes are not sent.

Figure 2-35 *AAL5 SDU Mode*

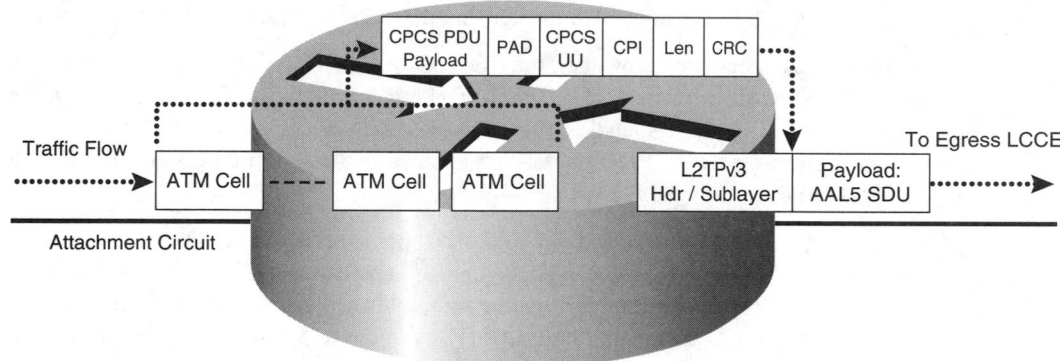

The egress LCCE performs the process shown in Figure 2-35 in reverse—it receives the L2TPv3 packets, decapsulates the AAL5 SDUs, reconstructs the AAL5 CPCS-PDUs, then disassembles the AAL5 CPCS-PDUs into ATM cells, and transmits them on the attachment circuit.

Figure 2-36 illustrates the encapsulation of AAL5 SDUs in L2TPv3 packets.

Figure 2-36 *L2TPv3 Encapsulation for AAL5 SDUs*

0										1										2										3	
0	1	2	3	4	5	6	7	8	9	0	1	2	3	4	5	6	7	8	9	0	1	2	3	4	5	6	7	8	9	0	1

IP Header [20 Bytes]
L2TPv3 Session Header

x	S	x	x	T	G	C	U	Sequence Number

AAL5 CPCS-SDU

The L2TPv3 packet shown in Figure 2-36 begins with the standard IP and L2TPv3 session headers. After the IP and L2TPv3 session headers comes the ATM-specific sublayer. The use of the ATM-specific sublayer is mandatory with AAL5 SDU mode.

When the ingress LCCE reassembles the AAL5 SDU, it discards the CPCS-PDU trailer consisting of the CPCS UU, CPI, Length, and CRC, as well as any padding (the PAD field)—see the section titled "ATM Operation, Cell, PDU, and SDU Formats," on page 67 for more information on these fields.

The T bit in the ATM-specific sublayer is set to 0 to indicate that this L2TPv3 packet carries a CPCS-SDU. A bit setting of 1 indicates that the packet carries an ATM admin cell.

As previously mentioned, however, the EFCI, CLP, and, if present, C/R (from the CPCS UU field) bit settings of the AAL5 CPCS-PDU are carried in the G, C, and U bit settings, respectively, of the ATM-specific sublayer in the L2TPv3 packet. The CPCS-SDU is extracted from the CPCS-PDU payload and placed in the AAL5 CPCS-SDU field of the L2TPv3 packet.

If the CPCS-SDU (contained in the CPCS-PDU payload) is greater than the L2TPv3 session MTU, the CPCS-SDU can be fragmented and carried in a number of L2TPv3 packets. The L2TPv3 packets carrying the first, intermediate, and final fragments of the CPCS-SDU are indicated using the B and E bits of the ATM-specific sublayer (see the explanation of Figure 2-30 earlier in this chapter), so that the egress LCCE can reassemble the CPCS-SDU (and then AAL5 CPCS-PDU).

As you will see by comparing Example 2-30 and Example 2-20, configuration of an AAL5 SDU mode L2TPv3 pseudowire is remarkably similar to that for an ATM VCC cell relay pseudowire (spot the difference!).

Example 2-30 *Configuration of an AAL5 SDU Mode L2TPv3 Pseudowire*

```
!
! On London.PE (line 1)
!
l2tp-class mjlnet.Class.To.Amsterdam
 digest secret mjlnet hash sha
!
pseudowire-class mjlnet.PW.To.Amsterdam
 encapsulation l2tpv3
 protocol l2tpv3 mjlnet.Class.To.Amsterdam
 ip local interface Loopback0
!
!
interface ATM1/0
 no ip address
 no ip directed-broadcast
 no atm enable-ilmi-trap
 no atm ilmi-keepalive
```

Example 2-30 *Configuration of an AAL5 SDU Mode L2TPv3 Pseudowire (Continued)*

```
pvc 6/100 l2transport (line 2)
 encapsulation aal5 (line 3)
 xconnect 172.16.1.3 1003 pw-class mjlnet.PW.To.Amsterdam (line 4)
 !
!
```

```
!
! On Amsterdam.PE (line 5)
!
l2tp-class mjlnet.Class.To.London
 digest secret mjlnet hash sha
!
pseudowire-class mjlnet.Class.To.London
 encapsulation l2tpv3
 protocol l2tpv3 mjlnet.Class.To.London
 ip local interface Loopback0
!
!
interface ATM1/0
 no ip address
 no ip directed-broadcast
 no atm enable-ilmi-trap
 no atm ilmi-keepalive
 pvc 6/100 l2transport (line 6)
  encapsulation aal5 (line 7)
  xconnect 172.16.1.1 1003 pw-class mjlnet.PW.To.London (line 8)
 !
!
```

The configuration for AAL5 SDU mode L2TPv3 pseudowire on London.PE and
Amsterdam.PE is shown from highlighted lines 1 to 4 and 5 to 8, respectively.

The **pvc** *vpi/vci* **l2transport** command (highlighted line 2) configures the VPI/VCI for a
PVC, and specifies that this PVC to be switched to a (L2TPv3) pseudowire. The **encapsulation
aal5** command (highlighted line 3) then configures ATM AAL5 encapsulation. This
command is the only difference with the configuration for an ATM VCC cell relay shown
in Example 2-20.

And finally, the **xconnect** *peer-ip-address vcid* **pw-class** *pseudowire-class* command in
highlighted line 4 then specifies that the PVC will be bound to the pseudowire with VC ID
1003, to peer LCCE/PE 172.16.1.3 (Amsterdam.PE), using pseudowire class
mjlnet.Class.To.Amsterdam.

The configuration on Amsterdam.PE is identical (highlighted lines 5 to 8), with the
exception of the peer IP address (172.16.1.1, London.PE) and pseudowire class name
(mjlnet.Class.To.London) configured using the **xconnect** command.

As shown in Example 2-31, you can verify the AAL5 SDU mode pseudowire using the
show atm vc command.

Example 2-31 *Verifying the AAL5 SDU Mode Pseudowire Using the* **show atm vc** *Command*

```
Amsterdam.PE#show atm vc
                 VCD /                                Peak Avg/Min Burst
   Interface     Name       VPI  VCI Type   Encaps    Kbps  Kbps Cells Sts
   1/0            1           6   100 PVC    AAL5      149760  N/A         UP
Amsterdam.PE#
```

The output of the **show atm vc** command confirms the VPI/VCI of the attachment circuit bound to the pseudowire (6/100), the encapsulation type (AAL5), and the circuit status (UP).

The other command that is useful for verifying AAL5 SDU mode L2TPv3 pseudowires is the old perennial, **show l2tun session** (see Example 2-32).

Example 2-32 *Verifying AAL5 SDU Mode L2TPv3 Pseudowires Using the* **show l2tun session** *Command*

```
London.PE#show l2tun session all
 Session Information Total tunnels 1 sessions 1
 Tunnel control packets dropped due to failed digest 0

Session id 5164 is up, tunnel id 33080
Call serial number is 135100005
Remote tunnel name is Amsterdam.PE
  Internet address is 172.16.1.3
  Session is L2TP signaled (line 1)
  Session state is established, time since change 00:01:53
    1 Packets sent, 0 received
    52 Bytes sent, 0 received
    Receive packets dropped:
      out-of-order:            0
      total:                   0
    Send packets dropped:
      exceeded session MTU:    0
      total:                   0
  Session vcid is 1003
  Session Layer 2 circuit, type is ATM AAL5, name is ATM1/0:6/100 (line 2)
  Circuit state is UP
    Remote session id is 13924, remote tunnel id 10630
  DF bit off, ToS reflect disabled, ToS value 0, TTL value 255
  No session cookie information available
  FS cached header information:
    encap size = 28 bytes
    00000000 00000000 00000000 00000000
    00000000 00000000 00000000
  Sequencing is off
London.PE#
```

Highlighted lines 1 and 2 contain the most pertinent information—highlighted line 1 shows that the pseudowire is L2TPv3 signaled, and highlighted line 2 shows that pseudowire type is AAL5 SDU mode.

Implementing L2TPv3 Pseudowire-Based L2VPNs Using Static Session Configuration

A second method of deploying L2TPv3 pseudowire-based L2VPNs is to use static session configuration. In this case, there is no dynamic session setup.

You can deploy static L2TPv3 sessions in a network in two ways:

- Static L2TPv3 sessions without a control connection
- Static L2TPv3 sessions with a control connection

These methods of deploying static L2TPv3 sessions are discussed in the following two sections.

Static L2TPv3 Sessions Without a Control Connection

The first method of deploying static L2TPv3 sessions is to configure them without a control connection.

Configuration consists of the following steps:

Step 1   Configure CEF.

Step 2   Configure a loopback interface to use as the pseudowire endpoint.

Step 3   Configure a pseudowire class.

Step 4   Bind attachment circuits to pseudowires.

These steps must be specified on both LACs between which pseudowires are configured.

The configuration for static L2TPv3 sessions without a control connection is almost identical to the configuration for dynamic L2TPv3 sessions, with the main difference being that you do not configure an L2TPv3 class.

Apart from the fact that you do not configure an L2TPv3 class, the only other difference is the method of binding attachment circuits to pseudowires (Step 4). This difference is discussed in detail in this section. See the section titled "Deploying L2TPv3 Pseudowires with Dynamic Session Setup" on page 42 for more information on configuration Steps 1 to 3.

Figure 2-37 shows a sample deployment of a static L2TPv3 session without a control connection.

Figure 2-37 *Sample Deployment of Static L2TPv3 Sessions Without a Control Connection*

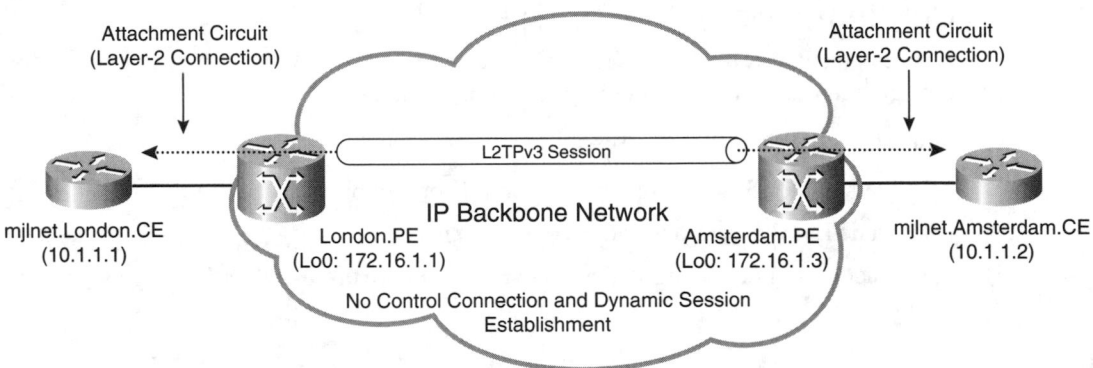

Example 2-33 shows the configuration corresponding to the deployment shown in Figure 2-37.

Example 2-33 *Deploying Static L2TPv3 Session Without a Control Connection*

```
!
hostname London.PE (line 1)
!
pseudowire-class l2tpv3.static.pw.class (line 2)
encapsulation l2tpv3
protocol none (line 3)
ip local interface Loopback0
!
interface FastEthernet1/0
!
interface FastEthernet1/0.100
 encapsulation dot1Q 100
 xconnect 172.16.1.3 2001 encapsulation l2tpv3 manual pw-class
   l2tpv3.static.pw.class (line 4)
 l2tp id 2001 1002 (line 5)
 l2tp cookie local 4 88888 (line 6)
 l2tp cookie remote 4 77777 (line 7)
!
!
!
hostname Amsterdam.PE (line 8)
!
pseudowire-class l2tpv3.static.pw.class (line 9)
encapsulation l2tpv3
protocol none (line 10)
ip local interface Loopback0
!
interface FastEthernet2/0
!
interface FastEthernet2/0.100
 encapsulation dot1Q 100
 xconnect 172.16.1.1 2001 encapsulation l2tpv3 manual pw-class
   l2tpv3.static.pw.class (line 11)
```

Example 2-33 *Deploying Static L2TPv3 Session Without a Control Connection (Continued)*

```
l2tp id 1002 2001 (line 12)
l2tp cookie local 4 77777 (line 13)
l2tp cookie remote 4 88888 (line 14)
!
!
```

Highlighted lines 1 to 7 show the configuration for London.PE.

In highlighted line 3, the **protocol none** command is configured within a pseudowire class called l2tpc3.static.pw.class. This command is crucial—it is the command that configures the PE router *not* to use dynamic session setup.

The **xconnect** *peer-pe-ip-address vcid* **encapsulation l2tpv3 manual pw-class** *pw-class-name* command is then used to bind interface Fast Ethernet 1/0.100 to a pseudowire with VC ID 2001 in highlighted line 4. The pseudowire class configured in highlighted line 2 (l2tpv3.static.pw.class) is specified with the **pw-class** parameter.

The **encapsulation l2tpv3 manual** keywords in the middle of the **xconnect** command syntax are used to specify that this is a static L2TPv3 session and allow the configuration of the commands shown in highlighted lines 5 to 7.

You might remember that when configuring dynamic L2TPv3 session setup the VC ID specified using the **xconnect** command must be consistent between PE routers for the same pseudowire. When you configure static L2TPv3 sessions, however, it is *possible* to configure different VC IDs because the VC ID is only used during dynamic session setup. Having said that, for the sake of consistency, it is certainly a good idea to configure consistent VC ID on PE routers for the same pseudowire.

Next, the **l2tp id** *local-session-id remote-session-id* command (highlighted line 5) is used to specify the local and remote L2TPv3 session IDs. These must be mirror images on peer PE routers for the same pseudowire.

The **l2tp cookie local** *size low-value* [*high-value*] and **l2tp cookie remote** *size low-value* [*high-value*] commands are configured in highlighted lines 6 and 7. These commands are used to specify local and remote cookie sizes (4 or 8 bytes in length), as well as local and remote cookie values. The *low-value* and *high-value* parameters are used to configure low-order and high-order 4 bytes of the cookie value. You only need to configure the high-order 4 bytes using the *high-value* parameter if you have specified an 8-byte cookie size.

The local and remote cookie sizes and values (both low order and high order) must mirror each other on peer PE routers for the same pseudowire.

The configuration of Amsterdam.PE (highlighted lines 8 to 14) is similar to that for London.PE, but there are one or two crucial differences—the session IDs and cookies specified in highlighted lines 12 to 14 are mirror images of those configured on London.PE in highlighted lines 5 to 7. As previously mentioned, these session IDs and cookie values must be mirror images on peer PE routers for the same pseudowire; otherwise, the pseudowire will not come up.

As with dynamic session establishment, you can use the **show l2tun session** command to examine the status of a manually configured L2TPv3 session.

Static L2TPv3 Sessions with a Control Connection

You might be looking at the title of this section and wondering what the point of configuring static L2TPv3 sessions with a control connection is. Well, the advantage of configuring a control connection with static L2TPv3 sessions is that you can still take advantage of the keepalive and authentication capabilities afforded by the control connection.

As far as configuration is concerned, it is the same as that discussed in the previous section, but with the exception that you must configure an L2TPv3 class.

Figure 2-38 illustrates a sample deployment of a static L2TPv3 session with a control connection.

Figure 2-38 *Sample Deployment of Static L2TPv3 Sessions with a Control Connection*

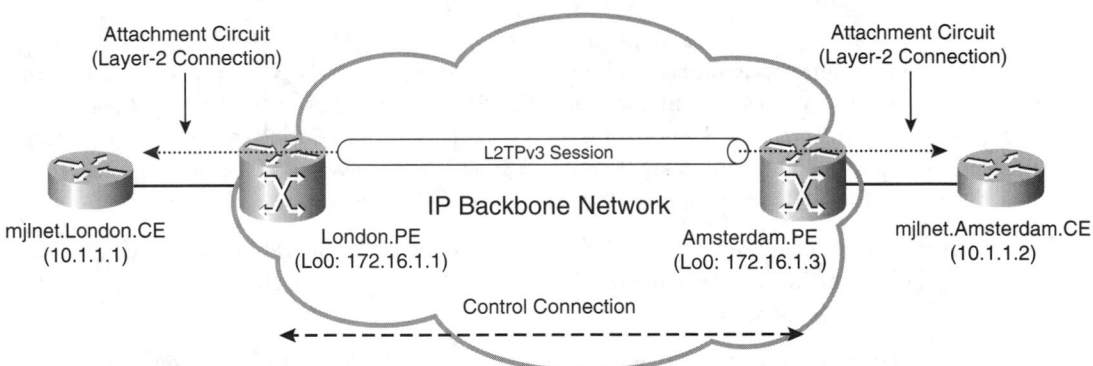

Example 2-34 shows the configuration of a static L2TPv3 session with a control connection (corresponding to the deployment in Figure 2-38).

Example 2-34 *Configuration of a Static L2TPv3 Session with a Control Connection*

```
!
hostname London.PE (line 1)
!
l2tp-class l2tpv3.static.class (line 2)
 hello 45 (line 3)
 digest secret mjlnet hash sha (line 4)
!
pseudowire-class l2tpv3.static.pw.class
encapsulation l2tpv3
protocol none
ip local interface Loopback0
```

Example 2-34 *Configuration of a Static L2TPv3 Session with a Control Connection (Continued)*

```
 !
 interface FastEthernet1/0
 !
 interface FastEthernet1/0.100
  encapsulation dot1Q 100
  xconnect 172.16.1.3 2001 encapsulation l2tpv3 manual pw-class
   l2tpv3.static.pw.class
  l2tp id 2001 1002
  l2tp cookie local 4 88888
  l2tp cookie remote 4 77777
  l2tp hello l2tpv3.static.class (line 5)
  !
```
```
 !
 hostname Amsterdam.PE (line 6)
 !
 l2tp-class l2tpv3.static.class (line 7)
  hello 45 (line 8)
  digest secret mjlnet hash sha (line 9)
 !
 pseudowire-class l2tpv3.static.pw.class
 encapsulation l2tpv3
 protocol none
 ip local interface Loopback0
 !
 interface FastEthernet2/0
 !
 interface FastEthernet2/0.100
  encapsulation dot1Q 100
  xconnect 172.16.1.1 2001 encapsulation l2tpv3 manual pw-class
   l2tpv3.static.pw.class
  l2tp id 1002 2001
  l2tp cookie local 4 77777
  l2tp cookie remote 4 88888
  l2tp hello l2tpv3.static.class (line 10)
  !
```

The first thing you might notice about the configurations of London.PE and Amsterdam.PE in Example 2-34 is that they are almost identical to those in Example 2-33.

So, what are the differences? Those of you with a keen eye may already have detected the addition of an L2TPv3 class to each configuration (the highlighting may be a bit of a giveaway)! An L2TPv3 class called l2tpv3.static.class is configured on London.PE in highlighted lines 2 to 4.

The **hello** *seconds* command is configured within the L2TPv3 class in highlighted line 3. This command configures the interval at which the PE router sends L2TPv3 Hello messages in the absence of any L2TPv3 data or control channel messages from its peer. If no acknowledgment is received from the peer, the control channel and session (pseudowire) are torn down.

NOTE   The default interval for L2TPv3 Hello messages is 60 seconds.

Highlighted line 4 shows the **digest secret** *password* [**hash** {**md5** | **sha**}] command. This command is used to configure authentication for the control channel using the specified password and hash algorithm.

The configuration of authentication is optional. Note that if authentication fails for the control channel then neither the control channel nor the L2TPv3 session(s) associated with it will come up. Make sure that the authentication password and hash algorithm are consistent between peer PE routers.

In highlighted line 5, the **l2tp hello** *l2tp-class-name* static session command is used to reference the L2TPv3 class that was configured in highlighted lines 2 to 4 (l2tpv3.static.class). An identical L2TPv3 class is configured on Amsterdam.PE in highlighted lines 7 to 9. This L2TPv3 class is then referenced for the static session in highlighted line 10.

You can again check the status of the L2TPv3 control connection and the static L2TPv3 session(s) using the **show l2tun session** command.

L2VPN Interworking with L2TPv3

By now, you know that it is possible to deploy L2TPv3 pseudowires with like attachment circuits. If you want to deploy pseudowires that connect attachment circuits of different types, however, you can use a feature called *L2VPN interworking*.

L2VPN interworking can be useful if, for example, a traditional L2VPN such as a Frame Relay VPN has been migrated to a service provider's IP backbone, and now a customer wants to take advantage of newer attachment circuit types such as Ethernet to connect new or existing sites to the VPN.

Figure 2-39 depicts L2VPN interworking.

L2VPN interworking can be implemented in two ways:

- Using Ethernet mode (pseudowire type 0x0005 [see Table 2-1])
- Using IP mode (pseudowire type 0x000B)

Ethernet mode and IP mode L2VPN interworking are discussed in the following two sections.

Figure 2-39 *L2VPN Interworking*

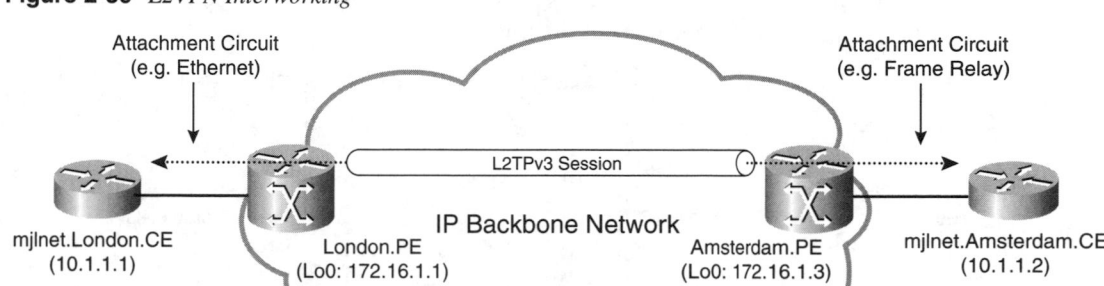

Ethernet Mode L2VPN Interworking with L2TPv3

In Ethernet mode interworking, the Ethernet attachment circuit is extended across the pseudowire between the PE routers. In this model, the interworking function (IWF) need only be performed on one PE router.

NOTE   Ethernet mode interworking can also be referred to as bridged mode interworking. The pseudowire type used with Ethernet mode is 0x0005 (Ethernet, see Table 2-1 on page 35).

Some of the main advantages and disadvantages of Ethernet mode interworking are as follows:

- It can be used to transport both IP and non-IP protocols (IPv4, IPv6, IPX, AppleTalk, and so on).

- Configuration for routing protocols such as Open Shortest Path First (OSPF) and Intermediate System-to-Intermediate System (IS-IS) is relatively simple with Ethernet mode.

- CE routers must be configured with Integrated Routing and Bridging (IRB) or Route Bridge Encapsulation (RBE) if the native service and the local attachment circuit type are different.

If you are using Ethernet mode L2VPN interworking, Ethernet frames that a PE router receives from a CE device are encapsulated in L2TPv3 and sent over the pseudowire to its peer PE router. A PE router receiving Ethernet frames over the pseudowire either just forwards these frames over the local attachment circuit to a CE device if the attachment circuit type is Ethernet, or encapsulates the Ethernet frames using the local attachment circuit encapsulation type if it is not Ethernet.

Figure 2-40 illustrates the operation of Ethernet mode L2VPN interworking.

Figure 2-40 *Ethernet Mode L2VPN Interworking*

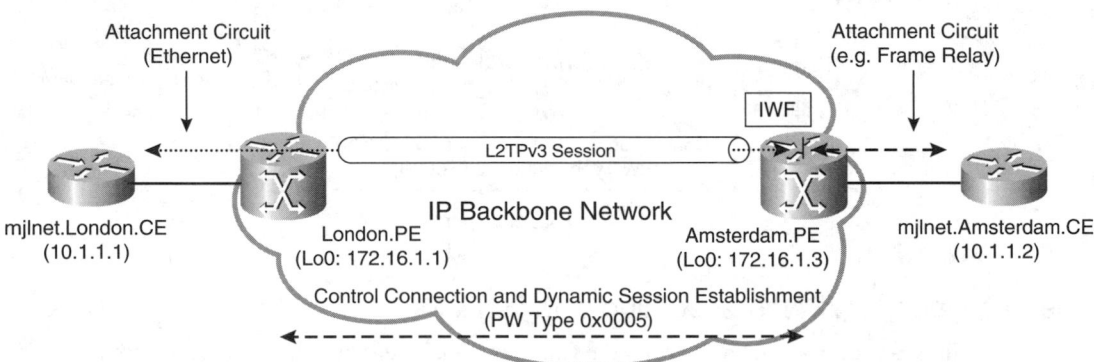

In Figure 2-40, mjlnet.London.CE transmits an Ethernet frame over the Ethernet attachment circuit to London.PE.

London.PE encapsulates the Ethernet frame received from mjlnet.London.CE in an L2TPv3 packet and transmits it to Amsterdam.PE.

Amsterdam.PE now has to forward the Ethernet frame over the attachment circuit to mjlnet.Amsterdam.CE, but the attachment circuit, in this example, uses a Frame Relay encapsulation. Amsterdam.PE performs an IWF and encapsulates the frame that it received over the L2TPv3 pseudowire from Beijing.PE in Frame Relay and sends it to mjlnet.Amsterdam.CE.

NOTE RFC 2427 describes the encapsulation (bridging) of 802.3/Ethernet over Frame Relay.

So far so good. But how does mjlnet.Amsterdam.CE handle the Ethernet over Frame Relay frames that it receives from Amsterdam.PE? To process these frames correctly, either a Bridge Virtual Interface (BVI) or RBE must be configured on mjlnet.Amsterdam.CE.

NOTE A BVI is used in conjunction with IRB. It is a virtual interface that that is associated with one of more physical (or logical) interfaces that are performing bridging via a bridge group.

RBE allows IEEE 802.3 or Ethernet II frames to be processed on a point-to-point routed interface. The point-to-point interface itself can be configured with an encapsulation such as PPP, Frame Relay, or ATM.

Traffic forwarding between mjlnet.Amsterdam.CE and mjlnet.London.CE occurs in the same way, but obviously in the opposite direction.

To understand L2VPN interworking, it is important to distinguish between the encapsulation used end-to-end between CE devices, and the encapsulation types used on the attachment circuits. The encapsulation used end to end between CE devices is sometimes referred to as the *native service*.

In Figure 2-40, the native service and attachment circuit encapsulation are the same on the link between mljnet.London.CE and London.PE (both Ethernet) but are different on the link between Amsterdam.PE and mjlnet.Amsterdam.CE (Ethernet and Frame Relay, respectively). The native service in Figure 2-40 is Ethernet.

At the time of this writing, you can use Ethernet mode L2VPN interworking with the following combinations of attachment circuits:

- Frame Relay to Ethernet
- Frame Relay to VLAN (802.1Q)
- Ethernet to VLAN (802.1Q)

Example 2-35 shows the configuration of Ethernet mode L2VPN interworking with Ethernet and VLAN attachment circuits (see Figure 2-40).

Example 2-35 *Configuration of Ethernet Mode Interworking with Frame Relay and Ethernet Attachment Circuits*

```
!
hostname London.PE (line 1)
!
l2tp-class l2tpv3.iw.class
 digest secret mjlnet hash sha
!
pseudowire-class l2tpv3.iw.pw.class
 encapsulation l2tpv3
 interworking ethernet (line 2)
 protocol l2tpv3 l2tpv3.iw.class
 ip local interface Loopback0
!
!
interface FastEthernet0/0 (line 3)
 xconnect 172.16.1.3 2001 pw-class l2tpv3.iw.pw.class
!
```
```
!
hostname Amsterdam.PE (line 4)
!
l2tp-class l2tpv3.iw.class
 digest secret mjlnet hash sha
!
pseudowire-class l2tpv3.iw.pw.class
 encapsulation l2tpv3
 interworking ethernet (line 5)
 protocol l2tpv3 l2tpv3.iw.class
```

continues

Example 2-35 *Configuration of Ethernet Mode Interworking with Frame Relay and Ethernet Attachment Circuits (Continued)*

```
 ip local interface Loopback0
 !
 !
 interface FastEthernet2/0
 !
 interface FastEthernet2/0.100 (line 6)
  encapsulation dot1Q 100 (line 7)
  xconnect 172.16.1.1 2001 pw-class l2tpv3.iw.pw.class
 !
```

The first thing you will notice about the configurations in Example 2-35 is that for the most part they resemble the configurations for like-to-like attachment circuits.

The significant difference in the configuration is the **interworking ethernet** command within the pseudowire class on London.PE (highlighted line 2) and Amsterdam.PE (highlighted line 5). This command is used to configure Ethernet mode interworking.

NOTE   The L2VPN interworking mode (Ethernet or IP) must match between peer PE routers; otherwise, interworking will not function.

IP Mode L2VPN Interworking with L2TPv3

In IP mode L2VPN interworking, both attachment circuits are locally terminated on their connected PE router, and the IWF is performed on both PE routers.

NOTE   IP mode interworking can also be called *routed mode interworking*. The pseudowire type used with IP mode interworking is 0x000B (IP Layer2 Transport, see Table 2-1).

Some of the main advantages and disadvantages of IP mode L2VPN interworking are as follows:

*   There is less packet overhead (it is more bandwidth efficient) than Ethernet mode because Layer 2 headers are not carried over the pseudowire.

*   Non-IP traffic cannot be carried.

*   Routing protocol (OSPF) configuration may be more complicated than when using Ethernet mode L2VPN interworking.

*   PE router configuration may be more complicated, particularly with respect to Address Resolution Protocol (ARP) mediation. *ARP mediation* is the process of discovering Layer 2 addresses when different address-resolution protocols are used on the attachment circuits (for example, ARP on one attachment circuit, and inverse ARP on the other attachment circuit).

When using IP mode interworking, a PE router extracts IP packets from frames received from the local CE device on the attachment circuit. The PE router then encapsulates these IP packets in L2TPv3 and sends them over the pseudowire to its peer PE router.

A PE router receiving IP packets from its peer PE router now encapsulates them using the local attachment circuit encapsulation type, and transmits them to its local CE device.

Figure 2-41 illustrates IP mode L2VPN interworking.

Figure 2-41 *IP Mode L2VPN Interworking*

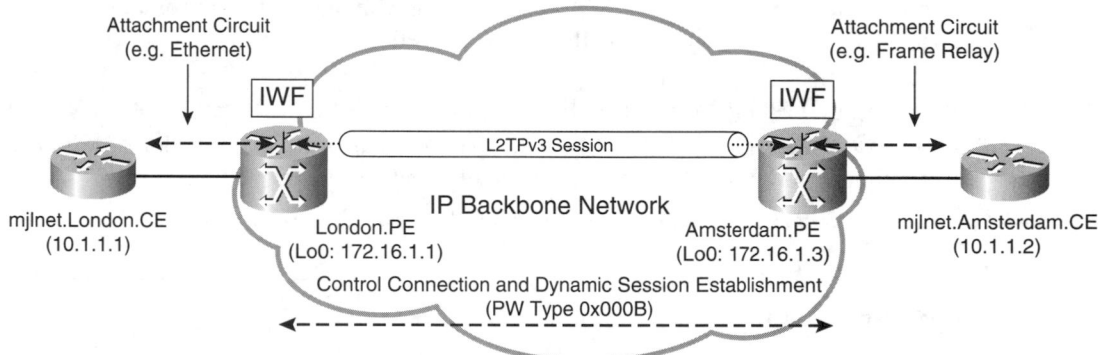

In Figure 2-41, mjlnet.London.CE forwards IPv4 packets in Ethernet frames over the attachment circuit to London.PE. London.PE extracts the IPv4 packets from the Ethernet frames, and forwards them over the pseudowire to Amsterdam.PE. Amsterdam.PE then encapsulates the IPv4 packets received over the pseudowire from London.PE in Frame Relay frames and sends them over the attachment circuit to mjlnet.Amsterdam.CE.

Traffic forwarding from mjlnet.Amsterdam.PE to mjlnet.London.PE occurs in the same manner, just in the opposite direction.

If you are wondering how non-IPv4 packets are forwarded between CE devices in IP mode L2VPN interworking, the simple answer is that they are not—non-IPv4 packets are not forwarded over the pseudowire but are instead dropped by PE routers. So, if you want to forward non-IPv4 packets over the pseudowire, do not use IP mode interworking; use Ethernet mode instead.

One other important consideration when using IP mode L2VPN interworking is that Layer 2 address resolution (ARP, inverse ARP, and so on) does not occur end to end between CE devices because the address-resolution protocols on the attachment circuits differ. Instead, if address resolution occurs at all, it occurs between a CE device and its local PE device.

The process of resolving Layer 2 addresses when address-resolution protocols used on attachment circuits are different is, as previously mentioned, called *ARP mediation*.

Configuring and Verifying IP Mode L2VPN Interworking with L2TPv3

You can use IP mode L2VPN interworking with L2TPv3 with the following combinations of attachment circuits (at the time of this writing):

- Frame Relay to Ethernet
- Frame Relay to VLAN (802.1Q)
- Frame Relay to PPP
- Ethernet to VLAN (802.1Q)

The configuration of IP mode L2VPN interworking with these different combinations of attachment circuits is discussed in the following sections.

IP Mode L2VPN Interworking Between Frame Relay and Ethernet or VLAN (802.1Q) Attachment Circuits

Example 2-36 shows the configuration of IP mode L2VPN interworking with Frame Relay and Ethernet attachment circuits.

Example 2-36 *Configuration of IP Mode Interworking with Frame Relay and Ethernet Attachment Circuits*

```
!
hostname London.PE
!
pseudowire-class L2VPN.IW.02.mjlnet.To.Amsterdam (line 1)
 encapsulation l2tpv3
 interworking ip (line 2)
 ip local interface Loopback1
!
interface FastEthernet0/0
 xconnect 172.16.1.3 2002 pw-class L2VPN.IW.02.mjlnet.To.Amsterdam (line 3)
 !
```

```
!
hostname Amsterdam.PE
!
frame-relay switching (line 4)
!
pseudowire-class L2VPN.IW.02.mjlnet.To.London (line 5)
 encapsulation l2tpv3
 interworking ip (line 6)
 ip local interface Loopback1
!
interface Serial4/3
 no ip address
 encapsulation frame-relay
 frame-relay interface-dlci 300 switched (line 7)
 frame-relay intf-type dce
!
connect L2.IW.London Serial4/3 300 l2transport (line 8)
 xconnect 172.16.1.1 2002 pw-class L2VPN.IW.02.mjlnet.To.London (line 9)
 !
!
```

Highlighted lines 1 to 3 in Example 2-36 show the configuration of IP mode L2VPN interworking on London.LCCE.

For the most part, the configuration is the same as regular Ethernet pseudowire configuration (compare with Example 2-10 on page 48). The difference is the addition of the **interworking ip** command within the pseudowire class.

Highlighted lines 4 to 9 show the configuration of IP mode interworking on Amsterdam.PE.

Again, for the most part, the configuration is the same as a regular DLCI-to-DLCI pseudowire configuration (see Example 2-18). But take a close look at highlighted line 3—the **interworking ip** command is used within the pseudowire class to specify that the pseudowire type is IP mode interworking.

If you examine highlighted lines 6 and 9, you can see that the **xconnect** command on London.PE specifies a VC ID of 2002 and points to Amsterdam.PE (172.16.1.3). The **xconnect** command on Amsterdam.PE specifies a VC ID of 2002 and points to London.PE (172.16.1.1).

Example 2-37 shows the configuration of mjlnet.Amsterdam.CE and mjlnet.London.CE.

Example 2-37 *Configuration of mjlnet.London.CE and mjlnet.Amsterdam.CE*

```
!
hostname mjlnet.London.CE
!
interface Ethernet 0 (line 1)
  description Connected to Amsterdam.PE
  ip address 10.1.1.1 255.255.255.0
!
```
```
!
hostname mjlnet.Amsterdam.CE
!
interface serial 0
  encapsulation frame-relay (line 2)
!
interface serial 0.1 point-to-point (line 3)
  description Connected to London.PE
  ip address 10.1.1.2 255.255.255.0
  frame-relay interface-dlci 300
!
```

Highlighted line 1 shows that an Ethernet interface is configured on mjlnet.London.CE for connectivity to London.PE. Note that a Frame Relay point-to-point subinterface is configured on mjlnet.Amsterdam.CE (see highlighted lines 2 and 3) for connectivity to Amsterdam.PE.

When configuring the Frame Relay encapsulation type on the CE device, you can choose either IETF or Cisco encapsulation (**encapsulation frame-relay** [**cisco** | **ietf**]).

As previously described, when using IP mode L2VPN interworking, address resolution (ARP, inverse ARP, and so on) does not occur end to end between CE devices. Instead, because attachment circuits are terminated on PE routers, the PE routers perform address resolution with local CE devices.

In Example 2-37, a Frame Relay point-to-point subinterface is used on mjlnet.Amsterdam.CE, and so the inverse ARP (RFC2390) is not used on the attachment circuit between mjlnet.Amsterdam.CE and Amsterdam.PE. If you want to use a multipoint interface then you can specify the remote CE device's IP address using the **frame-relay map ip** *remote-ce-ip-address dlci* [**broadcast**].

ARP (RFC826) is, however, used on the Ethernet attachment circuit between mjlnet.London.CE and London.PE.

In the case of Ethernet attachment circuits, the fact that address resolution does not occur end to end between CE devices (mjlnet.Amsterdam.CE and mjlnet.London.CE, in this example) means that PE routers (London.PE, here) must perform proxy ARP for remote CE devices. That is, PE routers must respond with their own MAC address when the local CE device sends an ARP Request message for the remote CE device's IP address.

Figure 2-42 illustrates proxy ARP on PE routers.

Figure 2-42 *Proxy ARP on PE Routers*

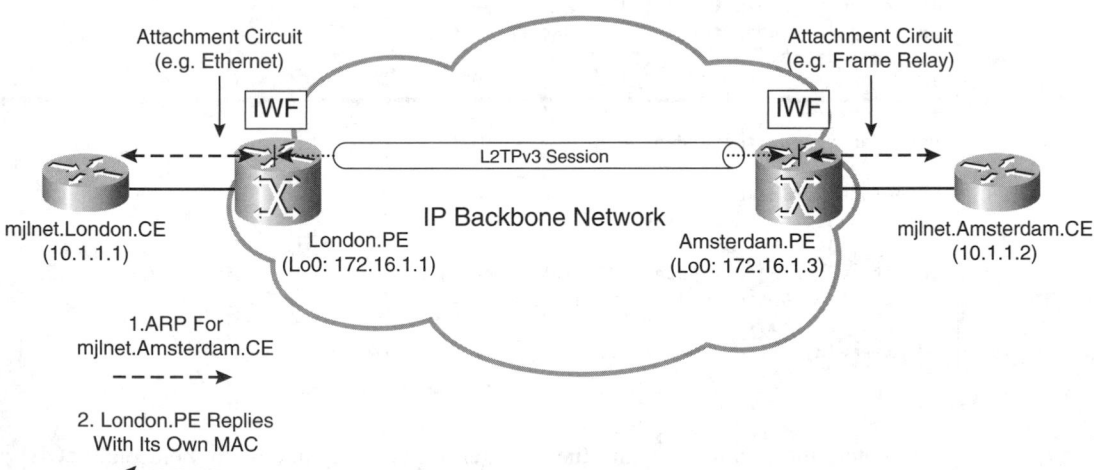

As shown in Figure 2-42, when London.PE receives an ARP Request for mjlnet. Amsterdam.CE's IP address, it responds with its own MAC address.

London.PE can learn mjlnet.London.CE's address via ARP, or by learning it from multicast/broadcast packets sent by mjlnet.London.CE. You can also optionally speed up the learning process by configuring the CE device to respond to ICMP Router Discovery Protocol (IRDP, RFC1256) Solicitation messages from London.PE.

If the CE device on the Ethernet attachment circuit is not configured for IRDP, it will not reply to the IRDP Router Solicitation messages from the PE router, and PE router will not learn the address of the connected CE device. If the PE router does not learn the address of connected CE device via IRDP, it drops traffic sent over the pseudowire to the connected CE device, until it can learn the addresses (which will only happen when the connected CE device starts sending traffic). So, configuring IRDP on the CE device ensures that there is not the (typically) temporary condition of the PE router dropping traffic destined for the connected CE device on the Ethernet attachment circuit.

Configuration of IRDP on CE devices on Ethernet attachment circuits can prove especially useful if a dynamic routing protocol such as OSPF is *not* configured on the CE devices. In this case, there will be no routing protocol transmissions from which the PE router can learn the CE device's address.

Figure 2-43 shows messages (IRDP Router Solicitation and IRDP Router Advertisement) sent between Amsterdam.PE and mjlnet.Amsterdam.CE when IRDP is configured.

Figure 2-43 *IRDP Messages Sent Between Amsterdam.PE and mjlnet.Amsterdam.CE*

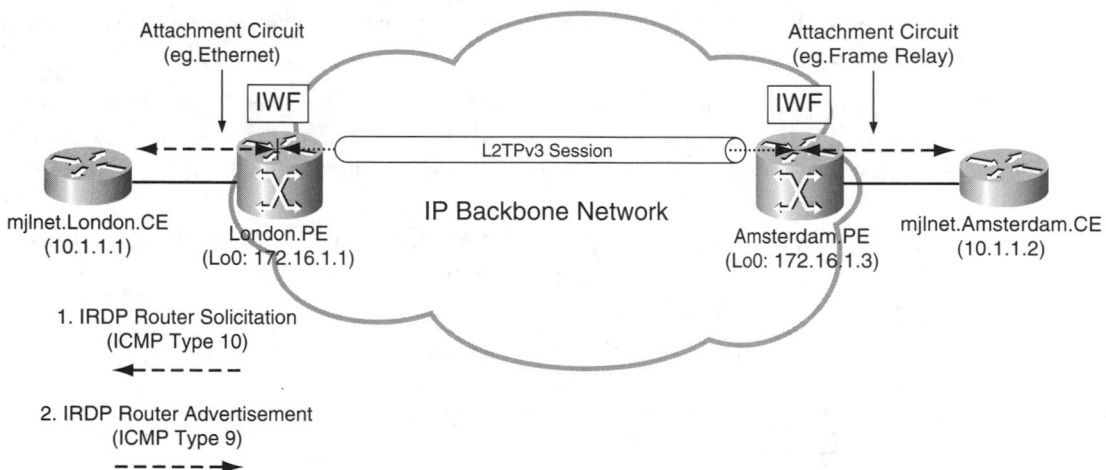

Example 2-38 shows the configuration of IRDP on mjlnet.London.CE.

Example 2-38 *Configuration of IRDP on mjlnet.London.CE*

```
interface e0
 ip address 10.1.1.1 255.255.255.0
 ip irdp (line 1)
 ip irdp maxadvertinterval 0 (line 2)
 !
```

The **ip irdp** command in highlighted line 1 is used to enable IDRP on the interface connected to Amsterdam.PE.

In highlighted line 2, the **ip irdp maxadvertinterval** *seconds* command is used to specify the maximum interval to send ICMP Router Advertisement messages. Because a maximum interval of 0 seconds is specified, advertisements are only sent in response to ICMP Router Solicitation messages from Amsterdam.PE.

Before finishing this particular section, it is important to discuss configuration differences when using Frame Relay and VLAN (802.1Q) attachment circuits.

Much of the configuration shown in Example 2-37 remains the same, with the only difference being the configuration of the attachment circuit on London.PE.

Example 2-39 shows the configuration of a VLAN attachment circuit on London.PE.

Example 2-39 *Configuration of a VLAN (8021Q) Attachment Circuit on London.PE*

```
!
interface FastEthernet0/0.1 (line 1)
 encapsulation dot1Q 100 (line 2)
 xconnect 172.16.1.3 2001 pw-class L2VPN.IW.02.mjlnet.To.Amsterdam
 !
```

In highlighted lines 1 and 2, 802.1Q encapsulation is configured on interface Fast Ethernet 0/0.1 for VLAN 100.

With the exception of the slight modification of the configuration of the attachment circuit on London.PE shown in Example 2-39, all other considerations discussed in the section (address resolution and so on) remain the same as for Ethernet attachment circuits.

IP Mode L2VPN Interworking Between Frame Relay and PPP Attachment Circuits

Example 2-40 shows the configuration of IP mode interworking between Frame Relay and PPP attachment circuits.

Example 2-40 *Configuration of IP Mode Interworking Between Frame Relay and PPP Attachment Circuits*

```
!
hostname London.PE
!
pseudowire-class L2VPN.IW.02.mjlnet.To.Amsterdam
 encapsulation l2tpv3
 interworking ip (line 1)
 ip local interface Loopback0
 !
 !
interface Serial2/0
 no ip address
 encapsulation ppp (line 3)
 xconnect 172.16.1.3 2002 pw-class L2VPN.IW.02.mjlnet.To.Amsterdam
 ppp ipcp address proxy 10.1.1.2 (line 3)
```

Example 2-40 *Configuration of IP Mode Interworking Between Frame Relay and PPP Attachment Circuits (Continued)*

```
!
!
hostname Amsterdam.PE
!
frame-relay switching (line 4)
!
pseudowire-class L2VPN.IW.02.mjlnet.To.Amsterdam
 encapsulation l2tpv3
 interworking ip (line 5)
 ip local interface Loopback0
!
!
interface Serial1/0
 no ip address
 encapsulation frame-relay (line 6)
 frame-relay intf-type dce
!
!
connect frame.to.ppp Serial1/0 50 l2transport
 xconnect 172.16.1.1 2002 pw-class L2VPN.IW.02.mjlnet.To.Amsterdam
!
```

You'll notice that again the main difference between the configurations shown in Example 2-40 and basic pseudowire configurations is the addition of the **interworking ip** command in the pseudowire class (see highlighted lines 1 and 5). One other important difference is the addition of the **ppp ipcp address proxy** *ip-address* command on London.PE.

The **ppp ipcp address proxy** *ip-address* command is used to configure the *remote* CE device's IP address (mjlnet.Amsterdam.CE, in this example), and it can be used because the LCP and, importantly, IP IPCP are negotiated between the CE device and the connected PE router (mjlnet.London.CE and London.PE respectively in this example), rather than end to end between the two CE devices. The PE router (London.PE) will supply the remote CE device's (mjlnet.Amsterdam.CE) IP address to the connected (local) CE router using an IPCP Address option during IPCP negotiation.

The Address option is an IPCP message component that can be used to communicate the IP address of a local system to a remote system. As already stated, if the **ppp ipcp address proxy** command is configured on the PE router, the PE router (London.PE) pretends to be the remote CE device (mjlnet.Amsterdam.CE) and supplies the remote CE's IP address during IPCP negotiation with the local CE device (mjlnet.London.CE). If the **ppp ipcp address proxy** command is not configured on the PE router, the Address option sent by the PE router during IPCP negotiation is empty (0.0.0.0)—this may or may not cause problems depending on the particular CE device type and vendor. Cisco CE routers take this empty Address option as a hint to supply an IP address from a pool, fail to find a configured address pool but then continue to forward traffic anyway. But, irrespective, it is probably a good idea to configure **ip ipcp address proxy** command on the PE router—it is better to be safe.

Figure 2-44 shows LCP and IPCP negotiation between the CE device and the connected PE router. You might like to contrast this regular PPP interworking where LCP and IPCP are negotiated between the CE devices at either end of the pseudowire (see Figure 2-19 on page 57).

Figure 2-44 *LCP and IPCP Are Negotiated Between the CE Device and the Connected PE Router*

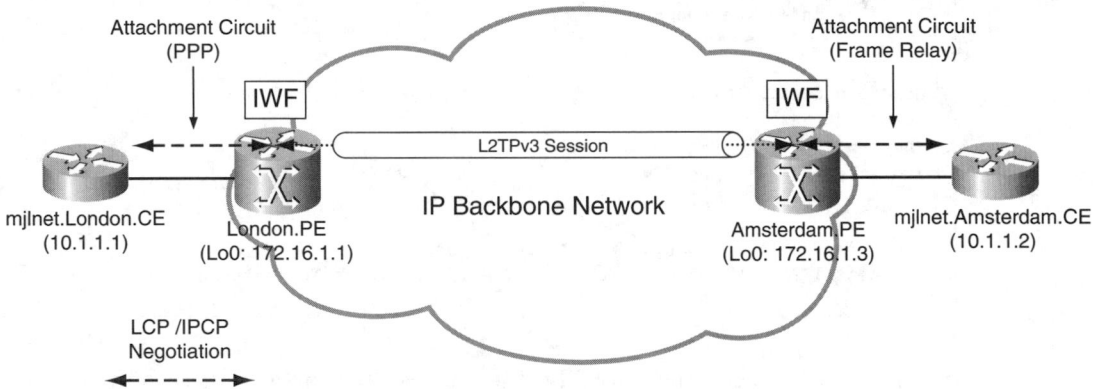

Example 2-41 shows the configuration of mjlnet.London.CE and mjlnet.Amsterdam.CE.

Example 2-41 *Configuration of mjlnet.London.CE and mjlnet.Amsterdam.CE*

```
!
hostname mjlnet.London.CE (line 1)
!
interface serial 0/0 (line 2)
 description Connected to London.PE
 encapsulation ppp (line 3)
 ip address 10.1.1.1 255.255.255.0
!
```
```
!
hostname mjlnet.Amsterdam.CE (line 4)
!
interface serial 1/0
 encapsulation frame-relay (line 4)
!
interface serial 1/0.1 point-to-point (line 6)
 description Connected to Amsterdam.PE
 ip address 10.1.1.2 255.255.255.0
 frame-relay interface-dlci 300
!
```

The configurations of mjlnet.London.CE and mjlnet.Amsterdam.CE are standard. The only thing to note is that a Frame Relay point-to-point subinterface is again configured on mjlnet.Amsterdam.CE (see highlighted line 6), thus ensuring that inverse ARP is not used.

If you want to use a multipoint interface, you can again specify the remote CE device's IP address using the **frame-relay map ip** *remote-ce-ip-address dlci* [**broadcast**].

NOTE   If you configure Frame Relay to PPP interworking, it is important to note that only a single PPP connection is supported for interworking with a single Frame Relay PVC—multipoint interworking is not supported.

IP Mode L2VPN Interworking with Ethernet and VLAN (802.1Q) Attachment Circuits   The configuration of IP mode L2VPN interworking with Ethernet and VLAN (802.1Q) attachments circuits is shown in Example 2-42.

Example 2-42 *Configuration of IP Mode L2VPN Interworking with Ethernet and VLAN (8021Q) Attachment Circuits*

```
!
hostname London.PE (line 1)
!
pseudowire-class L2VPN.IW.02.mjlnet.To.Amsterdam (line 2)
 encapsulation l2tpv3
 interworking ip (line 3)
 ip local interface Loopback1
!
interface FastEthernet0/0
!
interface FastEthernet1/0.1 (line 4)
 encapsulation dot1Q 100 (line 5)
 xconnect 172.16.1.3 2002 pw-class L2VPN.IW.02.mjlnet.To.Amsterdam (line 6)
 !
!
hostname Amsterdam.PE (line 7)
!
pseudowire-class L2VPN.IW.02.mjlnet.To.London (line 8)
 encapsulation l2tpv3
 interworking ip (line 9)
 ip local interface Loopback1
!
interface FastEthernet3/0
 xconnect 172.16.1.1 2002 pw-class L2VPN.IW.02.mjlnet.To.London (line 10)
 !
```

Highlighted lines 1 to 6 show the configuration of London.PE.

The **interworking ip** command in highlighted line 3 enables IP mode interworking (within pseudowire class L2VPN.IW.02.mjlnet.To.Amsterdam), and the commands in highlighted lines 4 and 5 are used to configure 802.1Q encapsulation on interface Fast Ethernet 1/0.1, and associated VLAN 500 with this interface.

In highlighted line 6, the **xconnect** command is used to bind interface Fast Ethernet 0/0.1 to the pseudowire with VC ID 2002, to Amsterdam.PE (172.16.1.3), using pseudowire class L2VPN.IW.02.mjlnet.To.Amsterdam. In highlighted lines 7 to 10, you can see the configuration of Amsterdam.PE.

Highlighted line 9 shows the **interworking ip** command, which again enables IP mode interworking (within pseudowire class L2VPN.IW.02.mjlnet.To.London), and in highlighted line 10, the **xconnect** command is used to bind interface Fast Ethernet 3/0 to a pseudowire with VC ID 2002 to London.PE, using pseudowire class L2VPN.IW.02.mjlnet.To.London.

As always, the attachment circuits are terminated on the PE routers, and ARP mediation is required to ensure that CE devices can perform address resolution for each other's address.

PE routers perform proxy ARP for the remote CE device's IP address. To speed up the PE routers' learning of their attached CE device's address, you can optionally configure IRDP on the CE devices.

Note that the configuration of IRDP is equally applicable to CE devices connected to PE routers via VLAN (802.1Q) attachment circuits.

Resolving MTU Issues with L2VPN Interworking

One important consideration when configuring L2VPN interworking is MTU sizes for the attachment circuits. You must ensure that the same MTU size is configured on the attachment circuits; otherwise, the pseudowire between the PE routers might not be established.

RFC3931 (L2TPv3) does not include a method of communicating attachment circuit MTUs between PE routers, but an *Interface MTU* AVP that can be used for this purpose has recently been added to L2TPv3. If PE routers do not support this AVP, and attachment circuit MTUs are not identical, the pseudowire can still be established. If PE routers support this AVP, and the attachment circuit MTUs are not identical, the pseudowire will not be established.

Irrespective of whether the PE routers support the Interface MTU AVP, it is a good idea to specify the lower of the two default attachment circuit MTUs as the MTU for the attachment circuit with the higher-default MTU. For example, when configuring interworking between Ethernet (default MTU 1500 bytes) and ATM (default MTU 4470 bytes) attachment circuits, you could configure the ATM attachment circuit with an MTU of 1500 bytes on both the PE router and the connected CE device. If attachment circuit MTUs are not the same, and the pseudowire is established, a certain proportion of traffic will be lost (traffic received by a CE device that has a packet size greater than the configured MTU).

If more than one circuit terminates on the same physical interface on a PE router, make sure that you only modify the MTU of the appropriate attachment circuit—for example, if you want to modify the MTU of a specific Frame Relay PVC rather than all the PVCs on a particular interface.

NOTE   It is worth noting that the **mtu** *bytes* differs from the **ip mtu** *bytes* command in that if you use the **mtu** command, the MTU size for all protocols is modified. If you configure the **ip mtu** command, on the other hand, only the MTU for IP is modified on the interface.

Routing Protocol Considerations with L2VPN Interworking

When deploying L2VPN interworking, it is important to carefully consider the configuration for certain routing protocols, including OSPF and IS-IS.

If you intend to configure IS-IS between CE routers when deploying L2VPN, it is important to bear in mind that IS-IS PDUs are not transported over IP. At the time of this writing, therefore, you cannot use IS-IS directly over a pseudowire between CE devices when using IP mode interworking. It can, however, be used with Ethernet mode interworking.

When configuring OSPF with IP mode interworking, it is important to ensure a consistent OSPF network type on CE devices; otherwise, an OSPF adjacency might not be established, and routing information might not be exchanged.

NOTE   It is important to note that, as with all forms of L2VPN (with the exception of PE routers that are performing simultaneous IPv6 protocol demultiplexing and IPv4 routing), PE routers do not participate in customer routing (they do not establish routing adjacencies, nor exchange routing information with CE devices).

For example, if you are using IP mode interworking with Frame Relay and Ethernet attachment circuits, the default OSPF network types on the CE devices will be different. The default OSPF network type on a Frame Relay multipoint interface will be *nonbroadcast* (*multiaccess*), and on a Frame Relay point-to-point subinterface it will be *point to point*. The default OSPF network type on an Ethernet interface is, however, broadcast.

One way around the issue of OSPF network type mismatches with IP mode L2VPN interworking is to configure a point-to-point OSPF network type on both CE devices. This OSPF network type is the default on Frame Relay point-to-point and PPP interfaces, but it must be manually specified on Ethernet, VLAN (802.1Q), and Frame Relay multipoint interfaces using the **ip ospf network point-to-point** command.

Figure 2-45 illustrates default OSPF network types on CE devices with Frame Relay and Ethernet attachment circuits.

Figure 2-45 *Default OSPF Network Types on CE Devices with IP Mode Interworking Using Frame Relay and Ethernet Attachment Circuits*

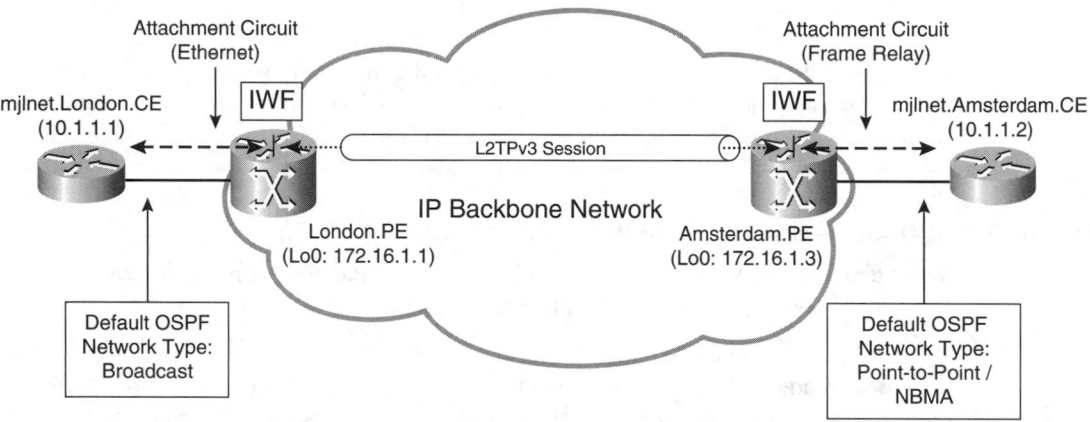

Transporting IPv6 over an IPv4 Backbone Using IPv6 Protocol Demultiplexing

With the growth in the deployment of IPv6, one important additional capability of L2TPv3 is its capability to transparently connect islands of IPv6 over an intervening IPv4 network. This capability is called *IPv6 protocol demultiplexing*, and its usage is illustrated in Figure 2-46. Note that only the IP addresses relevant to this example are shown.

Figure 2-46 *IPv6 Protocol Demultiplexing*

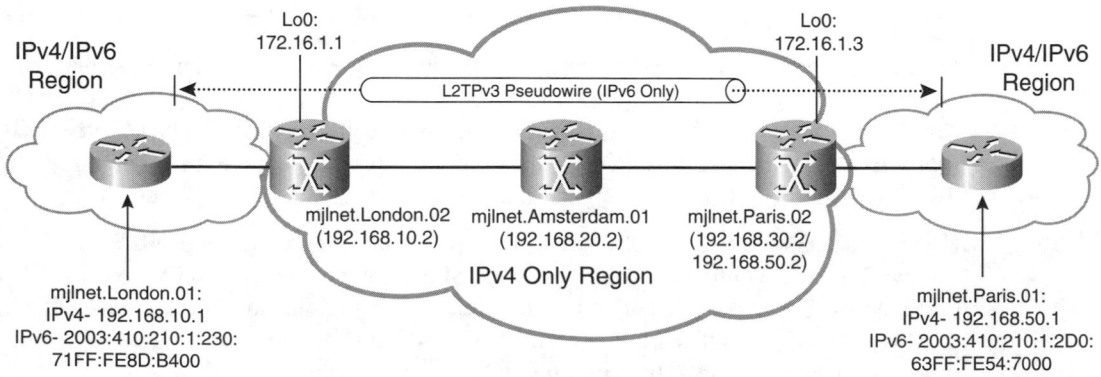

As illustrated in Figure 2-46, an L2TPv3 pseudowire provides IPv6 transport between routers mjlnet.London.01 and mjlnet.Paris.01 over an intervening IPv4 network.

When IPv4 traffic arrives at mjlnet.London.02 from mjlnet.London.01, it is not forwarded over the pseudowire, but is instead routed normally. When IPv6 traffic arrives at mjlnet.London.02 from mjlnet.London.01, on the other hand, it is forwarded over the pseudowire via mjlnet.Paris.02 to mjlnet.Paris.01.

The interface on mjlnet.London.02 that is connected to mjlnet.London.01, as well as the interface on mjlnet.Paris.02 that is connected to mjlnet.Paris.01, are configured with IPv4 addresses but not with IPv6 addresses. So, although mjlnet.London.01 and mjlnet.Paris.01 are *not* on the same IPv4 subnet, they are on the same IPv6 subnet (2003:410:210:1::/64), and the pseudowire provides transparent IPv6 transport.

Example 2-43 shows the relevant configuration on mjlnet.London.02 and mjlnet.Paris.02.

Example 2-43 *Configuration on mjlnet.London.01 and mjlnet.Paris.02*

```
!
hostname mjlnet.London.02 (line 1)
!
pseudowire-class l2tpv3.iw.pw.class
 encapsulation l2tpv3
 protocol l2tpv3 l2tpv3.iw.class
 ip local interface Loopback0
!
interface Serial3/0
 no ip address
 no ip directed-broadcast
 encapsulation frame-relay
 frame-relay intf-type dce
!
interface Serial3/0.1 multipoint
 ip address 192.168.10.2 255.255.255.0 (line 2)
 no ip directed-broadcast
 frame-relay map ip 192.168.10.1 200 broadcast
 frame-relay interface-dlci 200 (line 3)
   xconnect 172.16.1.3 2001 pw-class l2tpv3.iw.pw.class (line 4)
    match protocol ipv6 (line 5)
!
```

```
!
hostname mjlnet.Paris.02 (line 6)
!
pseudowire-class l2tpv3.iw.pw.class
 encapsulation l2tpv3
 protocol l2tpv3 l2tpv3.iw.class
 ip local interface Loopback0
!
interface Serial4/3
 no ip address
 no ip directed-broadcast
 encapsulation frame-relay
 frame-relay intf-type dce
!
interface Serial4/3.1 multipoint
 ip address 192.168.50.2 255.255.255.0 (line 7)
 no ip directed-broadcast
 frame-relay map ip 192.168.50.1 300 broadcast
 frame-relay interface-dlci 300 (line 8)
   xconnect 172.16.1.1 2001 pw-class l2tpv3.iw.pw.class (line 9)
    match protocol ipv6 (line 10)
!
```

Highlighted lines 2 to 4 show the relevant configuration on mjlnet.London.02. In highlighted line 2, an IPv4 address (192.168.10.2) is applied to interface serial 3/0.1, which is connected to mjlnet.London.01. Next, in highlighted line 3, the **frame-relay interface-dlci** *dlci* command is used to assign a DLCI (200) to the subinterface.

The **xconnect** command is then used to configure a pseudowire to 172.16.1.3 (mjlnet.Paris.02), with VC ID 2001, using L2TP pseudowire class l2tp.iw.pw.class.

Finally, the **match protocol ipv6** command configures IPv6 protocol demultiplexing on the interface. Any IPv6 (*not* IPv4) packets sent by mjlnet.London.01 toward mjlnet.London.02 will now be transparently forwarded over the pseudowire to 172.16.1.3 (mjlnet.Paris.02) and from there on to mjlnet.Paris.01. IPv4 packets will continue to be processed and routed regularly on mjlnet.London.02. The configuration on mljnet.Paris.02 (see highlighted lines 6 to 9) is almost identical.

The IPv4 address 192.168.50.2 is configured on interface serial 4/3.1 (the interface connected to mjlnet.Paris.01) in highlighted line 6. Notice that this IPv4 address is on a different subnet to that configured on interface serial 3/0.1 on mjlnet.London.02 (192.168.10.0/24, see highlighted line 2).

In highlighted line 7, DLCI 300 is then assigned to the interface. An L2TPv3 pseudowire to 172.16.1.1 (mjlnet.London.02) with VC ID 2001, using L2TP pseudowire class l2tpv3.iw.pw.class is configured in highlighted line 8.

The **match protocol ipv6** command is next used to configure IPv6 protocol demultiplexing on the interface (highlighted line 9). This command ensures that IPv6 packets received from mjlnet.Paris.01 are transparently forwarded over the pseudowire to mjlnet.London.02 (and onward to mjlnet.London.01). IPv4 packets received from mjlnet.Paris.01 are processed and routed normally and are not forwarded over the pseudowire.

So far so good. But what about the configuration of the routers connected to mjlnet.London.02 and mjlnet.Paris.02 (mjlnet.London.01 and mjlnet.Paris.01, respectively)? The configuration is unsurprisingly standard—no special configuration is required (see Example 2-44).

Example 2-44 *Configuration of mjlnet.London.01 and mjlnet.Paris.01*

```
!
hostname mjlnet.London.01 (line 1)
!
interface Serial4/3
 ip address 192.168.10.1 255.255.255.0 (line 2)
 encapsulation frame-relay
 ipv6 address 2003:410:210:1::/64 eui-64 (line 3)
 frame-relay map ipv6 2003:410:210:1:2D0:63FF:FE54:7000 200 broadcast
```

Example 2-44 *Configuration of mjlnet.London.01 and mjlnet.Paris.01 (Continued)*

```
 frame-relay map ip 192.168.10.2 200 broadcast
 !
```
```
 !
hostname mjlnet.Paris.01 (line 4)
 !
interface Serial2/0
 ip address 192.168.50.1 255.255.255.0 (line 5)
 encapsulation frame-relay
 ipv6 address 2003:410:210:1::/64 eui-64 (line 6)
 frame-relay map ipv6 2003:410:210:1:230:71FF:FE8D:B400 300 broadcast
 frame-relay map ip 192.168.50.2 200 broadcast
 !
```

The key points to notice in Example 2-44 are the IPv4 addresses (highlighted line 2 and 5) and the IPv6 addresses (highlighted lines 3 and 6) on mjlnet.London.01 and mjlnet.Paris.01.

The IPv4 addresses configured on mjlnet.London.01 and mjlnet.Paris.01 are obviously on different subnets (192.168.10.0/24 and 192.168.50.0/24, respectively). mjlnet.London.01 is on the same IPv4 subnet as mjlnet.London.02, and mjlnet.Paris.01 is on the same IPv4 subnet as mjlnet.Paris.02.

A quick comparison of the IPv6 addresses on mjlnet.London.01 and mjlnet.Paris.01, however, shows they are on the same subnet (2003:410:210:1::/64).

The functionality of the configuration shown in Example 2-43 is best illustrated by performing IPv4 and IPv6 traceroutes from mjlnet.London.01 to mjlnet.Paris.01, as demonstrated in Example 2-45.

Example 2-45 *IPv4 and IPv6 Traceroutes from mjlnet.London.01 and mjlnet.Paris.01*

```
mjlnet.London.01#
mjlnet.London.01#traceroute 192.168.50.1 (line 1)

Type escape sequence to abort.
Tracing the route to 192.168.50.1
  1 192.168.10.2 0 msec 0 msec 0 msec (line 2)
  2 192.168.20.2 20 msec 16 msec 20 msec (line 3)
  3 192.168.30.2 16 msec 16 msec 16 msec (line 4)
  4 192.168.50.1 28 msec 28 msec * (line 5)
mjlnet.London.01#
mjlnet.London.01#traceroute ipv6 2003:410:210:1:2D0:63FF:FE54:7000 (line 6)

Type escape sequence to abort.
Tracing the route to 2003:410:210:1:2D0:63FF:FE54:7000

  1 2003:410:210:1:2D0:63FF:FE54:7000 52 msec 52 msec 52 msec (line 7)
mjlnet.London.01#
```

In highlighted line 1, the IPv4 **traceroute** command is entered with destination mjlnet.Paris.01 (192.168.50.1).

The results of the traceroute are shown in highlighted lines 2 to 5, and as you can see the traceroute goes from mjlnet.London.01 via mjlnet.London.02 (192.168.10.2), mjlnet.Amsterdam.01 (192.168.20.2), and mjlnet.Paris.01 (192.168.30.2), to mjlnet.Paris.02 (192.168.50.1).

A similar IPv6 traceroute command (**traceroute ipv6** *destination-address*) is shown in highlighted line 6.

Highlighted line 7 shows the result of the IPv6 traceroute, and it is quite revealing—as you can see, no intermediate IPv6 hops exist on the path from mjlnet.London.01 to mjlnet.Paris.01 (2003:410:210:1:2D0:63FF:FE54:7000).

The difference in the output of the IPv4 and IPv6 traceroutes is, of course, due to the fact that mjlnet.London.02 and mjlnet.Paris.02 are configured to route IPv4 normally, while transparently forwarding IPv6 over the pseudowire.

NOTE   At the time of this writing, you can use IPv6 protocol demultiplexing only with Frame Relay (DLCI-to-DLCI) and Ethernet attachment circuits.

Provisioning Quality of Service for L2TPv3 Pseudowires

When designing and deploying L2TPv3 pseudowire based VPNs, it is important to take into account any QoS requirements.

For example, if you deploy Frame Relay transport over L2TPv3, you may want to make sure that Frame Relay traffic received on an attachment circuit with the DE bit set to 1 (see Figure 2-21 on page 61) is encapsulated in L2TPv3 packets with a less preferential type of service (ToS) marking in the IP packet headers than traffic received on an attachment circuit with the DE bit not set (0). After the ToS bytes in the IP headers of L2TPv3 packets are marked, routers in forwarding path between PE routers can handle these packets according to the marking contained within the ToS byte.

Figure 2-47 depicts the ToS byte in the IP packet header. As shown, the usage of the ToS byte has changed substantially since its original definition.

The ToS byte, as defined in RFC1349, can be described as follows:

- **Precedence field**—This 3-bit field indicates the priority of the packet.
- **ToS field**—This 4-bit field indicates how the network should handle the packet in relation to delay, throughput, reliability, and monetary cost considerations.
- **MBZ field**—This is a 1-bit field, and yes, you've guessed it, this field "must be 0."

The usage of the ToS byte as described in RFC1349 is now considered obsolete (although it is still used in some networks).

Figure 2-47 *ToS Byte in the IP Packet Header*

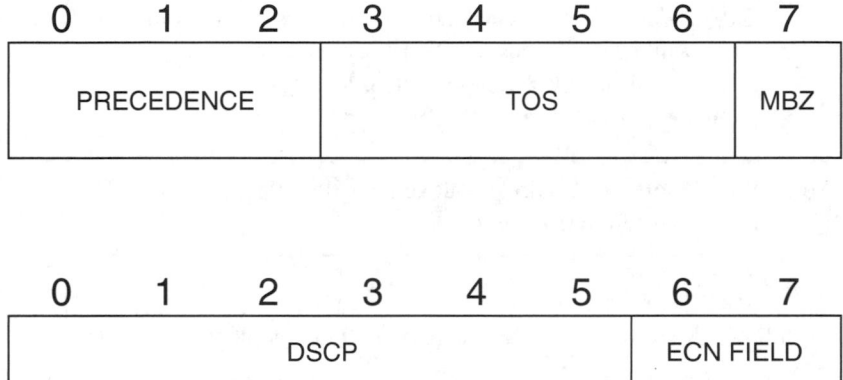

The ToS byte (Differentiated Services [DS] field), as described in RFC 2474 and RFC 3168, is as follows:

- **DSCP**—The Differentiated Service Code Point field (6 bits) indicates the per-hop behavior (PHB)—that is, the forwarding behavior (queuing, dropping, and so on) that should be accorded to the packet at each network hop.

- **ECN field**—The Explicit Congestion Notification field (2 bits) is, as the name suggests, used to indicate that congestion has been experienced in the network.

QoS configuration can consist of processes and mechanisms such as the following:

- **Traffic classification**—Differentiating between different traffic types. This usually takes place at the network edge.

- **Traffic marking**—This consists of indicating a desired QoS treatment by marking packets using fields such as the IP Precedence and DSCP fields in the IP packet header. Other fields used for marking *include* the 802.1p field in the VLAN (802.1Q) tag, as well as the Experimental (EXP) field in an MPLS label. Traffic is also usually marked at the network edge.

- **Traffic shaping and policing**—Shaping involves the buffering of traffic during periods of congestion before transmitting that traffic after congestion has abated. Policing, on the other hand, involves dropping, remarking, or simply transmitting excess traffic (traffic that exceeds a certain limit or rate). Shaping and policing usually take place at the edge of a network.

- **Traffic queuing**—Queuing provides the capability to prioritize and re-order traffic. Queuing can take place on any device in a QoS-enabled network.

- **Congestion avoidance**—This consists of the (selective) dropping of traffic when queues are becoming full. This selective dropping of traffic may cause (typically, TCP) senders to slow down the rate at which they send traffic over the network, which in turn will reduce congestion. You can configure congestion-avoidance mechanisms on any device in a QoS-enabled network.

NOTE   You can find more information about general QoS configuration in books such as *IP Quality of Service* from Cisco Press.

A QoS policy for L2TPv3 pseudowires can, for example, consist of the following:

- **QoS policy on PE routers**—This configuration may consist of classifying, marking, policing/shaping, queuing, and congestion avoidance.
- **QoS policy on P routers**—This configuration often consists of queuing, congestion avoidance, and so on.

Figure 2-48 illustrates an example QoS policy for L2TPv3 pseudowires.

Figure 2-48   *Example QoS Policy for L2TPv3 Pseudowires*

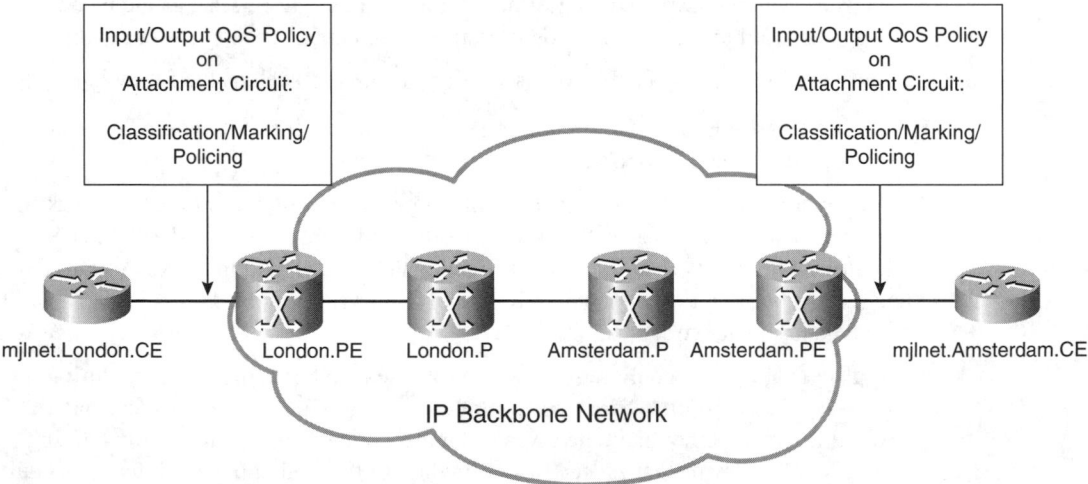

The example QoS policy in Figure 2-48 involves classification, marking, and policing on inbound traffic on attachment circuit interfaces of PE routers. In addition, the example policy includes classification, marking, and policing outbound on attachment circuits of PE routers. P routers (and the backbone-facing interfaces of PE routers) are configured to queue and selectively drop traffic based on the DCSP or IP precedence marking in the IP headers of L2TPv3 packets.

The following sections discuss the configuration of QoS policies for L2TPv3 pseudowires on PE routers.

Configuring an Input QoS Policy on (Ingress) PE Router Attachment Circuits

Input QoS policies on PE router attachment circuits can be used to map attachment circuit QoS policies to QoS policies used within the backbone network between PE routers, and involve the marking of the ToS byte in the IP headers of L2TPv3 packets.

There are three basic ways to mark the ToS byte of the IP headers of L2TPv3 packets:

- Use the **ip tos value** *value* command within the pseudowire class to ensure that the specified ToS value is carried in the ToS byte of the IP headers of L2TPv3 packets.

- Use the **ip tos reflect** within the pseudowire class to ensure the ToS byte value in IP packets received on an attachment circuit is copied to the ToS byte in the IP headers of L2TPv3 packets.

- Configure L2TPv3 tunnel marking via the Cisco Modular QoS CLI (MQC), using the **set ip dscp tunnel** *value* and **set ip precedence tunnel** *value* commands. The configured DSCP or IP precedence value is copied to the IP headers of L2TPv3 packets.

If all three methods of marking the ToS byte in the IP headers of L2TPv3 packets are configured, the order of precedence is as follows: **set ip dscp tunnel** *value* and **set ip precedence tunnel** *value*, **ip tos reflect**, and **ip tos value** *value*.

So, if either the **set ip dscp tunnel** *value* or **set ip precedence tunnel** *value* command is configured, its configuration will be imposed over any configuration of the **ip tos reflect** or **ip tos value** *value* commands. Similarly, if the **ip tos reflect** command is configured (but the **set ip dscp tunnel** *value* and **set ip precedence tunnel** *value* commands are not), its configuration will be imposed over any configuration of the **ip tos value** *value* command.

The following sections describe the use and configuration of the three methods of marking the IP header of L2TPv3 packets.

Using the **ip tos value** value and **ip tos reflect** Commands

Example 2-46 shows the configuration of the **ip tos value** *value* command within a pseudowire class.

Example 2-46 *Configuration of the* **ip tos value** *value Command*

```
pseudowire-class l2tpv3.pw.class
 ip tos value 160
```

In Example 2-46, the **ip tos value** *value* command is used to specify a value of 160 for the ToS byte of *all* L2TPv3 packets sent over pseudowires whose configuration is associated with the pseudowire class called l2tpv3.pw.class.

Figure 2-49 illustrates the effect of the configuration shown in Example 2-43.

Figure 2-49 *Effect of the Configuration Shown in Example 2-46*

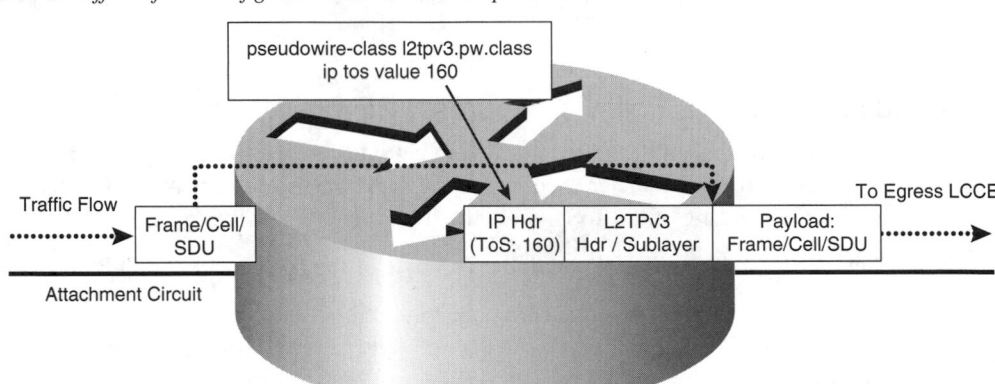

As shown in Figure 2-49, the value 160 is carried in the ToS byte of IP headers of L2TPv3 packets (this example value corresponds to an IP Precedence of 5 and a DSCP of 40 [see Figure 2-47]).

As described earlier in this chapter, a variation of the **ip tos value** *value* command is **ip tos reflect**. Example 2-47 shows its configuration.

Example 2-47 *Configuration of the* **ip tos reflect** *Command*

```
pseudowire-class l2tpv3.pw.class
  ip tos reflect
```

Figure 2-50 shows how the configuration in Example 2-47 affects the marking of the IP headers of L2TPv3 packets sent over the pseudowire.

Figure 2-50 *Effect of the Configuration Shown in Example 2-47*

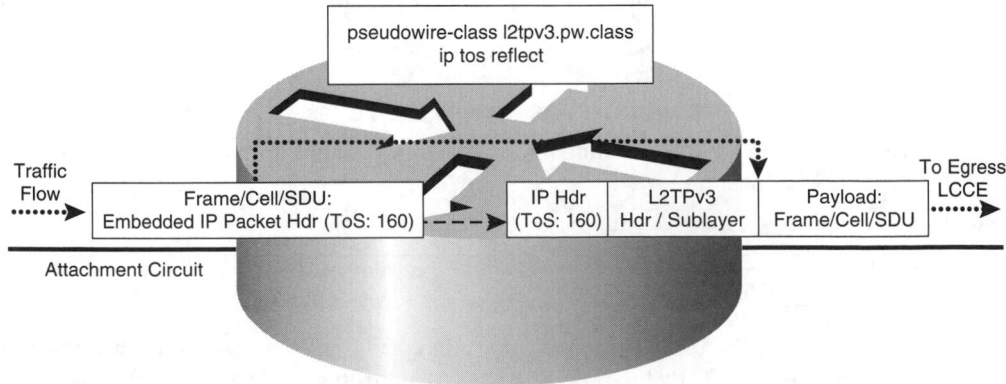

In the example in Figure 2-50, the value 160 is carried in the ToS byte of an IP header of a packet received on the attachment circuit. This value is copied into the IP header of the L2TPv3 packet because the **ip tos reflect** command is configured in the pseudowire class.

Configuring QoS for L2TPv3 Using L2TPv3 Tunnel Marking

A preferred method of marking the IP headers of L2TPv3 packets is to configure L2TPv3 tunnel marking.

The configuration of L2TPv3 tunnel marking consists of the following three steps:

Step 1   Configure a class map.

Step 2   Configure a policy map.

Step 3   Apply the policy map to an interface or VC.

These steps are detailed in the following sections.

Step 1: Configure a Class Map   A class map is used to specify how the traffic that you want to apply QoS tools to will be distinguished from all other traffic.

In the case of L2TPv3 pseudowires, you can match on a number of fields in the headers of frames or cells received on attachment circuits. Some of the fields that you can match on are as follows:

- **The DE bit in Frame Relay headers** (see Figure 2-21 on page 61)—You can match the DE bit using the **match fr-de** command within a class map.

- **The Cell Loss Priority (CLP) bit in ATM cell headers** (see Figure 2-26 on page 68)— Match the CLP bit using **match atm clp** command within a class map.

- **The 802.1p field (User Priority) in VLAN (802.1Q) headers** (see Figure 2-15 on page 50)—Use the **match cos** *cos-value* [*cos-value cos-value cos-value*] command to match up to four values in the 802.1p field of 802.1Q frames within a class map.

Example 2-48 shows the configuration of the **match not fr-de** command within a sample class map.

Example 2-48 *Configuration of the match not fr-de Command Within a Class Map*

```
!
class-map match-all l2tpv3.fr.de
  match not fr-de
!
```

The **class-map** [**match-all** | **match-any**] *class-map-name* command in Example 2-48 configures a class map called l2tpv3.fr.de. The **match-all** parameter is used to specify that in order for frames to match the class map all match conditions within the class map must be matched (there is only one match condition in this case).

Also in Example 2-48, the **match not fr-de** *value* command specifies that the DE field in Frame Relay headers must *not* be set (to 1) to fulfill this match condition.

Step 2: Configure a Policy Map

After you have configured the class map, you move on to the configuration of the policy map. The function of the policy map is to reference the class map and set values of the DSCP field or ToS byte in the IP headers of L2TPv3 packets.

Example 2-49 shows the configuration of a sample policy map.

Example 2-49 *Configuration of a Policy Map*

```
!
policy-map l2tpv3.policy
  class l2tpv3.fr.de
    set ip dscp tunnel 46
!
```

In Example 2-49, the **policy-map** *policy-map-name* command configures a sample policy map called l2tpv3.policy. The **class** {*class-map-name* | **class-default**} command references the class map condition(s) specified (in this example, class map l2tpv3.fr.de).

Finally, the **set ip dscp tunnel** *value* command is used to set the value of DSCP field in the IP headers of L2TPv3 packets if the conditions described in the class map, l2tpv3.fr.de, are matched.

As previously described, you can configure the **set ip precedence tunnel** *value* command instead of the **set ip dscp tunnel** *dscp-value* command if you want to set IP Precedence values rather than DSCP values in the IP header of L2TPv3 packets.

Step 3: Apply the Policy Map to an Interface or Virtual Circuit

The next step is to apply the policy map configured in Step 2 to the attachment circuit interface or VC (see Example 2-50).

Example 2-50 *Applying the Policy Map to an Attachment Circuit Interface*

```
!
interface Serial3/0
  service-policy input l2tpv3.policy
!
```

Example 2-50 uses the **service-policy input** *policy-map-name* command to apply the service policy configured in Step 2 to an interface.

It is important to note that a service policy that is used to configure the marking of IP headers of L2TPv3 packets can only be applied in an inbound direction (using the **service-policy input** command).

Configuring L2TPv3 Tunnel Marking Using Policing

Another way of marking the IP headers of L2TPv3 packets is in conjunction with the **police** {**cir** *cir*} [**bc** *conform-burst*] {**pir** *pir*} [**be** *peak-burst*] [**conform-action** *action* [**exceed-action** *action* [**violate-action** *action*]]] command. In this case, you can use **set-dscp-tunnel-transmit** *value* and **set-prec-tunnel-transmit** *value* as the *action* parameters in the **police** command syntax. These two action parameters can be used to set the DSCP and IP Precedence values in the IP headers of L2TPv3 packets respectively.

Example 2-51 shows an example marking of the IP header of L2TPv3 packets using the **police** command.

Example 2-51 *Marking of the IP Header of L2TPv3 Packets Using the **police** Command*

```
!
policy-map l2tpv3.policy (line 1)
 class class-default (line 2)
 police cir 32000 pir 64000 conform-action set-dscp-tunnel-transmit 46 exceed-action
  (line 3)
   set-dscp-tunnel-transmit 0 violate-action drop (line 4)
!
interface serial 3/0
 service-policy input l2tpv3.policy (line 5)
!
```

In Example 2-51, a policy map called l2tpv3.policy is configured (highlighted line 1). Then, in highlighted line 2, the **class class-default** command specifies a default traffic class that can be used for all traffic that does not match a configured class map.

The **police** command is configured in highlighted line 3, and it is used to specify a Committed Information Rate (CIR) of 32 kbps and a Peak Information Rate (PIR) of 64 kbps.

If traffic conforms to the CIR specified by the **police** command in Example 2-48 (**conform-action**), the IP header of the L2TPv3 packet is marked with a DSCP of 46; if traffic exceeds the CIR, the IP header is marked with a DSCP of 0 (**exceed-action**), and if traffic exceeds the PIR, the traffic is dropped (**violate-action**).

In highlighted line 5, the policy l2tpv3.policy is applied to attachment circuit interface in an inbound direction (**service-policy input**).

Configuring an Output QoS Policy on (Egress) PE Router Attachment Circuits

If you configure input QoS policies on the attachment circuits of PE routers, you will probably want to configure corresponding output policies on attachment circuits. These output policies will enable you to map backbone network QoS policies (represented by markings in the ToS byte of IP headers of L2TPv3 packets) to QoS policies and configurations on attachment circuits.

By configuring an output policy, you could, for example, ensure that the DSCP or IP Precedence carried in the IP headers of L2TPv3 packets is mapped back to a Frame Relay DE bit setting or an ATM CLP bit setting, as appropriate. You may also want to configure policing or shaping.

Figure 2-51 illustrates a sample output policy.

Figure 2-51 *Sample Output Policy*

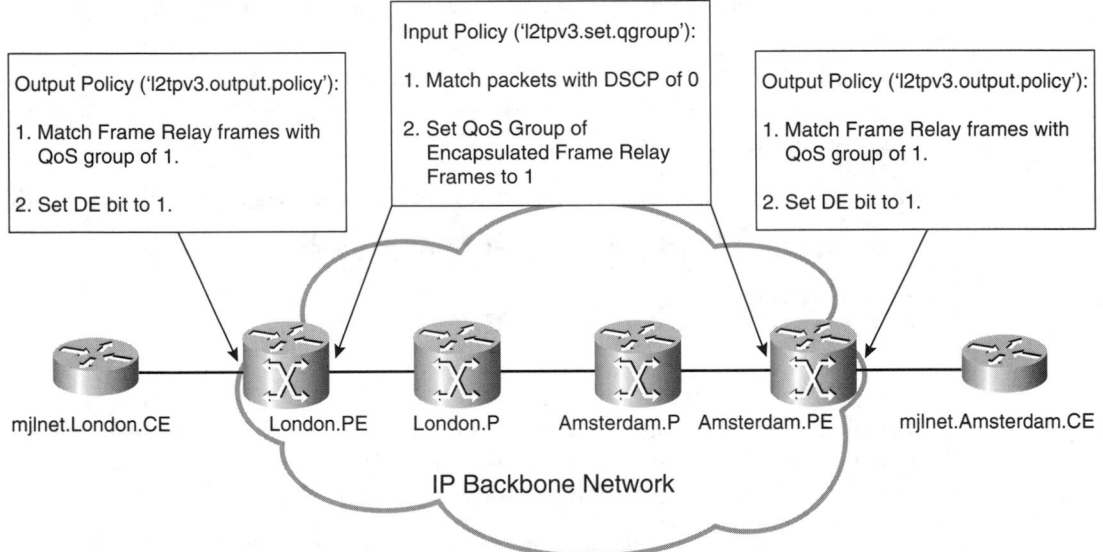

Example 2-52 shows an output policy on an attachment circuit (corresponding to Figure 2-51).

Example 2-52 *Sample Output Policy on an Attachment Circuit*

```
!
class-map match-all l2tpv3.dscp (line 1)
  match ip dcsp 0 (line 2)
!
policy-map l2tpv3.set.qgroup (line 3)
  class l2tpv3.dscp (line 4)
  set qos-group 1 (line 5)
!
interface Serial1/0
 description backbone interface
 service-policy input l2tpv3.set.qgroup (line 6)
!
!
class-map match-all qgroup1 (line 7)
  match qos-group 1 (line 8)
 !
 !
```

Example 2-52 *Sample Output Policy on an Attachment Circuit (Continued)*

```
policy-map l2tpv3.output.policy (line 9)
  class qgroup1 (line 10)
    set fr-de (line 11)
!
interface Serial3/0
  service-policy output l2tpv3.output.policy (line 12)
!
```

In highlighted line 1 and 2, a class map called l2tpv3.dscp is configured, and this class map matches (L2TPv3) packets that have a value of 0 in their DSCP field.

Lines 3 to 5 are used to configure a policy map called l2tpv3.set.group that references the class map l2tpv3.dscp, and sets the QoS group ID to 1 (for frames that are extracted from L2TPv3 packets). The QoS group ID can be used to help map certain QoS markings (a DSCP value of 0, in this example) on an input interface to corresponding QoS markings on an output interface.

The policy l2tpv3.set.qgroup is then applied in an inbound direction on interface serial 1/0 in highlighted line 6. Interface serial 1/0 is a backbone network interface and so is the interface on which this PE router receives L2TPv3 packets from its peer PE routers (via any P routers).

Lines 7 to 8 show the configuration of a second class map called qgroup1. This class map matches on Frame Relay frames (extracted from the L2TPv3 packets) that have a QoS group ID of 1. You will remember that frames extracted from L2TPv3 packets received on interface serial 1/0 with a DSCP value of 0 in their IP headers are marked with a QoS group ID of 1 (see highlighted lines 1 to 6).

A policy map called l2tpv3.output.policy is configured in highlighted lines 9 to 11. The policy references class map qgroup1 and specifies that any frames matching the conditions in that class map (the QoS group ID must be set to 1) will have the DE bit set when they are transmitted on an interface.

Finally, the policy map l2tpv3.output.policy is applied in an outbound direction to attachment circuit interface serial 3/0.

So, the effect of the configuration shown in Example 2-49 is as follows:

1 Frames contained within L2TPv3 packets received on backbone network interface serial 1/0 that have the DSCP field in their IP headers set to a value of 0 are marked with a QoS group ID of 1.

2 Frames extracted from the L2TPv3 packets that have a QoS group ID of 1 (those which were encapsulated in L2TPv3 packets with a value of 0 in the DCSP field of the IP header) have the DE bit set to 1 before being transmitted on attachment circuit interface serial 3/0.

You can use the **show policy-map** and **show policy-map interface** commands to check the configuration of the policy map and the effect of the policy map, respectively.

Avoiding Packet Fragmentation and Packet Drops with L2TPv3 Pseudowires

When you configure L2TPv3 pseudowires between PE routers across a backbone network, you must take account of the packet overhead that L2TPv3 adds to the frames, cells, and SDUs that it tunnels; otherwise, L2TPv3 session packets may be fragmented or even dropped by routers in the network path.

L2TPv3 session packets transport attachment circuit frames/cells/SDUs, and so the total size of L2TPv3 session packets is as follows:

- L2TPv3 session packet overhead is 36 bytes (maximum)
- The size of the attachment circuit frame/cell/SDU (carried in the L2TPv3 packet payload)

The L2TPv3 session packet overhead consists of the following:

- The outer IP header is 20 bytes.
- The L2TPv3 session header can be a variable size, depending on the presence and size of the cookie. Its maximum size is 12 bytes (with an 8-byte [64-bit] cookie).
- The (optional) Layer 2–specific sublayer, if present, is 4 bytes.

So assuming session data messages are carried directly over IP (protocol 115), the *maximum* L2TPv3 overhead is 36 bytes (20 + 12 + 4).

The L2TPv3 packet payload (carrying the attachment circuit frame, SDU, and so on) typically can be a maximum of the following size:

- The attachment circuit transport header, plus
- The attachment circuit MTU

NOTE   If you have configured ATM cell-relay, then the size of the L2TPv3 packet payload is 52 (the ATM cell size, minus the HEC) multiplied by the number of cell being concatenated (packed).

If you have configured an ATM cell relay pseudowire that can transport a maximum of 5 concatenated cells in each L2TPv3 session packet, the size of the payload is 52 * 5 = 260 bytes.

Figure 2-2 on page 31 illustrates the L2TPv3 session packet (data channel message).

So, if you want to transport an HDLC frame over the L2TPv3 pseudowire, the resulting L2TPv3 session packet size would be as follows:

- L2TPv3 session overhead: 36 bytes (maximum).

In the case of HDLC, the session overhead might be as little as 24 bytes if no cookie is used and sequencing is not configured (the [default] Layer 2–specific sublayer is only needed for HDLC if sequencing is configured).

- The size of the attachment circuit frame: 1504 bytes, consisting of the HDLC header (4 bytes), plus the attachment circuit MTU (1500 bytes).

The maximum size of L2TPv3 session packets carrying HDLC frames is 1540 bytes (36 + 1504). When you are transporting HDLC over L2TPv3 pseudowires, therefore, you must ensure that the MTU on all the backbone network links between PE routers can accommodate up to 1540 bytes if you do not want fragmentation or possible packet drops.

You might be wondering how L2TPv3 session packets can be fragmented or dropped. This can happen if the MTU of any of the links in the backbone network is less than the size of L2TPv3 session packets.

Fragmentation of L2TPv3 session packets occurs if *both* of the following conditions are met:

- An L2TPv3 session packet is larger than the outgoing interface MTU of a router in the path between PE routers.
- The Don't Fragment (DF) bit in the outer IP header is *not* set to 1.

Figure 2-52 illustrates fragmentation of an L2TPv3 session packet.

Figure 2-52 *Fragmentation of an L2TPv3 Session Packet*

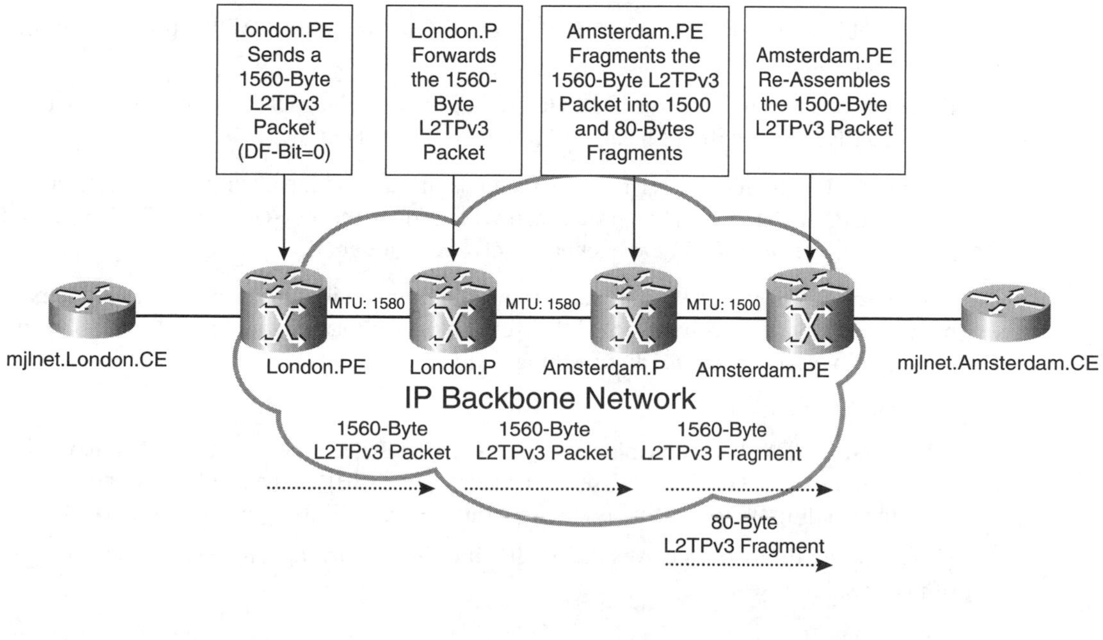

In Figure 2-52, London.PE sends a 1560-byte L2TPv3 packet with the DF bit not set (DF-bit=0) over the link to London.P. The MTU of outgoing interface is 1580 bytes; and because this MTU is greater than 1560 bytes, no fragmentation is necessary.

London.P forwards the packet over the link to Amsterdam.P. Again, no fragmentation is necessary because the outgoing interface (1580 bytes) is greater than the packet size (1560 bytes).

Amsterdam.P receives the packet, and because the packet (1560 bytes) is greater than the outgoing interface MTU (1500 bytes [to Amsterdam.PE]), it has to fragment the packet as follows:

- A 1500-byte packet (including the original IP packet header)
- An 80-byte packet (60 bytes, plus a new 20-byte IP header)

Amsterdam.P is able to fragment the packet because the DF bit is not set (DF-bit=0) in the IP packet header.

Amsterdam.P now forwards the two fragments to Amsterdam.PE, which has to reassemble them into the original 1580-byte packet.

So, what is the problem with the fragmentation of L2TPv3 session packets? The problem is that fragmented L2TPv3 session packets are reassembled on the receiving PE router. This packet reassembly may cause significant CPU overhead and reduce throughput.

If you want to avoid L2TPv3 session packet fragmentation, you can do the following:

- Configure the PE routers to set the DF bit to 1 in the outer IP header of L2TPv3 session packets.
- Enable Path MTU Discovery (PMTUD, RFC1191) for the L2TPv3 pseudowires on PE routers.

If the DF bit is set in the outer IP header of L2TPv3 session packets, routers in the path between PE routers will not be able to fragment the packets.

Setting the DF bit in the outer IP header sounds like a good idea; but if you don't also configure PMTUD for L2TPv3 pseudowires, some or, in the worst case, all L2TPv3 session packets may be dropped in the backbone network—not good.

The reason that some or even all packets may be dropped is that when a router in the path between PE routers receives an L2TPv3 session packet that is larger than the MTU of the outgoing interface, it *should* do two things:

- Drop the packet.
- Send an ICMP unreachable message (ICMP message type 3, code 4) back to the PE router that sent the L2TPv3 session packet. This ICMP unreachable message informs the sending PE router that is should reduce the size of the packets that it sends.

If the sending PE router receives the ICMP unreachable message, it should reduce the size of packets that it sends.

Figure 2-53 shows PMTUD for L2TPv3 pseudowires.

Figure 2-53 *PMTUD for L2TPv3 Pseudowires*

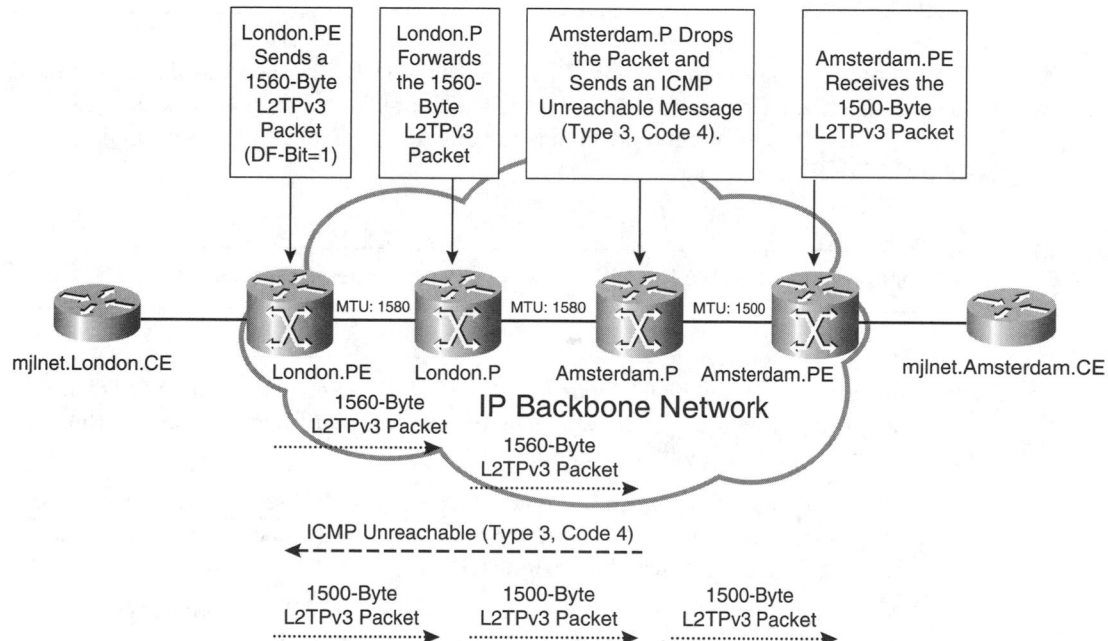

In Figure 2-53, London.PE sends a 1560-byte L2TPv3 packet with the DF bit in the IP header set to 1 (DF-bit=1). London.P forwards the packet because the outgoing interface MTU is greater than the packet size (1580 bytes > 1560 bytes).

Amsterdam.P receives the packet, and because the packet size is greater than the outgoing interface size (1560 bytes > 1500 bytes), it needs to fragment the packet. Unfortunately, the DF bit is set to 1 in the IP header, and so it drops the packet and sends an ICMP unreachable (type 3, code 4) message to London.PE.

London.PE receives the ICMP unreachable message and reduces the size of L2TPv3 packets that it sends to 1500 bytes. London.P and Amsterdam.P are both now able to forward these packets because the packet size is less than or equal to the outgoing interface sizes (1500 bytes < 1580 bytes, and 1500 bytes = 1500 bytes). Amsterdam.PE receives the unfragmented 1500-byte L2TPv3 packets.

Example 2-53 shows a configuration that sets the DF bit in the outer IP header of L2TPv3 session packets and enables PMTUD.

Example 2-53 *Setting the DF Bit in the Outer IP Header of L2TPv3 Session Packets and Enabling PMTUD*

```
pseudowire-class l2tpv3.Class.To.Amsterdam
 ip pmtu
 ip dfbit set
```

The **ip pmtu** command in Example 2-53 enables PMTUD, and the **ip dfbit set** command ensures that the DF bit is set in the outer IP header of L2TPv3 session packets. Note that these commands are configured within a pseudowire class (called, in this example, l2tpv3.Class.To.Amsterdam).

NOTE   It is not possible to enable PMTUD for statically configured L2TP sessions.

It seems that configuring the DF bit on L2TPv3 session packets and enabling PMTUD may solve all your problems as far as fragmentation and packet drops are concerned. But there are one or two problems with this solution:

- Routers in the path between PE routers that drop L2TPv3 session packets because they are too large must send ICMP unreachable (type 3, code 4) messages to the sending PE router. If they do not, PMTUD fails.

  Note, however, that most, if not all, routers will sent ICMP unreachables in this situation, unless they are explicitly configured not to do so.

- Any firewalls or other devices in the path between PE routers must permit ICMP unreachables (type 3, code 4); otherwise, PMTUD will fail.

Figure 2-54 illustrates PMTUD failure for L2TPv3 pseudowires. In Figure 2-54, London.PE sends a 1560-byte L2TPv3 session packet across the backbone network toward Amsterdam.PE. The DF bit is set in the IP header of this packet.

The packet sent by London.PE successfully crosses the link between London.PE and London.FW because the MTU on this link is 1580 bytes. London.FW then forwards the packet over the link to Amsterdam.P (the MTU on link is again 1580 bytes).

Amsterdam.P now drops the packet, however, because the packet (1560 bytes) is larger than the MTU of the interface connected to Amsterdam.PE (this interface has an MTU of 1500 bytes), *and* the DF bit is set to 1 in the outer IP header of the packet (Amsterdam.P cannot fragment the packet).

Figure 2-54 *PMTUD Failure for L2TPv3 Pseudowires*

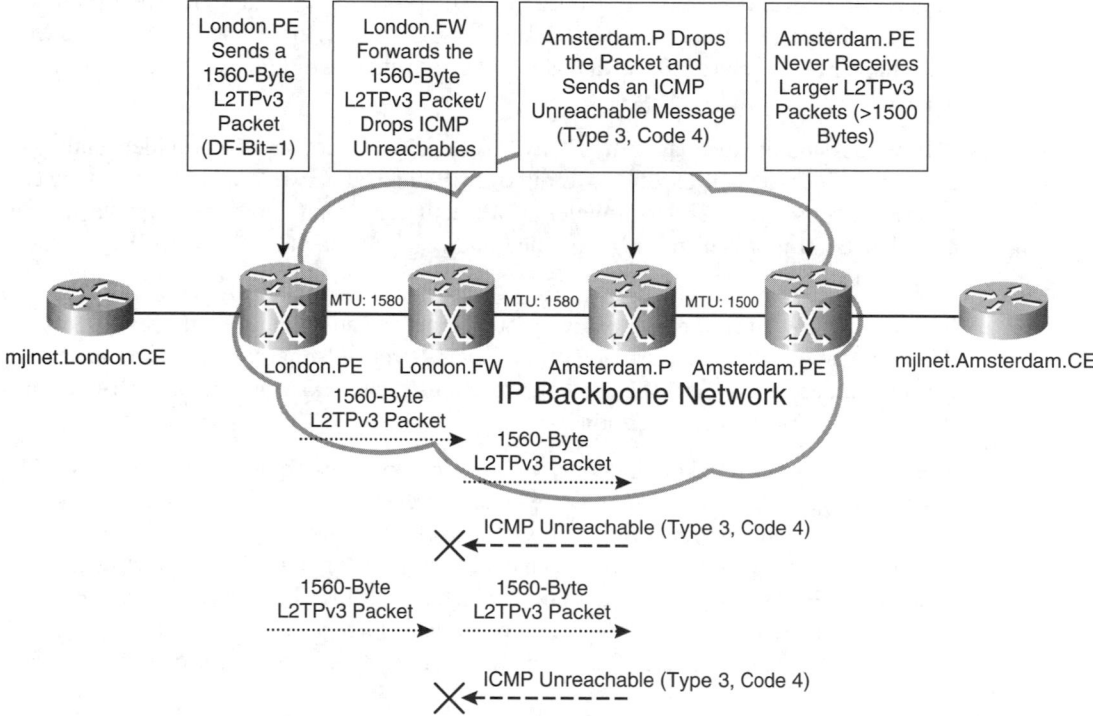

At this point, Amsterdam.P sends an ICMP unreachable message back toward London.PE. When the ICMP unreachable message arrives at London.FW, London.FW drops it because it has been configured to deny ICMP unreachable messages.

London.PE will now continue to send L2TPv3 session packets that may be too big to cross the backbone network to Amsterdam.PE, until that is, London.FW is reconfigured to permit ICMP unreachables. After London.FW has been reconfigured, London.PE will receive the ICMP unreachable messages and will therefore reduce the size of L2TPv3 session packets such they can cross the link between Amsterdam.P and Amsterdam.PE.

In conclusion, when you configure DF bit setting for L2TPv3 session packets in conjunction with enabling PMUTD (see Example 2-50), make sure that all routers in the path send ICMP unreachables (this should be the default) and that there are no firewalls or other devices between the PE routers that are blocking ICMP unreachable messages.

Summary

This chapter covered L2TPv3-based L2VPNs. L2TPv3 can be used to transport protocols such as Ethernet, Ethernet VLAN (802.1Q), HDLC, PPP, X.25, Frame Relay, and ATM. The chapter also explored the advantages and disadvantages of L2TPv3-based L2VPNs in detail.

Advantages and disadvantages of L2TPv3-based L2VPNs for service providers and enterprises include their capability to run over IP-enabled networks, the fact that they can be used to consolidate service provider infrastructure, the capability for enterprises to keep complete control of their routing, and their ability to transparently transport IPv6 traffic over an IPv4 backbone.

You learned how to configure L2TPv3 pseudowires and about the specific design and deployment considerations for each of the Layer 2 protocols that L2TPv3 can transport. It is essential to understand specific considerations such as ATM maximum cell-packing timeouts and OAM local emulation to successfully deploy L2TPv3 pseudowires.

The chapter also covered other deployment models and considerations such as L2VPN interworking, IPv6 protocol demultiplexing, the prevention of L2TPv3 packet fragmentation and dropping, as well as QoS. L2VPN interworking can be used to extend customers' legacy Layer 2 networks to include newer attachment circuit types such as Ethernet, whereas IPv6 protocol demultiplexing can considerably ease the implementation of IPv6 in a network. Finally, the prevention of packet fragmentation and the deployment of QoS mechanisms for L2TPv3 can help to ensure high-service QoS provider customers.

Review Questions

1 What types of networks can L2TPv3-based L2VPNs be deployed over?

2 What are some of the main advantages of VPWS L2VPNs (including those that are L2TPv3 based)?

3 Name five types of Layer 2 protocols that L2TPv3 can tunnel over packet-switched networks.

4 Which L2TPv3 deployment model applies in a pseudowire configuration?

5 What functions does the L2TPv3 control connection perform?

6 If an LCCE wants to request that an L2TPv3 session be torn down, what type of control message does it send?

7 What are some drawbacks of the deployment of static L2TPv3 sessions?

8 What types of control connection authentication can be used with L2TPv3?

9 Which Cisco IOS command enables you to bind attachment circuits to L2TPv3 pseudowires?

10 When an L2TPv3 pseudowire is used to transport PPP traffic, what part do the LACs take in PPP negotiation?

CHAPTER 3

Designing and Implementing AToM-Based Layer 2 VPNs

Any Transport over MPLS (AToM) allows the transport of Layer 2 protocols and connections over a Multiprotocol Label Switching (MPLS) backbone network. Transport over the MPLS backbone network is provided by encapsulating frames, cells, or Service Data Units (SDU), and transmitting them over a pseudowire.

If you have read Chapter 2, "Designing and Deploying L2TPv3-Based Layer 2 VPNs (L2VPN)," and you are thinking that all of this seems rather familiar, then you would be right—AToM pseudowires do a similar job to L2TPv3 pseudowires. The major difference is that L2TPv3 can transport Layer 2 protocols and connections over an IP backbone network, whereas AToM transports Layer 2 protocols and connections over an MPLS network.

Figure 3-1 illustrates the transport of Layer 2 protocols and connections over AToM pseudowires.

Figure 3-1   *Transport of Layer 2 Protocols and Connections over AToM Pseudowires*

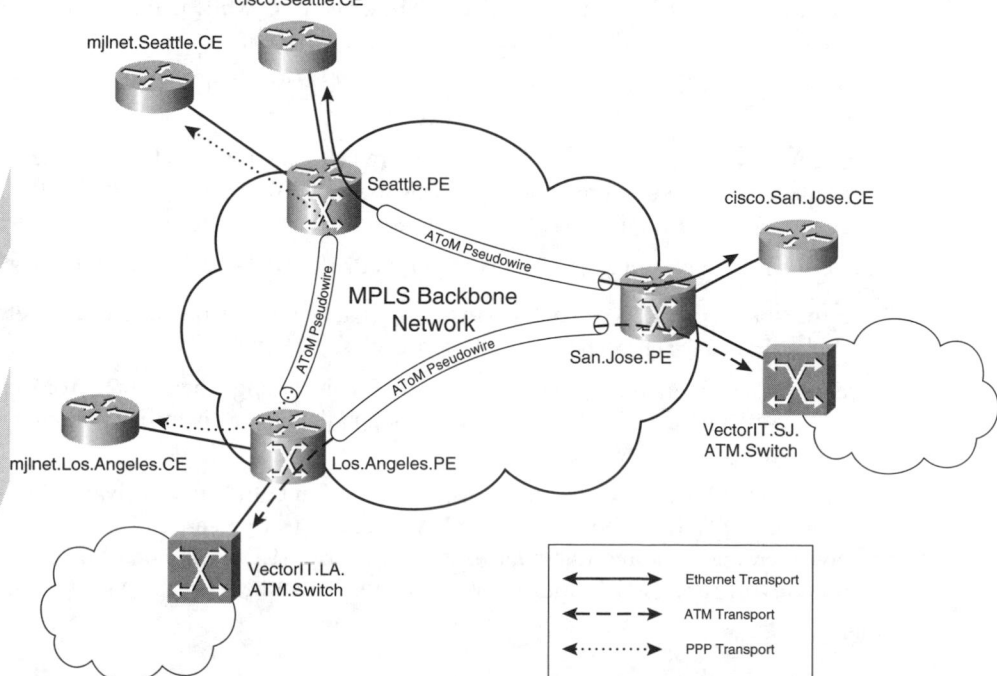

In Figure 3-1, ATM traffic is transported over an AToM pseudowire between VectorIT.LA .ATM.Switch and VectorIT.SJ.ATM.Switch; PPP traffic is transported over an AToM pseudowire between mjlnet.Los.Angeles.CE and mjlnet. Seattle.CE; and Ethernet traffic is transported over an AToM pseudowire between cisco.Seattle.CE and cisco.San.Jose.CE.

This chapter describes the design and implementation of AToM-based, pseudowire-based L2VPNs. But before looking at design and implementation, it is important to understand AToM pseudowire operation.

Benefits and Drawbacks of AToM-Based L2VPNs

Knowing that AToM pseudowires do a similar job to L2TPv3 pseudowires, you will not be surprised to learn that AToM-based L2VPNs share many advantages and disadvantages with L2TPv3-based L2VPNs.

Some of the main advantages for service providers implementing AToM-based L2VPNs are as follows:

- AToM-based L2VPNs are MPLS based, and are therefore deployed over an MPLS backbone network. It is possible to implement AToM over a Generic Routing Encapsulation (GRE) tunnel (and an IP backbone), but this is not a typical method of implementation.

- AToM allows the consolidation of service provider legacy and MPLS backbone networks. This consolidation of legacy and MPLS networks allows the service provider to save on operational and capital expenditure, while maintaining revenues for both legacy and IP/MPLS services.

- Service providers can use AToM to deploy both legacy Layer 2 (Frame Relay and so on) and newer Ethernet service offerings.

- Because AToM is MPLS based, a service provider can provision high service availability and traffic protection for AToM-based L2VPNs using MPLS traffic engineering (MPLS-TE) and MPLS-TE fast-reroute.

Some of the main advantages of AToM-based L2VPNs for enterprises are as follows:

- AToM-based L2VPNs can be used to transport non-IP protocols such as Internetwork Packet Exchange (IPX) between enterprise sites.

- Enterprises can maintain complete control of their routing when using AToM-based L2VPNs—Provider Edge (PE) routers do not participate in enterprise routing (unlike with MPLS Layer 3 VPNs).

- MPLS-based pseudowires can be used to provision both Virtual Private Wire Service (VPWS) and Virtual Private LAN Service (VPLS) architectures. Note, however, that although Label Distribution Protocol (LDP)-signaled MPLS pseudowires are used in both VPWS and VPLS architectures, the AToM command syntax described in this chapter is used for VPWS. For more information on VPLS, see Appendix A, "VPLS and IPLS Layer 2 VPNs."

Now that you understand the motivations behind the deployment of AToM-based L2VPNs, it is time to move on to a discussion of their underlying operation.

AToM Pseudowire Operation

When deploying AToM, it is essential to understand how pseudowires are set up, and how frames, cells, or SDUs received on attachment circuits are transported over pseudowires.

NOTE   AToM pseudowires are sometimes referred to as *Draft Martini* pseudowires because the original Internet drafts that defined LDP-signaled MPLS pseudowires were draft-martini-l2circuit-encap-mpls ("Encapsulation Methods for Transport of Layer 2 Frames over IP and MPLS Networks") and draft-martini-l2circuit-trans-mpls ("Transport of Layer 2 Frames over MPLS").

There are two channels, or planes, of communication for AToM pseudowires:

- **The control channel**—LDP messages are used to set up, maintain, and tear down AToM pseudowires.

- **The data channel**—Frames, cells, or SDUs received on an attachment circuit are encapsulated and sent over the pseudowire to the peer PE router.

Figure 3-2 illustrates overall packet formats for control channel and data channel packets used with AToM.

Figure 3-2   *Packet Formats for Control Channel and Data Channel Packets Used with AToM*

Control Plane Message (LDP)

IP Header
UDP/TCP Header (Port 646)
LDP PDU (LDP Header + LDP Message[s])

Data Plane Message

Tunnel Label(s)
PW (VC) Label
Optional Control Word
Payload

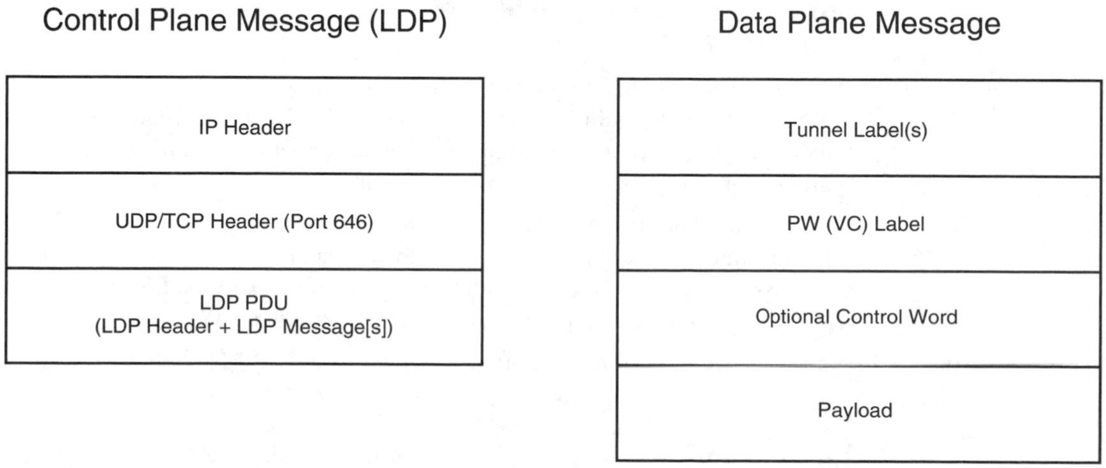

The sections that follow discuss control channel and data channel messages in more detail.

Control Channel Messages

As shown in Figure 3-2, an LDP message consists of the following elements:

- **An IP header and UDP or TCP header**—An LDP message is carried over either UDP or TCP, but in both cases, port 646 is used.

- **An LDP Protocol Data Unit (PDU)**—This consists of an LDP header, together with one or more LDP messages.

Figure 3-3 shows the format of the LDP header.

Figure 3-3 *LDP Header Format*

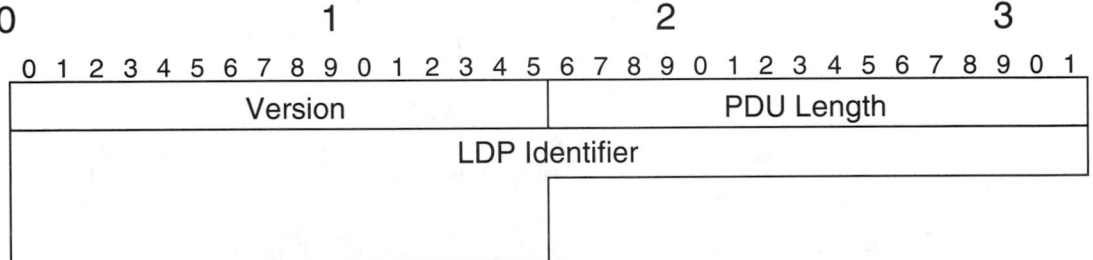

The LDP header (Figure 3-3) consists of three fields:

— **Version**—This specifies the version of LDP. At the time of this writing, there is only one version of LDP (version 1).

— **PDU Length**—This is the length of the PDU, with the exception of the Version and PDU Length fields.

— **LDP Identifier**—This field functions as a unique identifier of the label space of a Label Switching Router (LSR)/Provider Edge (PE) router. A label space is a pool of labels, and this pool can either be used for a particular interface or for a platform as a whole.

An LDP Identifier is 6 octets long, with the first 4 octets being a globally unique value (these 4 octets often correspond to an IP address), and the last 2 octets identifying the label space of the LSR. If a platform-wide label space is used, the last 2 octets are 0.

Figure 3-4 shows the LDP message format.

Figure 3-4   *LDP Message Format*

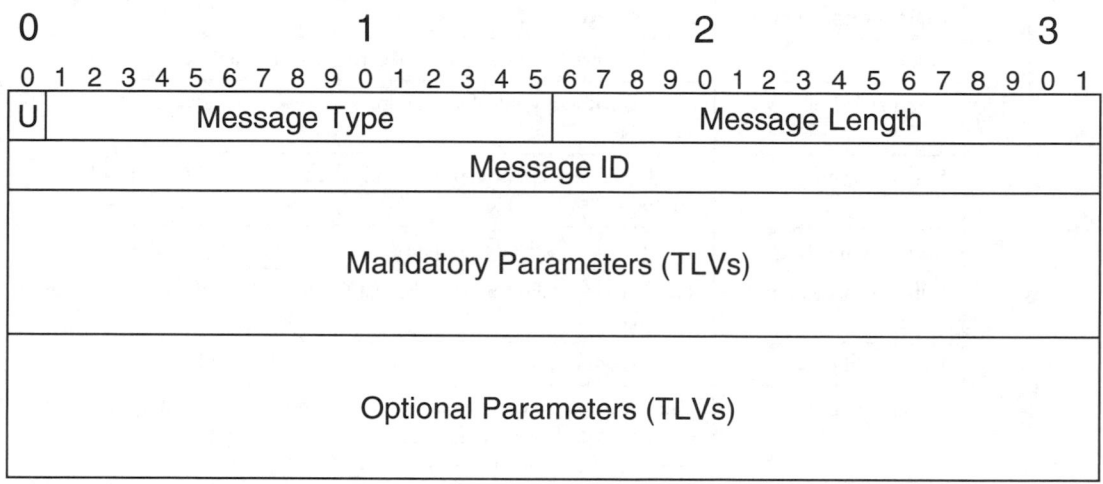

The LDP message format has the following fields:

- **U**—The Unknown message bit. This can be set either to 1 or 0.
- **Message Type**—The LDP message type. Table 3-1 shows possible LDP message types.
- **Message Length**—The length of the Message ID, Mandatory Parameters, and Optional Parameters fields.
- **Message ID**—This is an identifier for this message. This ID can be used in Notification messages to indicate the message to which they correspond.
- **Mandatory Parameters**—These are parameters that must be included with this message.
- **Optional Parameters**—These are parameters that may be included with this message.

Table 3-1   *LDP Message Types*

LDP Message Type	Description
Notification	This message is used to inform a peer of a significant event, such as an error.
Hello	Hello messages are exchanged as part of the LDP discovery process.
Initialization	These messages are exchanged during LDP session initialization.
Keepalive	Keepalive messages are used to verify that an LDP session is active.

continues

Table 3-1   *LDP Message Types (Continued)*

LDP Message Type	Description
Address	An LSR uses this message to advertise its interface addresses.
Address Withdraw	Used to withdraw interfaces addresses previously advertised in an Address message.
Label Mapping	Used to advertise Forwarding Equivalence Class (FEC) to label bindings.
Label Request	This message is used to request label bindings from LDP peers.
Label Abort Request	This is used to abort a label request (requested using a Label Request message).
Label Withdraw	Used to withdraw a previously advertised label binding.
Label Release	Used to communicate the fact that the sender no longer requires a label binding (which has already been advertised by an LDP peer or requested by the local LSR) .

As shown in Table 3-1, there are 11 possible LDP message types. These message types fall into 4 categories:

- **Discovery messages**—These messages are used by an LSR to announce its presence to other LSRs, and once announced, maintain that presence.

- **Session messages**—Session messages are used by LSRs to establish, maintain, and tear down LDP sessions.

- **Advertisement messages**—Advertisement messages are used to distribute, modify, and delete label bindings.

- **Error messages**—These messages are used to signal error information.

LDP discovery messages are sent over UDP (see Figure 3-2), but all other types of messages are sent over TCP.

Now that you are familiar with the overall LDP message format, it is time to take a look at AToM pseudowire setup, maintenance, and teardown.

AToM Pseudowire Setup

As previously mentioned, AToM uses LDP to set up, maintain, and tear down pseudowires.

Figure 3-5 illustrates AToM pseudowire setup.

Figure 3-5 *AToM Pseudowire Setup*

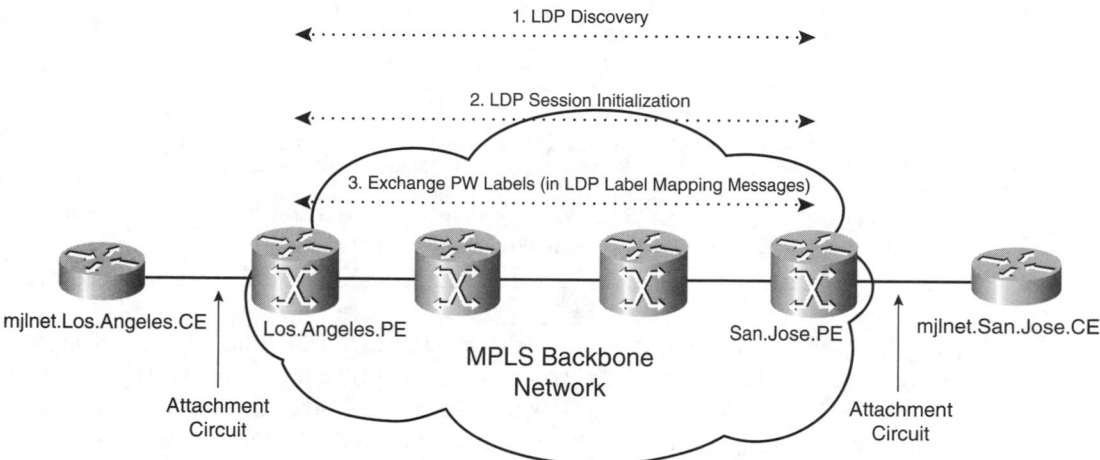

As you can see in Figure 3-5, AToM pseudowire setup consists of three steps:

Step 1   LDP discovery

Step 2   LDP session initialization (and establishment)

Step 3   LDP Label Mapping message (pseudowire [VC] label bindings)
exchange

LDP discovery consists of the exchange of Hello messages between the peer PE routers (the pseudowire endpoints). These Hello messages serve to make the PE routers aware of each other's existence.

LDP discovery can be performed in two different ways:

- **Basic discovery**—This is performed between directly connected peers (at the data link layer), and uses the *all routers on this subnet* multicast address of 224.0.0.2.

- **Extended discovery**—Extended discovery uses unicast (targeted Hello) transmission between peers.

In the case of LDP discovery between AToM PE routers, extended discovery is used because the peers are typically not directly connected.

In Example 3-1, you can see LDP extended discovery between peer Cisco PE routers.

Example 3-1 *LDP Extended Discovery Between Peer Cisco PE Routers*

```
San.Jose.PE#show mpls ldp discovery detail
 Local LDP Identifier:
    10.1.1.2:0
    Discovery Sources:
    Interfaces:
        Serial4/0 (ldp): xmit/recv
```

continues

Example 3-1 *LDP Extended Discovery Between Peer Cisco PE Routers (Continued)*

```
          Hello interval: 5000 ms; Transport IP addr: 10.1.1.2
          LDP Id: 10.1.1.4:0
           Src IP addr: 10.4.1.1; Transport IP addr: 10.1.1.4
          Hold time: 15 sec; Proposed local/peer: 15/15 sec
     Targeted Hellos: (line 1)
        10.1.1.2 -> 10.1.1.1 (ldp): active/passive, xmit/recv (line 2)
          Hello interval: 10000 ms; Transport IP addr: 10.1.1.2
          LDP Id: 10.1.1.1:0
           Src IP addr: 10.1.1.1; Transport IP addr: 10.1.1.1
          Hold time: 90 sec; Proposed local/peer: 90/90 sec
San.Jose.PE#
```

In highlighted lines 1 and 2, you can see that targeted LDP Hellos have been exchanged between the local PE router (10.1.1.2) and the remote PE router (10.1.1.1). This exchange of targeted Hellos is the basis of LDP extended discovery. Note that detailed, step-by-step information on verifying and troubleshooting AToM-based L2VPNs can be found in *Troubleshooting Virtual Private Networks* by Mark Lewis (Cisco Press).

After the PE routers are aware of each other, they can establish a transport connection and begin LDP session initialization.

During the session initialization process, the PE routers negotiate session parameters such as LDP version, label distribution method, and timers. After the initialization process is finished, an LDP session is established between the PE routers, and they are considered to be LDP peers.

You can use **show mpls ldp neighbor** *neighbor-ip-address* **detail** to examine LDP session information on Cisco PE routers, as demonstrated in Example 3-2.

Example 3-2 *Examining LDP Session Information*

```
San.Jose.PE#show mpls ldp neighbor 10.1.1.1 detail
    Peer LDP Ident: 10.1.1.1:0; Local LDP Ident 10.1.1.2:0 (line 1)
      TCP connection: 10.1.1.1.646 - 10.1.1.2.11008 (line 2)
      State: Oper; Msgs sent/rcvd: 18/19; Downstream; Last TIB rev sent 17 (line 3)
      Up time: 00:07:10; UID: 5; Peer Id 0; (line 4)
      LDP discovery sources:
       Targeted Hello 10.1.1.2 -> 10.1.1.1, active, passive;
        holdtime: infinite, hello interval: 10000 ms
      Addresses bound to peer LDP Ident:
        10.2.1.1      10.1.1.1
      Peer holdtime: 180000 ms; KA interval: 60000 ms; Peer state: estab
      Clients: Dir Adj Client
San.Jose.PE#
```

In Example 3-2, highlighted line 1, you can see the remote and local PE routers' LDP (router) IDs (10.1.1.1:0 and 10.1.1.2:0 respectively).

Highlighted line 2 shows that the LDP session has been established over a TCP connection. The TCP ports that the remote and local PE routers have opened for this TCP connection are 646 and 11008.

Highlighted lines 3 and 4 shows the LDP session state (operational [established]), the number of messages sent and received (18 and 19), the method of label distribution (unsolicited downstream), and the session uptime (7 minutes, 10 seconds).

The next step is for the PE routers to exchange LDP Label Mapping messages. These messages contain the pseudowire label bindings consisting of a FEC Type-Length-Value (TLV) and a Generic Label TLV (plus zero or more optional TLVs).

NOTE   Note that after LDP discovery and session initialization have taken place between peer PE routers, any number of pseudowires can be set up by exchanging LDP Label Mapping messages.

It is a good idea to take a closer look at the exchange of LDP Label Mapping messages during AToM pseudowire setup. Remember that these messages contain FEC and Generic Label TLVs.

Figure 3-6 depicts the FEC TLV.

Figure 3-6   *FEC TLV*

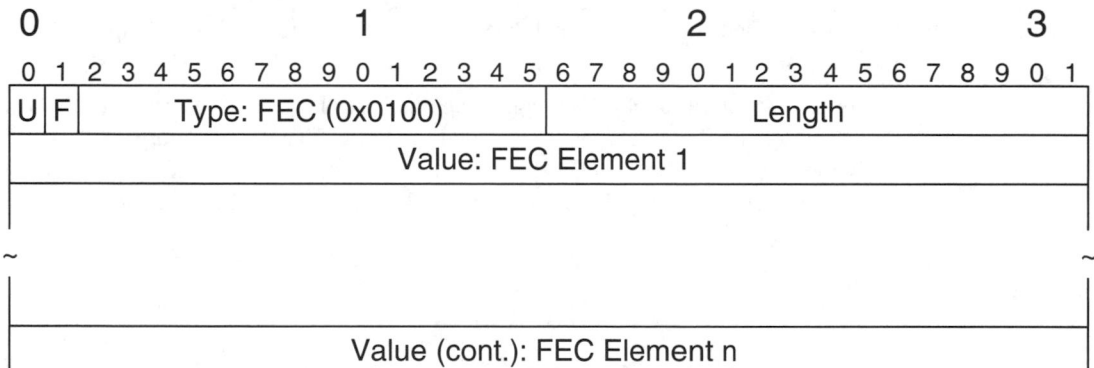

As shown in Figure 3-6, contents of the fields in the FEC TLV are as follows:

- **U and F**—The Unknown (U) and the Forward unknown (F) bits are both set to 0.
- **Type**—This is set to a value of 0x0100, indicating that this is an FEC TLV.
- **Length**—Indicates the length of the Value field (the FEC elements) in octets.
- **Value**—In the case of an FEC TLV, the Value field contains one or more FEC elements. In the case of LDP Label Mapping messages used with AToM, however, only one FEC element is included in an FEC TLV (the specific type of FEC element is discussed later in this section).

NOTE   Note that the format of the FEC TLV (U and F bits; Type, Length, and Value fields) is common to all LDP TLVs.

Figure 3-7 illustrates the Generic Label TLV.

Figure 3-7   *Generic Label TLV*

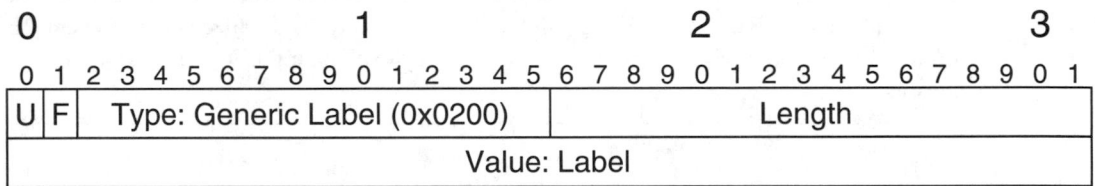

The Generic Label TLV can be described as follows:

- **U and F bits**—Both of these must be set to 0.

- **Type**—This field contains the value 0x0200, which indicates that this is a Generic Label FEC.

- **Length**—This indicates the length of the Value field.

- **Value**—This field contains a label. In the case of a pseudowire Label Mapping message, this field contains a PW (VC) label.

So far so good—an LDP Label Mapping message includes FEC and Generic Label TLVs. But what about the FEC element that is included in the FEC TLV (see Figure 3-6)? As previously mentioned, only one FEC element (called a pseudowire [PW] ID FEC element) is included when an LDP Label Mapping message is used with AToM, as illustrated in Figure 3-8.

Figure 3-8   *PW (VC) ID FEC Element*

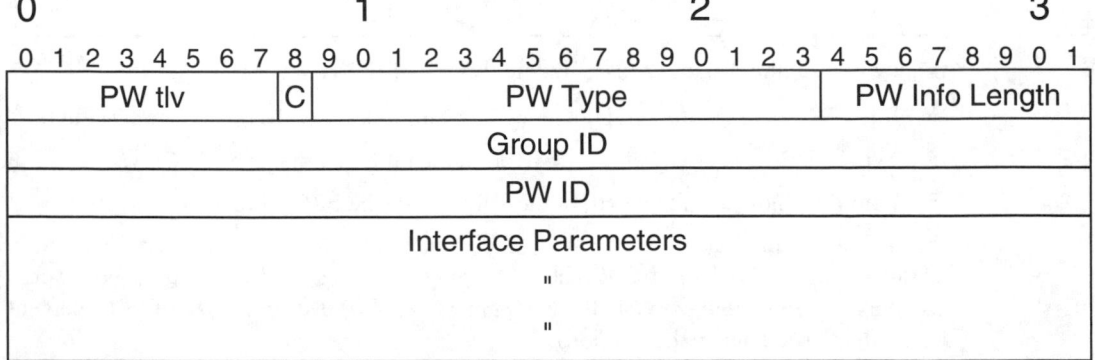

The PW ID FEC element consists of the following fields:

- **PW (VC) TLV**—This field contains the value of 128, indicating that this is a PW ID FEC element.

- **C bit**—This bit indicates whether a control word will be used with this pseudowire (will be included in pseudowire data channel packets [see Figure 3-2]). If the C bit is set to 1, a control word will be used; if the C bit is set to 0, a control word will not be used.

- **PW (VC) Type**—This indicates the pseudowire type as listed Table 3-2.

Table 3-2 *MPLS Pseudowire Types*

Pseudowire (PW/VC) Type	Description
0x0001	Frame Relay DLCI (Martini mode)
0x0002	ATM AAL5 SDU VCC transport
0x0003	ATM transparent cell transport
0x0004	Ethernet Tagged mode
0x0005	Ethernet
0x0006	High-Level Data Link Control (HDLC)
0x0007	PPP
0x0008	Synchronous Optical Network (SONET)/Synchronous Digital Hierarchy (SDH) Circuit Emulation Service over MPLS (CEM)
0x0009	ATM n-to-1 VCC cell transport
0x000A	ATM n-to-1 VPC cell transport
0x000B	IP Layer 2 Transport
0x000C	ATM 1-to-1 VCC Cell mode
0x000D	ATM 1-to-1 VPC Cell mode
0x000E	ATM AAL5 PDU VCC transport
0x000F	Frame Relay port mode
0x0010	SONET/SDH Circuit Emulation over Packet (CEP)
0x0011	Structure-agnostic E1 over Packet (SAToP)
0x0012	Structure-agnostic T1 (DS1) over Packet (SAToP)
0x0013	Structure-agnostic E3 over Packet (SAToP)
0x0014	Structure-agnostic T3 (DS3) over Packet (SAToP)
0x0015	CESoPSN basic mode

continues

Table 3-2 *MPLS Pseudowire Types (Continued)*

Pseudowire (PW/VC) Type	Description
0x0016	TDMoIP AAL1 mode
0x0017	CESoPSN TDM with CAS
0x0018	TDMoIP AAL2 mode
0x0019	Frame Relay DLCI

- **PW (VC) Info Length**—This field specifies the length of the PW ID and Interface Parameters fields (in octets).

- **Group ID**—The Group ID field contains a value that is used to represent a group of pseudowires.

  The Group ID can be used to group a number of pseudowires on an interface or virtual tunnel and can, for example, be useful when a PE router needs to withdraw labels for a number of pseudowires associated with a particular interface, or send a notification message that applies to a number of pseudowires associated with a particular interface.

- **PW (VC) ID**—This, together with the PW type, uniquely identifies an AToM pseudowire.

- **Interface Parameters**—This field is used to signal attachment circuit interface parameters such as maximum transmission unit (MTU) and interface description string.

  Figure 3-9 shows the format of the Interface Parameters field contained in the PW ID FEC element (also see Figure 3-8).

Figure 3-9 *Interface Parameters Field*

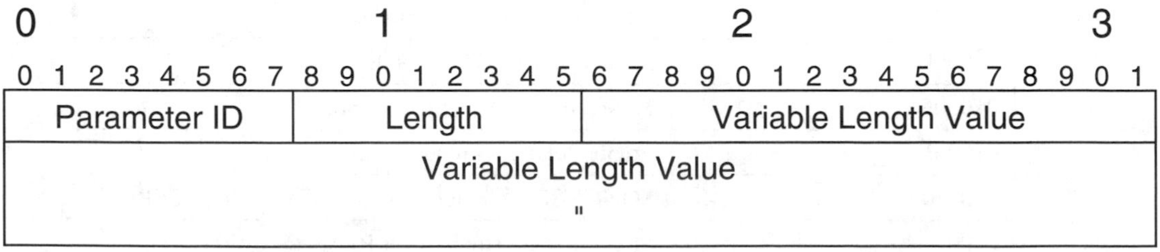

The components of the Interface Parameters field can be described as follows:

- **Parameter ID**—Identifies the type of interface parameter (interface MTU, description, and so on) contained in the Variable Length Value field.

- **Length**—Specifies the overall length of the Interface Parameters field, including Parameter ID and Length.

- **Variable Length Value**—Contains the actual data, whether the interface MTU, the interface description, or other interface parameter.

If you are a little confused about how all of these TLVs, FEC elements, and Interface Parameters fields fit together, take a look at Figure 3-10.

Figure 3-10 *Interrelationship Between FEC/Generic Label TLVs, PW ID FEC Element, and Interface Parameters Field*

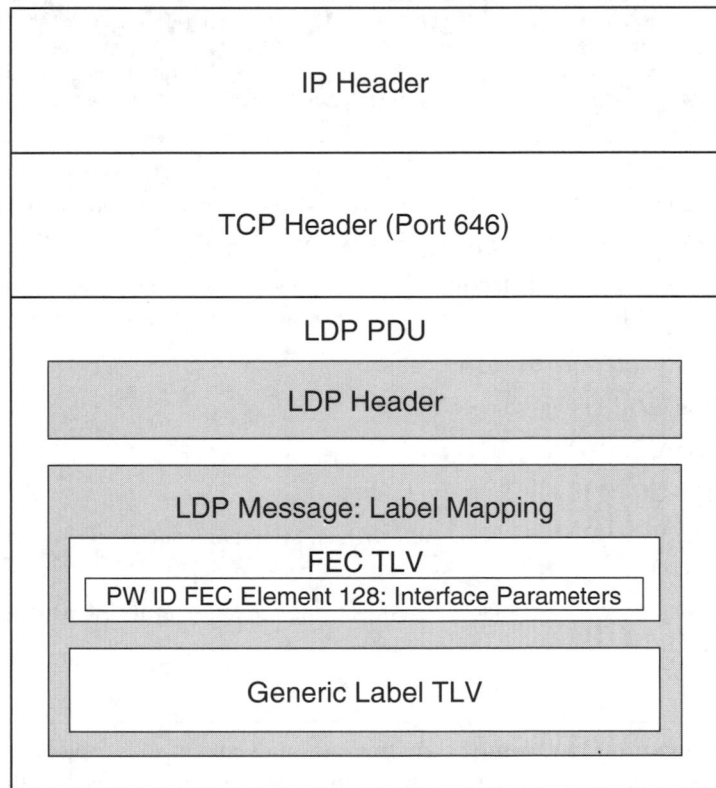

As shown in Figure 3-10, the LDP PDU consists of the following:

- An LDP header.
- An LDP message, which in this case is a Label Mapping message. The LDP Label Mapping message comprises the following:
  - An FEC TLV
  - A Generic Label TLV

Although not shown in Figure 3-10, the Label Mapping message may also contain zero or more optional parameter TLVs.

Finally, the FEC TLV contains a PW ID FEC element in its Interface Parameters field.

Example 3-3 shows the exchange of PW (VC) labels between peer Cisco PE routers.

Example 3-3   *Exchange of PW (VC) Labels Between Peer PE Routers*

```
San.Jose.PE#debug mpls l2transport signaling message
AToM LDP message debugging is on
San.Jose.PE#
*May 26 20:34:21.555: %LDP-5-NBRCHG: LDP Neighbor 10.1.1.1:0 is UP (line 1)
*May 26 20:34:21.555: AToM LDP [10.1.1.1]: Sending label mapping msg (line 2)
  vc type 6, cbit 1, vc id 1001, group id 0, vc label 21, status 0, mtu 1500 (line 3)
*May 26 20:34:21.835: AToM LDP [10.1.1.1]: Received label mapping msg, id 99 (line 4)
  vc type 6, cbit 1, vc id 1001, group id 3, vc label 21, status 0, mtu 1500 (line 5)
San.Jose.PE#
```

As you can see in Example 3-3, the LDP session has been established (highlighted line 1), and label bindings have been sent and received (highlighted lines 2 and 3).

A closer look at highlighted lines 2 and 3 shows some of the information contained in the PW (VC) ID FEC element (see Figure 3-8), such as the following:

- The VC (PW) type (6, see Table 3-2)
- The C bit setting
- The VC (PW) ID (1001)
- The Group ID (0)
- The VC (PW) label (21), status (0), and (attachment circuit) interface MTU (1500 bytes)

You can also view AToM label bindings using the **show mpls l2transport binding** command.

NOTE   The **debug mpls l2transport signaling message** command is used here for illustrative purposes only. Exercise caution when using **debug** commands because they can disrupt the operation of heavily loaded routers.

So that is pseudowire setup—now on to pseudowire status signaling.

AToM Status Signaling

LDP is not only used to setup pseudowires, it can also be used to signal pseudowire status. This can be important if, for example, one PE router wants to signal its peer PE router that its attachment circuit has changed state.

If a PE router wants to signal attachment circuit status changes to its peer PE router, it can use two different methods:

- It can send an LDP Label Withdraw message.
- It can send an LDP Notification message.

Signaling Attachment Circuit Status Changes with an LDP Label Withdraw Message

The LDP Label Withdraw message can be used to signal circuit down status.

Figure 3-11 shows the signaling of circuit down status using the LDP Label Withdraw message.

Figure 3-11   *Signaling Circuit Down Status Using the LDP Withdraw Message*

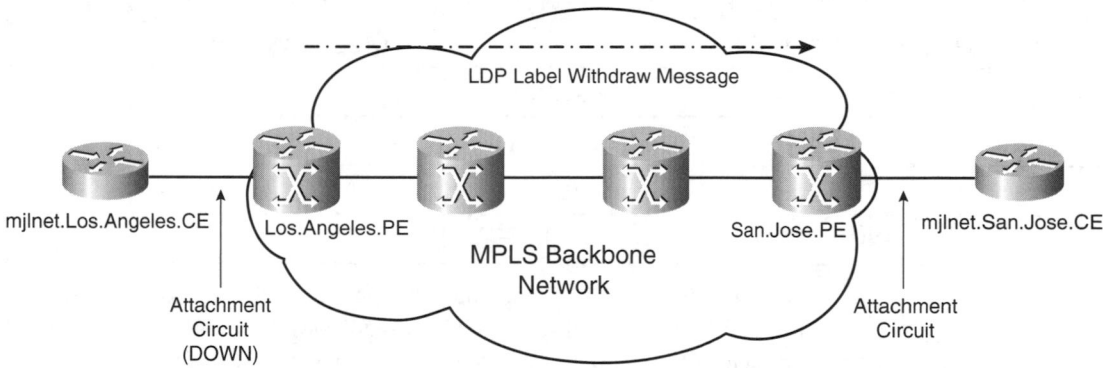

Example 3-4 shows the LDP Label Withdraw message being used to signal attachment circuit status between peer Cisco PE routers.

Example 3-4   *LDP Label Withdraw Message Being Used to Signal Pseudowire Status Between Peer Cisco PE Routers*

```
San.Jose.PE#debug mpls l2transport signaling message
AToM LDP message debugging is on
San.Jose.PE#
*May 26 21:48:54.279: AToM LDP [10.1.1.1]: Received label withdraw msg, id 279 (line 1)
   vc type 6, cbit 1, vc id 1001, group id 3, vc label 21, status 0, mtu 0 (line 2)
San.Jose.PE#
```

Highlighted line 1 shows that the local PE router has received an LDP Label Withdraw message from the remote PE router indicating an attachment circuit status change.

Signaling Attachment Circuit Status Changes with an LDP Notification Message

This alternative (and relatively recent) method of signaling status must be negotiated when LDP Label Mapping messages are exchanged during pseudowire setup (see Figure 3-5).

If the PE router initiating pseudowire setup supports status signaling using the LDP Notification message, it includes a PW Status TLV along with the FEC and Generic Label TLVs in the LDP Label Mapping message.

If the peer PE router also supports status signaling using the LDP Notification message, it also includes a PW Status TLV in the LDP Label Mapping message that it sends. If, on the other hand, *either* peer PE router does not include the PW Status TLV in the LDP Label Mapping message that it sends, both peer PE routers revert to using LDP Label Withdraw messages to signal status.

Figure 3-12 shows the format of the LDP Notification message used to signal pseudowire status.

Figure 3-12 *Format of the LDP Notification Message Used to Signal Status*

0										1										2										3	
0	1	2	3	4	5	6	7	8	9	0	1	2	3	4	5	6	7	8	9	0	1	2	3	4	5	6	7	8	9	0	1
0	Notification (0x0001)														Message Length																
Message ID																															
Status (TLV)																															
PW Status TLV																															
PW ID FEC																															

The key fields to notice in the LDP Notification message are the Status and PW Status TLVs, as well as the PW ID FEC element (see also Figure 3-8). Note that the PW ID FEC element does not include the Interface Parameters field when carried in the LDP Notification message.

A status code that indicates the status of the pseudowire is carried in the PW Status TLV. The PW ID FEC element is carried in the LDP Notification message to indicate the ID of the pseudowire (PW ID) or group (Group ID) to which the status code corresponds.

Table 3-3 shows possible PW status codes that can be carried in the PW Status TLV in the LDP Notification message.

Table 3-3 *Possible PW Status Codes Carried in the PW Status TLV*

(PW) Status Code	Description
0x00000000	Pseudowire forwarding (clear all failures)
0x00000001	Pseudowire not forwarding
0x00000002	Local attachment circuit (ingress) receive fault
0x00000004	Local attachment circuit (egress)transmit fault
0x00000008	Local PSN-facing PW (ingress) receive fault
0x00000010	Local PSN-facing PW (egress) transmit fault

As you can see in Table 3-3, the PW Status TLV can be used to signal a number of statuses. So, signaling pseudowire status using the LDP Notification message (including a PW Status TLV) is more flexible than signaling pseudowire status using the LDP Label Withdraw message because the LDP Label Withdraw message can only be used to signal attachment circuit down status.

Figure 3-13 illustrates negotiation of pseudowire status signaling (with the LDP Notification message) during LDP Label Mapping message exchange.

Figure 3-13 *Negotiation of Pseudowire Status Signaling (with the LDP Notification Message) During LDP Label Mapping Message Exchange*

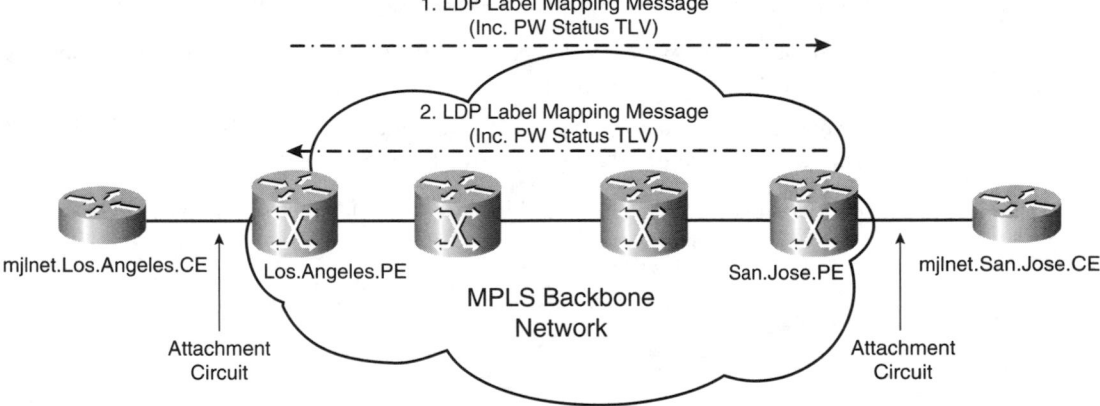

In Figure 3-13, both peer PE routers include the PW Status TLV in the LDP Label Mapping messages that they send, and this results in the PE routers using the LDP Notification message to signal pseudowire status.

Figure 3-14 shows the signaling of pseudowire status using the LDP Notification message.

Figure 3-14 *Signaling Pseudowire Status Using the LDP Notification Message*

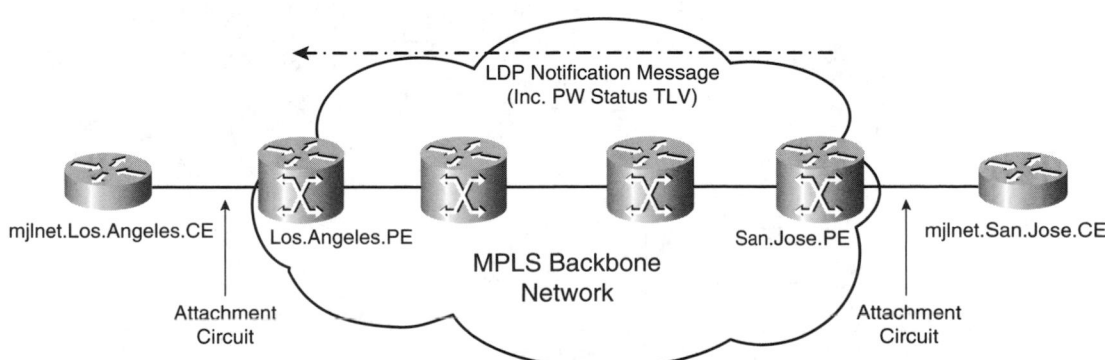

AToM Data Channel Packet Forwarding

The overall format of AToM data channel packets is shown in Figure 3-2 on page 139. As you can see, the packet format consists of the following:

- **One or more tunnel labels**—These tunnel labels can be advertised between adjacent PE and P routers (LSRs) using LDP, TDP, or RSVP-TE. Note, however, that the use of the Cisco-proprietary Tag Distribution Protocol (TDP) is now deprecated in MPLS networks.

- **A PW label**—This is also referred to as the *VC label* and serves as a demultiplexor that ensures that data channel packets are correctly associated with an attachment circuit.

  The PW label serves the same purpose as the session header (session ID and optional cookie) does with L2TPv3 pseudowires.

- **An optional control word**—This performs the same function as the service-specific sublayer with L2TPv3 pseudowires.

The PW label and the presence (or otherwise) of a control word are advertised in LDP Label Mapping messages exchanged during pseudowire setup.

Figure 3-15 depicts the transmission of AToM data channel packets.

Figure 3-15 *Transmission of AToM Data Channel Packets*

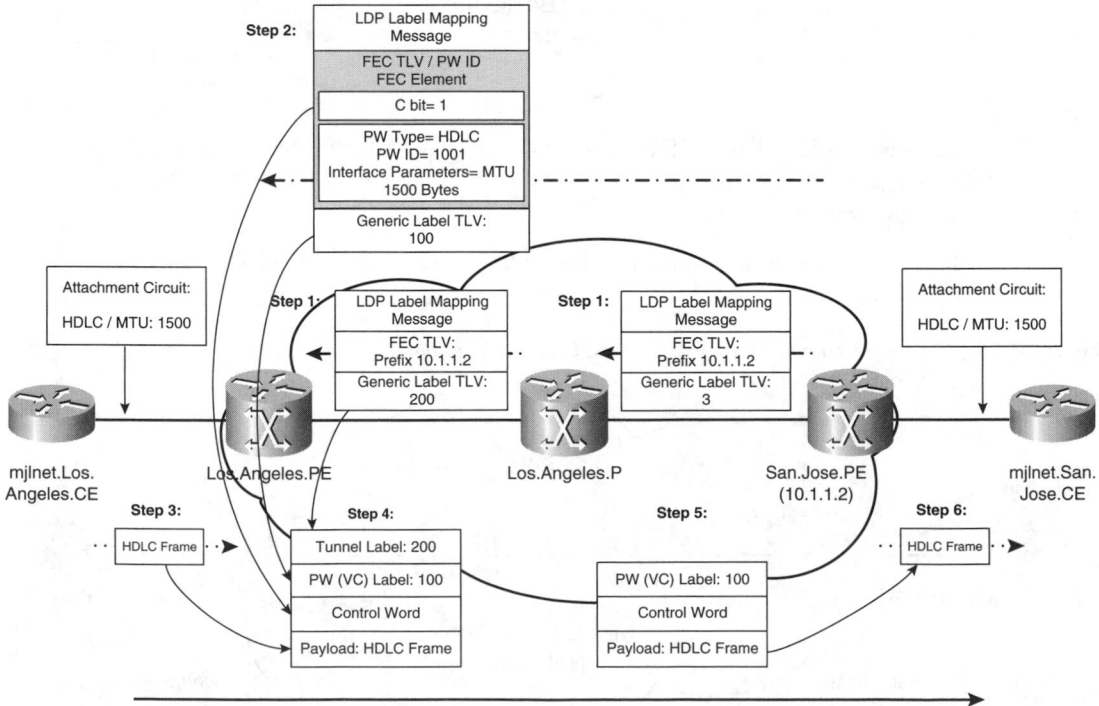

Figure 3-15 shows the transport of a AToM data channel packet across the MPLS backbone network between Los.Angeles.PE to San.Jose.PE (see the lower half of the figure), but it also shows how control channel packets (see the upper half of the figure) influence the form of data channel packets.

If you take a close look at Figure 3-15, you can see that the following events occur:

Step 1   San.Jose.PE advertises a (tunnel) label (3 [implicit-null]) corresponding to its IP address (10.1.1.2) to Los.Angeles.P using LDP.

Similarly, Los.Angeles.P advertises a (tunnel) label (200) corresponding to San.Jose.PE's IP address (10.1.1.2) to Los.Angeles.PE.

Step 2   San.Jose.PE sends an LDP Label Mapping message to Los.Angeles.PE. This message includes an FEC TLV (Figure 3-6) and a Generic Label TLV (Figure 3-7).

The FEC TLV includes a PW ID FEC element (Figure 3-8), with the C bit set to 1, the PW Type specified as High-Level Data Link Control (HDLC), the PW (VC) ID set to 1001, and the Interface Parameters, which specify an attachment circuit MTU of 1500.

The Generic Label TLV specifies a label value of 100 (this is the PW label).

Although not explicitly shown in Figure 3-15, Los.Angeles.PE also sends an LDP Label Mapping message to San.Jose.PE, and the pseudowire has been established.

Step 3   Los.Angeles.PE now receives an HDLC frame on the attachment circuit connected to mjlnet.Los.Angeles.CE.

Step 4   Los.Angeles.PE encapsulates the HDLC with a control word (this is included because the C bit was set to 1 in the PW ID FEC element in the LDP Label Mapping message in Step 2), a PW (VC) label (100, which was included in the Generic Label FEC in the LDP Label Mapping message sent in Step 2), and a tunnel label (200, which was received from Los.Angeles.P in Step 1). The purpose of the tunnel label is to transport the encapsulated frame to the egress PE router, which in this case is San.Jose.PE.

Los.Angeles.PE then sends the encapsulated HDLC frame to Los.Angeles.P.

Note that by default a control word is not required with an HDLC pseudowire. A control word is required only if sequencing is configured. Configuration of sequencing is discussed later in this chapter.

Step 5 Los.Angeles.P pops the tunnel label because the outgoing label (3, implicit-null) indicates that the egress PE router is the next hop (so, Los.Angeles.P performs a penultimate hop pop [PHP]).

Los.Angeles.P now forwards the encapsulated HDLC frame to San.Jose.PE.

Step 6 San.Jose.PE receives the encapsulated HDLC frame, and removes the PW (VC) label and the control word. The PW (VC) label indicates the local attachment circuit on which the encapsulated HDLC frame should be forwarded, and so San.Jose.PE then sends the HDLC frame to mjlnet.San.Jose.CE.

That is AToM data channel packet forwarding from Los.Angeles.PE to San.Jose.PE. Data channel packet forwarding from San.Jose.PE to Los.Angeles.PE happens in exactly the same manner, just in the opposite direction.

Now that you understand the background to AToM pseudowire operation, it is time to move on to AToM configuration.

Deploying AToM Pseudowires

As previously mentioned, a number of AToM pseudowire types can be configured on Cisco routers. These pseudowire types are as follows:

- Ethernet
- Ethernet VLAN (802.1Q)
- HDLC
- PPP
- Frame Relay
- ATM cell relay
- ATM AAL5-SDU
- IP Layer 2 transport

IP Layer 2 transport is discussed toward the end of this chapter, but all the other types listed are discussed in this section.

Implementing AToM Pseudowires for Ethernet Traffic Transport

Ethernet traffic can be transported over AToM pseudowires in two ways:

- Ethernet port (raw) mode
- Ethernet VLAN (802.1Q) mode

Before examining each of these methods of transporting Ethernet traffic, it might be worthwhile to re-acquaint yourself with Ethernet and Ethernet VLAN (802.1Q) frame formats. Figure 2-13 on page 47 and Figure 2-15 on page 50 illustrate these frame formats.

Now that you've reminded yourself of the Ethernet frame formats, its time to move on to configuration, starting with Ethernet port mode.

AToM Pseudowire Ethernet Port Transport

Before describing the configuration of Ethernet port transport, it is a good idea to take a look at the form of AToM data channel packets when used to transport Ethernet port frames. AToM data channel packets used to transport Ethernet frames conform to the general packet format shown in Figure 3-2, with the format of the optional control word shown in Figure 3-16.

Figure 3-16 *Optional Control Word for AToM Ethernet Port Transport*

0										1										2										3	
0	1	2	3	4	5	6	7	8	9	0	1	2	3	4	5	6	7	8	9	0	1	2	3	4	5	6	7	8	9	0	1

0 0 0 0	Reserved	Sequence Number

The control word used with Ethernet pseudowires consists of the following fields:

- **Reserved**—These bits are reserved for future use.

- **Sequence Number**—As the name suggests, this field contains a sequence number.

The control word is only included in AToM data channel packets used to transport Ethernet frames when sequencing is configured.

Figure 3-17 illustrates the encapsulation of an Ethernet frame received on an attachment circuit and its transmission on an AToM pseudowire (when using either Ethernet port or Ethernet VLAN [802.1Q] mode).

Figure 3-17 *Encapsulation of an Ethernet Frame and Its Transmission on an AToM Pseudowire*

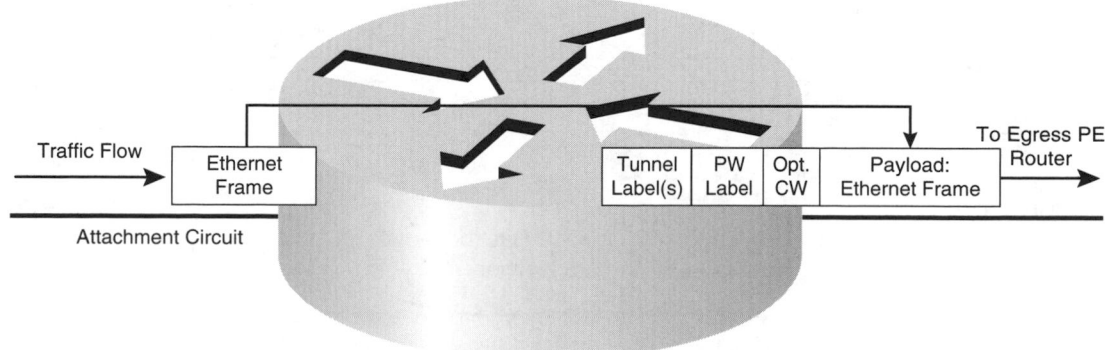

Ingress PE Router

When an Ethernet frame is received on an attachment circuit, the preamble and FCS are stripped from the frame; the tunnel label(s), pseudowire (PW) label, and optionally control word are prepended; and the resulting packet is transmitted to the egress PE router.

The egress PE router performs the same operations as the ingress PE router, just in reverse. It removes remaining labels (including the PW label), removes the control word, reconstructs the preamble and FCS, and then transmits the frame on the appropriate attachment circuit (as indicated by the PW label).

That is the theory, but how about configuration?

AToM Pseudowire Configuration on PE Routers

Configuration of an AToM pseudowire consists of the following general steps:

Step 1   Configure Cisco Express Forwarding (CEF).

Step 2   Configure a loopback interface to use as the pseudowire endpoint (and LDP router ID).

Step 3   Configure the label protocol.

Step 4   Configure MPLS on MPLS backbone interfaces.

Step 5   Configure the MPLS backbone interior gateway protocol (IGP), if not already configured.

Step 6   Configure a pseudowire class (optional).

Step 7   Bind attachment circuits to pseudowires.

Figure 3-18 shows the network topology for the Ethernet pseudowire configurations in this section.

Figure 3-18   *AToM Ethernet Pseudowire Topology*

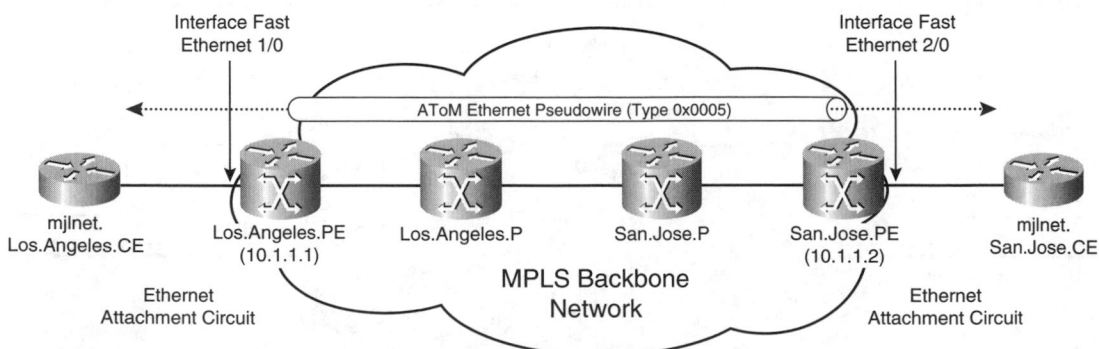

Example 3-5 shows an example configuration that encapsulates these steps on PE router Los.Angeles.PE.

Example 3-5 *Configuration of an Ethernet Port Mode AToM Pseudowire on Los.Angeles.PE*

```
!
hostname Los.Angeles.PE
!
ip cef (line 1)
!
mpls label protocol ldp (line 2)
!
mpls ldp router-id Loopback1 force (line 3)
!
interface Loopback1 (line 4)
 description LDP router id and PW endpoint
 ip address 10.1.1.1 255.255.255.255 (line 5)
!
interface FastEthernet1/0
 description Ethernet attachment circuit
 xconnect 10.1.1.2 1001 encapsulation mpls (line 6)
 no cdp enable
!
interface FastEthernet3/0
 description MPLS backbone network interface
 ip address 10.2.1.1 255.255.255.0
 mpls ip (line 7)
!
router ospf 100 (line 8)
 network 10.2.1.1 0.0.0.0 area 0 (line 9)
 network 10.1.1.1 0.0.0.0 area 0 (line 10)
 passive-interface Loopback1 (line 11)
!
!
```

Highlighted line 1 shows the **ip cef** command (Step 1 of the AToM pseudowire configuration process). This command enables CEF on the PE router. Certain platforms such as the 12000 series are capable of supporting distributed CEF—this can be enabled using the **ip cef distributed** command.

In highlighted line 2, **mpls label protocol ldp** enables you to specify that the label protocol to be used to advertise label bindings will be LDP (Step 3). Note that this command changes the label protocol used to signal tunnel labels from the default of TDP, but does not affect the protocol that is used to signal AToM pseudowire PW labels (it is always LDP) .

The **mpls ldp router-id** *interface* [**force**] command (highlighted line 3) is then used to ensure that the IP address configured on interface loopback 1 is used as the first four octets of the LDP (router) identifier that is carried in the LDP header (see Figure 3-3 on page 140).

Next, in highlighted lines 4 and 5, an IP address (10.1.1.1/32) is configured on interface loopback 1 (Step 2). This IP address is referenced by the **mpls ldp router-id** *interface* [**force**] command in highlighted line 3, and also serves as the pseudowire endpoint.

Highlighted line 6 shows the **xconnect** *peer-pe-ip-address pwid* **encapsulation mpls** command (Step 7). This command is configured on interface Fast Ethernet 1/0, and so binds this attachment circuit interface to a pseudowire to the specified peer PE router (using the peer's loopback [LDP ID] address), with the specified pseudowire ID (otherwise known as a VC ID), using MPLS encapsulation. The peer PE router is, in this example, San.Jose.PE (the other end of the Ethernet port mode pseudowire).

CAUTION   The pseudowire IDs (VC IDs) at either end of a pseudowire (configured using the **xconnect** command on peer PE routers) *must* match. If they do not match, pseudowire setup will fail.

The **mpls ip** command is then configured on interface Fast Ethernet 3/0 in highlighted line 7 (Step 4). This command is used to enable MPLS on this MPLS backbone network interface (this interface is connected to Los.Angeles.P in this example).

In highlighted lines 8 to 10, OSPF process 100 is configured using the **router ospf** *process-id* command, and OSPF is enabled on interfaces Fast Ethernet 3/0 (an MPLS backbone network interface) and loopback 1 using the **network** *ip-address wildcard-mask* **area** *area-id* command (Step 5). In highlighted line 11, interface loopback1 is configured as a passive interface (no OSPF packets will be sent on this interface).

Although OSPF is used as the backbone IGP in this particular example, it is important to understand that Intermediate System-to-Intermediate System (IS-IS) is also a popular choice as an MPLS backbone IGP. IS-IS and OSPF are by far the two most popular choices for an MPLS backbone IGP for a number of reasons, the most important of which is that they are the only two IGPs that currently support the necessary extensions for MPLS-TE.

CAUTION   Note that you must make sure that the PE routers have reachability to the IP address configured on the peer PE router's loopback interface (the pseudowire endpoint address as specified using the **xconnect** command). If there is no IP reachability between peer PE routers' loopback interfaces, pseudowire setup will fail.

That is a sample configuration, but you may have noticed the absence of any commands relating to a pseudowire class (Step 6) in Example 3-5. As previously mentioned, configuration of a pseudowire class is optional, but is essential if you are configuring AToM features such as sequencing and tunnel selection. For more information on the configuration of pseudowire classes, see the section on tunnel selection later in this chapter.

Example 3-6 shows the configuration for San.Jose.PE. Los.Angeles.PE and San.Jose.PE are the two ends of the Ethernet port mode pseudowire.

Example 3-6   *Configuration of an Ethernet Port Mode AToM Pseudowire on San.Jose.PE*

```
!
hostname San.Jose.PE
!
ip cef (line 1)
!
mpls label protocol ldp (line 2)
!
mpls ldp router-id Loopback1 force (line 3)
!
interface Loopback1 (line 4)
 description LDP router id and PW endpoint
 ip address 10.1.1.2 255.255.255.255 (line 5)
!
interface FastEthernet2/0
 description Ethernet attachment circuit
 xconnect 10.1.1.1 1001 encapsulation mpls (line 6)
 no cdp enable
!
interface FastEthernet4/0
 description MPLS backbone network interface
 ip address 10.4.1.2 255.255.255.0
 mpls ip (line 7)
!
router ospf 100 (line 8)
 network 10.4.1.2 0.0.0.0 area 0 (line 9)
 network 10.1.1.2 0.0.0.0 area 0 (line 10)
 passive-interface Loopback1 (line 11)
!
!
```

One quick look at the configuration in Example 3-6 will tell you that it is almost identical to that shown in Example 3-5. The only differences are the interface IP addresses and corresponding addresses specified using the OSPF **network** commands (highlighted lines 4, 5, 9, and 10), as well as the IP address specified using the **xconnect** command (highlighted line 6) .

The IP address specified using the **xconnect** command on San.Jose.PE (highlighted line 6) is the loopback interface IP address (LDP router ID) on Los.Angeles.PE.

You will also notice that the PW (VC) ID specified using the **xconnect** command (1001) is the same as that specified at the other end of the pseudowire, Los.Angeles.PE (see Example 3-5). Although not explicitly shown, the MTU on the attachment circuits at either end of the pseudowire (on interface Fast Ethernet 1/0 on Los.Angeles.PE (see Example 3-5), and on interface Fast Ethernet 2/0) is also identical—in this case, 1500 bytes. If either the PW ID or the attachment circuit MTU is not identical at both ends of the pseudowire, it will not become active.

Steps 1 to 6 of the configuration of PE routers are the same regardless of which type of Layer 2 protocol is being transported over AToM pseudowires. For that reason, these steps are not described again in subsequent sections dealing with the configuration of other pseudowire types (the completion of steps 1 to 6 is assumed).

Configuration on P Routers

Before finishing this section, it is worth taking a look at a sample configuration of a P router. The steps necessary to configure a P router are as follows:

Step 1 Configure CEF.

Step 2 Configure a loopback interface to use as the pseudowire endpoint (and LDP router ID).

Step 3 Configure the label protocol.

Step 4 Configure MPLS on MPLS backbone interfaces

Step 5 Configure the MPLS backbone IGP (if not already configured).

Example 3-7 shows the configuration of a P router, Los.Angeles.P.

Example 3-7 *Configuration of Los.Angeles.P*

```
!
hostname Los.Angeles.P
!
ip cef (line 1)
!
mpls label protocol ldp (line 2)
!
mpls ldp router-id Loopback1 force (line 3)
!
interface Loopback1
 description LDP router id
 ip address 10.1.1.3 255.255.255.255 (line 4)
!
interface FastEthernet1/0
 description MPLS backbone network interface
 ip address 10.2.1.2 255.255.255.0
 mpls ip (line 5)
!
interface Serial4/0
 description MPLS backbone network interface
 ip address 10.3.1.1 255.255.255.0
 mpls ip (line 6)
!
router ospf 100 (line 7)
 network 10.2.1.2 0.0.0.0 area 0 (line 8)
 network 10.3.1.1 0.0.0.0 area 0 (line 9)
 network 10.1.1.3 0.0.0.0 area 0 (line 10)
 passive-interface Loopback1 (line 11)
!
!
```

In highlighted lines 1 to 4, CEF is enabled (Step 1), LDP is specified as the label protocol (Step 3), interface loopback 1 is configured as the LDP router ID, and an IP address (10.1.1.3/32) is configured on interface loopback 1 (Step 2).

The **mpls ip** command is used to enable MPLS on MPLS backbone interfaces (interface Fast Ethernet [connected to Los.Angeles.PE] and interface serial 4/0 [connected to San.Jose.P]) in highlighted lines 5 and 6 (Step 4).

OSPF is then configured and enabled on MPLS backbone interfaces and interface loopback 1 in highlighted lines 7 to 11 (Step 5).

Note that the configuration of P routers is the same regardless of the type of Layer 2 protocols transported using AToM.

As you can see, the example configurations for Los.Angeles.PE, San.Jose.PE, and Los.Angeles.P use LDP to exchange tunnel label bindings and establish LSPs—MPLS-TE is not configured in this particular example, and RSVP-TE is not used to distribute tunnel label bindings.

AToM Pseudowire Ethernet VLAN (802.1Q) Transport

The (optional) control word used when transporting Ethernet VLAN (802.1Q) frames over an AToM pseudowire is identical to that used when transporting raw Ethernet frames (see Figure 3-16).

As with Ethernet port mode transport, when using Ethernet VLAN (802.1Q) transport, the ingress PE router removes the preamble and FCS before encapsulating the frame in an AToM data channel packet (see Figure 3-17). The egress PE router reconstitutes the preamble and FCS prior to forwarding an Ethernet frame on its local attachment circuit.

Figure 3-19 shows the topology for the Ethernet VLAN (802.1Q) pseudowire configurations covered in this section.

Figure 3-19 *AToM Ethernet VLAN (802.1Q) Pseudowire Topology*

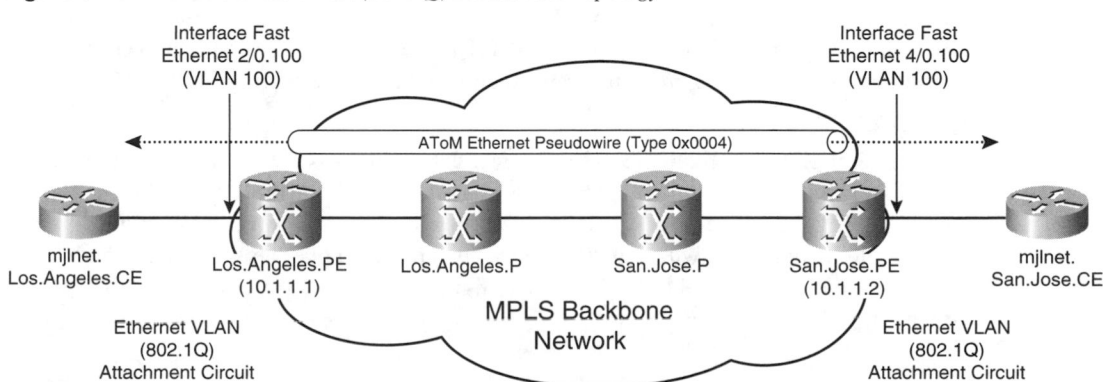

Example 3-8 shows the configuration of Ethernet VLAN (802.1Q) transport over an AToM pseudowire.

Example 3-8   *Configuration of Ethernet VLAN (8021Q) Transport over an AToM Pseudowire*

```
!
hostname Los.Angeles.PE
!
interface FastEthernet2/0.100 (line 1)
 encapsulation dot1Q 100 (line 2)
 xconnect 10.1.1.2 1002 encapsulation mpls (line 3)
!
```

```
!
hostname San.Jose.PE
!
interface FastEthernet4/0.100 (line 4)
 encapsulation dot1Q 100 (line 5)
 xconnect 10.1.1.1 1002 encapsulation mpls (line 6)
!
```

Highlighted lines 1 and 2 shows the configuration of subinterface Fast Ethernet 2/0.100 and the configuration of 802.1Q encapsulation for VLAN ID 100 (**encapsulation dot1q** *vlan-id*) on Los.Angeles.PE.

Subinterface Fast Ethernet 2/0.100 is then bound to a pseudowire to peer PE router 10.1.1.2 (San.Jose.PE), with PW (VC) ID 1002, using MPLS (AToM) encapsulation.

The corresponding peer PE router (San.Jose.PE) configuration is shown in highlighted lines 4 to 6.

In this case, subinterface 4/0.100 is configured in highlighted line 4, and 802.1Q encapsulation is configured for VLAN ID 100 in highlighted line 5.

In highlighted line 6, subinterface Fast Ethernet 4/0.100 is bound to a pseudowire to peer PE router 10.1.1.1 (Los.Angeles.PE), with PW (VC) ID 1002, using MPLS encapsulation.

So, the configuration of Ethernet VLAN (802.1Q) pseudowire is pretty similar to that for regular port mode Ethernet pseudowires. The main difference is that the **xconnect** command must be configured under an Ethernet subinterface with IEEE 802.1Q encapsulation.

One thing to notice in Example 3-8 is the fact that the VLAN ID configured using the **encapsulation dot1q** *vlan-id* command is identical on both PE routers (VLAN ID 100). If the VLAN ID is not identical, the PE routers have to perform a function known as VLAN ID rewrite. In this case, when an 802.1Q frame is received over a pseudowire, the VLAN ID is modified to be equal to the locally configured VLAN ID (refer to Figure 2-15 on page 50).

NOTE	With the exception of the 12000 series (with the 3-port Gigabit Ethernet card), VLAN rewrite is automatic if the VLAN ID is different at either end of the pseudowire.
	On the 12000 series with the 3-port Gigabit Ethernet card, however, you must configure the **remote circuit id** *remote-vlan-id* command in xconnect configuration mode (after configuring the **xconnect** command) on both PE routers.
	If (both peer) 12000 series PE routers are running 12.0(30)S or later, however, there is no need to configure the **remote circuit id** command (VLAN ID rewrite is automatic) .

Deploying AToM Pseudowires for HDLC and PPP Traffic Transport

When deploying AToM pseudowires for HDLC and PPP traffic transport, the control word is again optional in data channel packets, but can be used if sequencing is configured.

HDLC pseudowires can be used to transport HDLC or HDLC-like traffic, including older encapsulations such as X.25.

Figure 3-20 shows the optional control word for HDLC and PPP traffic transport.

Figure 3-20 *The Optional Control Word for HDLC and PPP Traffic Transport*

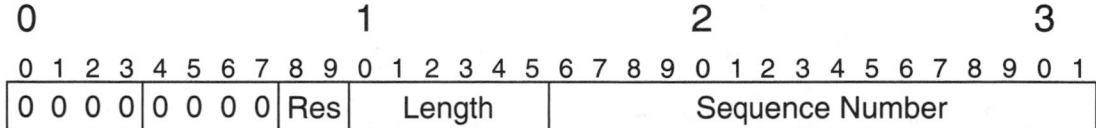

The fields of the HDLC control word can be described as follows:

- **The first 4 bits are set to 0**—This indicates a control word.
- **The next 4 bits are used for protocol specific flags**—In the case of HDLC and PPP transport, there are no are no flags, and so these bits are set to 0.
- **Reserved (Res)**—These bits are reserved for future use.
- **Length**—If the packet length, including the control word and the packet payload containing the HDLC or PPP frame, is less than 64 bytes, this field specifies the packet length. If the packet length is greater than or equal to 64 bytes, this field contains a value of 0.
- **Sequence Number**—This contains a sequence number.

Figure 3-21 shows the encapsulation of an HDLC or PPP frame in an AToM data channel packet as it is received on an attachment circuit.

Figure 3-21 *Encapsulation of an HDLC or PPP Frame in an AToM Data Channel Packet*

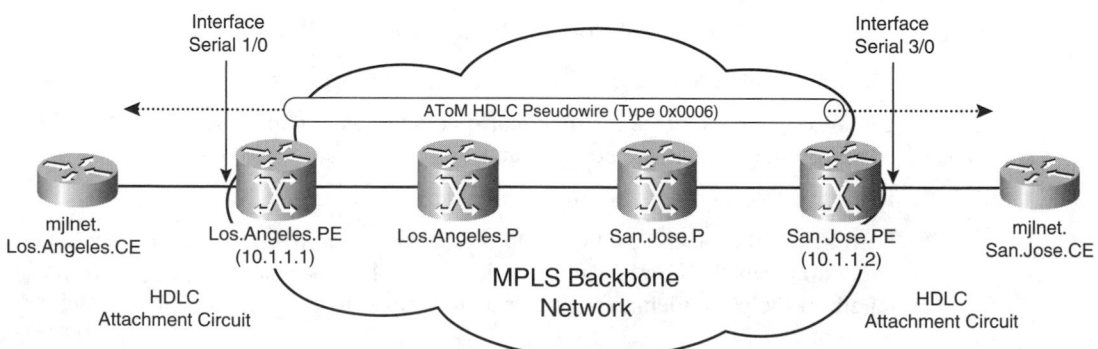

Ingress PE Router

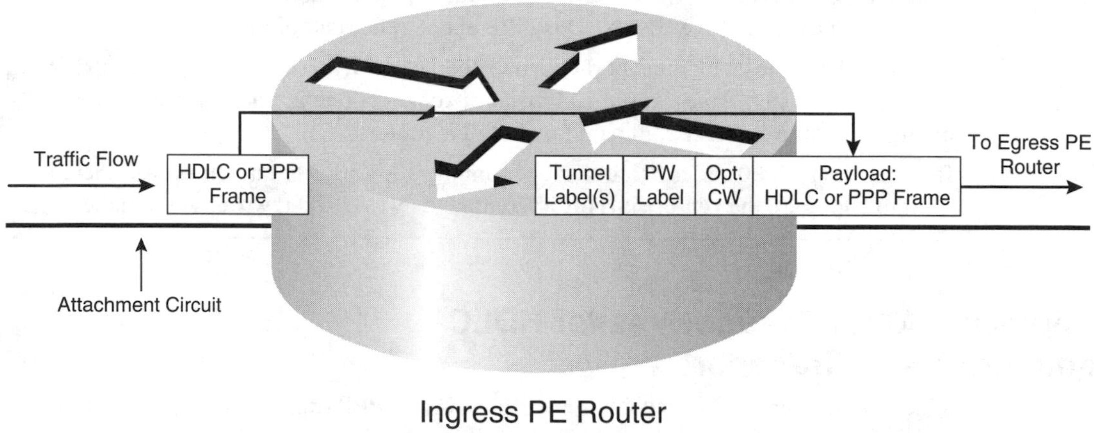

In Figure 3-21, an HDLC or PPP frame received on an attachment circuit is placed into the payload of an AToM data channel packet. Note that HDLC or PPP frames are carried in their entirety, with the exception of the flags and FCS fields (see Figure 2-16 and Figure 2-18 on pages xx and xx, respectively). Any bit stuffing is also undone prior to transmission of the frame over the pseudowire.

Example 3-9 shows a sample configuration for the transport of HDLC frames using an AToM pseudowire. This configuration corresponds to the sample topology shown in Figure 3-22.

Figure 3-22 *Sample Topology for Transport of HDLC Frames over an AToM Pseudowire*

As shown in Figure 3-22, an HDLC connection extends between mjlnet.Los.Angeles.CE and mjlnet.San.Jose.CE over the pseudowire between Los.Angeles.PE and San.Jose.PE. The pseudowire type is 0x0006 (see Table 3-2 on page 147).

Example 3-9 *Sample Configuration for the Transport of HDLC Frames Using an AToM Pseudowire*

```
!
hostname Los.Angeles.PE
!
interface Serial1/0
 encapsulation hdlc (line 1)
 xconnect 10.1.1.2 1002 encapsulation mpls (line 2)
 !
```
```
!
hostname San.Jose.PE
!
interface Serial3/0
 encapsulation hdlc (line 3)
 xconnect 10.1.1.1 1002 encapsulation mpls (line 4)
 !
```

As you can see in Example 3-9, the configuration of HDLC pseudowires is simple—all that is required (apart from Steps 1 to 6 described in the previous section) is to configure the **xconnect** *peer-pe-ip-address pwid* **encapsulation mpls** command under the HDLC attachment circuit interface.

In Example 3-9, **xconnect** command is configured under interface serial 1/0 and interface serial 3/0 on Los.Angeles.PE and San.Jose.PE, respectively.

The **xconnect** command on Los.Angeles.PE is used to bind the attachment circuit to a pseudowire to 10.1.1.2 (San.Jose.PE), with PW (VC) ID 1002, using MPLS (AToM) encapsulation.

Similarly, the **xconnect** command on San.Jose.PE is used to bind the attachment circuit to a pseudowire to 10.1.1.1 (Los.Angeles.PE), with PW (VC) ID 1002, using MPLS encapsulation.

You will also notice the **encapsulation hdlc** command configured under interface serial 1/0 on Los.Angeles.PE and serial 3/0 on San.Jose.PE. This command is actually a default and so is not really required—it is shown for illustrative purposes only.

You can verify AToM HDLC pseudowires using the **show mpls l2transport vc** *vcid* command, as shown in Example 3-10.

Example 3-10 *Verifying AToM HDLC Pseudowires Using the* **show mpls l2transport vc** *Command*

```
San.Jose.PE#show mpls l2transport vc 1002
Local intf    Local circuit    Dest address   VC ID   Status
------------  ----------------  --------------  ------  ----------- -----------
Se4/1         HDLC              10.1.1.1        1002    UP
San.Jose.PE#
```

As you can see in the highlighted line in Example 3-10, the pseudowire is associated with an attachment circuit on interface serial 4/1, the circuit type is HDLC, the remote endpoint (peer PE router) is 10.1.1.1, the VC (PW) ID is 1002, and the status is UP.

The configuration of AToM PPP pseudowires is similar to that for HDLC pseudowires. Example 3-11 shows the configuration of an AToM PPP pseudowire, and Figure 3-23 shows the topology to which the configuration corresponds.

Figure 3-23 *AToM PPP Pseudowire Topology*

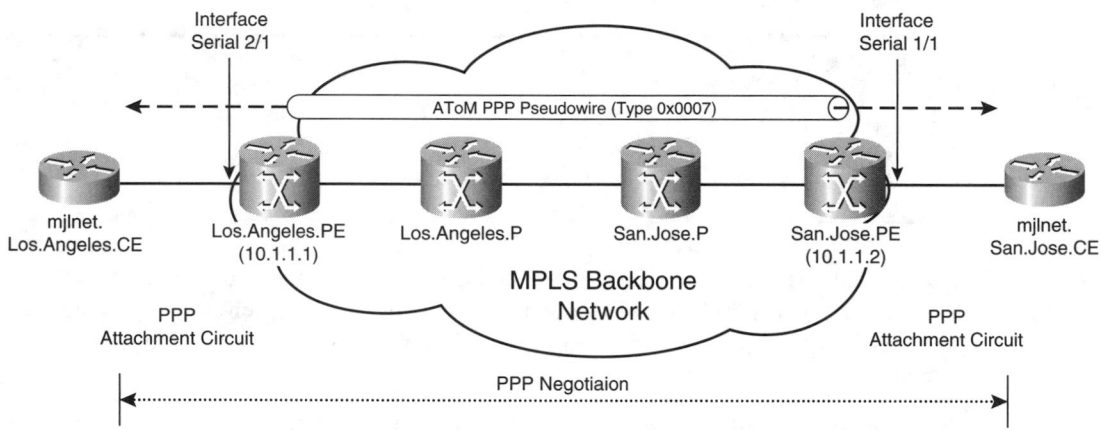

In Figure 3-23, an AToM PPP pseudowire is configured between Los.Angeles.PE and San.Jose.PE to transport a PPP connection between mjlnet.Los.Angeles.CE and mjlnet.San.Jose.CE.

One important thing to notice about Figure 3-23 is the fact that PPP negotiation (LCP, optional authentication, and NCP) takes place between CE devices—PE routers (Los.Angeles.PE and San.Jose.PE, in this example) do not take part in PPP negotiation.

Example 3-11 *Configuration of an AToM PPP Pseudowire*

```
!
hostname Los.Angeles.PE
!
interface Serial2/1
 encapsulation ppp (line 1)
 xconnect 10.1.1.2 1005 encapsulation mpls (line 2)
 !
 !
hostname San.Jose.PE
 !
interface Serial1/1
 encapsulation ppp (line 3)
 xconnect 10.1.1.1 1005 encapsulation mpls (line 4)
 !
```

As shown in Example 3-11, the **encapsulation ppp** command must be configured under the attachment circuit interface (see highlighted lines 1 and 3).

In highlighted line 2, the **xconnect** *peer-pe-ip-address pwid* **encapsulation mpls** command is used to bind the PPP attachment circuit to a pseudowire to 10.1.1.2 (San.Jose.PE), with PW (VC) ID 1005, using MPLS (AToM) encapsulation.

The **xconnect** command is also used in highlighted line 4 to bind the attachment circuit to a pseudowire to 10.1.1.1 (Los.Angeles.PE), with PW (VC) ID 1005, using MPLS encapsulation.

After you have configured an AToM PPP pseudowire, you can verify correct operation using the **show mpls l2transport vc** *vcid* command (see Example 3-12).

Example 3-12 *Verifying an AToM PPP Pseudowire Using the* **show mpls l2transport vc** *Command*

```
Los.Angeles.PE#show mpls l2transport vc 1005
Local intf   Local circuit     Dest address  VC ID    Status
------------ ----------------- --------------- -------- ----------- -----------
Se4/0        PPP               10.1.1.2      1005     UP
Los.Angeles.PE#
```

In the highlighted line in Example 3-12, you can see that the local attachment circuit (and pseudowire) type is PPP. You can also see that the circuit status is UP (active).

You can also examine PPP negotiation between the CE devices using the **debug ppp negotiation** command, as demonstrated in Example 3-13.

Example 3-13 *Examining PPP Negotiation Using the* **debug ppp negotiation** *Command*

```
mjlnet.Los.Angeles.CE#debug ppp negotiation
PPP protocol negotiation debugging is on
mjlnet.Los.Angeles.CE#
07:35:15: Se0 PPP: Treating connection as a dedicated line
07:35:15: Se0 PPP: Phase is ESTABLISHING, Active Open (line 1)
07:35:15: Se0 LCP: O CONFREQ [Closed] id 172 len 15
07:35:15: Se0 LCP:  AuthProto CHAP (0x0305C22305)
07:35:15: Se0 LCP:  MagicNumber 0x521443E6 (0x0506521443E6)
07:35:16: %SYS-5-CONFIG_I: Configured from console by console
07:35:17: Se0 LCP: TIMEout: State REQsent
07:35:17: Se0 LCP: O CONFREQ [REQsent] id 173 len 15
07:35:17: Se0 LCP:  AuthProto CHAP (0x0305C22305)
07:35:17: Se0 LCP:  MagicNumber 0x521443E6 (0x0506521443E6)
07:35:17: Se0 LCP: I CONFREQ [REQsent] id 169 len 15
07:35:17: Se0 LCP:  AuthProto CHAP (0x0305C22305)
07:35:17: Se0 LCP:  MagicNumber 0x01AC7A09 (0x050601AC7A09)
07:35:17: Se0 LCP: O CONFACK [REQsent] id 169 len 15
07:35:17: Se0 LCP:  AuthProto CHAP (0x0305C22305)
07:35:17: Se0 LCP:  MagicNumber 0x01AC7A09 (0x050601AC7A09)
07:35:17: Se0 LCP: I CONFACK [ACKsent] id 173 len 15
```

continues

Example 3-13 *Examining PPP Negotiation Using the* **debug ppp negotiation** *Command (Continued)*

```
07:35:17: Se0 LCP:  AuthProto CHAP (0x0305C22305)
07:35:17: Se0 LCP:  MagicNumber 0x521443E6 (0x0506521443E6)
07:35:17: Se0 LCP: State is Open (line 2)
07:35:17: Se0 PPP: Phase is AUTHENTICATING, by both
07:35:17: Se0 CHAP: O CHALLENGE id 77 len 42 from
 "mjlnet.Los.Angeles.CE" (line 3)
07:35:17: Se0 CHAP: I CHALLENGE id 64 len 39 from
 "mjlnet.San.Jose.CE" (line 4)
07:35:17: Se0 CHAP: O RESPONSE id 64 len 42 from
 "mjlnet.Los.Angeles.CE" (line 5)
07:35:17: Se0 CHAP: I RESPONSE id 77 len 39 from
 "mjlnet.San.Jose.CE" (line 6)
07:35:17: Se0 CHAP: O SUCCESS id 77 len 4 (line 7)
07:35:17: Se0 CHAP: I SUCCESS id 64 len 4 (line 8)
07:35:17: Se0 PPP: Phase is UP
07:35:17: Se0 IPCP: O CONFREQ [Closed] id 4 len 10
07:35:17: Se0 IPCP:  Address 192.168.1.1 (0x0306C0A80101)
07:35:17: Se0 CDPCP: O CONFREQ [Closed] id 5 len 4
07:35:17: Se0 IPCP: I CONFREQ [REQsent] id 6 len 10
07:35:17: Se0 IPCP:  Address 192.168.1.2 (0x0306C0A80102)
07:35:17: Se0 IPCP: O CONFACK [REQsent] id 6 len 10
07:35:17: Se0 IPCP:  Address 192.168.1.2 (0x0306C0A80102)
07:35:17: Se0 CDPCP: I CONFREQ [REQsent] id 7 len 4
07:35:17: Se0 CDPCP: O CONFACK [REQsent] id 7 len 4
07:35:17: Se0 IPCP: I CONFACK [ACKsent] id 4 len 10
07:35:17: Se0 IPCP:  Address 192.168.1.1 (0x0306C0A80101)
07:35:17: Se0 IPCP: State is Open (line 9)
07:35:17: Se0 CDPCP: I CONFACK [ACKsent] id 5 len 4
07:35:17: Se0 CDPCP: State is Open (line 10)
07:35:17: Se0 IPCP: Install route to 192.168.1.2
07:35:18: %LINEPROTO-5-UPDOWN: Line protocol on Interface Serial0, changed state
 to up (line 11)
mjlnet.Los.Angeles.CE#
```

Highlighted line 1 shows that the PPP phase is ESTABLISHING—this indicates that PPP negotiation is about to begin.

PPP negotiation then proceeds, and in highlighted line 2, the Link Control Protocol (LCP) state changes to OPEN, indicating that LCP negotiation has succeeded.

PPP authentication now begins, and in highlighted lines 3 to 8, mjlnet.Los.Angeles.CE and mjlnet.San.Jose.CE exchange Challenge Handshake Authentication Protocol (CHAP) messages over the pseudowire, and successfully authenticate each other.

Network Control Protocol (NCP) then begins, and you can see that IP Control Protocol (IPCP) and Cisco Discovery Protocol Control Protocol (CDPCP) negotiation has succeeded (their states change to Open in lines 9 and 10).

Finally, in highlighted line 11, the line protocol changes state to up.

Frame Relay Traffic Transport with AToM Pseudowires

Frame Relay is another Layer 2 traffic type that can be transported over AToM pseudowires. The two methods that support Frame Relay traffic transport are as follows:

- Frame Relay port mode
- Frame Relay DLCI-to-DLCI switching

The sections that follow discuss these two methods of Frame Relay traffic transport.

Frame Relay Port Mode Traffic Transport

The first method of transporting Frame Relay traffic using AToM is to configure an HDLC pseudowire. Remember that HDLC pseudowires can transport HDLC and HDLC-*like* traffic. If you compare the HDLC and Frame Relay frame formats (see Figures 2-16 and 2-21 on pages xx and xx), you will notice that the Frame Relay frame is based on the HDLC frame.

Figure 3-24 illustrates the transport of Frame Relay traffic over an HDLC pseudowire.

Figure 3-24 *Transport of Frame Relay Traffic over an HDLC Pseudowire*

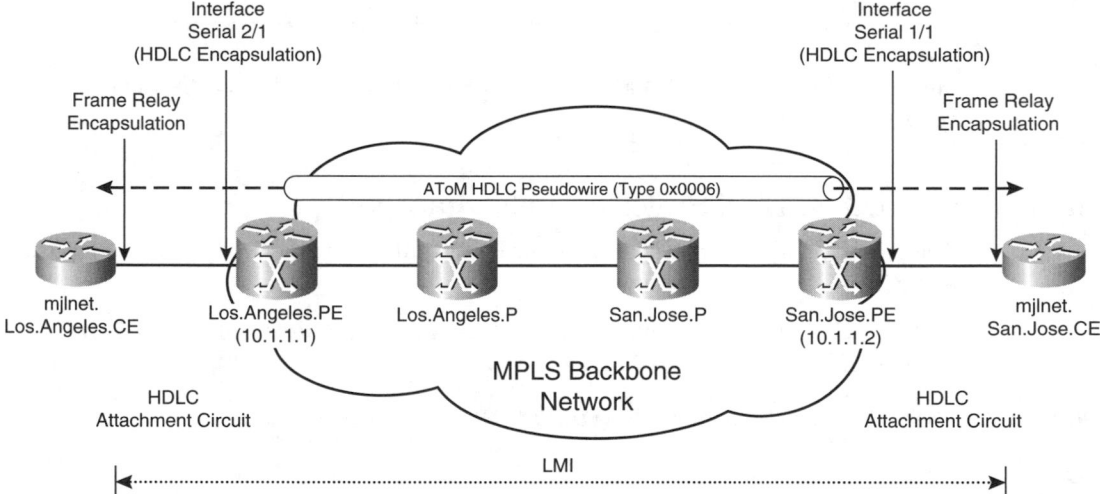

As shown in Figure 3-24, mjlnet.Los.Angeles.CE and mjlnet.San.Jose.CE are configured for Frame Relay encapsulation. The attachment circuit interfaces on Los.Angeles.PE and San.Jose.PE are configured for HDLC encapsulation, however.

As illustrated in Figure 3-24, if an HDLC pseudowire is used to transport Frame Relay traffic, the PE routers (Los.Angeles.PE and San.Jose.PE, in this example) do not participate in LMI—instead, LMI is signaled over the pseudowire between the CE devices.

The configuration of an HDLC pseudowire for Frame Relay traffic transport is shown in Example 3-9 on page 167—it is identical to the configuration of a regular HDLC pseudowire.

You can verify the status of an HDLC pseudowire using the **show mpls l2transport vc** *vcid* command, as shown in Example 3-10 on page 167.

You can also verify Frame Relay traffic transport on the CE devices using the **show frame-relay pvc** command, as demonstrated in Example 3-14.

Example 3-14 *Verifying Frame Relay Traffic Transport on CE Devices Using the show frame-relay pvc Command*

```
mjlnet.Los.Angeles.CE#show frame-relay pvc
PVC Statistics for interface Serial0 (Frame Relay DTE)
         Active    Inactive   Deleted    Static
Local       1         0          0          0
Switched    0         0          0          0
Unused      0         0          0          0
DLCI = 100, DLCI USAGE = LOCAL, PVC STATUS = ACTIVE, INTERFACE = Serial0 (line 1)
  input pkts 6        output pkts 6       in bytes 550
  out bytes 550       dropped pkts 0       in FECN pkts 0
  in BECN pkts 0       out FECN pkts 0      out BECN pkts 0
  in DE pkts 0        out DE pkts 0
  out bcast pkts 1     out bcast bytes 30
  pvc create time 00:02:54, last time pvc status changed 00:01:54
mjlnet.Los.Angeles.CE#
```

Highlighted line 1 shows that a Frame Relay PVC with DLCI 100 is active on interface serial 0.

Frame Relay DLCI-to-DLCI Switching Traffic Transport

The second method of transporting Frame Relay traffic over an AToM pseudowire is to use a DLCI-to-DLCI switching pseudowire.

Figure 3-25 shows the control word that is used with Frame Relay DLCI-to-DLCI switching.

Figure 3-25 *Control Word Used with Frame Relay DLCI-to-DLCI Switching*

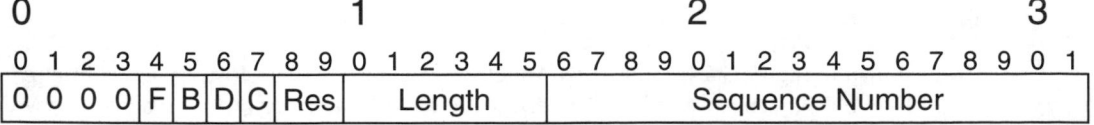

The fields in the control word are as follows:

- **The first 4 bits must be set to 0**—Indicates that this is pseudowire data.
- **The F (Forward Explicit Congestion Notification [FECN]) bit**—The setting of this bit should be copied from the FECN bit in the address field of the Frame Relay frame (see Figure 2-21 on page 61).

- **The B (Backward Explicit Congestion Notification [BECN])**—The setting of this bit should be copied from the BECN bit in the address field of the Frame Relay frame.

  It is worth noting that in earlier specifications the order of the B and F bits was reversed in the control word.

- **The D (Discard Eligibility [DE]) bit**—This should be copied from the DE bit in the address field of the Frame Relay frame.

- **The C (Command/Response [C/R]) bit**—This should be copied from the C/R bit of the Frame Relay frame.

- **Res**—These two bits are reserved for future use, and must be set to 0.

- **Length**—This field is useful when the AToM pseudowire transits a link that requires a certain minimum frame size.

  If the frame size is less than 64 octets (including the AToM data channel packet payload, plus the control word [see Figure 3-2]), the value contained Length field equals the length of the payload—this value allows the egress PE router to remove the padding that is added to ensure the minimum frame size. If the frame size is not less than 64 octets, the Length field is set to a value of 0.

- **Sequence Number**—When sequencing is enabled (a mechanism used to ensure the ordered delivery of pseudowire packets), this field contains a sequence number value.

Figure 3-26 illustrates the encapsulation of a Frame Relay frame received on an attachment circuit in an AToM data channel packet.

Figure 3-26 *Encapsulation of a Frame Relay Frame in an AToM Data Channel Packet*

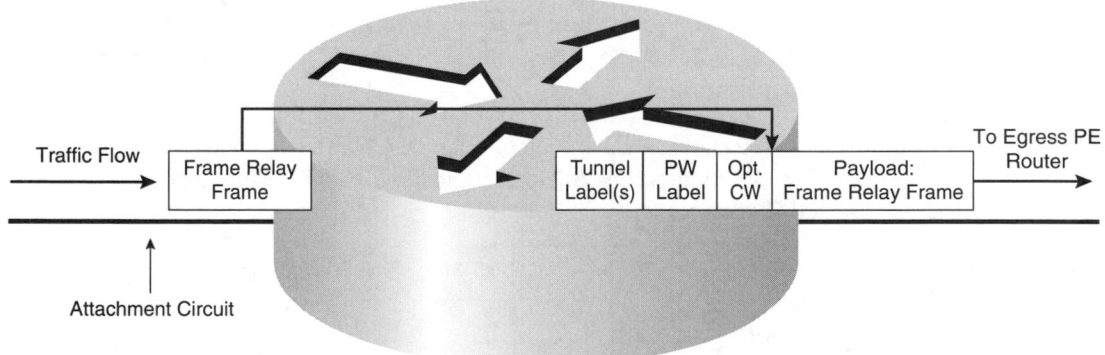

In Figure 3-26, a Frame Relay frame is received on an attachment circuit. The FECN, BECN, DE, and C/R bit setting are copied from the Frame Relay frame address field to the control word, and the frame itself is placed in the packet payload. PW (VC) and tunnel labels are added, and the packet is transmitted to the egress PE router.

Note that FECN, BECN, and DE bit settings in the control word can also be affected by configuration of the PE router (for example, the configuration of quality of service [QoS]).

When an AToM data channel packet containing a Frame Relay frame is received by the egress PE router, the process just described is performed in reverse, before the Frame Relay frame is transmitted to the connected CE device on the attachment circuit.

Example 3-15 shows the configuration of a Frame Relay DLCI-to-DLCI switching pseudowire between two PE routers. Figure 3-27 illustrates the corresponding network topology.

Figure 3-27 *Frame Relay DLCI-to-DLCI Pseudowire*

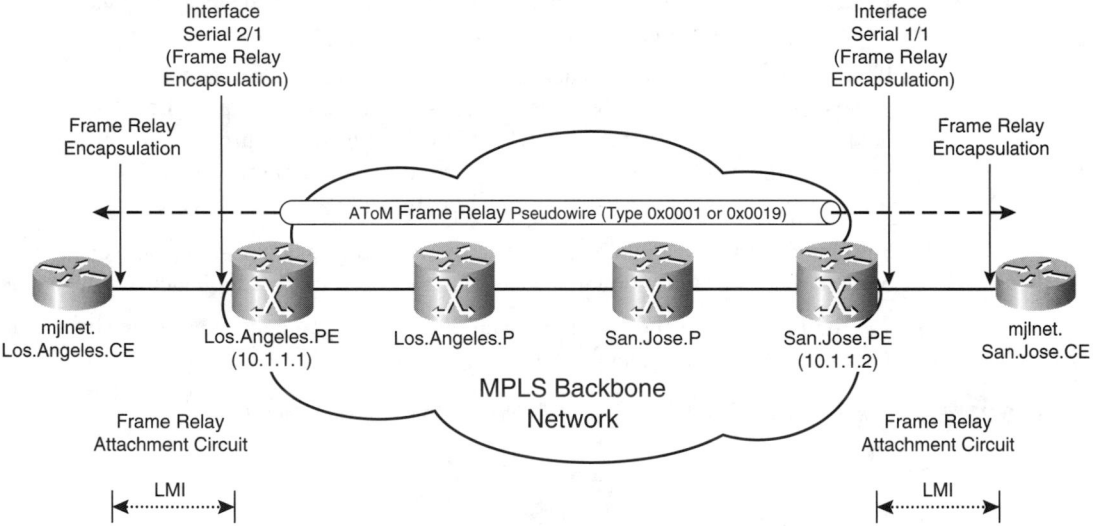

One particular thing to notice about Figure 3-27 is that unlike with Frame Relay port mode transport (Figure 3-24), when using Frame Relay DLCI-to-DLCI switching, LMI is terminated by the PE routers (Los.Angeles.PE and San.Jose.PE participate in LMI with their connected CE device).

Example 3-15 *Configuration of Frame Relay DLCI-to-DLCI Switching AToM Pseudowires*

```
!
hostname Los.Angeles.PE
!
frame-relay switching (line 1)
!
interface Serial2/1
 encapsulation frame-relay (line 2)
 frame-relay intf-type dce (line 3)
!
connect FR.DLCI.To.DLCI Serial2/1 100 l2transport (line 4)
 xconnect 10.1.1.2 1010 encapsulation mpls (line 5)
```

Example 3-15 *Configuration of Frame Relay DLCI-to-DLCI Switching AToM Pseudowires (Continued)*

```
!
!
hostname San.Jose.PE
!
frame-relay switching (line 6)
!
interface Serial1/1
 encapsulation frame-relay (line 7)
 frame-relay intf-type dce (line 8)
!
connect FR.DLCI.To.DLCI Serial1/1 100 l2transport (line 9)
 xconnect 10.1.1.1 1010 encapsulation mpls (line 10)
!
```

Highlighted lines 1 to 5 show the configuration of Los.Angeles.PE.

In highlighted line 1, the **frame-relay switching** command is used to configure the switching of Frame Relay PVCs.

The **encapsulation frame-relay** command in highlighted line 2 is used to configure Frame Relay encapsulation on the attachment circuit interface.

Following the **encapsulation frame-relay** command is the **frame-relay interface-type** **[dte | dte | nni]** command. In this example, the interface type is configured as User-to-Network Interface (UNI) data circuit terminating equipment (DCE) using the **dce** parameter. The **dte** and **nni** parameters can be used to configure the UNI data terminal equipment and Network-to-Network Interface (NNI) interface types, respectively.

After the encapsulation and interface type have been configured, the next step is to bind the attachment circuit to the AToM pseudowire using the **connect** and **xconnect** commands.

The **connect** *connection_name interface dlci* **l2transport** command in highlighted line 4 configures a locally significant connection name (FR.DLCI.To.DLCI, in this example) and associates that name with an attachment circuit interface (serial 2/1) and DLCI (100).

In highlighted line 5, the **xconnect** *peer-pe-ip-address pwid* **encapsulation mpls** command is used to bind the attachment circuit to a pseudowire to 10.1.1.2 (San.Jose.PE), with PW (VC) ID 1010, using MPLS (AToM) encapsulation.

The configuration of San.Jose.PE (highlighted lines 6 to 10) is similar to that for Los.Angeles.PE. The only differences are the interface name and IP address specified using the **connect** and **xconnect** commands.

The **connect** *connection_name interface dlci* **l2transport** command in highlighted line 9 is used to specify the connection name *FR.DLCI.To.DLCI,* interface serial 1/1, and DLCI 100.

In highlighted line 10, the **xconnect** command binds the attachment circuit interface (serial 1/1) to a pseudowire to 10.1.1.1 (Los.Angeles.PE), with PW (VC) ID 1010, using MPLS encapsulation.

One thing to note about the configurations of peer PE routers with Frame Relay DLCI-to-DLCI switching is that it is possible for different Frame Relay encapsulation types (Cisco or IETF RFC 1490) and LMI types (Cisco, ANSI, or ITU Q.933a) to be used at either end of the pseudowire.

To verify Frame Relay DLCI-to-DLCI AToM pseudowires, you can use the **show mpls l2transport vc** *vcid command* (see Example 3-16).

Example 3-16 *Verifying Frame Relay DLCI-to-DLCI AToM Pseudowires Using the* **show mpls l2transport vc** *Command*

```
San.Jose.PE#show mpls l2transport vc 1010
Local intf   Local circuit    Dest address   VC ID   Status
------------ ----------------- -------------- ------- ----------- ----------
Se1/1        FR DLCI 100       10.1.1.1       1010    UP
San.Jose.PE#
```

The highlighted line shows that a Frame Relay pseudowire with VC (PW) ID 1010 to 10.1.1.1 (the peer PE router) is in an UP state. This pseudowire is associated with local interface serial 1/1 and Frame Relay DLCI 100.

Using AToM Pseudowires to Transport ATM Traffic

There are a number of different methods of transporting ATM traffic over MPLS networks:

- **ATM port mode cell relay**—In this case, all ATM cells received on an attachment circuit are transport over the same pseudowire, irrespective of the values contained within the Virtual Path Indicator (VPI) or Virtual Channel Identifier (VCI) fields of the ATM headers (see Figure 2-26 on page 68).

    The AToM pseudowire type corresponding to ATM port mode cell relay is 0x0003 (see Table 3-2 on page 147).

- **ATM n-to-one cell relay**—In this mode, one or more ATM Virtual Circuit Connections (VCC) or Virtual Path Connections (VPC) are transported over the same pseudowire, as follows:

    — **ATM VCC mode n-to-one cell relay**—Cells corresponding to one or more VCCs are switched over the same pseudowire.

        An ATM VCC is an ATM connection where cells are switched based on the values contained in the VPI and VCI fields of the ATM cell header.

        The AToM pseudowire type corresponding to ATM VCC mode n-to-one cell relay is 0x0009.

    — **ATM VPC mode n-to-one cell relay**—Cells corresponding to one or more VPCs are transported over the same AToM pseudowire.

        An ATM VPC is an ATM connection where ATM cells are switched based on the value contained in the VPI field of the ATM cell header.

The pseudowire type corresponding to ATM VPC mode n-to-one cell relay is 0x000A.

- **ATM one-to-one cell relay**—In this case, one ATM VCC or VPC is transport over a pseudowire.

- **ATM AAL5 SDU mode**—The ingress PE router reassembles ATM Adaption Layer 5 Common Part Convergence Sublayer Service Data Unit (AAL5 CPCS-SDU, see Figure 2-27 on page 71) before transmitting them over the pseudowire in this mode.

  The pseudowire type for ATM AAL5 SDU mode is 0x0002.

- **ATM AAL5 PDU mode**—The ingress PE router assembles the AAL5 Protocol Data Unit (PDU) before transmitting it over the pseudowire.

NOTE   An important consideration when deploying AToM pseudowires for ATM traffic transport is OAM. As with L2TPv3 pseudowires, there are two methods of handling OAM cells: OAM cells can either be transported transparently over the pseudowire or terminated on the PE routers (if the **oam-ac emulation-enable** is configured).

For more information on the considerations for OAM, see the note in the section from Chapter 2 titled "Operations, Administration, and Management (OAM)" on page 71. OAM considerations for AToM pseudowires are the same as those described in Chapter 2.

Figure 3-28 illustrates the (optional) control word that is used with ATM transport.

Figure 3-28 *(Optional) Control Word Used with ATM Transport*

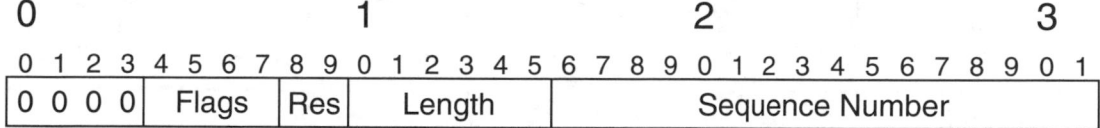

The fields of the control word are as follows:

- **4 bits set to zero**—These bits indicate pseudowire data.

- **Flags**—The significance of these bits is dependent on the particular transport type (see subsequent sections for details).

- **Res**—These bits are reserved for future use.

- **Length**—This field reflects the length of the packet if the packet length (payload, plus the control word) is less than 64 bytes. If the length is not less than 64 bytes, this field contains a value of 0.

- **Sequence Number**—This field contains a sequence number if sequencing is enabled for the pseudowire.

The specifics of ATM port mode and n-to-one cell relay, as well as AAL5 SDU mode transport over AToM pseudowires are discussed in the following two sections.

ATM Cell Relay

As already mentioned, there are two basic methods of transporting ATM cells over an AToM pseudowire:

- ATM port mode cell relay
- ATM VCC or VPC n-to-one cell relay

The sections that follow cover each method in more detail.

ATM Port Mode Cell Relay Transport over AToM Pseudowires

In ATM port mode cell relay, ATM cells received on the attachment circuit are transported over the pseudowire, without regard to the VCC or VPC to which they correspond (there is no match on the VPI or VCI fields in the ATM cell header).

Figure 3-29 depicts ATM port mode cell relay.

Figure 3-29 *ATM Port Mode Cell Relay*

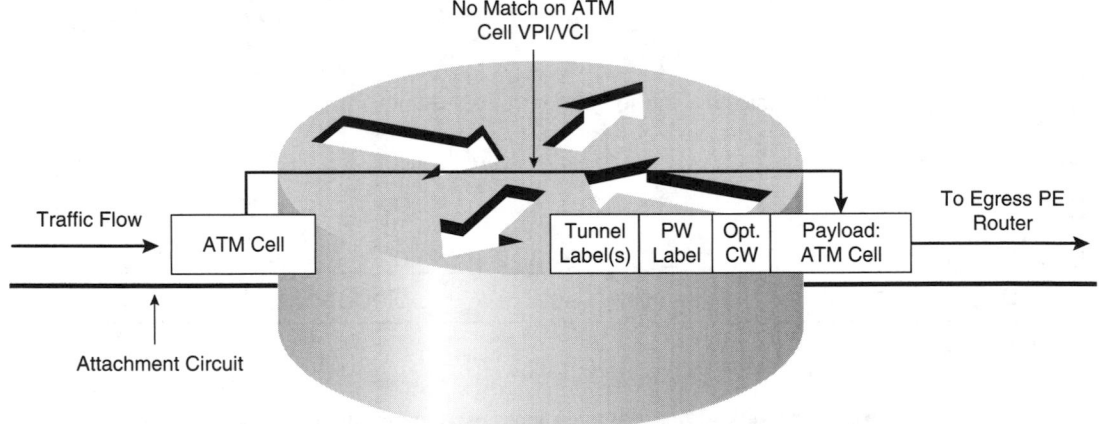

Ingress PE Router

As illustrated in Figure 3-29, when an ATM cell is received on the attachment circuit, it is placed in the payload of an AToM data channel packet that includes one or more tunnel labels, a PW (VC) label, and optionally a control word.

It is worth pointing out that the ATM cell with the exception of the Header Error Control (HEC) field (see Figure 2-26 on page 68) is carried in the AToM data channel packet.

Figure 3-30 shows a sample topology that illustrates ATM port mode cell relay pseudowire transport between two PE routers.

Figure 3-30 *ATM Port Mode Cell Relay Pseudowire Transport Between Two PE Routers*

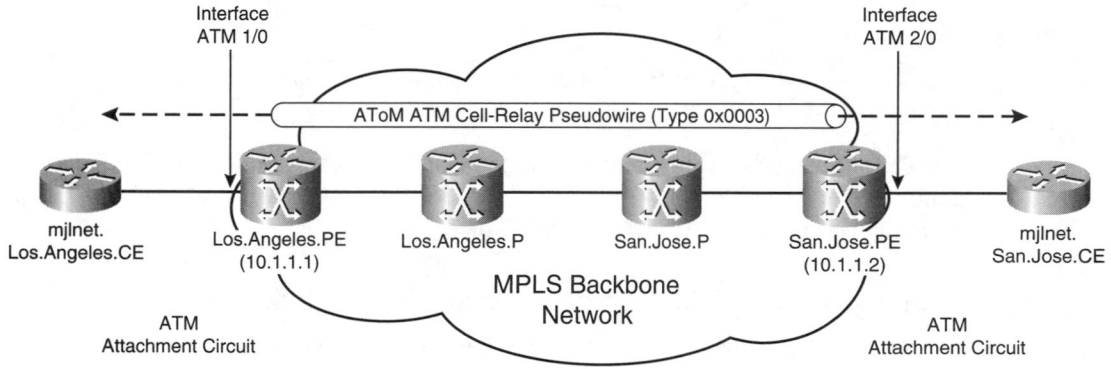

Example 3-17 shows the configuration of ATM port mode cell relay.

Example 3-17 *Configuration of ATM Port Mode Cell Relay*

```
!
hostname Los.Angeles.PE
!
interface ATM1/0
 xconnect 10.1.1.2 1015 encapsulation mpls (line 1)
!
```
```
!
hostname San.Jose.PE
!
interface ATM2/0
 xconnect 10.1.1.1 1015 encapsulation mpls (line 2)
!
```

The first thing that you will notice about the configurations shown in Example 3-17 is their relative simplicity—with the exception of Steps 1 to 6 described in the section titled "AToM Pseudowire Ethernet Port Transport" earlier in this chapter, the only command required is the **xconnect** command under the ATM interface.

In highlighted line 1, the **xconnect** *peer-pe-ip-address pwid* **encapsulation mpls** command binds the attachment circuit to a pseudowire to 10.1.1.2 (San.Jose.PE), with PW (VC) ID 1015, using MPLS encapsulation.

The **xconnect** command in highlighted line 2 binds the attachment circuit to a pseudowire to 10.1.1.1 (Los.Angeles.PE), with PW (VC) ID 1015, using MPLS encapsulation.

As shown in Example 3-18, after the pseudowire has been established, you can verify its operation using the **show mpls l2transport vc** *vcid* command.

Example 3-18 *Verifying ATM Port Mode Cell Relay*

```
San.Jose.PE#show mpls l2transport vc 1015
Local intf   Local circuit       Dest address   VC ID   Status
------------ ------------------- --------------- ------- ----------
AT1/0        ATM CELL ATM1/0     10.1.1.1        1015    UP
San.Jose.PE#
```

You can see that an ATM port mode cell relay AToM pseudowire with VC (PW) ID 1015 is configured to peer PE router 10.1.1.1. This pseudowire is associated with local attachment circuit interface ATM1/0, and it is in an UP state.

ATM n-to-One Cell Relay Transport over AToM Pseudowires

There are two methods of configuring VCC and VPC n-to-one cell relay transport:

- **Single cell relay**—This method allows the encapsulation of a single ATM cell in each AToM data channel packet as it is transmitted over the pseudowire.

- **Packed cell relay (cell packing)**—This allows the encapsulation of multiple ATM cells in each AToM data channel packet.

The sections that follow examine both methods in greater detail.

VCC and VPC N-to-One Cell Relay Transport with Single Cell Relay
Figure 3-31 illustrates ATM VCC and VPC single cell relay.

Figure 3-31 *ATM VCC and VPC Single Cell Relay*

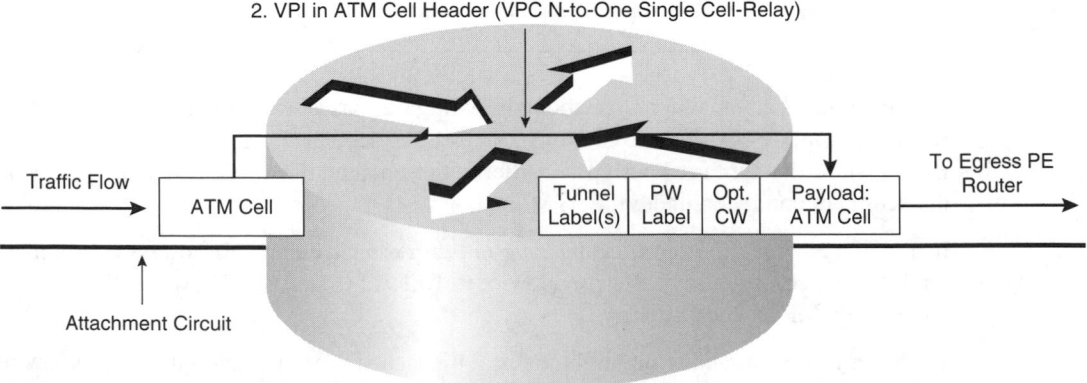

Match on Either:
1. VPI/VCI in ATM Cell Header (VCC N-to-One Single Cell-Relay)
2. VPI in ATM Cell Header (VPC N-to-One Single Cell-Relay)

Ingress PE Router

Figure 3-32 illustrates the AToM data channel packet format when using single cell relay.

Figure 3-32 *AToM Data Plan Packet Format When Using Single Cell Relay*

0										1										2										3	
0 1 2 3 4 5 6 7 8 9 0 1 2 3 4 5 6 7 8 9 0 1 2 3 4 5 6 7 8 9 0 1

Tunnel Label	Exp	S	TTL
PW Label	Exp	S	TTL
Control Word (Optional)			
VPI	VCI	PTI	C
ATM Payload (48 bytes)			
"			
"			
"			

In Figure 3-32, the AToM data channel packet consists of a tunnel label, a PW (VC) label, the control word (see Figure 3-28), and an ATM cell (VPI, VCI, PTI, C [CLP] bit, and ATM cell payload).

Note that although Figure 3-32 shows only one tunnel label, in reality (depending on the precise configuration) there may be more than one tunnel label.

VCC and VPC N-to-One Cell Relay Transport with Packed Cell Relay

Figure 3-33 illustrates the encapsulation of multiple ATM cells in an AToM data channel packet by the ingress PE router (packed cell relay).

Figure 3-33 *Encapsulation of Multiple ATM Cells by the Ingress PE Router (Packed Cell Relay)*

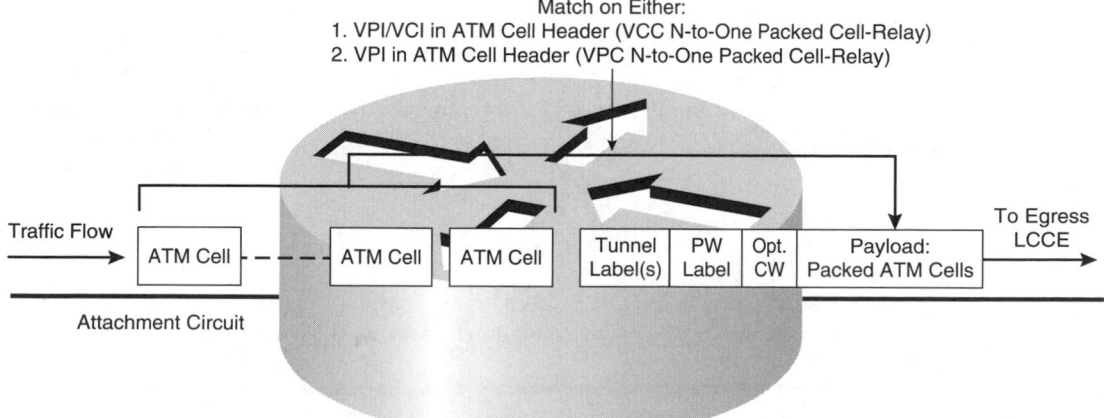

In Figure 3-33, a number of ATM cells are packed into the payload of a single AToM data channel packet.

Figure 3-34 illustrates the precise format of an AToM data channel packet when using ATM N-to-one packed cell relay.

Figure 3-34 *AToM Packet Format When Using Packed Cell Relay*

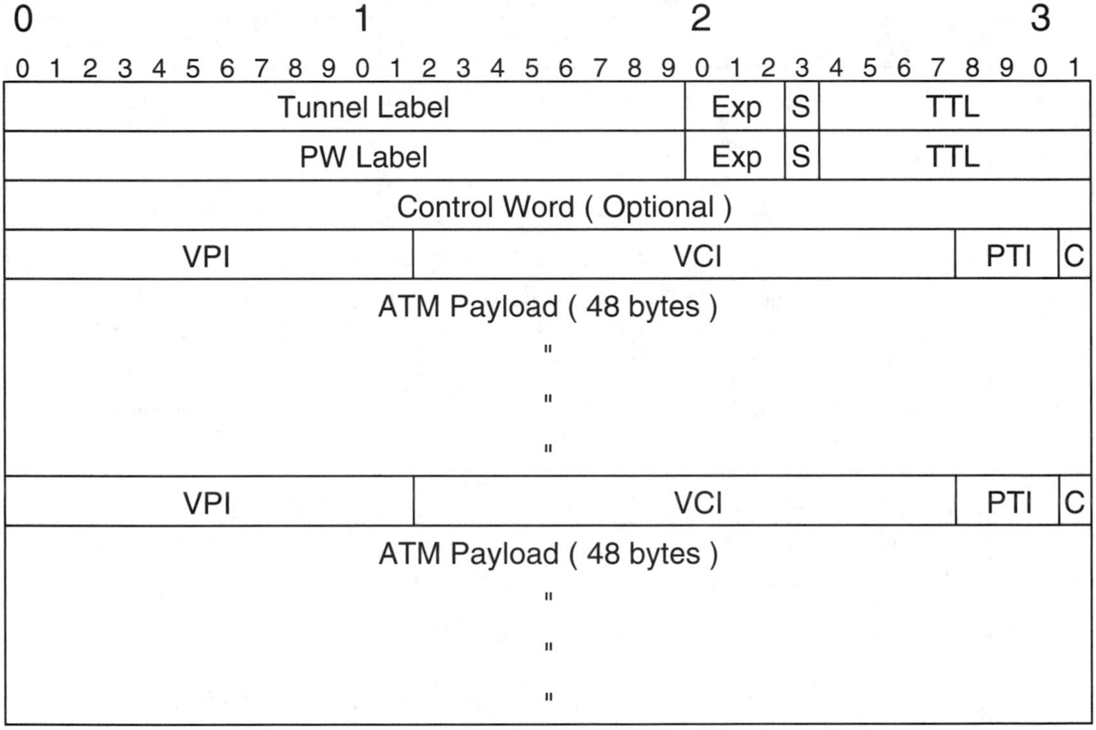

0	1	2	3
0 1 2 3 4 5 6 7 8 9	0 1 2 3 4 5 6 7 8 9	0 1 2 3 4 5 6 7 8 9	0 1

Tunnel Label		Exp	S	TTL
PW Label		Exp	S	TTL

Control Word (Optional)

VPI	VCI	PTI	C

ATM Payload (48 bytes)
"
"
"

VPI	VCI	PTI	C

ATM Payload (48 bytes)
"
"
"

The AToM packet shown in Figure 3-34 is the same as that shown in Figure 3-32, with the exception that multiple ATM cells are carried in the payload (two ATM cells, in this example).

That is the theory—now on to configuration.

Deploying ATM VCC N-to-One Cell Relay

Example 3-19 shows the configuration of ATM VCC n-to-one single cell relay. Figure 3-35 shows the corresponding network topology.

Figure 3-35 *ATM VCC N-to-One Cell Relay: Network Topology*

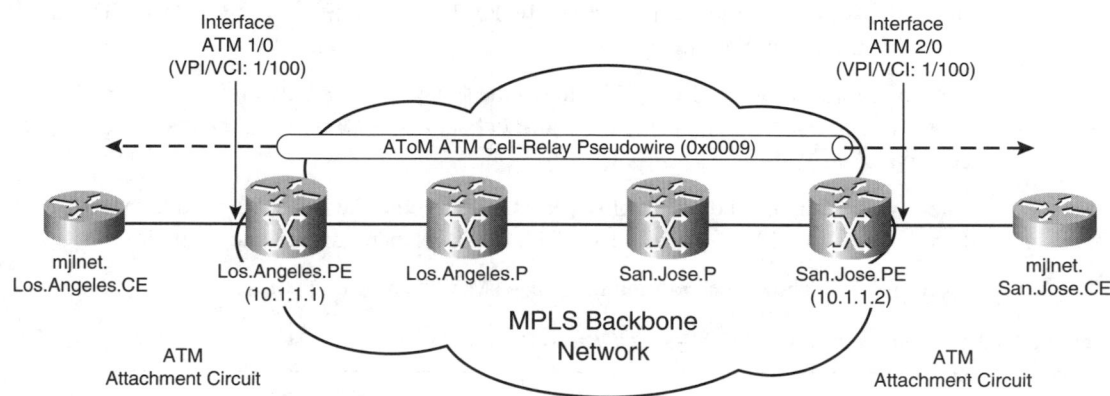

Example 3-19 *Configuration of ATM VCC N-to-One Single Cell Relay*

```
!
hostname Los.Angeles.PE
!
interface ATM1/0
!
interface ATM1/0.100 point-to-point
 pvc 1/100 l2transport (line 1)
 encapsulation aal0 (line 2)
 xconnect 10.1.1.2 1020 encapsulation mpls (line 3)
!
```

```
!
hostname San.Jose.PE
!
interface ATM2/0
!
interface ATM2/0.100 point-to-point
 pvc 1/100 l2transport (line 4)
 encapsulation aal0 (line 5)
 xconnect 10.1.1.1 1020 encapsulation mpls (line 6)
!
```

You can see the configuration of Los.Angeles.PE in highlighted lines 1 to 3, and the configuration of San.Jose.PE in highlighted lines 4 to 6.

The **pvc** *vpi/vci* **l2transport** command in highlighted line 1 specifies the VCI and VPI for the PVC (1 and 100, in this example), and configures the PVC as a PVC that will be switched to an AToM pseudowire.

In highlighted line 2, the **encapsulation aal0** command configures AAL0 encapsulation (cell relay).

Finally, the **xconnect** *peer-ip-address vcid* **encapsulation mpls** command in highlighted line 3 binds the PVC to a pseudowire to 10.1.1.2 (San.Jose.PE), with PW (VC) ID 1020, using MPLS encapsulation.

The configuration of San.Jose.PE is almost the same, with the only difference being the PE router IP address specified using the **xconnect** *peer-ip-address vcid* **encapsulation mpls** command.

The **xconnect** command on San.Jose.PE is used to bind the PVC to a pseudowire to Los.Angeles.PE (10.1.1.1), with PW (VC) ID 1020, using MPLS encapsulation.

Example 3-20 shows the configuration of ATM VCC n-to-one *packed* cell relay.

Example 3-20 *Configuration of ATM VCC N-to-One Packed Cell Relay*

```
!
hostname Los.Angeles.PE
!
interface ATM1/0
 atm mcpt-timers 100 200 300 (line 1)
!
interface ATM1/0.100 point-to-point
 pvc 1/100 l2transport
 encapsulation aal0
 cell-packing 3 mcpt-timer 1 (line 2)
 xconnect 10.1.1.2 1020 encapsulation mpls
!

!
hostname San.Jose.PE
!
interface ATM2/0
 atm mcpt-timers 100 200 300 (line 3)
!
interface ATM2/0.100 point-to-point
 pvc 1/100 l2transport
 encapsulation aal0
 cell-packing 3 mcpt-timer 1 (line 4)
 xconnect 10.1.1.1 1020 encapsulation mpls
!
```

The only differences between the configurations for packed cell relay shown in Example 3-20 and those for single cell relay in Example 3-19 are the **atm mcpt-timers** and **cell-packing** commands.

The **atm mcpt-timers** [*timeout-value-1 timeout-value-2 timeout-value-3*] command in highlighted lines 1 and 3 configures three maximum cell packing timeouts. These timeouts specify the maximum time that an ingress PE router will wait for ATM cells (to be packed into an AToM data channel packet [see Figure 3-33]) before sending the AToM data channel packet.

The **cell-packing** [*cells*] [**mcpt-timer** *timer*] command in highlighted lines 2 and 4 enables cell packing, and specifies the maximum number of cells that can be packed into a single

AToM data channel packet (specified using the *cells* parameter), as well as to specify one of the three timeouts configured using the **atm mcpt-timers** command (specified using the *timer* parameter).

In the configurations shown in Example 3-20, the **cell-packing** command specifies a maximum of three cells, as well as a maximum cell packing timeout of 100 microseconds (the first timeout specified using the **atm mcpt-timers** command).

This particular configuration means that the ingress PE router will pack a maximum of three ATM cells in a single AToM data channel packet, but will wait no more than 100 microseconds to receive these three cells. If three cells are not received in these 100 microseconds, the ingress PE router will transmit the AToM data channel packet with however many ATM cells have been received.

As shown in Example 3-21, you can verify ATM VCC n-to-one cell relay using the **show mpls l2transport vc** *vcid* command.

Example 3-21 *Verifying ATM VCC N-to-One Cell Relay Using the* **show mpls l2transport vc** *Command*

```
San.Jose.PE#show mpls l2transport vc 1020
Local intf   Local circuit        Dest address   VC ID    Status
------------ -------------------- --------------- -------- -----------
AT1/0.100    ATM VCC CELL 1/100   10.1.1.1        1020     UP
San.Jose.PE#
```

The highlighted line in Example 3-21 shows that an ATM VCC cell relay pseudowire has been set up to the peer PE router (10.1.1.1) with VC (PW) ID 1020. This pseudowire is associated with interface ATM1/0.100, and it is active (UP).

It is also possible to check packed cell relay using the **show atm cell-packing** command (see Example 3-22).

Example 3-22 *Verifying ATM VCC N-to-One Packed Cell Relay Using the* **show atm cell-packing** *Command*

```
San.Jose.PE#show atm cell-packing
                    average              average
   circuit     local nbr of cells   peer nbr of cells   MCPT
   type        MNCP rcvd in one pkt MNCP sent in one pkt (us)
ATM2/0.100  vc 1/100  3   2            3   2              100
San.Jose.PE#
```

The highlighted line in Example 3-22 shows the maximum number of cells that can be packed into a single AToM data channel packet on the local and peer PE routers (local MNCP/peer MNCP), the average number of cells that have been sent and received in one AToM data channel packet, and the maximum cell-packing timeout (MCPT).

Deploying ATM VPC N-to-One Cell Relay
In Example 3-23, you can find the configuration of ATM VPC n-to-one single cell relay. Figure 3-36 shows the corresponding network topology.

Figure 3-36 *ATM VPC N-to-One Cell Relay: Network Topology*

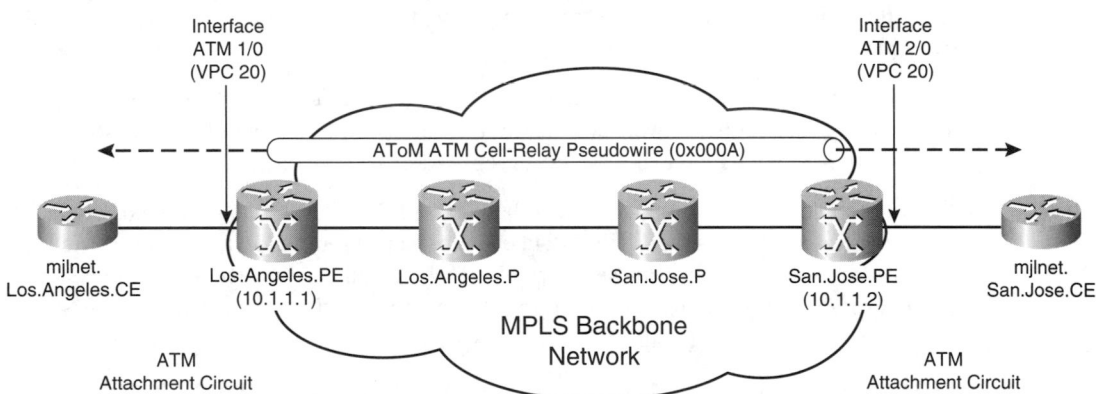

Example 3-23 *Configuration of ATM VPC N-to-One Single Cell Relay*

```
!
hostname Los.Angeles.PE
!
interface ATM1/0
 atm pvp 20 l2transport (line 1)
 xconnect 10.1.1.2 1030 encapsulation mpls (line 2)
 !
```
```
!
hostname San.Jose.PE
!
interface ATM2/0
 atm pvp 20 l2transport (line 3)
 xconnect 10.1.1.1 1030 encapsulation mpls (line 4)
 !
```

The first command in Example 3-23 is **atm pvp** *vpi* **l2transport** (highlighted lines 1 and 3). This command specifies that the Permanent Virtual Path (Connection) in question will be bound to a pseudowire. In this example, the PVP has a VPI of 20.

The second command is **xconnect** *peer-ip-address vcid* **encapsulation mpls.** In highlighted line 2, this command is used to bind the attachment circuit (PVP with VPI 20) to a pseudowire to San.Jose.PE (10.1.1.2), with PW (VC) ID 1030, using MPLS encapsulation.

The **xconnect** command is also used in highlighted line 4 to bind the attachment circuit on San.Jose.PE (PVP with VPI 20) to a pseudowire to Los.Angeles.PE (10.1.1.2), with PW (VC) ID 1030, using MPLS encapsulation.

Configuration of ATM VPC n-to-one packed cell relay takes advantage of the same command as ATM VCC n-to-one packed cell relay (see Example 3-24).

Example 3-24 *Configuration of ATM VPC N-to-One Packed Cell Relay*

```
!
hostname Los.Angeles.PE
!
interface ATM1/0
 atm mcpt-timers 200 300 400 (line 1)
 atm pvp 20 l2transport
 cell-packing 5 mcpt-timer 2 (line 2)
 xconnect 10.1.1.2 1030 encapsulation mpls
!
```
```
!
hostname San.Jose.PE
!
interface ATM2/0
 atm mcpt-timers 200 300 400 (line 3)
 atm pvp 20 l2transport
 cell-packing 5 mcpt-timer 2 (line 4)
 xconnect 10.1.1.1 1030 encapsulation mpls
!
```

In this example, the **atm mcpt-timers** command (highlighted lines 1 and 3) is used to configure timeouts of 200, 300, and 400 microseconds.

The **cell-packing** command specifies a maximum of 5 ATM cells in a single AToM data channel packet, and indicates a maximum timeout of 300 microseconds (the second timeout configured using the **atm mcpt-timers** command).

See the previous section for more information on the **atm mcpt-timers** and **cell-packing** commands.

Verification of ATM VPC n-to-one cell relay can begin with the **show mpls l2transport vc** *vcid* command (see Example 3-25).

Example 3-25 *Verification of ATM VPC N-to-One Cell Relay Using the* **show mpls l2transport vc** *Command*

```
San.Jose.PE#show mpls l2transport vc 1030
Local intf   Local circuit      Dest address   VC ID   Status
------------ ------------------ -------------- ------- ----------
AT1/0        ATM VPC CELL 20    10.1.1.1        1030    UP
San.Jose.PE#
```

The highlighted line in the output of the **show mpls l2transport vc** *vcid* command shows that attachment circuit interface ATM 1/0 and VPC with VPI 20 is bound to a pseudowire to peer PE router 10.1.1.1. This pseudowire has a VC (PW) ID of 1030, and its status is UP.

Implementing Advanced AToM Features

When deploying AtoM-based L2VPNs, you might want to take advantage of a number of advanced features, such as the following:

- **QoS**—A way of ensuring that traffic for AToM pseudowires receives prioritized forwarding treatment in the MPLS backbone network
- **Tunnel selection**—A method of forwarding AToM pseudowire traffic over MPLS-TE tunnels
- **L2VPN tunnel switching**—The ability to switch traffic received over one pseudowire to another pseudowire
- **L2VPN interworking**—A method of forwarding traffic over a pseudowire between different attachment circuit types
- **Local switching**—A method of allowing Layer 2 traffic to be forwarded between attachment circuits on the same PE router

The sections that follow examine the implementation of each of these features in greater detail.

Deploying AToM Pseudowire QoS

One common requirement when implementing AToM pseudowires is to configure QoS mechanisms on the PE and P routers to ensure that QoS requirements are met.

QoS requirements can include the following:

- Minimum bandwidth guarantees
- Maximum delay guarantees
- Maximum jitter (variable delay) guarantees
- Maximum packet loss guarantees

MPLS networks can support these requirements using QoS tools such traffic classification, marking, shaping, policing, queuing, and congestion avoidance. For more information on these mechanisms, see the section titled "Provisioning Quality of Service (QoS) for L2TPv3 Pseudowires" in Chapter 2.

As discussed in Chapter 2, certain QoS treatments such as queuing and dropping may be accorded to traffic at each hop in IP networks based on the values carried in the ToS or DSCP fields of the IP packet header (see Figure 2-46 on page 114). In MPLS networks, on the other hand, per-hop QoS treatments are based on the following:

- The value carried in the Experimental (EXP) bits of the MPLS shim header (label).

Figure 3-37 illustrates the MPLS shim header.

Figure 3-37 *The MPLS Shim Header*

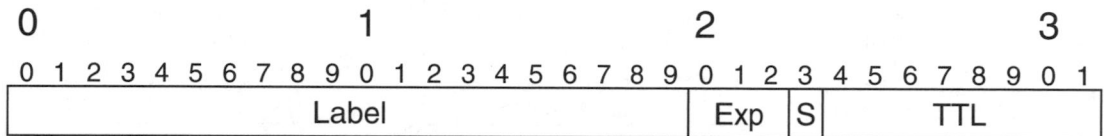

The MPLS shim header (label) consists of the following fields:

— **Label**—The label value.

— **Experimental (EXP) bits**—Used for experimental purposes. In practice, these bits are used for QoS.

— **Bottom-of-the-Stack (S)**—If set to 1, this is the final label in a label stack (which can consist of a number of labels).

— **Time-to-Live (TTL)**—Limits both the time that a labeled packet can exist in a network, as well as its forwarding scope.

When QoS treatments are based on the value carried in the EXP bits, the corresponding LSPs are known as *EXP-Inferred Per-Hop-Behavior Scheduling Class LSPs*, or (you'll be glad to know!) *E-LSPs*, for short.

• The MPLS label value itself.

When QoS treatments are based on the MPLS label value, the corresponding LSPs are referred to a *Label-Only-Inferred Per-Hop-Behavior Scheduling Class LSPs*, or *L-LSPs* for short.

This section focuses on provisioning QoS treatments for AToM pseudowire E-LSPs.

When you are provisioning QoS for AToM pseudowires, you need to consider QoS policy on PE routers, as well as (optionally) QoS policy on P routers.

QoS policy on PE routers may consist of a number of elements including classification, marking, queuing, policing, and shaping.

QoS policy on P routers may consist of elements such as queuing and congestion avoidance.

If you have read Chapter 2, this will all seem familiar—QoS policy for AToM pseudowires is similar to that for L2TPv3 pseudowires. One difference, however, is obviously the fact that marking of L2TPv3 pseudowire packets consists of the modification of the value contained in the ToS or DSCP field of IP packets (L2TPv3 packets are carried over IP). The marking of AToM pseudowire (data channel) packets consists of the modification of the value contained in the EXP field of the MPLS shim header.

Figure 3-38 shows a typical AToM pseudowire QoS policy.

Figure 3-38 *Typical AToM Pseudowire QoS Policy*

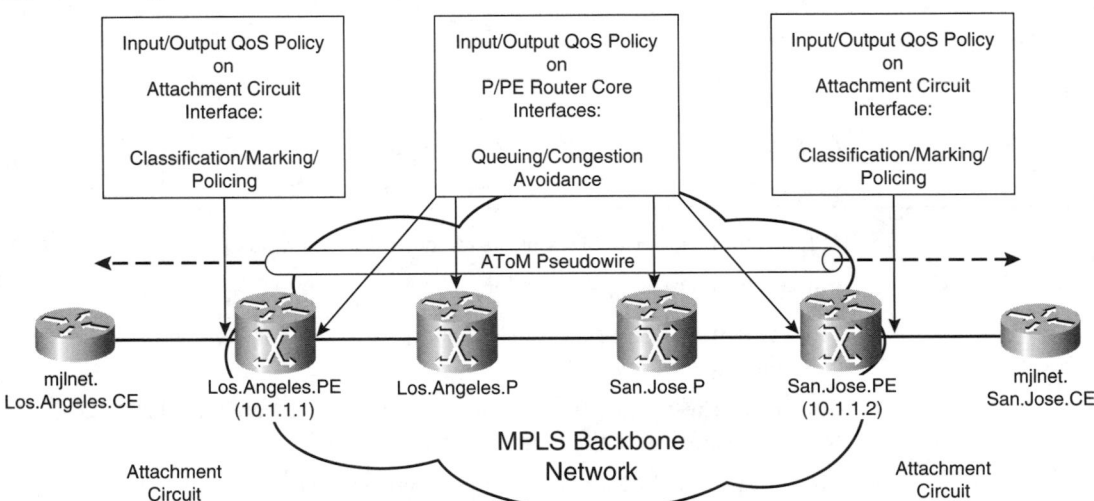

The QoS policies shown in Figure 3-38 consists of the following:

- Input and output QoS policies involving mechanisms such as classification, marking, and policing on PE router attachment circuit interfaces.

- Input and output QoS policies involving mechanisms such as queuing and congestion avoidance on P router interfaces, as well as output QoS policies on PE router MPLS backbone network (core) interfaces involving mechanisms such as queuing and congestion avoidance.

It is worth noting that some service providers choose not to configure specific QoS mechanisms on P routers if there is overprovisioning of bandwidth in the MPLS backbone network.

The remainder of this section focuses on the configuration of QoS policy on PE routers.

There are three steps that you must complete to configure an input QoS policy using the Cisco Modular QoS Command-Line Interface (MQC):

Step 1   Configure a class map using the **class-map** [**match-all** | **match-any**] *class-map-name* command.

Within a class map, it is possible to match certain fields within headers of certain Layer 2 frame/cell types received on attachment circuits. A number of fields can be matched within the headers of Layer 2 frames/cells received on attachment circuits, including the following:

— The Frame Relay Discard Eligibility (DE) bit using the **match fr-de** command

— The ATM Cell Loss Priority (CLP) bit using the **match atm clp** command

— The 802.1p field within the Ethernet 802.1Q header using the **match cos** command

Step 2   Configure a policy map using the **policy-map** *policy-map-name* command.

The class map is referenced within the policy map, and you can set the EXP bits in the MPLS shim header (label) by using the **set mpls experimental imposition** *value* command.

Note that the **set mpls experimental imposition** *value* command replaces the **set mpls experimental** *value* command in Cisco IOS Software Release 12.2(13)T.

Step 3   Apply the policy map to an interface or virtual circuit using the **service-policy** [**input** | **output**] *policy-map-name* command.

Example 3-26 shows the configuration of an example input QoS policy on a PE router (Los.Angeles.PE).

Example 3-26 *Configuration of an Example Input QoS Policy on a PE Router*

```
!
hostname Los.Angeles.PE
!
frame-relay switching
!
class-map match-all match.disc (line 1)
 match fr-de (line 2)
 !
 !
policy-map set.exp (line 3)
 class match.disc (line 4)
  set mpls experimental imposition 1 (line 5)
 class class-default (line 6)
  set mpls experimental imposition 4 (line 7)
 !
interface Serial2/1
 encapsulation frame-relay
 frame-relay intf-type dce
 service input set.exp (line 8)
 !
connect FR.DLCI.To.DLCI Serial2/1 100 l2transport
 xconnect 10.1.1.2 1010 encapsulation mpls
 !
```

In highlighted lines 1 and 2, the **class-map** [**match-all** | **match-any**] *class-map-name* and **match fr-de** commands are used to configure a class map named match.disc and match the DE bit within the Address field of Frame Relay frames (see Figure 2-21 on page 61).

The **policy-map** *policy-map-name* command is then used to configure a policy map called set.exp in highlighted line 3.

The **class** *class-name* command in line 4 links to the match.disc class map in highlighted lines 1 and 2.

In highlighted line 5, the **set mpls experimental imposition** *value* command sets the EXP field of the MPLS shim header (labels) of AToM data channel packets to a value of 1 if the encapsulated Frame Relay frame received on the attachment circuit has its DE bit set.

Highlighted lines 6 and 7 show the **class class-default** and **set mpls experimental imposition** *value* commands. The **class class-default** command is used to match on a default class (in this case, matching all frames that do *not* have their DE bit set to 1), and the **set mpls experimental imposition** *value* sets the EXP field of the MPLS shim header of AToM data channel packets to a value of 4 (if the encapsulated Frame Relay frame received on the attachment circuit does *not* have its DE bit set to 1).

Finally, in highlighted line 8, the **service-policy input** *policy-map-name* command is used to configure the policy map called set.exp (see line 3) on the attachment circuit in an inbound direction.

Figure 3-39 shows the effect of (part of) the configuration shown in Example 3-26.

Figure 3-39 *Input QoS Policy for AToM Pseudowires*

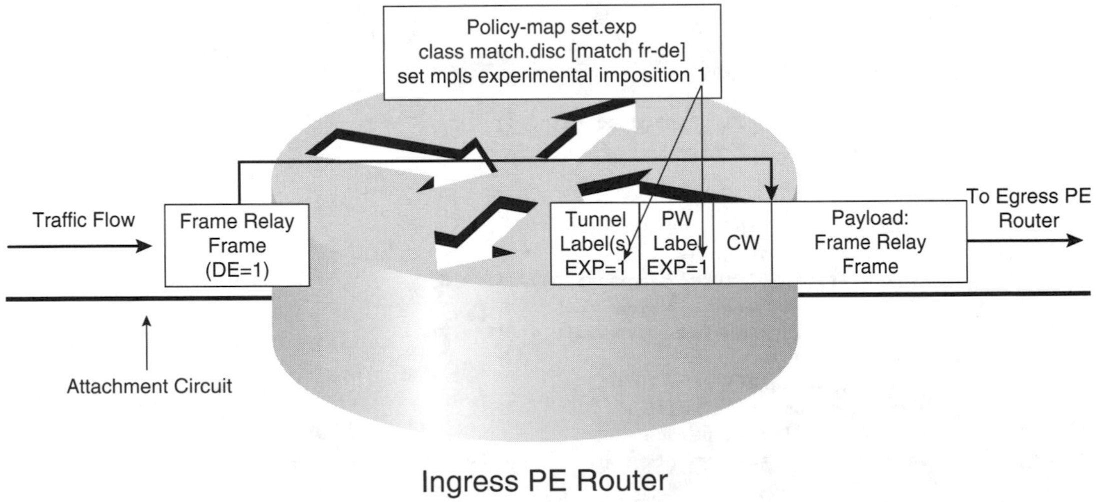

After the EXP bits of the MPLS shim header (labels) have been set, queuing and other QoS policies can be configured on the MPLS backbone interfaces of PE and P routers by matching on these bits (**match mpls experimental** *value* command) within a class map, and then configuring appropriate queuing and other QoS policies in a corresponding policy map.

NOTE   See the following URL for more information about queuing and other QoS mechanisms on Cisco devices:

http://www.cisco.com/en/US/tech/tk543/tsd_technology_support_category_home.html

See also Chapter 5, "Advanced MPLS Layer 3 VPN Deployment Considerations," for more information on the implementation and configuration of QoS for MPLS VPNs.

You can verify QoS policies using the **show policy-map** and **show policy-map interface** command.

Example 3-27 shows the output of the **show policy-map** command.

Example 3-27 **show policy-map** *Command Output*

```
Los.Angeles.PE#show policy-map
 Policy Map set.exp (line 1)
  Class match.disc (line 2)
    set mpls experimental imposition 1 (line 3)
  Class class-default (line 4)
    set mpls experimental imposition 4 (line 5)
San.Jose.PE#
```

Highlighted lines 1 to 5 show the configuration of the policy map called set.exp.

Example 3-28 shows the output of the **show policy-map interface** command.

Example 3-28 **show policy-map interface** *Command Output*

```
Los.Angeles.PE#show policy-map interface serial 2/1
 Serial2/1
 Service-policy input: set.exp (1038) (line 1)
  Class-map: match.disc (match-all) (1039/1) (line 2)
    18 packets, 1872 bytes
    5 minute offered rate 0 bps, drop rate 0 bps
    Match: fr-de (1040) (line 3)
    QoS Set
     mpls experimental imposition 1 (line 4)
      Packets marked 18 (line 5)
  Class-map: class-default (match-any) (1042/0) (line 6)
    615 packets, 47748 bytes
    5 minute offered rate 0 bps, drop rate 0 bps
    Match: any (1043) (line 7)
    615 packets, 47748 bytes
    5 minute rate 0 bps
    QoS Set
     mpls experimental imposition 4 (line 8)
      Packets marked 615 (line 9)
San.Jose.PE#
```

The output of the **show policy-map interface** command that a policy map called set.exp has been applied to interface serial 2/1 (highlighted line 1), and that there are two class maps called match.disc and class-default within the policy map (highlighted lines 2 and 6).

You can see that class map match.disc matches on frames that have their DE bit set to 1 (see highlighted line 3), and sets the MPLS EXP bits of AToM data channel packets encapsulating these frames to 1 (highlighted line 4). So far, 18 frames have been received on interface serial 2/1 with their DE bit set to 1 (see highlighted line 5).

In highlighted line 7, class map class-default matches on any other frames (those frames that do not have their DE bit set to 1), and sets the MPLS EXP bits of AToM data channel packets encapsulating these frames to 4 (highlighted line 8). 615 frames that do not have their DE bit set to 1 have been received on interface serial 4/1 so far.

So far in this section, QoS policies have been configured based on a *translation* between Layer 2 header settings and MPLS EXP bit settings. Another method of configuring a QoS policy for AToM pseudowires is to use the **police** {**cir** *cir*} [**bc** *conform-burst*] {**pir** *pir*} [**be** *peak-burst*] [**conform-action** *action* [**exceed-action** *action* [**violate-action** *action*]]] command.

When using the **police** command, you can specify a Committed Information Rate (CIR) and a Peak Information Rate (PIR), as well as actions if those rates are conformed to, exceeded, or violated.

In Example 3-29, you can see an example of a QoS policy configured using the **police** command.

Example 3-29 *Example of a QoS Policy for AToM Pseudowires Configured Using the* **police** *Command*

```
!
hostname Los.Angeles.PE
!
policy-map police.AC (line 1)
 class class-default (line 2)
 police cir 64000 pir 128000 conform-action set-mpls-exp-transmit 4 exceed-action (line 3)
  set-mpls-exp-transmit 1 violate-action drop (line 4)
 !
interface serial 2/1
 service-policy input police.AC (line 5)
 !
```

In highlighted lines 1 to 3, a policy map called police.AC is configured.

The **class class-default** command in highlighted line 2 is used to configure a default class for all traffic that does not match a configured class map (there is no configured class map, so the default class map matches all traffic).

A CIR of 64 kbps and a PIR of 128 kbps are configured using the **police** command in highlighted line 3.

When traffic received on the attachment circuit meets the CIR, AToM data channel packets that carry the traffic are assigned MPLS EXP bit settings of 4 (**set-mpls-exp-transmit 4**). When traffic exceeds the CIR, but not the PIR, AToM data channel packets that carry the traffic are assigned MPLS EXP bit settings of 1 (**set-mpls-exp-transmit 1**). When traffic exceeds the PIR, it is dropped (**violate-action drop**).

Tunnel Selection for AToM Pseudowires

Up to this point in the chapter, it has been assumed that AToM data channel packets are transported between PE routers using LDP-signaled tunnel labels (see Figure 3-15). LDP-signaled LSPs follow the IGP best path across a network between PE routers.

If you want AToM pseudowires to traverse MPLS-TE tunnels (using RSVP-TE-signaled tunnel labels) between PE routers, you can configure tunnel selection. Note that if used for tunnel selection, an MPLS-TE tunnel tail end must be the remote PE router.

Tunnel selection also enables you to specify an IP address or DNS name of a (remote) PE router. If you specify an IP address or DNS name, the IP address must correspond to the loopback interface on a peer PE router.

NOTE   The discussion of MPLS-TE in this section is not intended to be exhaustive. See the following website for more information of MPLS-TE:

http://www.cisco.com/warp/public/732/Tech/mpls/te/docs/

Configuring PE Routers for MPLS-TE Tunnel Selection for AToM Pseudowires

The steps necessary to configure MPLS-TE tunnel selection for AToM pseudowires on PE routers are as follows:

Step 1   Globally enable MPLS-TE.

Step 2   Enable MPLS-TE and specify reservable bandwidth on MPLS backbone network interfaces.

Step 3   Enable the MPLS backbone IGP for MPLS-TE.

Step 4   Configure the MPLS-TE tunnel interface.

Step 5   Configure an AToM pseudowire class.

Step 6   Bind the attachment circuit to the AToM pseudowire, and specify the pseudowire class.

Example 3-30 shows the configuration of tunnel selection for AToM pseudowires on PE routers.

Example 3-30 *Configuration of Tunnel Selection for AToM Pseudowires*

```
!
hostname Los.Angeles.PE
mpls traffic-eng tunnels (line 1)
!
pseudowire-class AToM.PWC.0001 (line 2)
 encapsulation mpls (line 3)
 preferred-path interface Tunnel1 disable-fallback (line 4)
!
 interface Tunnel1 (line 5)
 ip unnumbered Loopback1 (line 6)
 tunnel destination 10.1.1.2 (line 7)
 tunnel mode mpls traffic-eng (line 8)
 tunnel mpls traffic-eng priority 2 2 (line 9)
 tunnel mpls traffic-eng bandwidth 1000 (line 10)
 tunnel mpls traffic-eng path-option 1 explicit name AToM.Tun.1 (line 11)
!
interface FastEthernet2/0
 ip address 10.2.1.1 255.255.255.0
 mpls ip
 mpls traffic-eng tunnels (line 12)
 ip rsvp bandwidth 10000 10000 (line 13)
!
router ospf 100
 network 10.2.1.1 0.0.0.0 area 0
 network 10.1.1.1 0.0.0.0 area 0
 mpls traffic-eng router-id Loopback1 (line 14)
 mpls traffic-eng area 0 (line 15)
!
 ip explicit-path name AToM.Tun.1 enable (line 16)
 next-address 10.2.1.2 (line 17)
 next-address 10.5.1.2 (line 18)
 next-address 10.6.1.2 (line 19)
 next-address 10.7.1.2 (line 20)
 next-address 10.7.1.2 (line 21)
 next-address 10.1.1.2 (line 22)
!
!
connect FR.DLCI.To.DLCI Serial4/1 200 l2transport
 xconnect 10.1.1.1 1002 pw-class AToM.PWC.0001 (line 23)
 !
!
```

The configuration in Example 3-31 can be broken down as follows:

Step 1 Globally enable MPLS-TE:

In highlighted line 1, the **mpls traffic-eng tunnels** command is used to globally enable MPLS-TE on Los.Angeles.PE.

Step 2 Enable MPLS-TE and specify reservable bandwidth on MPLS backbone interfaces:

Highlighted lines 12 and 13 contain the **mpls traffic-eng tunnels** and **ip rsvp bandwidth** *interface-bandwidth single-flow-bandwidth* commands. The **mpls traffic-eng tunnels** command enables MPLS-TE on MPLS backbone interface Fast Ethernet 1/0, and the **ip rsvp bandwidth** command is used to specify the maximum reservable bandwidth for MPLS-TE tunnels on the interface.

Step 3 Enable the MPLS backbone IGP for MPLS-TE:

The **mpls traffic-eng router-id** *interface* command in highlighted line 14 is used to configure a unique MPLS-TE router ID for this router. In this case, the MPLS-TE router ID corresponds to the IP address configured on interface loopback 1.

In highlighted line 15, the **mpls traffic-eng** *area-id* command is used to enable the flooding of MPLS-TE information within the specified OSPF area.

If you are using IS-IS as your MPLS backbone IGP, you must specify the commands as follows:

```
router isis
  metric-style wide
  mpls traffic-eng router-id Loopback1
  mpls traffic-eng level-2
```

The **metric-style wide** command enables the router to advertise the 24- and 32-bit metrics necessary for MPLS-TE.

The **mpls traffic-eng {level-1 | level-2}** is used to enable the flooding of MPLS-TE information into the specified level.

Step 4 Configure the MPLS-TE tunnel interface:

Interface tunnel 1 is configured from highlighted line 5 to highlighted line 11. This interface is the MPLS-TE tunnel interface.

In highlighted line 6, the **ip unnumbered** *interface* command is used to configure an IP address on the tunnel interface. This IP address is "borrowed" from the interface loopback 1.

It is important to configure an IP address on an MPLS-TE tunnel interface—if one is not configured, no traffic is forwarded over the corresponding MPLS-TE tunnel.

The **tunnel destination** *ip-address* command in highlighted line 7 configures the ultimate destination of the MPLS-TE tunnel (the remote PE router [San.Jose.PE]).

Next, the **tunnel mode mpls traffic-eng** command (highlighted line 8) is used to enable MPLS traffic engineering on the tunnel interface.

Highlighted line 9 shows the **tunnel mpls traffic-eng priority** *setup-priority* [*hold-priority*]. This command is used to configure setup and hold priorities (here, 2 and 2) for the MPLS-TE tunnel. These priorities are used for call admission control (CAC)—tunnels with lower priorities take priority for reservable bandwidth during setup (there is a certain amount of reservable bandwidth on each MPLS-TE-enabled backbone interface on PE and P routers, and MPLS-TE tunnels might compete for that bandwidth).

The **tunnel mpls traffic-eng bandwidth** *bandwidth* command (highlighted line 10) is used to specify the amount of bandwidth that this MPLS-TE tunnel will attempt to reserve on interfaces along its path to the remote PE router. In this example, the amount of required bandwidth is 1000 kbps.

Finally, in highlighted line 11, the **tunnel mpls traffic-eng path-option** *number* **explicit name** {*path-name* | *path-number*} command configures an explicit hop-by-hop path across the network to the remote PE router (San.Jose.PE). The name of the explicit path is AToM.Tun.1.

Following the **mpls traffic-eng router-id** command is the **ip explicit-path** {**name** *word* | **identifier** *number*} [**enable** | **disable**] command (highlighted line 16). This command is used to begin configuration of an explicit MPLS-TE path across the MPLS backbone network. In this case, the path is assigned the name AToM.Tun.1.

In highlighted lines 17 to 22, the **next-address** *next-hop-address* command is used to configure the hop-by-hop path across the MPLS backbone network to (ultimately) the remote PE router (10.1.1.2, San.Jose.PE).

Step 5   Configure an AToM pseudowire class:

Highlighted lines 2 to 4 show the configuration of a pseudowire class called AToM.PWC.0001.

The **encapsulation mpls** command in highlighted line 3 configures MPLS (AToM) encapsulation for the pseudowire.

The **preferred path** [**interface tunnel** tunnel-number | **peer** {*ip address* | *host name*}] [**disable-fallback**] command (highlighted line 4) is used to specify that the AToM pseudowire should traverse an MPLS-TE tunnel (interface tunnel 1). Furthermore, the **disable-fallback** keywords are used to specify that, in this case, if the MPLS-TE tunnel is not available (it is down) then the AToM pseudowire should not traverse an LDP-signaled LSP.

Although not directly related to tunnel selection, it is worth noting here that one other command that can be configured under a pseudowire class for AToM is the **sequencing** command. This command can be used to enable sequencing for an AToM pseudowire (sequence numbers can be carried in the Control Word).

Step 6   Bind the attachment circuit to the AToM pseudowire, and specify the pseudowire class:

The **xconnect** *pe-ip-address* **pw-class** *pw-class-name* command (highlighted line 23) binds the attachment circuit to a pseudowire to 10.1.1.2 (San.Jose.PE) with PW (VC) ID 1002. It also links to a pseudowire class called AToM.PWC.0001.

Configuring P Routers for MPLS-TE

When using tunnel selection for AToM pseudowires with MPLS-TE tunnels, P routers must be configured for MPLS-TE.

The configuration of P routers for MPLS-TE is as follows:

Step 1   Globally enable MPLS-TE.

Step 2   Enable MPLS-TE and specify reservable bandwidth on MPLS backbone interfaces.

Step 3   Enable the MPLS backbone IGP for MPLS-TE.

Step 4   Configure the MPLS-TE tunnel interface.

If you are the observant type, you will have noticed that the configuration of P routers is a subset of the configuration of the PE router.

Example 3-31 shows an example configuration of a P router for MPLS-TE. For more information on the configuration, see the explanation of the configuration of the PE router.

Example 3-31 *Example Configuration of a P Router for MPLS-TE*

```
!
hostname Los.Angeles.P
!
mpls traffic-eng tunnels (line 1)
!
interface FastEthernet2/0
 ip address 10.2.1.2 255.255.255.0
 mpls ip
 mpls traffic-eng tunnels (line 2)
 ip rsvp bandwidth 10000 10000 (line 3)
!
interface Serial3/0
 ip address 10.3.1.1 255.255.255.0
 mpls ip
 mpls traffic-eng tunnels (line 4)
 ip rsvp bandwidth 10000 10000 (line 5)
!
!
```

continues

Example 3-31 *Example Configuration of a P Router for MPLS-TE (Continued)*

```
interface Serial4/0
 ip address 10.5.1.1 255.255.255.0
 mpls ip
 mpls traffic-eng tunnels (line 6)
 ip rsvp bandwidth 10000 10000 (line 7)
!
router ospf 100
 network 10.2.1.2 0.0.0.0 area 0
 network 10.3.1.1 0.0.0.0 area 0
 network 10.5.1.1 0.0.0.0 area 0
 mpls traffic-eng router-id Loopback1 (line 8)
 mpls traffic-eng area 0 (line 9)
!
```

Tunnel Selection for AtoM Pseudowires: Final Network Topology and Advantages

Figure 3-40 illustrates tunnel selection for AToM pseudowires.

Figure 3-40 *Tunnel Selection for AToM Pseudowires*

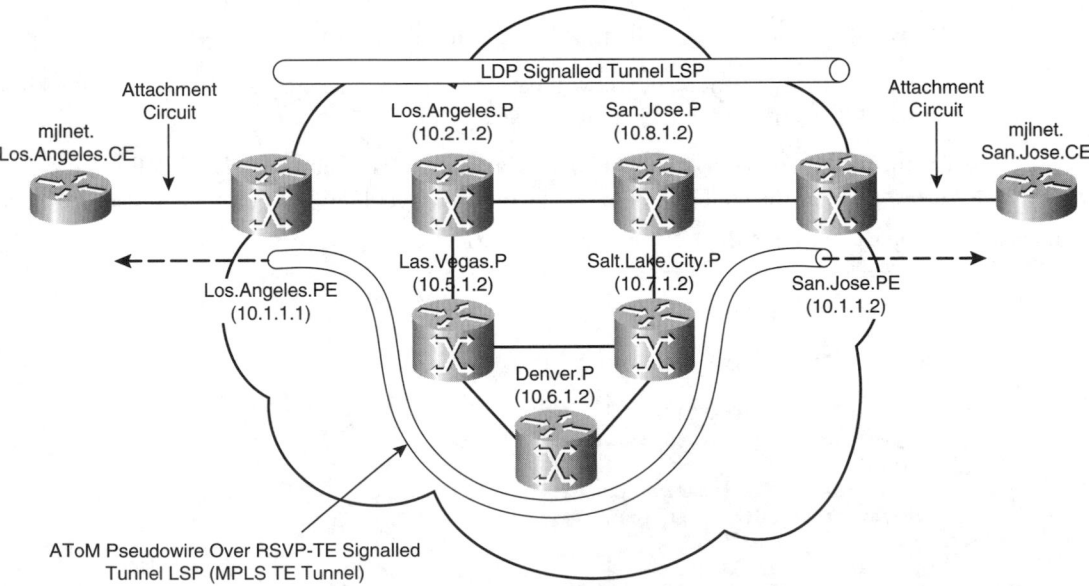

As shown in Figure 3-40, the configuration in Example 3-31 causes the AToM pseudowire to traverse an MPLS-TE (RSVP-TE signaled) tunnel from Los.Angeles.PE to San.Jose.PE (10.1.1.2) via Los.Angeles.P (10.2.1.2), Las.Vegas.P (10.5.1.2), Denver.P (10.6.1.2), Salt.Lake.City.P (10.7.1.2), and San.Jose.P (10.8.1.2).

Figure 3-40 also shows the LDP-signaled tunnel LSP between Los.Angeles.PE and San.Jose.PE via Los.Angeles.P and San.Jose.P (the shortest IGP path). The pseudowire does not traverse this LSP. If you remove **disable-fallback** keywords at the end of the

preferred-path command in highlighted line 4 in Example 3-31, the AToM pseudowire would traverse the LDP-signaled tunnel LSP in the event that the MPLS-TE tunnel failed.

Now, you might be looking at Figure 3-40 and wondering what the advantage of directing an AToM pseudowire over an MPLS-TE tunnel (using tunnel selection) is—after all, the LDP tunnel LSP traverses the shortest path between PE routers, and the RSVP-TE-signaled LSP (MPLS-TE tunnel) traverses a comparatively circuitous route between PE routers. The answer is that MPLS-TE enables you to take advantage of underutilized paths (bandwidth) in the MPLS backbone network, as well as enabling you to take advantage of features such as MPLS-TE fast-reroute.

MPLS-TE fast-reroute allows an MPLS-TE tunnel to fail over to an alternate route across an MPLS backbone network in the event of the failure of a node (router) or link in its primary path. This failover is fast, especially when compared to the failover times for LDP-signaled LSPs, and this fast failover can often be essential in maintaining service level agreements (SLA).

NOTE   For more information on MPLS-TE fast-reroute, see the following URL:

http://www.cisco.com/en/US/products/sw/iosswrel/ps1612/products_feature_
guide09186a00800809d4.html

Verifying MPLS-TE Tunnel Selection for AToM Pseudowires

You can use the **show mpls l2transport vc** *vcid* **detail** command to verify tunnel selection for AToM pseudowires (see Example 3-32).

Example 3-32 *Using the* **show mpls l2transport vc** *detail Command to Verify Tunnel Selection for AToM Pseudowires*

```
Los.Angeles.PE#show mpls l2transport vc 1002 detail
Local interface: Se4/1 up, line protocol up, FR DLCI 200 up
 Destination address: 10.1.1.2, VC ID: 1002, VC status: up
  Preferred path: Tunnel1, active (line 1)
  Default path: disabled
  Output interface: Tu1, imposed label stack {18 21} (line 2)
 Create time: 00:00:17, last status change time: 00:00:17
 Signaling protocol: LDP, peer 10.1.1.2:0 up
  MPLS VC labels: local 22, remote 16
  Group ID: local 0, remote 3
  MTU: local 1500, remote 1500
  Remote interface description:
 Sequencing: receive disabled, send disabled
 Sequence number: receive 0, send 0
 VC statistics:
  packet totals: receive 17, send 0
  byte totals:  receive 1274, send 0
  packet drops: receive 0, seq error 0, send 17
Los.Angeles.PE#
```

As shown in highlighted line 1, the preferred path for the pseudowire is via interface tunnel 1 (the MPLS-TE tunnel), and the tunnel is active.

Highlighted line 2 shows that the current output (outbound) interface for the pseudowire is interface tunnel 1. The label stack shown includes the tunnel label (18), and the PW (VC) label (21).

L2VPN Pseudowire Switching with AToM

The preceding sections in this chapter have described how to deploy AToM pseudowires over a single MPLS backbone network. But how about if you want to configure AToM pseudowires over more than one MPLS backbone network, or across autonomous system (service provider) boundaries? In this case, you have two choices:

- Configure AToM directly between PE routers in the separate networks or autonomous systems (AToM pseudowires between peer PE routers).

- Configure L2VPN pseudowire switching with AToM.

The problem with configuring AToM directly between PE routers (using the **xconnect** command to specify the remote PE router) is that the PE routers might belong to different service providers, and a direct pseudowire between the PE routers might cause security, as well as management and operations, concerns. L2VPN pseudowire switching, on the other hand, can help to ameliorate these concerns.

Figure 3-41 illustrates L2VPN pseudowire switching.

Figure 3-41 *L2VPN Pseudowire Switching*

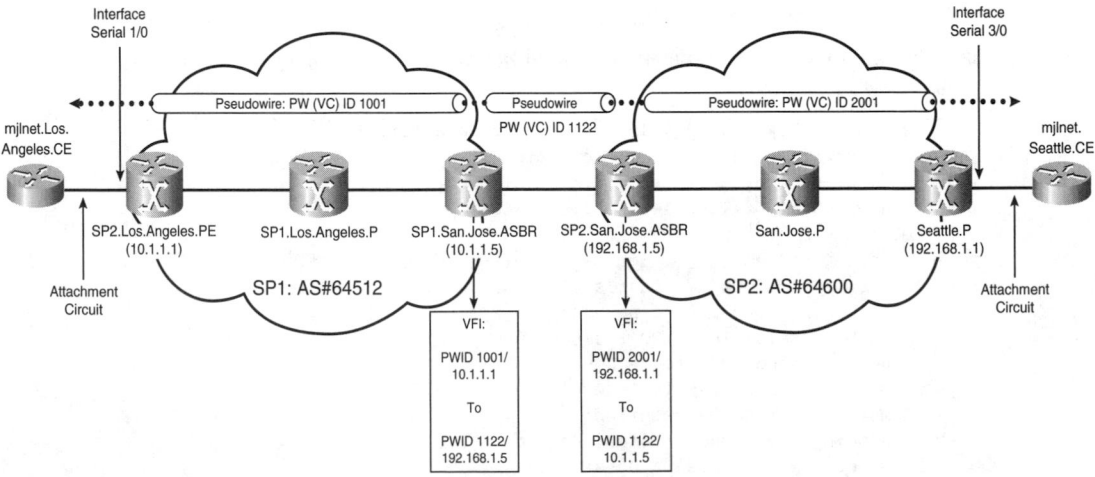

In Figure 3-41, Layer 2 connectivity is provided between mjlnet.Los.Angeles.CE and mjlnet.Seattle.CE. This connectivity is provided over the MPLS backbones of service providers SP1 and SP2.

Because connectivity is provided over the MPLS backbones of SP1 and SP2, these service providers have provisioned L2VPN pseudowire switching. L2VPN pseudowire switching is deployed on the Autonomous System Boundary Routers (ASBR) between the service providers' networks.

Precise pseudowire and L2VPN pseudowire switching configuration and traffic flow (mjlnet.Los.Angeles.CE to mjlnet.Seattle.CE in Figure 3-41) is as follows:

- SP1.Los.Angeles.PE is configured with a pseudowire with PW (VC) ID 1001. This pseudowire is used to transport Layer 2 traffic received on the attachment circuit to mjlnet.Los.Angeles.CE to SP1.San.Jose.ASBR.

- SP1.San.Jose.ASBR is configured with a point-to-point Layer 2 virtual forwarding interface (VFI). The function of this VFI is to switch Layer 2 traffic from the pseudowire to SP1.Los.Angeles.PE (PW [VC] ID 1001) to a pseudowire to SP2.San.Jose.ASBR (PW [VC] ID 1122).

- SP2.San.Jose.ASBR is configured with a point-to-point Layer 2 VFI. The function of this VFI is to switch Layer 2 traffic from the pseudowire to SP1.San.Jose.ASBR (PW [VC] ID 1122) and a pseudowire to SP2.Seattle.PE (PW [VC] ID 2001).

- SP2.Seattle.PE is configured with a pseudowire to SP2.San.Jose.ASBR (PW [VC] ID 2001). SP2.Seattle.PE switches traffic (from mjlnet.Los.Angeles.CE) received over the pseudowire to the attachment circuit mjlnet.Seattle.CE.

Traffic flow from mjlnet.Seattle.CE to mjlnet.Los.Angeles.CE is transported in the same manner, just in the opposite direction:

- SP2.Seattle.PE switches traffic received on the attachment circuit from mjlnet.Seattle.CE to the pseudowire to SP2.San.Jose.ASBR (PW [VC] ID 2001).

- SP2.San.Jose.ASBR is configured with a point-to-point Layer 2 VFI. This VFI switches Layer 2 traffic from the pseudowire to SP2.Seattle.PE (PW [VC] ID 2001) and a pseudowire to SP1.San.Jose.ASBR (PW [VC] ID 1122).

- SP1.San.Jose.ASBR is configured with a point-to-point Layer 2 VFI. This VFI switches Layer 2 traffic from the pseudowire to SP2.San.Jose.ASBR (PW [VC] ID 1122) to a pseudowire to SP1.Los.Angeles.PE (PW [VC] ID 1001).

- SP1.Los.Angeles.PE switches traffic received on the pseudowire with PW (VC) ID 1001 to SP1.San.Jose.ASBR to the attachment circuit to mjlnet.Los.Angeles.CE.

Example 3-33 shows the relevant configuration for SP1.Los.Angeles.PE and SP1.San.Jose.ASBR (see Figure 3-41).

Example 3-33 *Configurations for SP1.Los.Angeles.PE And SP1.San.Jose.ASBR*

```
!
hostname SP1.Los.Angeles.PE
!
mpls ldp router-id Loopback1 force
!
interface Loopback1
 ip address 10.1.1.1 255.255.255.255
!
interface Serial1/0
 xconnect 10.1.1.5 1001 encapsulation mpls (line 1)
!
```
```
!
hostname SP1.San.Jose.ASBR
!
l2 vfi VFI.To.SP2 point-to-point (line 2)
 neighbor 10.1.1.1 1001 encapsulation mpls (line 3)
 neighbor 192.168.1.5 1122 encapsulation mpls (line 4)
!
interface Loopback0
 ip address 10.1.1.5 255.255.255.255
!
interface Serial2/0
 ip address 172.16.1.1 255.255.255.0
 mpls bgp forwarding (line 5)
!
router bgp 64512
 no synchronization
 network 10.1.1.5 mask 255.255.255.255 (line 6)
 neighbor 172.16.1.2 remote-as 64600 (line 7)
 neighbor 172.16.1.2 send-label (line 8)
 no auto-summary
!
```

In highlighted line 1, the **xconnect** command in the configuration of SP1.Los.Angeles.PE binds the attachment circuit (interface serial 1/0) to a pseudowire to 10.1.1.5 (SP1.San.Jose.ASBR).

Highlighted lines 2 to 4 show the configuration of SP1.San.Jose.ASBR.

The **l2 vfi** *vfi-name* **point-to-point** command in highlighted line 2 configures a point-to-point VFI called VFI.To.SP2.

The **neighbor** {*ip-address*} {*vc-id*} {**encapsulation mpls** | **pw-class** *pw-class-name*} command in highlighted lines 3 and 4 configure pseudowire connections to 10.1.1.1 (SP1.Los.Angeles.PE) with PW (VC) ID 1001, and 192.168.1.5 (SP2.San.Jose.ASBR) with PW (VC) ID 1122.

In highlighted line 5, you can see the **mpls bgp forwarding** command. This command configures interface serial 2/0 (connected to SP2.San.Jose.PE) to label switch packets when labels are advertised by BGP. This command is essential to ensure that data channel packets can be label switched across the connection between SP1.San.Jose.ASBR and SP2.San.Jose.ASBR.

The **neighbor** *ip-address* **remote-as** *as-number* command in highlighted line 7 is used to configure a BGP neighbor relationship between the local router (SP1.San.Jose.ASBR) and the remote router (SP2.San.Jose.ASBR, 172.16.1.2 [its directly connected interface address]).

The **neighbor** *ip-address* **send-labels** command (highlighted line 8) configures the local router to send labels along with any routes advertised to the SP2.San.Jose.ASBR.

In highlighted line 6, the **network** *network-number* **mask** *network-mask* command is used to advertise the local loopback interface address (10.1.1.5/32) to SP2.San.Jose.ASBR. SP2.San .Jose.ASBR needs a route to this address because it is one of the endpoints of the pseudowire configured between the ASBRs (it is specified using the **neighbor** {*ip-address*} {*vc-id*} {**encapsulation mpls** | **pw-class** *pw-class-name*} command on SP2.San.Jose.ASBR).

Example 3-34 shows the relevant configuration for SP2.Seattle.PE and SP2.San.Jose.ASBR (see Figure 3-41).

Example 3-34 *Configurations SP2.Seattle.PE and SP2.San.JoseASBR*

```
!
hostname SP2.San.Jose.ASBR
!
l2 vfi VFI.To.SP1 point-to-point (line 1)
 neighbor 10.1.1.5 1122 encapsulation mpls (line 2)
 neighbor 192.168.1.1 2001 encapsulation mpls (line 3)
!
interface Loopback0
ip address 192.168.1.5 255.255.255.255
!
interface Serial4/0
 ip address 172.16.1.2 255.255.255.0
 mpls bgp forwarding (line 4)
!
router bgp 64600
 no synchronization
 network 192.168.1.5 mask 255.255.255.255 (line 5)
 neighbor 172.16.1.1 remote-as 64512 (line 6)
 neighbor 172.16.1.1 send-label (line 7)
 no auto-summary
!
```

```
!
hostname SP2.Seattle.PE
!
mpls ldp router-id Loopback1 force
!
interface Loopback1
 ip address 192.168.1.1 255.255.255.255
!
interface Serial3/0
 xconnect 192.168.1.5 2001 encapsulation mpls (line 8)
!
```

Highlighted lines 1 to 7 show the relevant configuration of SP2.San.Jose.ASBR. As you can see, it is similar to that for SP1.San.Jose.ASBR—the only real differences are the IP addresses and networks specified by the various commands.

Highlighted lines 1 to 3 show the configuration of a VFI called **VFI.To.SP1**. Within the VFI, the **neighbor** command is used to configure pseudowires to 10.1.1.5 (SP1.San.Jose.ASBR) and 192.168.1.5 (SP2.Seattle.PE).

Note that the pseudowire to 10.1.1.5 (SP1.San.Jose.ASBR) could not be built unless that address is advertised by SP1.San.Jose.ASBR (it is advertised—see Example 3-33, highlighted line 6).

The **mpls bgp forwarding** command (highlighted line 4) is again used to enable label switching when labels are advertised by BGP (here, on interface serial 4/0 [connected to SP1.San.Jose.PE]).

The **neighbor** *ip-address* **remote-as** *as-number* and **neighbor** *ip-address* **send-labels** commands in highlighted lines 5 and 6 are used to configure a BGP neighbor relationship between the local router (SP2.San.Jose.ASBR) and the remote router (SP1.San.Jose.ASBR, 172.16.1.1 [its directly connected interface address]), as well as configuring the local router to send labels along with any routes advertised to the SP1.San.Jose.ASBR.

Next, the **network** *network-number* **mask** *network-mask* command (highlighted line 7) is used to advertise the local loopback interface address (192.168.1.5/32) to SP1.San.Jose.ASBR. SP1.San.Jose.ASBR needs a route to this address because it is one of the endpoints of the pseudowire configured between the ASBRs (see Example 3-33, highlighted line 3).

The last highlighted command in Example 3-34 is the **xconnect** command on SP2.Seattle.PE (highlighted line 8). This command binds the local attachment circuit (interface serial 3/0) to a pseudowire with PW (VC) ID 2001 to SP2.San.Jose.ASBR (192.168.1.5).

After the configurations are up and running, you can verify the VFIs using the **show vfi** command, as demonstrated in Example 3-35.

Example 3-35 *Verifying the VFI Using the* **show vfi** *Command*

```
SP1.San.Jose.ASBR#show vfi
VFI name: VFI.T.SP2, type: point-to-point (line 1)
  Neighbors connected via pseudowires:
   Router ID    Pseudowire ID
   10.1.1.1     1001 (line 2)
   192.168.1.5  1122 (line 3)
SP1.San.Jose.ASBR#
```

Highlighted line 1 shows that the VFI name is VFI.T.SP2, and that the VFI type is point-to-point.

Highlighted lines 2 and 3 shows the pseudowires configured using the **neighbor** command within the VFI.

L2VPN Interworking with AToM Pseudowires

In Chapter 2, you saw how to configure both Ethernet and IP mode L2VPN interworking with L2TPv3 pseudowires. It is also possible to configure L2VPN interworking with AToM pseudowires in a similar manner.

NOTE   If you have not read (or cannot clearly remember!) the discussion of L2VPN interworking with L2TPv3 from Chapter 2, it is a good idea to read the section "L2VPN Interworking with L2TPv3" starting on page 98 before proceeding with this section.

L2VPN interworking can be supported with AToM in two ways (just like L2TPv3):

* **IP mode interworking**—In this mode of interworking, attachment circuits are terminated locally on PE routers. IP packets are forwarded over an AToM pseudowire, and the interworking function (IWF) is performed on both peer PE routers.

  IP mode interworking uses a type 0x000B AToM pseudowire (see Table 3-2).

  Figure 3-42 illustrates IP mode interworking with AToM.

Figure 3-42 *IP Mode L2VPN Interworking with AToM*

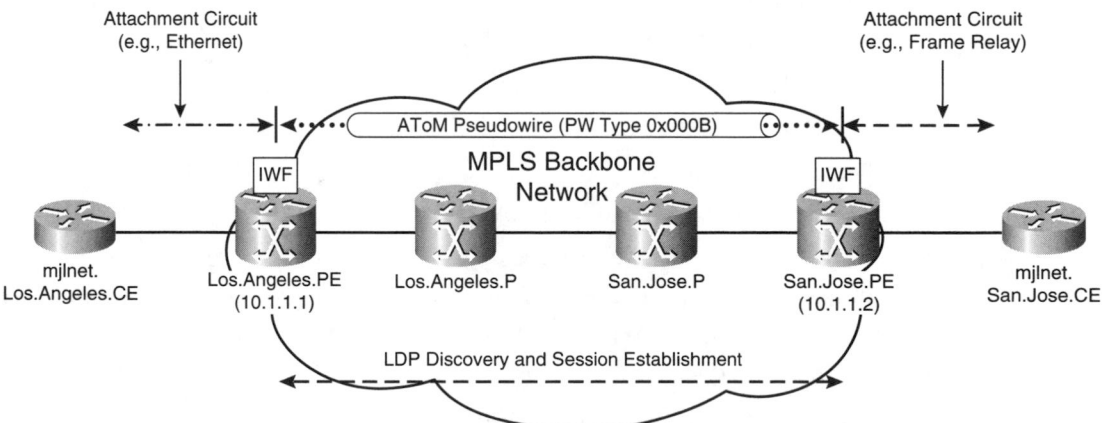

* **Ethernet mode interworking**—In Ethernet mode interworking, one of the attachment circuits is Ethernet, and this attachment circuit is extended over an AToM pseudowire from one PE router to its peer PE router.

Ethernet mode interworking uses a type 0x0005 AToM pseudowire.

Figure 3-43 shows Ethernet mode L2VPN interworking with AToM.

Figure 3-43 *Ethernet Mode L2VPN Interworking with AToM*

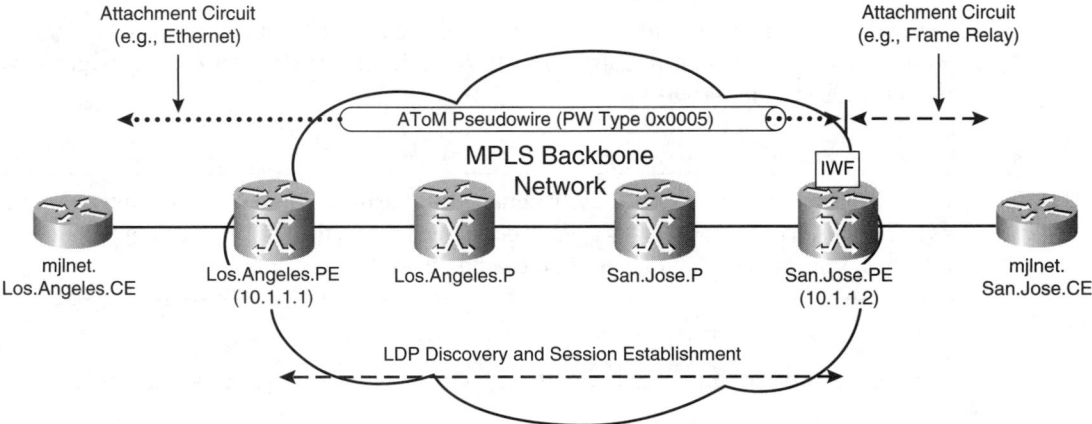

As previously stated, L2VPN interworking with L2TPv3 and AToM pseudowires is similar. The significant difference is the attachment circuit types supported with each pseudowire protocol.

At the time of this writing, the following attachment circuit type combinations are supported for IP mode L2VPN interworking with AToM pseudowires:

- Frame Relay to Ethernet
- Frame Relay to Ethernet VLAN (802.1Q)
- Frame Relay to PPP
- Frame Relay to ATM AAL5
- Ethernet to ATM AAL5
- Ethernet VLAN (802.1Q) to ATM AAL5
- Ethernet to Ethernet VLAN (802.1Q)

And the following attachment circuit type combinations are supported for L2VPN Ethernet mode interworking with AToM pseudowires:

- Frame Relay to Ethernet
- Frame Relay to Ethernet VLAN (802.1Q)
- Ethernet to ATM AAL5
- Ethernet VLAN (802.1Q) to ATM AAL5
- Ethernet to Ethernet VLAN (802.1Q)

Configuring Ethernet Mode L2VPN Interworking with AToM Pseudowires

Example 3-36 shows an example of the configuration of Ethernet mode L2VPN interworking using AToM (with Ethernet to Ethernet VLAN [802.1Q] attachment circuits). You might like to compare this to a similar configuration using L2TPv3 shown in Example 2-35 on page 101.

Example 3-36 *Sample Configuration of Ethernet Mode L2VPN Interworking Using AToM (with Ethernet and Ethernet VLAN [8021Q] Attachment Circuits)*

```
!
hostname Los.Angeles.PE
!
pseudowire-class atom.iw.pw.class (line 1)
 encapsulation mpls
 interworking ethernet (line 2)
!
interface FastEthernet0/0
 xconnect 10.1.1.2 2001 pw-class atom.iw.pw.class (line 3)
!
```
```
!
hostname San.Jose.PE
!
pseudowire-class atom.iw.pw.class (line 4)
 encapsulation mpls
 interworking ethernet (line 5)
!
interface FastEthernet2/0
!
interface FastEthernet2/0.100 (line 6)
 encapsulation dot1Q 100
 xconnect 10.1.1.1 2001 pw-class atom.iw.pw.class (line 7)
!
```

The relevant configuration of Los.Angeles.PE is shown in highlighted lines 1 to 3, and the relevant configuration of San.Jose.PE is shown in highlighted lines 4 to 7.

Notice that the configurations are similar to those for regular (like-to-like attachment circuit) AToM pseudowires.

The biggest difference between the configurations shown in Example 3-36 and those for regular AToM pseudowires is the addition of the **interworking ethernet** command within a pseudowire class (see highlighted lines 2 and 5). The **interworking ethernet** command is used to configure Ethernet mode interworking.

Configuring IP Mode L2VPN Interworking with AToM Pseudowires

Example 3-37 shows an example of the configuration of IP mode L2VPN interworking using AToM with Ethernet and Frame Relay attachment circuits. Compare this to the configuration using L2TPv3 shown in Example 2-36 on page 104.

Example 3-37 *Sample Configuration of IP Mode L2VPN Interworking Using AToM (with Ethernet and Frame Relay Attachment Circuits)*

```
!
hostname Los.Angeles.PE
!
pseudowire-class L2VPN.IW.02.mjlnet.To.San.Jose (line 1)
 encapsulation mpls
 interworking ip (line 2)
!
interface FastEthernet0/0
 xconnect 10.1.1.1 2002 pw-class L2VPN.IW.02.mjlnet.To.San.Jose (line 3)
 !
```

```
!
hostname San.Jose.PE
!
frame-relay switching
!
pseudowire-class L2VPN.IW.02.mjlnet.To.London (line 4)
 encapsulation mpls
 interworking ip (line 5)
!
interface Serial4/3
 no ip address
 encapsulation frame-relay
 frame-relay interface-dlci 300 switched
 frame-relay intf-type dce
!
connect L2.IW.London Serial4/3 300 l2transport
 xconnect 10.1.1.1 2002 pw-class L2VPN.IW.02.mjlnet.To.London (line 6)
 !
!
```

Highlighted lines 1 to 3 show the relevant configuration of LoS.Angeles.PE, and highlighted lines 4 to 6 show the relevant configuration of San.Jose.PE.

Again, the configurations shown in Example 3-37 are similar to those for regular AToM pseudowires. The key difference can again be found in the pseudowire class—the **interworking ip** command (highlighted lines 2 and 5) specifies that the pseudowire type is IP mode interworking.

Verifying L2VPN Interworking with AToM Pseudowires

You can verify L2VPN interworking with AToM using the **show mpls l2transport vc detail** command, as demonstrated in Example 3-38.

Example 3-38 *Verifying L2VPN Interworking with AToM Using the* **show mpls l2transport vc** *detail Command*

```
Los.Angeles.PE#show mpls l2transport vc 1002 detail
Local interface: Se2/1 up, line protocol up, FR DLCI 200 up
 MPLS VC type is Ethernet, interworking type is Ethernet (line 1)
 Destination address: 10.1.1.2, VC ID: 1002, VC status: up (line 2)
```

Example 3-38 *Verifying L2VPN Interworking with AToM Using the* **show mpls l2transport vc** *detail Command (Continued)*

```
   Preferred path: not configured
   Default path: active
   Tunnel label: 16, next hop point2point
   Output interface: Se2/0, imposed label stack {16 16}
 Create time: 00:00:22, last status change time: 00:00:22
 Signaling protocol: LDP, peer 10.1.1.2:0 up
   MPLS VC labels: local unassigned, remote 16
   Group ID: local unknown, remote 3
   MTU: local unknown, remote 1500
   Remote interface description:
 Sequencing: receive disabled, send disabled
 Sequence number: receive 0, send 0
 VC statistics:
   packet totals: receive 0, send 0
   byte totals:  receive 0, send 0
   packet drops: receive 0, seq error 0, send 0
San.Jose.PE#
```

Highlighted line 1 shows that the AToM PW (VC) type is Ethernet.

Highlighted line 2 shows that the VC (PW) ID is 1002, and that the pseudowire is up.

By this stage, you will have undoubtedly seen how similar the configurations for L2VPN interworking with AToM and L2TPv3 are. In fact, the main difference is the types of attachment circuit combinations supported by AToM and L2TPv3, respectively — at the time of this writing, AToM supports more combinations of attachment circuits than L2TPv3.

Considerations such as those involving MTU and routing protocol are identical when configuring L2VPN interworking with either AToM or L2TPv3. For more information, see the section "L2VPN Interworking With L2TPv3" in Chapter 2.

Configuring and Verifying Local Switching

Pseudowire technologies such as AToM and L2TPv3 allow the transport of Layer 2 protocols between attachment circuits across an intervening packet-switched network (PSN) network. But what if you want to switch Layer 2 protocols between attachment circuits on the same router? This is where a mechanism called *local switching* comes in.

Local switching does not itself require signaling and transport using mechanisms and protocols such as AToM and L2TPv3, but it is often required in the same networks where pseudowire technologies are deployed. That is why a discussion of local switching is included here.

Figure 3-44 illustrates local switching.

Figure 3-44 *Local Switching*

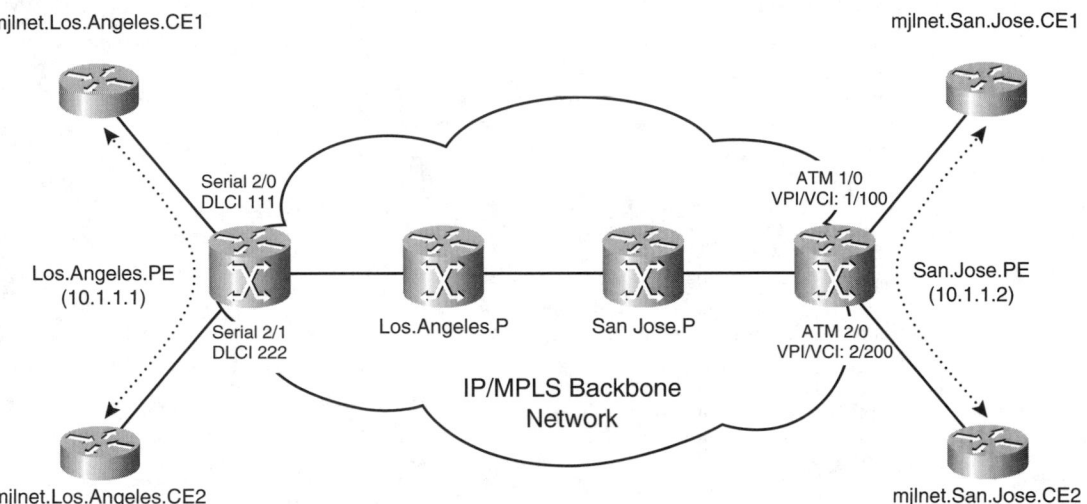

mjlnet.Los.Angeles.CE1

mjlnet.San.Jose.CE1

Serial 2/0
DLCI 111

ATM 1/0
VPI/VCI: 1/100

Los.Angeles.PE
(10.1.1.1)

San.Jose.PE
(10.1.1.2)

Serial 2/1
DLCI 222

Los.Angeles.P   San Jose.P

ATM 2/0
VPI/VCI: 2/200

IP/MPLS Backbone
Network

mjlnet.Los.Angeles.CE2

mjlnet.San.Jose.CE2

In Figure 3-44, on Los.Angeles.PE, a Frame Relay PVC with DLCI 111 on interface serial 2/0, is switched to a Frame Relay PVC with DLCI 222 on interface serial 2/1.

On San.Jose.PE, an ATM PVC with VPI/VCI 1/100 on interface ATM 1/0, is switched to an ATM PVC with VPI/VCI 2/200 on interface ATM 2/0.

Local switching enables the switching of frames or cells between different physical interfaces or circuits on the same physical interface. It is also possible to switch traffic between certain different types of interface and circuit such as ATM and Ethernet. This involves the use of an interworking function (IWF), which was discussed earlier in this chapter.

Local switching allows the switching of frames or cells between the following types of interfaces:

- Frame Relay interfaces
- ATM interfaces
- Ethernet or Ethernet VLAN (802.1Q) interfaces
- ATM and Ethernet/VLAN (802.1Q) interfaces
- ATM and Frame Relay interfaces

Local switching is configured using the **connect** command to specify the interfaces and circuits between which local switching should be performed.

Because of the relative simplicity of the configuration of local switching, this section contains some representative configurations, rather than examining each and every possible local switching scenario. What is important is to understand the **connect** command (you will soon have a good idea of its usage), as well as one or two special considerations for particular attachment circuit types.

Local Switching Between the Same Types of Physical Interfaces

Example 3-39 shows the configuration of local switching between Frame Relay interfaces.

Example 3-39 *Configuration of Local Switching Between Frame Relay Interfaces*

```
!
hostname Los.Angeles.PE
!
frame-relay switching (line 1)
!
interface Serial2/0
 encapsulation frame-relay
 frame-relay interface-dlci 111 switched (line 2)
 frame-relay intf-type dce
!
interface Serial2/1
 encapsulation frame-relay
 frame-relay interface-dlci 222 switched (line 3)
 frame-relay intf-type dce
!
connect Local.FR.Sw Serial2/0 111 Serial2/1 222 (line 4)
 !
!
```

The first command that you need when configuring local switching between Frame Relay interfaces is **frame-relay switching** (see highlighted line 1). This command enables switching for Frame Relay PVCs.

The optional **frame-relay interface-dlci** *dlci* **switched** command in highlighted lines 2 and 3 is used to create PVCs with the specified DLCIs, and indicate that those PVCs will be switched.

In highlighted line 4, the **connect** *connection-name interface dlci interface dlci* command is used to configure local switching between the two specified DLCIs on the specified interfaces.

It is worth noting that if you do not create PVCs using the **frame-relay interface-dlci** *dlci* **switched** command, they will automatically be created when you configure the **connect** *connection-name interface dlci interface dlci* command.

You can verify local switching for Frame Relay PVCs using the **show connection name** *connection-name* command, as demonstrated in Example 3-40.

Example 3-40 *Verifying Local Switching for Frame Relay PVCs*

```
Los.Angeles.PE#show connection name Local.FR.Sw
ID Name         Segment 1     Segment 2      State
===================================================================
1 Local.FR.Sw  Serial2/0 111  Serial2/1 222  UP
Los.Angeles.PE#
```

The highlighted line of output shows that a local switching connection with the name Local.FR.Sw and connection ID 1 has been configured between interface serial 2/0, DLCI 111, and interface serial 2/1, DLCI 222. The connection is in an UP state.

You can also use the **show frame-relay pvc** *dlci* command to examine the status of the individual PVCs.

If you want to configure local switching between ATM interfaces, you can choose between cell relay (AAL0) or AAL5 encapsulation.

In the case of cell relay, you can specify PVC or PVP mode local switching. Some platforms and linecards support cell packing with local switching.

Additionally, some platforms might require that VPI/VCI be the same on the interfaces between which you configure local switching with cell relay.

If the VPI/VCIs do not match between the interfaces, you must use AAL5 encapsulation. If you do configure AAL5 encapsulation, however, be aware that VPI/VCIs can only be different if OAM cells are not transported between the interfaces—if they are, VPI/VCIs must again match.

Example 3-41 shows the configuration of PVC mode local switching between ATM interfaces with AAL5 encapsulation.

Example 3-41 *Configuration of Local Switching Between ATM Interfaces*

```
!
hostname San.Jose.PE
!
interface atm 1/0
 pvc 1/100 l2transport (line 1)
 encapsulation aal5 (line 2)
!
interface atm 2/0
 pvc 2/200 l2transport (line 3)
 encapsulation aal5 (line 4)
!
connect Local.ATM.Sw_conn atm 1/0 1/100 atm 2/0 2/200 (line 5)
!
```

The **pvc** *vpi/vci* **l2transport** command in highlighted line 1 is used create a PVC with the specified VPI/VCI (1/100) on interface ATM 1/0, and indicate that the PVC is switched (rather than being terminated).

The **encapsulation aal5** command is then used to configure AAL5 encapsulation on the interface (highlighted line 2).

In highlighted lines 3 and 4, a switched PVC with VPI/VCI 2/200 is created on interface ATM 2/0.

In highlighted line 5, the **connect** *connection-name interface pvc interface pvc* command is used to configure local switching between the two specified PVCs on the specified interfaces (those created in highlighted lines 1 and 3).

If you want to configure cell relay rather than AAL5 encapsulation, you must configure the **encapsulation aal0** command rather than **encapsulation aal5** (see highlighted lines 2 and 4) .

NOTE   When configuring PVC mode local switching, it is optional to create PVCs using **pvc** *vpi/vci* **l2transport** command if you want to use cell relay (AAL0 encapsulation). This is because the appropriate PVCs are automatically configured with AAL0 encapsulation when the **connect** command is configured.

If you want to configure PVP mode local switching, you must configure the **atm pvp** *vpi* **l2transport** command instead of **pvc** *vpi/vci* **l2transport** (see highlighted lines 1 and 3).

After you have configured local switching between ATM interfaces, you can use the **show connection** command to verify that the connection is active, as demonstrated in Example 3-42.

Example 3-42 *Verifying Local Switching Between ATM Interfaces*

```
San.Jose.PE#show connection name Local.ATM.Sw
ID Name            Segment 1          Segment 2        State
=================================================================
1 Local.ATM.Sw    ATM1/0 1/00        ATM2/0 2/200     UP
San.Jose.PE#
```

As the highlighted line shows, a local switching connection named Local.ATM.Sw with connection ID 1 has been configured between a PVC with VPI/VCI 1/100 on interface ATM 1/0 and a PVC with VPI/VCI 2/200 on interface ATM 2/0. This connection is in an active (UP) state.

You can use the **show atm pvc** command to verify the individual PVCs. If you want to verify PVPs, you can use **show atm vp** command instead.

Local Switching Between Different Interfaces Types

Example 3-43 shows the configuration of local switching between ATM and Ethernet interfaces.

Local switching between ATM and Ethernet/Ethernet VLAN (802.1Q) interfaces requires an IWF on the router. This IWF can be either an Ethernet mode IWF or an IP mode IWF.

Example 3-43 *Configuration of Local Switching Between ATM and Ethernet Interfaces*

```
!
hostname San.Jose.PE
!
interface ATM1/0
 pvc 1/100 l2transport (line 1)
 encapsulation aal5snap (line 2)
 !
interface FastEthernet3/0
 !
connect Local.ATM.Eth.Sw ATM1/0 1/100 FastEthernet3/0 interworking ip (line 3)
 !
```

In highlighted line 1, the optional **pvc** *vpi/vci* **l2transport** command is used to configure a PVC with VPI/VCI 1/100 on interface ATM 1/0, and to specify that the PVC is switched.

In highlighted line 2, the **encapsulation [aal5snap | aal5mux]** command configures AAL5SNAP encapsulation.

The **connect** *connection-name interface vpi/vci interface* **interworking [ethernet | ip]** command is used to configure local switching between the specified ATM interface and PVC, and the specified Ethernet interface, using, in this example, IP mode interworking.

When you configure local switching between ATM and Ethernet interfaces, there are a few things to keep in mind.

If you do not manually configure a PVC using the **pvc** *vpi/vci* **l2transport** command, it is automatically created when you configure the **connect** command. However, the PVC is created with AAL5SNAP encapsulation.

You can use either Ethernet mode or IP mode interworking with ATM to Ethernet local switching (configured using the **connect** command). If you use Ethernet mode, you are restricted to using AAL5SNAP encapsulation on the ATM interface. If you use IP mode, however, you can choose either AAL5SNAP or AAL5MUX encapsulation on the ATM interface.

You can again verify local switching between ATM and Ethernet interfaces using the **show connection** command.

Before finishing this discussion of local switching between different interface types, it is worth pointing out one or two attachment-circuit-specific considerations:

- All the considerations for local switching between ATM and Ethernet interfaces are equally applicable to local switching between ATM and VLAN interfaces. In addition, it is worth noting that when VLAN frames are received on the Ethernet interface, the VLAN header is removed before the frames are forwarded.

- When you configure local switching between Frame Relay and ATM interfaces, the Discard Eligible (DE) bit setting in the Frame Relay frame header is not copied to the Cell Loss Priority (CLP) bit in the ATM cell header (and vice versa). Similarly, the Forward Explicit Congestion Notification (FECN) bit setting in the Frame Relay header is not copied to the Explicit Forward Congestion Indication (EFCI) bit in the ATM cell header (and vice versa).

Local Switching Between Circuits on the Same Interface

Local switching also allows the switching of frames, cells, or SDUs between circuits on the *same* physical interface as follows:

- Between Frame Relay PVCs on the same interface
- Between ATM PVCs or PVPs on the same interface

- Between Ethernet VLAN (802.1Q) subinterfaces associated with the same physical interface

Example 3-44 shows the configuration of local switching between Frame Relay PVCs on the same physical interface.

Example 3-44 *Configuration of Local Switching Between Frame Relay PVCs on the Same Physical Interface*

```
!
hostname Los.Angeles.PE
!
interface serial2/0
 encapsulation frame-relay
 frame-relay int-type nni
!
connect conn seria2/0 111 serial2/0 222
!
```

The first thing you will notice about the configuration in Example 3-44 is its simplicity. Apart from specifying Frame Relay encapsulation and interface type on the physical interface, the only other command that you need is **connect** *connection-name interface dlci interface dlci.*

Verification of local switching of circuits on the same physical interface can again be accomplished using the **show connection** or **show frame-relay pvc** commands.

Regardless of whether you are configuring local switching between the same or different physical interfaces or whether the interface/circuit types differ, you must keep in mind one or two final considerations:

- When configuring local switching, make sure that you configure identical MTU sizes on attachment circuit interfaces (if you do not, the circuits may come up, but traffic switching may fail).

  See the section "Resolving MTU Issues with L2VPN Interworking" on page 112 in Chapter 2 for more information on ensuring that MTU sizes are consistent on attachment circuits.

- Routing protocol configuration on CE routers might require careful consideration. See the section "Routing Protocol Considerations with L2VPN Interworking" on page 113 in Chapter 2.

Resolving AToM Data Channel Packet Drop Issues

Okay, so you have deployed your AToM pseudowires across your MPLS backbone network, and all seems well. Then you start to get complaints from customers about packet drops. This might be due to AToM data channel packet drops caused by an MTU size that is too small within the MPLS backbone network.

Figure 3-45 illustrates the dropping of AToM data channel packets within an MPLS
backbone network.

Figure 3-45 *AToM Data Channel Packet Drops Within an MPLS Backbone Network*

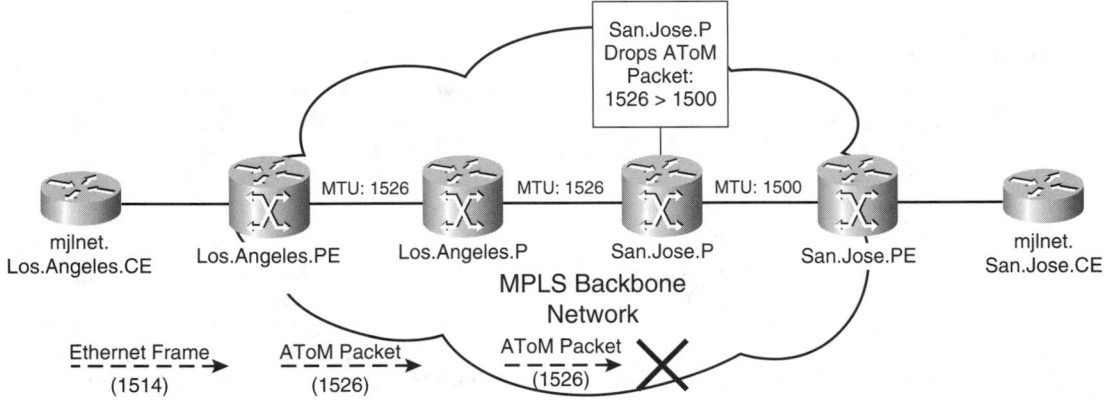

In Figure 3-45, Los.Angeles.PE receives a 1514-byte Ethernet frame (including a 14-byte
header) from mjlnet.Los.Angeles.CE. It encapsulates this frame in an AToM data channel
packet (see Figure 3-2 on page 139) and transmits the packet to Los.Angeles.P.

The size of the AToM data channel packet sent by Los.Angeles.PE to Los.Angeles.P is
1526 bytes, including the following:

- One tunnel label (4 bytes)
- PW (VC) label (4 bytes)
- (Optional) Control word (4 bytes)
- Encapsulated Ethernet frame (1514 bytes)

NOTE   Although the example in this section assumes one tunnel label, it is possible for more than
one tunnel label to be imposed on an AToM data channel packet.

If an LDP LSP (only) is used to transport AToM data channel packets across an MPLS
backbone between PE routers, there will be one tunnel label.

If there is an MPLS-TE tunnel between PE routers, and this is used to transport AToM data
channel packets, there will be one tunnel label.

If there is an MPLS-TE tunnel between P routers and the AToM pseudowire transits this tunnel,
there will be two tunnel labels (as AToM data channel packets cross the MPLS-TE tunnel).

If PE routers are in a back-to-back configuration, or are connected via a GRE tunnel (and
the AToM pseudowire transits the GRE tunnel), there will be no tunnel label—the egress
PE router will advertise an implicit-null label for the tunnel LSP (LDP is enabled on the
tunnel interface using the **mpls ip** command).

In Figure 3-45, Los.Angeles.PE is able to successfully transmit the AToM data channel packet to Los.Angeles.P because the packet is smaller than or, in this case, equal to that of Los.Angeles.PE's outgoing interface (AToM data channel packet size, 1526 bytes <= outgoing interface MTU, 1526 bytes).

Los.Angeles.P now transmits the packet over the link to San.Jose.P. Los.Angeles.P is able to successfully transmit the packet because the packet size is smaller than or equal to its outgoing interface MTU (AToM data channel packet size, 1526 bytes <= outgoing interface MTU, 1526 bytes).

San.Jose.P now pops the tunnel label (San.Jose.P is the penultimate hop), reducing the AToM data channel packet size to 1522 bytes.

Having popped the tunnel label, San.Jose.P now attempts to transmit the packet to San.Jose.PE, but fails. Hmm. What is going on here? San.Jose.P fails in its attempt to transmit the packet to San.Jose.PE because the packet size is greater than the outgoing interface MTU (AToM data channel packet size, 1522 bytes > outgoing interface MTU, 1500 bytes).

Working backward, you can work out that any customer Ethernet frame (received by Los.Angeles.PE or San.Jose.PE from mjlnet.Los.Angeles.CE or mjlnet.San.Jose.CE) that is larger than 1488 bytes will be dropped as it transits the MPLS backbone network (encapsulated in an AToM data channel packet) between PE routers. This is because the size of an AToM data channel packet encapsulating a 1489-byte Ethernet frame (*including a 14-byte header*) would be 1501 bytes:

- One tunnel label (4 bytes)
- PW (VC) label (4 bytes)
- (Optional) Control word (4 bytes)
- Encapsulated Ethernet frame (1489 bytes)

It is possible to identify and locate problems with small MTU sizes in an MPLS backbone network using commands such as **ping** and **ping mpls**.

Example 3-45 shows the output of a **ping** size sweep from a CE router.

Example 3-45 *Output of a Ping Size Sweep from a CE Router*

```
mjlnet.Los.Angeles.CE#ping
Protocol [ip]:
Target IP address: 192.168.1.2
Repeat count [5]: 50
Datagram size [100]:
Timeout in seconds [2]:
Extended commands [n]: y
Source address or interface:
Type of service [0]:
Set DF bit in IP header? [no]:
```

continues

Example 3-45 *Output of a Ping Size Sweep from a CE Router (Continued)*

```
Validate reply data? [no]:
Data pattern [0xABCD]:
Loose, Strict, Record, Timestamp, Verbose[none]:
Sweep range of sizes [n]: y
Sweep min size [36]: 1450
Sweep max size [18024]: 1500
Sweep interval [1]:
Type escape sequence to abort.
Sending 2550, [1450..1500]-byte ICMP Echos to 192.168.1.2, timeout is 2 seconds:
!!!!!!!!!!!!!!!!!!!!!!!!!!!!!!!!!!!!!!!!!!!!!..............
Success rate is 80 percent (60/75), round-trip min/avg/max = 1136/1151/1248 ms
mjlnet.Los.Angeles.CE#
```

As shown in Example 3-45, a ping size sweep (with packet sizes ranging from 1450 to 1500 bytes) reveals that although smaller packets successfully transit the AToM pseudowire across the MPLS backbone network, larger packets are dropped.

One way to track down the interface/link MTU that is causing packet drops is to use the **trace mpls** command. This command can display the Maximum Receive Unit (MRU—the maximum labeled packet size) at each hop across the MPLS backbone network.

You can also verify the MTU of a PE or P router (LSR) interface using the **show mpls interface** *interface* **detail** command, as demonstrated in Example 3-46.

Example 3-46 **show mpls interface** *interface* **detail** *Command Output on San.Jose.P*

```
San.Jose.P#show mpls interface serial 3/1 detail
Interface Serial3/1:
    IP labeling enabled (ldp)
    LSP Tunnel labeling not enabled
    BGP tagging not enabled
    Tagging operational
    Optimum Switching Vectors:
     IP to MPLS Turbo Vector
     MPLS Turbo Vector
    Fast Switching Vectors:
     IP to MPLS Fast Switching Vector
     MPLS Turbo Vector
    MTU = 1500
San.Jose.P#
```

You can see the MPLS MTU on interface serial 3/1 of San.Jose.P is 1500 bytes.

Now that you are sure of the location of the problem, you can modify the MPLS MTU using **mpls mtu** *bytes* command (see Example 3-47).

Example 3-47 *Modifying the MPLS MTU Using the* **mpls mtu** *Command*

```
San.Jose.P#conf t
Enter configuration commands, one per line. End with CNTL/Z.
San.Jose.P(config)#interface serial 3/1
San.Jose.P(config-if)#mpls mtu 1526
San.Jose.P(config-if)#end
San.Jose.P#
```

In the highlighted line in Example 3-47, the MPLS MTU on interface serial 3/1 is modified to 1526 bytes.

After the MPLS MTU has been modified, you can verify successful transport of larger packet sizes across the AToM pseudowire using again a ping sweep, as demonstrated in Example 3-48.

Example 3-48 *Output of a Ping Size Sweep from a CE Router After the MPLS MTU Has Been Modified*

```
mjlnet.Los.Angeles.CE#ping
Protocol [ip]:
Target IP address: 192.168.1.2
Repeat count [5]: 50
Datagram size [100]:
Timeout in seconds [2]:
Extended commands [n]: y
Source address or interface:
Type of service [0]:
Set DF bit in IP header? [no]:
Validate reply data? [no]:
Data pattern [0xABCD]:
Loose, Strict, Record, Timestamp, Verbose[none]:
Sweep range of sizes [n]: y (line 1)
Sweep min size [36]: 1450 (line 2)
Sweep max size [18024]: 1500 (line 3)
Sweep interval [1]:
Type escape sequence to abort.
Sending 2550, [1450..1500]-byte ICMP Echos to 192.168.1.2, timeout is 2 seconds:
!!!!!!!!!!!!!!!!!!!!!!!!!!!!!!!!!!!!!!!!!!!!!!!!!!!!!!!!!!!
Success rate is 100 percent (50/50), round-trip min/avg/max = 1136/1151/1248 ms
mjlnet.Los.Angeles.CE#
```

In highlighted line 3, you can see that larger packets now transit the MPLS backbone network (up to 1500 bytes).

When you are deploying AToM pseudowires, it is a good idea to calculate the maximum possible AToM data channel packet sizes for all pseudowires that you plan to deploy. After you have worked out the maximum possible packet size, you should (if necessary) modify the MPLS MTU on *all* interfaces within the MPLS backbone network to accommodate this packet size.

Summary

As discussed in this chapter, AToM pseudowires can be used to transport Layer 2 protocols such as Ethernet, Ethernet 802.1Q, HDLC, PPP, X.25, Frame Relay, and ATM (cell relay and AAL5) over an MPLS backbone network.

AToM-based L2VPNs share many of the advantages of L2TPv3-based L2VPNs—they enable the consolidation of service provider infrastructure and provide concomitant cost savings; they allow service providers to deploy Ethernet services over an MPLS backbone; they allow enterprises to maintain complete control of routing; and they permit the transport of non-IP protocols.

In this chapter, you learned basic AToM pseudowire configuration, as well as advanced features such as tunnel selection, L2VPN interworking, pseudowire switching, and QoS.

Advanced features allow service providers to implement AToM more optimally, more flexibly, and more scalably. Tunnel selection allows AToM pseudowires to transit MPLS-TE tunnels between PE routers. With L2VPN interworking, AToM-based L2VPNs can connect customer sites with disparate attachment circuit types. Service providers can deploy scalable inter-autonomous system AToM pseudowire transport using pseudowire switching.

Review Questions

1 Which protocol is used for AToM pseudowire control channel signaling?

2 What are the three steps of AToM pseudowire setup between peer PE routers (assuming an LDP session has not yet been established between PE routers)?

3 An AToM data channel packet typically consists of which elements?

4 Can TDP be used to signal the tunnel LSP? Can TDP be used to signal AToM PW/VC labels?

5 If an AToM HDLC pseudowire is used to transport Frame Relay (Frame Relay port mode), in what way do PE routers participate in LMI?

6 How can Layer 2 traffic to be forwarded between attachment circuits on the same PE router?

7 What is one method of configuring RVSP-TE signaled tunnel LSPs to transport AToM pseudowires between PE routers?

8 When transporting ATM cells over an AToM cell relay pseudowire, how is it possible to transport more than one ATM cell per AToM data channel packet?

9 How is it possible to connect dissimilar attachment circuit types over AToM pseudowires?

10 What are the two modes of L2VPN interworking?

CHAPTER 4

Designing MPLS Layer 3 Site-to-Site VPNs

Multiprotocol Label Switching (MPLS) Layer 3 VPNs are (predominantly) service-provider-provisioned VPNs that offer advantages such as any-to-any connectivity, support for real-time applications such as voice and video, and WAN routing simplicity for customers.

You can provision MPLS Layer 3 VPNs over an MPLS backbone network or an IP backbone network (using GRE, L2TPv3, or other tunneling technologies). Unless otherwise specified, this chapter assumes that they are provisioned over an MPLS backbone.

NOTE   MPLS Layer 3 VPNs are described in RFC 4364. They were formerly described in Internet Draft draft-ietf-l3vpn-rfc2547bis (RFC2547bis).

Figure 4-1 illustrates an MPLS backbone with two customer VPNs.

Figure 4-1   *Simple MPLS Layer 3 VPNs*

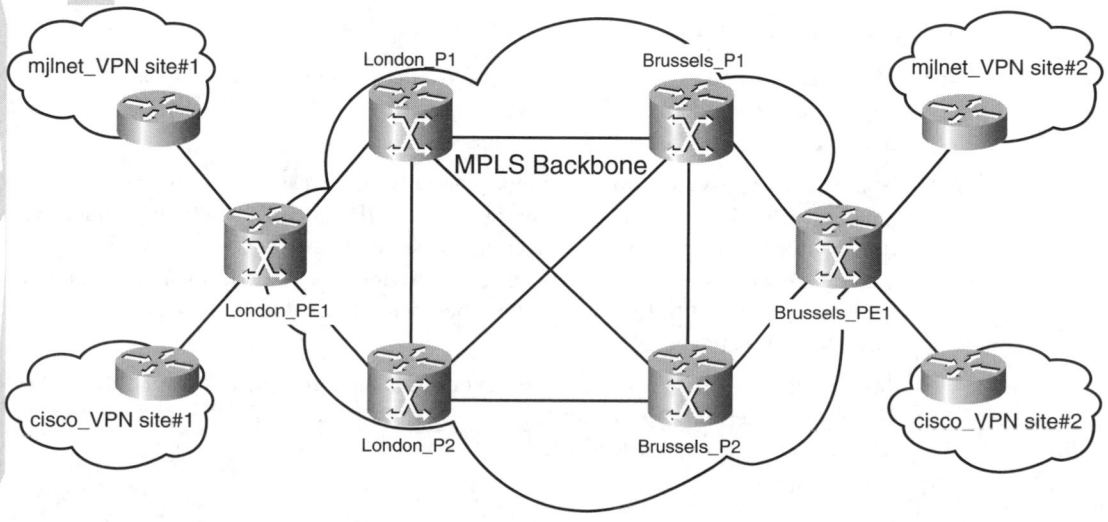

Figure 4-1 shows an MPLS backbone network and two customer VPNs:

- mjlnet_VPN
- cisco_VPN

Each customer VPN has two sites.

Advantages and Disadvantages of MPLS Layer 3 VPNs

As previously mentioned, MPLS Layer 3 VPNs have a number of significant advantages for service providers and enterprises alike. These advantages include the following:

- MPLS Layer 3 VPNs offer an extremely scalable VPN architecture that can scale to thousands of customer sites and VPNs.
- MPLS Layer 3 VPNs can be offered as a managed service by a service provider to enterprise customers, or implemented by enterprises themselves to provide clear partition between business units or services.
- MPLS Layer 3 VPNs allow an enterprise to simplify their WAN routing. Customer Edge (CE) routers need only peer with one or more Provider Edge (PE) routers (as well as Customer [C] routers) rather than with all the other CE routers in the VPN.
- MPLS Layer 3 VPNs allow any-to-any connectivity for enterprise customer sites, and can be configured to support quality of service (QoS) for real-time and business applications.
- MPLS traffic engineering (an associated technology) allows service providers to optimally utilize network bandwidth, and support tight service-level agreements (SLA) with fast failover (fast reroute) and guaranteed bandwidth.

Disadvantages of MPLS Layer 3 VPNs include the following:

- MPLS Layer 3 VPNs natively support IP traffic transport only. If customers want to support other protocols such as IPX, Generic Routing Encapsulation (GRE) tunnels must be configured between CE routers.
- Some service providers do not support native IP multicast traffic transport between sites in MPLS Layer 3 VPNs (native support for IP multicast can be implemented using Multicast VPNs [MVPN, covered in Chapter 5, "Advanced MPLS Layer 3 VPN Deployment Considerations"]). If a service provider does not offer native IP multicast transport, multicast traffic must be tunneled between customer sites by configuring GRE tunnels between CE routers.
- In an MPLS Layer 3 VPN, the customer does not have complete control of their WAN IP routing. CE routers at the customer VPN sites do not establish direct routing adjacencies, but must instead peer with PE routers.

- MPLS Layer 3 VPNs are trusted VPNs, and although they offer similar traffic segregation and security to that offered by Frame Relay and ATM, they do not natively (by default) offer the strong authentication and encryption of secure VPNs such as IPsec. If encryption and authentication are required, however, it is possible to protect VPN traffic in transit between PE routers using either IPsec (see Internet Draft draft-ietf-l3vpn-ipsec-2547) or end-to-end between CE devices.

Now that you understand the main advantages and disadvantages of MPLS Layer 3 VPNs, it is time to move on to a discussion of their operation.

MPLS Layer 3 VPNs Overview

As discussed in Chapter 1, "What Is a Virtual Private Network?" VPNs are often classified as one of the following types:

- **Overlay VPNs**—Customers and service providers do not exchange routing information. Instead, tunnels or circuits overlay the service provider network between CE devices

- **Peer VPNs**—Customer and service providers do exchange routing information.

IP Reachability in an MPLS Layer 3 VPN

MPLS Layer 3 VPNs conform to the peer model, but unlike other implementations of the peer model, routing and forwarding information for different customers is kept in entirely separate routing and forwarding tables called *VPN routing and forwarding tables* (VRF). Figure 4-2 illustrates the VRFs used to separate customer routing and forwarding information.

Figure 4-2 *VRFs Separate Customer Routing and Forwarding Information*

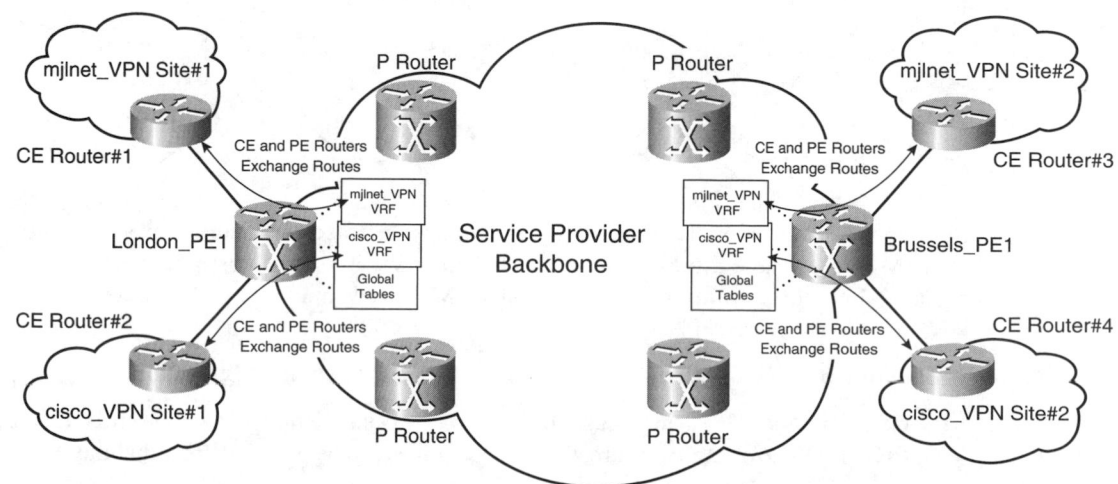

As you can see in Figure 4-2, there are two customers (VPNs), mjlnet_VPN and cisco_VPN. CE routers at mjlnet_VPN and cisco_VPN sites connect to PE routers London_PE1 and Brussels_PE1. PE routers London_PE1 and Brussels_PE1 exchange routing information with the CE routers (assuming that static routes are not used) and maintain routing and forwarding information relating to mjlnet_VPN and cisco_VPN in separate VRFs. PE routers also maintain global routing and forwarding tables, which contain routes to other PE and Provider (P) routers, as well as any Internet routes. P routers are connected only to PE routers and other P routers, not to customer sites.

Note that in an MPLS Layer 3 VPN, CE routers do not peer with each other and directly exchange routing information as they would when, for example, directly connected to each other via PVCs in a Frame Relay overlay VPN.

So, PE and CE routers are routing peers, and PE routers maintain customer VPN routing and forwarding information in VRFs. But, how is customer VPN routing information exchanged across the service provider backbone between PE routers? The answer is that the PE routers exchange customer VPN routes (and associated VPN labels [more on this later]) with each other using Multiprotocol Extensions to BGP (MP-BGP, RFC2858/draft-ietf-idr-rfc2858bis), as illustrated in Figure 4-3.

Figure 4-3   *PE Routers Exchange Customer VPN Routes and Associated VPN Labels Using MP-BGP*

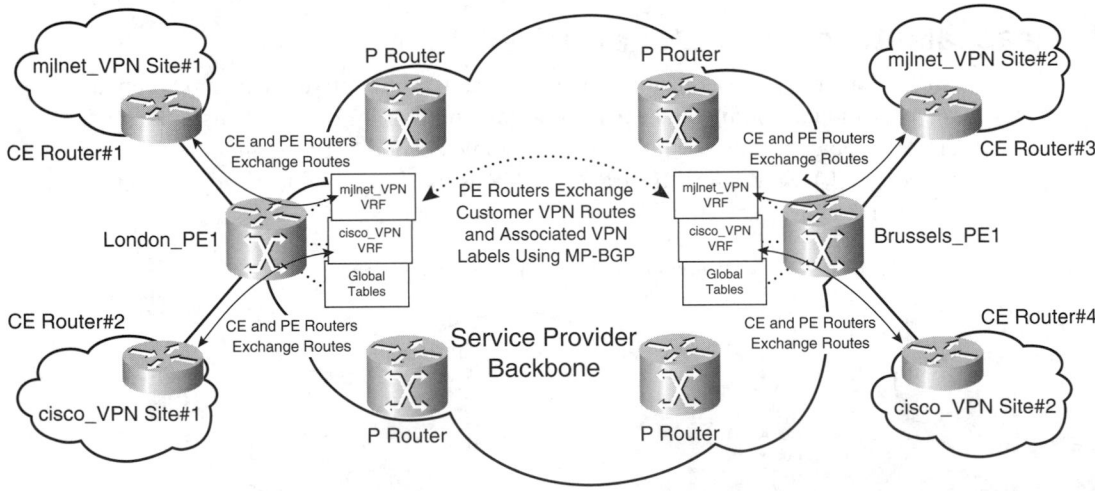

In Figure 4-3, PE routers London_PE1 and Brussels_PE1 exchange customer VPN routes using MP-BGP. These routes are then inserted into the appropriate customer VRF: mjlnet_VPN routes are inserted into the mjlnet_VPN VRF, and cisco_VPN routes are inserted into the cisco_VPN VRF.

The routing paradigm used in MPLS Layer 3 VPNs can be summarized as follows:

- CE and PE routers exchange customer VPN routes using routing protocols such as RIPv2, EIGRP, OSPF, or eBGP. Alternatively, static routes can be used for IP reachability.

- PE routers exchange customer VPN routes (and associated VPN labels) using MP-BGP. Note that route reflectors are often used in larger deployments. See Figure 3-37 in Chapter 3, "Designing and Implementing AToM-Based Layer 2 VPNs," for the exact format of the MPLS label (MPLS shim header).

- Different customer VPN routes are stored in separate VRFs.

So, for example, in Figure 4-3, the CE router at mjlnet_VPN site 1 sends local site routes to its attached PE router, London_PE1, using RIPv2, EIGRP, OSPF, or EBGP. These routes are inserted into the mjlnet_VPN VRF.

London_PE1 then advertises the mjlnet_VPN site 1 routes (and associated VPN labels) to Brussels_PE1 using MP-BGP. Brussels_PE1 inserts these routes into its mjlnet_VPN VRF.

Finally, Brussels_PE1 sends the mjlnet_VPN site 1 routes to the CE router at the mjlnet_VPN site 2 using the CE-PE routing protocol. The CE router at mjlnet_VPN site 2 now has IP reachability to the mjlnet_VPN site 1. IP reachability from mjlnet_VPN site 1 to mjlnet_VPN site 2 is accomplished in a similar fashion.

The CE router at mjlnet_VPN site 2 sends mjlnet_VPN site 2 routes to its attached PE router, Brussels_PE1. Brussels_PE1 inserts these routes into the mjlnet_VPN VRF. Brussels_PE1 now advertises the mjlnet_VPN site 2 routes (along with associated VPN labels) to London_PE1 using MP-BGP. London_PE1 inserts these routes into its mjlnet_VPN VRF.

Finally, London_PE1 sends the mjlnet_VPN site 2 routes to the CE router at mjlnet_VPN site 1 using the PE-CE routing protocol. The CE router at mjlnet_VPN site 2 now has IP reachability to mjlnet_VPN site 2.

Routes for the cisco_VPN are similarly advertised between CE routers across the service provider backbone: cisco_VPN CE routers sends routes to attached PE routers, and PE routers insert these routes into the cisco_VPN VRF; PE routers advertise cisco_VPN routes to each other using MP-BGP, and these routes are inserted into the cisco_VPN VRF; PE routers send routes to the remote cisco_VPN site to their attached cisco_VPN CE router using the PE-CE routing protocol.

So, that is route exchange and IP reachability, but what about user packet forwarding?

User Packet Forwarding Between MPLS Layer 3 VPN Sites

When a PE router receives a user packet from an attached CE router, it examines the destination address in the packet's IP header. The PE router will find a longest-match route in the customer VRF corresponding to the interface on which the user packet was received.

The VPN label associated with the route in the VRF will then be prepended to the user packet, and the packet will then be further encapsulated with another MPLS label (in a service provider backbone where MPLS is enabled), IP or GRE, L2TPv3, or IP/IPsec, and then forwarded across the backbone to the PE router that is attached to the VPN site to which the user packet is destined. This chapter assumes that the service provider backbone is MPLS enabled.

Figure 4-4 illustrates user packet forwarding between MPLS Layer 3 VPN sites.

Figure 4-4 *User Packet Forwarding Between MPLS Layer 3 Sites*

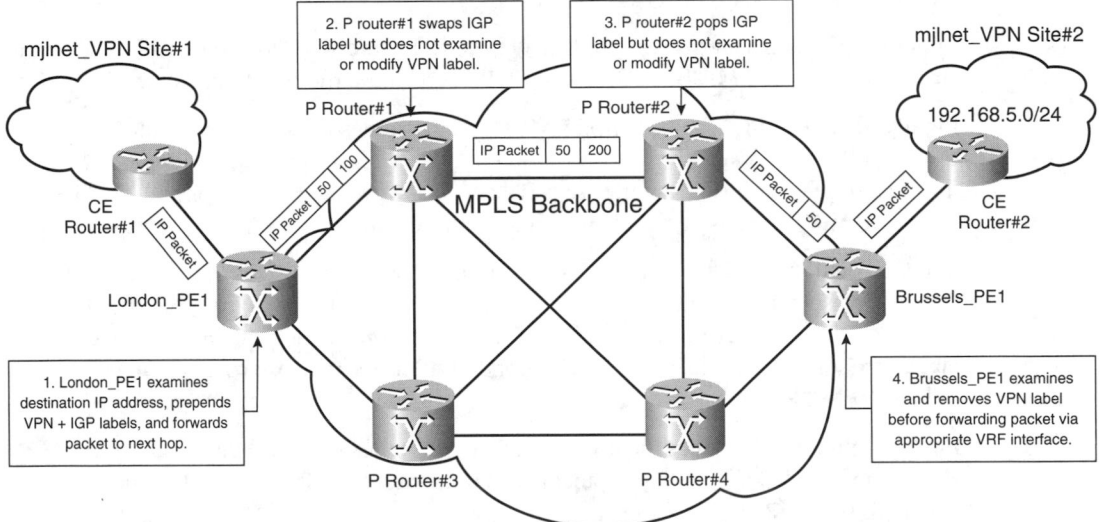

In Figure 4-4, a user packet is sent from mjlnet_VPN site 1 to network 192.168.5.0/24 at mjlnet_VPN site 2. When the user packet arrives at London_PE1 from CE Router #1, the PE router examines the destination IP address, finds the longest match in its mjlnet_VPN VRF (a VPN route to 192.168.5.0/24), and prepends the VPN label corresponding to the route 192.168.5.0/24 to the user packet. In this example, the VPN label has a value of 50.

It is important to reiterate where the VPN route and label came from. If you refer back to Figure 4-3, you can see that the PE routers exchange customer VPN routes and associated VPN labels. In this case, Brussels_PE1 has advertised a VPN route to 192.168.5.0/24 with VPN label 50 (a label value selected by Brussels_PE1) to London_PE1. The VPN label indicates the VRF or outgoing VRF interface on Brussels_PE1.

So, the user packet has arrived at London_PE1, London_PE1 has examined the destination IP address, found the longest-matching VPN route in the appropriate VRF (192.168.5.0/24 in mjlnet_VPN VRF in this example), and prepended the VPN label corresponding to this route (label 50 in this example).

The PE router must now encapsulate the packet with an additional MPLS label (if the service provider backbone is MPLS enabled), IP or GRE, L2TPv3, or IP/IPsec. In this example, the service provider backbone is MPLS enabled, and so London_PE1 prepends an additional MPLS label. The purpose of this additional (IGP) MPLS label or encapsulation is to ensure that the user packet can get from London_PE1 to Brussels_PE1. Remember that the already-prepended VPN label indicates the VRF or outgoing VRF interface on Brussels_PE1, but none of the P routers between PE routers London_PE1 and Brussels_PE1 has any knowledge of VPN labels. The IGP label, on the other hand, corresponds to a Label Switched Path (LSP) between PE routers London_PE1 and Brussels_PE1. In this case, the Label Distribution Protocol (LDP) is being used to signal IGP labels, and so the IGP label corresponds to the IGP route to Brussels_PE1 and in this example has a value of 100. This IGP label (100) is prepended to the user packet in addition to the VPN label (50).

NOTE   PE and P routers can signal (advertise) IGP labels to each other using the LDP, the Tag Distribution Protocol (TDP), or the Resource Reservation Protocol (RSVP). LDP- and TDP-signaled IGP labels correspond to IGP routes, and RSVP-signaled IGP labels correspond to traffic-engineered tunnels through the MPLS backbone network.

TDP is a legacy (Cisco proprietary) protocol, and its use is now deprecated in favor of LDP.

London_PE1 now forwards the labeled user packet to P Router #1. P Router #1 swaps IGP label 100 for IGP label 200 (which also corresponds to an IGP route to Brussels_PE1) and forwards the labeled packet to P Router #2. Note that P Router #1 does not examine or modify the VPN label (50).

P Router #2, being the penultimate hop in the LSP to Brussels_PE1, pops (removes) the IGP label (200) and forwards the labeled user packet to Brussels_PE1. At this stage, the label stack consists only of the VPN label (50).

Brussels_PE1 receives the labeled packet, pops the label stack (consisting of the VPN label), and based on the VPN label, either looks in the appropriate VRF for a route (in this case, mjlnet_VPN VRF) or just forwards the unlabeled user packet out of the VRF interface. The CE router at mjlnet_VPN site 2 now receives the unlabeled user packet and forwards it according to the regular IP routing paradigm.

A Detailed Examination of MPLS Layer 3 VPNs

The preceding section contained an overview of how routing and user packet forwarding work in an MPLS VPN, but now it is time to take a closer look at how each of these elements function.

Distinguishing Customer VPN Prefixes Using Route Distinguishers (RD)

As shown in Figure 4-3, PE routers advertise customer VPN routes and associated VPN labels to each other using MP-BGP. This seems simple enough, but what happens if two customers are using the same IP address space? Specifically, how can the PE routers distinguish between, say, network prefix 10.2.0.0/16 in mjlnet_VPN and network prefix 10.2.0.0/16 in cisco_VPN?

The issue of distinguishing between identical network prefixes in different customer VPNs is resolved by prepending an 8-byte *Route Distinguisher* (RD) to each route. An RD is simply a unique number that allows PE routers to distinguish between multiple otherwise identical network prefixes. By prepending an RD to an IPv4 network prefix, an entity called a *VPN-IPv4* (VPNv4) network prefix is created.

NOTE   A particular route can have only a single RD.

An RD is specified in three fields, as follows:

> Type field (2 bytes) + Administrator field + Assigned Number field

The length and semantics of the Administrator and Assigned Number fields are determined by the value contained in the Type field. If the Type field contains a value of 0, the Administrator field is 2 bytes long and carries an autonomous system number (ASN), and the Assigned Number field is a unique 4-byte value specified by the service provider:

> Type (0) + Administrator (2-byte ASN) + Assigned Number (unique 4-byte value)

If the Type field contains a value of 1, the Administrator is 4 bytes long and contains an IP address, and the Assigned Number field contains a unique 2-byte value specified by the service provider:

> Type (1) + Administrator (4-byte IP address) + Assigned Number (unique 2-byte value)

Finally, if the Type field contains a value of 2, the Administrator field is 4 bytes long and contains an ASN, and the Assigned Number field is 2 bytes long and contains a unique number assigned by the service provider:

> Type (2) + Administrator (4-byte ASN) + Assigned Number (unique 2-byte value)

Figure 4-5 illustrates the use of RDs to distinguish otherwise identical network prefixes.

Figure 4-5   *Use of RDs to Distinguish Otherwise Identical Network Prefixes*

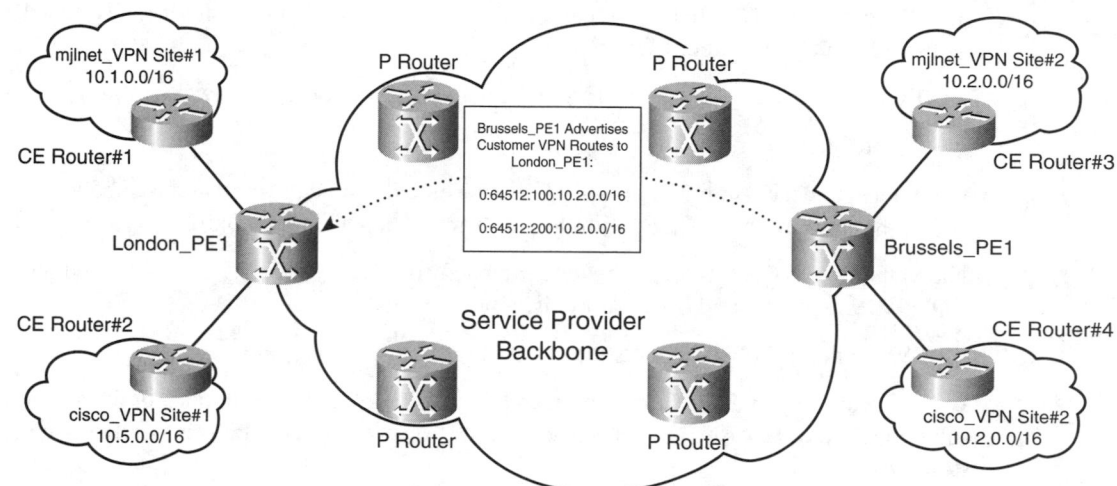

If you look closely at Figure 4-5, you can see that there are two VPNs: mjlnet_VPN and cisco_VPN. An overlap exists in IP address space in these two VPNs, with network prefix 10.2.0.0/16 being used at both mjlnet_VPN site 2 and cisco_VPN site 2.

Brussels_PE1 advertises the mjlnet_VPN site 2 prefix 10.2.0.0/16 and cisco_VPN site 2 prefix 10.2.0.0/16 as VPN-IPv4 addresses (each prefix has an RD prepended to it).

In this example, the RD 0:64512:100 (Type [0] + Administrator [ASN 64512] + Assigned Number [100]) is prepended to the mjlnet_VPN IPv4 prefix 10.2.0.0/16, giving the address 0:64512:100:10.2.0.0/16. The RD 0:64512:200 (Type [0] + Administrator [ASN 64512] + Assigned Number [200]) is prepended to the cisco_VPN IPv4 prefix 10.2.0.0/16, giving the VPN-IPv4 address 0:64512:200:10.2.0.0/16.

When London_PE1 receives the two VPN-IPv4 addresses, it does not consider the two as comparable addresses because the RDs differ (0:64512:100 versus 0:64512:200).

It is worth emphasizing at this point that an RD gives no indication as to the origin of a particular network prefix or the VRFs into which a prefix should be installed, but instead simply serves to identify separate network prefixes that would otherwise appear to be identical.

Using Route Targets (RT) to Control Customer VPN Route Distribution

So, PE routers use RDs to distinguish otherwise identical network prefixes. But how exactly are customer VPN routes advertised in BGP installed into the correct VRF(s) on the PE router that receives these routes? Customer routes received from other PE routers are installed into the correct VRF(s) based on a BGP extended community attribute called a *Route Target* (RT). One or more RTs are attached to a customer VPN-IPv4 route before it is advertised by one PE router to another PE router.

The BGP extended community is 8 bytes long and its format is as follows:

Type field + Value field

When the extended community is an RT, the Type field is 2 octets long and is subdivided into high- and low-order octets, with the low octet having a value of 0x02.

The Value field is 6 octets long when the extended community is an RT and is divided into Global Administrator and Local Administrator subfields:

Value field: Global Administrator + Local Administrator

When the high-order Type field octet in an RT is 0x00 or 0x02, the Global Administrator subfield contains an ASN, and the Local Administrator subfield contains a locally defined value.

When the high-order Type field octet is 0x01, the Global Administrator subfield contains an IP address, and the Local Administrator subfield contains a locally defined value.

Figure 4-6 illustrates the installation of customer VPN routes into VRFs based on RTs.

Figure 4-6   *Installation of Customer VPN Routes into VRFs Based on RTs*

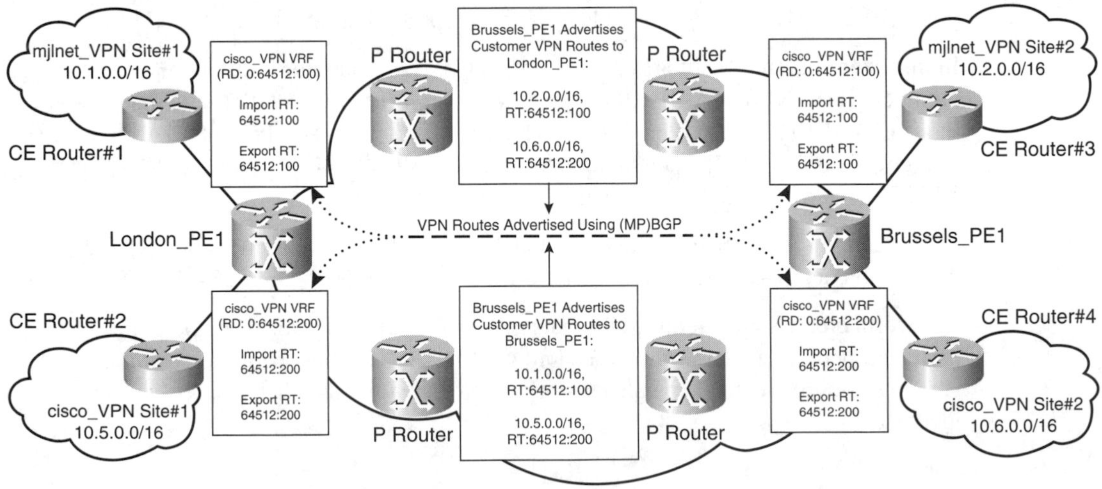

As Figure 4-6 shows, London_PE1 advertises VPN-IPv4 routes 10.1.0.0/16 with *export* RT 64512:100 and 10.5.0.0/16 with export RT 64512:200 to Brussels_PE1. Export RTs are RTs that are attached to routes before those routes are advertised by one PE router to other PE routers. The RTs in this example are in the format *ASN:xx* (Global Administrator:Local Administrator).

When Brussels_PE1 receives the VPN-IPv4 routes from London_PE1, it examines the RT(s) attached to each route, and as long as *one* attached RT matches an RT associated with a VRF, it installs that route into the VRF. The RT associated with a VRF for the purposes of VPN-IPv4 route installation is called an *import RT*.

So, because route 10.1.0.0/16 has RT 64512:100 attached to it, and import RT 64512:100 is associated with the mjlnet_VPN VRF on Brussels_PE1, route 10.1.0.0/16 is installed into that VRF. Route 10.1.0.0/16 is not, however, installed into the cisco_VPN VRF because the RT attached to the route (64512:100) is not an import RT associated with the cisco_VPN VRF.

Similarly, because route 10.1.0.0/16 has RT 64512:200 attached, it is installed into the cisco_VPN VRF. This is because the cisco_VPN VRF has import RT 64512:200 associated with it. This route is not installed into the mjlnet_VPN VRF, however, because the mjlnet_VPN VRF does not have RT 64512:200 associated with it.

Brussels_PE1 advertises VPN-IPv4 routes 10.2.0.0/16 with RT 64512:100 and 10.6.0.0/16 with RT 64512:200 to London_PE1.

Route 10.2.0.0/16 is installed into mjlnet_VPN VRF on London_PE1 because the RT attached to it (64512:100) is the same as the import RT associated with the mjlnet_VPN VRF. Route 10.6.0.0/16 is installed into the cisco_VPN VRF on London_PE1 because the RT attached to it (64512:200) is the same as the import RT associated with the cisco_VPN VRF on London_PE1.

You might have noticed that the RTs (64512:100 and 64512:200) in Figure 4-6 bear a striking resemblance to the RDs used in Figure 4-5 (0:64512:100 and 0:64512:200). It is quite common to configure the RDs and RTs associated with a particular set of VRFs to be the same in a full-mesh VPN (with any-to-any connectivity) for the sake of consistency. But, be sure to remember that there is no requirement that they be the same, and that, depending on the topology of a particular VPN, they may well differ (more on this later).

Deploying MPLS Layer 3 VPNs

Now that you understand the theory underlying MPLS Layer 3 VPNs, it is time to take a look at configuration. Figure 4-7 shows a sample network used to illustrate concepts and configuration discussed in this section.

The configuration of MPLS Layer 3 VPNs consists of three elements:

- The configuration of CE routers
- The configuration of PE routers
- The configuration of P routers

Figure 4-7 *Sample Network*

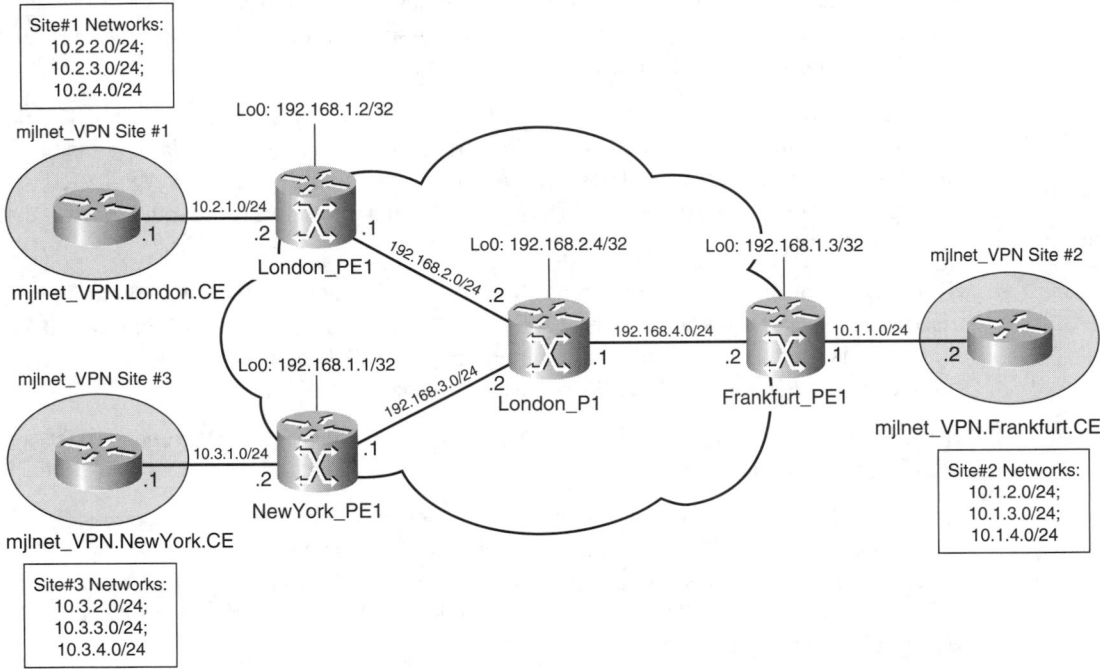

No special configuration is required for CE routers—you only need to configure either a dynamic routing protocol or static routes for reachability to other sites in the VPN. If you choose to configure a dynamic routing protocol, you must configure one of those currently supported on PE routers:

- RIP (Version 2)
- EIGRP
- OSPF
- eBGP

If you configure RIPv2, EIGRP, or OSPF, you must also be enable that protocol on the interface connected to the local PE router. If you configure eBGP, then you should configure the local PE router as an eBGP neighbor on the CE router.

Configuration of PE Routers

A number of steps are associated with the configuration of PE routers:

Step 1 Configure a loopback interface for use as the PE router's BGP router ID (and update source)/LDP router ID.

Step 2 Configure the LDP.

Step 3   Enable MPLS on interfaces connected to other PE or P routers.

Step 4   Configure the backbone network IGP (if not already configured).

Step 5   Configure MP-BGP for VPN-IPv4 route exchange with other PE routers or route reflectors.

Step 6   Configure the customer VRFs.

Step 7   Configure the customer VRF interfaces.

Step 8   Configure the customer VRF routing protocols or static routes.

Step 9   Redistribute the CE-PE routing protocol or static VRF routes into MP-BGP.

Step 1: Configure a Loopback Interface for Use as the PE Router's BGP Router ID/LDP Router ID

The first step when configuring an MPLS Layer 3 VPN PE router is to configure a loopback interface for use as the BGP router ID/update source and LDP router ID. Example 4-1 shows this configuration.

Example 4-1   *Configure a Loopback Interface for Use as the PE Router's BGP Router ID/LDP Router ID*

```
interface Loopback0
 ip address 192.168.1.2 255.255.255.255
```

It is important to ensure that the IP address mask is 32 bits long; failure to do so can, in certain circumstances, result in LSP failure (and traffic black-holing) across the MPLS backbone network.

Step 2: Configure LDP

Next you should configure LDP as the MPLS backbone label distribution protocol. The MPLS backbone label distribution protocol could actually be LDP, TDP, or RSVP. LDP is assumed throughout this chapter unless otherwise specified.

NOTE   For more information about the configuration of RSVP as the MPLS backbone label distribution protocol (with MPLS traffic engineering), see the following website:

http://www.cisco.com/en/US/products/sw/iosswrel/ps1829/
products_feature_guide09186a00800e955c.html

If you want to forward MPLS VPN traffic over MPLS traffic-engineering tunnels between P routers, you must enable LDP on the MPLS traffic-engineering tunnel interfaces using the **mpls ip** command.

Example 4-2 shows the configuration as LDP as the MPLS backbone network label distribution protocol.

Example 4-2 *Configure LDP*

```
mpls label protocol ldp
mpls ldp router-id Loopback0 force
```

In Example 4-2, LDP is configured as the label distribution protocol using the **mpls label protocol ldp** command. Interface loopback 0 (configured in Step 1) is then specified as the LDP router ID using the **mpls ldp router-id** *interface* [**force**] command. The **force** keyword ensures that the interface specified and no other interface becomes the LDP router ID.

To forward VPN packets over the MPLS backbone network, it is only necessary to advertise label bindings for PE routers' loopback interfaces addresses (their BGP update sources— these are the IGP labels used to forward packets between PE routers).

NOTE   If you have a large number of network prefixes in your MPLS backbone network, the advertisement of label bindings corresponding to these prefixes and the installation of the label bindings into the loopback interface (LFIB) will take time, and will affect LDP convergence after a failure. This can be a good reason to advertise only label bindings corresponding to PE routers' loopback interface addresses (BGP update sources).

If you choose to only advertise label bindings for PE routers' loopback interfaces, you can do so by using the configuration shown in Example 4-3.

Example 4-3 *Advertising Only Label Bindings for the PE Routers Loopback Interface (BGP Update Sources)*

```
no mpls ldp advertise-labels
mpls ldp advertise-labels for 10
access-list 10 permit 192.168.1.0 0.0.0.255
```

The **no mpls ldp advertise-labels** command in Example 4-3 enables you to disable the advertisement of LDP label bindings.

The advertisement of LDP bindings corresponding to prefixes specified in standard access list 10 is then enabled using the **mpls ldp advertise-labels for** *access-list* command.

In this example, **access-list 10** specifies only the IP addresses configured on the loopback interfaces of PE routers.

Step 3: Enable MPLS on Interfaces Connected to Other PE or P Routers

If you intend to transport MPLS VPN traffic over the backbone network between PE routers using MPLS LSPs (rather than IP/GRE, L2TPv3, or IPsec tunnels), you must enable MPLS on interface connected to other PE or P routers.

Example 4-4 shows the configuration of MPLS on a core interface connected to a PE or P router.

Example 4-4 *Enabling MPLS on Interfaces Connected to Other PE or P Routers*

```
interface Serial2/0
 mpls ip
```

The **mpls ip** command shown in Example 4-4 enables MPLS on the interface (in this case, interface serial 1/0).

Be sure to enable MPLS on all core network interfaces; otherwise, MPLS will not function on that interface.

NOTE   You should not enable MPLS on VRF interfaces unless you are configuring an MPLS VPN carriers' carrier architecture.

Step 4: Configure the Backbone Network IGP

Although you can use any IGP to advertise networks within the MPLS VPN backbone network, the two practical choices are Open Shortest Path First (OSPF) and Intermediate System-to-Intermediate System (IS-IS) because these two IGPs are the only two that currently support MPLS traffic engineering (MPLS-TE).

Configuring OSPF as the Backbone Network IGP

Example 4-5 shows a sample configuration for OSPF on the PE router.

Example 4-5 *Sample Configuration for OSPF as the MPLS VPN Backbone IGP*

```
router ospf 1
passive interface loopback0
network 192.168.1.1 0.0.0.0 area 0
network 192.168.2.0 0.0.0.255 area 0
```

The **router ospf** *process-id* command is used to enable OSPF.

The **network 192.168.2.1 0.0.0.0 area 0** command is used to enable OSPF on a core interface (connected to a P router) and to place this interface in OSPF area 0.

The **network 192.168.1.1 0.0.0.0 area 0** command is used to enable OSPF on interface loopback0 and to place the interface in OSPF area 0. This interface was configured in Step 1 and is the BGP update source and LDP router ID on this PE router.

It is important that you advertise the loopback interface in the backbone IGP; otherwise, this PE router cannot establish a BGP neighbor relationship with other PE routers (or route reflectors) and exchange VPN-IPv4 routes (using MP-BGP). In addition, if the LDP router ID is not advertised in the IGP, this PE router cannot establish LDP sessions with other PE and P routers and cannot exchange label bindings. If label bindings are not exchanged, LSPs will not be established between this PE router and other PE routers, and MPLS VPN traffic will not be transported over the MPLS VPN backbone.

The **passive-interface loopback0** command ensures that no OSPF packets are sent on interface loopback 0. It is not necessary to send OSPF packets because no neighbor relationships will be established on this interface.

Configuring IS-IS as the Backbone Network IGP

The other common option for an MPLS VPN backbone IGP is IS-IS. Example 4-6 shows a sample configuration.

Example 4-6   *Sample Configuration for IS-IS as the MPLS VPN Backbone IGP*

```
router isis
passive-interface Loopback0
 net 49.1234.0000.0000.0001.00
 is-type level-2-only
 metric-style wide
 !
interface serial2/0
 ip router isis
 !
```

The **router isis** command in Example 4-6 is used to enable IS-IS on the PE router. Next, the **passive-interface Loopback0** command enables IS-IS on the loopback interface and ensures that no IS-IS packets are sent on this interface. Following the **passive-interface** command is **net** *network-entity-title*. This command is used to specify the PE router's network entity title (a Network Service Access Point [NSAP]), consisting of an area ID, a system ID, and a selector.

In Example 4-6, the area ID is 49.1234, the system ID is 0000.0000.0001, and the selector is .00. Note that the system ID must be unique through the IS-IS areas and backbone, and the selector value must be .00.

The next command shown is **is-type level-2-only**. This command configures this PE router as a level 2 intermediate system (router) only. This command is optional, depending on the type of routing you want your PE router to perform.

The next command (**metric-style wide**) is again optional and is used to specify wide style metrics (24- or 32-bit metrics) for IS-IS on this router. Wide-style metrics are essential if you have any plans to deploy MPLS-TE in your network. If you do configure wide-style metrics using this command, make sure that all routers are configured to support wide-style metrics.

Finally, the **ip router isis** command is configured on core interfaces (serial 2/0 in this example). This command enables IS-IS routing for IP on the interface.

Now that you know how to configure OSPF and IS-IS on a PE router, you are probably wondering which is better. Unfortunately, there is no easy answer to this question—both work well in an MPLS VPN backbone, and both, as previously mentioned, support MPLS-TE. If you want to read a comparison of these two routing protocols to more fully inform your choice, you can find one at the following website:

http://www.nanog.org/mtg-0006/katz.html

Step 5: Configure MP-BGP for VPNv4 Route Exchange with Other PE Routers or Route Reflectors

The next step is the configuration of MP-BGP for VPNv4 route exchange with other PE routers or route reflectors. Example 4-7 shows the configuration of MP-BGP for VPNv4 route exchange.

Example 4-7 *Configuring MP-BGP for VPNv4 Route Exchange*

```
router bgp 65535
 no synchronization
 neighbor 192.168.1.1 remote-as 65535
 neighbor 192.168.1.1 update-source Loopback0
 no auto-summary
 !
 address-family vpnv4
 neighbor 192.168.1.1 activate
 neighbor 192.168.1.1 send-community extended
 exit-address-family
 !
```

The first command that is required when configuring MP-BGP between PE routers (or a PE router and a route reflector) is the **router bgp** *autonomous-system-number* command. This command is used to enable BGP on the PE router.

The **no synchronization** command enables you to disable synchronization between BGP and an IGP. The next command, **neighbor** *ip-address* **remote-as** *autonomous-system-number*, configures the IP address and ASN of the remote PE router or route reflector.

The **neighbor** *ip-address* **update-source** *interface* command configures the BGP update source to use with the remote PE router or route reflector. A loopback interface is used because a loopback interface never goes down.

Next comes the **no auto-summary** command. This command disables auto-summarization at major networks boundaries for routes redistributed into BGP using the **redistribute** command.

The **address-family vpnv4** command is then used to enter the VPNv4 address family configuration mode. The remote PE router (or route reflector) is then activated for VPNv4 route exchange (using MP-BGP) using the **neighbor** *ip-address* **activate** command.

Finally, the **neighbor** *ip-address* **send-community extended** enables the sending of BGP extended communities (including RTs). This command is configured by default for each neighbor that you activate for VPNv4 route exchange.

NOTE   If you want to enable the sending of standard BGP communities in addition to extended communities, you must configure the **neighbor** *ip-address* **send-community both** command.

You can verify BGP neighbor relationships and the capability to exchange MP-BGP (VPNv4) routes using the **show ip bgp neighbor** *ip-address*, as demonstrated in Example 4-8.

Example 4-8   *Using* **show ip bgp neighbor** *to Verify BGP Neighbor Relationships and Capability to Exchange MP-BGP (VPNv4) Routes*

```
London_PE1#show ip bgp neighbor 192.168.1.3
BGP neighbor is 192.168.1.3,  remote AS 65535, internal link
  BGP version 4, remote router ID 192.168.1.3
  BGP state = Established, up for 01:55:23 (line 1)
  Last read 00:00:22, hold time is 180, keepalive interval is 60 seconds
  Neighbor capabilities:
    Route refresh: advertised and received(new)
    Address family IPv4 Unicast: advertised and received
    Address family VPNv4 Unicast: advertised and received (line 2)
  Message statistics:
    InQ depth is 0
    OutQ depth is 0
! output omitted for brevity
```

Highlighted line 1 in Example 4-8 shows that the BGP state is Established—the neighbor relationship is in an up state, and routes can be exchanged.

Crucially, highlighted line 2 shows that both peers (the local and remote PE routers) support the advertisement of VPNv4 routes.

NOTE   You can find detailed information on verifying and troubleshooting MPLS Layer 3 VPNs in *Troubleshooting Virtual Private Networks* (Cisco Press).

Step 6: Configure the Customer VRFs

Configuration of customer VRFs is demonstrated in Example 4-9.

Example 4-9 *Configuring Customer VRFs*

```
ip vrf mjlnet_VPN
 rd 65535:100
 route-target export 65535:100
 route-target import 65535:100
 !
```

The **ip vrf** *vrf-name* command is used in Example 4-9 to configure a VRF named mjlnet_VPN. The VRF name is case sensitive and is locally significant only (although the same name is often used to configure all VRFs in a particular VPN).

The RD and RTs associated with the VRF are then configured using the **rd** *route-distinguisher* and **route-target** [**import** | **export** | **both**] *route-target-ext-community* commands.

In Example 4-9, the RD is configured as 65535:100, and both the import and export RTs are configured as 65535:100. Remember that although RDs and RTs are often configured identically (particularly when full-mesh connectivity is provisioned in a VPN), there is actually no requirement for this.

Step 7: Configure the Customer VRF Interfaces

After you have configured the customer VRFs, you can associate the interfaces on the PE router that are connected to the CE router(s) with the VRFs, as demonstrated in Example 4-10.

Example 4-10 *Configure the Customer VRF Interfaces*

```
interface Serial2/1
 ip vrf forwarding mjlnet_VPN
 ip address 10.1.1.2 255.255.255.0
```

The **ip vrf forwarding** *vrf-name* command in Example 4-10 is used to associate interface serial 2/1 with a customer VRF called mjlnet_VPN.

NOTE It is also possible to associate user packets with a VRF based on source IP address. For more information, see the following URL:

http://www.cisco.com/en/US/products/sw/iosswrel/ps5012/products_feature_guide09186a0080173d55.html

---

Now that you have configured a customer VRF and associated one or more interfaces with it, you can verify your configuration using the **show ip vrf detail** *vrf-name* command, as shown in Example 4-11.

Example 4-11 *Verifying VRF Configuration Using the* **show ip vrf detail** *Command*

```
London_PE1#show ip vrf detail mjlnet_VPN
VRF mjlnet_VPN; default RD 65535:100; default VPNID <not set> (line 1)
VRF Table ID = 1
  Interfaces:
    Serial2/1                  (line 2)
  Connected addresses are not in global routing table
  Export VPN route-target communities
    RT:65535:100               (line 3)
  Import VPN route-target communities
    RT:65535:100               (line 4)
  No import route-map
  No export route-map
CSC is not configured.
London_PE1#
```

In highlighted line 1, you can see that the RD for VRF mjlnet_VPN is 65535:100. Highlighted lines 3 and 4 show the import and export RTs (65535:100), and highlighted line 2 shows the interface associated with VRF mjlnet_VPN (interface serial 2/1).

Step 8: Configure the Customer VRF Routing Protocols or Static Routes for Connectivity Between Customer VPN Sites

You have a number of options as far as the routing protocols that can be used between CE and PE routers are concerned. The routing protocols that can be currently used as CE-PE routing protocols include the following:

- RIPv2
- EIGRP
- OSPF
- eBGP

You can also configure static routes for connectivity between customer VPN sites.

Configuring RIPv2 for Connectivity Between Customer VPN Sites

Example 4-12 shows the configuration of RIPv2 for site-to-site VPN connectivity.

Example 4-12 *Configuring RIPv2 for Site-to-Site VPN Connectivity*

```
router rip
 version 2
 !
 address-family ipv4 vrf mjlnet_VPN
```

Example 4-12 *Configuring RIPv2 for Site-to-Site VPN Connectivity (Continued)*

```
 version 2
 redistribute bgp 65535 metric 1
 network 10.1.1.0
 no auto-summary
 exit-address-family
!
```

As you can see, the configuration is fairly straightforward—the **router rip** command enables RIP, and the **version 2** command specifies RIP version 2.

The **address-family ipv4 vrf** *vrf-name* command is then used to enter the IPv4 address family configuration mode for a particular VRF (in this case, a VRF called mjlnet_VPN).

The **version 2** command is again used to specify RIP version 2. The address family inherits this command when version 2 is configured globally (directly under **router rip**).

Next comes the **redistribute bgp** *autonomous-system-number* **metric** [*metric* | **transparent**] command. This command is used to redistribute MP-BGP routes into RIPv2 (VPNv4 *received* by the local PE router from remote PE routers).

The RIPv2 metric (hop count) is carried in the BGP MED attribute when VPNv4 is advertised between PE routers. If you specify the **transparent** keyword when redistributing MP-BGP into RIPv2, the hop count from the remote PE router will be redistributed into RIPv2 on the local PE router. If you specify a metric, on the other hand, this will specify the hop count used for redistributed routes instead. In Example 4-12, a hop count of 1 is specified.

The **network** *ip-address* command is then used to specify the networks on which RIPv2 will be enabled. In this example, RIPv2 is enabled on network 10.1.1.0/24 (the network assigned to the link connected to the CE router).

The **no auto-summary** command is then used to disable auto-summarization of networks at major network boundaries. This command is configured by default.

Configuring EIGRP for Connectivity Between Customer VPN Sites

Example 4-13 shows the configuration of EIGRP as the PE-CE routing protocol.

Example 4-13 *Configuring EIGRP as the PE-CE Routing Protocol*

```
router eigrp 100
 !
 address-family ipv4 vrf mjlnet_VPN
 redistribute bgp 65535 metric 1000 1 255 1 1500
 network 10.1.1.0 0.0.0.255
 no auto-summary
 autonomous-system 200
 exit-address-family
 !
```

In Example 4-13, the **router eigrp** *autonomous-system-number* is used to enable EIGRP.

The **address-family ipv4 vrf** *vrf-name* command is again used to enter the IPv4 address family configuration mode. In this example, the VRF specified is mjlnet_VPN.

The next command, **redistribute bgp** *autonomous-system-number* [**metric** *metric*], is used to redistribute MP-BGP into EIGRP. It is important to configure a metric using this command or configure the **default-metric** command if remote VPN sites are in a different EIGRP autonomous system or use a different PE-CE routing protocol.

NOTE	Note that the EIGRP composite metric (bandwidth, delay, reliability, load, and MTU), as well as other information such as tag, ASN, and next hop, is carried in BGP extended communities (types 0x8800 to 0x8805).

The **network** *ip-address* [*wildcard-mask*] command enables EIGRP on the specified network(s) (links to the CE router).

The **no auto-summary** command is then used to disable auto-summarization of networks at major network boundaries. Again, this command is configured by default within the address family.

The next command (**autonomous-system** *autonomous-system-number*) specifies the customer ASN. This ASN must match that specified on the connected CE router; otherwise, they will not become EIGRP neighbors and exchange routes. Also, you should ensure that the same ASN is specified using this command on all PE routers in the VPN; otherwise, routes redistributed from MP-BGP will appear as external EIGRP routes.

Configuring OSPF for Connectivity Between Customer VPN Sites

Example 4-14 shows the configuration of OSPF for CE-PE routing.

Example 4-14 *Configuring OSPF as the CE-PE Routing Protocol*

```
router ospf 100 vrf mjlnet_VPN
 redistribute bgp 65535 subnets
 network 10.1.1.0 0.0.0.255 area 0
```

The first command shown in Example 4-14 (**router ospf** *process-id* **vrf** *vrf-name*) enables OSPF.

The **redistribute bgp** *autonomous-system-number* **subnets** command redistributes MP-BGP into OSPF. Do not forget the **subnets** keyword when configuring this command; otherwise, only major networks will be redistributed.

Finally, the **network** *network wildcard-mask* **area** *area-number* command enables OSPF on the PE-CE interface and places that interface in the specified OSPF area.

When OSPF is used as the PE-CE routing protocol at a number of sites for the same VPN, then, by default, type 1 and 2 (and 3) LSAs are translated into type 3 or 5 LSAs as they are advertised between sites. If the OSPF domain IDs (by default equal to the PE VRF OSPF process IDs/manually configured on the PEs using the **domain-id** command) are the same for different sites then type 1 and 2 LSAs are translated into type 3 LSAs as they are advertised between sites, but if domain IDs are different, then LSAs are translated into type 5 LSAs.

The fact that OSPF LSAs are translated between sites is important if there is a backdoor connection (not via the MPLS VPN backbone) between the two customer VPN sites because the backdoor link may be preferred over the connection via the MPLS VPN backbone network. In this case, if you want OSPF to prefer the connection over the MPLS VPN backbone network, you can configure a sham link.

Note that OSPF attributes such as domain ID, router ID, route type, and OSPF metric are advertised between PE routers using the BGP MED attribute and Extended Communities attributes.

You can find more information about the configuration of OSPF sham links at the following URL:

http://www.cisco.com/en/US/products/ps6604/products_white_paper09186a00800a8570.shtml

---

NOTE   Before finishing this section, it is important to mention one other consideration when configuring OSPF as the PE-CE routing protocol—prior to Cisco IOS Software Release 12.0(27)S, you could only configure 28 VRF OSPF processes on 1 PE router. With Cisco IOS Software Release 12.0(27)S and higher, the number of OSPF processes that you can configure is unlimited (within usual PE router memory and CPU constraints).

Configuring EBGP for Connectivity Between Customer VPN Sites

Example 4-15 shows the configuration of yet another option as the PE-CE routing protocol: eBGP.

Example 4-15 *Configuring eBGP as the PE-CE Routing Protocol*

```
router bgp 65535
 !
 address-family ipv4 vrf mjlnet_VPN
 neighbor 10.1.1.1 remote-as 64512
 neighbor 10.1.1.1 activate
 no auto-summary
 no synchronization
 exit-address-family
```

The **router bgp** *autonomous-system-number* command enables BGP on the PE router. After BGP has been enabled, the next step is to enter the IPv4 address family configuration mode for the appropriate VRF using the **address-family ip4 vrf** *vrf-name* command.

The **neighbor** *ip-address* **remote-as** *autonomous-system-number* command configures the IP address (BGP update source) and ASN of the CE router.

Next is **neighbor** *ip-address* **activate**. This command enables the exchange of BGP routing information with the specified neighbor.

The **no auto-summary** and **no synchronization** commands are shown next. These are defaults, and disable auto-summarization at major network boundaries for routes redistributed into BGP using the **redistribute** command and disable the requirement for synchronization with IGP routes.

Configuring Static Routes for Connectivity Between Customer VPN Sites

As a final option, you can configure static routes for IP reachability from a PE router to a customer VPN site. Example 4-16 shows the configuration of a static route for reachability from a PE router to a CE router.

Example 4-16 *Configuring Static VRF Routes for IP Reachability from a PE Router to a Customer Site*

```
ip route vrf mjlnet_VPN 10.2.2.0 255.255.255.0 10.2.1.1
```

In Example 4-16, the **ip route vrf** *vrf-name prefix mask* [*next-hop-address*] [*interface* [*interface-number*]] command configures a static route in a VRF called mjlnet_VPN to prefix 10.2.2.0/24 with next hop 10.2.1.1 (the interface of the connected CE router).

If you do want to use static routing for reachability across a customer VPN, you must configure static routes on not only PE routers, but also on the CE routers.

Step 9: Redistribute the PE-CE Routing Protocol / Static VRF Routes into MP-BGP

After you have configured the PE-CE routing protocol or static VRF routes, the next step is to redistribute the PE-CE routing protocol or static VRF routes into MP-BGP (for advertisement to remote PE routers).

Example 4-17 shows the configuration of redistribution of a CE-PE routing protocol into MP-BGP.

Example 4-17 *Configuring the Redistribution of a PE-CE Routing Protocol into MP-BGP*

```
router bgp 65535
address-family ipv4 vrf mjlnet_VPN
 redistribute eigrp 200
```

The **router bgp** *autonomous-system-number* enters router configuration mode for BGP.

The **address-family ipv4 vrf** *vrf-name* command enters IPv4 address family configuration mode for a VRF (in this example, VRF mjlnet_VPN).

Finally, the **redistribute eigrp** *autonomous-system-number* redistributes EIGRP (the PE-CE routing protocol in this example) into MP-BGP.

When redistributing EIGRP into MP-BGP, be sure to specify the EIGRP autonomous system number configured using the **autonomous-system** command (see the section "Configuring EIGRP for Connectivity Between Customer VPN Sites" for more information).

Other PE-CE routing protocols can be similarly redistributed into MP-BGP. OSPF can be redistributed using the **redistribute ospf** *process-id* **internal external 1 external 2** command (this command redistributes internal routes as well as type 1 and type 2 external OSPF routes). RIPv2 can be redistributed into MP-MP using the **redistribute rip** command.

Static VRF routes can be redistributed into MP-BGP using the **redistribute static** command. Note that you might also want to add the **redistribute connected** command. This might be necessary to ensure that the PE router advertises the PE-CE link (which may be useful for troubleshooting purposes).

Having redistributed the PE-CE routing or static VRF routes into MP-BGP, you can verify MP-BGP route exchange between PE routers using the **show ip bgp vpnv4 vrf** *vrf-name* command, as demonstrated in Example 4-18.

Example 4-18 *Verifying MP-BGP Route Exchange Between PE Routers Using the* **show ip bgp vpnv4 vrf** *Command*

```
London_PE1#show ip bgp vpnv4 vrf mjlnet_VPN
BGP table version is 52, local router ID is 192.168.1.2
Status codes: s suppressed, d damped, h history, * valid, > best, i - internal,
              r RIB-failure, S Stale
Origin codes: i - IGP, e - EGP, ? - incomplete
   Network          Next Hop          Metric LocPrf Weight Path
Route Distinguisher: 65535:100 (default for vrf mjlnet_VPN)
*>i10.1.1.0/24      192.168.1.3            0    100      0 ? (line 1)
*>i10.1.1.2/32      192.168.1.3            0    100      0 ? (line 2)
*>i10.1.2.0/24      192.168.1.3      1889792    100      0 ? (line 3)
*>i10.1.3.0/24      192.168.1.3      1889792    100      0 ? (line 4)
*>i10.1.4.0/24      192.168.1.3      1889792    100      0 ? (line 5)
*> 10.2.1.0/24      0.0.0.0                0         32768 ?
*> 10.2.1.1/32      0.0.0.0                0         32768 ?
*> 10.2.2.0/24      10.2.1.1         1889792         32768 ? (line 6)
*> 10.2.3.0/24      10.2.1.1         1889792         32768 ? (line 7)
*> 10.2.4.0/24      10.2.1.1         1889792         32768 ? (line 8)
London_PE1#
```

Highlighted lines 1 to 5 in Example 4-18 show VRF mjlnet_VPN routes advertised by Frankfurt_PE1. Notice that the next hop of the routes advertised by Frankfurt_PE1 is 192.168.1.3. IP address 192.168.1.3 is the Frankfurt_PE1's BGP update source (its loopback interface), and an IGP label binding corresponding to this address is required to forward VPN traffic to customer VPN routes 10.1.1.0/24, 10.1.1.2/32, 10.1.2.0/24, 10.1.3.0/24, and 10.1.4.0/24 across the MPLS VPN backbone to Frankfurt_PE1.

In highlighted lines 6 to 8, you can see customer VPN routes redistributed into MP-BGP on the local PE router.

You can also verify routes in a VRF routing table using the **show ip route vrf** *vrf-name* command, as shown in Example 4-19.

Example 4-19 *Verifying the VRF Routing Table Using the* **show ip route vrf** *Command*

```
London_PE1#show ip route vrf mjlnet_VPN
Routing Table: mjlnet_VPN
Codes: C - connected, S - static, I - IGRP, R - RIP, M - mobile, B - BGP
       D - EIGRP, EX - EIGRP external, O - OSPF, IA - OSPF inter area
       N1 - OSPF NSSA external type 1, N2 - OSPF NSSA external type 2
       E1 - OSPF external type 1, E2 - OSPF external type 2, E - EGP
       i - IS-IS, su - IS-IS summary, L1 - IS-IS level-1, L2 - IS-IS level-2
       ia - IS-IS inter area, * - candidate default, U - per-user static route
       o - ODR
Gateway of last resort is not set
     10.0.0.0/8 is variably subnetted, 10 subnets, 2 masks
C       10.2.1.1/32 is directly connected, Serial2/1
B       10.1.3.0/24 [200/1889792] via 192.168.1.3, 00:59:41 (line 1)
B       10.1.1.2/32 [200/0] via 192.168.1.3, 01:03:02 (line 2)
C       10.2.1.0/24 is directly connected, Serial2/1
B       10.1.2.0/24 [200/1889792] via 192.168.1.3, 00:59:41 (line 3)
D       10.2.2.0/24 [90/1889792] via 10.2.1.1, 00:56:01, Serial2/1 (line 4)
B       10.1.1.0/24 [200/0] via 192.168.1.3, 01:03:02 (line 5)
D       10.2.3.0/24 [90/1889792] via 10.2.1.1, 00:56:03, Serial2/1 (line 6)
D       10.2.4.0/24 [90/1889792] via 10.2.1.1, 00:56:03, Serial2/1 (line 7)
B       10.1.4.0/24 [200/1889792] via 192.168.1.3, 00:59:42 (line 8)
London_PE1#
```

In highlighted lines 1, 2, 3, 5, and 8, you can see customer VPN routes advertised by PE router Frankfurt_PE1 (192.168.1.3) using MP-BGP in VRF mjlnet_VPN.

Highlighted lines 4, 6, and 7 show customer VPN routes advertised to the local PE router by the connected CE router using the PE-CE routing protocol EIGRP.

Configuration of P Routers

The configuration of P routers consists of a subset of the configuration of PE routers:

Step 1 Configure a loopback interface for use as the P router's LDP router ID.

Step 2 Configure the LDP.

Step 3 Enable MPLS on interfaces connected to PE or other P routers.

Step 4 Configure the backbone network IGP (if not already configured).

Each of these configuration steps has previously been described. See the configuration guidelines from the previous section for more information.

Provisioning Route Distribution for VPN Topologies

Now that you know how to configure PE, P, and CE routers, it is important to consider how to design and deploy different customer VPN topologies, including the following:

- **Full mesh**—A full-mesh topology provides any site-to-any site in a customer VPN.

- **Hub and spoke**—In a hub-and-spoke topology, there is a central site or sites (called the *hub site[s]*). All other customer VPN sites (called *spoke sites*) can communicate directly with the central site or sites and must send traffic via the hub site(s) if they want to communicate with another spoke site.

- **Extranet connectivity**—In this topology, connectivity is provided between different VPNs.

A key fact to have remembered from the previous section is that if at least one of the RTs attached to a route (an export RT) is the same as one of the import RTs associated with a VRF, the route in question will be imported (installed) into the VRF.

The next three sections show you how to provision full-mesh, hub-and-spoke, and extranet MPLS VPNs by controlling the import of routes into VRFs based on RTs.

Full-Mesh Topology

In a full-mesh VPN, all the import and export RTs associated with a VPN (set of VRFs with connectivity) can be the same. Figure 4-8 illustrates route distribution between VRFs in a full-mesh MPLS Layer 3 VPN (a set of VRFs called mjlnet_VPN).

Figure 4-8 *Route Distribution Between VRFs in a Full-Mesh MPLS Layer 3 VPN*

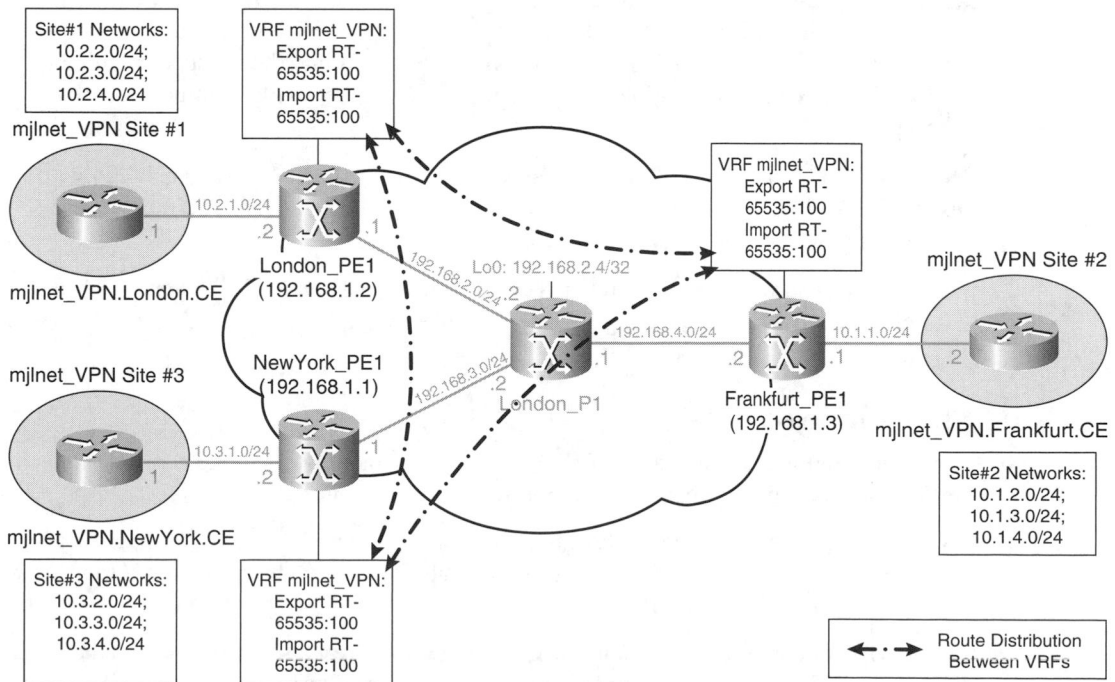

As shown in Figure 4-8, the mjlnet_VPN VRF on each PE router (London_PE1, Frankfurt_PE1, and New York_PE1) is configured with import and export RTs 65535:100. Example 4-20 shows the configuration of the mjlnet_VPN VRF on all three PE routers.

Example 4-20 *Configuration of mjlnet_VPN' VRF for Each PE Router in a Full-Mesh VPN Topology*

```
!
ip vrf mjlnet_VPN
 rd 65535:100
 route-target export 65535:100
 route-target import 65535:100
 !
```

The highlighted lines in Example 4-20 show that import and export RTs for the mjlnet_VPN VRF can be identical in a full-mesh VPN (in this example, 65535:100).

For example, London_PE1 advertises VPNv4 routes 10.2.2.0/24, 10.2.3.0/24, and 10.2.4.0/24 (from attached CE, mjlnet_VPN.London.CE) to Frankfurt_PE1 and New York_PE1 with an export route target of 65535:100. Because Frankfurt_PE1 and New York_PE1 have an import route target of 65535:100 configured for the mjlnet_VPN VRF, VPN routes 10.2.2.0/24, 10.2.3.0/24, and 10.2.4.0/24 are imported (installed) into Frankfurt_PE1's and New York_PE1's mjlnet_VPN VRFs.

Similarly, Frankfurt_PE1 advertises VPNv4 routes 10.1.2.0/24, 10.1.3.0/24, and 10.1.4.0/24 (from attached CE, mjlnet_VPN.Frankfurt.CE) with export RT 65535:100 to London_PE1 and New York_PE1, and each of them imports these routes into their respective mjlnet_VPN VRFs because their mjlnet_VPN VRFs are configured with an import RT of 65535:100.

New York_PE1 advertises VPNv4 routes 10.3.2.0/24, 10.3.3.0/24, and 10.3.4.0/24 with export RT 65535:100 to London_PE1 and Frankfurt_PE1, and they both import these routes into their mjlnet_VPN VRFs.

As you can see, route distribution between a set of VRFs in an MPLS Layer 3 VPN is straightforward when configuring full-mesh connectivity.

Hub-and-Spoke Topology

Route distribution between a set of VRFs in a VPN with hub-and-spoke connectivity is a little more complicated than that required for full-mesh connectivity.

When hub-and-spoke connectivity is required, two different RTs are required. One RT is used to identify routes (re)advertised from the hub site, and another is required to identify routes advertised from the spoke sites.

The PE router connected to the hub site CE router imports routes advertised from the spoke sites, and the PE routers connected to the spoke site CE routers import routes (re)advertised from the hub. Crucially, spoke sites do not import routes *directly* from other spoke sites.

In addition, it is important to note that the PE router connected to the hub site CE router requires two VRFs for the VPN, whereas the PE routers connected to the spoke site CE routers require only one VRF for the VPN.

Each of the VRFs on the PE router (connected to the hub site PE router) is associated with a separate interface that is connected to the hub site CE router. These separate interfaces can be logical (such as Frame Relay subinterfaces) or can be physical.

Figure 4-9 illustrates route distribution between VRFs in a hub-and-spoke MPLS Layer 3 VPN topology.

Figure 4-9   *Route Distribution in a Hub-and-Spoke MPLS Layer 3 VPN Topology*

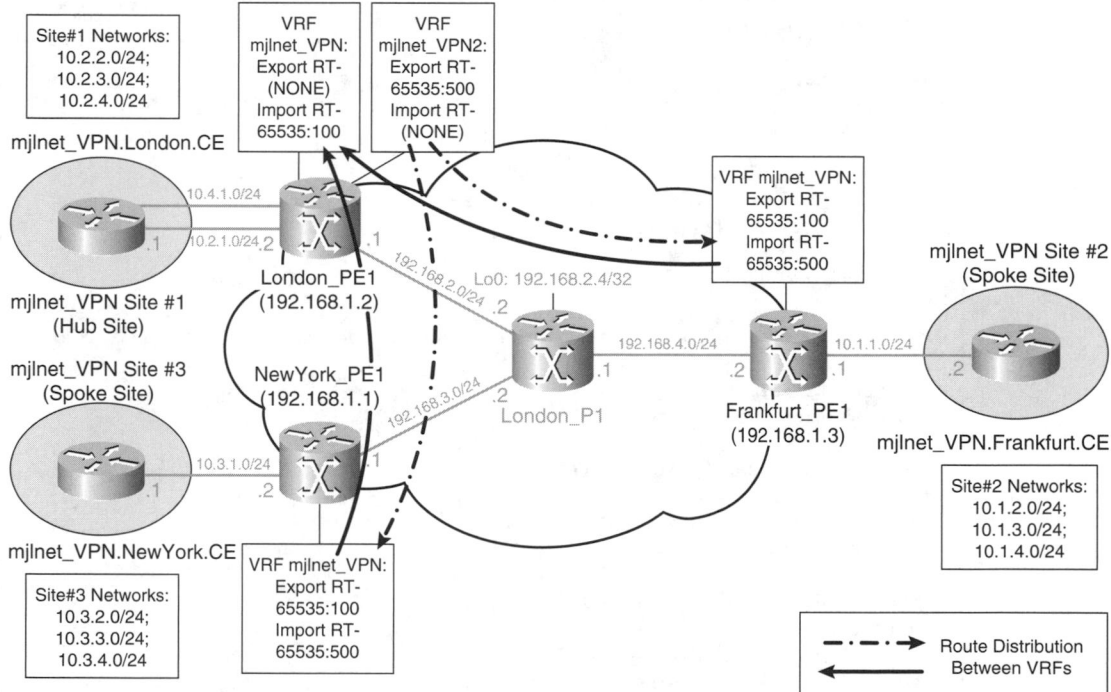

As you can see in Figure 4-9, two VRFs are configured for the VPN on London_PE1 (the PE router connected to the VPN hub site CE router). One VRF is called mjlnet_VPN1, and the other is called mjlnet_VPN2.

VRF mjlnet_VPN1 is configured with *import* RT 65535:100 but is *not* configured with an export RT. The purpose of this VRF is to import VPN routes from spoke sites. VRF mjlnet_VPN2 is configured with *export* RT 65535:500 but is *not* configured with an import RT. The purpose of this VRF is to export VPN routes to spoke sites.

The PE routers connected to the spoke site CE routers (Frankfurt_PE1 and NewYork_PE1) have a single VRF each for the VPN, called mjlnet_VPN. The import RT for these VRFs is

65535:500, which corresponds to the export RT for VRF mjlnet_VPN2 on London_PE1, and the export RT for these VRFs is 65535:100, which corresponds to the import RT for VRF mjlnet_VPN1 on London_PE1.

Example 4-21 shows the VRF configurations on PE routers London_PE1, Frankfurt_PE1, and NewYork_PE1. It also shows the interface configuration for London_PE1 for those interfaces connected to the hub site router.

Example 4-21 *VRF Configurations on PE Routers London_PE1, Frankfurt_PE1, and NewYork_PE1*

```
!
! PE router 'London_PE1' (connected to the hub-site CE router)
!
!
! VRF configuration
!
ip vrf mjlnet_VPN1
 rd 65535:100
 route-target import 65535:100
!
ip vrf mjlnet_VPN2
 rd 65535:500
 route-target export 65535:500
!
!
!
! Interface configuration (both subinterfaces are connected to the hub site router)
!
interface Serial2/1
 encapsulation frame-relay
!
interface Serial2/1.1 point-to-point
 ip vrf forwarding mjlnet_VPN1
 ip address 10.2.1.2 255.255.255.0
 frame-relay interface-dlci 100
!
interface Serial2/1.2 point-to-point
 ip vrf forwarding mjlnet_VPN2
 ip address 10.4.1.2 255.255.255.0
 frame-relay interface-dlci 200
!
!
! VRF configuration on PE router 'Frankfurt_PE1' (connected to a spoke site CE router)
ip vrf mjlnet_VPN
 rd 65535:100
 route-target export 65535:100
 route-target import 65535:500
!
!
! VRF configuration on PE router 'NewYork_PE1' (connected to a spoke site CE router)
ip vrf mjlnet_VPN
 rd 65535:100
 route-target export 65535:100
 route-target import 65535:500
!
```

Figure 4-10 illustrates VRF configuration and route distribution in one direction in a hub-and-spoke VPN.

Figure 4-10 *VRF Configuration and Route Distribution in One Direction in a Hub-and-Spoke VPN*

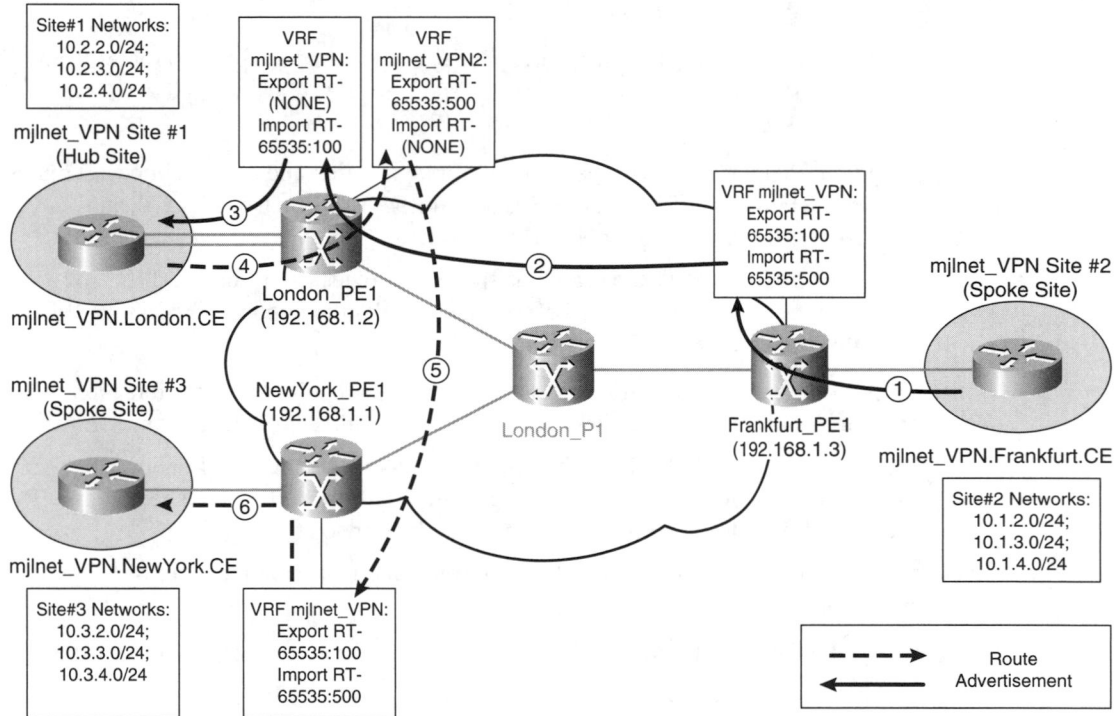

Route distribution from spoke site CE router mjlnet_VPN.Frankfurt.CE to spoke site CE router mjlnet_VPN.NewYork.PE via hub site CE router mjlnet_VPN.London.CE occurs as shown in Figure 4-10:

1   mjlnet_VPN.Frankfurt.CE advertises Frankfurt spoke site routes (10.1.2.0/24, 10.1.3.0/24, and 10.1.4.0/24) to PE router Frankfurt_PE1 using the PE-CE routing protocol (EIGRP in this example).

2   Frankfurt_PE1 installs these routes into VRF mjlnet_VPN. It then redistributes the Frankfurt spoke site routes into MP-BGP, attaches (export) RT 65535:100, and advertises them to London_PE1.

3   London_PE1 installs the Frankfurt spoke site routes into VRF mjlnet_VPN1 because the attached RT (65535:100) matches the import RT (65535:100).

London_PE1 then redistributes and advertises the Frankfurt spoke site routes (from VRF mjlnet_VPN1) to hub site CE router mjlnet_VPN.London.CE on subinterface serial 2/1.1 (on a Frame Relay PVC with DLCI 100) using the PE-CE routing protocol. Subinterface 2/1.1 is associated with VRF mjlnet_VPN1.

4 mjlnet_VPN.London.CE receives the Frankfurt site routes, and then re-advertises them back to London_PE1 (on a separate interface to that on which they were received). At the same time that mjlnet_VPN.London.CE re-advertises Frankfurt spoke site routes to London_PE1, it also advertises London hub site routes (10.2.2.0/24, 10.2.3.0/24, and 10.2.4.0/24).

5 London_PE1 receives the Frankfurt spoke site (and London hub site) routes from mjlnet_VPN.London.CE on subinterface 2/1.2 (on a PVC with DLCI 200). This interface is associated with VRF mjlnet_VPN2.

London_PE1 now redistributes the Frankfurt spoke site (and London hub site) routes (from VRF mjlnet_VPN2) into MP-BGP, attaches export RT 65535:500, and advertises them to PE router NewYork_PE1.

6 NewYork_PE1 receives the Frankfurt spoke site routes from London_PE1, and because the attached RT (65535:500) is the same as the import RT (65535:500), installs the routes into VRF mjlnet_VPN.

NewYork_PE1 then redistributes the spoke site 1 (and hub site) routes into the PE-CE routing protocol and advertises them to CE router mjlnet_VPN.NewYork.CE.

mjlnet_VPN.NewYork.CE receives the Frankfurt spoke site (and London hub site) routes and installs them into its routing table. The New York spoke site now has IP reachability to the Frankfurt spoke site (and the London hub site).

Figure 4-11 illustrates VRF configuration and route distribution in the other direction in a hub-and-spoke VPN.

Route distribution from the New York spoke site occurs in exactly the same way, just in the opposite direction:

1 mjlnet_VPN.NewYork.CE advertises New York spoke site routes (10.3.2.0/24, 10.3.3.0/24, and 10.3.4.0/24) to NewYork_PE1 using the PE-CE routing protocol.

2 NewYork_PE1 redistributes the New York spoke site routes into MP-BGP, attaches RT 65535:100, and advertises them to London_PE1.

3 London_PE1 receives the New York spoke site routes, and because the attached RT is the same as the import RT, installs the routes into VRF mjlnet_VPN1.

London_PE1 redistribute and advertises the routes to mjlnet_VPN.London.CE using the PE-CE routing protocol.

4 mjlnet_VPN.London.CE re-advertises the New York spoke site (and London hub site routes) to London_PE1 using the PE-CE routing protocol.

5 London_PE1 installs the New York spoke site routes into VRF mjlnet_VPN2.

London_PE1 redistributes the New York spoke site (plus London hub site) routes into MP-BGP, attaches export RT 65535:500, and advertises the routes to Frankfurt_PE1.

Figure 4-11 *VRF Configuration and Route Distribution in the Other Direction in a Hub-and-Spoke VPN*

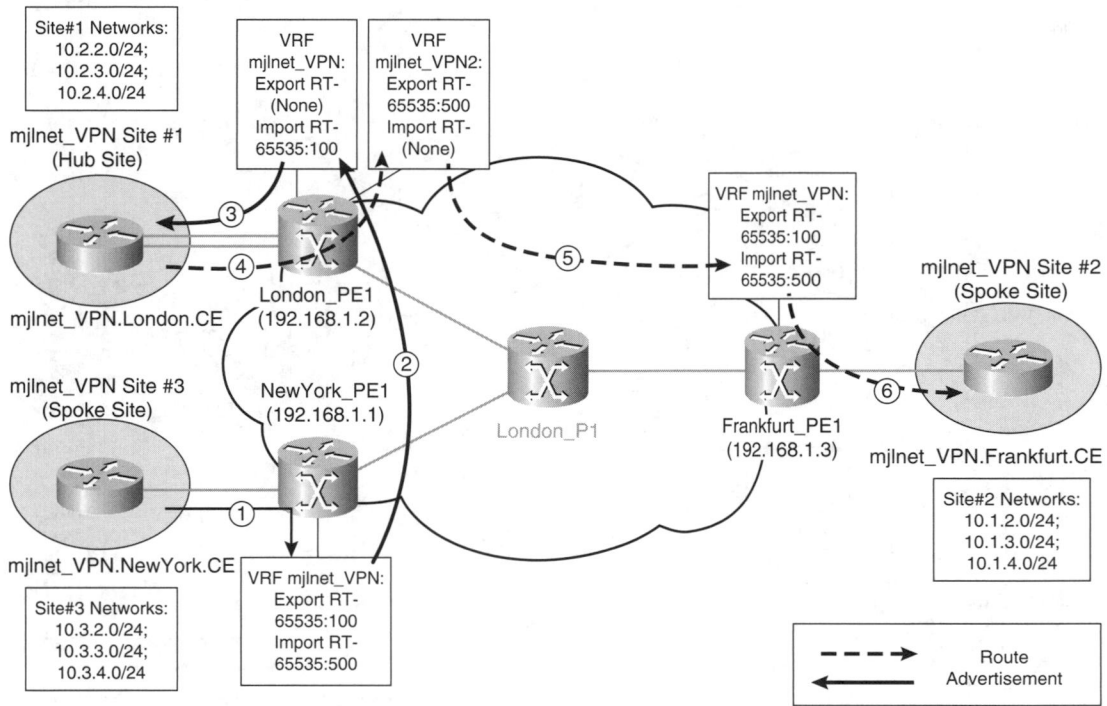

6 Frankfurt_PE1 installs the New York spoke site (and London hub site) routes into its mjlnet_VPN VRF because the attached RT (65535:500) is the same as the import RT for VRF mjlnet_VPN (65535:500).

Frankfurt_PE1 redistributes the New York spoke site (and London hub site) routes into the PE-CE routing protocol and advertises them to connected CE router mjlnet_VPN.Frankfurt.CE.

mjlnet_VPN.Frankfurt.CE receives the New York spoke site (and London hub site) routes and installs them into its routing table. The Frankfurt spoke site now has IP reachability to the New York spoke site (and the London hub site).

Because routes advertisement between spoke sites is via the hub site CE router, mjlnet_VPN.London.CE, spoke-to-spoke traffic also flows via the hub site CE router.

Figure 4-12 illustrates traffic flow in a hub-and-spoke MPLS VPN.

Figure 4-12 *Traffic Flow in a Hub-and-Spoke MPLS VPN*

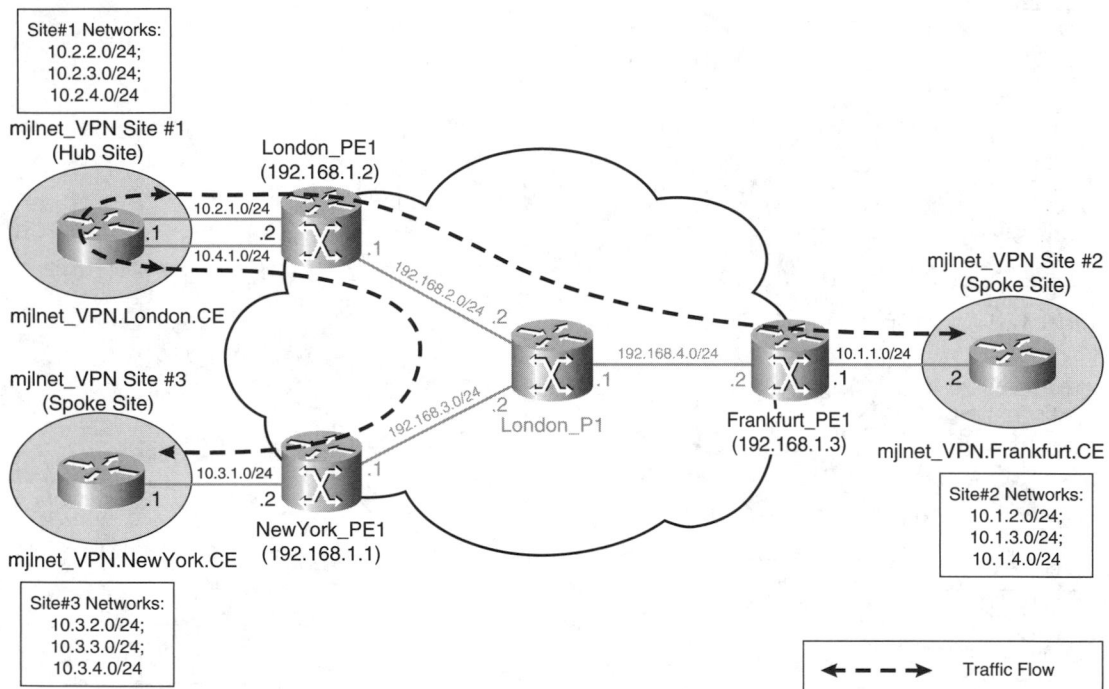

The traffic flow between the Frankfurt and NewYork spoke sites is illustrated by the output of the **traceroute** command between mjlnet_VPN.NewYork.CE and mjlnet_VPN.Frankfurt.CE, as shown in Example 4-22.

Example 4-22 traceroute *Command Output Showing Traffic Flow Between mjlnet_VPN.Frankfurt.CE and mjlnet_VPN.London.CE*

```
mjlnet_VPN.NewYork.CE#traceroute 10.1.2.1
Type escape sequence to abort.
Tracing the route to 10.1.2.1
  1 10.3.1.2 16 msec 16 msec 16 msec (line 1)
  2 10.4.1.1 64 msec 60 msec 60 msec (line 2)
  3 10.2.1.2 [AS 65535] 56 msec 212 msec 60 msec (line 3)
  4 10.1.1.2 [AS 65535] 120 msec *  120 msec (line 4)
mjlnet_VPN.NewYork.CE#
```

Highlighted line 1 shows the first hop (the VRF mjlnet_VPN interface on NewYork_PE1, 10.3.1.2) in the packets path.

In highlighted line 2, the packet reaches mjlnet_VPN.London.CE's interface connected to London_PE1's mjlnet_VPN2 (10.4.1.1).

Next, the packet reaches the VRF mjlnet_VPN1 interface on London_PE1 (10.2.1.2).

Finally, the packet reaches its destination, mjlnet_VPN.Frankfurt.CE (10.1.1.2). It is important to note that if you are using BGP as the PE-CE routing protocol in a hub-and-spoke environment and the BGP AS number is the same at multiple customer VPN sites then you'll need to configure the **neighbor** *hub-ce-ip-address* **as-override** and **neighbor** *hub-ce-ip-address* **allowas-in** commands on the PE router(s) connected to the hub site, and the **neighbor** *spoke-ce-ip-address* **as-override** command on PE router(s) connected to spoke sites. The **neighbor** *ip-address* **as-override** command ensures that CE routers will not drop routes from other VPN sites by replacing the AS number from one site with the service provider AS number in the BGP AS_PATH attribute, and the **neighbor** *ip-address* **allowas-in** command allows PE routers to accept spoke site routes re-advertised by the hub site (with the service provider's AS number in the AS_PATH attribute).

Extranet Topology

An extranet provides connectivity between organizations, as illustrated in Figure 4-13. Extranet connectivity can be provisioned over an MPLS VPN backbone using selective VPNv4 route distribution based on RTs.

Figure 4-13 *Extranet Connectivity*

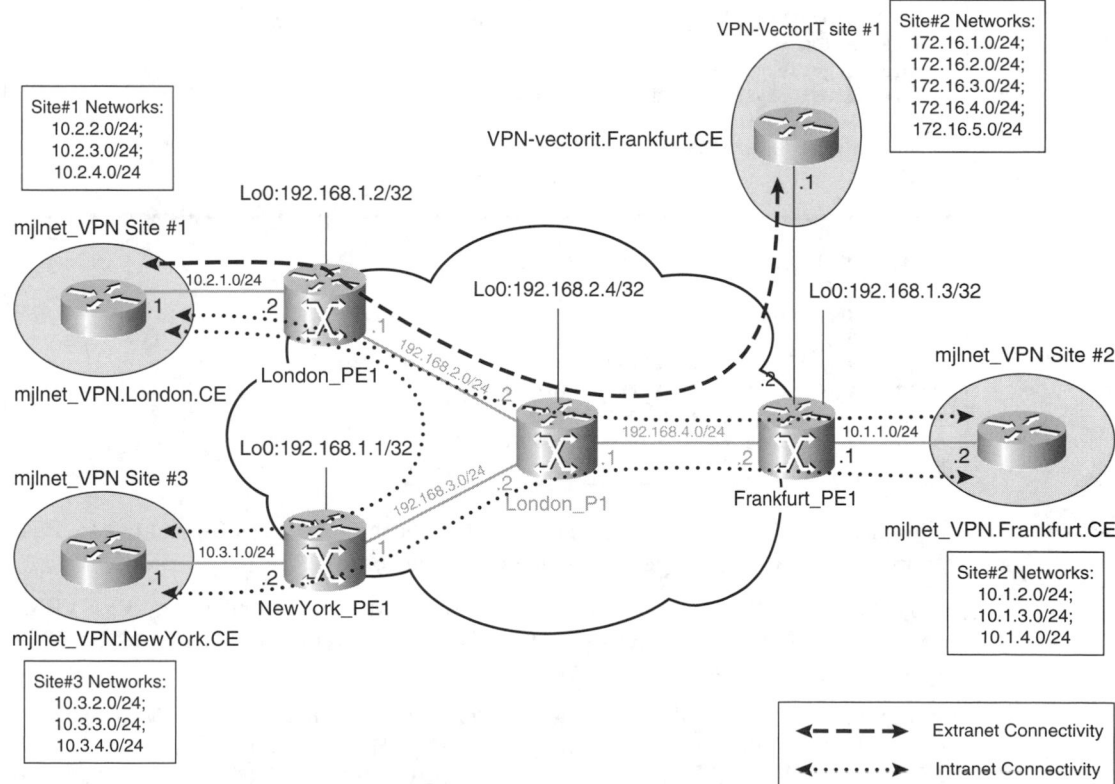

In Figure 4-13, extranet connectivity is provisioned between the London site of mjlnet_VPN (mjlnet_VPN.London.CE) and the Frankfurt site of VPN-VectorIT

(VPN-vectorit.Frankfurt.CE). There is no connectivity between any other sites in VPNs mjlnet_VPN and VPN-VectorIT.

To allow extranet connectivity between different MPLS Layer 3 VPNs, you can configure separate RTs on PE routers connected to the VPN sites between which you want to provision extranet connectivity.

In this example, extranet connectivity is provisioned between CE routers mjlnet_VPN.London.CE and VPN-vectorit.Frankfurt.CE, and so separate RTs for extranet connectivity are configured on the PE routers connected to thoseCE routers.

Example 4-23 shows the relevant configuration of the mjlnet_VPN VRF on London_PE1 (which is connected to mjlnet_VPN.London.CE) and VPN-vectorit VRF on Frankfurt_PE1 (which is connected to VPN-vectorit.Frankfurt.CE).

Example 4-23 *Configuration for PE Routers London_PE1 and Frankfurt_PE1*

```
!
! On London_PE1 (line 1)
!
ip vrf mjlnet_VPN
 rd 65535:100
 route-target export 65535:100
 route-target export 65535:600 (line 2)
 route-target import 65535:100
 route-target import 65535:700 (line 3)
 !
 !

 !
! On Frankfurt_PE1 (line 4)
 !
ip vrf VPN-vectorit
 rd 65535:200
 route-target export 65535:200
 route-target export 65535:700 (line 5)
 route-target import 65535:200
 route-target import 65535:600 (line 6)
 !
```

Highlighted lines 1 to 3 shows the configuration of the mjlnet_VPN VRF on London_PE1. Of particular relevance are the highlighted import and export RTs.

Import RT 65535:700 on London_PE1 is used to import *extranet* routes from VRF VPN-vectorit on Frankfurt_PE1 (it corresponds to the export RT configured on Frankfurt_PE1 shown in highlighted line 5).

Export RT 65535:600, on the other hand, is attached to *all* VRF mjlnet_VPN routes advertised to other PE routers (*including* Frankfurt_PE1) from London_PE1.

It is worth noting that RTs 65535:600 and 65535:700 are not configured on any other PE routers in the network, thus ensuring that extranet connectivity is *only* maintained between CE routers mjlnet_VPN.London.CE and VPN-vectorit.Frankfurt.CE.

Import and export RTs 65535:100 and 65535:200 shown in Example 4-23 are used to provision *intranet* connectivity for VPNs mjlnet_VPN and VPN-vectorit, respectively, and so are not discussed further in this section.

Example 4-24 shows the output of the **show ip route vrf** *vrf-name* command on PE router London_PE1.

Example 4-24 show ip route vrf *Command Output on PE Router London_PE1*

```
London_PE1#show ip route vrf mjlnet_VPN
Routing Table: mjlnet_VPN
Codes: C - connected, S - static, I - IGRP, R - RIP, M - mobile, B - BGP
       D - EIGRP, EX - EIGRP external, O - OSPF, IA - OSPF inter area
       N1 - OSPF NSSA external type 1, N2 - OSPF NSSA external type 2
       E1 - OSPF external type 1, E2 - OSPF external type 2, E - EGP
       i - IS-IS, su - IS-IS summary, L1 - IS-IS level-1, L2 - IS-IS level-2
       ia - IS-IS inter area, * - candidate default, U - per-user static route
       o - ODR
Gateway of last resort is not set
       172.16.0.0/24 is subnetted, 5 subnets
B         172.16.4.0 [200/0] via 192.168.1.3, 00:11:14 (line 1)
B         172.16.5.0 [200/0] via 192.168.1.3, 00:11:14 (line 2)
B         172.16.1.0 [200/0] via 192.168.1.3, 00:11:14 (line 3)
B         172.16.2.0 [200/0] via 192.168.1.3, 00:11:14 (line 4)
B         172.16.3.0 [200/0] via 192.168.1.3, 00:11:14 (line 5)
       10.0.0.0/8 is variably subnetted, 14 subnets, 2 masks
B         10.3.1.0/24 [200/0] via 192.168.1.1, 02:03:30
C         10.2.1.1/32 is directly connected, Serial2/1
B         10.1.3.0/24 [200/1889792] via 192.168.1.3, 00:11:15
B         10.1.1.2/32 [200/0] via 192.168.1.3, 00:11:15
C         10.2.1.0/24 is directly connected, Serial2/1
B         10.1.2.0/24 [200/1889792] via 192.168.1.3, 00:11:15
B         10.3.3.0/24 [200/0] via 192.168.1.1, 02:03:31
B         10.2.2.0/24 [20/0] via 10.2.1.1, 01:55:44
B         10.1.1.0/24 [200/0] via 192.168.1.3, 00:11:15
B         10.3.2.0/24 [200/0] via 192.168.1.1, 02:03:31
B         10.2.3.0/24 [20/0] via 10.2.1.1, 01:55:44
B         10.2.4.0/24 [20/0] via 10.2.1.1, 01:55:44
B         10.3.4.0/24 [200/0] via 192.168.1.1, 02:03:31
B         10.1.4.0/24 [200/1889792] via 192.168.1.3, 00:11:15
London_PE1#
```

As you can see in the output of the **show ip route vrf** *vrf-name* command on PE router London_PE1 (Example 4-24, highlighted lines 1 to 5), VPN-vectorit site 1 routes (172.16.1.0/24, 172.16.2.0/24, 172.16.3.0/24, 172.16.4.0/24, and 172.16.5.0/24) have been successfully imported into VRF mjlnet_VPN. You will notice that, as intended, only VPN-vectorit site 1 routes are imported into VRF mjlnet_VPN on London_PE1, and not any other VPN-vectorit routes.

The VPN-vectorit site 1 routes are then advertised via the PE-CE routing protocol (eBGP in this example) to mjlnet_VPN.London.CE, as shown by the output of the **show ip route** command in Example 4-25.

Example 4-25 show ip route *Command Output on CE Router mjlnet_VPN.London.CE*

```
mjlnet_VPN.London.CE#show ip route
Codes: C - connected, S - static, I - IGRP, R - RIP, M - mobile, B - BGP
       D - EIGRP, EX - EIGRP external, O - OSPF, IA - OSPF inter area
       N1 - OSPF NSSA external type 1, N2 - OSPF NSSA external type 2
       E1 - OSPF external type 1, E2 - OSPF external type 2, E - EGP
       i - IS-IS, L1 - IS-IS level-1, L2 - IS-IS level-2, ia - IS-IS inter area
       * - candidate default, U - per-user static route, o - ODR
Gateway of last resort is not set
     172.16.0.0/24 is subnetted, 5 subnets
B       172.16.4.0 [20/0] via 10.2.1.2, 00:10:14 (line 1)
B       172.16.5.0 [20/0] via 10.2.1.2, 00:10:14 (line 2)
B       172.16.1.0 [20/0] via 10.2.1.2, 00:10:14 (line 3)
B       172.16.2.0 [20/0] via 10.2.1.2, 00:10:14 (line 4)
B       172.16.3.0 [20/0] via 10.2.1.2, 00:10:14 (line 5)
     10.0.0.0/8 is variably subnetted, 10 subnets, 2 masks
B       10.1.3.0/24 [20/0] via 10.2.1.2, 00:10:14
B       10.1.1.2/32 [20/0] via 10.2.1.2, 00:10:14
B       10.1.2.0/24 [20/0] via 10.2.1.2, 00:10:14
C       10.2.1.0/24 is directly connected, Serial0
B       10.1.1.0/24 [20/0] via 10.2.1.2, 00:10:14
C       10.2.2.0/24 is directly connected, Loopback100
C       10.2.1.2/32 is directly connected, Serial0
C       10.2.3.0/24 is directly connected, Loopback101
C       10.2.4.0/24 is directly connected, Loopback102
B       10.1.4.0/24 [20/0] via 10.2.1.2, 00:10:16
mjlnet_VPN.London.CE#
```

Similarly, the output of the **show ip route vrf** *vrf-name* command on Frankfurt_PE1 (highlighted lines 1 to 4) shows that mjlnet_VPN site 1 routes (10.2.1.0/24, 10.2.2.0/24, 10.2.3.0/24, and 10.2.4.0/24) have been imported into the VPN-vectorit VRF.

Example 4-26 show ip route vrf *Command Output on PE Router Frankfurt_PE1*

```
Frankfurt_PE1#show ip route vrf VPN-vectorit
Routing Table: VPN-vectorit
Codes: C - connected, S - static, I - IGRP, R - RIP, M - mobile, B - BGP
       D - EIGRP, EX - EIGRP external, O - OSPF, IA - OSPF inter area
       N1 - OSPF NSSA external type 1, N2 - OSPF NSSA external type 2
       E1 - OSPF external type 1, E2 - OSPF external type 2, E - EGP
       i - IS-IS, su - IS-IS summary, L1 - IS-IS level-1, L2 - IS-IS level-2
       ia - IS-IS inter area, * - candidate default, U - per-user static route
       o - ODR
Gateway of last resort is not set
     172.16.0.0/16 is variably subnetted, 16 subnets, 2 masks
B       172.16.24.0/24 [200/0] via 192.168.1.2, 00:11:53
B       172.16.25.0/24 [200/0] via 192.168.1.2, 00:11:53
B       172.16.21.0/24 [200/0] via 192.168.1.2, 00:11:53
B       172.16.22.0/24 [200/0] via 192.168.1.2, 00:11:53
B       172.16.23.0/24 [200/0] via 192.168.1.2, 00:11:53
B       172.16.12.0/24 [200/0] via 192.168.1.1, 00:11:53
B       172.16.13.0/24 [200/0] via 192.168.1.1, 00:11:53
```

Example 4-26 show ip route vrf *Command Output on PE Router Frankfurt_PE1 (Continued)*

```
B        172.16.14.0/24 [200/0] via 192.168.1.1, 00:11:54
B        172.16.15.0/24 [200/0] via 192.168.1.1, 00:11:54
B        172.16.11.0/24 [200/0] via 192.168.1.1, 00:11:54
B        172.16.4.0/24 [20/0] via 172.16.1.2, 00:12:05
B        172.16.5.0/24 [20/0] via 172.16.1.2, 00:12:05
C        172.16.1.0/24 is directly connected, Serial4/2
B        172.16.2.0/24 [20/0] via 172.16.1.2, 00:12:05
B        172.16.3.0/24 [20/0] via 172.16.1.2, 00:12:05
C        172.16.1.2/32 is directly connected, Serial4/2
      10.0.0.0/24 is subnetted, 4 subnets
B        10.2.1.0 [200/0] via 192.168.1.2, 00:11:54 (line 1)
B        10.2.2.0 [200/0] via 192.168.1.2, 00:11:54 (line 2)
B        10.2.3.0 [200/0] via 192.168.1.2, 00:11:54 (line 3)
B        10.2.4.0 [200/0] via 192.168.1.2, 00:11:54 (line 4)
Frankfurt_PE1#
```

The mjlnet_VPN site 1 routes are advertised by Frankfurt_PE1 via the PE-CE routing protocol to VPN-vectorit.Frankfurt.CE. Notice that, as intended, mjlnet_VPN site 2 and site 3 routes have not been imported into VRF VPN-vectorit on Frankfurt_PE1.

Example 4-27 shows the mjlnet_VPN site 1 routes in the output of the **show ip route** command on VPN-vectorit.Frankfurt.CE (see highlighted lines 1 to 4).

Example 4-27 *Output of the* show ip route *Command on VPN-vectorit.Frankfurt.CE*

```
VPN-vectorit.Frankfurt.CE#show ip route
Codes: C - connected, S - static, I - IGRP, R - RIP, M - mobile, B - BGP
       D - EIGRP, EX - EIGRP external, O - OSPF, IA - OSPF inter area
       N1 - OSPF NSSA external type 1, N2 - OSPF NSSA external type 2
       E1 - OSPF external type 1, E2 - OSPF external type 2, E - EGP
       i - IS-IS, L1 - IS-IS level-1, L2 - IS-IS level-2, ia - IS-IS inter area
       * - candidate default, U - per-user static route, o - ODR
Gateway of last resort is not set
     172.16.0.0/16 is variably subnetted, 16 subnets, 2 masks
B        172.16.24.0/24 [20/0] via 172.16.1.1, 00:12:07
B        172.16.25.0/24 [20/0] via 172.16.1.1, 00:12:07
B        172.16.21.0/24 [20/0] via 172.16.1.1, 00:12:07
B        172.16.22.0/24 [20/0] via 172.16.1.1, 00:12:07
B        172.16.23.0/24 [20/0] via 172.16.1.1, 00:12:07
B        172.16.12.0/24 [20/0] via 172.16.1.1, 00:12:07
B        172.16.13.0/24 [20/0] via 172.16.1.1, 00:12:07
B        172.16.14.0/24 [20/0] via 172.16.1.1, 00:12:07
B        172.16.15.0/24 [20/0] via 172.16.1.1, 00:12:07
B        172.16.11.0/24 [20/0] via 172.16.1.1, 00:12:07
C        172.16.4.0/24 is directly connected, Loopback504
C        172.16.5.0/24 is directly connected, Loopback505
C        172.16.1.1/32 is directly connected, Serial0
C        172.16.1.0/24 is directly connected, Serial0
C        172.16.2.0/24 is directly connected, Loopback502
C        172.16.3.0/24 is directly connected, Loopback503
      10.0.0.0/24 is subnetted, 4 subnets
```

continues

Example 4-27 *Output of the* **show ip route** *Command on VPN-vectorit.Frankfurt.CE (Continued)*

```
B       10.2.1.0 [20/0] via 172.16.1.1, 00:12:08 (line 1)
B       10.2.2.0 [20/0] via 172.16.1.1, 00:12:08 (line 2)
B       10.2.3.0 [20/0] via 172.16.1.1, 00:12:08 (line 3)
B       10.2.4.0 [20/0] via 172.16.1.1, 00:12:08 (line 4)
VPN-vectorit.Frankfurt.CE#
```

As shown in Example 4-28, connectivity is then successfully tested between VPN-vectorit site 1 and mjlnet_VPN site 1 using **ping**.

Example 4-28 *Successfully Testing Connectivity Between VPN-vectorit Site 1 and mjlnet_VPN Site 1 Using ping*

```
VPN-vectorit.Frankfurt.CE#ping 10.2.1.1
Type escape sequence to abort.
Sending 5, 100-byte ICMP Echos to 10.2.1.1, timeout is 2 seconds:
!!!!!
Success rate is 100 percent (5/5), round-trip min/avg/max = 120/120/120 ms
VPN-vectorit.Frankfurt.CE#
```

So, extranet has been successfully provisioned between mjlnet_VPN site 1 and VPN-vectorit site 1.

The configuration shown in Example 4-23 will allow extranet connectivity, but it does not control exactly which prefixes should be distributed for extranet connectivity. The configuration allows the exchange of *all* mjlnet_VPN site 1 and VPN-vectorit site 1 routes between London_PE1 and Frankfurt_PE1.

If you want to have more selective control over the extranet routes exchanged between the mjlnet_VPN VRF and the VPN-vectorit VRF on London_PE1 and Frankfurt_PE1, you can configure export maps. Export maps can be used to control the attachment of (export) RTs to specific prefixes.

Example 4-29 shows the configuration of export maps on London_PE1 and Frankfurt_PE1 that ensure that only specific mjlnet_VPN site 1 and VPN-vectorit site 1 routes are exchanged for extranet connectivity.

Example 4-29 *Explicitly Controlling Extranet Routes Exchanged Between VRFs on PE Routers London_PE1 and Frankfurt_PE1*

```
!
! On London_PE1 (line 1)
!
ip vrf mjlnet_VPN
 rd 65535:100
 export map export-mjlnet-routes (line 2)
 route-target export 65535:100
 route-target import 65535:100
 route-target import 65535:700 (line 3)
!
route-map export-mjlnet-routes permit 10 (line 4)
 match ip address 50 (line 5)
```

Example 4-29 *Explicitly Controlling Extranet Routes Exchanged Between VRFs on PE Routers London_PE1 and Frankfurt_PE1 (Continued)*

```
  set extcommunity rt  65535:600 additive (line 6)
 !
 access-list 50 permit 10.2.1.0 (line 7)
 access-list 50 permit 10.2.2.0 (line 8)
  !
```
```
  !
 ! On Frankfurt_PE1 (line 9)
  !
 ip vrf VPN-vectorit
  rd 65535:200
  export map export-vectorit-routes (line 10)
  route-target export 65535:200
  route-target import 65535:200
  route-target import 65535:600 (line 11)
  !
 route-map export-vectorit-routes permit 10 (line 12)
  match ip address 50 (line 13)
  set extcommunity rt  65535:700 additive (line 14)
  !
 access-list 50 permit 172.16.1.0 (line 15)
 access-list 50 permit 172.16.2.0 (line 16)
  !
```

In highlighted line 2, an export map linking to a route map called **export-mjlnet-routes** is configured.

Highlighted lines 4 to 6 show the route map called **export-mjlnet-routes**.

The **match ip address** *access-list-number* command in highlighted line 5 matches prefixes specified in access list 50 (see highlighted line 7 and 8).

Then in highlighted line 6, the **set extcommunity rt** *extended-community-value* **additive** command is used to attach an *additional* RT (65535:600) to the prefixes specified in access list 50 before they are advertised to other PE routers. Besides RT 65535:600, RT 65535:100 is attached to these prefixes by the **route-target export** *route-target-ext-community* command.

It is important to include the **additive** keyword with the **set extcommunity rt** *extended-community-value* because if it is not included in the command syntax, RT 65535:600 will overwrite RT 65535:100 instead being added to it, and that would cause other mjlnet_VPN sites to lose connectivity to the networks specified in the access list (they are configured to import routes with an RT of 65535:100).

So, (export) RT 65535:600 is attached to mjlnet_VPN site 1 routes specified in access list 50. Now take a look at highlighted line 11. You will see that Frankfurt_PE1 is configured to import these routes into its VPN-vectorit VRF, and after they have been imported into VPN-vectorit, they are advertised to VPN-vectorit.Frankfurt.CE using the PE-CE routing protocol.

Frankfurt_PE1 is configured in a similar way to London_PE1 — an export map (highlighted line 10) references a route map called **export-vectorit-routes** (see highlighted lines 12 to 14). The **export-vectorit-routes** route map matches the prefixes specified in access list 50 (see highlighted lines 13, 15, and 16), and RT 65535:700 is attached to those prefixes (see highlighted line 14).

If you take a look at highlighted line 3, you can see that London_PE1 is configured to import routes with RT 65535:700 attached into the mjlnet_VPN VRF. These routes are then advertised to mjlnet_VPN.London.CE using the PE-CE routing protocol.

As shown in the output of the **show ip route** command in Example 4-30, mjlnet_VPN .London.CE now has IP reachability to VPN-vectorit site 1 networks 172.16.1.0/24 and 172.16.2.0/24 only.

Example 4-30 **show ip route** *Command Output on mjlnet_VPN.London.CE*

```
mjlnet_VPN.London.CE#show ip route
Codes: C - connected, S - static, I - IGRP, R - RIP, M - mobile, B - BGP
       D - EIGRP, EX - EIGRP external, O - OSPF, IA - OSPF inter area
       N1 - OSPF NSSA external type 1, N2 - OSPF NSSA external type 2
       E1 - OSPF external type 1, E2 - OSPF external type 2, E - EGP
       i - IS-IS, L1 - IS-IS level-1, L2 - IS-IS level-2, ia - IS-IS inter area
       * - candidate default, U - per-user static route, o - ODR
Gateway of last resort is not set
     172.16.0.0/24 is subnetted, 2 subnets
B       172.16.1.0 [20/0] via 10.2.1.2, 00:07:15
B       172.16.2.0 [20/0] via 10.2.1.2, 00:07:15
     10.0.0.0/8 is variably subnetted, 10 subnets, 2 masks
B       10.1.3.0/24 [20/0] via 10.2.1.2, 00:07:15
B       10.1.1.2/32 [20/0] via 10.2.1.2, 00:07:15
B       10.1.2.0/24 [20/0] via 10.2.1.2, 00:07:15
C       10.2.1.0/24 is directly connected, Serial0
B       10.1.1.0/24 [20/0] via 10.2.1.2, 00:07:15
C       10.2.2.0/24 is directly connected, Loopback100
C       10.2.1.2/32 is directly connected, Serial0
C       10.2.3.0/24 is directly connected, Loopback101
C       10.2.4.0/24 is directly connected, Loopback102
B       10.1.4.0/24 [20/0] via 10.2.1.2, 00:07:15
mjlnet_VPN.London.CE#
```

Similarly, as shown in Example 4-31, VPN-vectorit.Frankfurt.CE has IP reachability to mjlnet_VPN site 1 networks 10.2.1.0/24 and 10.2.2.0/24 only.

Example 4-31 **show ip route** *Command Output on VPN-vectorit.Frankfurt.CE*

```
VPN-vectorit.Frankfurt.CE#show ip route
Codes: C - connected, S - static, I - IGRP, R - RIP, M - mobile, B - BGP
       D - EIGRP, EX - EIGRP external, O - OSPF, IA - OSPF inter area
       N1 - OSPF NSSA external type 1, N2 - OSPF NSSA external type 2
       E1 - OSPF external type 1, E2 - OSPF external type 2, E - EGP
       i - IS-IS, L1 - IS-IS level-1, L2 - IS-IS level-2, ia - IS-IS inter area
       * - candidate default, U - per-user static route, o - ODR
```

Example 4-31 show ip route *Command Output on VPN-vectorit.Frankfurt.CE (Continued)*

```
Gateway of last resort is not set
     172.16.0.0/16 is variably subnetted, 16 subnets, 2 masks
B       172.16.24.0/24 [20/0] via 172.16.1.1, 00:08:05
B       172.16.25.0/24 [20/0] via 172.16.1.1, 00:08:05
B       172.16.21.0/24 [20/0] via 172.16.1.1, 00:08:05
B       172.16.22.0/24 [20/0] via 172.16.1.1, 00:08:05
B       172.16.23.0/24 [20/0] via 172.16.1.1, 00:08:05
B       172.16.12.0/24 [20/0] via 172.16.1.1, 00:08:20
B       172.16.13.0/24 [20/0] via 172.16.1.1, 00:08:20
B       172.16.14.0/24 [20/0] via 172.16.1.1, 00:08:20
B       172.16.15.0/24 [20/0] via 172.16.1.1, 00:08:20
B       172.16.11.0/24 [20/0] via 172.16.1.1, 00:08:20
C       172.16.4.0/24 is directly connected, Loopback504
C       172.16.5.0/24 is directly connected, Loopback505
C       172.16.1.1/32 is directly connected, Serial0
C       172.16.1.0/24 is directly connected, Serial0
C       172.16.2.0/24 is directly connected, Loopback502
C       172.16.3.0/24 is directly connected, Loopback503
     10.0.0.0/24 is subnetted, 2 subnets
B       10.2.1.0 [20/0] via 172.16.1.1, 00:08:07
B       10.2.2.0 [20/0] via 172.16.1.1, 00:08:07
VectorIT.Frank#
```

Another way of explicitly controlling the distribution of extranet routes is to use import maps. In this case, import maps are used to control which extranet routes are imported into a VRF.

Example 4-32 shows the configuration of import maps to control the import of extranet routes on London_PE1 and Frankfurt_PE1.

Example 4-32 *Configuring Import Maps to Control the Import of Extranet Routes on London_PE1 and Frankfurt_PE1*

```
!
! On London_PE1 (line 1)
!
ip vrf mjlnet_VPN
 rd 65535:100
 import map import-mjlnet-vectorit-routes (line 2)
 route-target export 65535:100
 route-target export 65535:600 (line 3)
 route-target import 65535:100 (line 4)
 route-target import 65535:700 (line 5)
!
route-map import-mjlnet-vectorit-routes permit 10 (line 6)
 match ip address 60 (line 7)
!
access-list 60 permit 172.16.1.0 (line 8)
access-list 60 permit 172.16.2.0 (line 9)
access-list 60 permit 10.0.0.0 0.255.255.255 (line 10)
!
! On Frankfurt_PE1 (line 11)
!
```

Example 4-32 *Configuring Import Maps to Control the Import of Extranet Routes on London_PE1 and Frankfurt_PE1 (Continued)*

```
ip vrf VPN-vectorit
 rd 65535:200
 import map import-vectorit-mjlnet-routes (line 12)
 route-target export 65535:200
 route-target export 65535:700 (line 13)
 route-target import 65535:200 (line 14)
 route-target import 65535:600 (line 15)
!
route-map import-vectorit-mjlnet-routes permit 10 (line 15)
 match ip address 60 (line 16)
!
access-list 60 permit 10.2.1.0 (line 17)
access-list 60 permit 10.2.2.0 (line 18)
access-list 60 permit 172.16.0.0 0.0.255.255 (line 19)
!
```

Highlighted line 2 shows an import map that references a route map called **import-mjlnet-vectorit-route**.

Route map **import-vectorit-mjlnet-routes** (highlighted lines 15 and 16) matches those VPNv4 routes specified in access list 60 (see highlighted lines 17 to 19).

The **access-list 60** command specifies mjlnet_VPN site 1 prefixes 10.2.1.0/24 and 10.2.2.0/24, as well as all VPN-vectorit prefixes (defined in highlighted line 19).

So, although highlighted line 3 and 4 permit the import of VPNv4 routes with RTs 65535:100 and 65535:700 attached, the import map ensures not only must prefixes have one of these RTs attached but they must also be one of those prefixes specified in access list 60.

You will also notice that *all* mjlnet_VPN site 1 routes are all advertised from London_PE1 with the attached (export) RT 65535:600 (see highlighted line 3).

The configuration on Frankfurt_PE1 is similar to that for London_PE1. Highlighted line 12 defines an import map that links to a route map called **import-vectorit-mjlnet-routes**. Route map **import-vectorit-mjlnet-routes** (highlighted lines 16 and 17) then matches those VPNv4 routes specified in access list 60 (see highlighted lines 18 to 20).

The **access-list 60** command specifies mjlnet_VPN site 1 prefixes 10.2.1.0/24 and 10.2.2.0/24, as well as all VPN-vectorit prefixes (defined in highlighted line 20). So, VPNv4 routes with the RTs specified in highlighted lines 14 and 15 (65535:200 and 65535:600) are imported into VRF VPN-vectorit as long as they are matched by the import map (and access list 60).

In highlighted line 13, you can see that *all* VPN-vectorit site 1 routes are advertised by Frankfurt_PE1 with attached (export) RT 65535:700.

In conclusion, the import map configuration shown in Example 4-32 has exactly the same effect in limiting the distribution of extranet routes between VPNs as the export map configuration shown in Example 4-29.

If you really want to be deterministic with regard to extranet route distribution and guard against the accidental distribution of the wrong routes between VPNs, it is possible to configure both export and import maps together. So, you could, for example, combine the export and import map configurations shown in Examples 4-29 and 4-32.

Before finishing this section, it is important to note that one common type of extranet VPN topology that can be configured using the techniques described in this section is a service provider management VPN. By exporting CE router loopback interface addresses to the management VPN VRF and management VPN subnet addresses to the customer VRFs, the service provider will be able to manage customer CE devices.

Preventing Routing Loops When Customer VPN Sites Are Multihomed

It is common for customer VPN sites to be dual homed to the service provider MPLS VPN backbone to provide redundant connectivity. In this case, however, it is important that PE routers be correctly configured to ensure that routing loops do not develop.

Figure 4-14 illustrates a routing loop that develops when a customer VPN site is dual homed to the service provider MPLS VPN backbone network.

Figure 4-14 *A Routing Loop When a Customer VPN Site Is Dual Homed to the Service Provider MPLS VPN Backbone Network*

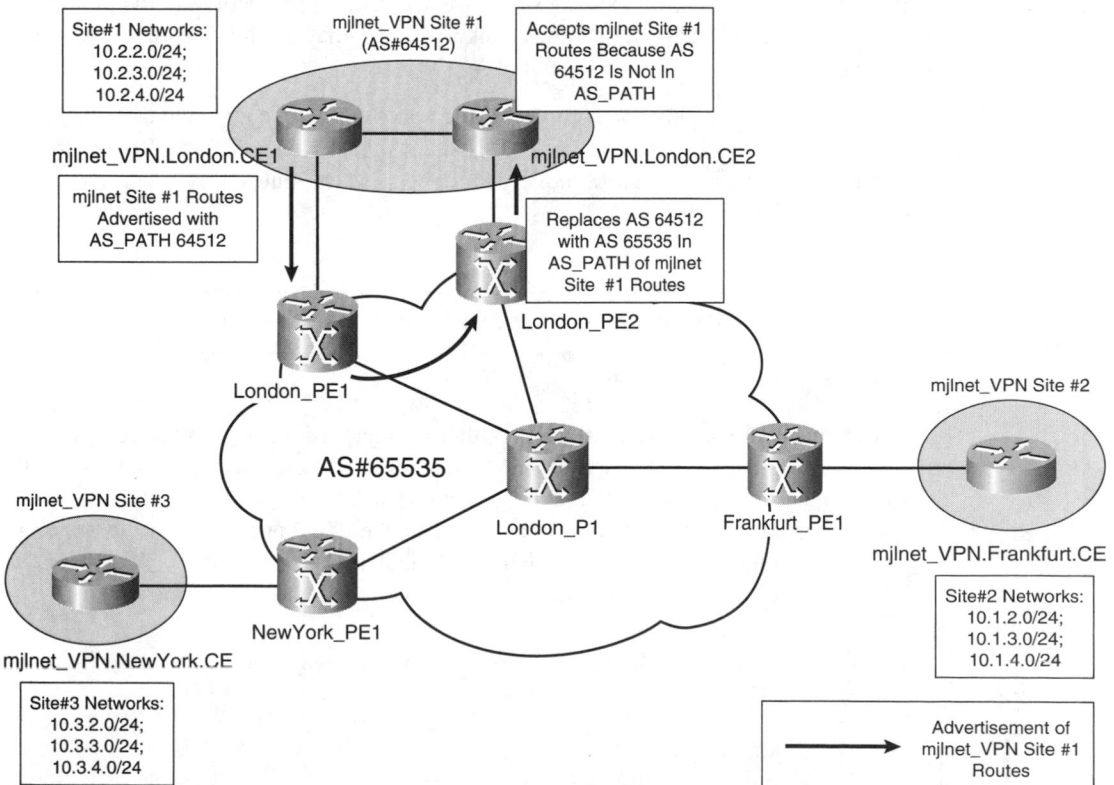

In Figure 4-14, mjlnet_VPN.London.CE1 and mjlnet_VPN.London.CE2 are advertising mljnet_VPN site 1 (London) routes to PE routes London_PE1 and London_PE2, respectively.

London_PE1 and London_PE2 then exchange VPNv4 routes (mjlnet_VPN site 1 routes). London_PE1 now advertises mjlnet_VPN site 1 routes (via London_PE2) to mjlnet_VPN.London.CE1, and London_PE2 advertises mjlnet_VPN site 1 routes (via London_PE1) to mjlnet_VPN.London.CE2.

At this point, mjlnet_VPN.London.CE1 has two sets of routes to mjlnet site 1 networks— it has local routes, and it has routes via London_PE1. Similarly, mjlnet_VPN.London.CE2 has two sets of routes to mjlnet_VPN site 1—it has local routes, and it has routes via London_PE2.

The mljnet_VPN site 1 routes that mjlnet_VPN.London.CE1 and mjlnet_VPN.London.CE2 have received via their connected PE router may, under certain circumstances, cause 1) suboptimal routing, 2) transitory routing loops, or 3) permanent routing loops.

These undesirable affects are *particularly* likely if the PE-CE routing protocol in use is eBGP because eBGP routes (which have an administrative distance of 20) will, by default, be preferred over iBGP routes (which have an administrative distance of 200) or IGP routes (which, with the exception of EIGRP summary routes, all have an administrative distance greater than 20). Irrespective of the PE-CE routing protocol, and the precise effects of the re-advertisement of routes back to the originating site, it is obviously not a good thing!

The way around this problem is to configure the attachment of an attribute called a *Site of Origin* (SoO) to VPNv4 routes. The SoO attribute is actually encoded as a Route Origin BGP extended community, and it uniquely identifies a set of routes advertised from a particular customer VPN site.

NOTE   The Route Origin BGP extended community is defined in RFC 4360.

If PE routers are so configured, an SoO attribute is attached to routes received *from* a customer VPN site, and routes advertised *to* that site are filtered so that any routes with an SoO attribute corresponding to that site are not sent. The effect of the attachment of SoO attributes, and filtering of routes based on attached SoO attributes, is illustrated in Figure 4-15. In Figure 4-15, mjlnet_VPN.London.CE1 advertises mljnet_VPN site 1 (London) routes to PE routes London_PE1.

Figure 4-15 *Effect of the SoO (Route Origin) Attributes*

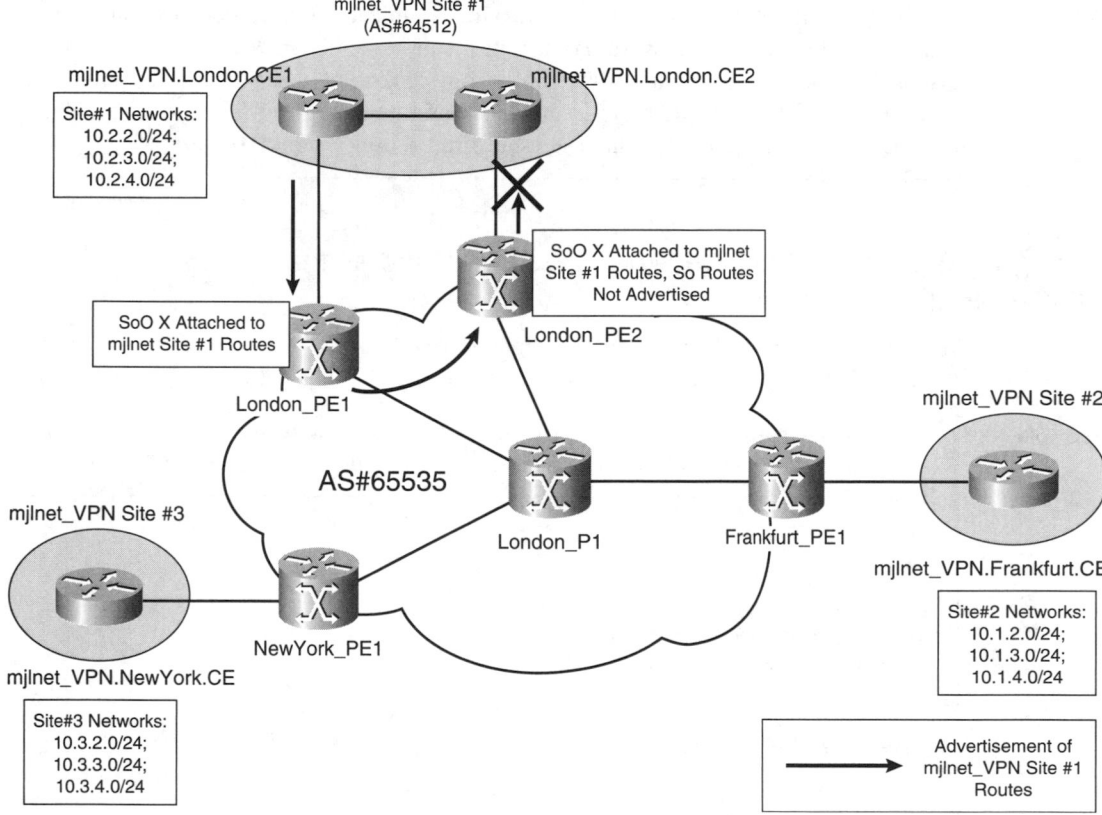

London_PE1 then advertises VPNv4 routes (including mjlnet_VPN site 1 routes) to London_PE2. London_PE2 would now usually advertise mjlnet_VPN site 1 routes to mjlnet_VPN.London.CE2, but because an SoO attribute corresponding to mjlnet_VPN site 1 is attached to the routes, they are not advertised to mjlnet_VPN.London.CE2.

The same process occurs with mjlnet_VPN site 1 routes advertised by mjlnet_VPN .London.CE2 via London_PE2—London_PE2 advertises VPNv4 routes (including the mjlnet_VPN site 1 routes) to London_PE1, but London_PE1 does not advertise these to mjlnet_VPN.London.CE1 because the routes have an attached SoO attribute corresponding to mjlnet_VPN site 1.

The method of configuring the SoO attribute differs slightly depending on whether the PE-CE routing protocol is eBGP. The next two sections examine configuration of the SoO attribute when eBGP is used as the PE-CE routing protocol and when another PE-CE routing is used.

NOTE   If the same BGP autonomous system is used at more than one customer VPN site, you must
configure the **neighbor** *ip-address* **as-override** command on PE routers to ensure that
CE routers do not drop routes from other sites. Unfortunately, in this case, CE routers will
also accept local site routes advertised back from PE routers (when the SoO attribute is *not*
configured on PE routers). The solution is to configure the SoO attribute to ensure that
CE routers will drop any local site routes advertised back from PE routers.

Configuring the SoO Attribute When eBGP Is Used as the PE-CE Routing Protocol

Example 4-33 shows the (relevant) configuration of London_PE1 when EBGP is used as
the PE-CE routing protocol.

Example 4-33 *Configuration of London_PE1 for the Attachment and Verification of BGP Routes with Attached SoO Extended BGP Community Attribute (When eBGP Is Used as the PE-CE Routing Protocol)*

```
!
! London_PE1 (line 1)
!
!
interface Serial2/1
 ip vrf forwarding mjlnet_VPN
 ip address 10.2.1.2 255.255.255.0
!
!
router bgp 65535 (line 2)
!
<output omitted>
!
 address-family ipv4 vrf mjlnet_VPN
 neighbor 10.2.1.1 remote-as 64512 (line 3)
 neighbor 10.2.1.1 activate (line 4)
 neighbor 10.2.1.1 as-override (line 5)
 neighbor 10.2.1.1 route-map set-soo in (line 6)
 no auto-summary
 no synchronization
 exit-address-family
!
route-map set-soo permit 10 (line 7)
 set extcommunity soo 65535:901 (line 8)
!
```

eBGP is configured as the PE-CE routing protocol between London_PE1 in highlighted
lines 3 and 4. Note that the ASN (64512) is used at all customer VPN sites in this example.

In highlighted lines 5, the **neighbor** *ip-address* **as-override** command is configured. This
command is necessary because, in this scenario, the same BGP autonomous system is being
used at all the customer VPN (mjlnet_VPN) sites.

Next, the **neighbor** *ip-address* **route-map** *map-name* **in** command is used to process BGP updates inbound from mjlnet_VPN.London.CE1 (see highlighted line 6) based on a route map called **set-soo**.

Highlighted lines 7 and 8 show the **set-soo** route map, which sets the SoO extended community attribute to 65535:901 on all BGP updates inbound from mjlnet_VPN.London.CE1.

As you can see in Example 4-34, the configuration of London_PE2 is almost identical.

Example 4-34 *Configuration of London_PE2 for the Attachment and Verification of BGP Routes with Attached SoO Extended BGP Community Attribute (When EBGP Is Used as the PE-CE Routing Protocol)*

```
!
! On London_PE2 (line 1)
!
interface Serial4/1
 ip vrf forwarding mjlnet_VPN
 ip address 10.1.1.1 255.255.255.0
!
router bgp 65535 (line 2)
 !
! output omitted for brevity
 !
 address-family ipv4 vrf mjlnet_VPN
 neighbor 10.1.1.2 remote-as 64512 (line 3)
 neighbor 10.1.1.2 activate (line 4)
 neighbor 10.1.1.2 as-override (line 5)
 neighbor 10.1.1.2 route-map set-soo in (line 6)
 no auto-summary
 no synchronization
 exit-address-family
 !
route-map set-soo permit 10 (line 7)
 set extcommunity soo 65535:901 (line 8)
 !
```

If you look closely (and compare to Example 4-33), you will see that the only difference in the configuration of London_PE2 is the IP address of the BGP neighbor (mjlnet_VPN.London.CE2) and the IP addressing applied to the VRF interface.

Also important, notice that the SoO (see highlighted line 8) is the same. The SoO *must* be the same for BGP updates received by PE routers from CE routers at the *same* site; otherwise, suboptimal routing and/or routing loops will not be prevented.

Now it is time to take a look at SoO in action. In Example 4-35, attachment of the SoO attribute to a sample mjlnet_VPN site 1 route (10.2.2.0/24) is verified on London_PE2 using the **show ip bgp vpnv4 vrf** *vrf-name network-address* command.

Example 4-35 *Verifying the SoO Extended Community Attribute Attached to a VPNv4 Route*

```
London_PE2#show ip bgp vpnv4 vrf mjlnet_VPN 10.2.2.0
BGP routing table entry for 65535:100:10.2.2.0/24, version 41
Paths: (1 available, best #1, table mjlnet_VPN)
  Not advertised to any peer
  64512
    192.168.1.2 (metric 30) from 192.168.1.2 (192.168.1.2) (line 1)
      Origin IGP, metric 0, localpref 100, valid, internal, best
      Extended Community: SoO:65535:901 RT:65535:100, (line 2)
      mpls labels in/out nolabel/24
London_PE2#
```

In highlighted line 1, you can see that this route has been advertised to London_PE2 by London_PE1 (192.168.1.2). London_PE1 received this route from mjlnet_VPN.London.CE1.

The SoO attribute is shown in highlighted line 2. As you can see, it is 65535:901.

The **debug ip bgp** *neighbor-ip-address* **updates** (see Example 4-36) shows what happens when London_PE2 advertises (route) updates to mjlnet_VPN.London.CE2.

Example 4-36 *London_PE2 Does Not Send mjlnet_VPN Site 1 Routes to mjlnet_VPN.London.CE2 (eBGP Is the PE-CE Routing Protocol)*

```
London_PE2#debug ip bgp 10.1.1.2 updates
BGP updates debugging is on for neighbor 10.1.1.2
London_PE2#
*Nov  1 23:02:55.339 UTC: %BGP-5-ADJCHANGE: neighbor 10.1.1.2 vpn vrf mjlnet_VPN Up
  len is 4
*Nov  1 23:02:55.343 UTC: BGP(4): 10.1.1.2 soo loop detected for 10.2.4.0/24 - sending
  unreachable (line 1)
*Nov  1 23:02:55.343 UTC: BGP(4): 10.1.1.2 soo loop detected for 10.2.3.0/24 - sending
  unreachable (line 2)
*Nov  1 23:02:55.343 UTC: BGP(4): 10.1.1.2 soo loop detected for 10.2.2.0/24 - sending
  unreachable (line 3)
*Nov  1 23:02:55.343 UTC: BGP(4): 10.1.1.2 soo loop detected for 10.2.1.0/24 - sending
  unreachable len is 5 (line 4)
London_PE2#undebug all
All possible debugging has been turned off
London_PE2#
```

As shown in highlighted lines 1 to 4, when London_PE2 processes mjlnet_VPN site 1 routes for advertisement to mjlnet_VPN.London.CE2, it detects a loop condition because the attached SoO attribute (65535:901) is the same as that configured for neighbor 10.1.1.2 (mjlnet_VPN.London.CE2). The updates are, therefore, not sent to mjlnet_VPN.London.CE2.

Note that, although not shown, the same thing happens when London_PE1 processes mjlnet_VPN site 1 routes for advertisement to mjlnet_VPN.London.CE1—it detects a loop condition and does not send the updates.

CAUTION **debug** commands are used in this chapter for illustrative purposes only. Always exercise caution when using **debug** commands in live networks because they can, in extreme cases, cause heavily loaded routers to crash.

Configuring the SoO Attribute When eBGP Is Not Used as the PE-CE Routing Protocol

The SoO extended community works in exactly the same way to prevent routing loops when eBGP is not used as the PE-CE routing protocol. There are, however, one or two differences as far as configuration of the PE routers is concerned.

Example 4-37 shows the configuration of London_PE1 for the attachment and verification of BGP routes with attached SoO extended BGP community attribute (when eBGP is not used as the PE-CE routing protocol).

Example 4-37 *Configuration of London_PE1*

```
!
! On London_PE1 (line 1)
!
interface Serial2/1
 ip vrf forwarding mjlnet_VPN
 ip vrf sitemap set-soo (line 2)
 ip address 10.2.1.2 255.255.255.0
!
router eigrp 100 (line 3)
 !
 address-family ipv4 vrf mjlnet_VPN (line 4)
 redistribute bgp 65535 metric 100 100 1 100 1500
 network 10.2.1.0 0.0.0.255
 no auto-summary
 autonomous-system 200
 exit-address-family
!
router bgp 65535 (line 5)
 !
<output omitted>
 !
 address-family ipv4 vrf mjlnet_VPN (line 6)
 redistribute eigrp 200
 no auto-summary
 no synchronization
 exit-address-family
!
route-map set-soo permit 10 (line 7)
 set extcommunity soo 65535:901 (line 8)
 !
```

The configuration of London_PE1 shown in Example 4-37 includes the configuration of EIGRP as the PE-CE routing protocol (see below highlighted lines 3 and 4). Below highlighted lines 5 and 6, BGP is configured as normal when using EIGRP as the PE-CE routing protocol.

If you compare the BGP IPv4 address family configuration for the mjlnet_VPN VRF with that shown in Example 4-33 (see highlighted line 6), you will immediately notice a key difference with regard to the application of the route map (**set-soo**) used to attach the SoO attribute—because EIGRP is used as the PE-CE routing protocol in Example 4-37, the route map cannot be applied using the **neighbor** *ip-address* **route-map** *map-name* **in** BGP command. Instead, the route map is applied at the VRF interface level using the **ip vrf sitemap** *map-name* command (see highlighted line 2).

The route map itself (**set-soo**) is configured in highlighted lines 7 and 8.

Example 4-38 shows the configuration of London_PE2 for the attachment and verification of BGP routes with attached SoO extended BGP community attributes (when eBGP is not used as the PE-CE routing protocol).

Example 4-38 *Configuration of London_PE2*

```
!
! On London_PE2 (line 1)
!
interface Serial4/1
 ip vrf forwarding mjlnet_VPN
 ip vrf sitemap set-soo (line 2)
 ip address 10.1.1.1 255.255.255.0
!
router eigrp 100 (line 3)
 !
address-family ipv4 vrf mjlnet_VPN (line 4)
  redistribute bgp 65535 metric 100 100 1 100 1500
  network 10.1.1.0 0.0.0.255
  no auto-summary
  autonomous-system 200
  exit-address-family
 !
router bgp 65535 (line 5)
 !
<output omitted>
 !
 address-family ipv4 vrf mjlnet_VPN (line 6)
 redistribute eigrp 200
 no auto-summary
 no synchronization
 exit-address-family
 !
route-map set-soo permit 10 (line 7)
 set extcommunity soo 65535:901 (line 8)
 !
```

The configuration of London_PE2 is almost identical to that for London_PE1. Again, it is essential that the SoO attribute configured in the route map (see highlighted line 8) be the same as that configured on London_PE1 (see Example 4-37, highlighted line 8) because the two PE routers are connected to the same site.

The **debug ip eigrp vrf** *vrf-name* command shows what happens when London_PE2 receives mjlnet site 1 routes from London_PE1 and prepares to advertise them to mjlnet_VPN.London.CE2 (see Example 4-39).

Example 4-39 *London_PE2 Does Not Send mjlnet Site 1 Routes to mjlnet_VPN.London.CE2 (EIGRP Is the PE-CE Routing Protocol)*

```
London_PE2#debug ip eigrp vrf mjlnet_VPN
IP-EIGRP Route Events debugging is on
London_PE2#
*Dec 25 23:38:48.939 UTC: IP-EIGRP(mjlnet_VPN:200): 10.1.1.0/24 - denied by SoO: loop
  detected (line 1)
*Dec 25 23:38:48.939 UTC: IP-EIGRP(mjlnet_VPN:200): 10.1.1.2/32 - denied by SoO: loop
  detected (line 2)
*Dec 25 23:38:48.939 UTC: IP-EIGRP(mjlnet_VPN:200): 10.1.2.0/24 - denied by SoO: loop
  detected (line 3)
*Dec 25 23:38:48.939 UTC: IP-EIGRP(mjlnet_VPN:200): 10.1.3.0/24 - denied by SoO: loop
  detected (line 4)
*Dec 25 23:38:48.939 UTC: IP-EIGRP(mjlnet_VPN:200): 10.1.4.0/24 - denied by SoO: loop
  detected (line 5)
London_PE2#undebug all
All possible debugging has been turned off
London_PE2#
```

Highlighted lines 1 to 5 show that when London_PE2 processes mjlnet site 1 routes for advertisement to mjlnet_VPN.London.CE2, it does not send them because it detects a loop condition. London_PE2 is able to detect a loop condition because the SoO extended attribute attached to the routes (65535:901) is the same as that configured on the interface connected to mjlnet_VPN.London.CE2.

London_PE1 similarly detects a loop condition when it processes mjlnet site 1 routes for advertisement to mjlnet_VPN.London.CE1 and therefore does not send them. That's SoO with EIGRP. If you are using OSPF as your PE-CE routing protocol, then you don't *need* SoO. This is because OSPF has it own loop prevention mechanisms, the Down Bit (carried in the Options field of the LSA header) and the VPN Route Tag (a special type of OSPF route tag), which don't require explicit configuration. If you use SoO in conjunction with OSPF it will prevent unnecessary non-loop, causing re-advertisement of routes, but it will also prevent the automatic repair of VPN sites that have become partitioned (in this case, when *not* using SoO, one part of the partitioned site will be able to reach the other part via the MPLS VPN backbone). So, many people choose not to use SoO when OSPF is the PE-CE routing protocol.

Implementing Internet Access for MPLS Layer 3 VPNs

When deploying MPLS Layer 3 VPNs, one common customer requirement is Internet access. Internet access can be provisioned in a number of ways, including the following:

- Using a separate global interface on PE routers
- Using route leaking between VRFs and the global routing table on PE routers
- Using a shared service VPN

These various approaches to providing Internet access are discussed in the following sections.

Providing Internet Access via Separate Global Interfaces on PE Routers

One method by which an MPLS Layer 3 VPN service provider can provide Internet access to its customers is to configure Internet connectivity via separate global interfaces on PE routers, as shown in Figure 4-16.

NOTE   The global interfaces on the PE router via which Internet access is provided can be either physical interfaces or logical interfaces (such as Frame Relay subinterfaces or GRE tunnel interfaces).

Figure 4-16 *Providing Internet Access via Separate Global Interfaces on PE Routers*

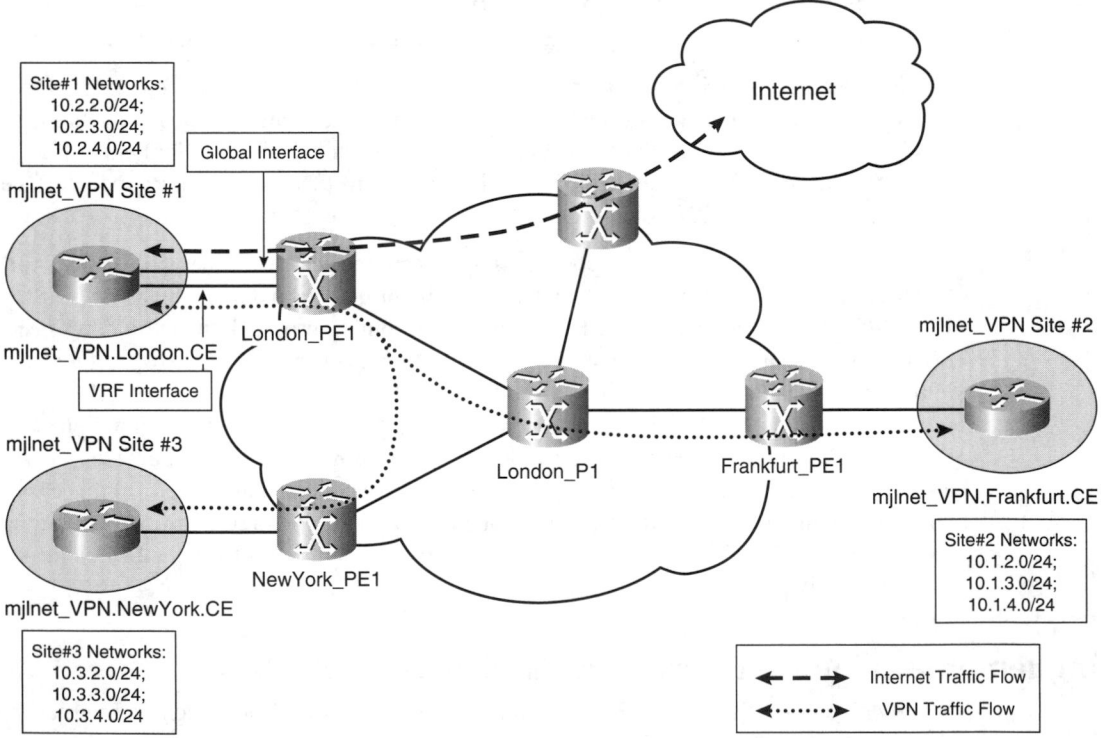

As shown in Figure 4-16, customers connect via separate physical or logical interfaces for Internet access. These interfaces are not associated with a VRF, but instead with the global routing table, which contains either a route to an Internet gateway router or the full Internet routing table.

In this scenario, Internet access can be provided from all customer sites or via a hub site CE router (see Figure 4-17). If access is provided via a hub site CE router, you must distribute a default route from the hub site to the spoke site routers (using the PE-CE routing protocol).

Figure 4-17 *Internet Access from All Customer Sites via a Separate Physical Interface on the Hub Site PE Router*

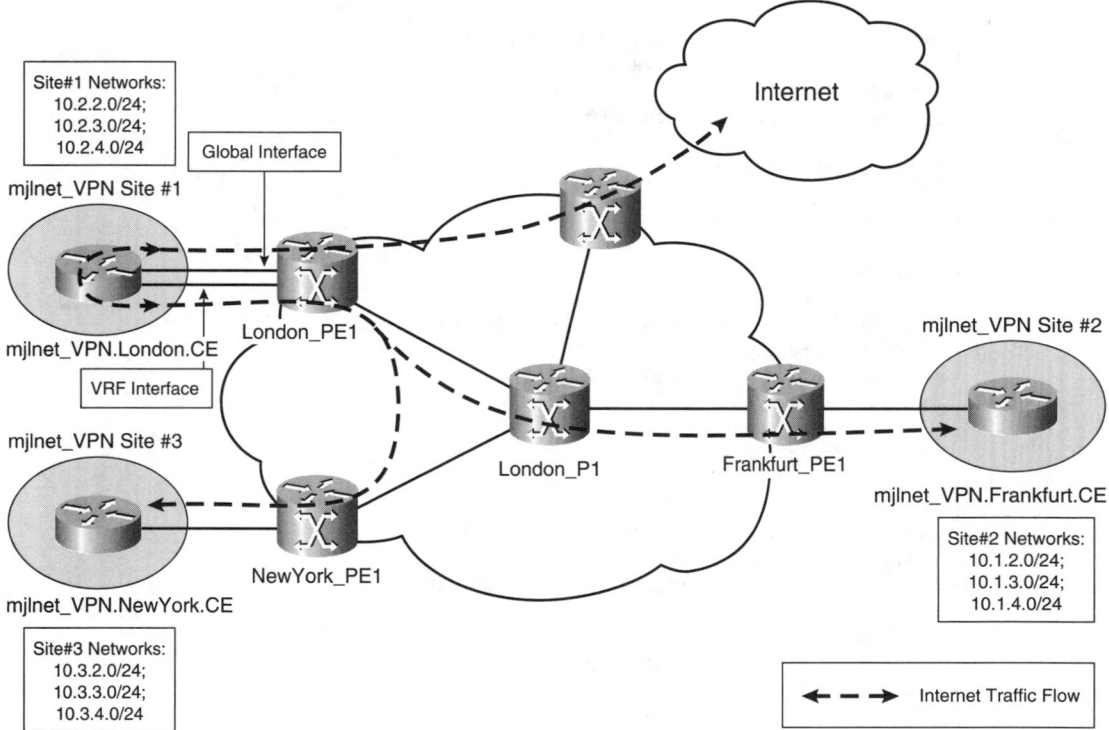

Example 4-40 shows the configuration of a PE router that is provisioned with a global interface for Internet connectivity and a VRF interface for VPN connectivity.

Example 4-40 *Configuration of a PE Router Provisioned with a Global Interface for Internet Connectivity and a VRF Interface for VPN Connectivity*

```
!
! On London_PE1 (line 1)
!
ip vrf mjlnet_VPN
 rd 65535:100
 route-target import 65535:100
!
interface Serial2/1
 encapsulation frame-relay
!
```

continues

Example 4-40 *Configuration of a PE Router Provisioned with a Global Interface for Internet Connectivity and a VRF Interface for VPN Connectivity (Continued)*

```
interface Serial2/1.1 point-to-point (line 2)
 description VRF Interface
 ip vrf forwarding mjlnet_VPN (line 3)
 ip address 10.2.1.2 255.255.255.0
 frame-relay interface-dlci 100
!
interface Serial2/1.2 point-to-point (line 4)
 description Global Interface
 ip address 10.4.1.2 255.255.255.0
 frame-relay interface-dlci 200
!
router eigrp 100 (line 5)
 !
 address-family ipv4
 no auto-summary
 exit-address-family
 !
 address-family ipv4 vrf mjlnet_VPN (line 6)
 redistribute bgp 65535
 network 10.2.1.0 0.0.0.255 (line 7)
 no auto-summary
 autonomous-system 200
 exit-address-family
!
router bgp 65535 (line 8)
 neighbor 10.4.1.1 remote-as 64512 (line 9)
 neighbor 192.168.1.3 remote-as 65535
 neighbor 192.168.1.3 update-source Loopback0
 !
 address-family ipv4
 neighbor 10.4.1.1 activate
 neighbor 192.168.1.3 activate
 default-information originate (line 10)
 no auto-summary
 no synchronization
 exit-address-family
 !
!
ip route 0.0.0.0 0.0.0.0 192.168.1.3 (line 11)
 !
```

In highlighted lines 2 and 3, Frame Relay subinterface 2/1.1 is configured and associated with the mjlnet_VPN VRF. This subinterface is used by the attached CE router for connectivity to other sites in the VPN.

Highlighted line 4 shows the configuration of a second Frame Relay subinterface (interface 2/1.2). This subinterface is not associated with any VRF and provides Internet connectivity for the attached CE router.

NOTE	Although VPN and Internet connectivity are provided via separate Frame Relay subinterfaces in Example 4-40, some customers' security policies may require the segregation of VPN and Internet traffic onto separate *physical* interfaces (and separate routers/firewalls).

Highlighted lines 5 to 7 show a standard configuration for EIGRP as the PE-CE routing protocol, and highlighted lines 8 to 11 show a sample configuration for Internet routing.

The **neighbor** *ip-address* **remote-as** *as-number* command, shown in highlighted line 9, is used to configure a BGP neighbor relationship with the CE router connected on global (Internet) interface 2/1.2. Highlighted line 11 shows the configuration of a static default route.

In highlighted line 10, the **default-information originate** command is used to redistribute the default route into BGP. This default route is advertised to the attached CE router to provide Internet reachability.

NOTE	Instead of configuring a static default route and advertising this to the attached CE router(s) using the **default-information originate** command, it is also possible to configure a static default route on the CE router or advertise full Internet routes to the attached CE router. The disadvantage of advertising full Internet routes is, of course, the memory and CPU overhead on the CE (and PE) router.

It is possible to configure Internet connectivity for a single central customer VPN site as shown Example 4-40 and then advertise a default route from the central site to the other sites in the customer VPN. The advantage of this method of configuring Internet access is that connectivity can be controlled via a single firewall or set of firewalls at the central site. Disadvantages are the fact that Internet access from other customer VPN sites would be indirect and that additional bandwidth would be required at the central site.

Alternatively, it is possible to configure each customer VPN site to access the Internet directly by configuring their attached PE router as shown in Example 4-16. The advantage of this method of configuring Internet access is that Internet access is direct from each customer VPN site. The disadvantage is that a firewall or set of firewalls would need to be configured and managed at each customer VPN site.

Providing Internet Access Using Route Leaking Between VRFs and the Global Routing Table on PE Routers

Another popular method of providing Internet access for MPLS Layer 3 VPNs is to configure route leaking between the VRFs and the global routing table on PE routers.

In this case, you configure a static VRF default route whose next hop is an Internet gateway that is reachable via the *global* routing table. This VRF default route is then redistributed into the PE-CE routing protocol to allow outbound Internet reachability for customer VPNs.

You must also configure a *global* static route or routes for reachability to customer VPN networks on the PE router(s). The global static route(s) should use a *VRF* interface as its outgoing interface and should be redistributed into global BGP to allow hosts on the Internet to reach customer networks.

Figure 4-18 illustrates configuration and traffic flow for Internet access using route leaking.

Figure 4-18 *Configuration and Traffic Flow for Internet Access Using Route Leaking*

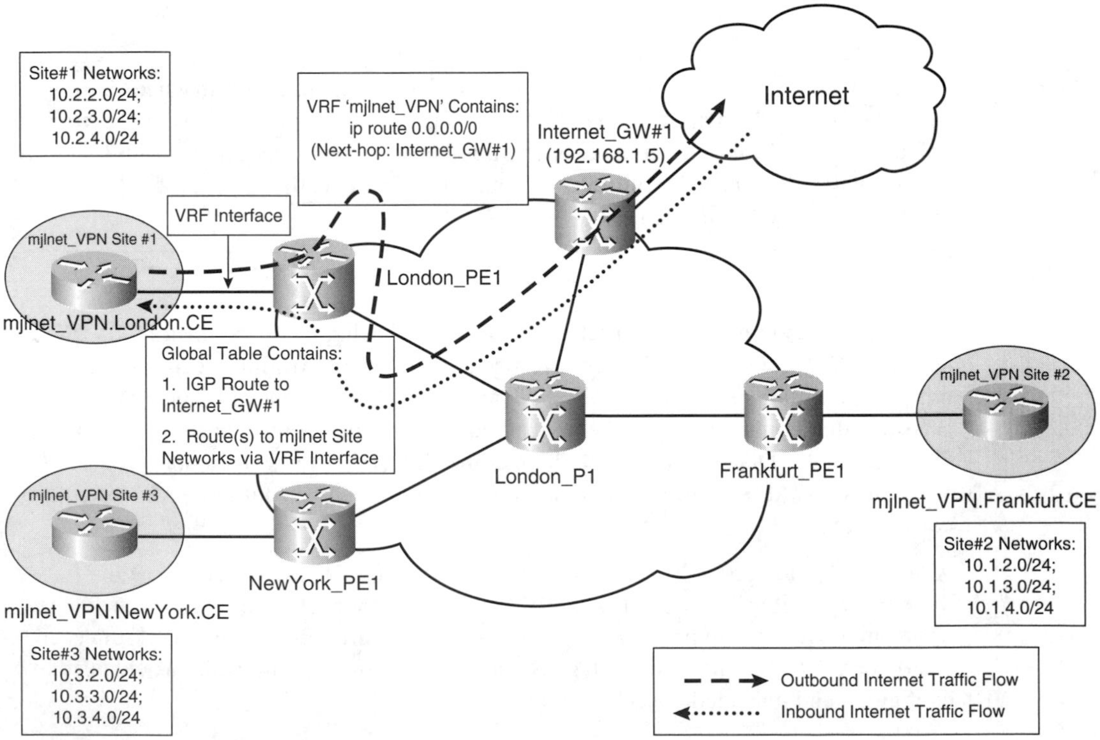

Figure 4-19 illustrates route distribution for Internet access using route leaking.

Figure 4-19 *Route Distribution for Internet Access Using Route Leaking*

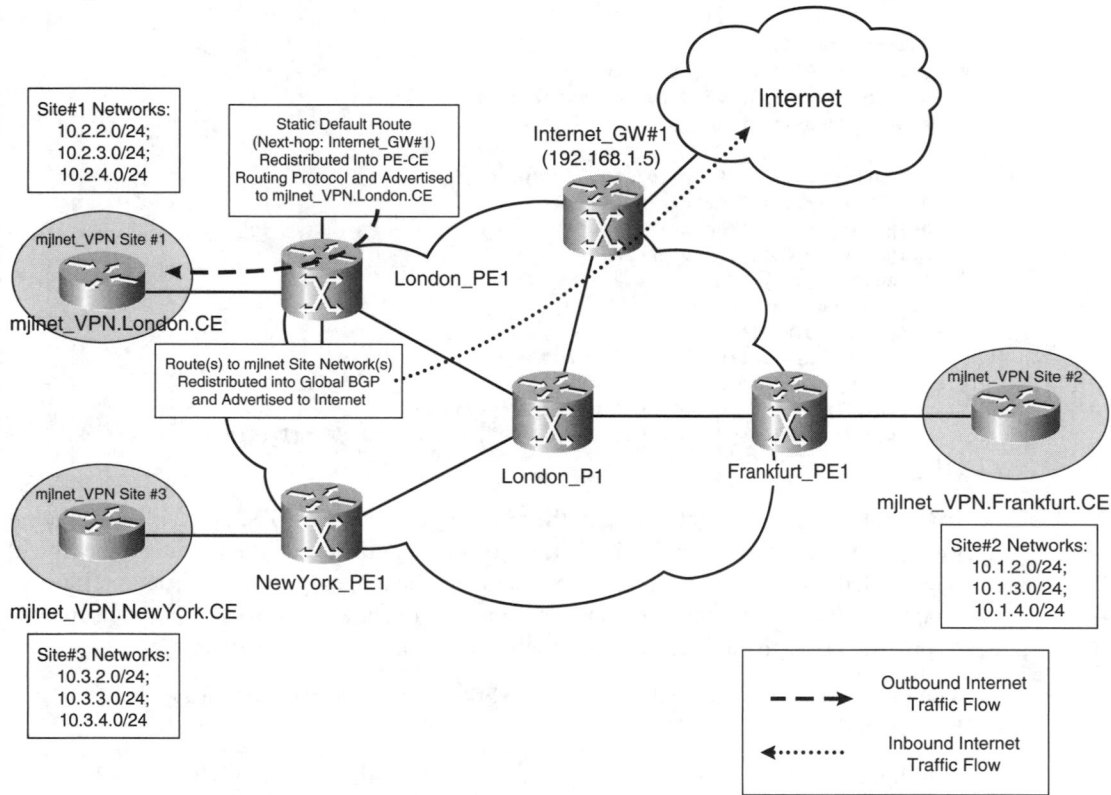

Example 4-41 shows the configuration of route leaking on a PE router.

Example 4-41 *Configuration of Route Leaking on a PE Router*

```
!
! On London_PE1 (line 1)
!
ip vrf mjlnet_VPN
 rd 65535:100
 route-target export 65535:100
 route-target import 65535:100
!
interface Serial2/1
 ip vrf forwarding mjlnet_VPN (line 2)
 ip address 10.2.1.2 255.255.255.0
!
router bgp 65535
 no synchronization
 redistribute static (line 3)
 neighbor 192.168.1.3 remote-as 65535
```

continues

Example 4-41 *Configuration of Route Leaking on a PE Router (Continued)*

```
  neighbor 192.168.1.3 update-source Loopback0
  no auto-summary
  !
  address-family vpnv4
  neighbor 192.168.1.3 activate
  neighbor 192.168.1.3 send-community extended
  exit-address-family
  !
  address-family ipv4 vrf mjlnet_VPN (line 4)
  neighbor 10.2.1.1 remote-as 64512
  neighbor 10.2.1.1 activate
  neighbor 10.2.1.1 as-override
  no auto-summary
  no synchronization
  network 0.0.0.0 (line 5)
  exit-address-family
 !
 ip route 10.2.0.0 255.255.0.0 Serial2/1 (line 6)
 ip route vrf mjlnet_VPN 0.0.0.0 0.0.0.0 192.168.1.3 global (line 7)
 !
```

In highlighted line 6, a static route to the mjlnet site 1 networks (10.2.0.0/24) is configured on London_PE1, with outgoing interface 2/1. Notice that this is a global static route (it will be installed into the global routing table) and that the outgoing interface is an interface associated with the mjlnet_VPN VRF (see highlighted line 2). The function of this route is to provide hosts on the Internet with reachability to mjlnet site 1 networks.

The global static route to mjlnet site 1 networks is then redistributed into global BGP in highlighted line 3.

Highlighted line 7 shows a static VRF default route, with a next hop (192.168.1.3) that is in the global routing table (as indicated by the **global** keyword). The function of this static VRF default route is to provide Internet reachability for mjlnet site 1 hosts.

In highlighted line 5, the **network** *network-address* command is used to redistribute the static VRF default route into the PE-CE routing protocol (eBGP in this example) for advertisement to the mjlnet site 1 CE router.

In Example 4-42, you can see in the output of the **show ip bgp** command on London_PE1 that the route to mjlnet site 1 (10.2.0.0/16) has been redistributed into global BGP.

Example 4-42 *Route to mjlnet Site 1 (10.2.0.0/16) Has Been Redistributed into Global BGP*

```
London_PE1#show ip bgp
BGP table version is 2, local router ID is 192.168.1.2
Status codes: s suppressed, d damped, h history, * valid, > best, i - internal,
              r RIB-failure, S Stale
Origin codes: i - IGP, e - EGP, ? - incomplete
   Network          Next Hop            Metric LocPrf Weight Path
*> 10.2.0.0/16      0.0.0.0                  0         32768 ?
London_PE1#
```

The output of the **show ip route vrf** *vrf-name* command on London_PE1 shows the static VRF default route (see Example 4-43).

Example 4-43 **show ip route vrf** *Command Output on London_PE1 Shows the Static VRF Default Route*

```
London_PE1#show ip route vrf mjlnet_VPN
Routing Table: mjlnet_VPN
Codes: C - connected, S - static, I - IGRP, R - RIP, M - mobile, B - BGP
       D - EIGRP, EX - EIGRP external, O - OSPF, IA - OSPF inter area
       N1 - OSPF NSSA external type 1, N2 - OSPF NSSA external type 2
       E1 - OSPF external type 1, E2 - OSPF external type 2, E - EGP
       i - IS-IS, su - IS-IS summary, L1 - IS-IS level-1, L2 - IS-IS level-2
       ia - IS-IS inter area, * - candidate default, U - per-user static route
       o - ODR
Gateway of last resort is 192.168.1.3 to network 0.0.0.0
     10.0.0.0/8 is variably subnetted, 14 subnets, 2 masks
B       10.3.1.0/24 [200/0] via 192.168.1.1, 00:14:21
C       10.2.1.1/32 is directly connected, Serial2/1
B       10.1.3.0/24 [200/1889792] via 192.168.1.3, 00:14:22
B       10.1.1.2/32 [200/0] via 192.168.1.3, 00:14:22
C       10.2.1.0/24 is directly connected, Serial2/1
B       10.1.2.0/24 [200/1889792] via 192.168.1.3, 00:14:22
B       10.3.3.0/24 [200/0] via 192.168.1.1, 00:14:22
B       10.2.2.0/24 [20/0] via 10.2.1.1, 00:14:28
B       10.1.1.0/24 [200/0] via 192.168.1.3, 00:14:22
B       10.3.2.0/24 [200/0] via 192.168.1.1, 00:14:22
B       10.2.3.0/24 [20/0] via 10.2.1.1, 00:14:28
B       10.2.4.0/24 [20/0] via 10.2.1.1, 00:14:28
B       10.3.4.0/24 [200/0] via 192.168.1.1, 00:14:22
B       10.1.4.0/24 [200/1889792] via 192.168.1.3, 00:14:22
S*   0.0.0.0/0 [1/0] via 192.168.1.3
London_PE1#
```

As previously mentioned, the next hop of the static VRF default route (192.168.1.3) is contained within the global routing table, as shown in the output of the **show ip route** command on London_PE1 in Example 4-44.

Example 4-44 *The Next Hop of the Static VRF Default Route (192.168.1.3) Is Contained Within the Global Routing Table*

```
London_PE1#show ip route
Codes: C - connected, S - static, I - IGRP, R - RIP, M - mobile, B - BGP
       D - EIGRP, EX - EIGRP external, O - OSPF, IA - OSPF inter area
       N1 - OSPF NSSA external type 1, N2 - OSPF NSSA external type 2
       E1 - OSPF external type 1, E2 - OSPF external type 2, E - EGP
       i - IS-IS, su - IS-IS summary, L1 - IS-IS level-1, L2 - IS-IS level-2
       ia - IS-IS inter area, * - candidate default, U - per-user static route
       o - ODR
Gateway of last resort is not set
     192.168.4.0/24 is variably subnetted, 2 subnets, 2 masks
i L2    192.168.4.0/24 [115/20] via 192.168.2.2, Serial2/0
```

continues

Example 4-44 *The Next Hop of the Static VRF Default Route (192.168.1.3) Is Contained Within the Global Routing Table (Continued)*

```
i L2    192.168.4.2/32 [115/20] via 192.168.2.2, Serial2/0
        10.0.0.0/16 is subnetted, 1 subnets
S       10.2.0.0 is directly connected, Serial2/1
        192.168.1.0/32 is subnetted, 4 subnets
i L2    192.168.1.1 [115/30] via 192.168.2.2, Serial2/0
i L2    192.168.1.3 [115/30] via 192.168.2.2, Serial2/0
C       192.168.1.2 is directly connected, Loopback0
i L2    192.168.1.4 [115/20] via 192.168.2.2, Serial2/0
        192.168.2.0/24 is variably subnetted, 2 subnets, 2 masks
C       192.168.2.2/32 is directly connected, Serial2/0
C       192.168.2.0/24 is directly connected, Serial2/0
        192.168.3.0/24 is variably subnetted, 2 subnets, 2 masks
i L2    192.168.3.2/32 [115/30] via 192.168.2.2, Serial2/0
i L2    192.168.3.0/24 [115/20] via 192.168.2.2, Serial2/0
London_PE1#
```

The **show ip route** command output on mjlnet_VPN.London.CE (see Example 4-45), reveals that the static VRF default route has been redistributed into the PE-CE routing protocol (eBGP) and advertised to mjlnet_VPN.London.CE.

Example 4-45 *The Static VRF Default Route Has Been Redistributed into the PE-CE Routing Protocol and Advertised to mjlnet_VPN.London.CE*

```
mjlnet_VPN.London.CE#show ip route
Codes: C - connected, S - static, I - IGRP, R - RIP, M - mobile, B - BGP
       D - EIGRP, EX - EIGRP external, O - OSPF, IA - OSPF inter area
       N1 - OSPF NSSA external type 1, N2 - OSPF NSSA external type 2
       E1 - OSPF external type 1, E2 - OSPF external type 2, E - EGP
       i - IS-IS, L1 - IS-IS level-1, L2 - IS-IS level-2, ia - IS-IS inter area
       * - candidate default, U - per-user static route, o - ODR
Gateway of last resort is 10.2.1.2 to network 0.0.0.0
       10.0.0.0/8 is variably subnetted, 14 subnets, 2 masks
B       10.3.1.0/24 [20/0] via 10.2.1.2, 00:14:35
B       10.1.3.0/24 [20/0] via 10.2.1.2, 00:14:35
B       10.1.1.2/32 [20/0] via 10.2.1.2, 00:14:35
B       10.1.2.0/24 [20/0] via 10.2.1.2, 00:14:35
C       10.2.1.0/24 is directly connected, Serial0
B       10.3.3.0/24 [20/0] via 10.2.1.2, 00:14:36
B       10.1.1.0/24 [20/0] via 10.2.1.2, 00:14:36
C       10.2.2.0/24 is directly connected, Loopback100
B       10.3.2.0/24 [20/0] via 10.2.1.2, 00:14:36
C       10.2.1.2/32 is directly connected, Serial0
C       10.2.3.0/24 is directly connected, Loopback101
C       10.2.4.0/24 is directly connected, Loopback102
B       10.3.4.0/24 [20/0] via 10.2.1.2, 00:14:36
B       10.1.4.0/24 [20/0] via 10.2.1.2, 00:14:36
B*  0.0.0.0/0 [20/0] via 10.2.1.2, 00:14:42
mjlnet_VPN.London.CE#
```

The advantage of using route leaking as a method of providing Internet connectivity to a customer VPN is that only one interface is required for customer VPN and Internet connectivity. The disadvantage is that customer VPN and Internet traffic is mixed on the PE-CE link, and this may not conform to some customers' security policies.

Providing Internet Access via a Shared Services VPN

Yet another method of providing Internet access for customer VPNs is to configure a shared services VPN, which is managed by the service provider. As the name suggests, a shared services VPN allows a number of customer VPNs to all access the Internet (or other common services) via a shared VPN. Figure 4-20 illustrates a shared services VPN.

Figure 4-20 *Internet Access via a Shared Services VPN*

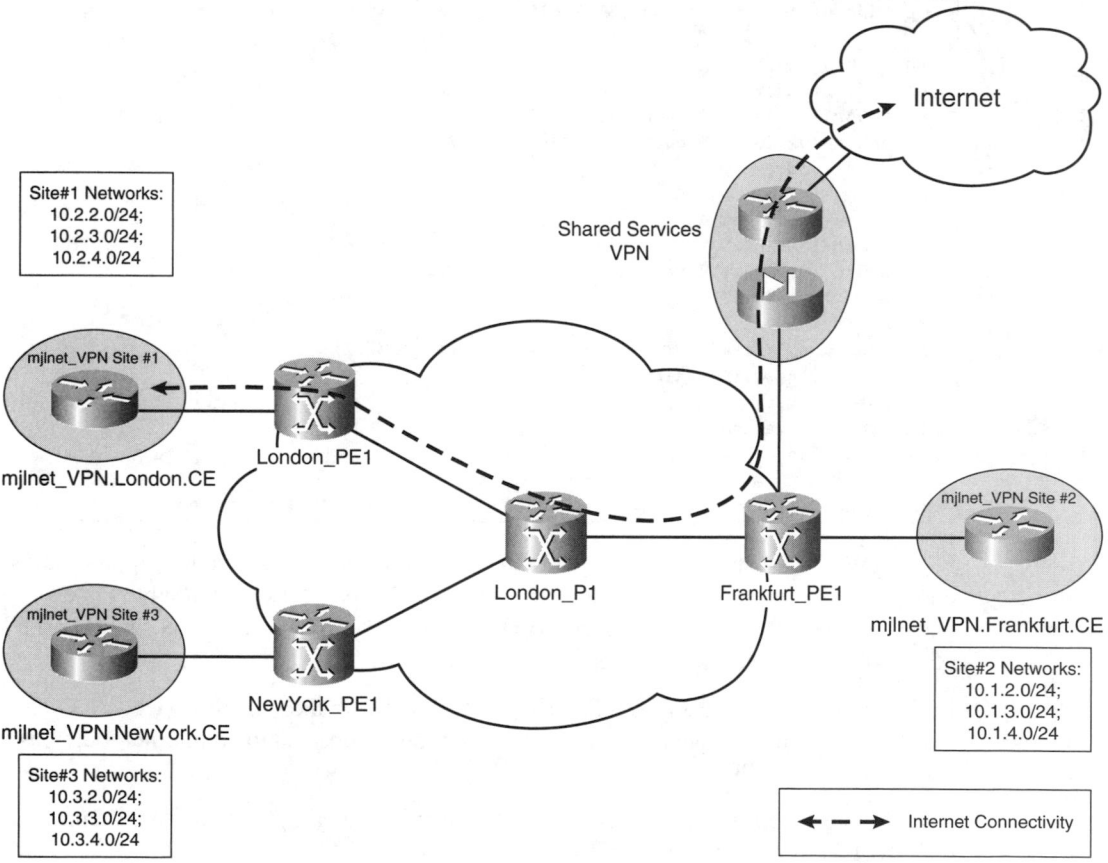

When providing Internet access via a shared services VPN, customer routes must be imported into the shared service VRF, and default routes must be exported from the shared services VRF and imported into the customers' VRFs. If this sounds familiar, it should be — a shared services VPN is a type of extranet VPN.

Example 4-46 shows the configuration of a shared service VRF on Frankfurt_PE1.

Example 4-46 *Configuring a Shared Services VRF on Frankfurt_PE1*

```
!
! On Frankfurt_PE1 (line 1)
!
ip vrf VPN-shared-services (line 2)
 rd 65535:300
 route-target export 65535:400
 route-target export 65535:700 (line 3)
 route-target import 65535:300
 route-target import 65535:600 (line 4)
!
interface Serial4/2
 ip vrf forwarding VPN-shared-services (line 5)
 ip address 172.16.1.1 255.255.255.0
!
router bgp 65535 (line 6)
 no synchronization
 neighbor 192.168.1.2 remote-as 65535
 neighbor 192.168.1.2 update-source Loopback0
 no auto-summary
 !
 address-family vpnv4
 neighbor 192.168.1.2 activate
 neighbor 192.168.1.2 send-community extended
 exit-address-family
 !
 address-family ipv4 vrf VPN-shared-services (line 7)
 redistribute static (line 8)
 no auto-summary
 no synchronization
 exit-address-family
 !
ip route vrf VPN-shared-services 0.0.0.0 0.0.0.0 172.16.1.2 (line 9)
```

Highlighted line 2 shows the configuration of a shared service VPN called, appropriately enough, VPN-shared-services. Notice the import and export RTs in highlighted lines 3 and 4—import RT 65535:700 is used to import routes from a customer VPN, and export RT 65535:600 is used to export routes to a customer VPN.

In highlighted line 5, interface serial 4/2 is associated with the shared services VRF. This interface is connected to a firewall, and that in turn is connected to an Internet router, as shown in Figure 4-20.

A static shared service VRF default route is configured in highlighted line 9 with a next hop (172.16.1.2) of the firewall connected via interface serial 4/2.

The default static route is redistributed in MP-BGP for advertisement to a customer VPN as shown in highlighted line 8.

Example 4-47 shows the configuration of London_PE1.

Example 4-47 *Configuration of London_PE1*

```
!
! On London_PE1 (line 1)
!
ip vrf mjlnet_VPN (line 2)
 rd 65535:100
 route-target export 65535:100
 route-target export 65535:600 (line 3)
 route-target import 65535:100
 route-target import 65535:700 (line 4)
!
interface Serial2/1
 ip vrf forwarding mjlnet_VPN
 ip address 10.2.1.2 255.255.255.0
!
router bgp 65535 (line 5)
 no synchronization
 neighbor 192.168.1.3 remote-as 65535
 neighbor 192.168.1.3 update-source Loopback0
 no auto-summary
 !
 address-family vpnv4
 neighbor 192.168.1.3 activate
 neighbor 192.168.1.3 send-community extended
 exit-address-family
 !
 address-family ipv4 vrf mjlnet_VPN (line 6)
 neighbor 10.2.1.1 remote-as 64512 (line 7)
 neighbor 10.2.1.1 activate (line 8)
 neighbor 10.2.1.1 as-override
 no auto-summary
 no synchronization
 exit-address-family
!
```

In highlighted lines 3 and 4, RTs are configured for the import and export of routes between customer VRF, mjlnet_VPN, and the common service VPN. The export RT (65535:600) is used to export mjlnet_VPN routes to the common services VPN (also see highlighted line 4, Example 4-46), and the import RT (65535:700) is used to import the default route from the common services VPN into the mjlnet_VPN VRF (see also highlighted line 3, Example 4-46).

In highlighted lines 7 and 8, eBGP is configured as the PE-CE routing protocol for the mjlnet_VPN VRF. In this example, therefore, the common services VPN default route is advertised to the attached CE router, mjlnet_VPN.London.CE, using eBGP.

NOTE   Although not used in the configurations shown in Example 4-46 and 4-47, import and/or export route maps can be used for more precise route distribution between the customer VPNs and the common services VPN.

See the section titled "Extranet Topology" for more information.

Example 4-48 shows the routing table on mjlnet_VPN.London.CE.

Example 4-48 *Routing Table on mjlnet_VPN.London.CE*

```
mjlnet_VPN.London.CE#show ip route
Codes: C - connected, S - static, I - IGRP, R - RIP, M - mobile, B - BGP
       D - EIGRP, EX - EIGRP external, O - OSPF, IA - OSPF inter area
       N1 - OSPF NSSA external type 1, N2 - OSPF NSSA external type 2
       E1 - OSPF external type 1, E2 - OSPF external type 2, E - EGP
       i - IS-IS, L1 - IS-IS level-1, L2 - IS-IS level-2, ia - IS-IS inter area
       * - candidate default, U - per-user static route, o - ODR
Gateway of last resort is 10.2.1.2 to network 0.0.0.0
       172.16.0.0/24 is subnetted, 1 subnets
B         172.16.1.0 [20/0] via 10.2.1.2, 00:03:03
       10.0.0.0/8 is variably subnetted, 14 subnets, 2 masks
B         10.3.1.0/24 [20/0] via 10.2.1.2, 00:03:03
B         10.1.3.0/24 [20/0] via 10.2.1.2, 00:03:03
B         10.1.1.2/32 [20/0] via 10.2.1.2, 00:03:03
B         10.1.2.0/24 [20/0] via 10.2.1.2, 00:03:03
C         10.2.1.0/24 is directly connected, Serial0/0
B         10.3.3.0/24 [20/0] via 10.2.1.2, 00:03:03
B         10.1.1.0/24 [20/0] via 10.2.1.2, 00:03:03
C         10.2.2.0/24 is directly connected, Ethernet1/0
B         10.3.2.0/24 [20/0] via 10.2.1.2, 00:03:03
C         10.2.1.2/32 is directly connected, Serial0
C         10.2.3.0/24 is directly connected, Ethernet1/1
C         10.2.4.0/24 is directly connected, Ethernet1/2
B         10.3.4.0/24 [20/0] via 10.2.1.2, 00:03:04
B         10.1.4.0/24 [20/0] via 10.2.1.2, 00:03:04
B*     0.0.0.0/0 [20/0] via 10.2.1.2, 00:03:04
mjlnet_VPN.London.CE#
```

The highlighted line shows the default route used for Internet access from mjlnet site 1.

NOTE   It is important to note that the configuration used to allow Internet access on London_PE1 (see Example 4-47) can be duplicated on each PE router connected to a customer VPN site to allow direct Internet access from each site via the shared services VPN.

The advantage of configuring a shared services VPN for customer VPN Internet access is that the customer can have direct Internet access from each site, without having to configure and manage any firewalls. The disadvantage is that customers will not have *direct* control over firewalls used to control access to and from the Internet to and from their VPNs.

Summary

This chapter examined the design and deployment of MPLS Layer 3 VPNs, their advantages and disadvantages, and the provisioning of a variety of VPN topologies.

In addition, this chapter discussed how to prevent routing loops when customer VPN sites are multihomed and how to configure Internet access.

MPLS Layer 3 VPNs offer a number of significant advantages to service providers and enterprises. MPLS Layer 3 VPNs offer an extremely scalable VPN architecture, provide any-to-any connectivity, support real-time and business applications, and allow enterprise customers to simplify their WAN routing. On the other hand, MPLS Layer 3 VPNs do not natively support the transport of non-IP protocols and require the configuration of MVPNs to provide *native* support for IP multicast.

Depending on customer requirements, MPLS Layer 3 VPNs can be flexibly configured to support full-mesh, hub-and-spoke, and extranet topologies. When designing MPLS Layer 3 VPNs where customer sites are multihomed, it is important to take into consideration loop prevention and, if necessary, correctly implement loop prevention measures using the SoO attribute. Internet connectivity can be supported for MPLS Layer 3 VPNs using a number of methods—via a separate global interface, using route leaking, or via a shared service VPN.

Review Questions

1 In an MPLS Layer 3 VPN, do CE routers exchange routing update directly with other CE routers, or with connected PE routers?

2 How do PE routers store customer routing and forwarding information?

3 How is customer routing information exchanged between PE routers?

4 In a simple MPLS Layer 3 VPN, with an MPLS-enabled backbone network where PE routers are not directly connected, how many labels are in the label stack of customer packets as they cross the backbone? What are the functions of those labels?

5 How can IGP labels be signaled in an MPLS network?

6 What is the function of the Route Distinguisher (RD)?

7 What is the function of the Route Target (RT)?

8 Typically, which two IGPs are used in MPLS networks?

9 Which BGP attribute can be used to prevent routing loops when customer sites are multihomed to the service provider MPLS VPN backbone?

10 What are three common methods of provisioning Internet access for MPLS Layer 3 VPN customers?

CHAPTER 5

Advanced MPLS Layer 3 VPN Deployment Considerations

Chapter 4, "Designing MPLS Layer 3 Site-to-Site VPNs," introduced MPLS Layer 3 VPNs and discussed common topologies and deployments. This chapter covers advanced deployment topologies, such as carriers' carrier (CSC) and inter-autonomous system, as well as other deployment considerations, such as multicast traffic transport.

The Carriers' Carrier Architecture

In Chapter 4, the customers of MPLS VPN service providers were considered to be enterprises, but it is also possible that the customer of a service provider might itself be a service provider. This might be the case if, for example, a smaller, customer service provider wanted to take advantage of a larger service provider's MPLS VPN backbone to connect its geographically dispersed points of presence (PoPs). The customer service provider might or might not in turn be offering MPLS Layer 3 VPN service to its own customers.

The backbone service provider that offers an MPLS VPN service to customer service providers is known as a *carriers' carrier* (CSC). The service provider that is a customer of the CSC is referred to in this section as a *CSC customer*. Figure 5-1 illustrates a carriers' carrier architecture.

In Figure 5-1, SP1 is the CSC and offers MPLS VPN connectivity to its customer, SP2. SP2 takes advantage of SP1's MPLS VPN backbone to connect two of its sites, SP2 New York and SP2 London. SP2, in turn, may then offer connectivity to its own customers (mjlnet, in Figure 5-1) via its own and SP1's backbone network.

One of the most important advantages of deploying a CSC architecture is the fact that routes external to the CSC customer (such as Internet and mjlnet destinations shown in Figure 5-1) need not be held on the CSC Provider Edge (PE) routers.

There are two basic CSC architectures:

- When MPLS is not enabled between CSC customer routers (packet forwarding is IP based).
- When MPLS is enabled between CSC customer routers (packet forwarding is MPLS based). When MPLS is enabled between CSC customer routers, the CSC customer can, in turn, offer MPLS VPN service to its customers.

Figure 5-1 *CSC Architecture*

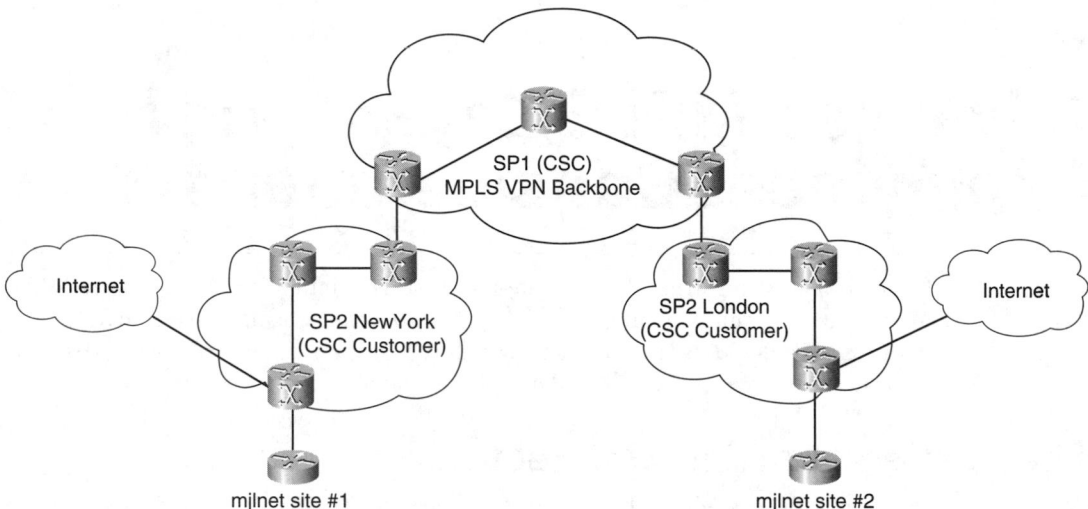

Note that irrespective of the CSC architecture, MPLS must be enabled between CSC PE and CSC Customer Edge (CE) routers.

The sections that follow examine both of these CSC architectures.

CSC Architecture When MPLS Is *Not* Enabled Within CSC Customer Sites

Figure 5-2 shows a CSC architecture when MPLS is not enabled within CSC customer sites.

Figure 5-2 *CSC Architecture When MPLS Is Not Enabled Within CSC Customer Sites.*

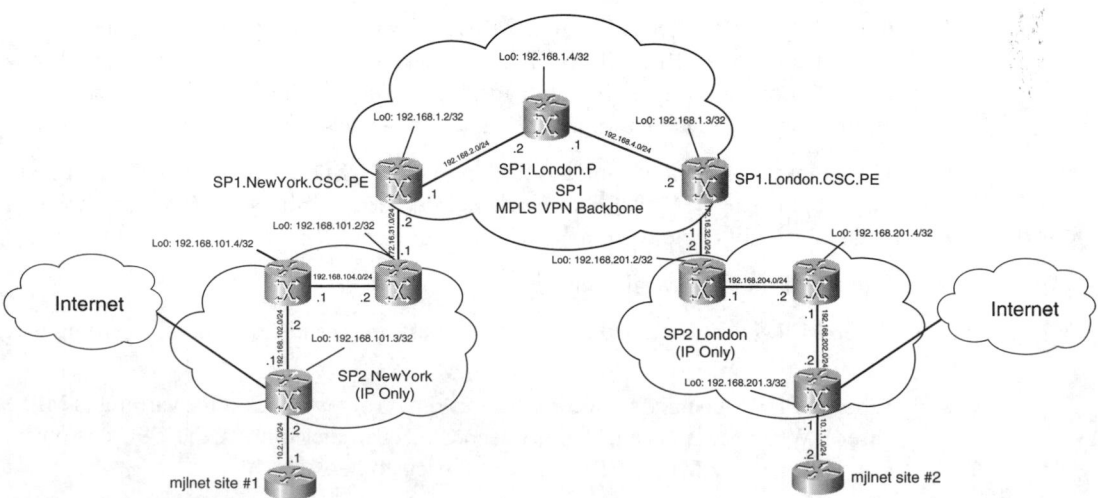

Two factors must be considered when discussing an MPLS CSC architecture (whether or not MPLS is enabled between routers within CSC customer sites):

- **Route advertisement**—How routes are advertised between sites
- **Packet forwarding**—How packets are forwarded between sites over the CSC MPLS VPN backbone network

Route advertisement and packet forwarding in a CSC architecture when MPLS is not enabled within the CSC customer sites are discussed in the following two sections.

Route Advertisement in a CSC Architecture When MPLS Is Not Enabled Within CSC Customer Sites

There are two important components of route advertisement in the CSC MPLS architecture:

- Advertisement of CSC customer *external* routes between CSC customer sites

  CSC customer external routes consist of the following:

  - CSC customer customers' routes (for example, the routes received from mjlnet sites 1 and 2 in Figure 5-2)
  - Any Internet routes

- Advertisement of CSC customer *internal* routes between CSC customer sites

  CSC customer internal routes consist of the following:

  - Routes to the border gateway protocol (BGP) *next hops* of CSC customer *external* routes (usually the loopback interfaces on CSC customer Autonomous System Boundary Routers [ASBRs]).
  - Routes to resources/networks internal to the CSC customer sites (management networks, shared services, and so on).

    Because reachability to resources within the CSC customer networks is provided using exactly the same mechanisms (either an interior gateway protocol [IGP] or static routes) used to advertise BGP next hops for external routes, the focus of discussion within this section is on providing reachability for the next hops of external BGP routes.

Now that you know what route advertisement consists of in a carriers' carrier MPLS VPN architecture, it's a good idea to take a look at an example. Figure 5-3 illustrates external and internal route advertisement between CSC customer sites.

The following two sections detail how external and internal routes are advertised between CSC customer sites.

Figure 5-3 *External and Internal Route Advertisement Between CSC Customer Sites*

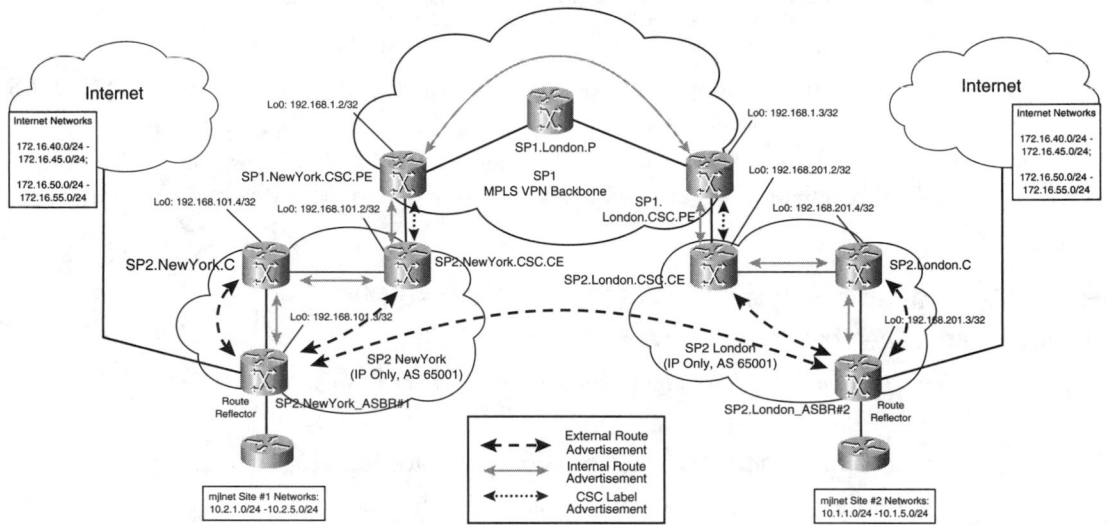

Advertising External Routes Between CSC Customer Sites

CSC customer external routes are advertised directly between CSC customer sites using BGP. If you take a close look at Figure 5-3, you can see that there is a BGP session directly between the ASBRs (SP2.NewYork_ASBR#1 and SP2.London_ASBR#2, which also function as route reflectors in this example) at customer SP2's New York and London sites. This BGP session is used to exchange CSC customer external routes.

As shown in Figure 5-3, SP2's external networks consist of the following:

- Internet networks 172.16.40.0/24 through 172.16.45.0/24 and 172.16.50.0/24 through 172.16.55.0/24. Note that these (private) networks, though not in reality routable on the public Internet, are used here for illustrative purposes.

- SP2 customer (mjlnet) site networks 10.1.1.0/24 through 10.1.5.0/24 and 10.2.1.0/24 through 10.2.5.0/24.

Example 5-1 shows the configuration of the BGP neighbor relationship between SP2.NewYork_ASBR#1 (192.168.101.3) and SP2.London_ASBR#2 (192.168.201.3) for the exchange of external routes.

Example 5-1 *Configuration of the BGP Neighbor Relationship Between SP2.NewYork_ASBR#1 and SP2.London_ASBR#2*

```
!
! On SP2.NewYork_ASBR#1
!
router bgp 65001
 no synchronization
 neighbor 192.168.201.3 remote-as 65001
 neighbor 192.168.201.3 update-source Loopback0
```

Example 5-1*Configuration of the BGP Neighbor Relationship Between SP2.NewYork_ASBR#1 and SP2.London_ASBR#2 (Continued)*

```
 neighbor 192.168.201.3 next-hop-self
 no auto-summary
```

```
!
! On SP2.London_ASBR#2
!
router bgp 65001
 no synchronization
 neighbor 192.168.101.3 remote-as 65001
 neighbor 192.168.101.3 update-source Loopback0
 neighbor 192.168.101.3 next-hop-self
!
```

As you can see, the configuration in Example 5-1 is standard—no special BGP configuration is required for the advertisement of external routes between CSC customer sites. Notice that the same autonomous system number is used at both CSC customer sites (65001), and so route exchange is via IBGP.

CAUTION   You *must* ensure that *all* routers (in the packet-forwarding path) within CSC customer sites possess external routes when MPLS is *not* enabled in the CSC customer networks. If some routers do not possess external routes, packet forwarding will fail (more on this later).

You can ensure that all routers possess external routes in a number of ways, including configuring a full mesh of BGP neighbors between CSC customer site routers or (in a more scalable configuration) configuring route reflectors at the CSC customer sites.

NOTE   SP2.NewYork_ASBR#1 and SP2.London_ASBR#2 are configured as route reflectors and to advertise routes directly between themselves in Example 5-3, but a more common real-world configuration would involve the advertisement of external routes between dedicated route reflectors at the CSC customer sites. In this case, all other CSC customer site routers (including ASBRs) would be route reflector clients.

For more information on the configuration of route reflectors, see the following URL:

http://www.cisco.com/en/US/products/sw/iosswrel/ps1828/products_configuration_guide_chapter09186a00800ca571.html#wp5155

External routes advertised between SP2.NewYork_ASBR#1 and SP2.London_ASBR#2 are not be installed into the routing tables of SP2 routers unless the next hops of these BGP routes are contained within their routing tables.

In this example, all routes received by SP2.NewYork_ASBR#1 and SP2.London_ASBR#2 from external peers (external customers and Internet peers) have their next hops reset using the **neighbor** *ip-address* **next-hop-self** BGP command, and so the next hop of the external routes correspond to the loopback interface addresses of the ASBRs, SP2.NewYork_ASBR#1 and SP2.London_ASBR#2.

In this example, therefore, in order for external routes to be installed into the routing tables of SP2 routers, loopback interface addresses of ASBRs must be advertised between SP2 sites. The loopback interface addresses are, as previously described, internal routes within the CSC customer sites, which brings us onto advertisement of internal routes between SP2 sites.

Advertising Internal Routes Between CSC Customer Sites

As previously mentioned, CSC customer site internal routes describe reachability to router loopback addresses (external route next hops) and other resources within the CSC customer sites. Internal routes are advertised between CSC customer sites via the CSC backbone network using any of the regular PE-CE routing protocols such as Open Shortest Path First (OSPF) or Intermediate System-to-Intermediate System (IS-IS). Alternatively, static routes can be configured on CSC PE and CE routers (and redistributed on the CSC CEs and PEs as appropriate).

In the example in this section, OSPF is the IGP used within both of the SP2 customer sites, and so this is also chosen as the PE-CE routing protocol on the connections between SP2.NewYork.CSC.CE and SP2.NewYork.CSC.PE, as well as SP2.London.CSC.CE and SP2.London.CSC.PE.

Example 5-2 shows the relevant interface and routing protocol configuration for SP2.NewYork.CSC.CE. Note that the configuration of router SP2.London.CSC.CE (not shown) is almost identical—only the IP addressing differs.

Example 5-2 *Interface and Routing Protocol Configurations for SP2.NewYork.CSC.CE*

```
!
! On SP2.NewYork.CSC.CE (line 1)
!
!
!
mpls label protocol ldp (line 2)
!
interface Serial1/1
 description To SP2.NewYork.CSC.PE
 ip address 172.16.31.1 255.255.255.0
 mpls ip (line 3)
!
!
router ospf 100 (line 4)
 passive-interface Loopback0
 network 172.16.31.0 0.0.0.255 area 0
 network 192.168.0.0 0.0.255.255 area 0
!
```

For the most part, the configuration shown in Example 5-2 is straightforward — the OSPF configuration beginning in highlighted line 4 enables OSPF on SP2 internal interfaces (192.168.0.0/16), and also on the interface connecting CSC CE and PE routers, SP2.NewYork.CSC.CE and SP2.NewYork.CSC.PE (interface serial 1/1 [172.16.31.0/24]).

There is, however, one seeming oddity with regard to the configuration of CSC CE SP2.NewYork.CSC.CE — Label Distribution Protocol (LDP) is enabled on the interface between SP2.NewYork.CSC.CE and SP1.NewYork.CSC.PE (see highlighted lines 2 and 3). LDP must be enabled between CSC PE and CE routers so that they can exchange label bindings for CSC customer internal routes (including the next hops of external routes). If a label distribution is not enabled, packet forwarding will fail.

NOTE   As an alternative to LDP, BGP may be used to distribute IPv4 label bindings between CSC PE and CE routers (many service providers prefer BGP). LDP, however, is assumed in this section.

More information on the use of BGP as a label distribution protocol for IPv4 can be found in the section "The Inter-Autonomous System/Interprovider MPLS VPN Architecture" later in this chapter (see in particular Examples 5-23 and 5-24).

It is worth mentioning here that if you do choose to use BGP, be careful to filter the routes that you send to the CSC PE router so that you do not include external routes as well as internal routes.

Example 5-3 shows the interface and routing protocol configuration for SP1.NewYork .CSC.PE. Again, the configuration of router SP1.London.CSC.PE (not shown) is almost the same, with the only difference being the IP addressing.

Example 5-3   *Interface and Routing Protocol Configurations for SP1.NewYork.CSC.PE*

```
!
! On SP1.NewYork.CSC.PE (line 1)
!
ip vrf VPN-sp2 (line 2)
 rd 65535:500
 route-target export 65535:500
 route-target import 65535:500
 !
interface Serial2/1
 ip vrf forwarding VPN-sp2 (line 3)
 ip address 172.16.31.2 255.255.255.0
 mpls ldp discovery transport-address interface (line 4)
 mpls ip (line 5)
 !
```

continues

Example 5-3   *Interface and Routing Protocol Configurations for SP1.NewYork.CSC.PE (Continued)*

```
router ospf 1 vrf VPN-sp2 (line 6)
 redistribute bgp 65535 subnets
 network 172.16.31.0 0.0.0.255 area 0
!
router bgp 65535 (line 7)
 no synchronization
 neighbor 192.168.1.3 remote-as 65535
 neighbor 192.168.1.3 update-source Loopback0
 no auto-summary
 !
 address-family vpnv4 (line 8)
 neighbor 192.168.1.3 activate
 neighbor 192.168.1.3 send-community extended
 exit-address-family
 !
 address-family ipv4 vrf VPN-sp2 (line 9)
 redistribute ospf 1 vrf VPN-sp2 match internal external 1 external 2
 no auto-summary
 no synchronization
 exit-address-family
!
```

The configuration of CSC PE router SP1.NewYork.CSC.PE is again pretty standard.

In highlighted line 2, a VPN routing and forwarding table (VRF) called VPN-sp1 is configured, and the interface connected to CSC CE router SP2.NewYork.CSC.CE (serial 2/1) is associated with this VRF using the **ip vrf forwarding** *vrf-name* command (see highlighted line 3).

In highlighted line 6, OSPF is enabled as the PE-CE routing protocol for VRF VPN-sp2. OSPF is configured on the interface connected to SP2.NewYork.CSC.CE (interface serial 2/1), and MP-BGP is redistributed into OSPF. Nothing special here.

Then in highlighted line 7, BGP is enabled and a neighbor relationship is configured with SP1.London.CSC.PE (192.168.1.3).

In highlighted line 8 and 9, MP-BGP is enabled for VPN-IPv4 route exchange with SP1.London.CSC.PE (see below highlighted line 8), and the PE-CE routing protocol OSPF is redistributed into MP-BGP (within the IPv4 VRF address family—see below highlighted line 9). Again, nothing special.

But take a look at highlighted lines 4 and 5. Here's where the configuration of the CSC architecture differs from regular MPLS VPN configuration on PE routers.

In highlighted line 5, LDP is enabled on the interface connected to SP2.NewYork.CSC.CE (LDP is automatically selected as the label protocol when configuring the **mpls ip** command on a VRF interface). Remember that LDP (or BGP) must be enabled between CSC CE and PE to ensure that label bindings for CSC customer internal routes are exchanged and packet forwarding does not fail.

NOTE	Note also the **mpls ldp discovery transport-address interface** in highlighted line 4. This command may be necessary on the VRF interface connected to the CSC CE (and also possibly on the CSC CE interface connected to the CSC PE) to ensure that an LDP transport connection can be successfully established between the CSC PE and CE and label bindings can be exchanged.
	By default, LDP uses the LDP router ID IP address (a loopback interface address or highest physical interface address) as the source/destination of its transport connection, but an LDP transport connection will fail if the CSC PE and CE do not have routes to each other's LDP router ID. There are a number of ways around this problem, but the easiest is to use the **mpls ldp discovery transport-address interface** command to configure LDP to use the (VRF) PE-CE interface address as the source/destination of its transport connection rather than the LDP router ID.

So, CSC customer internal routes are exchanged between sites in exactly the same way that customer routes are exchanged between sites in a standard (single service provider) MPLS VPN configuration.

Example 5-4 shows the output of the **show ip route** command on SP2.NewYork_ASBR#1 and SP2.London_ASBR#2.

Example 5-4 **show ip route** *Command Output on CSC Customer ASBRs SP2.NewYork_ASBR#1 and SP2.London_ASBR#2*

```
SP2.NewYork_ASBR#1#show ip route
Codes: C - connected, S - static, I - IGRP, R - RIP, M - mobile, B - BGP
       D - EIGRP, EX - EIGRP external, O - OSPF, IA - OSPF inter area
       N1 - OSPF NSSA external type 1, N2 - OSPF NSSA external type 2
       E1 - OSPF external type 1, E2 - OSPF external type 2, E - EGP
       i - IS-IS, su - IS-IS summary, L1 - IS-IS level-1, L2 - IS-IS level-2
       ia - IS-IS inter area, * - candidate default, U - per-user static route
       o - ODR

Gateway of last resort is not set

O    192.168.104.0/24 [110/65] via 192.168.102.2, 00:24:13, FastEthernet0/0
     172.16.0.0/16 is variably subnetted, 15 subnets, 2 masks
B       172.16.52.0/24 [200/0] via 192.168.201.3, 00:07:19 (line 1)
B       172.16.53.0/24 [200/0] via 192.168.201.3, 00:07:19 (line 2)
B       172.16.54.0/24 [200/0] via 192.168.201.3, 00:07:19 (line 3)
B       172.16.55.0/24 [200/0] via 192.168.201.3, 00:07:19 (line 4)
B       172.16.50.0/24 [200/0] via 192.168.201.3, 00:07:19 (line 5)
B       172.16.51.0/24 [200/0] via 192.168.201.3, 00:07:19 (line 6)
B       172.16.44.0/24 [20/0] via 172.16.20.1, 00:03:32 (line 7)
B       172.16.45.0/24 [20/0] via 172.16.20.1, 00:03:32 (line 8)
B       172.16.40.0/24 [20/0] via 172.16.20.1, 00:03:32 (line 9)
B       172.16.41.0/24 [20/0] via 172.16.20.1, 00:03:32 (line 10)
B       172.16.42.0/24 [20/0] via 172.16.20.1, 00:03:32 (line 11)
B       172.16.43.0/24 [20/0] via 172.16.20.1, 00:03:32 (line 12)
```

continues

Example 5-4 show ip route *Command Output on CSC Customer ASBRs SP2.NewYork_ASBR#1 and SP2.London_ASBR#2 (Continued)*

```
O IA    172.16.32.0/24 [110/114] via 192.168.102.2, 00:24:14, FastEthernet0/0
O IA    172.16.32.2/32 [110/114] via 192.168.102.2, 00:24:14, FastEthernet0/0
O       172.16.31.0/24 [110/113] via 192.168.102.2, 00:24:14, FastEthernet0/0
        192.168.201.0/32 is subnetted, 3 subnets
O IA    192.168.201.3 [110/290] via 192.168.102.2, 00:24:15,
   FastEthernet0/0 (line 13)
O IA    192.168.201.2 [110/162] via 192.168.102.2, 00:24:15,
   FastEthernet0/0 (line 14)
O IA    192.168.201.4 [110/226] via 192.168.102.2, 00:24:15,
   FastEthernet0/0 (line 15)
O IA 192.168.202.0/24 [110/289] via 192.168.102.2, 00:24:15, FastEthernet0/0
O IA 192.168.204.0/24 [110/225] via 192.168.102.2, 00:24:15, FastEthernet0/0
C    192.168.102.0/24 is directly connected, FastEthernet0/0
        192.168.101.0/32 is subnetted, 3 subnets
O       192.168.101.4 [110/2] via 192.168.102.2, 00:24:15,
   FastEthernet0/0 (line 16)
C       192.168.101.3 is directly connected, Loopback0 (line 17)
O       192.168.101.2 [110/66] via 192.168.102.2, 00:24:15, FastEthernet0/0 (line 18)
SP2.NewYork_ASBR#1#
```

```
SP2.London_ASBR#2#show ip route
Codes: C - connected, S - static, I - IGRP, R - RIP, M - mobile, B - BGP
       D - EIGRP, EX - EIGRP external, O - OSPF, IA - OSPF inter area
       N1 - OSPF NSSA external type 1, N2 - OSPF NSSA external type 2
       E1 - OSPF external type 1, E2 - OSPF external type 2, E - EGP
       i - IS-IS, su - IS-IS summary, L1 - IS-IS level-1, L2 - IS-IS level-2
       ia - IS-IS inter area, * - candidate default, U - per-user static route
       o - ODR, P - periodic downloaded static route

Gateway of last resort is not set

O IA 192.168.104.0/24 [110/288] via 192.168.202.1, 00:33:24, Serial0/0
        172.16.0.0/16 is variably subnetted, 15 subnets, 2 masks
B       172.16.52.0/24 [20/0] via 172.16.60.1, 00:08:53 (line 19)
B       172.16.53.0/24 [20/0] via 172.16.60.1, 00:08:53 (line 20)
B       172.16.54.0/24 [20/0] via 172.16.60.1, 00:08:53 (line 21)
B       172.16.55.0/24 [20/0] via 172.16.60.1, 00:08:53 (line 22)
B       172.16.50.0/24 [20/0] via 172.16.60.1, 00:08:53 (line 23)
B       172.16.51.0/24 [20/0] via 172.16.60.1, 00:08:53 (line 24)
B       172.16.44.0/24 [200/0] via 192.168.101.3, 00:14:22 (line 25)
B       172.16.45.0/24 [200/0] via 192.168.101.3, 00:14:22 (line 26)
B       172.16.40.0/24 [200/0] via 192.168.101.3, 00:14:22 (line 27)
B       172.16.41.0/24 [200/0] via 192.168.101.3, 00:14:22 (line 28)
B       172.16.42.0/24 [200/0] via 192.168.101.3, 00:14:22 (line 29)
B       172.16.43.0/24 [200/0] via 192.168.101.3, 00:14:22 (line 30)
O       172.16.32.0/24 [110/192] via 192.168.202.1, 00:33:25, Serial0/0
O IA    172.16.31.1/32 [110/193] via 192.168.202.1, 00:33:25, Serial0/0
O IA    172.16.31.0/24 [110/193] via 192.168.202.1, 00:33:25, Serial0/0
        192.168.201.0/32 is subnetted, 3 subnets
C       192.168.201.3 is directly connected, Loopback0 (line 31)
O       192.168.201.2 [110/129] via 192.168.202.1, 00:33:25, Serial0/0 (line 32)
O       192.168.201.4 [110/65] via 192.168.202.1, 00:33:25, Serial0/0 (line 33)
```

Example 5-4 **show ip route** *Command Output on CSC Customer ASBRs SP2.NewYork_ASBR#1 and SP2.London_ASBR#2 (Continued)*

```
       192.168.202.0/24 is variably subnetted, 2 subnets, 2 masks
C         192.168.202.0/24 is directly connected, Serial0/0
C         192.168.202.1/32 is directly connected, Serial0/0
O      192.168.204.0/24 [110/128] via 192.168.202.1, 00:33:26, Serial0/0
O IA 192.168.102.0/24 [110/298] via 192.168.202.1, 00:33:26, Serial0/0
       192.168.101.0/32 is subnetted, 3 subnets
O IA     192.168.101.4 [110/289] via 192.168.202.1, 00:33:26, Serial0/0 (line 34)
O IA     192.168.101.3 [110/299] via 192.168.202.1, 00:33:26, Serial0/0 (line 35)
O IA     192.168.101.2 [110/241] via 192.168.202.1, 00:33:26, Serial0/0 (line 36)
SP2.London_ASBR#2#
```

The first part of Example 5-4 shows the output of the **show ip route** command on SP2.NewYork_ASBR#1, with highlighted lines 1 to 18 showing CSC customer external and internal routes.

In highlighted lines 1 to 12, you can see external routes 172.16.50.0/24 through 172.16.55.0/24 and 172.16.40.0/24 through 172.16.45.0/24.

Highlighted lines 13 to 18 show the internal routes corresponding to CSC customer (SP2) router loopback interfaces. Of particular interest are the routes shown in highlighted lines 13 and 17 (192.168.201.3/32 and 192.168.101.3/32)—these two prefixes correspond to the loopback interface IP addresses on SP2.NewYork_ASBR#1 and SP2.London_ASBR#2 and are the next hops of the external BGP routes.

The output of the **show ip route** command on SP2.London_ASBR#2 is similar to that from SP2.NewYork_ASBR#1. Highlighted lines 19 to 36 show the external and internal routes.

You can see external routes in highlighted lines 19 to 30, and in highlighted lines 31 to 36, you can see internal routes corresponding to SP2 router loopback interface addresses. Again, the two most interesting internal routes are the prefixes shown in highlighted lines 31 and 35 (the loopback interfaces addresses of the ASBRs, which are the next-hop addresses for the external routes).

You can now see that SP2.NewYork_ASBR#1 and SP2.London_ASBR#2 have IP reachability (internal routes) to each other, as well as all CSC customer external destinations (external routes).

Before moving on to packet forwarding, it is important to just restate a few of the most important facts to remember about route advertisement in a CSC architecture when MPLS is *not* enabled in the CSC customer networks:

* CSC customer external routes provide IP reachability to destinations external to the CSC customer (external customers and/or Internet).

* CSC customer external routes are advertised directly between CSC customer sites using BGP.

- All routers within the CSC customer sites (in the IP forwarding path) *must* possess external routes otherwise packet forwarding will fail. You can ensure that all CSC customer routers contain external routes using a number of methods including configuring a BGP neighbor full mesh between CSC customer routers or preferably configuring route reflectors at CSC customer sites.

- CSC customer internal routes provide IP reachability to destinations within the CSC customer sites. Significantly, some internal routes (often loopback interface addresses on ASBRs) provide next-hop reachability for external BGP routes.

- CSC customer internal routes are advertised between CSC customer sites via the CSC backbone network. Standard PE-CE routing protocols can be used between CSC PE and CE routers.

Packet Forwarding in a CSC Architecture When MPLS Is Not Enabled Between Routers Within CSC Customer Sites

You must remember a few important things about packet forwarding in a CSC architecture when MPLS is not enabled between routers within CSC customer sites:

- Packet forwarding within the CSC customer sites is purely IP based.

- Packet forwarding between the CSC CEs and PEs is MPLS based.

- Packet forwarding within the CSC backbone network is MPLS based and conforms to the regular MPLS VPN backbone packet-forwarding paradigm.

To really understand how packet forwarding works in a CSC architecture, it is useful to examine how a packet is forwarded from a source in SP2's New York site to a destination *external* to SP2's London site.

Example 5-5 demonstrates how to use the **traceroute** command to examine packet forwarding hop by hop from source SP2.NewYork_ASBR#1 (SP's New York site) to destination IP address 172.16.51.1 (an Internet host reachable via SP2's London site [the direct Internet connection from SP2's New York site is down in this example]).

Example 5-5 *Traceroute from Source SP2.NewYork_ASBR#1 to Destination IP Address 172.16.51.1 (a Host on a Network External to SP2 Site 2).*

```
SP2.NewYork_ASBR#1#traceroute 172.16.51.1

Type escape sequence to abort.
Tracing the route to 172.16.51.1

  1 192.168.102.2 0 msec 0 msec 4 msec (line 1)
  2 192.168.104.2 16 msec 12 msec 16 msec (line 2)
  3 172.16.31.2 [MPLS: Label 32 Exp 0] 244 msec 328 msec 240 msec (line 3)
  4 192.168.2.2 [MPLS: Labels 19/25 Exp 0] 236 msec 228 msec 232 msec (line 4)
  5 172.16.32.1 [MPLS: Label 25 Exp 0] 204 msec 204 msec 208 msec (line 5)
  6 172.16.32.2 [MPLS: Label 18 Exp 0] 188 msec 188 msec 192 msec (line 6)
  7 192.168.204.2 88 msec 88 msec 88 msec (line 7)
  8 192.168.202.2 100 msec 100 msec 100 msec (line 8)
  9 172.16.60.1 115 msec 116 msec * (line 9)
SP2.NewYork_ASBR#1#
```

In highlighted lines 1 and 2, the packet is forwarded from SP2.NewYork_ASBR#1 to SP2.NewYork.C (192.168.102.2), and then from SP2.NewYork.C to SP2.NewYork.CSC.CE (192.168.104.2).

Notice that the output of the **traceroute** command does not show MPLS labels in highlighted lines 1 and 2. The lack of MPLS labels indicates that regular IP forwarding is used at each of these two hops (routers). The fact that IP forwarding is used is significant. It means that each of these two routers (in fact, all CSC customer site routers [in the packet-forwarding path]) *must* have knowledge of external routes (in this example, an external route to 172.16.51.1), otherwise packet forwarding will fail. So, as previously stated, CSC customer site routers must be configured as BGP peers to receive external routes.

In highlighted line 3, the packet is forwarded from SP2.NewYork.CSC.CE to SP1.NewYork.CSC.PE (172.16.31.2). Notice that an MPLS label (32) is shown in the output here. This label is *very* significant. It actually corresponds to the next hop of BGP route 172.16.51.0/24 (next hop 192.168.201.3 [SP2.London_ASBR#2]). You'll remember that Label Switching Routers (LSRs) do not (normally) assign labels to regular BGP routes but instead use the label corresponding to the next hops of those BGP routes.

The output of the **show mpls forwarding-table** command in Example 5-6 confirms that (outgoing) label 32 corresponds to prefix (next hop) 192.168.201.3.

Example 5-6   **show mpls forwarding-table** *Command Output*

```
SP2.NewYork.CSC.CE#show mpls forwarding-table
Local  Outgoing     Prefix           Bytes tag  Outgoing   Next Hop
tag    tag or VC    or Tunnel Id     switched   interface
16     Untagged     172.16.31.2/32   0          Se1/1      point2point
17     Untagged     192.168.104.1/32 0          Se1/0      point2point
18     Untagged     192.168.102.0/24 4656       Se1/0      point2point
19     Untagged     192.168.101.3/32 9547       Se1/0      point2point
20     Untagged     192.168.101.4/32 0          Se1/0      point2point
21     29           172.16.32.0/24   0          Se1/1      point2point
22     30           172.16.32.2/32   0          Se1/1      point2point
23     31           192.168.201.2/32 0          Se1/1      point2point
24     33           192.168.201.4/32 0          Se1/1      point2point
25     35           192.168.204.0/24 0          Se1/1      point2point
26     34           192.168.202.0/24 0          Se1/1      point2point
27     32           192.168.201.3/32 0          Se1/1      point2point
SP2.NewYork.CSC.CE#
```

The significance of the label (corresponding to the *next hop* of the external BGP route) pushed onto the packet in Example 5-5, highlighted line 3 is that it will allow the ingress CSC PE router, SP1.NewYork.CSC.PE, to forward the packet without having any knowledge of CSC customer external routes (including a route to destination 172.16.51.1).

For SP1.NewYork.CSC.PE to possess (assign) labels for next hop 192.168.201.3, all it needs to have is a route to this next hop. How does SP1.NewYork.CSC.PE get routes to the next hops of CSC customer external routes? It gets routes to next hops via the advertisement of CSC customer internal routes from SP2.London.CSC.CE to SP1.London.CSC.PE (advertised using the PE-CE routing protocol), and the advertisement of those routes from SP1.London.CSC.PE using MP-BGP.

In Example 5-5, highlighted line 4, the packet transits the link from SP1.NewYork.CSC.PE to SP1.London.P. Notice that SP1.NewYork.CSC.PE has swapped the label (32) for a label stack consisting of an IGP label (19) and a VPN label (25). The function of the IGP label is to get the packet from the ingress PE (SP1.NewYork.CSC.PE) to the egress PE (SP1.London.CSC.PE), and the function of the VPN label is to identify the outgoing interface or VRF on the egress PE.

Example 5-5 highlighted line 5 shows the packet as it transits the link from SP1.London.P to SP1.London.CSC.PE. SP1.London.P has popped the IGP label, leaving just the VPN label (it is the penultimate hop, so nothing unusual there).

Now to Example 5-5 highlighted line 6. This line shows the packet as it traverses the link between SP1.London.CSC.PE and SP2.London.CSC.CE. If you look closely, you can see that SP2.London.CSC.PE has removed the VPN label and pushed a label (18) corresponding to a route to next hop 192.168.201.3 (SP2.London_ASBR#2). SP1.London.CSC.PE is, like SP1.NewYork.CSC.PE, exchanging internal routes and corresponding label bindings with its connected CSC CE (SP2.London.CSC.CE).

In Example 5-5, highlighted lines 7 and 8, the packet traverses the links between SP2.London.CSC.CE and SP2.London.C, as well as SP2.London.C and SP2.London_ASBR#2. Neither of these highlighted lines shows an MPLS label, and so you know that SP2.London.CSC.CE and SP2.London.C used regular IP forwarding. Again, SP2.London.CSC.CE and SP2.London.C must possess external BGP routes to do this.

Then, in highlighted line 9, the packet is shown as it transits the connection between SP2.London_ASBR#2 and an external router. The output terminates at line 9 because the external router is directly connected to the destination IP address 172.16.51.1.

Figure 5-4 illustrates packet forwarding across the network from SP2.NewYork_ASBR#1 to external destination 172.16.51.1.

Figure 5-4 *Packet Forwarding Across the Network from SP2.NewYork_ASBR#1 to External Destination 172.16.51.1*

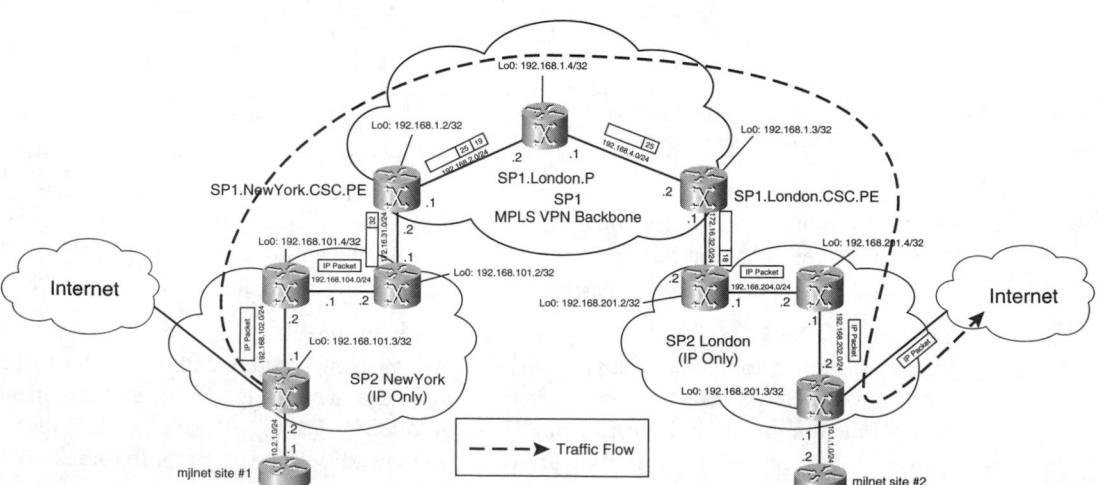

So, now you know how route advertisement and packet forwarding work in a CSC architecture when MPLS is not enabled in the CSC customer networks. But, how about if MPLS is enabled in CSC customer networks?

CSC Architecture When MPLS Is Enabled Within CSC Customer Sites

CSC customers gain two main advantages by enabling MPLS within their sites:

- CSC CE routers and nonedge routers (such as SP2.NewYork.C and SP2.London.C in Figure 5-5) no longer need external BGP routes.

- The CSC customer can offer MPLS VPN services to its own customers. This is sometimes called a *hierarchical VPN architecture*.

Figure 5-5 illustrates a CSC architecture when MPLS is enabled within CSC customer sites.

Figure 5-5   *A CSC Architecture When MPLS Is Enabled Within CSC Customer Sites*

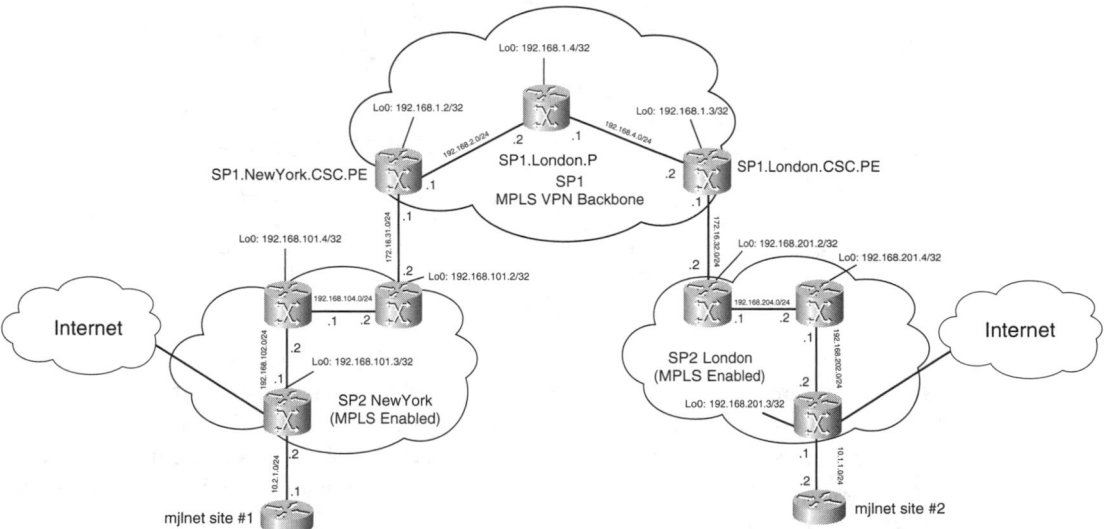

It is important to understand route advertisement and packet forwarding in a CSC architecture when MPLS is enabled in the CSC customer sites to understand why external routes are no longer required on some CSC customer routers, and why the CSC customer can now offer MPLS VPN services to its own customers.

Route Advertisement in a CSC Architecture When MPLS Is Enabled Within CSC Customer Sites

Route advertisement in a CSC architecture when MPLS is enabled within is much the same as when MPLS is not enabled within CSC customer sites, with (as previously mentioned) one key difference: External BGP routes no longer need to be advertised to CSC CE and nonedge CSC customer site routers.

Figure 5-6 illustrates external and internal route advertisement between CSC customer sites when MPLS is enabled at CSC customer sites. You might want to compare Figure 5-6 to Figure 5-3 (where MPLS is not enabled at the CSC customer sites).

Figure 5-6   *External and Internal Route Advertisement Between CSC Customer Sites (When MPLS Is Enabled CSC Customer Sites)*

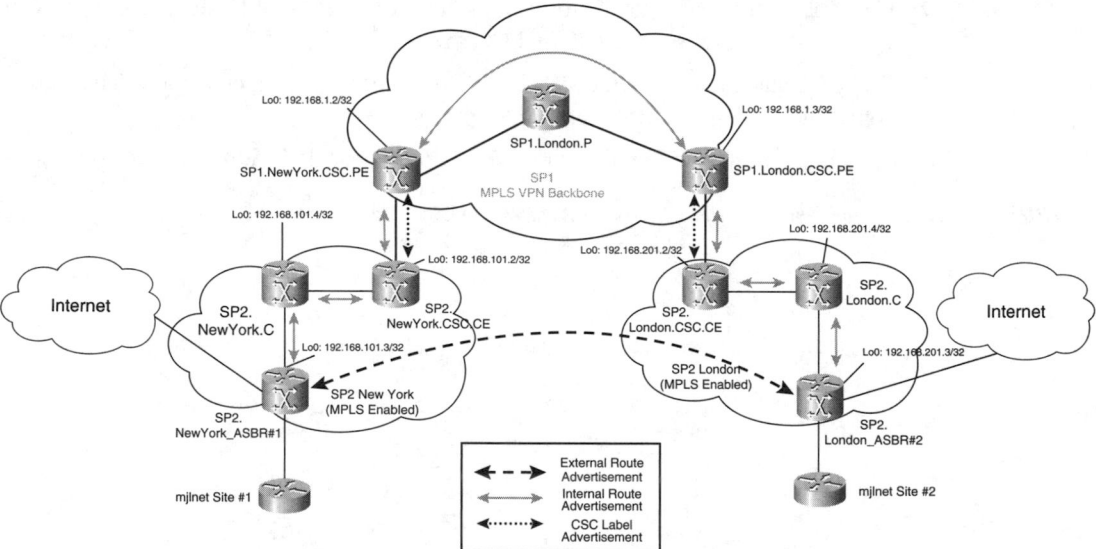

The reason that external routes are no longer required on CSC CE routers and nonedge CSC customer routers is that these routers now forward packets using MPLS. Just as with P routers in the standard MPLS VPN forwarding paradigm, CSC CE and nonedge CSC customer routers now only require internal routes (including routes to the next hops of external BGP routes) and label bindings corresponding to internal routes to successfully forward packets.

Therefore, the only configuration changes required when enabling MPLS in CSC customer sites are as follows:

- MPLS must be enabled (using the **mpls ip** command) on all CSC customer site router core-facing interfaces (those not facing external destinations).

- BGP configuration (that was required for *external* routes) can be removed on CSC CE routers (assuming that BGP is not the PE-CE routing protocol) and nonedge CSC customer site routers (with the exception of that on route reflectors!).

  Routers connected to external destinations (ASBRs) still require BGP configuration (and external routes) because they are required to perform regular IP packet forwarding to and from external networks.

NOTE	Although it cannot be used as the label protocol between CSC PE and CE routers, it is possible to use Tag Distribution Protocol (TDP) to advertise label bindings between LSRs within CSC customer sites.
	Note, however, that the use of Cisco's proprietary TDP is deprecated in favor of IETF standard LDP.

Packet Forwarding in a CSC Architecture When MPLS Is Enabled Between Routers Within CSC Customer Sites

When MPLS is enabled within CSC customer sites, CSC customer site routers forward packets using MPLS. Forwarding within the CSC backbone network is exactly the same as when MPLS is not enabled within CSC customer sites.

Example 5-7 demonstrates using the **traceroute** command to examine packet forwarding hop by hop from source SP2.NewYork_ASBR#1 (SP2's New York site) to destination IP address 172.16.51.1 (a host on a network external to SP2's London site).

Example 5-7 *Traceroute from Source SP2.NewYork_ASBR#1 to Destination IP Address 172.16.51.1 When MPLS Is Enabled Within CSC Customer Sites*

```
SP2.NewYork_ASBR#1#traceroute 172.16.51.1

Type escape sequence to abort.
Tracing the route to 172.16.51.1

  1 192.168.102.2 [MPLS: Labels 26 Exp 0] 548 msec 388 msec 388 msec (line 1)
  2 192.168.104.2 [MPLS: Labels 24 Exp 0] 372 msec 368 msec 520 msec (line 2)
  3 172.16.31.2 [MPLS: Labels 32 Exp 0] 352 msec 356 msec 352 msec (line 3)
  4 192.168.2.2 [MPLS: Labels 19/35 Exp 0] 344 msec 344 msec 340 msec (line 4)
  5 172.16.32.1 [MPLS: Labels 35 Exp 0] 320 msec 384 msec 316 msec (line 5)
  6 172.16.32.2 [MPLS: Labels 25 Exp 0] 304 msec 304 msec 300 msec (line 6)
  7 192.168.204.2 [MPLS: Labels 20 Exp 0] 288 msec 288 msec 288 msec (line 7)
  8 192.168.202.2 220 msec 220 msec 224 msec (line 8)
  9 172.16.60.1 130 msec * 132 msec (line 9)
SP2.NewYork_ASBR#1
```

If you compare the output in Example 5-7 to that shown in Example 5-5 (when MPLS is not enabled within the CSC customer sites), you can see in highlighted lines 1, 2, and 7 that the difference is that the packet is now forwarded using MPLS (note the MPLS labels) between CSC customer site routers.

In highlighted line 1, the packet is forwarded between routers SP2.NewYork_ASBR#1 and SP2.NewYork.C.

Highlighted line 2 shows the packet as it is forwarded between routers SP2.NewYork.C and SP2.NewYork.CSC.CE.

From highlighted line 3 to 6, the packet is forwarded from SP2.NewYork.CSC.CE across the CSC backbone network to SP2.London.CSC.CE. Forwarding across the CSC backbone network is unchanged from Example 5-5 (when MPLS is not enabled within CSC customer sites).

In highlighted line 7, the packet is forwarded between routers SP2.London.CSC.CE and SP2.London.C.

Then in highlighted line 8, the packet is forwarded between SP2.London.C and SP2.London_ASBR#2.

Finally, the packet is forwarded between routers SP2.London_ASBR#2 and the external router that is connected to host 172.16.51.1.

Figure 5-7 shows packet forwarding across the network from SP2.NewYork_ASBR#1 to external destination 172.16.51.1 when MPLS is enabled within CSC customer sites.

Figure 5-7 *Packet Forwarding Across the Network from SP2.NewYork_ASBR#1 to External Destination 172.16.51.1 When MPLS Is Enabled Within Sites*

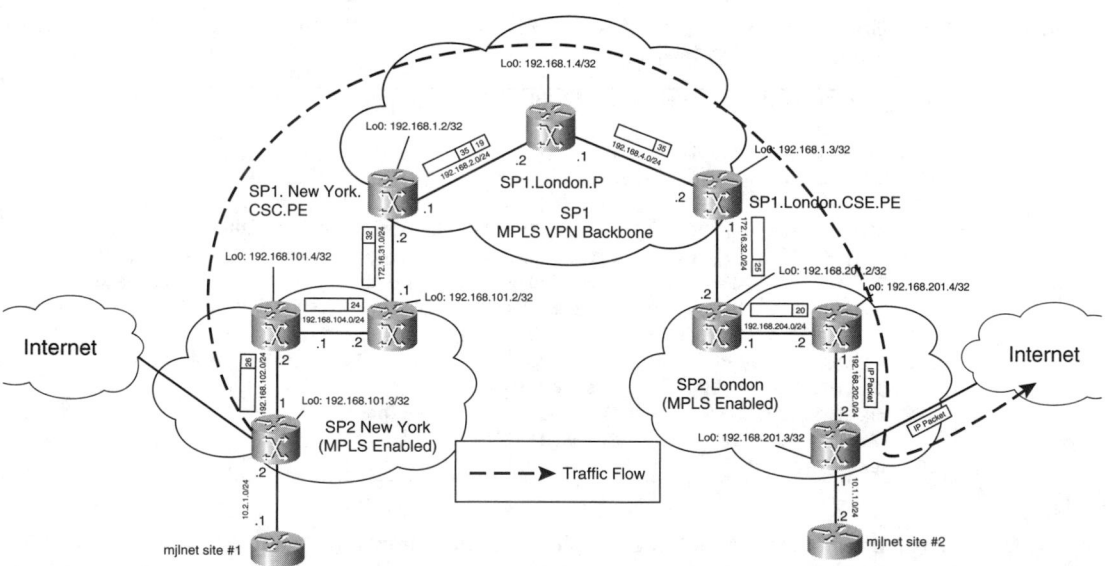

Enabling Hierarchical VPNs in a CSC Architecture

As previously mentioned, one major advantage of enabling MPLS within CSC customer sites is that the CSC customer can now offer MPLS VPN service to its customers.

In this case, route advertisement remains that same as previously described (when MPLS is enabled within CSC customers), with one key difference—MP-BGP must be enabled between ASBR/PEs connected to the CSC customer's MPLS VPN-enabled customers to advertise VPN-IPv4 routes.

Figure 5-8 shows hierarchical VPNs.

Figure 5-8   *Hierarchical VPNs*

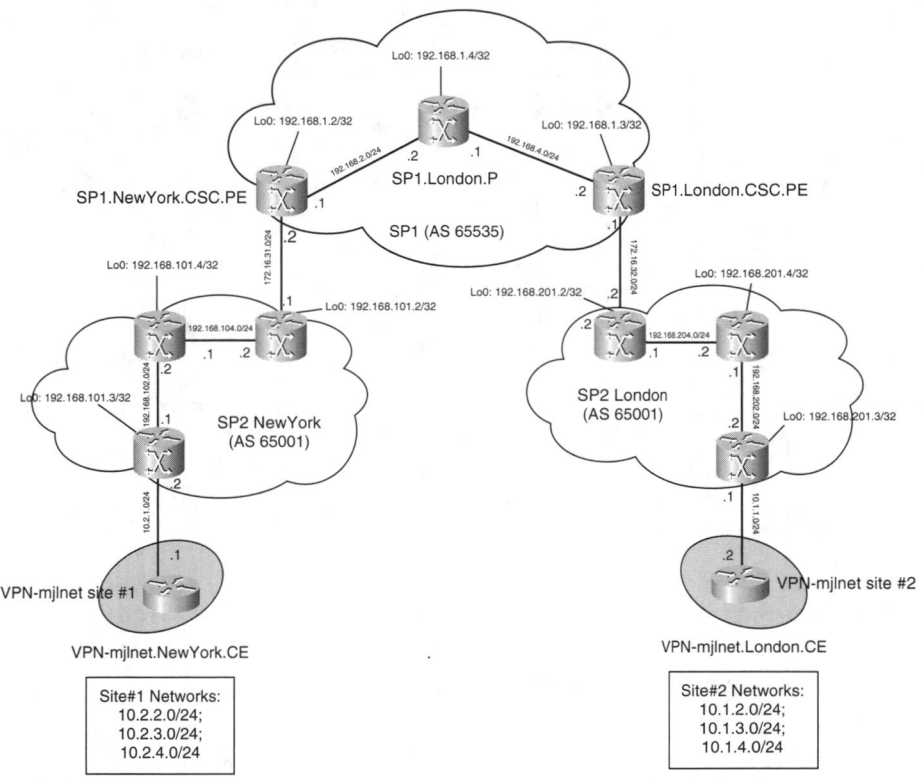

As you can see in Figure 5-8, connectivity for VPN-mjlnet is provisioned over the SP2 (and SP1) network.

Figure 5-9 shows route and label advertisement in hierarchical VPNs.

Example 5-8 shows the configuration of SP2.NewYork_ASBR#1/PE when hierarchical VPNs are enabled. SP2.NewYork_ASBR#1/PE is connected to VPN-mjlnet site 1.

Note that the configuration of SP2.London_ASBR#2/PE (connected to VPN-mjlnet site 2) is almost identical, with the only difference being IP address configuration.

Figure 5-9 *Route and Label Advertisement in Hierarchical VPNs*

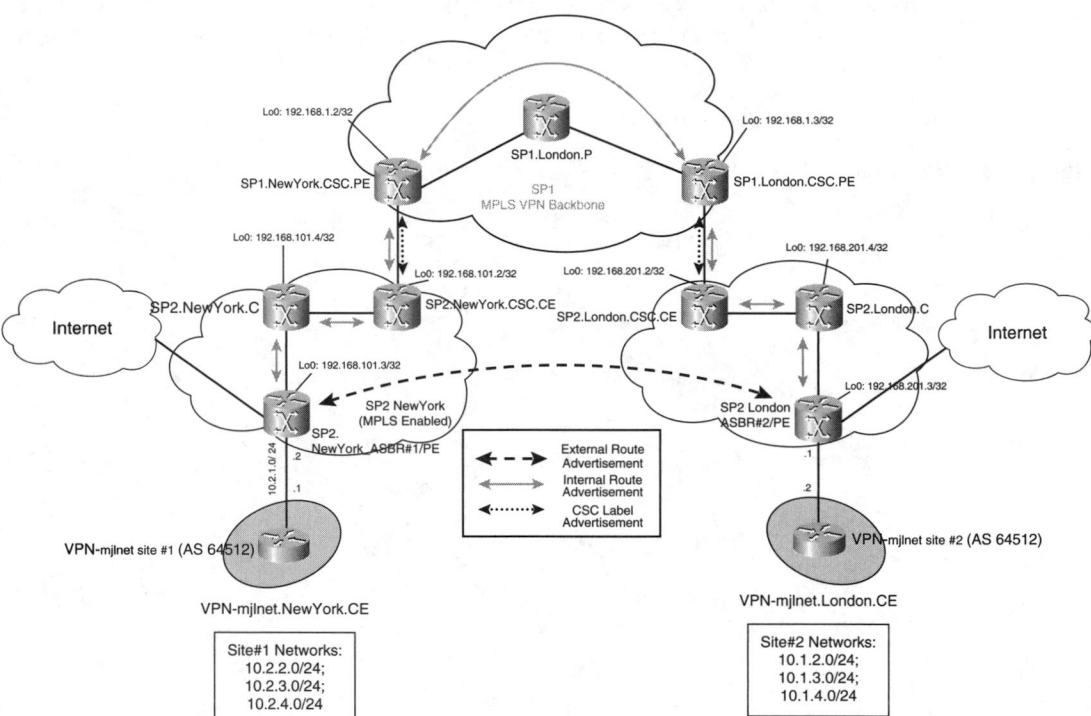

Example 5-8 *Configuration of SP2.NewYork_ASBR#1/PE When Hierarchical MPLS VPNs Are Enabled*

```
!
! On SP2.NewYork_ASBR#1/PE# (line 1)

!
ip vrf VPN-mjlnet (line 2)
 rd 65535:100
 route-target export 65535:100
 route-target import 65535:100
!
!
interface Serial1/1 (line 3)
 ip vrf forwarding VPN-mjlnet
 ip address 10.2.1.2 255.255.255.0
!
router bgp 65001 (line 4)
 no synchronization
 neighbor 192.168.201.3 remote-as 65001
```

Example 5-8 *Configuration of SP2.NewYork_ASBR#1/PE When Hierarchical MPLS VPNs Are Enabled (Continued)*

```
 neighbor 192.168.201.3 update-source Loopback0
 no auto-summary
 !
 address-family vpnv4 (line 5)
 neighbor 192.168.201.3 activate
 neighbor 192.168.201.3 send-community extended
 exit-address-family
 !
 address-family ipv4 vrf VPN-mjlnet (line 6)
 neighbor 10.2.1.1 remote-as 64512
 neighbor 10.2.1.1 activate
 neighbor 10.2.1.1 as-override
 no auto-summary
 no synchronization
 exit-address-family
!
```

Highlighted lines 1 and 2 show the configuration of VRF VPN-mjlnet and the association of interface serial 1/1 with VRF VPN-mjlnet.

In highlighted lines 3, BGP is enabled on SP2.NewYork_ASBR#1/PE.

Then, in highlighted line 4, MP-BGP is enabled for the advertisement of VPN-IPv4 routes between CSC customer sites, and in highlighted line 5, an IPv4 address family is configured for VRF VPN-mjlnet.

Notice that in this example (below highlighted line 6), the PE-CE routing protocol for VPN VPN-mjlnet is BGP. The customer (mjlnet) autonomous system is 64512, and because the same autonomous system is being used at mjlnet sites 1 and 2, the **neighbor** *ip-address* **as-override** is required to ensure that routes are not dropped.

So that is route advertisement for hierarchical VPNs. Now on to packet forwarding.

Example 5-9 demonstrates using the **traceroute** command to examine packet forwarding between VPN mjlnet sites 1 and 2.

Example 5-9 *Traceroute Output from VPN mjlnet Site 1 to VPN mjlnet Site 2*

```
VPN-mjlnet.NewYork.CE#traceroute 10.1.2.1

Type escape sequence to abort.
Tracing the route to 10.1.2.1

  1 10.2.1.2 4 msec 0 msec 0 msec (line 1)
  2 192.168.102.2 [MPLS: Labels 26/29 Exp 0] 548 msec 388 msec 388 msec (line 2)
  3 192.168.104.2 [MPLS: Labels 24/29 Exp 0] 372 msec 368 msec 520 msec (line 3)
  4 172.16.31.2 [MPLS: Labels 32/29 Exp 0] 352 msec 356 msec 352 msec (line 4)
  5 192.168.2.2 [MPLS: Labels 19/35/29 Exp 0] 344 msec 344 msec 340 msec (line 5)
```

continues

Example 5-9 *Traceroute Output from VPN mjlnet Site 1 to VPN mjlnet Site 2 (Continued)*

```
 6 172.16.32.1 [MPLS: Labels 35/29 Exp 0] 320 msec 384 msec 316 msec (line 6)
 7 172.16.32.2 [MPLS: Labels 25/29 Exp 0] 304 msec 304 msec 300 msec (line 7)
 8 192.168.204.2 [MPLS: Labels 20/29 Exp 0] 288 msec 288 msec 288 msec (line 8)
 9 10.1.1.1 [AS 65001] [MPLS: Label 29 Exp 0] 220 msec 220 msec 224 msec (line 9)
10 10.1.1.2 [AS 65001] 136 msec *  136 msec (line 10)
VPN-mjlnet.NewYork.CE#
```

Highlighted line 1 shows the packet as it transits the link between CE router VPN-mjlnet.NewYork.CE and SP2.NewYork_ASBR#1/PE.

In highlighted line 2, the packet crosses the connection between SP2.NewYork_ASBR#1/PE and SP2.NewYork.C. Notice that SP2.NewYork_ASBR#1/PE has pushed two labels onto the packet, an IGP label (26) and a VPN label (29). This VPN label identifies the outgoing interface or VRF on the egress PE router, SP2.London_ASBR#2/PE.

In highlighted line 3, the packet crosses the link between SP2.NewYork.C and SP2.NewYork.CSC.CE. Notice that the IGP label has been swapped (it is now label 24), but the VPN label (29) is unchanged.

From highlighted line 4 to highlighted line 7, the packet transits between routers SP2.NewYork.CSC.CE and SP2.London.CSC.CE via the CSC backbone network. Notice that the original VPN label (29) is maintained in the label stack and is not popped.

The packet then crosses the link between SP2.London.CSC.CE and SP2.London.C in highlighted line 8, and in highlighted line 9, it reaches router SP2.London_ASBR#1/PE. Again, notice that the original VPN label (29) has been maintained in the label stack.

Finally, in highlighted line 10, the packet is forwarded (unlabeled) to VPN-mjlnet.London.CE and its destination IP address 10.1.2.1.

Even though the sources and destinations are different, it is interesting to compare Example 5-7 (where a non-VPN packet is forwarded between MPLS-enabled CSC customer sites) to Example 5-9 (where hierarchical VPNs have been configured). You can see that the main body of each output is the same, with the only difference being the addition of an extra (VPN) label (label 29, in Example 5-9).

Figure 5-10 shows packet forwarding across the network from VPN-mjlnet site 1 to destination VPN-mjlnet site 2 when hierarchical VPNs are configured.

Figure 5-10   *Packet Forwarding Across the Network from mjlnet Site 1 to mjlnet Site 2 When Hierarchical VPNs Are Configured*

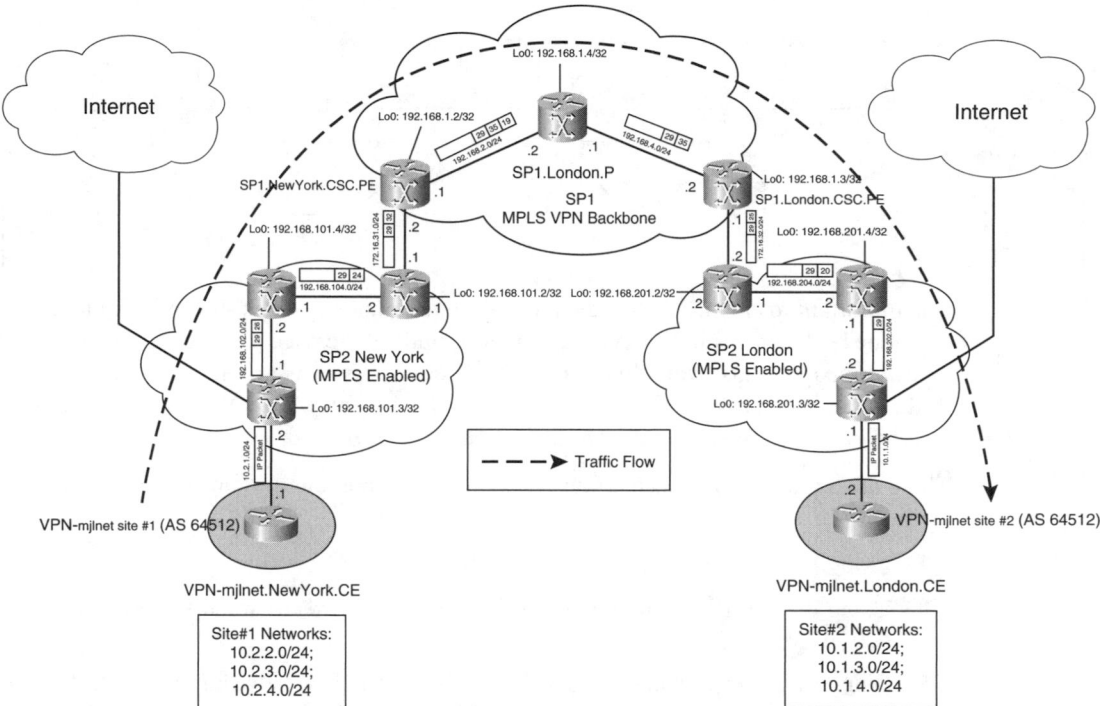

The Inter-Autonomous System/Interprovider MPLS VPN Architecture

If a customer VPN has some of its sites connected to one autonomous system, but other of its sites connected to other autonomous systems, the basic MPLS VPN architecture involving a single autonomous system will clearly not be capable of providing MPLS VPN connectivity between all customer VPN sites. In this case, an extended MPLS VPN architecture known as the *inter-autonomous system* or *multi-autonomous system* MPLS VPN architecture is required.

Figure 5-11 illustrates customer VPN site connectivity in an inter-autonomous system MPLS VPN architecture.

Figure 5-11 *Customer VPN Site Connectivity in an Inter-Autonomous System MPLS VPN Architecture*

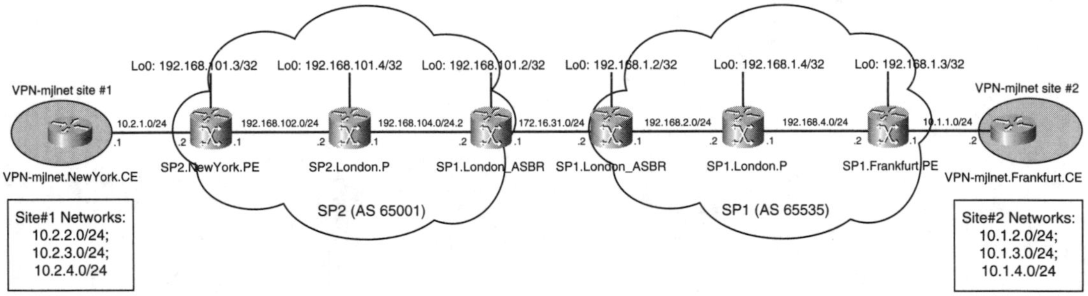

It is important to emphasize that the multiple autonomous systems shown in Figure 5-11 might be belong to a single service provider or multiple service providers. If the multiple autonomous systems over which MPLS VPN connectivity is provided belong to multiple service providers, this inter-autonomous system MPLS VPN architecture can also be called an *interprovider MPLS VPN architecture*.

There are a number of ways to provision an inter-autonomous system MPLS VPN architecture:

- Using VRF-to-VRF connectivity at ASBRs
- Using the advertisement of labeled VPN-IPv4 (VPNv4) between ASBRs with MP-eBGP
- Using the advertisement of labeled VPN-IPv4 (VPNv4) between route reflectors in different autonomous systems with multihop MP-eBGP

The following three sections examine each of these methods of provisioning inter-autonomous system MPLS VPN connectivity in detail.

VRF-to-VRF Connectivity at ASBRs

This model for inter-autonomous system MPLS VPN connectivity has the following characteristics:

- Each ASBR is configured as a PE router and regards its peer ASBR as a CE router.
- VRFs must be configured on ASBRs, and a separate logical or physical interface must be provisioned for each VRF.

Figure 5-12 shows the configuration of an inter-autonomous system MPLS VPN architecture using VRF-to-VRF connectivity at ASBRs.

The advantage of configuring inter-autonomous system MPLS VPNs using VRF-to-VRF connectivity at ASBRs is the simplicity of both route/label advertisement and packet forwarding.

Figure 5-12 *Configuration of an Inter-Autonomous System MPLS VPN Architecture Using VRF-to-VRF Connectivity at ASBRs*

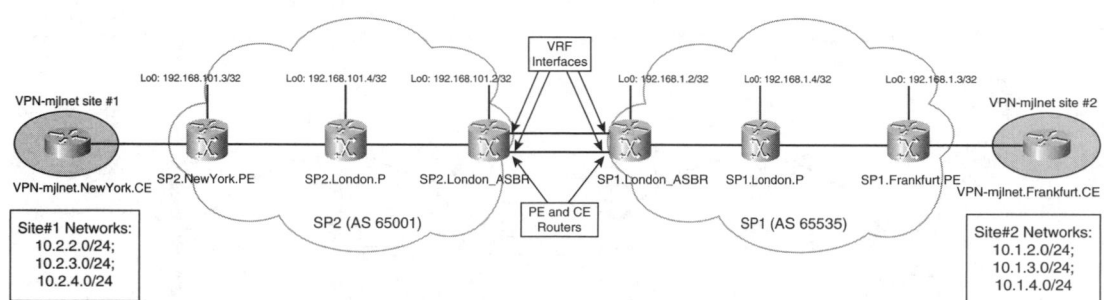

A major disadvantage is scalability. When provisioning inter-autonomous system MPLS VPNs using VRF-to-VRF connectivity at ASBRs, as already mentioned, VRFs must be configured on ASBRs, and a separate logical or physical interface must be configured and associated with each VRF. These limitations mean that it can often be impractical to deploy this model for inter-autonomous system MPLS VPN connectivity when there are more than a small number of VPNs (VRFs).

To understand the deployment of an inter-autonomous system MPLS VPN architecture using VRF-to-VRF connectivity at ASBRs, it is again important to examine route and label advertisement, as well as packet forwarding.

Route and Label Advertisement Between Autonomous Systems When Deploying Inter-Autonomous System MPLS VPNs VRF-to-VRF Connectivity at ASBRs

Route and label advertisement when deploying inter-autonomous system MPLS VPNs VRF-to-VRF connectivity at ASBRs is straightforward. As previously mentioned, each ASBR is configured as a PE router and treats the remote ASBR as a CE router.

Route and label advertisement when using this model for inter-autonomous system connectivity is as follows:

- PE routers advertise customer VPN site (VPN-IPv4) routes and associated VPN labels to their local ASBR (either directly or via a route reflector).

- ASBRs exchange customer VPN site routes using the configured PE-CE routing protocol. Alternatively, static VRF routes can be configured on ASBRs for connectivity to customer VPN sites in the remote autonomous system.

  Note that ASBRs do not exchange VPN-IPv4 routes or labels because, as previously discussed, each ASBR acts as a PE router and regards the remote ASBR as a CE router.

Figure 5-13 illustrates route and label advertisement when deploying inter-autonomous system MPLS VPNs VRF-to-VRF connectivity at ASBRs.

Figure 5-13 *Route and Label Advertisement When Deploying Inter-Autonomous System MPLS VPNs VRF-to-VRF Connectivity at ASBRs*

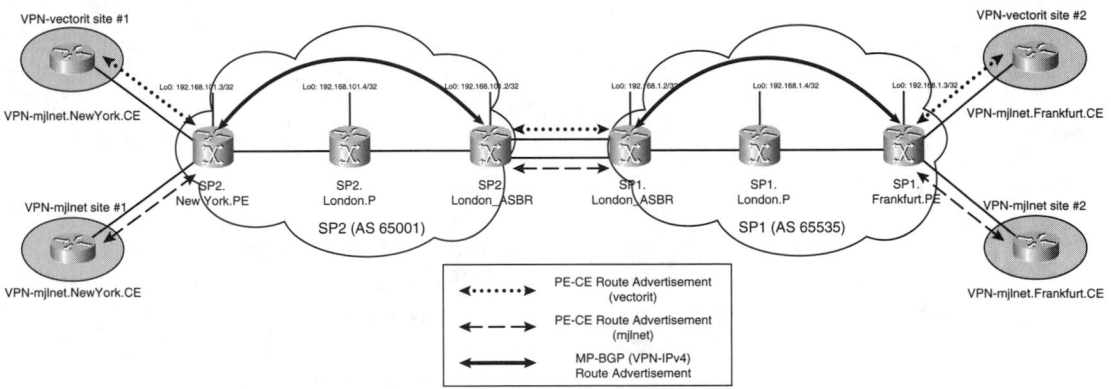

Example 5-10 shows the configuration of SP2.London_ASBR.

Example 5-10 *Configuration of SP2.London_ASBR When Deploying Inter-Autonomous System MPLS VPNs VRF-to-VRF Connectivity at ASBRs*

```
!
! On SP2.London_ASBR (line 1)
!
ip vrf VPN-mjlnet (line 2)
 rd 65001:100
 route-target export 65001:100
 route-target import 65001:100
!
ip vrf VPN-vectorit (line 3)
 rd 65001:200
 route-target export 65001:200
 route-target import 65001:200
!
!
interface Serial1/1
 encapsulation frame-relay
!
interface Serial1/1.1 point-to-point (line 4)
 ip vrf forwarding VPN-mjlnet
 ip address 172.16.27.1 255.255.255.0
 frame-relay interface-dlci 100
!
interface Serial1/1.2 point-to-point (line 5)
 ip vrf forwarding VPN-vectorit
 ip address 172.16.26.1 255.255.255.0
 frame-relay interface-dlci 200
!
!
```

Example 5-10 *Configuration of SP2.London_ASBR When Deploying Inter-Autonomous System MPLS VPNs VRF-to-VRF Connectivity at ASBRs (Continued)*

```
router bgp 65001 (line 6)
 no synchronization
 neighbor 192.168.101.3 remote-as 65001
 neighbor 192.168.101.3 update-source Loopback0
 no auto-summary
 !
 address-family vpnv4 (line 7)
 neighbor 192.168.101.3 activate
 neighbor 192.168.101.3 send-community extended
 exit-address-family
 !
 address-family ipv4 vrf VPN-vectorit (line 8)
 redistribute connected
 neighbor 172.16.26.2 remote-as 65535
 neighbor 172.16.26.2 activate
 no auto-summary
 no synchronization
 exit-address-family
 !
 address-family ipv4 vrf VPN-mjlnet (line 9)
 redistribute connected
 neighbor 172.16.27.2 remote-as 65535
 neighbor 172.16.27.2 activate
 no auto-summary
 no synchronization
 exit-address-family
 !
```

As you can see in Example 5-10, the configuration of SP2.London_ASBR is much in line with standard PE router configuration.

Highlighted lines 2 and 3 define two VRFs—VPN-mjlnet and VPN-vectorit.

Then, below highlighted lines 6 and 7, a BGP neighbor relationship is configured with SP2.NewYork.PE (192.168.101.3), and MP-BGP is enabled for VPN-IPv4 route exchange.

Below highlighted lines 8 and 9, BGP is configured as the PE-CE routing protocol for both VRF VPN-vectorit and VRF VPN-mjlnet, with the BGP peer (CE) for PE-CE route exchange specified as 172.16.26.2 (SP1.London_ASBR) and 172.16.27.2 (also SP1.London_ASBR), respectively. Remember that in this configuration each ASBR acts as both a PE and a CE router.

NOTE   It is possible to use any of the standard PE-CE routing protocols for route exchange between ASBRs, but BGP is usually preferred because it is already almost exclusively used for inter-autonomous system route exchange.

An important part of the configuration of SP2.London_ASBR can be seen below highlighted lines 4 and 5. Below these two highlighted lines, you can see the configuration of two separate Frame Relay subinterfaces, both of which connect to SP1.London_ASBR. Interface serial 1/1.1 is associated with VRF VPN-mjlnet and is used for route exchange and packet forwarding for VPN-mjlnet between ASBRs. Interface serial 1/1.2, on the other hand, is associated with VRF VPN-vectorit and is used for route exchange and packet forwarding for VPN-vectorit between ASBRs.

Highlighted lines 4 and 5 illustrate one of the scalability issues when deploying inter-autonomous system MPLS VPN VRF-to-VRF connectivity at ASBRs—a separate logical or physical interface is required on each ASBR for each VRF. If you plan to configure inter-autonomous system connectivity for a large number of MPLS VPNs, the configuration of logical or physical interface can quickly get out of hand.

As shown in Example 5-11, the configuration of SP1.London_ASBR is almost identical to that of SP2.London_ASBR.

Example 5-11 *Configuration of SP1.London_ASBR When Deploying Inter-Autonomous System MPLS VPNs VRF-to-VRF Connectivity at ASBRs*

```
!
! On SP1.London_ASBR (line 1)
!
ip vrf VPN-mjlnet (line 2)
 rd 65535:100
 route-target export 65535:100
 route-target import 65535:100
!
ip vrf VPN-vectorit (line 3)
 rd 65535:200
 route-target export 65535:200
 route-target import 65535:200
!
interface Serial2/1
 encapsulation frame-relay
!
interface Serial2/1.1 point-to-point (line 4)
 ip vrf forwarding VPN-mjlnet
 ip address 172.16.27.2 255.255.255.0
 frame-relay interface-dlci 100
!
interface Serial2/1.2 point-to-point (line 5)
 ip vrf forwarding VPN-vectorit
 ip address 172.16.26.2 255.255.255.0
 frame-relay interface-dlci 200
!
!
router bgp 65535 (line 6)
 no synchronization
 neighbor 192.168.1.3 remote-as 65535
 neighbor 192.168.1.3 update-source Loopback0
 no auto-summary
 !
```

Example 5-11 *Configuration of SP1.London_ASBR When Deploying Inter-Autonomous System MPLS VPNs VRF-to-VRF Connectivity at ASBRs (Continued)*

```
address-family vpnv4 (line 7)
neighbor 192.168.1.1 activate
neighbor 192.168.1.1 send-community extended
exit-address-family
!
address-family ipv4 vrf VPN-vectorit (line 8)
redistribute connected
neighbor 172.16.26.1 remote-as 65001
neighbor 172.16.26.1 activate
no auto-summary
no synchronization
exit-address-family
!
address-family ipv4 vrf VPN-mjlnet (line 9)
redistribute connected
neighbor 172.16.27.1 remote-as 65001
neighbor 172.16.27.1 activate
no auto-summary
no synchronization
exit-address-family
!
```

Highlighted lines 2 and 3 show the configuration of two VRFs—VPN-mjlnet and VPN-vectorit.

Highlighted lines 4 and 5 show the configuration of two Frame Relay subinterfaces associated with the VRFs.

Below highlighted lines 6 and 7, a BGP neighbor relationship is configured with SP1.Frankfurt.PE (192.168.1.3), and MP-BGP is enabled for VPN-IPv4 route exchange.

Finally, below highlighted lines 8 and 9, BGP is configured as the PE-CE routing protocol for VRF VPN-vectorit and VRF VPN-mjlnet. The BGP peer (CE) for PE-CE route exchange is specified as 172.16.26.1 (SP2.London_ASBR) and 172.16.27.1 (also SP2.London_ASBR), respectively.

In Example 5-12, an examination of the output of the **show ip route vrf** *vrf-name* command on SP2.London_ASBR and SP1.London_ASBR shows that customer VPN routes are successfully exchanged between autonomous systems.

Example 5-12 **show ip route vrf** *Command Output on SP2.London_ASBR and SP1.London_ASBR*

```
SP2.London_ASBR#show ip route vrf VPN-mjlnet

Routing Table: VPN-mjlnet
Codes: C - connected, S - static, I - IGRP, R - RIP, M - mobile, B - BGP
       D - EIGRP, EX - EIGRP external, O - OSPF, IA - OSPF inter area
       N1 - OSPF NSSA external type 1, N2 - OSPF NSSA external type 2
       E1 - OSPF external type 1, E2 - OSPF external type 2, E - EGP
       i - IS-IS, su - IS-IS summary, L1 - IS-IS level-1, L2 - IS-IS level-2
```

continues

Example 5-12 **show ip route vrf** *Command Output on SP2.London_ASBR and SP1.London_ASBR (Continued)*

```
           ia - IS-IS inter area, * - candidate default, U - per-user static route
           o - ODR

Gateway of last resort is not set

     10.0.0.0/24 is subnetted, 9 subnets
B       10.1.3.0 [20/0] via 172.16.27.2, 00:35:44 (line 1)
B       10.2.1.0 [200/0] via 192.168.101.3, 00:50:40
B       10.1.2.0 [20/0] via 172.16.27.2, 00:35:44 (line 2)
B       10.2.2.0 [200/0] via 192.168.101.3, 00:50:40
B       10.1.1.0 [20/0] via 172.16.27.2, 00:35:44 (line 3)
B       10.2.3.0 [200/0] via 192.168.101.3, 00:50:40
B       10.2.4.0 [200/0] via 192.168.101.3, 00:50:40
B       10.1.4.0 [20/0] via 172.16.27.2, 00:35:44 (line 4)
C       172.16.27.0 is directly connected, Serial1/1.1
SP2.London_ASBR#
```

```
SP1.London_ASBR#show ip route vrf VPN-mjlnet

Routing Table: VPN-mjlnet
Codes: C - connected, S - static, I - IGRP, R - RIP, M - mobile, B - BGP
       D - EIGRP, EX - EIGRP external, O - OSPF, IA - OSPF inter area
       N1 - OSPF NSSA external type 1, N2 - OSPF NSSA external type 2
       E1 - OSPF external type 1, E2 - OSPF external type 2, E - EGP
       i - IS-IS, su - IS-IS summary, L1 - IS-IS level-1, L2 - IS-IS level-2
       ia - IS-IS inter area, * - candidate default, U - per-user static route
       o - ODR

Gateway of last resort is not set

     10.0.0.0/24 is subnetted, 9 subnets
B       10.1.3.0 [200/0] via 192.168.1.3, 02:03:22
B       10.2.1.0 [20/0] via 172.16.27.1, 00:36:54 (line 5)
B       10.1.2.0 [200/0] via 192.168.1.3, 02:03:22
B       10.2.2.0 [20/0] via 172.16.27.1, 00:36:54 (line 6)
B       10.1.1.0 [200/0] via 192.168.1.3, 02:03:22
B       10.2.3.0 [20/0] via 172.16.27.1, 00:36:54 (line 7)
B       10.2.4.0 [20/0] via 172.16.27.1, 00:36:54 (line 8)
B       10.1.4.0 [200/0] via 192.168.1.3, 02:03:22
C       172.16.27.0 is directly connected, Serial2/1.1
SP1.London_ASBR#
```

Highlighted lines 1 to 4 show the VPN-mjlnet site 2 routes on SP2.London_ASBR.

Highlighted lines 5 to 8 show the VPN-mjlnet site 1 routes on SP1.London_ASBR.

Packet Forwarding Between Autonomous Systems When Deploying Inter-Autonomous System MPLS VPNs VRF-to-VRF Connectivity at ASBRs

Example 5-13 shows the packet forwarding between VPN-mjlnet site 1 (VPN-mjlnet.NewYork.CE) and VPN-mjlnet site 2 (host 10.1.2.1) as provided by the output of the **traceroute** command.

Example 5-13 *Packet Forwarding Between mjlnet Site 1 (VPN-mjlnet.NewYork.CE) and mjlnet Site 2 (Host 10.1.2.1)*

```
VPN=mjlnet.NewYork.CE#traceroute 10.1.2.1

Type escape sequence to abort.
Tracing the route to 10.1.2.1

 1 10.2.1.2 4 msec 4 msec 0 msec (line 1)
 2 192.168.102.2 [MPLS: Labels 17/26 Exp 0] 96 msec 100 msec 100 msec (line 2)
 3 172.16.27.1 [AS 65001] [MPLS: Label 26 Exp 0] 36 msec 36 msec 36 msec (line 3)
 4 172.16.27.2 [AS 65001] 36 msec 32 msec 32 msec (line 4)
 5 192.168.2.2 [MPLS: Labels 19/23 Exp 0] 188 msec 184 msec 188 msec (line 5)
 6 10.1.1.1 [AS 65001] [MPLS: Label 23 Exp 0] 120 msec 120 msec 120 msec (line 6)
 7 10.1.1.2 [AS 65001] 80 msec *  120 msec (line 7)
VPN-mjlnet.NewYork.CE#
```

The packet is forwarded from VPN-mjlnet.NewYork.CE to SP2.NewYork.PE in highlighted line 1.

In highlighted line 2, the packet transits the connection between SP2.NewYork.PE and SP2.London.P. The two label stack here consists of an IGP label (17) and a VPN label (26).

Next, the packet crosses the link between SP2.London.P and SP2.London_ASBR. Notice that the IGP label has been popped, and only the VPN label (26) remains.

The packet then crosses the link between SP2.London_ASBR and SP1.London_ASBR in highlighted line 4. It is important to note that the packet is unlabeled as it crosses this link (no surprise there—remember it is a PE-to-CE link).

In highlighted line 5, the packet crosses the connection between SP1.London_ASBR and SP1.Frankfurt.P. Once again, the packet is prepended with a two-label stack consisting of an IGP label (19) and a VPN label (23).

The packet transits the link between SP1.Frankfurt.P and SP1.Frankfurt.PE in highlighted line 6. The IGP label has been popped, but the VPN label (23) is unchanged.

In highlighted line 7, the unlabeled packet crosses the link between SP1.Frankfurt.PE and VPN-mjlnet.Frankfurt.CE.

Figure 5-14 shows packet forwarding from VPN-mjlnet.NewYork.CE (mjlnet site 1) to host 10.1.2.1 (a host at mjlnet site 2).

The output of the **traceroute** command in Example 5-14 shows packet forwarding between VPN-mjlnet site 2 (VPN-mjlnet.Frankfurt.CE) and VPN-mjlnet site 1 (host 10.2.2.1).

Highlighted lines 1 shows the packet as it transits the link between VPN-mjlnet.Frankfurt.CE and SP1.Frankfurt.PE.

In highlighted line 2, the packet crosses the link between SP1.Frankfurt.PE and SP1.Frankfurt.P. The label stack consists of an IGP label (18) and a VPN label (30).

Figure 5-14 *Packet Forwarding from VPN-mjlnet.NewYork.CE (mjlnet Site 1) to Host 10.1.2.1 (a Host at mjlnet Site 2)*

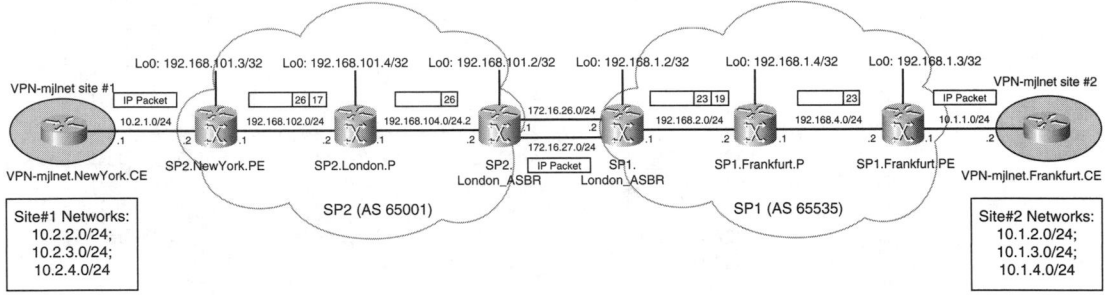

Example 5-14 *Packet Forwarding Between mjlnet Site 2 (VPN-mjlnet.Frankfurt.CE) and mjlnet Site 1 (Host 10.2.2.1)*

```
VPN-mjlnet.Frankfurt.CE#traceroute 10.2.2.1

Type escape sequence to abort.
Tracing the route to 10.2.2.1

  1 10.1.1.1 16 msec 16 msec 16 msec (line 1)
  2 192.168.4.1 [MPLS: Labels 18/30 Exp 0] 256 msec 156 msec 156 msec (line 2)
  3 172.16.27.2 [AS 65535] [MPLS: Label 30 Exp 0] 88 msec 88 msec 88 msec (line 3)
  4 172.16.27.1 [AS 65535] 68 msec 60 msec 64 msec (line 4)
  5 192.168.104.1 [MPLS: Labels 18/20 Exp 0] 152 msec 152 msec 152 msec (line 5)
  6 10.2.1.2 [AS 65535] [MPLS: Label 20 Exp 0] 144 msec 272 msec 148 msec (line 6)
  7 10.2.1.1 [AS 65535] 76 msec * 80 msec (line 7)
VPN-mjlnet.Frankfurt.CE#
```

The packet then crosses the connection between SP1.Frankfurt.P and SP1.London_ASBR in highlighted line 3. The IGP label has been popped, but the VPN label (30) is unmodified.

The packet now passes over the link between SP1.London_ASBR and SP2.London_ASBR (see highlighted line 4). Notice that the packet is unlabeled as it crosses this link (again, it is a PE-to-CE link).

Highlighted line 5 shows the packet as it transits the connection between SP2.London_ ASBR and SP2.London.P. The label stack here consists of an IGP label (18) and a VPN label (20).

In highlighted line 6, the packet transits the link between SP2.London.P and SP2.NewYork.PE. The IGP label has been popped, but the VPN label (20) in unchanged.

Finally, highlighted line 7 shows the packet as it passes over the link between SP2.NewYork.PE and VPN-mjlnet.NewYork.CE.

Figure 5-15 illustrates packet forwarding from VPN-mjlnet.Frankfurt.CE (VPN-mjlnet site 2) to host 10.2.2.1 (a host at VPN-mjlnet site 1).

Figure 5-15 *Packet Forwarding from VPN-mjlnet.Frankfurt.CE (mjlnet Site 2) to Host 10.2.2.1 (a Host at mjlnet Site 1)*

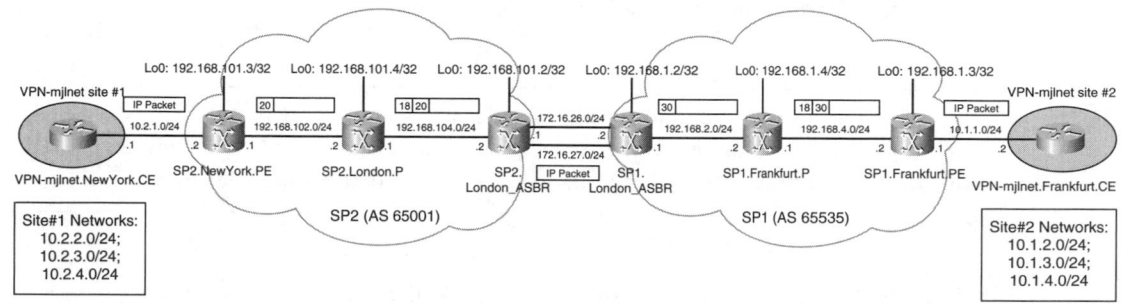

Advertisement of Labeled VPN-IPv4 (VPNv4) Between ASBRs Using MP-eBGP

A second method of provisioning inter-autonomous system MPLS VPN connectivity is to configure the advertisement of labeled customer VPN-IPv4 routes between ASBRs, as shown in Figure 5-16.

Figure 5-16 *Advertisement of Customer VPN-IPv4 Routes Between ASBRs*

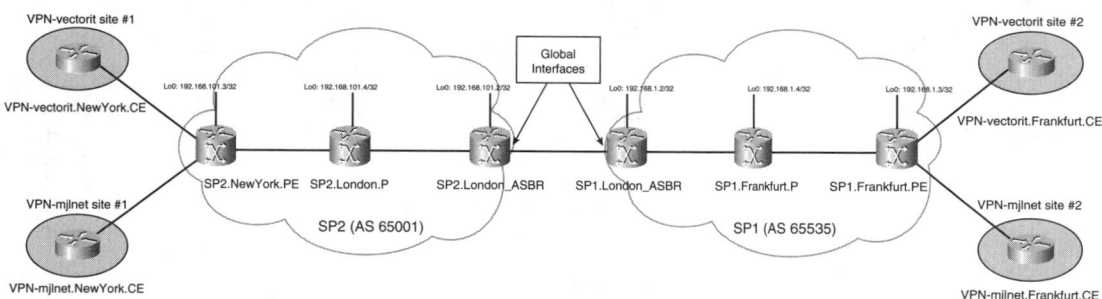

This method of provisioning inter-autonomous system connectivity is more scalable than configuring back-to-back VRFs because there is no need to configure VRFs on the ASBRs, and there is no need to configure separate logical or physical interfaces between ASBRs.

The next two sections examine route and label advertisement between autonomous systems, as well as packet forwarding between MPLS VPN sites.

Route and Label Advertisement Between Autonomous Systems When Deploying Inter-Autonomous System MPLS VPNs Using MP-eBGP Between ASBRs

When using this method of configuring inter-autonomous system MPLS VPNs, PE routers advertise VPN-IPv4 routes to their local ASBRs. ASBRs in the different autonomous systems exchange VPN-IPv4 routes (using MP-eBGP), and then advertise these VPN-IPv4 routes to PE routers in their local autonomous system.

NOTE   Note that the advertisement of VPN-IPv4 routes between PE routers and their local ASBRs might not be direct. Instead, you can configure route reflectors and PE routers and ASBRs (as route reflector clients) and then exchange routes with the route reflectors.

When VPN-IPv4 routes are advertised between ASBRs, a VPN label representing each route is also advertised to the remote ASBR. These VPN labels are used to forward customer VPN packets over the ASBR-to-ASBR link.

Figure 5-17 illustrates inter-autonomous system MPLS VPNs configured with the advertisement of labeled VPN-IPv4 (VPNv4) between ASBR using MP-eBGP.

Figure 5-17   *Inter-Autonomous System MPLS VPNs Configured with Advertisement of Labeled VPN-IPv4 (VPNv4) Between ASBR Using MP-eBGP*

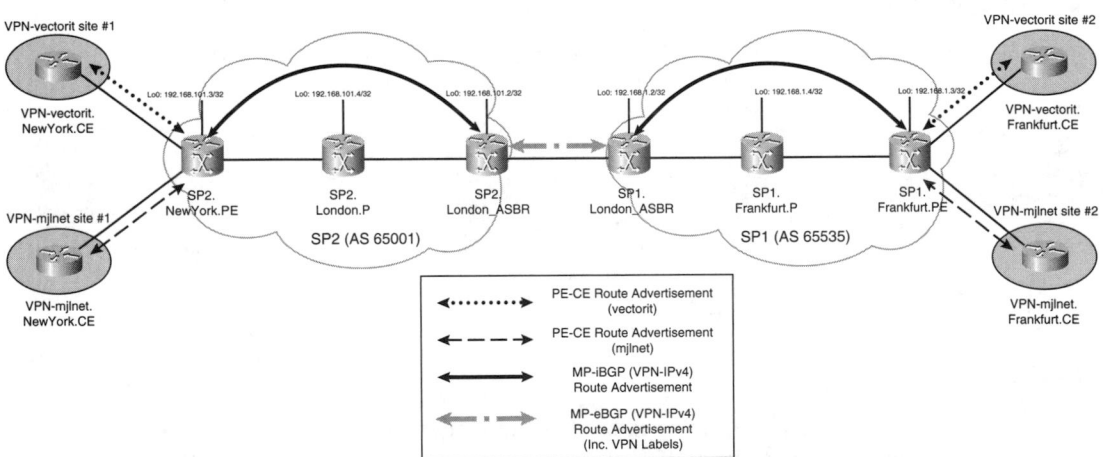

In Figure 5-17, route and label advertisement from VPN-mjlnet.NewYork.CE (VPN-mjlnet site 1) and VPN-vectorit.NewYork.CE (VPN-vectorit site 1) to VPN-mjlnet.Frankfurt.CE (VPN-mjlnet site 2) and VPN-vectorit.Frankfurt.CE (VPN-vectorit site 2) is as follows:

1   VPN-mjlnet.NewYork.CE and VPN-vectorit.NewYork.CE advertise VPN-mjlnet and VPN-vectorit site 1 routes to SP2.NewYork.PE using PE-CE routing protocols.

2   SP2.NewYork.PE advertises VPN-mjlnet and VPN-vectorit VPN site 1 (VPN-IPv4) routes and associated VPN labels to SP2.London_ASBR.

3   SP2.London_ASBR then advertises mjlnet and vectorit site 1 (VPN-IPv4) routes and associated VPN labels to SP1.London_ASBR. The VPN labels advertised with the VPN-IPv4 routes will allow SP1.London_ASBR to forward VPN-mjlnet and VPN-vectorit user packets across the connection to SP2.London_ASBR.

4 SP1.London_ASBR now advertises the VPN-mjlnet and VPN-vectorit site 1 (VPN-IPv4) routes and associated VPN labels (received from SP2.London_ASBR) to SP1.Frankfurt.PE.

5 Finally, SP1.Frankfurt.PE advertises the VPN-mjlnet and VPN-vectorit site 1 routes to VPN-mjlnet.Frankfurt.CE and VPN-vectorit.Frankfurt.CE, respectively, using PE-CE routing protocols.

Route advertisement from VPN-mjlnet.Frankfurt.CE (VPN-mjlnet site 2) and VPN-vectorit. Frankfurt.CE (VPN-vectorit site 2) to VPN-mjlnet.NewYork.CE (VPN-mjlnet site 1) and VPN-vectorit.NewYork.CE is similar:

1 VPN-mjlnet.Frankfurt.CE (VPN-mjlnet site 2) and VPN-vectorit.Frankfurt.CE (VPN-vectorit site 2) advertise VPN-mjlnet and VPN-vectorit site 2 routes to SP1.Frankfurt.PE using PE-CE routing protocols.

2 SP1.Frankfurt.PE then advertises VPN-mjlnet and VPN-vectorit site 2 (VPN-IPv4) routes and associated VPN labels to SP1.London_ASBR.

3 SP1.London_ASBR advertises VPN-mjlnet and VPN-vectorit site 2 (VPN-IPv4) and associated VPN labels to SP2.London_ASBR. These VPN labels will allow SP2.London_ASBR to forward mjlnet VPN packets over the link to SP1.London_ASBR.

4 SP2.London_ASBR now advertises the VPN-mjlnet and VPN-vectorit site 2 (VPN-IPv4) routes and associated VPN labels (received from SP1.London_ASBR) to SP2.NewYork.PE.

5 Finally, SP2.NewYork.PE advertises the VPN-mjlnet and VPN-vectorit site 2 routes to VPN-mjlnet.NewYork.CE and VPN-vectorit.NewYork.CE, respectively, using PE-CE routing protocols.

Now that you know how route advertisement works, it is time to take a look at the configuration of ASBRs SP2.London_ASBR and SP1.London_ASBR.

Example 5-15 shows the configuration of SP2.London_ASBR when using the advertisement of labeled VPN-IPv4 (VPNv4) between ASBRs with MP-eBGP for inter-autonomous system MPLS VPN connectivity.

Example 5-15 *Configuration of SP2.London_ASBR*

```
!
! On SP2.London_ASBR (line 1)
!
interface Serial1/1
 ip address 172.16.31.1 255.255.255.0
 mpls bgp forwarding (line 2)
!
!
router ospf 100
 log-adjacency-changes
 redistribute connected subnets (line 3)
 passive-interface Loopback0
 network 192.168.0.0 0.0.255.255 area 0
!
```

continues

Example 5-15 *Configuration of SP2.London_ASBR (Continued)*

```
router bgp 65001
 no synchronization
 no bgp default route-target filter (line 4)
 neighbor 172.16.31.2 remote-as 65535 (line 5)
 neighbor 192.168.101.3 remote-as 65001 (line 6)
 neighbor 192.168.101.3 update-source Loopback0
 no auto-summary
 !
 address-family vpnv4
 neighbor 172.16.31.2 activate (line 7)
 neighbor 172.16.31.2 send-community extended
 neighbor 192.168.101.3 activate (line 8)
 neighbor 192.168.101.3 send-community extended
 exit-address-family
 !
```

The **mpls bgp forwarding** command in highlighted line 2 is used to enable interface serial 1/1 (directly connected to SP2.London_ASBR) to receive MPLS packets when labels are advertised by BGP. This command is required on directly connected ASBR-to-ASBR interfaces and is *automatically* enabled by BGP when VPN-IPv4 route exchange is configured between ASBRs on directly connected interfaces/neighbors (so there's no need to explicitly configure the command in this example).

In highlighted line 3, the network between the SP2.London_ASR and SP1.London_ASBR (172.16.31.0/24) is redistributed into the IGP (OSPF) used within the SP2 autonomous system using the **redistribute connected subnets** command.

The **redistribute connected subnets** command is necessary because the VPN-IPv4 routes advertised from SP1.London_ASBR have a next hop of 172.16.31.2 (SP1.London_ASBR's directly connected interface address). If the network between the ASBRs (including the next-hop address of 172.16.31.2) is not redistributed into the IGP, VPN-IPv4 routes will not be installed into the VRFs on local PE routers.

NOTE   Another method of ensuring next-hop reachability for VPN-IPv4 routes is to use the **neighbor** *ip-address* **next-hop-self** command to modify the next hop of VPN-IPv4 address of VPN-IPv4 routes as they are advertised to PE routers or route reflectors within the SP2 autonomous system.

One particularly important command can be seen in highlighted line 4 (**no bgp default route-target filter**). This command is important because no VRFs are configured on SP2.London_ASBR. Normally, if a router receives VPN-IPv4 routes whose route targets do not match the import route targets configured within a VRF, the router drops them. In this case, of course, because no VRFs are configured on SP2.London_ASBR, it would normally drop *all* VPN-IPv4 routes—not what you want! The **no bgp default route-target filter** command ensures that VPN-IPv4 routes received by SP2.London_ASBR from SP1.London_ASBR are not dropped.

In highlighted lines 5 and 6, BGP neighbor relationships are configured with SP1.London_ASBR (172.16.31.2) and SP2.NewYork.PE (192.168.101.3).

MP-BGP (VPN-IPv4) route exchange is then enabled with SP1.London_ASBR and SP2.NewYork.PE in highlighted lines 7 and 8.

Example 5-16 shows the configuration of SP1.London_ASBR when using an advertisement of a labeled VPN-IPv4 (VPNv4) between ASBRs with MP-eBGP for inter-autonomous system MPLS VPN connectivity.

Example 5-16 *Configuration of SP1.London_ASBR*

```
!
! On SP1.London_ASBR (line 1)
!
interface Serial2/1
 ip address 172.16.31.2 255.255.255.0
 mpls bgp forwarding (line 2)
!
router isis
 net 49.1234.0000.0000.0001.00
 is-type level-2-only
 metric-style wide
 mpls traffic-eng router-id Loopback0
 mpls traffic-eng level-2
 redistribute connected (line 3)
!
router bgp 65535
 no synchronization
 no bgp default route-target filter (line 4)
 neighbor 172.16.31.1 remote-as 65001 (line 5)
 neighbor 192.168.1.3 remote-as 65535 (line 6)
 neighbor 192.168.1.3 update-source Loopback0
 no auto-summary
 !
 address-family vpnv4
 neighbor 172.16.31.1 activate (line 7)
 neighbor 172.16.31.1 send-community extended
 neighbor 192.168.1.3 activate (line 8)
 neighbor 192.168.1.3 send-community extended
 exit-address-family
!
```

Highlighted line 2 shows the configuration of the **mpls bgp forwarding** command on the interface (serial 2/1) directly connected to SP2.London_ASBR.

In highlighted line 3, the network between SP1.London_ASBR and SP2.London_ASBR is redistributed into the IGP (IS-IS) used within the SP1 autonomous system using the **redistribute connected** command (this again provides next-hop reachability for MP-BGP routes).

The **no bgp default route-target filter** command in highlighted line 4 is used to ensure that SP1.London_ASBR does not drop VPN-IPv4 routes received from SP2.London_ASBR (there are no VRFs configured on this router).

Highlighted lines 5 and 6 shows the configuration of BGP neighbor relationships with SP2.London_ASBR (172.16.31.1) and SP1.Frankfurt.PE (192.168.1.3) highlighted lines 7 and 8 show the enabling of MP-BGP (VPN-IPv4) route exchange for these same peers.

NOTE   The configuration of PE routers SP2.NewYork.PE and SP1.Frankfurt.PE is standard (see the section "Configuration of PE Routers" in Chapter 4 for more information). Each PE router either peers with its local ASBR directly to exchange VPN-IPv4 routes or peers with a route reflector (which also peers with its local ASBR[s]).

As Example 5-17 demonstrates, you can see (VPN-IPv4) route advertisement between SP2.London_ASBR and SP1.London_ASBR by examining the output of the **show ip bgp vpnv4 all** command.

Example 5-17 *Viewing Route Advertisement Between SP2.London_ASBR and SP1.London_ASBR*

```
SP2.London_ASBR#show ip bgp vpnv4 all
BGP table version is 18, local router ID is 192.168.101.2
Status codes: s suppressed, d damped, h history, * valid, > best, i - internal,
              r RIB-failure, S Stale
Origin codes: i - IGP, e - EGP, ? - incomplete

   Network          Next Hop          Metric LocPrf Weight Path
Route Distinguisher: 65535:100
*> 10.1.1.0/24      172.16.31.2                       0 65535 64512 I (line 1)
*> 10.1.2.0/24      172.16.31.2                       0 65535 64512 i (line 2)
*> 10.1.3.0/24      172.16.31.2                       0 65535 64512 i (line 3)
*> 10.1.4.0/24      172.16.31.2                       0 65535 64512 i (line 4)
*>i10.2.1.0/24      192.168.101.3         0     100   0 64512 i (line 5)
*>i10.2.2.0/24      192.168.101.3         0     100   0 64512 i (line 6)
*>i10.2.3.0/24      192.168.101.3         0     100   0 64512 i (line 7)
*>i10.2.4.0/24      192.168.101.3         0     100   0 64512 i (line 8)
SP2.London_ASBR#
```

```
SP1.London_ASBR#show ip bgp vpnv4 all
BGP table version is 18, local router ID is 192.168.1.2
Status codes: s suppressed, d damped, h history, * valid, > best, i - internal,
              r RIB-failure, S Stale
Origin codes: i - IGP, e - EGP, ? - incomplete

   Network          Next Hop          Metric LocPrf Weight Path
Route Distinguisher: 65535:100
*>i10.1.1.0/24      192.168.1.3           0     100   0 64512 i (line 9)
*>i10.1.2.0/24      192.168.1.3           0     100   0 64512 i (line 10)
*>i10.1.3.0/24      192.168.1.3           0     100   0 64512 i (line 11)
*>i10.1.4.0/24      192.168.1.3           0     100   0 64512 i (line 12)
*> 10.2.1.0/24      172.16.31.1                       0 65001 64512 i (line 13)
```

Example 5-17 *Viewing Route Advertisement Between SP2.London_ASBR and SP1.London_ASBR (Continued)*

```
*> 10.2.2.0/24        172.16.31.1                    0 65001 64512 i (line 14)
*> 10.2.3.0/24        172.16.31.1                    0 65001 64512 i (line 15)
*> 10.2.4.0/24        172.16.31.1                    0 65001 64512 i (line 16)
SP1.London_ASBR#
```

Highlighted lines 1 to 8 show the output of the **show ip bgp vpnv4 all** command on
SP2.London_ASBR.

In highlighted lines 1 to 4, you can see VPN-mjlnet site 2 routes. Notice the next hop for
these routes (172.16.31.2)—these routes have been received from SP1.London_ASBR
(172.16.31.2).

Then, in highlighted lines 5 to 8, you can see VPN-mjlnet site 1 routes received from
SP2.NewYork.PE (192.168.101.3).

Highlighted lines 9 to 16 show the output of the **show ip bgp vpnv4 all** command on
SP1.London_ASBR.

Highlighted lines 9 to 12 show VPN-mjlnet site 2 routes received from PE router
SP1.Frankfurt.PE (192.168.1.3).

Highlighted lines 13 to 16 show the VPN-mjlnet site 1 routes received from
SP2.London_ASBR (172.16.31.1).

Packet Forwarding Between Autonomous Systems When Deploying Inter-Autonomous System MPLS VPNs Using MP-eBGP Between ASBRs

Packet forwarding in an inter-autonomous system MPLS VPN can be examined using the
traceroute command.

Example 5-18 demonstrates using the **traceroute** command to examine packet forwarding
hop by hop from VPN-mjlnet site 1 (VPN-mjlnet.NewYork.CE) to VPN-mjlnet site 2
(host 10.1.2.1).

Example 5-18 *Traceroute Results from mjlnet Site 1 (VPN-mjlnet.NewYork.CE) to mjlnet Site 2 (Host 10.1.2.1)*

```
VPN-mjlnet.NewYork.CE#traceroute 10.1.2.1

Type escape sequence to abort.
Tracing the route to 10.1.2.1

  1 10.2.1.2 0 msec 4 msec 4 msec (line 1)
  2 192.168.102.2 [MPLS: Labels 19/29 Exp 0] 336 msec 244 msec 240 msec (line 2)
  3 192.168.104.2 [MPLS: Labels 16/29 Exp 0] 224 msec 224 msec 224 msec (line 3)
  4 172.16.31.2 [MPLS: Label 29 Exp 0] 204 msec 204 msec 204 msec (line 4)
  5 192.168.2.2 [MPLS: Labels 19/26 Exp 0] 192 msec 196 msec 192 msec (line 5)
  6 10.1.1.1 [AS 65001] [MPLS: Label 26 Exp 0] 128 msec 128 msec 220 msec (line 6)
  7 10.1.1.2 [AS 65001] 88 msec *  84 msec (line 7)
VPN-mjlnet.NewYork.CE#
```

The packet crosses the link from VPN-mjlnet.NewYork.CE to SP2.NewYork.PE in highlighted line 1.

In highlighted lines 2 and 3, the packet transits the links from SP2.NewYork.PE to SP2.London.P and SP2.London.P to SP2.London_ASBR.

Notice the label stacks in highlighted lines 2 and 3 (19/29 and 16/29). The outer label in each stack (19 and 16, respectively) is an IGP label, and inner label (29) is a VPN label. The VPN label (29) does not change as the packet is forwarded to SP2.London_ASBR.

In highlighted line 4, the packet crosses the link between SP2.London_ASBR and SP1.London_ASBR.

Take a close look at the label stack in highlighted line 4—it consists of only the VPN label (29). This VPN label was advertised by SP1.London_ASBR to SP2.London_ASBR, and it corresponds to the VPN-IPv4 (VPN-mjlnet site 2) route 10.1.2.0/24. VPN label 29 is therefore included in the label stack forwarded with the packet in highlighted lines 2 and 3.

Highlighted line 5 shows the packet as it crosses the link between SP1.London_ASBR and SP1.Frankfurt.P. Notice that the VPN label has been swapped here—SP1.London_ASBR has swapped VPN label 29 for VPN label 26, and an IGP label (19) has been pushed onto the stack. The function of the IGP label is to transport the packet to the egress PE router (SP1.Frankfurt.PE), and the function of the VPN label (26) is to identify the VRF or outgoing interface on the egress PE router.

The packet then crosses the link from SP1.Frankfurt.P to (egress PE router) SP1.Frankfurt.PE in highlighted line 6. The IGP label has been popped here (because SP1.Frankfurt.PE is the penultimate hop LSR), but the VPN label (26) remains unchanged.

Finally, in highlighted line 7, the unlabeled packet transits the link from SP1.Frankfurt.PE to VPN-mjlnet.Frankfurt.CE.

Figure 5-18 shows packet forwarding from VPN-mjlnet site 1 (VPN-mjlnet.NewYork.CE) to mjlnet site 2 (host 10.1.2.1).

Figure 5-18 *Packet Forwarding from VPN-mjlnet Site 1 (VPN-mjlnet.NewYork.CE) to mjlnet Site 2 (host 10.1.2.1)*

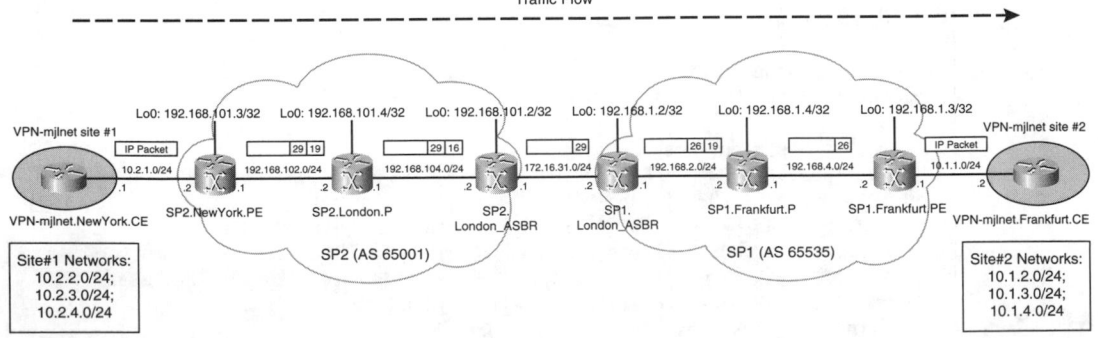

Example 5-19 shows a traceroute in the opposite direction from VPN-mjlnet site 2 (VPN-mjlnet.Frankfurt.CE) to VPN-mjlnet site 1 (host 10.2.2.1).

Example 5-19 *traceroute Results from mjlnet Site 2 (VPN-mjlnet.Frankfurt.CE) to mjlnet Site 1 (Host 10.2.2.1).*

```
VPN-mjlnet.Frankfurt.CE#traceroute 10.2.2.1

Type escape sequence to abort.
Tracing the route to 10.2.2.1

  1 10.1.1.1 16 msec 20 msec 16 msec (line 1)
  2 192.168.4.1 [MPLS: Labels 22/21 Exp 0] 212 msec 208 msec 264 msec (line 2)
  3 192.168.2.1 [MPLS: Labels 17/21 Exp 0] 192 msec 192 msec 192 msec (line 3)
  4 172.16.31.1 [MPLS: Label 21 Exp 0] 168 msec 168 msec 168 msec (line 4)
  5 192.168.104.1 [MPLS: Labels 18/23 Exp 0] 152 msec 152 msec 152 msec (line 5)
  6 10.2.1.2 [AS 65535] [MPLS: Label 23 Exp 0] 148 msec 148 msec 148 msec
  7 10.2.1.1 [AS 65535] 84 msec *  80 msec
VPN-mjlnet.Frankfurt.CE#
```

Highlighted line 1 shows the packet as it is forwarded from VPN-mjlnet.Frankfurt.CE to SP1.Frankfurt.PE.

In highlighted lines 2 and 3, the packet is forwarded between routers SP1.Frankfurt.PE and SP1.Frankfurt.P, as well as SP1.Frankfurt.P and SP1.London_ASBR.

The outer label in the label stacks (22 and 17, respectively) in highlighted lines 2 and 3 is the IGP label used to forward the packet to SP1.London_ASBR. The inner label (21) is a VPN label and is unchanged as the packet is forwarded to SP2.London_ASBR.

In highlighted line 4, the packet is forwarded to SP2.London_ASBR.

The VPN label shown in highlighted line 4 (21) was advertised by SP2.London_ASBR to SP1.London_ASBR and corresponds to VPN-IPv4 (VPN-mjlnet site 1) route 10.2.2.0/24. SP1.London_ASBR advertised this VPN label to SP1.Frankfurt.PE along with VPN-IPv4 route 10.2.2.0/24.

In highlighted line 5, the packet is forwarded over the link between SP2.London_ASBR and SP2.London.P. Note that VPN label 21 has been swapped for VPN label 23, and an IGP label (18) has been pushed onto the label stack. The function of the IGP label is, of course, to forward the packet to the egress PE router (SP2.NewYork.PE), and the function of the VPN label is to identify the VRF or outgoing interface on the egress PE router.

Figure 5-19 illustrates packet forwarding from VPN-mjlnet site 2 (VPN-mjlnet.Frankfurt.CE) to VPN-mjlnet site 1 (host 10.2.2.1).

Figure 5-19 *Packet Forwarding from mjlnet Site 2 (VPN-mjlnet.Frankfurt.CE) to mjlnet Site 1 (Host 10.2.2.1)*

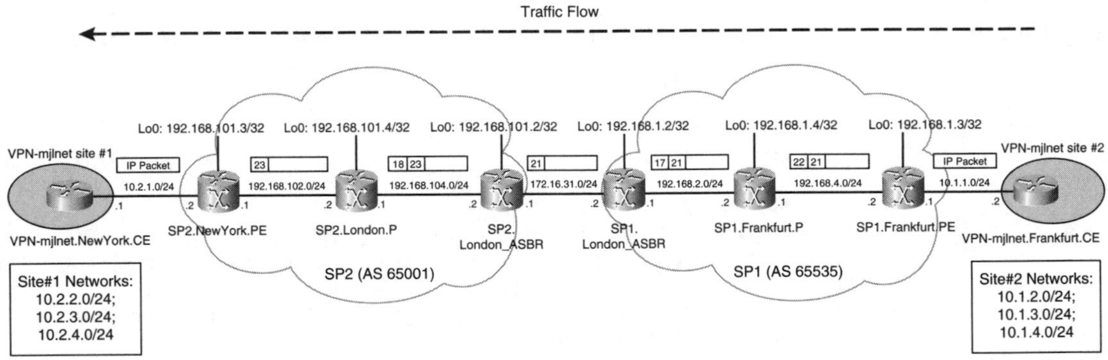

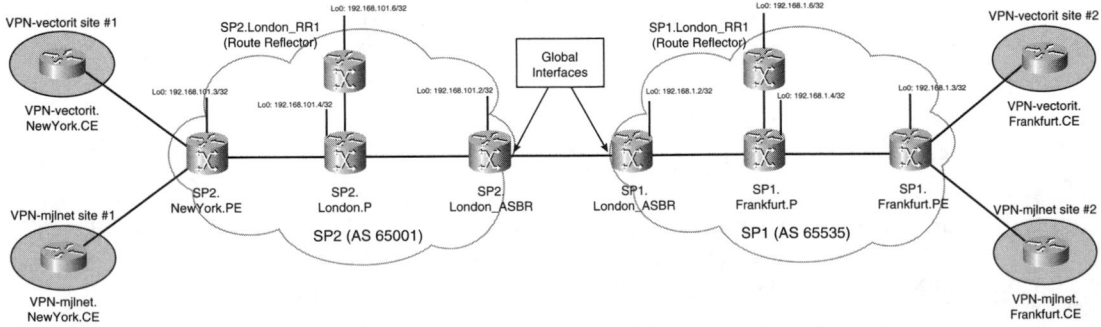

Advertisement of Labeled VPN-IPv4 (VPNv4) Between Route Reflectors in Separate Autonomous Systems Using Multihop MP-eBGP

A third method of provisioning inter-autonomous system MPLS VPN connectivity is to configure the advertisement of customer VPN-IPv4 routes and associated labels between route reflectors in the separate autonomous systems, as illustrated in Figure 5-20.

Figure 5-20 *Deploying Inter-Autonomous System MPLS VPNs with the Advertisement of Labeled VPN-IPv4 (VPNv4) Between Route Reflectors in Separate Autonomous Systems Using Multihop MP-eBGP*

The advantage of deploying inter-autonomous system MPLS VPNs with the advertisement of labeled VPN-IPv4 between route reflectors in separate autonomous systems is that it is more scalable than the other two methods of deploying inter-autonomous system MPLS VPNs. It is more scalable because the route reflectors are often out of the packet forwarding path between MPLS VPN sites and because ASBRs do not have to maintain VPN-IPv4 routes.

There are two disadvantages of deploying inter-autonomous system MPLS VPNs using this method:

- From a configuration and management perspective, it is more complex than the other two methods.

- It requires the advertisement of PE router addresses between autonomous systems, which might not be acceptable.

When discussing the deployment of inter-autonomous system MPLS VPNs with the advertisement of labeled VPN-IPv4 (VPNv4) between route reflectors in the separate autonomous systems, it is again useful to firstly discuss route and label advertisement between autonomous systems and then to discuss packet forwarding between MPLS VPN sites.

Route and Label Advertisement When Deploying Inter-Autonomous System MPLS VPNs with the Advertisement of Labeled VPN-IPv4 Between Route Reflectors in the Separate Autonomous Systems

When configuring inter-autonomous system MPLS VPNs using the advertisement of labeled VPN-IPv4 between route reflectors, it is important to ensure that the following routes are advertised:

- **VPN-IPv4 routes**—VPN-IPv4 routes and associated VPN labels must be advertised between route reflectors in the separate autonomous systems.

- **Routes to the next-hops of VPN-IPv4 routes**—In this model, the next-hops of the VPN-IPv4 routes are the loopback interface addresses of PE routers from which the routes are originally advertised.

  Routes to the next-hops must be advertised between autonomous systems otherwise remote VPN-IPv4 routes will not be installed in the routing tables (VRFs) of PE routers.

Advertisement of VPN-IPv4 routes and routes to the next hops of VPN-IPv4 routes is discussed in the following two sections.

Advertisement of VPN-IPv4 Routes (and Associated VPN Labels)

The advertisement of VPN-IPv4 routes is straightforward:

1 CE routers advertise local site routes to their connected PE router using the PE-CE routing protocol (if one is configured).

2 The PE routers advertise local customer VPN site (VPN-IPv4) routes to their local autonomous system route reflectors.

3 The route reflectors in the separate autonomous system exchange customer VPN site (VPN-IPv4) routes.

4 Route reflectors advertise remote autonomous system customer VPN site (VPN-IPv4) routes to PE routers in their local autonomous system.

5 PE routers advertise remote customer VPN site routes to their attached CE routers using the PE-CE routing protocol (if one is configured).

Figure 5-21 illustrates the advertisement of VPN-IPv4 routes between autonomous systems when deploying inter-autonomous system MPLS VPNs using MP-eBGP between route reflectors in separate autonomous systems.

Figure 5-21 *Advertisement of VPN-IPv4 Routes Between Autonomous Systems When Deploying Inter-Autonomous System MPLS VPNs Using MP-eBGP Between Route Reflectors in Separate Autonomous Systems*

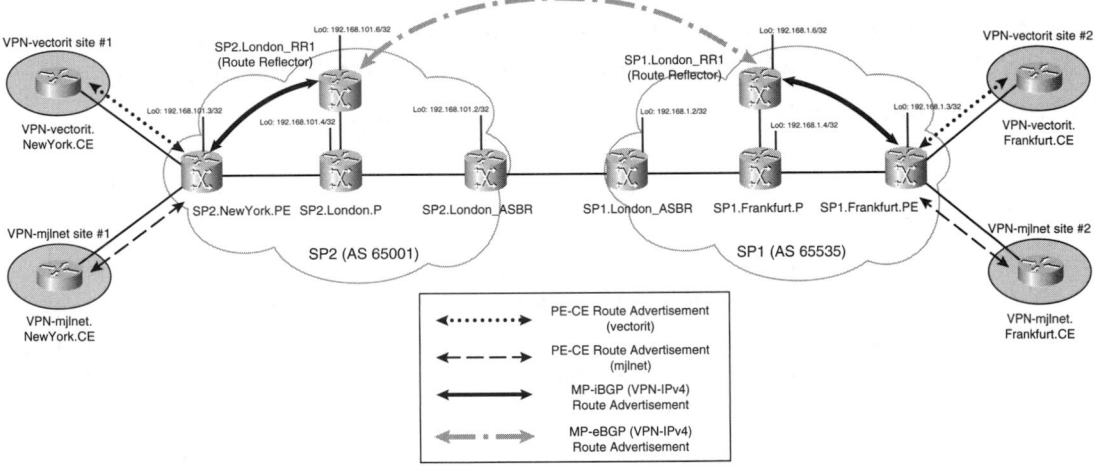

Example 5-20 shows the configuration of route reflector SP2.London_RR1.

Example 5-20 *Configuration of Route Reflectors SP2.London_RR1.*

```
!
! On SP2.London_RR1 (line 1)
!
router bgp 65001
 no synchronization
 no bgp default ipv4-unicast
 no bgp default route-target filter (line 2)
 bgp cluster-id 100
 neighbor 192.168.1.6 remote-as 65535 (line 3)
 neighbor 192.168.1.6 ebgp-multihop 255 (line 4)
 neighbor 192.168.1.6 update-source Loopback0 (line 5)
 neighbor 192.168.101.3 remote-as 65001 (line 6)
 neighbor 192.168.101.3 update-source Loopback0 (line 7)
 no auto-summary
!
```

Example 5-20 *Configuration of Route Reflectors SP2.London_RR1. (Continued)*

```
address-family vpnv4
 neighbor 192.168.1.6 activate (line 8)
 neighbor 192.168.1.6 next-hop-unchanged (line 9)
 neighbor 192.168.1.6 send-community extended
 neighbor 192.168.101.3 activate (line 10)
 neighbor 192.168.101.3 route-reflector-client (line 11)
 neighbor 192.168.101.3 send-community extended
 no auto-summary
 exit-address-family
 !
```

In highlighted line 2, the **no bgp default route-target filter** command is used to ensure that VPN-IPv4 routes are not dropped by SP2.London_RR1. This command is essential because no VRFs are configured on SP2.London_RR1.

In highlighted lines 3 to 5, a BGP neighbor relationship is configured with SP1.London_RR1 (192.168.1.6). Note, in particular, the command in highlighted line 4 (**neighbor** *ip-address* **ebgp-multihop** *ttl*). This command is required because the neighbor relationship between the route reflectors in the separate autonomous systems is not formed over a direct connection but is formed over multiple network hops. You can specify the maximum number of hops between the route reflectors using the *ttl* argument.

Next, highlighted lines 6 and 7 show the configuration of a BGP neighbor relationship to the PE router in the local autonomous system. In this example, there is only one PE router, SP2.NewYork.PE (192.168.101.3).

In highlighted line 8, MP-BGP is enabled for the exchange of VPN-IPv4 (VPNv4) routes with SP1.London_RR1 (192.168.1.6).

Highlighted line 9 shows the configuration of the **neighbor** *ip-address* **next-hop-unchanged** command. By default, the IP address of the route reflector is used as the next-hop address of VPN-IPv4 routes advertised to route reflectors in separate autonomous systems (default eBGP behavior), but this is undesirable in this scenario because it would cause all customer VPN packets to be forwarded via the route reflector. The **neighbor** *ip-address* **next-hop-unchanged** command ensures that the original next-hop address of VPN-IPv4 routes (the route originating PE router [SP2.NewYork.PE]) is maintained when the routes are advertised. This way, customer VPN packets are forwarded directly between PE routers (rather than via route reflectors).

Highlighted lines 10 and 11 show that MP-BGP is enabled for the exchange of VPN-IPv4 with the local PE router, SP2.NewYork.PE, and SP2.NewYork.PE is configured as a route reflector client.

Notice that an MP-BGP neighbor relationship is not configured with the local ASBR (SP2.London_ASBR). This is because the ASBR is not required to exchange VPN-IPv4 routes with the remote autonomous system.

The configuration of route reflector SP1.London_RR1 (see Example 5-21) is similar to that for SP2.London_RR1.

Example 5-21 *Configuration of Route Reflectors SP1.London_RR1*

```
!
! On SP1.London_RR1 (line 1)
!
router bgp 65535
 no synchronization
 no bgp default ipv4-unicast
 no bgp default route-target filter (line 2)
 bgp cluster-id 100
 neighbor 192.168.1.3 remote-as 65535 (line 3)
 neighbor 192.168.1.3 update-source Loopback0 (line 4)
 neighbor 192.168.101.6 remote-as 65001 (line 5)
 neighbor 192.168.101.6 ebgp-multihop 255 (line 6)
 neighbor 192.168.101.6 update-source Loopback0 (line 7)
 no auto-summary
 !
 address-family vpnv4
 neighbor 192.168.1.3 activate (line 8)
 neighbor 192.168.1.3 route-reflector-client (line 9)
 neighbor 192.168.1.3 send-community extended
 neighbor 192.168.101.6 activate (line 10)
 neighbor 192.168.101.6 next-hop-unchanged (line 11)
 neighbor 192.168.101.6 send-community extended
 no auto-summary
 exit-address-family
 !
```

The **no bgp default route-target filter** (highlighted line 2) is again used to ensure that SP1.London_RR1 does not drop VPN-IPv4 routes.

Highlighted lines 3 to 7 show the configuration of BGP neighbor relationships for SP1.Frankfurt.PE (192.168.1.3) and SP2.London_RR1 (192.168.101.6).

In highlighted lines 8 and 9, MP-BGP is enabled for VPN-IPv4 route exchange with SP1.Frankfurt.PE, and SP1.Frankfurt.PE is configured as a route reflector client.

In highlighted lines 10 and 11, MP-BGP is enabled for VPN-IPv4 route exchange with SP2.London_RR1, and SP1.London_RR1 is configured not to modify original VPN-IPv4 route next hops as these routes are advertised to SP2.London_RR1.

Example 5-22 shows the exchange of VPN-IPv4 routes between SP2.London_RR1 and SP1.London_RR1 as provided in the output of the **show ip bgp vpnv4 all**.

Example 5-22 **show ip bgp vpnv4 all** *Command Output on SP2.London_RR1 and SP1.London_RR1*

```
SP2.London_RR1#show ip bgp vpnv4 all
BGP table version is 19, local router ID is 192.168.101.6
Status codes: s suppressed, d damped, h history, * valid, > best, i - internal
Origin codes: i - IGP, e - EGP, ? - incomplete
```

Example 5-22 **show ip bgp vpnv4 all** *Command Output on SP2.London_RR1 and SP1.London_RR1 (Continued)*

```
   Network            Next Hop         Metric LocPrf Weight Path
   Route Distinguisher: 65535:100
   *> 10.1.1.0/24      192.168.1.3                          0 65535 64512 I (line 1)
   *> 10.1.2.0/24      192.168.1.3                          0 65535 64512 i (line 2)
   *> 10.1.3.0/24      192.168.1.3                          0 65535 64512 i (line 3)
   *> 10.1.4.0/24      192.168.1.3                          0 65535 64512 i (line 4)
   *>i10.2.1.0/24      192.168.101.3        0    100        0 64512 i (line 5)
   *>i10.2.2.0/24      192.168.101.3        0    100        0 64512 i (line 6)
   *>i10.2.3.0/24      192.168.101.3        0    100        0 64512 i (line 7)
   *>i10.2.4.0/24      192.168.101.3        0    100        0 64512 i (line 8)
   SP2.London_RR1#
```

```
SP1.London_RR1#show ip bgp vpnv4 all
BGP table version is 19, local router ID is 192.168.1.6
Status codes: s suppressed, d damped, h history, * valid, > best, i - internal
Origin codes: i - IGP, e - EGP, ? - incomplete

   Network            Next Hop         Metric LocPrf Weight Path
   Route Distinguisher: 65535:100
   *>i10.1.1.0/24      192.168.1.3          0    100        0 64512 i (line 9)
   *>i10.1.2.0/24      192.168.1.3          0    100        0 64512 i (line 10)
   *>i10.1.3.0/24      192.168.1.3          0    100        0 64512 i (line 11)
   *>i10.1.4.0/24      192.168.1.3          0    100        0 64512 i (line 12)
   *> 10.2.1.0/24      192.168.101.3                        0 65001 64512 i (line 13)
   *> 10.2.2.0/24      192.168.101.3                        0 65001 64512 i (line 14)
   *> 10.2.3.0/24      192.168.101.3                        0 65001 64512 i (line 15)
   *> 10.2.4.0/24      192.168.101.3                        0 65001 64512 i (line 16)
   SP1.London_RR1#
```

Highlighted lines 1 to 8 show the output of the **show ip bgp vpnv4 all** command on
SP2.London_RR1.

Highlighted lines 1 to 4 show the VPN-IPv4 (VPN-mjlnet site 2) routes received by
SP2.London_RR1 from SP1.London_RR1 (192.168.1.6).

Then, in highlighted lines 5 to 8, you can see VPN-IPv4 (VPN-mjlnet site 1) routes received
by SP2.London_RR1 from SP2.NewYork.PE (192.168.101.3).

The same routes are, of course, shown in the output of the **show ip bgp vpnv4 all** command
on SP1.London_RR1.

Highlighted lines 9 to 12 show VPN-IPv4 (VPN-mjlnet site 2) routes received from
SP1.Frankfurt.PE (192.168.1.3), and highlighted lines 13 to 16 show VPN-IPv4 (VPN-
mjlnet site 1) routes received from SP2.London_RR1 (192.168.101.6).

Before moving on, it is worth taking another look at the VPN-IPv4 routes advertised
between route reflectors (see highlighted line 1 to 4 and 9 to 12). Notice that the next hops
of these routes are not the route reflectors from which the routes were received (SP2.London_
RR1 [192.168.101.6] and SP1.London_RR1 [192.168.1.6], as they normally would be), but
are instead the original next hops (the PE routers that originally advertised the routes,
SP2.NewYork.PE [192.168.101.3] and SP1.Frankfurt.PE [192.168.1.3]). The fact that the

next hops are the original PE router addresses is because the **neighbor** *ip-address* **next-hop-unchanged** command is configured on each route reflector.

Advertisement of Routes to the Next Hops of VPN-IPv4 Routes (and Routes to Route Reflectors)

The advertisement of route to the next hops of the VPN-IPv4 routes, as well as routes to route reflectors is as follows:

1   The next hops of VPN-IPv4 routes (PE router loopback interface addresses), as well as routes to route reflectors, are advertised in the *local* autonomous system IGP to the *local* ASBR.

   Note that routes to route reflectors are exchanged between autonomous systems so that route reflectors can establish BGP neighbor relationships between themselves.

2   Routes to next hops (*local* PE routers) and routes to *local* route reflectors are redistributed into BGP at the *local* ASBR.

3   ASBRs exchange BGP routes to local next hops (PE routers) and route reflectors, as well as associated labels. These labels are used to forward packets across the ASBR-to-ASBR link.

4   ASBRs redistribute BGP routes to *remote* next hops (PE routers) and route reflectors into the *local* IGP. This redistribution must be carefully controlled to ensure that instability in the remote autonomous system is not imported into the local autonomous system.

5   PE routers receive IGP routes to *remote* next hops (PE routers), and route reflectors receive IGP routes to remote route reflectors.

   The receipt of IGP routes to remote next hops allows PE routers to install VPN-IPv4 routes to remote customer sites into their VRFs (remember that a router must have reachability to the next hop of [MP-]BGP routes before it can install those routes into a routing table).

Figure 5-22 shows the advertisement of routes to next hops (PE routers) when deploying inter-autonomous system MPLS VPNs using MP-eBGP between route reflectors in separate autonomous systems.

Example 5-23 shows the configuration of ASBR SP2.London_ASBR.

Highlighted line 2 in Example 5-23 shows the **mpls bgp forwarding** command. As previously explained, this command is used to enable the interface (connected to the remote ASBR) to receive MPLS packets when labels are advertised using BGP.

Routes to next hops (PE routers) and route reflectors in the remote autonomous system are then redistributed into the local IGP (OSPF) using the **redistribute** command in highlighted line 3.

Figure 5-22 *Advertisement of Routes to Next Hops (PE Routers) Between Autonomous Systems When Deploying Inter-Autonomous System MPLS VPNs Using MP-eBGP Between Route Reflectors in Separate Autonomous Systems*

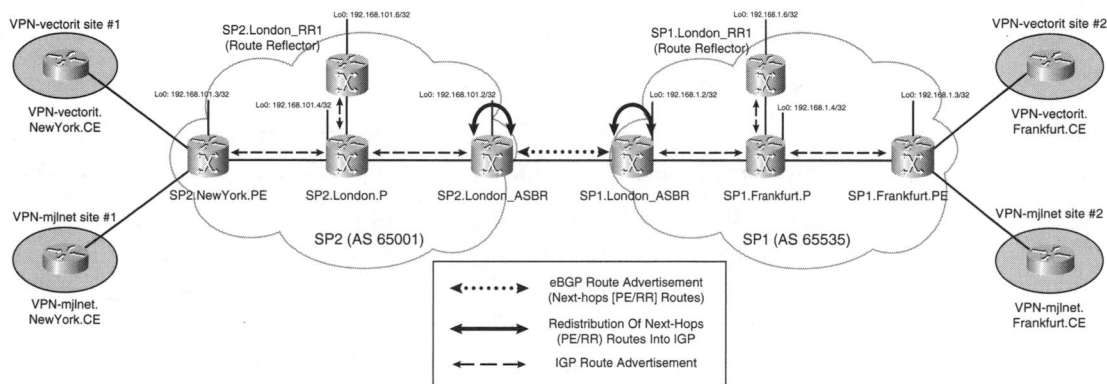

Example 5-23 *Relevant Configuration of Route Reflectors SP2.London_ASBR*

```
!
! On SP2.London_ASBR (line 1)
!
interface Serial1/1
 ip address 172.16.31.1 255.255.255.0
 mpls bgp forwarding (line 2)
!
router ospf 100
 redistribute bgp 65001 subnets route-map filter-sp2 (line 3)
 passive-interface Loopback0
 network 192.168.0.0 0.0.255.255 area 0
!
router bgp 65001
 neighbor 172.16.31.2 remote-as 65535 (line 4)
 !
 address-family ipv4
 neighbor 172.16.31.2 activate (line 5)
 neighbor 172.16.31.2 route-map filter-sp2 in (line 6)
 neighbor 172.16.31.2 route-map filter-sp1 out (line 7)
 neighbor 172.16.31.2 send-label (line 8)
 no auto-summary
 no synchronization
 network 192.168.101.3 mask 255.255.255.255 (line 9)
 network 192.168.101.6 mask 255.255.255.255 (line 10)
 exit-address-family
!
access-list 10 permit 192.168.101.6 (line 11)
access-list 10 permit 192.168.101.3 (line 12)
!
access-list 20 permit 192.168.1.3 (line 13)
access-list 20 permit 192.168.1.6 (line 14)
!
route-map filter-sp2 permit 10 (line 15)
```

continues

Example 5-23 *Relevant Configuration of Route Reflectors SP2.London_ASBR (Continued)*

```
  match ip address 20 (line 16)
  match mpls-label (line 17)
 !
route-map filter-sp1 permit 10 (line 18)
  match ip address 10 (line 19)
  set mpls-label (line 20)
 !
```

Notice that **redistribute** command in highlighted line 3 links to a route map called **filter-sp2**.

The route map itself is shown in highlighted lines 15 to 17. In highlighted line 16, IP prefixes specified in access list 20 (see highlighted lines 13 and 14) are matched, and then in highlighted line 17, the **match mpls-label** command is used to ensure that only if routes have an associated label will they be redistributed.

Note that access list 20 (highlighted lines 13 and 14) specifies routes to remote autonomous system next hops (SP1.Frankfurt.PE [192.168.1.3]) and route reflectors (SP1.London_RR1 [192.168.1.6]).

A BGP neighbor relationship with SP1.London_ASBR (172.16.31.2) is configured in highlighted line 4.

In highlighted line 5, SP1.London_ASBR is enabled for IPv4 route exchange, and then in highlighted line 6, the route map **filter-sp2** is applied to filter routes advertised by SP1.London_ABSR2 (the route map is applied in an inbound direction).

You may notice that the route map specified in highlighted line 6 (**filter-sp2**) is the same one utilized in highlighted line 3 to control routes redistributed into the local IGP.

In highlighted line 7, the route map **filter-sp1** is applied to filter routes advertised from SP2.London_ASBR to SP1.London_ASBR (the route map is applied in an outbound direction).

Route map **filter-sp1** is configured from highlighted line 18 to 20. In highlighted line 19, IP prefixes specified in access list 10 are matched, and in highlighted line 20, the **set mpls-label** command is used to ensure that a label is assigned to each prefix specified in access list 10.

Access list 10 specifies routes to local autonomous system next hops (SP2.NewYork.PE [192.168.101.3]) and route reflectors (SP2.London_RR1 [192.168.101.6]).

The **neighbor** *ip-address* **send-label** command in highlighted line 8 is used to ensure that labels are sent with BGP routes advertised to SP1.London_ASBR.

Finally, in highlighted lines 9 and 10, routes to SP2.NewYork.PE (192.168.101.3) and SP2.London_RR1 (192.168.101.6) are redistributed into BGP using the **network** *network-number* [**mask** *network-mask*] command. These are the routes that are advertised to SP1.London_ASBR.

The configuration of SP1.London_ASBR is similar to that for SP2.London_ASBR, as you can see in Example 5-24.

Example 5-24 *Relevant Configuration of Route Reflectors SP1.London_ASBR*

```
!
! On SP1.London_ASBR (line 1)
!
interface Serial2/1
 ip address 172.16.31.2 255.255.255.0
 mpls bgp forwarding (line 2)
!
router isis
 net 49.1234.0000.0000.0001.00
 is-type level-2-only
 metric-style wide
 mpls traffic-eng router-id Loopback0
 mpls traffic-eng level-2
 redistribute bgp 65535 route-map filter-sp1 (line 3)
!
router bgp 65535
 neighbor 172.16.31.1 remote-as 65001 (line 4)
 !
 address-family ipv4
 neighbor 172.16.31.1 activate (line 5)
 neighbor 172.16.31.1 route-map filter-sp1 in (line 6)
 neighbor 172.16.31.1 route-map filter-sp2 out (line 7)
 neighbor 172.16.31.1 send-label (line 8)
 no auto-summary
 no synchronization
 network 192.168.1.3 mask 255.255.255.255 (line 9)
 network 192.168.1.6 mask 255.255.255.255 (line 10)
 exit-address-family
!
access-list 10 permit 192.168.1.3 (line 11)
access-list 10 permit 192.168.1.6 (line 12)
!
access-list 20 permit 192.168.101.6 (line 13)
access-list 20 permit 192.168.101.3 (line 14)
!
route-map filter-sp2 permit 10 (line 15)
 match ip address 10 (line 16)
 set mpls-label (line 17)
!
route-map filter-sp1 permit 10 (line 18)
 match ip address 20 (line 19)
 match mpls-label (line 20)
!
```

The **mpls bgp forwarding** command in highlighted line 2 has already been described.

The **redistribute** command in highlighted line 3 is again used to redistribute remote autonomous system next hop (PE router) and route reflector routes into the local IGP (IS-IS).

The **redistribute** command links to route map filter-sp1, which is defined in highlighted lines 18 to 20.

Route map **filter-sp1** matches routes to SP2.NewYork.PE (192.168.101.3) and SP2.London_RR1 (192.168.101.6) as specified in access list 20 (see highlighted lines 13 and 14).

In highlighted line 4, a BGP neighbor relationship is configured with SP2.London_ASBR (172.16.31.1).

In highlighted lines 5 and 6, SP2.London_ASBR is enabled for IPv4 route exchange, and route map filter-sp1 is applied inbound to the connection.

Route map filter-sp1 is configured in highlighted lines 18 to 20. It matches routes to SP2.NewYork.PE and SP2.London_RR1 (defined in access list 20, see highlighted lines 13 and 14) and specifies that routes matched must have an associated label.

Highlighted lines 7 and 8 configure an outbound route map for routes advertised to SP2.London_ASBR (route map filter-sp2) and specify that a label should be sent along with each route advertised.

Route map filter-sp2 is defined in highlighted lines 15 to 17. It matches routes configured in access list 10 (routes to SP2.Frankfurt.PE [192.168.1.3] and SP2.London_RR1 [192.168.1.6]), specifies that a label must be assigned to each of these routes.

Routes to SP1.Frankfurt.PE and SP1.London_RR1 are redistributed into BGP in highlighted lines 9 and 10. These routes are advertised to SP2.London_RR1.

NOTE   Notice that SP2.London_ASBR and SP1.London_ASBR are configured to exchange IPv4 routes (plus associated labels) only. They are not configured to exchange VPN-IPv4 routes—remember that VPN-IPv4 route exchange occurs only between route reflectors.

So that is configuration. Now it is time to verify route and label advertisement between the ASBRs using the **show ip bgp** and **show ip bgp labels** commands.

Example 5-25 shows the output of the **show ip bgp** and **show ip bgp labels** commands on SP2.London_ASBR.

Example 5-25 show ip bgp *and* show ip bgp labels *Command Output on SP2.London_ASBR*

```
SP2.London_ASBR#show ip bgp
BGP table version is 33, local router ID is 192.168.101.2
Status codes: s suppressed, d damped, h history, * valid, > best, i - internal,
              r RIB-failure, S Stale
Origin codes: i - IGP, e - EGP, ? - incomplete

   Network          Next Hop          Metric LocPrf Weight Path
*> 192.168.1.3/32   172.16.31.2           30            0 65535 I (line 1)
*> 192.168.1.6/32   172.16.31.2           30            0 65535 i (line 2)
*> 192.168.101.3/32 192.168.104.1         59        32768 i (line 3)
*> 192.168.101.6/32 192.168.104.1        113        32768 i (line 4)
SP2.London_ASBR#
```

Example 5-25 show ip bgp *and* show ip bgp labels *Command Output on SP2.London_ASBR (Continued)*

```
SP2.London_ASBR#show ip bgp labels
   Network            Next Hop        In label/Out label
   192.168.1.3/32    172.16.31.2      23/22 (line 5)
   192.168.1.6/32    172.16.31.2      24/23
   192.168.101.3/32 192.168.104.1     22(from LDP)/nolabel
   192.168.101.6/32 192.168.104.1     20(from LDP)/nolabel

SP2.London_ASBR#
```

The output of the **show ip bgp** command on SP2.London_ASBR (highlighted lines 1 to 4) shows routes to SP1.Frankfurt.PE (192.168.1.3) and SP1.London_RR1 (192.168.1.6), as well as routes to SP2.NewYork.PE (192.168.101.3) and SP2.London_RR1 (192.168.101.6). The routes to SP2.NewYork.PE and SP2.London_RR1 were redistributed into BGP on SP2.London_ASBR from the local IGP, and the routes to SP1.Frankfurt.PE and SP1.London_RR1 were received from SP1.London_ASBR.

In the output of the **show ip bgp labels** command (highlighted line 5), you can see the label (22) assigned to route 192.168.1.3 (SP1.Frankfurt.PE) by SP1.London_ASBR and advertised to SP2.London_ASBR.

This label (22) is significant because it corresponds to the next hop (SP1.Frankfurt.PE) for VPN-mjlnet site 2 (VPN-IPv4) routes advertised by SP1.Frankfurt.PE to SP2.NewYork.PE via route reflectors SP1.London_RR1 and SP2.London_RR1. This label will be used to forward packets going from VPN-mjlnet site 1 to VPN-mjlnet site 2 across the link between SP2.London_ASBR to SP1.London_ASBR.

Example 5-26 shows the output of the **show ip bgp** and **show ip bgp labels** commands on SP1.London_ASBR.

Highlighted lines 1 to 4 show the output of the **show ip bgp** command on SP1.London_ASBR.

You can see routes to SP1.Frankfurt.PE (192.168.1.3), SP1.London_RR1 (192.168.1.6), SP2.NewYork.PE (192.168.101.3), and SP2.London_RR1 (192.168.101.6). Routes to SP1.Frankfurt.PE and SP1.London_RR1 were redistributed from the local IGP into BGP, and the routes to SP2.NewYork.PE and SP2.London_RR1 were received from SP2.London_ASBR.

Example 5-26 show ip bgp *and* show ip bgp labels *Command Output on SP1.London_ASBR*

```
SP1.London_ASBR#show ip bgp
BGP table version is 7, local router ID is 192.168.1.2
Status codes: s suppressed, d damped, h history, * valid, > best, i - internal,
              r RIB-failure, S Stale
Origin codes: i - IGP, e - EGP, ? - incomplete

   Network            Next Hop          Metric LocPrf Weight Path
*> 192.168.1.3/32    192.168.2.2           30          32768 i (line 1)
*> 192.168.1.6/32    192.168.2.2           30          32768 i (line 2)
```

continues

Example 5-26 **show ip bgp** *and* **show ip bgp labels** *Command Output on SP1.London_ASBR (Continued)*

```
*> 192.168.101.3/32 172.16.31.1           59           0 65001 i (line 3)
*> 192.168.101.6/32 172.16.31.1          113           0 65001 i (line 4)
SP1.London_ASBR#
```
```
SP1.London_ASBR#show ip bgp labels
   Network          Next Hop       In label/Out label
   192.168.1.3/32   192.168.2.2     22(from LDP)/nolabel
   192.168.1.6/32   192.168.2.2     23(from LDP)/nolabel
   192.168.101.3/32 172.16.31.1     25/22 (line 5)
   192.168.101.6/32 172.16.31.1     24/20

SP1.London_ASBR#
```

The output of the **show ip bgp labels** command shows the label (22) assigned to route
192.168.101.3 (SP2.NewYork.PE) by SP2.London_ASBR and advertised to SP1.London_
ASBR. Label 22 will be used to forward packets from VPN-mjlnet site 2 to VPN-mjlnet
site 1 across the link from SP1.London_ASBR to SP2.London_ASBR.

Packet Forwarding When Deploying Inter-Autonomous System MPLS VPNs Using MP-eBGP Between Route Reflectors in Separate Autonomous Systems

Packet forwarding between customer sites is best illustrated by using **traceroute**.

In Example 5-27, the **traceroute** command is used to examine packet forwarding from
VPN-mjlnet.NewYork.CE (VPN-mjlnet site 1) to host 10.1.4.1 (at VPN-mjlnet site 2).

Example 5-27 *Packet Forwarding from VPN-mjlnet.NewYork.CE (mjlnet Site 1) to Host 10.1.4.1 (at mjlnet Site 2)*

```
VPN-mjlnet.NewYork.CE#traceroute 10.1.4.1

Type escape sequence to abort.
Tracing the route to 10.1.4.1

  1 10.2.1.2 4 msec 0 msec 0 msec (line 1)
  2 192.168.102.2 [MPLS: Labels 23/28 Exp 0] 244 msec 244 msec 244 msec (line 2)
  3 192.168.104.2 [MPLS: Labels 24/28 Exp 0] 224 msec 240 msec 224 msec (line 3)
  4 172.16.31.2 [MPLS: Labels 22/28 Exp 0] 208 msec 212 msec 208 msec (line 4)
  5 192.168.2.2 [MPLS: Labels 18/28 Exp 0] 192 msec 192 msec 196 msec (line 5)
  6 10.1.1.1 [AS 65001] [MPLS: Label 28 Exp 0] 128 msec 128 msec 124 msec (line 6)
  7 10.1.1.2 [AS 65001] 84 msec *  84 msec (line 7)
VPN-mjlnet.NewYork.CE#
```

Highlighted line 1 shows the packet as it is forwarded over the link between
VPN-mjlnet.NewYork.CE and SP2.NewYork.PE.

In highlighted line 2, the packet crosses the link from SP2.NewYork.PE and SP2.London.P.
The label stack here consists of an IGP label (23) and a VPN label (28). The VPN label
was advertised along with its associated VPN-mjlnet site 2 route 10.1.4.0/24 from
SP1.Frankfurt.PE via the route reflectors to SP2.NewYork.PE.

The packet then transits the link from SP2.London.P to SP2.London_ASBR in highlighted line 3. Notice that the IGP label has been swapped, but that the VPN label remains the same (28).

Highlighted line 4 shows the packet as it transits the link from SP2.London_ASBR to SP1.London_ASBR. Notice that the outer label used to forward the packet is the one advertised by SP1.London_ASBR (see Example 5-25, highlighted line 5). The VPN label (28) again remains unchanged.

In highlighted line 5, the packet is forwarded over the link from SP1.London_ASBR to SP1.Frankfurt.P. The IGP label is 18, and the VPN label is again unchanged (28).

The packet then transits the link from SP1.Frankfurt.P to SP1.Frankfurt.PE in highlighted line 6. The IGP label is popped, but the VPN label remains the same (28).

In highlighted line 7, the unlabeled packet crosses the link from SP1.Frankfurt.PE to VPN-mjlnet.Frankfurt.CE.

Figure 5-23 shows packet forwarding from VPN-mjlnet.NewYork.CE (mjlnet site 1) to host 10.1.4.1 (a host at VPN-mjlnet site 2).

Figure 5-23 *Packet Forwarding from VPN-mjlnet.NewYork.CE (mjlnet Site 1) to Host 10.1.4.1 (a Host at mjlnet Site 2)*

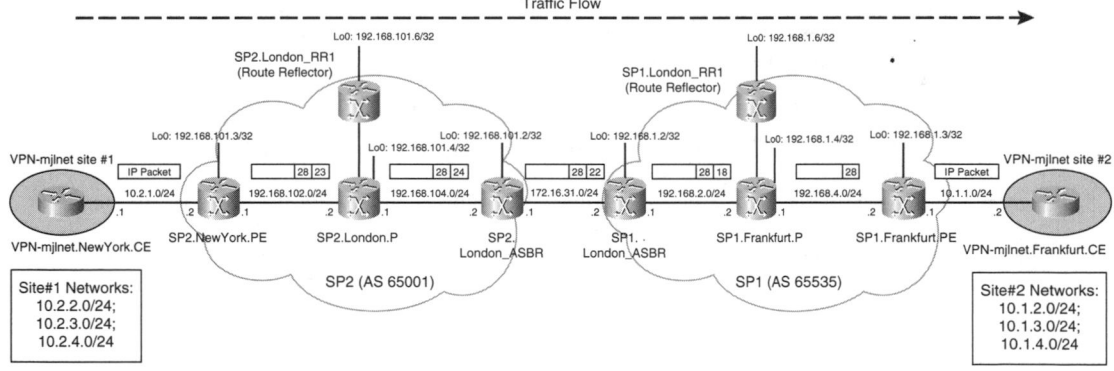

Packet forwarding from VPN-mjlnet.Frankfurt.CE (VPN-mjlnet site 2) to host 10.2.4.1 (a host at VPN-mjlnet site 1) is similar, as illustrated in Example 5-28.

Example 5-28 *Packet Forwarding from VPN-mjlnet.Frankfurt.CE (mljnet Site 2) to Host 10.2.4.1 (at mjlnet Site 1)*

```
VPN-mjlnet.Frankfurt.CE#traceroute 10.2.4.1

Type escape sequence to abort.
Tracing the route to 10.2.4.1

 1 10.1.1.1 16 msec 16 msec 16 msec (line 1)
 2 192.168.4.1 [MPLS: Labels 23/23 Exp 0] 212 msec 212 msec 208 msec (line 2)
 3 192.168.2.1 [MPLS: Labels 25/23 Exp 0] 188 msec 188 msec 188 msec (line 3)
 4 172.16.31.1 [MPLS: Labels 22/23 Exp 0] 228 msec 172 msec 172 msec (line 4)
 5 192.168.104.1 [MPLS: Labels 22/23 Exp 0] 152 msec 152 msec 156 msec (line 5)
 6 10.2.1.2 [AS 65535] [MPLS: Label 23 Exp 0] 320 msec 148 msec 152 msec (line 6)
 7 10.2.1.1 [AS 65535] 80 msec * 80 msec (line 7)
VPN-mjlnet.Frankfurt.CE#
```

The packet crosses the link from VPN-mjlnet.Frankfurt.CE to SP1.Frankfurt.PE in highlighted line 1.

Next, the packet is forwarded between SP1.Frankfurt.PE and SP1.Frankfurt.P (highlighted line 2). The label stack here consists of an IGP label (23) and a VPN label (23). The VPN label corresponds to VPN-mjlnet site 1 route 10.2.4.0/24 and was advertised to SP1.Frankfurt.PE by SP2.NewYork.PE via the route reflectors.

In highlighted line 3, the packet transits the link from SP1.Frankfurt.P to SP1.London_ ASBR. The IGP label is swapped, but the VPN label remains the same (23).

Highlighted line 4 shows the packet as it crosses the link between SP1.London_ASBR and SP2.London_ASBR. Notice that the outer label (22) is the label advertised by SP2.London_ASBR to SP1.London_ASBR (see Example 5-26, highlighted line 5). The VPN label (23) is again unchanged.

SP2.London_ASBR forwards the packet to SP2.London.P in highlighted line 5. The outer label is an IGP label (22), and the inner (VPN) label is unchanged (23).

The packet now crosses the link from SP2.London.P to SP2.NewYork.PE (highlighted line 6). The IGP label has been popped, whereas the VPN label (23) is again unmodified.

Then, in highlighted line 7, the unlabeled packet transits the link between SP2.NewYork.PE and VPN-mjlnet.NewYork.CE.

Figure 5-24 illustrates packet forwarding from VPN-mjlnet.Frankfurt.CE (VPN-mjlnet site 2) to host 10.2.4.1 (a host at VPN-mjlnet site 1).

Figure 5-24 *Packet Forwarding from VPN-mjlnet.Frankfurt.CE (mjlnet Site 2) to Host 10.2.4.1 (a Host at mjlnet Site 1)*

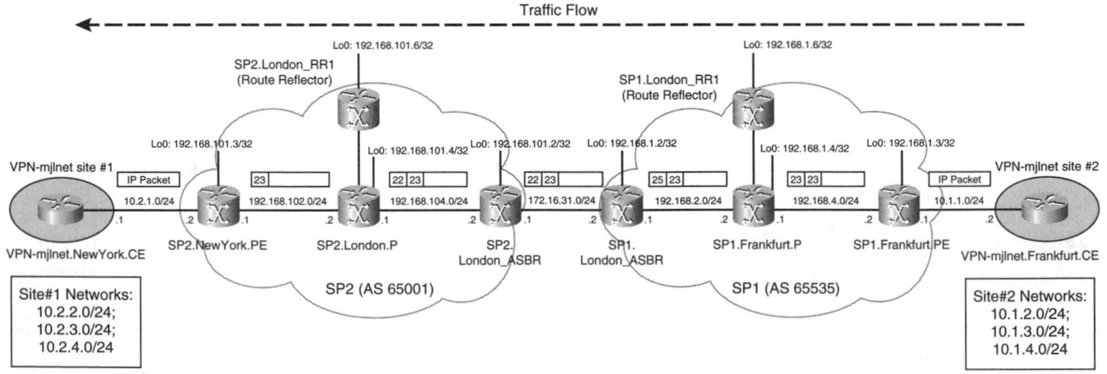

Supporting Multicast Transport in MPLS Layer 3 VPNs

Although the base specification for MPLS Layer 3 VPNs specifies mechanisms that facilitate the forwarding of unicast traffic between customer VPN sites, it does not specify mechanisms to facilitate the forwarding the of multicast traffic.

Point-to-Point GRE Tunnels

In the absence of a native mechanism to support multicast traffic transport in an MPLS Layer 3 VPN environment, the traditional method of supporting multicast between customer sites has been to configure point-to-point Generic Routing Encapsulation (GRE) tunnels between CE routers, as illustrated in Figure 5-25.

Figure 5-25 *Multicast Forwarding Between Customer Sites Using Point-to-Point GRE Tunnels*

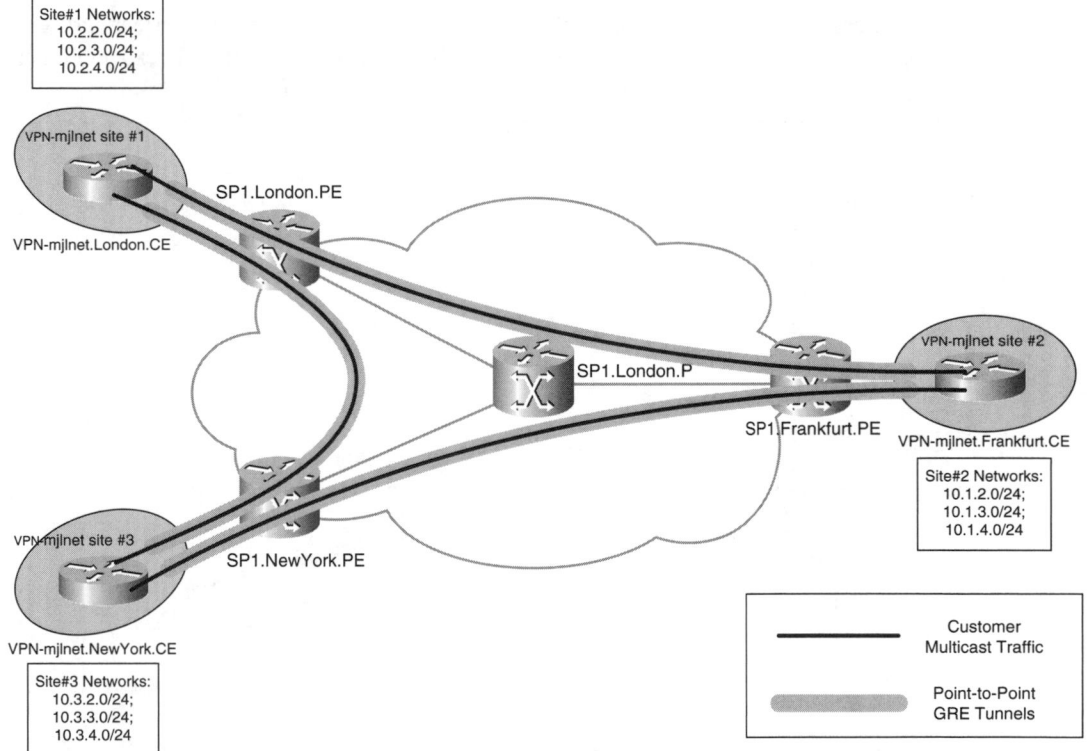

The advantage of using point-to-point GRE tunnels to transport multicast traffic between customer VPN sites is that it is not necessary to enable multicast transport within the service provider core network.

One major disadvantage of using point-to-point GRE tunnels is the fact that a mesh of tunnels is necessary to transport multicast traffic between CE routers, and if any site to any site multicast transport is required then the number of GRE tunnels required is $n(n-1)/2$ (where n is the number of sites). If there are 5 sites, you need 10 tunnels; if there are 50 sites, you need 1225 tunnels; and if there are 100 sites, you need 4950 tunnels. So, configuring point-to-point GRE tunnels between CE routers is an inherently unscalable solution.

Another problem with configuring point-to-point GRE tunnels between CE routers is the fact that this causes the unicast and multicast forwarding paths to be incongruent—CE routers receive unicast traffic on their physical interface connected to a PE router but receive multicast on their GRE tunnel interfaces. The fact that forwarding paths are incongruent means that without careful configuration of CE routers, reverse-path forwarding (RPF) checks fail, and multicast traffic is dropped (see Figure 5-26).

NOTE   RFP checks ensure that multicast traffic is received on the interface that corresponds to the shortest path to the source. If the unicast routing table is used for RPF checks and unicast and multicast forwarding paths are incongruent, multicast traffic will be dropped.

Figure 5-26 *Incongruent Traffic Forwarding May Cause Multicast Traffic to Be Dropped by CE Routers*

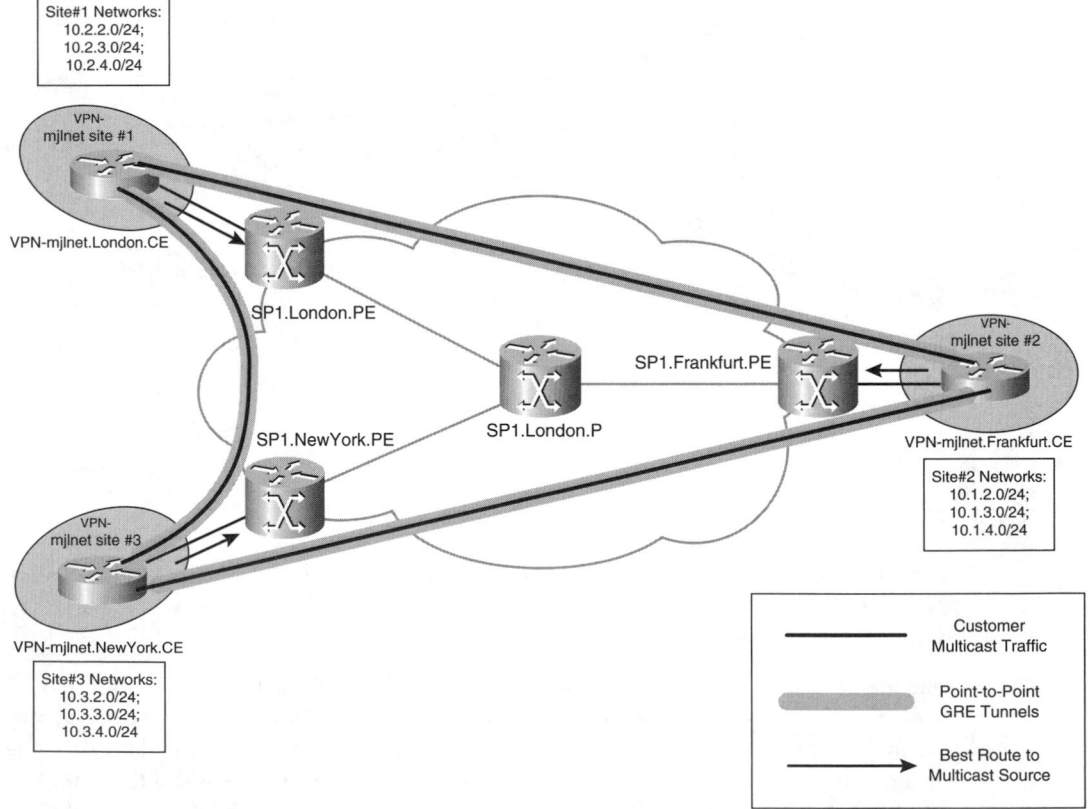

The simplest method of ensuring that CE routers do not drop multicast traffic when unicast and multicast forwarding paths are incongruent is to configure static multicast routes (**ip**

mroute *source-address mask* **tunnel** *interface-number*). The static multicast route will be used for RPF checking, and will ensure that CE routers do not drop multicast traffic.

In summary, point-to-point GRE tunnels between CE routers do not offer a truly viable solution for the transport of multicast traffic between customer VPN sites.

Multicast VPNs (MVPN)

If point-to-point GRE tunnels are not a viable solution for multicast traffic transport, then what is? The answer is multicast VPNs (MVPN).

NOTE   Multicast transport in MPLS Layer 3 VPNs is described in Internet Draft draft-rosen-vpn-mcast at the time of this writing. MVPN is based on this Internet Draft.

MVPN avoids both of the major disadvantages of point-to-point GRE tunnels between CE routers:

- No special configuration is required on CE routers (no point-to-point GRE tunnels are required).

- CE routers receive multicast traffic on the same interface as unicast traffic, thereby ensuring that no special configuration is required to ensure that RPF checks succeed on CE routers.

There are a number of important components and considerations when deploying MVPN, including the following:

- The multicast domain (MD)
- The multicast VRF (MVRF)
- The multicast tunnel (MT) and multicast tunnel interface (MTI)
- Protocol Independent Multicast (PIM) adjacencies
- Multicast distribution trees (MDT)
- RPF checks in an MVPN

The following section discuss these components and considerations.

The Multicast VRF and Multicast Domain

An MD is a grouping of MVRFs on PE routers (and possibly ASBRs, when inter-autonomous system MVPN is configured) that send multicast traffic to and receive multicast from each other. An MVRF consists of multicast and forwarding tables corresponding to a VRF.

Figure 5-27 shows an MD.

Figure 5-27 *Multicast Domain*

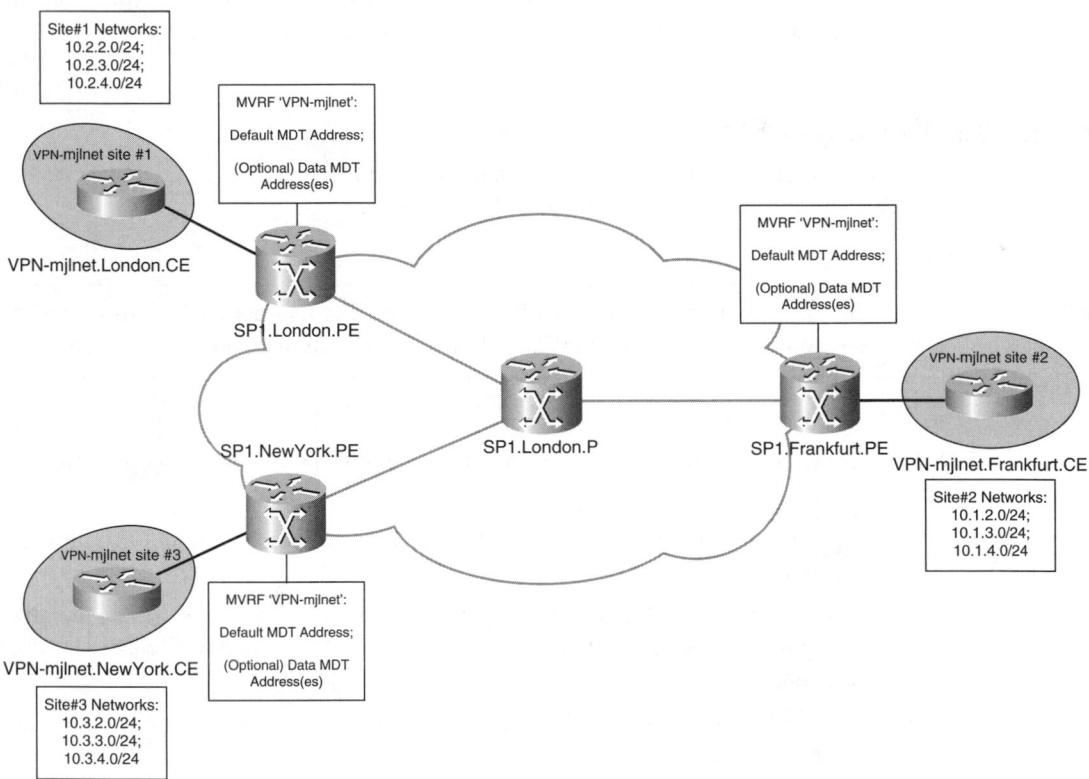

As shown in Figure 5-27, SP1.London.PE, SP1.NewYork.PE, and SP1.Frankfurt.PE are all configured with an MVRF corresponding to customer VPN VPN-mjlnet, and these MVRFs comprise one MD.

When an MVRF is configured on a PE router, an MTI is created, which allows the forwarding of multicast traffic between the local MVRF and other (remote) MVRFs in an MD. Unicast traffic is not forwarded over the MTI.

Customer multicast packets sent on the MTI are encapsulated in GRE, with the GRE packet source IP address being the BGP update source of the PE router and the destination address being a multicast address specific to the MD. The type of service (ToS) settings in customer multicast packets are copied to the outer IP packet header (IP/GRE).

Figure 5-28 shows the form of packets send on the MTI.

NOTE   At the time of writing, GRE encapsulation is the only option for packets sent on the MTI. Internet Draft draft-rosen-vpn-mcast discusses the encapsulation of customer multicast traffic sent over the MT using GRE, IP, or MPLS.

Figure 5-28 *Packets Sent on the MTI*

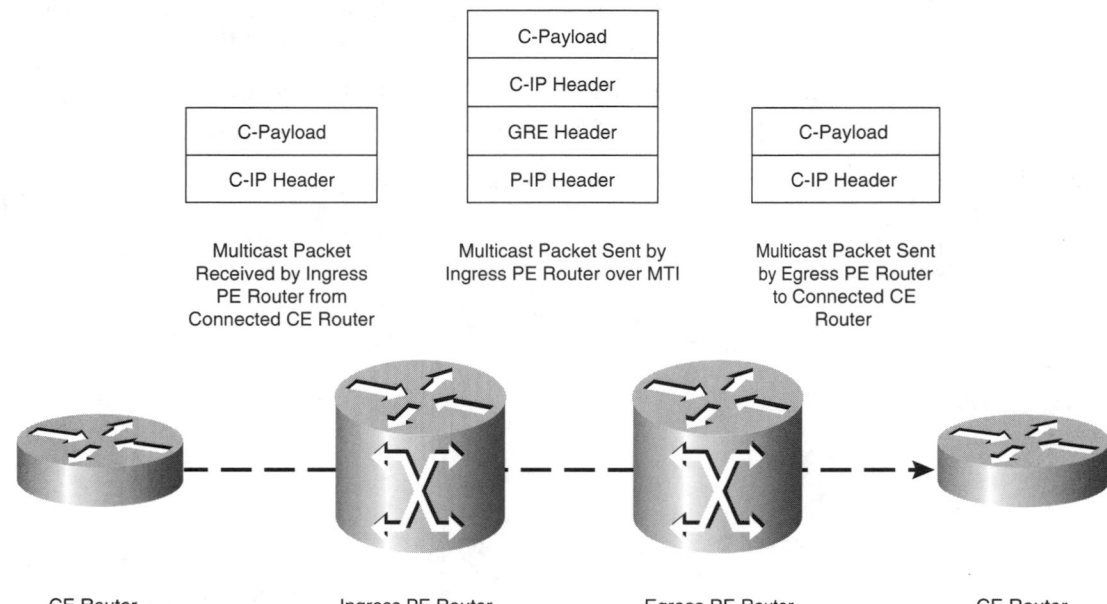

Figure 5-28 shows a customer multicast packet (called a *C-Packet*) arriving at the ingress PE router from a connected CE router.

As previously discussed, when a C-packet is sent over the MT, it is encapsulated in GRE, with the outer IP header having a source IP address being the BGP update source of the sending PE router and the destination IP address being one corresponding to the particular MD and being significant only in the service provider backbone. Because IP addresses in the outer header are significant only in the service provider backbone, the outer header is shown as the *P-IP Header* in Figure 5-28.

The encapsulated C-packet arrives at the egress PE router. Because more than one MVRF may be configured on the egress PE router, the destination IP address contained in the P-IP header is used to determine the correct MVRF. After the correct MVRF has been determined, the egress PE router decapsulates the C-packet (removes the P-IP/GRE headers) and forwards the C-packet to the connected CE router.

The Default and Data MDTs

You now know that customer multicast packets are encapsulated when sent between PE routers and that the destination IP address contained in P-IP header is a multicast address. It is important to understand the multicast addresses used.

When an MD is configured, a multicast tree called the default multicast distribution tree (MDT) is automatically built between PE routers configured to participate in an MD.

When you configure a PE router to participate in an MD, it becomes a source (root) for the default MDT as well as being a receiver (leaf) for the default MDT. So, each PE router participating in an MD is both a root and a leaf node of the default MDT.

Multicast traffic sent over the default MDT by one PE router in an MD is received by all the other PE routers in that MD, as shown in Figure 5-29.

Figure 5-29 *Multicast Transmission over the Default MDT*

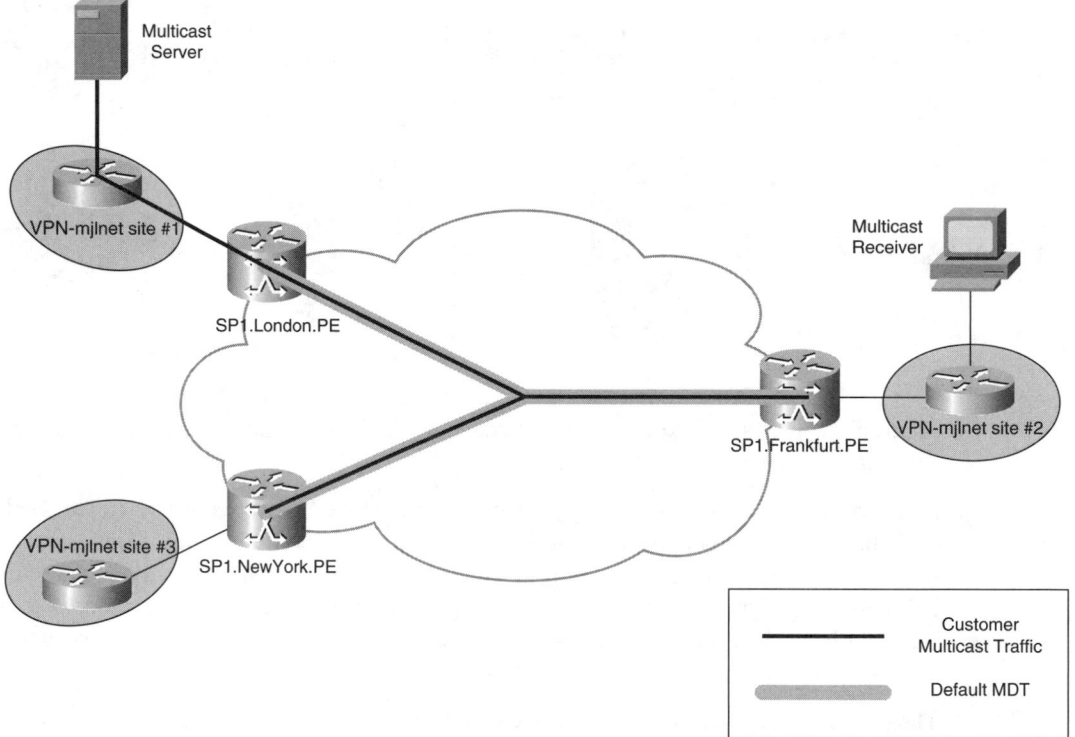

By default, all multicast traffic sent between customer sites in an MVPN is sent over the default MDT corresponding to that MVPN (MD). That includes all PIM control traffic, all PIM sparse mode multicast group traffic, and all PIM dense mode multicast group traffic.

You gain a number of advantages by sending all MVPN multicast traffic over a default MDT, including the following:

- The default MDT aggregates all customer multicast group traffic, and by extension multicast state in the service provider core network.

  Because all customer multicast traffic for a particular MVPN is (by default) tunneled using a single multicast group address, core PE and P routers only need to maintain default MDT routing and forwarding information (multicast state information) for the specific MD, rather than multicast state for each individual multicast group address used within a customer MVPN.

- The default MDT can be used to transport all multicast traffic types (traffic for sparse, dense, and source-specific multicast mode groups).

Unfortunately, there is one significant disadvantage of using the default MDT to transport all customer MVPN multicast traffic—all customer MVPN traffic is sent to *all* PE routers in the MD regardless of whether the site to which a PE router is connected has any multicast receivers for the particular multicast group in question. Figure 5-30 illustrates this issue.

Figure 5-30 *Multicast Transport over the Default MDT*

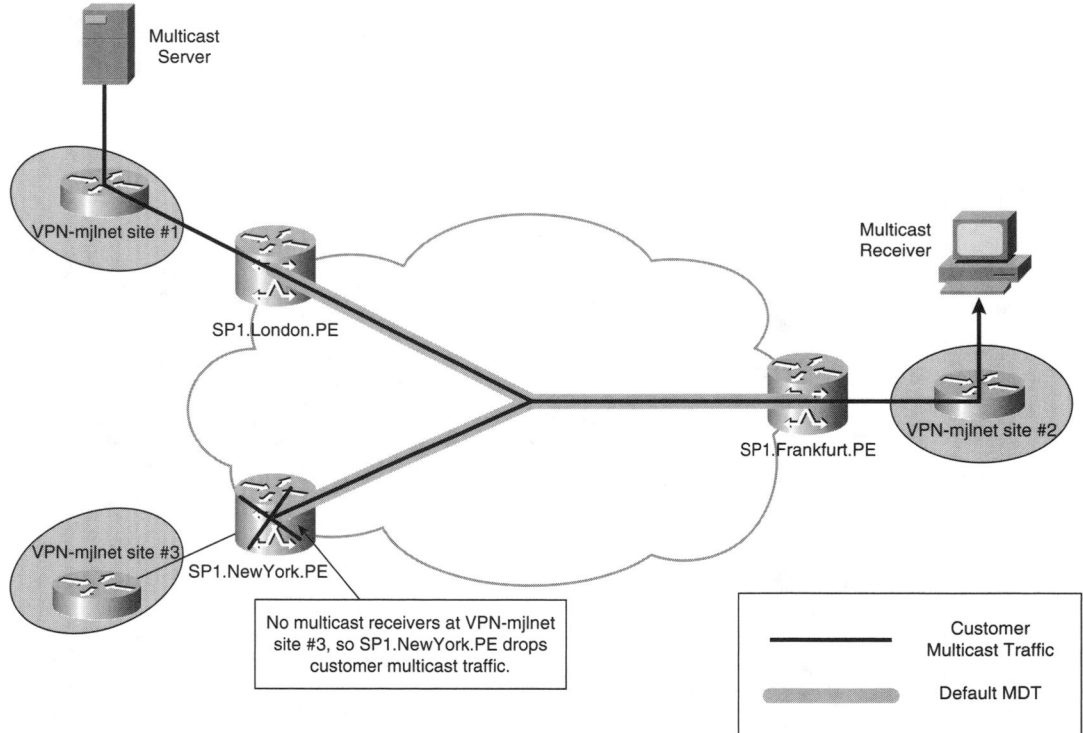

As you can see, there are receivers for the customer multicast group at VPN-mjlnet site 2 (Frankfurt), but there are no receivers at site 3 (New York). Notice, however, that traffic from the source at site 1 (London) is transported over the default MDT to all PE routers in the MD, including SP1.NewYork.PE (connected to site 3).

The default MDT, therefore, provides suboptimal multicast transport if there are not receivers for all customer MVPN groups at all sites. What is the solution to the issue of suboptimal multicast traffic transport? The answer is the configuration of data MDTs.

NOTE   Configuration of data MDTs is optional.

The difference between a default MDT and a data MDT is that a data MDT is constructed only between the PE connected to a high-bandwidth customer multicast source and other PE routers in the MD that are connected to sites at which there are multicast receivers for the multicast group in question. PE routers connected to sites at which there are no receivers do not join the data MDT.

Figure 5-31 illustrates a data MDT.

Figure 5-31 *Data MDT*

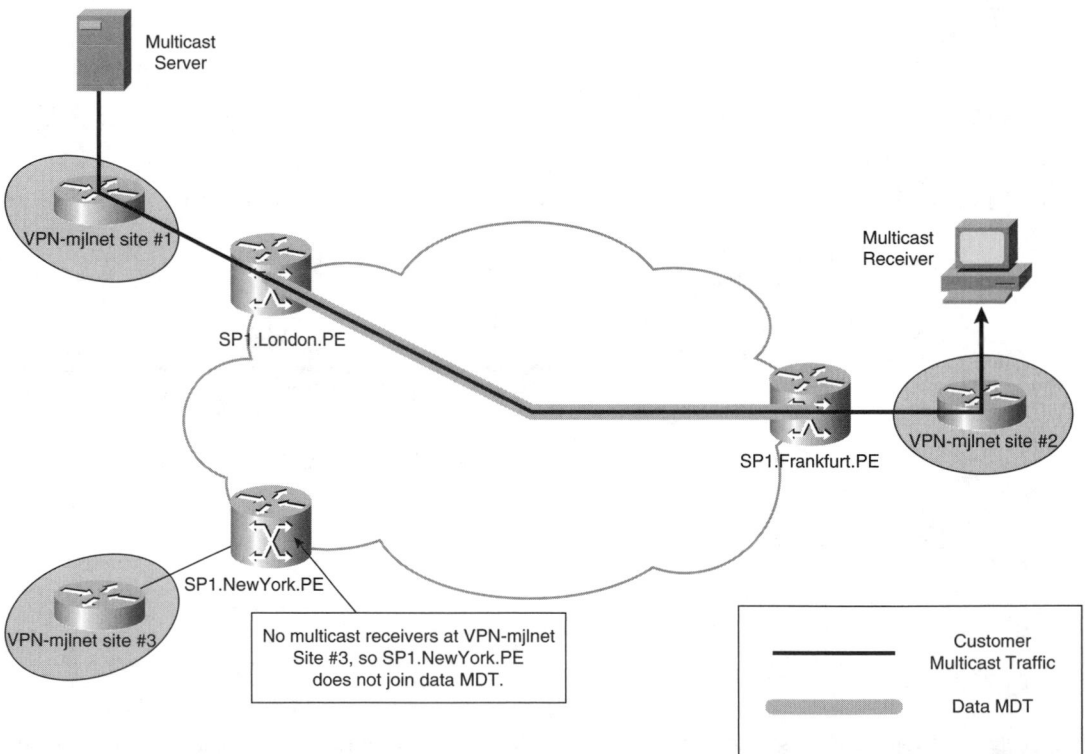

As previously mentioned, data MDTs are constructed for high-bandwidth multicast groups (high bandwidth traffic flows that correspond to [S, G] entries in the MVRF). The decision as to what constitutes a high-bandwidth multicast source is determined by the service provider—the amount of bandwidth that a multicast source needs to be sending to trigger the creation of a data MDT is configurable (on PE routers). The source can be sending as little as 1 kbps or as much as 4294967 kbps.

You might be wondering how exactly data MDTs are constructed in the service provider network. After all, unlike default MDTs where each PE router is both a root and leaf in the MDT, data MDTs are only constructed between the PEs that are connected to sites where there are receivers for a certain customer multicast group and the PE connected to the site where the source for that group resides (via a Rendezvous Point [RP] if PIM Sparse Mode [PIM-ISM] or bi-directional PIM mode is used in the provider backbone).

So, the leaf PEs in this case (those connected to sites where there are receivers) need to discover the root of the data MDT (the PE which is connected to the site at which the source is located) as well as other information, such as customer multicast flow information, so that they can join the MDT. To ensure that leaf PEs can discover the address of the PE connected to the source, a new message (Type Length Value [TLV]), called an *MDT Join*, has been introduced (see Figure 5-32).

Figure 5-32 *MDT Join Message*

The root PE router sends the MDT Join to all PE routers in the MD over the default MDT. The root PE router encapsulates the MDT Join message in UDP with port 3232 using destination IP address 224.0.0.13 (ALL-PIM-ROUTERS), with the MDT Join message fields described as follows:

- **Type**—This field contains a value of 1, indicating that this message is an MDT Join.
- **Length**—The total length of the message, not including IP and UDP headers. The length of the MDT Join is 16 bytes.
- **Reserved**—Reserved for future use.
- **C-source**—The customer multicast source IP address.
- **C-group**—The customer multicast group address.
- **P-group**—The multicast group address that the root PE router will use to send data MDT traffic.

So, the root PE advertises the customer multicast source and group addresses as well as the multicast group address the root PE router will use encapsulate the customer multicast flow to other PE routers in the MD using the MDT Join message, and *interested* PE routers (those connected to sites where there are receivers) join the data MDT either via the RP if PIM Sparse mode or bi-directional mode is used for data MDTs in the provider backbone, or directly to the root PE if PIM Source Specific Multicast (SSM) is used for data MDTs in the provider backbone. Noninterested PE routers (those connected to sites where there are no receivers) cache the MDT Join message information, which allows these to then quickly join the data MDT if a receiver comes on line at the connected customer VPN site.

The root PE router for the data MDT begins sending customer multicast traffic over the data MDT 3 seconds after sending the MDT Join, thus giving leaf PE routers time to join the data MDT.

Figure 5-33 shows data MDT setup.

Figure 5-33 *Leaf PE Routers Join the Data MDT*

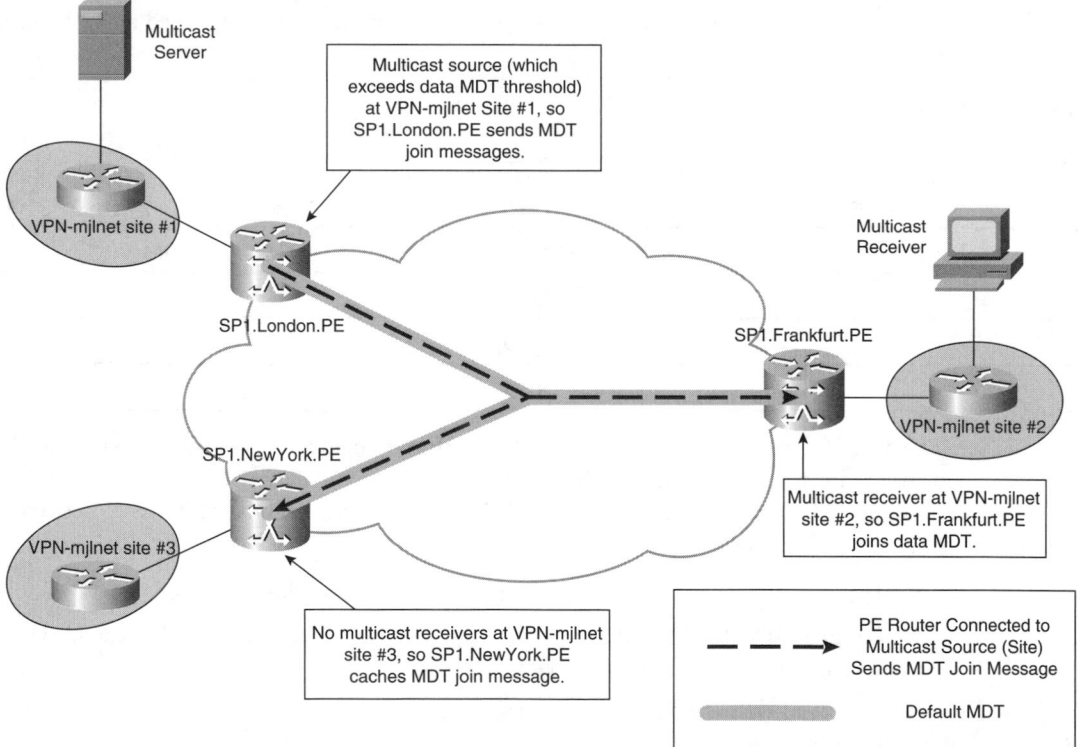

It is worth noting that the root PE for a data MDT resends the MDT Join message over the default MDT every 60 seconds as long as the customer multicast source is sending traffic over the configured bandwidth threshold. If an interested PE router does not receive an MDT Join for the data MDT for 3 minutes, it deletes the corresponding multicast state information.

Also, if the customer multicast traffic rate drops below the configured threshold, this traffic remains on the data MDT for up to 60 seconds before transferring back to the default MDT. This means that oscillations in the rate at which customer multicast traffic is sent will not cause data MDTs to be created, destroyed, and created again in quick succession.

As you now know, the advantage of data MDTs is that they optimize multicast traffic flow in the service provider core network because only interested PE routers receive multicast traffic.

The disadvantage of data MDTs is that more multicast state is required in the service provider core network (there are more multicast groups).

Before finishing this section, it is important to note that PIM control traffic and dense mode multicast traffic remains on the default MDT and is never sent over a data MDT.

PIM Adjacencies

When designing and deploying MVPNs, it is important to understand the PIM adjacencies that are formed between CE, PE, and P routers.

In an MVPN, the service provider core network is transparent to customer routers. PE routers establish PIM adjacencies with CE routers in the appropriate MVRF context, so the PIM instances corresponding to each customer (MVRF) are logically separate on PE routers. PE routers also establish PIM adjacencies with other PE routers in the same MD over the MT, the MT is treated by the VPN (VRF) specific PIM instances as a LAN interface, and PIM LAN behavior is implemented on the MT. Finally, PE routers establish global PIM adjacencies with P routers.

Figure 5-34 illustrates MVPN PIM adjacencies.

Figure 5-34 *MVPN PIM Adjacencies*

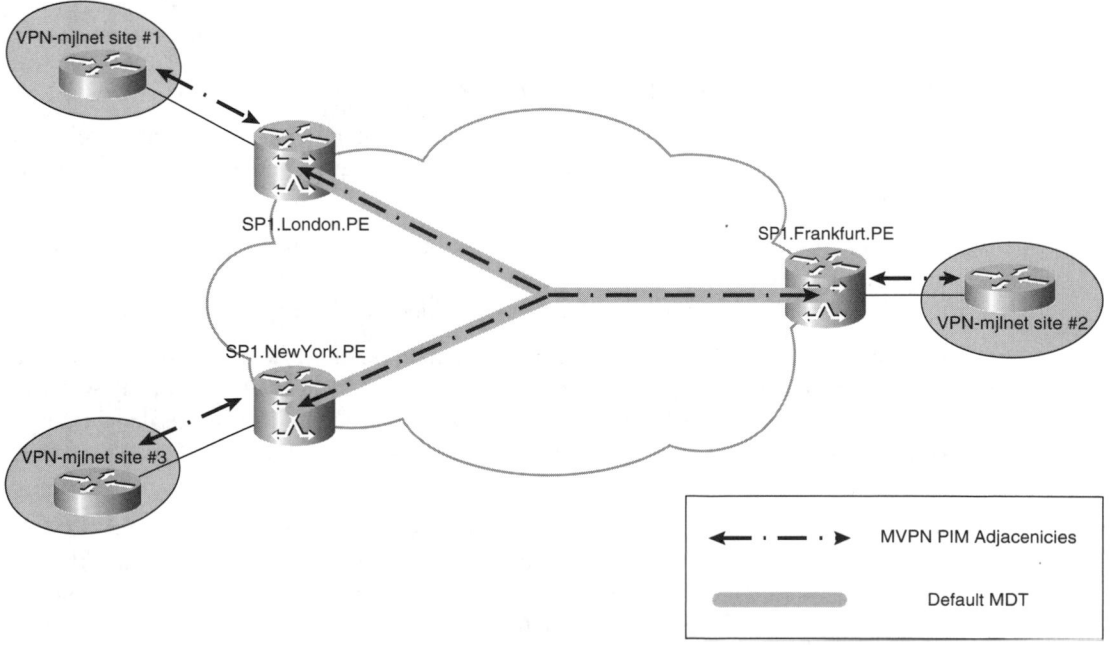

Figure 5-35 illustrates global PIM adjacencies.

Figure 5-35 *Global PIM Adjacencies*

Global PIM
Adjacencies

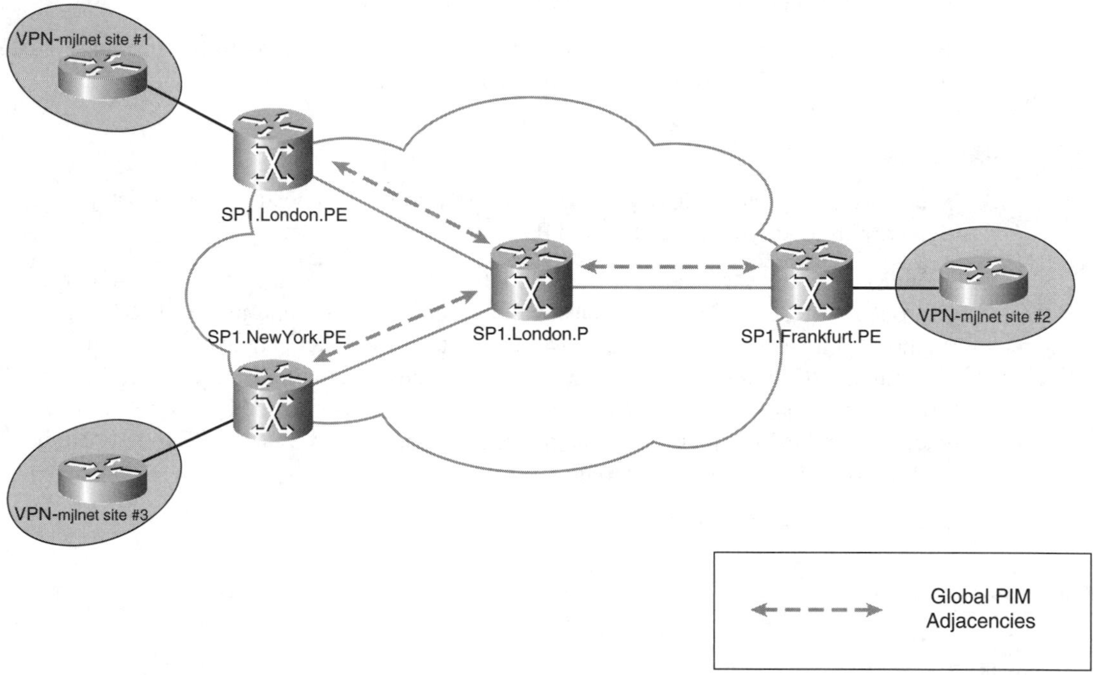

Reverse-Path Forwarding Checks in the MVPN

RPF checks are used in multicast networks to ensure that multicast packets are received on the correct interface. The correct interface is that which corresponds to the best path back to the multicast source.

By default, the RPF check is based on information contained within the unicast routing table. In regular IP networks, using the unicast routing table for RPF checks works well, but using the unicast routing table can cause problems on PE routers in an MVPN.

You will remember that in an MVPN, customer multicast traffic is transported over the MT between PE routers. Unicast traffic, on the other hand, is forwarded over Label Switched Paths (LSP) or L2TPv3/GRE/IPsec tunnels between PE routers. This means that the unicast routes to customer multicast sources are reachable via LSPs or L2TPv3/GRE/IPsec tunnels across the service provider core network.

For example, in the MPLS VPN backbone network shown in Figure 5-36, the customer multicast source (10.2.1.1) is reachable via an LSP to SP1.London.PE from SP1.Frankfurt.PE. The LSP to SP1.London.PE is the regular unicast path back to the source, as dictated by a route contained in the unicast routing table.

The problem with the fact that the best route back to the customer multicast source is via an LSP to SP1.London.PE is that when customer multicast traffic arrives at SP1.Frankfurt.PE over the MT, and if the regular RPF check is applied, this multicast traffic would be dropped (multicast traffic is received on the MT, but the best route back to the multicast source is via the physical interface and over the LSP).

Figure 5-36 *Customer Multicast Source Is Reachable via an LSP to SP1.London.PE*

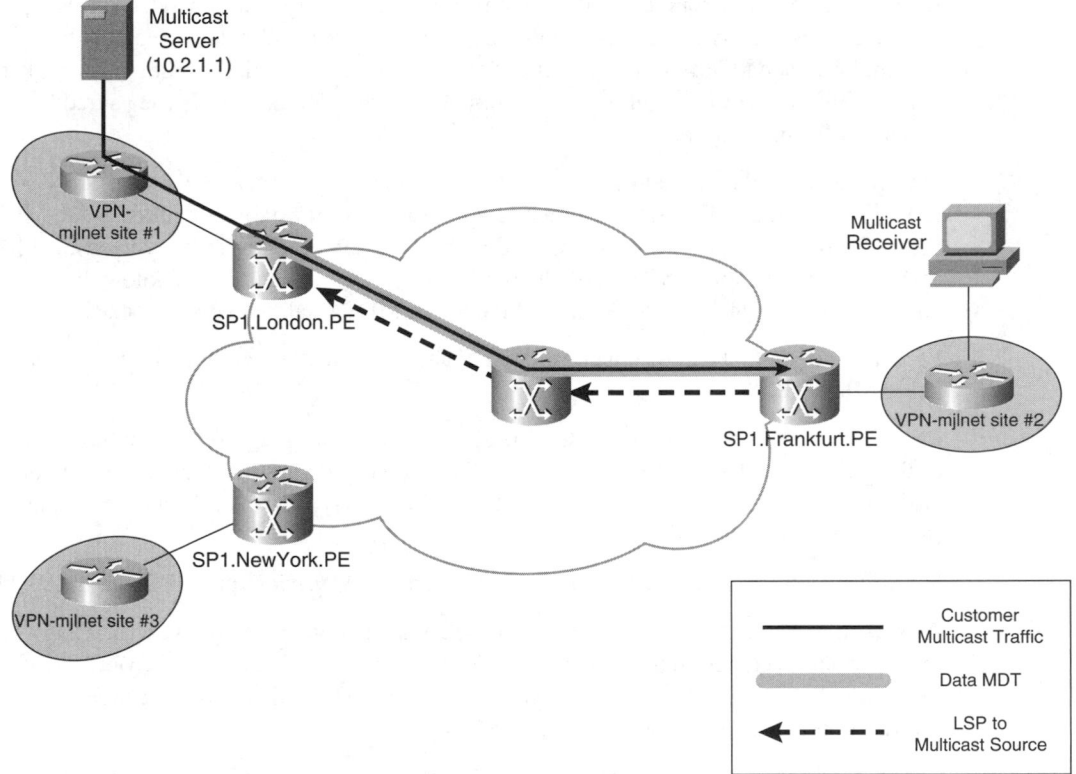

Thankfully, the multicast RPF check has been slightly modified for use in an MVPN—if the interface corresponding to the best route to the source is not via an interface associated with the VRF, the MTI is instead considered to be the interface corresponding to the best route to the source for multicast traffic. By using the MTI as the RPF interface, customer multicast traffic received on the MT can now be accepted by PE routers and forwarded onward to the appropriate connected customer site.

Configuring PIM Between PE and P Routers in the Service Provider MPLS VPN Backbone Network

PIM must be enabled within the service provider MPLS VPN backbone network, but the exact choice of configuration is flexible. It is possible, for example, to configure PIM sparse mode (PIM-SM), bidirectional PIM, and PIM source-specific multicast (PIM-SSM).

If you configure PIM-SM in the service provider core network, you need one or more rendezvous points (RP).

If you use PIM-SSM, on the other hand, no RPs are required. The advantage of having no RPs is that it removes possible points of failure from the network (the RPs), reduces the complexity of the multicast configuration in the core network, and reduces multicast forwarding delay because (initially) multicast traffic is sent over a shared tree rooted at the RP in a PIM-SM environment. PIM-SSM is often particularly recommended for data MDTs because otherwise a large number of unique multicast (P-) addresses may be required for each MD. Furthermore, in order that amount of multicast routing state is kept to a minimum on P routers, it is often recommended that default MDTs use shared trees (such as PIM bidirectional trees).

If PIM-SM or bi-directional PIM is used to establish a default MDT, PE routers only need to know the default MDT (P-group) address in order to start establishing the default MDT (other PE routers' addresses can then be discovered when PIM traffic is received). If PIM-SSM is used to establish MDTs, on the other hand, every PE router must know the source address of every other PE router in the MD before MDT establishment can start.

PE routers in an MD can discover each other's addresses by signaling this information using MP-BGP.

Prior to Cisco IOS Software Release 12.0(29)S, PE routers signal this information (as well as the default MDT group address) using a BGP update containing extended community attribute 0x0009 and an MP_REACH_NRLI attribute. A type 0x0002 Route Distinguisher (RD) is carried in the update.

Figure 5-37 illustrates PE router auto-discovery in Cisco IOS versions prior to Release 12.0(29).

As shown in Figure 5-37, PE routers in the MD that are configured to use PIM-SSM use the information carried in the BGP update to directly join the default MDT (rooted at other PE routers). If a PE router is not configured to use PIM-SSM, it simply caches the information contained in the update message.

The method of distribution of the default MDT information used prior to Cisco IOS Release 12.0(29)S is limited to a single autonomous system.

In Cisco IOS Software Release 12.0(29)S, a new BGP address family (subsequent address family indicator [SAFI] 66) is used to signal default MDT information between PE routers (see Figure 5-38).

| NOTE | Cisco IOS Software Release 12.0(29)S is backward compatible with previous Cisco IOS versions for the advertisement of default MDT information. |

Figure 5-37 *Signaling of the Default MDT Group Address and Root Address in Cisco IOS Software Prior to Release 12.0(29)*

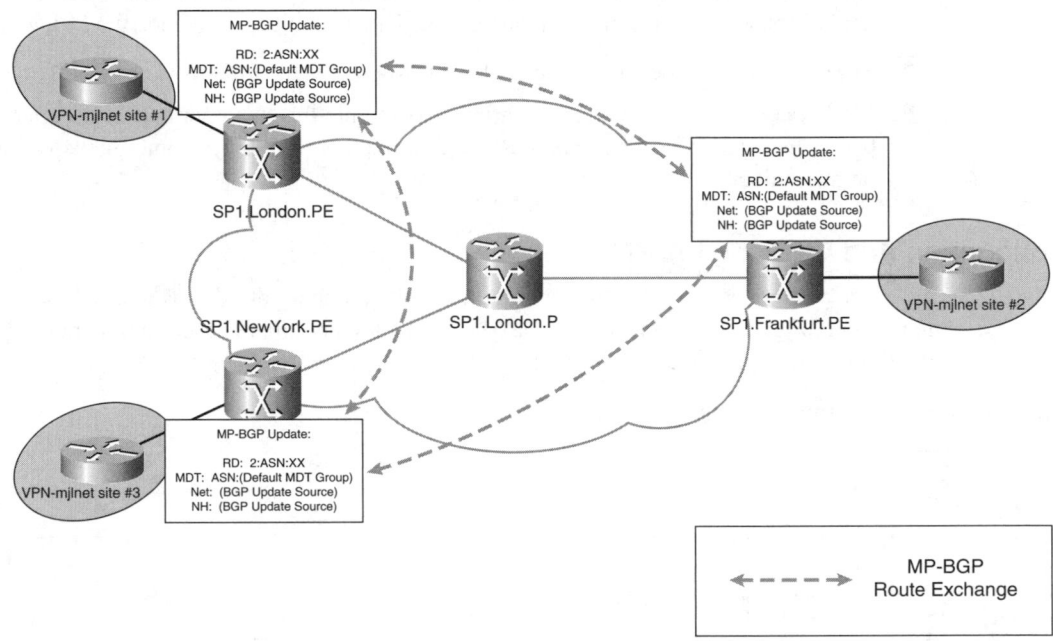

Figure 5-38 *MDT SAFI MP_REACH_NRLI*

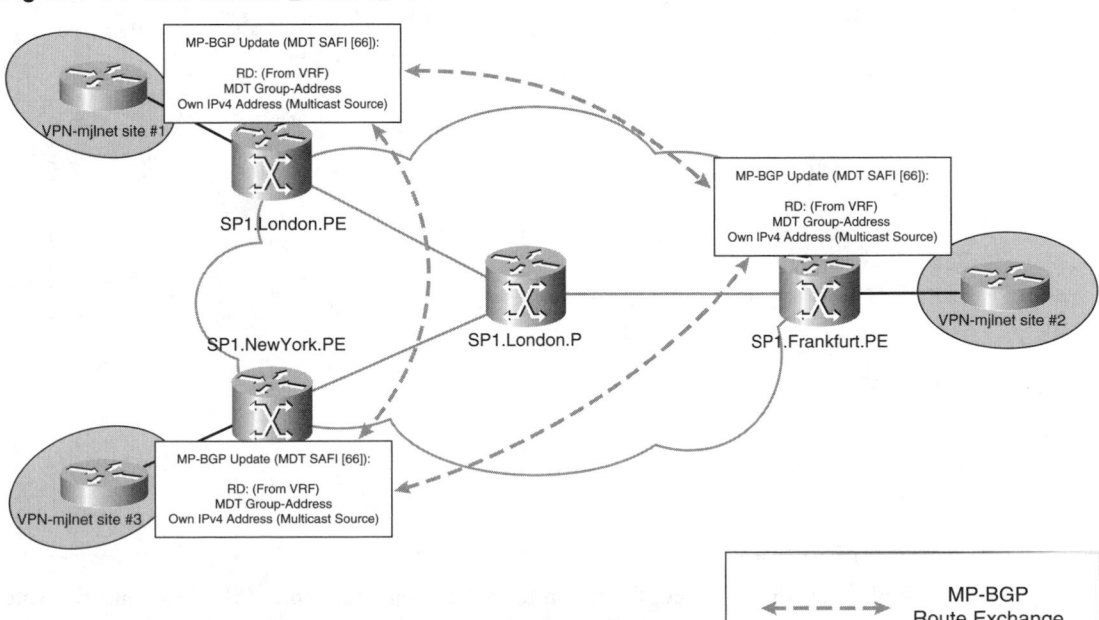

Advantages of Deploying MVPN

MVPN has a number of advantages when compared to using a mesh of GRE tunnels between CE routers to transport multicast traffic. These advantages include the following:

- MVPN is scalable because a mesh of point-to-point GRE tunnels is not required.

- MVPN does not require special configuration within the customer network (either on C or CE routers). Existing multicast configuration within the customer network can be maintained.

Configuring and Verifying MVPN

Now that you know how MVPN works in theory, it is time to take a look at how it works in practice. Figure 5-39 shows a sample MVPN deployment that is used to illustrate configurations throughout this section.

Figure 5-39 *Sample MVPN Deployment*

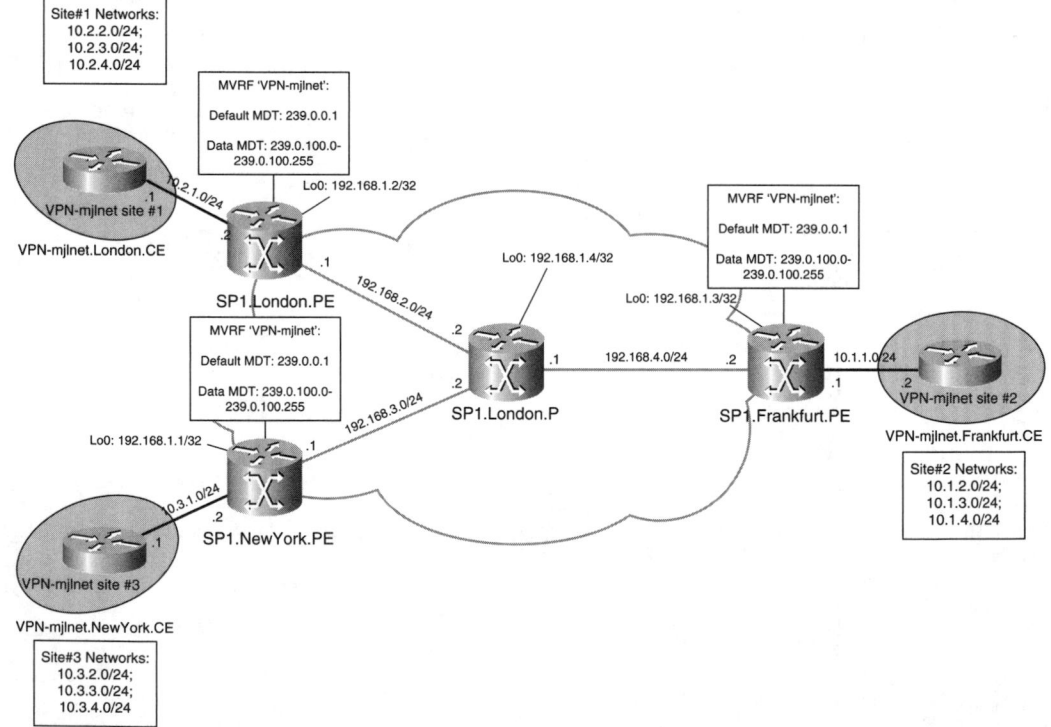

Configuring MVPN

Example 5-29 shows the configuration for MVPN on a PE router (SP1.London.PE). Note that the configuration for MVPN on SP1.Frankfurt.PE and SP1.NewYork.PE is the same for MVPN.

Example 5-29 *Configuration for MVPN on SP1.London.PE*

```
!
! On SP1.London.PE (line 1)
!
ip vrf VPN-mjlnet (line 2)
 rd 65535:100
 route-target export 65535:100
 route-target import 65535:100
 mdt default 239.0.0.1 (line 3)
 mdt data 239.0.100.0 0.0.0.255 threshold 1 (line 4)
!
ip multicast-routing (line 5)
ip multicast-routing vrf VPN-mjlnet (line 6)
!
interface Loopback0
ip address 192.168.1.2 255.255.255.255
ip pim sparse-dense-mode
!
interface Serial2/0
 ip address 192.168.2.1 255.255.255.0
 ip pim sparse-mode (line 7)
 tag-switching ip
!
interface Serial2/1
 ip vrf forwarding VPN-mjlnet (line 8)
 ip address 10.2.1.2 255.255.255.0
 ip pim sparse-dense-mode (line 9)
!
router bgp 65535 (line 10)
 no synchronization
 neighbor 192.168.1.1 remote-as 65535
 neighbor 192.168.1.1 update-source Loopback0
 neighbor 192.168.1.3 remote-as 65535
 neighbor 192.168.1.3 update-source Loopback0
 no auto-summary
 !
 address-family ipv4 mdt (line 11)
 neighbor 192.168.1.1 activate (line 12)
 neighbor 192.168.1.3 activate (line 13)
 exit-address-family
 !
 address-family vpnv4
 neighbor 192.168.1.1 activate
 neighbor 192.168.1.1 send-community extended
 neighbor 192.168.1.3 activate
 neighbor 192.168.1.3 send-community extended
 exit-address-family
 !
 address-family ipv4 vrf VPN-mjlnet
 neighbor 10.2.1.1 remote-as 64512
 neighbor 10.2.1.1 activate
 neighbor 10.2.1.1 as-override
```

continues

Example 5-29 *Configuration for MVPN on SP1.London.PE (Continued)*

```
 no auto-summary
 no synchronization
 exit-address-family
 !
ip pim ssm range 50 (line 14)
 !
access-list 50 permit 239.0.0.0 0.0.255.255 (line 15)
 !
```

In highlighted line 3, the default MDT address for VRF VPN-mjlnet is configured as 239.0.0.1 using the **mdt default** *group-address* command. The default MDT address must match between all VRFs in the MVPN (all VPN-mjlnet VRFs configured on all PE routers).

The MTI for the MPVN is created by the **mdt default** *group-address* command. The source address of default MDT (P-) packets will be the BGP update source address (the loopback interface), and the destination address will be the configured group address.

The address range for data MDTs is configured in highlighted line 4 (239.0.100.0 to 239.0.100.255) using the **mdt data** *group-address-range wildcard-bits* [**threshold** *bandwidth-threshold-value* [**list** *access-list*]] command. Remember that the data MDTs are optional but recommended if customers have high-bandwidth multicast sources that send traffic over the MPLS VPN backbone network.

The group address range configured using the **mdt data** *group-address-range wildcard-bits* [**threshold** *threshold-value* [**list** *access-list*]] constitutes a pool of addresses from which data MDT groups are chosen. A data MDT group address is chosen when traffic for a particular customer multicast group (that matches the addresses specified in the access list) exceeds the configured threshold. The source address for a data MDT's (P-) packets is the BGP update source, and the destination address corresponds to the group address selected from the configured data MDT group address range.

NOTE   Recommended practice dictates that all MDT group addresses (P-group addresses) be in the range of administratively scoped multicast addresses (that is, 239.0.0.0 to 239.255.255.255 [see RFC2365]). This will ensure that if the service provider is providing Internet multicast service the MDT group addresses will not overlap.

In highlighted line 5, the **ip multicast-routing** command is used to enable IP multicast on the SP1.London.PE. The **ip multicast-routing vrf** *vrf-name* command is used to enable IP multicast for VRF VPN-mjlnet in highlighted line 6.

Next, the **ip pim sparse-mode** command is used to enable PIM sparse mode on an MPLS VPN backbone interface (an interface connected to a P router/other PE router) in highlighted line 7. Note that in this example, SSM is used within the SP1 MPLS VPN backbone network, but if you choose to enable PIM sparse mode with auto-RP, you will need to configure PIM sparse-dense mode using the **ip pim sparse-dense mode** command.

Also notice the **ip pim-sparse-dense mode** command configured on interface Loopback0 (the MP-BGP update source). Make sure that you enable PIM on the MP-BGP update source; otherwise, MVPN will fail to operate correctly.

NOTE   The **ip pim autorp listener** global configuration mode command can be used from Cisco IOS version 12.2(7) to enable auto-RP to operate on PIM sparse mode interfaces.

Highlighted line 9 shows the **ip pim sparse-dense** mode command on a VRF VPN-mjlnet interface. The PIM mode that is enabled on VRF interfaces will depend on the customer multicast configuration, but the configuration of the **ip pim sparse-dense mode** command on VRF interfaces allows the greatest flexibility.

In highlighted line 11, the **address-family ipv4 mdt** command is used to enter the IPv4 MDT address family configuration mode.

Then, in highlighted lines 12 and 13, the **neighbor** *ip-address* **activate** command is used within the IPv4 MDT address family to enable the signaling of default MDT source address and group address with the specified PE routers using the new BGP subsequent address family (SAFI 66). Remember that the signaling of the source address of the default MDT is only necessary when using SSM within the MPLS VPN backbone network.

NOTE   The **address-family ipv4 mdt** command was added in Cisco IOS Software Release 12.0(29)S.

The **ip pim ssm range** *access-list* command (highlighted line 14) is used to define the range of multicast addresses to be used for SSM within the MPLS VPN backbone. In this case, the actual multicast addresses are specified using **access-list 50** in highlighted line 15 (multicast address range 239.0.0.0 to 239.0.255.255).

The **ip pim ssm range** command is necessary only when using SSM in the MPLS VPN backbone. Make sure that the range of multicast addresses specified using this command includes those group addresses configured using the **mdt default** and **mdt data** commands when using SSM for default and data MDTs.

As shown in Example 5-30, the configuration required on P routers (SP1.London.P) to support MVPN is much simpler than that required for PE routers.

The **ip multicast-routing** command in highlighted line 2 is used to enable global multicast on SP1.London.P.

Example 5-30 *Configuration Required on P Routers to Support MVPN*

```
!
! On SP1.London.P (line 1)
!
ip multicast-routing (line 2)
!
interface FastEthernet0/0
 ip address 192.168.3.2 255.255.255.0
 ip pim sparse-mode (line 3)
 tag-switching ip
!
interface Serial1/0
 ip address 192.168.2.2 255.255.255.0
 ip pim sparse-mode (line 4)
 tag-switching ip
!
interface Serial1/1
 ip address 192.168.4.1 255.255.255.0
 ip pim sparse-mode (line 5)
 tag-switching ip
!
ip pim ssm range 50 (line 6)
!
access-list 50 permit 239.0.0.0 0.0.255.255 (line 7)
!
```

In highlighted lines 3, 4, and 5, the **ip pim sparse-mode** command is used to enable PIM sparse mode on the interfaces connected to other P routers and PE routers. Again, if auto-RP is used in the MPLS VPN backbone, you must configure the **ip pim sparse-dense-mode** command or (in Cisco IOS Software Release 12.2(7) and later) configure the **ip pim autorp listener** global configuration mode command to enable auto-RP to operate on PIM sparse mode interfaces.

In this example, PIM SSM is used within the MPLS VPN backbone, and the **ip pim ssm range** *access-list* command shown in highlighted line 6 is used to define the range of multicast addresses to be used for SSM. The multicast addresses are specified using **access-list 50** (see highlighted line 7) and include those group addresses configured using the **mdt default** and **mdt data** commands on the PE routers.

Verifying PIM Adjacencies

PE routers maintain global PIM adjacencies with P routers (and with any directly connected PE routers) as well as MVRF PIM adjacencies with other PE routers on their MTIs and with directly connected CE routers on their VRF interfaces. You can display global PIM adjacencies using the **show ip pim neighbors** command, as shown in Example 5-31.

Example 5-31 *Verifying Global PIM Neighbors Using the* **show ip pim neighbors** *Command*

```
SP1.London.PE#show ip pim neighbors
PIM Neighbor Table
Neighbor          Interface              Uptime/Expires     Ver   DR
Address                                                           Priority/Mode
192.168.2.2       Serial2/0              00:06:12/00:01:26 v2    1 /
SP1.London.PE#
```

As you can see, SP1.London.PE has one global PIM neighbor on core MPLS VPN backbone interface serial 2/0 (SP1.London.P, 192.168.2.2).

On the other hand, SP1.London.PE has three MVRF VPN-mjlnet PIM adjacencies (see Example 5-32).

Example 5-32 *Verifying MVRF PIM Neighbors Using the* **show ip pim vrf** *Command*

```
SP1.London.PE#show ip pim vrf VPN-mjlnet neighbor
PIM Neighbor Table
Neighbor          Interface              Uptime/Expires     Ver   DR
Address                                                           Priority/Mode
10.2.1.1          Serial2/1              00:06:30/00:01:44 v2    1 /
192.168.1.1       Tunnel0                00:02:35/00:01:37 v2    1 / V
192.168.1.3       Tunnel0                00:04:03/00:01:38 v2    1 / DR V
SP1.London.PE#
```

The three MVRF VPN-mjlnet PIM adjacencies are with 10.2.1.1 (VPN-mjlnet.London.CE on interface serial 2/1), with 192.168.1.1 (SP1.NewYork.PE on interface tunnel 0 [the MTI]), and with 192.168.1.3 (SP1.Frankfurt.PE on interface tunnel 0 [MTI]). If you are wondering why there are no MVRF PIM adjacencies on core MPLS VPN backbone interfaces (interface serial 2/0), remember that MVRF PIM adjacencies are only established with remote PE routers on their MTIs and with CE routers on VRF interfaces.

Although not shown here, SP1.Frankfurt.PE and SP1.NewYork.PE similarly each maintain two PIM adjacencies over their MTIs (with the other two PE routers) and a single PIM adjacency with the directly connected CE router (VPN-mjlnet.Frankfurt.CE and VPN-mjlnet.NewYork.CE, respectively).

Example 5-33 shows the PIM neighbor table on SP1.London.P.

Example 5-33 *The PIM Neighbor Table on SP1.London.P*

```
SP1.London_P#show ip pim neighbor
PIM Neighbor Table
Neighbor          Interface              Uptime/Expires     Ver   DR
Address                                                           Priority/Mode
192.168.3.1       FastEthernet0/0        00:07:36/00:01:31 v2    1 /
192.168.2.1       Serial1/0              00:08:23/00:01:15 v2    1 /
192.168.4.2       Serial1/1              00:08:02/00:01:33 v2    1 /
SP1.London_P#
```

SP1.London.P has PIM neighbors on interface Fast Ethernet 0/0 (192.168.3.1, SP1.NewYork.PE), serial 1/0 (192.168.2.1, SP1.London.PE), and serial 1/1 (192.168.4.2, SP1.Frankfurt.PE).

Verifying the Signaling of the Default MDT

As previously mentioned, PE routers running Cisco IOS Software Release 12.0(29)S and later can advertise the source and group addresses used for the default MDT with the MDT SAFI.

You can verify the negotiation of the MDT SAFI capability between PE routers with the **show ip bgp neighbors** [*neighbor-address*] command, as demonstrated for SP1.London.PE in Example 5-34.

Example 5-34 *Verifying Negotiation of the MDT SAFI Capability Between PE Routers*

```
SP1.London.PE#show ip bgp neighbors 192.168.1.3 | begin MDT
   Address family IPv4 MDT: advertised and received
   Address family VPNv4 Unicast: advertised and received
  Message statistics:
   InQ depth is 0
   OutQ depth is 0
                        Sent        Rcvd
   Opens:                 1           1
   Notifications:         0           0
   Updates:               0           8
   Keepalives:           23          23
   Route Refresh:         0           0
   Total:                30          32
  Default minimum time between advertisement runs is 5 seconds

<output omitted>

SP1.London.PE#
```

The highlighted line shows that MDT SAFI capability has been negotiated with SP1.Frankfurt.PE. The word *advertised* indicates that the local PE router (SP1.London.PE) supports this capability and has advertised this to SP1.NewYork.PE. The word *received* indicates that SP1.NewYork.PE supports this capability and has advertised this to the local PE router.

Again, although not shown here, all PE routers are running Cisco IOS Software Release 12.0(29)S or later and similarly negotiate MDT SAFI capability with each other. The PE routers then advertise source and destination default MDT addresses to each other.

You can verify default MDT groups using the **show ip bgp ipv4 mdt all** command, as demonstrated for SP1.London.PE in Example 5-35. As seen in highlighted line 1, the RD associated with the MDT default group advertised between PE routers for VRF VPN-mjlnet is 65535:100.

Example 5-35 *Verifying Default MDT Groups*

```
SP1.London.PE#show ip bgp ipv4 mdt all
BGP table version is 5, local router ID is 192.168.1.2
Status codes: s suppressed, d damped, h history, * valid, > best, i - internal,
              r RIB-failure, S Stale
Origin codes: i - IGP, e - EGP, ? - incomplete

   Network          Next Hop            Metric LocPrf Weight Path
Route Distinguisher: 65535:100 (default for vrf VPN-mjlnet) (line 1)
*>i192.168.1.1/32   192.168.1.1              0    100      0 ? (line 2)
*> 192.168.1.2/32   0.0.0.0                           0 ? (line 3)
*>i192.168.1.3/32   192.168.1.3              0    100      0 ? (line 4)
SP1.London_PE#
```

In highlighted lines 2 to 4, you can see the default MDT source addresses advertised by each of the three PE routers in the VPN-mjlnet multicast domain (192.168.1.1 [SP1.NewYork.PE], 192.168.1.2 [SP1.London.PE, the local PE router], and 192.168.1.3 [SP1.Frankfurt.PE]).

You can use the **show ip bgp ipv4 mdt all** *ip-address* command to see more information regarding default MDT advertisement between PE routers, as demonstrated in Example 5-36 for SP1.London.PE.

Example 5-36 *Displaying More Information Regarding Default MDT Advertisement Between PE Routers*

```
SP1.London.PE#show ip bgp ipv4 mdt all 192.168.1.1
BGP routing table entry for 65535:100:192.168.1.1/32, version 5 (line 1)
Paths: (1 available, best #1, table IPv4-MDT-BGP-Table)
  Not advertised to any peer
  Local
    192.168.1.1 (metric 30) from 192.168.1.1 (192.168.1.1)
      Origin incomplete, metric 0, localpref 100, valid, internal, best,
      MDT group address: 239.0.0.1 (line 2)

SP1.London.PE#
```

```
SP1.London.PE#show ip bgp ipv4 mdt all 192.168.1.3
BGP routing table entry for 65535:100:192.168.1.3/32, version 4 (line 3)
Paths: (1 available, best #1, table IPv4-MDT-BGP-Table)
  Not advertised to any peer
  Local
    192.168.1.3 (metric 30) from 192.168.1.3 (192.168.1.3)
      Origin incomplete, metric 0, localpref 100, valid, internal, best,
      MDT group address: 239.0.0.1 (line 4)

SP1.London.PE#
```

Highlighted lines 1 and 2 show that SP1.NewYork.PE is advertising source 192.168.1.1 for default MDT group address 239.0.0.1.

In highlighted lines 3 and 4, you can see that SP1.Frankfurt.PE is advertising source 192.168.1.3 for default MDT group 239.0.0.1.

Verifying Multicast Traffic Flow

You can verify multicast traffic flow across the MPLS VPN backbone by examining the multicast routing table on PE and P routers using the **show ip mroute** command.

Example 5-37 shows the output of the **show ip mroute** command on SP1.London.PE.

Example 5-37 *Multicast Routing Table on SP1.London.PE*

```
SP1.London.PE#show ip mroute
IP Multicast Routing Table
Flags: D - Dense, S - Sparse, B - Bidir Group, s - SSM Group, C - Connected,
       L - Local, P - Pruned, R - RP-bit set, F - Register flag,
       T - SPT-bit set, J - Join SPT, M - MSDP created entry,
       X - Proxy Join Timer Running, A - Candidate for MSDP Advertisement,
       U - URD, I - Received Source Specific Host Report, Z - Multicast Tunnel,
       Y - Joined MDT-data group, y - Sending to MDT-data group
       V - RD & Vector, v - Vector
Outgoing interface flags: H - Hardware switched, A - Assert winner
 Timers: Uptime/Expires
 Interface state: Interface, Next-Hop or VCD, State/Mode

(192.168.1.1, 239.0.0.1), 00:02:01/00:02:57, flags: sTIZ (line 1)
  Incoming interface: Serial2/0, RPF nbr 192.168.2.2
  Outgoing interface list:
    MVRF VPN-mjlnet, Forward/Sparse, 00:02:01/00:00:58

(192.168.1.2, 239.0.0.1), 00:05:52/00:03:17, flags: sTZ (line 2)
  Incoming interface: Loopback0, RPF nbr 0.0.0.0
  Outgoing interface list:
    Serial2/0, Forward/Sparse, 00:03:51/00:02:35

(192.168.1.3, 239.0.0.1), 00:03:31/00:02:56, flags: sTIZ (line 3)
  Incoming interface: Serial2/0, RPF nbr 192.168.2.2
  Outgoing interface list:
    MVRF VPN-mjlnet, Forward/Sparse, 00:03:31/00:00:00

(192.168.1.1, 239.0.100.0), 00:01:49/00:02:57, flags: sTIZ (line 4)
  Incoming interface: Serial2/0, RPF nbr 192.168.2.2
  Outgoing interface list:
    MVRF VPN-mjlnet, Forward/Sparse, 00:01:49/00:01:11

(192.168.1.2, 239.0.100.0), 00:01:29/00:03:27, flags: sTZ (line 5)
  Incoming interface: Loopback0, RPF nbr 0.0.0.0
  Outgoing interface list:
    Serial2/0, Forward/Sparse, 00:01:29/00:02:34 (line 6)

(*, 224.0.1.40), 00:05:56/00:02:56, RP 0.0.0.0, flags: DCL
  Incoming interface: Null, RPF nbr 0.0.0.0
  Outgoing interface list:
    Loopback0, Forward/Sparse, 00:05:54/00:02:56

SP1.London.PE#
```

Highlighted lines 1, 2, and 3 show the default MDT source and group addresses advertised by PE routers SP1.NewYork.PE, SP1.London.PE (the local PE router), and SP1.Frankfurt.PE. Take a close look at the flags shown—note, in particular, the **s** flag, which indicates that these multicast routing table entries correspond to SSM groups, and the **Z** flag, which indicates that these entries are MDT entries and that packets corresponding to these entries should be sent and received on the MTI.

Highlighted lines 4 and 5 show entries for data MDTs (192.168.1.1, 239.0.100.0 and 192.168.1.2, 239.0.100.0). Notice that the outgoing interface list for SSM group 192.168.1.2, 239.0.100.0 contains interface serial 2/0. This is because a (high-bandwidth) source at VPN-mjlnet site 1 (London) is sending traffic on this data MDT over the MPLS VPN backbone.

Example 5-38 shows the multicast routing table on SP1.London.PE.

Example 5-38 *Multicast Routing Table on SP1.London.PE*

```
SP1.London.P#show ip mroute
IP Multicast Routing Table
Flags: D - Dense, S - Sparse, B - Bidir Group, s - SSM Group, C - Connected,
       L - Local, P - Pruned, R - RP-bit set, F - Register flag,
       T - SPT-bit set, J - Join SPT, M - MSDP created entry,
       X - Proxy Join Timer Running, A - Candidate for MSDP Advertisement,
       U - URD, I - Received Source Specific Host Report, Z - Multicast Tunnel,
       Y - Joined MDT-data group, y - Sending to MDT-data group
Outgoing interface flags: H - Hardware switched
 Timers: Uptime/Expires
 Interface state: Interface, Next-Hop or VCD, State/Mode

(192.168.1.1, 239.0.0.1), 00:04:25/00:03:25, flags: sT (line 1)
  Incoming interface: FastEthernet0/0, RPF nbr 192.168.3.1
  Outgoing interface list:
    Serial1/0, Forward/Sparse, 00:04:25/00:03:07
    Serial1/1, Forward/Sparse, 00:04:25/00:03:25

(192.168.1.2, 239.0.0.1), 00:06:14/00:03:25, flags: sT (line 2)
  Incoming interface: Serial1/0, RPF nbr 192.168.2.1
  Outgoing interface list:
    Serial1/1, Forward/Sparse, 00:06:14/00:03:25
    FastEthernet0/0, Forward/Sparse, 00:06:14/00:02:59

(192.168.1.3, 239.0.0.1), 00:05:54/00:03:15, flags: sT (line 3)
  Incoming interface: Serial1/1, RPF nbr 192.168.4.2
  Outgoing interface list:
    Serial1/0, Forward/Sparse, 00:05:54/00:03:07
    FastEthernet0/0, Forward/Sparse, 00:05:54/00:02:58

(192.168.1.1, 239.0.100.0), 00:04:11/00:03:26, flags: sT (line 4)
  Incoming interface: FastEthernet0/0, RPF nbr 192.168.3.1
  Outgoing interface list:
    Serial1/0, Forward/Sparse, 00:04:11/00:03:15

(192.168.1.2, 239.0.100.0), 00:03:52/00:03:25, flags: sT (line 5)
  Incoming interface: Serial1/0, RPF nbr 192.168.2.1
```

continues

Example 5-38 *Multicast Routing Table on SP1.London.PE (Continued)*

```
       Outgoing interface list:
         FastEthernet0/0, Forward/Sparse, 00:03:52/00:03:12

      (*, 224.0.1.40), 00:15:58/stopped, RP 0.0.0.0, flags: DCL
       Incoming interface: Null, RPF nbr 0.0.0.0
       Outgoing interface list:
         Serial1/0, Forward/Sparse, 00:07:46/00:00:00

    SP1.London.P#
```

Highlighted lines 1, 2, and 3 show the three SSM groups corresponding to the default MDT sourced from PE routers SP1.NewYork.PE (192.168.1.1), SP1.London.PE (192.168.1.2), and SP1.Frankfurt.PE (192.168.1.3). Notice that the outgoing interface list for each default MDT contains the interfaces toward the other two PE routers (and the incoming interface list contains the interface toward the source PE router).

For example, the default MDT sourced from address 192.168.1.1 (SP1.NewYork.PE) has an outgoing interface list containing interfaces Serial1/0 (toward SP1.London.PE) and Serial1/1 (toward SP1.Frankfurt.PE). The incoming interface list contains interface FastEthernet0/0 (toward SP1.NewYork.PE).

In highlighted line 4, you can see a data MDT with source address 192.168.1.1 and group address 239.0.100.0. If you look at the outgoing interface list, you can see that it contains interface Serial1/0 (toward SP1.London.PE), and the incoming interface list contains interface FastEthernet0/0 (toward SP1.NewYork.PE). So, there is a (high-bandwidth) source at VPN-mjlnet site 3 (New York) that is sending multicast traffic to a receiver at VPN-mjlnet site 1 (London) over this data MDT.

Finally, highlighted line 5 shows a data MDT with source address 192.168.1.2 (SP1.London.PE) and group address 239.0.100.0. The outgoing interface list for this group contains interface FastEthernet0/0 (toward SP1.NewYork.PE), and the incoming interface list contains interface Serial1/0 (toward SP1.London.PE). You can conclude from this information that there is a (high-bandwidth) multicast source at VPN-mjlnet site 1 (London) that is sending traffic to a receiver at VPN-mjlnet site 3 (New York) over this data MDT.

Implementing QoS for MPLS Layer 3 VPNs

One element of MPLS Layer 3 VPN design and deployment that is becoming more and more important is quality of service (QoS). The deployment of QoS can allow an MPLS VPN backbone network to support the tight service level requirements for applications such as voice and video.

Two popular QoS deployment models used by MPLS VPN service providers are to

- Configure QoS mechanisms at the edge (between CE and PE routers) with no QoS configuration in the core (between PE and P routers).
- Configure QoS mechanisms both at the edge and in the core.

QoS is often configured at the edge because of the typical scarcity of bandwidth there. In the core, on the other hand, some service providers simply overprovision the amount of bandwidth such that even during failure scenarios, bandwidth is still plentiful and service levels can still be guaranteed even for applications such as voice and video. Other service providers consider that overprovisioning of bandwidth is too expensive and so deploy QoS configuration to ensure that they can still guarantee service levels with less core bandwidth.

Figure 5-40 illustrates the QoS deployment models for MPLS VPN service providers.

Figure 5-40 *QoS Deployment Models for MPLS VPN Service Providers*

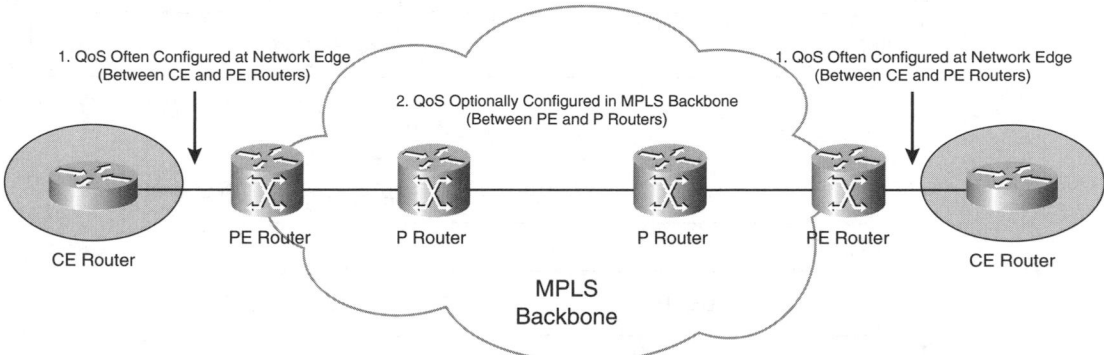

Service provider backbone (core) QoS design can comprise two overall elements:

- **QoS configuration to support transmission performance**—This ensures that traffic is appropriately prioritized during periods of network congestion (application traffic with tight service requirements is prioritized over other traffic during congestion). Application service requirements can consist of elements such as maximum packet loss, maximum delay, maximum jitter (variable delay), and minimum bandwidth.

- **Configuration to ensure service availability**—This ensures that during (partial) network failure scenarios, the service provider can continue to guarantee service availability for critical applications.

To provide (adequate) transmission performance, a service provider can implement a Differentiated Service (DiffServ, RFC2475) architecture in their backbone network. In a DiffServ architecture, packets are marked using packet fields such as the type of service (ToS) byte, Differentiated Service (DS) field, or MPLS Experimental (EXP) bits. These packet markings then indicate to routers in the path what level and type of service (queuing, bandwidth, selective dropping, and so on) they should offer to the packets.

Figure 5-41 shows the ToS byte, DS field, and MPLS EXP bits. As shown in Figure 5-41, the three EXP bits form part of the MPLS shim header (also see Figure 3-37 on page 189).

Figure 5-41 *ToS Byte, DS Field, and MPLS EXP Bits*

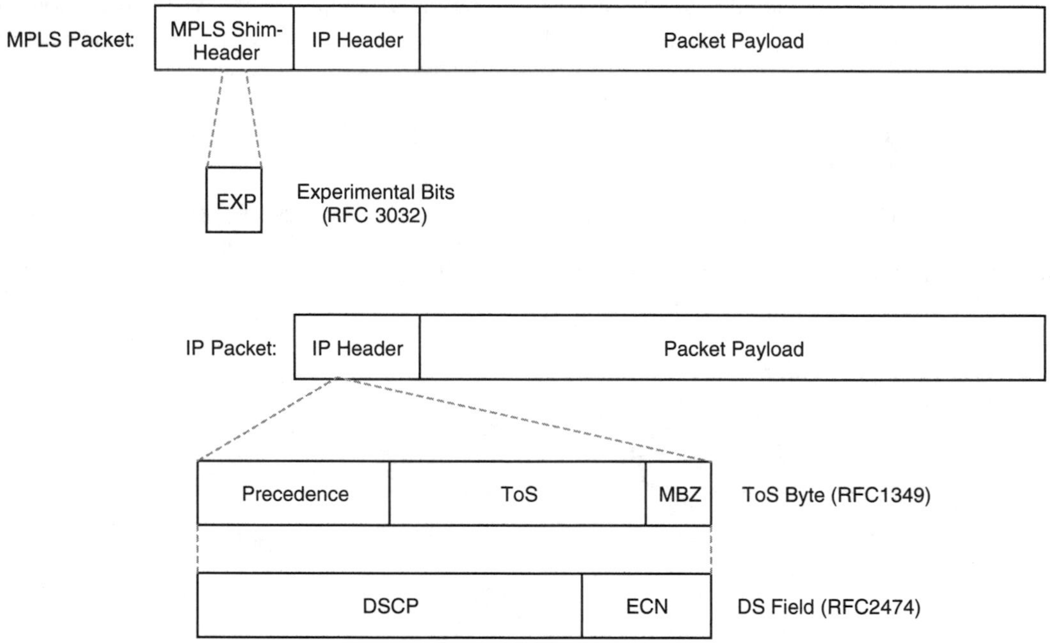

The fields of the ToS byte are defined in RFC1349 as follows:

- **Precedence**—This 3-bit field defines the relative importance or priority of a packet.

- **ToS**—This 4-bit field describes how the network should make tradeoffs between throughput, delay, reliability, and cost.

- **MBZ**—This bit is unused and *must be zero*.

The use of the DS field has replaced that of the ToS byte in most networks. Its elements are described in RFCs 2474 and 3168 as follows:

- **DSCP (Differentiated Service Code Point)**—This 6-bit field defines the Per-Hop Behavior (PHB), an externally observable forwarding behavior (QoS treatment) applied by a network device to packets marked with certain DSCP values. There are four DiffServ PHBs:

  - **Best Effort (BE)**—Indicated when all 6 bits of the DSCP field are zero. No specific QoS treatment is specified for this PHB (it is best effort!).

  - **Class Selector (CS)**—Used for backward compatibility with IP Precedence. When using the CS PHB, the last (least-significant) 3 bits of the DSCP field are zero.

  - **Assured Forwarding (AF, RFC 2597)**—Specifies four queuing classes and three drop thresholds (likelihoods of packets being dropped). When using AF, the first (most-significant) 3 bits of the DSCP field indicate the queuing class (which can be 1 to 4), and the next 2 bits indicate the drop threshold (which can be 1 to 3). AF PHB names are written in the format AF*xy*, where *x* is the queuing class, and *y* is the drop threshold.

— **Expedited Forwarding (EF, RFC 3246)**—Specifies a single low-delay, -jitter, and-packet-loss QoS treatment with a certain bandwidth guarantee. This is typically used to ensure QoS for voice traffic.

- **ECN (Explicit Congestion Notification)**—This 2-bit field defines a method by which network congestion can be communicated to hosts.

As described in RFC3270 (*Multi-Protocol Label Switching (MPLS) Support of Differentiated Services*), QoS markings can be indicated in two ways in an MPLS network:

- **Based on the value carried in the MPLS shim header EXP bits**—In this case, the corresponding LSPs are referred to as EXP-Inferred Per-Hop-Behavior Scheduling Class LSPs (E-LSP).

- **Based on the MPLS label value itself**—In this case, the corresponding LSPs are called Label-Only-Inferred Per-Hop-Behavior Scheduling Class LSPs (L-LSP). L-LSPs are, at present, only deployed in cell mode MPLS networks.

As previously mentioned, the backbone QoS design for service providers might also include mechanisms used to help ensure high service availability. MPLS traffic engineering (MPLS-TE), MPLS DiffServ-aware traffic engineering (MPLS DS-TE), and MPLS-TE fast reroute can be used to support service availability and transmission performance. MPLS-TE is beyond the scope of this book, but you can find more information in *Traffic Engineering with MPLS* (Cisco Press).

The sections that follow focus on the implementation of DiffServ QoS configuration in the MPLS backbone network.

MPLS DiffServ Tunneling Models

RFC3270 discusses two models for implementing DiffServ tunneling—the Pipe Model and the Uniform Model. These two tunneling models allow integration or separation of customer and service provider DiffServ domains. A DiffServ domain is a set of network devices that apply a consistent set of QoS treatments based on a common set of PHBs.

Pipe Model/Short Pipe Model

A Pipe Model architecture ensures that customer and service provider DiffServ domains are separate. Figure 5-42 shows an example of a Pipe Model architecture implemented in an MPLS backbone.

In Figure 5-42, the customer DiffServ domain comprises mjlnet_VPN sites 1 and 2; the service provider DiffServ domain comprises the devices in the MPLS backbone, including PE and P routers.

Figure 5-42   *MPLS DiffServ Pipe Model Ensures That Customer and Service Provider DiffServ Domains Are Separate*

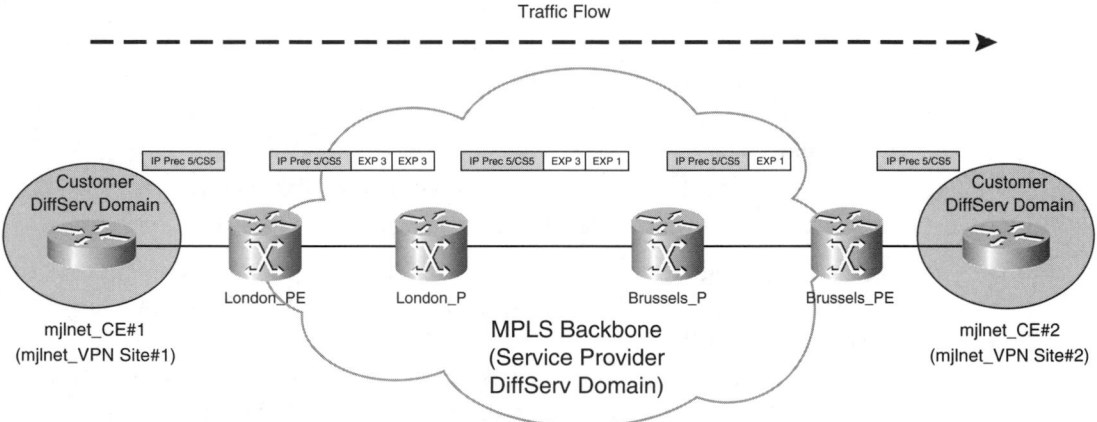

In the Pipe Model, when a customer packet arrives at ingress PE router London_PE from mjlnet_CE#1, the IP Precedence/DSCP marking in the IP header (in this example, IP Precedence 5/CS 5) is not copied to the MPLS EXP bits of the labels that are imposed on the packet (VPN and IGP labels). Instead, the PE router is configured to mark the MPLS EXP bits according to whatever QoS policy is configured in the service provider DiffServ domain, which in this example means that the packet is marked with MPLS EXP 3.

Next, London_PE forwards the packet to London_P, at which point, the MPLS EXP bits of the top (of stack) label are re-marked to 1 (this might be due to the amount of traffic arriving from London_PE exceeding a certain rate).

London_P then sends the packet to Brussels_P, which (being the penultimate hop) pops the IGP label, copies the MPLS EXP bit setting of the IGP label (1) to the VPN label, and forwards the packet Brussels_PE.

Finally, Brussels_PE removes the VPN label, and sends the unlabeled packet on to mjlnet_CE#2.

The key thing to notice here is that the IP Precedence/DSCP value of the unlabeled packet as it arrives at mjlnet_CE#2 (IP Precedence 5/CS5) is the same as that when the packet was sent from mjlnet_CE#1 to London_PE. So, irrespective of the marking (and any remarking of) MPLS EXP bit settings, the customer packet IP Precedence/DSCP value remains unchanged.

At this point, it is important to note that there are actually two varieties of Pipe Model architecture—the "standard" Pipe Model and the Short Pipe Model. The difference between these two models relates to the QoS forwarding treatment (queuing, shaping, and so on) on the egress interface of the egress PE router (the PE-CE interface). Figure 5-43 illustrates this difference.

Figure 5-43 *Pipe Model and Short Pipe Model*

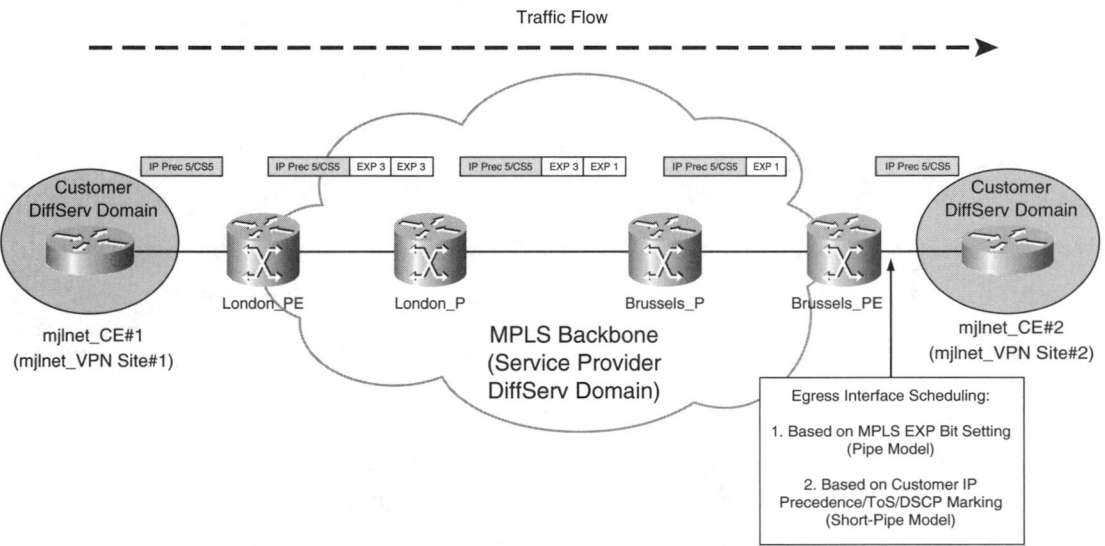

As shown in Figure 5-43, when using the Pipe Model, the QoS scheduling (queuing, shaping, and so on) on the egress interface (PE-CE interface) of the egress PE router is based on the MPLS EXP bit setting of the packet—in Figure 5-43, this would mean that the egress interface QoS forwarding treatment was based on an MPLS EXP bit setting of 1.

When using, the Short Pipe Model, on the other hand, the egress interface QoS forwarding treatment is based on the customer IP packet's IP Precedence/DSCP value, which in Figure 5-43 is IP Precedence 5 (CS5).

Uniform Model

When using the Uniform Model, customer QoS markings are reflected in the MPLS EXP bit settings of the labels imposed on customer packet by the ingress PE router, and the MPLS EXP bit settings are reflected in the IP Precedence of the customer IP packets by the egress PE router.

As illustrated in Figure 5-44, when using the Uniform Model, ingress PE router London_PE copies the IP Precedence of customer packets (5) to the MPLS EXP bits of the IGP and VPN labels that it imposes (MPLS EXP bit setting 5).

London_PE now forwards the packet to London_P which, in this example, re-marks the MPLS EXP bit settings of the IGP label to a value of 1 (from a value of 5). London_P then sends the packet onward to Brussels_P.

Figure 5-44 *Uniform Model*

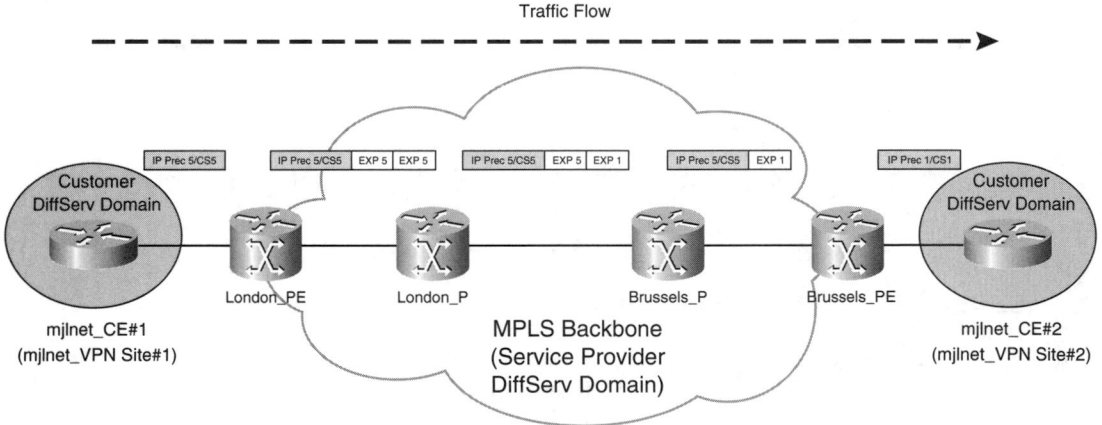

Brussels_P pops the IGP label, copies the MPLS EXP bit setting of the IGP label (1) to the VPN label, and then forwards the packet to Brussels_PE.

Finally, Brussels_PE removes the VPN label and copies the MPLS EXP bit setting (1) to the IP Precedence field of the customer packet. Brussels_PE then sends the packet to mjlnet_CE#2.

So, the crucial difference between Uniform and Pipe models is the behavior of the ingress and egress PE routers.

When using the Pipe Model (or Short Pipe Model), the ingress PE router does not copy the IP Precedence of customer packets that it receives from its connected CE router to the MPLS EXP bit settings of labels that it imposes on the packets, and the egress PE router does not copy the MPLS EXP bit setting to the IP Precedence of customer packets that it transmits to its connected CE router.

When using the Uniform Model, on the other hand, the ingress PE router copies the IP Precedence of the customer packets that it receives from its connected CE router to the MPLS EXP bit settings of labels that it imposes, and the egress PE router copies the MPLS EXP bit settings to the IP Precedence field of customer packets that it transmits to its connected CE router.

Configuring MPLS QoS on Cisco Routers

Now that you understand the DiffServ tunneling models that can be implemented in an MPLS network, it is time to move on to configuration. This section describes the configuration of MPLS DiffServ Pipe Model, Short Pipe Model, and Uniform Model architectures.

Implementing an MPLS DiffServ Pipe Model Architecture

Implementation of an MPLS DiffServ Pipe Model architecture consists of the configuration of PE routers and P routers.

The configuration of PE routers comprises the following steps:

Step 1   Configure and apply an edge policy to apply in an input direction to the PE router's interface connected to CE routers.

Step 2   Configure and apply a core policy to apply in an output direction to the PE router's core interfaces (connected to P or PE routers).

Example 5-39 shows the configuration of a sample edge policy.

Example 5-39 *Configuration of a Sample Edge Policy*

```
!
class-map match-any Edge-Control (line 1)
match ip dscp cs6
class-map match-any Edge-Voice (line 2)
match ip dscp ef
class-map match-any Edge-Streaming-Video (line 3)
match ip dscp af41
class-map match-any Edge-Priority-Apps (line 4)
match ip dscp af21 af22 af23 af31 af32 af33
class-map match-any Edge-Other-Apps (line 5)
match ip dscp af11 af12 af13
class-map match-any Edge-Default (line 6)
match ip dscp default
!
!
policy-map Edge-Policy-In (line 7)
  class Edge-Control (line 8)
   set mpls experimental imposition 3
  class Edge-Voice (line 9)
   set mpls experimental imposition 5
  class Edge-Streaming-Video (line 10)
   set mpls experimental imposition 4
  class Edge-Priority-Apps (line 11)
   set mpls experimental imposition 3
  class Edge-Other-Apps (line 12)
   set mpls experimental imposition 2
  class Edge-Default (line 13)
   set mpls experimental imposition 2
 !
 !
interface Serial1/0
ip vrf forwarding mjlnet_VPN
 ip address 172.16.10.1 255.255.255.0
 service-policy input Edge-Policy-In (line 14)
 !
```

In highlighted lines 1 to 6, six class maps are configured using the **class-map [match-all | match-any]** *class-map-name* command. The class maps are variously named Edge-Control, Edge-Voice, Edge-Streaming-Video, Edge-Priority-Apps, Edge-Other-Apps, and Edge-Default.

These class maps match traffic according to the DSCP setting in its IP header. So, for example, any traffic with a DSCP setting of Expedited Forwarding (EF) is matched by the Edge-Voice class map (highlighted line 2), and any traffic with a DSCP setting of Assured Forwarding 41 (AF41) is matched by the Edge-Streaming-Video class map (highlighted line 3).

Other class maps are used to match the following:

- **Edge-Control**—This matches (transit) traffic marked with Class Selector (CS)/IP Precedence 6.
- **Edge-Priority-Apps**—This matches traffic marked with DSCP code points AF21, AF22, AF23, AF31, AF32, and AF33.
- **Edge-Other-Apps**—This matches packets with DSCP settings AF11, AF12, and AF13.
- **Edge-Default**—This matches packets with DSCP setting default (000000).

Highlighted lines 7 to 13 show a policy map used to define QoS treatments for traffic matched by the class maps in highlighted lines 1 to 6.

The **policy-map** *policy-map-name* command (highlighted line 7) is used to configure a policy map called Edge-Policy-In that references the class maps using the **class** *class-map-name* command and defines QoS policy for traffic matched by the various class maps.

So, for example, the **class Edge-Voice** command (highlighted line 9) references the class map called Edge-Voice (highlighted line 2) and then sets the MPLS EXP bits for labels that are imposed on this traffic as it transmitted across the MPLS backbone to 5 using the **set mpls experimental imposition** *mpls-exp-value* command. There are three MPLS EXP bits, and so the valid bit settings (values) are 0 to 7.

NOTE   The **set mpls experimental imposition** command replaces the **set mpls experimental** command in Cisco IOS Software Release 12.2(13)T.

The policy map called Edge-Policy-In is also used to mark other packets as follows:

- **Edge-Control (highlighted line 8)**—The policy map marks packets matched by this class map with MPLS EXP bit setting 3.
- **Edge-Streaming-Video (highlighted line 10)**—Packets matched by this class map are marked with MPLS EXP bit setting 4.
- **Edge-Priority-Apps (highlighted line 11)**—Packets matched by this class map are marked with MPLS EXP bit setting 3.

- **Edge-Other-Apps (highlighted line 12)**—Packets matched by this class map are marked with MPLS EXP bit setting 2.

- **Edge-Default (highlighted line 13)**—Packets matched by this class map are marked with MPLS EXP bit setting 2.

Having configured class maps and a policy map, the next step is to apply the policy map to the PE-CE interface.

The policy map called Edge-Policy-In is applied in an input direction on the PE-CE interface Serial 1/0 using the **service-policy** [**input | output**] *policy-map-name* command. This means that policy map Edge-Policy-In will be applied to any traffic received on the interface from the connected CE router.

It is worth noting that Edge-Policy-In simply classifies customer packets according to their DSCP markings (DSCP). This type of input PE-CE interface QoS policy is very trusting (DSCP values are trusted) and therefore would typically be seen if the service provider is also managing the CE routers. If the service provider is not managing the CE routers, more sophisticated classification and/or policing of customer traffic would typically be required on the PE router (based on IP addresses, TCP/UDP ports and so on). Some service providers also choose to police customer traffic received from CE routers, and then set the MPLS EXP bits for traffic according to whether the traffic has conformed to or exceeded a specified rate (using the **police** *bps* [*burst-normal*] [*burst-max*] **conform-action set-mpls-experimental-imposition-transmit** *value* **exceed-action set-mpls-experimental-imposition-transmit** *value* [**violate-action** *action*]).

So, QoS policy for traffic received by the ingress PE router on the PE-CE interface is now taken care of. But, it is also important to configure QoS policy on the PE router's PE-P router interface.

Example 5-40 shows the configuration of a sample QoS policy for PE-P interfaces.

Example 5-40 *Configuration of a Sample QoS Policy for PE-P Interfaces*

```
!
class-map match-any Core-Control (line 1)
  match ip dscp cs6
  match mpls experimental topmost 6
class-map match-any Core-Voice (line 2)
  match mpls experimental topmost 5
class-map match-any Core-Streaming-Video (line 3)
  match mpls experimental topmost 4
class-map match-any Core-Apps (line 4)
  match mpls experimental topmost 3
!
!
policy-map Core-Policy (line 5)
  class Core-Control (line 6)
   bandwidth percent 3
  class Core-Voice (line 7)
   priority percent 25
  class Core-Video (line 8)
   bandwidth percent 10
```

continues

Example 5-40 *Configuration of a Sample QoS Policy for PE-P Interfaces (Continued)*

```
  class Core-Apps (line 9)
   bandwidth percent 25
   random-detect
  class class-default (line 10)
   bandwidth percent 37
   random-detect
 !
 interface FastEthernet2/0
  ip address 10.10.10.1 255.255.255.0
  max-reserved-bandwidth 100 (line 11)
  service-policy output Core-Policy (line 12)
 !
```

Highlighted lines 1 to 4 in Example 5-40 show the configuration of four class maps that explicitly match traffic with a variety of MPLS EXP bit settings as well as DSCP CS6.

For example, the Core-Voice class map (highlighted line 2) matches any traffic with MPLS EXP bit setting 5 in the topmost label in the label stack using the **match mpls experimental topmost** *mpls-exp-value* command. If you look back at Example 5-39 (highlighted line 9), you can see that the Edge-Policy-In policy map referenced class map Edge-Voice and set the MPLS EXP bits to 5 for customer traffic received on the PE-CE interface that matches this class map. So, class map Core-Voice will match labeled customer voice traffic.

Other class maps in Example 5-40 match traffic as follows:

- **Core-Control (highlighted line 1)**—Matches packets with DSCP setting CS6 (IP Precedence 6) or MPLS EXP bit setting 6.

  This class map matches control traffic such as BGP and LDP. Cisco routers mark control traffic using CS 6 (IP Precedence 6).

  It is worth mentioning that Cisco routers ensure that (most types of) locally generated control traffic is not dropped (or dropped last) by using an internal mechanism called PAK_PRIORITY. PAK_PRIORITY is a flag that specifies the importance of packets as they are queued within a router.

  You can find more information about PAK_PRIORITY at the following URL:

  http://www.cisco.com/warp/public/105/rtgupdates.html

- **Core-Streaming-Video (highlighted line 3)**—Matches labeled packets with MPLS EXP bit setting 4.

- **Core-Apps (highlighted line 4)**—Matches labeled packets MPLS EXP bit setting 3.

In highlighted lines 5 to 10 in Example 5-40, you can see the configuration of a policy map called Core-Policy. The policy map references the class maps configured in highlighted lines 1 to 4 and configures queuing, assigns link bandwidth, and specifies congestion avoidance.

In the case of the Core-Voice class (highlighted line 7), the **priority percent** *percentage* command is used to configure Low Latency Queuing (LLQ). LLQ provides a priority queue for Class-Based Weighted Fair Queuing (CBWFQ), and this priority queue ensures that delay-sensitive traffic (such as voice) is transmitted before other types of traffic in other queues. In this example, the **percent** keyword is used to specify that 25 percent of link bandwidth is allocated to traffic in the priority queue during periods of congestion.

Policy map Core-Policy also specifies the following policies:

- **Core-Control (highlighted line 6)**—This class map is referenced, and 3 percent of link bandwidth is assigned to this traffic type using the **bandwidth percent** *percentage* command.

- **Core-Video (highlighted line 8)**—10 percent of link bandwidth is assigned to traffic matched by this class map.

- **Core-Apps (highlighted line 9)**—25 percent of link bandwidth is assigned to traffic matched by this class map. Additionally, the **random-detect** command configures Weight Random Early Detection (WRED), a mechanism that provides congestion avoidance by selectively dropping packets during periods of congestion.

- **class-default (highlighted line 10)**—37 percent of link bandwidth is assigned and WRED is specified for this class.

In highlighted line 11 in Example 5-40, the **max-reserved-bandwidth** *percent* command configures the maximum bandwidth that can be reserved on interface FastEthernet 2/0 (a core interface connected to London_P) to 100 percent (the default is 75 percent).

Finally, the **service-policy output** *policy-map-name* command is used to apply the policy map called Core-Policy (configured in highlighted lines 5 to 10) to the interface. Note that because the policy map called Core-Policy assigns a total 100 percent of link bandwidth, it is essential to configure the **max-reserved-bandwidth 100** command; otherwise, it is not possible to apply the policy to the interface.

So far, so good. The configuration in Example 5-39 classifies and marks customer traffic received by PE routers from the connected CE router. And, the configuration in Example 5-40 matches and specifies queuing treatment/bandwidth assignments/congestion avoidance for the (labeled) customer traffic as it is sent from the PE routers to P routers.

Now it is time to consider what QoS policy is required on the P routers. In fact, the configuration shown in Example 5-40 can also be applied to P router interfaces (again in an output direction). This configuration ensures consistent QoS treatment for customer traffic as it crosses the links between PE and P routers.

The only element of the Pipe Model architecture that remains is the configuration of the PE router to ensure that QoS treatment on PE-CE interfaces for packets sent to connected CE routers is based on MPLS EXP bit settings (rather than the underlying customer packet DSCP values/IP Precedence).

Example 5-41 and Example 5-42 provide a sample configuration (in two parts) to ensure that QoS treatment on PE-CE interfaces for packets sent to connected CE routers is based on MPLS EXP bit settings.

Example 5-41 *Configuration of a Sample QoS Policy on the Egress PE Router (Part 1)*

```
!
class-map match-any EXP5 (line 1)
  match mpls experimental topmost 5
class-map match-any EXP4 (line 2)
  match mpls experimental topmost 4
class-map match-any EXP3 (line 3)
  match mpls experimental topmost 3
class-map match-any EXP2 (line 4)
  match mpls experimental topmost 2
!
!
policy-map Set-QoS-Group (line 5)
  class EXP5 (line 6)
   set qos-group 5
  class EXP4 (line 7)
   set qos-group 4
  class EXP3 (line 8)
   set qos-group 3
  class EXP2 (line 9)
   set qos-group 2
!
interface FastEthernet2/0
ip address 10.10.10.1 255.255.255.0
 service policy input Set-QoS-Group (line 10)
!
```

The class maps in highlighted lines 1 to 4 (EXP1, EXP2, EXP3, and EXP4) match MPLS EXP bit settings 1 to 4.

The policy map configured in highlighted lines 5 to 9 (Set-QoS-Group) references the class maps configured in highlighted lines 1 to 4 and sets the QoS group value to the same value as the MPLS EXP bit setting (QoS group 5 is set for packets whose MPLS EXP bit setting is 5, and so on).

The QoS group is a Cisco router internal placeholder used here to temporarily store the MPLS EXP bit setting of packets that arrive at the PE router from P routers. This placeholder is necessary because the MPLS EXP bit settings are lost when MPLS labels are removed after the packets are received on the PE-P interface—remember that the output QoS treatment on the PE-CE interface must correspond to the MPLS EXP bit setting in a Pipe Model architecture, so it is essential not to lose these values.

Finally, the policy map is applied in an input direction to the core interface (connected to a P router) in highlighted line 10.

NOTE	When you want every MPLS EXP bit setting to be written to a corresponding QoS group value (MPLS EXP 5 = QoS group 5, MPLS EXP 4 = Qos group 4, and so on) it is possible to achieve this more efficiently using the **set qos-group mpls exp topmost** command (under class class-default in a policy map).

Example 5-42 shows the second half of the configuration necessary to ensure the output QoS treatment on the PE-CE interface corresponds to the packets' MPLS EXP bit settings.

Example 5-42 *Configuration of a Sample QoS Policy on the Egress PE Router (Part 2)*

```
!
class-map match-any QoSGroup5 (line 1)
   match qos-group 5
class-map match-any QoSGroup4 (line 2)
   match qos-group 4
class-map match-any QoSGroup3 (line 3)
   match qos-group 3
class-map match-any QoSGroup2 (line 4)
   match qos-group 2
 !
 !
policy-map Edge-Policy-Out (line 5)
   class QoSGroup5 (line 6)
    priority percent 25
   class QoSGroup4 (line 7)
    bandwidth percent 10
   class QoSGroup3 (line 8)
    bandwidth percent 25
    random-detect
   class class-default (line 9)
    bandwidth percent 37
    random-detect
 !
interface Serial1/0
ip vrf forwarding mjlnet_VPN
 ip address 172.16.10.1 255.255.255.0
 max-reserved-bandwidth 100 (line 10)
 service-policy output Edge-Policy-Out (line 11)
 !
```

Highlighted lines 1 to 4 show the configuration of 4 class maps that match the QoS groups set by the Set-QoS-Group policy map configured previously in Example 5-41 (highlighted lines 5 to 9).

A policy map called Edge-Policy-Out is then configured in highlighted lines 5 to 9. This policy map references the class maps configured in highlighted lines 1 to 4 and specifies bandwidth assignments and congestion avoidance (WRED) for traffic corresponding to the various classes. So, for example, traffic with QoS group value 5 (MPLS EXP bit setting 5) is allocated 25 percent of link bandwidth, and traffic with QoS group 4 (MPLS EXP 4) is allocated 10 percent of link bandwidth.

The **max-reserved-bandwidth 100** command is used to allow the reservation of 100 percent of link bandwidth, and the policy map is applied in an output direction to the PE-CE interface in highlighted lines 11 and 12, respectively.

The important concept to understand from the configuration in Examples 5-41 and 5-42 is how to preserve the MPLS EXP bit settings of packets using QoS groups. Notice that for the sake of simplicity (and focus on MPLS EXP to QoS group mapping), policy map Edge-Policy-Out uses exactly the same QoS treatments as specified in policy map Core-Policy back in Example 5-40. In certain cases (such as on slower Frame Relay access connections), the QoS treatment applied to packets sent by the PE router to a connected CE router might, for example, involve traffic shaping and/or link fragmentation and interleave (LFI).

Figure 5-45 shows the application of the QoS policies shown in Examples 5-39 to 5-42 to PE and P routers.

Figure 5-45 *Application of QoS Policies to PE and P Routers for Pipe Model Architecture*

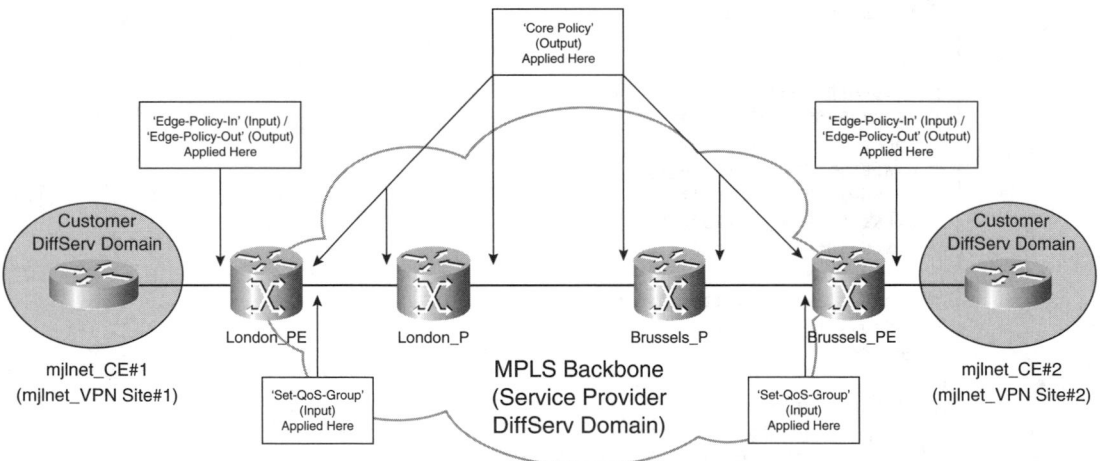

NOTE	More information on generic QoS configuration such as traffic shaping and LFI can be found in books such as *IP Quality of Service* (by Cisco Press).

Implementing an MPLS DiffServ Short Pipe Model Architecture

Now that you understand the configuration of a Pipe Model architecture, you'll find that the implementation of a Short Pipe Model architecture is pretty simple.

You will remember that the only difference between a Short Pipe Model architecture and a Pipe Model architecture is the output QoS treatment on the PE-CE interface of the PE routers (the QoS treatment is based on the IP Precedence/DSCP markings of the customer packets rather than the MPLS EXP bit settings [see Figure 5-43]).

The only difference from a configuration perspective, therefore, is that you do not need the Set-QoS-Group input policy (which preserves the MPLS EXP bit settings), and the Edge-Policy-Out policy map should be configured to match customer packet IP Precedence/ DSCP markings rather QoS groups. Other QoS policies described in the previous section still apply.

Example 5-43 shows the configuration of Edge-Policy-Out so that it matches IP Precedence/DSCP markings of customer packets rather than QoS groups.

Example 5-43 *Configuration of Edge-Policy-Out*

```
!
class-map match-any Edge-Control (line 1)
match ip dscp cs6
class-map match-any Edge-Voice (line 2)
match ip dscp ef
class-map match-any Edge-Streaming-Video (line 3)
match ip dscp af41
class-map match-any Edge-Priority-Apps (line 4)
match ip dscp af21 af22 af23 af31 af32 af33
class-map match-any Edge-Other-Apps (line 5)
match ip dscp af11 af12 af13
class-map match-any Edge-Default (line 6)
match ip dscp default
!
!
policy-map Edge-Policy-Out (line 7)
  class Edge-Control (line 8)
    priority percent 3
  class Edge-Voice (line 9)
    bandwidth percent 25
  class Edge-Streaming-Video (line 10)
    bandwidth percent 10
  class Edge-Priority-Apps (line 11)
    bandwidth percent 15
    random-detect dscp-based
  class Edge-Other-Apps (line 12)
    bandwidth percent 10
    random-detect dscp-based
  class class-default (line 13)
    bandwidth percent 37
    random-detect dscp-based
!
interface Serial1/0
ip vrf forwarding mjlnet_VPN
 ip address 172.16.10.1 255.255.255.0
 max-reserved-bandwidth 100 (line 14)
 service-policy output Edge-Policy-Out (line 15)
!
```

Class maps matching customer packet IP Precedence/DSCP markings are shown in highlighted lines 1 to 6. You will notice that these class maps are actually the same as those shown in Example 5-39.

The Edge-Policy-Out policy map is then configured from highlighted line 7 to 13. The policy map references the class maps configured in highlighted lines 1 to 6, and specifies queuing, assigns bandwidths, and configures congestion avoidance (WRED).

Notice that the **dscp-based** keyword has been added to the **random-detect** command (which configures WRED) in this example. The effect of the **dscp-based** keyword is to allow WRED to take into account AF drop precedences when selectively dropping packets. So, packets with a drop precedence of 3 (AFx3) would be dropped earlier than packets within the same class with a drop precedence of 2 (AFx2), and packets with a drop precedence of 2 would be dropped earlier than packets within the same class with a drop precedence of 1 (AFx1).

Figure 5-46 shows the application of Short Pipe Model QoS policies to PE and P routers.

Figure 5-46 *Application of Short Pipe Model QoS Policies to PE and P Routers*

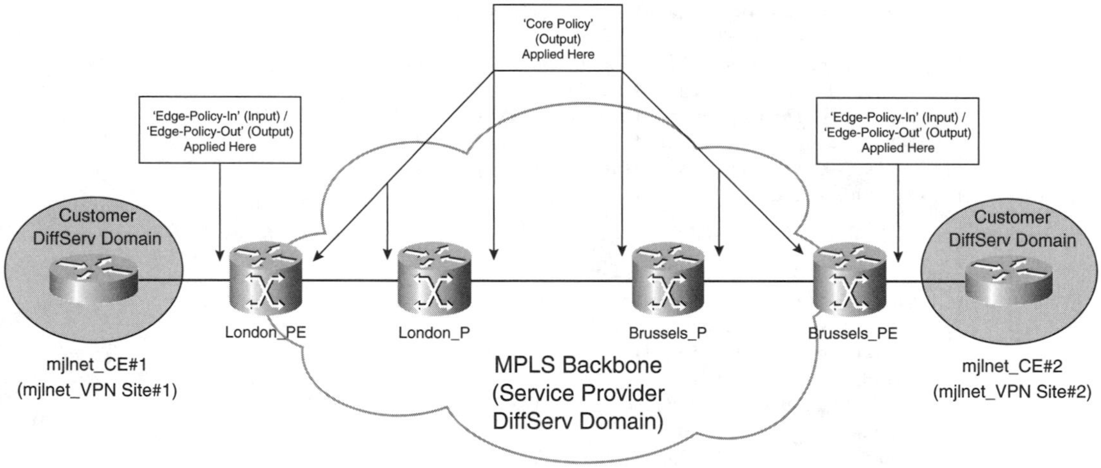

So, that is the Short Pipe Model. Now on to the Uniform Model.

Implementing an MPLS DiffServ Uniform Model Architecture

The configuration of a Uniform Model architecture differs from that of a Pipe or Short Pipe Model in the following ways:

- The IP Precedence/DSCP CS must be copied to the MPLS EXP bit setting at ingress PE routers.

- The MPLS EXP bit setting must be copied to the IP Precedence/DSCP CS at egress PE routers.

The copying of the IP Precedence/DSCP CS to the MPLS EXP bits on ingress PE routers is actually simple because this is the default behavior for Cisco routers (no explicit configuration is required).

Example 5-44 shows a sample configuration used to copy the MPLS EXP bit setting to the IP Precedence/DSCP CS field of customer packets on the (egress) PE router.

Example 5-44 *Sample Configuration to Copy MPLS EXP Bit Setting to IP Precedence/DSCP CS Field of Customer Packets on the (Egress) PE Router*

```
!
policy-map Set-QoS-Group (line 1)
  class class-default (line 2)
    set qos-group mpls exp topmost
!
policy-map Set-IP-Prec (line 3)
  class class-default (line 4)
    set precedence qos-group
!
!
interface FastEthernet2/0
ip address 10.10.10.1 255.255.255.0
 service policy input Set-QoS-Group (line 5)
!
!
interface Serial1/0
ip vrf forwarding mjlnet_VPN
 ip address 172.16.10.1 255.255.255.0
service-policy output Set-IP-Prec (line 6)
!
```

Highlighted lines 1 and 2 show the creation of a policy map called Set-QoS-Group. The purpose of this policy is to match all traffic and set the QoS group for each packet to the same value as the MPLS EXP bit setting of that packet (achieved using the **set qos-group mpls exp topmost** command). So, a packet that is received with MPLS EXP bit setting 5 will have its QoS group set to 5.

Another policy map called Set-IP-Prec is configured in highlighted lines 3 and 4. This policy again matches all traffic and sets the IP Precedence/DSCP CS of the packet to be the same as the corresponding QoS group (achieved using the **set precedence qos-group** command).

In highlighted lines 5 and 6, the Set-QoS-Group policy map is applied in an input direction to a core interface (connected to a P router), and the Set-IP-Prec policy map is applied in an output direction to a PE-CE interface (connected to a CE router).

The effect of the configuration in Example 5-44 is that the MPLS EXP of incoming labeled packets on the core interface is copied to QoS groups, and the QoS group values are then copied back to the IP Precedence of the corresponding unlabeled packets as they are transmitted on the PE-CE interface to the connected CE router.

Figure 5-47 shows the application of Uniform Model QoS policies to PE and P routers.

Figure 5-47 *Application of Uniform Model QoS Policies to PE and P Routers*

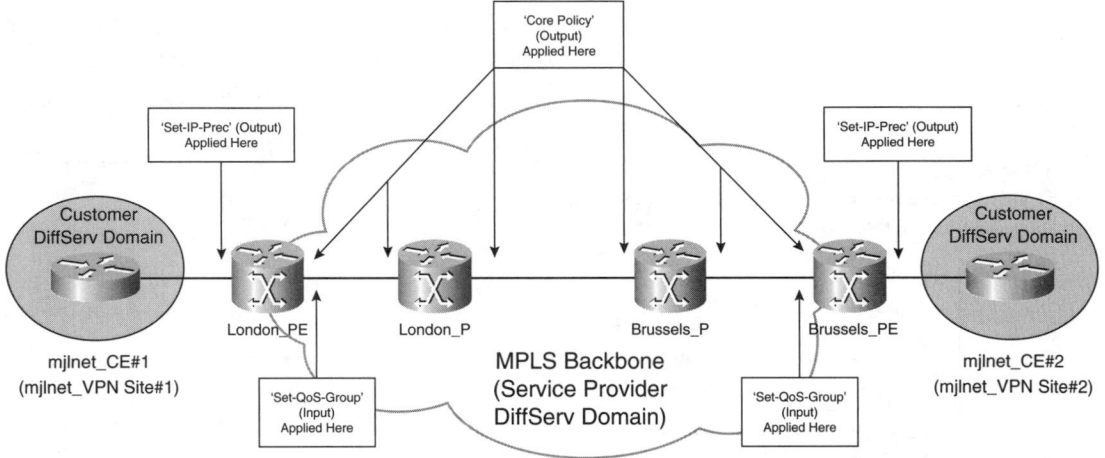

Supporting IPv6 Traffic Transport in MPLS Layer 3 VPNs Using 6VPE

So far in this book, it has been assumed that traffic transiting between customer MPLS Layer 3 VPN sites consists of IPv4 packets. But, what if customers (also) want to send IPv6 traffic between their VPN sites? In this case, an extension to the standard MPLS Layer 3 VPN model (RFC 4364/RFC2547bis) can be used to support customer IPv6 route exchange and traffic transport. This extension to the basic MPLS Layer 3 VPN model is called *6VPE*.

NOTE   6VPE should not be confused with another mechanism called 6PE. 6PE (IPv6 Provider Edge Router) does not support IPv6 route exchange and traffic transport between customer VPN sites. Instead, it offers global reachability between IPv6 domains via an IPv4/MPLS backbone network.

For more information on 6PE, refer to the following URL:

http://www.cisco.com/en/US/products/sw/iosswrel/ps1835/products_data_
sheet09186a008052edd3.html

Figure 5-48 illustrates 6VPE. In this figure, there are two IPv6-enabled VPN sites, mjlnet_VPN sites 1 and 2. PE routers London_PE1 and Brussels_PE1 maintain IPv6 VRFs corresponding to mjlnet_VPN sites 1 and 2.

Figure 5-48 *6VPE*

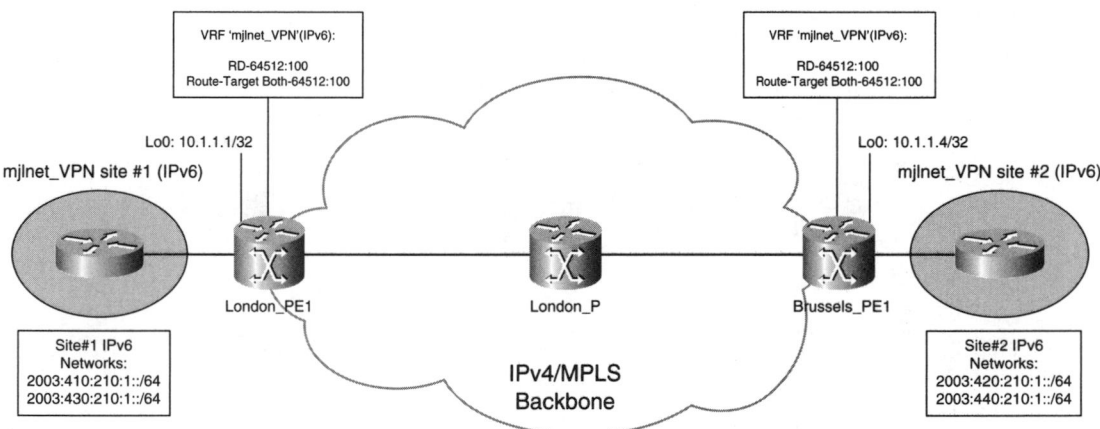

6VPE does not require the deployment of IPv6 in the service provider backbone network. IPv6 routes are exchanged between CE and PE routers and between PE routers (using a new VPN-IPv6 address family with MP-BGP [AFI=2, SAFI=128]). P routers, however, do not need to be IPv6 enabled, and this fact enables service providers to smoothly introduce IPv6 MPLS Layer 3 VPNs without too much disruption.

To understand 6VPE more fully, it is necessary to examine how routes are exchanged and how packets are forwarded. These elements of 6VPE are described in the following two sections.

6VPE Route Exchange

As previously mentioned, 6VPE introduces a new VPN-IPv6 address family that is similar to the VPN-IPv4 address family used with IPv4 MPLS Layer 3 VPNs.

As with IPv4 MPLS Layer 3 VPNs, in IPv6 MPLS Layer 3 VPNs, the PE and CE router exchange IPv6 routes using regular IPv6-capable routing protocols (BGP, OSPFv3, RIPng, IS-IS) or can alternatively use static routes. PE routers redistribute customer IPv6 routes into MP-BGP and advertise these routes via MP-BGP to their peer 6VPE PE routers. Customer routes are stored in the normal way in VRFs on PE routers.

The BGP routing updates used to advertise customer IPv6 routes between PE routers indicate the VPN-IPv6 address family and include and RD, route target(s), a VPN label, and a next hop (per prefix).

The next hop of the customer IPv6 routes as they are advertised between PE routers is this:

    ::FFFF:<IPv4_address [update_source]>.

Figure 5-49 depicts route exchange with 6VPE.

Figure 5-49 *Route Exchange with 6VPE*

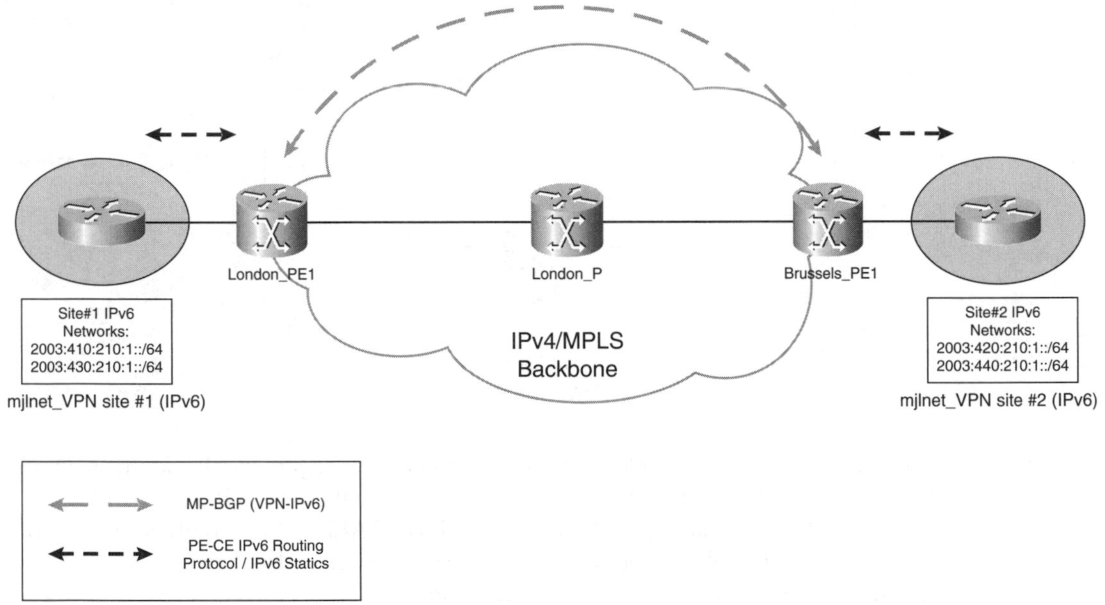

As shown in Figure 5-49, London_PE1 and Brussels_PE1 exchange IPv6 routes with the CE routers at mjlnet_VPN site 1 and 2, respectively, using a PE-CE IPv6 routing protocol. Alternatively, IPv6 static routes can be used. London_PE1 and Brussels_PE1 redistribute the IPv6 routes received from their connected CE routers (or IPv6 static routes) into MP-BGP, and then exchange these routes over the MPLS backbone network.

When a PE router receives customer IPv6 routes advertised in MP-BGP by another PE router, it extracts the IPv4 address from the next hop and looks for this address in the global IPv4 routing table. This address is the update source of the PE router that advertised the routes, and after the PE router that received the routes has found the address in the routing table, it attempts to find a corresponding IGP label (and LSP) to this address. If both a route to the IPv4 address/update source (and metric) and an IGP label are found, the customer IPv6 routes are inserted into the customer IPv6 VRF.

6VPE Data Packet Forwarding

When an ingress PE router receives an IPv6 data packet from a CE router, it does a lookup in the IPv6 VRF associated with the PE-CE router interface, and assuming that it finds a valid route, prepends the appropriate VPN label and IGP label onto the IPv6 data packet and forwards it over the MPLS backbone to the egress PE router. The IGP label is, as usual, used to transport the data packet to the egress PE router, and the VPN label is used by the egress PE router to associate the data packet with the appropriate IPv6 VRF. The egress PE router removes the VPN label and forwards the unlabeled IPv6 packet to the connected CE router.

Figure 5-50 shows IPv6 data packet forwarding with 6VPE.

Figure 5-50 *IPv6 Data Packet Forwarding with 6VPE*

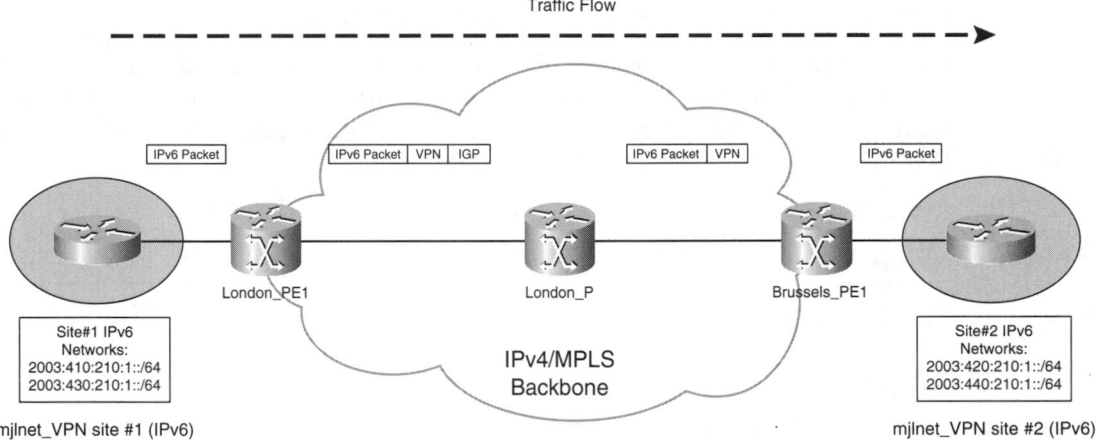

The CE router at mjlnet_VPN site 1 forwards an IPv6 packet to London_PE1. London_PE1 then encapsulates this packet using a VPN label and an IGP label and transmits the labeled packet to London_P. London_P, being the penultimate hop, pops the IGP label and forwards the packet to Brussels_PE1 (the VPN label is unchanged). Finally, Brussels_PE1 removes the VPN label and forwards the IPv6 packet to mjlnet_VPN site 2.

Configuring and Verifying 6VPE

If you have a reasonable understanding of the configuration MPLS Layer 3 VPNs for IPv4 (you should by now!), you will find the configuration of 6VPE straightforward.

The configuration steps for 6VPE on PE routers are as follows:

Step 1 Enable IPv6 routing and IPv6 CEF.

Step 2 Configure MP-BGP for VPN-IPv6/VPN-IPv4 route exchange with other PE routers or route reflectors.

Step 3 Configure the customer IPv6 VRFs.

Step 4 Configure the customer VRF interfaces.

Step 5 Configure the customer VRF (PE-CE) IPv6 routing protocols or static IPv6 routes.

Step 6 Redistribute the CE-PE routing protocol or static VRF routes into MP-BGP (and vice-versa, as appropriate).

Note that it is assumed that a loopback interface has already been configured for use as the PE router's BGP router ID/LDP router ID, that LDP is already configured, that MPLS is already enabled on interfaces connected to other PE or P routers, and that the backbone IGP is already configured. More information on these tasks is contained in the section "Configuration of PE Routers" in Chapter 4. It is also assumed that P routers are already configured as described in the section "Configuration of P Routers," also in Chapter 4 (remember that IPv6 does not need to be enabled on P routers).

Before taking a look at a configuration example, it is worth noting that 6VPE can be configured on PE routers that are also configured for IPv4 MPLS Layer 3 VPNs. And, as you will see, it is even possible to configure VRF interfaces to support both IPv4 and IPv6 (VRF interfaces can be IPv4 only, IPv6 only, or IPv4/IPv6).

Example 5-45 shows a sample 6VPE configuration for two (peer) PE routers.

Example 5-45 *Sample 6VPE Configuration for Two (Peer) PE Routers*

```
!
hostname London_PE1 (line 1)
!
ip cef
ipv6 unicast-routing (line 2)
ipv6 cef (line 3)
!
!
vrf definition mjlnet_VPN (line 4)
 rd 64512:100
 route-target export 64512:100
 route-target import 64512:100
 !
 address-family ipv4
 exit-address-family
 !
 address-family ipv6
 exit-address-family
 !
 !
 !
mpls ldp router-id Loopback0 force
mpls label protocol ldp
 !
 !
interface Loopback0
 ip address 10.1.1.1 255.255.255.255
 !
 !
interface Serial2/0 (line 5)
 description Customer VRF interface
 vrf forwarding mjlnet_VPN
 ip address 172.16.4.1 255.255.255.0
 ipv6 address 2003:410:210:1::/64 eui-64
 !
interface Serial2/3
 description backbone interface
```

Example 5-45 *Sample 6VPE Configuration for Two (Peer) PE Routers (Continued)*

```
 ip address 10.20.10.1 255.255.255.0
 ip router isis
 mpls ip
 !
 !
 ! Core IGP configuration (line 6)
 !
 router isis
  net 49.0001.0000.0000.0001.00
  is-type level-2-only
  metric-style wide
  passive-interface Loopback0
 !
 !
 ! PE-CE IPv4 routing protocol configuration (line 7)
 !
 router rip
  version 2
  !
  address-family ipv4 vrf mjlnet_VPN
  redistribute bgp 64512 metric transparent
  network 172.16.0.0
  no auto-summary
  exit-address-family
 !
 !
 !
 router bgp 64512 (line 8)
  no synchronization
  neighbor 10.1.1.4 remote-as 64512
  neighbor 10.1.1.4 update-source Loopback0
  no auto-summary
  !
  address-family vpnv6 (line 9)
  neighbor 10.1.1.4 activate
  neighbor 10.1.1.4 send-community both
  exit-address-family
  !
  address-family vpnv4 (line 10)
  neighbor 10.1.1.4 activate
  neighbor 10.1.1.4 send-community both
  exit-address-family
  !
 !
  address-family ipv4 vrf mjlnet_VPN (line 11)
  redistribute connected
  redistribute rip
  no auto-summary
  no synchronization
  exit-address-family
  !
  address-family ipv6 vrf mjlnet_VPN (line 12)
```

continues

Example 5-45 *Sample 6VPE Configuration for Two (Peer) PE Routers (Continued)*

```
 redistribute connected
 redistribute static
 no synchronization
 exit-address-family
!
!
!
! IPv6 static route for PE-CE reachability
!
ipv6 route vrf mjlnet_VPN 2003:430:210:1::/64 Serial2/0 (line 13)
!
```
```
!
hostname Brussels_PE1 (line 14)
!
!
ip cef
ipv6 unicast-routing (line 15)
ipv6 cef (line 16)
!
!
vrf definition mjlnet_VPN (line 17)
 rd 64512:100
 route-target export 64512:100
 route-target import 64512:100
 !
 address-family ipv4
 exit-address-family
 !
 address-family ipv6
 exit-address-family
!
!
mpls ldp router-id Loopback0 force
mpls label protocol ldp
!
!
interface Loopback0
 ip address 10.1.1.4 255.255.255.255
!
!
interface Serial3/0
 description backbone interface
 ip address 10.20.30.2 255.255.255.0
 ip router isis
 mpls ip
!
!
!
interface Serial3/3 (line 18)
 description Customer VRF interface
 vrf forwarding mjlnet_VPN
 ip address 172.16.8.1 255.255.255.0
```

Example 5-45 *Sample 6VPE Configuration for Two (Peer) PE Routers (Continued)*

```
ipv6 address 2003:420:210:1::/64 eui-64
!
!
! Core IGP configuration (line 19)
!
router isis
 net 49.0001.0000.0000.0003.00
 is-type level-2-only
 metric-style wide
 passive-interface Loopback0
!
!
! PE-CE IPv4 routing protocol configuration (line 20)
!
router rip
 version 2
 !
 address-family ipv4 vrf mjlnet_VPN
 redistribute bgp 64512 metric transparent
 network 172.16.0.0
 no auto-summary
 exit-address-family
!
!
!
router bgp 64512
 no synchronization
 bgp log-neighbor-changes
 neighbor 10.1.1.1 remote-as 64512
 neighbor 10.1.1.1 update-source Loopback0
 no auto-summary
 !
 address-family vpnv6
 neighbor 10.1.1.1 activate
 neighbor 10.1.1.1 send-community both
 exit-address-family
 !
 address-family vpnv4
 neighbor 10.1.1.1 activate
 neighbor 10.1.1.1 send-community both
 exit-address-family
 !
!
 address-family ipv4 vrf mjlnet_VPN
 redistribute connected
 redistribute rip
 no auto-summary
 no synchronization
 exit-address-family
 !
 address-family ipv6 vrf mjlnet_VPN
 redistribute connected
 redistribute static
```

continues

Example 5-45 *Sample 6VPE Configuration for Two (Peer) PE Routers (Continued)*

```
 no synchronization
 exit-address-family
!
!
! IPv6 static route for PE-CE reachability
!
ipv6 route vrf mjlnet_VPN 2003:440:210:1::/64 Serial3/3 (line 21)
!
!
```

The configuration of PE router London_PE1 begins in highlighted line 1. The **ipv6 unicast-routing** and **ipv6 cef** commands in highlighted lines 2 and 3 are used to enable IP6 routing and enable CEF for IPv6, respectively.

Below highlighted line 4, you can see the configuration of an IPv4/IPv6 VRF. The **vrf definition** *vrf-name* command is used to configure a VRF, which in this case is called mjlnet_VPN.

Next, the RD and RTs are defined as usual using the **rd** and **route-target** commands.

The **address-family** [**ipv4** | **ipv6**] command is then used to specify whether this VRF will be an IPv6 or an IPv4/IPv6 VRF. In this example, because the **address-family** command is used to specify both IPv4 and IPv6, VRF mjlnet_VPN will be an IPv4/IPv6 VRF.

Note that if you want to use different RTs for IPv4 and IPv6, you should specify these within the appropriate address families rather than globally under the VRF definition.

A customer VRF interface is configured starting in highlighted line 5. Notice that both IPv4 and IPv6 addresses are applied to this interface, and that this interface is associated with the VRF created in highlighted line 4 (using the **vrf forwarding** *vrf-name* command).

Configuration of BGP begins in highlighted line 8, and below highlighted lines 9 and 10, MP-BGP is configured for VPN-IPv6 (VPNv6) and VPN-IPv4 (VPNv4) route exchange with peer PE router 10.1.1.4 (Brussels_PE1) using the **address-family** {**vpnv6** | **vpnv4**} and **neighbor** *ip-address* activate commands.

Below highlighted lines 11 and 12, IPv4 RIP (the VRF mjlnet_VPN IPv4 PE-CE routing protocol) and IPv6 static routes (used for VRF mjlnet_VPN IPv6 PE-to-customer site reachability) are redistributed into MP-BGP using the **redistribute** command under the VPN-IPv4 and VPN-IPv6 address families (**address-family** {**ipv4** | **ipv6**} **vrf** *vrf-name*). Notice that in this example, connected (VRF) interface addresses are also redistributed into MP-BGP.

Finally, in highlighted line 13, an IPv6 VRF static route (VRF mjlnet_VPN) is configured for PE router to customer site reachability using the **ipv6 route vrf** *vrf-name customer-site-ipv6-prefix* {*ipv6-next-hop* | *output-vrf-interface*}.

Note that if you want to use BGP for PE-CE IPv6 reachability, you should configure and activate the CE router as a BGP neighbor under the VPN-IPv6 address family (**address-family ipv6 vrf** *vrf-name,* **neighbor** *ce-ipv6-address* **remote-as** *as-number,* **neighbor** *ce-ipv6-address* **activate**).

The configuration of peer PE router Brussels_PE1 begins in highlighted line 14. Notice that the only real differences are the IP addresses (interfaces, BGP neighbors [10.1.1.1, London_PE1], routes) configured using the various commands—logically, the configuration is identical to that for London_PE1.

So, that's configuration.

You can use a number of commands to verify 6VPE, including **show ipv6 route vrf** *vrf-name,* **show bgp vpnv6 unicast vrf** *vrf-name,* **show bgp vpnv6 unicast vrf** *vrf-name* **labels,** and **show ipv6 cef vrf** *vrf-name.*

Example 5-46 shows the output of the **show ipv6 route vrf** *vrf-name* command on PE router London_PE1.

Example 5-46 **show ipv6 route vrf** *Command Output on PE Router London_PE1*

```
London_PE1#show ipv6 route vrf mjlnet_VPN
 IPv6 Routing Table - mjlnet_VPN - 6 entries
 Codes: C - Connected, L - Local, S - Static, U - Per-user Static route
        B - BGP, R - RIP, I1 - ISIS L1, I2 - ISIS L2
        IA - ISIS interarea, IS - ISIS summary
        O - OSPF Intra, OI - OSPF Inter, OE1 - OSPF ext 1, OE2 - OSPF ext 2
        ON1 - OSPF NSSA ext 1, ON2 - OSPF NSSA ext 2
 C   2003:410:210:1::/64 [0/0]
      via Serial2/0, directly connected
 L   2003:410:210:1:2D0:63FF:FE54:7000/128 [0/0]
      via Serial2/0, receive
 B   2003:420:210:1::/64 [200/0] (line 1)
      via 10.1.1.4%Default-IP-Routing-Table, indirectly connected
 S   2003:430:210:1::/64 [1/0] (line 2)
      via Serial2/0, directly connected
 B   2003:440:210:1::/64 [200/0] (line 3)
      via 10.1.1.4%Default-IP-Routing-Table, indirectly connected
 L   FF00::/8 [0/0]
      via Null0, receive
London_PE1#
```

Highlighted lines 1 and 3 show two routes to IPv6 networks at the mjlnet_VPN Brussels site. Notice that these two routes are BGP routes, and that the next hop of these routes is 10.1.1.4. 10.1.1.4 is the (IPv4) BGP update source on Brussels_PE1.

In highlighted line 2, notice that there is a static route to an IPv6 network at the connected mjlnet_VPN London site.

The **show bgp vpnv6 unicast vrf** *vrf-name* command supplies more information about the VPN-IPv6 routes (see Example 5-47).

Example 5-47 show bgp vpnv6 unicast vrf *Command Output*

```
London_PE1#show bgp vpnv6 unicast vrf mjlnet_VPN
BGP table version is 9, local router ID is 10.1.1.1
Status codes: s suppressed, d damped, h history, * valid, > best, i - internal,
              r RIB-failure, S Stale
Origin codes: i - IGP, e - EGP, ? - incomplete

   Network          Next Hop         Metric LocPrf Weight Path
Route Distinguisher: 64512:100 (default for vrf mjlnet_VPN)
*> 2003:410:210:1::/64
                    ::                       0         32768 ?
*>i2003:420:210:1::/64
                    ::FFFF:10.1.1.4          0    100     0 ? (line 1)
*> 2003:430:210:1::/64
                    ::                       0         32768 ?
*>i2003:440:210:1::/64
                    ::FFFF:10.1.1.4          0    100     0 ? (line 2)
London_PE1#
```

Highlighted lines 1 and 2 show the two VPN-IPv4 routes received from Brussels_PE1 for VRF mjlnet_VPN. Notice the format of the next hops of these routes (::FFFF:<IPv4_address [update_source]>).

As shown in Example 5-48, you can see the VPN labels associated with VPN-IPv6 routes using the **show bgp vpnv6 unicast vrf** *vrf-name* **labels** command.

Example 5-48 *Verifying VPN Labels Associated with VPN-IPv6 Routes*

```
London_PE1#show bgp vpnv6 unicast vrf mjlnet_VPN labels
   Network          Next Hop      In label/Out label
Route Distinguisher: 64512:100 (mjlnet_VPN)
   2003:410:210:1::/64
                    ::                  23/nolabel
   2003:420:210:1::/64
                    ::FFFF:10.1.1.4 nolabel/23
   2003:430:210:1::/64
                    ::                  24/nolabel
   2003:440:210:1::/64
                    ::FFFF:10.1.1.4 nolabel/24

London_PE1#
```

The VPN labels associated with VPN-IPv6 routes 2003:420:210::/64 and 2003:440:210 :1::/64 (advertised by Brussels_PE1 to London_PE1) are 23 and 24, respectively.

If you want to see the complete label stack that will be imposed on customer IPv6 data packets as they transit the MPLS backbone network between PE routers, you can use the **show ipv6 cef vrf** *vrf-name* command (see Example 5-49).

Example 5-49 *Verifying the Label Stack for 6VPE Data Packets*

```
London_PE1#show ipv6 cef vrf mjlnet_VPN
::/0
  no route
2003:410:210:1::/64
  attached to Serial2/0
2003:410:210:1:2D0:63FF:FE54:7000/128
  attached to Serial2/0, receive
2003:420:210:1::/64
  nexthop 10.20.10.2 Serial2/3 label 18 23 (line 1)
2003:430:210:1::/64
  attached to Serial2/0
2003:440:210:1::/64
  nexthop 10.20.10.2 Serial2/3 label 18 24 (line 2)
FF00::/8
  attached to Null0, receive
London_PE1#
```

Highlighted line 1 shows that the label stack imposed on customer IPv6 data packets by London_PE1 as they transit the MPLS backbone toward Brussels_PE1 and mjlnet_VPN site 2 network 2003:420:210:1::/64 consists of labels 18 (the IGP label) and 23 (the VPN label). The IGP label (18) corresponds to a route to 10.1.1.4 (Brussels_PE1's BGP update source).

Similarly, in highlighted line 2, you can see that the label stack imposed on customer IPv6 data packets destined for network 2003:440:210:1::/64 consists of labels 18 (the IGP label) and 24 (the VPN label).

Summary

This chapter examined the design and deployment of advanced MPLS Layer 3 VPN models such as CSC and inter-autonomous system architectures.

The CSC VPN architecture can be used to support customer service providers that want to take advantage of another service provider's MPLS backbone to connect their geographically dispersed sites. Customer service providers can, in turn, offer MPLS VPN service to their own customers.

The inter-autonomous system architecture, on the other hand, allows service providers to extend MPLS VPNs beyond a single autonomous system. If more than one service provider cooperates to provide MPLS VPNs over their autonomous systems, this architecture can be called an interprovider architecture.

MVPN, MPLS QoS, and 6VPE were also described in this chapter.

MVPN allows an MPLS VPN service provider to offer "native" IP multicast transport between customer VPN sites rather than having to provision a mesh of point-to-point GRE tunnels. For this reason, MVPN is considered to be a much more scalable solution for multicast transport.

The deployment of QoS for MPLS VPNs is becoming more and more important for service providers. MPLS DiffServ tunneling models offer the service provider the capability to either separate or integrate its own DiffServ domain with customer DiffServ domains. Pipe and Short Pipe DiffServ tunneling models ensure that service provider and customer DiffServ domains are separate. The Uniform DiffServ tunneling model allows the integration of service provider and customer DiffServ domains.

Finally, 6VPE allows service providers to offer IPv6 traffic transport between customer VPN sites. 6VPE closely conforms to the standard IPv4 MPLS Layer 3 VPN architecture and can be relatively easily deployed because it is not necessary to configure IPv6 on P routers.

Review Questions

1 In which type of MPLS Layer 3 VPN architecture does the backbone service provider offer an MPLS VPN service to customer service providers?

2 How are internal routes are advertised between CSC customer sites via the carriers' carrier backbone network?

3 How are label bindings advertised between CSC PE and CE routers?

4 How are external routes advertised in a CSC architecture?

5 What type of MPLS Layer 3 VPN network architecture is required if a customer VPN has some of its sites connected to one autonomous system but other sites connected to other autonomous systems?

6 What are the three methods of provisioning an inter-autonomous system MPLS VPN architecture?

7 Describe the label stack that is prepended to packets as they cross inter-autonomous system links in an inter-autonomous system MPLS VPN architecture when using VRF-to-VRF connectivity at ASBRs.

8 What is the effect of the **no bgp default route-target filter** command?

9 What are the two common methods of supporting IP multicast transport between customer sites in an MPLS Layer 3 VPNs?

10 What are the main advantages of using MVPN when compared to point-to-point GRE tunnels?

CHAPTER 6

Deploying Site-to-Site IPsec VPNs

IPsec provides security services to IP, and it has become an extremely popular way to provision site-to-site and remote access VPNs. In a site-to-site VPN, IPsec tunnels are built between an organization's sites, and all traffic is authenticated and/or encrypted as it passes over the intervening network.

Depending on connectivity requirements and other considerations, site-to-site IPsec VPNs can be deployed in full-mesh, partial-mesh, or hub-and-spoke architectures, as shown in Figure 6-1.

Figure 6-1   *Full-Mesh, Partial-Mesh, and Hub-and-Spoke IPsec VPN Architectures*

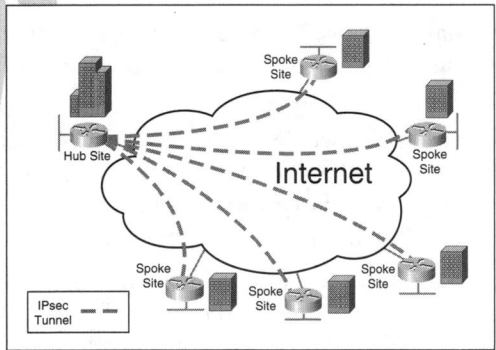

Hub-and-Spoke

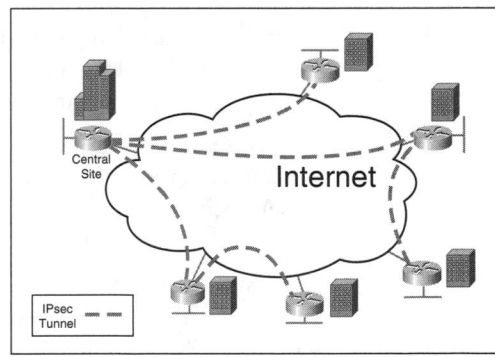

Partial-Mesh

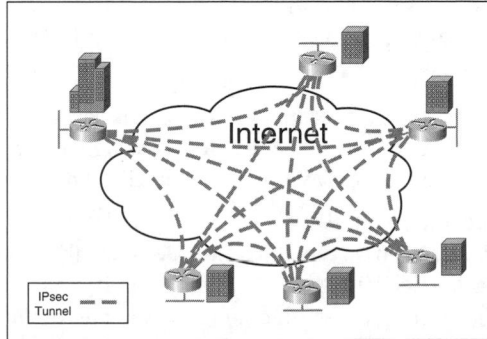

Full-Mesh

As illustrated in Figure 6-1, in a hub-and-spoke architecture, spoke (remote) sites are connected to a hub (central) site via IPsec tunnels. Spoke-to-spoke connectivity is provided via the hub site. In a partial-mesh architecture, not all remote sites have direct connectivity to the central site. Finally, in a full-mesh architecture, all sites have direct connectivity to each other.

When designing and deploying IPsec VPNs, it is essential to have a solid grasp of the underlying technology and configuration. This chapter introduces IPsec and discusses site-to-site VPN configuration.

Advantages and Disadvantages of IPsec Site-to-Site VPNs

Before deciding whether to deploy an IPsec site-to-site VPN, it is important to take a look at their advantages and disadvantages:

- IPsec VPNs (properly configured) permit highly secure (encrypted and authenticated) site-to-site connectivity.

- IPsec site-to-site VPNs can be deployed by an enterprise or offered as a managed service by a service provider.

- IPsec VPNs can be implemented over any IP-enabled backbone network, including the Internet. The fact that IPsec VPNs can be deployed over the Internet can also make their implementation attractive from a cost perspective.

- Enterprises that deploy and manage a site-to-site IPsec VPN will have complete control of their WAN routing. This is in contrast to a Multiprotocol Label Switching (MPLS) Layer 3 VPN, where Customer Edge (CE) routers must exchange routing information with Provider Edge (PE) routers (assuming dynamic routing is configured).

- IPsec site-to-site VPNs built using standard IPsec tunnels might be difficult to scale because an IPsec tunnel needs to be provisioned between each pair of IPsec VPN gateways. IPsec site-to-site VPNs using standard IPsec tunnels are particularly difficult to scale if full-mesh (any-to-any) connectivity is required.

  Although site-to-site VPNs using standard IPsec tunnels may be difficult to scale, technologies such as Dynamic Multipoint VPNs (DMVPN) allow much greater scalability.

- To make IPsec VPNs as secure as possible, it is necessary to use digital signature (digital certificate) authentication. The use of digital signature authentication mandates the deployment of a Public Key Infrastructure (PKI) that must be carefully managed.

- Dynamic routing in an IPsec site-to-site VPN (using standard point-to-point IPsec tunnel configuration) is typically more complex than that in an MPLS Layer 3 VPN—because each IPsec VPN gateway must be an IP routing peer of each other IPsec VPN gateway (assuming full-mesh connectivity), whereas in an MPLS Layer 3 VPN, each

CE router is an IP routing peer with directly connected PE routers and not every other CE router in the VPN. Note, however, that where meshed-connectivity is provided using Dynamic Multipoint VPN (DMVPN), spoke site routers become routing peers only with the hub site router(s) and not other spoke site routers.

- Currently, standard IPsec does not provide support for multiprotocol and IP multicast traffic. Support for multiprotocol and IP multicast traffic can be provisioned using Generic Routing Encapsulation (GRE) tunnels or (in the case of IP multicast) virtual tunnel interfaces (VTI).

- IPsec can impose high CPU overhead on VPN gateways (due to the processing necessary for packet encryption/decryption and authentication). High CPU overhead can be alleviated by using hardware accelerators (this is often a good idea in live deployments, especially on hub-site routers).

Having examined some of the main advantages and disadvantages of IPsec site-to-site VPNs, it is now time to discuss their underlying operation.

IPsec: A Security Architecture for IP

IPsec protects IPv4 and IPv6 traffic as it transits a network between end hosts or security gateways.

NOTE   In this book, the term *security gateway* or simply *gateway* refers to Cisco routers, PIX Firewalls, Adaptive Security Appliances (ASA), or VPN concentrators that provide IPsec security services to end hosts or other devices on internal networks as they communicate with end hosts or other devices on external networks.

The terms *IPsec peer* and *IPsec device* refer to IPsec-enabled end hosts or security gateways.

IPsec consists of a number of elements, including the following:

- Cryptographic algorithms
- Security protocols
- Security associations
- IPsec databases
- SA and key management techniques

These elements together provide the following security services to IP:

- **Access control**—IPsec can control access to resources such as an end host or networks behind a security gateway.

- **Connectionless integrity**—IPsec can detect modifications to IP packets regardless of the order in which they are sent or received. If an attacker modifies packets in transit between IPsec-enabled hosts or security gateways, these packets are dropped by the receiving host or security gateway.

- **Data origin authentication**—IPsec verifies that messages that are received were transmitted by a supposed sender and not by another source masquerading as the supposed sender. Packets sent by an attacker are dropped by IPsec-enabled hosts or security gateways.

  Note that connectionless integrity and data origin authentication are collectively known as *authentication*.

- **Replay protection**—Replay protection ensures that IPsec-enabled hosts or security gateways drop any duplicate IPsec packets that they receive.

- **Data confidentiality**—Data confidentiality hides data and prevents it from being disclosed to an attacker. IPsec uses encryption algorithms to provide data confidentiality.

- **Limited traffic flow confidentiality**—In some cases, even if an attacker is unable to determine the exact nature of protected data, he/she might still find information such as identities of communicating devices, the frequency of transmission, and even packet sizes useful. IPsec provides limited protection against an attacker being able to obtain this information.

Cryptographic Algorithms

IPsec relies on a number of cryptographic algorithms to authenticate and encrypt user packets, including the following:

- Authentication algorithms
- Encryption algorithms
- Public key cryptographic algorithms

The sections that follow discuss these algorithm types in greater detail.

Authentication Algorithms

In IPsec, a number of hash algorithms provide connectionless integrity and data origin authentication (authentication). These algorithms are discussed in this section.

Hash Algorithms

A hash algorithm is a type of cryptographic algorithm that takes a message of an *arbitrary length* as its input and produces a *fixed-length* output value that is characteristic of the message input and no other message. The output value produced by a hash algorithm is variously called a hash value, a fingerprint, or a message digest.

Two common hash algorithms are Message Digest 5 (MD5) and the Secure Hash Algorithm (SHA-1). MD5 produces a 128-bit hash, and SHA-1 produces a 160-bit hash.

As an example of the operation of a hash algorithm, the message "Comparing, Designing, and Deploying Virtual Private Networks by Mark Lewis" produces the output hash value (in hexadecimal) of 0x164727408b1e20f1c97b6952b1cb425c4ffa8864 using SHA-1, and the message "Troubleshooting Virtual Private Networks by Mark Lewis" produces the output hash value 0xecaae55ceff1d90ebff79def877796e033538f4a using SHA-1.

Cryptographic hash algorithms have two important characteristics:

- It should be computationally infeasible to find two different messages that produce the same output hash value.

  So, for example, it should be infeasible that you could find another message that would produce the hash value 0x164727408b1e20f1c97b6952b1cb425c4ffa8864 (the hash value produced by the input message "Comparing, Designing, and Deploying Virtual Private Networks by Mark Lewis") using the SHA-1 algorithm.

- It is not possible to reverse the hash algorithm to produce the original (input) message from the hash value. So, given only the hash value 0x164727408b1e20f1c97b6952b1 cb425c4ffa8864, it would not be possible to find out that the original message was "Comparing, Designing, and Deploying Virtual Private Networks by Mark Lewis."

NOTE   See the following URL if you would like to try out the MD5 and SHA-1 hash algorithms yourself:

http://block111.servehttp.com/hash

http://pajhome.org.uk/crypt/md5/

Now, because a hash algorithm provides a fingerprint of a message, you might think that if a host or security gateway simply sends a hash value along with a message this would be enough to ensure that an attacker would not be able to tamper with that message. But this is not the case. Figure 6-2 illustrates transmission of a message with its corresponding hash value.

To keep the following example as simple to follow as possible, hash values for the messages "Comparing, Designing, and Deploying Virtual Private Networks by Mark Lewis" and "Troubleshooting Virtual Private Networks by Mark Lewis" have been truncated to 16 bits (4 hexadecimal numerals).

In Figure 6-2, the London gateway transmits a message ("Comparing, Designing, and Deploying Virtual Private Networks by Mark Lewis") along with its corresponding (truncated) SHA-1 hash value, 0x1647.

If an attacker modifies the message to be "Troubleshooting Virtual Private Networks," the Paris gateway will detect this when it receives the message, as shown in Figure 6-3.

Figure 6-2 *"Authenticating" a Message with a Hash Value*

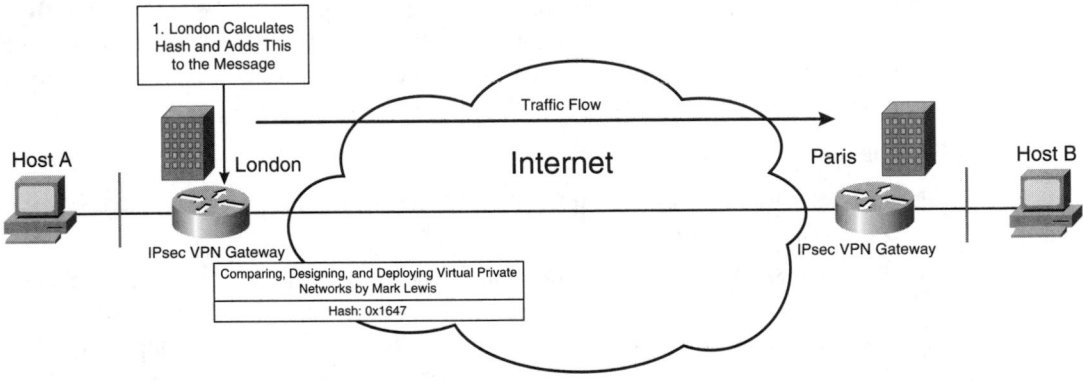

Figure 6-3 *An Attacker Modifies the Message*

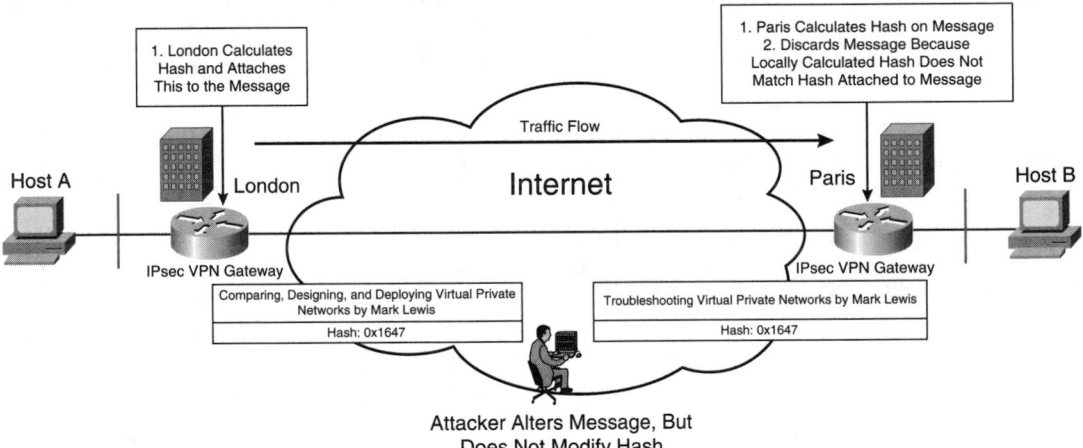

In Figure 6-3, the London gateway calculates a hash value for "Comparing, Designing, and Deploying Virtual Private Networks by Mark Lewis" (truncated to 0x1647) and attaches this hash value to the message before sending the message to the Paris gateway.

An attacker alters the message to "Troubleshooting Virtual Private Networks by Mark Lewis" as it transits the Internet to the Paris gateway. The Paris gateway then receives the message (now "Troubleshooting Virtual Private Networks by Mark Lewis") and calculates a hash value (truncated to 0xecaa). The locally calculated hash value (0xecaa) does not match the attached hash value (0x1647, which corresponds to the message "Comparing, Designing, and Deploying Virtual Private Networks by Mark Lewis"), and so the Paris gateway drops the message.

At this point, it might appear that a hash algorithm can prevent an attacker altering a message; however, unfortunately, that is not the case (see Figure 6-4).

Figure 6-4 *An Attacker Modifies the Message and the Hash Value*

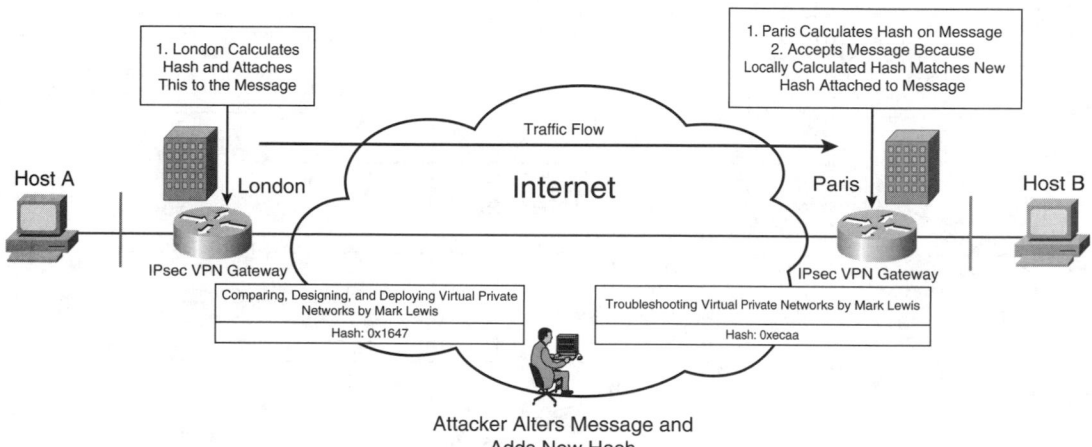

In Figure 6-4, the London gateway calculates a hash value for "Comparing, Designing, and Deploying Virtual Private Networks by Mark Lewis" (truncated to 0x1647), and attaches this hash value to the message. The London gateway then sends the message to the Paris gateway.

The attacker intercepts and alters the message (to "Troubleshooting Virtual Private Networks by Mark Lewis") *and* adds the new hash value 0xecaa (which corresponds to the message "Troubleshooting Virtual Private Networks by Mark Lewis").

Finally, the Paris gateway receives the message ("Troubleshooting Virtual Private Networks by Mark Lewis") and calculates a hash value (truncated to 0xecaa). The locally calculated hash value (0xecaa) matches the attached hash value (0xecaa), and so the Paris gateway accepts the message.

So, if the attacker alters the attached hash value at the same time as altering the message itself, the message will be accepted by the receiving gateway. Clearly, a simple hash value is not enough to protect a message from tampering.

Message Authentication Code (MAC) and Hashed Message Authentication Code (HMAC) Algorithms

As stated in the previous section, a simple hash value is not enough to ensure that a message is not tampered with in transit between IPsec-enabled hosts or security gateways.

What is needed is to add something else (apart from the message itself) as an input to the hash algorithm such that only the sending and receiving hosts or security gateways can correctly calculate and verify the hash value. This something is a *shared key*. If the attacker does not know the shared key, any attempt to modify the message or the hash or both will result in the receiving gateway discarding the message, as shown in Figure 6-5.

Figure 6-5 *An Attacker Modifies the Message and the Hash*

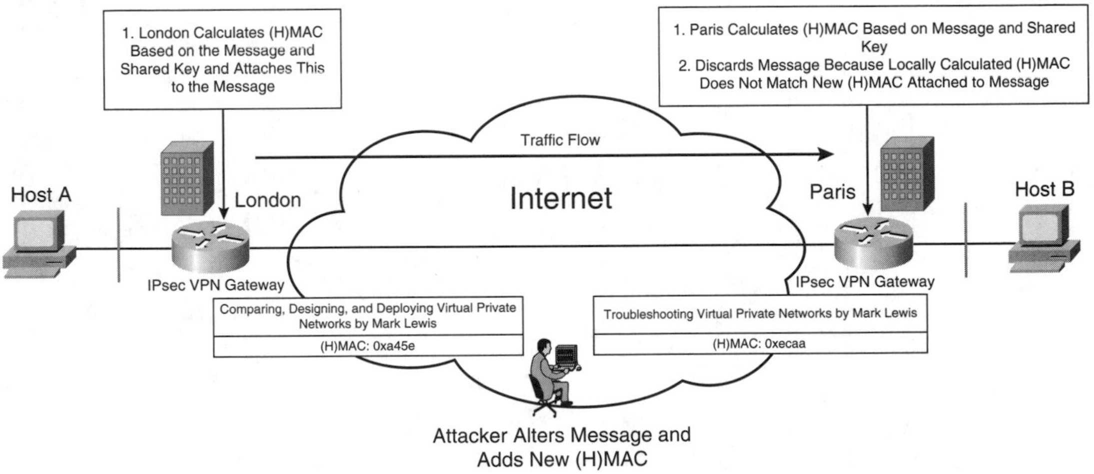

Notice in Figure 6-5 that the hash value calculated by the London gateway (0xa45e) no longer corresponds to the output of the regular SHA-1 hash algorithm. The output of regular SHA-1 for the "Comparing, Designing, and Deploying Virtual Private Networks by Mark Lewis" message is (when truncated to 16 bits) 0x1647. This difference in hash values (0xa45e and 0x1647) is due to the addition of a shared key as an input to the SHA-1 hash algorithm.

A hash algorithm that uses the message and a shared key as inputs is known as a Message Authentication Code (MAC) algorithm.

One further characteristic of a MAC (apart from ensuring that a message cannot been tampered with) is that a receiver can use it for data origin authentication (to verify that a specific sender did, indeed, send the message). The MAC can be used for data origin authentication because only the sender and receiver know the shared key and can correctly calculate MACs. If an attacker attempts to modify a MAC, the receiver will detect this attempt because the attacker does not possess the shared key.

However, that is not quite the end of the story. Regular MD5 and SHA-1 have been shown to be vulnerable to attack, and so IPsec uses a strengthened MAC algorithm called a *Hashed Message Authentication Code* (HMAC). Figure 6-6 illustrates an HMAC algorithm.

Two HMACs algorithms that are often used with IPsec are MD5-HMAC-96 and SHA-HMAC-96. Whereas regular MD5 produces a 128-bit output and SHA-1 produces a 160-bit output, MD5-HMAC-96 and SHA-HMAC-96 both produce a truncated output of 96 bits. One advantage of this truncation of output is that less information is available to an attacker, and so the attacker has less chance of being able to successfully crack the HMAC.

NOTE   MAC and HMAC algorithms are often referred to simply as *hash algorithms*.

Figure 6-6   *HMAC Algorithm*

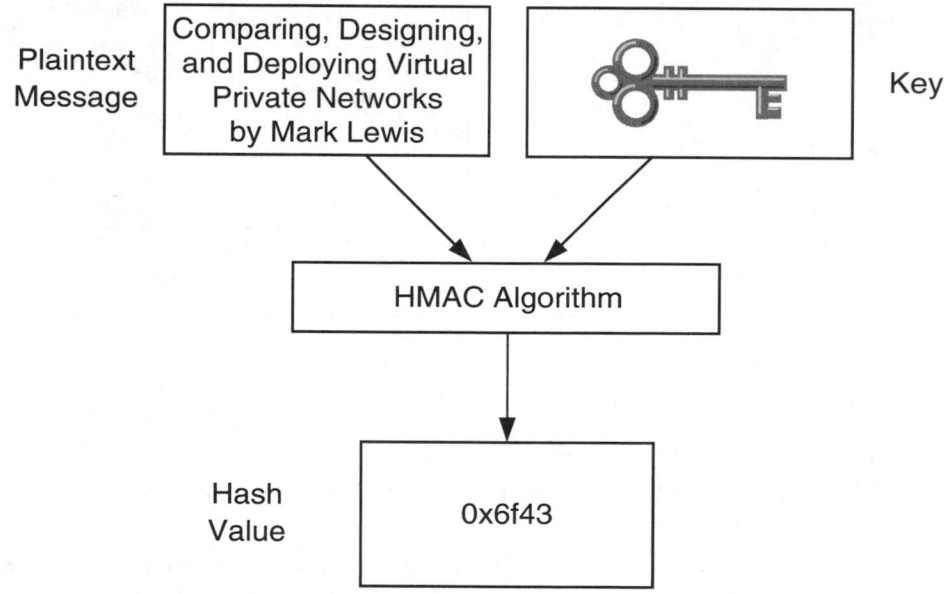

Encryption Algorithms

Encryption is a process by which data is rendered incomprehensible to anyone other than those allowed to view that data. Data in its unencrypted form is known as *plaintext* or *cleartext*. Data in its encrypted form is known as *ciphertext*.

The process of *encryption* changes a plaintext to a ciphertext; the process of changing the ciphertext back to its unencrypted plaintext form is known as *decryption*.

IPsec uses symmetric encryption algorithms for bulk encryption of data. Symmetric encryption algorithms use a key as an input (along with a plaintext) to produce a ciphertext. The *same* key is used as an input (with the ciphertext) to reproduce the plaintext. So, when one IPsec VPN gateway encrypts data with a certain key, another gateway will require that same key to decrypt the data.

Figure 6-7 illustrates encryption and decryption using a symmetric encryption algorithm.

Figure 6-7   *Encryption and Decryption Using a Symmetric Encryption Algorithm*

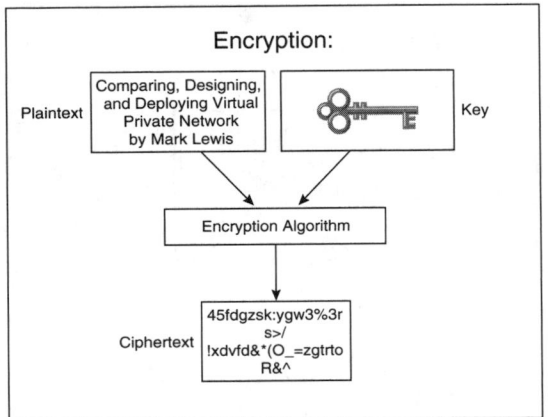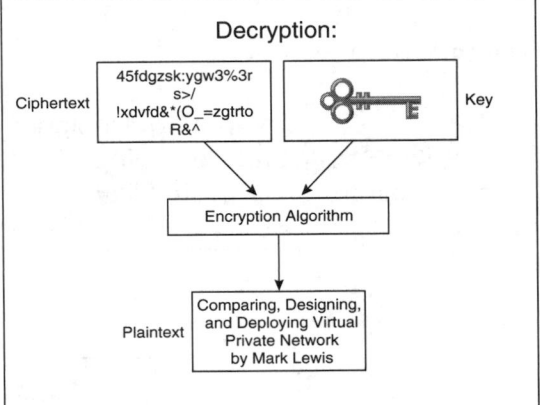

The main characteristics of symmetric encryption algorithms are as follows:

- The same key is required for encryption and decryption.
- The ciphertext is compact.
- Symmetric encryption algorithms are relatively fast and can therefore be used for bulk encryption.
- Key management and distribution is complex. IPsec peers must use the same key, and so distribution of keys in a large-scale network can be challenging.

There are two types of symmetric encryption algorithms:

- Block ciphers
- Stream ciphers

The sections the follow describe each symmetric encryption algorithm in more detail.

Block Ciphers

Block ciphers encrypt and decrypt a block of plaintext or ciphertext at one time and can operate in a number of modes, including the following:

- Electronic Codebook (ECB) mode
- Cipher-Block Chaining (CBC) mode
- Cipher Feedback (CFB) mode
- Output Feedback (OFB) mode

In ECB mode, each block of plaintext is encrypted independently. One disadvantage of ECB mode is that any two blocks of identical plaintext will produce identical ciphertext. So, for example, the plaintext block "Hello" would always produce the same ciphertext block.

In ECB mode, an attacker might then be able to analyze patterns of identical blocks of ciphertext within the complete ciphertext. In addition, a ciphertext produced using ECB mode might be vulnerable to cut-and-paste attacks (the substitution of blocks of ciphertext).

The CBC, CFB, and OFB modes of operation introduce an element of feedback into the encryption of any given block of plaintext.

In CBC mode, prior to encryption, each block of plaintext is first XOR'd (exclusive OR'd) with the ciphertext corresponding to the previous block of data. Because there is no previous block of data, the *first* block of plaintext is first XOR'd with a special random value called an initialization vector (IV) prior to encryption.

Figure 6-8 illustrates encryption using CBC mode (with, in this example, an eight-character block size).

Figure 6-8   *Encryption Using CBC Mode*

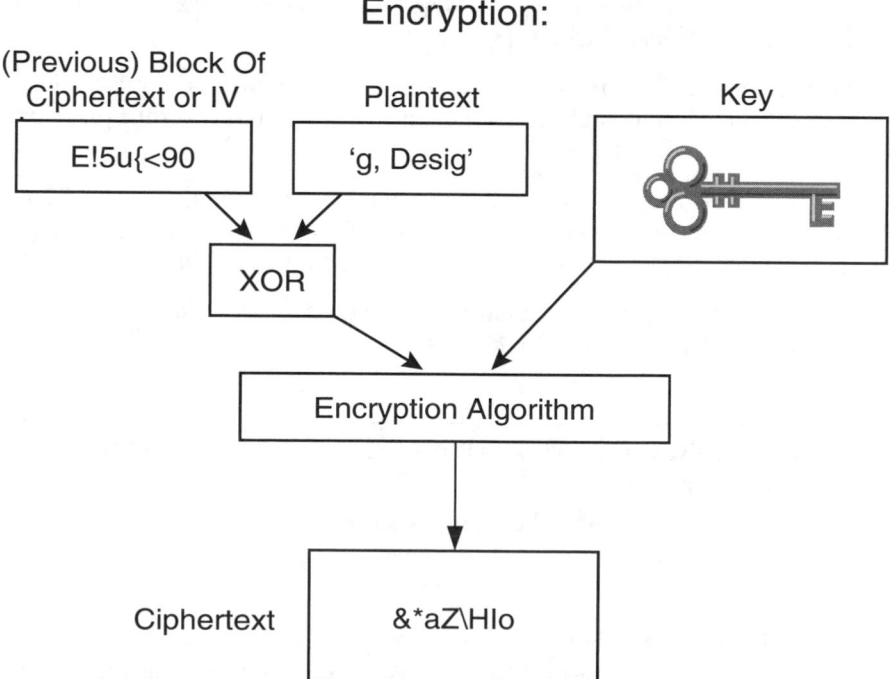

In Figure 6-8, the first block of eight characters of the message "Comparing, Designing, and Deploying Virtual Private Networks by Mark Lewis" ("Comparin") has already been encrypted, producing the ciphertext E!5u{<90. Note that the first block of plaintext was XOR'd with the (random) IV before being input into the encryption algorithm.

The next block of eight characters of plaintext ("g, Desig") is then XOR'd with the ciphertext produced by the previous block of data (E!5u{<90). The resulting data is then input into the encryption algorithm along with the (symmetric) encryption key, producing the &*aZ\Hlo ciphertext.

The process of encrypting each block is continued until all the blocks of characters in the message have been encrypted. If the final block of data in the plaintext does not equal the encryption algorithm's block size, it is padded prior to encryption.

Two examples of block ciphers are the Data Encryption Standard (DES) and the Advanced Encryption Standard (AES). The U.S. National Institute of Standards and Technology has published both of these algorithms as Federal Information Processing Standards (FIPS), and each can operate in CBC mode.

DES encrypts/decrypts 64-bit blocks of plaintext/ciphertext at a time and uses a 64-bit key. For parity, 8 bits of the key are used, and so the effective key length is 56 bits.

Triple DES (3DES) is a derivation of the DES algorithm that uses different keys to (typically) encrypt, then decrypt, and finally encrypt each block of plaintext. 3DES has an effective key length of 168 bits (3 * 56 bits).

DES has in recent years proved to be vulnerable to brute-force attacks. In a brute-force attack, each possible key is tried in an attempt to recover the plaintext from a ciphertext.

Although 3DES currently remains secure, it is slow, and so in 1997, NIST initiated a competition to find a replacement for DES. In October 2000, the Rijndael algorithm was selected as the winner of the competition and in 2001 was published as a FIPS.

AES encrypts/decrypts 128-bit blocks of plaintext/ciphertext in one go, and can use key lengths of 128 bits, 192 bits, or 256 bits.

NOTE   If you would like to see a block cipher (AES) in action, you might like to download the following Flash animation:

http://www.esat.kuleuven.ac.be/~rijmen/rijndael/Rijndael_Anim_exe.zip

Stream Ciphers

Stream ciphers, in contrast to block ciphers, operate on the plaintext (usually) a single bit at a time. Stream ciphers are fast—usually faster than block ciphers.

Examples of stream ciphers are RC4 and the Software Encryption Algorithm (SEAL). RC4 was designed by Ron Rivest, and SEAL was designed by Phil Rogaway and Don Coppersmith and is optimized for 32-bit processors.

Public Key Cryptographic Algorithms

In the previous two sections, symmetric cryptographic algorithms (that require the sender and receiver of a message to be in possession of the same key) were discussed. Public key (asymmetric) cryptographic algorithms differ from symmetric cryptographic algorithms in a number of ways, the most fundamental of which is that a *pair* of keys is required (one public, one private), rather than the single key required for symmetric cryptographic algorithms.

Public key algorithms have a number of characteristics, including the following:

- Public key algorithms are much slower than symmetric algorithms and are therefore not suitable for bulk encryption.

- The ciphertext produced by public key algorithms is not compact.

- Public key algorithms do not have the same key distribution and management problems as symmetric algorithms. Key distribution consists of the publication of each device's public key.

- Public key algorithms can variously be used for encryption, for digital signatures, and for symmetric key exchange.

Some popular public key algorithms are the Diffie-Hellman; Rivest, Shamir, and Addlemen (RSA); the Digital Signature Algorithm (DSA); and ElGamal. Diffie-Hellman is used for key exchange, RSA and ElGamal can be used for encryption or digital signatures, and DSA can, as the name suggests, be used to create digital signatures.

Encryption Using Public Key Algorithms

As previously discussed, symmetric encryption algorithms use the same key for both encryption and decryption, but public key algorithms use one key for encryption and another for decryption.

Public key algorithms require a public key and a mathematically associated private key. Any data encrypted using the public key must be decrypted using the corresponding private key. Similarly, any data encrypted with the private key must be decrypted using the corresponding public key.

Any data encrypted using the public key cannot be decrypted using the public key, and any data encrypted using the private key cannot be decrypted using the private key. Figures 6-9 and 6-10 illustrate public key encryption.

Figure 6-9 *Encryption with the Private Key, and Decryption with the Corresponding Public Key*

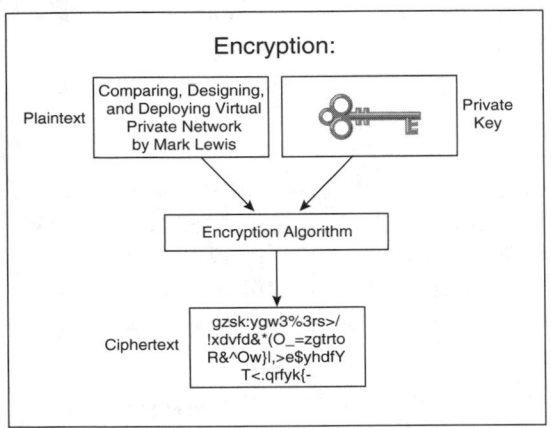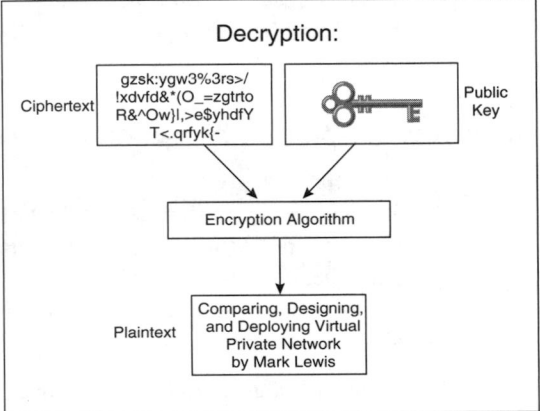

Figure 6-10 *Encryption with the Public Key, and Decryption with the Corresponding Private Key*

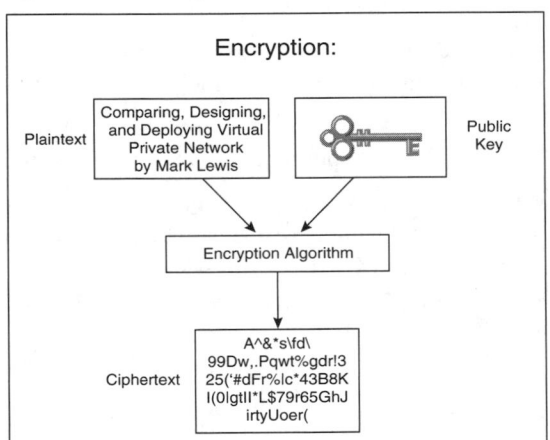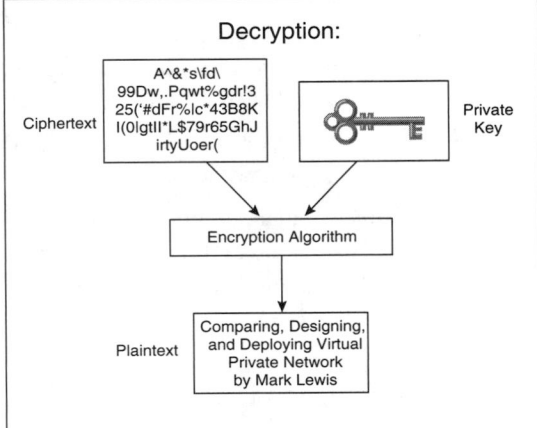

Digital Signatures

Digital signatures are *encrypted hash values* and can be used to prove that a particular entity sent, authorized, or vouches for a certain communication. Figure 6-11 shows an example of the use of a digital signature.

Figure 6-11 *Using a Digital Signature*

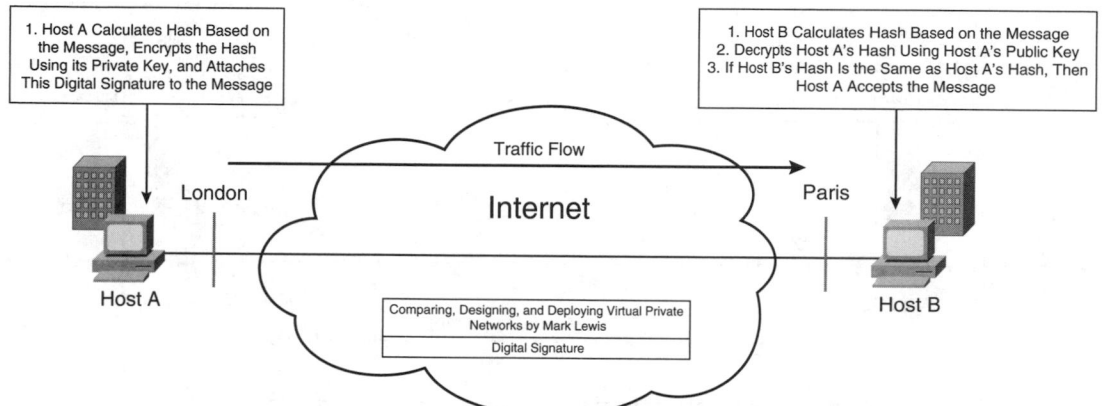

In Figure 6-11, Host A calculates a hash value on the message "Comparing, Designing, and Deploying Virtual Private Networks by Mark Lewis" and then encrypts this hash using its *private key*, giving a digital signature.

Host A attaches this digital signature to the message (signs the message) and sends it to the Host B. Host B now calculates its own hash value on the message. It then decrypts the hash value from Host A using Host A's *public key*. If Host B's and Host A's hash values match, Host B accepts the message.

If the hash values match, the Host B gateway knows two things:

- That the message has not been tampered with. If the message had been tampered with, the hash value calculated by Host B would not match the (encrypted) hash value sent by Host A.

- That the message could only have been sent by Host A. The digital signature consists of a hash value encrypted using Host A's private key (which only Host A has, assuming that it has not been compromised); so if the hash value can be successfully decrypted using the Host A's public key, it must have come from Host A.

Key Exchange with Diffie-Hellman

Diffie-Hellman is a public key algorithm that allows two peers to establish a secret key that only they know while communicating over an insecure channel such as the Internet. Diffie-Hellman relies on modular exponentiation. Figure 6-12 illustrates a Diffie-Hellman exchange.

Figure 6-12 *Diffie-Hellman Exchange*

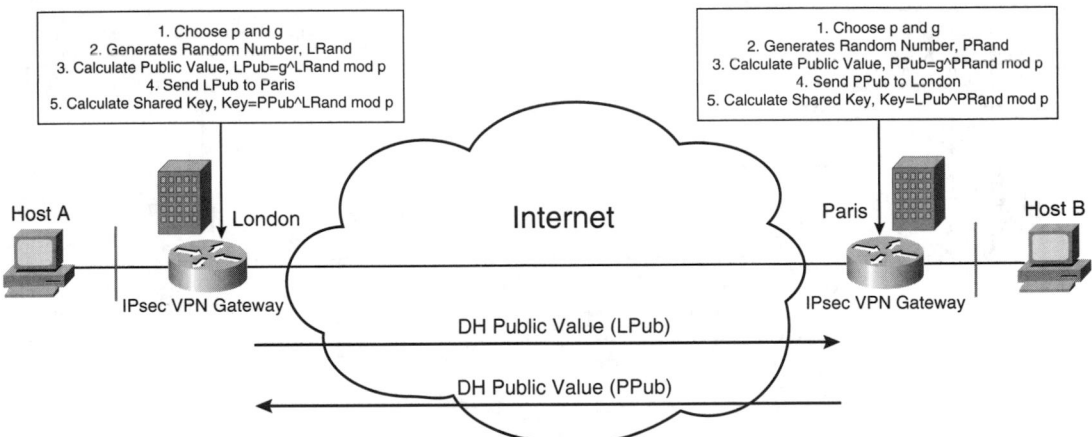

In Figure 6-12, the following events occur:

1 London and Paris select a large prime number (p) and a generator number (g). The numbers p and g are not secret values and can be known publicly.

2 London and Paris each select a random number. London's random number is called LRand, and Paris's random number is called PRand.

3 London and Paris calculate public values. London public value is calculated as follows: LPub=g^LRand mod p. Paris's public value is calculated as follows: PPub=g^PRand mod p.

4 London and Paris exchange their public values, LPub and PPub.

5 London and Paris calculate the shared key. London calculates the shared key as follows: shared key=PPub^LRand mod P. Paris calculates the shared key as follows: shared key=LPub^PRand mod p.

Security Protocols: AH and ESP

IPsec uses two security protocols, the Authentication Header (AH) and the Encapsulating Security Payload (ESP). The following two sections discuss AH and ESP.

Authentication Header (AH)

AH is a packet header that provides the following security services:

- Connectionless integrity
- Data origin authentication
- Optional replay protection

AH is IP protocol 51.

Figure 6-13 shows the AH header format.

Figure 6-13 *AH Header Format*

0	1	2	3
0 1 2 3 4 5 6 7	8 9 0 1 2 3 4 5	6 7 8 9 0 1 2 3	4 5 6 7 8 9 0 1
Next Header	Payload Len	RESERVED	
Security Parameters Index (SPI)			
Sequence Number Field			
Integrity Check Value-ICV (variable)			

AH fields have the following functions:

- **Next Header**—This indicates the type of header that comes after the AH header (for example, a value of 6 is contained in this field if the next header is TCP).

- **Payload Length**—The length of the AH in 32-bit words minus 2.

- **Reserved**—This is reserved for future use.

- **Security Parameter Index (SPI)**—This is used by the receiving gateway to identify the security association (SA, described later in this chapter) to which this packet corresponds.

- **Sequence Number**—A per-packet counter that allows replay protection to be enabled.

- **Integrity Check Value (ICV)**—A cryptographic value (hash) corresponding to the user packet being protected. The receiving IPsec VPN gateway uses the ICV to authenticate the packet.

AH can operate in two modes:

- Transport mode

- Tunnel mode

In transport mode, the AH header is inserted between the original IP header and header of the next protocol (such as TCP, UDP, or ICMP) of the user packet being protected. Figure 6-14 shows AH transport mode.

In AH transport mode, the whole packet is authenticated except any mutable fields in the original IP header (fields that may change during transit between IPsec-enabled hosts or security gateways). Mutable fields *include* Time-To-Live (TTL), Type of Service (ToS), and Header Checksum.

Figure 6-14 *AH Transport Mode*

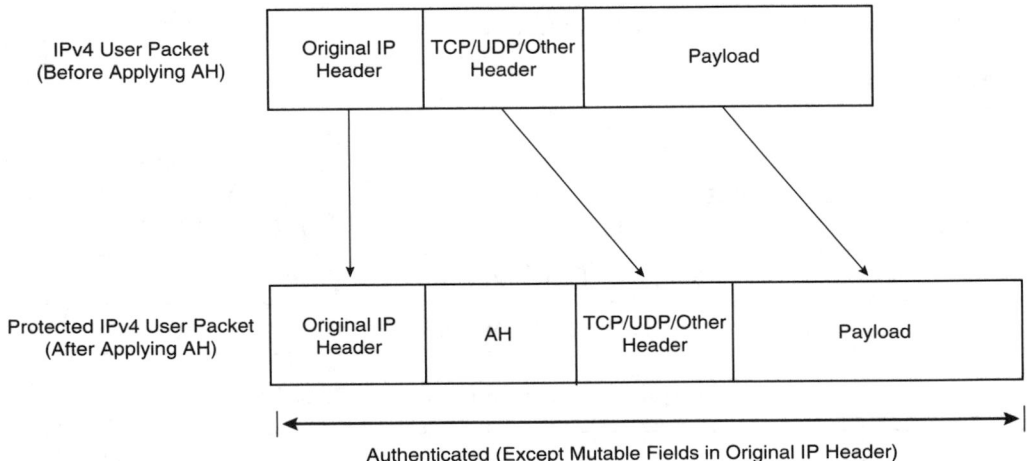

Typically, AH transport mode is used to protect user packets as they transit a network between IPsec-enabled end hosts or devices. It is also possible, however, for security gateways to use AH transport mode to protect tunneling protocols such as GRE, and Layer Two Tunneling Protocol (L2TP).

In tunnel mode, the AH header along with a new IP header are prepended to the user packet being protected. Figure 6-15 shows AH tunnel mode.

Figure 6-15 *AH Tunnel Mode*

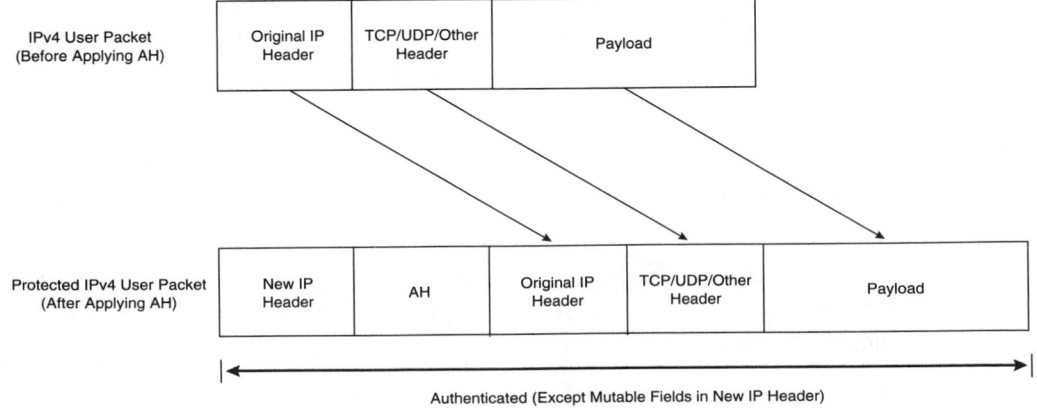

In AH tunnel mode, the whole packet is authenticated except mutable fields in the new IP header. AH tunnel mode can be used to protect user packets as they transit a network between end hosts, but it is typically used to protect user packets as they transit a network between security gateways.

So, that is the theory. However, it is definitely worth taking a look at what happens in practice. Figure 6-16 shows a sample IPsec VPN.

Figure 6-16 *Sample IPsec VPN*

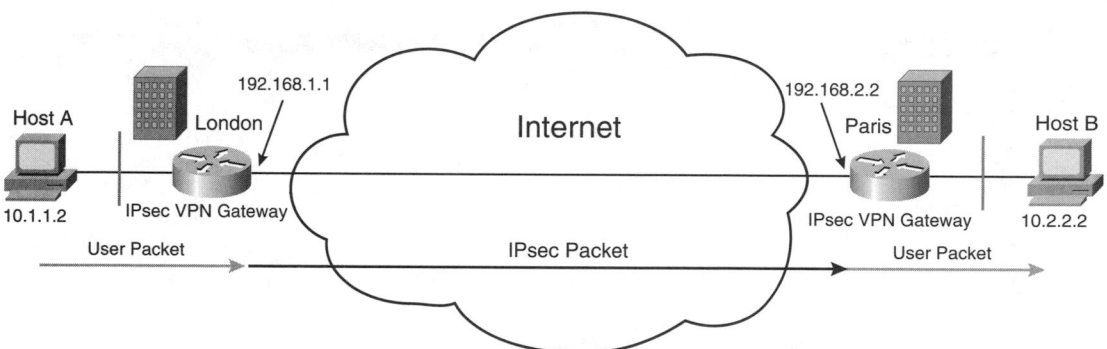

In Figure 6-16, Host A (10.1.1.2) sends a user packet to Host B (10.2.2.2). When the user packet arrives at the London gateway (192.168.1.1), it is encapsulated in IPsec (AH).

The IPsec packet then transits the Internet to the Paris gateway (192.168.2.2). The Paris gateway decapsulates the user packet (by authenticating it and removing the AH header) and sends it onward to Host B.

Figure 6-17 shows the packet capture of the packet sent from Host A to Host B. The packet was captured at a point between the London and Paris IPsec VPN gateways. Highlighted line 2 in Figure 6-17 shows that this is an AH packet.

If you take look at the line directly above highlighted line 2, you can see that the new (outer) IP header. This new IP header includes source and destination IP addresses 192.168.1.1 (the London gateway) and 192.168.2.2 (the Paris gateway).

If you look below highlighted line 2, you can see another IP header (source address 10.1.1.2 [Host A], destination address 10.2.2.2 [Host B]). This is the original IP header of the encapsulated user packet.

Below the original IP header, you can see an Internet Control Message Protocol (ICMP) header. In fact, this is the ICMP header of a ping packet from Host A to Host B.

Figure 6-17 *AH Packet Capture*

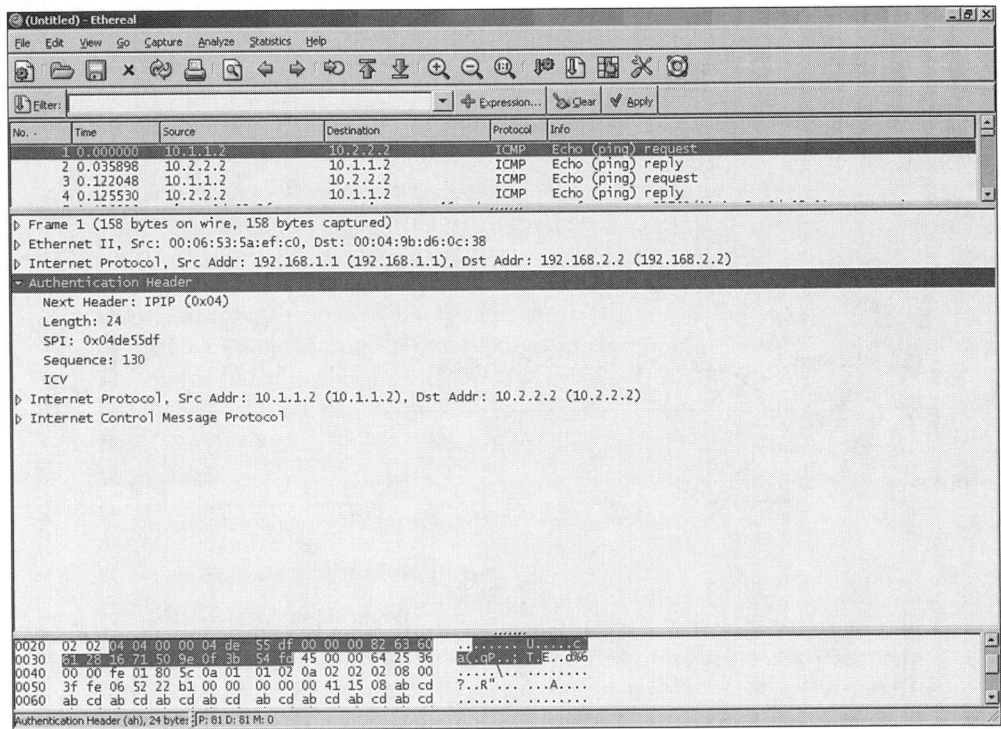

So, there are two IP headers—a new IP header and an original IP header. This is an AH tunnel mode packet (see Figure 6-15).

Directly below highlighted line 2, you can see the fields in the AH header:

- The Next Header field shows that the next header after the AH header in the packet is IPIP (0x04). This indicates that the next header is the original IP header.

- The (Payload) Length field contains a value of 24.

- The SPI field contains a value of 0x04de55df. This value identifies the AH SA on the Paris gateway and will enable the Paris gateway to correctly process (authenticate) the packet when it arrives.

- The Sequence (number) field contains a value of 130.

- The value contained in the ICV field is not explicitly shown.

Encapsulating Security Payload (ESP)

ESP is a packet header that provides the following:

- Connectionless integrity

- Data origin authentication

- Optional replay protection
- Data confidentiality
- Limited traffic flow confidentiality (available only in tunnel mode)

Notice that ESP provides all the same security services as AH, as well as data and limited traffic flow confidentiality. For this reason, AH is now rarely used. ESP is IP protocol 50. Figure 6-18 shows the ESP header (and trailers).

Figure 6-18 *ESP Header Format*

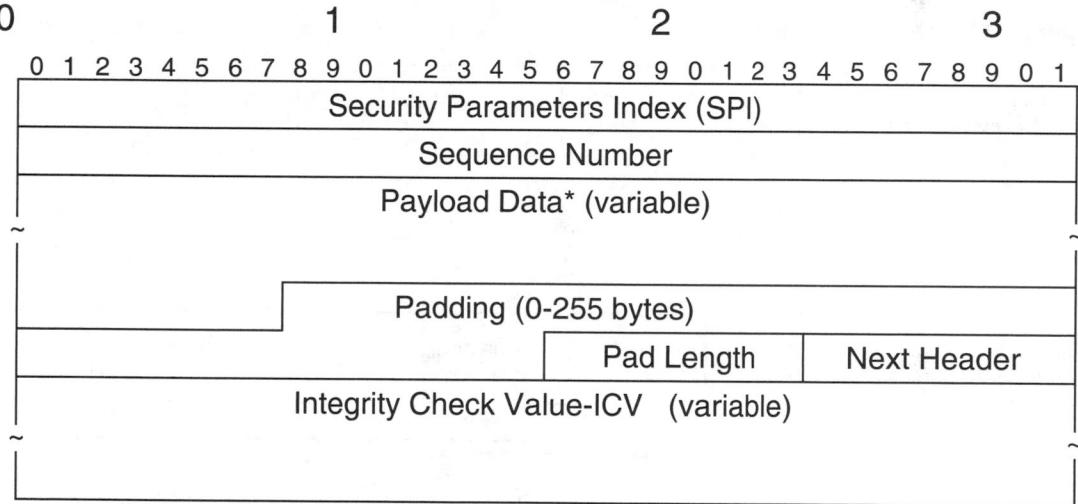

Many of the fields in the ESP header have the same function as those in the AH. Fields not already described have the following functions:

- **Payload Data**—This is the user packet data. This field may also contain Initialization Vector (IV) and Traffic Flow Confidentiality (TFC) padding. Some encryption algorithms use an IV to encrypt the first block of user packet data. TFC padding is used to hide user traffic flow characteristics such as user packet size.

- **Padding**—Used to ensure that user packet data is a multiple of a certain number of bytes (this may be required by the encryption algorithm that you use) and to ensure that the Pad Length and Next Header fields are right aligned with a 4-byte boundary within the overall packet.

- **Pad Length**—Indicates the number of bytes in the Padding field.

- **ICV**—This is an optional field and has the same function as the ICV contained within the AH. The ICV field is present only if ESP authentication is configured.

ESP also operates in two modes:

- Transport mode
- Tunnel mode

In ESP transport mode, the ESP header is inserted between the original IP header of the user packet and the header of the next layer protocol of the user packet being protected. In addition, a variable-length ESP trailer (consisting of the Padding, Pad Length, and Next Header fields), and optionally an ESP ICV field, is appended to the packet. Figure 6-19 illustrates ESP transport mode.

Figure 6-19 *ESP Transport Mode*

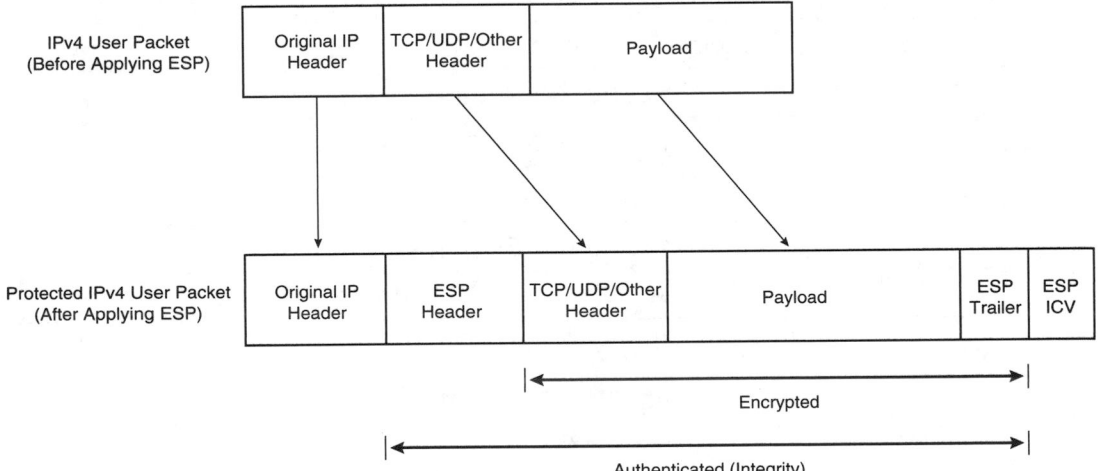

As you can see in Figure 6-19, if ESP authentication is configured, the initial ESP header (including the SPI and Sequence Number fields), TCP/UDP/Other Header, Payload, and ESP Trailer fields are all authenticated. Notice that the original header is not authenticated, unlike when using AH (see Figure 6-14). If ESP encryption is configured, the TCP/UDP/Other Header, Payload, and ESP Trailer fields are all encrypted.

ESP transport mode is usually used to protect user traffic between IPsec-enabled end hosts or other devices, although it may also be used to protect GRE, L2TP, or other tunnels between security gateways.

Figure 6-20 illustrates ESP tunnel mode. In ESP tunnel mode, a new IP header and ESP header are prepended to the user packet, and an ESP trailer and (if ESP authentication is configured) an ESP ICV are appended to the user packet. If ESP authentication is configured, the ESP header, the entire user packet, and the ESP trailer are authenticated.

Figure 6-20 *ESP Tunnel Mode*

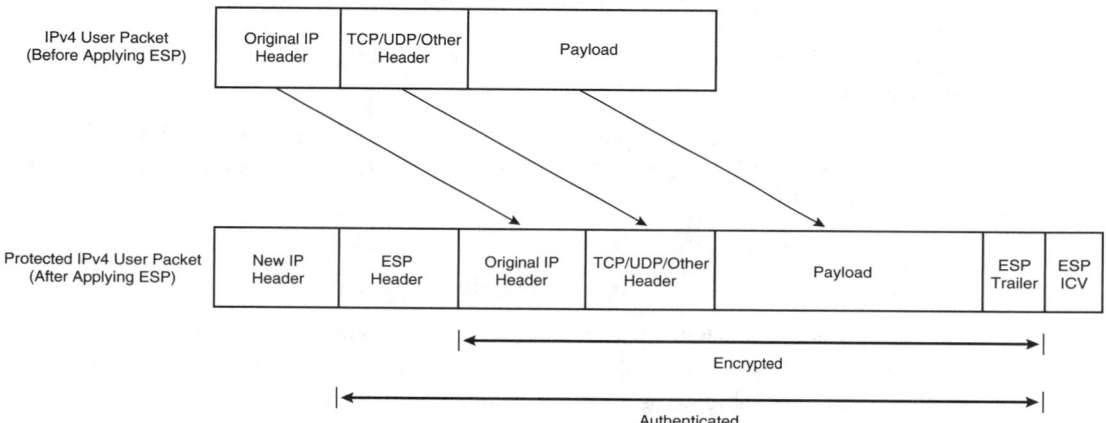

If ESP encryption is configured, the ESP header, entire user packet, and the ESP trailer are encrypted. Now it is time to see how ESP works in practice.

Figure 6-21 shows an ESP tunnel mode packet captured in transit between the London and Paris gateways shown in Figure 6-16. Again, Host A sends a user packet to Host B, and this user packet is encapsulated in ESP by the London gateway and transmitted to the Paris gateway.

Figure 6-21 *ESP Packet Capture*

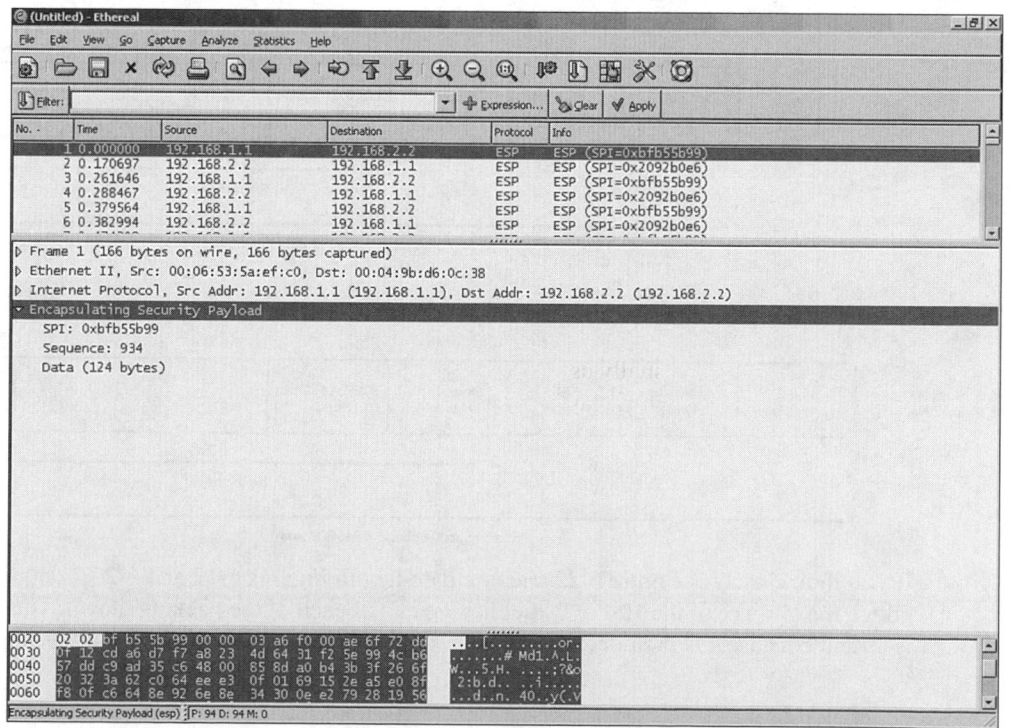

If you look just above highlighted line 2, you can see the new (outer) IP header, with source address 192.168.1.1 (London) and destination address 192.168.2.2 (Paris).

In highlighted line 2, you can see the ESP header. Looking just below highlighted line 2, you can see the fields in the (initial) ESP header:

- The SPI field contains a value of 0xbfb55b99. This identifies the ESP SA on the Paris gateway and will enable the Paris gateway to correctly process (authenticate and/or decrypt) the packet.
- The Sequence Number field contains a value of 934.

After the SPI and Sequence Number fields, Figure 6-21 shows 124 bytes of data.

If you are wondering what happened to the encapsulated user packet from Host A, as well as the Padding, Pad Length, and Next Header fields (collectively referred to as the ESP trailer), refer back to Figure 6-20. In this example, ESP encryption is configured, and so the encapsulated user packet and ESP trailer are all encrypted.

AH and ESP Together

It is possible to configure both AH and ESP protection for a single user traffic flow. In this case, AH and ESP headers are included, as shown in Figure 6-22.

Figure 6-22 *AH/ESP Transport and Tunnel Modes*

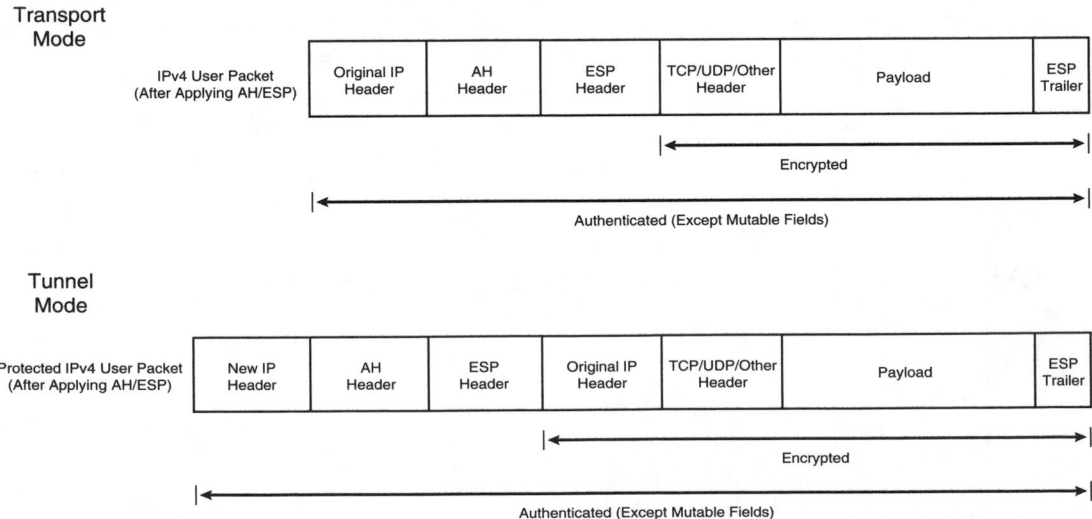

If you look closely at Figure 6-22 and compare it with Figures 6-19 and 6-20, you might notice the absence of the ESP ICV field at the end of each of the packets shown. The field is absent because it is included only if ESP authentication is enabled. If you are using AH authentication, there is no point also using ESP authentication (although it is *possible* to configure both AH and ESP authentication for a single traffic flow).

Figure 6-23 shows an AH/ESP tunnel mode packet captured between the London and Paris gateways shown in Figure 6-16.

Figure 6-23 *AH/ESP Tunnel Mode Packet Capture*

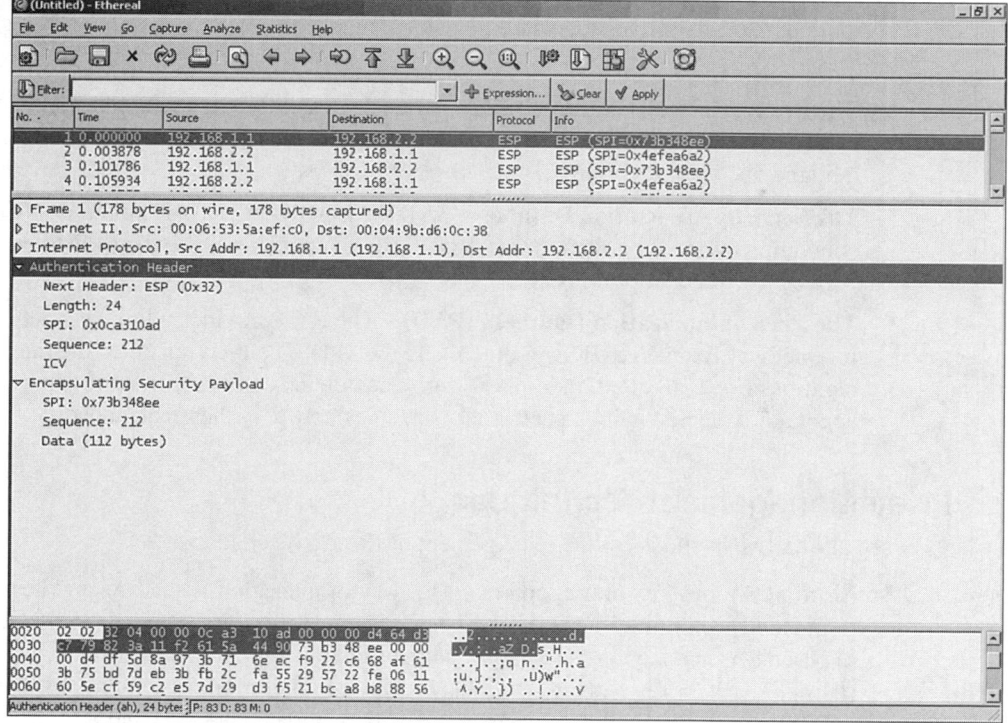

Highlighted line 2 shows the AH header. Directly below that are the AH header fields. Note, in particular, the Next Header field—this indicates the protocol in the following header (in this case, ESP).

After the AH header fields is the ESP header. One thing to note here is the SPI (0x73b348ee); if you compare this to the SPI in the AH header (0x0ca310ad), you can see that they differ. The SPIs differ because they correspond to different SAs. The AH header SPI will enable the Paris gateway to correctly authenticate the packet, and the ESP header SPI will enable the Paris gateway to correctly decrypt the packet.

Security Associations

An IPsec SA is unidirectional in nature and defines how traffic for a particular traffic flow is to be protected by IPsec. An IPsec SA is identified by an SPI and includes information such as security protocol, security protocol mode, cryptographic algorithms, and SA lifetime.

A particular traffic flow may be protected by one or more SAs. For example, if AH is specified for authentication and ESP is specified for encryption, traffic protection will involve two SAs. Because IPsec SAs are unidirectional, a *minimum* of two IPsec SAs are required to protect user traffic in both directions between a pair of IPsec VPN gateways.

IPsec Databases

IPsec defines three databases to ensure that IP traffic is correctly processed (with regard to IPsec):

- **The Security Policy Database (SPD)**—This database specifies traffic that should be protected by IPsec and traffic that should bypass IPsec. The SPD is consulted for all inbound and outbound traffic.

- **The Security Association Database (SAD or SADB)**—The SAD contains an entry containing information related to each IPsec SA and interfaces to the SPD to ensure correct IPsec packet processing.

- **The Peer Authorization Database (PAD)**—The PAD provides a link between the Internet Key Exchange (IKE) protocol and the SPD. The PAD specifies the range of identities (for example, IP addresses) for which the IPsec device is authorized to negotiate IPsec SAs with a peer; it also specifies how to authenticate a peer.

SA and Key Management Techniques

IPsec allows two methods for the management of IPsec SAs and keys:

- **Manual SA and key management**—One way of managing IPsec SAs and keys is to manually configure SAs and keying material on IPsec peers. Manual configuration of IPsec SAs and keying material is analogous to the configuration of static routes (though much more involved), and just like the configuration of static routes, the manual configuration of IPsec SAs and keying material is not scalable

- **Automated SA and key management through the IKE protocol**—The IKE protocol allows IPsec peers to dynamically authenticate each other, generate keying material, and negotiate IPsec SAs.

  There are two versions of IKE: IKE Version 1 (IKEv1) and IKE Version 2 (IKEv2). IKEv1 is defined in RFCs 2407, 2408, and 2409, and IKEv2 is defined in RFC 4306. IKEv2 improves the efficiency and security of IKE and adds extra functionality to the base protocol specification.

IKEv1

IKEv1 is made up of elements of a number of protocols:

- **The Secure Key Exchange Mechanism (SKEME)**—Describes a versatile key exchange technique

- **The Oakley Key Determination Protocol**—Describes a series of key exchange techniques (modes), as well as Perfect Forward Secrecy, identity protection, and authentication

- **The Internet Security Association and Key Management Protocol (ISAKMP)**—Describes a framework for authentication and key exchange

IKEv1 negotiation is divided into two phases and three modes. In phase 1, IPsec peers establish an IKE SA. This IKE SA is used to protect phase 2 negotiations, which are then used to negotiate IPsec SAs.

IKEv1 phase 1 can be negotiated using main mode or aggressive mode. IKEv1 phase 2, on the other hand, is negotiated using quick mode. It is worth noting that the IKE SA negotiated during phase 1 is bidirectional, but IPsec SAs negotiated during phase 2 are unidirectional.

IKE Phase 1 Main Mode Negotiation

So, the purpose of IKEv1 phase 1 is to establish an IKE SA between two IPsec peers. But, how exactly is this accomplished? During IKE phase 1, the two IPsec peers exchange three pairs of messages, giving a total of six messages. The function of these messages is as follows:

- **First pair of messages (messages 1 and 2)**—These are used to negotiate IKE policy parameters, such as the hash algorithm, encryption algorithm, and method of authentication. These parameters are specified using the **crypto isakmp policy** *priority* command.

- **Second pair of messages (messages 3 and 4)**—These are used to exchange Diffie-Hellman public values and nonces (random numbers).

  The Diffie-Hellman exchange allows the IPsec peers to agree a shared secret key. The nonce values are used as keying material in the calculation of session keys on the IPsec peers.

  The IPsec peers now generate the first of four session keys called SKEYID. A further three session keys (SKEYID_d, SKEYID_a, and SKEYID_e) are then calculated using SKEYID. IKE phase 2 keys are derived from SKEYID_d. IPsec peers authenticate and encrypt remaining IKE phase 1 and phase 2 messages that they send to each other using SKEYID_a and SKEYID_e.

- **Third pair of messages (messages 5 and 6)**—These messages are used to exchange identities and authenticate the IPsec peers to each other.

Phase 1 is now complete, and an IKE SA has been established between the IPsec peers.

Figure 6-24 illustrates IKE main mode negotiation between IPsec VPN gateways.

Figure 6-24 *IKE Main Mode Negotiation*

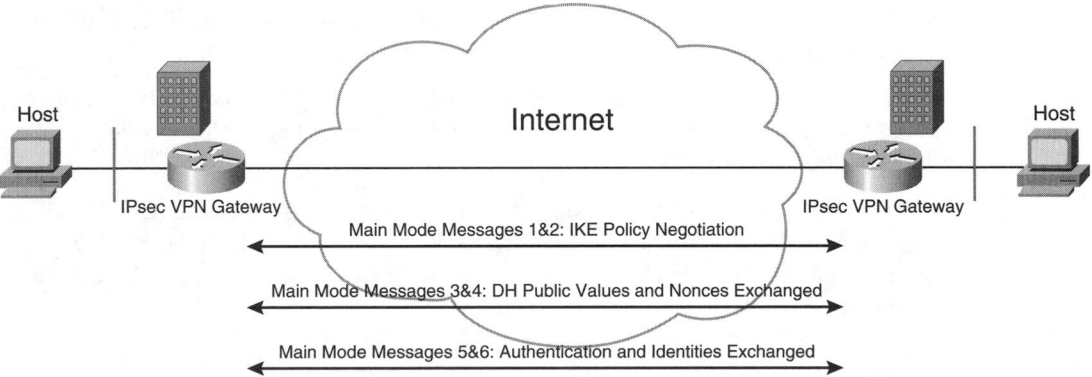

Before finishing this section, it is worth taking a look at the three methods that IPsec peers can use to authenticate each other during IKE negotiation:

- **Preshared keys**—A statically configured key that must be identical on peer IPsec gateways.

- **Encrypted nonces**—As the name suggests, this involves the encryption of a nonce with the public key of the peer IPsec VPN gateway. Each peer must possess the other peer's public key prior to IKE negotiation.

- **Digital signatures (using digital certificates)**—A digital signature (a hash encrypted using a private key) of certain pieces of information is created and exchanged by the IPsec peers. Each peer then verifies the digital signature on the information using the public key of the other peer.

  Each IPsec peer must not only possess the public key of the other peer but also be sure that the public key is, in fact, the correct public key and not the public key of an imposter. To ensure that the public keys can be trusted, each IPsec obtains a signed digital certificate from a certificate authority (CA). A digital certificate is an association between an identity (name) and public key. A CA is a third party trusted by each IPsec peer.

  Figure 6-25 illustrates IPsec VPN gateways enrolling with a CA and obtaining a digital certificate.

Figure 6-25 *Enrolling with a CA and Obtaining a Digital Certificate*

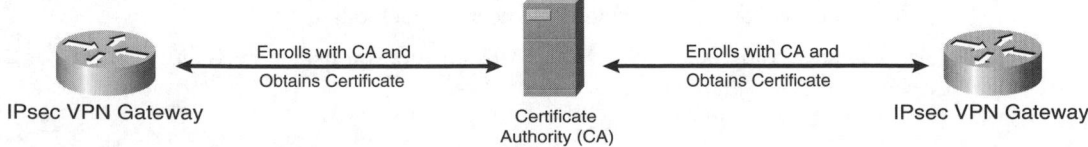

During IKE negotiation, IPsec peers exchanges certificates and in this way obtain the public key of the other peer. Because the certificate is signed by a mutually trusted CA (or CA hierarchy), each IPsec peer can be sure that the public key that it has received from its peer during IKE negotiation is the real public key.

If a certificate becomes invalid for reasons such as key compromise, it is also possible to revoke that certificate. The CA can periodically publish a list of revoked certificates called a Certificate Revocation List (CRL) or make information about revoked certificates available via protocols such as the Online Certificate Status Protocol (OCSP).

IPsec VPN gateways verify the revocation status of peer gateways' certificates during IKE negotiation. If a peer's certificate is found to be invalid (revoked or otherwise invalid), IKE negotiation fails. For more information on digital certificate authentication, see Chapter 7, "Scaling and Optimizing IPsec VPNs."

IKE Phase 1 Aggressive Mode Negotiation

An alternative to main mode negotiation is aggressive mode negotiation. Aggressive mode negotiation consists of three messages rather than the six messages used in main mode.

Aggressive mode negotiation is quicker but is less secure than main mode. It is less secure than main mode because the IPsec identities are exchanged unencrypted. As previously discussed, in main mode negotiation, identities are sent during the third exchange of messages (messages five and six), which are encrypted using session key SKEYID_e.

The three messages exchanged during aggressive mode negotiation can be described as follows:

- **Message 1**—This message is sent by the initiator and consists of all the information contained in the initiator's first two messages used for main mode negotiation (IKE policy proposals, Diffie-Hellman public value, and nonce) as well as the initiator's identity.

  Note that the initiator is the IPsec peer that initiates IKE negotiation, and the responder is the other IPsec peer.

- **Message 2**—This message is sent by the responder and consists of all the information contained in all three main mode messages sent by the responder (IKE policy acceptance, Diffie-Hellman public value, nonce, and responder's identity). This message also serves to authenticate the responder to the initiator.

- **Message 3**—This message is sent by the initiator and serves to authenticate the initiator to the responder.

Figure 6-26 illustrates IKE aggressive mode negotiation.

Figure 6-26 *IKE Aggressive Mode Negotiation*

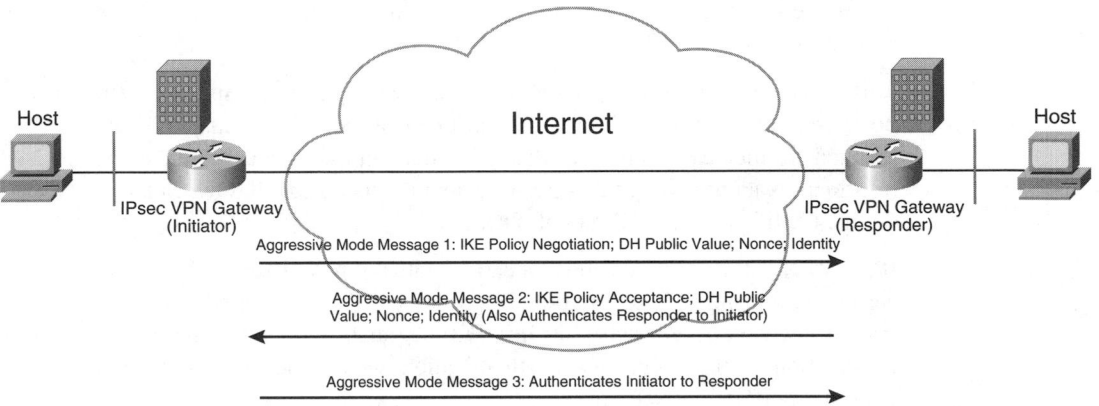

IKE Phase 2 Quick Mode Negotiation

When IKE phase 1 negotiation is complete, phase 2 can begin. The purpose of IKE phase 2 negotiation is, as previously described, to established IPsec SAs. These IPsec SAs are then used to protect user traffic as it transits the intervening network between the IPsec peers.

IKE phase 2 negotiation consists of three messages:

- **Message 1**—This message is sent by the initiator and contains IPsec SA proposals such as encryption algorithm, hashing algorithm, and IPsec lifetime. IPsec proposals (transforms) are configured using the **crypto ipsec transform-set** command.

- **Message 2**—This message serves to accept one of the IPsec proposals sent in message 1.

- **Message 3**—This message serves as an acknowledgment of message 2.

Messages 1 and 2 also contain additional keying material (nonces) to be used for the IPsec SAs. Keying material can be used for the authentication key of an AH SA or for the authentication key and/or encryption key for an ESP SA. It is also worth noting that if Perfect Forward Secrecy (PFS) is enabled using the **set pfs** command, extra Diffie-Hellman public values are also exchanged in messages 1 and 2.

Usually, keying material used for IPsec SAs is (partially) derived from the Diffie-Hellman public values exchanged during IKE phase 1. If you want more security, however, you can enable PFS and thereby ensure that IPsec keying material is based on Diffie-Hellman values exchanged during phase 2.

If the IPsec peers are gateways negotiating SAs on behalf of end hosts, messages 1 and 2 also contain (proxy) identities. These identities differ from those exchanged during phase 1. Phase 1 identities serve to identify the IPsec peers themselves. Phase 2 identities, on the other hand, describe the traffic to be protected by the IPsec SAs (defined using crypto access lists).

All IKE phase 2 messages are protected using the session keys SKEYID_e and SKEYID_a, which are generated during phase 1.

Figure 6-27 illustrates IKE phase 2 (quick mode) negotiation.

Figure 6-27 *IKE Phase 2 (Quick Mode) Negotiation*

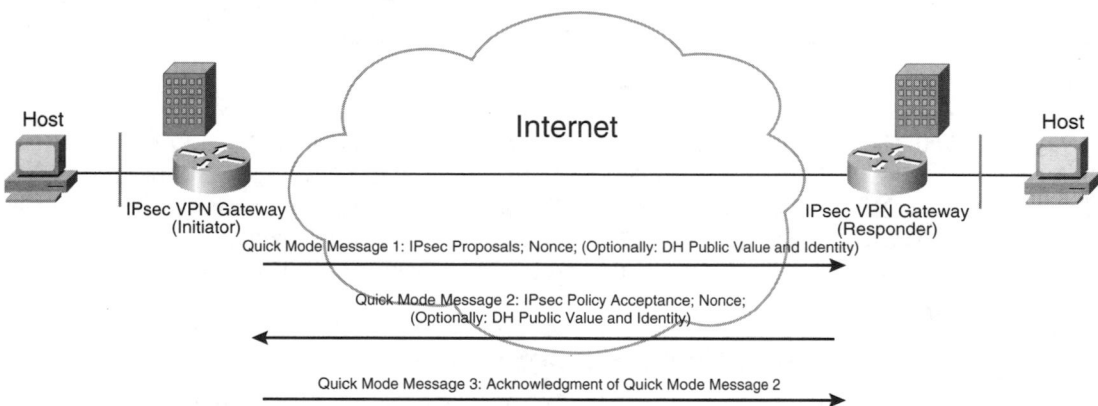

IKEv2

The IKEv2 base specification includes all the functionality of IKEv1 as well as additional functionality that was tacked on to IKEv1, such as NAT traversal and legacy authentication. IKEv2 also includes improvements in overall efficiency and security.

IKEv2 preserves most of the features of IKEv1, including the two negotiation phases. In IKEv2 phase 1, the IPsec peers negotiate algorithms, establish a secret session key, authenticate each other, and establish an IKE SA—just like IKEv1. In IKEv2, however, the first IPsec SA is also established during phase 1. In IKEv2, IPsec SAs associated with an IKE SA are known as *child SAs*.

Figure 6-28 illustrates a typical IKEv2 phase 1 negotiation sequence. In Figure 6-28, the initiator and responder exchange two pairs of IKEv2 Request and Response messages. The purpose of the first pair of messages (Request 1/Response 1) is used to negotiate cryptographic algorithms such as encryption algorithm and Diffie-Hellman group. The second pair of Request and Response messages (Request 2/Response 2) is used to exchange identities and authenticate the IPsec peers and to negotiate the first IPsec SA.

Figure 6-28 *IKEv2 Phase 1 Negotiation*

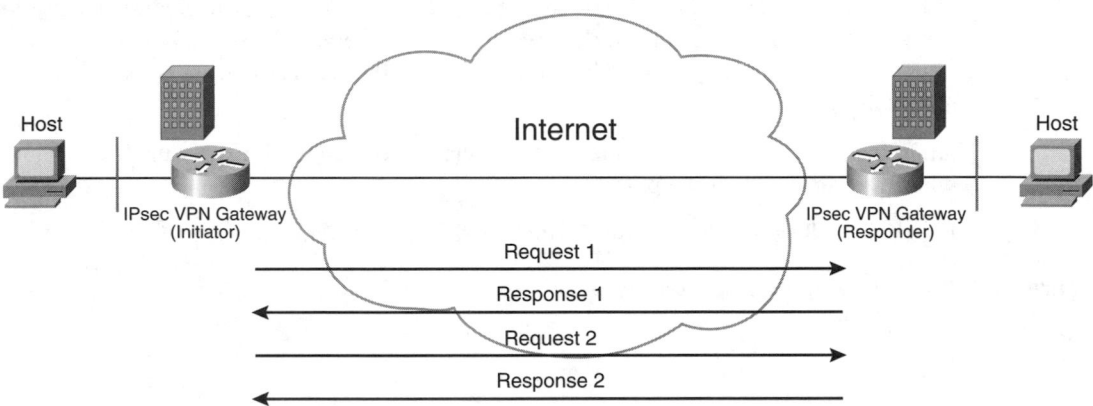

In IKEv2, phase 2 is responsible for negotiating any *further* child IPsec SAs that may be required. These additional child IPsec SAs are negotiated using additional pairs of IKE Request and Response messages. Additional IKEv2 Request and Response messages can also be used for sending informational messages. These informational messages can be for purposes such as informing an IPsec peer of the deletion of an IPsec SA.

Putting It All Together: IPsec Packet Processing

Now that you have seen all of the components, it is time to take a look at outbound and inbound user packet processing on an IPsec VPN gateway.

Outbound Processing

Figure 6-29 illustrates outbound processing of user packets from the inside interface to the outside interface of an IPsec VPN gateway. In Figure 6-29, the IPsec VPN gateway receives a user packet on its inside interface. The gateway checks the packet against the SPD to determine whether the packet should be discarded, should bypass IPsec and be forwarded, or should be protected by IPsec.

The user packet is discarded if the SPD indicates that this should be the case. If the SPD indicates that the user packet should bypass IPsec, the packet is forwarded out of the outside interface.

If the SPD indicates that the user packet should be protected by IPsec, the SAD is consulted for an IPsec SA. If no corresponding IPsec SA exists in the SAD, IKE negotiation is initiated with the remote IPsec peer (assuming that automated SA and key management is enabled and that IKE negotiation is authorized by the PAD). If IKE negotiation is successful, one or more IPsec SAs are installed into the SAD.

Figure 6-29 *Outbound Processing of User Packets*

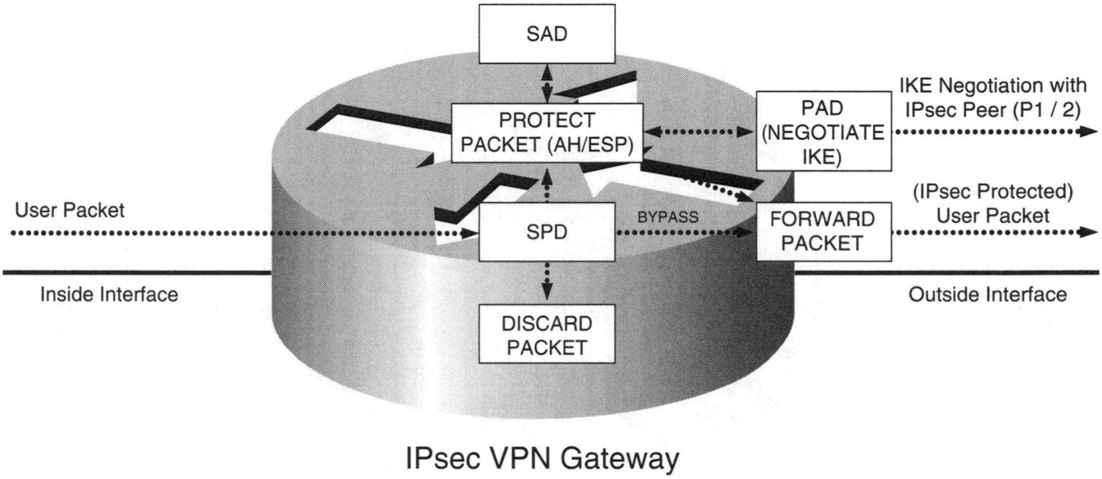

IPsec VPN Gateway

The user packet is then encapsulated (protected) according to the SA in the SAD (using AH or ESP). If only one SA (AH or ESP *only*) corresponds to the user packet, the packet is forwarded on the outside interface.

If more than one SA corresponds to the user packet (for example, AH *in addition to* ESP), the SAD is again consulted, and the packet is again encapsulated (protected) according to the additional SA (or SAs).

After all IPsec SAs corresponding to the user packet have been processed, the packet is forwarded out of the outside interface to the peer IPsec gateway.

Inbound Processing

Figure 6-30 shows IPsec processing of packets received on the outside interface of an IPsec VPN gateway. As shown in Figure 6-30, the IPsec VPN gateway receives a packet on the outside interface.

If the packet is not IPsec protected, the packet is processed according to the SPD. If the SPD specifies that the packet should bypass IPsec, the packet is forwarded out of the inside interface. If the packet is an ICMP packet addressed to the gateway (for example, as ping packet), it is passed to the ICMP process. If the SPD does not specify that the packet should bypass IPsec, and the packet is not an ICMP packet, it is discarded.

If the packet received on the outside interface is an IPsec packet, IPsec protection (AH or ESP header) is removed by referencing the correct SA in the SAD using the SPI in the AH/ESP header.

Figure 6-30 *Inbound Processing of Packets*

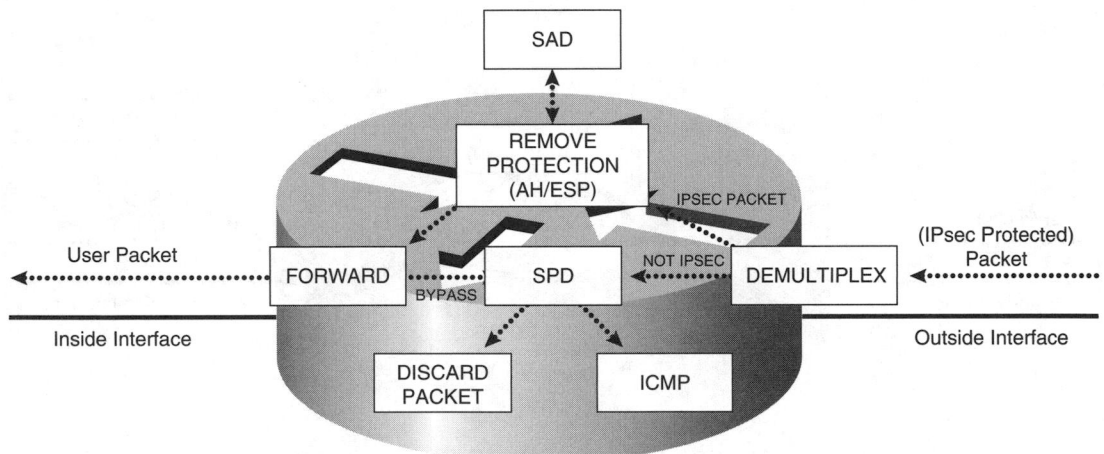

IPsec VPN Gateway

If the packet is protected by more than one IPsec header (for example, ESP in addition to AH), the SAD is again consulted and the IPsec protection is removed.

After all IPsec protection has been removed, the user packet is forwarded out of the inside interface.

Deploying IPsec VPNs: Fundamental Considerations

When deploying an IPsec VPN, there are a number of fundamental considerations, including the following:

- IKE policies (assuming automated SA and key management)
- IPsec transforms
- Crypto access lists
- Crypto map
- Transport of multiprotocol and multicast traffic
- Manual SA and key management
- Special considerations, including whether IPsec tunnels will traverse NAT devices or firewalls

These considerations are discussed in the remainder this chapter. The sample topology shown in Figure 6-31 is used to illustrate the various concepts discussed.

Figure 6-31 *Sample IPsec VPN Topology*

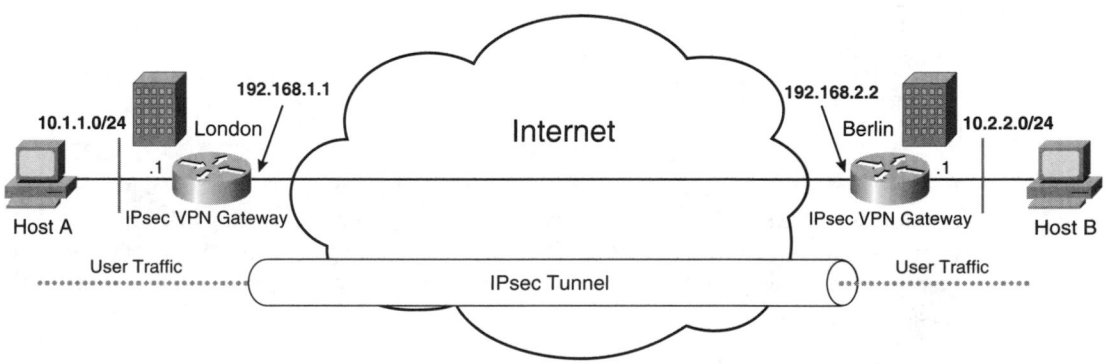

Selecting and Configuring IKE Policies for Automated SA and Key Management

When deploying IPsec VPNs with IKE, it is important to select the appropriate IKE parameters such as method of authentication and encryption algorithm to ensure that the VPN is both secure and scalable. IKE parameters are collectively known as a protection suite.

As previously mentioned, the purpose of IKE is to allow IPsec peers (IPsec VPN gateways) to dynamically authenticate each other, negotiate cryptographic parameters, and agree on session keys.

Selecting the Appropriate Method of IKE Authentication

Cisco routers can support three methods of authentication for IKE:

- Preshared key authentication
- Encrypted nonce authentication
- Digital signature authentication

The sections that follow cover these methods of authentication in greater detail.

IKE Preshared Key Authentication

You can configure IKE preshared key authentication on all Cisco devices that support IPsec.

Example 6-1 shows configuration of an IKE (ISAKMP) preshared key on a Cisco IOS router using the **crypto isakmp key** *keystring* **address** *peer-address* [*mask*] command.

Example 6-1 *Configuring Preshared Key Authentication*

```
London#conf t
Enter configuration commands, one per line. End with CNTL/Z.
London(config)#crypto isakmp key 1tdsKre*7:'W12345sQw'#%5 address 192.168.2.2
London(config)#exit
London#
```

In Example 6-1, the preshared key is 1tdsKre*7: 'W12345sQw'#%5, and the peer's IP address is 192.168.2.2. The preshared key is an alphanumeric string and must be configured *identically* on peer IPsec VPN gateways. If the preshared key is not configured identically on peer IPsec VPN gateways, IKE authentication will fail, and the IPsec tunnel(s) will not come up.

The **address** parameter is used to specify the identity of the remote IPsec peer in the form of an IP address.

Normally, you specify one preshared key per remote IPsec VPN gateway. Having one preshared per remote gateway is best from a security perspective, but with a large number of remote gateways administration can become burdensome.

It is possible to specify a wildcard address (0.0.0.0) rather than a specific IP address. If you specify a wildcard address, a remote host with *any* IP address can establish an IPsec tunnel using the configured preshared key. Example 6-2 illustrates configuration of a wildcard preshared key.

Example 6-2 *Configuring a Wildcard Preshared Key*

```
London#conf t
Enter configuration commands, one per line. End with CNTL/Z.
London(config)#crypto isakmp key 4$pe&89fHPi*90oic;:atv!(:1 address 0.0.0.0
London(config)#exit
London#
```

Although wildcard preshared keys can occasionally be useful, you should be aware of the security risks. A regular preshared key can only be used by the IPsec VPN gateway specified (for example, 192.168.2.2 in Example 6-2). But when you configure a wildcard preshared key, an attacker with any IP address can connect to the IPsec VPN gateway if he/ she is able to find out the preshared key (something that is quite possible if you choose a *weak* preshared key).

It is worth taking a closer look at the preshared keystring itself. Notice that in Example 6-1 the keystring is pretty random (1tdsKre*7: 'W12345sQw'#%5). The (relative) randomness of the keystring is deliberate—if the keystring is easily guessable, it is weak and vulnerable to attack. So, make sure that your preshared keys are long, random strings of lower- and uppercase characters, numbers, and punctuation.

It is possible to launch brute-force attacks against weak preshared keys, especially if you use aggressive mode for phase 1 IKE negotiation. If you use main mode for IKE phase 1 negotiation, it is more difficult but still possible for an attacker to recover a weak preshared key.

Do not be lulled by the strength of cryptographic algorithms such as SHA-1, 3DES, and AES, thinking that it does not matter whether preshared keys are (relatively) random. Preshared keys can be the weak link that undermines IPsec as a whole.

NOTE   The vulnerability of weak preshared keys has been extensively documented. For more information, refer to the following sites:

http://www.ernw.de/download/pskattack.pdf

http://www.cisco.com/warp/public/707/cisco-sn-20030422-ike.html

---

Now that you know how vulnerable weak preshared keys can be to attack, it is useful to list some recommendations for using preshared key authentication:

- Don't! If possible, use digital signature authentication instead. See the section "IKE Digital Signature Authentication" later in this chapter for more information.

- Make sure that your preshared keys are as random as possible (as previously described).

- Use a unique preshared key between each pair of IPsec peers.

  Do not use wildcard or group preshared keys, if possible. Wildcard and group preshared keys are particularly vulnerable to attack because a specific preshared key is not tied to a specific peer identity (such as an IP address or fully qualified domain name).

- Cisco routers use main mode for IKE phase 1 negotiations by default. However, if a remote IPsec peer initiates aggressive mode to a Cisco router, the Cisco router will switch to aggressive mode.

  If you do not need aggressive mode, you can disable it using the **crypto isakmp aggressive-mode disable** command, as shown in Example 6-3. This command is available in Cisco IOS Software Release 12.3(1) and higher.

Example 6-3   *Disabling IKE Aggressive Mode*

```
London#conf t
Enter configuration commands, one per line. End with CNTL/Z.
London(config)#crypto isakmp aggressive-mode disable
London(config)#exit
London#
```

Make sure that you do not disable IKE aggressive mode if you are deploying remote access IPsec VPNs with Cisco VPN clients or Cisco Easy VPN clients. Both Cisco VPN clients and Easy VPN clients may require IKE aggressive mode negotiation.

- By default, preshared keys are stored in cleartext in IPsec VPN gateway configuration files.

  Do not overlook the possibility of an attacker gaining access to printouts of IPsec VPN gateway configuration files or IPsec VPN gateway configuration files stored on a file server. Make sure that distribution of printouts of IPsec VPN gateway configuration files is restricted and that file servers are properly secured. In addition, if you are running Cisco IOS Software Release 12.3(2)T or higher, you can encrypt preshared keys within your IPsec VPN gateway configuration files.

Example 6-4 shows the encryption of preshared keys in a configuration file.

Example 6-4 *Encrypting Preshared Keys in a Configuration File*

```
London#show running-config | begin crypto isakmp key
crypto isakmp key cisco address 192.168.1.1 (line 1)
!
London#conf t
Enter configuration commands, one per line. End with CNTL/Z.
London(config)#key config-key password-encrypt psk123encrypt (line 2)
London(config)#password encryption aes (line 3)
London(config)#exit
London#
London#show running-config | begin crypto isakmp key
crypto isakmp key 6 ShGXJ][_TOLdGHTPFg[U_EMQff_ address 192.168.1.1 (line 4)
!
!
```

Highlighted line 1 shows that the preshared key is cisco. Note that this is a weak preshared key and is used for illustrative purposes only.

In highlighted lines 2, a master key that will be used to encrypt all preshared keys within the configuration file is configured using the **key config-key password-encrypt** [*master-key*] command. In this example, the master key is psk123encrypt. The master key is not stored within the configuration file and cannot be obtained by users that connect to the router.

In highlighted line 3, the **password encryption aes** command is used to enable encryption of preshared keys within the configuration file using the AES.

Finally, in highlighted line 4, you can see the preshared key in its encrypted form within the configuration file.

IKE Encrypted Nonce Authentication

The second option for IKE authentication is encrypted nonce authentication.

NOTE	Encrypted nonce authentication can be configured only on Cisco routers, and not on PIX Firewalls, ASA 5500s, or VPN 3000 concentrators.

In you want to use encrypted nonce authentication, you must complete the following tasks on each IPsec VPN gateway:

- Configure the IPsec VPN gateway's host name and domain name.
- Generate RSA keys.
- Configure public keys from peer IPsec VPN gateways.

You can configure an IPsec VPN gateway's host name and IP domain name using the **hostname** *hostname* and **ip domain-name** *domain-name* commands, as demonstrated in Example 6-5.

Example 6-5 *Configuring the Host Name and IP Domain Name*

```
London#conf t
Enter configuration commands, one per line. End with CNTL/Z.
London(config)#hostname London
London(config)#ip domain-name mjlnet.com
London(config)#exit
London#
```

In Example 6-5, an IPsec VPN gateway's host name and domain name are configured as London and mjlnet.com, respectively. The host name and domain name are concatenated into the fully qualified domain name (FQDN) London.mjlnet.com.

After you have configured the host name and domain name, the next step is to generate RSA keys on the IPsec VPN gateway using the **crypto key generate rsa** [**usage-keys** | **general-keys**] [*key-pair-label*] command, as demonstrated in Example 6-6.

Example 6-6 *Generating RSA Keys on an IPsec VPN Gateway*

```
London#conf t
Enter configuration commands, one per line. End with CNTL/Z.
London(config)#crypto key generate rsa (line 1)
The name for the keys will be: London.mjlnet.com (line 2)
Choose the size of the key modulus in the range of 360 to 2048 for your
 General Purpose Keys. Choosing a key modulus greater than 512 may take
 a few minutes.
How many bits in the modulus [512]: 1024 (line 3)
% Generating 1024 bit RSA keys ...[OK]
London(config)#exit
London#
```

In highlighted line 1, the **crypto key generate rsa** command is used to generate RSA general usage keys (keys that can be used for either signing or encryption). If you specify the **usage-keys** keyword, separate keys are generated for encryption and signing.

The message shown in highlighted line 2 indicates that the name assigned to the key pair (public and private keys) will be London.mjlnet.com (the FQDN). The default name assigned to the key pair is the FQDN, but if you do want to assign a different name to a key pair, you can specify it using the *key-pair-label* parameter when you use the **crypto key generate rsa** command.

Highlighted line 3 specifies a key size (modulus) of 1024 bits. You can specify a key modulus of 360 to 2048 bits. The shorter the key modulus, the less secure the key pair is, so recommended practice is that you use a minimum key modulus of 1024 bits.

After you have generated RSA keys on your IPsec VPN gateways, the next step is to exchange the peer gateways' public keys and paste them into the configuration of the IPsec VPN gateways.

For example, after you have generated RSA keys on the London and Berlin gateways (see Figure 6-31), you should paste the public key(s) from the Berlin gateway into the configuration of the London gateway and the public key(s) of the London gateway into the configuration of the Berlin gateway.

In Figures 6-32, 6-33, and 6-34, the public key of the Berlin gateway is displayed, and then it is copied and pasted into the configuration of the London gateway.

In Figure 6-32, the **show crypto key mypubkey rsa** command is used to display the public key of the Berlin gateway. This public key is copied.

Figure 6-32 *Displaying and Copying the Public Key of the Berlin IPsec VPN Gateway*

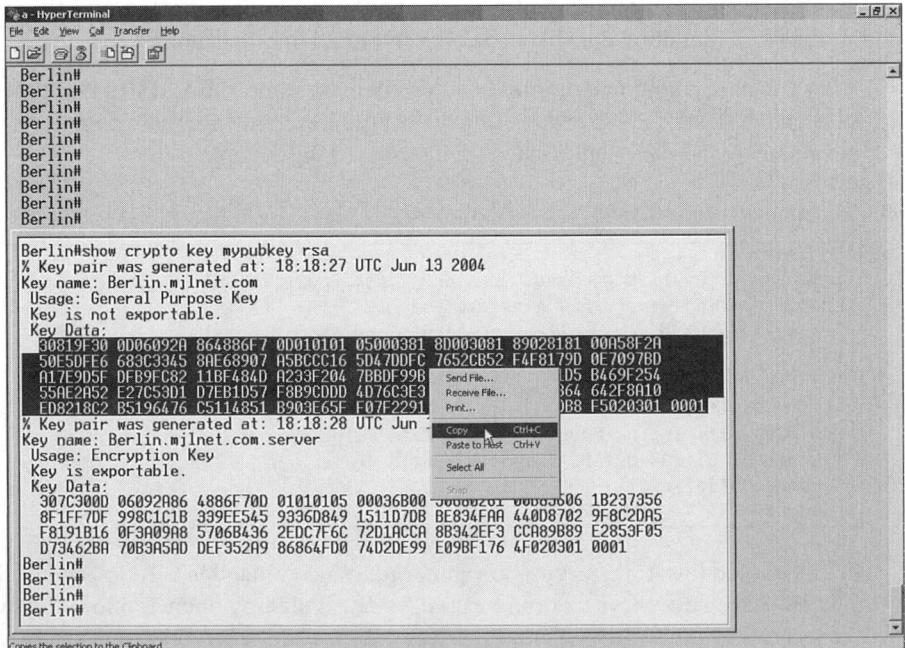

In Figure 6-33, the **crypto key pubkey-chain rsa** command is used on the London IPsec VPN gateway to enter the public key configuration mode.

Figure 6-33 *Preparing to Paste Berlin's Public Key into the Configuration of the London IPsec VPN Gateway*

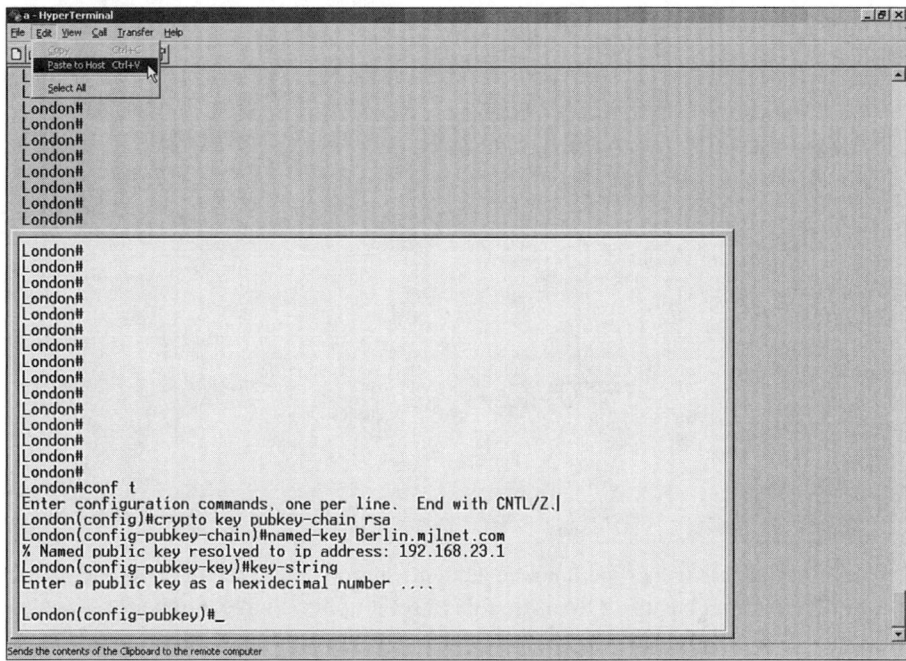

The **named-key** *key-name* command is then used to specify the name (FQDN) of the key to be manually configured (in this example, Berlin.mjlnet.com).

Finally, the **key-string** command is used to enter the mode in which the public key from the peer gateway (Berlin in this example) can be pasted into the configuration.

As shown in Figure 6-34, after the **key-string** command has been entered, the public key of the remote gateway is pasted, and the **quit** command is used to exit public key configuration mode.

You might be thinking to yourself that IKE encrypted nonce authentication looks like a lot of hard work, especially if you have a large number of gateways in your VPN. Well, you are right; it is a lot of hard work (imagine copying and pasting all those public keys), and that is the reason that it is not a common method of IKE authentication.

So, when might you use encrypted nonce authentication? Well, you might *possibly* use it if you are concerned about weak preshared keys but you do not want to go to the trouble of deploying the PKI necessary to enable digital signature authentication.

Figure 6-34 *Berlin's Public Key Is Pasted to the London IPsec VPN Gateway*

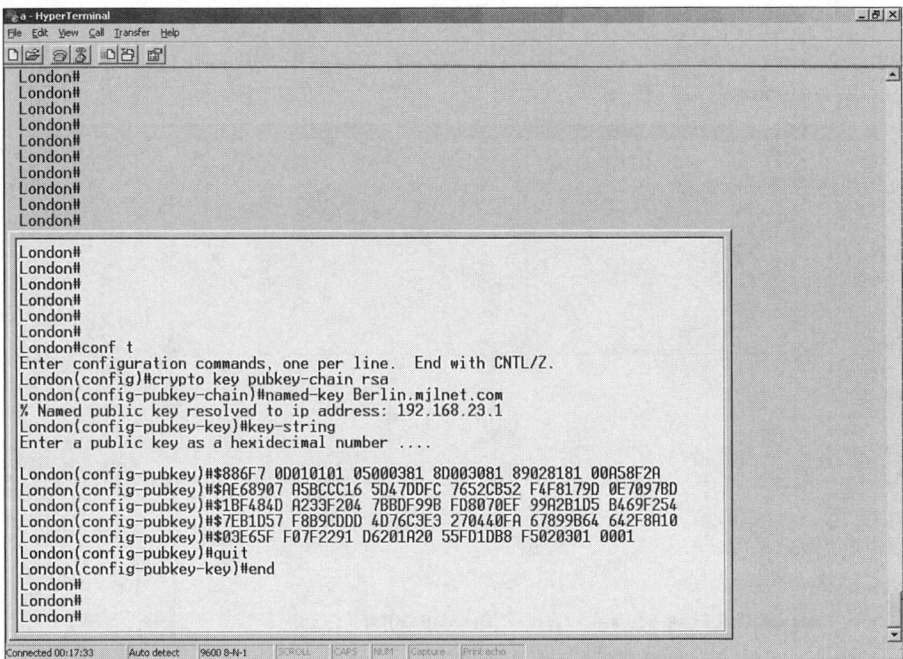

In summary, IKE encrypted nonce authentication is more secure than preshared key authentication, but it is a lot of trouble to set it up for a large number of IPsec peers. Most people opt for preshared key authentication (while avoiding weak preshared keys) or, much better, use digital signature authentication.

IKE Digital Signature Authentication

The third and final method of IKE authentication is RSA digital signature authentication using digital certificates.

You must complete a number of steps on each IPsec VPN gateway if you want to use digital signature authentication in your IPsec VPN:

Step 1 Set the time on the IPsec VPN gateways.

Step 2 Configure the IPsec VPN gateways' host names and IP domain names.

Step 3 Generate RSA keys on the IPsec VPN gateways.

Step 4 Declare the CA.

Step 5 Authenticate the CA.

Step 6 Enroll the IPsec VPN gateways with the CA.

These steps are examined in the sections that follow.

Step 1: Set the Time on the IPsec VPN Gateways

Ensuring that the time is correctly set on IPsec VPN gateways is important when using digital signature authentication. Certificates are valid for a certain time period only, and if the time is not set correctly, IKE authentication may fail, and gateways may not even be able to obtain a certificate from a CA in the first place.

So, now that you know how important time is for digital signature authentication, what are the options for ensuring accurate time on the gateways? There are two options:

- Manually setting the time on each IPsec VPN gateway
- Setting the time on IPsec VPN gateways using the Network Time Protocol (NTP)

These methods of ensuring accurate time are discussed in the following two sections.

Manually Setting the Time on Each IPsec VPN Gateway   To ensure accurate time on IPsec VPN gateways by manually setting them, use the **clock set** *hh:mm:ss day month year* command to manually set the clock, as demonstrated in Example 6-7.

Example 6-7 *Manually Setting the System Clock*

```
London#clock set 11:33:00 june 14 2004
```

Also, be sure to set the time zone using the **clock timezone** *zone hours-offset* [*minutes-offset*] command, as demonstrated in Example 6-8.

Example 6-8 *Setting the Time Zone*

```
London#conf t
Enter configuration commands, one per line. End with CNTL/Z.
London(config)#clock timezone GMT 0
London(config)#exit
London#
```

In Example 6-8, the time zone is set to be GMT (Greenwich mean time), with an offset of 0 hours from universal time coordinated (UTC).

Disadvantages of manually setting time of the IPsec VPN gateways are that it is easy to make a simple error and if the systems in question do not have hardware clocks, the time will reset in the event of a reboot.

Setting the Time on IPsec VPN Gateways Using NTP   Another option for ensuring accurate time on the gateways in an IPsec VPN is to use NTP.

The advantages of NTP are that you can be sure that all the gateways in the VPN will have accurate time (assuming that the NTP server[s] has accurate time), and that even if a gateway is rebooted it will resynchronize its time with an NTP server.

The disadvantage of NTP is that an NTP server (or preferably servers) is required.

Use the **ntp server** *ip-address* command to allow a gateway to synchronize its time to an NTP server, as demonstrated in Example 6-9.

Example 6-9   *Specifying an NTP Server Using the ntp server Command*

```
London#conf t
Enter configuration commands, one per line. End with CNTL/Z.
London(config)#ntp server 10.10.10.99
London(config)#exit
London#
```

In Example 6-9, a gateway is configured to synchronize its time to NTP server 10.10.10.99.

One important consideration when using NTP is to ensure that IPsec VPN gateways synchronize their clocks with a trusted time source. It is possible for an attacker to carry out a denial-of-service attack by getting gateways to synchronize their time with a bogus time source. In this case, IKE authentication can fail if the bogus time is outside the validity period of the gateways' certificates. In addition, gateways with revoked certificates might be able continue to participate in the VPN.

To ensure that gateways synchronize their clocks with a trusted time source, you can use NTP authentication, as demonstrated in Example 6-10.

Example 6-10   *Configuring NTP Authentication*

```
London#conf t
Enter configuration commands, one per line. End with CNTL/Z.
London(config)#ntp authenticate
London(config)#ntp authentication-key 1 md5 mjlnet
London(config)#ntp trusted-key 1
London(config)#ntp server 10.10.10.99 key 1
London(config)#exit
London#
```

The **ntp authenticate** command in Example 6-10 enables NTP authentication.

The **ntp authentication-key** *key-number* **md5** *key-string* command specifies MD5 NTP authentication with, in this example, the key string **mjlnet**. Note that **mjlnet** is not a secure choice of authentication key and is used here for illustrative purposes only. In live deployments, you should choose a random string of up to eight characters.

After the authentication key has been configured, the **ntp trusted-key** *key-number* command specifies the trusted NTP key. The key number must match with that specified using the **ntp authentication-key** command.

The **ntp server** *ip-address* **key** *key-value* command then configures the IP address of an NTP server, and specifies that the gateway will synchronize its time to that server only if the server's NTP packets can be authenticated with the previously specified trusted key (**mjlnet** in this example).

NOTE   If you decide to use NTP in your IPsec VPN, it is important that it be deployed in a scalable, highly available, and secure manner. A good starting point for obtaining more information concerning NTP deployment is the following white paper:

http://www.cisco.com/en/US/tech/tk869/tk769/technologies_white_paper 09186a0080117070.shtml

Step 2: Configure the IPsec VPN Gateways' Host Names and IP Domain Names   Having set the time on the IPsec VPN gateways, the next step is to configure their IP domain names, as well host names if they have not already been configured.

Example 6-11 demonstrates configuration of the IP domain name.

Example 6-11 *Configuring an IP Domain Name*

```
London#conf t
Enter configuration commands, one per line. End with CNTL/Z.
London(config)#ip domain-name mjlnet.com
London(config)#exit
London#
```

The IP domain name of IPsec VPN gateway London is configured in Example 6-11 using the **ip domain-name** *name* command.

If you have not already configured a host name on your IPsec VPN gateways, now is the time to do it using the **hostname** *name* global configuration mode command.

The IPsec VPN gateways' host name and IP domain name are concatenated to produce an FQDN.

Step 3: Generate RSA Keys on the IPsec VPN Gateways   Next are the IPsec VPN gateways' RSA keys.

Use the **crypto key generate rsa** command to generate RSA keys, as demonstrated in Example 6-12.

Example 6-12 *Generating RSA Keys on the IPsec VPN Gateways*

```
London#conf t
Enter configuration commands, one per line. End with CNTL/Z.
London(config)#crypto key generate rsa
The name for the keys will be: London.mjlnet.com
Choose the size of the key modulus in the range of 360 to 2048 for your
  General Purpose Keys. Choosing a key modulus greater than 512 may take
    a few minutes.
How many bits in the modulus [512]: 1024
% Generating 1024 bit RSA keys ...[OK]
London(config)#exit
London#
```

Notice that the name associated with the RSA key pair generated using the **crypto key generate** command is, by default, the FQDN of the gateway. Also, notice that a key length (modulus) of 1024 bits is specified. The minimum recommended length for RSA keys is 1024 bits.

You can verify the RSA keys using the **show crypto key mypubkey rsa** command, as demonstrated in Example 6-13.

Example 6-13 *Verifying RSA Keys*

```
London#show crypto key mypubkey rsa
% Key pair was generated at: 12:14:20 GMT Jun 14 2004
Key name: London.mjlnet.com (line 1)
 Usage: General Purpose Key (line 2)
 Key is not exportable.
 Key Data:
  30819F30 0D06092A 864886F7 0D010101 05000381 8D003081 89028181 00C6CED9 (line 3)
  C6887913 A661D773 C200DB17 0BF83826 30371342 18EF2CCD F691BB36 62E91B5D (line 4)
  17C9B4F9 4F1CCDE4 15A4F80F 3288D6E9 C193701A 246CEAE6 CCEDD551 C577A7C8 (line 5)
  EE247482 37F2166D 7B0C21E5 6BD038E9 4D48210B 799CF399 1097B323 BD8E9776 (line 6)
  C2533CDE 3B1ED52B B49A364C 895C5BC3 9BB6D517 671677D5 2A5CC996
   BF020301 0001 (line 7)
% Key pair was generated at: 12:26:36 GMT Jun 14 2004
Key name: London.mjlnet.com.server
 Usage: Encryption Key
 Key is not exportable.
 Key Data:
  307C300D 06092A86 4886F70D 01010105 00036B00 30680261 009A2365 E55C3BC9
  742995EC FDB3DFDF 1AF1EE36 D05D3ABF 749282A7 4C8D152E 78DA88D4 2B25178C
  04A3209E 1008ED55 6B1A82AB 2A7C49BA 86005839 06517310 4B95C487 6D2D3666
  ADFA28BF 84BADB77 3F92A3D7 6F061F73 B5ABAB9E 19A472C3 0B020301 0001
London#
```

Highlighted line 1 shows the RSA public key name London.mjlnet.com.

Highlighted line 2 shows that the key is for general purposes (encryption and signing).

The key itself is then shown in highlighted lines 3 to 7.

Step 4: Declare the CA   You are almost ready to obtain the IPsec VPN gateway's certificate from the CA, but there are one or two remaining steps before you can do that—the first of which is to declare the CA.

Declaring the CA involves a number of things, including specifying a name for the CA, specifying the mode to be used for certificate enrollment, and configuring the URL to use when enrolling with the CA.

Before declaring the CA, make sure that the CA's name is mapped locally on the gateway using the **ip host** *name ip-address* command or resolvable via DNS.

Example 6-14 declares CA mjlnetcertsrv.

Example 6-14 *Declaring the CA*

```
London#conf t
Enter configuration commands, one per line. End with CNTL/Z.
London(config)#crypto pki trustpoint mjlnetcertsrv (line 1)
London(ca-trustpoint)#enrollment mode ra (line 2)
London(ca-trustpoint)#enrollment url
 http://mjlnetcertsrv:80/certsrv/mscep/mscep.dll (line 3)
London(ca-trustpoint)#revocation-check none (line 4)
London(ca-trustpoint)#end
London#
```

In highlighted line 1, the **crypto pki trustpoint** *name* command configures a locally significant name for a CA and enters ca-trustpoint configuration mode.

NOTE   The **crypto pki trustpoint** command replaces the **crypto ca trustpoint**, **crypto ca identity**, and **crypto ca trusted-root** commands. The **pki** keyword also replaces the **ca** keyword in a number of commands in more recent versions of Cisco IOS Software.

The **enrollment mode ra** command shown in highlighted line 2 configures the gateway to enroll with the CA using the registration authority (RA) enrollment mode. Check with your CA administrator about the enrollment mode that you should configure.

Next is the **enrollment url** *url* command (highlighted line 3). This command configures the URL to be used for Simple Certificate Enrollment Protocol (SCEP) enrollment with the CA. SCEP is a protocol that supports operations such as certificate enrollment, revocation, certificate access, and CRL access.

Verify the correct enrollment URL with your CA administrator.

NOTE   It is also possible to enroll with a CA either manually or using TFTP if your CA does not support SCEP. Check Cisco.com for more information.

In highlighted line 4, the **revocation-check** *method1* [*method2*[*method3*]] command specifies how the gateway should check whether peer IPsec VPN gateways' certificates have been revoked. You can specify up to three methods for the gateway to use for certificate revocation checking. If more than one method is specified, each method is tried in turn.

In Example 6-14, the **none** keyword is specified, so the local gateway will check a CRL if one is cached in memory, but will not download a CRL from a CRL Distribution Point (CDP). The **revocation-check none** command replaces the **crl optional** command.

Other keywords (methods) that you can specify with the **revocation-check** command are **ocsp** and **crl**. If you specify the **ocsp** keyword, OCSP is used to check certificate revocation status, via the OSCP responder (server) specified in the Authority Information Access (AIA) extension of a certificate (it is also possible to specify the OCSP responder manually, and override that contained in the AIA, by using the **ocsp url** *url* command in the trustpoint configuration mode). If you specify the **crl** keyword, the gateway will attempt to download a CRL from the CDP specified in a certificate.

If you specify either the **ocsp** or **crl** keyword alone (for example, **revocation-check oscp**), the local gateway attempts to verify certificate status by using OCSP or by downloading a CRL as appropriate; if it is unable to contact the OCSP responder or download the CRL, however, the revocation check will not succeed, and IKE authentication will fail.

A best-effort certificate revocation check can be configured by specifying the **none** keyword after the **crl** or **ocsp** keywords. So, for example, if you specify the **revocation-check crl none** command, the local gateway will attempt to download a CRL and verify the certificate's status; if it is unable to download the CRL, however, it will accept the certificate, and IKE authentication will succeed.

The **revocation-check crl none** command replaces the **crl best-effort** command.

NOTE   If you specify either the **none** keyword alone or use best-effort certificate revocation checking (as previously discussed), it is possible for IKE authentication to succeed even if a certificate has been revoked.

On the other hand, if you specify either the **ocsp** or **crl** keyword alone, it is possible for an attacker to conduct a denial-of-service attack on your IPsec VPN by targeting the OSCP responder(s) or CDP(s) and making them unavailable to the IPsec VPN gateways. In this case, if the OSCP responder or CDP is unavailable, IKE authentication will fail *throughout* the IPsec VPN.

So, be sure you carefully weigh the options when configuring the **revocation-check** command.

Step 5: Authenticate the CA   The penultimate step before you can enroll your IPsec VPN gateways is to authenticate the CA by obtaining its certificate, as illustrated in Figure 6-35.

Figure 6-35 *Authenticating the CA*

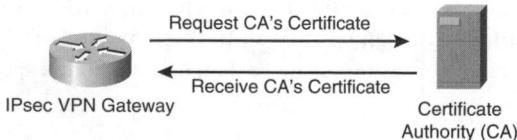

Use the **crypto pki authenticate** *name* command to authenticate the CA, as demonstrated in Example 6-15, where the *name* parameter is that specified when declaring the CA (see Example 6-14).

Example 6-15 *Authenticating the CA*

```
London#conf t
Enter configuration commands, one per line. End with CNTL/Z.
London(config)#crypto pki authenticate mjlnetcertsrv
Certificate has the following attributes:
Fingerprint: 54C151AE FFF125FD BD4FB4D7 D26AD8CA
% Do you accept this certificate? [yes/no]: y
Trustpoint CA certificate accepted.
London(config)#exit
London#
```

In Example 6-15, the CA's certificate is downloaded from the CA.

At this point, you can choose to either accept or reject the CA's certificate. If the fingerprint displayed (highlighted in Example 6-15) matches the fingerprint visible to the CA administrator, you should accept the certificate.

After the CA's certificate has been downloaded, you can verify the CA's certificate using the **show crypto pki certificate** command, as demonstrated in Example 6-16.

Example 6-16 *Verifying the CA's Certificate*

```
London#show crypto pki certificate
CA Certificate
 Status: Available
 Certificate Serial Number: 48B8A34E0C6A09A7447B8CBDD77C3A81
 Certificate Usage: Signature
 Issuer:
  CN = mjlnet.ca1
   OU = Engineering
   O = MJL Network Solutions
   L = London
   ST = none
   C = UK
   EA = admin@mjlnet.com
 Subject:
  CN = mjlnet.ca1
   OU = Engineering
   O = MJL Network Solutions
   L = London
   ST = none
   C = UK
   EA = admin@mjlnet.com
 CRL Distribution Point:
  http://mjl-certsrv-acs/CertEnroll/mjlnet.ca1.crl
 Validity Date:
  start date: 13:20:22 UTC Mar 25 2004
  end  date: 13:29:01 UTC Mar 25 2009
 Associated Trustpoints: mjlnetca
London#
```

For more information about the fields in the certificate shown in Example 6-16, see the section titled "The X.509 Certificate" in Chapter 7.

NOTE   You can also manually add (or delete) a CA's certificate in hexadecimal format using the **certificate ca** *certificate-serial-number* command within the certificate chain configuration mode. You can enter the certificate chain configuration mode using the **crypto pki certificate chain** *name* command from global configuration mode.

Step 6: Enroll the IPsec VPN Gateways with the CA   The final step is to enroll the IPsec VPN gateway with the CA. During enrollment, the gateway obtains a signed certificate from the CA for each RSA key pair that you generated, as illustrated in Figure 6-36.

Figure 6-36 *Enrolling with the CA and Obtaining a Certificate*

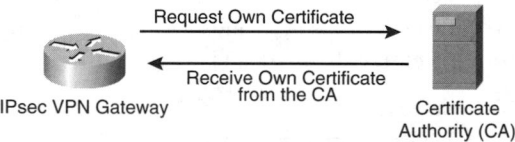

You can use the **crypto pki enroll** *name* command to enroll with the CA, as demonstrated in Example 6-17. The name should be the same as you specified using the **crypto pki trustpoint** command (see Example 6-14).

Example 6-17 *Enrolling with the CA*

```
London#conf t
Enter configuration commands, one per line. End with CNTL/Z.
London(config)#crypto pki enroll mjlnetcertsrv
%
% Start certificate enrollment ..
% Create a challenge password. You will need to verbally provide this
  password to the CA Administrator to revoke your certificate.
  For security reasons your password will not be saved in the configuration.
  Please make a note of it.
Password: (line 1)
Re-enter password: (line 2)
% The fully-qualified domain name in the certificate will be: London.mjlnet.com
% The subject name in the certificate will be: London.mjlnet.com (line 3)
% Include the router serial number in the subject name? [yes/no]: no (line 4)
% Include an IP address in the subject name? [no]: (line 5)
Request certificate from CA? [yes/no]: yes (line 6)
% Certificate request sent to Certificate Authority
% The certificate request fingerprint will be displayed.
% The 'show crypto ca certificate' command will also show the fingerprint.
London(config)#  Fingerprint: DEEFAF09 8FC3C7D3 1F26ACE8 87E7238F
```

Example 6-17 *Enrolling with the CA (Continued)*

```
Jun 14 11:37:18.859: CRYPTO_PKI: status = 102:
 certificate request pending (line 7)
Jun 14 11:37:40.215: CRYPTO_PKI: status = 102: certificate request pending
Jun 14 11:38:42.175: %CRYPTO-6-CERTRET: Certificate received from Certificate
 Authority (line 8)
London(config)#exit
London#
```

As you can see in Example 6-17, when you issue the **crypto pki enroll** command, you are asked to enter a password (highlighted lines 1 and 2) and then asked whether you want to include the router serial number (highlighted line 4) and IP address (highlighted line 5) in the certificate.

The CA administrator may ask you to supply the challenge password in the event that you need to revoke the certificate, so make sure you note this.

The serial number referred to in highlighted line 4 is not the certificate serial number (see the section "The X.509 Certificate" in Chapter 7 for more on this), but instead the gateway's internal board serial number.

If you want to include an IP address in the certificate (see highlighted line 5), make sure it is the IP address of the outside interface to which the crypto map is applied, or if the crypto map is applied to multiple interfaces, the IP address specified with the **crypto map local-address** command.

Be careful if you do decide to include an IP address in the certificate because if you do change the IP address on the outside interface (or the IP address referred to with the **crypto map local-address** command), IKE authentication will fail for the IPsec VPN gateway in question. In this case, you need to re-enroll the gateway with the CA, and obtain a new certificate, or change the IP address on the outside interface (or the IP address referred to with the **crypto map local-address** command) back to its original form.

Notice the subject name shown in highlighted line 3—the gateway's FQDN is, by default, included as the subject name in the gateway's certificate.

The certificate is requested from the CA in highlighted line 6, and then in highlighted line 7 you can see that the certificate request is pending.

The CA administrator then approves the certificate, and in highlighted line 8 the gateway receives its certificate.

You can verify the certificate using the **show crypto pki certificate** command, as demonstrated in Example 6-18 (only the relevant output is shown).

Example 6-18 *Verifying the IPsec VPN Gateway's Certificate*

```
London#show crypto pki certificates
Certificate
 Status: Available
```

continues

Example 6-18 *Verifying the IPsec VPN Gateway's Certificate (Continued)*

```
 Certificate Serial Number: 617C2FE2000000000012
 Certificate Usage: General Purpose
 Issuer:
  cn=mjlnet.ca1
  ou=Engineering
  o=MJL Network Solutions
  l=London
  st=none
  c=UK
  ea=admin@mjlnet.com
 Subject:
  Name: London.mjlnet.com
  hostname=London.mjlnet.com
 CRL Distribution Points:
  http://mjlnet-ca/CertEnroll/mjlnet.ca1.crl
 Validity Date:
  start date: 11:07:22 GMT Jun 14 2004
  end  date: 11:17:22 GMT Jun 14 2005
  renew date: 00:00:00 GMT Jan 1 1970
 Associated Trustpoints: mjlnetcertsrv
```

The status of the IPsec VPN gateway's certificate is listed as Available, which indicates that the (signed) certificate has been received from the CA. For more information on the various fields in the certificate, see the section "The X.509 Certificate" in Chapter 7.

Phew! All done. But, just in case you are not satisfied with the contents of your certificate, and if you prefer not to go through the dialog shown Example 6-17 (entering a password, specifying a serial number, and so on), it is possible to configure this information in advance within the crypto ca-trustpoint mode, as shown in Example 6-19.

Example 6-19 *Specifying Answers to the Certificate Enrollment Dialog, as Well as Certificate Fields*

```
London#conf t
Enter configuration commands, one per line. End with CNTL/Z.
London(config)#crypto pki trustpoint mjlnetcertsrv
London(ca-trustpoint)#usage ike (line 1)
London(ca-trustpoint)#subject-name C=GB, O=MJL Network Solutions,
 OU=Engineering (line 2)
London(ca-trustpoint)#ip-address 192.168.1.1 (line 3)
London(ca-trustpoint)#serial-number (line 4)
London(ca-trustpoint)#password cisco (line 5)
London(ca-trustpoint)#end (line 6)
London#
```

The **usage** *method1* [*method2* [*method3*]] command in highlighted line 1 specifies the usage of the certificate (in this case, IKE).

In highlighted line 2, the **subject-name** command specifies the X.500 Distinguished Name (DN) to be used in the Subject Name field of the certificate. In this example, the country (C) is GB, the Organization (O) is MJL Network Solutions, and the organizational unit (OU) is Engineering.

Highlighted line 3 specifies the IP address 192.168.1.1 using the **ip-address** *address* command. This IP address is included in the Subject Name field of the certificate. Make sure that you follow the guidelines discussed earlier in this section if you do decide to include an IP address in the certificate.

Next is the **serial-number** command (see highlighted line 4). This command specifies that the internal board serial number should be included in the certificate. Again, the serial number is included in the Subject Name field of the certificate. If you do not want to include the gateway's serial number in the certificate, you can specify this using the **serial-number none** command.

The challenge password is specified in highlighted line 5. This password must be supplied to the CA administrator if you need to revoke the certificate at a later date. The password specified in this example (cisco) is not secure and is used for illustrative purposes only.

CAUTION   Make sure that you save your configuration using the **copy running-config startup-config** command after you have generated RSA keys, authenticated the CA, and enrolled with the CA.

If you do not save your configuration, information will be lost, and you will have to repeat these processes.

Automating Enrollment with the CA   Now that you know how to enroll with the CA manually, it is useful to take a look at how this process can be automated. The auto-enrollment feature enables you to preconfigure your IPsec VPN gateway with enrollment parameters, and it will then automatically enroll with the CA. If you are configuring a large number of IPsec VPN gateways, this can really be a time saver.

Example 6-20 shows the configuration necessary to enable auto-enrollment.

Example 6-20 *Configuring an IPsec VPN Gateway for Auto-Enrollment with the CA*

```
!
crypto pki trustpoint mjlnetcertsrv
 enrollment mode ra
 enrollment url http://mjlnetcertsrv:80/certsrv/mscep/mscep.dll
 usage ike
 serial-number none
 ip-address 192.168.1.1
 password 7 121A0C041104
 subject-name C=GB, O=mjlnet, OU=engineering
 revocation-check crl
 rsakeypair London.mjlnet.com 1024 (line 1)
 auto-enroll (line 2)
!
```

Almost all of the commands shown in Example 6-20 should already be familiar, but there are one or two new commands.

In highlighted line 2, you can see the **auto-enroll** [*percent*] [**regenerate**] command. This command configures the gateway to automatically generate RSA keys and enroll with the CA on reboot using the parameters specified.

The optional **rsakeypair** *key-label* [*key-size* [*encryption-key-size*]] command (highlighted line 1) specifies which key pair you want to associate with the certificate as well as (optionally) the key size.

The **rsakeypair** command is important because, by default, the **auto-enroll** command generates 512-bit RSA keys prior to enrolling with the CA. By configuring the **rsakeypair** command, you can specify the RSA key size (the minimum recommended is 1024 bits).

There is one process that must be completed manually on the gateway before auto-enrollment can begin—you must manually authenticate the CA (as discussed in the section "Step 5: Authenticate the CA"). If you forget to authenticate the CA, the message shown in Example 6-21 displays.

Example 6-21 *Message Displayed If You Forget to Authenticate the CA*

```
% Time to Re-enroll trust_point mjlnetcertsrv
% You must authenticate the Certificate Authority before you can enroll with it.
```

Automating Re-Enrollment with the CA

Okay, your IPsec VPN gateways now have their certificates, and you can relax, right? Well, you can for a while—specifically until your gateways' certificates expire. If you have manually enrolled the gateways with the CA, when the certificates expire you have to go through the entire enrollment process again on each and every gateway.

Luckily (or maybe not so luckily), the **auto-enroll** [*percentage*] [**regenerate**] command allows your gateways to re-enroll with the CA automatically when the original certificate expires, saving you a lot of time and trouble manually re-enrolling gateways with the CA.

If you specify the *percentage* parameter with the **auto-enroll** command, you can control the point at which the gateway re-enrolls with the CA. For example, if you specify 90 percent, the gateway will re-enroll with the CA when the current certificate reaches the point at which 90 percent of its validity has expired.

By specifying a re-enrollment percentage, you can help to ensure that certificate enrollment is seamless, and that the gateway is not left with an old and invalid certificate that would cause IKE authentication failure.

Furthermore, you can specify the **regenerate** keyword with the **auto-enroll** command if you want the gateway to generate a new RSA key pair when it re-enrolls with the CA. This can be useful because some CAs require a new key pair for re-enrollment.

Example 6-22 shows the configuration of the **auto-enroll** command with the *percentage* parameter and **regenerate** keyword.

Example 6-22 *Specifying the percentage Parameter and regenerate Keyword with the auto-enroll Command*

```
London#conf t
Enter configuration commands, one per line. End with CNTL/Z.
London(config)#crypto ca trustpoint mjlnetcertsrv
London(ca-trustpoint)#auto-enroll 90 regenerate
London(ca-trustpoint)#end
London#
```

In Example 6-22, the **auto-enroll** command specifies a re-enrollment percentage of 90 percent. When the existing certificate reaches 90 percent of its validity period, the gateway will attempt to re-enroll with the CA.

Because the **regenerate** keyword is also specified with the **auto-enroll** command in Example 6-22, the gateway will generate a new RSA key pair every time it re-enrolls with the CA.

Selecting Cryptographic Parameters for IKE Policies

After you have configured the IKE authentication method, the next step is to configure IKE policies.

IKE policies are made up of cryptographic parameters, and are configured using the **crypto isakmp policy** *priority* command. You can configure multiple IKE policies each with a different priority (from 1 to 10000). Somewhat confusingly, lower numbered policies have a higher priority, with IKE policy 1 having the highest priority of all.

A default IKE policy is automatically created with priority 65535. This policy includes all of the default IKE policy parameters discussed in this section.

During IKE phase 1, IPsec peers negotiate IKE policies, starting with the highest-priority (lowest-numbered) policy, until either the peers find a matching policy and IKE negotiation succeeds or they do not find a match and IKE negotiation fails.

An IKE policy (ISAKMP policy) is made up of the following elements:

- Encryption algorithm
- Diffie-Hellman group
- Hash algorithm
- Authentication method
- IKE lifetime

Configuring an Encryption Algorithm for an IKE Policy

You can specify three encryption algorithms in an IKE policy:

- DES 56-bit encryption (the default)
- 3DES 168-bit encryption
- AES 128-bit, 192-bit, or 256-bit encryption

Use the **encryption** {**des** | **3des** | **aes** | **aes 192** | **aes 256**} ISAKMP configuration mode command to configure an encryption algorithm, as demonstrated in Example 6-23.

The default encryption algorithm is DES.

Example 6-23 *Configuration of an IKE Protection Suite*

```
London#conf t
Enter configuration commands, one per line. End with CNTL/Z.
London(config)#crypto isakmp policy 10
London(config-isakmp)#encryption 3des
London(config-isakmp)#end
London#
```

Example 6-23 specifies 3DES as the encryption algorithm within IKE policy 10.

Table 6-1 shows the **encryption** command options.

Table 6-1 *IKE Encryption Configuration*

Keyword	Function	Notes
des	56-bit DES encryption*	Insecure; Default
3des	168-bit 3DES encryption*	Secure
aes	128-bit AES encryption*	Secure
aes 192	192-bit AES encryption*	Secure
aes 256	256-bit AES encryption*	Secure

*For more information on encryption algorithms, see the section titled "Encryption Algorithms" later in chapter

Configuring a Diffie-Hellman Group for an IKE Policy

The next step is to configure the Diffie-Hellman group.

You can configure one of three Diffie-Hellman groups within IKE policies:

- **Group 1**—A 768-bit prime modulus group (the default)
- **Group 2**—A 1024-bit prime modulus group
- **Group 5**—A 1536-bit prime modulus group

Diffie-Hellman group 5 is the most secure of the three groups but causes the most processing overhead. Diffie-Hellman group 1, on the other hand, is the least secure but causes the least overhead.

Use the **group** {1 | 2 | 5} command to configure the Diffie-Hellman group within an IKE policy, as demonstrated in Example 6-24.

Example 6-24 *Configuring the Diffie-Hellman Group*

```
London#conf t
Enter configuration commands, one per line. End with CNTL/Z.
London(config)#crypto isakmp policy 10
London(config-isakmp)#group 2
London(config-isakmp)#end
London#
```

In Example 6-24, a 1024-bit Diffie-Hellman group is configured for IKE policy 10.

Table 6-2 summarizes **group** command options.

Table 6-2   *IKE Diffie-Hellman Group Configuration*

Keyword	Function
1	768-bit Diffie-Hellman group
	(Default) Not recommended by NIST
2	1024-bit Diffie-Hellman group
5	1536 Diffie-Hellman group

Configuring a Hash Algorithm for an IKE Policy

Next is the hash algorithm. This is used to authenticate IKE messages sent between IPsec peers.

Again, there is a choice of algorithms:

- MD5, HMAC variant
- SHA-1, HMAC variant (the default)

For more information regarding hash algorithms, see the section "Configuring IPsec Transform Sets" later in this chapter.

Specify the hash algorithm to be used with an IKE policy using the **hash** {**sha** | **md5**} command, as demonstrated in Example 6-25.

The default hash algorithm is SHA-1.

Example 6-25 *Configuring the Hash Algorithm Group*

```
London#conf t
Enter configuration commands, one per line. End with CNTL/Z.
London(config)#crypto isakmp policy 10
London(config-isakmp)#hash md5
London(config-isakmp)#end
London#
```

The **hash** command is used in Example 6-25 to specify MD5 as the hash algorithm to be used within IKE policy 10.

Table 6-3 shows **hash** command options.

Table 6-3   *IKE Policy Hash Algorithm Configuration*

Keyword	Function	Notes
sha	SHA-1 (HMAC variant) authentication*	1. Considered to be secure
		2. Slightly slower than MD5
		3. Default algorithm
md5	MD5 (HMAC variant) authentication*	Considered to be secure

*See the section "Hash Algorithms" later in this chapter for more information on hash algorithms

Configuring an Authentication Method for an IKE Policy

You must also specify the method of peer authentication within the IKE policy. The method of authentication can be, as previously described, the following:

- Preshared keys
- Encrypted nonces
- Digital signatures (the default)

Use the **authentication** {**rsa-sig** | **rsa-encr** | **pre-share**} command to configure the method of authentication to be used by an IKE policy, as demonstrated in Example 6-26.

Example 6-26 *Configuring the Method of Authentication*

```
London#conf t
Enter configuration commands, one per line. End with CNTL/Z.
London(config)#crypto isakmp policy 10
London(config-isakmp)#authentication pre-share
London(config-isakmp)#end
London#
```

In Example 6-26, the **authentication** command specifies preshared key authentication.

Table 6-4 shows the **authentication** command options.

Table 6-4   *IKE Authentication Configuration*

Keyword	Function	Notes
rsa-sig	RSA digital signature authentication	1. Secure 2. Scalable 3. Default method of authentication
rsa-encr	RSA encrypted nonce authentication	1. Secure 2. Not scalable
pre-share	Preshared key authentication	1. Not secure with weak preshared keys 2. Not scalable

Configuring an IKE SA Lifetime for an IKE Policy

The final parameter that you can configure with an IKE policy is the IKE SA lifetime. When this lifetime expires, the IPsec peers renegotiate IKE phase 1.

As shown in Example 6-27, use the **lifetime** *seconds* command to configure the IKE SA lifetime. The lifetime can range from 60 seconds to 86400 seconds, with the default lifetime being 86400 seconds (24 hours).

Example 6-27 *Configuring the Method of Authentication*

```
London#conf t
Enter configuration commands, one per line. End with CNTL/Z.
London(config)#crypto isakmp policy 10
London(config-isakmp)#lifetime 43200
London(config-isakmp)#end
London#
```

Many people choose to leave the IKE SA lifetime at the default value of 86400. It is worth noting, however, that the longer the lifetime, the less secure the SA is. The SA is less secure with a longer lifetime because with a longer lifetime an attacker has more time to collect encrypted traffic and subject it to cryptanalysis (attempt to recover the plaintext). However, a shorter IKE lifetime causes IPsec peers to have to renegotiate IKE more often.

So, in a particularly sensitive environment, you *may* choose to configure a shorter IKE SA lifetime.

CAUTION   Make sure that you configure IPsec peers with identical IKE SA lifetimes. If you do not, IKE negotiation may fail.

Table 6-5 shows the **lifetime** command options.

Table 6-5 *IKE Lifetime Configuration*

Keyword	Function	Notes
seconds	IKE SA Lifetime	Ranges from 60 to 86400 seconds (default is 86400)

Sample IKE Policy

Before finishing this section, it is worth taking a look at a complete sample IKE policy, as shown in Example 6-28.

Example 6-28 *A Complete Sample IKE Policy*

```
crypto isakmp policy 10
 encr 3des
 group 2
 lifetime 43200
 !
```

The sample IKE policy in Example 6-28 specifies 3DES as the encryption algorithm, SHA-1 as the hash algorithm (the default), Diffie-Hellman group 2, digital signature authentication (the default), and an IKE SA lifetime of 43200 seconds (12 hours). Note that default parameters are not shown in Example 6-28.

It is generally a good idea to configure identical IKE policies for all peers in an IPsec VPN, but sometimes (particularly when configuring an extranet) it is possible that you might require one IKE policy for most peers and another policy for one or two other peers.

If you do require multiple IKE policies, you can simply configure these with different priority numbers, as shown in Example 6-29.

Example 6-29 *Multiple IKE Policies*

```
 !
crypto isakmp policy 10
 encr 3des
 group 5
 !
crypto isakmp policy 20
 hash md5
 authentication pre-share
 !
```

In Example 6-29, IKE policy 10 specifies RSA digital signature authentication (the default), 3DES encryption, the SHA-1 hash algorithm (the default), and Diffie-Hellman group 5.

IKE policy 20 specifies preshared key authentication, DES encryption (the default), the MD5 hash algorithm, and Diffie-Hellman group 1 (the default). IKE policy 20 is relatively insecure because it utilizes DES.

Selecting and Configuring IPsec Transforms

After you have configured the IKE policy or policies, the next step is to specify cryptographic parameters for the IPsec transform set(s). The cryptographic parameters specified in an IPsec transform set are used as the parameters for the IPsec SAs negotiated with the remote IPsec peer during IKE phase 2. The parameters that you can specify in an IPsec transform set are as follows:

- Security protocol(s) and mode
- Hash algorithm
- Encryption algorithm
- Compression algorithm

Some common considerations when selecting parameters for IPsec transform sets are as follows:

- What kind of user traffic do you want to protect, and how do you want it to be protected?
- How strong must encryption be? How long must the user traffic remain confidential?
- What volume of traffic do you want to encrypt?
- What kind of platform will you be using for your IPsec VPN gateways? Will you be using hardware crypto accelerators?
- What version of Cisco IOS will your IPsec VPN gateways be running? What encryption algorithms can the version of Cisco IOS Software that your gateways will be running support?

Ideally, the final two considerations are informed by the first three considerations. However, your IPsec VPN might need to be constructed using existing hardware, and available versions of Cisco IOS Software might be limited by U.S. government export controls.

Selecting Security Protocols in an IPsec Transform Set

You can specify two security protocols in the IPsec transform set:

- Authentication Header (AH)
- Encapsulating Security Payload (ESP)

As previously described, AH provides message authentication, whereas ESP can provide message authentication and/or encryption.

Selecting Hash Algorithms in an IPsec Transform Set

As with IKE policies, there are two hash algorithms available with IPsec transform sets:

- MD5, HMAC variant
- SHA-1, HMAC variant

The MD5 algorithm generates a 128-bit hash, and the SHA-1 algorithm generates a 160-bit hash. As previously mentioned, regular MD5 and SHA-1 have been shown to be (theoretically) vulnerable to attack.

NOTE   For more information on possible attacks on regular MD5 and SHA-1, refer to the following links:

ftp://ftp.rsasecurity.com/pub/cryptobytes/crypto2n2.pdf

http://www.schneier.com/blog/archives/2005/02/cryptanalysis_o.html

http://www.rsasecurity.com/rsalabs/node.asp?id=2834

As previously discussed, HMAC variants of MD5 and SHA-1 differ from regular MD5 and SHA-1 in that a secret key is used as an additional input of the MD5 hash function. HMAC also adds cryptographic strength to the MD5 and SHA-1 hash function. HMAC-MD5 and HMAC-SHA-1 do not, however, significantly degrade the performance of the regular MD5 and SHA-1.

It is important to note that the HMAC variants of MD5 and SHA-1 (HMAC-MD5 and HMAC-SHA-1) have *not* to date been shown to be vulnerable to attack.

In IPsec, the 128-bit and 160-bit hashes produced by HMAC-MAC and HMAC-SHA-1 are truncated to a 96-bit length.

So, in summary

- Regular MD5 and SHA-1 are vulnerable to attack.
- To date, neither HMAC-MD5 nor HMAC-SHA-1 have been shown to be vulnerable to attack.
- HMAC-SHA-1 is perceived to be more secure than HMAC-MD5 because of the longer key and hash produced by SHA-1 (160 bits, as opposed to 128 bits for MD5).
- HMAC-SHA-1 is slower than HMAC-MD5.

Selecting Encryption Algorithms for Use with ESP

You can specify a number of encryption algorithms for use with ESP:

* DES
* 3DES
* AES (128 bit, 192 bit, and 256 bit)
* The Software Encryption Algorithm (SEAL)

DES (including 3DES) and AES are block ciphers, and SEAL is a stream cipher. Block ciphers operate on blocks of plaintext (original unencrypted data) bits at one time, and stream ciphers (usually) operate on plaintext a single bit at a time.

The DES, 3DES, AES, and SEAL algorithms have the following key sizes:

* **DES**—56 bits
* **3DES**—168 bits
* **AES**—128 bits, 192 bits, and 256 bits
* **SEAL**—160 bits

The most important considerations when deciding which encryption algorithm to use is the security of the encryption algorithm.

The security of 56-bit DES has been questioned since its publication by the U.S. National Institute of Standards and Technology (NIST, formerly called the National Bureau of Standards [NBS]). In 1999, 56-bit DES was publicly cracked in 22 hours and 15 minutes during RSA Data Security's DES Challenge III. 56-bit DES is not considered secure.

NOTE	For more information on cracking DES, see the following URL:
	http://www.eff.org/Privacy/Crypto/Crypto_misc/DESCracker/

With a 168-bit key length, 3DES is much more secure than 56-bit DES. Standard 3DES uses two keys and involves the encryption of the plaintext with the first key, the decryption with the second key, and then encryption once again with a third key. The main disadvantage of 3DES is that it is slow when run in software.

AES is the successor to DES (and 3DES), and is the result of an open competition run by NIST beginning in January 1997, and culminating in the selection of the Rijndael algorithm (one of the initial 15 candidate algorithms) as the AES.

NIST used a number of evaluation criteria for the selection of the AES algorithm:

- Security (the most important criterion)
- Costs, including computational efficiency and program size
- Algorithm and implementation characteristics, including versatility (ability to be implemented on diverse platforms), key agility (key setup time), and simplicity

So, AES was designed from the ground up to be secure and computationally efficient (fast, with relatively low overhead). In addition, and with particular relevance for IPsec, AES offers fast key setup. Fast key setup is important to applications such as IPsec because keys can often change.

The final encryption algorithm that you can use with your IPsec transform sets on Cisco routers is SEAL. SEAL is used with Stream Cipher ESP (SC/ESP), a nonstandard extension to ESP that enables the use of stream ciphers with IPsec.

SEAL uses a 160-bit key, is optimized to run in software, but is not supported if a hardware encryption accelerator is present. SC/ESP (including when used with SEAL) mandates the use of authentication to prevent certain kinds of attacks that are specifically related to the use of stream ciphers with IPsec. If you attempt to configure SEAL without authentication, you will receive an error message.

Two advantages of using SEAL encryption are its speed (SEAL is fast—measured as being 16.9 times faster than DES in certain sample tests) and the reduced size of SEAL encrypted packets when compared to those encrypted using DES and AES.

Selecting Compression in an IPsec Transform Set

Encryption of plaintext produces a seemingly random ciphertext. Unfortunately, compression algorithms look for common patterns in data, and because a ciphertext by definition contains no common patterns, ciphertext cannot be compressed. In fact, *compression* of ciphertext can result in an expansion of the original data!

The upshot of the fact that ciphertext cannot be compressed is that data link layer compression algorithms do not work with the network layer encryption provided by IPsec. So, is it possible to use compression with IPsec? Yes, compression is possible, but it must take place prior to encryption.

The IP Payload Compression Protocol (IPComp or PCP) was designed to address the problem of the ineffectiveness of data link layer compression protocols when applied to encrypted data. When using PCP, data is compressed before it is encrypted.

PCP, just like AH and ESP, is an IP protocol in its own right (IP protocol 108). Two compression algorithms are specified for use with PCP: Lempel-Ziv-Stac (LZS) and Deflate. On Cisco routers, you can configure LZS, which can give a maximum compression ratio of 2:1 depending on the data being compressed.

The compression algorithm used between IPsec peers is negotiated using IKE, and this information is stored as a PCP SA.

IPsec adds a large amount of overhead to a user packet (for more on this, see the section "Fragmentation Considerations in an IPsec VPN" in Chapter 7) and on low-speed lines this can cause a considerable impact on throughput. PCP may, therefore, be a solution for improving throughput on low-speed links.

Note that some hardware accelerators support LZS; if LZS runs in software, however, it can add considerable processor overhead to an IPsec VPN gateway.

Configuring IPsec Transform Sets

Use the **crypto ipsec transform-set** *transform-set-name transform1* [*transform2*] [*transform2*] [*transform3*] [*tranform4*] to configure transforms (IPsec cryptographic algorithms and parameters) for IPsec tunnels.

It is *possible* to configure a total of four transforms (algorithms) within an IPsec transform set:

- One AH
- Two ESP (one authentication, plus one encryption)
- One compression

However, four transforms would necessarily include an AH (authentication) transform and an ESP authentication transform. Configuration of two authentication transforms within one transform set is nonsensical, and so the practical limit for the number of transforms within a transform set is three:

- One authentication (whether AH or ESP)
- One encryption
- One compression

Cryptographic algorithms and parameters configured using the **crypto ipsec transform-set** command are used by the IPsec (and PCP) SAs negotiated during IKE phase 2.

Table 6-6 summarizes IPsec transforms that you can configure using the **crypto ipsec transform-set** command.

Table 6-6   *IPsec Transforms*

Security/ Compression Protocol	Hash Algorithm	Encryption Algorithm	Compression Algorithm	Function	Notes
AH	ah-md5-hmac			AH MD5 (HMAC variant) authentication	Authenticates whole packet, including outer IP header[1]

continues

Table 6-6   *IPsec Transforms (Continued)*

Security/ Compression Protocol	Hash Algorithm	Encryption Algorithm	Compression Algorithm	Function	Notes
	ah-sha-hmac			AH SHA-1 (HMAC variant) authentication	1. Authenticates whole packet, including outer IP header[1] 2. More secure/processor intensive than MD5-HMAC
ESP	esp-md5-hmac			ESP MD5 (HMAC variant) authentication	Authenticates whole packet, excluding the outer IP header
	esp-sha-hmac			ESP SHA-1 (HMAC variant) authentication	1. Authenticates whole packet, excluding outer IP header 2. More secure/processor intensive than MD5-HMAC
		esp-null		ESP null encryption. Authentication, but no encryption	N/A
		esp-des		ESP 56-bit DES encryption	1. *Not* secure 2. Slow (especially in software)
		esp-3des		ESP 168-bit 3DES encryption	1. Secure 2. Slow (especially in software) 3. Subject to U.S. export controls
		esp-aes		ESP 128-bit AES encryption	1. Secure 2. Successor to DES as NIST standard 3. Available in Cisco IOS Release 12.2(13)T 4. Subject to U.S. export controls

Table 6-6   *IPsec Transforms (Continued)*

Security/ Compression Protocol	Hash Algorithm	Encryption Algorithm	Compression Algorithm	Function	Notes
		esp-aes 192		ESP 192-bit AES encryption	Same as for ESP 128-bit AES encryption
		esp-aes 256		ESP 256-bit AES encryption	Same as for ESP 128-bit AES encryption
		esp-seal		ESP 160-bit SEAL encryption	1. Secure[2] 2. Fast 3. Available in Cisco IOS Release 12.3(7)T 4. Not supported with hardware accelerators 5. Smaller packet sizes than DES/AES 6. Implemented with nonstandard SC/ESP 7. SC/ESP mandates the use of authentication 8. Subject to U.S export controls
IPComp / PCP			comp-lzs	LZS compression	1. Option on low-speed links 2. Processor intensive in software

[1]The value of authenticating the outer IP header is often questioned

[2]Has not been subject to the same level of cryptanalysis as DES and AES, but is generally regarded as being secure

Example 6-30 shows the configuration of a sample IPsec transform set with ESP SHA-1 authentication and ESP 128-bit AES encryption.

Example 6-30 *Sample IPsec Transform Set*

```
London#conf t
Enter configuration commands, one per line. End with CNTL/Z.
London(config)#crypto ipsec transform-set mjlnettransform esp-aes esp-sha-hmac
London(cfg-crypto-trans)#end
London#
```

It is worth noting the possible single transforms or combinations of transforms that you can use in a single transform set:

- AH authentication alone
- ESP, DES, or AES encryption alone
- AH authentication together with ESP encryption
- ESP authentication together with ESP encryption (most common)

LZS compression can be used with all of these transforms.

As you can see, it is possible to configure ESP, DES, or AES encryption without authentication in an IPsec transform set. Although this might be possible, it is not generally a good idea—in certain circumstances ESP encryption SAs (without ESP or AH authentication) are vulnerable to *cut-and-paste* attacks. Cut-and-paste attacks involve the substitution of certain parts of IPsec packets and can result in an attacker being able to recover unencrypted messages (plaintext). So, use either ESP or AH authentication with ESP, DES, or AES encryption.

There are also one or two transforms that you cannot use:

- ESP authentication alone
- SEAL encryption alone

When configuring your IPsec transform sets, it is possible to configure the IPsec security protocol mode using the **mode {tunnel | transport}** command, as demonstrated in Example 6-31.

Example 6-31 *Configuring Security Protocol Modes*

```
London#conf t
Enter configuration commands, one per line. End with CNTL/Z.
London(config)#crypto ipsec transform-set mjlnettransform esp-aes esp-sha-hmac
London(cfg-crypto-trans)#mode transport
London(cfg-crypto-trans)#end
London#
```

The highlighted line shows the specification of transport mode for use with IPsec transform set mjlnettransform.

If you do not specify an IPsec security protocol mode, the default is tunnel mode. In tunnel mode, user packets are entirely encapsulated and protected by IPsec and a new IP header is added, whereas in transport mode the payload is encapsulated and protected by IPsec, but a new IP packet header is not added.

Typically, tunnel mode is the mode used for IPsec VPNs, although transport mode may be used if a GRE tunnel is being used to carry multiprotocol and multicast traffic. See the section "Using GRE Tunnels to Carry Multiprotocol and Multicast Traffic Across the IPsec VPN" later in this chapter for more information on GRE tunnels.

Designing and Configuring Crypto Access Lists

In IPsec, traffic *selectors* define the traffic that is to be protected by an SA. Traffic selectors consist of a number of items, including the following:

- Source and destination IP addresses
- Next layer protocol (for example, ICMP, GRE, TCP, UDP)
- Source and destination ports, if applicable

On Cisco routers, traffic selectors are configured using crypto access lists. Crypto access lists are extended access lists that are then specified in a crypto map.

Example 6-32 shows a sample crypto access list.

Example 6-32 *Sample Crypto Access List*

```
London#conf t
Enter configuration commands, one per line. End with CNTL/Z.
London(config)#access-list 101 permit ip 10.1.1.0 0.0.0.255 10.2.2.0 0.0.0.255
London(config)#exit
London#
```

In Example 6-32, access list 101 specifies all IP traffic from source network 10.1.1.0/24 to destination network 10.2.2.0/24.

In this case, all IP traffic from network 10.1.1.0/24 to network 10.2.2.0/24 will be protected using the algorithms specified in the IPsec transform set. Also, all IP traffic received from network 10.2.2.0/24 destined for 10.1.1.0/24 must be protected using the algorithms specified in the IPsec transform set—if it is not, it will be dropped.

The output of the **show crypto ipsec sa** command in Example 6-33 shows the IPsec SAs corresponding to the crypto access list configured in Example 6-32.

Example 6-33 *IPsec SAs with One Line in the Crypto Access List*

```
London#show crypto ipsec sa
interface: Serial1/0
  Crypto map tag: mjlnetmap, local addr. 192.168.1.1
  protected vrf:
  local  ident (addr/mask/prot/port): (10.1.1.0/255.255.255.0/0/0) (line 1)
  remote ident (addr/mask/prot/port): (10.2.2.0/255.255.255.0/0/0) (line 2)
  current_peer: 192.168.2.2:500
   PERMIT, flags={origin_is_acl,}
  #pkts encaps: 4, #pkts encrypt: 4, #pkts digest: 4
  #pkts decaps: 4, #pkts decrypt: 4, #pkts verify: 4
  #pkts compressed: 0, #pkts decompressed: 0
  #pkts not compressed: 0, #pkts compr. failed: 0
  #pkts not decompressed: 0, #pkts decompress failed: 0
  #send errors 1, #recv errors 0
   local crypto endpt.: 192.168.1.1, remote crypto endpt.: 192.168.2.2
   path mtu 1500, media mtu 1500
```

continues

Example 6-33 *IPsec SAs with One Line in the Crypto Access List (Continued)*

```
         current outbound spi: 64095EF9
         inbound esp sas: (line 3)
         spi: 0xCA9C1822(3399227426)
          transform: esp-aes esp-sha-hmac , (line 4)
          in use settings ={Tunnel, }
          slot: 0, conn id: 2000, flow_id: 7, crypto map: mjlnetmap
          crypto engine type: Software, engine_id: 1
          sa timing: remaining key lifetime (k/sec): (4542627/3575)
          ike_cookies: 966D547F ADD7F649 1E32E5D2 E3AA6BD7
          IV size: 16 bytes
          replay detection support: Y
         inbound ah sas:
         inbound pcp sas:
         outbound esp sas: (line 5)
         spi: 0x64095EF9(1678335737)
          transform: esp-aes esp-sha-hmac , (line 6)
          in use settings ={Tunnel, }
          slot: 0, conn id: 2001, flow_id: 8, crypto map: mjlnetmap
          crypto engine type: Software, engine_id: 1
          sa timing: remaining key lifetime (k/sec): (4542627/3573)
          ike_cookies: 966D547F ADD7F649 1E32E5D2 E3AA6BD7
          IV size: 16 bytes
          replay detection support: Y
         outbound ah sas:
         outbound pcp sas:
London#
```

Highlighted lines 1 and 2 show the traffic selectors configured in the crypto access list in Example 6-32.

Highlighted lines 3 and 4 show the inbound ESP SA (with ESP AES encryption and SHA-1 authentication). Then, in highlighted lines 5 and 6, you can see the outbound ESP SA (again with AES encryption and SHA-1 authentication).

It is a good idea to specify the traffic that you want to protect in as few lines as possible (often just one line). Each **permit** statement in a crypto access list causes separate SAs to be negotiated between IPsec peers. For example, the crypto access list shown in Example 6-34 results in the negotiation of the IPsec SAs shown in the output of the **show crypto ipsec sa** command in Example 6-35.

Example 6-34 *Crypto Access List with Two Lines*

```
access-list 101 permit icmp 10.1.1.0 0.0.0.255 10.2.2.0 0.0.0.255
access-list 101 permit ip 10.1.1.0 0.0.0.255 10.2.2.0 0.0.0.255
```

Example 6-35 *IPsec SAs Corresponding to the Access List Shown in Example 6-34*

```
London#show crypto ipsec sa
interface: Serial1/0
  Crypto map tag: mjlnetmap, local addr. 192.168.1.1
  protected vrf:
```

Example 6-35 *IPsec SAs Corresponding to the Access List Shown in Example 6-34 (Continued)*

```
local ident (addr/mask/prot/port): (10.1.1.0/255.255.255.0/0/0) (line 1)
remote ident (addr/mask/prot/port): (10.2.2.0/255.255.255.0/0/0) (line 2)
current_peer: 192.168.2.2:500
 PERMIT, flags={origin_is_acl,}
#pkts encaps: 6, #pkts encrypt: 6, #pkts digest: 6
#pkts decaps: 0, #pkts decrypt: 0, #pkts verify: 0
#pkts compressed: 0, #pkts decompressed: 0
#pkts not compressed: 0, #pkts compr. failed: 0
#pkts not decompressed: 0, #pkts decompress failed: 0
#send errors 1, #recv errors 0
 local crypto endpt.: 192.168.1.1, remote crypto endpt.: 192.168.2.2
 path mtu 1500, media mtu 1500
 current outbound spi: B6CC7F94
 inbound esp sas: (line 3)
 spi: 0x674B911B(1733005595)
  transform: esp-aes esp-sha-hmac ,
  in use settings ={Tunnel, }
  slot: 0, conn id: 2002, flow_id: 15, crypto map: mjlnetmap
  crypto engine type: Software, engine_id: 1
  sa timing: remaining key lifetime (k/sec): (4416744/3476)
  ike_cookies: 966D547F 66B1A334 1E32E5D2 12CD70EC
  IV size: 16 bytes
  replay detection support: Y
 inbound ah sas:
 inbound pcp sas:
 outbound esp sas: (line 4)
 spi: 0xB6CC7F94(3066855316)
  transform: esp-aes esp-sha-hmac ,
  in use settings ={Tunnel, }
  slot: 0, conn id: 2003, flow_id: 16, crypto map: mjlnetmap
  crypto engine type: Software, engine_id: 1
  sa timing: remaining key lifetime (k/sec): (4416742/3474)
  ike_cookies: 966D547F 66B1A334 1E32E5D2 12CD70EC
  IV size: 16 bytes
  replay detection support: Y
 outbound ah sas:
 outbound pcp sas:
protected vrf:
local ident (addr/mask/prot/port): (10.1.1.0/255.255.255.0/1/0) (line 5)
remote ident (addr/mask/prot/port): (10.2.2.0/255.255.255.0/1/0) (line 6)
current_peer: 192.168.2.2:500
 PERMIT, flags={origin_is_acl,}
#pkts encaps: 4, #pkts encrypt: 4, #pkts digest: 4
#pkts decaps: 4, #pkts decrypt: 4, #pkts verify: 4
#pkts compressed: 0, #pkts decompressed: 0
#pkts not compressed: 0, #pkts compr. failed: 0
#pkts not decompressed: 0, #pkts decompress failed: 0
#send errors 1, #recv errors 0
 local crypto endpt.: 192.168.1.1, remote crypto endpt.: 192.168.2.2
 path mtu 1500, media mtu 1500
 current outbound spi: 66B63AD9
```

continues

Example 6-35 *IPsec SAs Corresponding to the Access List Shown in Example 6-34 (Continued)*

```
     inbound esp sas: (line 7)
     spi: 0xC783E6A2(3347310242)
      transform: esp-aes esp-sha-hmac ,
      in use settings ={Tunnel, }
      slot: 0, conn id: 2000, flow_id: 13, crypto map: mjlnetmap
      crypto engine type: Software, engine_id: 1
      sa timing: remaining key lifetime (k/sec): (4414367/3468)
      ike_cookies: 966D547F 66B1A334 1E32E5D2 12CD70EC
      IV size: 16 bytes
      replay detection support: Y
     inbound ah sas:
     inbound pcp sas:
     outbound esp sas: (line 8)
     spi: 0x66B63AD9(1723218649)
      transform: esp-aes esp-sha-hmac ,
      in use settings ={Tunnel, }
      slot: 0, conn id: 2001, flow_id: 14, crypto map: mjlnetmap
      crypto engine type: Software, engine_id: 1
      sa timing: remaining key lifetime (k/sec): (4414367/3467)
      ike_cookies: 966D547F 66B1A334 1E32E5D2 12CD70EC
      IV size: 16 bytes
      replay detection support: Y
     outbound ah sas:
     outbound pcp sas:
London#
```

Highlighted lines 1 and 2 in Example 6-35 show traffic selectors corresponding to the second line of the crypto access list in Example 6-34.

Note the protocol (**prot**) and port numbers shown at the end of highlighted lines 1 and 2 (**/0/0**). The 0s indicate that the traffic selectors specify IP but no specific IP protocol or port.

Highlighted lines 3 and 4 show the ESP SAs associated with the traffic selectors specified in the second line of the crypto access list in Example 6-34.

Then, in highlighted lines 5 and 6, you can see traffic selectors corresponding to the first line in the crypto access list. Notice the protocol and port (**/1/0**) at the end of highlighted lines 5 and 6. The 1 indicates the IP protocol number (ICMP).

Finally, in highlighted lines 7 and 8, you can see the ESP SAs corresponding to the traffic selectors specified in the first line of the crypto access in Example 6-34.

So, keep the number of crypto access list lines (**permit** statements) to a minimum or you will end up with unnecessary IPsec SAs between IPsec peers.

It is worth saying that there are one or two reasons that might justify configuration of multiple permit statements in a crypto access list—see the section "Designing QoS for IPsec VPNs" in Chapter 7 on page 656 for more information.

If you want to explicitly exclude some traffic from being protected by IPsec, just specify this traffic using a **deny** statement or statements at the beginning of your crypto access lists.

Note that crypto access lists should be mirrored between peer IPsec VPN gateways.
Example 6-36 shows the crypto access lists that would be configured on the London and
Berlin gateways (refer back to Figure 6-31).

Example 6-36 *Crypto Access Lists Should Be Mirrored Between Peer IPsec VPN Gateways*

```
!
! Crypto access list on London
!
access-list 101 permit ip 10.1.1.0 0.0.0.255 10.2.2.0 0.0.0.255
!
```
```
!
! Crypto access list on Berlin
!
access-list 101 permit ip 10.2.2.0 0.0.0.255 10.1.1.0 0.0.0.255
!
```

It is actually possible to configure crypto access lists that are not mirrored between IPsec
VPN gateways, but this results in just one IPsec VPN gateway being able to initiate an
IPsec VPN tunnel, as well as IPsec traffic drops.

NOTE   For more information on crypto access lists that are not mirrored between peer IPsec VPN
gateways (and the problems they can cause), refer to Chapter 8 of *Troubleshooting Virtual
Private Networks* (Cisco Press). *Troubleshooting Virtual Private Networks* includes in-
depth information on troubleshooting all typical and not-so-typical issues with IPsec VPNs.

Pulling Everything Together with a Crypto Map

Now that you have designed your IKE policies, IPsec transform sets, and crypto access
lists, it is time to configure your crypto map. The function of the crypto map is to pull
together the IKE policies, IPsec transform sets, and crypto access lists into a form that can
then be applied to an interface.

Example 6-37 illustrates the configuration of a crypto map using the **crypto map** *map-
name seq-num* **ipsec-isakmp** [**dynamic** *dynamic-map-name*] [**discover**] command.

Example 6-37 *Configuration of a Crypto Map*

```
London#conf t
Enter configuration commands, one per line. End with CNTL/Z.
London(config)#crypto map mjlnetcmap 10 ipsec-isakmp
London(config-crypto-map)#set peer 192.168.2.2
London(config-crypto-map)#set transform-set mjlnettransform
London(config-crypto-map)#match address 101
London(config-crypto-map)#end
London#
```

In Example 6-37, a crypto map called mjlnetcmap is configured on IPsec VPN gateway London. Within the crypto map, the **set peer [hostname | ip-address]** command specifies the host name or IP address of the IPsec peer (in this case, IP address 192.168.2.2).

The **set transform-set** *transform-set-name* [*transform-set-name2.....transform-set-name6*] then specifies that the IPsec transform set named mjlnettransform will be used to protect user traffic with peer 192.168.2.2. It is possible to specify up to six possible transform sets. If multiple transform sets are specified, a common transform set will be negotiated with the peer during IPsec tunnel setup (in IKE phase 2).

Finally, the crypto access list is specified using the **match address** [*access-list-number | name*] command. In this example, **access-list number 101** is specified.

One other option that you can configure within a crypto map is PFS. Normally, keys used to encrypt and authenticate IPsec packets are derived from the IKE phase 1 Diffie-Hellman shared secret key. If the IKE phase 1 Diffie-Hellman shared secret key is discovered, this can lead to the compromise of all IPsec packets. If you specify PFS, however, a new Diffie-Hellman exchange takes place during IKE phase 2 (quick mode), and this exchange is used to derive the keys used to encrypt and authenticate IPsec packets. The result of using PFS is that the compromise of the IKE phase 1 Diffie-Hellman shared secret key cannot lead directly to the compromise of keys used to encrypt and authenticate IPsec packets.

So, the advantage of PFS is increased security, but the disadvantage is some additional processing overhead whenever a new IPsec SA is negotiated during IKE phase 2.

You can configure PFS using the **set pfs [group1 | group2 | group5]** under the crypto map, as shown in Example 6-38.

Example 6-38 *Configuring PFS Within the Crypto Map*

```
London#conf t
Enter configuration commands, one per line. End with CNTL/Z.
London(config)#crypto map mjlnetcmap 10 ipsec-isakmp
London(config-crypto-map)#set pfs group2
London(config-crypto-map)#end
London#
```

Example 6-38 shows the configuration of PFS using Diffie-Hellman group 2 (1024 bit).

If multiple IPsec peers connect over the same outside interface, you can specify multiple entries in a particular crypto map using different crypto map sequence numbers, as demonstrated in Example 6-39.

Example 6-39 *Configuration of Multiple Entries in a Crypto Map*

```
!
crypto map mjlnetcmap 10 ipsec-isakmp
 set peer 192.168.2.2
```

Example 6-39 *Configuration of Multiple Entries in a Crypto Map (Continued)*

```
 set transform-set mjlnettransform
 match address 101
crypto map mjlnetcmap 20 ipsec-isakmp
 set peer 192.168.3.3
 set transform-set mjlnettransform
 match address 102
!
```

After you have configured a crypto map, you can apply it to the (outside) interface to which IPsec peers will connect. Example 6-40 demonstrates application of a crypto map to an interface.

Example 6-40 *Application of a Crypto Map to an Interface*

```
!
interface Serial1/0
 ip address 192.168.1.1 255.255.255.0
 crypto map mjlnetcmap
!
```

In Example 6-40, the crypto map is applied to the outside interface serial 1/0.

Complete IPsec VPN Gateway Configurations

Now that you understand the main elements of the configuration of an IPsec VPN gateway, it is useful to take a look at the complete configurations of peer IPsec VPN gateways London and Berlin (see Example 6-41 and refer back to Figure 6-31).

Example 6-41 *Complete Configurations for IPsec VPN Gateways London and Berlin*

```
London#show running-config
Building configuration...
Current configuration : 7701 bytes
!
version 12.3
!
!
! IPsec gateway's host name and IP domain name
!
hostname London
!
ip domain name mjlnet.com
!
!
! Crypto pki trustpoint - enrollment parameters, certificate fields, and auto
! (re-)enrollment
!
```

continues

Example 6-41 *Complete Configurations for IPsec VPN Gateways London and Berlin (Continued)*

```
crypto pki trustpoint mjlnetcertsrv
 enrollment mode ra
 enrollment url http://mjlnetcertsrv:80/certsrv/mscep/mscep.dll
 usage ike
 serial-number none
 ip-address 192.168.1.1
 password 7 1104130919171F
 subject-name C=GB, O=mjlnet, OU=engineering
 revocation-check crl none
 rsakeypair London.mjlnet.com
 auto-enroll 90 regenerate
!
!
! Gateway's and CA's Certificates
!
crypto pki certificate chain mjlnetcertsrv
 certificate 613240F1000000000018
 308204A9 30820453 A0030201 02020A61 3240F100 00000000 18300D06 092A8648
 86F70D01 01050500 30819931 1F301D06 092A8648 86F70D01 09011610 61646D69
! <text omitted>
 quit
 certificate ca 48B8A34E0C6A09A7447B8CBDD77C3A81
 30820304 308202AE A0030201 02021048 B8A34E0C 6A09A744 7B8CBDD7 7C3A8130
 0D06092A 864886F7 0D010105 05003081 99311F30 1D06092A 864886F7 0D010901
! <text omitted>
 quit
!
!
! IKE policy
!
crypto isakmp policy 10
 encr 3des
 group 2
!
!
! IPsec transform set
!
crypto ipsec transform-set mjlnettransform esp-3des esp-sha-hmac
!
!
! Crypto map
!
crypto map mjlnetmap 10 ipsec-isakmp
 set peer 192.168.2.2
 set transform-set mjlnettransform
 match address 101
!
!
! Outside interface
!
interface Serial1/0
```

Example 6-41 *Complete Configurations for IPsec VPN Gateways London and Berlin (Continued)*

```
  ip address 192.168.1.1 255.255.255.0
  crypto map mjlnetmap
 !
 !
 ! Inside interface
 !
interface FastEthernet3/0
  ip address 10.1.1.1 255.255.255.0
 !
 !
 ! Route to the Berlin gateway
 !
ip route 0.0.0.0 0.0.0.0 192.168.1.2
 !
 !
 ! Crypto access list
 !
access-list 101 permit ip 10.1.1.0 0.0.0.255 10.2.2.0 0.0.0.255
 !
 !
 ! NTP with authentication
 !
ntp authentication-key 1 md5 09414405170003 7
ntp authenticate
ntp trusted-key 1
ntp server 10.10.10.99 key 1
 !
end
```
```
Berlin#show running-config
Building configuration...
Current configuration : 7109 bytes
 !
version 12.3
 !
 !
 ! IPsec gateway's host name and IP domain name
 !
hostname Berlin
 !
ip domain name mjlnet.com
 !
 !
 ! Crypto pki trustpoint - enrollment parameters, certificate fields, and auto
 ! (re-)enrollment
 !
crypto pki trustpoint mjlnetcertsrv
  enrollment mode ra
  enrollment url http://mjlnetcertsrv:80/certsrv/mscep/mscep.dll
  usage ike
  serial-number none
```

continues

Example 6-41 *Complete Configurations for IPsec VPN Gateways London and Berlin (Continued)*

```
 ip-address 192.168.2.2
 password 7 0009190A0A5E1F
 subject-name C=GB, O=mjlnet, OU=engineering
 revocation-check crl none
 rsakeypair Berlin.mjlnet.com
 auto-enroll 90 regenerate
!
!
! Gateway's and CA's certificates
!
crypto pki certificate chain mjlnetcertsrv
 certificate 612A9069000000000019
  308204A9 30820453 A0030201 02020A61 2A906900 00000000 19300D06 092A8648
  86F70D01 01050500 30819931 1F301D06 092A8648 86F70D01 09011610 61646D69
! <text omitted>
 quit
 certificate ca 48B8A34E0C6A09A7447B8CBDD77C3A81
  30820304 308202AE A0030201 02021048 B8A34E0C 6A09A744 7B8CBDD7 7C3A8130
  0D06092A 864886F7 0D010105 05003081 99311F30 1D06092A 864886F7 0D010901
! <text omitted>
 quit
!
!
! IKE policy
!
crypto isakmp policy 10
 encr 3des
 authentication pre-share
 group 2
!
!
! IPsec transform set
!
crypto ipsec transform-set mjlnettransform esp-3des esp-sha-hmac
!
!
! Crypto map
!
crypto map mjlnetmap 10 ipsec-isakmp
 set peer 192.168.1.1
 set transform-set mjlnettransform
 match address 101
!
!
! Inside interface
!
interface FastEthernet1/0
 ip address 10.2.2.1 255.255.255.0
!
!
! Outside interface
!
```

Example 6-41 *Complete Configurations for IPsec VPN Gateways London and Berlin (Continued)*

```
interface Serial4/0
 ip address 192.168.2.2 255.255.255.0
 crypto map mjlnetmap
 !
 !
 ! Route to the London gateway
 !
 ip route 0.0.0.0 0.0.0.0 192.168.2.1
 !
 !
 ! Crypto access list
 !
 access-list 101 permit ip 10.2.2.0 0.0.0.255 10.1.1.0 0.0.0.255
 !
 !
 ! NTP with authentication
 !
 ntp authentication-key 1 md5 1104130919171F 7
 ntp authenticate
 ntp trusted-key 1
 ntp server 10.10.10.99 key 1
 !
 end
```

Transporting Multiprotocol and Multicast Traffic over an IPsec VPN

Standard IPsec can transport and protect unicast IP traffic, but it cannot at present natively transport and protect multiprotocol or multicast traffic. One workaround for this problem is to configure a GRE tunnel between peer IPsec VPN gateways. Multiprotocol and multicast traffic is transported over the GRE tunnel, and the GRE tunnel is in turn protected by IPsec.

If you want to transport IP unicast and multicast traffic (but not multiprotocol traffic), another option is to configure virtual tunnel interfaces (VTI). VTIs were introduced in Cisco IOS Software Release 12.3(14)T.

Configuring GRE/IPsec Tunnels

Figure 6-37 illustrates an IPsec-protected GRE tunnel between IPsec VPN gateways.

Figure 6-37 *IPsec Protected GRE Tunnel Between IPsec VPN Gateways*

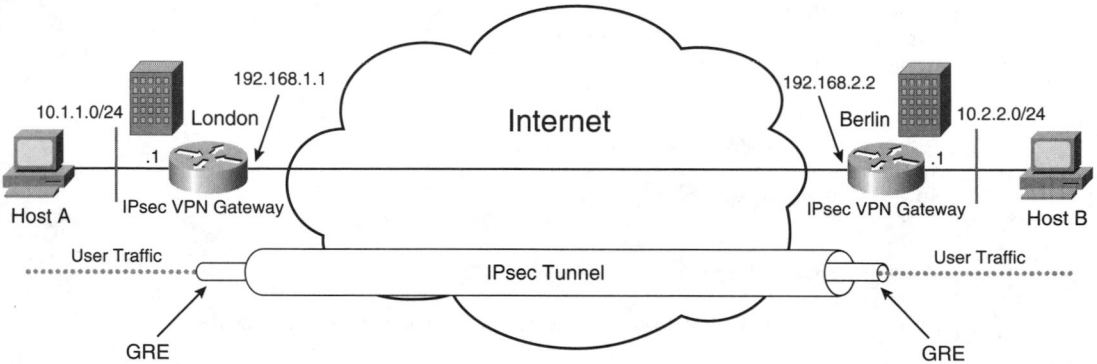

Configuration of IPsec-protected GRE tunnels involves the following steps:

Step 1 Configure the GRE tunnel interfaces.

Step 2 Configure the routing protocol or static routes.

Step 3 Configure the IKE policies.

Step 4 Configure the IPsec transforms sets.

Step 5 Configure the crypto access lists.

Step 6 Configure and apply the crypto maps.

These steps are discussed in detail in the following sections.

Step 1: Configure the GRE Tunnel Interfaces

The first step is to configure the GRE tunnel interfaces on the IPsec VPN gateways.

Example 6-42 shows the configuration of GRE tunnel interfaces on two IPsec VPN gateways depicted in Figure 6-37, London and Berlin.

Example 6-42 *Configuring GRE Tunnel Interfaces for Multiprotocol and Multicast Traffic Transport*

```
!
! On London
!
interface Tunnel0
 ip address 10.3.3.1 255.255.255.0
 ipx network 3000
 ip pim sparse-dense-mode
 tunnel source 192.168.1.1
 tunnel destination 192.168.2.2
 !
 !
! On Berlin
!
interface Tunnel0
```

Example 6-42 *Configuring GRE Tunnel Interfaces for Multiprotocol and Multicast Traffic Transport (Continued)*

```
 ip address 10.3.3.2 255.255.255.0
 ipx network 3000
 ip pim sparse-dense-mode
 tunnel source 192.168.2.2
 tunnel destination 192.168.1.1
 !
```

The GRE tunnel interface is configured on the London gateway with a tunnel source IP address of 192.168.1.1 (its outside physical interface) and a destination IP address of 192.168.2.2 (the outside physical interface [tunnel source] on the Berlin gateway).

The GRE tunnel interface on Berlin is configured in a similar manner. The tunnel source IP address is configured as 192.168.2.2 (its outside interface), and the tunnel destination IP address is 192.168.1.1 (the outside interface [tunnel source] on London).

If you have multiple outside physical interfaces, you might want to configure a loopback interface (**interface loopback** *interface-number*) on each IPsec VPN gateway to act as the source address for the GRE tunnel.

If you do use loopback interfaces as the source IP address of GRE tunnels, make sure that you specify the loopback interface on the IPsec VPN gateways using the **crypto map** *crypto-map-name* **local-address** *interface* (for example, **crypto map mjlnetcmap local-address Loopback0**) command to ensure that IKE negotiation succeeds between the IPsec VPN gateways. Also, if you are using preshared keys, make sure you specify the peer's loopback interface address using the **crypto isakmp key** *key-string* **address** *peer-ip-address* and crypto map **set peer** *ip-address* commands.

Step 2: Configure the Routing Protocol or Static Routes

After you have configured the GRE tunnel interfaces, you can configure a routing protocol for IP reachability over the GRE tunnels between sites, as shown in Example 6-43.

Example 6-43 *Configuring EIGRP for IP Reachability Between IPsec VPN Sites*

```
!
! On London
!
router eigrp 100 (line 1)
 network 10.1.1.0 0.0.0.255 (line 2)
 network 10.3.3.0 0.0.0.255 (line 3)
 no auto-summary
 !
 !
! On Berlin
!
router eigrp 100 (line 4)
 network 10.2.2.0 0.0.0.255 (line 5)
 network 10.3.3.0 0.0.0.255 (line 6)
 no auto-summary
 !
```

In Example 6-43, EIGRP is configured for IP reachability between the London and Berlin sites.

In highlighted lines 1 to 3, EIGRP autonomous system 100 is configured on the London gateway, and EIGRP is enabled on the inside network (10.1.1.0/24) as well as on the GRE tunnel interface (10.3.3.0/24).

Then, in highlighted lines 4 to 6, EIGRP autonomous system 100 is configured on Berlin, and EIGRP is enabled on the inside network (10.2.2.0/24) as well as on the GRE tunnel interface (10.3.3.0/24).

The routing protocol should be enabled on the GRE tunnel interfaces and on inside interfaces (where appropriate), but it should not be enabled on the outside physical interface for reachability between tunnel endpoints.

NOTE   If the same routing protocol (instance) is configured on the GRE tunnel interface and on the outside physical interface (for reachability between the GRE tunnel endpoints), the GRE tunnel will be disabled.

The GRE tunnel interface is disabled because the best route to the GRE tunnel destination is via the GRE tunnel itself, and the gateway attempts to send GRE tunnel packets over the GRE tunnel itself. That is not going to work!

You could also choose to configure static IP routes for IP reachability between sites. In this case, you can configure the outbound interface of the static routes as the GRE tunnel interface, as shown in Example 6-44.

Example 6-44 *Configuring Static Routes for IP Reachability Between IPsec VPN Sites*

```
!
! On London
!
ip route 10.2.2.0 255.255.255.0 Tunnel0 (line 1)
!
!
! On NewYork
!
ip route 10.1.1.0 255.255.255.0 Tunnel0 (line 2)
!
```

In Example 6-44, highlighted line 1, a static route to the Berlin site network (10.2.2.0/24) via the GRE tunnel interface is configured on the London gateway.

Then, in highlighted line 2, a static route to the London site network (10.1.1.0/24) via the GRE tunnel interface is configured on the Berlin site network.

When you are choosing whether to use a dynamic routing protocol or static routes for IP reachability, remember that static routes are inherently unscalable. The administrative and management overhead of maintaining and troubleshooting a large number of static routes is often considered prohibitive.

Step 3: Configure the IKE Policies

After you have configured either a dynamic routing protocol or static routes, the next step is to configure the IKE (ISAKMP) policies on the gateways. There are no special considerations for GRE tunnels, and so the IKE policies should be configured as discussed in the section "Selecting and Configuring IKE Policies" earlier in this chapter.

Step 4: Configure the IPsec Transform Sets

Next are IPsec transform sets. You should configure these as described in the section "Selecting and Configuring IPsec Transform Sets" earlier in this chapter.

It is worth noting that you can choose to configure IPsec transport mode when configuring IPsec protection for GRE tunnels. One advantage of using transport mode is that you save 20 bytes of overhead when compared to using tunnel mode because a new outer IP header is not required (compare Figures 6-14, 6-15, 6-19, and 6-20).

Step 5: Configure the Crypto Access Lists

Following the configuration of the IPsec transform sets, you can configure the crypto access list (see Example 6-45).

Example 6-45 *Configuring a Crypto Access List for a GRE Tunnel*

```
!
! On London
!
access-list 101 permit gre host 192.168.1.1 host 192.168.2.2 (line 1)
!
!
! On Berlin
!
access-list 101 permit gre host 192.168.2.2 host 192.168.1.1 (line 2)
!
```

Highlighted line 1 shows the crypto access list configured on London. Notice that the source and destination addresses (192.168.1.1 and 192.168.2.2, respectively) are the GRE tunnel endpoints (GRE tunnel interface source addresses). Also, notice that GRE is specified as the protocol within the crypto access list.

In highlighted line 2, you can see the crypto access list on Berlin. The idea is the same— source and destination addresses correspond to the GRE tunnel endpoints. Again, GRE is specified as the protocol within the crypto access list.

Step 6: Configure and Apply Crypto Maps

To a great extent, configuring and applying crypto maps is as described in the section "Pulling Everything Together with a Crypto Map."

There is one important consideration, however—if your gateways are running Cisco IOS Software prior to Release 12.2(13)T, you must apply the crypto map to the outside interfaces *and* the GRE tunnel interfaces. If your gateways are running Cisco IOS Software Release 12.2(13)T or higher, you need to apply the crypto map only to the outside physical interfaces.

NOTE   It is also possible to use the **tunnel protection** command to apply IPsec protection to a GRE tunnel. This command is discussed further in Chapter 7.

Complete IPsec VPN Gateway Configurations with GRE Tunnel for Multiprotocol and Multicast Traffic Transport

Again, it is useful to examine the complete configurations of peer IPsec VPN gateways London and Berlin with GRE tunnel for multiprotocol and multicast traffic transport. Example 6-46 shows these configuration (see Figure 6-37 for the physical topology).

Example 6-46 *Complete Configurations for IPsec VPN Gateways London and Berlin with GRE Tunnels for Multiprotocol and Multicast Traffic Transport*

```
London#show running-config
Building configuration...
Current configuration : 7757 bytes
!
version 12.3
!
!
! IPsec gateway's host name and IP domain name
!
hostname London
!
ip domain name mjlnet.com
!
!
! IP multicast and IPX configuration (example only)
!
ip multicast-routing
ipx routing 0050.2afe.0800
ipx internal-network 1000
!
!
! Crypto pki trustpoint - enrollment parameters, certificate fields, and auto
! (re-)enrollment
!
```

Example 6-46 *Complete Configurations for IPsec VPN Gateways London and Berlin with GRE Tunnels for Multiprotocol and Multicast Traffic Transport (Continued)*

```
crypto pki trustpoint mjlnetcertsrv
 enrollment mode ra
 enrollment url http://mjlnetcertsrv:80/certsrv/mscep/mscep.dll
 usage ike
 serial-number none
 ip-address 192.168.1.1
 password 7 1104130919171F
 subject-name C=GB, O=mjlnet, OU=engineering
 revocation-check crl none
 rsakeypair London.mjlnet.com
 auto-enroll 90 regenerate
!
!
! Gateway's and CA's certificates
!
crypto pki certificate chain mjlnetcertsrv
 certificate 613240F1000000000018
 308204A9 30820453 A0030201 02020A61 3240F100 00000000 18300D06 092A8648
 86F70D01 01050500 30819931 1F301D06 092A8648 86F70D01 09011610 61646D69
! <text omitted>
 quit
 certificate ca 48B8A34E0C6A09A7447B8CBDD77C3A81
 30820304 308202AE A0030201 02021048 B8A34E0C 6A09A744 7B8CBDD7 7C3A8130
 0D06092A 864886F7 0D010105 05003081 99311F30 1D06092A 864886F7 0D010901
! <text omitted>
 quit
!
!
! IKE policy
!
crypto isakmp policy 10
 encr 3des
 group 2
!
!
! IPsec transform set
!
crypto ipsec transform-set mjlnettrans esp-3des esp-sha-hmac
!
!
! Crypto map
!
crypto map mjlnetmap 10 ipsec-isakmp
 set peer 192.168.2.2
 set transform-set mjlnettrans
 match address 101
!
!
! GRE tunnel interface
!
```

continues

Example 6-46 *Complete Configurations for IPsec VPN Gateways London and Berlin with GRE Tunnels for Multiprotocol and Multicast Traffic Transport (Continued)*

```
interface Tunnel0
 ip address 10.3.3.1 255.255.255.0
 ip pim sparse-dense-mode
 ipx network 3000
 tunnel source 192.168.1.1
 tunnel destination 192.168.2.2
!
!
! Outside interface
!
interface Serial1/0
 ip address 192.168.1.1 255.255.255.0
 crypto map mjlnetmap
!
!
! Inside interface
!
interface FastEthernet3/0
 ip address 10.1.1.1 255.255.255.0
 ip pim sparse-dense mode
!
!
! Dynamic routing protocol for reachability over the GRE tunnel
!
router eigrp 100
 network 10.1.1.0 0.0.0.255
 network 10.3.3.0 0.0.0.255
 no auto-summary
!
!
! Route to the Berlin gateway (outside interface)
!
ip route 0.0.0.0 0.0.0.0 192.168.1.2
!
!
! Crypto access list
!
access-list 101 permit gre host 192.168.1.1 host 192.168.2.2
!
!
! NTP with authentication
!
ntp authentication-key 1 md5 09414405170003 7
ntp authenticate
ntp trusted-key 1
ntp server 10.10.10.99 key 1
!
end
Berlin#show running-config
Building configuration...
Current configuration : 7437 bytes
!
```

Example 6-46 *Complete Configurations for IPsec VPN Gateways London and Berlin with GRE Tunnels for Multiprotocol and Multicast Traffic Transport (Continued)*

```
version 12.3
!
!
! IPsec gateway's host name and IP domain name
!
hostname Berlin
!
ip domain name mjlnet.com
!
!
! IP multicast and IPX configuration (example only)
!
ip multicast-routing
ip cef
ipx routing 0004.9bd6.0c00
ipx internal-network 2000
!
!
! Crypto pki trustpoint - enrollment parameters, certificate fields, and auto
! (re-)enrollment
!
crypto pki trustpoint mjlnetcertsrv
 enrollment mode ra
 enrollment url http://mjlnetcertsrv:80/certsrv/mscep/mscep.dll
 usage ike
 serial-number none
 ip-address 192.168.2.2
 password 7 0009190A0A5E1F
 subject-name C=GB, O=mjlnet, OU=engineering
 revocation-check crl none
 rsakeypair Berlin.mjlnet.com
 auto-enroll 90 regenerate
!
!
! Gateway's and CA's certificates
!
crypto pki certificate chain mjlnetcertsrv
 certificate 612A9069000000000019
 308204A9 30820453 A0030201 02020A61 2A906900 00000000 19300D06 092A8648
 86F70D01 01050500 30819931 1F301D06 092A8648 86F70D01 09011610 61646D69
! <text omitted>
 quit
 certificate ca 48B8A34E0C6A09A7447B8CBDD77C3A81
 30820304 308202AE A0030201 02021048 B8A34E0C 6A09A744 7B8CBDD7 7C3A8130
 0D06092A 864886F7 0D010105 05003081 99311F30 1D06092A 864886F7 0D010901
! <text omitted>
 quit
!
!
! IKE policy
!
```

continues

Example 6-46 *Complete Configurations for IPsec VPN Gateways London and Berlin with GRE Tunnels for Multiprotocol and Multicast Traffic Transport (Continued)*

```
crypto isakmp policy 10
 encr 3des
group 2
!
!
! IPsec transform set
!
crypto ipsec transform-set mjlnettrans esp-3des esp-sha-hmac
!
!
! Crypto map
!
crypto map mjlnetmap 10 ipsec-isakmp
 set peer 192.168.1.1
 set transform-set mjlnettrans
 match address 101
!
!
! GRE tunnel interface
!
interface Tunnel0
 ip address 10.3.3.2 255.255.255.0
 ip pim sparse-dense-mode
 ipx network 3000
 tunnel source 192.168.2.2
 tunnel destination 192.168.1.1
!
!
! Inside interface
!
interface FastEthernet1/0
 ip address 10.2.2.1 255.255.255.0
 ip pim sparse-dense mode
!
!
! Outside interface
!
interface Serial4/0
 ip address 192.168.2.2 255.255.255.0
 crypto map mjlnetmap
!
!
! Dynamic routing protocol for reachability over the GRE tunnel
!
router eigrp 100
 network 10.2.2.0 0.0.0.255
 network 10.3.3.0 0.0.0.255
 no auto-summary
!
!
! Route to the London gateway (outside interface)
!
```

Example 6-46 *Complete Configurations for IPsec VPN Gateways London and Berlin with GRE Tunnels for Multiprotocol and Multicast Traffic Transport (Continued)*

```
ip route 0.0.0.0 0.0.0.0 192.168.2.1
!
!
! Crypto access list
!
access-list 101 permit gre host 192.168.2.2 host 192.168.1.1
!
!
! NTP with authentication
!
ntp authentication-key 1 md5 1104130919171F 7
ntp authenticate
ntp trusted-key 1
ntp server 10.10.10.99 key 1
!
End
```

Configuring VTIs

The configuration of VTIs is similar to that for IPsec-protected GRE tunnels.

Example 6-47 shows the configuration on the Berlin and London IPsec VPN gateways using, in this case, preshared key authentication. Note that only the relevant configuration is shown.

Example 6-47 *Configurations for IPsec VPN Gateways London and Berlin with VTIs for IP Unicast and Multicast Traffic Transport*

```
!
hostname London
!
!
! IP multicast configuration (example only)
!
ip multicast-routing
ip cef
!
!
! IKE policy
!
crypto isakmp policy 10
 encr 3des
 authentication pre-share
 group 2
!
!
! Preshared key
!
```

continues

Example 6-47 *Configurations for IPsec VPN Gateways London and Berlin with VTIs for IP Unicast and Multicast Traffic Transport (Continued)*

```
crypto isakmp key mjlnet address 0.0.0.0 0.0.0.0
!
!
! IPsec transform set
!
crypto ipsec transform-set vti.trans esp-3des esp-sha-hmac
!
!
! IPsec profile
!
crypto ipsec profile vti.prof
 set transform-set vti.trans
!
!
! Virtual tunnel interface (VTI)
!
interface Tunnel0
 ip address 10.3.3.1 255.255.255.0
 ip pim sparse-dense-mode
 tunnel source 192.168.1.1
 tunnel destination 192.168.2.2
 tunnel mode ipsec ipv4
 tunnel protection ipsec profile vti.prof
!
!
! Outside interface
!
interface Serial1/0
 ip address 192.168.1.1 255.255.255.0
!
!
! Inside interface
!
interface FastEthernet3/0
 ip address 10.1.1.1 255.255.255.0
 ip pim sparse-dense mode
!
! Dynamic routing protocol for reachability over the VTI
!
router eigrp 100
network 10.1.1.0 0.0.0.255
 network 10.3.3.0 0.0.0.255
no auto-summary
!
!
! Route to the Berlin gateway (outside interface)
!
ip route 192.168.2.0 255.255.255.0 192.168.1.2
!
!
```

Example 6-47 *Configurations for IPsec VPN Gateways London and Berlin with VTIs for IP Unicast and Multicast Traffic Transport (Continued)*

```
hostname Berlin
!
!
! IP multicast configuration (example only)
!
ip multicast-routing
!
!
! IKE policy
!
crypto isakmp policy 10
 encr 3des
 authentication pre-share
 group 2
!
!
! Preshared key
!
crypto isakmp key mjlnet address 0.0.0.0 0.0.0.0
!
!
! IPsec transform set
!
crypto ipsec transform-set vti.trans esp-3des esp-sha-hmac
!
!
! IPsec profile
!
crypto ipsec profile vti.prof
 set transform-set vti.trans
!
!
! Virtual tunnel interface (VTI)
!
interface Tunnel0
 ip address 10.3.3.2 255.255.255.0
 ip pim sparse-dense-mode
 tunnel source 192.168.2.2
 tunnel destination 192.168.1.1
 tunnel mode ipsec ipv4
 tunnel protection ipsec profile vti.prof
!
!
! Inside interface
!
interface FastEthernet1/0
 ip address 10.2.2.1 255.255.255.0
 ip pim sparse-dense mode
!
!
```

continues

Example 6-47 *Configurations for IPsec VPN Gateways London and Berlin with VTIs for IP Unicast and Multicast Traffic Transport (Continued)*

```
! Outside interface
!
interface Serial4/0
 ip address 192.168.2.2 255.255.255.0
 !
 !
! Dynamic routing protocol for reachability over the VTI
 !
router eigrp 100
network 10.2.2.0 0.0.0.255
 network 10.3.3.0 0.0.0.255
 no auto-summary
 !
 !
! Route to the London gateway (outside interface)
 !
ip route 192.168.1.0 255.255.255.0 192.168.2.1
 !
```

If you compare the configurations shown in Example 6-46 and 6-47, you will see quite a number of similarities. Apart from the obvious difference in the method of IKE phase 1 authentication (digital signature authentication versus preshared key authentication), the other major differences are the configuration of the VTIs and the IPsec profiles in Example 6-47.

The configuration of the VTI consists of many of the same commands used to configure a GRE tunnel (**tunnel source**, **tunnel destination**, and so on). Some of the commands that are used to configure VTIs are new, however. The **tunnel mode ipsec ipv4** command configures the tunneling mode as IPsec and the transport protocol as IPv4. The **tunnel protection ipsec profile** *profile-name* command associates the tunnel interface with an IPsec profile (which provides IPsec protection). The IPsec profile in this example is called vti.prof.

The IPsec profile itself (vti.prof) is configured using the **crypto ipsec profile** *profile-name* command. Within the IPsec profile, an IPsec transform set (vti.trans) is specified using the **set transform-set** *transform-set-name*.

The IKE policy, preshared key, and transform set (vti.trans) are configured in the normal way using the **crypto isakmp policy**, **crypto isakmp key**, and **crypto ipsec transform-set** commands.

The **show ip eigrp neighbors** command can be used to verify the EIGRP neighbor relationship over the VTI (see Example 6-48).

Example 6-48 *Verifying the EIGRP Neighbor Relationship over the VTI Using the show ip eigrp neighbors Command*

```
London#show ip eigrp neighbors
IP-EIGRP neighbors for process 100
H  Address          Interface     Hold Uptime  SRTT  RTO Q Seq
                                  (sec)    (ms)    Cnt Num
0  10.3.3.2         Tu0            10 00:42:20 1062 5000 0 4
London#
```

As you can see, IPsec VPN gateway London has an EIGRP neighbor relationship with IPsec VPN gateway Berlin (10.3.3.2) over the VTI (Tu0).

As shown in Example 6-49, you can verity the PIM neighbor relationship using the **show ip pim neighbor** command.

Example 6-49 *Verifying the PIM Neighbor Relationship over the VTI Using the show ip pim neighbor Command*

```
London#show ip pim neighbor
PIM Neighbor Table
Neighbor       Interface       Uptime/Expires  Ver  DR
Address                                             Prio/Mode
10.3.3.2       Tunnel0         00:38:57/00:01:40 v2  1 / S
London#
```

The output of the **show ip pim neighbor** command shows that a PIM neighbor relationship has also been established over the VTI with Berlin.

Manual SA and Key Management

As discussed earlier in this chapter, there are two ways of managing SAs and session keys with IPsec:

- You can automate it using IKE.
- You can manually configure your SAs and session keys.

Manual session key configuration does have a number of disadvantages, including the following:

- Configuring and troubleshooting manual session keys is laborious. These factors render manual configuration unsuitable for all but the smallest VPN deployments.
- Anti-relay mechanisms for AH and ESP are not supported with manual SA and key management.
- Manual key management is not supported with hardware accelerators.

Now that you know why you would not want to deploy it, it is worth taking a look at the one or two exceptions when the configuration of manual session keys might prove useful:

- If an IPsec peer does not support IKE, configuration of manual session keys is a solution. Note, however, that all Cisco devices that support IPsec also support IKE.

- It is a possible solution if there is a firewall or other device in the path between IPsec VPN gateways that blocks IKE. In this case, the best option is to reconfigure the device blocking IKE, but manual session keys are a possible solution if reconfiguration is not possible.

Okay, on to configuration. Figure 6-38 and Example 6-50 show the configuration of manual session keys on peer IPsec VPN gateways, London and Berlin.

Figure 6-38 *Configuring IPsec Manual Session Keys*

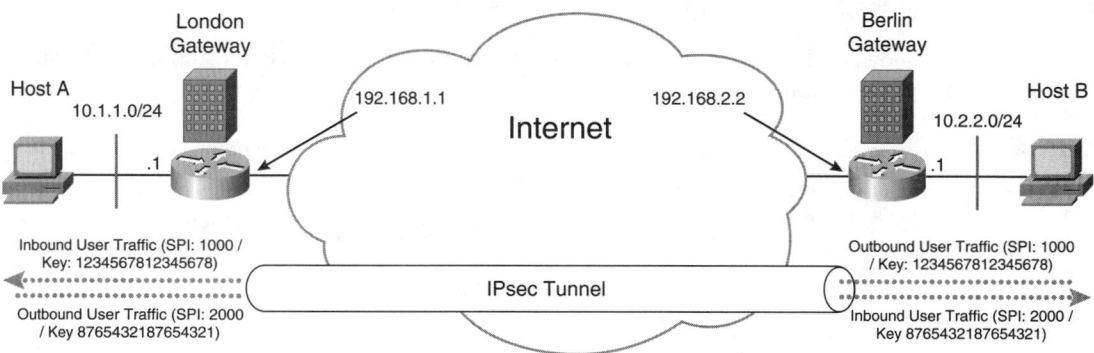

Example 6-50 *Configuring IPsec Manual Session Keys*

```
!
! On London
!
no crypto isakmp enable (line 1)
!
!
crypto ipsec transform-set mjlnettransform esp-des (line 2)
!
crypto map mjlnetcmap 10 ipsec-manual (line 3)
 set peer 192.168.2.2
 set session-key inbound esp 1000 cipher 1234567812345678 (line 4)
 set session-key outbound esp 2000 cipher 8765432187654321 (line 5)
 set transform-set mjlnettransform
 match address 101
!
!
access-list 101 permit ip 10.1.1.0 0.0.0.255 10.2.2.0 0.0.0.255
!
!
! On Berlin
!
no crypto isakmp enable
!
!
crypto ipsec transform-set mjlnettransform esp-des
!
```

Example 6-50 *Configuring IPsec Manual Session Keys (Continued)*

```
crypto map mjlnetcmap 10 ipsec-manual
 set peer 192.168.1.1
 set session-key inbound esp 2000 cipher 8765432187654321 (line 6)
 set session-key outbound esp 1000 cipher 1234567812345678 (line 7)
 set transform-set mjlnettransform
 match address 101
!
!
access-list 101 permit ip 10.2.2.0 0.0.0.255 10.1.1.0 0.0.0.255
!
```

The configuration of the London gateway begins with the command **no crypto isakmp enable** (highlighted line 1). This command disables IKE.

In highlighted line 2, you can see a regular IPsec transform set. Note, however, that it only includes ESP DES encryption. You will know by now that this is a weak transform—it specifies 56-bit DES (an insecure encryption algorithm), and it does not include authentication (it is vulnerable to cut-and-paste attacks). In a live network, you should include authentication in the transform set and if possible specify a stronger encryption algorithm.

The **crypto map** *map-name seq-number* **ipsec-manual** command in highlighted line 3 is then used to specify that IKE will not be used to establish IPsec SAs. Within the crypto map, two session keys are specified using the **set session-key** {**inbound|outbound**} **esp spi** *hex-key-string* [**authenticator** *hex-key-string*] command (see highlighted lines 4 and 5).

The **set session-key** command in highlighted line 4 configures the SPI (1000) and ESP key (1234567812345678) for IPsec packets *inbound* from the Berlin gateway to the London gateway. The SPI is specified in decimal (a value from 256 to 4,294,967,295), and the key is specified in hexadecimal.

The **set session-key** command in highlighted line 5, on the other hand, configures the SPI (2000) and ESP key (8765432187654321) for IPsec packets sent by London and *outbound* to the Berlin gateway.

Because ESP authentication is not specified in the IPsec transform in this example, the **authenticator** keyword is not required with the **set session-key** command. If you do specify ESP authentication, make sure that you configure the **authenticator** keyword and associated *hex-key-string* parameter. The **authenticator** keyword is used to configure the key string (in hexadecimal) to be used for ESP authentication.

The key that you specify can be 8, 16, or 20 bytes long, depending on the following requirements:

- If you specify DES encryption in the IPsec transform set, the key must be at least 8 bytes long.
- If you specify MD5 authentication, the key must be at least 16 bytes long.
- If you specify SHA-1 authentication, the key must be at least 20 bytes long.

If you configure AH in your IPsec transforms, you can specify the AH SPIs and keys in a similar way using the **set session-key** {**inbound|outbound**} **ah** *spi hex-key-string* command.

The configuration of the Berlin gateway is almost identical, but there are one or two slight differences.

The **set session-key** command in highlighted line 6 configures the SPI (2000) and ESP key (8765432187654321) for IPsec packets *inbound* from the London gateway. Parameters in this line *must* match those for IPsec packets outbound from the London gateway (see highlighted line 5).

The **set session-key** command in highlighted line 5 configures the SPI (1000) and ESP key (1234567812345678) for IPsec packets sent by the Berlin gateway and *outbound* to the London gateway. Parameters in this line *must* match those for IPsec packets inbound to the London gateway (see highlighted line 4).

So, configuration of manual session keys is fairly simple, but their usage is limited by the disadvantages discussed earlier in this section.

Deploying IPsec VPNs with NAT/PAT

If there is a Network Address Translation (NAT) or Port Address Translation (PAT) device in the path between IPsec peers in your IPsec VPN, you must carefully configure either the IPsec peers or the NAT/PAT device to ensure that IPsec operates correctly and does not break. This section examines how NAT/PAT devices can break IPsec, and how you can get around this. Figure 6-39 shows a sample IPsec VPN topology used to illustrate some of the concepts discussed in this section.

Figure 6-39 *Sample IPsec VPN Topology*

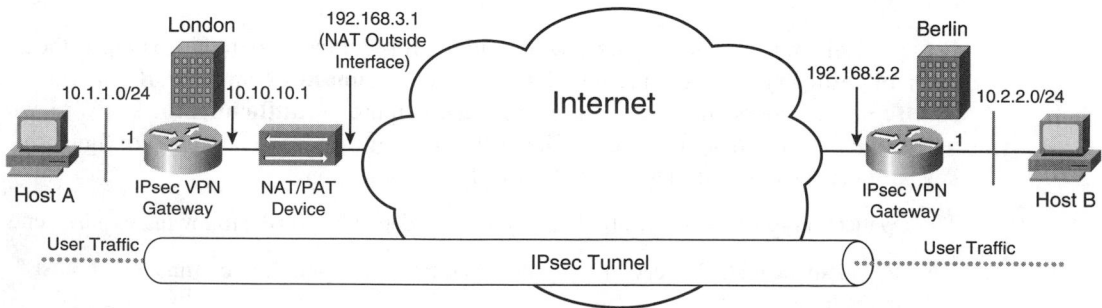

As you can see in Figure 6-39, the only difference to the reference topology used throughout the rest this chapter is the addition of a NAT/PAT device in front of the London IPsec VPN gateway.

How NAT/PAT Breaks IPsec

So, NAT can break IPsec, but how exactly can this happen? NAT/PAT can break IPsec in a number of ways, including the following:

- NAT/PAT can cause IKE negotiation initiated by IPsec peers on outside networks to fail.
- NAT/PAT can cause rekeying to fail when NAT/PAT is based on IKE cookies.
- NAT/PAT can break IP address IKE identifier verification.
- NAT/PAT can cause IPsec peers to drop ISAKMP traffic.
- NAT/PAT causes IPsec devices to drop all AH traffic.
- NAT/PAT devices might not translate ESP packets.
- NAT/PAT based on SPI selection can cause ESP packets to be dropped.
- NAT/PAT translation timeouts can cause ESP traffic to be dropped.
- NAT/PAT can cause TCP/UDP header checksum verification to fail when TCP/UDP traffic is transported over ESP.
- NAT/PAT can cause applications with embedded IP addresses to fail.
- Unintentional NAT of user packets can cause these packets not to be sent over the IPsec tunnel.

To understand how you can get around problems with NAT/PAT, it is a good idea to examine each problem in a little more depth.

NAT/PAT Can Cause IKE Negotiation Initiated by IPsec Peers on Outside Networks to Fail

NAT/PAT devices must be specifically configured to accept IKE negotiation initiated by IPsec peers on outside networks. This is because there is usually a default requirement with NAT devices that address translation be initiated by devices on the inside network.

A simple method of allowing outsides IPsec devices to initiate IKE negotiation with inside IPsec devices when using standard (one-to-one) NAT is to configure a static NAT translation. So, for example, in Figure 6-39 a static translation would allow the Berlin gateway to initiate IKE negotiation through the NAT/PAT device to the London gateway.

Example 6-51 shows the configuration of a static NAT translation to allow outside IPsec gateways to initiate IKE negotiation to an inside IPsec gateway.

Example 6-51 *Configuring a Static NAT Translation on the NAT Device to Allow Outside IPsec Gateways to Initiate IKE Negotiation with an Inside IPsec Gateway*

```
!
! NAT device configuration
!
! Interface s2/0 is the NAT inside address
!
interface Serial2/0
 ip address 10.10.10.2 255.255.255.0
 ip nat inside
!
! Interface serial 2/1 is the NAT outside address
!
interface Serial2/1
 ip address 192.168.3.1 255.255.255.0
 ip nat outside
!
! The static NAT translation here allows the Berlin gateway to initiate IPsec
! connections to the London gateway.
!
ip nat inside source static 10.10.10.1 192.168.3.5
!
```

The highlighted line shows a static NAT translation of London's inside local address (10.10.10.1) to the inside global address 192.168.3.5.

Do not forget to configure the remote gateway (Berlin in this example) to use the local gateway's inside *global* address as appropriate (see Example 6-52).

Example 6-52 *Configuring the Remote Gateway (Berlin) to Use the Local Gateway's Inside Global Address*

```
!
! Remote gateway's (Berlin's) configuration
!
crypto isakmp policy 10
 hash md5
 authentication pre-share
crypto isakmp key cisco address 192.168.3.5 (line 1)
!
!
crypto ipsec transform-set mjlnettrans esp-des esp-md5-hmac
!
crypto map mjlnetmap 10 ipsec-isakmp
 set peer 192.168.3.5 (line 2)
 set transform-set mjlnettrans
 match address 101
!
```

In Example 6-52, highlighted line 1, the inside global address of London gateway (192.168.3.5) is specified using the **crypto isakmp key** and **set peer** commands.

If you are using PAT rather than standard (one-to-one) NAT, the configuration differs slightly, as shown in Example 6-53.

Example 6-53 *Configuring a Static Translation on a PAT Device to Allow Outside IPsec Gateways to Initiate IKE Negotiation with an Inside IPsec Gateway*

```
!
! PAT device configuration
!
! Interface s2/0 is the NAT inside address
!
interface Serial2/0
 ip address 10.10.10.2 255.255.255.0
 ip nat inside
!
!
! Interface serial 2/1 is the NAT outside address
!
interface Serial2/1
 ip address 192.168.3.1 255.255.255.0
 ip nat outside
!
!
! The static translations here allows the Berlin gateway to initiate IPsec
! connections to the London gateway.
!
ip nat inside source list 10 interface Serial2/1 overload
ip nat inside source static esp 10.10.10.1 interface Serial2/1 (line 1)
ip nat inside source static udp 10.10.10.1 500 interface Serial2/1 500 (line 2)
!
access-list 10 permit 10.10.10.0 0.0.0.255
!
```

The **ip nat inside source static esp** *inside_local_address_of_gateway* **interface** *outside_interface* command in highlighted line 1 is used to allow the translation of ESP tunnel mode traffic for an IPsec tunnel to the specified inside local address. So, in this example, the destination address of ESP packets that the Berlin gateway sends to the London gateway is translated from the inside global address 192.168.3.1 (the IP address applied to interface serial 2/1) to the inside local address 10.10.10.1 (London's outside interface IP address).

The **ip nat inside source static udp** *inside_local_address_of_gateway* **500 interface** *outside_interface* **500** command (highlighted line 2) similarly allows the translation of ISAKMP traffic (UDP port 500) to the specified inside local address. In this example, the destination address of ISAKMP packets that the Berlin gateway sends are translated from the inside global address 192.168.3.1 (the IP address applied to interface serial 2/1) to the inside local address 10.10.10.1 (London).

Again, you should configure the remote gateway to use the local gateway's inside *global* address as appropriate (see Example 6-52). In this case, the local gateway's inside global address is 192.168.3.1 (the IP address of interface serial 2/1 on the NAT device [see Example 6-53]).

NAT/PAT Can Cause Rekeying to Fail When NAT/PAT Is Based on IKE Cookies

Instead of translating UDP ports, some NAT/PAT devices use ISAKMP cookies to demultiplex IKE traffic inbound on the outside interface and identify individual IPsec peers to which this traffic is bound. Cookies are unique identifiers used during IKE phase 1 to make denial-of-service attacks more difficult.

If a NAT/PAT device uses ISAKMP cookies to demultiplex IKE traffic, then during rekeying (when different cookies are typically used) NAT/PAT may fail.

NAT/PAT Might Break IP Address IKE Identifier Verification

When you use IP addresses as IKE (ISAKMP) identifiers, your IKE identifier verification might fail, and ISAKMP packets might be dropped. Verification might fail because NAT/PAT modifies IP addresses in the IP header.

NAT/PAT Can Cause IPsec Peers to Drop ISAKMP Traffic

When there are multiple IPsec peers behind a PAT device, all of which are negotiating IKE SAs to the same responder, that responder must be able to accept ISAKMP packets with a source port other than UDP port 500 if the PAT device translates the source port of ISAKMP packets (from UDP port 500). This is because the PAT device translates the source UDP port of ISAKMP packets from each IPsec peer to a unique value (so that it can distinguish the individual flows/IPsec peers). However, translation of UDP source ports does mean that the responder must be able to accept (and respond to) ISAKMP packets from source UDP ports other than UDP port 500.

During rekeying, the responder must also use the unique UDP port that identifies each individual IPsec peer behind the PAT device as the UDP destination port for ISAKMP packets. If the responder does not do this, rekeying may fail.

Figure 6-40 illustrates translation of the UDP port for ISAKMP packets. In Figure 6-40, the UDP port for ISAKMP packets from hosts A, B, and C (all IKE initiators) is translated from port 500 to X, Y, and Z, respectively. This translation of UDP source port numbers allows the PAT device to distinguish ISAKMP traffic inbound from the IKE responder.

So, for example, when IKE traffic from Host A to the IKE responder is received on the PAT device, it translates the UDP *source* port from 500 to X. The IKE responder then sends IKE traffic to Host A using UDP *destination* port X, and because this UDP port is unique, the PAT device is able to distinguish that this traffic should be sent to Host A (and not Hosts B and C).

Figure 6-40 *PAT Device Translates ISAKMP Source Port Numbers*

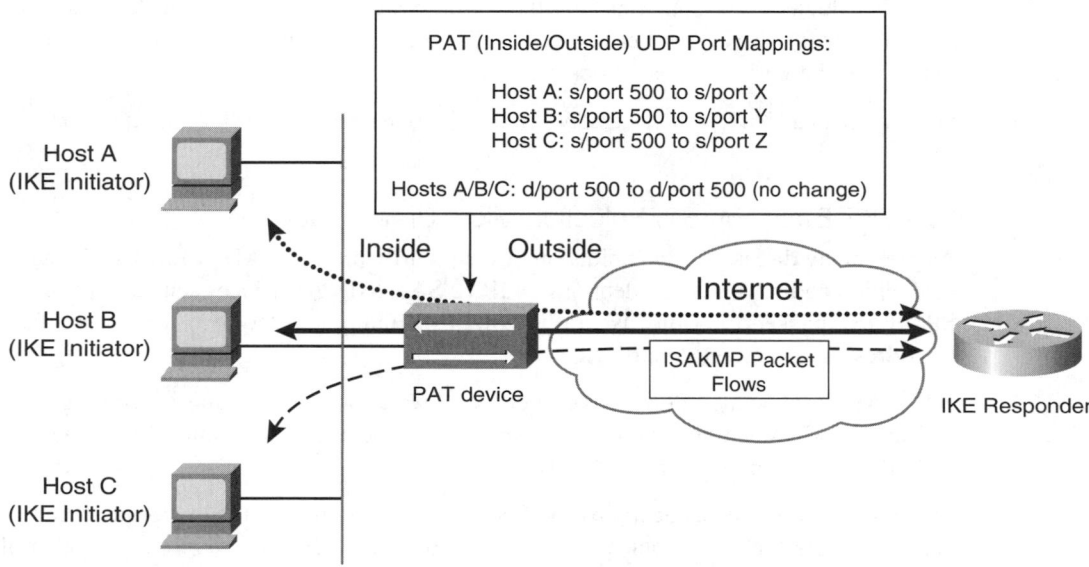

It is worth noting that some PAT devices do not translate UDP port 500 because of the inability of some IPsec devices to handle ISAKMP traffic on UDP ports other than 500.

NAT/PAT Causes IPsec Devices to Drop All AH Traffic

If AH is used to protect IP traffic (whether in transport *or* tunnel mode), the whole packet is authenticated, including the outer IP header. NAT/PAT, by definition, translates the outer header IP address(es), and that causes the AH integrity check to fail.

Figure 6-41 illustrates the failure of the AH integrity check.

Figure 6-41 *NAT Causes the AH Integrity Check to Fail*

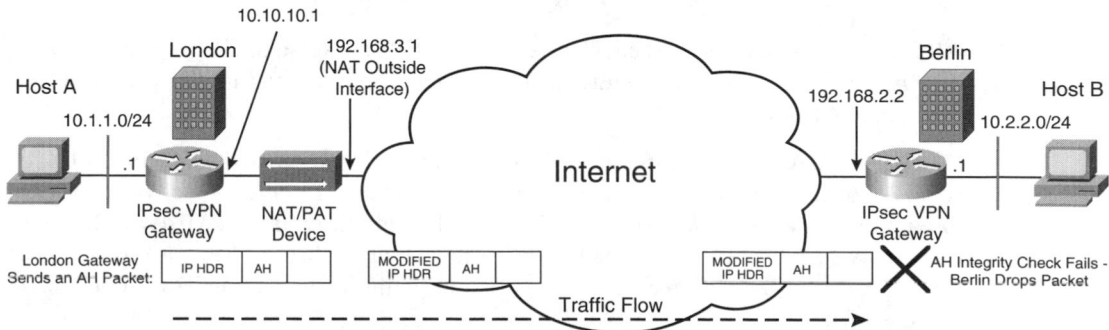

In Figure 6-41, the London gateway sends an AH packet to the Berlin gateway. The NAT/PAT device in the path translates the IP address(es) in the outer IP header, and when the AH packet arrives at the Berlin gateway, this translation causes the AH integrity check to fail, and the Berlin gateway drops the packet.

So, if there is a NAT/PAT device between two IPsec devices, use ESP rather than AH.

NAT/PAT Based on SPI Selection Might Break IPsec

As previously discussed, a combination of the security protocol (AH or ESP), SPI, and destination address uniquely identifies an IPsec SA. NAT/PAT devices sometimes use the SPI of ESP packets to distinguish traffic flows from multiple IPsec peers and ensure that IP addresses are correctly translated.

NAT/PAT based on the SPI of ESP packets often works well, but it can sometimes go wrong. Before examining how it can go wrong, it is useful to first examine exactly how NAT/PAT based on SPI works.

SPIs are assigned independently by the IPsec devices and then communicated to IPsec peers during IKE phase 2 (quick mode) negotiation. So, one host will inform the other of the SPI to use when sending traffic to it for a particular IPsec SA. Because all phase 2 messages are encrypted, it is impossible for a PAT device to find out SPI values from IKE negotiation.

PAT devices can translate the IP addresses for ESP packets by making a "best guess" based on which inside host (or other device) has *recently* negotiated IKE and sent ESP packets.

Figure 6-42 illustrates how a PAT device can handle ESP packet translation using SPIs. In Figure 6-42, Host A negotiates IKE with the IPsec gateway. During phase 2 negotiation, Host A informs the IPsec gateway that it should use SPI 0x11111111 when sending ESP packets to Host A, and the IPsec gateway informs Host A that should use SPI 0x22222222 when sending ESP packets to the IPsec gateway. The phase 2 negotiation is encrypted so the PAT device has no way of knowing that Host A has assigned SPI 0x11111111 and that the IPsec gateway has assigned SPI 0x22222222.

After IKE negotiation is finished, Host A sends an ESP packet to the IPsec gateway (using SPI 0x22222222). Then shortly after that, the IPsec gateway sends an ESP packet to Host A via the PAT device.

When the PAT device receives the ESP packet, the destination IP address is 192.168.1.1 (the PAT overload IP address), and the SPI is 0x11111111. The PAT device then does a lookup into its translation table for the SPI (and IP addresses). If the PAT device has not previously seen the SPI, it makes a best guess and assumes that this SPI corresponds to an IPsec SA negotiated via a recent IKE negotiation (in this case, between Host A and the IPsec gateway).

Figure 6-42 *NAT/PAT Based on SPIs*

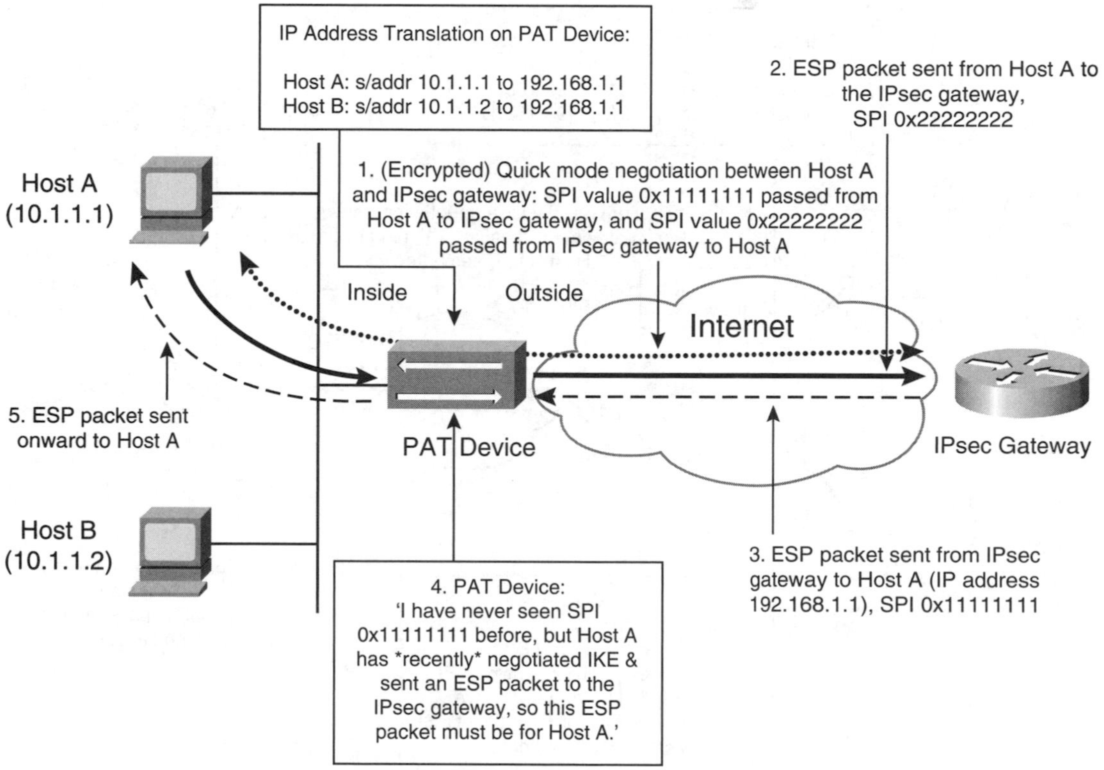

IP Address Translation on PAT Device:

Host A: s/addr 10.1.1.1 to 192.168.1.1
Host B: s/addr 10.1.1.2 to 192.168.1.1

2. ESP packet sent from Host A to the IPsec gateway, SPI 0x22222222

Host A
(10.1.1.1)

1. (Encrypted) Quick mode negotiation between Host A and IPsec gateway: SPI value 0x11111111 passed from Host A to IPsec gateway, and SPI value 0x22222222 passed from IPsec gateway to Host A

Inside   Outside

Internet

5. ESP packet sent onward to Host A

PAT Device

IPsec Gateway

Host B
(10.1.1.2)

3. ESP packet sent from IPsec gateway to Host A (IP address 192.168.1.1), SPI 0x11111111

4. PAT Device:
'I have never seen SPI 0x11111111 before, but Host A has *recently* negotiated IKE & sent an ESP packet to the IPsec gateway, so this ESP packet must be for Host A.'

Having determined that the ESP packet should go to Host A, the PAT device translates the destination IP address of the ESP packet from 192.168.1.1 (the inside global address) to 10.1.1.1 (the inside local address [Host A]) and sends the packet onward to Host A.

So, NAT/PAT based on SPIs can work well. But if two (or more) inside IPsec devices attempt to negotiate IKE with the same peer IPsec device at the same time, this can lead to communication failure.

Figure 6-43 illustrates a communication failure when two devices on the inside of the PAT device simultaneously attempt to negotiate IKE with the same IPsec peer. In Figure 6-43, Hosts A and B simultaneously negotiate IKE with the IPsec gateway. During IKE phase 2 negotiation, Host A informs the IPsec gateway that it should use SPI 0x11111111 when transmitting ESP packets to Host A. Host B informs the IPsec gateway that it should use SPI 0x55555555 when transmitting ESP packets to Host B. Immediately after negotiating IKE phase 2, Hosts A and B both send ESP packets to the IPsec gateway (not shown).

Figure 6-43 *NAT/PAT Based on SPIs Fails*

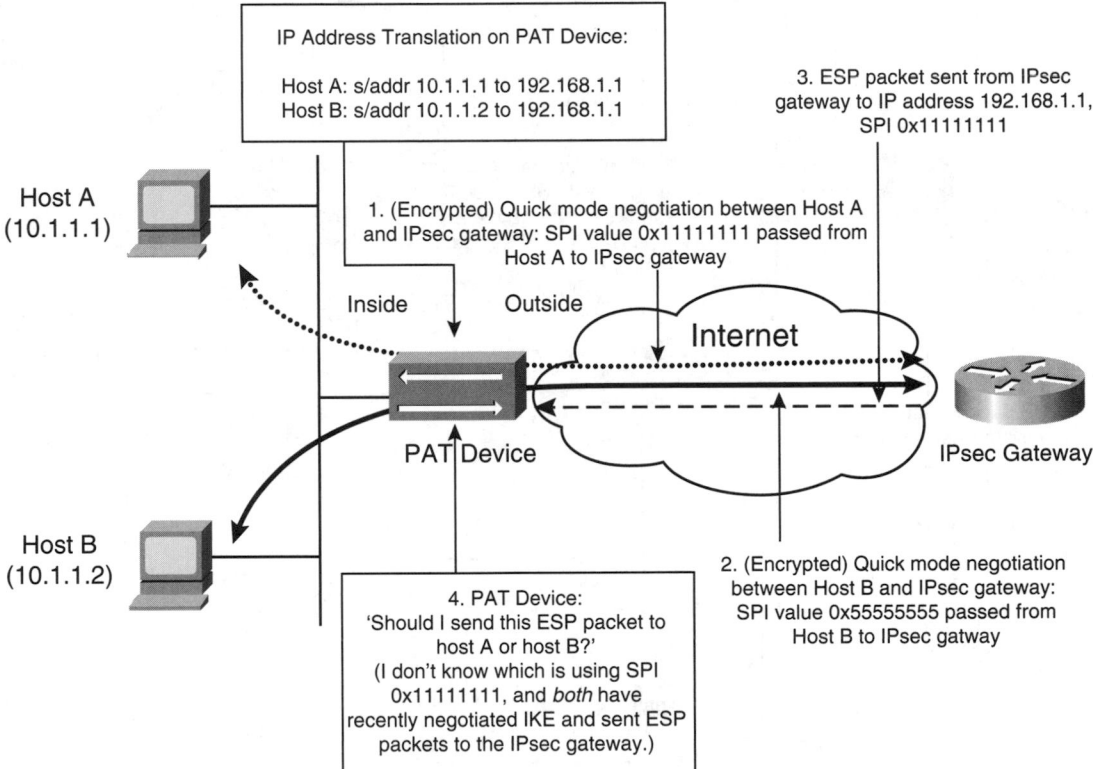

The IPsec gateway then sends an ESP packet to Host A, the header of which contains SPI 0x11111111. When it arrives at the PAT device, the PAT device looks up the SPI in its translation table, and when it finds no existing translation for that particular SPI (from that particular IPsec gateway), the PAT device checks to see which inside devices have recently negotiated IKE with the IPsec gateway. Unfortunately, both Host A and Host B have recently negotiated IKE phase 2 with the IPsec gateway, and so the PAT device has no idea where to send the packet.

NAT/PAT Devices Might Not Translate ESP Packets

Some NAT/PAT devices will only translate UDP- or TCP-based traffic. In this case, ESP traffic will simply be dropped.

NAT/PAT Translation Timeouts Can Cause IPsec Traffic to be Dropped

NAT translations may time out before IPsec SAs. In this case, IPsec traffic will be black-holed!

Figure 6-44 illustrates IPsec packets dropped when the NAT translation times out before the IPsec SA.

Figure 6-44 *NAT Translation Times Out Before the IPsec SA*

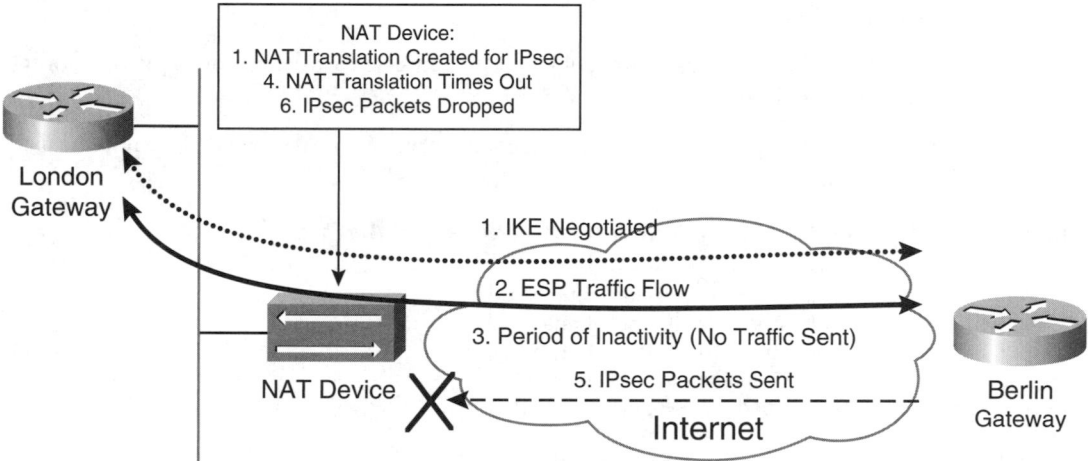

In Figure 6-44, the London and Berlin gateways negotiate IKE and then exchange ESP packets. At this point, NAT translations exist on the NAT device for IPsec traffic between the London and Berlin gateways.

A period of inactivity then ensues, during which no traffic is sent between the London and Berlin gateways. This period of inactivity causes the NAT translations on the NAT device to time out. The Berlin gateway then sends an IPsec packet to the London gateway, but the NAT device drops the packet because the NAT translation has already timed out.

NAT/PAT Can Cause TCP/UDP Header Checksum Verification to Fail When TCP/UDP Traffic Is Transported over ESP

TCP and UDP include a checksum to ensure the integrity of segments transmitted over a network. The checksum computation performed by TCP and UDP includes not only the TCP or UDP header and data but also a 12-byte "pseudo-header." This pseudo-header includes the source and destination IP addresses and ensures the TCP or UDP segment has not been delivered to the wrong destination. Normally, when a NAT device modifies IP addresses in the IP header, it updates the TCP checksum as appropriate.

In transport mode IPsec, the pseudo-header included in checksum calculation includes IP addresses from the outer IP header. Unfortunately, when a NAT device translates IP addresses in the outer header, it cannot update the checksums in the TCP or UDP headers because they are protected by ESP. This means that checksum verification fails on the receiving IPsec peer, and packets may be dropped.

NAT/PAT Can Cause Applications with Embedded IP Addresses to Fail

If IP addresses are embedded into the payload of an IP packet and the packets are protected by ESP, the IP addresses embedded in the payload will not be translated by a NAT/PAT device, and applications that rely on the IP addresses in the payload being correctly translated will not function correctly.

FTP is a good example of a protocol where IP addresses are carried in the payload of the packet (with **FTP PORT** and **PASV** commands).

Figure 6-45 shows how IP addresses embedded in an ESP packet payload are not translated by a NAT device.

Figure 6-45 *IP Addresses Embedded in IPsec Packet Payloads Are Not Translated by NAT*

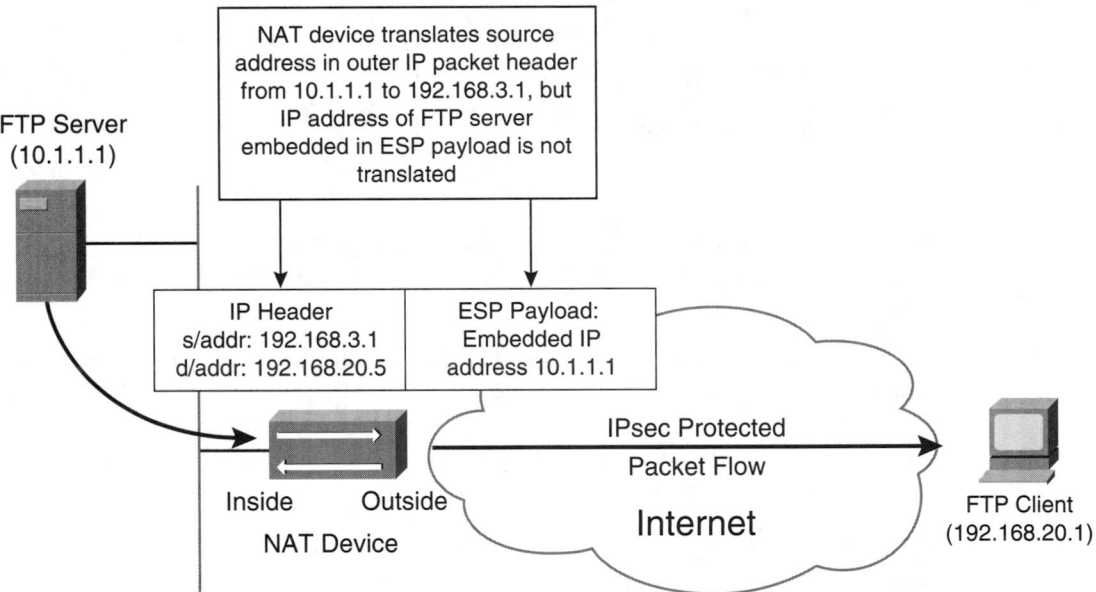

In Figure 6-45, the FTP server sends an ESP packet to the FTP client. The NAT device translates the source address of the packet from 10.1.1.1 to 192.168.3.1 but is unable to modify the IP address (10.1.1.1) embedded in the ESP packet payload. Because the NAT device does not translate the embedded IP address, communication fails.

Unintentional NAT'ing of User Packets Can Cause These Packets Not to Be Sent over the IPsec Tunnel

If you configure NAT on an IPsec VPN gateway, you must be careful not to unintentionally NAT user packets that should be sent over an IPsec tunnel. In this case, user packets may not be sent over the tunnel, as illustrated in Figure 6-46.

Figure 6-46 *Unintentionally NAT'ing User Packets Causes Them Not to Be Sent over the IPsec Tunnel*

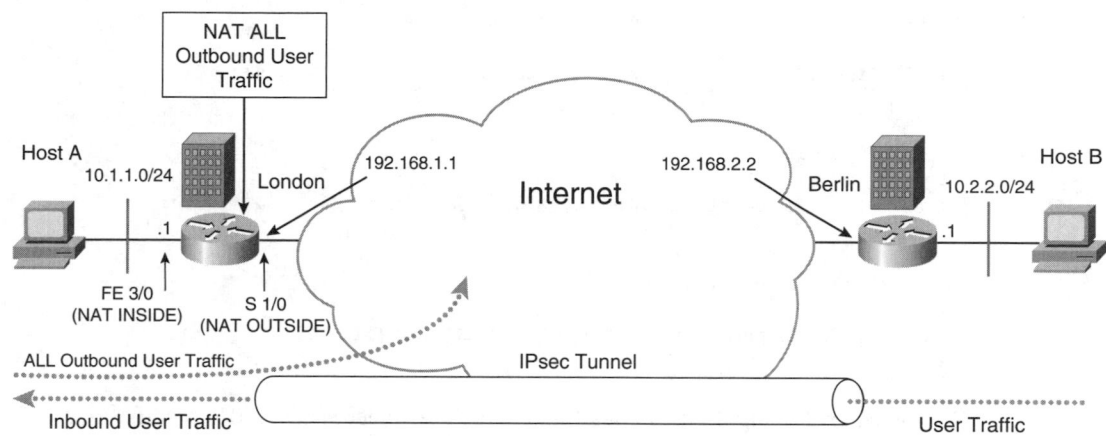

In Figure 6-46, (inbound) user traffic from the Berlin site is sent over the IPsec tunnel and successfully received at the London site.

No user traffic from network 10.1.1.0/24 to network 10.2.2.0/24 is sent over the IPsec tunnel, however.

Example 6-54 shows the configuration of the London gateway. Only the relevant configuration is shown.

Example 6-54 *London Gateway's Configuration*

```
!
! Crypto map
!
crypto map mjlnetmap 10 ipsec-isakmp
 set peer 192.168.2.2
 set transform-set mjlnettrans
 match address 101 (line 1)
!
!
! NAT outside interface
!
interface Serial1/0
 ip address 192.168.1.1 255.255.255.0
 ip nat outside
 crypto map mjlnetmap
!
!
! NAT inside interface
!
interface FastEthernet3/0
 ip address 10.1.1.1 255.255.255.0
 ip nat inside
!
!
```

continues

Example 6-54 *London Gateway's Configuration (Continued)*

```
! NAT inside source list specifies access list 102
!
ip nat inside source list 102 interface Serial1/0 overload (line 2)
!
!
! Crypto access list
!
access-list 101 permit ip 10.1.1.0 0.0.0.255 10.2.2.0 0.0.0.255 (line 3)
!
!
! Addresses to be NAT'ed
!
access-list 102 permit ip 10.1.1.0 0.0.0.255 any (line 4)
!
```

As you can see in highlighted lines 1 and 3, the crypto access list (101) specifies that all user (IP) traffic outbound from network 10.1.1.0/24 to network 10.2.2.0/24 should be sent over the IPsec tunnel.

But, no traffic outbound from network 10.1.1.0/24 to network 10.2.2.0/24 is being sent over the IPsec tunnel, as shown in the output of the **show crypto engine connections active** command (see Example 6-55).

Example 6-55 *No Outbound Traffic Is Sent over the IPsec Tunnel*

```
London#show crypto engine connections active
  ID Interface     IP-Address    State Algorithm        Encrypt Decrypt
   2 Serial1/0     192.168.1.1    set  HMAC_MD5+DES_56_CB     0   0
2000 Serial1/0     192.168.1.1    set  HMAC_MD5+DES_56_CB     0  45
2001 Serial1/0     192.168.1.1    set  HMAC_MD5+DES_56_CB     0   0
London#
```

The first highlighted line shows the inbound IPsec SA corresponding to the IPsec tunnel. As you can see, 45 packets have been decrypted—these are inbound user packets from the Berlin site (10.2.2.0/24).

The second highlighted line shows the outbound IPsec SA corresponding to the IPsec tunnel. No user packets from network 10.1.1.0/24 to network 10.2.2.0/24 have been sent using this IPsec SA (this is indicated by the 0 in the Encrypt column).

The reason that no user traffic (from network 10.1.1.0/24 to network 10.2.2.0/24) has been sent outbound over the IPsec tunnel is revealed if you take a look back at highlighted lines 2 and 4 in Example 6-54.

Highlighted line 2 in Example 6-54 shows that the source IP address of all user traffic specified in access list 102 (shown in highlighted line 4 in Example 6-54) is translated to the IP address configured on interface serial 1/0 (192.168.1.1).

The crypto access list specifies that all user traffic from (source) network 10.1.1.0/24 to (destination) network 10.2.2.0/24 should be sent over the IPsec tunnel, but the NAT source list specifies that the source IP address of all user traffic from source 10.1.1.0/24 should be translated to IP address 192.168.1.1.

Unfortunately, NAT happens before IPsec, so by the time any user traffic from source network 10.1.1.0/24 is matched against the crypto access list, the source IP address has already been translated (to 192.168.1.1), it does not match the source addresses in the crypto access list (10.1.1.0/24), and it is therefore not sent over the IPsec tunnel.

To solve this issue, when configuring NAT on an IPsec gateway, you must be careful to ensure that user traffic that should be sent over that IPsec tunnel is not unintentionally NAT'ed.

Access list 102 (which defines addresses to be NAT'ed [see highlighted line 4, Example 6-54]) is then modified to ensure that user traffic from network 10.1.1.0/24 to network 10.2.2.0/24 is sent over the IPsec tunnel, as shown in Example 6-56.

Example 6-56 *Bypassing NAT for User Traffic from Network 10.1.1.0/24 to Network 10.2.2.0/24*

```
London#conf t
Enter configuration commands, one per line. End with CNTL/Z.
London(config)#no access-list 102 (line 1)
London(config)#access-list 102 deny
 ip 10.1.1.0 0.0.0.255 10.2.2.0 0.0.0.255 (line 2)
London(config)#access-list 102 permit ip 10.1.1.0 0.0.0.255 any (line 3)
London(config)#exit
London#
```

In highlighted line 1, access list 102 is deleted.

Then, in highlighted lines 2 and 3, access list 102 is reconfigured to deny user traffic from network 10.1.1.0/24 to network 10.2.2.0 (the user traffic specified in the crypto access list [see Example 6-54, highlighted line 3]), and permit all other user traffic from network 10.1.1.0/24.

The effect of this reconfiguration is that user traffic that should be sent over the IPsec tunnel (as defined in the crypto access list) bypasses NAT. Because this user traffic bypasses NAT, it now correctly matches the crypto access list and is sent over the IPsec tunnel. All other user traffic from network 10.1.1.0/24 to any other destination is still NAT'ed.

In Example 6-57, the output of the **show crypto engine connections active** command shows that outbound traffic from the network 10.1.1.0/24 to network 10.2.2.0/24 is now sent over the IPsec tunnel.

Example 6-57 *Outbound Traffic from Network 10.1.1.0/24 to Network 10.2.2.0/24 Is Now Sent over the IPsec Tunnel*

```
London#show crypto engine connections active
  ID Interface      IP-Address     State Algorithm           Encrypt  Decrypt
   1 Serial1/0      192.168.1.1    set   HMAC_MD5+DES_56_CB   0        0
2000 Serial1/0      192.168.1.1    set   HMAC_MD5+DES_56_CB   0        121
2001 Serial1/0      192.168.1.1    set   HMAC_MD5+DES_56_CB   121      0
London#
```

The first highlighted line shows inbound user traffic that has been sent over the IPsec tunnel from the Berlin site (121 packet decrypted).

The second highlighted line shows outbound user traffic that has been sent over the IPsec tunnel to the Berlin site (121 packet encrypted).

Figure 6-47 illustrates the effect of modifying access list 102.

Figure 6-47 *User Traffic from Network 10.1.1.0/24 to Network 10.2.2.0/24 Is Now Sent over the IPsec Tunnel*

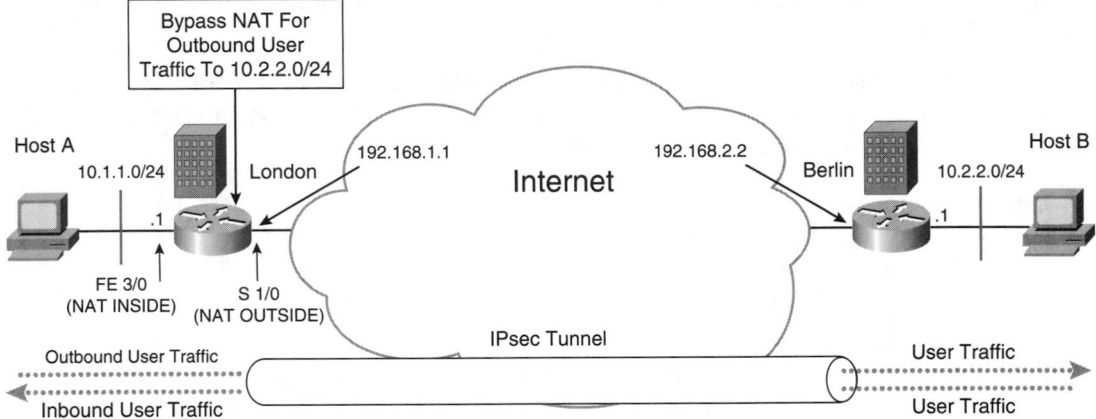

So, now you know how to bypass dynamic NAT for user traffic that should be sent over an IPsec tunnel. But, how about bypassing static NAT?

Example 6-58 shows the configuration necessary to bypass static NAT for user traffic that should be sent over an IPsec tunnel. This configuration relates to the topology shown in Figures 6-46 and 6-47.

Example 6-58 *Bypassing Static NAT for User Traffic That Should Be Sent over the IPsec Tunnel*

```
!
! Loopback interface that is used to bypass static NAT for user traffic that should be
! sent over the IPsec tunnel
!
interface Loopback0 (line 1)
 ip address 100.1.1.1 255.255.255.0
!
!
! NAT inside interface (route map 'bypass.static.nat' configured here)
!
interface FastEthernet3/0
 ip address 10.1.1.1 255.255.255.0
 ip nat inside
 ip route-cache policy
 ip policy route-map bypass.static.nat (line 2)
!
!
```

Example 6-58 *Bypassing Static NAT for User Traffic That Should Be Sent over the IPsec Tunnel (Continued)*

```
! Static NAT entry
!
ip nat inside source static 10.1.1.2 192.168.1.3 (line 3)
!
!
! Access list 103 specifies user traffic that should bypass static NAT
!
access-list 103 permit ip host 10.1.1.2 10.2.2.0 0.0.0.255 (line 4)
!
!
! Route map 'bypass.static.nat' defines user traffic that should bypass static NAT
! (references access list 103), and sets the next-hop for this traffic as 100.1.1.2
! (an IP address on the same subnet as interface Loopback 0)
!
route-map bypass.static.nat permit 10 (line 5)
 match ip address 103 (line 6)
 set ip next-hop 100.1.1.2 (line 7)
!
```

The static NAT entry in highlighted line 3 specifies that the source address 10.1.1.2 should be translated to address 192.168.1.3.

Route map **bypass.static.nat** in highlighted lines 5 through 7 ensures that all traffic matching access list 103 (highlighted line 4) should be routed via the IP address 100.1.1.2 (an IP address on the same subnet as interface Loopback 0 [see highlighted line 1]). The route map is then applied to the inside interface in highlighted line 2.

Now, the effect of routing all user traffic matching access list 103 (host address 10.1.1.2 to network 10.2.2.0/24) via next hop 100.1.1.2 is that this traffic bypasses the static NAT entry (highlighted line 3). The user traffic specified in access list 103 then matches the crypto access list (which matches all traffic from network 10.1.1.0/24 to network 10.2.2.0/24), and it is sent over the IPsec tunnel.

Getting Around Issues with NAT/PAT and IPsec Tunnels

As described in the previous sections, NAT/PAT can break IPsec in a number of ways. This section describes and summarizes possible solutions that will allow you configure IPsec tunnels when there is a NAT device in the path between IPsec peers.

To allow IPsec tunnels to traverse NAT/PAT devices, you can do the following:

- Configure static NAT entries to allow IPsec gateways on the outside network to initiate IKE. See the section "NAT/PAT Can Cause IKE Negotiation Initiated by IPsec Peers on Outside Networks to Fail" for more information on this solution.

- Use an IPsec-aware NAT/PAT device. As described in the sections "NAT/PAT Can Cause Rekeying to Fail When NAT/PAT Is Based on IKE Cookies" and "NAT/PAT Based on SPI Selection Can Cause ESP Packets to Be Dropped," IPsec-aware NAT/PAT devices are not perfect, but they do often work well.

Cisco IOS Software Release 12.2(13)T and 12.2(15)T introduce support for ESP through PAT on Cisco routers. See the following URLs for more information on this feature:

http://www.cisco.com/en/US/products/sw/iosswrel/ps1839/products_feature_guide09186a0080110c03.html

http://www.cisco.com/en/US/products/sw/iosswrel/ps1839/products_feature_guide09186a00801541de.html

- Use ESP tunnel mode rather than transport mode. Tunnel mode can resolve issues with IKE identifiers and TCP/UDP checksums.

  The TCP/UDP checksum issue does not affect tunnel mode because in this mode the pseudo-header includes source and destination IP addresses taken not from the new outer IP header, but from the original IP header which is not modified by NAT (see Figure 6-20).

  Another way of resolving the UDP/TCP checksum issue is to configure GRE over IPsec. In this case, user packets are encapsulated in GRE, and UDP/TCP checksums are therefore not affected by NAT.

- Use ESP rather than AH. Remember that AH is incompatible with NAT/PAT.

- Use IPsec NAT traversal/transparency. This feature allows IPsec devices to detect NAT/PAT devices during IKE phase 1 and encapsulate IKE/ESP traffic in UDP (using port 4500).

  NAT traversal/transparency is a comprehensive solution and resolves issues with NAT/PAT devices not translating ESP packets, resolves issues with TCP/UDP checksums, and resolves the issue of IPsec peers dropping ISAKMP packets that do not use UDP port 500.

  NAT traversal/transparency is available in Cisco IOS Software Release 12.2(13)T and is enabled by default. If for some reason you do not want to use NAT traversal/transparency, you can use the **no crypto ipsec nat-transparency udp-encapsulation** global configuration mode command.

  Note that NAT traversal is included in the base specification for IKEv2.

  NAT traversal is an industry standard, but on Cisco ASA 5500s and VPN 3000 concentrators it is also possible to configure Cisco proprietary UDP or TCP encapsulation for IPsec on a user-defined port.

- Use keepalives or a dynamic routing protocol to ensure that dynamic NAT/PAT translation timeouts do not cause IPsec traffic to be dropped (assuming the keepalive/update interval is less than the NAT/PAT translation timeout).

  Use the **crypto isakmp nat keepalive** *seconds* global configuration mode command to configure IPsec peers to send NAT keepalives at the interval specified.

Alternatively, use GRE tunnel keepalives (assuming that you have configured a GRE tunnel to carry multiprotocol and multicast traffic) or ISAKMP keepalives to ensure that NAT/PAT translations do not time out.

You can configure GRE keepalives using the **keepalive** *seconds* [*retries*] command under a GRE tunnel interface.

You can configure ISAKMP keepalives using the **crypto isakmp keepalive** *seconds* [*retries*] command.

Finally, you could also configure a dynamic routing protocol over a GRE/IPsec tunnel. Because dynamic routing protocols periodically send keepalives and/or updates, this ensures that NAT/PAT translations do not time out.

- Perform NAT before IPsec to allow applications that use embedded IP addresses to function correctly.

  If the IPsec device is placed in front of the NAT device, or NAT is performed on the IPsec device itself (assuming NAT processing before IPsec), applications function correctly because NAT is also able to translate embedded IP addresses.

- Bypass NAT for user traffic that should be sent over an IPsec tunnel, if appropriate.

  See the section "Unintentional NAT'ing of User Packets Can Cause These Packets Not to Be Sent over the IPsec Tunnel" for more information on this solution.

Allowing IPsec to Traverse a Firewall

If there is a firewall in front of an IPsec VPN gateway (as shown in Figure 6-48), you must be careful to ensure that IPsec traffic is allowed through the firewall.

Figure 6-48 *Firewall in Front of an IPsec VPN Gateway*

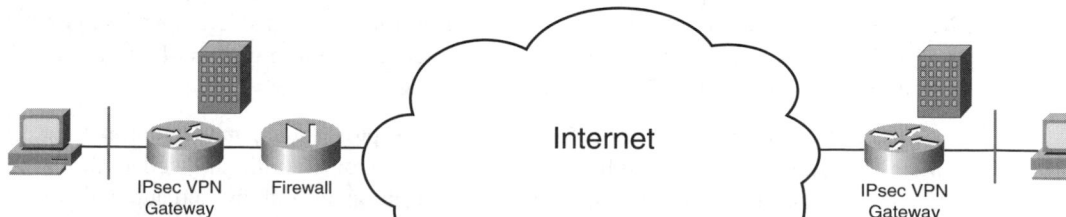

The protocols and ports that you might need to allow through a firewall (depending on your precise configuration) are as follows:

- AH, IP protocol 51.
- ESP, IP protocol 50.
- IKE (ISAKMP), UDP port 500.
- If you are using standard NAT traversal/transparency, allow UDP port 4500.
- If you have configured Cisco proprietary UDP or TCP encapsulation for IPsec on a Cisco VPN concentrator, allow this user-defined UDP or TCP port.
- If the IPsec tunnel terminates on the firewall, allow user traffic protocols and ports. User protocols and ports need to be permitted because IPsec traffic is processed twice on an outside interface: once in its IPsec encapsulated form, and once when IPsec encapsulation has been removed.

Summary

IPsec can be used to build site-to-site and remote access VPNs. Site-to-site VPNs can be deployed in hub-and-spoke, partial-mesh, and full-mesh architectures.

IPsec consists of various elements such as cryptographic algorithms, security protocols, security associations, IPsec databases, and SA and key management techniques.

Cryptographic algorithms include authentication algorithms such as hash and MAC algorithms, as well as encryption algorithms such as block and stream ciphers.

IPsec includes two basic security protocols, AH and ESP. AH provides connectionless integrity, data origin authentication, and optional replay protection. ESP offers connectionless integrity, data origin authentication, optional replay protection, data confidentiality, and limited traffic flow confidentiality.

SA and key management can be either manual or automated. Manual SA and key management involves static configuration, whereas automated SA and key management involves the use of the IKE protocol.

When designing IPsec VPNs, there are a number of important considerations, including IKE policies, IPsec transforms, crypto access lists, crypto maps, transport of multiprotocol and multicast traffic, and NAT/PAT and firewall traversal.

Important design decisions include the selection of cryptographic parameters for IKE policies, including method of authentication and encryption algorithm as well as choice of IPsec transforms, including security protocols, encryption algorithms, and authentication algorithms.

If multiprotocol or IP multicast transport is required, there are two choices: IPsec-protected GRE tunnels (for multiprotocol and IP multicast) and VTIs (for IP multicast).

Finally, it is crucial to consider the issues involving the presence of NAT devices between IPsec VPNs gateways, and, in addition, possible solutions to those issues.

Issues involving the presence of NAT devices *include* the fact that IKE may fail if the initiator is on the outside; the fact that NAT/PAT may cause rekeying to break when NAT/PAT is based on IKE cookies; the fact that NAT/PAT devices cause IPsec peers to drop AH traffic; and the fact that translation timeouts may cause ESP traffic to be dropped.

Solutions to some of the problems with NAT/PAT include configuring static NAT entries, using IPsec-aware NAT/PAT devices, using ESP tunnel mode rather than transport mode, using ESP rather than AH, using NAT traversal/transparency, and using ISAKMP or GRE keepalives.

Review Questions

1 IPsec consists of what elements?

2 What services does IPsec provide to IP?

3 What are the main characteristics of symmetric encryption algorithms?

4 What are the two types of symmetric encryption algorithms?

5 What are the characteristics of public key algorithms?

6 What security services do AH and ESP provide?

7 What is an IPsec security association (SA)?

8 What is the function of IKE?

9 What are some common considerations when selecting parameters for IPsec transform sets?

CHAPTER 7

Scaling and Optimizing IPsec VPNs

Chapter 6, "Deploying Site-to-Site IPsec VPNs," introduced IPsec VPNs. This chapter looks at how to scale IPsec VPNs using technologies such as Tunnel Endpoint Discovery (TED) and Dynamic Multipoint VPN (DMVPN), how IPsec VPNs can support quality of service (QoS), and how to avoid performance degradation caused by IPsec packet fragmentation.

Scaling IPsec Virtual Private Networks

As you saw in Chapter 6, IPsec tunnels are inherently point to point. The fact that the tunnels are point to point means that there are a number of challenges to be faced when scaling IPsec VPNs to a large number of sites. These challenges can be best illustrated by taking a look at the network shown in Figure 7-1.

The network in Figure 7-1 consists of six sites. If you want direct connectivity between all sites (a full-mesh topology) you need at least $n(n - 1)/2$ IPsec tunnels (pairs of security associations [SA]), where n is the number of sites. For 6 sites, that means 15 tunnels. Not too bad, but what if you have 200 sites? That is a mere 19,900 tunnels!

Some of the major considerations when scaling IPsec VPNs are as follows:

- The maximum number of IPsec tunnels that can be configured on a device
- The amount of configuration necessary
- The type of Internet Key Exchange (IKE) authentication that you use

Each type of device has a finite limit to the number of IPsec tunnels that it can support. This limit depends on a number of factors, including the following:

- The power of the device's CPU
- The amount of memory installed in the device
- Whether a hardware accelerator is installed into the device
- The cryptographic algorithms that you intend to use in your IPsec VPN
- The volume (and packet sizes) of traffic that is expected to pass over each IPsec tunnel

Figure 7-1 *Sample Topology*

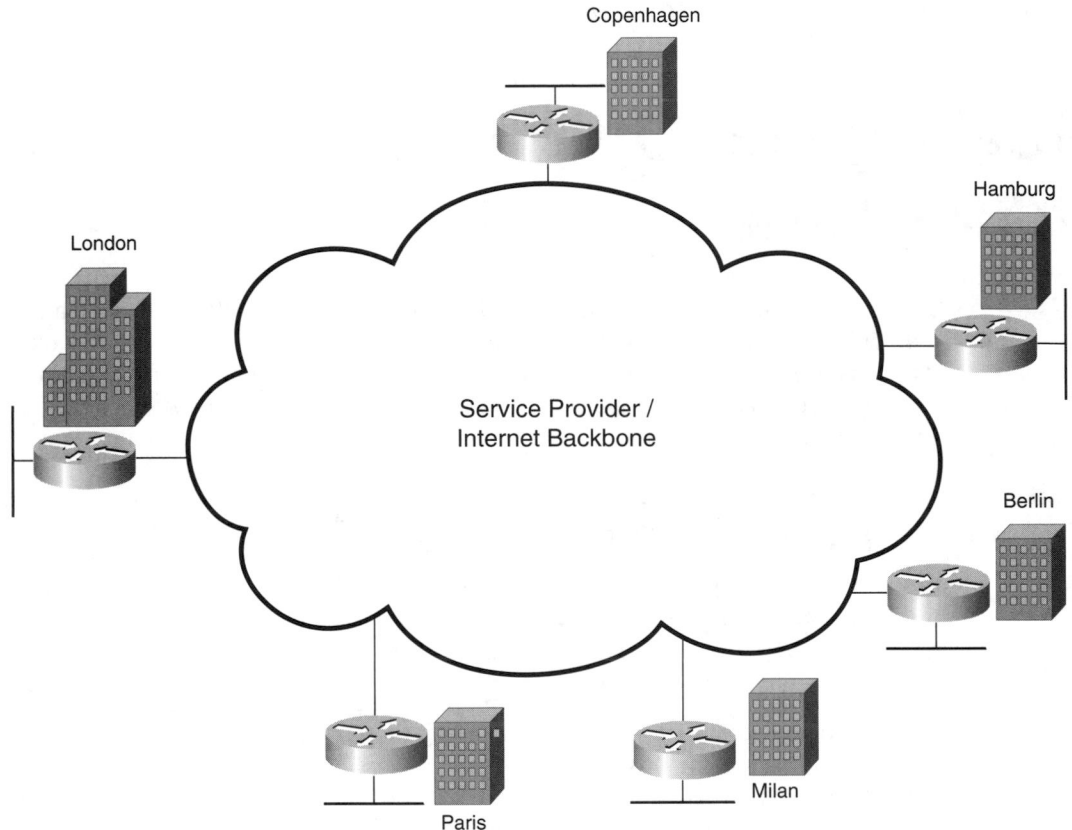

Because devices are constantly changing and new ones are being introduced, no limits are specified here. One useful document to use as a *starting point* when considering the number of IPsec tunnels that can be supported by a particular device can be found in the data sheet "Cisco IPSec and SSL VPN Solutions" located at the following URL:

> http://www.cisco.com/en/US/netsol/ns340/ns394/ns171/
> netbr09186a00801f0a72.html

NOTE   Note that the preceding URL contains performance data of devices tested under ideal conditions (there were no other processes running on the router, the packet sizes were fixed, there was a following wind, and so on).

The amount of configuration is also a key factor to consider when designing IPsec VPNs. It would be extremely laborious, for example, to manually configure the 19,900 IPsec tunnels mentioned in the previous example.

So, manual configuration of each IPsec tunnel is fine for small deployments, but for large-scale installations it is clearly impractical.

Another important consideration is the type of IKE authentication that you use. If you use a unique preshared key for each pair of gateways, and you require direct connectivity between all VPN sites, you need $n(n-1)/2$ preshared keys—15 preshared keys for an IPsec VPN with 6 sites, but 19,900 preshared keys for an IPsec VPN with 200 sites.

The sections that follow examine ways to reduce the number of IPsec tunnels required, reducing the amount of configuration, and scaling IKE authentication.

Reducing the Number of IPsec Tunnels Required in a VPN

A traditional solution for the problem of the exponential growth in the number of IPsec tunnels is to deploy a hub-and-spoke architecture, such as that illustrated in Figure 7-2.

Figure 7-2   *Hub-and-Spoke Network Architecture*

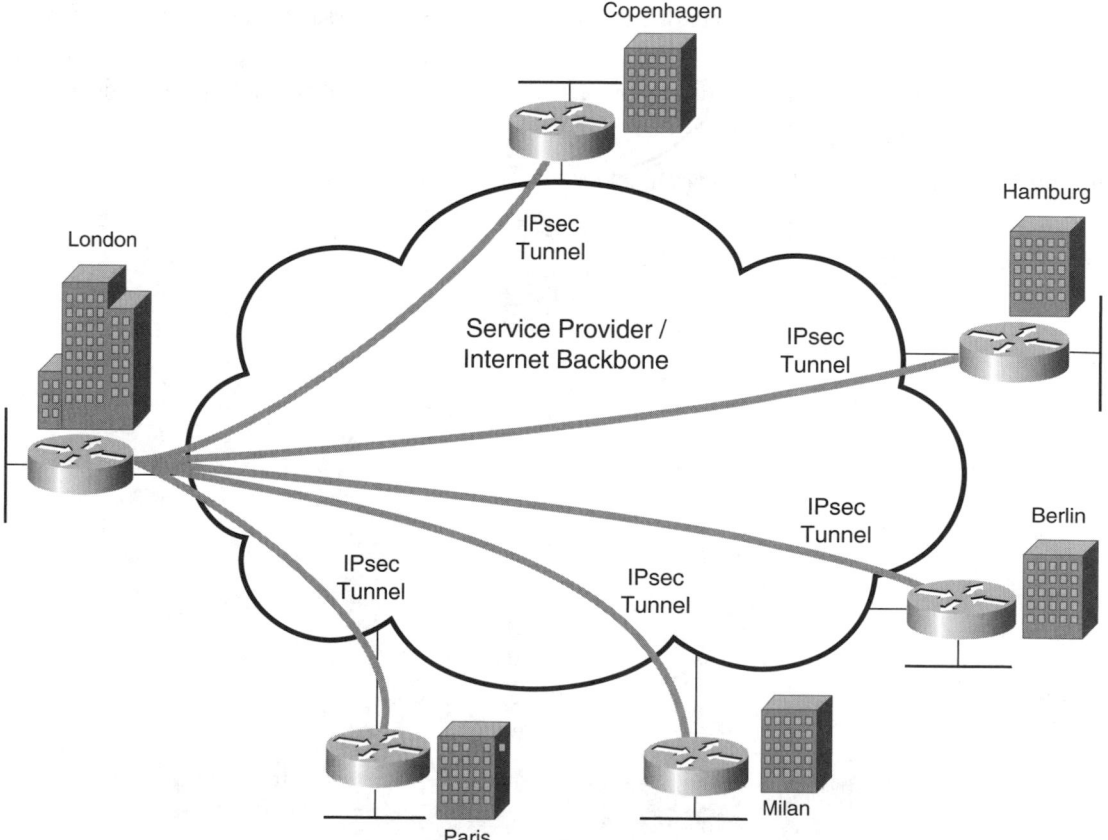

The advantage of the hub-and-spoke architecture becomes pretty clear just by looking at Figure 7-2—the number of IPsec tunnels is now $n - 1$. So, for the 6-site VPN shown in Figure 7-2, you need 5 tunnels—a significant reduction of the 15 tunnels required for a full mesh. For a 200-site VPN, 199 tunnels are required—a huge reduction on the 19,900 tunnels required for a full mesh.

There are, however, a number of drawbacks and considerations with the hub-and-spoke topology in comparison to the full-mesh topology:

- Traffic latency is increased for spoke-to-spoke user traffic because it must transit the hub site. Traffic latency will be of particular concern if you are deploying real-time or delay-sensitive applications such as voice and video.

- Because spoke-to-spoke traffic must transit the hub router, the amount of bandwidth required at the hub site is increased. The amount of bandwidth required at the hub site depends on the amount of spoke-to-hub traffic and spoke-to-spoke traffic.

- The CPU and memory overhead is increased on the hub site router because the hub site router must decrypt and then re-encrypt traffic as it transits between spoke sites.

- There is a finite limit to the number of IPsec tunnels that a single hub site router can support.

One way to get around *some* of the limitations listed in the previous section is to extend the hub-and-spoke architecture so that it becomes a hierarchical hub-and-spoke architecture, such as that illustrated in Figure 7-3.

Figure 7-3 *Hierarchical Hub-and-Spoke IPsec VPN*

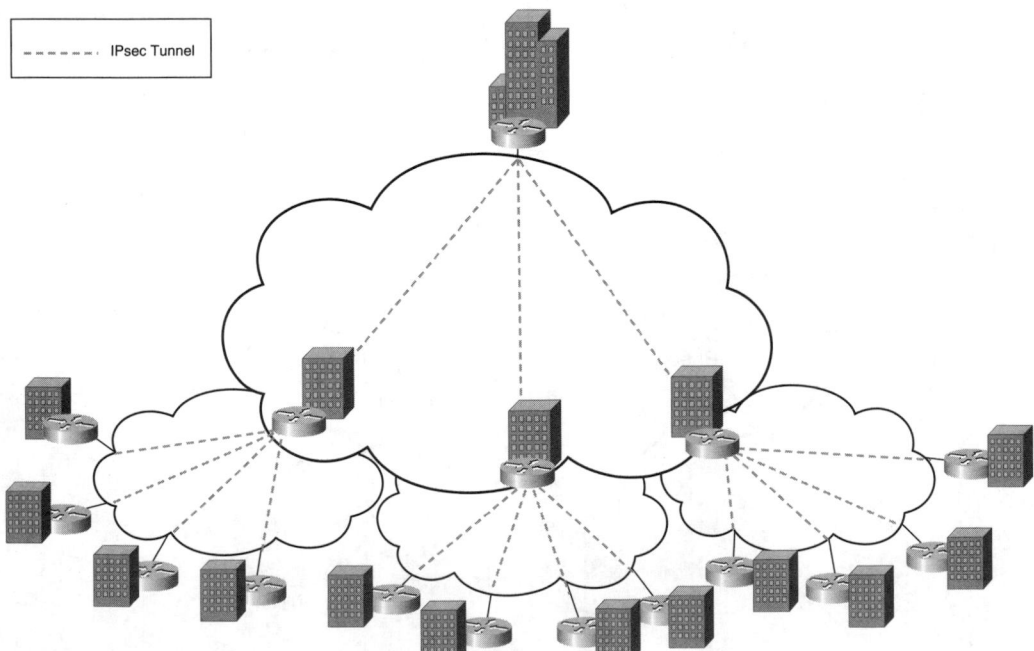

In Figure 7-3, there are three levels of hierarchy:

- The access layer (the bottom-most level)
- The distribution layer (the mid level)
- The core layer (the top level)

This type of hierarchical model is well understood and widely deployed. If you split the network into three levels of hierarchy based on traffic flow and geography, the VPN can scale to a much greater degree than the simple hub-and-spoke architecture described previously.

The hierarchical hub-and-spoke architecture alleviates two of the main concerns with the simple hub-and-spoke model:

- It alleviates the CPU and memory overhead on a single hub router. The VPN architecture is now distributed, and CPU and memory overhead should be distributed over a number of (regional) hub routers.

- The number of IPsec tunnels that each of the (regional) hub site routers must support is much smaller than the number that would otherwise have to be supported by a single-hub site router.

Reducing IPsec VPN Configuration Complexity with TED and DMVPN

One of the challenges when scaling an IPsec VPN to include a large number of IPsec VPN gateways is the sheer amount of configuration required on each gateway as the VPN grows.

In a full-mesh IPsec VPN with 250 gateways, for example, each gateway normally requires 249 static crypto map entries (1 for each other gateway). When a new gateway is added to an IPsec VPN, the new gateway must be configured with crypto map entries to support each of the existing gateways. And a new crypto map entry must be added on each existing IPsec VPN gateway.

So, in large-scale full-mesh IPsec VPNs, a large amount of configuration is normally required. This configuration can prove difficult to manage and troubleshoot.

If you want to reduce the amount of configuration on each IPsec gateway, you have two possible solutions:

- Tunnel Endpoint Discovery
- Dynamic Multipoint VPN

TED and DMVPN are discussed in detail in the following two sections.

Tunnel Endpoint Discovery (TED)

TED is a Cisco proprietary enhancement for IKE that enables IPsec peers to dynamically discover each other and then proceed with phase 1 and 2 IKE negotiation. If the peers already have an IKE SA in place, IKE phase 1 negotiation can be skipped, and the peers can jump straight to phase 2 negotiation.

Because TED dynamically discovers remote peers, static configuration of peers is not required. Instead of static configuration, a dynamic crypto map is configured on each TED-enabled IPsec peer.

Figure 7-4 shows the operation of TED.

Figure 7-4 *TED Operation*

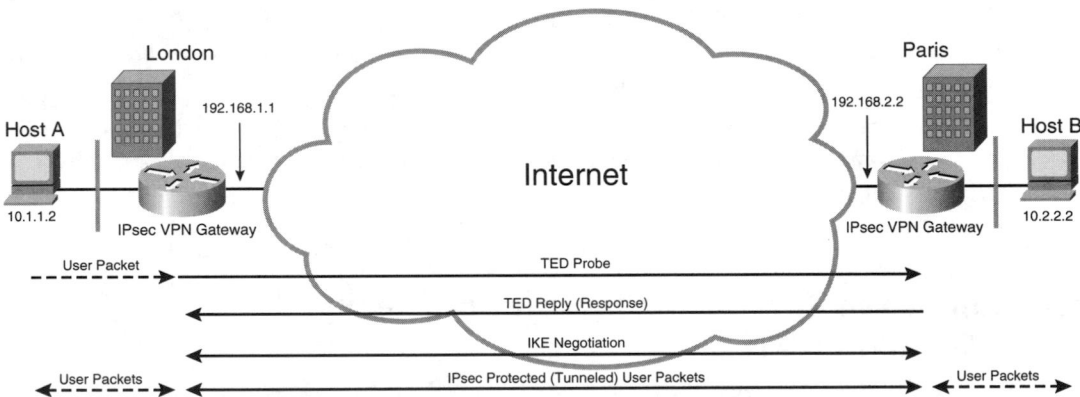

In Figure 7-4, Host A at the London site sends a user packet to Host B at the Paris site.

The London gateway intercepts the user packet from Host A and checks whether there is an IPsec SA corresponding to the packet. There is no existing IPsec SA, so the London gateway drops the packet from Host A and sends a TED Probe packet toward Host B. The TED Probe packet is an unencrypted ISAKMP packet and uses the same source and destination IP addresses as the original user packet (in this case, the source IP address is 10.1.1.2 [Host A], and the destination IP address is 10.2.2.2 [Host B]).

The Paris gateway intercepts the TED Probe packet and, after it has checked that the Probe corresponds to traffic that should be protected by IPsec (Host A's and B's IP addresses), the Paris gateway sends a TED Reply (response) packet to the London gateway. The TED Reply is also an unencrypted ISAKMP packet.

The London gateway receives the TED Reply and verifies that the TED Reply corresponds to the TED Probe that it sent. After the London gateway has verified this, the London gateway initiates IKE negotiation with the Paris gateway, IPsec tunnel setup completes as normal, and user packets can be transmitted over the IPsec tunnel between Host A and Host B.

Example 7-1 shows the configuration of the London and Paris IPsec VPN gateways.

Example 7-1 *Configuration of TED on the London and Paris Gateways*

```
London#show running-config
Building configuration...
!
! London gateway's configuration
!
!
! IKE (ISAKMP) Policy
!
crypto isakmp policy 10
 hash md5
 authentication pre-share
!
!
! Wildcard Pre-Shared Key
!
crypto isakmp key cisco address 0.0.0.0 0.0.0.0 (line 1)
!
!
! IPsec Transform Set
!
crypto ipsec transform-set mjlnettransform esp-des esp-md5-hmac
!
!
! Dynamic Crypto Map Entry
!
crypto dynamic-map mjlnetted 10 (line 2)
 set transform-set mjlnettransform
 match address 101
!
!
! Parent Crypto Map Entry
!
crypto map mjlnetcmap 10 ipsec-isakmp dynamic mjlnetted discover (line 3)
!
!
! Outside Interface
!
interface Serial1/0
 ip address 192.168.1.1 255.255.255.0
 crypto map mjlnetcmap (line 4)
!
!
! Inside Interface
!
interface FastEthernet3/0
 ip address 10.1.1.1 255.255.255.0
!
!
! Crypto Access List
!
access-list 101 permit ip 10.1.1.0 0.0.0.255 10.2.2.0 0.0.0.255
!
```

continues

Example 7-1 *Configuration of TED on the London and Paris Gateways (Continued)*

```
Paris#show running-config
Building configuration...
!
! Paris gateway's configuration
!
!
! IKE (ISAKMP) Policy
!
crypto isakmp policy 10
 hash md5
 authentication pre-share
!
!
! Wildcard Pre-Shared Key
!
crypto isakmp key cisco address 0.0.0.0 0.0.0.0 (line 5)
!
!
! IPsec Transform Set
!
crypto ipsec transform-set mjlnettrans esp-des esp-md5-hmac
!
!
! Dynamic Crypto Map Entry
!
crypto dynamic-map mjlnetted 10 (line 6)
 set transform-set mjlnettrans
 match address 101
!
!
! Parent Crypto Map Entry
!
crypto map mjlnetcmap 10 ipsec-isakmp dynamic mjlnetted discover (line 7)
!
!
! Inside Interface
!
interface FastEthernet1/0
 ip address 10.2.2.1 255.255.255.0
!
!
! Outside Interface
!
interface Serial2/0
 ip address 192.168.2.2 255.255.255.0
 crypto map mjlnetcmap (line 8)
!
!
! Crypto Access List
!
access-list 101 permit ip 10.2.2.0 0.0.0.255 10.1.1.0 0.0.0.255
!
!
```

In highlighted line 1, you can see a wildcard preshared key (**crypto isakmp key** *keystring* **address 0.0.0.0 0.0.0.0**). This wildcard preshared allows all other gateways in the VPN (including Paris) to connect to the London gateway.

As discussed in Chapter 6, wildcard preshared keys can be insecure, so if you configure TED, it is a good idea to use Rivest, Shamir, and Adlemen (RSA) digital signature authentication (using digital certificates).

Line 2 shows the **crypto dynamic-map** *dynamic-map-name dynamic-seq-num* command. This command is used to configure a dynamic crypto map entry (called, in this example, mjlnetted).

Dynamic crypto maps are similar to regular (static) crypto maps but allow a gateway to accept connections from peers even if not all parameters are known in advance. In this case, the IP addresses of remote gateways are not known in advance. Notice that the dynamic crypto map does not require the configuration of the **set peer** command, which is used with regular crypto maps to specify the IP address or host name of remote gateways.

The **crypto map** *map-name seq-num* **ipsec-isakmp dynamic** *dynamic-map-name* **discover** command shown in line 3 is used to configure a parent crypto map entry (called mjlnetcmap here), which links to the dynamic crypto map entry in line 2. The parent crypto map is applied to the outside interface (see line 4).

The parent crypto map entry called mjlnetcmap links to the dynamic crypto map entry mjlnetted. The **discover** keyword enables TED for use with the crypto map.

Lines 5, 6, 7, and 8 show the configuration of the wildcard preshared key, dynamic crypto map entry, and parent crypto map on the Paris gateway. Notice that their configuration on the Paris gateway is identical to that for the London gateway.

And that is it—pretty simple really. But, it really does reduce the amount of configuration required in large-scale IPsec VPNs because individual crypto map entries are no longer required for each remote gateway.

So, TED can help to reduce the amount of configuration required on IPsec VPN gateways— a major benefit. However, there is one drawback to TED—the addresses of hosts on the inside interfaces of IPsec VPN gateways (using IP addresses specified in the crypto access lists) must use globally routable IP addresses. That is, routers and other devices in the path between IPsec VPN gateways must have routes to the IP addresses specified in your crypto access lists.

In Figure 7-4, for example, networks 10.1.1.0/24 and 10.2.2.0/24 (including the addresses of Hosts A and B) must be reachable from the routers in the backbone network.

If your IPsec VPN is deployed over the Internet, addresses specified in your crypto access lists must be public (globally routable) IP addresses.

Dynamic Multipoint Virtual Private Network (DMVPN)

As discussed previously in the section "Reducing the Number of IPsec Tunnels Required in a VPN," one problem in a hub-and-spoke IPsec VPN where there is spoke-to-spoke traffic is that this traffic must transit the hub site. Spoke-to-spoke traffic puts additional demands on the hub site (gateway), both in terms of bandwidth requirements and packet processing (additional decrypt and encrypt). Furthermore, spoke-to-spoke traffic transiting the hub site incurs additional delay, which might cause problems with real-time applications such as voice and video.

One solution to these problems is to configure point-to-point IPsec tunnels between the spoke sites, but this just gives you a full or partial mesh of static IPsec tunnels. The amount of configuration required on the gateways then grows quickly because you need one tunnel interface per remote gateway, one crypto access list per remote gateway and (usually) one crypto map statement for each remote gateway.

The entry of the configuration on the gateways is onerous enough, but the additional configuration complexity also makes management and troubleshooting that much more difficult—imagine wading through hundreds of lines of configuration looking for a single mistake! Not pleasant.

A much more scalable solution to the problem of spoke-to-spoke traffic and configuration complexity is Cisco-proprietary DMVPN. DMVPN was introduced in Cisco IOS Software Release 12.2(13)T.

One main advantage of DMVPN is that it dramatically reduces the amount of configuration on hub and spoke site gateways (when compared to a traditional hub-and-spoke and full/partial-mesh architectures). Additional benefits include the following:

- Spoke-to-spoke tunnels are dynamically created on an as-needed basis and do not require explicit configuration.

- Direct spoke-to-spoke tunnels created in a DMVPN environment reduce spoke site-to-spoke site latency.

- CPU and memory overhead is reduced on the hub site gateway(s) because spoke-to-spoke traffic does not now need to transit the hub (in any significant volume).

- Because spoke-to-spoke traffic does not transit the hub, bandwidth requirements at the hub site are reduced.

Before making a decision to deploy DMVPN, it is important to fully understand how it works and how it is configured. These subjects are discussed in the following two sections.

How DMVPN Works

So, DMVPN provides an answer to the problem of IPsec VPN configuration scalability, but how exactly does it work? The fundamentals of DMVPN are remarkably simple.

DMVPN is based on the Next Hop Resolution Protocol (NHRP), which is described in RFC2332. NHRP provides mechanisms that allow a source host or a router connected to a nonbroadcast multiaccess (NBMA) network to determine the network layer and associated NBMA address of either the destination host or router, or the NBMA address of the egress router that is closest to the destination host or router.

DMVPN modifies this paradigm slightly by using NHRP to enable a source DMVPN gateway to determine the *physical* interface IP address of the DMVPN gateway closest to a destination. The source DMVPN gateway then dynamically builds a Generic Routing Encapsulation (GRE)/IPsec tunnel directly to the DMVPN gateway closest to the destination. After the tunnel is built, the source DMVPN gateway forwards user traffic directly to the destination site.

So, that is a high-level description of DMVPN. To explain how DMVPN works in detail, it is a good idea to start with the sample topology shown in Figure 7-5.

Figure 7-5   *Sample DMVPN Topology*

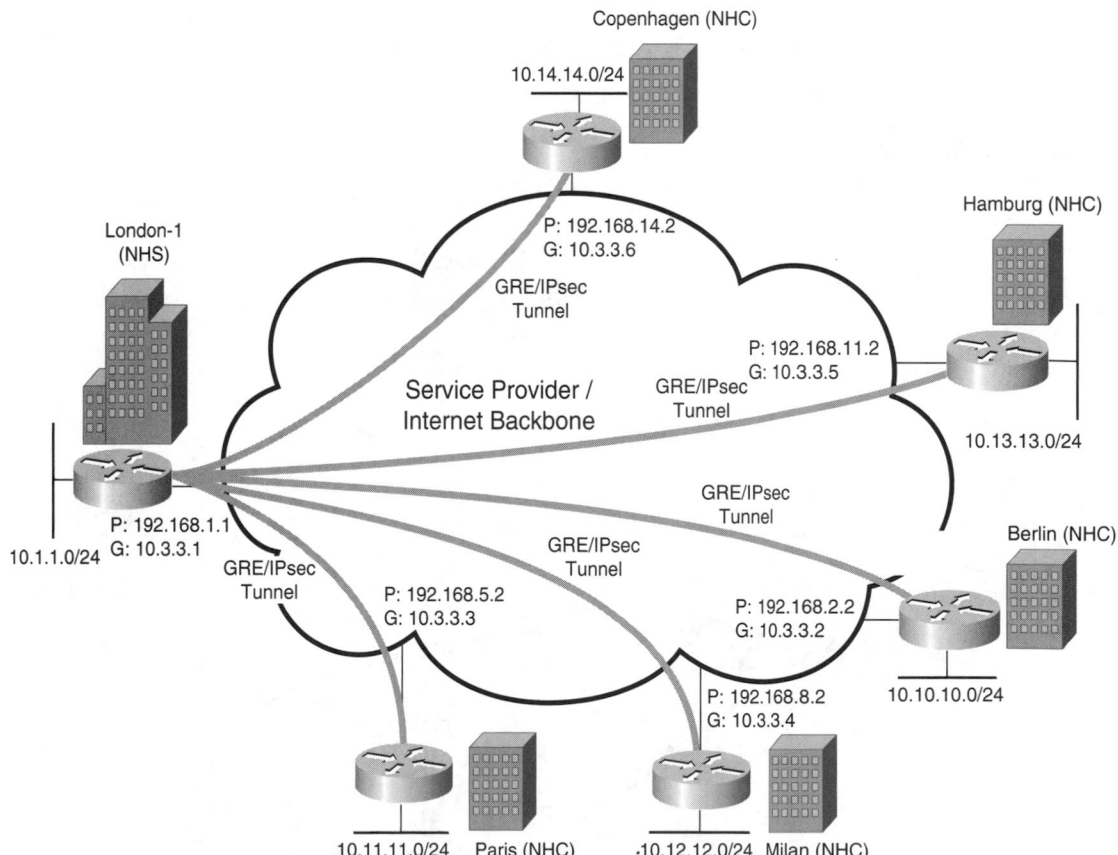

As you can see in Figure 7-5, there are six sites in the DMVPN: the hub site in London; and spoke sites in Copenhagen, Hamburg, Berlin, Milan, and Paris.

Each of the spoke site gateways automatically initiates an IPsec-protected GRE tunnel configured to the London-1 hub site gateway as soon as it is switched on (or initially configured for DMVPN). In Figure 7-5, the letter *G* indicates IP addresses applied to gateway GRE tunnel interfaces, and the letter *P* indicates IP addresses applied to physical interfaces. The physical IP addresses are routable over the service provider backbone/Internet.

In this scenario, the gateway at the London (hub) site is configured as a Next Hop Server (NHS), and the spoke site gateways are configured as Next Hop Clients (NHC).

Each of the spoke site gateways (the NHCs) sends an NHRP Registration Request message to the London-1 gateway (the NHS) on startup. The purpose of these Registration Request messages is to notify the NHS of the NHCs' physical and GRE tunnel interface addresses. The NHS (London) caches these physical to GRE tunnel address mappings, and responds to the NHCs with a Registration Reply message.

If configured to do so, the NHS also adds broadcast/multicast mappings for spoke sites when they register. These multicast mappings allow multicast traffic such as routing protocol traffic to be sent over the tunnels between the hub-and-spoke sites.

Figure 7-6 illustrates the NHRP registration process.

Figure 7-6   *The NHRP Registration Process*

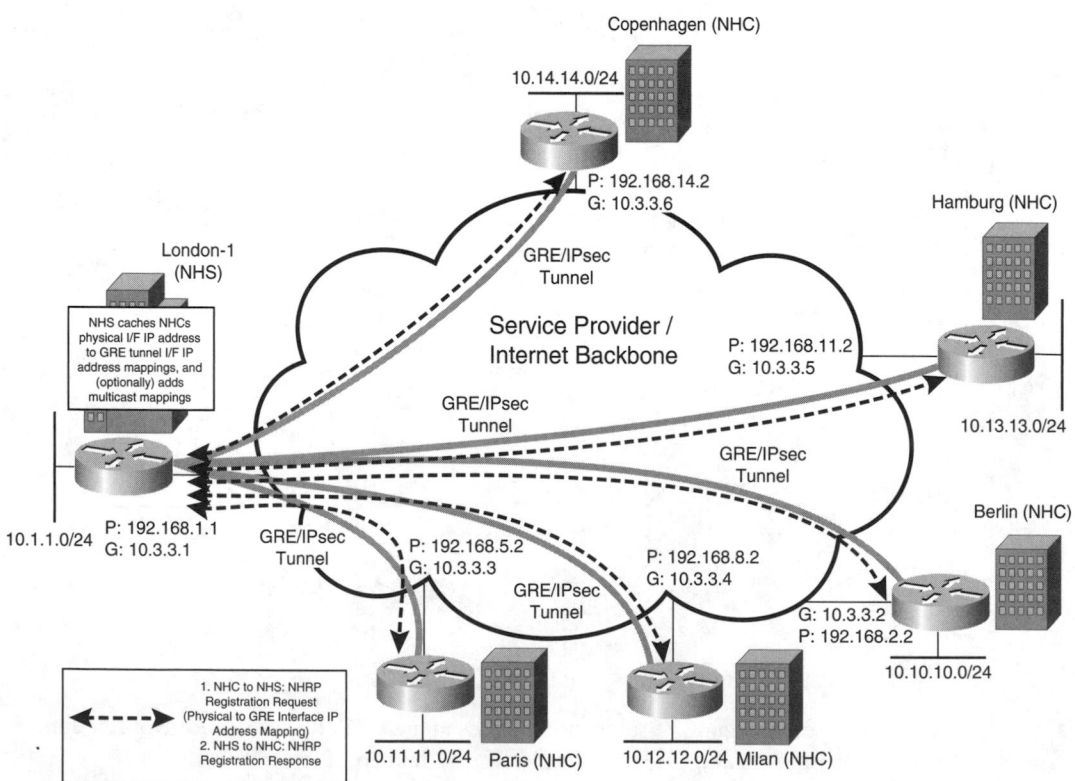

The NHS (hub site gateway) caches the NHCs' physical interface to GRE tunnel interface address mappings. So, after all the NHCs (spoke site gateways) have registered with the NHS, the NHS's cache will be as shown in Table 7-1.

Table 7-1   *NHS's Cache After All NHCs Register*

NHC	Physical Interface Address	GRE Tunnel Interface Address
Copenhagen	192.168.14.2	10.3.3.6
Hamburg	192.168.11.2	10.3.3.5
Berlin	192.168.2.2	10.3.3.2
Milan	192.168.8.2	10.3.3.4
Paris	192.168.5.2	10.3.3.3

Now what happens if one of the spoke site gateways needs to send some traffic to another spoke site? Imagine that the Paris gateway receives a packet from host 10.11.11.1 (on its local LAN) destined for host 10.13.13.1 at the Hamburg site.

In this case, the Paris gateway finds a route to destination 10.13.13.0/24 in its routing table with a next hop of 10.3.3.5 (the GRE tunnel interface address of the Hamburg gateway). So, the Paris gateway has the next-hop address (10.3.3.5), but because this next-hop address is not a globally routable IP address, the Paris router needs to find the globally routable IP address (the physical interface IP address) of the gateway to which the GRE tunnel interface address 10.3.3.5 belongs.

At this point, the Paris gateway checks its local cache of NHRP mappings and finds no mapping for next-hop address 10.3.3.5. The Paris gateway then sends a NHRP Resolution Request message to the London-1 gateway (the NHS) requesting the physical interface (globally routable) address to which the next-hop (GRE tunnel interface) address 10.3.3.5 corresponds.

The London-1 gateway looks in its NHRP cache (see Table 7-1), finds that physical interface address 192.168.11.2 corresponds to next-hop address 10.3.3.5, and sends this information back to the Paris gateway in an NHRP Resolution Reply message. The Paris gateway enters this information in its NHRP cache.

The Paris gateway now has all the information it needs (a globally routable physical interface address), and so builds an IPsec protected GRE (GRE/IPsec) tunnel directly to the Hamburg gateway. After the tunnel has been built, packets from host 10.11.11.1 at the Paris site can be sent directly to host 10.13.13.1 at the Hamburg site.

Figure 7-7 illustrates dynamic setup of the IPsec/GRE tunnel from the Paris gateway to the Hamburg gateway.

Figure 7-7 *Dynamic IPsec/GRE Tunnel Setup from the Paris Gateway to the Hamburg Gateway*

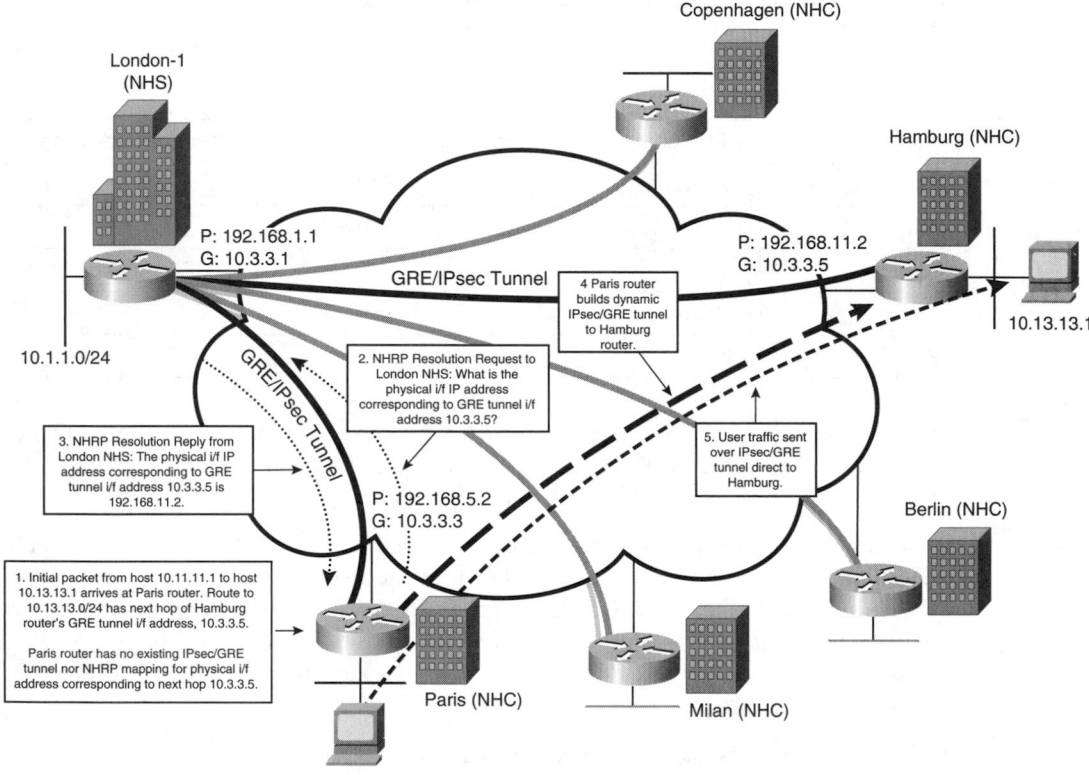

You might be wondering what happens to data traffic sent from host 10.11.11.1 (at the Paris site) to host 10.13.13.1 (at the Hamburg site) while the Paris gateway is in the process of setting up the IPsec/GRE tunnel directly to the Hamburg gateway. The initial few packets are, in fact, sent between the Paris and Hamburg sites via the London-1 gateway.

The IPsec/GRE tunnel between the Paris and Hamburg gateways remains in place as long as there is traffic passing over it, and for an additional (configurable) idle period. After this idle period has passed without any more traffic passing over the tunnel, it is torn down. If either gateway subsequently needs to send traffic to the other, an IPsec/GRE tunnel must again be dynamically built as previously described.

Deploying a DMVPN Architecture

When deploying a DMVPN, you must configure two types of devices:

- Hub site gateway(s)
- Spoke site gateways

Configuration of these two DMVPN device types is discussed in the following sections.

Configuring the DMVPN Hub Site Gateway

The first step in deploying the single hub router DMVPN architecture (as shown in Figure 7-5) is to configure the hub site gateway (the NHS).

Hub site gateway configuration involves the following steps:

Step 1 Configure the IKE policy (including authentication).

Step 2 Configure the IPsec transform set.

Step 3 Configure the IPsec profile.

Step 4 Configure common parameters on the multipoint GRE (mGRE) tunnel interface.

Step 5 Configure the routing protocol for site-to-site reachability.

The first two steps have already been described in Chapter 6, and so are not discussed further here. See Chapter 6 for more information.

Steps 3, 4, and 5 are discussed further in the following sections.

It is worth noting that although this section discusses the configuration of a single DMVPN hub site gateway, it is possible to configure redundant hub site gateways in a DMVPN. Configuration of redundant hub site gateways in a DMVPN is discussed in the section "High Availability with DMVPN" later in this chapter.

Step 3: Configure the IPsec Profile A crypto profile is a way to bring together a number of IPsec policy settings that can then be referenced elsewhere in a configuration file. Although a crypto profile is similar to a crypto map, it is not possible to specify either a crypto access list or a peer address within a crypto profile.

Example 7-2 shows the configuration of the crypto profile.

Example 7-2 *Configuration of a Crypto Profile*

```
!
crypto ipsec profile mjlnetprofile
 set transform-set mjlnettransform
!
```

In Example 7-2, the **crypto ipsec profile** *name* command is used to configure a profile called mjlnetprofile.

The **set transform-set** *transform-set-name* command is then used to specify an IPsec transform set called mjlnettransform.

When using DMVPN, GRE/IPsec tunnels are automatically built, with the crypto access lists and (spoke) peer addresses being automatically derived from NHRP mappings.

Step 4: Configure Common Parameters on the mGRE Tunnel Interface   After the IPsec profile has been configured, the next step is to configure common parameters on the mGRE tunnel interface.

Assuming one DMVPN, you need to configure one mGRE tunnel interface on the hub gateway no matter how many spoke gateways there are.

The configuration of the mGRE tunnel interface consists of several steps:

1   Configure the IP address.

2   Configure NHRP parameters.

3   Configure tunnel parameters.

4   Associate the tunnel interface with the IPsec profile.

Example 7-3 shows the configuration of the mGRE tunnel interface.

Example 7-3   *Configuration of the mGRE Tunnel Interface on the Hub Site Gateway*

```
!
interface Tunnel0
 ip address 10.3.3.1 255.255.255.0
 ip nhrp authentication mjlnet
 ip nhrp map multicast dynamic
 ip nhrp network-id 1234
 tunnel source 192.168.1.1
 tunnel mode gre multipoint
 tunnel key 5678
 tunnel protection ipsec profile mjlnetprofile
!
```

The **ip address** *ip-address mask* command is used to configure the IP address 10.3.3.1/24 on tunnel interface 0 in Example 7-3.

The **ip nhrp authentication** *string* command is used to configure an authentication string for DMVPN gateways. This string must be identical for all gateways in a particular DMVPN.

Next is the **ip nhrp map multicast dynamic** command. This command allows the hub gateway to automatically add spoke gateways to its NHRP multicast mapping table. This is necessary to ensure that dynamic routing protocols (that send multicast traffic) work correctly over the DMVPN.

The **ip nhrp network-id** *number* command is then used to configure the NHRP network ID. The NHRP network ID uniquely identifies the NHRP network, and must be configured identically on all gateways in the same DMVPN.

The **tunnel source** {*ip-address* | *interface-type interface-number*} command is used to configure the source IP address of the tunnel.

One thing to notice in Example 7-3 is the absence of the **tunnel destination** command. This command is required when configuring point-to-point GRE tunnels but not when configuring mGRE tunnels.

The tunnel mode is then configured as mGRE using the **tunnel mode gre multipoint** command.

The **tunnel key** *key-number* command is used to configure an ID key for the tunnel interface. This ID key, together with the authentication string and network ID specified with the **ip nhrp authentication** and **ip nhrp network-id** commands, is used to map NHRP and tunnel packets to this particular mGRE interface. The tunnel key must be configured identically on all gateways for a particular DMVPN.

The final command configured on the tunnel interface is **tunnel protection ipsec profile** *name*. This associates the IPsec profile configured in Step 3 with the tunnel interface.

TIP

Although not shown in Example 7-3, one other command that you might want to add to the configuration is **ip nhrp holdtime** *seconds*. You can use this command to configure the number of seconds that addresses are advertised as valid in authoritative NHRP responses. The default value is 7200 seconds (2 hours), but a much more practical value for DMVPN is 300 to 600 seconds. It is a good idea to add this command on all routers in a DMVPN.

Step 5: Configure the Routing Protocol for Site-to-Site Reachability   Having configured the mGRE tunnel interface, the next step is to configure the routing protocol for site-to-site reachability.

You can use a number of routing protocols for site-to-site reachability in a DMVPN, the most popular of which are the following:

- OSPF
- EIGRP
- RIP

Configuration of these routing protocols on a DMVPN hub site gateway is discussed in the following three sections.

OSPF   If you decide to use Open Shortest Path First (OSPF) for site-to-site reachability, be sure to enable OSPF on the mGRE interface and the inside interfaces (as appropriate). You must also ensure that the hub gateway is configured as the OSPF Designated Router (DR). If there is more than one hub site gateway, make sure that another hub site gateway is configured as the Backup Designated Router (BDR). Finally, make sure that all gateways in the DMVPN are configured to use the OSPF broadcast network type on their mGRE tunnel interfaces.

Example 7-4 provides a sample configuration of OSPF on a hub site gateway.

Example 7-4 *Sample Configuration of OSPF for Site-to-Site Reachability*

```
!
router ospf 100
 network 10.1.1.0 0.0.0.255 area 0
 network 10.3.3.0 0.0.0.255 area 0
 !
interface Tunnel0
 ip ospf priority 100
 ip ospf network broadcast
 !
```

In Example 7-4, the **router ospf** *process-id* command is used to enable OSPF process 100, and the **network** *network* [*wildcard-mask*] **area** *area-number* command is used to enable OSPF area 0 on the inside interface (10.1.1.1, in this example), and the mGRE tunnel interface (10.3.3.1, in this example).

The **ip ospf priority** *priority* command is then configured on the mGRE interface. This command must be used to specify high (higher than spoke site) priority values on hub site gateways' mGRE interfaces, thus ensuring that hub site gateways become the DR and BDR. In fact, it is a good idea to specify an OSPF priority value of 0 on spoke site gateways' mGRE interfaces, so that the spoke site gateways can never become the DR or BDR.

Finally, the **ip ospf network broadcast** command is used to specify the OSPF broadcast network type on the hub site gateways' mGRE interfaces. This command allows GRE/IPsec tunnels to be built directly between spoke sites for spoke site-to-spoke site user traffic.

EIGRP   When using Enhanced Interior Gateway Routing Protocol (EIGRP) for site-to-site reachability, you should enable EIGRP on the mGRE tunnel interface and inside interfaces (as appropriate). You must also disable IP split horizon and IP next-hop-self on the mGRE tunnel interface.

Example 7-5 provides a sample configuration of EIGRP on a hub site gateway.

Example 7-5 *Sample Configuration of EIGRP for Site-to-Site Reachability*

```
!
router eigrp 100
 network 10.1.1.0 0.0.0.255
 network 10.3.3.0 0.0.0.255
 no auto-summary
 !
 !
interface Tunnel0
 no ip next-hop-self eigrp 100
 no ip split-horizon eigrp 100
 !
```

In Example 7-5, the **router eigrp** *autonomous-system* command is used to enable EIGRP autonomous system 100, and the **network** *network* [*wildcard-mask*] command is used to enable EIGRP on the hub site gateway's inside interface (10.1.1.1 in this example), and on the mGRE tunnel interface (10.3.3.1 in this example).

The **no auto-summary** command in Example 7-5 ensures that networks are not auto-summarized at major network boundaries.

The **no ip split-horizon eigrp** *autonomous-system-number* command disables IP split horizon for EIGRP, thus allowing the hub site to re-advertise routes received on its mGRE interface from one spoke site to other spoke sites on the same interface. This command allows spoke site-to-spoke site reachability.

The **no ip next-hop-self eigrp** *autonomous-system-number* command is used to ensure that all EIGRP routes that are received from one spoke site are re-advertised to other spoke sites with their original (spoke site) IP next hop. Re-advertisement of routes by the hub site with their original spoke site IP next hop is important to ensure that spoke sites build GRE/IPsec tunnels directly between themselves for spoke site-to-spoke site user traffic.

RIP   Configuration of Routing Information Protocol (RIP) for site-to-site reachability in a DMVPN is relatively easy. You must simply enable RIP on the mGRE interface and inside interfaces (as appropriate), and disable IP split horizon on the mGRE tunnel interface.

Example 7-6 provides a sample RIP configuration for a hub site gateway.

Example 7-6   *Sample Configuration of RIP for Site-to-Site Reachability*

```
!
router rip
 version 2
 network 10.0.0.0
 no auto-summary
!
!
interface Tunnel0
 no ip split-horizon
!
```

In Example 7-6, the **router rip** and **version 2** commands are used to enable RIP Version 2. The **network** *network* and **no auto-summary** commands are then used to enable RIP on the mGRE (10.3.3.1) and inside (10.1.1.1) interfaces and disable auto-summarization of routes at major network boundaries respectively.

The **no ip split-horizon** command is used to disable IP split horizon on the mGRE tunnel interface and allow the hub site to re-advertise routes received on the mGRE interface from one spoke site to other spoke sites on the same interface. This command ensures spoke site-to-spoke site reachability. Note that because the hub site automatically re-advertises spoke site routes with their original IP next hop when using RIP, spoke sites will automatically build GRE/IPsec tunnels directly between themselves for spoke site-to-spoke site user traffic.

Complete Sample Hub Site Gateway DMVPN Configuration   Example 7-7 shows a sample hub site gateway DMVPN configuration. Only the relevant portions of the configuration are shown.

Example 7-7   *Complete Sample Hub Site Gateway DMVPN Configuration*

```
London-1#show running-config
Building configuration...
Current configuration : 2546 bytes
!
! IKE policy
!
crypto isakmp policy 10
 authentication pre-share
!
!
! Wildcard pre-shared key
!
crypto isakmp key mjlnet address 0.0.0.0 0.0.0.0
!
!
! IPsec transform set
!
crypto ipsec transform-set mjlnettransform esp-3des esp-sha-hmac
!
!
! IPsec profile
!
crypto ipsec profile mjlnetprofile
 set transform-set mjlnettransform
!
!
! mGRE tunnel interface
!
interface Tunnel0
 ip address 10.3.3.1 255.255.255.0
 no ip next-hop-self eigrp 100
 ip nhrp authentication mjlnet
 ip nhrp map multicast dynamic
 ip nhrp network-id 1234
 no ip split-horizon eigrp 100
 tunnel source 192.168.1.1
 tunnel mode gre multipoint
 tunnel key 5678
 tunnel protection ipsec profile mjlnetprofile
!
!
! Inside interface
!
interface FastEthernet0/0
 ip address 10.1.1.1 255.255.255.0
!
!
```

Example 7-7   *Complete Sample Hub Site Gateway DMVPN Configuration (Continued)*

```
! Outside interface
!
interface Serial1/0
 ip address 192.168.1.1 255.255.255.0
 !
 !
 ! EIGRP for site-to-site reachability
 !
router eigrp 100
 network 10.1.1.0 0.0.0.255
 network 10.3.3.0 0.0.0.255
 no auto-summary
 !
 !
```

Although most of the configuration as been previously explained, notice that the highlighted line shows that a wildcard preshared key is used for IKE authentication. This wildcard preshared key is used for illustrative purposes only.

Configuring the DMVPN Spoke Site Gateways

After the hub site gateway has been configured, you can move on to configuring spoke site gateways.

The configuration of spoke site gateways comprises five steps:

Step 1   Configure the IKE policy (including authentication).

Step 2   Configure the IPsec transform set.

Step 3   Configure the crypto map or IPsec profile.

Step 4   Configure common parameters on the GRE tunnel interface.

Step 5   Configure the routing protocol for site-to-site reachability.

Configuration of spoke site gateways is, as you can see, similar to that for the hub site gateway. There are, however, one or two differences when configuring the GRE tunnel interface and configuring the routing protocol for site-to-site reachability.

Configuring Common Parameters on the GRE Tunnel Interface of Spoke Site Gateways   You have two choices when configuring the GRE tunnel interface on a spoke site gateway:

- You can configure point-to-point GRE tunnel interfaces.
- You can configure multipoint GRE tunnel interfaces.

Although an mGRE tunnel is required on spoke site gateways to support the transport of user traffic directly between spoke sites, point-point-point tunnels can be useful if spoke sites have not yet been upgraded to Cisco IOS Software Release 12.2(13)T or later. If you do configure point-to-point GRE tunnels on spoke site gateways, spoke-to-spoke user traffic is transported via the hub site.

Example 7-8 shows the configuration of a point-to-point GRE tunnel interface on a spoke site gateway running a Cisco IOS version prior to 12.2(13)T.

Example 7-8 *Configuration of a Point-to-Point GRE Tunnel Interface on a Spoke Site Gateway*

```
!
interface Tunnel0
 ip address 10.3.3.3 255.255.255.0
 ip nhrp authentication mjlnet
 ip nhrp map 10.3.3.1 192.168.1.1 (line 1)
 ip nhrp network-id 1234
 ip nhrp nhs 10.3.3.1 (line 2)
 tunnel source 192.168.2.2
 tunnel destination 192.168.1.1 (line 3)
 tunnel key 5678
 crypto map mjlnetmap (line 4)
!
```

Some of the commands shown in Example 7-8 were described in the previous section, and so are not discussed here. Commands that have not been previously described are highlighted in Example 7-8.

Highlighted line 1 shows the **ip nhrp map** *physical-ip-address gre-tunnel-interface-ip-address* command. This command is used to build an NHRP mapping of the hub gateway's outside physical interface IP address to its GRE tunnel interface IP address. In this example, the IP address configured on the hub gateway's physical interface is 192.168.1.1, and the IP address configured on its mGRE tunnel interface is 10.3.3.1.

Line 2 shows the **ip nhrp nhs** *nhs-gre-interface-ip-address* command, which is used to specify the (mGRE tunnel interface) IP address of the NHS. The NHS is the hub site gateway.

The **tunnel destination** {*hostname* | *ip-address*} command shown in line 3 then specifies the GRE tunnel destination. In this case, the tunnel destination is the hub site gateway's GRE tunnel source address (192.168.1.1, its outside physical interface).

Finally, the **crypto map** *map-name* in line 4 applies a crypto map to the GRE tunnel interface. Because the configuration shown in Example 7-8 applies to spoke site gateways running Cisco IOS versions prior to 12.2(13)T, you must apply a crypto map to the GRE tunnel interface in addition to the outside physical interface. See the section "Transporting Multiprotocol and Multicast Traffic over an IPsec VPN" in Chapter 6 for more details on the configuration and application of a crypto map for a point-to-point GRE tunnel.

The configuration of an mGRE tunnel interface on a spoke site gateway differs slightly, as shown in Example 7-9. In this case, the spoke site gateway is running Cisco IOS Software Release 12.2(13)T or later.

Example 7-9 *Configuration of an mGRE Tunnel Interface on a Spoke Site Gateway*

```
!
interface Tunnel0
 ip address 10.3.3.3 255.255.255.0
 ip nhrp authentication mjlnet
 ip nhrp map 10.3.3.1 192.168.1.1
 ip nhrp map multicast 192.168.1.1
 ip nhrp network-id 1234
 ip nhrp nhs 10.3.3.1
 tunnel source 192.168.2.2
 tunnel mode gre multipoint
 tunnel key 5678
 tunnel protection ipsec profile mjlnetprofile
!
```

There are three main differences when compared to the configuration of point-to-point GRE tunnel interfaces on spoke site gateways:

- The GRE tunnel interface is configured to use GRE multipoint mode using the **tunnel mode gre multipoint** command.

- The **tunnel protection ipsec profile** command is used apply an IPsec profile.

- Because an IPsec profile is applied to the mGRE tunnel interface, a crypto map is not required.

For more information on these commands, as well as the configuration of the IPsec profile, see the previous section, "Configuring the DMVPN Hub Site Gateway."

Configuring the Routing Protocol for Site-to-Site Reachability on the Spoke Site Gateways   The configuration of the routing protocol for site-to-site reachability on the spoke site gateways is again similar to that on hub site gateways. The differences are as follows:

- When using OPSF for site-to-site reachability, you should configure an OSPF priority of 0 on the GRE tunnel interfaces of all spoke site gateways using the **ip opsf priority 0** command. This command ensures that spoke gateways cannot become the OSPF DR or BDR.

- When using EIGRP, you should *not* disable IP split horizon using the **no ip split-horizon eigrp** command, nor configure the **no ip next-hop-self eigrp** command on the GRE tunnel interfaces of spoke gateways. This is because spoke site gateways are not required to re-advertise routes that they receive from other gateways.

- If you use RIP, you should *not* disable IP split horizon on the GRE tunnel interfaces of spoke gateways. Again, this is because spoke gateways are not required to re-advertise routes that they receive from other gateways.

Complete Sample Spoke Site Gateway DMVPN Configuration   Example 7-10
shows a sample spoke site gateway configuration (with an mGRE tunnel interface). Note
that only relevant portions of the configuration are shown.

Example 7-10 *Complete Sample Spoke Site Gateway DMVPN Configuration*

```
Berlin#show running-config
Building configuration...
Current configuration : 2546 bytes
!
! IKE policy
!
crypto isakmp policy 10
 authentication pre-share
!
!
! Wildcard pre-shared key
!
crypto isakmp key mjlnet 0.0.0.0 0.0.0.0
!
!
! IPsec transform set
!
crypto ipsec transform-set mjlnettransform esp-3des esp-sha-hmac
!
!
! IPsec profile
!
crypto ipsec profile mjlnetprofile
 set transform-set mjlnettransform
!
!
! mGRE tunnel interface
!
interface Tunnel0
 ip address 10.3.3.3 255.255.255.0
 ip nhrp authentication mjlnet
 ip nhrp map 10.3.3.1 192.168.1.1
 ip nhrp map multicast 192.168.1.1
 ip nhrp network-id 1234
 ip nhrp nhs 10.3.3.1
 tunnel source 192.168.2.2
 tunnel mode gre multipoint
 tunnel key 5678
 tunnel protection ipsec profile mjlnetprofile
!
!
! Inside interface
!
interface FastEthernet2/0
 ip address 10.10.10.1 255.255.255.0
!
!
```

Example 7-10 *Complete Sample Spoke Site Gateway DMVPN Configuration (Continued)*

```
! Outside interface
!
interface FastEthernet2/0
 ip address 192.168.2.2 255.255.255.0
!
!
! EIGRP for site-to-site reachability
!
router eigrp 100
 network 10.2.2.0 0.0.0.255
 network 10.3.3.0 0.0.0.255
no auto-summary
!
!
```

Note that the wildcard preshared key shown in the highlighted line is used for illustrative purpose only. See Chapter 6 for more information on wildcard preshared keys.

Configuring DMVPN on Spoke Site Gateways with Dynamically Assigned IP Addresses
The configuration shown in Example 7-10 is applicable to spoke site gateways whose outside physical interface IP addresses are statically assigned, but it is possible to configure DMVPN on spoke site gateways whose IP addresses are dynamically assigned. This feature can prove useful when spoke sites do not have a statically assigned address, but instead rely on the assignment of an IP address by their local ISP's Dynamic Host Configuration Protocol (DHCP) server.

Example 7-11 shows the configuration of a spoke site gateway configured with a point-to-point GRE tunnel when it is using DHCP for address assignment.

Example 7-11 *Configuration of a Point-to-Point GRE Tunnel Interface on a Spoke Site Gateway When Using DHCP for Address Assignment*

```
!
! Configures the local source IP address for IPsec and IKE traffic
!
crypto map mjlnetmap local-address FastEthernet 1/0 (line 1)
!
!
! Crypto map
!
crypto map mjlnetmap 10 ipsec-isakmp
 set peer 192.168.1.1
 set security-association level per-host (line 2)
 set transform-set mjlnettransform
 match address 101
!
!
! Point-to-point GRE tunnel interface
!
```

Example 7-11 *Configuration of a Point-to-Point GRE Tunnel Interface on a Spoke Site Gateway When Using DHCP for Address Assignment (Continued)*

```
interface Tunnel0
 ip address 10.3.3.3 255.255.255.0
 ip nhrp authentication mjlnet
 ip nhrp map 10.3.3.1 192.168.1.1
 ip nhrp network-id 1234
 ip nhrp nhs 10.3.3.1
 tunnel source FastEthernet1/0 (line 3)
 tunnel destination 192.168.1.1
 tunnel key 5678
 crypto map mjlnetmap
!
!
! Outside interface
!
interface FastEthernet 1/0
 ip address dhcp (line 4)
 crypto map mjlnetmap
!
!
! Crypto access list
!
access-list 101 permit gre 192.168.2.0 0.0.0.255 host 192.168.1.1 (line 5)
 !
```

Most of the configuration shown in Example 7-11 has already been discussed, but the highlighted lines have special significance.

In highlighted line 1, the **crypto map** *map-name* **local-address** *interface-id* command is used to configure the local source IP address to be used for all IPsec and IKE traffic.

The crypto access list in line 5 differs slightly from that regularly used for a point-to-point GRE tunnel (see the section "Transporting Multiprotocol and Multicast Traffic over an IPsec VPN" in Chapter 6). If you take a closer look at the source IP address, you will notice that it is not a host address (the specific GRE tunnel source IP address, as would normally be the case), but instead an IP address range (192.168.2.0/24). The reason that it is an address range is that the local ISP DHCP server might assign any one of the IP addresses in this range to the spoke gateway (it corresponds to the DHCP server[s]' scope).

Now take a look at the command in line 2 (**set security-association level per-host**). This command ensures that IPsec SAs are negotiated on a per-host basis.

In the absence of the **set security-association level per-host**, the spoke gateway would negotiate IPsec SAs with the hub site gateway using source IP address 192.168.2.0/24 and destination IP address 192.168.1.1 as its traffic selectors (traffic selectors specify what traffic should be protected by IPsec). But in reality, the spoke gateway only needs to negotiate IPsec SAs with a *single* source IP address in the range 192.168.2.0/24 (whatever single IP address that the DHCP server assigns to the spoke gateway). So, the **set security-association level per-host** command ensures that IPsec SAs are negotiated with the hub site gateway using whatever *single* IP address the DHCP assigns (for example, 192.168.2.5) and 192.168.1.1 as the traffic selectors.

The **tunnel source FastEthernet 1/0** command in line 3 is used to specify the outside interface *name* as the tunnel source rather than a fixed IP address. It is important to specify the interface name rather than a fixed IP address because it is uncertain which IP address the DHCP server will assign to the spoke gateway (again, it could any single IP address in a range).

In line 4, you can see the **ip address dhcp** [**client-id** *interface-name*] [**hostname** *hostname*] command. This configures the spoke gateway to request an IP address for its outside interface from a DHCP server. The **client-id** and **hostname** parameters are used to specify nondefault values for DHCP options 61 and 12, respectively. DHCP options 61 and 12 are carried in DHCPDISCOVER messages sent by the spoke gateway to the DHCP server and by default carry the MAC address of the interface to which the **ip address dhcp** command is applied and the router host name, respectively. Check with your ISP to determine whether you need to specify nondefault values for DHCP options 61 and 12.

Okay, that is the configuration for a spoke gateway configured with a point-to-point GRE tunnel. But, how about the configuration for a spoke gateway with an mGRE tunnel?

Example 7-12 shows the configuration for a spoke gateway with an mGRE tunnel.

Example 7-12 *Configuration of an mGRE Tunnel Interface on a Spoke Site Gateway When Using DHCP for Address Assignment*

```
!
interface Tunnel0
 ip address 10.3.3.3 255.255.255.0
 ip nhrp authentication mjlnet
 ip nhrp map 10.3.3.1 192.168.1.1
 ip nhrp map multicast 192.168.1.1
 ip nhrp network-id 1234
 ip nhrp nhs 10.3.3.1
 tunnel source FastEthernet1/0 (line 1)
 tunnel mode gre multipoint
 tunnel key 5678
 tunnel protection ipsec profile mjlnetprofile
 !
 !
 ! Outside interface
 !
interface FastEthernet 1/0
 ip address dhcp (line 2)
 !
```

If you compare Example 7-12 to Example 7-10, you will notice only two differences — the outside interface name is specified using the **tunnel source** command (see highlighted line 1), and the **ip address dhcp** command is configured on the outside interface (see highlighted line 2).

Because an IPsec profile is used when configuring an mGRE tunnel interface, and the crypto access list is automatically derived by the gateway, you do not need to worry about configuring a crypto map or a crypto access list when using an mGRE tunnel interfaces on spoke gateways.

Scaling IPsec VPNs with Digital Signature Authentication

As discussed in Chapter 6, three options exist for IKE authentication on Cisco routers:

- Preshared key authentication
- Encrypted nonce authentication
- Digital signature authentication

All three options work fine for small-scale IPsec VPNs. In fact, preshared key authentication, because of the relative ease with which it can be configured, is probably the most popular option for smaller VPNs. As VPNs begin to grow, however, IKE authentication using both preshared keys and encrypted nonces becomes less and less viable.

One problem with preshared key authentication as VPNs grow is key management.

It is a good idea to use a unique preshared key between each pair of IPsec gateways because if you use the same (wildcard) preshared key between all gateways, the compromise of a single IPsec gateway compromises the whole VPN. On the other hand, if a unique preshared key is used between each pair of IPsec gateways, the compromise of a single preshared key only compromises a single pair of routers. If a unique preshared key is compromised, it is a relatively simple task to modify that key on the two affected IPsec gateways. If you use the same preshared key on all IPsec gateways and the preshared key is compromised, it is a much more laborious task to modify the key on all the IPsec gateways. And during the period that you are modifying the preshared key, the entire VPN will be down.

So, to ensure the security of your VPN, you need to use a unique preshared key for each pair of IPsec gateways. The problem with using unique preshared keys, however, is that the number of keys grows dramatically as the number of IPsec gateways in the VPN grows.

If you require full-mesh connectivity in your VPN, you need $n(n-1)/2$ keys (where n is the total number of IPsec gateways). If you have 5 IPsec gateways, for example, you need 10 preshared keys. If you have 10 IPsec gateways, you need 45 preshared keys. And if you have 100 IPsec gateways, you need 4950 preshared keys.

Figure 7-8 illustrates the number of preshared keys required in a full-mesh topology with five sites.

Figure 7-8   *Number of Preshared Keys Required in a Full-Mesh Topology*

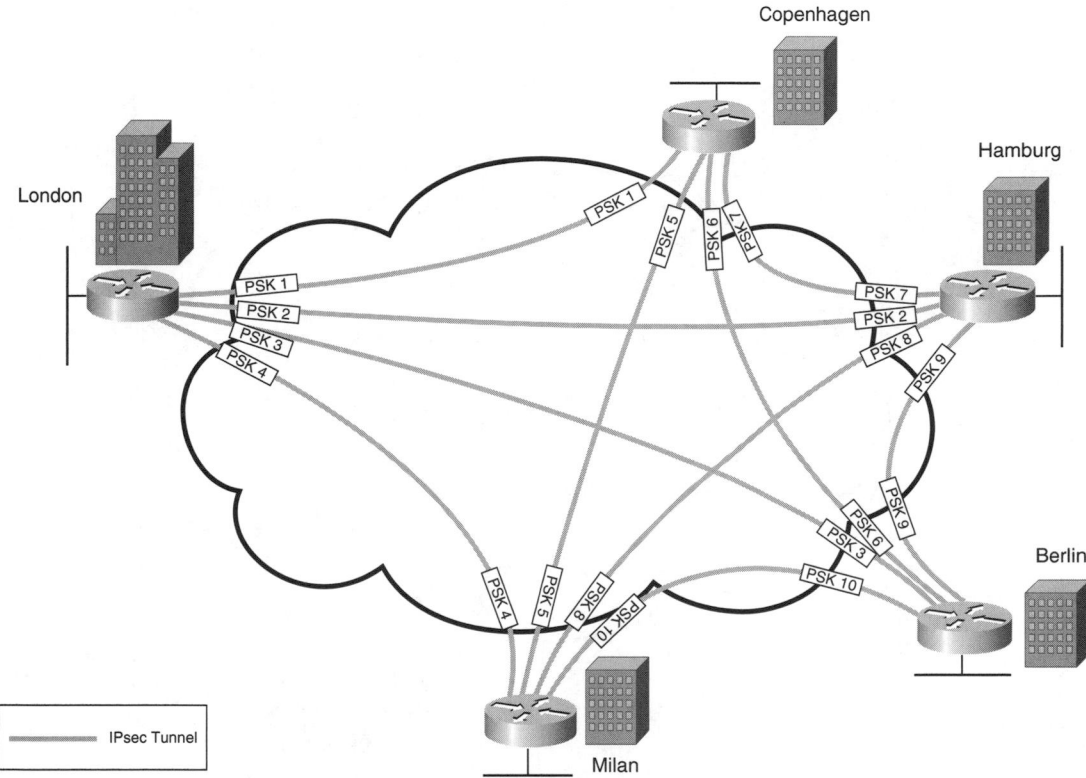

There are five IPsec gateways (sites) in the network shown in Figure 7-8. The number of IPsec tunnels and preshared keys (PSK) is, therefore, $5(5 - 1)/2 = 10$.

If you choose a hub-and-spoke topology (with one hub gateway), you need s preshared keys, where s is the number of spoke gateways. So, for 5 spoke gateways, you need 5 preshared keys; for 10 spoke gateways, you need 10 preshared keys; and for 100 spoke gateways, you need 100 preshared keys.

Figure 7-9 shows the total number of preshared keys in a hub-and-spoke topology.

If you have redundant hub site gateways at a single site, the number of preshared keys is $h * s$, where h is the number of hub site gateways, and s is the total number of spoke site gateways. So, with 2 hub site gateways and 5 spoke gateways, you need $2 * 5 = 10$ preshared keys. With 2 hub site gateways and 100 spoke gateways, you need $2 * 100 = 200$ preshared keys.

Figure 7-9 *Number of Preshared Keys Required in a Hub-and-Spoke Topology*

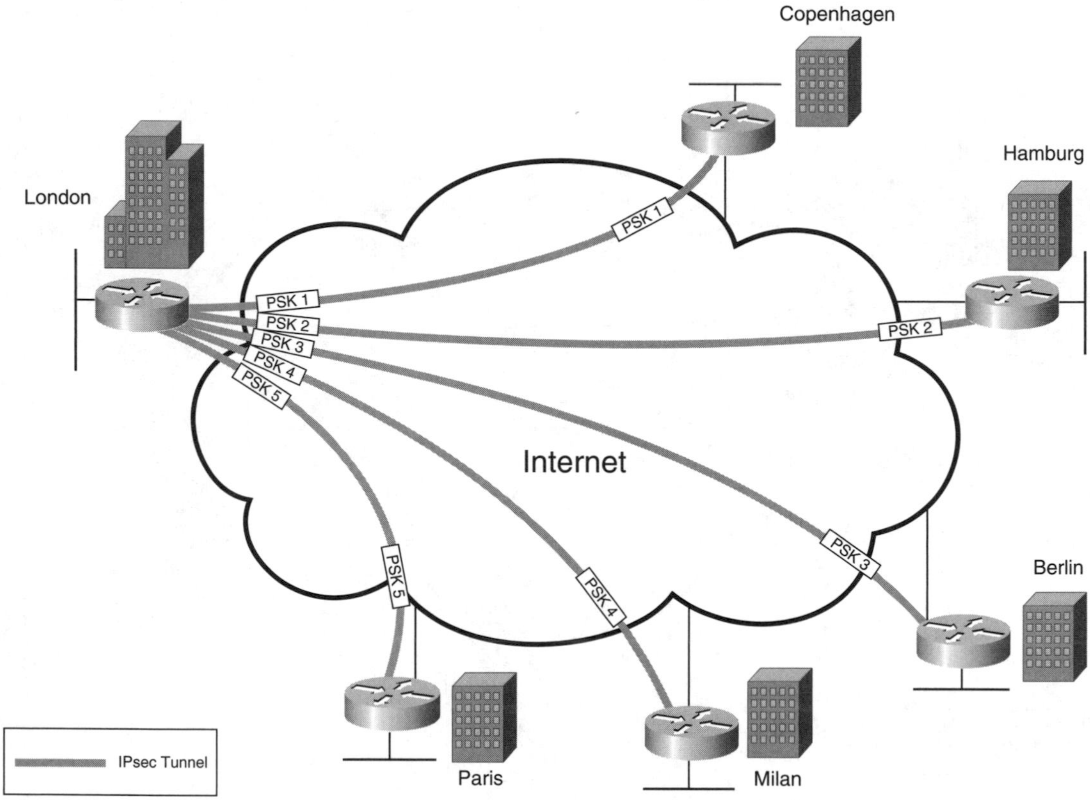

Administrating a large number of preshared keys can be laborious and time-consuming. And, when you need to add a new gateway to the VPN, it might not be as simple as you might imagine. If your VPN is fully meshed, not only will you need to configure the new gateway with a preshared key for each of the existing gateways, you will also need to revisit each existing gateway and configure a new preshared key for the new gateway. If you are using a hub-and-spoke topology, things are easier—you only need to add a preshared key or keys for the hub gateway or gateways on the new device as well as a preshared key for the new device on the hub gateway or gateways.

Figure 7-10 illustrates the addition a new gateway to a fully meshed IPsec VPN with preshared key authentication.

In Figure 7-10, a new site (Paris) is added to an existing IPsec VPN. This addition requires the configuration of five preshared keys on the new gateway, as well as the configuration of one new preshared key on each of the existing IPsec VPN gateways.

So, preshared key authentication can quickly become a burden as a VPN grows, and that means it does not scale for large VPNs.

Figure 7-10 *Addition of New Gateway to Fully Meshed IPsec VPN with Preshared Key Authentication*

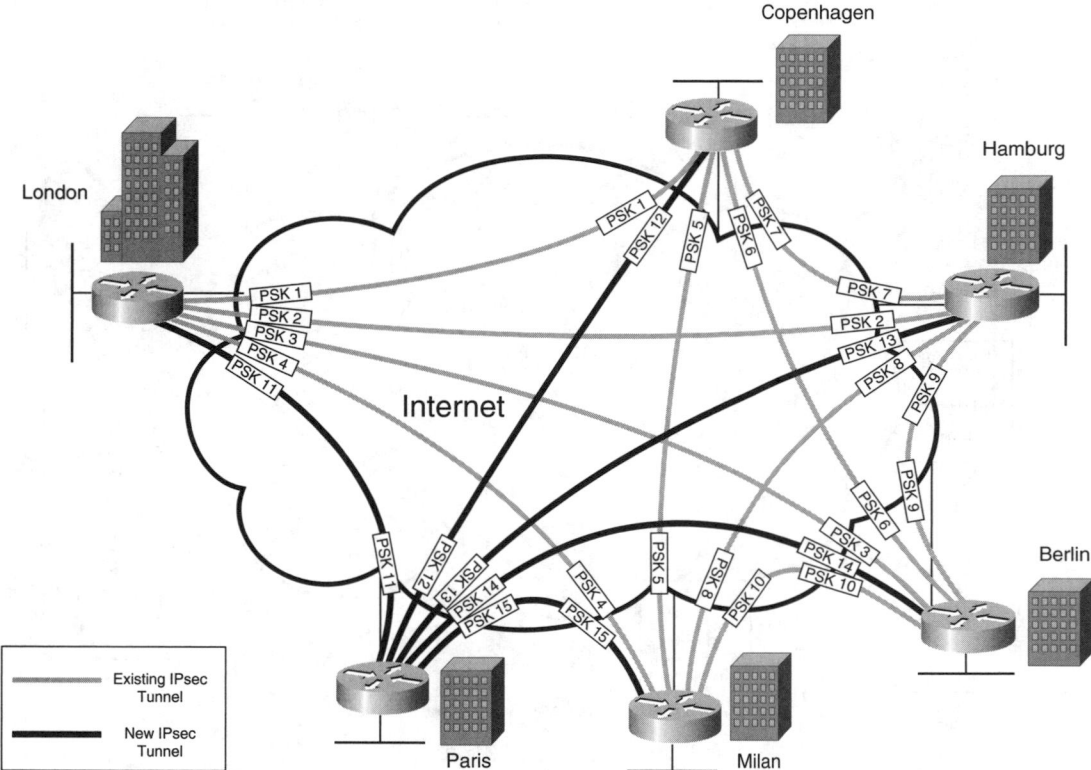

Preshared key authentication might not scale well, but how about encrypted nonce authentication? As previously discussed in the section "IKE Encrypted Nonce Authentication" in Chapter 6, when configuring encrypted nonce authentication, you need to manually configure each IPsec gateway with the public key (or keys) of every other IPsec gateway. So, although you do not have the problem of a huge number of keys in a full mesh (as you would with unique preshared keys), you still need to configure each IPsec gateway with the public keys of each other gateway.

The number of public keys that you need to configure on each gateway in a full-mesh topology is equal to $n - 1$ (assuming you are using general-usage keys), where n is the total number of IPsec gateways. In a hub-and-spoke topology, you need to configure the hub site gateway with $n - 1$ public keys and the spoke gateways with the public key of the hub gateway (or gateways).

Figure 7-11 shows the number of public keys required in a fully meshed IPsec VPN with encrypted nonce authentication.

Figure 7-11 *Fully Meshed IPsec VPN with Encrypted Nonce Authentication*

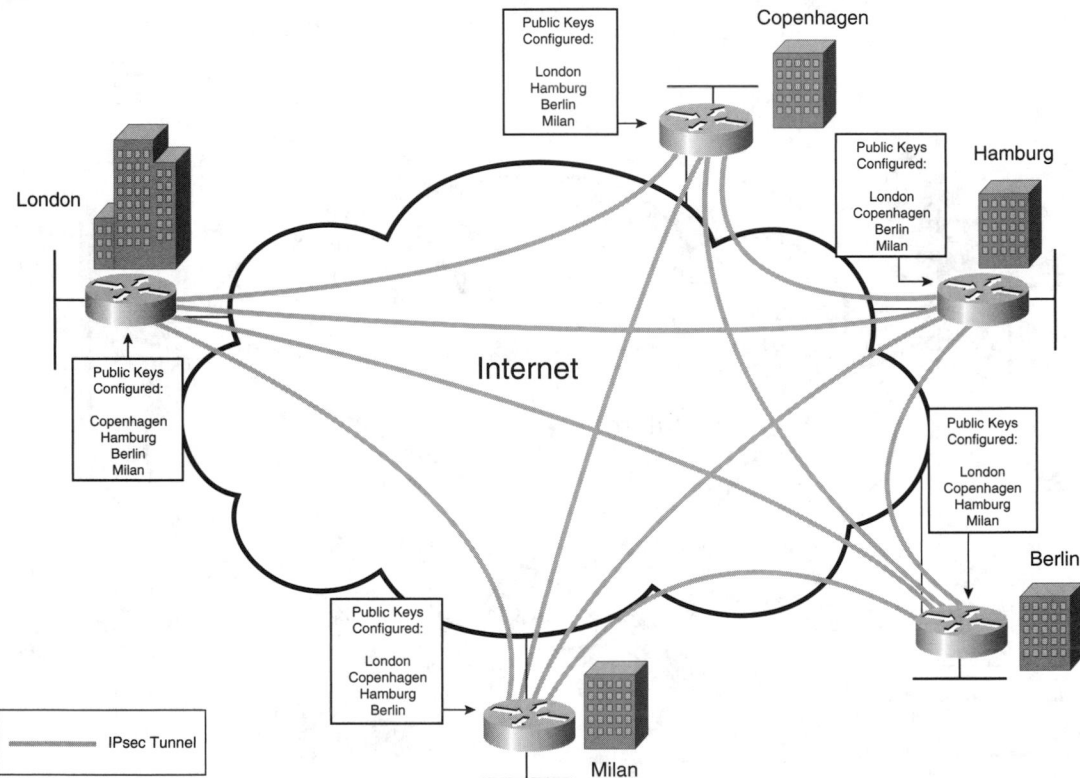

When you are using encrypted nonce authentication and you add a new gateway to a full-mesh VPN, you need to configure the new gateway with the public keys of all the other gateways in the network, and revisit all the existing gateways in the VPN to add the public key of new gateway. If you add a spoke gateway in a hub-and-spoke VPN, you need to configure the gateway with the public key of the hub site gateway or gateways. Furthermore, if you are using separate keys for signing and encryption, you need to configure twice as many public keys on each gateway in the VPN.

Figure 7-12 illustrates the addition of a new IPsec gateway to a fully meshed VPN with encrypted nonce authentication. This figure shows the addition of a new IPsec gateway (Paris) to a fully meshed IPsec VPN. In this example, gateway Paris must be configured with the public keys of all the existing IPsec gateways in the VPN. Additionally, the existing IPsec gateway must be configured with the public key of the Paris gateway.

The manual configuration of public keys on gateways is a time-consuming process, and encrypted nonce authentication is therefore not a practical option for large-scale IPsec VPNs.

Figure 7-12 *Addition of New Gateway to Fully Meshed IPsec VPN with Encrypted Nonce Authentication*

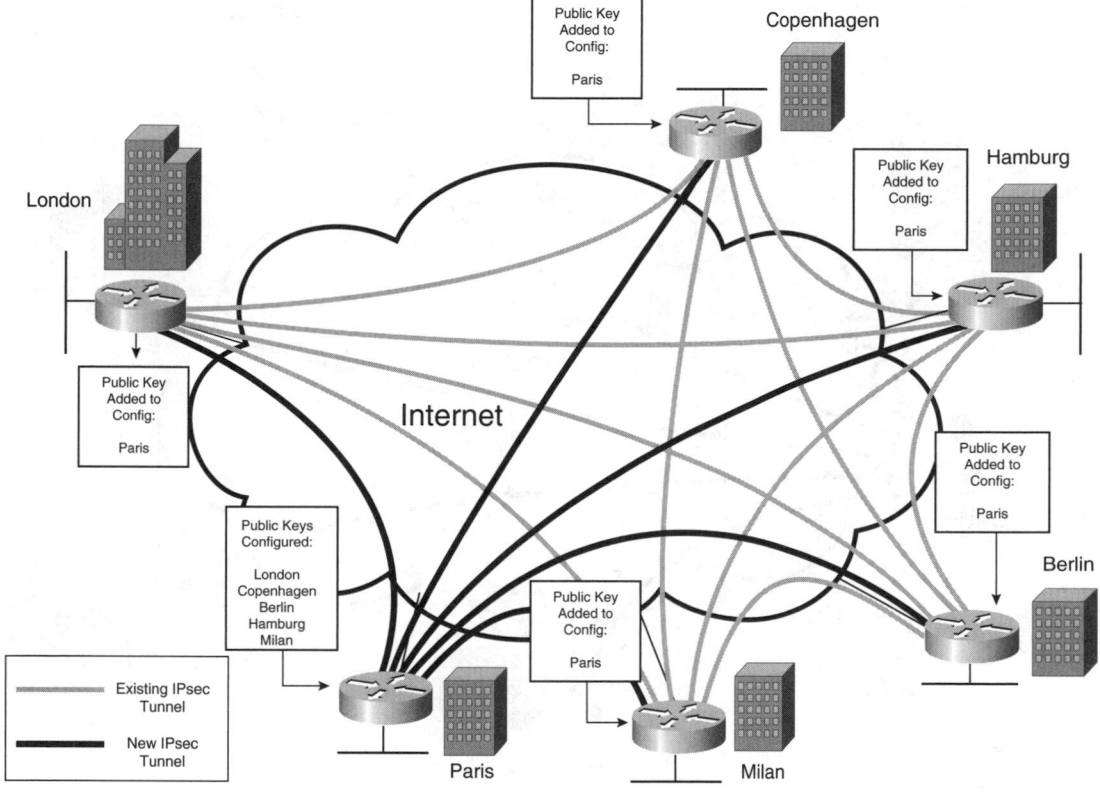

So, if preshared key and encrypted nonce authentication are not scalable, how about digital signature authentication? When using digital signature authentication, each IPsec peer enrolls with a (trusted) certificate authority (CA), obtains a certificate, and then during IKE negotiation, certificates are automatically exchanged. These certificates are used by IPsec VPN gateways to authenticate each other.

Figure 7-13 illustrates a fully meshed IPsec VPN with digital signature authentication.

In Figure 7-13, the London, Copenhagen, Hamburg, Berlin, and Milan gateways each enroll with the CA and obtain a certificate.

When a new gateway is added to the VPN with digital signature authentication, it simply has to enroll with the CA and obtain a certificate before it can establish IPsec tunnels with other gateways in the VPN. Great! There is no need to manually configure gateways with the keys of other gateways. Digital signature authentication (using digital certificates) is therefore much more scalable than both preshared key or encrypted nonce authentication.

Figure 7-13 *Fully Meshed IPsec VPN with Digital Signature Authentication*

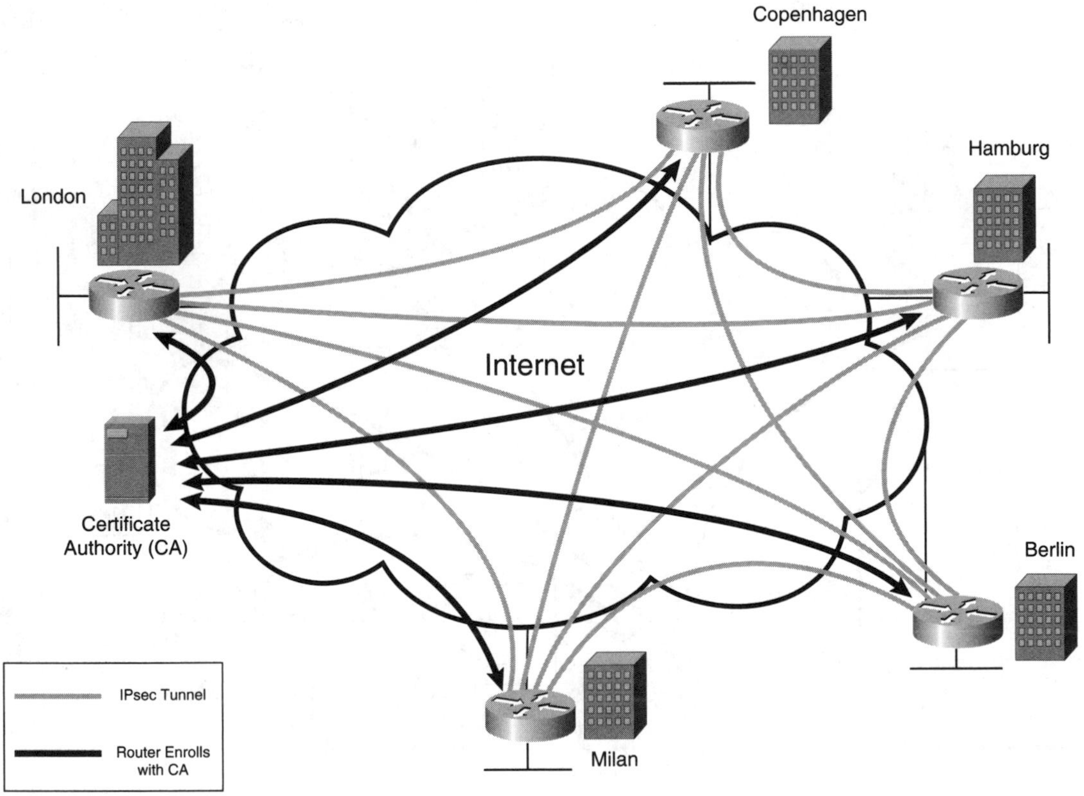

Figure 7-14 illustrates the addition of a new gateway to a fully meshed VPN with digital signature authentication.

The Paris gateway is added to the IPsec VPN in Figure 7-14. Before the Paris gateway can establish IPsec tunnel with existing gateways in the VPN, it just has to enroll with the CA and obtain a certificate.

You might be asking yourself, "If digital signature authentication is so much more scalable than either preshared key or encrypted nonce authentication, why not use it in all IPsec VPNs deployments, both large and small?" The answer to this question is that digital signature authentication requires a Public Key Infrastructure (PKI), and the deployment of a PKI can be complex.

Figure 7-14 *Addition of New Gateway to Fully Meshed IPsec VPN with Digital Signature Authentication*

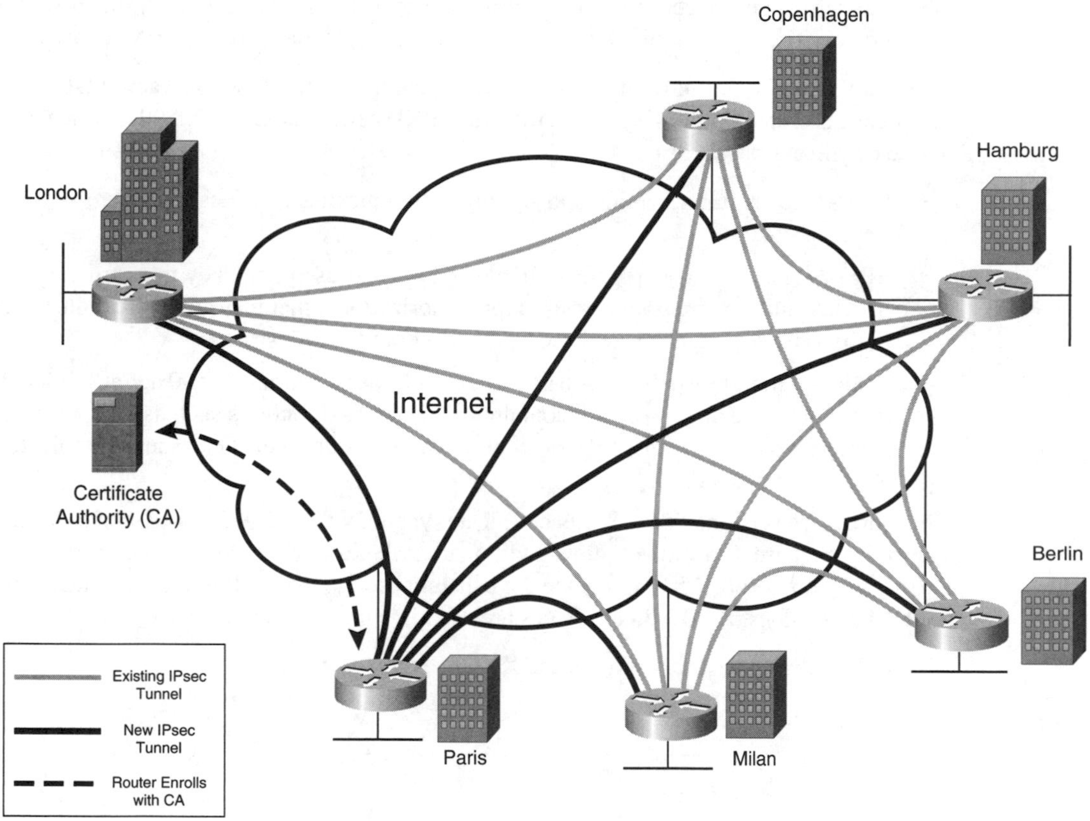

Background to PKI Deployment

Before considering the deployment of a PKI, it is essential to examine (in more detail) some of the background for a PKI, including the following:

- X.509 certificates
- Certificate revocation
- PKI components
- PKI trust models commonly deployed with IPsec VPNs

These elements are discussed in the sections that follow.

X.509 Certificates

A digital certificate is a certificate in electronic form that binds an end-entity identity with a public key. The end entity in question could, for example, be an IPsec VPN gateway.

There are several types of (digital) certificates, including Pretty Good Privacy (PGP) certificates, Simple Public Key Infrastructure (SPKI) certificates, and X.509 certificates. These certificate standards can be described as follows:

- **PGP**—A way of encrypting and signing e-mail messages or files for secure transmission.

- **SPKI**—A set of standards for a simple and easy-to-use public key infrastructure. SPKI certificates are primarily used for authorization rather than authentication. SPKI has not, however, gained wide acceptance within the industry.

- **X.509**—Originally defined as part of the X.500 specifications. X.500 defines a global, distributed directory structure containing the names of entities such as computers, printers, and people. In a PKI, an X.500 directory stores certificates and Certificate Revocation Lists (CRL).

There are three versions of the X.509 certificate. Versions 1 and 2 X.509 certificates lacked flexibility because they did not allow additional attributes to be included. Version 3 certificates, on the other hand, include the capability to include additional attributes in the form of extensions. X.509v3 certificates are used in conjunction with IPsec.

Figure 7-15 illustrates the format of the X.509 version 3 certificate.

Figure 7-15 *X.509 Version 3 Certificate*

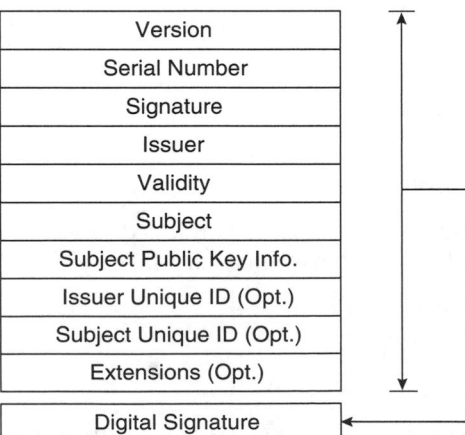

The fields of the X.509v3 certificate can be defined as follows:

- **Version**—The version of X.509 certificate, here 3.

- **Serial Number**—A positive integer that identifies this certificate. The serial number is unique for each certificate issued by a particular CA.

- **Signature**—The algorithm (hash and signature algorithm) used to calculate the digital signature that is appended to the certificate. A common combination is the SHA-1 hashing algorithm and the RSA encryption algorithm (remember that a signature is an encrypted hash).

- **Issuer**—A unique Distinguished Name (DN) that identifies the issuer of the certificate (a CA). A DN is a hierarchical name composed of a number of attributes such as e-mail address (E or EA), country (C), state or province name (ST), locality (L), organization (O), organizational unit (OU), and common name (CN).

Figure 7-16 shows some example DNs.

Figure 7-16 *Example DNs*

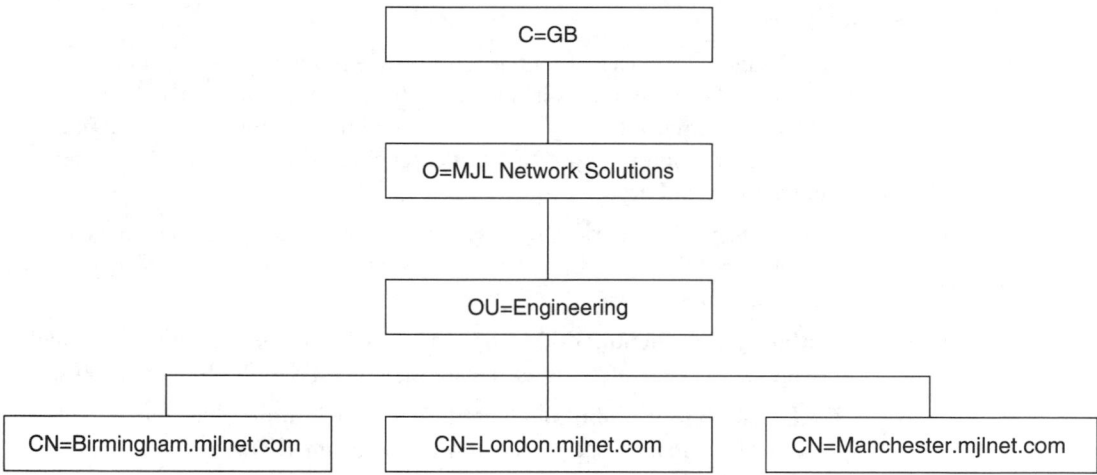

The DNs for the three entities shown in Figure 7-16 are C=GB, O=MJL Network Solutions, OU=Engineering, CN=Birmingham.mjlnet.com; C=GB, O=MJL Network Solutions, OU=Engineering, CN=London.mjlnet.com; and C=GB, O=MJL Network Solutions, OU=Engineering, CN=Manchester.mjlnet.com, respectively.

- **Validity**—The period during which the certificate can be considered valid, unless the certificate has been revoked. The Validity field includes a sequence of two dates and times—the date/time when the certificate's validity begins, and the date/time when certificate's validity ends. These times are represented as universal time coordinated (UTC) time (Zulu or Greenwich mean time), or generalized time (a standard ASN.1 type for variable-precision representation of time).

RFC3280 specifies that UTC time must be used for validity periods up to the year 2049, and generalized time for validity periods from the year 2050.

- **Subject**—This field contains the DN of the entity associated with the public key carried in this certificate (the certificate owner). The subject name may also be carried in the subjectAltName extension.

- **Subject Public Key Info**—This field carries the public key and identifies the algorithm used with key (including the modulus [bit length]). Examples of algorithms include RSA and DSA.

- **Issuer Unique Identifier**—This optional field is carried only in Versions 2 and 3 certificates and ensures that the issuer can still be uniquely identified even if an issuer name in the Issuer field is reused.

- **Subject Unique Identifier**—This optional field is also carried only in Versions 2 and 3 certificates, and ensures that the subject can still be uniquely identified even if a name in the Subject field is reused.

- **Extensions**—Extensions are optional, and can only be included when using Version 3 certificates. There are a large number possible extensions, including the following:

  — **Key Usage**—Defines restrictions to the usage of the key included in the certificate. Possible usages include encipherment (encryption) and digital signature (signing). If a key can be used for either encipherment or digital signatures, the **show crypto ca certificates** command shows the Key Usage field as General Purpose.

  — **Subject Key Identifier**—Uniquely identifies a certificate that contains a particular public key. This extension is useful when a certificate owner possesses several keys.

  — **Authority Key Identifier**—Identifies a public key corresponding to a particular private key. This identifier is used when an issuer has multiple signing keys.

  — **CRL Distribution Point(s)**—Identifies how CRL information can be obtained (where an IPsec VPN gateway can get a CRL).

  — **Authority Information Access**—Indicates how to obtain CA information and services such as online validation services. If you are using the Online Certificate Status Protocol (OCSP) for certificate revocation status checks in your IPsec VPN, the OCSP Responder (server) is specified in this field.

  — **Subject Alternative Name**—Alternative names that are bound to the subject of the certificate. Examples of alternative names include DNS name, IP address, and e-mail address.

- **Digital Signature**—Algorithm ID and encrypted hash (signature) of the certificate data.

  End-entity certificates are signed by the certificate issuing CA (the CA encrypts a hash of the certificate using its private key). The root CA signs its own certificate.

  Algorithms used to calculate the hash of certificates include SHA-1.

Okay, that is the theory. Figures 7-17 and 7-18 show a certificate issued to an IPsec VPN gateway (as seen on the certificate issuing CA).

Figure 7-17   *Certificate Issued to a Gateway (First Half)*

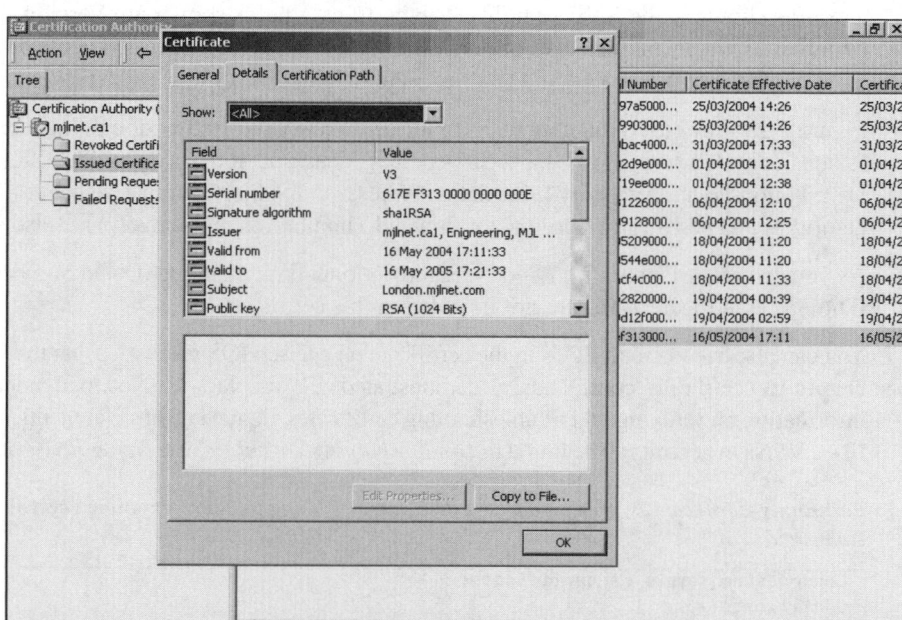

Figure 7-18   *Certificate Issued to a Gateway (Second Half)*

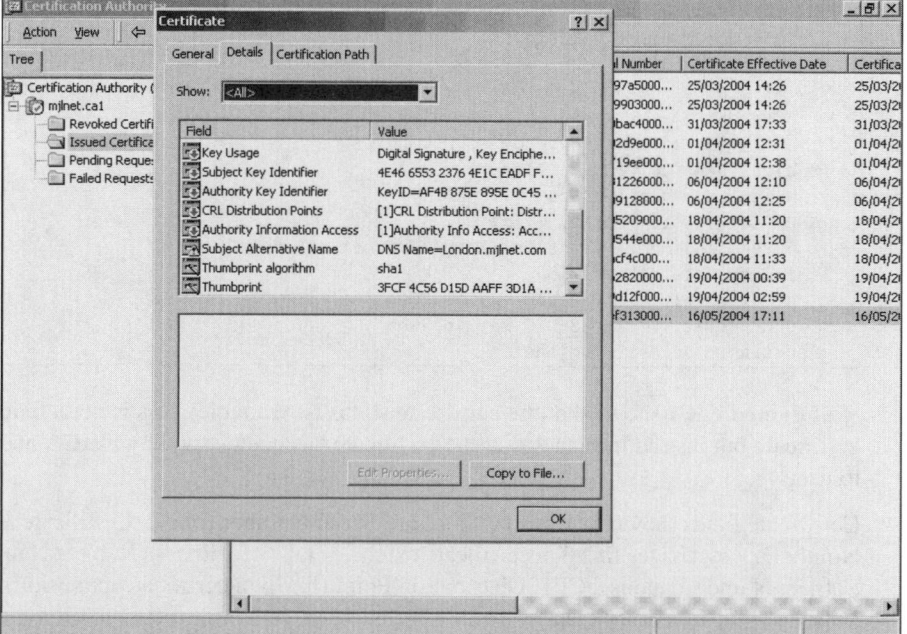

Figure 7-17 shows the first half of the certificate issued to a gateway called London.mjlnet .com (as shown in the Subject field). The certificate fields shown are Version, Serial Number, Signature (algorithm), Issuer, Validity (shown as its two constituent parts, Valid from, and Valid to), Subject, and (Subject) Public Key (Info).

Figure 7-18 shows the remaining fields of the certificate issued to London.mjlnet.com. Fields (extensions) shown are Key Usage, Subject Key Identifier, Authority Key Identifier, CRL Distribution Points, Authority Information Access, and Subject Alternative Name. The hash algorithm and hash (Thumbprint algorithm and Thumbprint, respectively) are also shown.

As you can see in Figures 7-17 and 7-18, the optional Issuer Unique ID and Subject Unique ID fields (see Figure 7-15) are not included in this certificate.

You can also view certain fields in the certificate on a Cisco IOS gateway using the **show crypto ca certificates** commands, as demonstrated in Example 7-13. Note that much more information on verifying and troubleshooting certificates, digital signature authentication, and IPsec VPNs in general can be found in *Troubleshooting Virtual Private Networks* (Cisco Press).

Example 7-13 *End-Entity Certificate as Seen on a Cisco IOS Gateway Using the* **show crypto ca certificates** *Command*

```
London#show crypto ca certificates
Certificate
  Status: Available (line 1)
  Certificate Serial Number: 617EF31300000000000E (line 2)
  Key Usage: General Purpose (line 3)
  Issuer: (line 4)
    CN = mjlnet.ca1
    OU = Engineering
    O = MJL Network Solutions
    L = London
    ST = none
    C = UK
    EA =<16> admin@mjlnet.com
  Subject Name Contains: (line 5)
    Name: London.mjlnet.com
  CRL Distribution Point: (line 6)
    http://mjl-certsrv-acs/CertEnroll/mjlnet.ca1.crl
  Validity Date: (line 7)
    start date: 16:11:33 UTC May 16 2004
    end   date: 16:21:33 UTC May 16 2005
  Associated Identity: mjlnetca
```

Highlighted line 1 shows that the certificate status is Available. This is not a field in the certificate but instead indicates that the certificate has been issued by the CA and is ready to use.

Certificate fields shown in Example 7-13 are Serial Number (line 2, Certificate Serial Number), Key Usage (line 3, a certificate extension), Issuer (line 4), Subject Name (line 5, Subject Name Contains), CRL Distribution Point (line 6, a certificate extension), and Validity (line 7, Validity Date).

Certificate Revocation

Although certificates are valid for the period specified in their Validity field, it is possible for them to be revoked before their validity period ends.

Certificates can be revoked for a number of reasons, including the following:

- The private key corresponding to the public key contained within the certificate has been compromised. This might occur if an unauthorized person gained access to an entity.

- The CA that issued the certificate has been compromised.

- The affiliation of the entity has changed. If the entity were a network device, this would, for example, happen when a division of company that owned the network device was sold to another company.

When certificates are revoked, this information must be communicated to end entities so that communications are not compromised. In the case of an IPsec VPN, a gateway performing RSA digital signature authentication (during IKE negotiation) checks whether the certificate of its peer has been revoked. If the peer's certificate has been revoked, and the gateway is able to access this information, IKE authentication fails.

Because certificates are revoked on the CA, there must be some mechanisms that allow end entities to access certificate revocation information. Two popular mechanisms that allow end entities to access this information are as follows:

- **CRLs**—Signed lists of revoked certificates.

- **OCSP**—End entities verify the status of a certificate on-the-fly by querying a device known as an OCSP Responder.

The two sections that follow discuss CRLs and OSCP.

CRLs   CAs can periodically make CRLs available to end entities. In an IPsec VPN, IPsec peers either download these CRLs and cache them, or download them as needed during IKE negotiation. It is also possible for a CA to delegate the issuance of CRLs to a trusted authority. In this case, the CRL is called an indirect CRL.

A complete CRL is a list of all revoked certificates within a particular scope. The scope of a CRL usually conforms to all those certificates issued by a particular CA but may include certificates issued by multiple CAs. Delta CRLs may also be issued. These list only those certificates whose status has changed since the issuance of the last complete CRL.

To ensure that certificate revocation information contained within a CRL is fresh, one important consideration is the frequency that CRLs are published. If the CRL is published once a week, for example, it is possible for IPsec devices with revoked certificates to establish IPsec tunnels with other devices for up to one week after their certificates have been revoked. In sensitive environments, it is important to ensure that CRLs are published at sufficiently short intervals such that the risk of devices with revoked certificates establishing IPsec tunnels is reduced as much as possible.

There are two CRL versions. Version 1 CRLs have a number of drawbacks, including a lack of flexibility. Version 2 CRLs address the drawbacks of version 1 CRLs. Figure 7-19 illustrates the format of a version 2 CRL.

Figure 7-19 *Version 2 CRL Format*

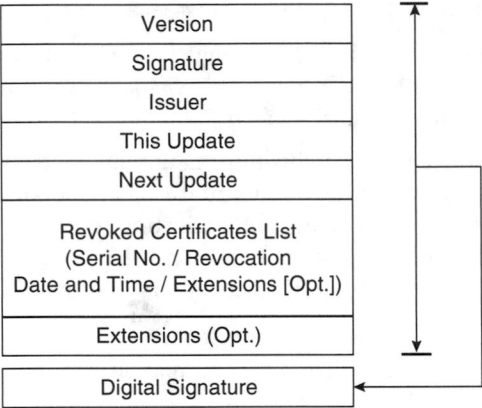

The fields of the version 2 CRL are as follows:

- **Version**—Describes the version of the CRL (2).
- **Signature**—Algorithm ID for algorithm used to digitally sign the certificate.
- **Issuer Name**—DN of the entity that signed and issued this CRL. As previously mentioned, this entity is usually a CA.
- **This Update**—The issue date of this CRL. This is represented as either UTC time or generalized time.
- **Next Update**—The date before which the next CRL will be issued.
- **Revoked Certificates**—This field is present only if one or more certificates have been revoked. If one or more certificates have been revoked, each revoked certificate's serial number is listed here, along with the date/time when the certificate was revoked.

In version 2 CRLs, optional extensions containing additional information may be included for each *entry* in the list of revoked certificates.

CRL entry extensions include the following:

— **(CRL) Reason Code**—The reason that the certificate was revoked. Possible reasons include key compromise, CA compromise, a change of affiliation of the entity, the certificate having been superseded, and a temporary certificate hold (suspension).

— **Invalidity Date**—The date on which it is known or suspected that a certificate or (private) key associated with the certificate became invalid or was compromised. This may be earlier than the date that the certificate was actually revoked.

- **Extensions**—Extensions to the CRL *as a whole* rather than a particular entry in the CRL. These extensions allow additional information to be included with the CRL. Possible extensions include the following:

— **Authority Key Identifier**—Allows the end entity to identify the correct public key associated with the private key that a CRL issuer used to sign the CRL. This is important when there are multiple public keys corresponding to a CRL issuer (when it has multiple public/private key pairs).

— **Issuer Alternative Name**—Alternative names for the issuer of the CRL. Types of alternative name include e-mail address, IP address, and DNS name.

— **CRL Number**—An increasing sequence number that allows end entities to easily determine when one CRL supersedes another.

Figure 7-20 shows a version 2 CRL (on the publishing CA).

Figure 7-20 *Version 2 CRL*

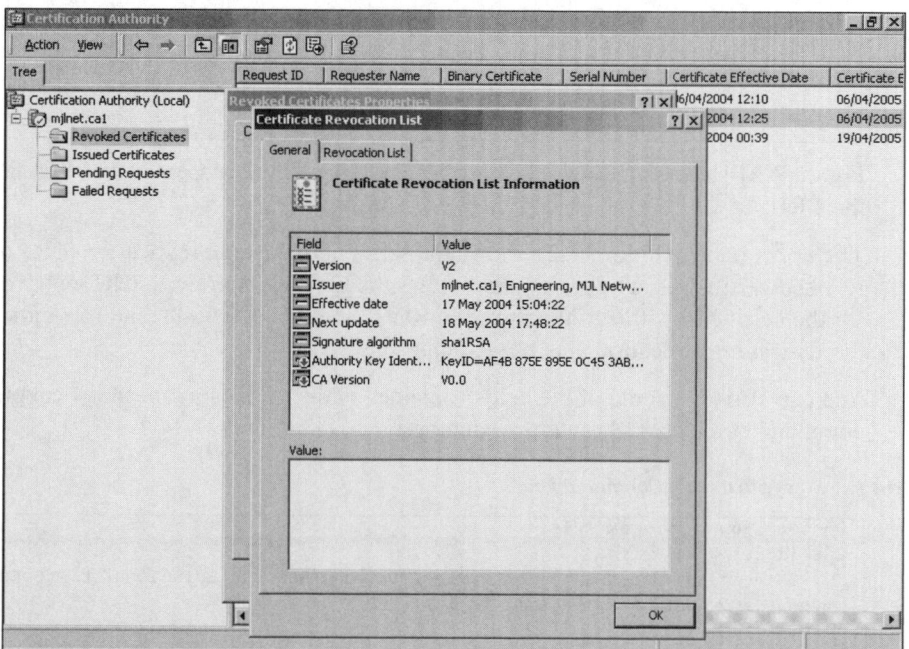

In Figure 7-20, you can see the Version, Issuer, This Update (Effective Date), Next Update, Signature (algorithm), and two extensions to the CRL (Authority Key Identifier and CA Version). Note that CA Version is a Microsoft-specific extension that specifies how many times the CA has been renewed and how many signing keys the CA possesses.

Figure 7-21 shows the individual CRL entries in the Revoked Certificates List field of the CRL.

Figure 7-21 *Individual CRL Entries*

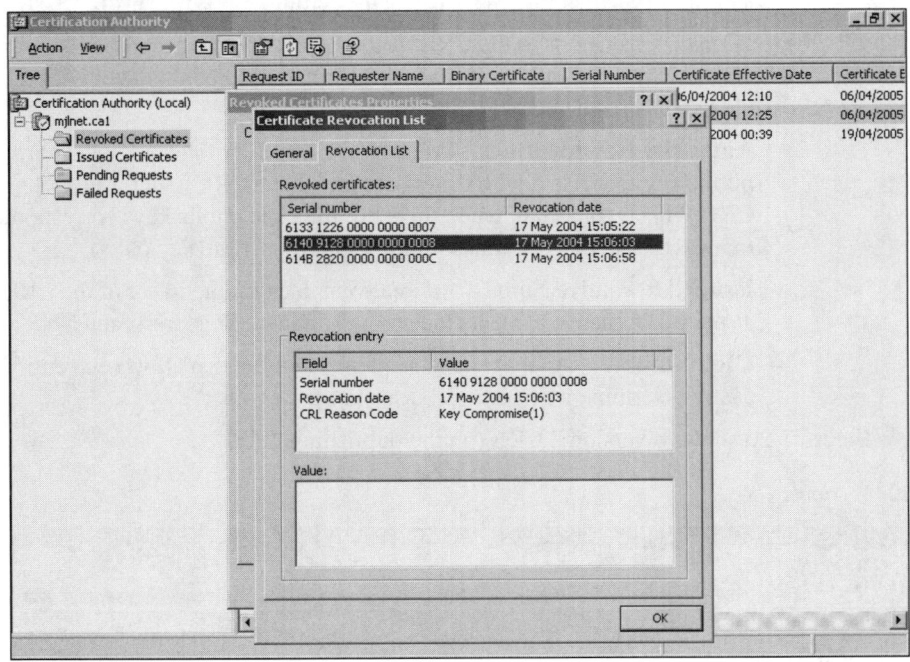

Figure 7-21 shows three revoked certificates in the Revoked Certificates List field of the CRL.

The upper pane in Figure 7-21 shows the serial numbers and revocation dates of the revoked certificates. The lower pane shows the CRL Reason Code CRL entry extension for the certificate with serial number 6140 9128 0000 0000 0008, and this indicates that the reason for revocation was Key Compromise.

You can also view some of the fields contained in the CRL using the **show crypto ca crls** command on Cisco IOS routers, as demonstrated in Example 7-14.

Example 7-14 show crypto ca crls *Command Output*

```
London#show crypto ca crls
CRL Issuer Name: (line 1)
    CN = mjlnet.ca1, OU = Engineering, O = MJL Network Solutions, L = London, ST
= none, C = UK, EA =<16> admin@mjlnet.com
```

Example 7-14 show crypto ca crls *Command Output (Continued)*

```
      LastUpdate: 14:04:22 UTC May 17 2004 (line 2)
      NextUpdate: 16:48:22 UTC May 18 2004 (line 3)
      Retrieved from CRL Distribution Point: (line 4)
        http://mjl-certsrv-acs/CertEnroll/mjlnet.ca1.crl
  London#
```

Highlighted line 1 shows the Issuer (CRL Issuer Name) field of the CRL. Lines 2 and 3 then show the Last Update and Next Update fields of the CRL. Finally, line 4 shows the CRL Distribution Point (CDP) from which the CRL was obtained.

Online Certificate Status Protocol (OCSP)   As previously mentioned, end entities can verify the status of a certificate by querying an OCSP Responder.

The OCSP Responder can be either the CA that issued the certificate in question or another authorized Responder designated by the CA. If you are use an authorized Responder, this device must hold a special certificate issued by the CA that indicates that this device is authorized to issue OCSP responses on behalf of the CA.

To find out the status of a certificate, an OCSP client (an end entity such as an IPsec VPN gateway) sends an OCSP Request message to the OCSP Responder. The Responder replies with an OCSP Response message. The Request message indicates the certificate for which revocation status is required, and the Response message indicates one of three statuses:

- **Good**—The certificate has not been revoked.
- **Revoked**—The certificate has been revoked (either permanently or temporarily [the certificate status is "on hold"]). If the private key for a particular CA has been compromised, the OCSP Responder may also indicate a revoked status for all certificates issued by that CA.
- **Unknown**—The OCSP Responder does not know about the certificate.

Figure 7-22 illustrates OCSP functionality. In this figure, the London and New York IPsec VPN gateways are negotiating IKE phase 1. During IKE phase 1, London and New York exchange certificates. At this point, they both request the revocation status of the other's certificate by sending an OCSP Request message to the OCSP Responder. The OCSP Responder informs London of the status of New York's certificate, and New York of the status of London's certificate using OCSP Response messages. Assuming that each IPsec VPN gateway receives an OCSP Response message indicating that the status of its peer's certificate is Good, IKE negotiation can continue, and an IPsec tunnel can be established between the two peers.

Figure 7-22 *OCSP Functionality*

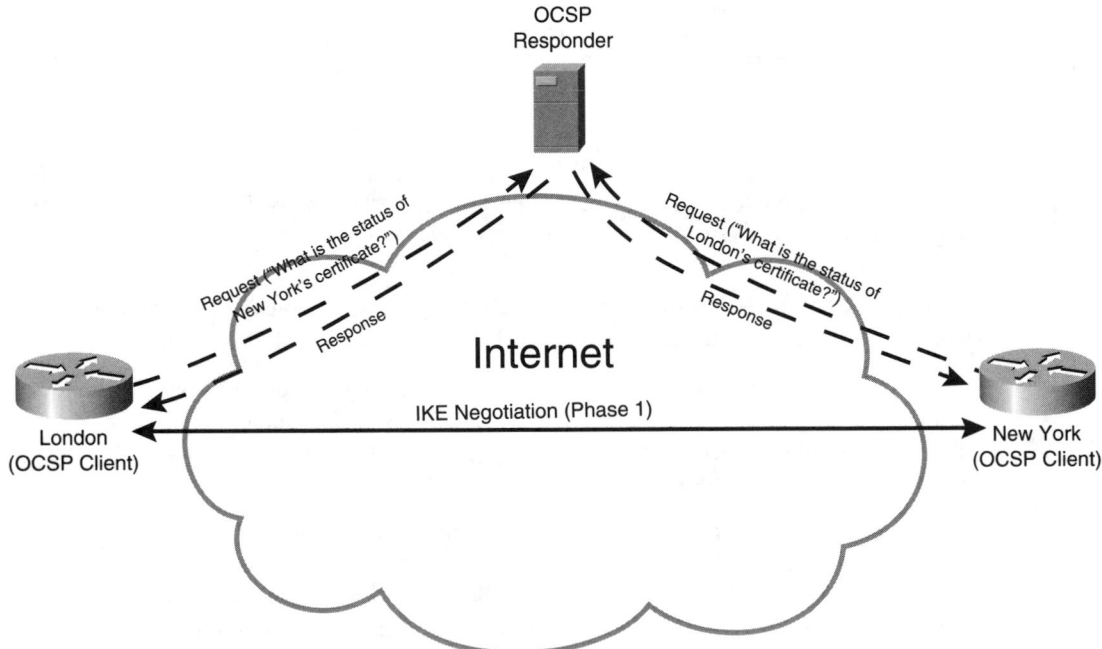

OCSP has a number of important advantages over CRLs, including the following:

- The evaluation of certificate validity is centralized on the OCSP Responder. When you are using CRLs, each IPsec peer must download a CRL or CRLs and locally evaluate the status of certificates received from IPsec peers.

- Certificate revocation status obtained using OCSP is fresh (assuming that the OCSP Responder has access to current certificate revocation information). The information contained in CRLs, on the other hand, can often be stale. The extent to which the information contained in a CRL is stale depends on the frequency that the CA publishes the CRL.

- The amount of network bandwidth required to verify a certificate's status using OCSP is insignificant. CRLs can grow to be large, and the amount of network bandwidth that is required to allow an end entity to download a CRL can become significant.

OCSP is particularly useful in environments, such as those involving financial transactions, where the freshest possible certificate revocation information in required.

PKI Components

IKE digital signature authentication requires the deployment of a PKI. But what does a PKI consist of exactly? As the name suggests, a PKI consists of all the infrastructure elements or components necessary to enable public key security services in a network and allow automated identification, authentication, access control, and authorization. In an IPsec VPN, the PKI allows devices such as gateways (called *end entities* in PKI terminology) to authenticate each other, and help to ensure the integrity and confidentiality of data as it transits the network.

The PKI components include the following:

- End entities
- CA
- Registration authority (RA)
- Certificate repository
- CRL issuer

NOTE   It is possible for a single system to fulfill the responsibilities of more than one of the PKI components listed above (with the exception of end entities).

Figure 7-23 illustrates the relationship of the various PKI components to each other.

Figure 7-23 *Relationship of PKI Components to Each Other*

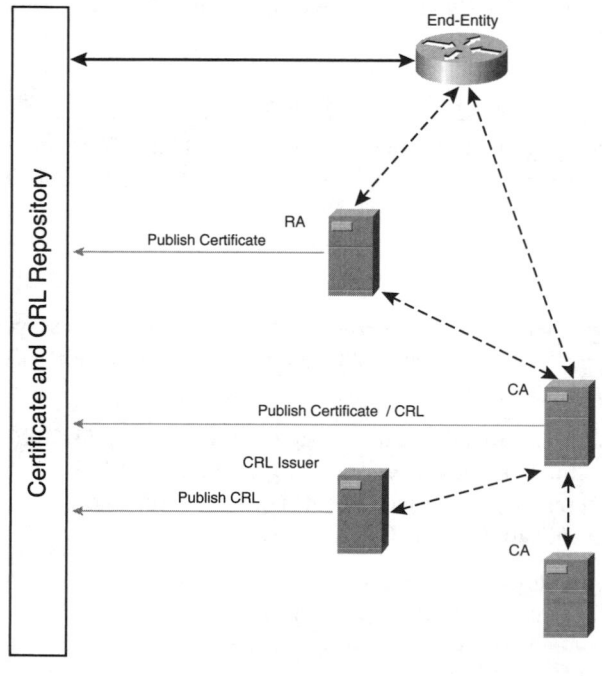

The sections the follow discuss the PKI components in greater detail.

End Entity
An end entity is a user or subject of a certificate. So, in an IPsec VPN, IPsec VPN gateways are all end entities (assuming they are using IKE digital signature authentication).

Certificate Authority (CA)
A CA is responsible for certifying an association of an entity identity (name) with a public key. This association is carried in a digital certificate, and a CA certifies this association by digitally signing the certificate. What a CA is doing by signing a certificate is saying, "I certify that this public key corresponds to (is owned by) this identity (entity)."

The important thing to remember about CAs and digital certificates is that the end entities in a PKI trust a CA, and because a CA certifies the association of entity identity and public key in certificates, entities also trust these certificates. So, if an IPsec VPN gateway trusts a certain CA, it also trusts certificates issued (and signed) by that CA.

Digital certificates are analogous to passports. Because immigration personnel around the world trust the passport agency that has issued your passport, they also (after they are satisfied that it is genuine) trust the identity given in your passport (name and so on).

Figure 7-24 illustrates an end entity (IPsec VPN gateway) enrolling with a CA and obtaining a certificate using SCEP.

NOTE   SCEP relies on Public Key Cryptography Standards (PKCS) #7 and #10. PKCS#7 provides a general syntax for data that may have cryptography applied to it, and PKCS#10 provides a syntax for certification requests.

In Figure 7-24, the Hamburg gateway sends a SCEP certificate enrollment request message to the CA. Note that the Hamburg gateway has already obtained the CA's certificate at this point (via HTTP Get and Response messages).

In this example, the CA is configured to manually authenticate the end entity, and so the CA responds to the certificate enrollment request from Hamburg with a PENDING response message. This PENDING response message indicates that the certificate enrollment request is awaiting authentication by the CA administrator.

The Hamburg gateway periodically polls the CA using GetCertInitial messages, and the CA replies to these polling messages by sending PENDING response messages.

Figure 7-24   *An End Entity Enrolls with a CA Using SCEP*

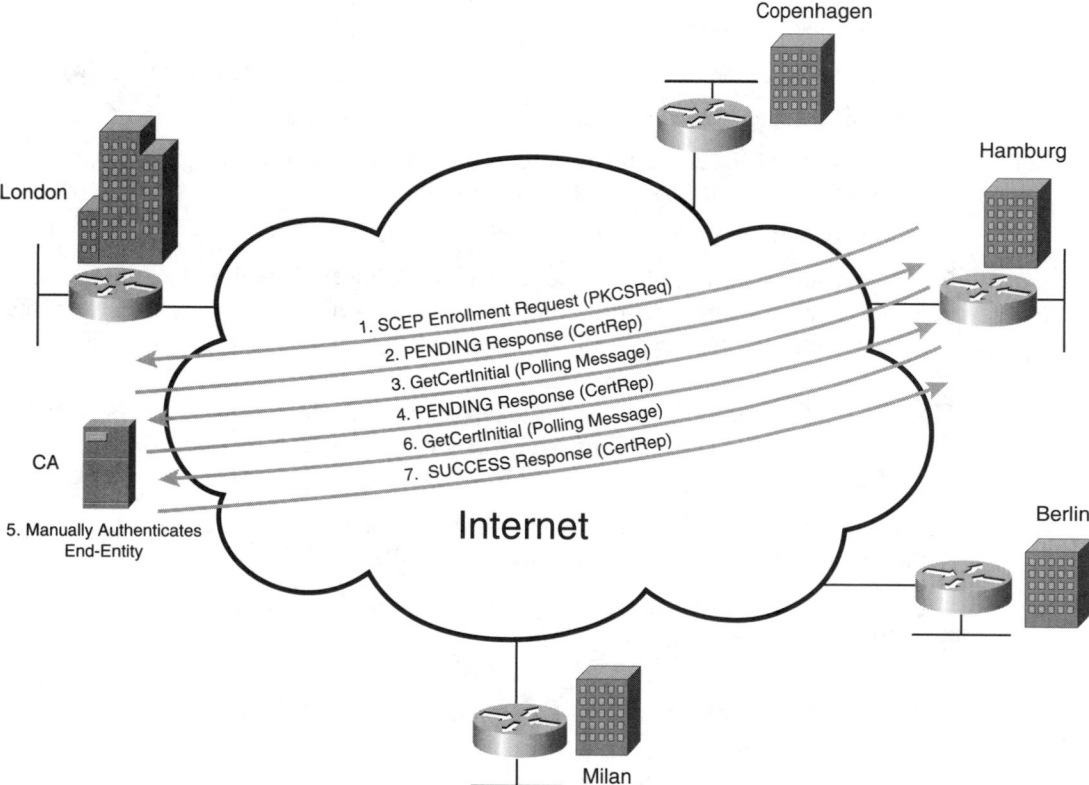

The CA administrator then manually authenticates the certificate enrollment request from Hamburg (which could be done by calling the Hamburg gateway administrator, for example), and when the Hamburg gateway next polls the CA, the CA now replies with a SUCCESS message. This SUCCESS message contains the Hamburg gateway's certificate signed by the CA.

It is worth noting that the CA can also be configured to automatically approve certificate requests, in which case the SCEP certificate enrollment request message sent by the Hamburg gateway in Figure 7-24 would simply be followed by a SUCCESS message sent by the CA. Also, if the certificate enrollment request is rejected, the CA can send a FAILURE message (rather than a SUCCESS message).

Other important responsibilities of the CA include reissuing certificates when they expire and revoking certificates that have become invalid.

Registration Authority (RA)   An RA is an optional component of a PKI to which some of the functions of the CA can be delegated. Functions that may be delegated to the RA include the following:

- Initial verification of the identity information supplied by the end entity
- Authentication of the end entity via a challenge password
- Verifying that the end entity is in possession of the private key corresponding to the public key submitted (Proof of Possession [POP])
- Initiation of end-entity certification with the CA

It is important to note that an RA is never responsible for the issuance of certificates or CRLs. Also, a human may perform some of the RA's functions such as verification of the end entity's identification, especially in a high-security environment.

Certificate Repository   A certificate repository is an online system (or systems) that is responsible for storing certificates and CRLs. End entities can then obtain certificates and CRLs from this repository.

Certificate repositories often consist of a distributed database accessed via protocols such as the Lightweight Directory Access Protocol (LDAP) or SCEP.

The location of the certificate repository can be indicated via certificate extensions such as the CRL Distribution Point (CDP).

CRL Issuer   A CRL issuer is an optional system to which the CA delegates the publishing of CRLs.

PKI Trust Models Commonly Deployed with IPsec VPNs

A PKI is a trust infrastructure. An end entity trusts a CA and therefore also trusts certificates signed by that CA (as long as those certificates have not been revoked). Figure 7-25 illustrates this simple trust model.

In Figure 7-25, the Berlin and Hamburg gateways enroll with CA1, and each obtain a signed certificate. Berlin and Hamburg then want to set up an IPsec tunnel, and so negotiate IKE. During IKE negotiation, Berlin and Hamburg exchange certificates, and because each trusts CA1, they also trust each other's certificates (because they are signed by CA1).

Figure 7-25 *Simple PKI Trust Model*

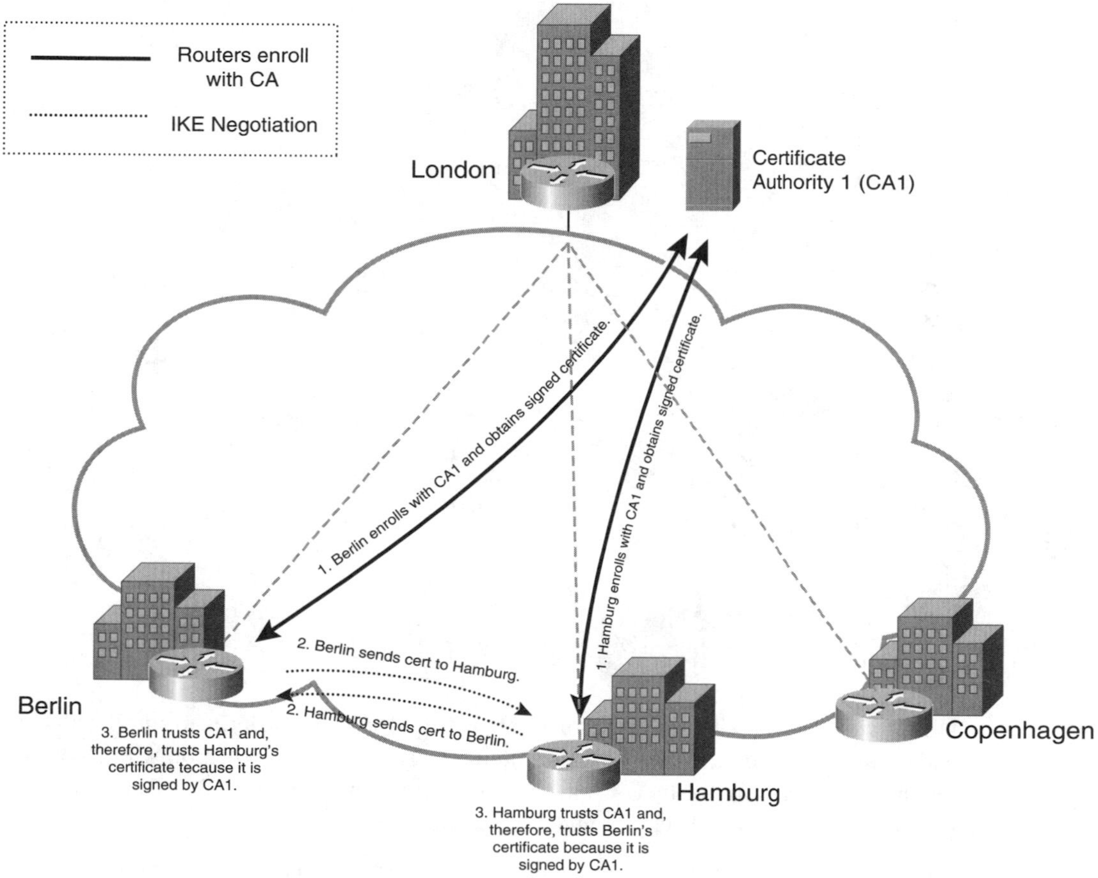

So far so good, but what happens if peer IPsec gateways are enrolled with different CAs? Figure 7-26 illustrates this situation.

In Figure 7-26, Berlin enrolls with CA1 and obtains a certificate signed by CA1. Leipzig enrolls with CA2 and obtains a certificate signed by CA2.

Berlin and Leipzig then commence IKE negotiation, and exchange certificates. Unfortunately, Berlin rejects Leipzig's certificate because it is signed by CA2 and Berlin has no trust relationship with CA2. Similarly, Leipzig rejects Berlin's certificate because it has no trust relationship with CA1.

Figure 7-26 *Peer IPsec VPN Gateways Are Enrolled with Different CAs*

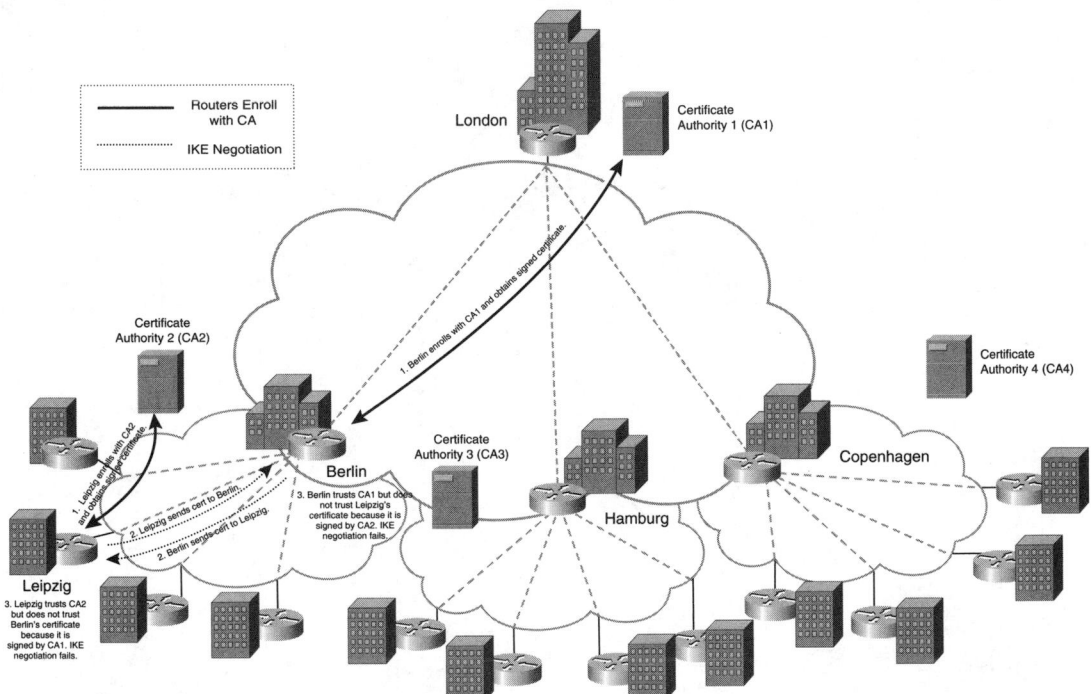

Hmm? How can this situation be resolved? One way would be for Berlin to enroll with CA2 and obtain a certificate signed by CA2. Alternatively, Leipzig could enroll with CA1 and obtain a certificate signed by CA1. In Cisco IOS Software Release 12.2(2)T and later, it is possible for a gateway to support multiple certificates.

So, in Figure 7-26, you could, for example, enroll Berlin with CA2 in addition to CA1. Berlin could then establish IPsec tunnels with other gateways enrolled with CA1 or other gateways enrolled with CA2 (including Leipzig). In certain situations, such as extranet topologies, support for multiple certificates is useful, but there is a simpler solution to the situation shown in Figure 7-26.

If you reexamine Figure 7-26, you will notice that the problem is one of trust—Berlin does not trust CA2 and Leipzig does not trust CA1. One way of getting round this problem, however, is to get CA1 and CA2 to trust each other. In this case, Berlin would trust Leipzig's certificate because the CA that it is enrolled with (CA1) would trust CA2. Also, Leipzig would trust Berlin's certificate because the CA it is enrolled with (CA2) would trust CA1.

To get CA1 and CA2 to trust each other you can cross-certify the two CAs. Figure 7-27 illustrates this trust relationship.

Figure 7-27 *Cross-Certification of CAs*

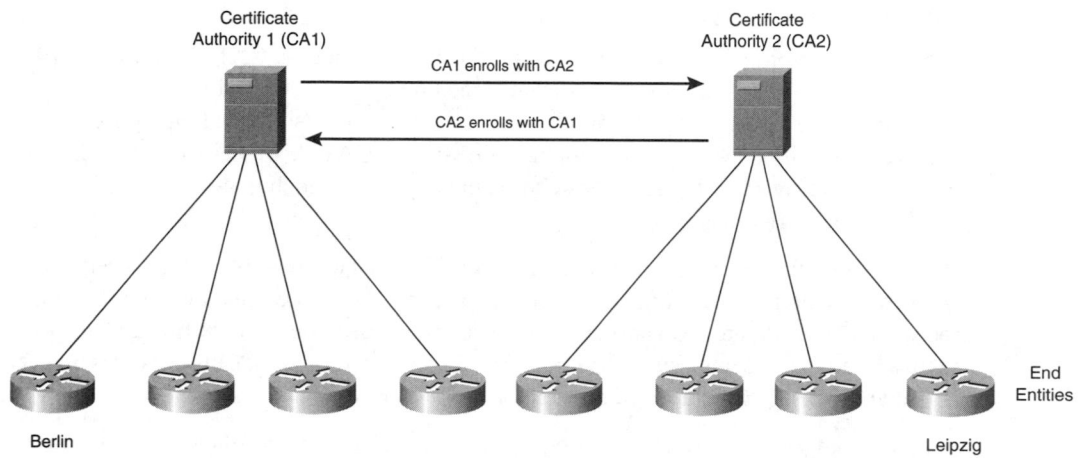

In Figure 7-27, CA1 and CA2 enroll with each other and are therefore cross-certified. Because the CAs are cross-certified, the end entities enrolled with each of the CAs then trust the certificates of end entities enrolled with the other CA. So, in Figure 7-27, Berlin would trust Leipzig's certificate and vice-versa.

Figure 7-28 illustrates cross-certified CAs deployed in an IPsec VPN.

Figure 7-28 *Cross-Certified CAs Deployed in an IPsec VPN*

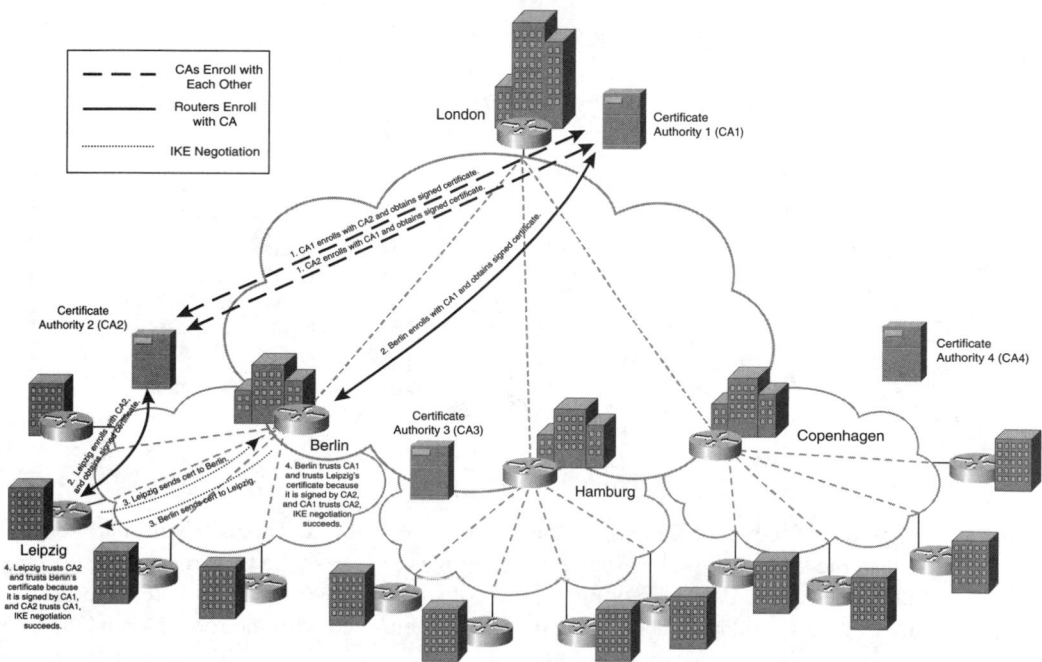

In Figure 7-28, CA1 and CA2 enroll with each other and obtain signed certificates (they are cross-certified).

Berlin then enrolls with CA1 and obtains a certificate signed by CA1. Similarly, Leipzig enrolls with CA2 and obtains a certificate signed by CA2. Berlin and Leipzig exchange certificates during IKE negotiation. Berlin trusts CA1, and also trusts Leipzig's certificate because it is signed by CA2, which in turn is trusted by CA1. Also, Leipzig trusts CA2, and also trusts Berlin's certificate because it is signed by CA1, which in turn is trusted by CA2. IKE negotiation succeeds.

So, cross-certification would also work, in theory. Note that it is possible for cross-certification to be used within a single organization or department, but more often than not it is used between CAs in different organizations or departments. Because cross-certification involves a trust relationship being established right across organizations, or departments, this model should only be deployed after careful consideration of its implications.

Another way to enable Berlin and Leipzig to trust each other's certificates is to create a *subordinated* CA hierarchy (also called a *strict* CA hierarchy). In a cross-certification model, CAs enroll with each other, and neither CA is subordinate to the other. In a subordinated hierarchy, however, there is a single *root* CA, and other CAs in the hierarchy are subordinate to that root CA.

Figure 7-29 illustrates a subordinated CA hierarchy.

Figure 7-29 *Subordinated CA Hierarchy*

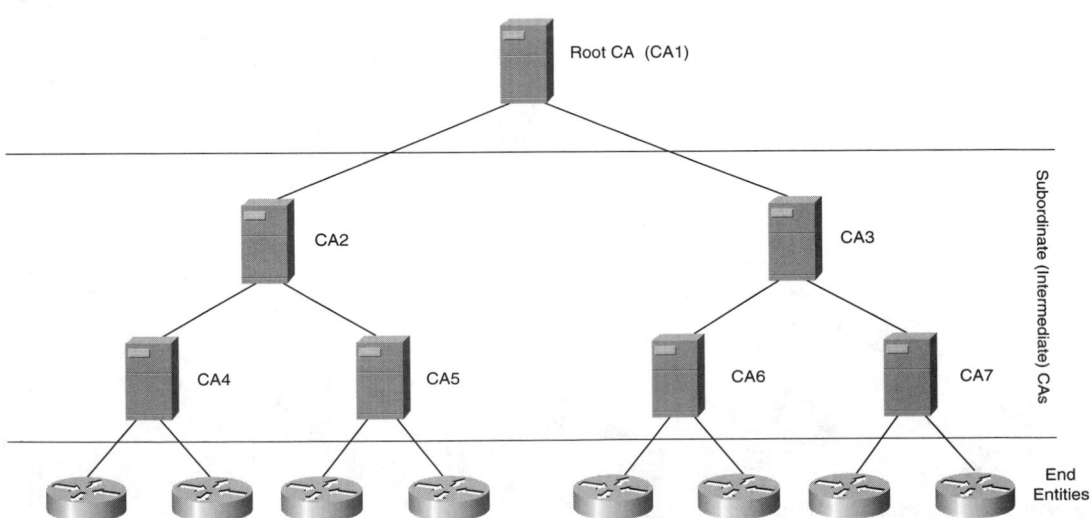

At the top of the subordinated CA hierarchy is the root CA. This is the ultimate source of trust in the hierarchy, and as such it is sometimes known as the trust root or trust anchor. Below the root CA are zero or more levels of subordinate (or intermediate) CAs. The subordinate CAs directly below the root CA are enrolled with the root CA, and the CAs below that level are enrolled with the CAs directly below the root CA. Finally, at the bottom level of the hierarchy, there are the end entities. The end entities are enrolled with the CAs directly above them in the CA hierarchy.

Figure 7-30 illustrates a subordinated CA hierarchy deployed with an IPsec VPN.

Figure 7-30 *Subordinated CA Hierarchy Deployed in an IPsec VPN*

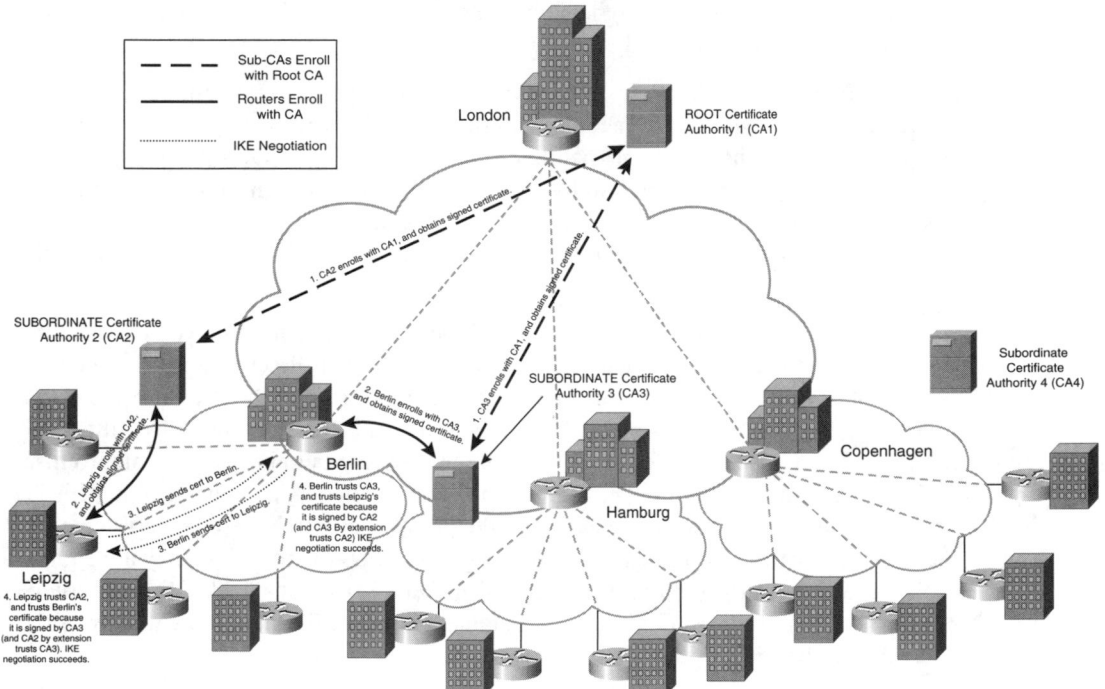

In Figure 7-30, CA2 and CA3 enroll with and obtain certificates from root CA, CA1. CA2 and CA3 are now in a position to issue certificates to end entities (or even other CAs in the next level of the CA hierarchy). In this case, there are no CAs below CA2 and CA3 in the CA hierarchy, and so CA2 and CA3 issue certificates to end entities.

Berlin and Leipzig now enroll with and obtain certificates from CA3 and CA2, respectively. After they have obtained their certificates, Berlin and Leipzig begin IKE negotiation and exchange certificates. Berlin trusts Leipzig's certificate because it was issued by CA2, a CA whose certificate was issued in turn by CA1. Berlin trusts CA1 because Berlin's certificate was issued by CA3, whose certificate was issued in turn by CA1. So, in other words, Berlin trusts Leipzig's certificate because there is an extended trust relationship between CA3 and CA2 via CA1. Leipzig trusts Berlin's certificate because there is again an extended trust relationship between CA2 and CA3 via CA1.

In simple terms, Berlin says to Leipzig, "I trust you (and your certificate) because your certificate was issued by CA2 and CA2 is trusted by CA1 (CA1 issued CA2's certificate).

My own certificate was issued by CA3, which in turn trusts CA1. So, if CA1 trusts CA2 (which issued your [Leipzig's] certificate), and CA3 trusts CA1, your (Leipzig's) certificate is good enough for me." Leipzig (if it could speak!) would say something similar to Berlin.

Although there are only two levels of hierarchy in CA hierarchy shown in Figure 7-30, it is (theoretically) possible to have as many levels in the hierarchy as you like. So, CA2 and CA3 could issue certificates to other subordinate CAs, and they in turn could either issue certificates to other CAs or end entities.

In a subordinated CA hierarchy, one advantage is that you can take the root CA off line—either physically disconnect it from the network, or power it down, or both. The root CA is only responsible for issuing certificates to *directly* subordinated CAs (that is, CAs in the next level of hierarchy), not to end entities. So, in Figure 7-30, the root CA will issue certificates only to CA2 and CA3 (and CA4). It is possible for the root CA to issue certificates to end entities, but that breaks the strict hierarchy, so it is not a good idea.

After the root CA has issued certificates to directly subordinate CAs, you can take it off line until it needs to issue another certificate to another directly subordinate CA. Being able to take the root CA off line is important because of the nature of the trust relationships in a subordinated CA hierarchy—in a subordinated hierarchy, all trust relationships rely on the root CA. If the root CA's private (signing) key is compromised, and all certificates issued by the root CA and subordinate CA become invalid. This is because a hacker/cracker in possession of the private key can issue fake certificates that are indistinguishable from genuine certificates issued by the root CA (they are signed with the genuine but compromised root CA's private key). So, a hacker/cracker could easily issue him- or herself with a certificate and build an IPsec tunnel with any of the gateways in the IPsec VPN.

A compromise of the root CA's private key is the most disastrous scenario, but a compromise of the private key of any of the subordinate CAs would compromise the certificates of any subordinate CAs and end entities below *that* CA (only). If you refer back to Figure 7-29, the compromise of CA2's private key, for example, would compromise the certificates of CA4, CA5, and all the end entities enrolled with CA4 and CA5. The certificates of CA1, CA3, CA6, CA7, and all end entities enrolled with CA6 and CA7 would, however, not be affected if the private key of CA2 were compromised.

Because of the risk of compromise of the private keys of CAs, CA private keys are often protected using a Hardware Security Module (HSM). An HSM is separate device that provides physical isolation and tamper protection for the CA's private key(s).

Before finishing this section, it is worth emphasizing that the PKI trust model is completely independent of the network topology. So, it is possible to deploy a subordinated CA hierarchy in a full-mesh (nonhierarchical) IPsec VPN.

Deploying the PKI for an IPsec VPN: Considerations

Now that you understand the background to a PKI, it is time to take a brief look at some of the considerations that you must make *before* deploying a PKI for your IPsec VPN. Considerations include the following:

- Whether the present *or* predicted future size of your IPsec VPN would justify the use of IKE digital signature authentication and the associated deployment of a PKI.

  When considering whether to use IKE digital signature authentication, and deploying a PKI, one consideration is the size of your present IPsec VPN as well as the potential size of your future IPsec VPN. If the VPN consists of *or* will in the future consist of more than a few gateways, preshared key and encrypted nonce IKE authentication might not be viable (for administrative reasons).

- Whether security considerations would justify the use of IKE digital signature authentication and the associated deployment of a PKI.

  As you already know, preshared key IKE authentication is not as secure as digital signature authentication, especially when using weak preshared keys. Security considerations may dictate that you use digital signature authentication and deploy an associated PKI.

- The choice of hardware and software to support your PKI.

  Cisco gateways support a wide range of CAs, but the choice of software and hardware for your PKI (hardware/software for RA/CAs) can be bewildering.

- Whether the setup and administration of your PKI should be insourced or outsourced.

  If the IT staff do not have the time or the expertise to deploy and support a PKI, you might consider outsourcing this. However, the outsourcing of a PKI requires that your organization be satisfied with an associated (partial) loss of control and security of your VPN.

- What PKI trust model you should deploy.

  There a number of PKI trust models, but which one should you deploy? The subordinated hierarchical model described in the previous section is the most commonly deployed and works well in support of an IPsec VPN.

- Whether the PKI used to support IKE digital signature authentication for your IPsec VPN should be dedicated for this purpose only or should be part of the overall organization's PKI (encompassing e-mail security and so on).

  Although the PKI used to support an IPsec VPN can be part of a larger overall PKI, many organizations choose to deploy a separate dedicated PKI for the VPN. By choosing to deploy a separate, dedicated PKI, you can simplify administration and help to ensure security of the VPN.

Simplifying PKI Deployment with the IOS Certificate Server

The deployment of a PKI can be complex. One way to simplify its deployment is to configure a Cisco IOS Software certificate server.

The Cisco IOS certificate server was introduced in Cisco IOS Software Release 12.3(4)T and has a number of advantages, including the following:

- It provides a basic PKI in support of IKE digital signature authentication in an IPsec VPN.
- It simplifies the choice of hardware and software for a PKI.

    The Cisco IOS certificate server is an integrated component of Cisco IOS Software Release 12.3(4)T and later. Support for this feature on a particular router platform can be verified using the Cisco IOS Feature Navigator (login required):

    http://tools.cisco.com/ITDIT/CFN/jsp/index.jsp

- It eases the requirement to retrain IT staff or outsource deployment and administration of a PKI

    Assuming that IT staff are already familiar with the Cisco IOS command-line interface, it is a simple task to train them to deploy and administer a Cisco IOS certificate server.

- It provides support for a subordinated CA hierarchy

    The initial release of the Cisco IOS certificate server in Cisco IOS Software Release 12.3(4)T supported only one level of CA hierarchy (see Figure 7-29). Support for additional levels of hierarchy was added in Cisco IOS Software Release 12.3(14)T.

- It provides a dedicated PKI for the IPsec VPN.

You must consider a number of tasks when deploying a Cisco IOS certificate server, including the following:

- Determining the Cisco IOS certificate server deployment model
- Configuring the Cisco IOS certificate server
- Administrating the Cisco IOS certificate server

The following three sections examine these tasks in detail.

Determining the Cisco IOS Certificate Server Deployment Model

Before you can deploy a Cisco IOS certificate server, you must decide whether you want to configure it as an integrated element of an IPsec VPN gateway or to deploy it as a separate device.

In the case of a small VPN (with a small number of certificates, and therefore a small CRL), it is possible to deploy the Cisco IOS certificate server as an integrated element of an IPsec VPN gateway.

When deployed in a small hub-and-spoke IPsec VPN, the Cisco IOS certificate server is typically deployed as an integrated element of a hub site gateway. If the VPN is full mesh, the Cisco IOS certificate server can potentially be deployed as an integrated element of any of the IPsec VPN gateways.

The choice of which Cisco IOS router to use as the certificate server depends largely on the (free) CPU and memory capacity of the routers in the VPN. You should always ensure that the Cisco IOS certificate server is deployed on a router with plenty of spare memory and CPU capacity (the router is relatively lightly loaded) and that this router is easily accessible from all of the gateways in the IPsec VPN. You should also take into account additional bandwidth requirements at the site where the certificate server is deployed, particularly if there are a large number of IPsec VPN gateways and the CRL grows to a large size.

Assuming that files (including the CRL) are stored locally, the router configured as the Cisco IOS certificate server will not only need to be available to issue certificates to new gateways and to renew existing gateways' certificates, but also to provide the CRL to gateways when they negotiate IKE and need to verify the revocation status of peer gateways' certificates.

Figure 7-31 illustrates the deployment of an integrated Cisco IOS certificate server in a small-scale IPsec VPN.

Figure 7-31 *Deploying a Cisco IOS Certificate Server as an Integrated Element of an IPsec VPN Router*

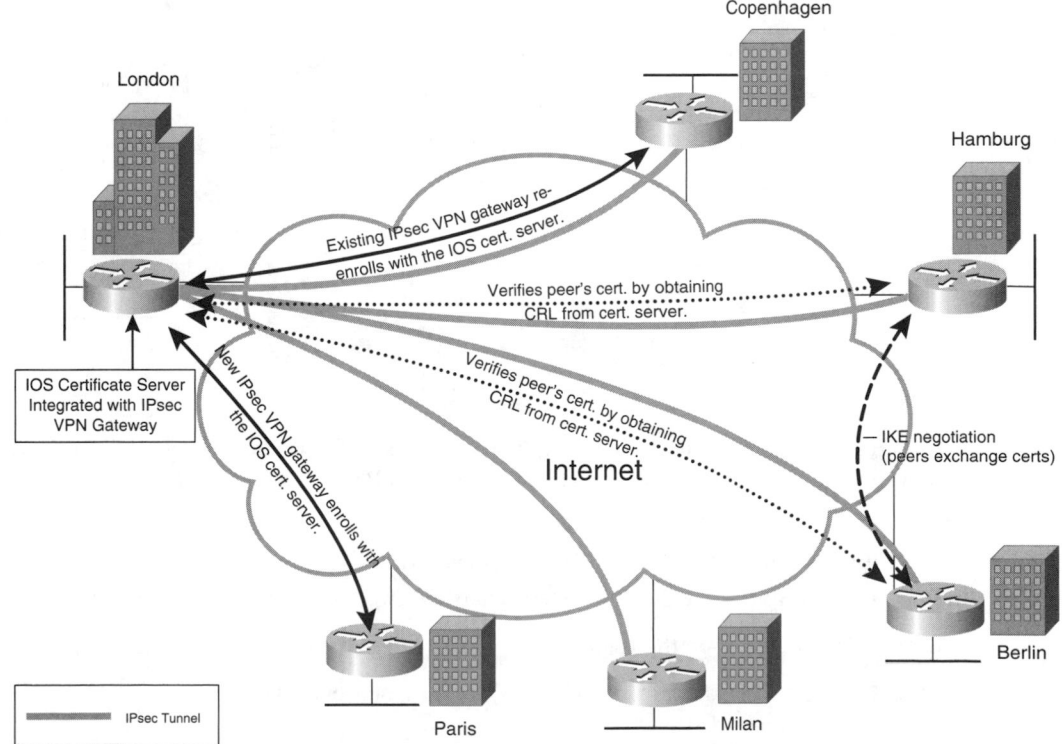

As illustrated in Figure 7-31, an integrated Cisco IOS certificate server needs to be able to enroll new gateways, re-enroll existing gateways, and make a CRL available to gateways negotiating IKE and verifying the revocation status of peer gateways' certificates.

The alternative to deploying a Cisco IOS certificate server as an integrated element of an IPsec VPN gateway is to deploy a Cisco IOS certificate server as a separate dedicated device, as illustrated in Figure 7-32.

Figure 7-32 *Deploying a Cisco IOS Certificate Server as a Separate Device in an IPsec VPN*

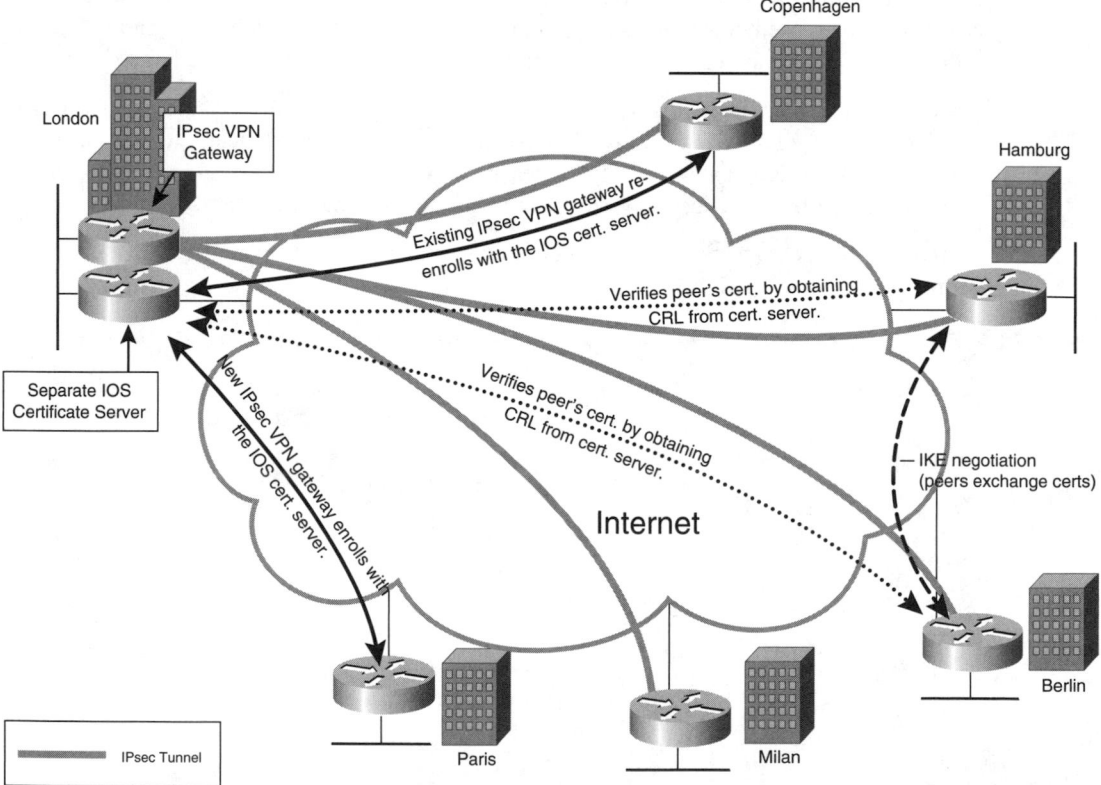

In Figure 7-32, a separate device is deployed as a Cisco IOS certificate server. Deployment of a separate device ensures that the hub site IPsec VPN gateway is not too heavily loaded.

Configuring a Cisco IOS Certificate Server

Basic configuration of a Cisco IOS certificate server consists of the following seven steps:

Step 1 Set the time on the router.

Step 2 Generate and export the Cisco IOS certificate server key pair (recommended).

Step 3   Configure the HTTP server (recommended).

Step 4   Configure the Cisco IOS certificate server's database parameters.

Step 5   Configure certificate attributes.

Step 6   Specify the CRL lifetime.

Step 7   Enable the Cisco IOS certificate server.

The following seven sections describe the configuration of a Cisco IOS certificate server.

Step 1: Set the Time on the Router

The first step in the configuration of the Cisco IOS certificate server is to set the time. You can either set the clock using the **clock set** command or you can configure the Network Time Protocol (NTP).

The **clock set** command should only be used if your router has a hardware clock, because otherwise the time will be lost whenever the router is reloaded. Configuration of NTP is discussed in detail in the section "Setting the Time on IPsec VPN Gateways Using NTP" in Chapter 6. Note that you cannot enable a Cisco IOS certificate server if you have not first set the time on the router.

Finally, it is a good idea to set the time zone using the **clock timezone** and **clock summer-time** commands.

Step 2: Generate and Export the Cisco IOS Certificate Server Key Pair (Recommended)

After you have set the time, the next step is to generate and export the Cisco IOS certificate server's public/private key pair, as demonstrated in Example 7-15.

Example 7-15 *Generating the Cisco IOS Certificate Server's Key Pair*

```
London(config)#crypto key generate rsa general-keys label mjlnetca modulus 2048
  exportable
The name for the keys will be: mjlnetca
% The key modulus size is 2048 bits
% Generating 2048 bit RSA keys ...[OK]
London(config)#exit
London#
```

In the highlighted line, the **crypto key generate rsa general-keys label** *key-label* **modulus** *modulus* **exportable** command is used to generate a public/private keys pair for the Cisco IOS certificate server with a modulus of 2048 bits.

The *key-label* parameter is used to specify a label for the key pair, and the **exportable** keyword ensures that the **exportable** flag is set and that the key pair can be backed up. In the event that the Cisco IOS certificate server fails catastrophically, the backed-up key pair can be used to re-create the certificate server on another Cisco IOS router.

Recommended best practice dictates that you should specify a modulus of at least 1024 bits for the certificate server's key pair. Remember the certificate server's private key is used to sign the certificates that it issues to end entities (gateways), and the key modulus dictates the security of that signature.

You can then verify the RSA key pair using the **show crypto key mypubkey rsa** command, as shown in Example 7-16.

Example 7-16 *Verifying the RSA Key Pair*

```
London#show crypto key mypubkey rsa
% Key pair was generated at: 19:22:28 UTC May 22 2004
Key name: mjlnetca
 Usage: General Purpose Key
 Key is exportable.
 Key Data:
  30820122 300D0609 2A864886 F70D0101 01050003 82010F00 3082010A 02820101
  00C7E22A AB04B6BB 5A6AEF00 89DBC028 FD1F92DF 63376ABB 09D7B1A7 8EAED052
  1E990469 2AECF141 62DCD3D7 2C7C51E3 EE3D5196 1317B3EC F990C7DF 8A5430E7
  EF96171B B5DA9C09 65802EA9 A4703266 10CF52A6 141EC102 070976B3 1BC745E6
  B0390D84 4BD6EA88 E74011FE 3FB5B6FF A4AD3DE7 7F381646 CEBE37EB C1D201DC
  4DB0E7F3 86604680 ECB2AB14 4FB217CB 6A91906B FC2DCD08 0745C3EE 8E38A3BB
  C012C706 862E4C8C 0769D607 3B3E79C9 8FB47F17 F0BBDFDD 9844F1E2 CA63C9D2
  DAC83351 48101112 EA002934 49679B7E E29C7B48 B4EE84CC B6E6C19A 6624A4B8
  F5091652 0FA1E84C AF84CDF8 87F55DEB 82638A09 96758ED8 547FBA5D BE35E4A1
  BD020301 0001
% Key pair was generated at: 19:22:30 UTC May 22 2004
```

As you can see in the highlighted line, the key pair is marked as exportable, allowing it to be backed up.

After the key pair has been generated, you can back it up to a variety of locations, including a Flash memory card, an FTP server, and a TFTP server, using the **crypto key export rsa** *key-label* **pem url** *url* {**3des** | **des**} *passphrase* command. This command backs up the keys pair in a Privacy Enhanced Mail (PEM) format, to a specified location (URL), encrypted using the specified algorithm (either DES or 3DES) with the specified passphrase. Note that PEM (base64) format is just an ASCII form of the original binary certificate.

Note that it is not mandatory to manually generate a public/private key pair (as shown in Example 7-15), but if you do not, when you enable the Cisco IOS certificate server (Step 3) the router will automatically generate a 1024-bit key pair that is not exportable.

Example 7-17 demonstrates exporting the key pair to a Flash disk.

Example 7-17 *Exporting the RSA Key*

```
Router(config)#crypto key export rsa mjlnetca pem url disk0: 3des mjlnetvpn (line 1)
% Key name: mjlnetca
 Usage: General Purpose Key
Exporting public key...
Destination filename [mjlnetca.pub]? (line 2)
Writing file to disk0:mjlnetca.pub
Exporting private key...
Destination filename [mjlnetca.prv]? (line 3)
Writing file to disk0:mjlnetca.prv
```

Highlighted line 1 in Example 7-17 shows that the RSA key pair is encrypted using 3DES with the passphrase mjlnetvpn, and exported to Flash disk 0. The key label identifies the key pair to export (in this example, mjlnetca), which must be the same as that specified when generating the key pair using the **crypto key generate rsa general-keys label** *key-label* **modulus** *modulus* **exportable** command.

Highlighted lines 2 and 3 show the destination filenames of the public and private keys, respectively. For the reasons previously described, you should ensure that the certificate server's private key is stored securely.

Step 3: Configure the HTTP Server (Recommended)   Now that the key, pair has been backed up, you can move on to configuring the HTTP server, as shown in Example 7-18.

Example 7-18 *Configuring the HTTP Server*

```
London#conf t
London(config)#ip http server
London(config)#exit
London#
```

The **ip http server** command in the highlighted line is used to enable the HTTP server on the router.

The **ip http server** command is essential if you want to allow certificate enrollment requests from end-entity routers to be transmitted to the certificate server using SCEP (which operates over HTTP). If you do not configure the HTTP server on the certificate server, end entities can only enroll with the certificate server manually using PKCS#10.

Step 4: Configure the Cisco IOS Certificate Server's Database Parameters   The next step is to configure certificate server database parameters, as demonstrated in Example 7-19. The certificate server database stores information related to certificates issued by the certificate server.

Example 7-19 *Configuring the Cisco IOS Certificate Server's Database Parameters*

```
London#conf t
London(config)#crypto pki server mjlnetca (line 1)
London(cs-server)#database url tftp://10.10.10.9 (line 2)
London(cs-server)#database level complete (line 3)
London(cs-server)#database username mjlnet password cisco (line 4)
```

The **crypto pki server** *cs-label* command in line 1 is used to enter certificate server configuration mode. The *cs-label* must exactly match the *key-label* specified in the **crypto key generate rsa general-keys label** *key-label* **modulus** *modulus* **exportable** (shown in Example 7-15).

In line 2, the **database url** *root-url* command is used to specify the location to which certificate server database entries (including certificates issued to end entities) will be written. In this example, certificate server database entries will be written to a TFTP server at IP address 10.10.10.9.

CAUTION   Make sure that if you do specify an external server as the location for database files that this server is reachable from the Cisco IOS certificate server. If the external server is unreachable, you will be unable to enable the Cisco IOS certificate server (see Step 7).

The certificate database can be located on any file system support by the router (for example, FTP, TFTP, and Flash), but you should ensure that the file system specified can support (potentially) a large number of read and write operations and has sufficient storage for a large number of certificates (assuming a large number of IPsec routers in the VPN).

If you choose to locate the database on an external server, seriously consider configuring an IPsec tunnel between the Cisco IOS certificate server and the external server to protect communications with that external server.

Although storing certificate server database files on an external server is attractive, carefully consider all the advantages and disadvantages of doing this.

Advantages of storing database files on an external server include the fact that there is generally a greater amount storage space available and the fact that files can be backed up periodically using the server's regular backup processes.

Disadvantages of storing database files on an external server include the fact that if the server is unavailable (off line) and the **revocation-check crl none** or **crl optional** commands are *not* configured on IPsec VPN gateways, IKE phase 1 negotiation may fail between these peers (and IPsec tunnel will not be established). Note, however, that if the server is unavailable and the **revocation-check crl none** or **crl optional** commands are configured on IPsec VPN routers, IPsec VPN routers with revoked certificates may be able to negotiate IKE phase 1 and establish IPsec tunnels with other IPsec VPN routers. For more information on the **revocation-check** command, see the section "Step 4: Declare the Certificate Authority (CA)" in Chapter 6.

The next command (shown in line 3) is **database level {minimal | names | complete}**. This command dictates the form of information written to the certificate server database.

If the minimal level is specified using the **database level minimal** command, a minimum amount information is written to the database. This minimum amount of information consists of a file named *cs-label*.ser, which holds the serial number of the previously issued certificate.

If the names level is specified using the **database level names** command, the subject names in human-readable and distinguished encoding rules (DER) form (a way of encoding certificate fields) as well as serial numbers of certificates are written to the database in files named *cs-label*.cnm. Subject names and serial numbers are necessary for administrators to locate a specific certificate in the database and revoke it, if required. Certificate expiration dates and certificate states (valid or revoked) can also be written to the *cs-label*.cnm file.

Finally, if the complete level is specified using the **database level complete** command, complete certificates are written to the database. In this case, each certificate is stored in binary form in an individual file named *certificate-serial-number*.cer. Depending on the number of certificates issued, the complete level can potentially cause a large number of files to be written to the database storage location.

The complete level should be specified only if the database location is an external database (such as an FTP or TFTP sever), it is anticipated that only a small number of certificates will be issued (that there will only be a small number of IPsec routers in the VPN), or the local router file system has a great deal of spare file system memory capacity and the file system can support a large number of write operations.

In line 4, the **database** {**username** *username* | **password** *password*} command is used to specify a username and password to access the certificate database. This protects against an attacker who attempts to modify the .ser and .crl files in the database. If these files are illegally modified or deleted, the Cisco IOS certificate server may stop issuing certificates.

The username and password specified using the **database** {**username** *username* | **password** *password*} command are no substitute, however, for good server security and an IPsec tunnel to protect communications between the Cisco IOS certificate server and an external database server. Note that the username and password specified in highlighted line 4 are not secure and are used for illustrative purposes only!

Step 5: Configure Certificate Attributes
After the certificate server database has been configured, you can begin to configure certain attributes of the certificates that the Cisco IOS certificate server will issue.

Example 7-20 shows configuration of certificate attributes. Note that certificate attributes are specified in certificate server configuration mode.

Example 7-20 *Configuring Certificate Attributes*

```
London(cs-server)#issuer-name C=GB, O=MJL Network Solutions, OU=Engineering,
  CN=mjlnetca.mjlnet.com (line 1)
London(cs-server)#lifetime ca-certificate 1825 (line 2)
London(cs-server)#lifetime certificate 365 (line 3)
London(cs-server)#cdp-url http://mjlnetcrlrepos.com/mjlnetca.crl (line 4)
```

The DN of the issuer (the Cisco IOS certificate server itself) is specified in line 1 using the **issuer-name** *DN-string* command. The issuer DN is included in the issuer field of the X.509 certificates issued by the certificate server. For more information on DNs, see the section, "X.509 Certificates" earlier in this chapter.

The lifetime of the certificate server's X.509 certificate is then specified using the **lifetime ca-certificate** *days* command. The default lifetime of the certificate server's certificate is 1095 days (3 years) and can be from 1 to 1825 days (5 years). The lifetime specified using this command is used to derive the Validity field of the certificate server's own X.509 certificate.

Note that the certificate server's certificate will be self-signed if the Cisco IOS certificate server is a root CA.

The next step is to specify the lifetime of X.509 certificates issued by the certificate server to gateways (or other CAs) using the **lifetime certificate** *days* command (line 3). The lifetime specified using this command is used to derive the Validity field of certificates issued by the certificate server.

Finally, the location of the CRL distribution point (CDP) is specified using the **cdp-url** *url* command. Because of the additional overhead that would otherwise be required on the Cisco IOS certificate server, if you are deploying a large-scale IPsec VPN you should specify an external server using this command. If you do not specify a CDP using this command, the X.509 certificate CDP extension will not be included in certificates issued to end entities, but (assuming that the HTTP server is configured) Cisco IOS IPsec gateways will be able to obtain the CRL via SCEP from the Cisco IOS certificate server. The CRL, whether stored locally on the Cisco IOS certificate server or on an external server, has the file name *cs-label*.crl.

Other information contained in other fields in the X.509 certificates issued to end entities (or CAs) is specified by the end entities (or CAs) themselves during certificate enrollment.

For more information on X.509 certificate fields, see the section "The X.509 Certificates" earlier in this chapter.

Step 6: Specify the CRL Lifetime
Next, you should specify the lifetime of the CRL issued by the Cisco IOS certificate server using the **lifetime crl** *hours* command, as shown in Example 7-21. Again, this command is specified in certificate server configuration mode.

Example 7-21 *Configuring the CRL Lifetime*

```
London(cs-server)#lifetime crl 72
```

In Example 7-21, a CRL lifetime of 72 hours (3 days) is specified, and so the Cisco IOS certificate server will publish a new CRL every 72 hours. The default CRL lifetime is 168 hours (1 week), and the maximum lifetime that can be specified is 336 hours (2 weeks).

As previously mentioned, the CRL publishing interval (CRL lifetime) is a key consideration when configuring your certificate server. It is possible for an IPsec VPN gateway with a revoked certificate to build IPsec tunnels to other IPsec VPN gateways during the period between the revocation of its certificate and the time at which the next CRL is published.

Step 7: Enable the Cisco IOS Certificate Server

The configuration of the Cisco IOS certificate server is now complete, and it can be enabled using the **no shutdown** command in certificate server configuration mode, as shown in Example 7-22.

Example 7-22 *Enabling the Cisco IOS Certificate Server*

```
London(cs-server)#no shutdown
% Once you start the server, you can no longer change some of
% the configuration.
Are you sure you want to do this? [yes/no]: y
!!!!!!!!
Loading mjlnetca.ser from 10.10.10.9 (via FastEthernet3/0): !
[OK - 32 bytes]
Loading mjlnetca.crl from 10.10.10.9 (via FastEthernet3/0): !
[OK - 416 bytes]
% Certificate Server enabled.
London(cs-server)#end
London#
```

In Example 7-22, the Cisco IOS certificate server is enabled using the **no shutdown** certificate server configuration mode command.

After the Cisco IOS certificate server has been enabled, you can verify its configuration and status using the **show crypto pki server** command, as shown in Example 7-23.

Example 7-23 *Using the show crypto pki server Command to Verify Cisco IOS Certificate Server Configuration and Status*

```
London#show crypto pki server
Certificate Server mjlnetca:
    Status: enabled, configured (line 1)
    Issuer name: C=GB, O=MJL Network Solutions, OU=Engineering, CN=mjlnetca (line 2)
    CA cert fingerprint: 40B54845 6984A34E 8CCD75FF 1A6BAE95 (line 3)
    Granting mode is: manual (line 4)
    Last certificate issued serial number: 0x1 (line 5)
    CA certificate expiration timer: 19:24:02 UTC Jul 30 2009 (line 6)
    CRL NextUpdate timer: 19:24:04 UTC Aug 3 2004 (line 7)
    Current storage dir: tftp://10.10.10.9 (line 8)
    Database Level: Complete - all issued certs written as <serialnum>.cer (line 9)
London#
```

In highlighted line 1, you can see that the Cisco IOS certificate server has been enabled. Line 2 shows the issuer DN for certificates issued by this Cisco IOS certificate server. Then in line 3, you can see the fingerprint of the Cisco IOS certificate server's certificate.

The certificate issuing mode is shown in line 4 (in this case, manual). The serial number of the last certificate issued is shown in line 5. In line 6, you can see the date and time at which the Cisco IOS certificate server's own certificate will expire.

Line 7 shows the date and time when the next CRL will be published. The location of the Cisco IOS certificate server's database is shown in line 8. Finally, in line 9, you can see the database level configured on the Cisco IOS certificate server (complete, in this example).

NOTE   The default enrollment URL for a Cisco IOS certificate server is http://*IOS-certificate-server-name-or-IP-address*:80. The *default* enrollment mode is CA (the **enrollment mode ra** command is not required on gateways enrolling with the Cisco IOS certificate server, by default).

The enrollment URL if you enroll from a Cisco VPN 3000 or a Cisco VPN client is http://*IOS-Certificate-server-name-or-IP-address*/cgi-bin/pkiclient.exe

---

Approving, Rejecting, Revoking, and Manually Requesting Certificates

The main responsibility of the certificate server administrator is approving, rejecting, revoking, and manually requesting certificates. These responsibilities are detailed in this section.

Approving and Rejecting Certificate Requests   End entities request certificates from the certificate server during enrollment. The certificate server administrator must either approve or reject those certificate requests.

An administrator can either manually grant SCEP certificate requests or use a preshared to pre-authorize certificate requests.

You can use the **crypto pki server** *cs-label* **grant** {**all** | *transaction-id*} command to manually grant (issue) certificates requested using SCEP. The *cs-label* that you specify must match that used when configuring the certificate server (see Example 7-19). If you specify the **all** keyword with this command, all pending certificate requests will be granted (issued); and if you specify a particular *transaction-id*, only the certificate request associated with the particular transaction ID will be granted.

Before you grant a certificate, you can verify its transaction ID using the **crypto pki server** *cs-label* **info requests** command.

Example 7-24 shows the granting of a certificate using the **crypto pki server** *cs-label* **grant** {**all** | *transaction-id*}.

Example 7-24 *Manually Granting a Certificate Using the* **crypto pki server** *Command*

```
London#crypto pki server mjlnetca info requests (line 1)
Enrollment Request Database:
RA certificate requests:
 ReqID  State      Fingerprint                    SubjectName
 --------------------------------------------------------------
```

Example 7-24 *Manually Granting a Certificate Using the* **crypto pki server** *Command (Continued)*

```
Router certificates requests:
ReqID  State      Fingerprint                        SubjectName
-------------------------------------------------------------------
1      pending    235A10BFCB166B85A96D5CA2E817A5D5
  hostname=Berlin.mjlnet.com (line 2)
London#
London#crypto pki server mjlnetca grant 1 (line 3)
!!!!!!
London#
```

In Example 7-24, the **crypto pki server** *cs-label* **info requests** command is used to verify the transaction ID of a certificate request (see highlighted line 1).

In line 2, you can see that one certificate request from Berlin.mjlnet.com is pending, and it has transaction ID (ReqID) 1.

The **crypto pki server** *cs-label* **grant** {**all** | *transaction-id*} command is then used in line 3 to grant the certificate.

It is also possible to automatically grant all certificate requests by specifying the **grant auto** command in certificate configuration mode, as demonstrated in Example 7-25.

Example 7-25 *Enabling the Cisco IOS Certificate Server*

```
London(config)#crypto pki server mjlnetca
London(cs-server)#grant auto
% This will cause all certificate requests to be automatically granted.
Are you sure you want to do this? [yes/no]: y
London(cs-server)#
```

Be careful when considering the use of the **grant auto** command to ensure that it conforms to your organization's security policy. Remember that if you do choose to use it, any and all certificates requests will be granted—which could lead to a serious security issue if an attacker is able to request a certificate from the certificate server.

If you want to reject a particular certificate request or all pending certificate requests, you can use the **crypto pki server** *cs-label* **reject** {**all** | *transaction-id*} command. Again, the *cs-label* parameter must match that specified when configuring the certificate server. The **all** keyword or *transaction-id* parameter can be used to specify that all pending certificate requests are rejected or that only the certificate request associated with a particular certificate request (*transaction-id*) is rejected.

NOTE   If certificate requests are not granted within an hour, they will expire.

The other method of granting certificate requests is to pre-authorize them using a preshared key (challenge password). In this case, you can use the **crypto pki server** *cs-label*

password generate [*minutes*] command to generate a challenge password that when specified by the end entity during certificate enrollment will ensure that the request is automatically granted by the certificate server. This password is a one-time password (it cannot be used repeatedly) and will ensure only that a certificate is automatically granted if it is used within the time period specified (in minutes). If you use the **crypto pki server** *cs-label* **password generate** [*minutes*] command to generate another password before the previous password is used, the previous password becomes invalid and can no longer be used.

Example 7-26 shows the configuration of the **crypto pki server** *cs-label* **password generate** [*minutes*] command.

Example 7-26 *Configuration of the* **crypto pki server** *Command*

```
London#crypto pki server mjlnetca password generate 60
% New password is 98C5D08456937BA1, valid for 60 minutes
London#
```

The **crypto pki server** *cs-label* **password generate** [*minutes*] command is used in Example 7-26 to generate a password (98C5D08456937BA1) that is valid for 60 minutes.

Revoking Certificates   If for some reason (such as the compromise of an IPsec VPN gateway) a certificate needs to be revoked, you can use the **crypto pki server** *cs-label* **revoke** *certificate-serial-number* command to accomplish this, as shown in Example 7-27. Note that the *cs-label* must again match that specified when configuring the Cisco IOS certificate server, and the certificate serial number must be specified in hexadecimal.

Example 7-27 *Using the* **crypto pki server** *Command to Revoke a Certificate*

```
London#crypto pki server mjlnetca revoke 0x03
!!
London#
```

In Example 7-27, the certificate with serial number 0x03 is revoked.

You can also verify the Cisco IOS certificate server's CRL using the **crypto pki server** *cs-label* **info crl** command (see Example 7-28). The CRL is only published at the interval specified using the **lifetime crl** command (see Example 7-21), and so revoked certificates will not immediately be included on the CRL unless their revocation happens to coincide with the certificate server publishing the CRL.

Example 7-28 *Using the* **crypto pki server** *Command to Verify the Cisco IOS Certificate Server's CRL*

```
London#crypto pki server mjlnetca info crl
Certificate Revocation List:
    Issuer: c=GB,o=MJL Network Solutions,ou=Engineering,cn=mjlnetca
    This Update: 20:35:36 UTC Jul 31 2004
    Next Update: 20:35:36 UTC Aug 3 2004
```

Example 7-28 *Using the* **crypto pki server** *Command to Verify the Cisco IOS Certificate Server's CRL (Continued)*

```
   Number of CRL entries: 1 (line 1)
   CRL size: 438 bytes
Revoked Certificates:
   Serial Number: 0x03 (line 2)
   Revocation Date: 20:35:36 UTC Jul 31 2004 (line 3)
London#
```

Highlighted line 1 shows that there is 1 entry in the CRL, and lines 2 and 3 shows the serial number and revocation date/time of the revoked certificate.

Manually Requesting Certificates   It is possible to manually request certificates for end entities via the Cisco IOS certificate server command line. This is useful if an IPsec VPN gateway is unable to request a certificate using SCEP.

To manually request a certificate via base64-encoded (base64 encodes files into ASCII text format) or a PEM-formatted PKCS#10 certificate request, you can use the **crypto pki server** *cs-label* **request pkcs10** {**url** *url* | **terminal**} command. Once again, the *cs-label* should be the same as that specified when configuring the certificate server. You can specify a file system such as FTP, TFTP, or Flash (using the *url* parameter) from which to import the certificate request, or you can simply specify that it should be imported via the console using cut and paste with the **terminal** keyword.

Ensuring High Availability in an IPsec VPN

When designing an IPsec VPN, one of the most important considerations is high availability, particularly in a hub-and-spoke topology. Ensuring high availability in an IPsec VPN means that resources are constantly available from spoke sites, even in the event of the failure of a single gateway at a hub site.

Figure 7-5 on page 533 illustrates the importance of high availability. The crucial thing to notice about the hub-and-spoke topology shown is that the hub site gateway is a single point of failure. That is, if the hub site gateway fails, spoke-to-hub site connectivity fails, as well as any site-to-site connectivity via the hub site. It is worth pointing out that even if you are using DMVPN, and spoke-to-spoke traffic is transported directly between spoke sites, the hub site gateway remains a single point of failure for spoke-to-spoke traffic because it functions as the NHS for the DMVPN (if the NHS goes down, the spoke sites will no longer be able to dynamically build tunnels between themselves).

There are several approaches to ensuring high availability in an IPsec VPN, the two most popular of which are as follows:

- Configuring high availability with HSRP
- Configuring high availability with GRE

These two approaches are described in the sections that follow.

High Availability with HSRP

One way of provisioning high availability at a hub site is by configuring a Hot Standby Routing Protocol (HSRP) group between redundant IPsec gateways. HSRP allows a group of routers to share virtual IP and MAC addresses. Traffic from end hosts or other network devices can then be forwarded to the virtual IP (and MAC) address, and as long as one of the routers in the HSRP group is in an up state, traffic continues to be forwarded.

When HSRP is used to provide IPsec high availability, remote IPsec gateways build IPsec tunnels to the *HSRP virtual IP address* rather than an IP address that corresponds to a single head-end (hub site) IPsec gateway. As long as one of the head-end IPsec gateways is in an up state, traffic continues to be forwarded to and from remote IPsec gateways.

Figure 7-33 illustrates IPsec high availability with HSRP.

Figure 7-33 *IPsec High Availability with HSRP*

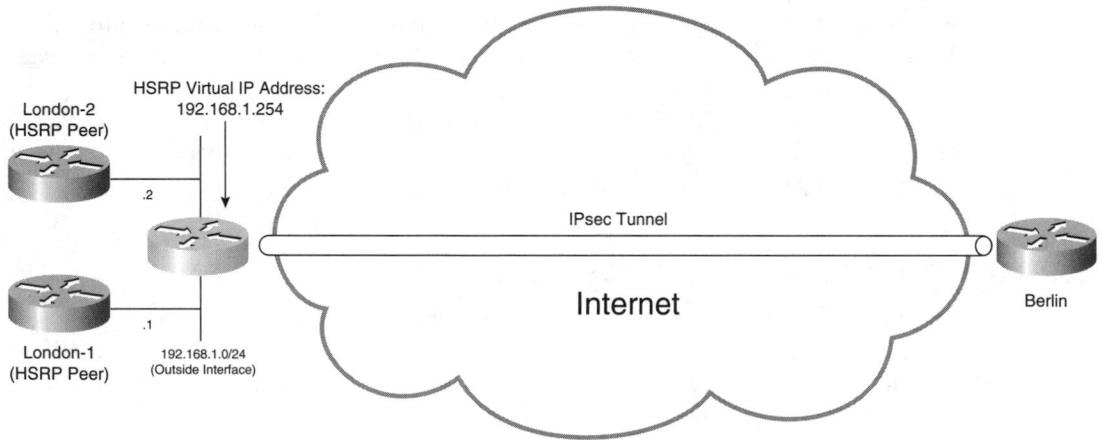

In Figure 7-33, gateways London-1 and London-2 constitute an HSRP group (on their outside interfaces) with a virtual IP address of 192.168.1.254. The remote Berlin IPsec gateway builds an IPsec tunnel to the HSRP virtual address rather than the individual IP addresses assigned to London-1 and London-2 (192.168.1.1 and 192.168.1.2, respectively). In this case, the active HSRP peer in the group is actually the endpoint of the IPsec tunnel. In the event that the active HSRP router (gateway) fails, the standby router takes over as the IPsec tunnel endpoint.

Okay, so the tunnel endpoint fails over to the HSRP standby router in the event of a failure of the active HSRP router. But, how exactly does this process occur? Does the tunnel failover without any loss of user data traffic, or will there be some kind of service interruption?

The answer to both of these questions depends on whether the routers in the HSRP group are configured for stateless or stateful IPsec high availability with HSRP.

Stateless IPsec High Availability

If head-end gateways London-1 and London-2 (see Figure 7-33) are configured for stateless IPsec high availability, no IPsec state information is replicated from the active HSRP peer to the standby HSRP peer. This means that if the existing active HSRP router London-1 (which maintains the IPsec SAs in its SADB) fails, remote IPsec gateway Berlin detects the failure via IKE (ISAKMP) keepalives and re-initiates IKE negotiation with the new active HSRP peer, London-2.

The renegotiation of SAs does mean that *some* user traffic is dropped. The failover time and associated amount of user traffic dropped depends, to a great extent, on the HSRP holdtime (the amount of time before the standby HSRP peer becomes active) and the IKE keepalive interval.

The IKE keepalive interval is specified using the **crypto isakmp keepalive** *seconds* [**periodic**] command. This command enables a mechanism that sends IKE keepalive messages at the time interval specified.

Figure 7-34 illustrates stateless IPsec high availability failover.

Figure 7-34 *Stateless IPsec High Availability Failover*

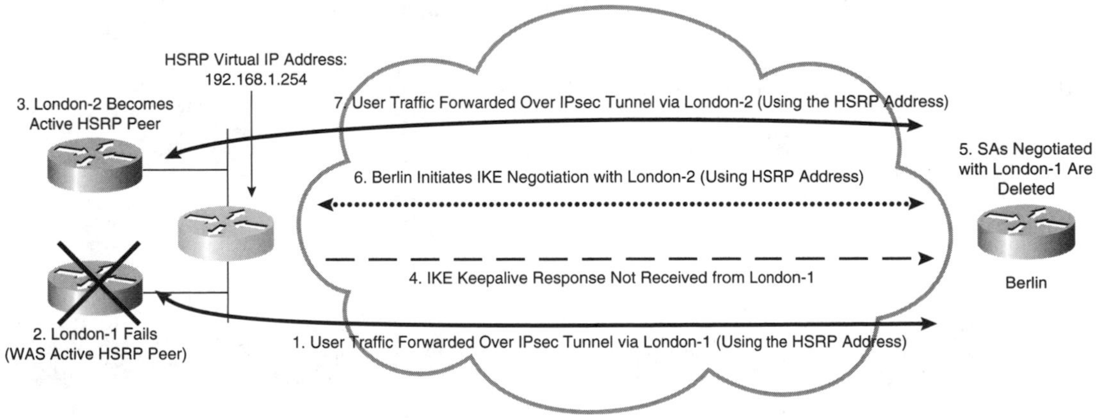

In Figure 7-34, the following events occur:

1 User traffic is forwarded over an IPsec tunnel via London-1. London-1 is the active HSRP active, and the HSRP virtual IP address (192.168.1.254) is the tunnel endpoint address.

2 London-1 fails.

3 London-2 detects the failure of London-1 and becomes the active HSRP peer.

4 London-1 fails to respond to IKE keepalives from Berlin.

5 Berlin deletes SAs negotiated with London-1.

6 When it needs to send more user traffic to the London site, Berlin initiates IKE negotiation with London-2 (via the HSRP virtual IP address, 192.168.1.254).

7 When IKE negotiation is complete, Berlin forwards user traffic over the new IPsec tunnel to London-2.

That is the theory.

Stateless IPsec high availability can be configured in two ways:

- Stateless IPsec high availability with reverse route injection (RRI)
- Stateless IPsec high availability with HSRP on the inside interface

These two methods of configuration are discussed in the following sections.

Stateless IPsec High Availability with RRI

When stateless IPsec high availability is using with RRI, a static route to the remote network is injected into the routing table on the *active* HSRP peer. This static route is then (optionally) redistributed into a routing protocol such as EIGRP and advertised to other routers on the inside interface.

Figure 7-35 illustrates stateless IPsec high availability with RRI.

Figure 7-35 *Stateless IPsec High Availability with RRI*

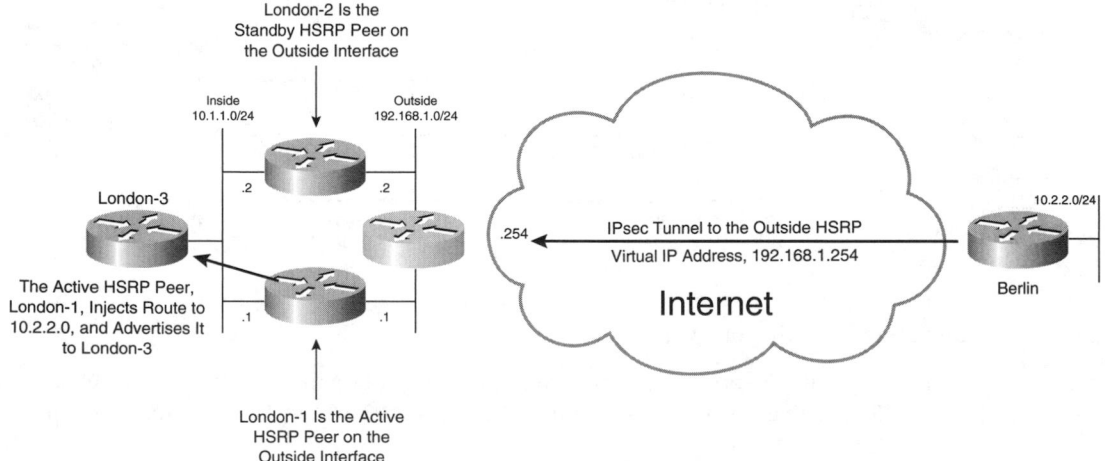

Example 7-29 shows the configuration of Berlin.

Example 7-29 *Configuration of Berlin for Stateless IPsec High Availability*

```
Berlin#show running-config
Building configuration...
!
hostname Berlin
!
!
crypto isakmp policy 10
 hash md5
 authentication pre-share
crypto isakmp key cisco address 192.168.1.254 (line 1)
crypto isakmp keepalive 10 (line 2)
!
crypto ipsec transform-set mjlnettransform esp-des esp-md5-hmac
!
crypto map mjlnetmap 10 ipsec-isakmp
 set peer 192.168.1.254 (line 3)
 set transform-set mjlnettransform
 match address 101
!
!
! Outside interface
!
interface FastEthernet0/0
 ip address 192.168.2.2 255.255.255.0
 crypto map mjlnetmap
!
!
! Inside interface
!
interface FastEthernet1/0
 ip address 10.2.2.1 255.255.255.0
!
ip route 0.0.0.0 0.0.0.0 192.168.2.1
!
access-list 101 permit ip 10.2.2.0 0.0.0.255 10.1.1.0 0.0.0.255
!
!
```

The first thing to notice about the configuration of Berlin is that there is little out of the ordinary. But, take a look at highlighted lines 1 and 3—the peer IP address specified is the HSRP virtual IP address (see Figure 7-35). Also notice line 2—the **crypto isakmp keepalive** *seconds* command configures Berlin to send IKE (ISAKMP) keepalives (every 10 seconds in this case).

Example 7-30 shows the configuration of London-1.

Example 7-30 *Configuration of London-1 for Stateless IPsec High Availability with RRI*

```
London-1#show running-config
Building configuration...
!
hostname London-1
!
crypto isakmp policy 10
 authentication pre-share
crypto isakmp key cisco address 192.168.2.2
crypto isakmp keepalive 10 (line 1)
!
crypto ipsec transform-set mjlnettransform esp-des esp-sha-hmac
!
crypto map mjlnetmap 10 ipsec-isakmp
 set peer 192.168.2.2
 set transform-set mjlnettransform
 match address 101
 reverse-route (line 2)
!
!
! Inside interface
!
interface FastEthernet0/0
 ip address 10.1.1.1 255.255.255.0
!
!
! Outside interface
!
interface FastEthernet3/0
 ip address 192.168.1.1 255.255.255.0
 standby 20 ip 192.168.1.254 (line 3)
 standby 20 priority 120 (line 4)
 standby 20 preempt (line 5)
 standby 20 name ipsecfailover2 (line 6)
 standby 20 track FastEthernet0/0 50 (line 7)
 crypto map mjlnetmap redundancy ipsecfailover2 (line 8)
!
router eigrp 100
 redistribute static (line 9)
 network 10.1.1.0 0.0.0.255
 no auto-summary
!
access-list 101 permit ip 10.1.1.0 0.0.0.255 10.2.2.0 0.0.0.255 (line 10)
!
```

Highlighted line 1 shows the **crypto isakmp keepalive** *seconds* command. This command configures London-1 to send an IKE keepalive message every 10 seconds.

In line 2, the **reverse-route** command is configured within crypto map mjlnetmap. This command enables RRI, and when used with a static crypto map injects a static route or routes derived from the destination address(es) specified in the crypto access list. In this example, a static route to prefix 10.2.2.0/24 (specified as the destination address in the crypto access list shown in highlighted line 10) is injected into the routing table when London-1 is the active HSRP peer. This static route is then redistributed into EIGRP (the dynamic routing protocol used at the London site in this example), as shown in highlighted line 9.

In lines 3 to 5, HSRP group 20 with virtual IP address 192.168.11.254 is configured (**standby 20 ip 192.168.11.254**), an HSRP priority of 120 is assigned to London-1 (**standby 20 priority 120**), and London-1 is configured to preempt other HSRP peers to become the active HSRP router in the event that it has a higher priority (**standby 20 preempt**).

In lines 6 and 8, the HSRP group name ipsecfailover2 is configured for HSRP group 20 (**standby 20 name ipsecfailover2**), and then the HSRP group is linked to the crypto map mjlnetmap using the HSRP group name (**crypto map mjlnetmap redundancy ipsecfailover2**). These two commands allow remote IPsec peers (such as Berlin) to build IPsec tunnels to London-1 using the HSRP virtual IP address 192.168.1.254 (assuming that London-1 is the active HSRP peer).

The final command in the HSRP group configuration is shown in line 7. The command **standby 20 track FastEthernet0/0 50** configures London-1 to reduce its own HSRP priority by 50 (from 120 to 70) in the event that inside interface FastEthernet 0/0 goes down.

In line 9, the static route(s) injected into the routing table via RRI are redistributed into EIGRP using the **redistribute static** command. EIGRP is the routing protocol used at the London site in this example.

Line 10 in Example 7-30 shows the crypto access list. Notice the destination address specified here (10.2.2.0). 10.2.2.0/24 is the network at the Berlin site.

Example 7-31 shows the configuration of London-2.

Example 7-31 *Configuration of London-2 for Stateless IPsec High Availability with RRI*

```
London-2#show running-config
Building configuration...
!
hostname London-2
!
crypto isakmp policy 10
 authentication pre-share
crypto isakmp key cisco address 192.168.2.2
crypto isakmp keepalive 10
!
crypto ipsec transform-set mjlnettransform esp-des esp-sha-hmac
!
crypto map mjlnetmap 10 ipsec-isakmp
 set peer 192.168.2.2
 set transform-set mjlnettransform
 match address 101
```

continues

Example 7-31 *Configuration of London-2 for Stateless IPsec High Availability with RRI (Continued)*

```
 reverse-route
!
!
! Inside interface
!
interface FastEthernet1/0
 ip address 10.1.1.2 255.255.255.0
!
!
! Outside interface
!
interface FastEthernet2/0
 ip address 192.168.1.2 255.255.255.0
 standby 10 priority 110
 standby 10 ip 192.168.1.254
 standby 10 preempt
 standby 10 name mjlnetfailover
 standby 10 track FastEthernet1/0 50
 crypto map mjlnetmap redundancy mjlnetfailover
!
router eigrp 100
 redistribute static
 network 10.1.1.0 0.0.0.255
 no auto-summary
!
!
access-list 101 permit ip 10.1.1.0 0.0.0.255 10.2.2.0 0.0.0.255
!
```

The configuration of London-2 shown in Example 7-31 is almost identical to that for London-1, with one significant difference. As shown in the highlighted line, London-2 is configured with an HSRP priority of 110. Because London-1 is configured with an HSRP priority of 120 (see Example 7-30, highlighted line 4), London-1 will be the active HSRP router in normal operation. If either London-1 or its inside interface (see Example 7-30, highlighted line 7) fails, London-2 will take over as both the active HSRP peer and, *after IKE re-negotiation*, as the endpoint of the IPsec tunnel to Berlin.

As shown in Figure 7-35, London-1 is initially the active HSRP peer at the London site. This is confirmed using the **show standby** command, as demonstrated in Example 7-32.

Example 7-32 **show standby brief** *Command Output on London-1*

```
London-1#show standby brief
                     P indicates configured to preempt.
                     |
Interface   Grp Prio P State   Active       Standby       Virtual IP
Fa3/0        10  120 P Active   local        192.168.1.2   192.168.1.254
London-1#
```

As the highlighted line indicates, London-1 is the active HSRP peer (its state is Active), and London-2 (192.168.1.2) is the standby HSRP peer.

Because London-1 is initially the active HSRP, it is also initially the endpoint of the IPsec tunnel from Berlin. This can be confirmed using the **show crypto isakmp sa** and **show crypto ipsec sa** commands, as demonstrated in Example 7-33.

Example 7-33 *IKE and IPsec SAs on London-1 Prior to Its Failure*

```
London-1#show crypto isakmp sa
dst              src             state        conn-id   slot
192.168.1.254    192.168.2.2     QM_IDLE           1       0 (line 1)
London-1#
London-1#show crypto ipsec sa
interface: FastEthernet0/0
   Crypto map tag: mjlnetmap, local addr. 192.168.1.254
   local  ident (addr/mask/prot/port): (10.1.1.0/255.255.255.0/0/0)
   remote ident (addr/mask/prot/port): (10.2.2.0/255.255.255.0/0/0)
   current_peer: 192.168.2.2:500
    PERMIT, flags={origin_is_acl,}
   #pkts encaps: 10, #pkts encrypt: 10, #pkts digest 10
   #pkts decaps: 10, #pkts decrypt: 10, #pkts verify 10
   #pkts compressed: 0, #pkts decompressed: 0
   #pkts not compressed: 0, #pkts compr. failed: 0
   #pkts not decompressed: 0, #pkts decompress failed: 0
   #send errors 0, #recv errors 0
    local crypto endpt.: 192.168.1.254, remote crypto endpt.: 192.168.2.2
    path mtu 1500, media mtu 1500
    current outbound spi: 2153037B
    inbound esp sas: (line 2)
      spi: 0xDAA97EB8(3668541112)
        transform: esp-des esp-sha-hmac ,
        in use settings ={Tunnel, }
        slot: 0, conn id: 2000, flow_id: 1, crypto map: mjlnetmap
        sa timing: remaining key lifetime (k/sec): (4607997/1562)
        IV size: 8 bytes
        replay detection support: Y
    inbound ah sas:
    inbound pcp sas:
    outbound esp sas: (line 3)
      spi: 0x2153037B(559088507)
        transform: esp-des esp-sha-hmac ,
        in use settings ={Tunnel, }
        slot: 0, conn id: 2001, flow_id: 2, crypto map: mjlnetmap
        sa timing: remaining key lifetime (k/sec): (4607998/1562)
        IV size: 8 bytes
        replay detection support: Y
    outbound ah sas:
    outbound pcp sas:
London-1#
```

Highlighted line 1 shows that an IKE (ISAKMP) SA has been established with Berlin (192.168.2.2). Below lines 2 and 3, you can see the inbound and outbound IPsec (ESP) SAs established with Berlin in the output of the **show crypto ipsec sa** command.

It is also worth confirming that London-1 is injecting a static route corresponding to the destination address in the crypto access list (the Berlin site network, 10.2.2.0/24). This is confirmed using the **show ip route** command, as demonstrated in Example 7-34.

Example 7-34 show ip route *Command Output on London-1*

```
London-1#show ip route
Codes: C - connected, S - static, R - RIP, M - mobile, B - BGP
       D - EIGRP, EX - EIGRP external, O - OSPF, IA - OSPF inter area
       N1 - OSPF NSSA external type 1, N2 - OSPF NSSA external type 2
       E1 - OSPF external type 1, E2 - OSPF external type 2
       i - IS-IS, L1 - IS-IS level-1, L2 - IS-IS level-2, ia - IS-IS inter area
       * - candidate default, U - per-user static route, o - ODR
       P - periodic downloaded static route
Gateway of last resort is not set
C    192.168.11.0/24 is directly connected, Ethernet3/0
     10.0.0.0/24 is subnetted, 3 subnets
D       10.1.3.0 [90/156160] via 10.1.1.10, 00:37:58, FastEthernet0/0
S       10.2.2.0 [1/0] via 192.168.2.2
C       10.1.1.0 is directly connected, FastEthernet0/0
London-1#
```

As you can see, a static route to the Berlin site network (10.2.2.0/24) is indeed being injected into the routing table on London-1 by RRI.

The output of the **show ip route** command in Example 7-35 shows that the route has been redistributed into EIGRP and advertised to London-3.

Example 7-35 show ip route *Command Output on London-3*

```
London-3#show ip route
Codes: C - connected, S - static, I - IGRP, R - RIP, M - mobile, B - BGP
       D - EIGRP, EX - EIGRP external, O - OSPF, IA - OSPF inter area
       N1 - OSPF NSSA external type 1, N2 - OSPF NSSA external type 2
       E1 - OSPF external type 1, E2 - OSPF external type 2, E - EGP
       i - IS-IS, L1 - IS-IS level-1, L2 - IS-IS level-2, ia - IS-IS inter area
       * - candidate default, U - per-user static route, o - ODR
       P - periodic downloaded static route
Gateway of last resort is not set
     10.0.0.0/24 is subnetted, 3 subnets
C       10.1.3.0 is directly connected, Loopback0
D EX    10.2.2.0 [170/281856] via 10.1.1.1, 00:00:08, Vlan1
C       10.1.1.0 is directly connected, Vlan1
London-Cat1#
```

In Example 7-35, you can see a route to the Berlin network via London-1 (10.1.1.1).

So, that is the state of play on London-1 and London-3.

The next step is to check the IKE and IPsec SAs on London-2 using the **show crypto isakmp sa** and **show crypto ipsec sa** commands, as demonstrated in Example 7-36.

Example 7-36 show crypto isakmp sa *and* show crypto ipsec sa *Command Output on London-2*

```
London-2#show crypto isakmp sa (line 1)
dst               src              state         conn-id    slot
London-2#
London-2#show crypto ipsec sa (line 2)
interface: FastEthernet2/0
    Crypto map tag: mjlnetmap, local addr. 192.168.1.254
   local  ident (addr/mask/prot/port): (10.1.1.0/255.255.255.0/0/0)
   remote ident (addr/mask/prot/port): (10.2.2.0/255.255.255.0/0/0)
   current_peer: 192.168.2.2:500
     PERMIT, flags={origin_is_acl,}
    #pkts encaps: 0, #pkts encrypt: 0, #pkts digest 0
    #pkts decaps: 0, #pkts decrypt: 0, #pkts verify 0
    #pkts compressed: 0, #pkts decompressed: 0
    #pkts not compressed: 0, #pkts compr. failed: 0
    #pkts not decompressed: 0, #pkts decompress failed: 0
    #send errors 0, #recv errors 0
     local crypto endpt.: 192.168.1.254, remote crypto endpt.: 192.168.2.2
     path mtu 1500, media mtu 1500
     current outbound spi: 0
     inbound esp sas: (line 3)
     inbound ah sas:
     inbound pcp sas:
     outbound esp sas: (line 4)
     outbound ah sas:
     outbound pcp sas:
London-2#
```

Highlighted line 1 shows the **show crypto isakmp sa** command. The output of this command shows that there is, as expected, no IKE SA with Berlin initially.

Line 2 shows the **show crypto ipsec sa** command, and again, as expected, below lines 3 and 4 you can see that no IPsec (ESP) SAs have been established to Berlin.

Okay, so London-1 is the HSRP active peer and the endpoint of the IPsec tunnel from Berlin. Next, take a look at what happens when London-1 fails.

Example 7-37 shows the output of the **debug crypto isakmp** command on Berlin when London-1 fails (only the relevant output is shown).

Example 7-37 debug crypto isakmp *Command Output on Berlin When London-1 Fails*

```
Berlin#debug crypto isakmp
Crypto ISAKMP debugging is on
Berlin#
*Jun 25 13:11:16.739: ISAKMP (0:1): incrementing error counter on sa:
  PEERS_ALIVE_TIMER
*Jun 25 13:11:16.739: ISAKMP (1): sending packet to 192.168.1.254 (I) QM_IDLE
```

continues

Example 7-37 debug crypto isakmp *Command Output on Berlin When London-1 Fails (Continued)*

```
*Jun 25 13:11:16.739: ISAKMP (0:1): purging node 106163783
*Jun 25 13:11:18.739: ISAKMP (0:1): incrementing error counter on sa:
  PEERS_ALIVE_TIMER
*Jun 25 13:11:18.739: ISAKMP (0:1): peer not responding! (line 1)
*Jun 25 13:11:18.739: ISAKMP (0:1): phase 1 going away; let's be paranoid. (line 2)
*Jun 25 13:11:18.739: ISAKMP (0:1): Bring down phase 2's (line 3)
*Jun 25 13:11:18.739: ISAKMP (0:1): That phase 1 was the last one of its kind.
  Taking phase 2's with us. (line 4)
```

In highlighted line 1, Berlin reports that London-1 is not responding to IKE (ISAKMP) keepalives. In lines 2, 3, and 4, Berlin removes the phase 1 (IKE/ISAKMP) and phase 2 (IPsec) SAs associated with London-1.

London-2 now takes over as the active HSRP peer, as demonstrated in the output of the **show standby brief** command in Example 7-38.

Example 7-38 show standby brief *Command Output on London-2 After London-1 Fails*

```
London-2#show standby brief
                     P indicates configured to preempt.
                     |
Interface   Grp Prio P State   Active     Standby      Virtual IP
Fa2/0        10  100 P Active   local      unknown      192.168.1.254
London-2#
```

In the highlighted line, you can see that the HSRP state on London-2 is now Active.

Because London-2 is now the active HSRP peer, the RRI feature causes a static route to the Berlin network (10.2.2.0, specified as the destination address in the crypto access list) to be injected into the local routing table.

You can verify the presence of the route to network 10.2.2.0/24 using the **show ip route** command, as demonstrated in Example 7-39.

Example 7-39 *Static Route Is Now Injected into the Routing Table on London-2*

```
London-2#show ip route
Codes: C - connected, S - static, R - RIP, M - mobile, B - BGP
       D - EIGRP, EX - EIGRP external, O - OSPF, IA - OSPF inter area
       N1 - OSPF NSSA external type 1, N2 - OSPF NSSA external type 2
       E1 - OSPF external type 1, E2 - OSPF external type 2
       i - IS-IS, L1 - IS-IS level-1, L2 - IS-IS level-2, ia - IS-IS inter area
       * - candidate default, U - per-user static route, o - ODR
       P - periodic downloaded static route
Gateway of last resort is not set
C    192.168.11.0/24 is directly connected, FastEthernet2/0
     10.0.0.0/24 is subnetted, 3 subnets
D       10.1.3.0 [90/156160] via 10.1.1.10, 00:54:09, FastEthernet1/0
S       10.2.2.0 [1/0] via 192.168.2.2
C       10.1.1.0 is directly connected, FastEthernet1/0
London-2#
```

So, London-1 is down, Berlin has removed IKE and IPsec SAs associated with London-1, and London-2 has taken over as the active HSRP peer.

Some user traffic destined for the London site now arrives at Berlin, and because there is no existing IPsec tunnel to the London site (because London-1 went down and the IPsec SAs were removed), Berlin now initiates IKE negotiation with London-2 using the HSRP virtual IP address (192.168.1.254).

After IKE negotiation has finished, the output of the **show crypto isakmp sa** and **show crypto ipsec sa** command is as shown in Example 7-40.

Example 7-40 **show crypto isakmp sa** *and* **show crypto ipsec sa** *Command Output on London-2 After Berlin Has Negotiated IKE with London-2*

```
London-2#show crypto isakmp sa
dst              src              state        conn-id    slot
192.168.1.254   192.168.2.2      QM_IDLE          1        0 (line 1)
London-2#show crypto ipsec sa
interface: FastEthernet2/0
    Crypto map tag: mjlnetmap, local addr. 192.168.1.254
   local  ident (addr/mask/prot/port): (10.1.1.0/255.255.255.0/0/0)
   remote ident (addr/mask/prot/port): (10.2.2.0/255.255.255.0/0/0)
   current_peer: 192.168.2.2:500
    PERMIT, flags={origin_is_acl,}
   #pkts encaps: 10, #pkts encrypt: 10, #pkts digest 10
   #pkts decaps: 10, #pkts decrypt: 10, #pkts verify 10
   #pkts compressed: 0, #pkts decompressed: 0
   #pkts not compressed: 0, #pkts compr. failed: 0
   #pkts not decompressed: 0, #pkts decompress failed: 0
   #send errors 0, #recv errors 0
    local crypto endpt.: 192.168.1.254, remote crypto endpt.: 192.168.2.2
    path mtu 1500, media mtu 1500
    current outbound spi: 22661DC4
    inbound esp sas: (line 2)
     spi: 0x86F96FA5(2264493989)
       transform: esp-des esp-sha-hmac ,
       in use settings ={Tunnel, }
       slot: 0, conn id: 2000, flow_id: 1, crypto map:
mjlnetmap
       sa timing: remaining key lifetime (k/sec): (4607997/3147)
       IV size: 8 bytes
       replay detection support: Y
    inbound ah sas:
    inbound pcp sas:
    outbound esp sas: (line 3)
     spi: 0x22661DC4(577117636)
       transform: esp-des esp-sha-hmac ,
       in use settings ={Tunnel, }
       slot: 0, conn id: 2001, flow_id: 2, crypto map: mjlnetmap
       sa timing: remaining key lifetime (k/sec): (4607998/3147)
       IV size: 8 bytes
```

continues

Example 7-40 **show crypto isakmp sa** *and* **show crypto ipsec sa** *Command Output on London-2 After Berlin Has Negotiated IKE with London-2 (Continued)*

```
         replay detection support: Y
      outbound ah sas:
      outbound pcp sas:
London-2#
```

Highlighted line 1 shows the output of the **show crypto isakmp sa** command on London-2. As you can see, an IKE SA has been established with Berlin (192.168.2.2).

Below lines 2 and 3, you can see that inbound and outbound IPsec (ESP) SAs have been negotiated with Berlin.

Stateless IPsec High Availability with HSRP on the Inside Interface

The other way to configure stateless IPsec high availability is with inside and outside HSRP groups, as illustrated in Figure 7-36.

Figure 7-36 *Stateful IPsec High Availability Failover with Inside and Outside HSRP Groups*

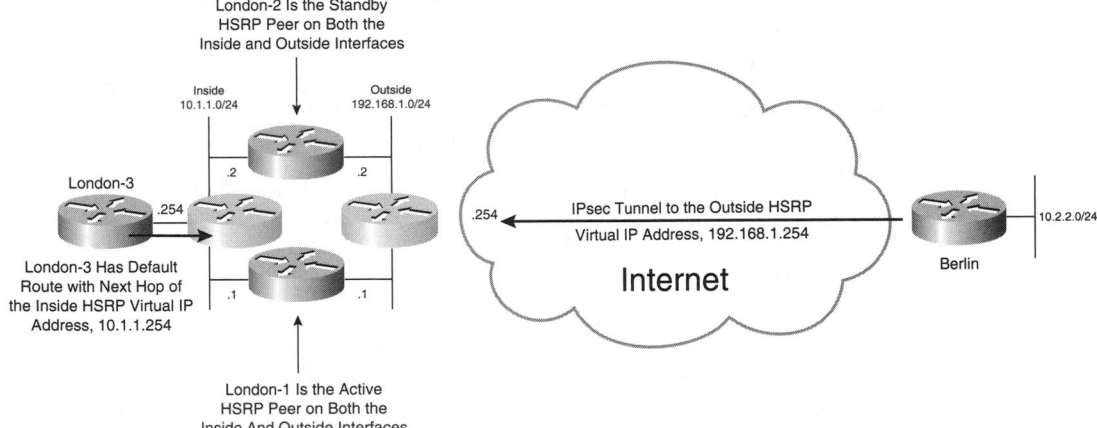

In Figure 7-36, Berlin has established an IPsec tunnel to the outside HSRP virtual IP address, 192.168.1.254. Because London-1 is the active HSRP peer on the outside interface, it is the endpoint of the IPsec tunnel.

An HSRP group is also configured on London-1 and London-2's *inside* interfaces. London-3 has a default route to the inside HSRP virtual IP address 10.1.1.254, and because London-1 is also the active HSRP peer on the inside interface, user traffic *outbound* to the Berlin network is forwarded via London-1.

Example 7-41 shows the configuration of London-1.

Example 7-41 *Configuration of London-1 for Stateless IPsec High Availability*

```
London-1#show running-config
Building configuration...
!
hostname London-1
!
crypto isakmp policy 10
 authentication pre-share
crypto isakmp key cisco address 192.168.2.2
crypto isakmp keepalive 10
 !
 !
crypto ipsec transform-set mjlnettransform esp-des esp-sha-hmac
 !
crypto map mjlnetmap 10 ipsec-isakmp
 set peer 192.168.2.2
 set transform-set mjlnettransform
 match address 101
 !
 !
 ! Inside interface
 !
interface FastEthernet0/0
 ip address 10.1.1.1 255.255.255.0
 standby 10 ip 10.1.1.254 (line 1)
 standby 10 priority 120 (line 2)
 standby 10 preempt (line 3)
 standby 10 name ipsecfailover1 (line 4)
 standby 10 track FastEthernet3/0 50 (line 5)
 !
 !
 ! Outside interface
 !
interface FastEthernet3/0
 ip address 192.168.1.1 255.255.255.0
 standby 20 ip 192.168.1.254
 standby 20 priority 120
 standby 20 preempt
 standby 20 name ipsecfailover
 standby 20 track FastEthernet0/0 50
 crypto map mjlnetmap redundancy ipsecfailover
 !
access-list 101 permit ip 10.1.1.0 0.0.0.255 10.2.2.0 0.0.0.255
 !
```

The configuration of London-1 with HSRP on the inside interface (FastEthernet 0/0) is similar to that with RRI (see Example 7-30)—the only difference is the obvious removal of RRI (and EIGRP) and the configuration of HSRP on the inside interface.

Highlighted lines 1 to 5 shows the HSRP configuration on the inside interface.

The configuration of inside interface FastEthernet 0/0 is similar to that for outside interface FastEthernet 3/0. Notice in line 2 that the HSRP priority on the inside interface (120, configured using the **standby** [*group-number*] **priority** *priority* command) is identical to that configured on outside interface FastEthernet 3/0. The configuration of consistent HSRP priorities on inside and outside interfaces is important, and ensures that when London-1 is the active HSRP peer on the outside interface, it will also be the active HSRP peer on the inside interface. If one router is not the active HSRP on both inside and outside interfaces, user traffic will be black-holed (dropped).

Figure 7-37 illustrates the black-holing of user traffic when one router is not the active HSRP peer on both interfaces.

Figure 7-37 *User Traffic Is Black-Holed if One Router Is Not the Active HSRP Peer on Both Interfaces*

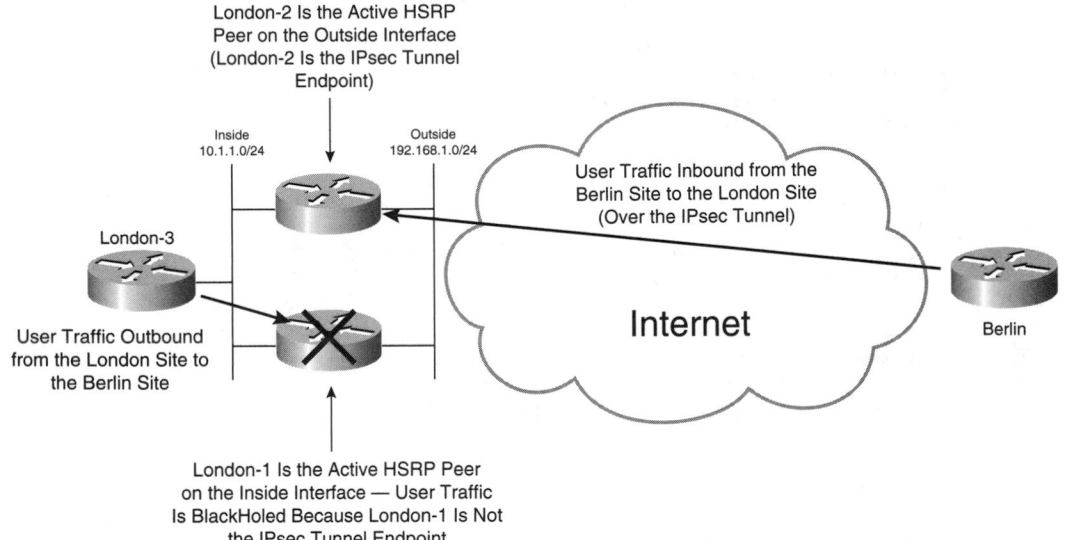

In Figure 7-37, London-1 is the active HSRP peer on its inside interface, and London-2 is the active HSRP peer on the outside interface. User traffic *inbound* from the Berlin site to the London site is forwarded via London-2 because London-2 is the active HSRP peer on the outside interface.

User traffic *outbound* from the London site is forwarded via London-1 because London-1 is the active HSRP peer on the inside interface. Because London-1 is not the endpoint of the IPsec tunnel to the Berlin site (it is not the active HSRP peer on the outside interface), user traffic is block-holed on London-1. Not good.

To ensure that user traffic is not black-holed, you must ensure that one router is the active HSRP peer on both inside and outside interfaces.

Figure 7-38 illustrates user traffic flow when one router is the active HSRP on both interfaces.

Figure 7-38 *User Traffic Is Not Black-Holed If One Router Is the Active HSRP Peer on Both Interfaces*

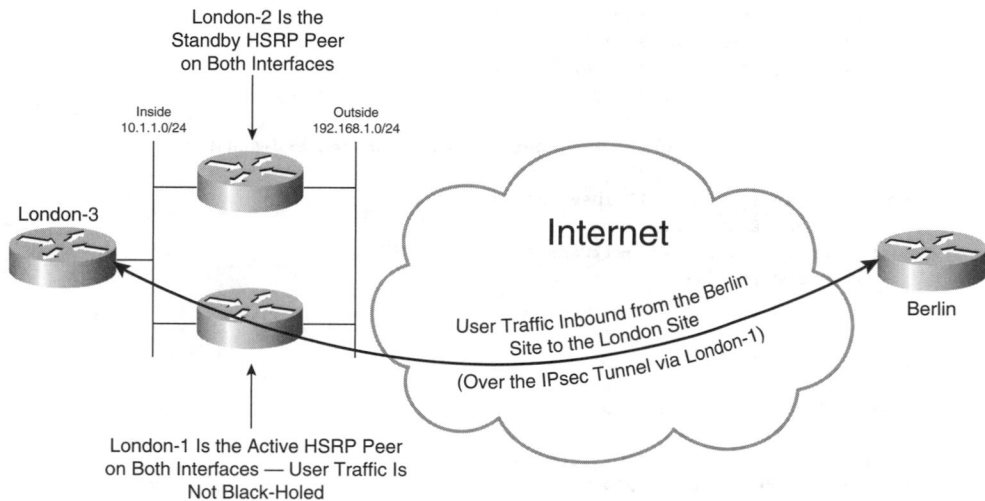

In Figure 7-38, London-1 is the active HSRP peer on both inside and outside interfaces, and is therefore responsible for forwarding both inbound and outbound user traffic. User traffic is therefore not black-holed.

Highlighted lines 1 and 3 in Example 7-41 show the **standby** [*group-number*] **ip** [*virtual-IP-address*] and **standby** [*group-number*] **preempt** commands. Both of these commands have been previously described, but note that the **standby** [*group-number*] **ip** *virtual-IP-address* command here configures a virtual IP address for the inside HSRP group of 10.1.1.254.

In highlighted line 4 in Example 7-41, the **standby** [*group-name*] **name** command is used to specify the HSRP name on the inside interface (ipsecfailover1 in this example).

The **standby** [*group-number*] **track** command on the inside interface (highlighted line 5 in Example 7-41) is used to track the status of the *outside* interface. This command ensures that if the outside interface goes down the HSRP priority on London-1's inside interface will be reduced by 50 (from the default priority of 120 to 70), and because London-2 will then have a higher priority on the outside interface (HSRP priority of 110), London-2 will become active on the inside. If London-1's outside interface goes down, London-2 will also, of course, be the active HSRP peer on the outside interface, and so user traffic will not be black-holed.

Example 7-42 shows the configuration of London-2.

Example 7-42 *Configuration of London-2 for Stateless IPsec High Availability*

```
London-2#show running-config
Building configuration...
!
hostname London-2
!
```

continues

Example 7-42 *Configuration of London-2 for Stateless IPsec High Availability (Continued)*

```
crypto isakmp policy 10
 authentication pre-share
crypto isakmp key cisco address 192.168.2.2
crypto isakmp keepalive 10
!
crypto ipsec transform-set mjlnettransform esp-des esp-sha-hmac
!
crypto map mjlnetmap 10 ipsec-isakmp
 set peer 192.168.2.2
 set transform-set mjlnettransform
 match address 101
!
!
! Inside interface
!
interface FastEthernet1/0
 ip address 10.1.1.2 255.255.255.0
 standby 10 priority 110 (line 1)
 standby 10 ip 10.1.1.254
 standby 10 preempt
 standby 10 name ipsecfailover1
 standby 10 track FastEthernet2/0 50
!
!
! Outside interface
!
interface FastEthernet2/0
 ip address 192.168.1.2 255.255.255.0
 standby 10 priority 110 (line 2)
 standby 20 ip 192.168.1.254
 standby 20 preempt
 standby 20 name ipsecfailover2
 standby 20 track FastEthernet1/0 50
 crypto map mjlnetmap redundancy ipsecfailover2
!
access-list 101 permit ip 10.1.1.0 0.0.0.255 10.2.2.0 0.0.0.255
!
```

As you can see, the configuration of London-2 is almost identical to that for London-1. But, there are one or two differences. As you can see in highlighted lines 1 and 2, an HSRP priority of 110 is configured on both the inside and outside interfaces of London-2. Again, it is important that the HSRP priority be consistent on inside and outside interfaces to ensure that traffic is not black-holed. The HSRP priority on London-2 (110) is lower than that configured on London-1 (120), and so in normal operation, London-1 will be the active HSRP peer and IPsec tunnel endpoint.

When stateless IPsec high availability is configured with HSRP on the inside interface, London-3 should be configured with a default route (or specific a static route to the remote site network, 10.2.2.0/24) with a next hop of the inside HSRP group's virtual IP address. Example 7-43 shows the routing table on London-3.

Example 7-43 *Routing Table on London-3 When Stateless IPsec High Availability with HSRP on the Inside Interface Is Configured on London-1 and London-2*

```
London-3#show ip route
Codes: C - connected, S - static, I - IGRP, R - RIP, M - mobile, B - BGP
       D - EIGRP, EX - EIGRP external, O - OSPF, IA - OSPF inter area
       N1 - OSPF NSSA external type 1, N2 - OSPF NSSA external type 2
       E1 - OSPF external type 1, E2 - OSPF external type 2, E - EGP
       i - IS-IS, L1 - IS-IS level-1, L2 - IS-IS level-2, ia - IS-IS inter area
       * - candidate default, U - per-user static route, o - ODR
       P - periodic downloaded static route
Gateway of last resort is 10.1.1.254 to network 0.0.0.0
     10.0.0.0/24 is subnetted, 2 subnets
C       10.1.3.0 is directly connected, Loopback0
C       10.1.1.0 is directly connected, Vlan1
S*   0.0.0.0/0 [1/0] via 10.1.1.254
London-3#
```

The highlighted line indicates a static default route with a next hop of the inside HSRP group's virtual IP address. Because the next hop is the HSRP virtual IP address on the inside network, outbound user traffic will be forwarded via London-1 or London-2 depending on which is the active HSRP peer.

Stateful IPsec High Availability

Stateless IPsec high availability is fine if you can tolerate losing a certain amount of user traffic as IKE is renegotiated when the (previously) active HSRP router fails. But, what if you cannot or do not want to tolerate this loss of user traffic? The solution is stateful IPsec high availability.

Remember that when using stateless IPsec high availability, standby HSRP peers do not maintain any IPsec state. That is, standby HSRP peers do not maintain IKE or IPsec SA information. The lack of IPsec state on the standby HSRP peer is the reason that IKE must be renegotiated, and some user traffic is lost.

When using stateful IPsec high availability, IPsec state, including IKE and IPsec SAs, is replicated to the standby HSRP peer, and so failover is instantaneous, and little user traffic is lost.

Figure 7-39 illustrates failover of the IPsec tunnel from the active HSRP peer to the standby HSRP peer when using stateful IPsec high availability.

Figure 7-39 *Stateful IPsec High Availability Failover*

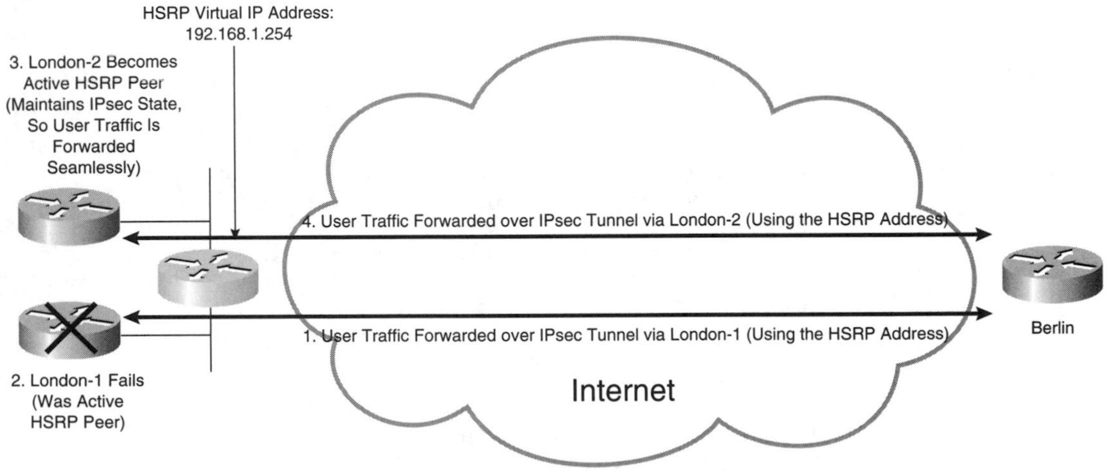

In Figure 7-39, the following sequence of events occurs:

1 User traffic is being forwarded over an IPsec tunnel from Berlin via London-1 using the HSRP virtual IP address (192.168.1.254). London-1 is the active HSRP peer.

2 London-1 then fails.

3 London-2 takes over as the active HSRP peer.

4 User traffic is now forwarded over an IPsec tunnel from Berlin via London-2 using the HSRP virtual IP address. Because IPsec state is maintained on London-2, it is able to take over as the endpoint of the IPsec tunnel seamlessly, and little or no user traffic is lost.

As already mentioned, the reason that failover is seamless when using stateful IPsec high availability is that IPsec state is replicated to the standby HSRP peer. Failover with IPsec state replication is achieved via the stateful switchover (SSO) mechanism.

NOTE   It is also possible to configure IPsec high availability using the State Synchronization Protocol (SSP). SSP was intended to provide stateful failover for IPsec only, whereas SSO can provide stateful failover for a number of protocols, including IPsec. SSO is the preferred method of provisioning IPsec high availability.

There are a few limitations and considerations with stateful IPsec high availability (at the time of this writing):

• Active and standby HSRP peers must run identical Cisco IOS versions.

- The HSRP groups configured on inside and outside interfaces must be configured to track the other interface. That is, the HSRP group on the outside interface must be configured to track the inside interface, and the HSRP group on the inside interface must be configured to track the outside interface.

- The IP addresses configured on the outside and inside interfaces on HSRP peers must be consistently either higher or lower than those of other peers. IP addresses must be configured in this way to ensure that if an HSRP router is the active peer on the outside interface, it will also be the active peer on the inside interface. If a router is the active HSRP peer on the outside interface but not on the inside interface, traffic forwarding will fail (traffic would be black-holed).

- It is a good idea to configure PortFast on ports of switches that connect active and standby HSRP peers on their inside and outside interfaces.

Figure 7-40 illustrates the configuration of stateful IPsec high availability with RRI.

Figure 7-40 *Stateful IPsec High Availability Failover with RRI*

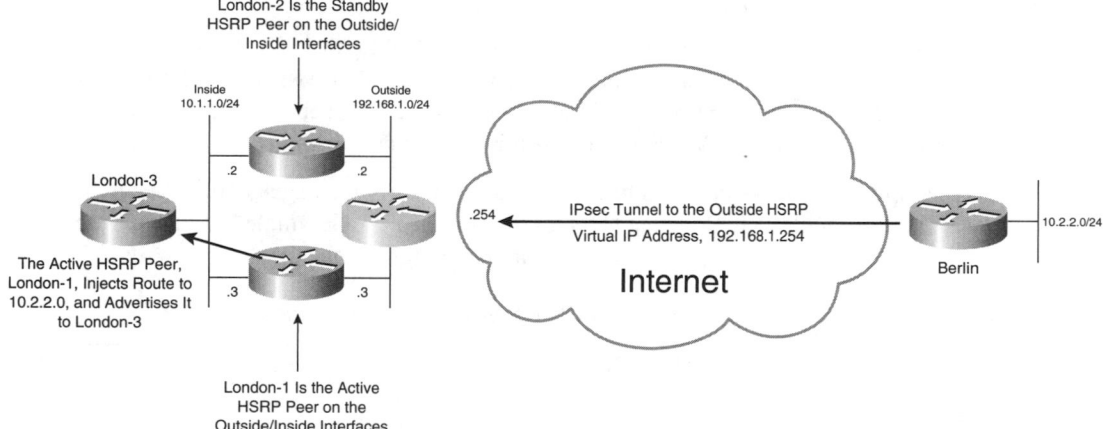

In Figure 7-40, there is an IPsec tunnel between Berlin and the outside HSRP virtual IP address, 192.168.1.254. Because London-1 is the active HSRP peer, London-1 is endpoint of the IPsec tunnel. Additionally, London-1, being the active HSRP peer, injects a static route to the Berlin network (10.2.2.0/24) into its routing table (using RRI) and then redistributes the route into a dynamic routing protocol and advertises it to London-3.

If you do not want to use a dynamic routing protocol between the inside router (London-3) and the HSRP peers (London-1 and London-2), you can instead configure a static route on the inside router to the remote network with its next hop being the HSRP virtual IP address on the inside interfaces of the HSRP peers, as illustrated in Figure 7-41.

In Figure 7-41, Berlin has established an IPsec tunnel to the outside HSRP virtual IP address, 192.168.1.254. Because London-1 is the active HSRP peer on the outside interface, it is the endpoint of the IPsec tunnel.

Figure 7-41 *Stateful IPsec High Availability Failover with Static Route(s) Configured on the Inside Router for Reachability to Remote Networks*

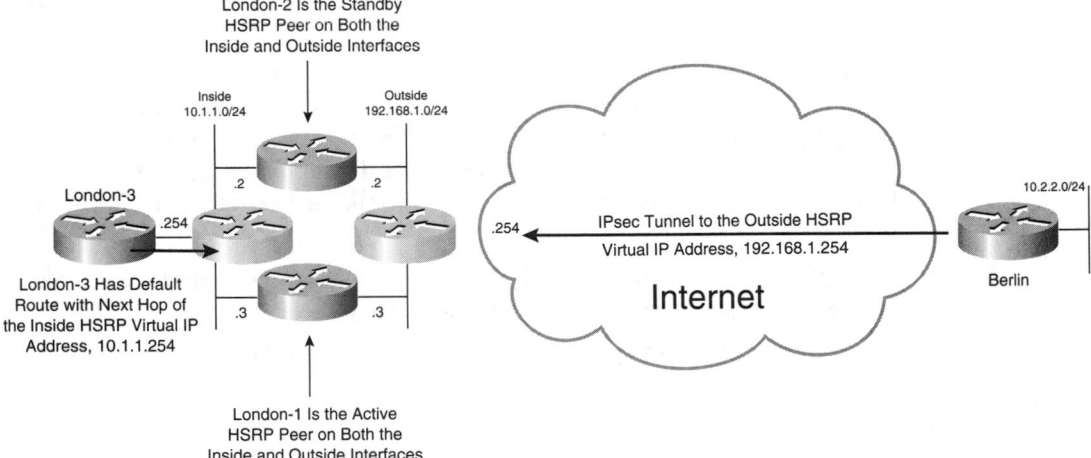

An HSRP group is also configured on London-1's and London-2's inside interfaces. London-3 has a default route with a next hop of the inside HSRP virtual IP address 10.1.1.254, and because London-1 is also the active HSRP peer on the inside interface, user traffic outbound to the Berlin network is forwarded via London-1.

Example 7-44 shows the configuration of London-1 when using stateful IPsec high availability with RRI. Note that some of the commands in Example 7-44 have been previously described and so are not reexamined in this section.

Example 7-44 *Configuration of London-1 for Stateful IPsec High Availability with RRI*

```
London-1#show running-config
Building configuration...
!
hostname London-1
!
!
redundancy inter-device (line 1)
 scheme standby ipsecfailover1 (line 2)
 security ipsec sso-ipsec (line 3)
!
!
ipc zone default (line 4)
 association 1 (line 5)
  no shutdown (line 6)
  protocol sctp (line 7)
   local-port 4000 (line 8)
    local-ip 10.1.1.3 (line 9)
   remote-port 4000 (line 10)
    remote-ip 10.1.1.2 (line 11)
!
```

Example 7-44 *Configuration of London-1 for Stateful IPsec High Availability with RRI (Continued)*

```
!
crypto isakmp policy 10 (line 12)
 authentication pre-share
crypto isakmp key mjlnet address 0.0.0.0 0.0.0.0 no-xauth (line 13)
!
!
crypto ipsec transform-set mjlnettransform esp-des esp-sha-hmac (line 14)
crypto ipsec transform-set ssotransform esp-aes esp-sha-hmac (line 15)
!
crypto ipsec profile sso-ipsec (line 16)
 set transform-set ssotransform (line 17)
!
!
crypto map mjlnetmap redundancy replay-interval inbound 1000
   outbound 20000 (line 18)
crypto map mjlnetmap 10 ipsec-isakmp (line 19)
 set peer 192.168.100.10
 set transform-set mjlnettransform
 match address 101
 reverse-route (line 20)
!
!
interface FastEthernet0/0
 description Inside interface
 ip address 10.1.1.3 255.255.255.0
 standby delay reload 120 (line 21)
 standby 20 ip 10.1.1.254 (line 22)
 standby 20 preempt (line 23)
 standby 20 name ipsecfailover1 (line 24)
 standby 20 track FastEthernet1/0 (line 25)
!
interface FastEthernet1/0
 description Outside interface
 ip address 192.168.1.3 255.255.255.0
 standby delay reload 120 (line 26)
 standby 10 ip 192.168.1.254 (line 27)
 standby 10 preempt (line 28)
 standby 10 name ipsecfailover2 (line 29)
 standby 10 track FastEthernet0/0 (line 30)
 crypto map mjlnetmap redundancy ipsecfailover2 stateful (line 31)
!
!
!
router ospf 100
 redistribute static metric 10 subnets (line 32)
 network 10.1.1.0 0.0.0.255 area 0
!
ip route 0.0.0.0 0.0.0.0 192.168.1.10 (line 33)
!
access-list 101 permit ip 10.1.1.0 0.0.0.255 10.2.2.0 0.0.0.255
!
```

Highlighted lines 1 to 3 show the configuration of redundancy.

The **redundancy inter-device** command in highlighted line 1 is used to begin the configuration of interdevice redundancy.

In line 2, the **scheme standby** *standby-group-name* command configures the redundancy scheme (standby [HSRP]) and links to the standby (HSRP) group name configured on London-1's inside interface (**ipsecfailover1**).

Line 3 shows the **security ipsec** *profile-name* command. This command links to an IPsec profile that is used to protect SSO information as it is exchanged between the redundancy group (London-1 and London-2). The **security ipsec** command is recommended but is not absolutely essential if you are sure that the interfaces on which SSO information is exchanged are secure.

The configuration of the interdevice communication protocol (IPC) is shown in lines 4 to 11.

The **ipsec zone default** command (line 4) begins the configuration of IPC and enters IPC zone configuration mode.

In line 5, the **association 1** command is used to specify an IPC association between London-1 and London-2.

The **protocol sctp** command (line 7) then configures the Stream Control Transmission Protocol (SCTP, RFC2960) as the transport protocol for communication between London-1 and London-2.

Next, the **local-port** *local-port-number*, **local-ip** *ip-address*, **remote-port** *remote-port-number*, and **remote-ip** *ip-address* commands in lines 8 to 11 are used to configure the local SCTP port, local device interface IP address (inside interface), remote SCTP port, and remote device interface IP address (inside interface), respectively. The local SCTP port number should be the same as the remote SCTP port on the peer device (London-2 in this case), and the remote SCTP port number should be the same as the local SCTP port number on the peer device.

The **no shutdown** command in line 6 then enables London-1 to begin communication with London-2.

Lines 12 to 14 show the configuration of the IKE (ISAKMP) policy, preshared key, and IPsec transform set (used to encrypt and authenticate traffic sent between London and Berlin).

In line 15, an IPsec transform set is configured to encrypt and authenticate SSO traffic as it is exchanged between London-1 and London-2.

The **crypto ipsec profile** *profile-name* command (line 16) begins the configuration of an IPsec profile that is used to protect SSO traffic, and the **set transform-set** *transform-set-name* command (line 17) references the transform set configured in line 15.

The intervals at which IPsec anti-replay information is replicated between London-1 and London-2 is now specified in line 18 using the **crypto map** *map-name* **redundancy replay-interval inbound** *in-value* **outbound** *out-value* command.

The *in-value* and *out-value* parameters are used to configure the number of inbound and outbound IPsec packets (received from/sent to the remote IPsec peer) that are processed before the anti-replay information is sent to the standby peer in the redundancy group.

The crypto map is then configured beginning in line 19, and the **reverse-route** command (line 20) is then used to inject a static route to the remote network (Berlin's inside network) on the active peer in the redundancy group.

Configuration of the HSRP groups on London-1's inside interface (FastEthernet 0/0) is next.

In line 21, you can see the command **standby** [*group-number*] **delay minimum** [*min-delay*] **reload** [*reload-delay*], which ensures that if a router interface that was previously in a down state comes up, or the router is reloaded, it does not immediately become the active HSRP peer (assuming its HSRP priority or IP address would cause this) but instead waits for the periods specified. These waiting periods ensure that HSRP packets are received from HSRP peers before any HSRP state change to active.

Next are the **standby** *group-number* **ip** *ip-address* and **standby** *group-number* **preempt** (lines 22 and 23) commands. These commands are used to configure the virtual IP address and preemption for the HSRP group, respectively.

The **standby** [*group-number*] **name** *group-name* command in line 24 configures the inside interface HSRP group name (ipsecfailover1 in this example).

The final command on inside interface FastEthernet 0/0 is **standby** [group-number] **track** *interface* (line 25). This command configures London-1 to monitor the status of the *outside* interface (FastEthernet1/0 in this example) and decrements the (default) *inside* HSRP priority of 100 by 10 if the outside interface goes down. 10 is the default decrement, and so it is not shown.

Lines 26 to 30 show the configuration of HSRP on the outside interface (FastEthernet 1/0). The key differences with the HSRP configuration of the inside interface are (obviously) the HSRP virtual IP address, as well as the HSRP group name (ipsecfailover2 as opposed to ipsecfailover1 on the inside interface). Also notice that the **standby** *group-number* **track** *interface* command is used in this case to track the *inside* interface and decrement the (default) *outside* HSRP priority of 100 by 10 if the inside interface goes down.

The result of the HSRP interface tracking configuration on the inside and outside interfaces is that either London-1 or London-2 will always be the active HSRP peer for *both* inside and outside interfaces.

If one router (either London-1 or London-2) is not the active HSRP peer on both inside and outside interfaces, user traffic might be black-holed (dropped).

Figure 7-42 illustrates the black-holing of user traffic when one router is not the active HSRP peer on both interfaces.

Figure 7-42 *User Traffic Is Black-Holed If One Router Is Not the Active HSRP Peer on Both Interfaces*

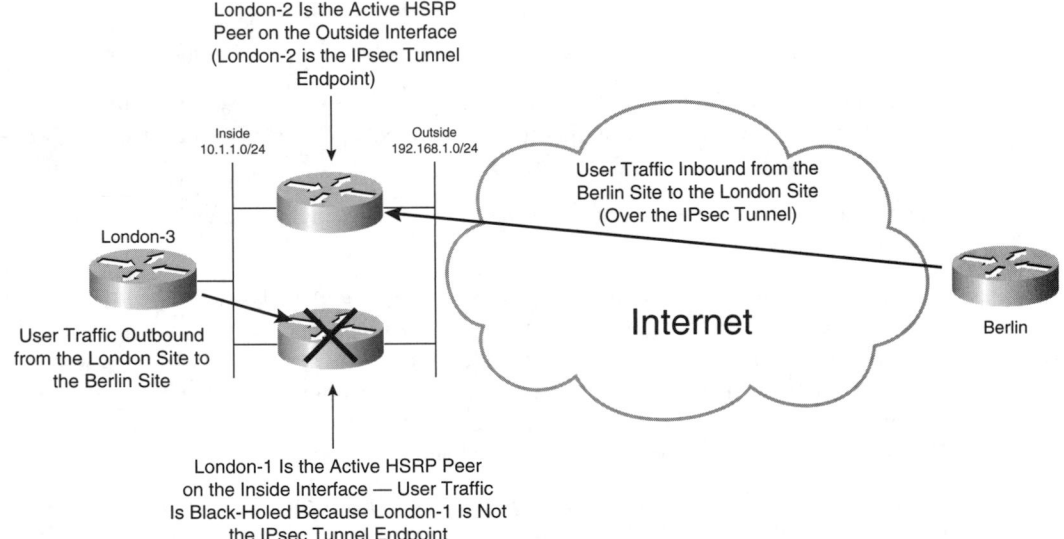

In Figure 7-42, London-1 is the active HSRP peer on its inside interface, and London-2 is the active HSRP peer on the outside interface. User traffic inbound from the Berlin site to the London site is forwarded via London-2 because London-2 is the active HSRP peer on the outside interface. User traffic outbound from the London site is forwarded via London-1 because London-1 is the active HSRP peer on the inside interface. Because London-1 is not the endpoint of the IPsec tunnel to the Berlin site (it is not the active HSRP peer on the outside interface), user traffic is black-holed on London-1.

So, to ensure that user traffic is not black-holed, you must ensure that one router is the active HSRP peer on both inside and outside interfaces (which is the effect of the configurations in Examples 7-44 and 7-45).

Figure 7-43 illustrates user traffic flow when one router is the active HSRP peer on both interfaces.

In Figure 7-43, London-1 is the active HSRP peer on both inside and outside interfaces, and is therefore responsible for forwarding both inbound and outbound user traffic. User traffic is not black-holed.

Returning to the configuration in Example 7-44, the **crypto map** *map-name* [**redundancy** *standby-group-name* [**stateful**]] command in highlighted line 31 binds the crypto map configured in highlighted line 19 to the redundancy group and specifies that failover will be stateful. Note that the standby group name configured using this command must match that specified using the **standby name** command (ipsecfailover2).

Figure 7-43 *User Traffic Is Not Black-Holed If One Router Is the Active HSRP Peer on Both Interfaces*

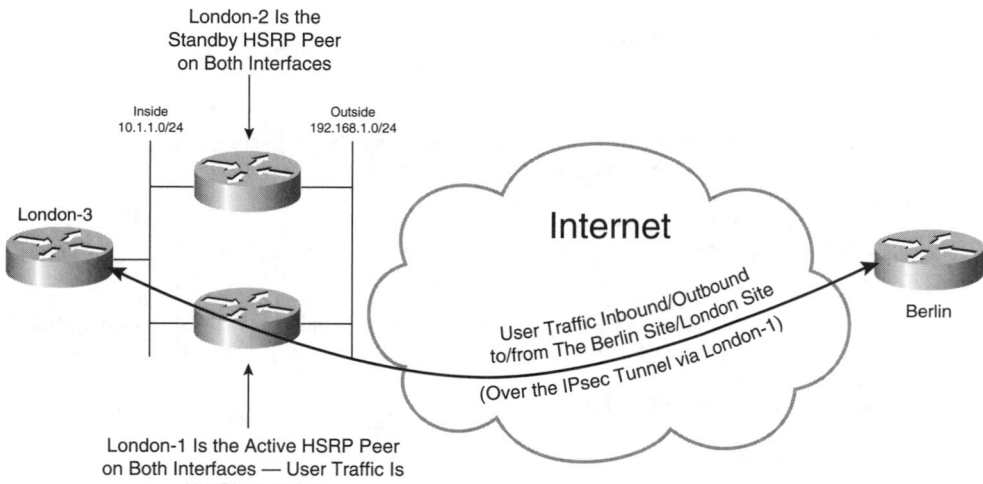

Highlighted line 32 in Example 7-44 shows the redistribution of the static route to the Berlin network (which is injected into routing table via RRI on the active HSRP peer) into the routing protocol used on the inside network (OSPF in this example).

In highlighted line 33, a static default route is used to provide reachability to Berlin.

Example 7-45 shows the configuration of London-2.

Example 7-45 *Configuration of London-2 for Stateful IPsec High Availability with RRI*

```
London-2#show running-config
Building configuration...
!
hostname London-2
!
!
redundancy inter-device
 scheme standby ipsecfailover1
 security ipsec sso-ipsec
!
!
ipc zone default
 association 1
  no shutdown
  protocol sctp
   local-port 4000
    local-ip 10.1.1.2 (line 1)
   remote-port 4000
    remote-ip 10.1.1.3 (line 2)
!
!
```

continues

Example 7-45 *Configuration of London-2 for Stateful IPsec High Availability with RRI (Continued)*

```
crypto isakmp policy 10
 authentication pre-share
crypto isakmp key mjlnet address 0.0.0.0 0.0.0.0 no-xauth
!
!
crypto ipsec transform-set mjlnettransform esp-des esp-sha-hmac
crypto ipsec transform-set ssotransform esp-aes esp-sha-hmac
!
crypto ipsec profile sso-ipsec
 set transform-set ssotransform
!
!
crypto map mjlnetmap redundancy replay-interval inbound 1000 outbound 20000
crypto map mjlnetmap 10 ipsec-isakmp
 set peer 192.168.100.10
 set transform-set mjlnettransform
 match address 101
reverse-route
!
!
interface FastEthernet0/0
 description Inside interface
 ip address 10.1.1.2 255.255.255.0 (line 3)
standby delay reload 120
 standby 20 ip 10.1.1.254
 standby 20 preempt
 standby 20 name ipsecfailover1
 standby 20 track FastEthernet2/0
!
interface FastEthernet2/0
 description Outside interface
 ip address 192.168.1.2 255.255.255.0 (line 4)
standby delay reload 120
 standby 10 ip 192.168.1.254
 standby 10 preempt
 standby 10 name ipsecfailover2
 standby 10 track FastEthernet0/0
 crypto map mjlnetmap redundancy ipsecfailover2 stateful
!
!
router ospf 100
redistribute static metric 10 subnets
 network 10.1.1.0 0.0.0.255 area 0
!
!
ip route 0.0.0.0 0.0.0.0 192.168.1.10
!
access-list 101 permit ip 10.1.1.0 0.0.0.255 10.2.2.0 0.0.0.255
 !
```

To a great extent, the configuration of London-2 is the same as that for London-1.
The only differences are the local and remote device IP addresses configured in

highlighted lines 1 and 2, and the IP addresses configured on the inside and outside interfaces in lines 3 and 4.

That is the configuration of stateful IPsec high availability with RRI. Now it is time to see what happens in operation.

Initially, London-1 is the active HSRP peer and is active as far as SSO is concerned. This is verified using the **show standby brief** and **show redundancy states** commands, as demonstrated in Example 7-46.

Example 7-46 *Confirming That London-1 Is the Active HSRP Peer on Its Outside Interfaces*

```
London-1#show standby brief
                     P indicates configured to preempt.
                   |
Interface   Grp Prio P State    Active    Standby      Virtual IP
Fa0/0        20  100 P Active   local     10.1.1.2     10.1.1.254 (line 1)
Fa1/0        10  100 P Active   local     192.168.1.2  192.168.1.254 (line 2)
London-1#
London-1#
London-1#show redundancy states
       my state = 13 -ACTIVE (line 3)
     peer state = 8   -STANDBY HOT (line 4)
           Mode = Duplex
        Unit ID = 0

     Split Mode = Disabled
   Manual Swact = Enabled
 Communications = Up

   client count = 8
 client_notification_TMR = 30000 milliseconds
         RF debug mask = 0x0

London-1#
```

Highlighted line 1 shows that the HSRP state on London-1's inside interface (FastEthernet 0/0) is Active. The IP of the standby HSRP peer is also shown (London-2, 10.1.1.2), along with the HSRP virtual IP address (10.1.1.254).

In line 2, you can also see that the HSRP state on London-1's outside interface (FastEthernet 1/0) is Active. The IP address of the standby HSRP peer is again shown (London-2, 192.168.1.2) as well as the virtual IP address (192.168.1.254).

The virtual IP address on the outside interface is used as the IPsec tunnel endpoint, and because London-1 is the active HSRP peer on the outside, London-1 terminates the IPsec tunnel.

The output of the **show redundancy states** command (lines 3 and 4) confirms that the local router is active and that the peer (London-2) is in a hot-standby state.

When using stateful IPsec high availability, IPsec state is maintained on both the active HSRP peer (London-1) and the standby HSRP peer (London-2). This is clearly illustrated in the output of the **show crypto isakmp ha active** and **show crypto ipsec sa** commands in Example 7-47.

Example 7-47 show crypto isakmp ha active *and* show crypto ipsec sa *Command Output on London-1*

```
London-1#show crypto isakmp sa active
dst             src             state          conn-id slot status
192.168.1.254   192.168.100.10  QM_IDLE            2      0 ACTIVE (line 1)

London-1#
London-1#
London-1#show crypto ipsec sa active

interface: FastEthernet1/0
    Crypto map tag: mjlnetmap, local addr 192.168.1.254

   protected vrf: (none)
   local  ident (addr/mask/prot/port): (10.1.1.0/255.255.255.0/0/0)
   remote ident (addr/mask/prot/port): (10.2.2.0/255.255.255.0/0/0)
   current_peer 192.168.100.10 port 500
     PERMIT, flags={origin_is_acl,}
    #pkts encaps: 4, #pkts encrypt: 4, #pkts digest: 4
    #pkts decaps: 5, #pkts decrypt: 5, #pkts verify: 5
    #pkts compressed: 0, #pkts decompressed: 0
    #pkts not compressed: 0, #pkts compr. failed: 0
    #pkts not decompressed: 0, #pkts decompress failed: 0
    #send errors 0, #recv errors 0

     local crypto endpt.: 192.168.1.254, remote crypto endpt.:
       192.168.100.10 (line 2)
     path mtu 1500, ip mtu 1500
     current outbound spi: 0xC8A8EE8C(3366514316)

     inbound esp sas: (line 3)
      spi: 0xDFC85091(3754446993)
        transform: esp-des esp-sha-hmac ,
        in use settings ={Tunnel, }
        conn id: 2005, flow_id: SW:5, crypto map: mjlnetmap
        sa timing: remaining key lifetime (k/sec): (4449849/3032)
            HA KB life last checkpointed at (k): (4449850)
        IV size: 8 bytes
        replay detection support: Y
        Status: ACTIVE

     inbound ah sas:

     inbound pcp sas:

     outbound esp sas: (line 4)
      spi: 0xC8A8EE8C(3366514316)
        transform: esp-des esp-sha-hmac ,
```

Example 7-47 show crypto isakmp ha active *and* show crypto ipsec sa *Command Output on London-1*

```
                    in use settings ={Tunnel, }
                    conn id: 2006, flow_id: SW:6, crypto map: mjlnetmap
                    sa timing: remaining key lifetime (k/sec): (4449849/3031)
                         HA KB life last checkpointed at (k): (4449850)
                    IV size: 8 bytes
                    replay detection support: Y
                    Status: ACTIVE

             outbound ah sas:

             outbound pcp sas:
London-1#
```

Highlighted line 1 shows the IKE SAs for which London-1 is currently the active peer. In this case, London-1 is active for an IKE (ISAKMP) SA with IPsec peer 192.168.100.10 (Berlin). IKE SA information shown includes IKE state (QM_IDLE—IKE phase 1 is complete, and phase 2 [quick mode] is in an idle state).

Below lines 3 and 4, you can see the inbound and outbound IPsec (ESP) SAs established between the HSRP virtual IP address 192.168.1.254 (London-1, as the HSRP active peer), and 192.168.100.10 (Berlin, see line 2).

Because London-1 and London-2 are configured as stateful IPsec high-availability peers, IKE and IPsec SA information is replicated from the active HSRP peer, London-1, to the standby HSRP peer, London-2. You can verify this replication of SA information using the **show crypto isakmp ha standby** and **show crypto ipsec sa standby** commands on London-2, as demonstrated in Example 7-48.

Example 7-48 show crypto isakmp ha standby *and* show crypto ipsec sa *Command Output on London-2*

```
London-2#show crypto isakmp sa standby
dst                 src              state         conn-id slot status
192.168.1.254     192.168.100.10     QM_IDLE           2     0 STDBY (line 1)

London-2#
London-2#
London-2#show crypto ipsec sa standby

interface: FastEthernet2/0
    Crypto map tag: mjlnetmap, local addr 192.168.1.254

    protected vrf: (none)
    local  ident (addr/mask/prot/port): (10.1.1.0/255.255.255.0/0/0)
    remote ident (addr/mask/prot/port): (10.2.2.0/255.255.255.0/0/0)
    current_peer 192.168.100.10 port 500
      PERMIT, flags={origin_is_acl,}
     #pkts encaps: 0, #pkts encrypt: 0, #pkts digest: 0
     #pkts decaps: 0, #pkts decrypt: 0, #pkts verify: 0
     #pkts compressed: 0, #pkts decompressed: 0
```

continues

Example 7-48 show crypto isakmp ha standby *and* show crypto ipsec sa *Command Output on London-2 (Continued)*

```
         #pkts not compressed: 0, #pkts compr. failed: 0
         #pkts not decompressed: 0, #pkts decompress failed: 0
         #send errors 0, #recv errors 0

          local crypto endpt.: 192.168.1.254, remote crypto endpt.: 192.168.100.10
          path mtu 1500, ip mtu 1500
          current outbound spi: 0xC8A8EE8C(3366514316)

         inbound esp sas: (line 2)
          spi: 0xDFC85091(3754446993)
            transform: esp-des esp-sha-hmac ,
            in use settings ={Tunnel, }
            conn id: 2005, flow_id: SW:5, crypto map: mjlnetmap
            sa timing: remaining key lifetime (k/sec): (4131229/2938)
                 HA KB life last update received (k): (4131229)
            IV size: 8 bytes
            replay detection support: Y
            Status: STANDBY (line 3)

         inbound ah sas:

         inbound pcp sas:

         outbound esp sas: (line 4)
          spi: 0xC8A8EE8C(3366514316)
            transform: esp-des esp-sha-hmac ,
            in use settings ={Tunnel, }
            conn id: 2006, flow_id: SW:6, crypto map: mjlnetmap
            sa timing: remaining key lifetime (k/sec): (4131229/2937)
                 HA KB life last update received (k): (4131229)
            IV size: 8 bytes
            replay detection support: Y
            Status: STANDBY (line 5)

         outbound ah sas:

         outbound pcp sas:
London-2#
```

Highlighted line 1 shows the IKE SAs for which London-2 is currently the standby peer. IKE SA information is replicated from the active peer, London-1.

Below line 2, you can see that the inbound IPsec (ESP) SA has again been replicated to London-2 from London-1. Line 3 shows that this SA is in a standby state.

Similarly, in lines 4 and 5, you can see the outbound IPsec (ESP) SA, and the fact that it is in a standby state.

Okay, so HSRP and IPsec state replication are operating as expected. But how about RRI? Example 7-49 shows the output of the **show ip route** command on London-3 when London-1 is the active HSRP peer.

Example 7-49 *IP Routing Table on London-1 When London-1 Is the Active HSRP Peer*

```
London-3#show ip route
Codes: C - connected, S - static, I - IGRP, R - RIP, M - mobile, B - BGP
       D - EIGRP, EX - EIGRP external, O - OSPF, IA - OSPF inter area
       N1 - OSPF NSSA external type 1, N2 - OSPF NSSA external type 2
       E1 - OSPF external type 1, E2 - OSPF external type 2, E - EGP
       i - IS-IS, L1 - IS-IS level-1, L2 - IS-IS level-2, ia - IS-IS inter area
       * - candidate default, U - per-user static route, o - ODR

Gateway of last resort is not set

     10.0.0.0/8 is variably subnetted, 4 subnets, 2 masks
O E2    10.1.1.2/32 [110/10] via 10.1.1.3, 00:09:44, Ethernet0
O E2    10.2.2.0/24 [110/10] via 10.1.1.3, 00:03:17, Ethernet0
C       10.1.1.0/24 is directly connected, Ethernet0
O E2    10.1.1.1/32 [110/10] via 10.1.1.2, 00:09:44, Ethernet0
     192.168.1.0/32 is subnetted, 1 subnets
O E2    192.168.1.10 [110/10] via 10.1.1.3, 00:03:17, Ethernet0
London-3#
```

The highlighted line indicates that a route to network 10.2.2.0/24 (Berlin) has been installed into London-3's routing table. Notice that the route is via 10.1.1.3 (London-1, the active HSRP peer).

All well and good—everything seems to be operating as expected with London-1 as the active HSRP peer. Now take a look at what happens when London-1 fails.

When London-1 fails, the messages shown in Example 7-50 are logged on London-2.

Example 7-50 *Messages Logged on London-2 When London-1 Fails*

```
London-2#
*Nov 16 22:39:10.363: %HSRP-6-STATECHANGE: FastEthernet0/0 Grp 20
  state Standby -> Active (line 1)
*Nov 16 22:39:10.363: %HSRP-6-STATECHANGE: FastEthernet2/0 Grp 10
  state Standby -> Active (line 2)
*Nov 16 22:39:10.367: %CRYPTO-5-IKE_SA_HA_STATUS: IKE sa's if any,
  for vip  192.168.1.254 will change from STANDBY to ACTIVE (line 3)
*Nov 16 22:39:10.371: %CRYPTO-5-IPSEC_SA_HA_STATUS: IPSec sa's if any,
  for vip  192.168.1.254 will change from STANDBY to ACTIVE (line 4)
London-2#
```

In line 1, the HSRP state changes from standby to active on London-2's interface FastEthernet 0/0. So, London-2 is now the active HSRP peer on the inside interface.

In line 2, London-2 takes over as the active HSRP peer on its outside interface (FastEthernet 2/0).

London-2 takes over as the active device for IKE on the HSRP virtual IP address 192.168.1.254 in line 3.

Then, in line 4, London-2 takes over as the active device for IPsec on the HSRP virtual IP address 192.168.1.254. London-2 is now the endpoint of the IPsec tunnel to Berlin.

London-2 is the IPsec tunnel endpoint, and because IPsec state has been maintained on London-2, it is ready to seamlessly forward user traffic over the IPsec tunnel without having to renegotiate IKE with Berlin.

A quick check of the IKE and IPsec SAs using the **show crypto isakmp ha active** and **show crypto ipsec sa active** commands confirms that the SAs are now active on London-2, as demonstrated in Example 7-51.

Example 7-51 show crypto isakmp ha active *and* show crypto ipsec sa *Command Output on London-2*

```
London-2#show crypto isakmp sa active
dst              src             state        conn-id slot status
192.168.1.254    192.168.100.10   QM_IDLE            2    0 ACTIVE (line 1)

London-2#
London-2#
London-2#show crypto ipsec sa active

interface: FastEthernet2/0
    Crypto map tag: mjlnetmap, local addr 192.168.1.254

   protected vrf: (none)
   local  ident (addr/mask/prot/port): (10.1.1.0/255.255.255.0/0/0)
   remote ident (addr/mask/prot/port): (10.2.2.0/255.255.255.0/0/0)
   current_peer 192.168.100.10 port 500
     PERMIT, flags={origin_is_acl,}
    #pkts encaps: 0, #pkts encrypt: 0, #pkts digest: 0
    #pkts decaps: 0, #pkts decrypt: 0, #pkts verify: 0
    #pkts compressed: 0, #pkts decompressed: 0
    #pkts not compressed: 0, #pkts compr. failed: 0
    #pkts not decompressed: 0, #pkts decompress failed: 0
    #send errors 0, #recv errors 0

     local crypto endpt.: 192.168.1.254, remote crypto endpt.: 192.168.100.10
     path mtu 1500, ip mtu 1500
     current outbound spi: 0xC8A8EE8C(3366514316)

     inbound esp sas: (line 2)
      spi: 0xDFC85091(3754446993)
        transform: esp-des esp-sha-hmac ,
        in use settings ={Tunnel, }
        conn id: 2005, flow_id: SW:5, crypto map: mjlnetmap
        sa timing: remaining key lifetime (k/sec): (3815107/2209)
            HA KB life last checkpointed at (k): (3815107)
        IV size: 8 bytes
        replay detection support: Y
        Status: ACTIVE (line 3)

     inbound ah sas:
```

Example 7-51 show crypto isakmp ha active *and* show crypto ipsec sa *Command Output on London-2*

```
      inbound pcp sas:

      outbound esp sas: (line 4)
        spi: 0xC8A8EE8C(3366514316)
          transform: esp-des esp-sha-hmac ,
          in use settings ={Tunnel, }
          conn id: 2006, flow_id: SW:6, crypto map: mjlnetmap
          sa timing: remaining key lifetime (k/sec): (3815107/2207)
               HA KB life last checkpointed at (k): (3815107)
          IV size: 8 bytes
          replay detection support: Y
          Status: ACTIVE (line 5)

      outbound ah sas:

      outbound pcp sas:
London-2#
```

Highlighted line 1 confirms that London-2 is now the active peer for the IKE SA established to Berlin (192.168.100.10).

Below lines 2 and 4, you can see the inbound and outbound IPsec (ESP) SAs established with Berlin. Lines 3 and 5 show that these SAs are now in an active state.

A look at the routing table on London-3 reveals that London-2 (10.1.1.2) is now the next hop of the route to the Berlin network (10.2.2.0/24) (see Example 7-52).

Example 7-52 *IP Routing Table on London-2 When London-2 Has Taken Over as the Active HSRP Peer*

```
London-3#show ip route
Codes: C - connected, S - static, I - IGRP, R - RIP, M - mobile, B - BGP
       D - EIGRP, EX - EIGRP external, O - OSPF, IA - OSPF inter area
       N1 - OSPF NSSA external type 1, N2 - OSPF NSSA external type 2
       E1 - OSPF external type 1, E2 - OSPF external type 2, E - EGP
       i - IS-IS, L1 - IS-IS level-1, L2 - IS-IS level-2, ia - IS-IS inter area
       * - candidate default, U - per-user static route, o - ODR

Gateway of last resort is not set

     10.0.0.0/8 is variably subnetted, 3 subnets, 2 masks
O E2    10.2.2.0/24 [110/10] via 10.1.1.2, 00:00:14, Ethernet0 (line 1)
C       10.1.1.0/24 is directly connected, Ethernet0
O E2    10.1.1.1/32 [110/10] via 10.1.1.2, 00:00:14, Ethernet0
     192.168.1.0/32 is subnetted, 1 subnets
O E2    192.168.1.10 [110/10] via 10.1.1.2, 00:00:15, Ethernet0
mjlnet.Los.Angeles.CE#
London-2#
```

In the highlighted line, you can see a route to the Berlin network. London-2 is now the active HSRP peer, so RRI is injecting a static route to the Berlin network, and this route is being redistributed and advertised to London-3.

High Availability with GRE

An alternative method of provisioning high availability for IPsec VPNs is to use GRE tunnels. High availability for IPsec VPNs using GRE can be provisioned in two ways:

- Using point-to-point GRE tunnels
- Using multipoint GRE tunnels (with DMVPN)

The following two sections examine high availability with GRE tunnels.

High Availability with Point-to-Point GRE Tunnels

One way to ensure high availability for IPsec VPNs is to configure two point-to-point GRE tunnels from each spoke site, with one GRE tunnel terminating on one hub site gateway, and the other GRE tunnel terminating on another hub site gateway.

Figure 7-44 illustrates high availability with point-to-point GRE tunnels for a single-spoke gateway.

Figure 7-44   *High Availability with Point-to-Point GRE Tunnels*

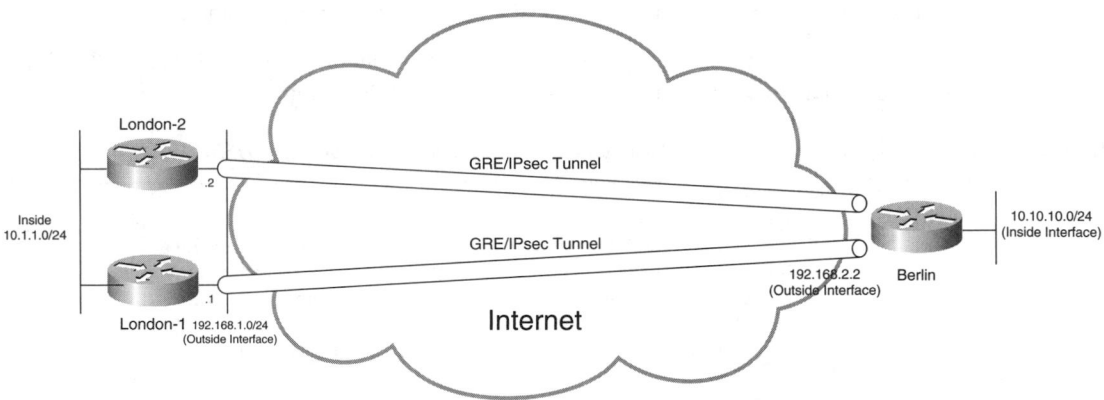

In Figure 7-44, the Berlin gateway is configured with one point-to-point GRE tunnel to the London-1 gateway and one point-to-point GRE tunnel to the London-2. Both GRE tunnels are constantly in an up state, and so if either London-1 or London-2 fails, the spoke Berlin gateway maintains connectivity to the London site via the other hub site London gateway.

Figure 7-45 shows point-to-point GRE tunnels from a number of spoke site gateways.

In Figure 7-45, the Berlin, Paris, and Milan spoke gateways each have two GRE tunnels configured, one to the London-1 hub site gateway and one to the London-2 hub site gateway.

Figure 7-45 *High Availability with Point-to-Point GRE Tunnels from a Number of Spoke Site Gateways*

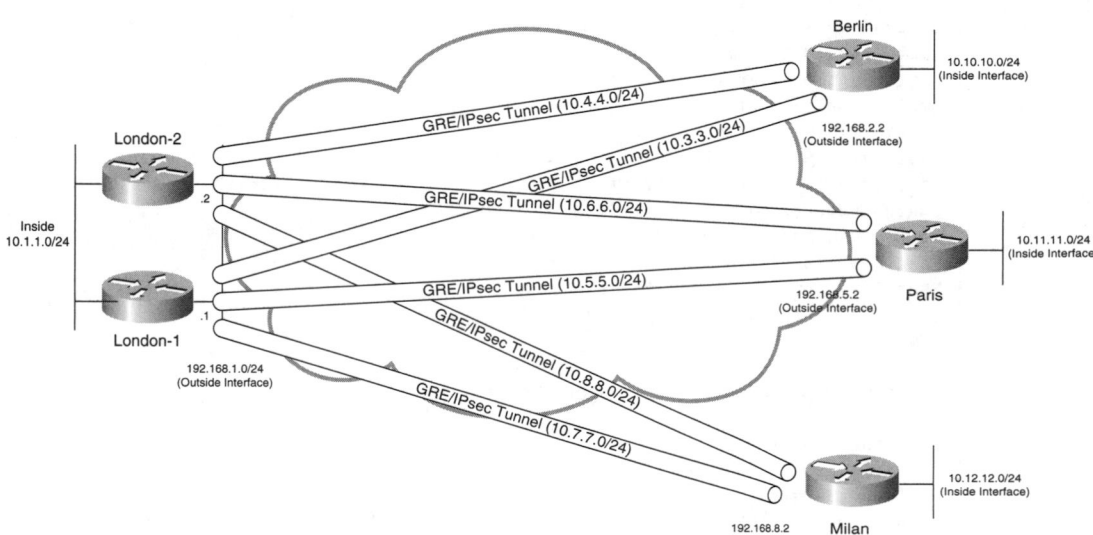

Example 7-53 shows the configuration of the London-1 and London-2 hub site gateways.

Example 7-53 *Configuration of the London-1 and London-2 Hub Site Gateways*

```
London-1#show running-config
Building configuration...
!
! London-1 gateway configuration
!
!
! IKE policy
!
crypto isakmp policy 10
 authentication pre-share
!
!
! Pre-shared keys (one per spoke gateway)
!
crypto isakmp key mjlnet1 address 192.168.2.2
crypto isakmp key mjlnet2 address 192.168.5.2
crypto isakmp key mjlnet3 address 192.168.8.2
!
!
! IPsec transform set
!
crypto ipsec transform-set mjlnettrans esp-3des esp-sha-hmac
!
!
! Crypto map entries (one per spoke gateway)
!
```

continues

Example 7-53 *Configuration of the London-1 and London-2 Hub Site Gateways (Continued)*

```
crypto map mjlnetmap 10 ipsec-isakmp
 set peer 192.168.2.2
 set transform-set mjlnettrans
 match address 101
crypto map mjlnetmap 20 ipsec-isakmp
 set peer 192.168.5.2
 set transform-set mjlnettrans
 match address 102
crypto map mjlnetmap 30 ipsec-isakmp
 set peer 192.168.8.2
 set transform-set mjlnettrans
 match address 103
!
!
! Point-to-point GRE tunnel interfaces (one per spoke gateway)(line 1)
!
interface Tunnel0
 description To Berlin
 ip address 10.3.3.1 255.255.255.0
 tunnel source 192.168.1.1
 tunnel destination 192.168.2.2
!
interface Tunnel1
 description To Paris
 ip address 10.5.5.1 255.255.255.0
 tunnel source 192.168.1.1
 tunnel destination 192.168.5.2
!
interface Tunnel2
 description To Milan
 ip address 10.7.7.1 255.255.255.0
 tunnel source 192.168.1.1
 tunnel destination 192.168.8.2
!
!
! Inside interface
!
interface FastEthernet3/0
 ip address 10.1.1.1 255.255.255.0
!
!
! Outside interface
!
interface Serial1/0
 ip address 192.168.1.1 255.255.255.0
 crypto map mjlnetmap
!
!
! Routing protocol configuration (enable on GRE tunnel interfaces and inside
! interfaces as appropriate) (line 2)
!
router eigrp 100
```

Example 7-53 *Configuration of the London-1 and London-2 Hub Site Gateways (Continued)*

```
 network 10.1.1.0 0.0.0.255
 network 10.3.3.0 0.0.0.255
 network 10.5.5.0 0.0.0.255
 network 10.7.7.0 0.0.0.255
 no auto-summary
!
!
! Crypto access lists (one per GRE tunnel)
!
access-list 101 permit gre host 192.168.1.1 host 192.168.2.2
access-list 102 permit gre host 192.168.1.1 host 192.168.5.2
access-list 103 permit gre host 192.168.1.1 host 192.168.8.2
!
!
end
```

```
London-2#show running-config
Building configuration...
!
! London-2 gateway configuration
!
!
! IKE policy
!
crypto isakmp policy 10
 authentication pre-share
!
!
! Pre-shared keys (one per spoke gateway)
!
crypto isakmp key mjlnet address 192.168.2.2
crypto isakmp key mjlnet address 192.168.5.2
crypto isakmp key mjlnet address 192.168.8.2
!
!
! IPsec transform set
!
crypto ipsec transform-set mjlnettrans esp-3des esp-sha-hmac
!
!
! Crypto map entries (one per spoke gateway)
!
crypto map mjlnetmap 10 ipsec-isakmp
 set peer 192.168.2.2
 set transform-set mjlnettrans
 match address 101
crypto map mjlnetmap 20 ipsec-isakmp
 set peer 192.168.5.2
 set transform-set mjlnettrans
 match address 102
crypto map mjlnetmap 30 ipsec-isakmp
 set peer 192.168.8.2
```

continues

Example 7-53 *Configuration of the London-1 and London-2 Hub Site Gateways (Continued)*

```
 set transform-set mjlnettrans
 match address 103
!
!
! Point-to-point GRE tunnel interface (one per spoke gateway) (line 3)
!
interface Tunnel0
 description To Berlin
 ip address 10.4.4.1 255.255.255.0
 tunnel source 192.168.1.2
 tunnel destination 192.168.2.2
!
interface Tunnel1
 description To Paris
 ip address 10.6.6.1 255.255.255.0
 tunnel source 192.168.1.2
 tunnel destination 192.168.5.2
!
interface Tunnel2
 description To Milan
 ip address 10.8.8.1 255.255.255.0
 tunnel source 192.168.1.2
 tunnel destination 192.168.8.2
!
!
! Inside interface
!
interface FastEthernet0/0
 ip address 10.1.1.10 255.255.255.0
!
!
! Outside interface
!
interface Serial2/0
 ip address 192.168.1.2 255.255.255.0
 crypto map mjlnetmap
!
!
! Routing protocol configuration (enable on GRE tunnel interfaces and inside
! interfaces as appropriate) (line 4)
!
router eigrp 100
 network 10.1.1.0 0.0.0.255
 network 10.4.4.0 0.0.0.255
 network 10.6.6.0 0.0.0.255
 network 10.8.8.0 0.0.0.255
 no auto-summary
!
!
! Crypto access lists (one per GRE tunnel)
!
access-list 101 permit gre host 192.168.1.2 host 192.168.2.2
```

Example 7-53 *Configuration of the London-1 and London-2 Hub Site Gateways (Continued)*

```
access-list 102 permit gre host 192.168.1.2 host 192.168.5.2
access-list 103 permit gre host 192.168.1.2 host 192.168.8.2
!
!
end
```

As you can see in Example 7-53, the configuration of the London-1 and London-2 hub site gateways is pretty standard. If you find the configuration confusing, you might like to refresh your memory by referring back to the section "Using GRE Tunnels to Carry Multiprotocol and Multicast Traffic Across the IPsec VPN" in Chapter 6.

Notice below highlighted lines 1 and 3 that London-1 and London-2 are configured with one point-to-point GRE tunnel interface per spoke site. Also, notice that EIGRP is configured on the GRE tunnel and inside interfaces of London-1 and London-2 for site-to-site reachability (see below lines 2 and 4). It is also possible to configure another dynamic routing protocol such as OSPF or even use static routes for site-to-site reachability.

Example 7-54 shows the configuration of a spoke site gateway (the Berlin gateway in this example).

Example 7-54 *Configuration of the Berlin Spoke Site Gateway*

```
Berlin#show running-config
Building configuration...
!
! Berlin gateway configuration
!
!
! IKE policy
!
crypto isakmp policy 10
 authentication pre-share
!
!
! Pre-shared keys (one per hub site gateway)
!
crypto isakmp key mjlnet address 192.168.1.1
crypto isakmp key mjlnet address 192.168.1.2
!
!
! IPsec transform set
!
crypto ipsec transform-set mjlnettrans esp-3des esp-sha-hmac
!
!
! Crypto map entries (one per hub site gateway)
!
```

continues

Example 7-54 *Configuration of the Berlin Spoke Site Gateway (Continued)*

```
crypto map mjlnetmap 10 ipsec-isakmp
 set peer 192.168.1.1
 set transform-set mjlnettrans
 match address 101
crypto map mjlnetmap 20 ipsec-isakmp
 set peer 192.168.1.2
 set transform-set mjlnettrans
 match address 102
!
!
! Point-to-point GRE tunnel interface (One per hub site gateway) (line 1)
!
interface Tunnel0
 description To London-1
 ip address 10.3.3.2 255.255.255.0
 tunnel source 192.168.2.2
 tunnel destination 192.168.1.1
!
interface Tunnel1
 description To London-2
 ip address 10.4.4.2 255.255.255.0
 tunnel source 192.168.2.2
 tunnel destination 192.168.1.2
!
!
! Inside interface
!
interface FastEthernet1/0
 ip address 10.10.10.1 255.255.255.0
!
!
! Outside interface
!
interface FastEthernet2/0
 ip address 192.168.2.2 255.255.255.0
 crypto map mjlnetmap
!
!
! Routing protocol configuration (enable on GRE tunnel interfaces and inside
! interfaces as appropriate) (line 2)
!
router eigrp 100
 network 10.10.10.0 0.0.0.255
 network 10.3.3.0 0.0.0.255
 network 10.4.4.0 0.0.0.255
 no auto-summary
!
!
! Crypto access lists (one per GRE tunnel)
!
```

Example 7-54 *Configuration of the Berlin Spoke Site Gateway (Continued)*

```
access-list 101 permit gre host 192.168.2.2 host 192.168.1.1
access-list 102 permit gre host 192.168.2.2 host 192.168.1.2
!
!
!
end
```

Below highlighted line 1, you can see the configuration of one GRE tunnel interface per hub site gateway. Then, below highlighted line 2, you can see the configuration of EIGRP on the inside interface and the GRE tunnel interfaces for site-to-site reachability.

The base configurations shown in Examples 7-53 and 7-54 are a good starting point; if asymmetric routing and out-of-order packets are to be avoided, however, you need to add one or two optimizations.

Asymmetric routing and out-of-order packets are caused because of the equal-cost routes that result with the base configurations shown in Examples 7-53 and 7-54. These equal-cost routes are shown in the output of the **show ip route** command on the Berlin gateway in Example 7-55.

Example 7-55 **show ip route** *Command Output Shows Two Equal-Cost Routes*

```
Berlin#show ip route
Codes: C - connected, S - static, R - RIP, M - mobile, B - BGP
       D - EIGRP, EX - EIGRP external, O - OSPF, IA - OSPF inter area
       N1 - OSPF NSSA external type 1, N2 - OSPF NSSA external type 2
       E1 - OSPF external type 1, E2 - OSPF external type 2
       E1 - OSPF external type 1, E2 - OSPF external type 2
       ia - IS-IS inter area, * - candidate default, U - per-user static route
       o - ODR, P - periodic downloaded static route
Gateway of last resort is 192.168.2.1 to network 0.0.0.0
     10.0.0.0/24 is subnetted, 8 subnets
D       10.12.12.0 [90/310172416] via 10.4.4.1, 01:07:47, Tunnel1 (line 1)
                   [90/310172416] via 10.3.3.1, 01:07:47, Tunnel0 (line 2)
D       10.11.11.0 [90/310070016] via 10.4.4.1, 01:07:54, Tunnel1 (line 3)
                   [90/310070016] via 10.3.3.1, 01:07:54, Tunnel0 (line 4)
C       10.10.10.0 is directly connected, FastEthernet1/0
D       10.8.8.0 [90/310044416] via 10.4.4.1, 01:15:38, Tunnel1
D       10.7.7.0 [90/310044416] via 10.3.3.1, 01:15:38, Tunnel0
D       10.6.6.0 [90/310044416] via 10.4.4.1, 01:15:38, Tunnel1
D       10.5.5.0 [90/310044416] via 10.3.3.1, 01:15:38, Tunnel0
C       10.4.4.0 is directly connected, Tunnel1
C       10.3.3.0 is directly connected, Tunnel0
D       10.1.1.0 [90/297246976] via 10.4.4.1, 01:15:39, Tunnel1 (line 5)
                 [90/297246976] via 10.3.3.1, 01:15:39, Tunnel0 (line 6)
C    192.168.2.0/24 is directly connected, FastEthernet2/0
S*   0.0.0.0/0 [1/0] via 192.168.2.1
Berlin#
```

Highlighted lines 1 and 2 show equal-cost routes via the London-2 and London-1 to the Milan inside network (10.12.12.0/24). Lines 3 and 4 show equal-cost routes via the London-2 and London-1 to the Paris inside network (10.11.11.0/24). Lines 5 and 6 show equal-cost routes via the London-2 and London-1 to the London inside network (10.1.1.0/24).

You might think that the load balancing produced by the equal-cost routes is beneficial, but it might produce asymmetric routing (outbound and inbound traffic follows different paths) and packet re-ordering problems (if per-packet load balancing is used), as illustrated in Figure 7-46.

Figure 7-46 *Asymmetric Routing in the VPN*

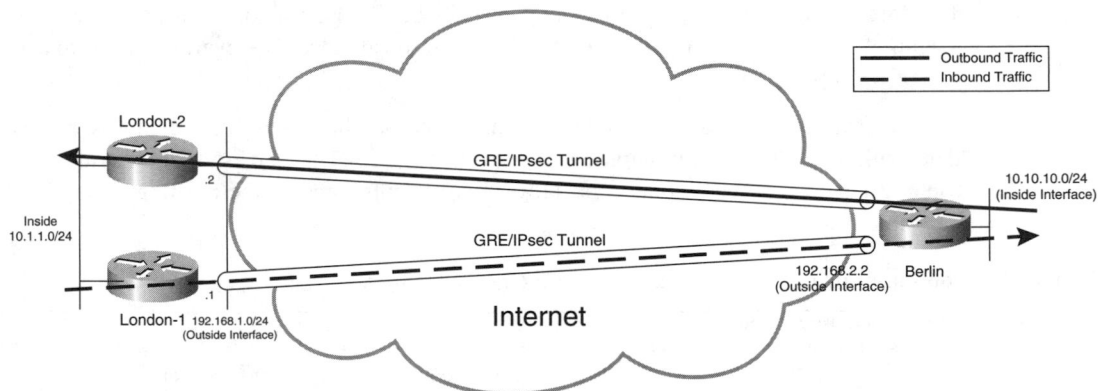

In Figure 7-46, outbound traffic from the Berlin site follows the path over the GRE/IPsec tunnel via the London-2 gateway, and inbound traffic to the Berlin site follows the path over the GRE/IPsec tunnel via London-1 gateway.

Note that although Figure 7-46 illustrates only traffic flow between the Berlin and London sites, asymmetric routing affects all traffic flows, including those to and from the Paris and Milan sites via the London site.

The alternative to load balancing and possible asymmetric routing and packet re-ordering is to configure primary and backup paths to each destination such that all traffic (both outbound and inbound) follows the same primary path in normal operation but can fail over to the backup path in the event of a failure of the primary path.

To configure primary and backup paths for user traffic, you need to modify routing protocol metrics.

In this example, EIGRP is the routing protocol, and so you can configure primary and backup paths for all *outbound* traffic by modifying the delay (a constituent of the composite EIGRP metric) on one of the tunnels on the Berlin gateway, such that one path is preferred over the other, as demonstrated in Example 7-56.

Example 7-56 *Modifying the Delay Metric on One of the Tunnel Interfaces on Berlin*

```
Berlin#conf t
Enter configuration commands, one per line.  End with CNTL/Z.
Berlin(config)#interface tunnel1
Berlin(config-if)#delay 50001
Berlin(config-if)#end
Berlin#
```

In Example 7-56, the delay is modified on interface tunnel 1 to a value of 50001 (tens of microseconds). The delay on the tunnel 0 interface remains at the default value of 50000 (tens of microseconds), and so the tunnel 0 interface becomes the preferred (primary) path for all outbound traffic from the Berlin gateway, as shown in the output of the **show ip route** command in Example 7-57.

Example 7-57 *London-1 Gateway Is Now the Primary for All Outbound Traffic from the Berlin Gateway*

```
Berlin#show ip route
Codes: C - connected, S - static, R - RIP, M - mobile, B - BGP
       D - EIGRP, EX - EIGRP external, O - OSPF, IA - OSPF inter area
       N1 - OSPF NSSA external type 1, N2 - OSPF NSSA external type 2
       E1 - OSPF external type 1, E2 - OSPF external type 2
       i - IS-IS, su - IS-IS summary, L1 - IS-IS level-1, L2 - IS-IS level-2
       ia - IS-IS inter area, * - candidate default, U - per-user static route
       o - ODR, P - periodic downloaded static route
Gateway of last resort is 192.168.2.1 to network 0.0.0.0
     10.0.0.0/24 is subnetted, 8 subnets
D       10.12.12.0 [90/310172416] via 10.3.3.1, 00:00:06, Tunnel0 (line 1)
D       10.11.11.0 [90/310070016] via 10.3.3.1, 00:00:06, Tunnel0 (line 2)
C       10.10.10.0 is directly connected, FastEthernet1/0
D       10.8.8.0 [90/310046976] via 10.3.3.1, 00:00:06, Tunnel0
D       10.7.7.0 [90/310044416] via 10.3.3.1, 00:00:06, Tunnel0
D       10.6.6.0 [90/310046976] via 10.3.3.1, 00:00:06, Tunnel0
D       10.5.5.0 [90/310044416] via 10.3.3.1, 00:00:06, Tunnel0
C       10.4.4.0 is directly connected, Tunnel1
C       10.3.3.0 is directly connected, Tunnel0
D       10.1.1.0 [90/297246976] via 10.3.3.1, 00:00:08, Tunnel0 (line 3)
C    192.168.2.0/24 is directly connected, FastEthernet2/0
S*   0.0.0.0/0 [1/0] via 192.168.2.1
Berlin#
```

As you can see in highlighted lines 1, 2, and 3, the primary path outbound to networks 10.1.1.0/24, 10.11.11.0/24, and 10.12.12.0/24 is now via the London-1 gateway (tunnel 0).

Okay, that is outbound traffic, but how about inbound traffic to 10.10.10.0/24 (the local inside network at the Berlin site)?

If you take a look at the output of the **show ip route** command on the Paris gateway as shown in Example 7-58, you can see that there are still two paths to the 10.10.10.0/24 network.

Example 7-58 *Two Paths Still Exist to the 10.10.10.0/24 Network from the Paris Gateway*

```
Paris#show ip route
Codes: C - connected, S - static, I - IGRP, R - RIP, M - mobile, B - BGP
       D - EIGRP, EX - EIGRP external, O - OSPF, IA - OSPF inter area
       N1 - OSPF NSSA external type 1, N2 - OSPF NSSA external type 2
       E1 - OSPF external type 1, E2 - OSPF external type 2, E - EGP
       i - IS-IS, su - IS-IS summary, L1 - IS-IS level-1, L2 - IS-IS level-2
       ia - IS-IS inter area, * - candidate default, U - per-user static route
       o - ODR, P - periodic downloaded static route
Gateway of last resort is 192.168.5.1 to network 0.0.0.0
C    192.168.5.0/24 is directly connected, Ethernet0/0
     10.0.0.0/24 is subnetted, 8 subnets
D       10.10.10.0 [90/310046976] via 10.6.6.1, 00:08:50, Tunnel1
                   [90/310046976] via 10.5.5.1, 00:08:50, Tunnel0
D       10.7.7.0 [90/310044416] via 10.5.5.1, 00:34:21, Tunnel0
D       10.8.8.0 [90/310044416] via 10.6.6.1, 00:34:22, Tunnel1
D       10.3.3.0 [90/310044416] via 10.5.5.1, 00:34:21, Tunnel0
D       10.4.4.0 [90/310044416] via 10.6.6.1, 00:34:22, Tunnel1
D       10.1.1.0 [90/297246976] via 10.6.6.1, 00:34:38, Tunnel1
                 [90/297246976] via 10.5.5.1, 00:34:38, Tunnel0
C       10.12.12.0 is directly connected, Loopback100
C       10.11.11.0 is directly connected, Ethernet0/1
C       10.6.6.0 is directly connected, Tunnel1
C       10.5.5.0 is directly connected, Tunnel0
S*   0.0.0.0/0 [1/0] via 192.168.5.1
Paris#
```

The highlighted lines verify that two equal-cost routes still exist from the Paris gateway (via London) to the Berlin inside network (10.10.10.0/24). So, any traffic outbound from the Paris site and *inbound* to the Berlin site (10.10.10.0/24) will be split over interfaces tunnel 0 and tunnel 1.

To ensure that traffic inbound to the Berlin site is not load balanced, but instead sent over the tunnel via the London-1 to the Berlin gateway (thereby ensuring symmetric routing), the **delay** command can again used. This time the **delay** command is used to specify a delay of 50001 on the London-2 gateway tunnel interface connected to the Berlin gateway, as shown in Example 7-59.

Example 7-59 *Modifying the Delay Metric on Interface Tunnel 0 on London-2*

```
London-2#conf t
Enter configuration commands, one per line.  End with CNTL/Z.
London-2(config)#interface tunnel 0
London-2(config-if)#delay 50001
London-2(config-if)#end
London-2#
```

After the **delay** command has been used to modify the EIGRP metric on London-2, the London-1 gateway is preferred for all traffic inbound to the Berlin site because the default delay on the tunnel interface on London-1 is lower than that configured on London-2 (50000 < 50001). This is shown in the output of the **show ip route** command on the Paris gateway in Example 7-60.

Example 7-60 *London-1 Gateway Is Preferred for (Inbound) Traffic to the Berlin Site*

```
Paris#show ip route
Codes: C - connected, S - static, I - IGRP, R - RIP, M - mobile, B - BGP
       D - EIGRP, EX - EIGRP external, O - OSPF, IA - OSPF inter area
       N1 - OSPF NSSA external type 1, N2 - OSPF NSSA external type 2
       E1 - OSPF external type 1, E2 - OSPF external type 2, E - EGP
       i - IS-IS, su - IS-IS summary, L1 - IS-IS level-1, L2 - IS-IS level-2
       ia - IS-IS inter area, * - candidate default, U - per-user static route
       o - ODR, P - periodic downloaded static route
Gateway of last resort is 192.168.5.1 to network 0.0.0.0
C    192.168.5.0/24 is directly connected, Ethernet0/0
     10.0.0.0/24 is subnetted, 8 subnets
D       10.7.7.0 [90/310044416] via 10.5.5.1, 00:34:21, Tunnel0
D       10.8.8.0 [90/310044416] via 10.6.6.1, 00:34:22, Tunnel1
D       10.4.4.0 [90/322844416] via 10.6.6.1, 00:00:05, Tunnel1
D       10.10.10.0 [90/310046976] via 10.5.5.1, 00:00:05, Tunnel0 (line 1)
D       10.3.3.0 [90/310044416] via 10.5.5.1, 00:00:05, Tunnel0
D       10.12.12.0 [90/297246976] via 10.5.5.1, 00:00:05, Tunnel0 (line 2)
                   [90/297246976] via 10.6.6.1, 00:00:05, Tunnel1 (line 3)
D       10.1.1.0 [90/297246976] via 10.5.5.1, 00:00:05, Tunnel0 (line 4)
                 [90/297246976] via 10.6.6.1, 00:00:05, Tunnel1 (line 5)
C       10.6.6.0 is directly connected, Tunnel1
C       10.5.5.0 is directly connected, Tunnel0
C       10.11.11.0 is directly connected, Ethernet0/1
S*   0.0.0.0/0 [1/0] via 192.168.5.1
Paris#
```

In highlighted line 1, you can see that traffic for the 10.10.10.0/24 (Berlin site) network is now sent only via the London-1 gateway (via tunnel 0).

Figure 7-47 illustrates the symmetric outbound and inbound traffic flow for the Berlin gateway now that the delay metric has been modified on the Berlin gateway and the London-2 gateway.

Figure 7-47 *Symmetric Routing in the VPN*

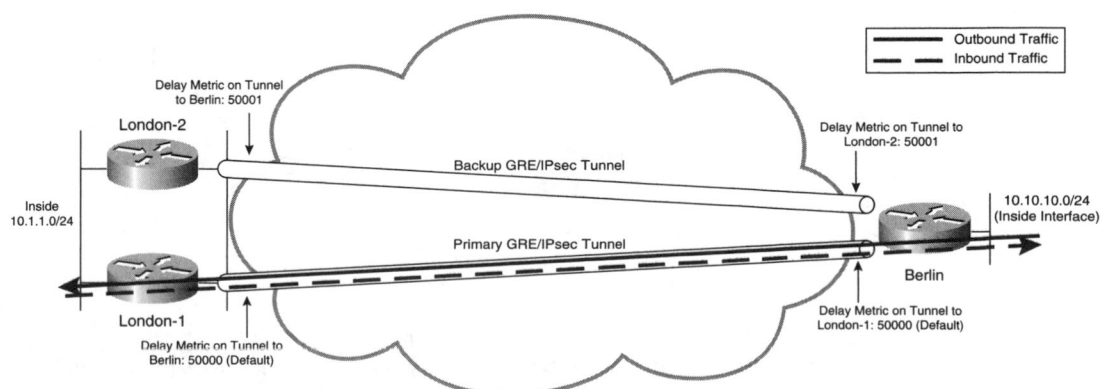

As you can see in Figure 7-47, all outbound and inbound traffic is now sent over the primary GRE/IPsec tunnel via London-1 in normal operation. If the London-1 gateway should fail, however, all traffic fails over to the GRE/IPsec tunnel via the London-2 gateway.

You might also notice in Example 7-60 that the Paris gateway is still load balancing traffic for the 10.1.1.0/24 and 10.12.12.0/24 networks across its two GRE tunnels (via London-1 and London-2). To ensure that all traffic in the IPsec VPN uses a primary path via the London-1 gateway, it would be necessary to modify the delay metric on the Paris and Milan gateways (as demonstrated on the Berlin gateway in Example 7-56). In addition, it would be necessary to modify the delay metric on the tunnel interfaces on the London-2 that connect to the Paris and Milan spoke site such that all inbound traffic to the Paris and Milan sites also goes via the London-1 gateway (as demonstrated for traffic inbound to the Berlin site in Example 7-59).

So, load balancing inbound and outbound traffic over tunnels from a *particular* spoke gateway is usually a bad idea, but it is still possible to load balance traffic to multiple hub site gateways, as illustrated in Figure 7-48.

Figure 7-48 *Load Balancing to Hub Site Gateways*

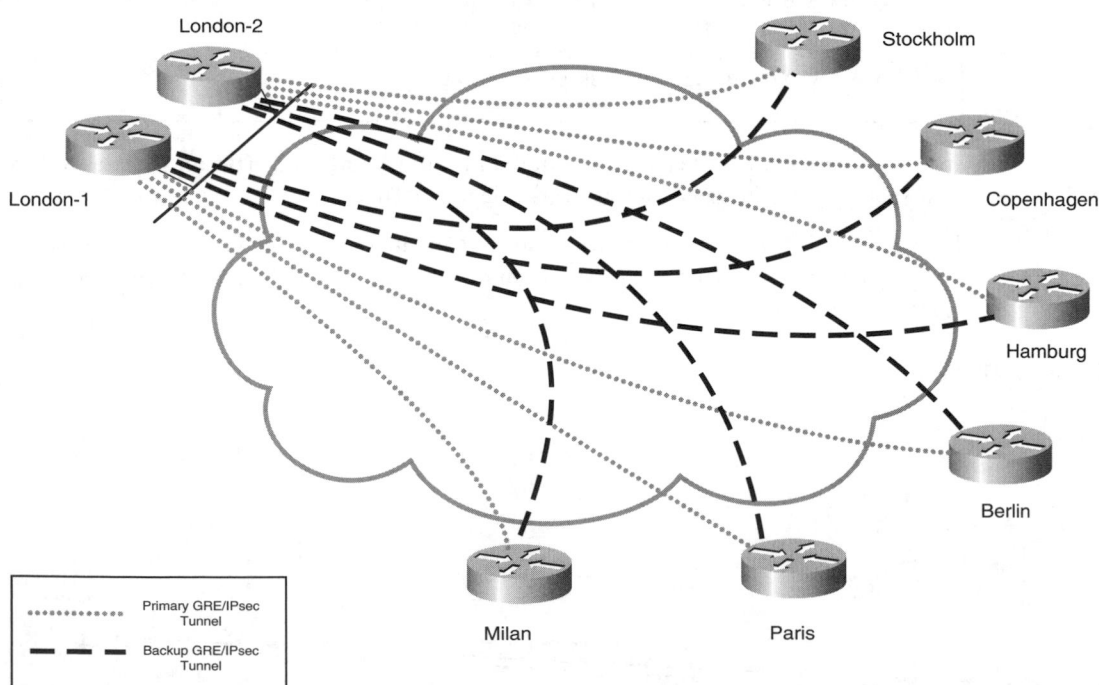

In Figure 7-48, the Stockholm, Copenhagen, and Hamburg gateways' primary GRE/IPsec tunnels terminate on the London-2 hub site gateway. Their backup GRE/IPsec tunnels terminate on the London-1 gateway.

The Berlin, Paris, and Milan gateways' primary GRE/IPsec tunnels terminate on the London-1 gateway, and their backup GRE/IPsec tunnels terminate on the London-2 gateway.

So, in normal operation for the IPsec VPN shown in Figure 7-48, traffic would be evenly load balanced between the London-1 and London-2 gateways. If one of the hub site gateways were to fail, all traffic would be transported via the remaining hub site gateway or gateways.

One advantage of using GRE/IPsec tunnels for high availability is that GRE/IPsec tunnels can be used to provide high availability where hub site gateways are co-located *or* when hub site gateways are located at geographically dispersed sites.

Figure 7-49 illustrates using GRE/IPsec tunnels for high availability when hub site gateways are geographically dispersed.

Figure 7-49 *High Availability with GRE/IPsec Tunnels When Hub Site Gateways Are Geographically Dispersed*

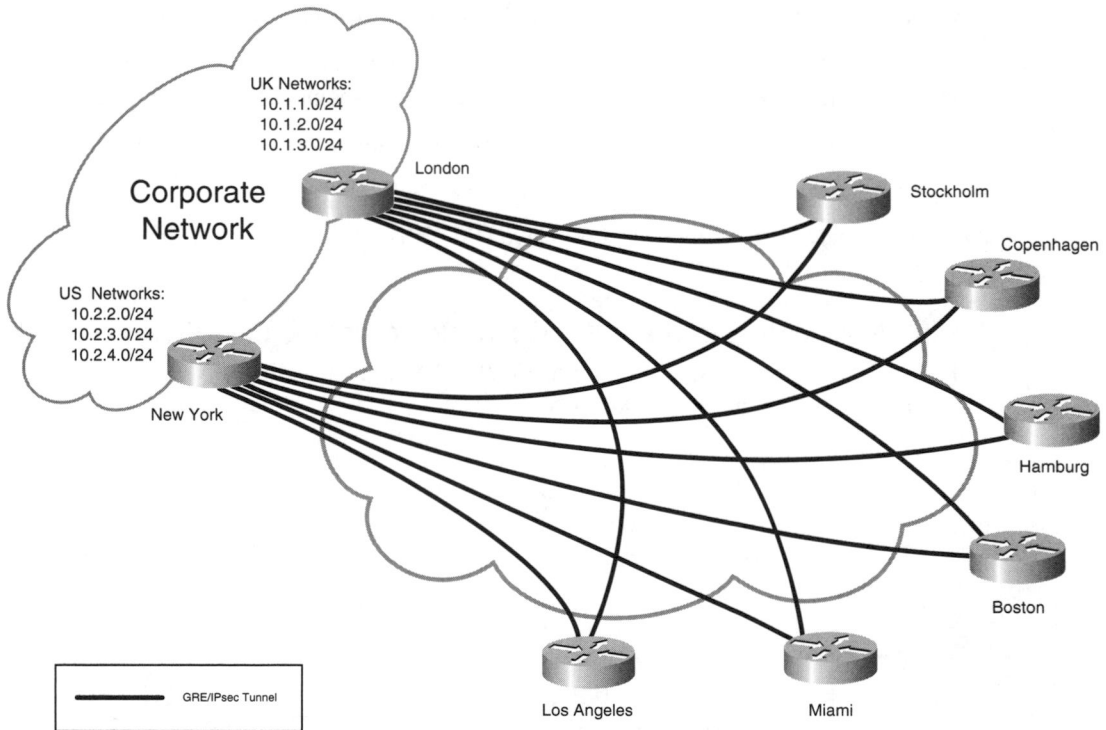

In Figure 7-49, all spoke site gateways are connected to the London and New York hub site gateways via GRE/IPsec tunnels.

In this case, it is usually unnecessary to configure the primary and backup GRE/IPsec tunnels by modifying routing protocol metrics, because traffic will naturally be routed over the tunnel that provides the shortest path to a particular destination (assuming you use a dynamic routing protocol).

For example, in Figure 7-49, traffic from the Los Angeles site destined for one of the U.S. networks (10.2.2.0/24, 10.2.3.0/24, and 10.2.4.0/24) would normally be routed over the GRE/IPsec tunnel via the New York hub site gateway (because of the shorter routing protocol path). If the New York gateway were to go down, however, traffic from the Los Angeles site destined for one of the U.S. networks would be routed via the London gateway (the longer routing protocol path).

High Availability with DMVPN

As you saw in the preceding section, point-to-point GRE/IPsec tunnels can work well as a solution for providing high availability in an IPsec VPN. But, as previously discussed, the use of point-to-point GRE/IPsec tunnels does not scale well (because of the amount of configuration required).

A more scalable solution for high availability with GRE/IPsec is to use DMVPN.

In this case, the hub site gateways are configured with multipoint GRE (mGRE) interfaces, and the spoke site gateways are configured with either point-to-point GRE or mGRE interfaces.

There are two ways to configure DMVPN for high availability:

- The gateways are connected over one DMVPN.
- The gateways are connected over two DMVPNs.

High Availability with Gateways Connected over One DMVPN

Figure 7-50 illustrates the configuration of DMVPN for high availability with all gateways connected over one network (DMVPN).

Figure 7-50 *High Availability with One DMVPN*

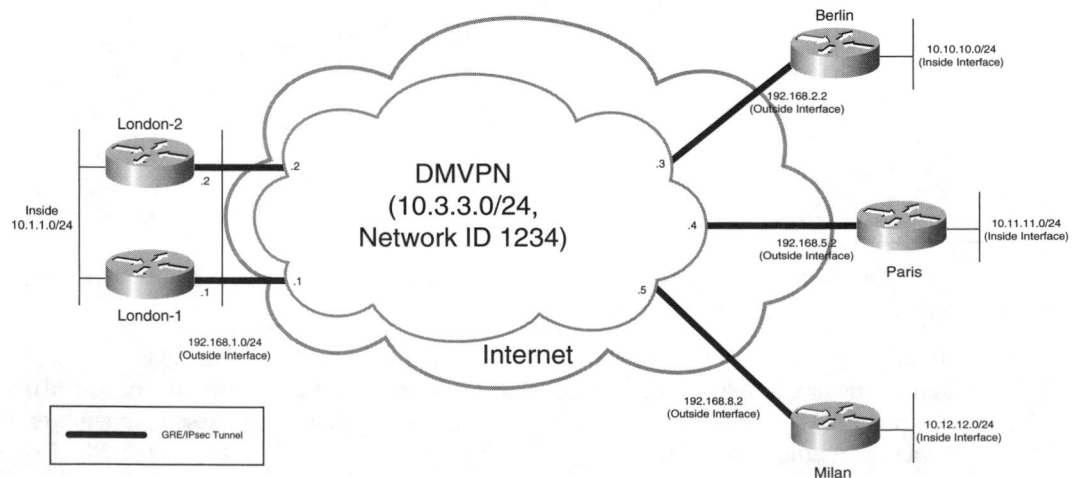

In Figure 7-50, the London-1, London-2, Berlin, Paris, and Milan sites are all connected over one DMVPN (network 10.3.3.0/24, NHRP network ID 1234).

Example 7-61 shows the configuration required on the London-1 and London-2 hub site gateways when using one DMVPN (IP network 10.3.3.0/24, and NHRP network ID 1234).

Example 7-61 *Configuration of the London-1 and London-2 Hub site Gateways When Using One DMVPN*

```
London-1#show running-config
Building configuration...
!
! London-1 gateway configuration
!
!
! IKE policy
!
crypto isakmp policy 10
 authentication pre-share
!
!
! Wildcard pre-shared key
!
crypto isakmp key mjlnet address 0.0.0.0 0.0.0.0
!
!
! IPsec transform set
!
crypto ipsec transform-set mjlnettrans esp-3des esp-sha-hmac
!
!
! IPsec profile
!
crypto ipsec profile mjlnetprofile
 set transform-set mjlnettrans
!
!
! mGRE tunnel interface
!
interface Tunnel0
 ip address 10.3.3.1 255.255.255.0 (line 1)
 no ip next-hop-self eigrp 100
 ip nhrp authentication mjlnet
 ip nhrp map multicast dynamic
 ip nhrp map 10.3.3.2 192.168.1.2
 ip nhrp map multicast 192.168.1.2
 ip nhrp network-id 1234
 ip nhrp nhs 10.3.3.2
 no ip split-horizon eigrp 100
 tunnel source 192.168.1.1
 tunnel mode gre multipoint
 tunnel key 5678
 tunnel protection ipsec profile mjlnetprofile
!
!
```

continues

Example 7-61 *Configuration of the London-1 and London-2 Hub site Gateways When Using One DMVPN (Continued)*

```
! Inside interface
!
interface FastEthernet0/0
 ip address 10.1.1.1 255.255.255.0
!
!
! Outside interface
!
interface Serial1/0
 ip address 192.168.1.1 255.255.255.0
!
!
! EIGRP for site-to-site reachability (line 2)
!
router eigrp 100
 passive-interface Ethernet3/0
 network 10.1.1.0 0.0.0.255
 network 10.3.3.0 0.0.0.255
 no auto-summary
!
```
```
London-2#show running-config
Building configuration...
!
! London-2 gateway configuration
!
!
! IKE policy
!
crypto isakmp policy 10
 authentication pre-share
!
!
! Wildcard pre-shared key
!
crypto isakmp key mjlnet address 0.0.0.0 0.0.0.0
!
!
! IPsec transform set
!
crypto ipsec transform-set mjlnettrans esp-3des esp-sha-hmac
!
!
! IPsec profile
!
crypto ipsec profile mjlnetprofile
 set transform-set mjlnettrans
!
!
! mGRE tunnel interface
!
```

Example 7-61 *Configuration of the London-1 and London-2 Hub site Gateways When Using One DMVPN (Continued)*

```
interface Tunnel0
 ip address 10.3.3.2 255.255.255.0 (line 3)
 no ip next-hop-self eigrp 100
 ip nhrp authentication mjlnet
 ip nhrp map multicast dynamic
 ip nhrp map 10.3.3.1 192.168.1.1
 ip nhrp map multicast 192.168.1.1
 ip nhrp network-id 1234
 ip nhrp nhs 10.3.3.1
 no ip split-horizon eigrp 100
 delay 50001 (line 4)
 tunnel source 192.168.1.2
 tunnel mode gre multipoint
 tunnel key 5678
 tunnel protection ipsec profile mjlnetprofile
!
!
! Inside interface
!
interface FastEthernet0/0
 ip address 10.1.1.10 255.255.255.0
!
!
! Outside interface
!
interface Serial2/0
 ip address 192.168.1.2 255.255.255.0
!
!
! EIGRP for site-to-site reachability (line 5)
!
router eigrp 100
 network 10.1.1.0 0.0.0.255
 network 10.3.3.0 0.0.0.255
 no auto-summary
!
```

Most of the configuration of the London-1 and London-2 gateways shown in Example 7-61 should be pretty familiar. If you are unsure as to basic DMVPN configuration, see the section "Dynamic Multipoint Virtual Private Network (DMVPN)" earlier in this chapter. Notice that only one tunnel interface is required on London-1 and London-2 (irrespective of the number of spoke sites).

Of particular significance is the fact that the London-1 and London-2 gateways are configured as NHSs for the DMVPN. If either London-1 or London-2 should fail, spoke gateways will simply use the remaining hub site gateway/NHS to access resources at the London site and to resolve the addresses of other spoke gateways.

Notice in highlighted lines 1 and 3 that the London-1 and London-2 hub site gateways are on the same DMVPN (network 10.3.3.0/24).

EIGRP is configured on London-1 and London-2 below highlighted lines 2 and 5. EIGRP provides IP reachability between all the sites in the DMVPN. Note that EIGRP is used for illustrative purposes only, and any routing protocol could be used for site-to-site reachability.

One other important command to note is the **delay** command configured on the mGRE tunnel interface on London-2 (see highlighted line 4). This command ensures that the path via the London-1 gateway is preferred for all traffic outbound from the London site to the spoke sites. The path via the London-1 gateway is preferred because the delay on the London-2 gateway is higher (50001 > 50000 [the default delay on London-1's GRE interface]), and so the composite EIGRP metric via the London-1 gateway is lower. Should the London-1 gateway go down, however, all traffic outbound to the spoke sites would simply fail over to the London-2 gateway.

Note that if you use OSPF as you routing protocol for site-to-site reachability, you can use the **ip ospf cost** interface configuration mode command to ensure that one of the hub site gateways is preferred over the other for outbound traffic to spoke sites (by configuring a lower OSPF cost on the preferred hub site gateway's tunnel interface).

Another important thing to notice in the configuration of London-1 and London-2 is the inclusion of the **ip nhrp map**, **ip nhrp map multicast**, and **ip nhrp nhs** commands on their mGRE tunnel interfaces. These commands are used to configure London-1 as a client of London-2, and London-2 as a client of London-1—this will ensure that there is direct connectivity between London-1 and London-2, and that the routing protocol will function correctly.

Now on to the configuration of the spoke gateways. Example 7-62 shows the configuration of the Berlin gateway with one DMVPN.

Example 7-62 *Configuration of the Berlin Spoke Gateway with One DMVPN*

```
Berlin#show running-config
Building configuration...
!
! Berlin gateway configuration
!
!
! IKE policy
!
crypto isakmp policy 10
 authentication pre-share
!
!
! Wildcard pre-shared key
!
crypto isakmp key mjlnet 0.0.0.0 0.0.0.0
!
!
! IPsec transform set
!
```

Example 7-62 *Configuration of the Berlin Spoke Gateway with One DMVPN (Continued)*

```
crypto ipsec transform-set mjlnettrans esp-3des esp-sha-hmac
!
!
! IPsec profile
!
crypto ipsec profile mjlnetprofile
 set transform-set mjlnettrans
!
!
! mGRE tunnel interface
!
interface Tunnel0
 ip address 10.3.3.3 255.255.255.0
 ip nhrp authentication mjlnet
 ip nhrp map 10.3.3.1 192.168.1.1 (line 1)
 ip nhrp map multicast 192.168.1.1 (line 2)
 ip nhrp map multicast 192.168.1.2 (line 3)
 ip nhrp map 10.3.3.2 192.168.1.2 (line 4)
 ip nhrp network-id 1234
 ip nhrp nhs 10.3.3.1 (line 5)
 ip nhrp nhs 10.3.3.2 (line 6)
 tunnel source 192.168.2.2
 tunnel mode gre multipoint
 tunnel key 5678
 tunnel protection ipsec profile mjlnetprofile
!
!
! Inside interface
!
interface FastEthernet2/0
 ip address 10.10.10.1 255.255.255.0
!
!
! Outside interface
!
interface FastEthernet2/0
 ip address 192.168.2.2 255.255.255.0
!
!
! EIGRP for site-to-site reachability
!
router eigrp 100
 network 10.2.2.0 0.0.0.255
 network 10.3.3.0 0.0.0.255
 distance 95 10.3.3.2 0.0.0.0 10 (line 7)
 no auto-summary
!
!
access-list 10 permit any (line 8)
!
!
```

Once again, much of the configuration of the Berlin spoke gateway is standard DMVPN configuration. As shown in highlighted lines 1 through 6, however, the **ip nhrp map**, **ip nhrp map multicast**, and **ip nhrp nhs** commands are duplicated. These three commands are used to configure the NHS on the Berlin gateway, and because there are two NHSs in this example (London-1 [192.168.1.1/10.3.3.1] and London-2 [192.168.1.2/10.3.3.2]), the configuration is duplicated.

Also, take a look at highlighted line 7—the **distance** *admin-distance ip-address wildcard-mask access-list* command here is used to apply an administrative distance of 95 to *any routes* (as specified by access list 10 in highlighted line 8) received from hub site gateway 10.3.3.2 (London-2). Because the default administrative distance for (internal) EIGRP routes is 90, this means that routes received from hub site gateway 10.3.3.1 (London-1) will be preferred over routes received from 10.3.3.2 (London-2), and so traffic *outbound* from the Berlin spoke gateway to the London site will traverse the London-1 hub site gateway.

It is worth noting that the **delay** command cannot be used on the GRE interface on the Berlin gateway (as it was in the previous section) to ensure that outbound traffic takes the path via the London-1 gateway because the interface here is *multipoint*, and so any delay that was configured would affect *all paths* via the interface (to all gateways [London-1 and London-2]).

Remember that the **delay** command applied to the tunnel interface on London-2 (see highlighted line 4, Example 7-61) causes traffic inbound from the London site to the Berlin site also to traverse the London-1 gateway. So, the **delay** command on London-2 and the **distance** command on the Berlin gateway cause inbound and outbound traffic to traverse the London-1 gateway, giving symmetric routing.

Note that the **distance** command can also be used if you use OSPF as your routing protocol for site-to-site reachability. In this case, you can specify an administrative distance greater than 110 (the default administrative distance for OSPF routes) for OSPF routes received from the backup hub site gateway so that routes received from the primary hub site gateway will be preferred.

So, for example, the **distance 112 10.3.3.2 0.0.0.0 10** command (configured on spoke site gateways in OSPF router configuration mode) would ensure that all routes (specified by access list 10) received from the London-2 gateway (10.3.3.2) were given an administrative distance of 112, and that routes received from the London-1 gateway (with a default administrative distance of 110) would therefore be preferred for outbound traffic.

Figure 7-51 illustrates the traffic flow when the delay of 50001 is configured on London-2 (see highlighted line 4, Example 7-61), and the **distance** command is configured on the Berlin gateway (see highlighted line 7, Example 7-62).

Figure 7-51 shows that in normal operation, all traffic inbound to and outbound from the Berlin site flows via the London-1 gateway.

Figure 7-51 *Symmetric Routing in the VPN with One DMVPN*

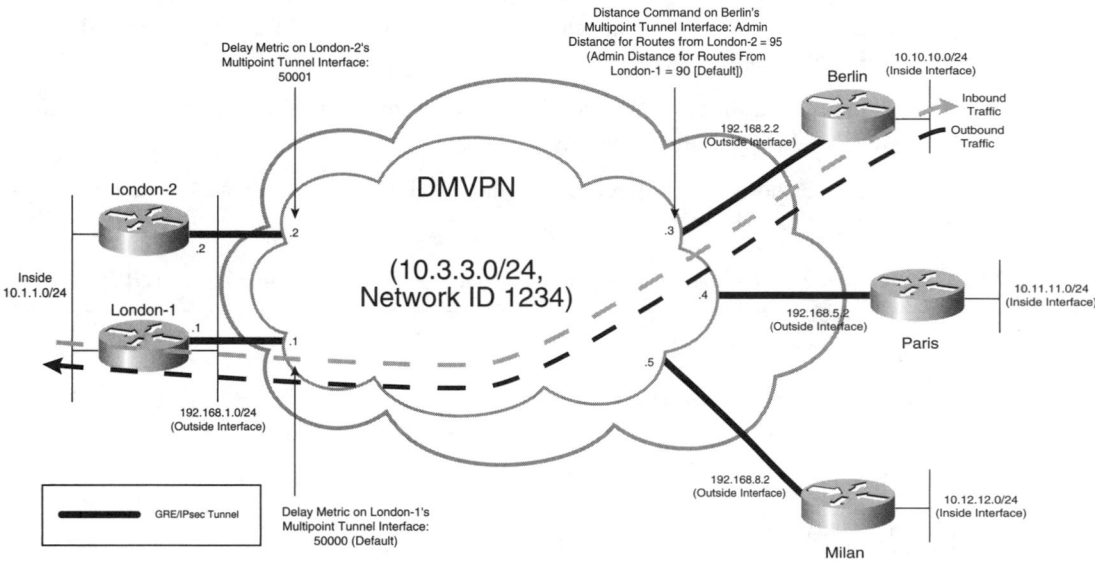

High Availability with Gateways Connected over Two DMVPNs

Another way of provisioning high availability with DMVPN is to configure two DMVPNs, one connected to each hub site gateway, as illustrated in Figure 7-52.

Figure 7-52 *High Availability with Two DMVPNs*

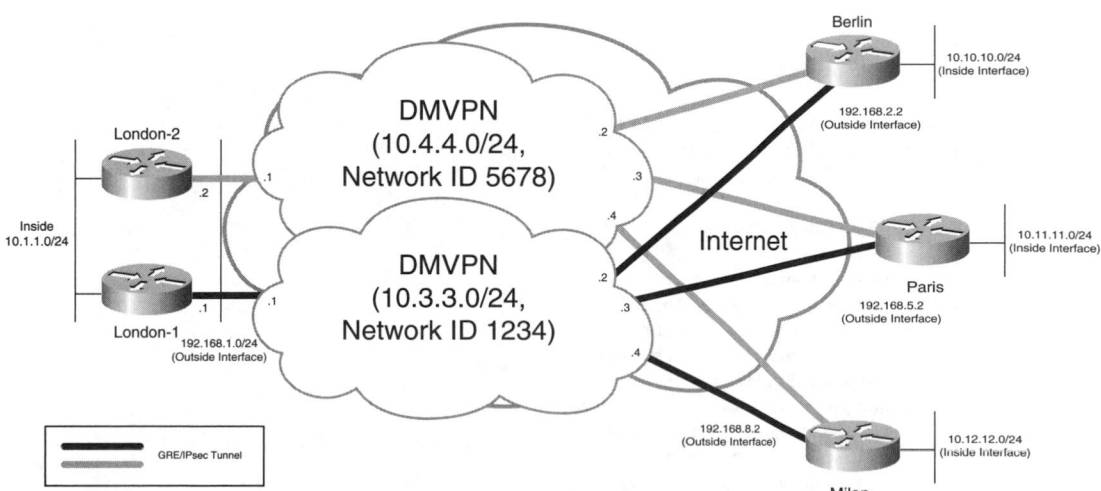

As you can see in Figure 7-52, each of the spoke gateways (Berlin, Paris, and Milan) are connected to two DMVPNs, one with London-1 as its NHS (IP network 10.3.3.0/24, and NHRP network ID 1234) and one with London-2 as its NHS (IP network 10.4.4.0/24, and NHRP network ID 5678).

The advantage of using two DMVPNs is that control of user traffic is easier than when using a single DMVPN for high availability.

Example 7-63 shows the configuration of the London-1 and London-2 hub site gateways when using two DMVPNs.

Example 7-63 *Configuration of the London-1 and London-2 Hub site Gateways When Using Two DMVPNs*

```
London-1#show running-config
Building configuration...
!
! London-1 gateway configuration
!
!
! IKE policy
!
crypto isakmp policy 10
 authentication pre-share
!
!
! Wildcard pre-shared key
!
crypto isakmp key mjlnet address 0.0.0.0 0.0.0.0
!
!
! IPsec transform set
!
crypto ipsec transform-set mjlnettrans esp-3des esp-sha-hmac
!
!
! IPsec profile
!
crypto ipsec profile mjlnetprofile
 set transform-set mjlnettrans
!
!
! mGRE tunnel interface
!
interface Tunnel0
 ip address 10.3.3.1 255.255.255.0 (line 1)
 no ip next-hop-self eigrp 100
 ip nhrp authentication mjlnet
 ip nhrp map multicast dynamic
 ip nhrp network-id 1234 (line 2)
 no ip split-horizon eigrp 100
 tunnel source 192.168.1.1
 tunnel mode gre multipoint
 tunnel key 5678
```

Example 7-63 *Configuration of the London-1 and London-2 Hub site Gateways When Using Two DMVPNs (Continued)*

```
 tunnel protection ipsec profile mjlnetprofile
!
!
! Inside interface
!
interface FastEthernet0/0
 ip address 10.1.1.1 255.255.255.0
!
!
! Outside interface
!
interface Serial1/0
 ip address 192.168.1.1 255.255.255.0
!
!
! EIGRP for site-to-site reachability
!
router eigrp 100
 passive-interface Ethernet3/0
 network 10.1.1.0 0.0.0.255
 network 10.3.3.0 0.0.0.255
 no auto-summary
!
!
!
End
```

```
London-2#show running-config
Building configuration...
!
! London-2 gateway configuration
!
!
! IKE policy
!
crypto isakmp policy 10
 authentication pre-share
!
!
! Wildcard pre-shared key
!
crypto isakmp key mjlnet address 0.0.0.0 0.0.0.0
!
!
! IPsec transform set
!
crypto ipsec transform-set mjlnettrans esp-3des esp-sha-hmac
!
!
! IPsec profile
!
```

continues

Example 7-63 *Configuration of the London-1 and London-2 Hub site Gateways When Using Two DMVPNs (Continued)*

```
crypto ipsec profile mjlnetprofile
 set transform-set mjlnettrans
 !
 !
 ! mGRE tunnel interface
 !
interface Tunnel0
 ip address 10.4.4.1 255.255.255.0 (line 3)
 no ip next-hop-self eigrp 100
 ip nhrp authentication mjlnet
 ip nhrp map multicast dynamic
 ip nhrp network-id 5678 (line 4)
 no ip split-horizon eigrp 100
 delay 50001 (line 5)
 tunnel source 192.168.1.2
 tunnel mode gre multipoint
 tunnel key 1234
 tunnel protection ipsec profile mjlnetprofile
 !
 !
 ! Inside interface
 !
interface FastEthernet0/0
 ip address 10.1.1.10 255.255.255.0
 !
 !
 ! Outside interface
 !
interface Serial2/0
 ip address 192.168.1.2 255.255.255.0
 !
 !
 ! EIGRP for site-to-site reachability
 !
router eigrp 100
 network 10.1.1.0 0.0.0.255
 network 10.4.4.0 0.0.0.255
 no auto-summary
 !
 !
 !
 end
```

The configuration of the London-1 and London-2 hub site gateways is much the same as that shown in Example 7-61. If you look at highlighted lines 1 to 4, however, you will see that London-1 and London-2 are now connected to separate DMVPNs. London-1 is connected to the DMVPN with network ID 1234, and using IP network 10.3.3.0/24. London-2, on the other hand, is connected to the DMVPN with network ID 5678, and using IP network 10.4.4.0/24.

Highlighted line 5 shows the **delay 50001** command, which configures a delay of 50001 on the tunnel 0 interface of the London-2 gateway and causes traffic *outbound* from the London site to follow the path via the London-1 gateway (50001 > 50000 [the default delay on the tunnel 0 interface on London-1]).

Example 7-64 shows the configuration of spoke gateway Berlin with two DMVPNs.

Example 7-64 *Configuration of the Berlin Spoke Gateway with Two DMVPNs*

```
Berlin#show running-config
Building configuration...
!
! Berlin gateway configuration
!
!
! IKE policy
!
crypto isakmp policy 10
 authentication pre-share
!
!
! Wildcard pre-shared key
!
crypto isakmp key mjlnet address 0.0.0.0 0.0.0.0
!
!
! IPsec transform set
!
crypto ipsec transform-set mjlnettrans esp-3des esp-sha-hmac
!
!
! IPsec profile
!
crypto ipsec profile mjlnetprofile
 set transform-set mjlnettrans
!
!
! mGRE tunnel interface for DMVPN with network id 1234/IP network 10.3.3.0/24
!
interface Tunnel0 (line 1)
 ip address 10.3.3.2 255.255.255.0
 ip nhrp authentication mjlnet
 ip nhrp map 10.3.3.1 192.168.1.1
 ip nhrp map multicast 192.168.1.1
 ip nhrp network-id 1234
 ip nhrp nhs 10.3.3.1
 tunnel source Loopback100 (line 2)
 tunnel mode gre multipoint
 tunnel key 5678
 tunnel protection ipsec profile mjlnetprofile
!
!
```

continues

Example 7-64 *Configuration of the Berlin Spoke Gateway with Two DMVPNs (Continued)*

```
! mGRE tunnel interface for DMVPN with network id 5678/IP network 10.4.4.0/24
!
interface Tunnel1 (line 3)
 ip address 10.4.4.2 255.255.255.0
 ip nhrp authentication mjlnet
 ip nhrp map 10.4.4.1 192.168.1.2
 ip nhrp map multicast 192.168.1.2
 ip nhrp network-id 5678
 ip nhrp nhs 10.4.4.1
 delay 50001 (line 4)
 tunnel source Loopback101 (line 5)
 tunnel mode gre multipoint
 tunnel key 1234
 tunnel protection ipsec profile mjlnetprofile
!
!
! Loopback interface 100 for use as interface tunnel 0 source address
!
interface Loopback100 (line 6)
 ip address 192.168.6.1 255.255.255.255
!
!
! Loopback interface 101 for use as interface tunnel 1 source address
!
interface Loopback101 (line 7)
 ip address 192.168.6.2 255.255.255.255
!
!
! Inside interface
!
interface FastEthernet1/0
 ip address 10.10.10.1 255.255.255.0
!
!
! Outside interface
!
interface FastEthernet2/0
 ip address 192.168.2.2 255.255.255.0
!
!
! EIGRP for site-to-site reachability
!
router eigrp 100
 passive-interface FastEthernet1/0
 network 10.2.2.0 0.0.0.255
 network 10.3.3.0 0.0.0.255
 network 10.4.4.0 0.0.0.255
 no auto-summary
!
!
!
end
```

Notice in highlighted lines 1 and 3 the configuration of tunnel interfaces 0 and 1. Tunnel interface 0 connects to the DMVPN with network ID 1234 and IP network 10.3.3.0/24, and tunnel interface 1 connects to the DMVPN with network id 5678 and IP network 10.4.4.0/24.

Also notice that the tunnel source address for tunnel interfaces 0 and 1 correspond to loopback interfaces 100 and 101, respectively (see highlighted lines 2, 5, 6, and 7). When using two DMVPNs, you must use separate tunnel source addresses with each tunnel interface; otherwise, your DMVPNs will not function correctly. And, make sure that the tunnel source addresses (here, those configured on loopback interfaces 100 and 101) are globally reachable (they can be reached from the other gateways in the DMVPN).

In highlighted line 4 you can see the **delay 50001** command configured on tunnel interface 1. I am sure you can guess the function of this command, but to reiterate, its function is to ensure that traffic *outbound* from the Berlin site uses the tunnel 0 interface via London-1 gateway (the DMVPN with network ID 1234 and IP network 10.3.3.0/24). Outbound traffic uses the path via the London-1 gateway because the tunnel 0 interface (to London-1) has a lower delay than the tunnel 1 interface (50000 < 50001).

Figure 7-53 illustrates the traffic flow outbound from and inbound to the Berlin site with two DMVPNs.

Figure 7-53 *Traffic Flow with Two DMVPNs*

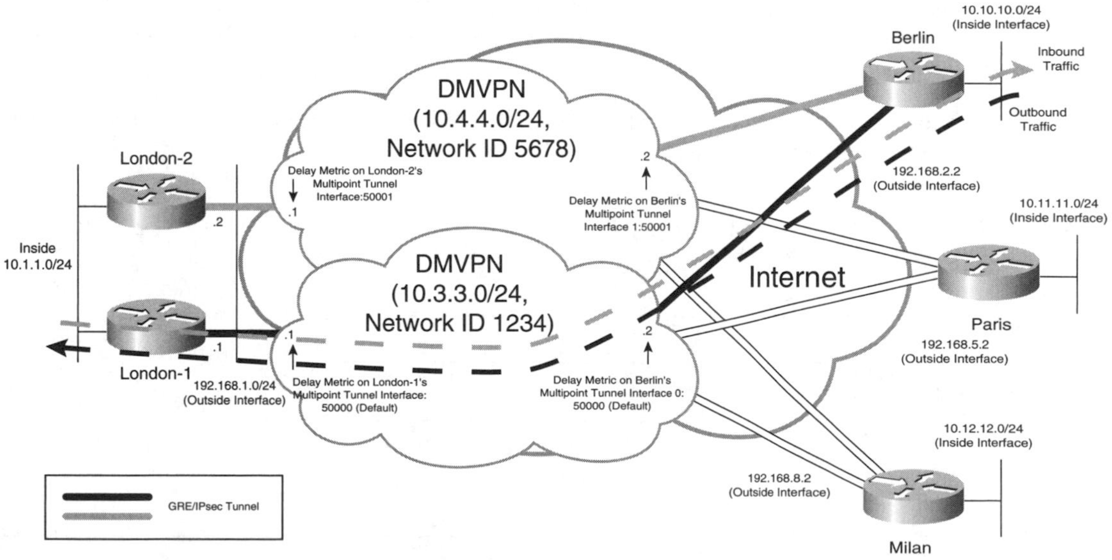

As illustrated in Figure 7-53, all traffic outbound from and inbound to the Berlin site flows via the London-1 gateway in normal operation. In the event that London-1 fails, user traffic will fail over to the London-2 gateway.

Designing QoS for IPsec VPNs

Quality of service (QoS) describes a number of mechanisms that prioritize some traffic over other traffic. QoS is sometimes known as "managed unfairness."

As previously described, you can implement QoS in a network in two ways:

- Using the Differentiated Services (DiffServ) model
- Using the Integrated Services (IntServ) model

There are important considerations when using DiffServ and/or IntServ in an IPsec VPN, as described in the following two sections.

Using DiffServ in an IPsec VPN

RFC2401 specifies that the contents of the type of service (ToS) or Differentiated Services (DS) field in the IP header of a protected user packet must be copied to the outer header of a tunnel mode IPsec packet. The ToS or DS field is maintained in the outer IP header of an IPsec transport mode packet.

NOTE   Copying of the ToS/DS field is supported in all Cisco IOS releases that support IPsec. Copying of the ToS/DS field is also supported in PIX software release 5.1 and later and VPN 3000 concentrator software release 3.5 and later.

Figure 7-54 illustrates the copying of the ToS/DS field from the protected user packet to the outer IP header of an IPsec tunnel mode packet.

Figure 7-54 *Copying of the ToS/DS Field from the Protected User Packet to the Outer IP Header of an IPsec Tunnel Mode Packet*

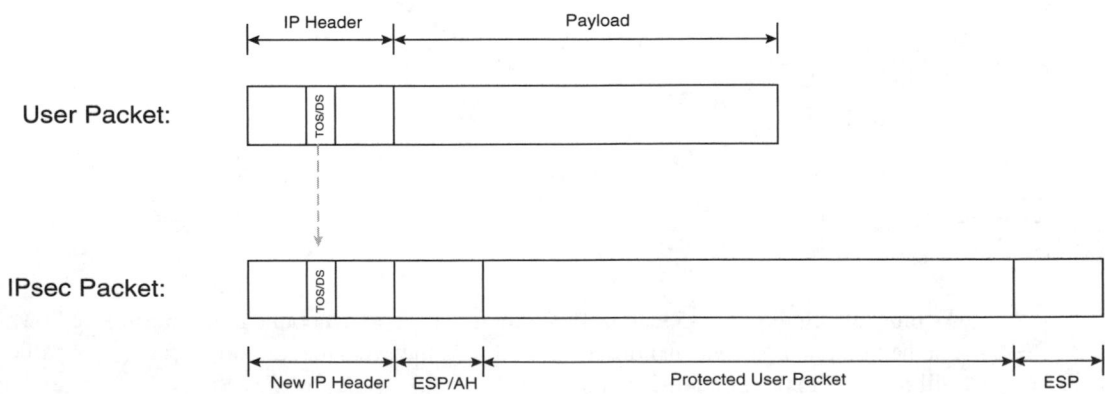

When deploying QoS in an IPsec VPN, it is important to consider that after a user packet has been encapsulated in IPsec (producing an IPsec packet), much if not all information that could be used to classify a packet is unavailable.

Information from the original user packet IP header that is maintained or copied to the outer IP header of an IPsec packet is as follows:

- **Transport mode**—All information is maintained except the IP protocol number that is modified to reflect the (initial) security protocol (ESP/AH). Note that the IP protocol number indicates the protocol such as TCP, UDP, ESP, or AH that comes directly after the IP header.

- **Tunnel mode**—The ToS/DS field is copied from the encapsulated user packet IP header.

See Figure 7-67 later in this chapter to see the IP header.

Figure 7-55 illustrates classification of IPsec packets on router in the path between IPsec VPN gateways.

Figure 7-55 *Router Between the IPsec VPN Gateways Tries to Classify an IPsec Packet*

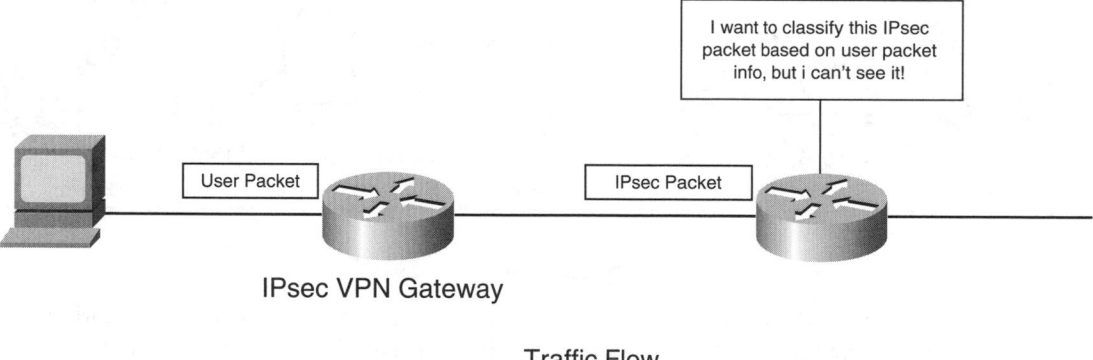

In Figure 7-55, the IPsec VPN gateway encapsulates a user packet with IPsec, and when that packet arrives at the next-hop router, it is unable to classify the packet using user packet information because this information is hidden by IPsec.

So, if you want to classify packets based on user packet information such as IP protocol number, TCP port number, or UDP port number, you should classify and mark the ToS/DS field of the packet prior to IPsec encapsulation in normal operation.

In Figure 7-55, for example, if you want to classify and mark the packet based on user packet information such as IP protocol, TCP port number, or UDP port number, you must do it on the IPsec VPN gateway.

In any network (including an IPsec VPN), classification and marking of user packets should be performed as close the packets' source as possible. Some user applications and end devices such as IP phones may mark user packets by default.

In some customer-managed IPsec VPNs, it might be acceptable to trust the ToS/DS field marking performed by user applications and end devices. In many customer-managed and most if not all provider-managed IPsec VPNs, however, it is necessary to reclassify and re-mark user packets on an IPsec VPN gateway. IPsec VPN gateways, therefore, often function as a QoS trust boundary between the customer network and the service provider network.

After packets have been classified and marked, and if the IPsec VPN is provisioned over a private service provider network, intermediate devices between IPsec VPN gateways can schedule (queue) packets without having to reclassify those packets.

Figure 7-56 shows typical classification, marking, and scheduling of packets in an IPsec VPN provisioned over a private service provider backbone network.

Figure 7-56 *Classification, Marking, and Scheduling of Packets in an IPsec VPN Provisioned over a Private Service Provider Network*

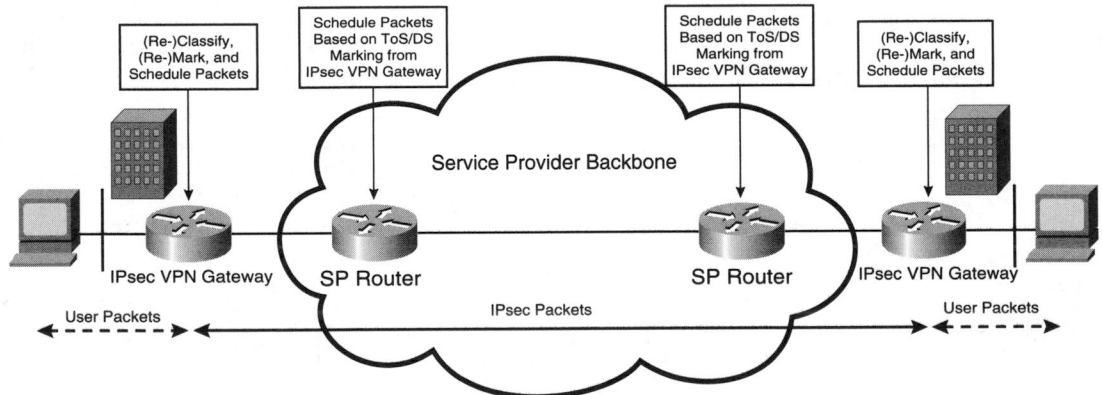

In Figure 7-56, the IPsec VPN gateways are responsible for classifying and marking packets, and the service provider routers then schedule IPsec packets based on the (ToS/DS) marking performed on the IPsec VPN gateways.

Note that IPsec VPN gateways and service provider routers shown in Figure 7-56 might also perform traffic shaping and policing, respectively.

If the IPsec VPN is provisioned over the public Internet, intermediate devices between IPsec VPN gateways will not typically schedule packets based on marking done on IPsec VPN gateways.

Figure 7-57 shows typical scheduling of packets in an IPsec VPN provisioned over the public Internet. As Figure 7-57 shows, ISP routers do not schedule packets based on any marking performed on IPsec VPN gateways.

Although it is possible to configure traffic shaping on IPsec VPN gateways where the IPsec VPN is provisioned over the Internet, IPsec VPNs provisioned over the public Internet provide best-effort service, with no guarantees.

Figure 7-57 *Scheduling of Packets in an IPsec VPN Provisioned over the Public Internet*

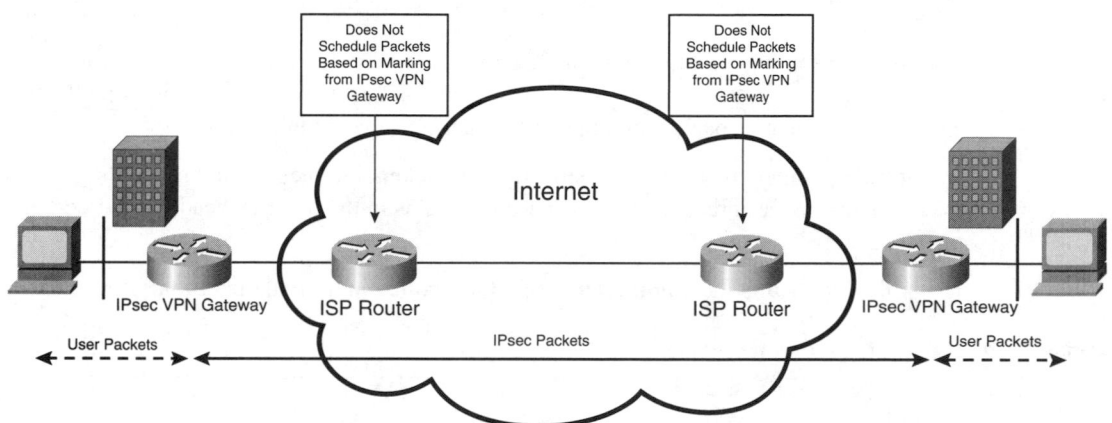

Configuring QoS with the qos pre-classify Command

If you want to classify, mark, and schedule packets on IPsec VPN gateways, you must carefully configure the IPsec VPN gateways. Careful configuration of the IPsec VPN gateways is necessary because when packets are encapsulated in IPsec, the information that is available to help you classify packets is, as previously mentioned, limited.

Figure 7-58 illustrates information available to classify packets on IPsec VPN gateways.

Figure 7-58 *Information Available for the Classification of Packets on IPsec VPN Gateways*

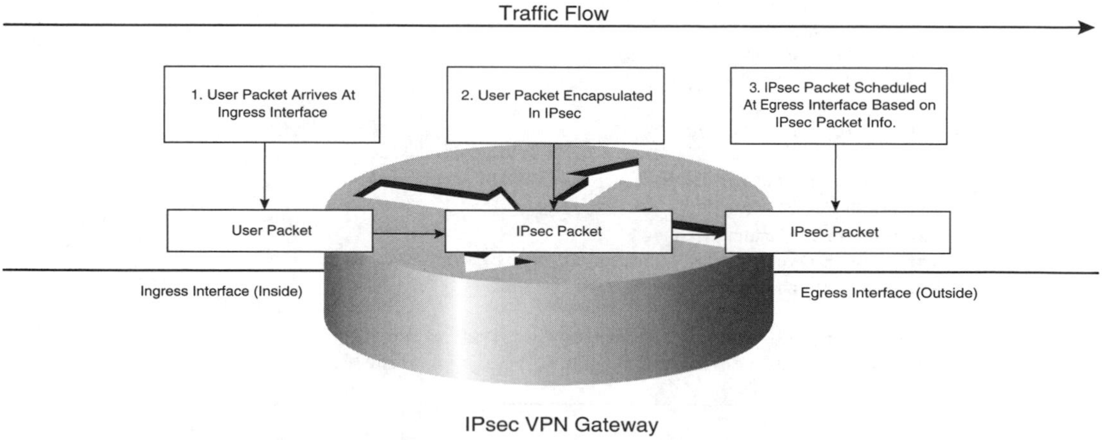

As you can see in Figure 7-58, if you want to classify and mark packets based on user packet layer information, such as TCP or UDP port, in normal operation you have to do it on the IPsec VPN gateway's ingress interface (prior to the user packets being encapsulated by IPsec).

In normal operation, classification on the egress interface of an IPsec VPN gateway can only be based on information in the outer header of IPsec packets—remember that IPsec encapsulated the user packet, and most user packet information is hidden.

In normal operation, therefore, classification of packets for queuing and scheduling mechanisms on the egress interface is based on fields in the outer IP header of IPsec packets.

Example 7-65 shows the configuration of a QoS policy in normal operation.

Example 7-65 *QoS Policy in Normal Operation*

```
London#show running-config
Building configuration...
Current configuration : 2546 bytes
!
version 12.3
!
class-map match-all critical-data (line 1)
 match access-group 199
class-map match-any real-time-traffic (line 2)
 match ip rtp 16384 16383
 match access-group 198
!
!
policy-map voice-data-policy (line 3)
  class critical-data
   set ip dscp 25
   bandwidth percent 40
  class real-time-traffic
   set ip dscp ef
   priority percent 30
  class class-default
   set ip dscp default
   bandwidth percent 30
!
interface Serial1/0
 ip address 192.168.1.1 255.255.255.0
 max-reserved-bandwidth 100
 service-policy output voice-data-policy (line 4)
 crypto map mjlnetmap
!
access-list 198 permit tcp any any eq 1720 (line 5)
access-list 199 permit tcp any any eq telnet (line 6)
 !
```

Highlighted lines 1, 2, 3, and 4 show the configuration of a sample Class-Based Weighted Fair Queuing (CBWFQ) policy called voice-data-policy and its application to egress (outside) interface serial 1/0 of an IPsec VPN gateway.

The CBWFQ policy defines three traffic classes:

- **critical-data**—Matches traffic specified in access list 199 (see highlighted line 6)
- **real-time-traffic**—Matches voice traffic (Real Time Transport Protocol [RTP] traffic on even ports in UDP port range 16384 and 32767) and call signaling traffic as specified in access list 198 (see highlighted line 5)
- **class-default**—Matches all other IP traffic

NOTE   The specific QoS policy shown in Example 7-65 is used for illustrative purposes only and is not necessarily recommended for live deployments. QoS policy will vary according to the requirements of each particular IPsec VPN.

Traffic matching all three classes in the CBWFQ policy is sent across the IPsec VPN, and the **show policy-map interface** *interface-name* command is used to verify traffic matching the three traffic classes in the CBWFQ policy, as shown in Example 7-66.

Example 7-66 *Verifying Traffic Matching the CBWFQ Policy*

```
London#show policy-map interface serial 1/0
 Serial1/0
  Service-policy output: voice-data-policy
    Class-map: critical-data (match-all)
      0 packets, 0 bytes
      5 minute offered rate 0 bps, drop rate 0 bps
      Match: access-group 199
      QoS Set
        dscp 25
          Packets marked 0 (line 1)
      Queueing
        Output Queue: Conversation 265
        Bandwidth 40 (%)
        Bandwidth 617 (kbps) Max Threshold 64 (packets)
        (pkts matched/bytes matched) 0/0
        (depth/total drops/no-buffer drops) 0/0/0
    Class-map: real-time-traffic (match-any)
      0 packets, 0 bytes
      5 minute offered rate 0 bps, drop rate 0 bps
      Match: ip rtp 16384 16383
        0 packets, 0 bytes
        5 minute rate 0 bps
      Match: access-group 198
        0 packets, 0 bytes
        5 minute rate 0 bps
      QoS Set
        dscp ef
```

continues

Example 7-66 *Verifying Traffic Matching the CBWFQ Policy (Continued)*

```
               Packets marked 0 (line 2)
        Queueing
          Strict Priority
          Output Queue: Conversation 264
          Bandwidth 30 (%)
          Bandwidth 463 (kbps) Burst 11575 (Bytes)
          (pkts matched/bytes matched) 0/0
          (total drops/bytes drops) 0/0
      Class-map: class-default (match-any)
        1904 packets, 218399 bytes
        5 minute offered rate 12000 bps, drop rate 0 bps
        Match: any
        QoS Set
          dscp default
            Packets marked 1866 (line 3)
        Queueing
          Output Queue: Conversation 266
          Bandwidth 30 (%)
          Bandwidth 463 (kbps) Max Threshold 64 (packets)
          (pkts matched/bytes matched) 1892/219756
          (depth/total drops/no-buffer drops) 0/0/0
London#
```

In highlighted lines 1 and 2, you can see that there no packets have matched the critical-data and real-time-traffic classes, and in highlighted line 3 that 1866 packets have matched the class-default class.

Hmm? What is going on here? Traffic matching the critical-data and real-time-traffic classes is definitely being sent over the IPsec VPN, but it is not being matched by the CBWFQ policy.

The answer is that because the CBWFQ policy is applied to the egress interface, traffic that would otherwise match the critical-data and real-time-traffic classes is already encapsulated by IPsec by the time it reaches the IPsec VPN's egress interface, and so it does not in fact match the critical-data and real-time-traffic classes. Instead, all (IPsec) traffic matches the class-default class.

So, the problem is that when user packets are encapsulated in IPsec, most information (including TCP and UDP port numbers) is unavailable for matching.

From Cisco IOS Software Release 12.1(5)T or later on the 7200 platform, and from Cisco IOS Software Release 12.2(2)T on 2600 or 3600 platforms, however, it is possible to get around this problem of unavailable user packet information using the **qos pre-classify** command.

The **qos pre-classify** command allows an IPsec VPN gateway to temporarily store Layer 3 and 4 information from original user packets so that the corresponding IPsec-encapsulated packets can be classified, queued, and scheduled on the egress (outside) interface according to the original Layer 3 and 4 information.

Figure 7-59 illustrates the effect of the **qos pre-classify** command.

Figure 7-59 *Effect of the* **qos pre-classify** *Command*

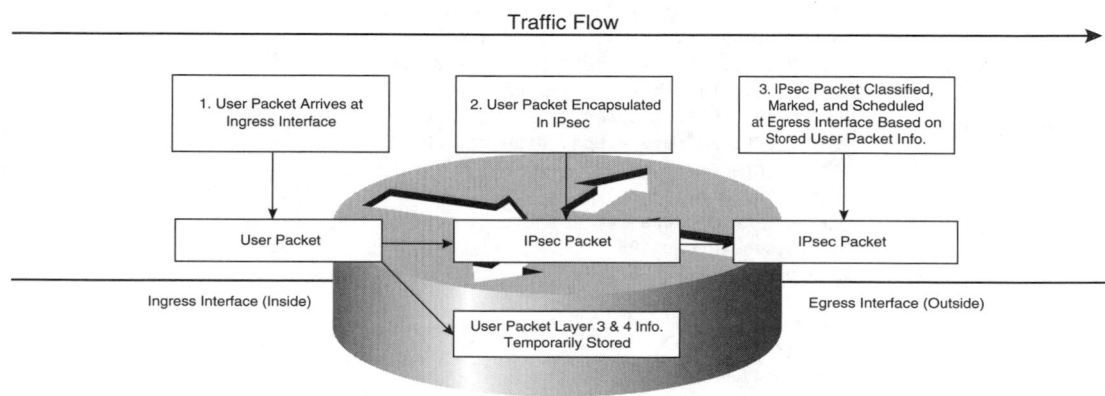

In this example, a plain IPsec tunnel (without GRE) is being used, and so the **qos pre-classify** command is applied within the crypto map, as shown in Example 7-67. Note that only relevant configuration is shown.

Example 7-67 *Verifying Traffic Matching the CBWFQ Policy*

```
London#conf t
Enter configuration commands, one per line.  End with CNTL/Z.
London(config)#crypto map mjlnetmap 10 ipsec-isakmp
London(config-crypto-map)#qos pre-classify
London(config-crypto-map)#end
London#
```

After the **qos pre-classify** command has been configured, traffic matches the critical-data and real-time-traffic classes within the CBWFQ policy, as shown in the output of the **show policy-map interface** command in Example 7-68.

Example 7-68 *Verifying Traffic Matching the CBWFQ Policy*

```
London#show policy-map interface serial 1/0
 Serial1/0
  Service-policy output: voice-data-policy
    Class-map: critical-data (match-all)
      5534 packets, 863304 bytes
      5 minute offered rate 13000 bps, drop rate 0 bps
      Match: access-group 199
      QoS Set
        dscp 25
          Packets marked 5534 (line 1)
      Queueing
```

continues

Example 7-68 *Verifying Traffic Matching the CBWFQ Policy (Continued)*

```
                 Output Queue: Conversation 265
                 Bandwidth 40 (%)
                 Bandwidth 617 (kbps) Max Threshold 64 (packets)
                 (pkts matched/bytes matched) 5534/863304
                 (depth/total drops/no-buffer drops) 0/0/0
        Class-map: real-time-traffic (match-any)
          5285 packets, 613060 bytes
          5 minute offered rate 0 bps, drop rate 0 bps
          Match: ip rtp 16384 16383
            0 packets, 0 bytes
            5 minute rate 0 bps
          Match: access-group 198
            5285 packets, 613060 bytes
            5 minute rate 0 bps
          QoS Set
            dscp ef
              Packets marked 5285 (line 2)
          Queueing
            Strict Priority
            Output Queue: Conversation 264
            Bandwidth 30 (%)
            Bandwidth 463 (kbps) Burst 11575 (Bytes)
            (pkts matched/bytes matched) 5285/613060
            (total drops/bytes drops) 0/0
        Class-map: class-default (match-any)
          6431 packets, 737805 bytes
          5 minute offered rate 0 bps, drop rate 0 bps
          Match: any
          QoS Set
            dscp default
              Packets marked 6271
          Queueing
            Output Queue: Conversation 266
            Bandwidth 30 (%)
            Bandwidth 463 (kbps) Max Threshold 64 (packets)
            (pkts matched/bytes matched) 6271/727304
            (depth/total drops/no-buffer drops) 0/0/0
London#
```

As you can see in highlighted lines 1 and 2, packets are now matching the critical-data and real-time-data classes and are marked and scheduled accordingly.

If you are using GRE tunnels to carry multiprotocol or multicast traffic, you must apply the **qos pre-classify** command within the crypto map *and* on the GRE tunnel interface, as shown in Example 7-69. Note that only relevant configuration is shown.

Example 7-69 *Configuring the qos pre-classify Command with GRE/IPsec Tunnels*

```
 !
 crypto map mjlnetmap 10 ipsec-isakmp
  set peer 192.168.2.2
  set transform-set mjlnettrans
  match address 101
  qos pre-classify (line 1)
 !
 interface Tunnel0
  ip address 10.3.3.1 255.255.255.0
  qos pre-classify (line 2)
  tunnel source 192.168.1.1
  tunnel destination 192.168.2.2
 !
```

In highlighted lines 1 and 2, the **qos pre-classify** command is configured under the crypto map and tunnel interface respectively.

If you are using mGRE tunnels with DMVPN, you only need to apply the **qos pre-classify** command on the mGRE tunnel interface, as shown in Example 7-70. Note that only relevant configuration is shown.

Example 7-70 *Configuring the* **qos pre-classify** *Command with mGRE/IPsec Tunnels*

```
 !
 interface Tunnel0
  ip address 10.3.3.1 255.255.255.0
  ip nhrp authentication mjlnet
  ip nhrp map multicast dynamic
  ip nhrp network-id 1234
  no ip split-horizon eigrp 100
  qos pre-classify
  tunnel source 192.168.1.1
  tunnel mode gre multipoint
  tunnel key 5678
  tunnel protection ipsec profile mjlnetprofile
 !
```

The highlighted line shows where the **qos re-classify** command is configured under the mGRE tunnel interface.

Before finishing this section, it is worth noting that you cannot configure the **qos pre-classify** command in conjunction with legacy priority queuing (configured using the **priority-list** and **priority-group** command).

IPsec Anti-Replay Considerations with QoS

One feature of IPsec that you can implement in conjunction with both AH and ESP is protection against duplicate IPsec packets sent by an attacker. Protection against duplicate packets is known as *replay protection* and when implemented causes a receiving IPsec

VPN gateway to just drop duplicate IPsec packets. Replay protection can have implications in an IPsec VPN where packet scheduling based on ToS or DS field values (such as IP Precedence or Differentiated Services Code Point [DSCP]) is implemented in the backbone network between IPsec VPN gateways.

IPsec uses unique packet sequence numbers to protect against replay attacks. Each packet associated with a particular SA is sent with a unique sequence number, and the sequence number increases by one every time an IPsec VPN gateway sends a packet for that IPsec SA.

Figure 7-60 illustrates IPsec packet sequence numbers.

Figure 7-60 *IPsec Packet Sequence Numbers*

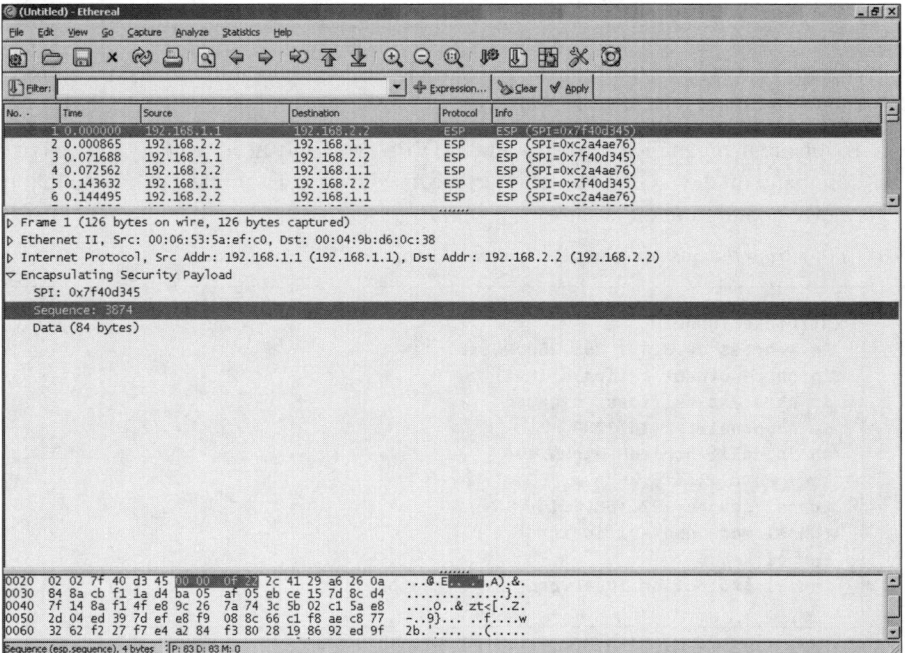

In the first highlighted line in Figure 7-60, you can see an ESP packet sent from IPsec VPN gateway 192.168.1.1 to IPsec VPN gateway 192.168.2.2. Notice the SPI of 0x7f40d345, which (together with the security protocol [ESP] and destination IP address) uniquely identifies the IPsec SA.

In the second highlighted line in Figure 7-60, you can see that the sequence number associated with this ESP packet is 3874.

If replay protection is implemented on a packet receiving IPsec VPN gateway, it maintains a sliding relay window. This replay window dictates whether the receiving IPsec VPN gateway will accept or discard IPsec packets that it receives.

Figure 7-61 illustrates the IPsec Replay Window. Note that a 10-packet replay window is used for illustrative purposes only.

Figure 7-61 *IPsec Replay Window*

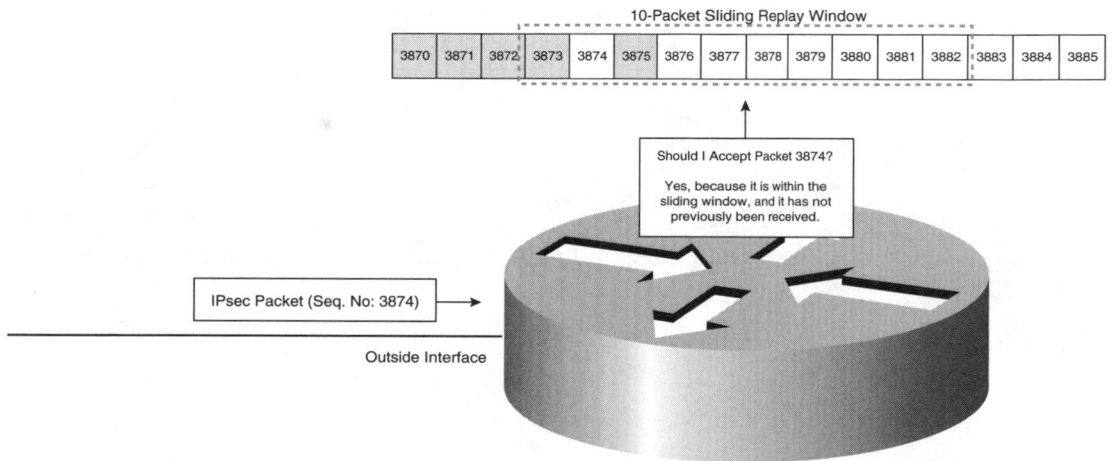

In Figure 7-61, the IPsec VPN gateway is implementing a 10-packet replay window. The gateway receives an IPsec packet with sequence number 3874, and because it is within the sliding window (from sequence number 3873 to 3882) and the gateway has not already received a packet with sequence number 3874, the gateway accepts the packet. Sequence numbers of packets that the gateway has already received are shaded gray in Figure 7-61.

In Figure 7-61, if the gateway were to receive an IPsec packet with sequence number of 3872, it would drop it because it would not be within the replay window. If the gateway were to receive an IPsec packet with sequence number of 3875, it would drop it because a packet with that sequence number has already been received.

If an IPsec VPN gateway receives a packet whose sequence number is to the right of the current window (has a sequence number which is greater than the largest current sequence number encompassed by the replay window), after the gateway has authenticated that packet, it shifts the replay window to the right to encompass the newly received packet.

NOTE   Although Figure 7-61 shows a 10-packet replay window, an IPsec replay window must be at least 32 packets, and preferably 64 packets.

Cisco IOS routers implement a 64-packet replay window, and Cisco PIX firewalls implement a 32-packet replay window.

Replay protection works well when IPsec packets are received in roughly the same order as they are sent by the transmitting IPsec VPN gateway. If IPsec packets become re-ordered in the backbone network between IPsec VPN gateways, this can cause the receiving IPsec VPN gateway to drop some IPsec packets, as illustrated in Figure 7-62.

Figure 7-62 *Re-Ordering Causes IPsec Packet Drops*

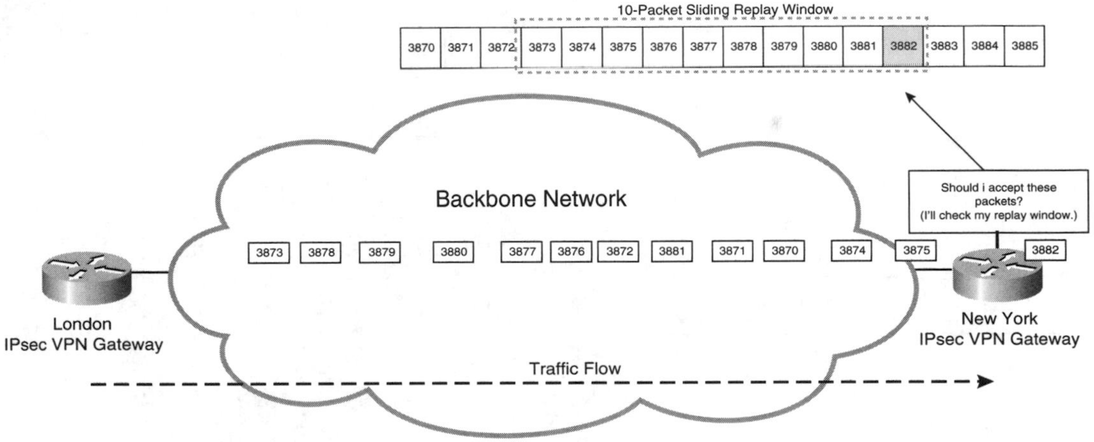

In Figure 7-62, the London IPsec VPN gateway sends 13 IPsec packets (with sequence numbers 3870 to 3882) in (correct) sequence to the New York gateway. Unfortunately, the IPsec packets become re-ordered in the backbone network, and the first packet that the New York gateway receives is IPsec packet with sequence number 3882.

When it receives packet 3882, the New York gateway shifts the (10-packet) replay window to the right to encompass packet 3882.

The New York gateway now receives the other 12 packets, but drops packets 3870, 3871, and 3872 because they do not fall within the (10-packet) replay window.

Although the extreme packet re-ordering shown in Figure 7-62 is unlikely, it is easy to see how packet re-ordering could result in some IPsec packets being dropped.

The big question is, how can packet re-ordering occur? One common cause of packet re-ordering is QoS packet scheduling in the backbone network between IPsec VPN gateways. If QoS is implemented in the backbone, some traffic will be prioritized over other traffic, and this inevitably leads to packet re-ordering.

The good news is that although packet re-ordering can occur when QoS is implemented in a backbone network, it is likely that the only packets dropped will be low-priority packets. This is because high-priority packets will travel faster over the backbone network; low-priority packets will travel more slowly. Some low-priority packets might, therefore, be outside (to the left of) the replay window when they are received on an IPsec VPN gateway.

If you do find that packets loss due to QoS scheduling in the backbone network is a problem, it is possible to overcome this by ensuring that separate IPsec SAs (and therefore separate replay windows) are negotiated for different traffic types. If you configure separate lines (traffic selectors) for *different* traffic types in your crypto access list, separate IPsec SAs are negotiated between IPsec VPN gateways for these traffic types. It would be possible, for example, to specify one line in your crypto access list to match all UDP traffic, and another line to match all TCP traffic, and each of these lines would be negotiated as a separate IPsec SA.

Note that IKEv1 does not allow the configuration of *identical* traffic selectors (defined in separate lines in crypto access lists) for IPsec SAs associated with *separate* quality of service. For example, in IKEv1 you cannot specify two identical traffic selectors for source IP address 10.1.1.0/24 and destination IP address 10.2.2.0/24, with one of the traffic selectors associated with an IPsec SA for DSCP 46 (Expedited Forwarding [EF]) and the other associated with an IPsec SA for DSCP 25.

IKEv2, on the other hand, specifies that identical traffic selectors may be used for separate IPsec SAs, each of which can be used, for example, for a separate QoS.

As a final note on packet re-ordering and replay protection, it is worth stating that replay protection is mandatory for the IPsec VPN gateways when sending IPsec packets (sequence numbers must be included in the packets), but that replay protection is not mandatory for the IPsec VPN gateways receiving IPsec packets (it is not mandatory for a receiver to implement a replay window).

Cisco routers implement a replay window for IPsec SAs except for ESP when authentication is not specified.

TIP   Beginning with Cisco IOS Software Release 12.3(14)T, it is possible to change the replay window size or even disable it using the **crypto ipsec security-association replay window-size** and **crypto ipsec security-association replay disable** global configuration mode commands (which affect all SAs), or the **set security-association replay window-size** and **set security-association replay disable** commands within a crypto map (which affect only those SAs associated with that crypto map).

Think carefully before changing the replay window size (the default is there for a good reason), and think especially carefully before disabling it.

Use the **show crypto ipsec sa** command to verify replay protection as shown in Examples 7-71 (IPsec SAs with authentication) and 7-72 (IPsec ESP SAs without authentication).

Example 7-71 *Verifying Replay Protection for IPsec SAs (with Authentication)*

```
London#show crypto ipsec sa
interface: Serial1/0
   Crypto map tag: mjlnetmap, local addr. 192.168.1.1
   protected vrf:
   local  ident (addr/mask/prot/port): (10.1.1.0/255.255.255.0/0/0)
   remote ident (addr/mask/prot/port): (10.2.2.0/255.255.255.0/0/0)
   current_peer: 192.168.2.2:500
     PERMIT, flags={origin_is_acl,}
    #pkts encaps: 485, #pkts encrypt: 485, #pkts digest: 485
    #pkts decaps: 484, #pkts decrypt: 484, #pkts verify: 484
    #pkts compressed: 0, #pkts decompressed: 0
    #pkts not compressed: 0, #pkts compr. failed: 0
    #pkts not decompressed: 0, #pkts decompress failed: 0
```

continues

Example 7-71 *Verifying Replay Protection for IPsec SAs (with Authentication) (Continued)*

```
     #send errors 6, #recv errors 0
     local crypto endpt.: 192.168.1.1, remote crypto endpt.: 192.168.2.2
     path mtu 1500, media mtu 1500
     current outbound spi: E5C7FCD
     inbound esp sas: (line 1)
      spi: 0x6BAC2CF5(1806445813)
        transform: esp-des esp-md5-hmac ,
        in use settings ={Tunnel, }
        slot: 0, conn id: 2000, flow_id: 1, crypto map: mjlnetmap
        crypto engine type: Software, engine_id: 1
        sa timing: remaining key lifetime (k/sec): (4493187/2247)
        ike_cookies: A0585410 105DCC1E 90A62179 A82ADF45
        IV size: 8 bytes
        replay detection support: Y
      spi: 0x8690C4AD(2257634477)
        transform: esp-des esp-md5-hmac ,
        in use settings ={Tunnel, }
        slot: 0, conn id: 2002, flow_id: 3, crypto map: mjlnetmap
        crypto engine type: Software, engine_id: 1
        sa timing: remaining key lifetime (k/sec): (4406361/2245)
        ike_cookies: A0585410 105DCC1E 90A62179 A82ADF45
        IV size: 8 bytes
        replay detection support: Y (line 2)
     inbound ah sas:
     inbound pcp sas:
     outbound esp sas: (line 3)
      spi: 0x74C8114A(1959268682)
        transform: esp-des esp-md5-hmac ,
        in use settings ={Tunnel, }
        slot: 0, conn id: 2001, flow_id: 2, crypto map: mjlnetmap
        crypto engine type: Software, engine_id: 1
        sa timing: remaining key lifetime (k/sec): (4493187/2245)
        ike_cookies: A0585410 105DCC1E 90A62179 A82ADF45
        IV size: 8 bytes
        replay detection support: Y
      spi: 0xE5C7FCD(240943053)
        transform: esp-des esp-md5-hmac ,
        in use settings ={Tunnel, }
        slot: 0, conn id: 2003, flow_id: 4, crypto map: mjlnetmap
        crypto engine type: Software, engine_id: 1
        sa timing: remaining key lifetime (k/sec): (4406360/2244)
        ike_cookies: A0585410 105DCC1E 90A62179 A82ADF45
        IV size: 8 bytes
        replay detection support: Y (line 4)
     outbound ah sas:
     outbound pcp sas:
London#
```

In highlighted lines 1 to 4, you can see that replay protection (shown as replay detection support) is supported (replay detection support: Y) for both inbound and outbound IPsec SAs (when receiving and sending IPsec packets) when the IPsec SAs specify authentication.

Example 7-72 *Verifying Replay Protection IPsec ESP Without Authentication*

```
London#show crypto ipsec sa
interface: Serial1/0
    Crypto map tag: mjlnetmap, local addr. 192.168.1.1
   protected vrf:
   local  ident (addr/mask/prot/port): (10.1.1.0/255.255.255.0/0/0)
   remote ident (addr/mask/prot/port): (10.2.2.0/255.255.255.0/0/0)
   current_peer: 192.168.2.2:500
     PERMIT, flags={origin_is_acl,}
    #pkts encaps: 42, #pkts encrypt: 42, #pkts digest 0
    #pkts decaps: 26, #pkts decrypt: 26, #pkts verify 0
    #pkts compressed: 0, #pkts decompressed: 0
    #pkts not compressed: 0, #pkts compr. failed: 0
    #pkts not decompressed: 0, #pkts decompress failed: 0
    #send errors 1, #recv errors 0
     local crypto endpt.: 192.168.1.1, remote crypto endpt.: 192.168.2.2
     path mtu 1500, media mtu 1500
     current outbound spi: 7D0
     inbound esp sas: (line 1)
      spi: 0x3E8(1000)
        transform: esp-des ,
        in use settings ={Tunnel, }
        slot: 0, conn id: 2001, flow_id: 1, crypto map: mjlnetmap
        no sa timing
        IV size: 8 bytes
        replay detection support: N (line 2)
     inbound ah sas:
     inbound pcp sas:
     outbound esp sas: (line 3)
      spi: 0x7D0(2000)
        transform: esp-des ,
        in use settings ={Tunnel, }
        slot: 0, conn id: 2000, flow_id: 2, crypto map: mjlnetmap
        no sa timing
        IV size: 8 bytes
        replay detection support: N (line 4)
     outbound ah sas:
     outbound pcp sas:
London#
```

Highlighted lines 1 to 4 show that replay protection is not supported (replay detection support: N) for both inbound and outbound IPsec ESP SAs when authentication is not specified.

Other Considerations When Provisioning QoS for an IPsec VPN

There are a number of other considerations to take into account when provisioning QoS for an IPsec VPN. These considerations are as follows:

- RSVP does not work between IPsec VPN gateways because IPsec hides information about user traffic flows (such as Layer 4 information).

- The compressed RTP (cRTP) does not work with IPsec. In normal operation, cRTP compresses the IP, UDP, and RTP headers such that a G.729 packet is reduced from a total size of 60 bytes to 23 bytes. Unfortunately, the UDP and RTP headers (plus the IP header in IPsec tunnel mode) are hidden by IPsec, and so are unavailable for compression.

- Prior to Cisco IOS Software Release 12.2(13)T, IPsec supported a single first-in, first-out (FIFO) queue. This single crypto queue can impact delay-sensitive traffic when the crypto engine is congested because voice packets can get stuck behind large data packets in the FIFO queue.

  Cisco IOS Software Release 12.2(13)T introduced a Low Latency Queue (LLQ) for IPsec. This LLQ ensures that high-priority traffic such as voice is guaranteed bandwidth and is encrypted before data traffic.

  Figure 7-63 illustrates the single FIFO crypto queue prior to Cisco IOS Software Release 12.2(13)T, and the dual LLQ and FIFO queues in Cisco IOS Software Release 12.2(13)T and later.

Figure 7-63 *Crypto Engine FIFO and LLQ Queues*

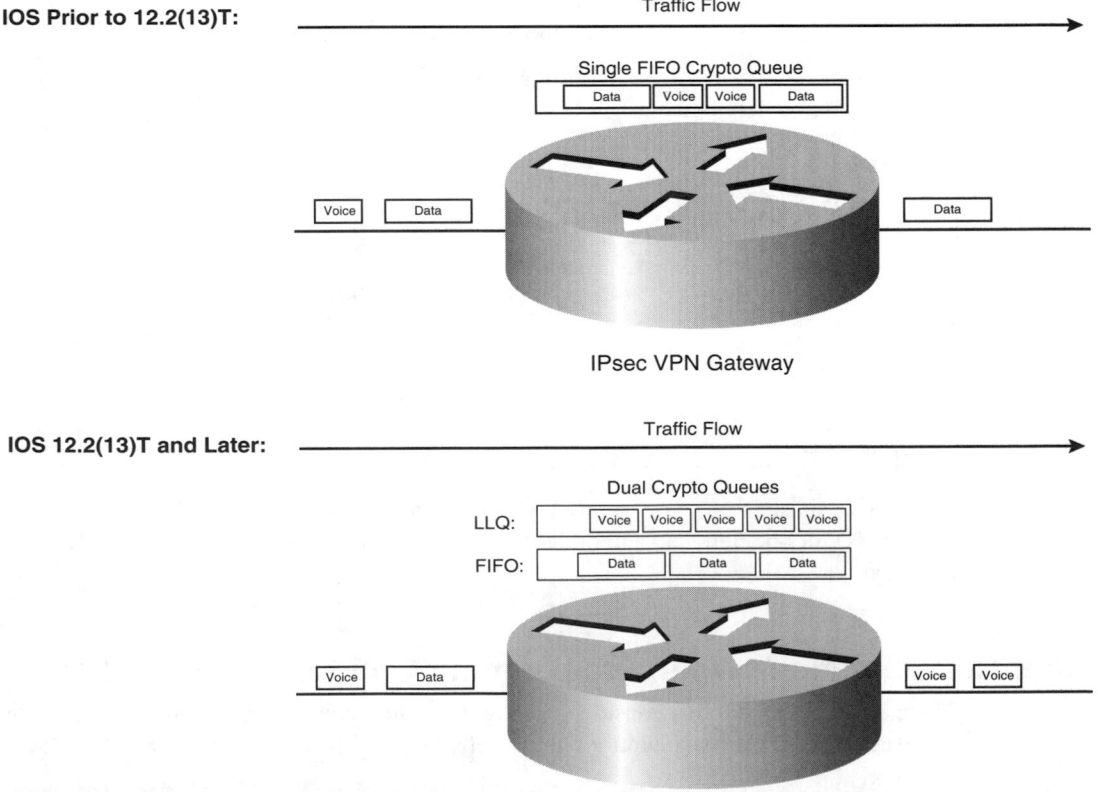

MTU and Fragmentation Considerations in an IPsec VPN

One important consideration when deploying an IPsec VPN is how to deal with maximum transmission unit (MTU) and fragmentation issues caused by large IPsec packets. This is because IPsec adds considerable overhead to the IP packets that it encapsulates.

IPsec Packet Overhead

When user data packets are transmitted over an IPsec VPN, IPsec adds considerable overhead. The exact amount of overhead added by IPsec depends on a number of factors, including the following:

- The security protocols (and cryptographic algorithms) that you use.
- Whether you use transport or tunnel mode.
- Whether you have configured a GRE tunnel to transport multicast and multiprotocol traffic. Note that this section assumes use of *point-to-point* GRE tunnels for multicast and multiprotocol traffic transport.

Figure 7-64 illustrates the overhead added by an IPsec VPN gateway to a user packet as the user packet is sent over an IPsec tunnel.

Figure 7-64 *Overhead by an IPsec VPN Gateway*

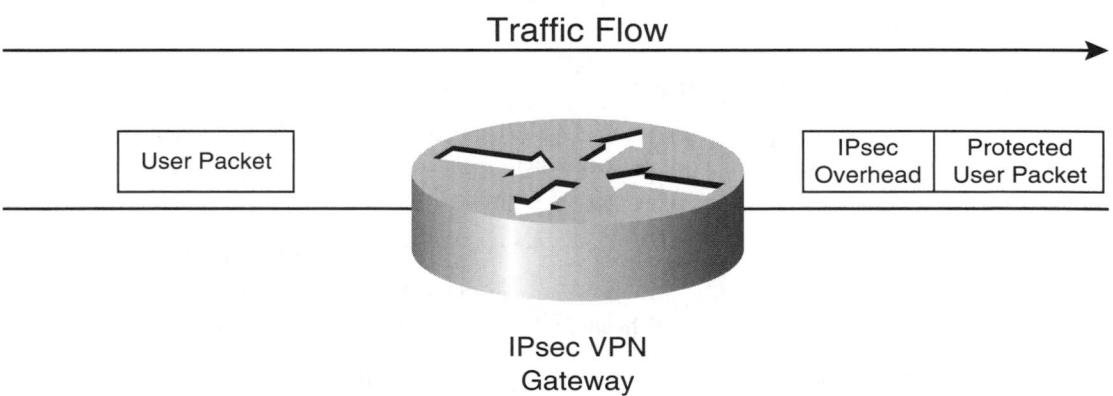

The following sections examine the factors that affect the amount of overhead added by IPsec.

Overhead Added by Security Protocols

One determinant of the IPsec overhead are the security protocols (AH/ESP) that you configure in your IPsec transform set.

If you take look at Figure 6-13 on page 423, you can see that AH adds the following:

16 bytes (the Next header, AH payload length, Reserved, SPI, and Sequence Number fields) + the variable number of bytes added by the Integrity Check Value (ICV) field.

So, the AH is 16 bytes plus the number of bytes added by the variable-length ICV field long.

Calculating the amount of overhead added by ESP is more complicated, as you see by looking at the ESP header in Figure 6-18 on page 427.

As shown in Figure 6-18, the Security Parameter Index (SPI) field adds 4 bytes, the Sequence Number field adds 4 bytes, synchronization data (such as an Initialization Vector [IV]) in the Payload field adds a variable number of bytes, the Padding field can add from 0 to 255 bytes, the Pad Length field adds 1 byte, the Next Header field adds 1 byte, and the Authentication Data field adds a variable number of bytes.

So, that is 10 bytes (SPI, Sequence Number, Pad Length, and Next Header) plus the number of bytes added by the variable-length synchronization data, Padding field, and Authentication Data fields.

Overhead Added in Transport and Tunnel Modes

If you refer back to Figures 6-14, 6-15, 6-19, and 6-20 on pages 424, 428, and 429, you can see that in tunnel mode an additional (new) IP header is prepended to the packet. The length of an IP header is variable; in almost all cases, however, it is 20 bytes. In transport mode, however, no additional IP header is added.

Overhead Added by a GRE Tunnel

If you have configured a point-to-point GRE tunnel to carry multicast and multiprotocol traffic, this usually (assuming that optional fields are not present) adds 24 additional bytes of overhead. The 24 bytes are made up of the following:

The GRE header itself (4 bytes) + an additional IP header (20 bytes)

mGRE adds 28 bytes of overhead because of the additional 4-byte Key field (which is not typically included in the GRE header when using a point-to-point tunnel).

Figure 7-65 illustrates the overhead added by (point-to-point) GRE.

Figure 7-65 *Overhead Added by GRE*

New IP Header (20 bytes)	GRE Header (4 bytes)	User Packet

Calculating Total Overhead

As you can see, calculating the precise overhead added to user packets when they are transmitted over an IPsec VPN is complicated, particularly in relation to the overhead added by AH and ESP. Table 7-2, however, shows the overhead added when using AH and/ or ESP (in tunnel and transport modes) and a variety of cryptographic algorithms to a user packet size of 1500 bytes sent over an IPsec or GRE/IPsec VPN tunnel.

Table 7-2   *IPsec VPN Packet Sizes*

Security Protocol	P-P GRE Tunnel	MD5	SHA-1	DES	3DES	SEAL	AES (128)	Packet Size
AH/ESP (Tunnel)		x		x				1564
		x			x			1564
		x				x		1556
		x					x	1572
			x	x				1564
			x		x			1564
			x			x		1556
			x				x	1572
ESP (Tunnel)		x		x				1552
		x			x			1552
		x				x		1544
		x					x	1560
			x	x				1552
			x		x			1552
			x			x		1544
			x				x	1560
AH/ESP (Tunnel)	x	x		x				1588*
	x	x			x			1588*
	x	x				x		1580*
	x	x					x	1604*
	x		x	x				1588*

continues

Table 7-2 *IPsec VPN Packet Sizes (Continued)*

Security Protocol	P-P GRE Tunnel	MD5	SHA-1	DES	3DES	SEAL	AES (128)	Packet Size
	x		x		x			1588*
	x		x			x		1580*
	x		x				x	1604*
ESP (Tunnel)	x	x		x				1576*
	x	x			x			1576*
	x	x				x		1568*
	x	x					x	1592*
	x		x	x				1576*
	x		x		x			1576*
	x		x			x		1568*
	x		x				x	1592*
AH/ESP (Transport)	x	x		x				1572*
	x	x			x			1572*
	x	x				x		1560*
	x	x					x	1588*
	x		x	x				1572*
	x		x		x			1572*
	x		x			x		1560*
	x		x				x	1588*
ESP (Transport)	x	x		x				1560*
	x	x			x			1560*
	x	x				x		1548*
	x	x					x	1576*
	x		x	x				1560*
	x		x		x			1560*
	x		x			x		1548*
	x		x				x	1576*

*Includes point-to-point GRE tunnel overhead

Table 7-2 is fairly self-explanatory, but to give a few examples, highlighted line 1 shows that when you configure an IPsec tunnel mode transform set with AH MD5 authentication and ESP 3DES encryption, the IPsec packet size that results is 1564 bytes (the original 1500 bytes, *plus* 64 bytes of IPsec overhead).

Highlighted line 2 shows that when you configure an IPsec tunnel mode transform set with ESP MD5 authentication and DES encryption, the IPsec packet size that results is 1552 bytes (the original 1500 bytes, plus 52 bytes of IPsec overhead).

Finally, highlighted line 3 shows that when you configure an IPsec transport mode transform set with ESP MD5 authentication and DES encryption to protect a point-to-point GRE tunnel, the GRE/IPsec packet size that results is 1560 bytes (the original 1500 bytes, plus 60 bytes of GRE/IPsec overhead).

It is worth emphasizing again that Table 7-2 shows the overhead that results for a 1500-byte user packet, but the overhead does vary according to the user packet size. So, for example, if you configure an IPsec transport mode transform set with ESP MD5 authentication and DES encryption to protect a GRE tunnel, the GRE/IPsec packet sizes that results for user packet sizes of 500 and 1000 bytes are 560 and 1056 bytes, respectively. Compare these with the resulting 1560 GRE/IPsec packet size shown in Table 7-2, highlighted line 3, for an original user packet size of 1500.

You might be slightly mystified as to why a 500-byte user packet incurs more overhead than a 1000-byte user packet (60 bytes versus 56 bytes). The reason is the Padding field in the ESP header (see Figure 6-18 on page 427). As previously described, the length of this field must be such that the payload (including the additional IP/GRE headers if applicable), plus any padding is a multiple of the block size of the encryption algorithm (64 bits for DES, in this example), and the Pad Length and Next Header fields are right-aligned with a 4-byte word. The upshot of all this is that *some* smaller user packet sizes might incur slightly more overhead than larger user packet sizes.

Ensuring That Large IPsec Packets Are Not Fragmented or Dropped

Okay, so now you know that IPsec (and GRE) can add considerable overhead to user packets. This overhead can cause large (larger than the path maximum transmission unit [PMTU]) IPsec or GRE/IPsec packets to be dropped or fragmented (broken into smaller pieces).

NOTE   An interface MTU is the maximum packet size in bytes that can be transmitted out of an interface.

The MTU between two devices over an intervening network is called the *path MTU*.

If IPsec packets are dropped, this is clearly not good; but, why is fragmentation bad? The answer to this question is that fragmentation of IPsec packets can cause high processor and memory overhead and reduce overall throughput on the IPsec packet-receiving IPsec VPN gateway.

High processor/memory overhead and lower throughput is caused on the receiving IPsec VPN gateway because it has to reassemble fragmented IPsec packets using process switching before it can decapsulate (authenticate and decrypt) them. Performance is impacted even if you use a hardware accelerator card because IPsec packets have to be reassembled before they can be sent to the hardware accelerator.

Before discussing how to ensure that IPsec packets are not dropped or fragmented, it is useful to look at the exactly how fragmentation and packet drops can occur in an IPsec VPN.

Fragmentation of IPsec packets and IPsec packet drops are discussed in the next two sections. These sections reference the sample IPsec VPN topology shown in Figure 7-66.

Figure 7-66 *Sample IPsec VPN Topology*

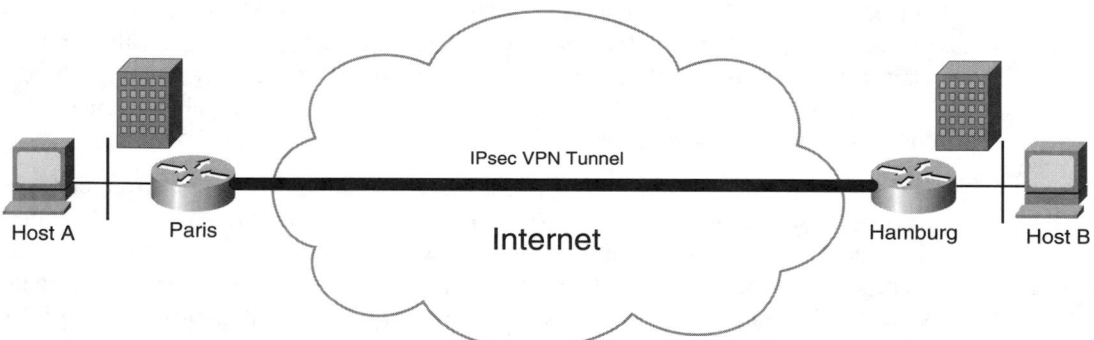

In Figure 7-66, an IPsec VPN is configured between the Paris IPsec VPN gateway and the Hamburg IPsec VPN gateway. Host A is located at the Paris site, and Host B is located at the Hamburg site.

Fragmentation of IPsec and GRE/IPsec Packets

As previously discussed, if IPsec packets are fragmented, the receiving IPsec VPN gateway has to reassemble the fragments, and this causes high overhead and lowers IPsec VPN throughput.

Fragmentation of IPsec (and other IP) packets occurs when the Don't Fragment (DF) bit is cleared in the outer IP header of IPsec packets, and these packets are larger than the path or outgoing interface MTU.

Prior to Cisco IOS Software Release 12.1(11b)E, Cisco IOS IPsec VPN gateways fragment IPsec packets when the packet size is larger than the path MTU. Routers in the path between IPsec VPN gateways fragment IPsec packets when they are larger than their outgoing interface MTU.

The DF bit is contained within the IP packet header, and, as the name suggests, it controls whether network devices are allowed to fragment an IP packet. If the DF bit is set (1), network devices cannot fragment the packet, and if the DF bit is cleared (0), network devices can fragment the packet.

Figure 7-67 illustrates the IPv4 packet header.

Figure 7-67 *IPv4 Packet Header*

0									1										2										3	
0	1	2	3	4	5	6	7	8	9	0	1	2	3	4	5	6	7	8	9	0	1	2	3	4	5	6	7	8	9	0	1

Version	IHL	Type of Service	Total Length
Identification		Flags	Fragment Offset
Time to Live	Protocol	Header Checksum	
Source Address			
Destination Address			
Options			Padding

Notice in Figure 7-67 the apparent absence of a DF bit. In fact, it is the middle of the three bits contained within the Flags field.

Now that you know how fragmentation can occur, it is worth taking a look at one or two examples involving the fragmentation of plain (without GRE) IPsec packets and the fragmentation of GRE/IPsec packets.

Fragmentation of Plain IPsec Packets

The default behavior for IPsec is to copy (or maintain) the DF-bit setting from the IP header of the user packet to the (outer) IP header of the IPsec packet.

In this example, a large, plain IPsec packet is fragmented as it crosses an IPsec VPN. Note that an IPsec tunnel mode transform with ESP MD5 authentication and DES encryption is used in this example.

Figure 7-68 illustrates fragmentation of a large, plain IPsec packet. Host A (10.1.1.2) sends a 1500-byte user packet (with the DF bit *not* set in the IP header) to Host B (10.2.2.1). The Paris gateway encapsulates it in IPsec, which adds 52 bytes for a total IPsec packet size of 1552 bytes (see Table 7-2). Because the path MTU to the Hamburg gateway (which is initially equal to the MTU of the outgoing link from the Paris gateway to the ISP1 router) is only 1500 bytes, the Paris gateway has to fragment the IPsec packet. The DF bit is not set (it is copied or maintained from the user packet IP header), and so the Paris gateway goes ahead and fragments the 1552-byte packet into a 1500-byte fragment and a 72-byte fragment.

Figure 7-68 *Fragmentation of a Large IPsec Packet*

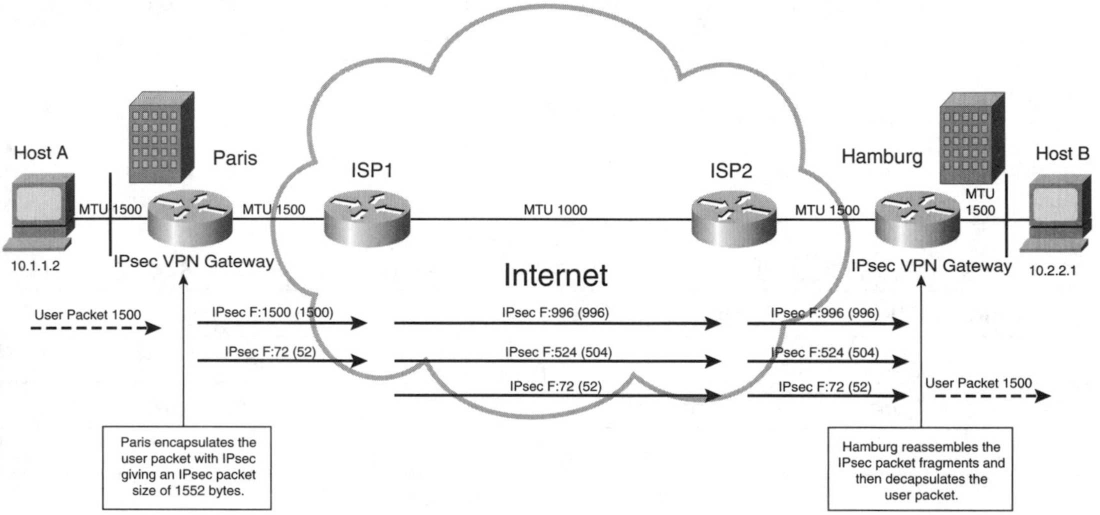

Example 7-73 shows the fragmentation of the 1552-byte IPsec packet by the Paris gateway.

CAUTION   The **debug ip packet** (**detail**) command can cause high processor overhead and is used here
for illustrative purposes only.

Example 7-73 *Fragmentation of the 1552-Byte IPsec Packet on the Paris IPsec VPN Gateway*

```
Paris#debug ip packet detail
IP packet debugging is on (detailed)
Paris#
*May 28 03:08:48.059: datagramsize=1514, IP 126: s=10.1.1.2 (Ethernet3/0),
  d=10.2.2.1 (Serial1/0), g=192.168.1.2, totlen 1500, fragment 0, fo 0,
  forward (line 1)
*May 28 03:08:48.059:        ICMP type=8, code=0
*May 28 03:08:48.063: datagramsize=1504, IP 384: s=192.168.1.1 (Ethernet3/0),
  d=192.168.2.2 (Serial1/0), totlen 1500, fragment 1, fo 0, sending fragment,
  proto=50 (line 2)
*May 28 03:08:48.063: datagramsize=24, IP 384: s=192.168.1.1 (Ethernet3/0),
  d=192.168.2.2 (Serial1/0), totlen 72, fragment 0, fo 1480,
  sending last fragment (line 3)
Paris
```

In highlighted line 1, the Paris gateway receives the 1500-byte user packet from Host A.
The IP packet length is shown as the totlen parameter (this is actually the Total Length field
in the IP header [see Figure 7-67]).

Then, in highlighted lines 2 and 3, the Paris gateway sends the 1500- and 72-byte packet fragments (see the totlen field in each of these lines) onward toward the ISP1 router.

Hold on, you might be thinking, 1500 plus 72 is 1572—that is 20 bytes more than the original IPsec packet size of 1552 bytes. When the 1552-byte IPsec packet is broken into 1500-byte and 52-byte fragments, the 1500-byte fragment includes the original (though slightly modified) IP packet header from the 1552-byte IPsec packet, but the 52-byte fragment does not include an IP header. Without an IP header, the 52-byte fragment cannot be transmitted, and so the Paris gateway adds a new (20-byte) IP header to the 52-byte fragment, giving a total of 72 bytes.

Note that the **datagramsize** parameter shown in Example 7-73 specifies the datagram size including Layer 2 headers (such as Ethernet and PPP).

Figure 7-69 illustrates the fragmentation of the 1552-byte IPsec packet on the Paris IPsec gateway.

Figure 7-69 *Fragmentation of the 1552-Byte IPsec Packet on the Paris IPsec VPN Gateway*

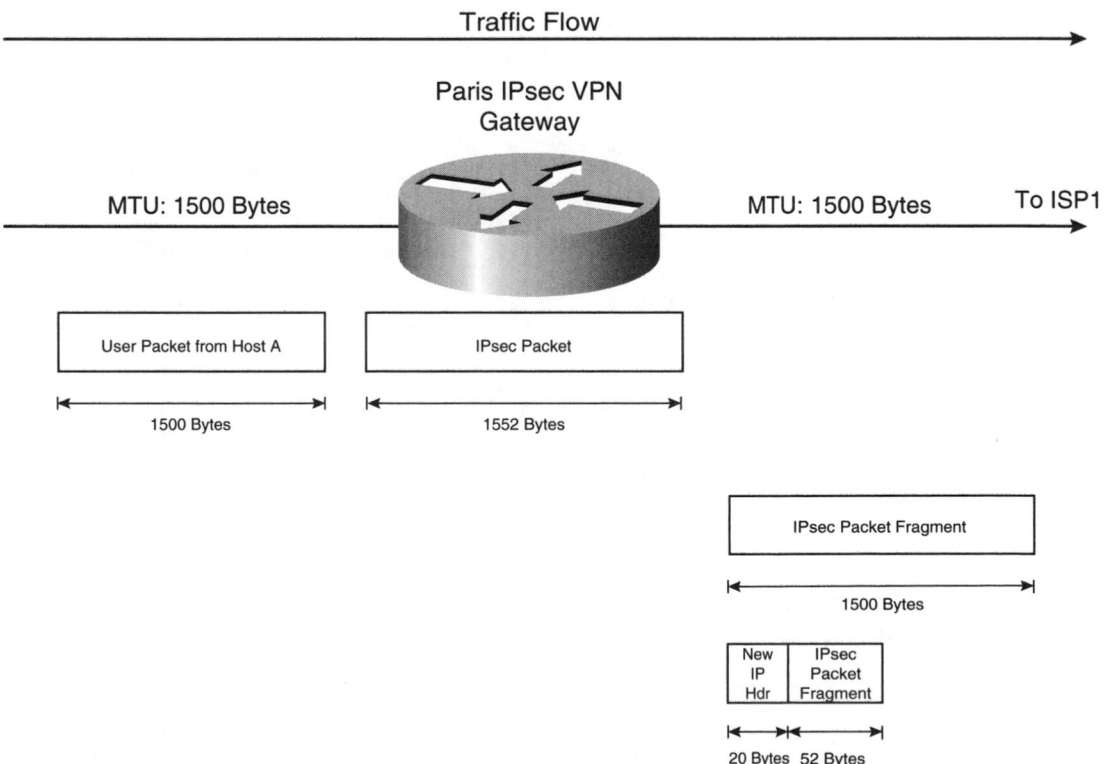

The ISP1 router now receives the 1500- and 72-byte IPsec packet fragments from the Paris IPsec VPN gateway. It forwards the 72-byte fragment to the ISP2 router unmodified, but there is a problem with the 1500-byte fragment—it is bigger than ISP1's outgoing interface MTU of 1000 bytes.

Note that the 1000-byte MTU between the ISP1 and ISP2 routers does not correspond to any particular link type, and is used for illustrative purposes only.

At this point, the ISP1 router fragments the 1500-byte fragment into two further fragments of 996 bytes and 524 bytes. Again, the second of these two fragments (524 bytes) includes a new 20-byte IP header, so the total number of bytes in these two fragments is 996 + 524 = 1520 bytes.

So, now three fragments constitute the original 1552-byte IPsec packet:

- A 996-byte fragment
- A 524-byte fragment
- A 72-byte fragment

Example 7-74 shows the fragmentation of the 1552-byte IPsec packet on the ISP1 router.

Example 7-74 *Fragmentation of the 1500-Byte IPsec Packet Fragment on the ISP1 Router*

```
ISP1#debug ip packet detail
IP packet debugging is on (detailed)
ISP1#
*Jul 20 12:38:56.347: datagramsize=1504, IP 384: s=192.168.1.1 (Serial2/0),
   d=192.168.2.2 (Serial2/1), g=192.168.3.2, totlen 1500, fragment 1, fo 0,
   forward, proto=50 (line 1)
*Jul 20 12:38:56.351: datagramsize=1000, IP 384: s=192.168.1.1 (Serial2/0),
   d=192.168.2.2 (Serial2/1), totlen 996, fragment 1, fo 0, sending fragment,
   proto=50 (line 2)
*Jul 20 12:38:56.351: datagramsize=528, IP 384: s=192.168.1.1 (Serial2/0),
   d=192.168.2.2 (Serial2/1), totlen 524, fragment 1, fo 976,
   sending fragment (line 3)
*Jul 20 12:38:56.359: datagramsize=76, IP 384: s=192.168.1.1 (Serial2/0),
   d=192.168.2.2 (Serial2/1), g=192.168.3.2, totlen 72, fragment 0, fo 1480,
   forward (line 4)
ISP1#
```

In highlighted line 1, the ISP1 router receives the 1500-byte fragment from the Paris gateway.

Then, in highlighted lines 2 and 3, the ISP1 router fragments the 1500-byte packet into the 996-byte and 524-byte fragments and sends them onward to the ISP2 router.

Finally, in highlighted line 4, the ISP1 router forwards the 72-byte fragment to the ISP2 router.

Figure 7-70 illustrates the fragmentation of the 1500-byte IPsec fragment on the ISP1 router.

Figure 7-70 *Fragmentation of the 1500-Byte IPsec Packet Fragment on the ISP1 Router*

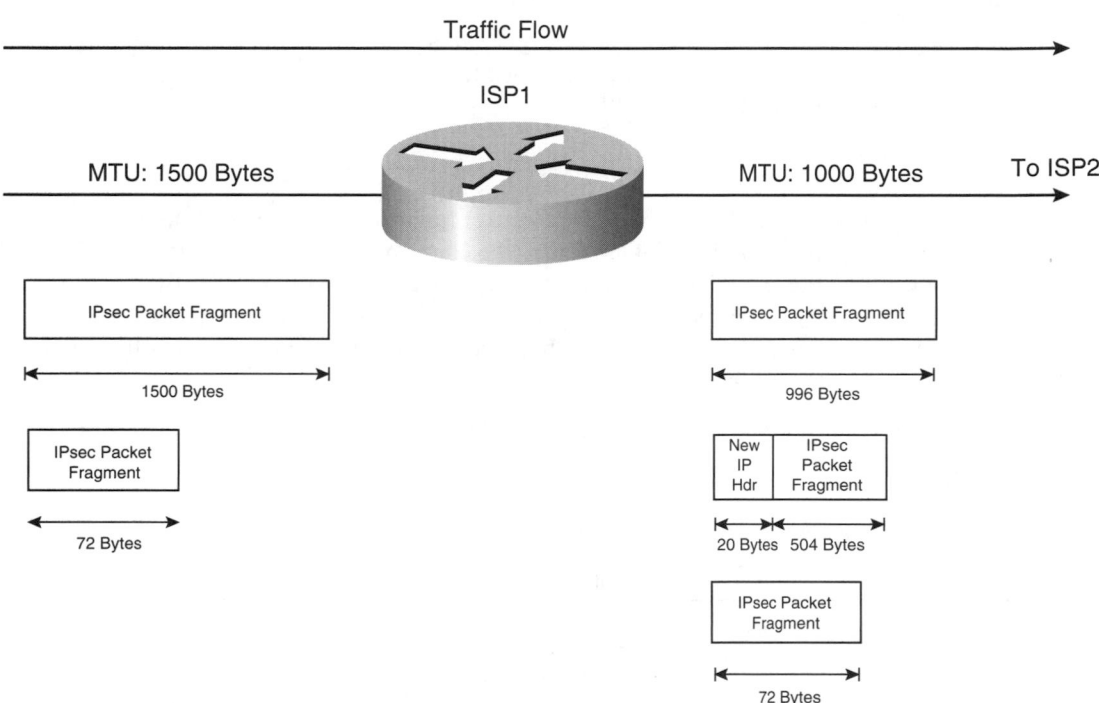

The ISP2 router forwards the three fragments unmodified to the Hamburg IPsec VPN gateway (all three fragments are smaller than ISP2's outgoing interface MTU of 1500 bytes).

Finally, the Hamburg gateway reassembles the fragments, decapsulates the user packet (removes the IPsec encapsulation) and forwards the packet to Host B, as shown in Example 7-75.

Example 7-75 *Hamburg Gateway Reassembles the Fragments and Decapsulates the Packet*

```
Hamburg#debug ip packet detail
IP packet debugging is on (detailed)
Hamburg#
*May 28 17:04:53.491: IP: recv fragment from 192.168.1.1 offset 0 bytes (line 1)
*May 28 17:04:53.555: IP: recv fragment from 192.168.1.1 offset 976 bytes (line 2)
*May 28 17:04:53.567: IP: recv fragment from 192.168.1.1
  offset 1480 bytes (line 3)
*May 28 17:04:53.567: datagramsize=1552, IP 271: s=192.168.1.1 (Serial4/0),
  d=192.168.2.2 (Serial4/0), totlen 1552, fragment 0, fo 0, rcvd 3,
  proto=50 (line 4)
*May 28 17:04:53.567: datagramsize=1500, IP 73: s=10.1.1.1 (Serial4/0),
  d=10.2.2.1 (FastEthernet1/0), g=10.2.2.1, totlen 1500, fragment 0, fo 0,
  forward (line 5)
```

continues

Example 7-75 *Hamburg Gateway Reassembles the Fragments and Decapsulates the Packet (Continued)*

```
*May 28 17:04:53.571:      ICMP type=8, code=0
*May 28 17:04:53.571: datagramsize=1514, IP 73: s=10.1.1.1 (Serial4/0),
  d=10.2.2.1 (FastEthernet1/0), totlen 1500, fragment 0, fo 0,
  sending full packet (line 6)
*May 28 17:04:53.571:      ICMP type=8, code=0
Hamburg#
```

In highlighted lines 1 to 3, the 3 IPsec packet fragments are received (recv) on the Hamburg gateway. In highlighted line 4, the Hamburg gateway reassembles the IPsec packet (1552 bytes). The Hamburg gateway then decapsulates the 1500-byte user packet (removes the IPsec encapsulation by authenticating and decrypting the packet) in highlighted line 5. And finally, in highlighted line 6, the Hamburg gateway forwards the user packet to Host B.

Figure 7-71 illustrates IPsec packet reassembly and decapsulation on the Hamburg gateway.

Figure 7-71 *IPsec Packet Reassembly and Decapsulation on the Hamburg Gateway*

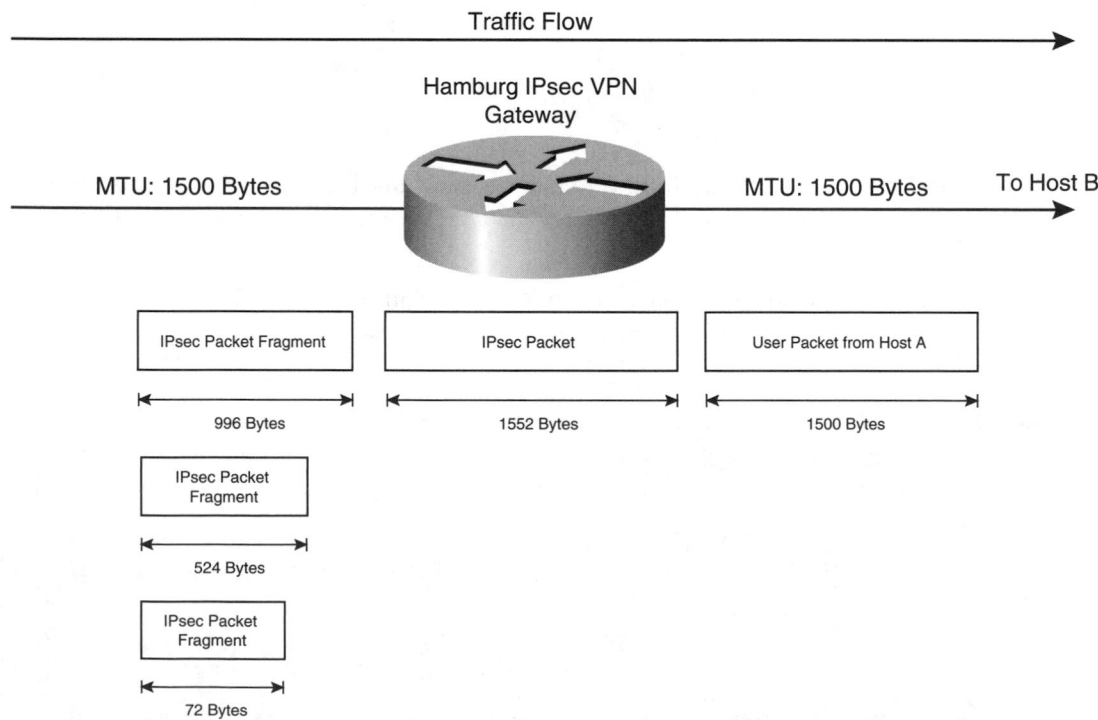

So, all seemingly well and good—Host B has successfully received the packet from Host A. But, there is that one major problem with packet reassembly on the receiving IPsec VPN gateway (Hamburg in this example)—as previously mentioned, packet reassembly is process switched, and this incurs high processor overhead on the receiving gateway and reduces packet throughput.

Fragmentation of GRE/IPsec Packets

The default behavior for GRE tunnels is *not* to copy the DF bit setting from the encapsulated packet to the outer GRE tunnel IP header. Because the DF bit is not set on GRE packets, this means that by default the DF bit is not set in the outer IP header of GRE/IPsec packets because IPsec copies the DF bit setting from the GRE packet.

Note that an IPsec transport mode transform with ESP MD5 authentication and DES encryption is used in this example.

Figure 7-72 illustrates the fragmentation of a large GRE packets before it is encapsulated in IPsec.

Figure 7-72 *Fragmentation of a 1500-Byte IPsec Packet After It Is Encapsulated in IPsec*

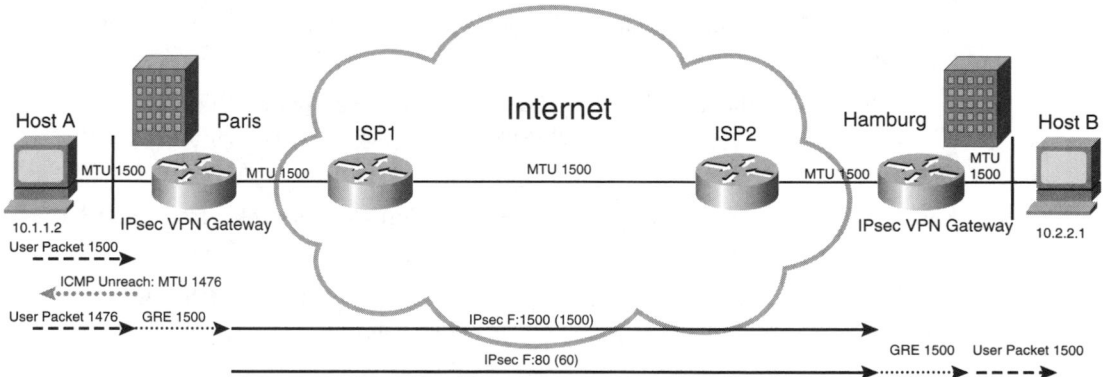

In Figure 7-72, Host A sends a 1500-byte user packet (with the DF bit set) to Host B. The 1500-byte user packet arrives at the Paris IPsec VPN gateway, but the user packet size is greater than the MTU on the GRE tunnel (1500 > 1476). The GRE tunnel MTU is automatically set to the outgoing link MTU (1500 bytes, the link to the ISP1 router) *minus* the total GRE overhead (24 bytes).

Because the 1500-byte user packet is larger than the GRE tunnel interface MTU (1476 bytes) and the DF bit is set in the user packet, the user packet is dropped.

The Paris gateway then sends an ICMP unreachable message (type 3, code 4) to Host A. The purpose of this message is to inform Host A that the Paris gateway needs to fragment the 1500-byte user packet, but that the DF bit is set. The ICMP unreachable also contains the MTU of the GRE tunnel (1476 bytes).

Host A now sends a 1476-byte packet to Host B. The packet arrives at the Paris gateway, and is encapsulated in GRE, adding 24 bytes for a total of 1500 bytes. The DF bit is *not*, however, copied from the user packet IP header (this is the default behavior for GRE). Host A dynamically reduces the size of the packet that it sends (from 1500 bytes to 1476 bytes) because it is using a mechanism called Path MTU Discovery (PMTUD). PMTUD is discussed more fully in the next section.

In this example, the 1500-byte GRE packet is now encapsulated in IPsec using an IPsec transport mode transform with ESP MD5 authentication and DES encryption. If you refer back to Table 7-2, you can see that the overhead for this IPsec transform is 60 bytes for a 1500-byte packet. So, the total IPsec packet size is now 1560 bytes.

Because the IPsec packet size is greater than the path MTU (which is initially set the outgoing interface MTU to the ISP1 router), the IPsec packet is fragmented into a 1500-byte fragment and an 80-byte fragment. The second fragment includes, as previously described, a new 20-byte IP header, which gives the 80-byte total (60 bytes plus 20 bytes for the new IP header). The Paris gateway is able to fragment the IPsec packet because the DF bit is not set in the GRE packet.

The Paris gateway then sends the two fragments across the network to the Hamburg gateway. In this example, the MTU on the links between the ISP1 and ISP2 routers, and the ISP2 and Hamburg gateway is 1500 bytes, so no further fragmentation is required.

When the two fragments arrive at the Hamburg gateway, it reassembles the 1560-byte IPsec packet and decapsulates the 1500-byte GRE packet (by authenticating and decrypting it).

Finally, the Hamburg gateway decapsulates the 1476-byte user packet from Host A (by removing the GRE headers) and sends it to Host B.

So, sending large (larger than the path MTU) GRE/IPsec packets with the DF bit not set results in IPsec packet reassembly on the receiving gateway.

PMTUD and IPsec Packet Drops

You have already seen that fragmentation results if the DF bit is not set in IPsec and GRE/IPsec packets. This section shows how you can use PMTUD to reduce or eliminate fragmentation.

PMTUD is a mechanism that, as the name suggests, allows a host or network device to dynamically discover the lowest MTU along a path to a destination. PMTUD relies on four factors:

- The DF bit must be set in packets sent by a host or network device. Almost all hosts and network devices support PMTUD, and so the DF bit is almost always set on TCP/IP user packets.

- If a device in the path between a packet source and destination determines that a packet needs to be fragmented (because it is larger than the device's outgoing interface MTU), but that the DF bit is set, the device must send an ICMP unreachable message (type 3, code 4) back to the packet source.

  The purpose of this ICMP unreachable message is to inform the packet source that fragmentation is required but that the DF bit is set. The ICMP unreachable message should also include the next hop MTU (the MTU of the outgoing interface on the network device that sent the ICMP unreachable).

- Devices such as firewalls must not block ICMP unreachable (type 3, code 4) messages.

- The host or device that sends packets must dynamically reduce the size of packets that it sends in response to any ICMP unreachable (type 3, code 4) messages that it receives. As previously mentioned, almost all hosts and network devices support PMTUD, and so will dynamically reduce the size of packets that they send in response to ICMP unreachable messages.

Again, a couple of examples are used to illustrate the concept.

PMTUD with Plain IPsec Packets

This section shows the interaction between PMTUD and plain IPsec packets.

Figure 7-73 illustrates interaction between PMTUD and plain IPsec packets. Note that an IPsec tunnel mode transform with ESP MD5 authentication and DES encryption is used in this example.

Figure 7-73 *Interaction Between PMTUD and Plain IPsec Packets*

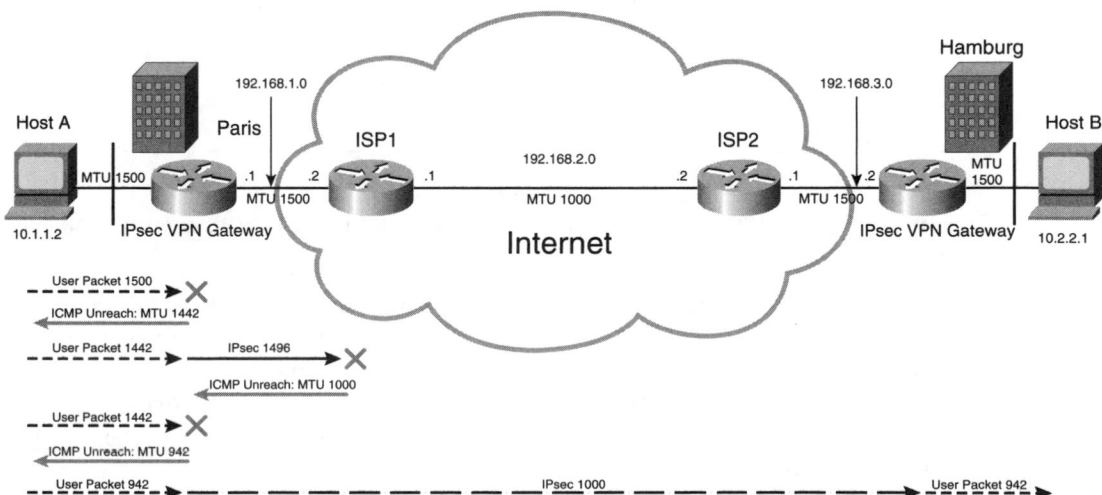

In Figure 7-73, Host A sends a 1500-byte user packet (with the DF bit set) to Host B via the Paris gateway. The IPsec overhead (52 bytes) will increase the overall packet size of the packet to 1552 bytes, and because this is greater than the *current* path MTU (1552 bytes > 1500 bytes), the Paris gateway drops Host A's packet and sends an ICMP unreachable message back to Host A. This ICMP unreachable message lets Host A know that the Paris gateway needs to fragment the packet from Host A, but that the DF bit is set in the packet header.

Included in the ICMP unreachable message sent by the Paris gateway to Host A is the path MTU *minus* the overhead that would be imposed by IPsec. The Paris gateway effectively uses the ICMP unreachable message to tell Host A the packet size that Host A can send without Paris needing to fragment it.

The Paris gateway (and in fact, any IPsec gateway), records the path MTU to the destination IPsec gateway (Hamburg in this example) and the MTU of its outgoing interface (to ISP1 in this case) in the SADB. The contents of the SADB after Host A has sent its first packet (1500 bytes) can be viewed using the **show crypto ipsec sa** command, as shown in Example 7-76. Only the relevant portion of the output is shown.

Example 7-76 **show crypto ipsec sa** *Command Output After Host A Has Sent Its First Packet*

```
Paris#show crypto ipsec sa
interface: Serial1/0
   Crypto map tag: mjlnetmap, local addr. 192.168.1.1
   protected vrf:
   local  ident (addr/mask/prot/port): (10.1.1.0/255.255.255.0/0/0)
   remote ident (addr/mask/prot/port): (10.2.2.0/255.255.255.0/0/0)
   current_peer: 192.168.2.2:500
     PERMIT, flags={origin_is_acl,}
   #pkts encaps: 11, #pkts encrypt: 11, #pkts digest 11
   #pkts decaps: 11, #pkts decrypt: 11, #pkts verify 11
   #pkts compressed: 0, #pkts decompressed: 0
   #pkts not compressed: 0, #pkts compr. failed: 0
   #pkts not decompressed: 0, #pkts decompress failed: 0
   #send errors 1, #recv errors 0
    local crypto endpt.: 192.168.1.1, remote crypto endpt.: 192.168.2.2
    path mtu 1500, media mtu 1500
     current outbound spi: C4A03648
```

In the highlighted line, you can see the path MTU (1500 bytes) and the local outgoing interface (media) MTU. It is worth noting that the path MTU can be dynamically updated by the IPsec gateway.

Figure 7-74 shows a packet capture of the ICMP unreachable message sent by the Paris IPsec VPN gateway to Host A. The first highlighted line in Figure 7-74 shows the ICMP unreachable message sent from the Paris gateway (10.1.1.1) to Host A (10.1.1.2). If you look in the pane below the first highlighted line, you can see the packet detail, specifically that the ICMP message is a type 3 (destination unreachable), code 4 (fragmentation needed [but DF bit set]).

Figure 7-74 *ICMP Unreachable Message Sent by the Paris IPsec VPN Gateway to Host A*

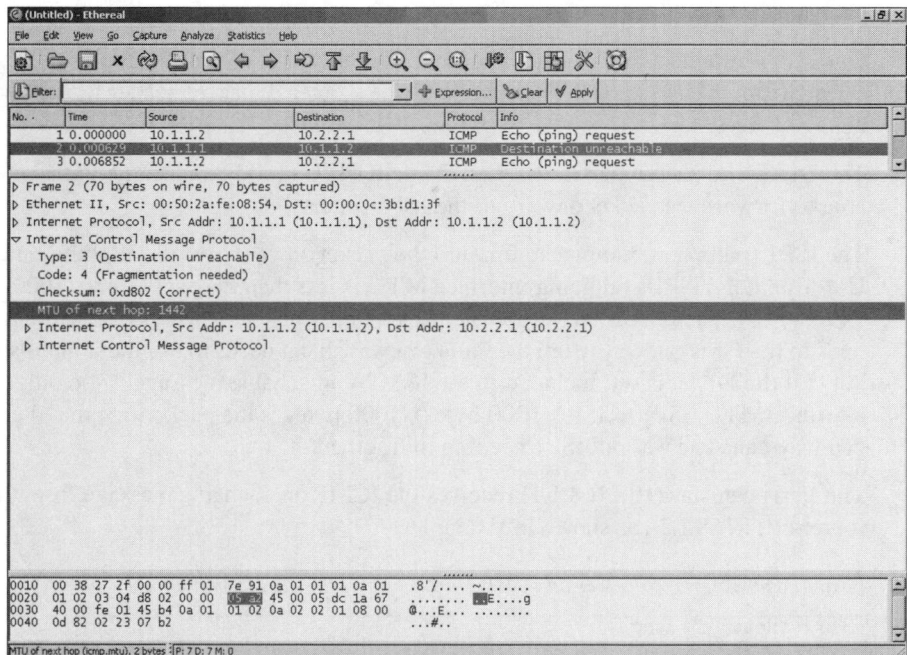

In the second highlighted line in Figure 7-74, you can see that the MTU of the next hop (that is, the path MTU on the Paris gateway) minus the IPsec overhead is included in the ICMP message.

Before describing the rest of the packet, take a closer look at the second highlighted line. In particular, look at the MTU reported by the Paris gateway as the next-hop MTU—it is 1442 bytes. Hold on a second, you might be thinking, shouldn't this be 1448 bytes (1500 – 52 [the overhead added to a 1500-byte user packet by ESP MD5 authentication and DES encryption])? Well, no—the maximum overhead that can be added to a user packet for the IPsec transform used in this example is 58 bytes, so the Paris gateway simply informs Host A of maximum possible overhead rather than the overhead for a specific user packet size (1500 bytes, in this example). This is a good idea—if the Paris gateway did not signal a 1442-byte MTU, it might have to continually inform Host A of different MTU sizes depending on the size of user packets sent by Host A (because the IPsec overhead varies according to the user packet size).

Host A now sends another packet to Host B via the Paris gateway. This packet is 1442 bytes rather than 1500 bytes—Host A is using PMTUD, and so has dynamically adjusted the size of the packet in response to the ICMP unreachable message sent by the Paris gateway.

The Paris gateway adds the IPsec encapsulation (specifically ESP), giving a total packet size of 1442 + 54 (IPsec overhead) = 1496. If you are wondering what happened to the 52 bytes of overhead, remember that the 52 bytes is the overhead that applies to a 1500-byte user packet, not a 1442-byte user packet (IPsec overhead varies according to user packet size).

One other important fact to remember here is that the Paris gateway copies the DF bit setting from the user packet IP header to the new outer IP packet header (this is the *default* behavior for IPsec).

The 1496-byte packet size is less than the path MTU (1500), and so the Paris gateway is able to forward the packet onward to the ISP1 router.

The ISP1 router now attempts to forward the packet onward over its outgoing link to ISP2. Unfortunately, ISP1's outgoing interface MTU is less than the packet size (1000 bytes < 1496 bytes). The ISP1 router drops the packet and sends an ICMP unreachable message back to the Paris gateway to tell the Paris gateway that it needs to fragment the IPsec packet but that the DF bit is set. Included in the ICMP unreachable message is the outgoing interface MTU (ISP1 to ISP2, 1000 bytes). 1000 bytes is the packet size that the Paris gateway can send without ISP1 needing to fragment it.

The Paris gateway (192.168.1.1) receives the ICMP unreachable message from the ISP1 router (192.168.1.2), as shown in Example 7-77.

Example 7-77 *Paris IPsec Gateway Receives an ICMP Unreachable Message from the ISP1 Router*

```
Paris#debug ip icmp
ICMP packet debugging is on
Paris#
*May 26 06:58:25.923: ICMP: dst (192.168.1.1) frag. needed and DF set
  unreachable rcv from 192.168.1.2
```

As shown in Example 7-78, the Paris gateway has now updated the path MTU in its SADB.

Example 7-78 *Paris IPsec VPN Gateway Updates the Path MTU in Its SADB*

```
Paris#show crypto ipsec sa
interface: Serial1/0
    Crypto map tag: mjlnetmap, local addr. 192.168.1.1
   local  ident (addr/mask/prot/port): (10.1.1.0/255.255.255.0/0/0)
   remote ident (addr/mask/prot/port): (10.2.2.0/255.255.255.0/0/0)
   current_peer: 192.168.2.2
     PERMIT, flags={origin_is_acl,}
    #pkts encaps: 1, #pkts encrypt: 1, #pkts digest 1
    #pkts decaps: 0, #pkts decrypt: 0, #pkts verify 0
    #pkts compressed: 0, #pkts decompressed: 0
    #pkts not compressed: 0, #pkts compr. failed: 0, #pkts decompress failed: 0
    #send errors 1, #recv errors 0
     local crypto endpt.: 192.168.1.1, remote crypto endpt.: 192.168.2.2
     path mtu 1000, media mtu 1500
     current outbound spi: C92A9FF3
```

As you can see, the Paris gateway has updated the path MTU to be 1000 bytes (which is the MTU signaled in the ICMP unreachable sent by the ISP1 router).

You might be surprised to learn that the Paris gateway does not immediately send an ICMP unreachable message to inform Host A of the new path MTU. There is a good reason for this—the ICMP unreachable message from the ISP1 router does not contain enough information to allow the Paris gateway to work out that the IPsec packet which the ISP1 router dropped encapsulated a user packet from Host A (any number of hosts at the Paris site could be sending traffic over the IPsec tunnel).

Host A now sends another packet (its third). This packet again has a size of 1442 bytes. Because the Paris gateway has updated the path MTU in its SADB to 1000 (as shown in Example 7-78), it now sends another ICMP unreachable message to Host A specifying a next-hop MTU of 942. Again, this MTU is the path MTU of 1000 minus the maximum overhead of 58 bytes.

Figure 7-75 shows a packet capture of the second ICMP unreachable message sent by the Paris IPsec VPN gateway to Host A.

Figure 7-75 *Second ICMP Unreachable Message Sent by the Paris IPsec VPN Gateway to Host A*

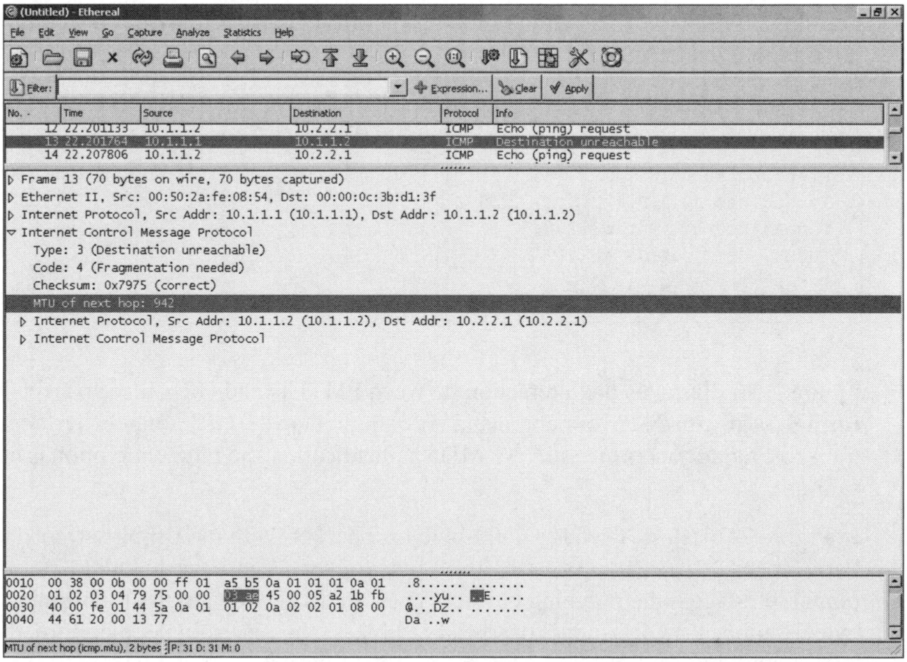

In the second highlighted line in Figure 7-75, you can see that the next-hop MTU specified in the ICMP unreachable message that the Paris gateway sent to Host A is 942 bytes.

Finally, Host A sends a 942-byte packet to Host B. The Paris gateway encapsulates this packet with IPsec, giving a total packet size of 1000 bytes (the overhead for a 942-byte packet is 58 bytes). The Paris gateway forwards the IPsec packet to ISP1, which can now forward it over the link to ISP2.

ISP2 then forwards the IPsec packet over the link to the Hamburg gateway (the ISP2 to Hamburg gateway link has a link MTU of 1500 bytes, so no problem there).

The Hamburg gateway decapsulates the 942-byte user packet from Host A (by authenticating and decrypting it) and forwards it to Host B.

Success!

PMTUD with GRE/IPsec Packets

You can also copy the DF bit setting from the encapsulated user packet and enable PMTUD for GRE packets by configuring the **tunnel path-mtu discovery** command on the GRE tunnel. Having the DF bit set is one of the factors that PMTUD relies on to function correctly.

Remember that by default the DF bit setting is not copied from the user packet to the GRE packet, and so PMTUD (which relies on the DF bit being set) is disabled.

Example 7-79 shows the configuration of the **tunnel path-mtu discovery** command on a GRE tunnel interface.

Example 7-79 *GRE Tunnel Configured with the* **tunnel path-mtu discovery** *Command*

```
interface Tunnel0
 ip address 10.3.3.1 255.255.255.0
 tunnel source 192.168.1.1
 tunnel destination 192.168.2.2
 tunnel path-mtu-discovery
!
```

Figure 7-76 illustrates the interaction between PMTUD and GRE/IPsec packets when the **tunnel path-mtu discovery** command is configured on the GRE tunnel interface. An IPsec transport mode transform with ESP MD5 authentication and DES encryption is used in this example.

In Figure 7-76, Host A sends a 1500-byte user packet (with the DF bit set) to Host B. The Paris IPsec VPN gateway drops the 1500-byte packet because the default MTU on the GRE tunnel interface is the outgoing physical interface MTU (toward the ISP1 router [1500 bytes]) minus the GRE tunnel overhead (24 bytes). In this example, therefore, the default GRE tunnel interface MTU is 1476 bytes (1500 bytes–24 bytes). The Paris gateway sends an ICMP unreachable message to Host A specifying the MTU of the GRE tunnel interface (1476 bytes).

Host A then sends a 1476-byte user packet to Host B. The Paris gateway encapsulates the user packet in GRE, giving a total GRE packet size of 1500 bytes (1476 bytes + 24 bytes).

Figure 7-76 *Interaction Between PMTUD and GRE/IPsec Packets When the* **tunnel path-mtu discovery**
Command Is Configured on the GRE Tunnel Interface

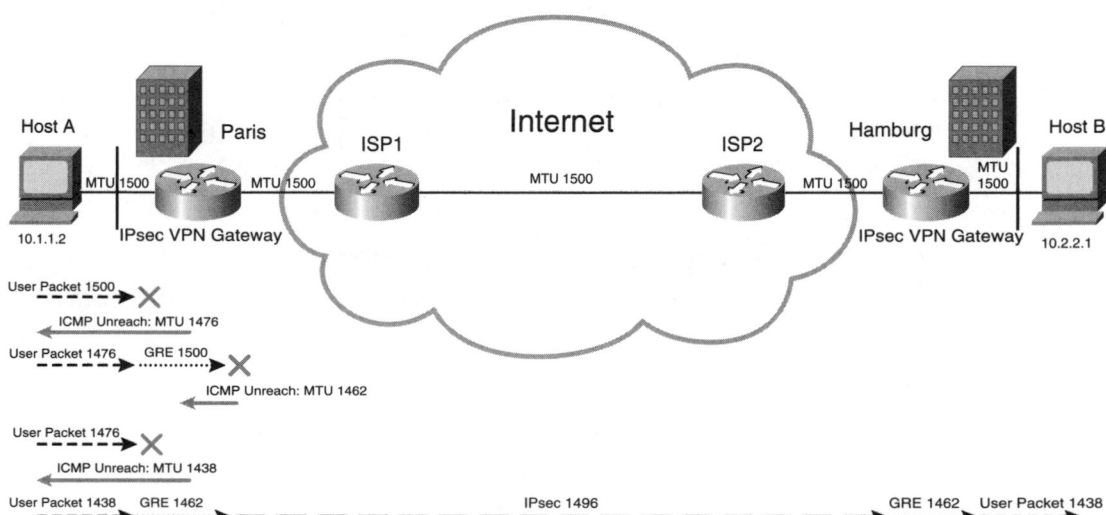

Unfortunately, the 1500-byte GRE packet size plus the IPsec overhead is greater than the outgoing interface MTU (1500 bytes). The Paris gateway, therefore, drops the GRE packet, and sends an ICMP unreachable message *internally* to GRE informing it that the effective MTU of the outgoing interface is 1462 bytes. This 1462-byte effective MTU size takes into account the maximum IPsec overhead of 38 bytes for the IPsec transform used in this example.

The MTU of the GRE tunnel is now adjusted to 1438 bytes (1462 bytes – 24 bytes [GRE overhead] = 1438 bytes), as shown in the Example 7-80.

Example 7-80 *MTU of the GRE Tunnel Is Now Adjusted to 1438 Bytes*

```
Paris#debug tunnel
Tunnel Interface debugging is on
Paris#
*May 29 04:47:26.183: Tunnel0: dest 192.168.2.2, received frag needed
  (mtu 1462), adjusting soft state MTU from 0 to 1438
Paris#
```

Note that the **debug tunnel** command is used here for illustrative purposes only.

Host A now sends another 1476-byte user packet. The Paris gateway drops the packet and sends an ICMP unreachable message to Host A specifying the new MTU of the GRE tunnel interface (1438 bytes).

Host A then sends a 1438-byte user packet. The Paris gateway encapsulates the user packet in GRE (giving a GRE packet size of 1462 bytes) and then encapsulates the GRE packet in IPsec (giving a total GRE/IPsec packet size of 1496 bytes).

The IPsec packet transits the network to the Hamburg IPsec VPN gateway. The Hamburg IPsec VPN gateway decapsulates the 1462-byte GRE packet (by authenticating and decrypting it), decapsulates the 1438-byte user packet (by removing the GRE header), and forwards the user packet to Host B.

So, if you configure the **tunnel path-mtu discovery** command on a GRE tunnel, and the DF bit is set in user packets, GRE/IPsec packets are not fragmented as they cross the intervening network between IPsec VPN gateways.

User Packets Are Dropped When PMTUD Is Broken

So, fragmentation is bad, but PMTUD solves all your problems, right? Unfortunately, no.

As previously described, PMTUD relies on a number factors. It is worth just briefly reiterating these:

- The DF bit must be set in packets sent by a host or network device.
- If a device in the path between a packet source and destination determines that a packet needs to be fragmented but that the DF bit is set, it must send an ICMP unreachable message (type 3, code 4) back to the packet source.
- Devices such as firewalls must not block ICMP unreachable messages (type 3, code 4).
- The host or device that sends packets must dynamically reduce the size of packets that it sends in response to ICMP unreachable (type 3, code 4) messages that it receives.

If just one of the factors listed does not operate as described, PMTUD will not work correctly, and large IPsec packets will be dropped.

The most common cause of PMTUD breaking is a misconfigured firewall dropping ICMP unreachable (type 3, code 4) messages. Figure 7-77 illustrates a scenario in which a misconfigured firewall causes PMTUD to break.

Figure 7-77 *Misconfigured Firewall Causes PMTUD to Break*

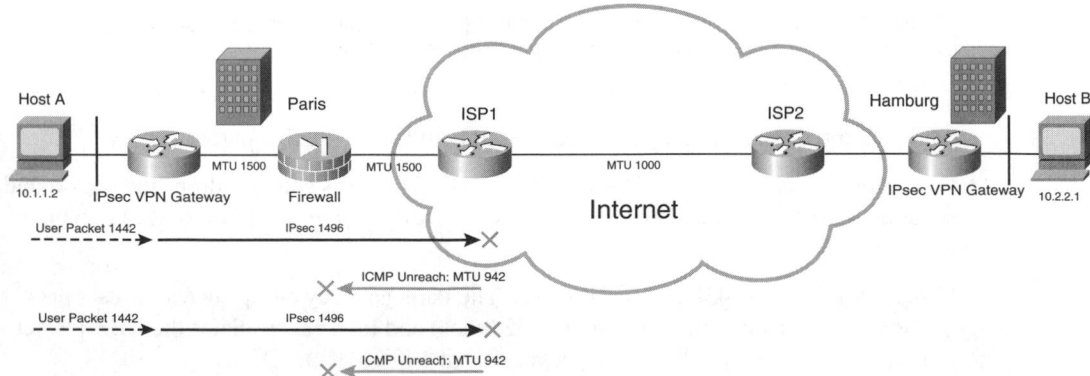

In Figure 7-77, Host A sends a 1442-byte packet (with the DF bit set) to the Paris IPsec VPN gateway. The Paris gateway encapsulates the packet in IPsec and forwards the packet to firewall, which then forwards the packet on to the ISP1 router. The ISP1 drops the IPsec packet because it is too large (larger than its outgoing interface MTU) and the DF bit is set. At this point, the ISP1 router sends an ICMP unreachable message to the Paris gateway, but this ICMP unreachable message is blocked by the firewall.

Because the ICMP message from the ISP1 router is blocked by the firewall, the Paris gateway is unaware that it should reduce the size of packets that it sends. And, because the Paris gateway is unaware that it should reduce the size of packets it sends, it does not in turn inform Host A (via an ICMP unreachable message) that Host A should reduce the size of packets that Host A sends. Host A, therefore, continues sending packets that are too large, the Paris gateway continues to encapsulate them in IPsec, and the ISP1 router continues to drop them. Not good!

Solutions for IPsec Packet Fragmentation and Drops

There are two "evils" as far as large IPsec packets are concerned:

- **Fragmentation**—This causes performance degradation on the receiving IPsec VPN gateway, and a concomitant reduction in packet throughput. If IPsec packets are fragmented, application performance may be impacted.
- **IPsec packet drops**—If IPsec traffic is dropped because PMTUD is broken, applications may not work at all.

What can you do against these twin "evils?" There are a number of solutions, including the following:

- Ensuring that end hosts send smaller user packets
- Fixing PMTUD if it is broken
- Using prefragmentation for IPsec packets if it is available in the version of IOS that you are using
- As a last resort, and if you are faced with a choice between IPsec packet fragmentation and IPsec packet drops, choosing the lesser of the two "evils" and allowing fragmentation

These solutions are discussed in more detail in the following four sections.

It is worth noting that to solve issues with fragmentation or packet drops, you *might* need to implement more than one of the solutions described.

Solution 1: Ensuring That End Hosts Send Smaller User Packets

Perhaps the best solution for fragmentation and IPsec packet drops is for end hosts to send smaller user packets, such that even with the added IPsec or GRE/IPsec overhead the resulting IPsec or GRE/IPsec packets are smaller than or equal to the path MTU. In this case, packets will neither be fragmented nor dropped.

It is possible to either manually configure end hosts to send smaller packets or indirectly get them to send smaller packets.

The article "Adjusting IP MTU, TCP MSS, and PMTUD on Windows and Sun Systems" on Cisco.com summarizes a number of useful references that tell you how to manually configure Windows and Sun hosts to send smaller packet sizes. Manually configuring end hosts to send smaller packets is, however, often impractical.

Two other ways to get end hosts to send smaller packets are to configure the **ip mtu** or **ip tcp adjust-mss** commands on IPsec VPN gateways.

Configuring the ip mtu Command on GRE Tunnel Interfaces   If PMTUD is functioning correctly between end hosts and their *local* IPsec VPN gateway, you can use the **ip mtu** command to limit the size of IP packets that these end hosts send.

You can configure the **ip mtu** command on the GRE tunnel interface as shown in Example 7-81.

Example 7-81 *Configuring the* **ip mtu** *Command on a GRE Tunnel Interface*

```
interface Tunnel0
 ip address 10.3.3.1 255.255.255.0
 ip mtu 1418
 tunnel source 192.168.1.1
 tunnel destination 192.168.2.2
 tunnel path-mtu-discovery
```

In Example 7-81, the **ip mtu** command is used to specify a GRE tunnel MTU of 1418 bytes.

Now, if you remember, the *default* MTU for a GRE tunnel interface is the MTU of the outgoing physical interface minus the GRE tunnel overhead of 24 bytes. So, if the outgoing physical interface has an MTU of 1500, the MTU of the GRE tunnel will, by default, be 1476 bytes (1500 − 24 = 1476).

As you saw in Figure 7-72, assuming an outgoing interface MTU of 1500 bytes, if a 1476-byte user packet is sent on a GRE tunnel interface, fragmentation will still result after the GRE *and* IPsec overhead have been added (1476 + 24 [GRE] + IPsec overhead > 1500).

In Example 7-81, the **ip mtu 1418** command ensures that even after the GRE and IPsec overhead (with an IPsec tunnel mode ESP authentication and encryption transform set in this example) have been added the overall packet size will still be less than 1500 bytes (actually, 1496 bytes).

Table 7-3 summarizes guideline maximum MTU sizes that you can configure on the GRE tunnel interfaces of IPsec VPN gateways using the **ip mtu** command such that with the added GRE and IPsec overhead, user packets will not require fragmentation. Table 7-3 assumes an outgoing physical interface MTU of 1500 bytes on the IPsec VPN gateway.

Table 7-3   *Maximum Values That Can Be Configured on a GRE Tunnel Interface with the* **ip mtu** *Command*

IPsec Transform (Mode)	IP MTU on GRE Tunnel
AH/ESP (Tunnel)	1406
ESP (Tunnel)	1418
AH/ESP (Transport)	1426
ESP (Transport)	1438

NOTE   When using mGRE tunnel interfaces with DMVPN, a good guideline MTU to configure on the interfaces is 1400 bytes (although you can obviously tweak this based on specific requirements).

Configuring the ip tcp adjust-mss Command on the GRE Tunnel or *Inside Physical Interface*   The **ip tcp adjust-mss** command was introduced in Cisco IOS Software Release 12.2(4)T and can be used to configure gateways to dynamically adjust the TCP maximum segment size (MSS) in SYN and SYN/ACK packets (segments) sent by end hosts. Peer devices exchange SYN and SYN/ACK messages during TCP connection establishment.

The MSS is the largest amount of data, *excluding* the TCP and IP headers (20 bytes + 20 bytes = 40 bytes), that a device such as an end host will send using TCP. During TCP connection establishment, a host can optionally inform its peer of the MSS it can receive in the SYN or SYN/ACK packet it sends. If a host does not specify an MSS, its peer will infer an MSS of 536 bytes.

A host will send data segments no larger than the smaller value of the MSS value specified by its peer and the MTU of its own interface (minus 40 bytes for the TCP and IP headers). So, for example, if the MSS specified by a peer host is 1460 bytes, and the MTU of the local host's interface is 1410, the local host will use an MSS of 1370 (the local interface MTU of 1410 bytes minus TCP/IP headers [40 bytes]).

The **ip tcp adjust-mss** command allows a gateway to dynamically modify the MSS in SYN and SYN/ACK packets sent by end hosts (if the MSS sent by a host is greater than the MSS specified using the **ip tcp adjust-mss** command). This command ensures that end hosts do not send (TCP/IP) packets larger than the MSS specified plus 40 bytes (the TCP and IP headers).

You can configure the **ip tcp adjust-mss** command on either the GRE tunnel interface (if you have one configured) or *inside* physical interface of an IPsec VPN gateway.

In Example 7-82, the **ip tcp adjust-mss** command is configured on a GRE tunnel interface. In this example, the **ip tcp adjust-mss** command configures the gateway to dynamically adjust the TCP MSS in SYN and SYN/ACK packets to a value of 1378 bytes. TCP/IP packets sent by end hosts will, therefore, not exceed 1418 bytes (including TCP/IP headers).

Example 7-82 *Configuring the* **ip tcp adjust-mss** *Command on a GRE Tunnel Interface*

```
interface Tunnel0
 ip address 10.3.3.1 255.255.255.0
 ip tcp adjust-mss 1378
 tunnel source 192.168.1.1
 tunnel destination 192.168.2.2
 !
```

Figure 7-78 illustrates the function of the **ip tcp adjust-mss** command.

Figure 7-78 *Function of the* **ip tcp adjust-mss** *Command*

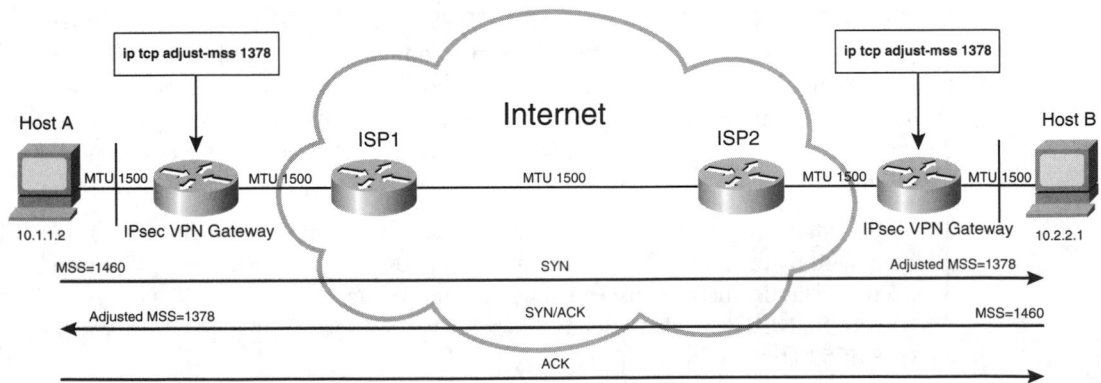

In Figure 7-78, Host A sends a TCP SYN to Host B. The SYN packet specifies an MSS of 1460 bytes. The Paris IPsec VPN gateway intercepts the SYN packet and dynamically adjusts the MSS value contained within it to a value of 1378 bytes. Host B then receives the SYN.

Host B sends a TCP SYN/ACK to Host A. This SYN/ACK specifies an MSS of 1460 bytes. The Hamburg gateway intercepts the SYN/ACK packet and dynamically adjusts the MSS value contained within it to a value of 1378 bytes. Host A then receives the SYN/ACK.

Finally, Host A sends an ACK packet to Host B, and the TCP connection is established.

Host A will now not send a TCP data segment larger than 1378 bytes to Host B (a total IP packet size of 1418 bytes, including the [40-byte] TCP/IP headers). And Host B will also not send a data segment of more than 1378 bytes to Host A (again, a total IP packet size of 1418 bytes, including TCP/IP headers).

Although it is a good idea to configure the **ip tcp adjust-mss** command on both IPsec VPN gateways (as shown in Figure 7-78), it is *possible* to configure this command on just one of the gateways to achieve the same result. You might want to configure the **ip tcp adjust-mss** command on just one gateway if the other gateway has an older Cisco IOS version that does not support this command.

Solution 2: Fixing PMTUD If It Is Broken

If you suspect that user or IPsec packets are being dropped because PMTUD is broken, the best course of action is, of course, to fix PMTUD.

Fixing PMTUD might involve doing one or more of the following things:

- Ensuring that end hosts are configured to support PMTUD (most, if not all, should).
- Configuring the **tunnel path-mtu discovery** command on a GRE tunnel, as discussed in the section "PMTUD with GRE/IPsec Packets" earlier in this chapter.
- Reconfiguring a network device to send ICMP unreachable messages (type 3, code 4). Although unlikely, check for the presence of the **no ip unreachables** command, which prevents a network device from sending ICMP unreachables. ICMP unreachables can be reenabled by configuring the **ip unreachables** command.
- Reconfiguring devices such as firewalls to permit ICMP unreachable (type 3, code 4) messages. Misconfigured firewalls are the most common cause of PMTUD breaking.

Be sure to check that PMTUD is operating correctly both between end hosts and their local IPsec VPN gateway and between IPsec VPN gateways. You can partially verify this by pinging a remote host using large packets (greater than the path MTU) with the DF bit set and ensuring that ICMP unreachable messages (type 3, code 4) are received back from intermediate network devices. Check that ICMP unreachables are received using, for example, a packet sniffer, or if testing from a Cisco router by using (with caution) the **debug ip packet** [**detailed**] command.

Solution 3: Using Prefragmentation for IPsec Packets

One useful feature that you can use with Cisco routers is prefragmentation for IPsec VPNs. This feature was introduced in Cisco IOS Software Release 12.1(11b)E and allows an IPsec VPN gateway to fragment large user packets (which do *not* have their DF bit set) *before* IPsec encapsulation, if the gateway calculates that the packet *including* IPsec overhead would exceed the MTU.

The upshot of the prefragmentation for IPsec VPNs feature is that fragmented user packets are reassembled on the destination end hosts rather than the receiving IPsec VPN gateway. Because IPsec VPN gateways do not have to reassemble IPsec packets, VPN performance and throughput can be greatly improved.

NOTE   The performance of end hosts is not (generally) noticeably affected by IP packet reassembly.

Figure 7-79 illustrates prefragmentation for IPsec VPNs when the DF bit is set in large user packets. An IPsec tunnel mode transform with ESP authentication and DES encryption is used in this example.

Figure 7-79 *Prefragmentation for IPsec VPNs When the DF Bit Is Set in Large User Packets*

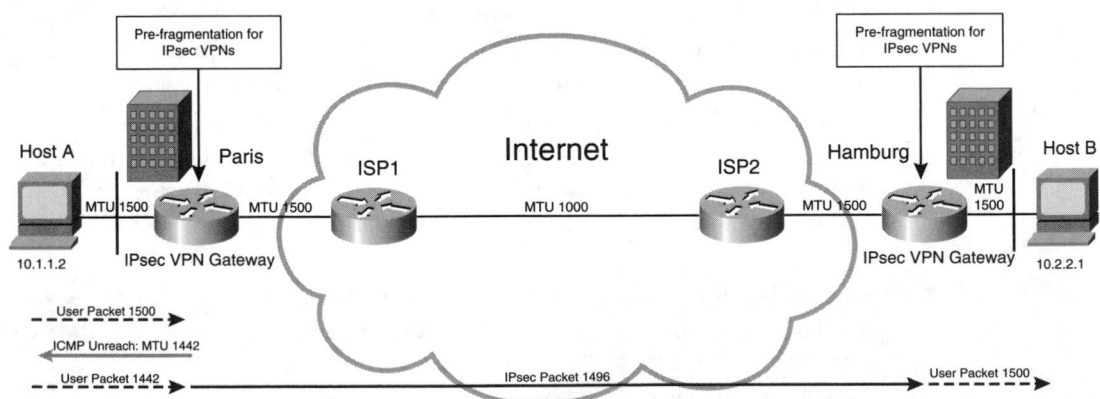

In Figure 7-79, Host A sends a 1500-byte user packet with the DF bit set to Host B. Because the user packet plus the IPsec overhead would be greater than the path MTU to the Hamburg IPsec VPN gateway, the Paris VPN gateway sends an ICMP unreachable (type 3, code 4) message back to Host A. This ICMP unreachable message specifies an MTU of 1442 bytes.

Host A then sends a 1442-byte user packet to Host B. The Paris gateway encapsulates it with IPsec and sends the IPsec packet to the Hamburg gateway. The IPsec packet is 1496 bytes long.

The Hamburg gateway receives the IPsec packet, decapsulates the user packet, and sends it onward to Host B.

As you can see, if the DF bit is set in large user packets, the IPsec VPN gateway does not (by default) fragment the packet even if prefragmentation for IPsec is enabled.

Figure 7-80 illustrates prefragmentation for IPsec VPNs when the DF bit is *not* set in large user packets.

Figure 7-80 *Prefragmentation for IPsec VPNs When the DF Bit Is Not Set in Large User Packets*

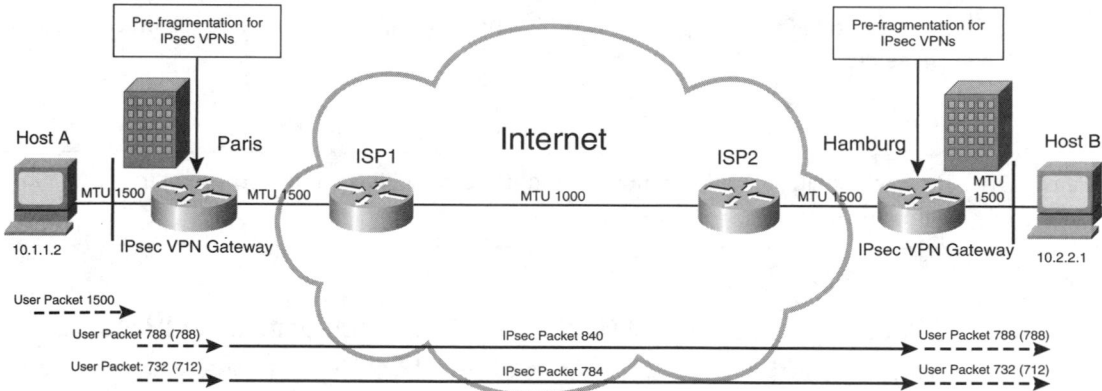

In Figure 7-80, Host A sends a 1500-byte user packet with the DF bit *not* set to Host B. Because the user packet plus the IPsec overhead would exceed the MTU, the Paris gateway fragments the user packet into (roughly equal sized) 788-byte and 732-byte fragments. The 732-byte fragment includes a new 20-byte IP header.

Note that the prefragmentation feature causes large packets to be broken into roughly equal-sized fragments. This helps to prevent the further fragmentation of fragments-as illustrated in Figure 7-68 earlier in this chapter.

The Paris gateway then encapsulates each user packet fragment into a separate IPsec packet and transmits them to the Hamburg gateway.

The Hamburg gateway receives the two IPsec packets, decapsulates each, and sends the two user packet fragments separately on to Host B. Crucially, packet reassembly is *not* required on the Hamburg gateway.

Host B then reassembles the two user packet fragments.

Prefragmentation is enabled by default in Cisco IOS versions that support this feature. If, for any reason, you do want to configure fragmentation *after* IPsec encapsulation (the only kind of fragmentation available prior to Cisco IOS Software Release 12.1(11b)E), use the **crypto ipsec fragmentation after-encryption** global (affecting all interfaces) or interface (affecting a particular interface) configuration mode command. To reenable fragmentation before IPsec encapsulation (prefragmentation), use the **crypto ipsec fragmentation before-encryption** global or interface configuration mode command.

Note that if one gateway is running Cisco IOS Software Release 12.1(11b)E or later, but its peer is running an older version, you can still take advantage of this feature on the gateway running Cisco IOS Software Release 12.1(11b)E or later. In this case, IPsec traffic will be fragmented before encryption in one direction, and after encryption in the other direction across the IPsec VPN.

NOTE   Prefragmentation is only supported with IPsec tunnel mode transforms, not transport mode transforms.

Solution 4: As a Very Last Resort, Allowing Fragmentation of IPsec Packets

In the event that PMTUD is broken between peer IPsec VPN gateways (and IPsec packets are being dropped), as a last resort it is possible to clear the DF bit in *all* tunnel mode IPsec packets sent by an IPsec VPN gateway. Even if encapsulated user packets have their DF bit set, the DF bit is cleared in the outer IP header.

The upside to clearing the DF bit is that IPsec packets will not be dropped. The downside is that by clearing the DF bit in all IPsec packets you allow fragmentation of IPsec packets, and that means IPsec packet reassembly, and the concomitant performance and throughput degradation on the receiving IPsec VPN gateway. But at least the IPsec packets will get through.

You can use the **crypto ipsec df-bit clear** command to clear the DF bit on IPsec packets. This command can be configured in global configuration mode to clear the DF bit in IPsec packets sent on all interfaces. Alternatively, you can configure this command on a specific interface if you only want the DF bit in packets sent on that interfaces to be cleared.

Example 7-83 shows the configuration of the **crypto ipsec df-bit clear** command on a specific interface.

Example 7-83 **crypto ipsec df-bit clear** *Command Is Configured on a Specific Interface*

```
interface Serial1/0
 ip address 192.168.1.1 255.255.255.0
 crypto map mjlnetmap
 crypto ipsec df-bit clear
 !
```

If you do decide to use the **crypto ipsec df-bit clear** command, you should selectively configure it on IPsec VPN gateways. Configure it on a gateway only if IPsec packets (with the DF bit set) transmitted from that gateway are being dropped due to a break in PMTUD (and for some reason it cannot be fixed).

As already mentioned, you can only use the **crypto ipsec df-bit clear** command to clear the DF bit in tunnel mode IPsec packets. But, it is also possible to indirectly ensure that the DF bit is cleared in transport mode IPsec packets. If you are using a transport mode transform, you can configure a route map on the *inside* interface of an IPsec VPN gateway to clear the DF bit in user packets. Because the DF bit setting of user packets is copied or maintained in IPsec packets by default, the route map also ensures that the DF bit is cleared in transport mode IPsec packets. Again, you should only configure route maps to clear the DF bit in user packets where absolutely necessary.

Example 7-84 shows the configuration of a route map to clear the DF bit of user packets on the inside interface of an IPsec gateway.

Example 7-84 *Route Map to Clear the DF Bit on User Packets Configured on the Inside Interface of an IPsec VPN Gateway*

```
 !
 access-list 199 permit ip 10.1.1.0 0.0.0.255 10.2.2.0 0.0.0.255 (line 1)
 !
 route-map clear.user.packet.df.bits permit 10 (line 2)
  match ip address 199
  set ip df 0
 !
 interface FastEthernet1/0
  description Inside Interface
  ip address 10.1.1.1 255.255.255.0
  ip policy route-map clear.user.packet.df.bits (line 3)
 !
```

In highlighted line 1, access list 199 matches all user packets from inside network 10.1.1.0/24 going to destination network 10.2.2.0/24. In highlighted line 2, route map clear.user.packet.df.bits matches the user packets defined in access list 199, and clears the DF bit in these packets. Finally, in highlighted line 3, route map clear.user.packet.df.bits is applied to the inside interface of the IPsec VPN gateway.

Summary

This chapter discussed methods for scaling and optimizing IPsec VPNs.

A number of topologies can be provisioned for IPsec VPNs, including full-mesh, partial-mesh, hub-and-spoke, and hierarchical IPsec VPNs. Each topology has its own applications and characteristics.

Two of the main problems when scaling IPsec VPNs are the amount of configuration that is necessary on IPsec VPN gateways and the provisioning of IKE authentication. The amount of configuration can be reduced using technologies such as TED and DMVPN. By using digital signature authentication, you can scale IKE authentication.

Another issue that concern when designing IPsec VPNs is high availability—it is important that hub sites are highly available to ensure constant resource access from spoke sites. High availability can be provided in IPsec VPNs using a variety of techniques, including configuring multiple IPsec peer with IKE keepalives, using HSRP, and using GRE tunnels.

Fragmentation can cause high processor and memory overhead on IPsec VPN gateways and should be avoided if at all possible. This chapter introduced a number of techniques for avoiding fragmentation in an IPsec VPN, including ensuring that end hosts send smaller packets, fixing PMTUD, and using prefragmentation for IPsec.

This chapter also discussed provisioning QoS in IPsec VPNs. Provisioning QoS in an IPsec VPN can be problematical because after user packets are encapsulated by IPsec, information that might otherwise be used to classify traffic is hidden. It may be important when provisioning QoS in an IPsec VPN to consider anti-replay mechanisms. These mechanisms can, in some cases, cause IPsec packets to be dropped.

Review Questions

1 Assuming that you are using IKE preshared key authentication, and that a unique preshared key is used between each pair of gateways, how many unique preshared keys are required for an IPsec VPN consisting of 10 gateways? How many (end-entity) certificates are required if IKE RSA digital signature authentication is used instead?

2 What are two common ways to reduce the amount of configuration on gateways in an IPsec VPN?

3 What protocol does DMVPN rely on to provide direct spoke site-to-spoke site connectivity?

4 What type of certificate is used for RSA digital signature authentication with IPsec?

5 What are two methods that a Cisco IOS router can use to check the revocation status of a certificate?

6 What are the three main ways to configure high availability in an (IOS) IPsec VPN?

7 Why is fragmentation of IPsec packets undesirable?

8 What ToS/DS value does an IPsec VPN gateway include in the outer header of an IPsec packet by default?

9 Why might packets associated with the same IPsec SA be dropped if they are subject to different QoS treatment in an intervening network between IPsec VPN gateways?

10 What are some common ways to prevent fragmentation of IPsec packets?

PART III

Remote Access VPNs

CHAPTER 8

Designing and Implementing L2TPv2 and L2TPv3 Remote Access VPNs

In Chapter 2, "Designing and Deploying L2TPv3-Based Layer 2 VPNs (L2VPN)," you saw how Layer Two Tunneling Protocol version 3 (L2TPv3) can be used to transport a number of Layer 2 protocols in a site-to-site configuration. This chapter shows how L2TPv2 (RFC2661) and L2TPv3 (RFC3931) can be used to provide home workers, telecommuters, or "road warriors" with access to a corporate or other organization network.

Figure 8-1 depicts L2TP remote access VPNs.

Figure 8-1 *L2TP Remote Access VPNs*

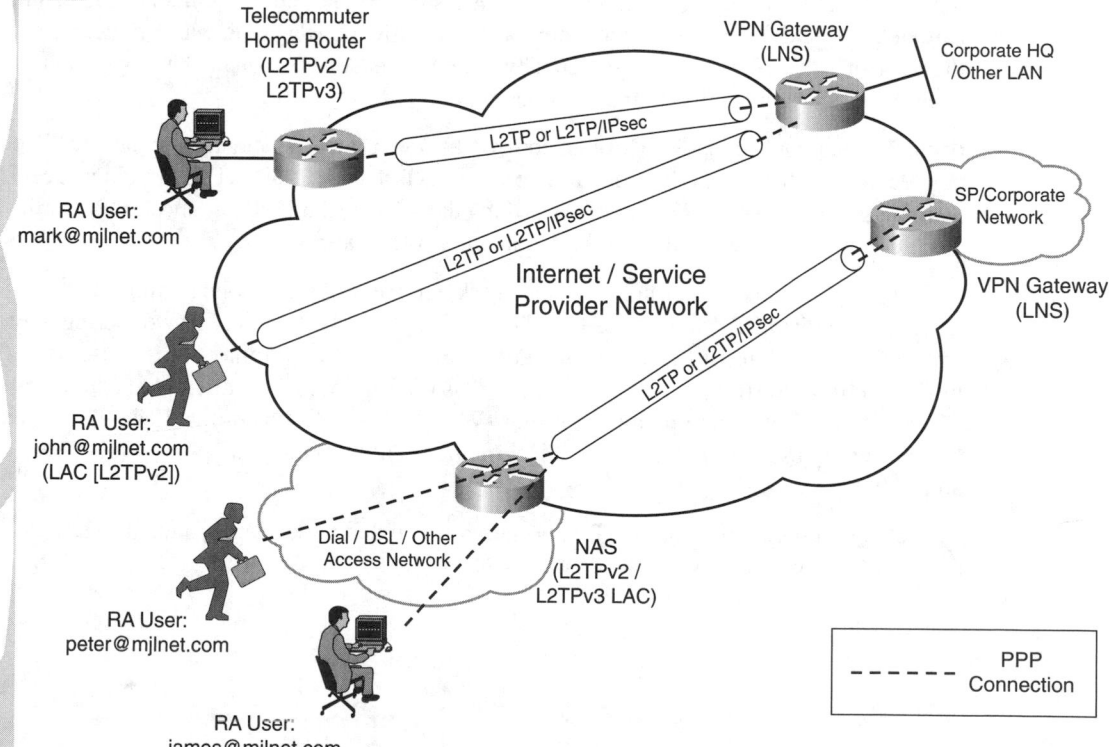

L2TP can be used to provide remote access in two different ways:

- **Voluntary/client-initiated tunnel mode**—In this mode, PPP connections are tunneled over L2TP directly to a remote VPN gateway called an *L2TP Network Server* (LNS) from a remote access client or client router.

  The key point to note is that the PPP connection and L2TP tunnel are terminated on the same device when using voluntary/client-initiated tunnel mode.

- **Compulsory/NAS-initiated tunnel mode**—In this mode, remote users connect to a Network Access Server (NAS) called an *L2TP Access Concentrator* (LAC), and PPP frames (to and from the remote access users) are tunneled via L2TP to an LNS.

  In this mode, the LAC does not terminate PPP connections (at least PPP connections that are transported over the L2TP tunnel).

In Figure 8-1, remote access users mark@mjlnet.com and john@mjlnet.com are taking advantage of L2TP voluntary/client-initiated tunnel mode to connect to a corporate VPN gateway (LNS).

mark@mjlnet.com is a telecommuter, and uses a small home router to tunnel traffic to and from a VPN gateway. john@mjlnet.com, on the other hand, is a "road warrior" who uses the built-in L2TP/IPsec (L2TP protected by IPsec) client software on his laptop to connect over an Internet connection to the VPN gateway.

peter@mjlnet.com and james@mjlnet.com, on the other hand, do not *directly* use L2TP to connect to a VPN gateway. Instead, they connect via PPP (over dialup, DSL, or other access technologies) to a service provider LAC, which then tunnels both PPP connections over the same compulsory/NAS-initiated L2TP tunnel to a VPN gateway.

In Figure 8-1, telecommuter home router (mark@mjlnet.com) and john@mjlnet.com are labeled 'L2TPv2/L2TPv3' and 'LAC [L2TPv2]' respectively. You may be wondering why two different versions of L2TP are used depending on whether a remote access user is mobile (a 'road-warrior') or a telecommuter. This is because, to date, all implementation of L2TP included with host operating systems (Windows/Mac OS X) utilize L2TPv2, while Cisco routers (used in Figure 8-1 for telecommuter remote access) support both L2TPv2 and L2TPv3.

This chapter concentrates on L2TPv2 because of its much wider deployment as a remote access VPN protocol.

Benefits and Drawbacks of L2TP Remote Access VPNs

When deciding whether you want to deploy remote access L2TP VPNs, it is important to understand their benefits and drawbacks, and how they compare to other widely deployed remote access VPN types such as IPsec and Secure Sockets Layer (SSL).

The benefits and drawbacks of L2TP remote access VPNs include the following:

- L2TP can be used to transport multiprotocol traffic such as IP, IPX, and AppleTalk (over PPP).

  Neither IPsec nor SSL natively provide multiprotocol support, although as discussed in Chapter 5, "Advanced MPLS Layer 3 VPN Deployment Considerations," multiprotocol traffic transport is sometimes supported in an IPsec site-to-site VPN configuration by using Generic Routing Encapsulation (GRE)/IPsec tunnels.

  If you are planning to support multiprotocol traffic transport over L2TP, however, it is a good idea to ensure that the VPN gateway that you choose supports these protocols (Cisco VPN 3000 concentrators support IP only, whereas Cisco routers support IP, IPX, AppleTalk, and other protocols depending on the version of Cisco IOS Software).

- PPP, which is tunneled over L2TP, allows flexible negotiation of options such as user authentication protocols, compression, and IP addresses.

  Mechanisms such as Extended Authentication within IKE (Xauth), Hybrid Authentication Mode for IKE, Challenge/Response Authentication of Cryptographic Keys (CRACK), and the ISAKMP Configuration Method (Mode Config) can be used to provide similar functionality with IPsec.

- Windows VISTA, XP, and 2000, and MacOS X include a built-in L2TP/IPsec client. L2TP VPN client software is also available for other operating systems.

- L2TP can be used to transport multicast traffic. This contrasts with protocols such as IPsec that do not, at the time of this writing, transport multicast traffic in a remote access configuration.

- L2TP offers a flexible method for service providers to back haul large numbers of remote access users' PPP connections from a NAS (or other aggregation device) across an intervening network to an LNS. Neither IPsec nor SSL provide this type of functionality.

- L2TP remote access VPNs are completely Internet Engineering Task Force (IETF) standards based.

- L2TP's native security is weak, and consists simply of control connection/tunnel authentication and hidden attribute-value pairs (AVP).

  Additional security may be provided by protecting the L2TP tunnel with IPsec (RFC3193).

- L2TP/IPsec can add considerable overhead to encapsulated PPP packets. L2TPv2 itself typically adds 40 bytes of overhead (IP + UDP + L2TP headers), and on top of that, IPsec adds even more overhead. The precise amount of overhead depends on a number of factors—see Chapter 7, "Scaling and Optimizing IPsec VPNs," for more information.

- Last but not least, L2TP/IPsec remote access VPNs are sometimes thought of as being difficult to implement. This can certainly be true if, for example, your remote access clients are Windows 2000 workstations and you want to use preshared key authentication with IPsec (more on this later). If your remote access client workstations are Windows XP, however, implementation is much easier.

Before going on to the design and implementation of L2TP remote access VPNs, it is essential that you understand the operation of both voluntary tunnel mode and compulsory tunnel mode L2TP configurations.

The following section discusses the operation of L2TP voluntary/client-initiated mode.

Operation of L2TP Voluntary/Client-Initiated Tunnel Mode

Voluntary tunnel mode can be implemented in one of two basic configurations:

- **L2TP with PPP user authentication (without IPsec protection)**—In this case, users are authenticated by the LNS using PPP authentication protocols such as Password Authentication Protocol (PAP) and Challenge Handshake Authentication Protocol (CHAP, Data traffic transported over the L2TP tunnel is not encrypted (unless MPPE is negotiated for PPP payload encryption), and so communication is vulnerable to packet-capture tools such as network sniffers.

  Figure 8-2 illustrates L2TP with PPP user authentication (without IPsec protection).

Figure 8-2 *L2TP with PPP User Authentication (Without IPsec Protection)*

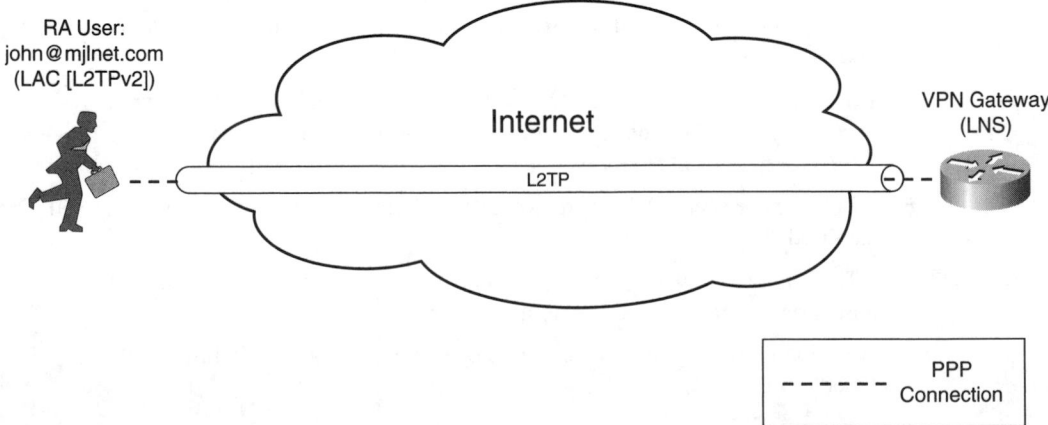

In Figure 8-2, remote access user john@mjlnet.com connects to a VPN gateway (LNS) over an L2TP tunnel without IPsec protection. Security consists of only PPP authentication of the *user* himself (there is no authentication of the *machine* the user uses to connect to the VPN gateway).

- **L2TP over IPsec (L2TP/IPsec) with PPP user authentication**—In this case, IPsec can be used to both authenticate and encrypt L2TP tunnel traffic. Users connecting to the LNS over the tunnel are authenticated using PPP authentication protocols such as PAP and CHAP. This option is considered to be (depending on the specific configuration of IPsec) much more secure than L2TP without IPsec.

  Figure 8-3 shows L2TP over IPsec (L2TP/IPsec) with PPP user authentication.

Figure 8-3   *L2TP over IPsec with PPP User Authentication*

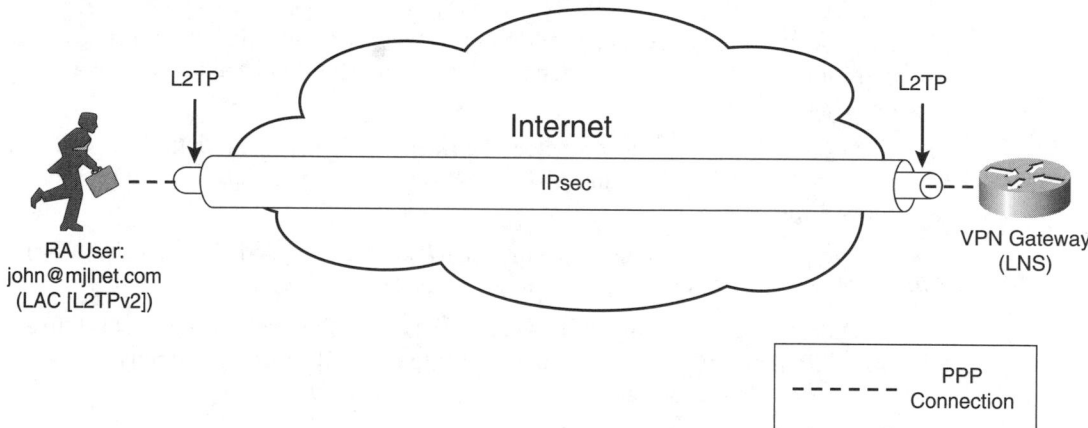

When remote access user john@mjlnet.com connects to the VPN gateway (LNS) over an IPsec-protected L2TP tunnel (L2TP/IPsec), the *machine* that the user is using is authenticated using preshared keys or digital signatures (digital certificates) during IKE (phase 1) negotiation, and *user* john@mjlnet.com himself is authenticated during PPP negotiation (PPP authentication).

Even when using L2TP/IPsec, it is important to ensure that users themselves are authenticated in addition to the machine that they are using. This is because if the user is not authenticated, someone who steals a VPN user's machine could easily establish connectivity to a VPN gateway.

L2TPv2 Message Formats and Message Types

To understand L2TP tunnel setup, it is important to understand the L2TP message format and message types. Figure 8-4 shows the L2TPv2 message header format.

Figure 8-4 *L2TPv2 Message Header Format*

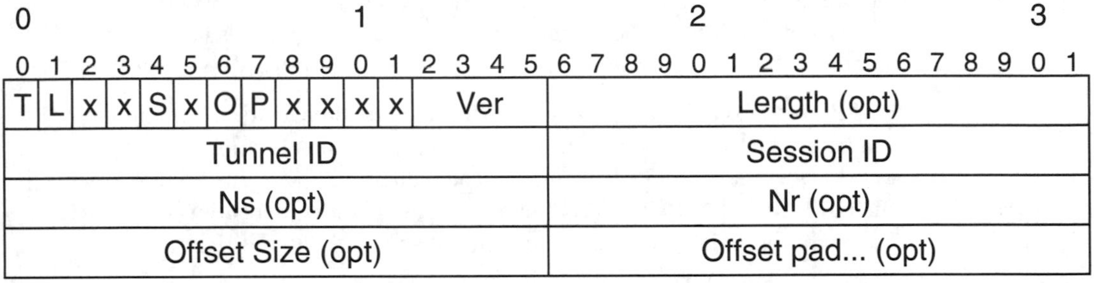

```
 0                   1                   2                   3
 0 1 2 3 4 5 6 7 8 9 0 1 2 3 4 5 6 7 8 9 0 1 2 3 4 5 6 7 8 9 0 1
┌─┬─┬─┬─┬─┬─┬─┬─┬─┬─┬─┬─┬───────┬───────────────────────────────┐
│T│L│x│x│S│x│O│P│x│x│x│x│  Ver  │           Length (opt)        │
├─┴─┴─┴─┴─┴─┴─┴─┴─┴─┴─┴─┴───────┼───────────────────────────────┤
│           Tunnel ID           │           Session ID          │
├───────────────────────────────┼───────────────────────────────┤
│            Ns (opt)           │            Nr (opt)           │
├───────────────────────────────┼───────────────────────────────┤
│         Offset Size (opt)     │        Offset pad... (opt)    │
└───────────────────────────────┴───────────────────────────────┘
```

The fields in the L2TPv2 message header have the following functions:

- The Type (T) bit indicates the type of L2TPv2 message—0=data message, and 1=control message. Data session messages carry user data (PPP frames) and control messages are used to set up, maintain, and tear down the L2TP tunnel or session.

- The Length (L) bit indicates whether the Length field is present in this L2TPv2 message header. The L bit must be set to 1 (and the Length field must be present) for control messages.

- The Sequence (S) bit dictates whether the Next Sent (Ns) and Next Received (Nr) fields are present in this L2TPv2 message header.

- The Offset (O) is used to specify whether the Offset Size field is present (1=Offset Size field is present). The O bit must be set to 0, and the Offset field must not be present for control messages.

- The Priority (P) bit specifies whether this L2TPv2 message should be prioritized. When this bit is set to 1, the L2TPv2 message should be prioritized.

- The Version (Ver) field indicates the version of L2TP. This must be set to 2 to indicate L2TPv2.

- The Length field, if present, specifies the total length of the L2TPv2 message in octets.

- The Tunnel ID is a unique, locally significant identifier of a tunnel or control connection between L2TPv2 peers (a LAC and an LNS).

- The Session ID is a unique, locally significant identifier for a data session between L2TPv2 peers (a LAC and an LNS). A data session carries user data (PPP frames).

  Note that in voluntary tunnel mode there is one data session (PPP connection) per tunnel; in compulsory tunnel mode, however, there are usually many data sessions per L2TPv2 tunnel.

- The Ns and Nr fields, if present, carry the packet sequencing information.
- The Offset Size field, if present, dictates the number of octets in the Offset Pad.
- The Offset Pad field is used to pad the L2TPv2 message up to the beginning of the L2TPv2 message payload.

Figure 8-5 shows the overall format of L2TPv2 messages.

Figure 8-5   *Overall Format of L2TPv2 Messages*

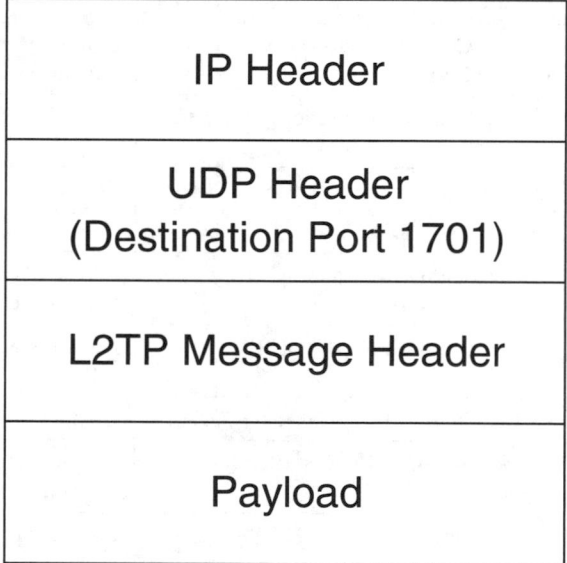

As shown in Figure 8-5, the overall L2TPv2 message format consists of an IP header, followed by a UDP header (with its destination port set to be 1701), followed by the L2TPv2 message header (shown in Figure 8-4) and a payload. If this is a data message (T bit=0), the payload contains a PPP frame. If this is a control message (T bit=1), the payload contains a number of AVPs, which indicate the specific type of control message, as well as carrying other information relevant to the control message.

Note that one type of L2TPv2 message, called a *Zero-Length-Body Ack* (ZLB Ack), does not include a payload.

Now that you know how L2TPv2 messages are constructed, it is time to take a look at specific L2TPv2 control message types as described in Table 8-1.

Table 8-1   *L2TPv2 Control Message Types*

Message Type Value	Message	Description
1	Start-Control-Connection-Request (SCCRQ)	Initiates control connection establishment
2	Start-Control-Connection-Reply (SCCRP)	Control connection establishment
3	Start-Control-Connection-Connected (SCCCN)	Completes control connection establishment
4	Stop-Control-Connection-Notification (StopCCN)	Control connection teardown
5	(Reserved)	(Reserved)
6	Hello (HELLO)	Control connection keepalive
7	Outgoing-Call-Request (OCRQ)	Initiates data session establishment (outgoing call)
8	Outgoing-Call-Reply (OCRP)	Data session establishment (outgoing call)
9	Outgoing-Call-Connected (OCCN)	Completes data session (outgoing call)
10	Incoming-Call-Request (ICRQ)	Initiates data session establishment (incoming call)
11	Incoming-Call-Reply (ICRP)	Data session establishment (incoming call)
12	Incoming-Call-Connected (ICCN)	Completes data session (incoming call)
13	(Reserved)	(Reserved)
14	Call-Disconnect-Notify (CDN)	Data session teardown
15	WAN-Error-Notify (WEN)	Error reporting
16	Set-Link-Info	PPP session control

L2TP/IPsec Remote Access VPN Setup (Voluntary/Client-Initiated Tunnel Mode)

Figure 8-6 shows how L2TP/IPsec remote access VPNs are set up.

Figure 8-6   *L2TP/IPsec Remote Access VPN Setup*

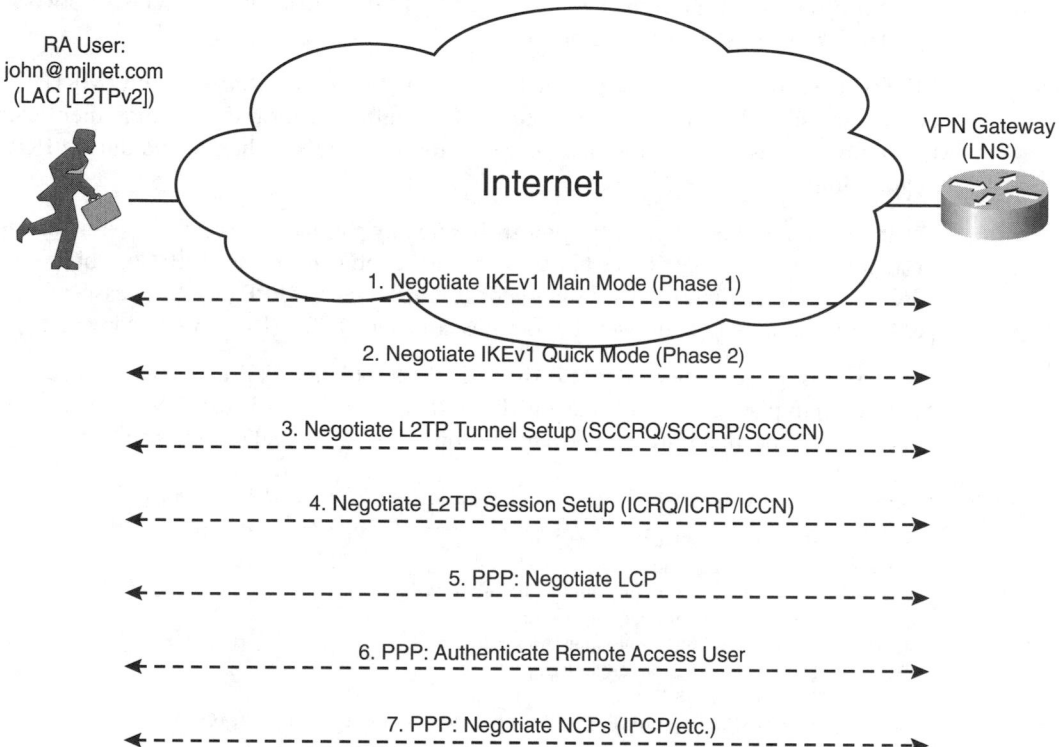

In Figure 8-6, you can see that the first stage in the setup of an L2TP/IPsec remote access VPN is the negotiation of IKE between the remote access client and the VPN gateway (Steps 1 and 2). Internet Key Exchange (IKE) is used to negotiate cryptographic parameters and algorithms, exchange keying material, and authenticate IPsec peers. For more information on IKE, see Chapter 6, "Deploying Site-to-Site IPsec VPNs."

NOTE   Obviously, if IPsec is not configured to protect the L2TP tunnel, IKE negotiation (Steps 1 and 2 in Figure 8-6) does not take place.

Note that Windows L2TP/IPsec clients initiate IKEv1 main mode (rather than aggressive mode) phase 1 negotiation, followed by phase 2 quick mode negotiation.

After IKE negotiation has completed successfully, L2TP tunnel setup begins (Step 3). This consists of the exchange of SCCRQ, SCCRP, and SCCCN messages (see Table 8-1).

Following L2TP tunnel setup is L2TP session setup (Step 4). This comprises the exchange of ICRQ, ICRP, and ICCN messages.

Finally, PPP negotiation takes place (Steps 5, 6, and 7). PPP negotiation begins with Link Control Protocol (LCP) negotiation, followed by PPP authentication, and then Network Control Protocol (NCP) negotiation.

LCP is used to negotiate link parameters such as Maximum Receive Unit (MRU), compression, and authentication protocol. PPP authentication is used to authenticate the remote access *user* (rather than the machine, which is authenticated during IKE negotiation).

During NCP negotiation, network protocols, and any parameters associated with network protocols can be negotiated. The most commonly negotiated NCP is the IP Control Protocol (IPCP), which facilitates the negotiation of IP transport over PPP as well as associated parameters such as IP addresses, IP compression, and DNS/WINS server addresses.

Okay, so that's the theory. Now it is time to take a look at L2TP/IPsec remote access VPN setup in practice—as demonstrated in Examples 8-1 to 8-3 from a VPN gateway's perspective. Note that only the relevant portion of the command output is shown.

Example 8-1 *L2TP/IPsec Remote Access VPN Setup: IKE Negotiation (Steps 1 and 2 in Figure 8-6)*

```
mjlnet.VPN.Gateway.03#debug crypto isakmp
Crypto ISAKMP debugging is on
mjlnet.VPN.Gateway.03#debug vpdn l2x-events
L2X protocol events debugging is on
mjlnet.VPN.Gateway.03#debug ppp negotiation
PPP protocol negotiation debugging is on
mjlnet.VPN.Gateway.03#
*Jun 5 19:49:06.291: ISAKMP (0:0): received packet from 192.168.1.1
 dport 500 sport
 500 Global (N) NEW SA
*Jun 5 19:49:06.291: ISAKMP:(0:0:N/A:0):Input = IKE_MESG_FROM_PEER, IKE_MM_EXCH
*Jun 5 19:49:06.291: ISAKMP:(0:0:N/A:0):Old State = IKE_READY
New State = IKE_R_MM1 (line 1)
*Jun 5 19:49:06.291: ISAKMP:(0:0:N/A:0): processing SA payload. message ID = 0
*Jun 5 19:49:06.291: ISAKMP:(0:0:N/A:0): processing vendor id payload
*Jun 5 19:49:06.291: ISAKMP:(0:0:N/A:0): vendor ID seems Unity/DPD but major 228
 mismatch
*Jun 5 19:49:06.291: ISAKMP:(0:0:N/A:0): processing vendor id payload
*Jun 5 19:49:06.291: ISAKMP:(0:0:N/A:0): vendor ID seems Unity/DPD but major 194
 mismatch
*Jun 5 19:49:06.291: ISAKMP:(0:0:N/A:0): processing vendor id payload
*Jun 5 19:49:06.291: ISAKMP:(0:0:N/A:0): vendor ID seems Unity/DPD but major 123
 mismatch
*Jun 5 19:49:06.291: ISAKMP:(0:0:N/A:0): vendor ID is NAT-T v2
*Jun 5 19:49:06.291: ISAKMP:(0:0:N/A:0): processing vendor id payload
*Jun 5 19:49:06.291: ISAKMP:(0:0:N/A:0): vendor ID seems Unity/DPD but major 184
 mismatch
*Jun 5 19:49:06.291: ISAKMP: Looking for a matching key for 192.168.1.1 in default :
 success
*Jun 5 19:49:06.291: ISAKMP:(0:0:N/A:0):found peer pre-shared key matching
 192.168.1.1
```

Example 8-1 *L2TP/IPsec Remote Access VPN Setup: IKE Negotiation (Steps 1 and 2 in Figure 8-6) (Continued)*

```
*Jun 5 19:49:06.291: ISAKMP:(0:0:N/A:0): local preshared key found
<output omitted>
*Jun 5 19:49:06.295: ISAKMP:(0:0:N/A:0):Checking ISAKMP transform 4 against
 priority 1 policy
*Jun 5 19:49:06.295: ISAKMP:   encryption DES-CBC
*Jun 5 19:49:06.295: ISAKMP:   hash SHA
*Jun 5 19:49:06.295: ISAKMP:   default group 1
*Jun 5 19:49:06.295: ISAKMP:   auth pre-share
*Jun 5 19:49:06.295: ISAKMP:   life type in seconds
*Jun 5 19:49:06.295: ISAKMP:   life duration (VPI) of 0x0 0x0 0x70 0x80
*Jun 5 19:49:06.295: ISAKMP:(0:0:N/A:0):atts are acceptable. Next payload is 3
<output omitted>
*Jun 5 19:49:06.323: ISAKMP:(0:1:SW:1): sending packet to 192.168.1.1 my_port 500
 peer_port 500 (R) MM_SA_SETUP
*Jun 5 19:49:06.323: ISAKMP:(0:1:SW:1):Input = IKE_MESG_INTERNAL,
 IKE_PROCESS_COMPLETE
*Jun 5 19:49:06.323: ISAKMP:(0:1:SW:1):Old State = IKE_R_MM1
 New State = IKE_R_MM2 (line 2)
*Jun 5 19:49:06.371: ISAKMP (0:134217729): received packet from 192.168.1.1
 dport 500 sport 500 Global (R) MM_SA_SETUP
*Jun 5 19:49:06.371: ISAKMP:(0:1:SW:1):Input = IKE_MESG_FROM_PEER, IKE_MM_EXCH
*Jun 5 19:49:06.371: ISAKMP:(0:1:SW:1):Old State = IKE_R_MM2
 New State = IKE_R_MM3 (line 3)
*Jun 5 19:49:06.371: ISAKMP:(0:1:SW:1): processing KE payload. message ID = 0
*Jun 5 19:49:06.403: ISAKMP:(0:1:SW:1): processing NONCE payload. message ID = 0
*Jun 5 19:49:06.403: ISAKMP: Looking for a matching key for 192.168.1.1 in default :
 success
*Jun 5 19:49:06.403: ISAKMP:(0:1:SW:1):found peer pre-shared key matching
 192.168.1.1
*Jun 5 19:49:06.407: ISAKMP:(0:1:SW:1):SKEYID state generated
*Jun 5 19:49:06.407: ISAKMP:received payload type 17
*Jun 5 19:49:06.407: ISAKMP:received payload type 17
*Jun 5 19:49:06.407: ISAKMP:(0:1:SW:1):Input = IKE_MESG_INTERNAL,
 IKE_PROCESS_MAIN_MODE
*Jun 5 19:49:06.407: ISAKMP:(0:1:SW:1):Old State = IKE_R_MM3
 New State = IKE_R_MM3
*Jun 5 19:49:06.407: ISAKMP:(0:1:SW:1): sending packet to 192.168.1.1 my_port 500
 peer_port 500 (R) MM_KEY_EXCH
*Jun 5 19:49:06.407: ISAKMP:(0:1:SW:1):Input = IKE_MESG_INTERNAL,
 IKE_PROCESS_COMPLETE
*Jun 5 19:49:06.407: ISAKMP:(0:1:SW:1):Old State = IKE_R_MM3
 New State = IKE_R_MM4 (line 4)
*Jun 5 19:49:06.423: ISAKMP (0:134217729): received packet from 192.168.1.1
 dport 500 sport 500 Global (R) MM_KEY_EXCH
*Jun 5 19:49:06.423: ISAKMP:(0:1:SW:1):Input = IKE_MESG_FROM_PEER, IKE_MM_EXCH
*Jun 5 19:49:06.423: ISAKMP:(0:1:SW:1):Old State = IKE_R_MM4
 New State = IKE_R_MM5 (line 5)
*Jun 5 19:49:06.423: ISAKMP:(0:1:SW:1): processing ID payload. message ID = 0
*Jun 5 19:49:06.423: ISAKMP (0:134217729): ID payload
 next-payload : 8
 type         : 1
```

continues

Example 8-1 *L2TP/IPsec Remote Access VPN Setup: IKE Negotiation (Steps 1 and 2 in Figure 8-6) (Continued)*

```
 address      : 192.168.1.1
 protocol     : 0
 port         : 0
 length       : 12
*Jun 5 19:49:06.423: ISAKMP:(0:1:SW:1):: peer matches *none* of the profiles
*Jun 5 19:49:06.423: ISAKMP:(0:1:SW:1): processing HASH payload. message ID = 0
*Jun 5 19:49:06.423: ISAKMP:(0:1:SW:1):SA authentication status:
 authenticated
*Jun 5 19:49:06.423: ISAKMP:(0:1:SW:1):SA has been authenticated with 192.168.1.1
*Jun 5 19:49:06.423: ISAKMP: Trying to insert a peer 10.40.10.1/192.168.1.1/500/,
 and inserted successfully.
*Jun 5 19:49:06.423: ISAKMP:(0:1:SW:1):Input = IKE_MESG_INTERNAL,
 IKE_PROCESS_MAIN_MODE
*Jun 5 19:49:06.423: ISAKMP:(0:1:SW:1):Old State = IKE_R_MM5
 New State = IKE_R_MM5
*Jun 5 19:49:06.423: ISAKMP:(0:1:SW:1):SA is doing pre-shared key authentication
 using id type ID_IPV4_ADDR
*Jun 5 19:49:06.423: ISAKMP (0:134217729): ID payload
 next-payload : 8
 type         : 1
 address      : 10.40.10.1
 protocol     : 17
 port         : 500
 length       : 12
*Jun 5 19:49:06.423: ISAKMP:(0:1:SW:1):Total payload length: 12
*Jun 5 19:49:06.427: ISAKMP:(0:1:SW:1): sending packet to 192.168.1.1 my_port 500
 peer_port 500 (R) MM_KEY_EXCH
*Jun 5 19:49:06.427: ISAKMP:(0:1:SW:1):Input = IKE_MESG_INTERNAL,
 IKE_PROCESS_COMPLETE
*Jun 5 19:49:06.427: ISAKMP:(0:1:SW:1):Old State = IKE_R_MM5 New State =
 IKE_P1_COMPLETE (line 6)
*Jun 5 19:49:06.427: ISAKMP:(0:1:SW:1):Input = IKE_MESG_INTERNAL, IKE_PHASE1_COMPLETE
*Jun 5 19:49:06.427: ISAKMP:(0:1:SW:1):Old State = IKE_P1_COMPLETE New State =
 IKE_P1_COMPLETE (line 7)
*Jun 5 19:49:06.451: ISAKMP (0:134217729): received packet from 192.168.1.1 dport 500
 sport 500 Global (R) QM_IDLE
*Jun 5 19:49:06.451: ISAKMP: set new node -1715998770 to QM_IDLE (line 7)
*Jun 5 19:49:06.451: ISAKMP:(0:1:SW:1): processing HASH payload. message ID = -
 1715998770
*Jun 5 19:49:06.451: ISAKMP:(0:1:SW:1): processing SA payload. message ID = -
 1715998770
*Jun 5 19:49:06.451: ISAKMP:(0:1:SW:1):Checking IPSec proposal 1
*Jun 5 19:49:06.451: ISAKMP: transform 1, ESP_3DES
*Jun 5 19:49:06.451: ISAKMP: attributes in transform:
*Jun 5 19:49:06.451: ISAKMP:   SA life type in seconds
*Jun 5 19:49:06.451: ISAKMP:   SA life duration (VPI) of 0x0 0x0 0xE 0x10
*Jun 5 19:49:06.451: ISAKMP:   SA life type in kilobytes
*Jun 5 19:49:06.451: ISAKMP:   SA life duration (VPI) of 0x0 0x3 0xD0 0x90
*Jun 5 19:49:06.451: ISAKMP:   encaps is 2 (Transport)
*Jun 5 19:49:06.455: ISAKMP:   authenticator is HMAC-MD5
*Jun 5 19:49:06.455: ISAKMP:(0:1:SW:1):atts are acceptable.
<output omitted>
```

Example 8-1 *L2TP/IPsec Remote Access VPN Setup: IKE Negotiation (Steps 1 and 2 in Figure 8-6) (Continued)*

```
*Jun 5 19:49:06.707: ISAKMP:(0:1:SW:1): Creating IPSec SAs
*Jun 5 19:49:06.707:    inbound SA from 192.168.1.1 to 10.40.10.1 (f/i) 0/0
  (proxy 192.168.1.1 to 10.40.10.1)
*Jun 5 19:49:06.707:    has spi 0xCAB64693 and conn_id 2000 and flags 4
*Jun 5 19:49:06.707:    lifetime of 3600 seconds
*Jun 5 19:49:06.707:    lifetime of 250000 kilobytes
*Jun 5 19:49:06.707:    has client flags 0x0
*Jun 5 19:49:06.707:    outbound SA from 10.40.10.1 to 192.168.1.1 (f/i) 0/0
  (proxy 10.40.10.1 to 192.168.1.1)
*Jun 5 19:49:06.707:    has spi -1967707474 and conn_id 2001 and flags C
*Jun 5 19:49:06.707:    lifetime of 3600 seconds
*Jun 5 19:49:06.707:    lifetime of 250000 kilobytes
*Jun 5 19:49:06.707:    has client flags 0x0
*Jun 5 19:49:06.707: ISAKMP:(0:1:SW:1): sending packet to 192.168.1.1 my_port 500
  peer_port 500 (R) QM_IDLE
*Jun 5 19:49:06.707: ISAKMP:(0:1:SW:1):Node -1715998770, Input = IKE_MESG_FROM_IPSEC,
  IKE_SPI_REPLY
*Jun 5 19:49:06.707: ISAKMP:(0:1:SW:1):Old State = IKE_QM_SPI_STARVE New State =
  IKE_QM_R_QM2 (line 8)
*Jun 5 19:49:06.715: ISAKMP (0:134217729): received packet from 192.168.1.1 dport 500
  sport 500 Global (R) QM_IDLE
*Jun 5 19:49:06.715: ISAKMP:(0:1:SW:1):deleting node -1715998770 error FALSE reason
  "QM done (await)"
*Jun 5 19:49:06.715: ISAKMP:(0:1:SW:1):Node -1715998770, Input = IKE_MESG_FROM_PEER,
  IKE_QM_EXCH
*Jun 5 19:49:06.715: ISAKMP:(0:1:SW:1):Old State = IKE_QM_R_QM2 New State =
  IKE_QM_PHASE2_COMPLETE (line 9)
```

Highlighted lines 1 and 2 indicate that the remote access VPN client and the VPN gateway
have exchanged the first two messages in the IKE main mode exchange (states MM1 and
MM2). The purpose of these two messages is to agree on an IKE policy (cryptographic
parameters and algorithms).

Now that an IKE policy has been negotiated, the remote access VPN client and VPN
gateway exchange the third and fourth messages in the IKE main mode exchange (indicated
by the MM3 and MM4 states in highlighted lines 3 and 4). These messages are used to
exchange keying material.

Highlighted lines 5 and 6 indicate that the fifth and sixth main mode messages have been
exchanged (states MM5 and MM6). These messages are used to authenticate the IPsec peers.
Note that during the exchange of messages 5 and 6, the remote access VPN client machine
(but not the user of the machine) is authenticated by the VPN gateway (and vice versa).

Highlighted line 7 shows that IKE phase 1 is complete. IKE phase 2 (quick mode) is about
to begin.

Highlighted lines 8, 9, and 10 indicate that the remote access VPN client and VPN gateway
have exchanged three quick mode (IKE phase 2) messages. During this quick mode
exchange, the peers negotiate the IPsec policy (cryptographic parameters and algorithms)
that will be used to protect L2TP.

L2TPv2 tunnel and session setup (Steps 3 and 4 in Figure 8-6) can begin (see Example 8-2).

Example 8-2 *L2TP/IPsec Remote Access VPN Setup: L2TP Tunnel and Session Setup (Steps 3 and 4 in Figure 8-6)*

```
*Jun 5 19:49:06.731: L2TP: I SCCRQ from markxp1 tnl 3 (line 1)
*Jun 5 19:49:06.731: Tnl 12726 L2TP: Tunnel Authorization started for host markxp1
*Jun 5 19:49:06.731: Tnl 12726 L2TP: New tunnel created for remote markxp1, address
 192.168.1.1
*Jun 5 19:49:06.731: L2X: Requested security for socket, UDP socket info: local
 10.40.10.1(1701), remote 192.168.1.1(1701)
*Jun 5 19:49:06.731: Tnl 12726 L2TP: O SCCRP to markxp1 tnlid 3 (line 2)
*Jun 5 19:49:06.731: Tnl 12726 L2TP: Control channel retransmit delay set to 1
 seconds
*Jun 5 19:49:06.735: Tnl 12726 L2TP: Tunnel state change from idle to wait-ctl-reply
*Jun 5 19:49:06.735: Tnl 12726 L2TP: Socket MTU changed to 1462
*Jun 5 19:49:06.735: Tnl 12726 L2TP: Secure socket up event
*Jun 5 19:49:06.743: Tnl 12726 L2TP: I SCCCN from markxp1 tnl 3 (line 3)
*Jun 5 19:49:06.743: Tnl 12726 L2TP: Tunnel state change from wait-ctl-reply to
 established
*Jun 5 19:49:06.743: Tnl 12726 L2TP: SM State established
*Jun 5 19:49:06.743: Tnl 12726 L2TP: I ICRQ from markxp1 tnl 3 (line 4)
*Jun 5 19:49:06.743: Tnl/Sn 12726/3 L2TP: Session state change from idle to
 wait-connect
*Jun 5 19:49:06.743: Tnl/Sn 12726/3 L2TP: Accepted ICRQ, new session created
*Jun 5 19:49:06.743: uid:2 Tnl/Sn 12726/3 L2TP: O ICRP to markxp1 3/1 (line 5)
*Jun 5 19:49:06.743: Tnl 12726 L2TP: Control channel retransmit delay set to 1
 seconds
*Jun 5 19:49:06.767: uid:2 Tnl/Sn 12726/3 L2TP: I ICCN from markxp1 tnl 3,
 cl 1 (line 6)
*Jun 5 19:49:06.767: uid:2 Tnl/Sn 12726/3 L2TP: Session state change from
 wait-connect to wait-for-service-selection-iccn
```

Highlighted lines 1 to 3 show the exchange of SCCRQ, SCCRP, and SCCCN messages between the remote access VPN client and the VPN gateway. L2TPv2 control connection establishment has been completed.

By the way, you might notice the machine name (as distinct from the username) of the remote access VPN client in the highlighted lines (markxp1).

ICRQ, ICRP, and ICCN messages are then exchanged in highlighted lines 4 to 6. These messages comprise L2TPv2 session setup.

The L2TPv2 tunnel and session have now both been established, and in Example 8-3, PPP negotiation between the remote access VPN client and the VPN gateway begins (Steps 5 to 7 in Figure 8-6).

Example 8-3 *L2TP/IPsec Remote Access VPN Setup: PPP Negotiation (Steps 5 to 7 in Figure 8-6)*

```
*Jun 5 19:49:06.767: ppp2 PPP: Using vpn set call direction
*Jun 5 19:49:06.767: ppp2 PPP: Treating connection as a callin
*Jun 5 19:49:06.767: ppp2 PPP: Phase is ESTABLISHING, Passive Open (line 1)
*Jun 5 19:49:06.767: ppp2 LCP: State is Listen
*Jun 5 19:49:06.895: ppp2 LCP: I CONFREQ [Listen] id 0 len 21
```

Example 8-3 *L2TP/IPsec Remote Access VPN Setup: PPP Negotiation (Steps 5 to 7 in Figure 8-6) (Continued)*

```
*Jun 5 19:49:06.895: ppp2 LCP: MRU 1400 (0x01040578)
*Jun 5 19:49:06.895: ppp2 LCP: MagicNumber 0x1B24034B (0x05061B24034B)
*Jun 5 19:49:06.895: ppp2 LCP: PFC (0x0702)
*Jun 5 19:49:06.895: ppp2 LCP: ACFC (0x0802)
*Jun 5 19:49:06.895: ppp2 LCP: Callback 6 (0x0D0306)
<output omitted>
*Jun 5 19:49:06.919: ppp2 LCP: State is Open
*Jun 5 19:49:06.919: ppp2 PPP: Phase is AUTHENTICATING, by this end (line 2)
*Jun 5 19:49:06.919: ppp2 CHAP: O CHALLENGE id 1 len 42 from "mjlnet.VPN.Gateway.03"
*Jun 5 19:49:06.923: ppp2 LCP: I IDENTIFY [Open] id 4 len 18 magic 0x1B24034B
MSRASV5.10
*Jun 5 19:49:06.927: ppp2 LCP: I IDENTIFY [Open] id 5 len 23 magic 0x1B24034B MSRAS-
0-MARKXP1
*Jun 5 19:49:06.927: ppp2 CHAP: I RESPONSE id 1 len 25 from
 "mark@mjlnet.com" (line 3)
*Jun 5 19:49:06.927: ppp2 PPP: Phase is FORWARDING, Attempting Forward
*Jun 5 19:49:06.927: ppp2 PPP: Phase is AUTHENTICATING, Unauthenticated User
*Jun 5 19:49:06.931: ppp2 PPP: Phase is FORWARDING, Attempting Forward
*Jun 5 19:49:06.931: Vi2.1 Tnl/Sn 12726/3 L2TP: Session state change from
 wait-for-service-selection-iccn to established
*Jun 5 19:49:06.931: Vi2.1 PPP: Phase is AUTHENTICATING, Authenticated User
*Jun 5 19:49:06.931: Vi2.1 CHAP: O SUCCESS id 1 len 4
*Jun 5 19:49:06.931: Vi2.1 PPP: Phase is UP (line 4)
*Jun 5 19:49:06.931: Vi2.1 IPCP: O CONFREQ [Closed] id 1 len 10
*Jun 5 19:49:06.935: Vi2.1 IPCP: Address 10.40.10.1 (0x03060A0A0A48)
*Jun 5 19:49:06.935: Vi2.1 PPP: Process pending ncp packets
*Jun 5 19:49:06.959: Vi2.1 CCP: I CONFREQ [Not negotiated] id 6 len 10
*Jun 5 19:49:06.959: Vi2.1 CCP: MS-PPC supported bits 0x01000001 (0x120601000001)
*Jun 5 19:49:06.959: Vi2.1 LCP: O PROTREJ [Open] id 2 len 16 protocol CCP
 (0x80FD0106000A120601000001)
*Jun 5 19:49:06.959: Vi2.1 IPCP: I CONFREQ [REQsent] id 7 len 34
*Jun 5 19:49:06.959: Vi2.1 IPCP: Address 0.0.0.0 (0x030600000000)
*Jun 5 19:49:06.959: Vi2.1 IPCP: PrimaryDNS 0.0.0.0 (0x810600000000)
*Jun 5 19:49:06.963: Vi2.1 IPCP: PrimaryWINS 0.0.0.0 (0x820600000000)
*Jun 5 19:49:06.963: Vi2.1 IPCP: SecondaryDNS 0.0.0.0 (0x830600000000)
*Jun 5 19:49:06.963: Vi2.1 IPCP: SecondaryWINS 0.0.0.0 (0x840600000000)
*Jun 5 19:49:06.963: Vi2.1 AAA/AUTHOR/IPCP: Start. Her address 0.0.0.0, we want
 0.0.0.0
*Jun 5 19:49:06.963: Vi2.1 AAA/AUTHOR/IPCP: Done. Her address 0.0.0.0, we want
 0.0.0.0
*Jun 5 19:49:06.963: Vi2.1 IPCP: Pool returned 10.20.10.1
<output omitted>
*Jun 5 19:49:06.979: Vi2.1 IPCP: State is Open (line 5)
*Jun 5 19:49:06.979: Vi2.1 IPCP: Install route to 10.20.10.1
*Jun 5 19:49:06.979: Vi2.1 IPCP: Add link info for cef entry 10.20.10.1
mjlnet.VPN.Gateway.03#
```

Highlighted line 1 shows that the PPP phase is ESTABLISHING—LCP negotiation is about to begin. Then, in highlighted line 2, the LCP negotiation is complete, and the PPP phase changes to AUTHENTICATING. PPP authentication is next.

If you take a look at the remote access VPN client's CHAP response in highlighted line 3, you can see the remote access VPN client's *username* (rather than machine name) is mark@mjlnet.com.

The PPP phase changes to UP in highlighted line 4. This indicates that user authentication has completed successfully, and NCP is ready to start.

Highlighted line 5 shows that the IPCP state has changed to OPEN—IPCP negotiation has completed successfully, and IP communication can begin between the remote access VPN client and the VPN gateway.

You might be interesting to note the type of remote access VPN client involved in the VPN setup shown in Examples 8-1 to 8-3. There is a hint to its type between highlighted lines 2 and 3 in Example 8-3—there is an LCP Identification (IDENTIFY) message, which shows MSRASV5.10. This is a fairly hefty hint, and in fact, the remote access VPN client is a Windows XP workstation.

Implementing L2TP Voluntary/Client-Initiated Tunnel Mode Remote Access VPNs

As previously mentioned, voluntary (client-initiated) tunnel mode can be used to implement remote access VPNs between client workstations/routers and a VPN gateway.

It is important to review the function of each element and protocol when using L2TP/IPsec to tunnel traffic between remote access client workstations and a VPN gateway:

- **IPsec**—IPsec is used to protect the L2TP tunnel.

  Two types of (IKE) authentication are used with IPsec (in an L2TP voluntary/client-initiated tunnel mode deployment):

  — **Preshared key (PSK) authentication**—A PSK is an alphanumeric string which must be identical on both the remote access VPN client workstation and the VPN gateway.

  — **Digital signature (digital certificate) authentication**—In this case, the remote access client workstation/router and the VPN gateway must both be enrolled with (both possess a digital certificate from) the same certificate authority (CA) or CA hierarchy.

- **L2TP**—L2TP is used to tunnel PPP frames between the remote access client workstation/router and the VPN gateway.

- **PPP**—PPP frames carry IP or other network protocols between the remote access VPN client workstation/router and the VPN gateway. Protocols such as the CHAP or the Microsoft Challenge Handshake Protocol versions 1 and 2 (MS-CHAPv1 and v2) can also be used during PPP negotiation for user authentication.

Reading the preceding list, you will have noticed that two components are used for authentication when using L2TP/IPsec: IPsec and PPP. As previously discussed, the difference is that IPsec (IKE) authentication is used to authenticate the remote access client workstation, and PPP authentication is used to authenticate the user of the remote access client workstation. Authentication of the user of a remote access client workstation is important; otherwise, anyone with access to the workstation (including someone who has stolen the workstation) could authenticate himself with the VPN gateway.

The following two sections discuss the configuration of L2TP/IPsec remote access VPNs with PSK authentication and with digital signature authentication.

Configuring PSK Authentication for L2TP/IPsec Voluntary Tunnel Mode VPNs

The advantage of configuring PSK authentication with L2TP/IPsec is that it is relatively simple when compared to the configuration of digital signature (digital certificate) authentication with L2TP/IPsec. The disadvantage of PSK authentication is that it is not as secure as digital signature authentication.

There are two parts to the configuration of PSK authentication with L2TP/Ipsec:

- Configuration of the VPN gateway
- Configuration of the remote access VPN clients

The sections that follow cover these aspects of configuring PSK authentication with L2TP/IPsec.

Configuring a Cisco VPN 3000 Concentrator as an L2TP/IPsec VPN Gateway for PSK Authentication

The configuration of a Cisco VPN 3000 concentrator as an L2TP/IPsec VPN gateway consists of a number of steps:

Step 1 Configure an address pool (or other method of IP address assignment).

Step 2 Configure the base group.

Step 3 Configure L2TP/IPsec remote access client *user* accounts.

Step 4 Modify IPsec parameters such as IKE and IPsec security association (SA) proposals (optional).

Step 1: Configure an Address Pool

Addresses from within an IP address pool are assigned to remote access VPN client workstation during PPP (specifically, IPCP) negotiation. Figure 8-7 illustrates address pool configuration.

Figure 8-7 *Address Pool Configuration*

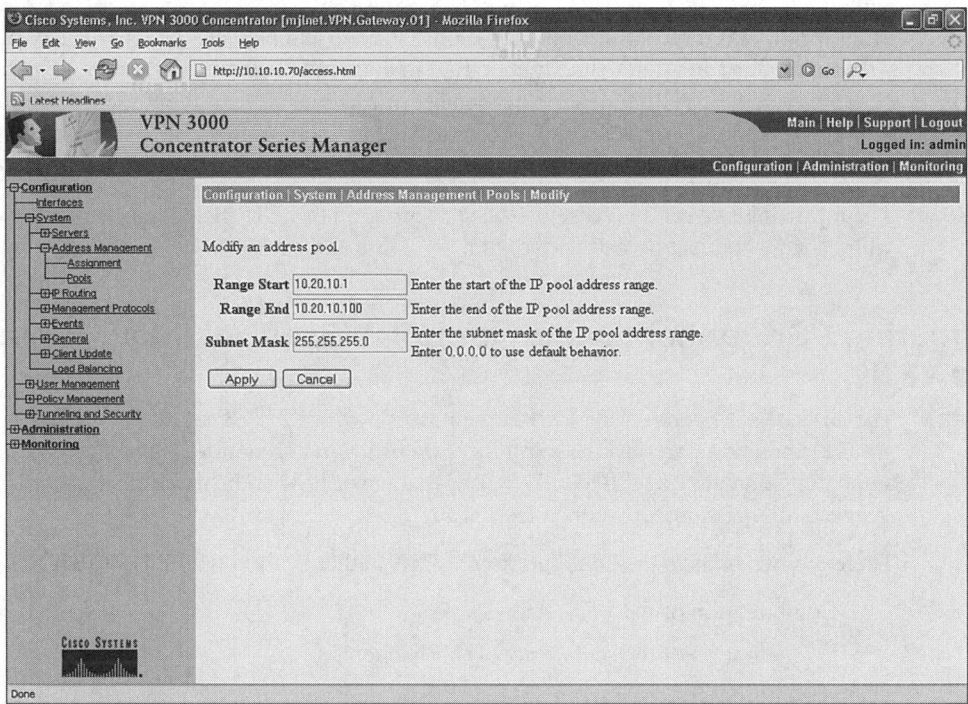

In Figure 8-5, an IP address pool that starts with 10.20.10.1 and ends with 10.20.10.100 is configured. An associated subnet mask of 255.255.255.0 is configured with the address pool. Notice that the IP address pool is configured under **Configuration > System > Address Management > Pools**.

It is also possible to assign IP addresses to remote access clients using an authentication server (such as a Remote Authentication Dial-In User Service [RADIUS] server) or by using a Dynamic Host Configuration Protocol (DHCP) server. Furthermore, it is possible to allow remote access clients to specify their own IP addresses. These methods of IP address assignment can be configured under **Configuration > System > Address Management > Assignment**.

Now you might be asking yourself what the IP address assigned by the VPN concentrator to the remote access client is used for. The answer is that it is applied to a *VPN tunnel interface*. This means that the remote access client will have one or more IP addresses assigned to physical interfaces, as well as the IP address assigned by the VPN concentrator that is applied to the remote access client's *VPN tunnel interface* (a PPP adapter on Windows systems).

Figure 8-8 shows the output of the **ipconfig /all** command on a Windows XP remote access client workstation after an L2TP/IPsec VPN tunnel has been established with a Cisco VPN concentrator. This output illustrates the assignment of an IP address to a VPN tunnel interface.

Figure 8-8   *Output of the* **ipconfig /all** *Command on a Windows XP Remote Access Client Workstation*

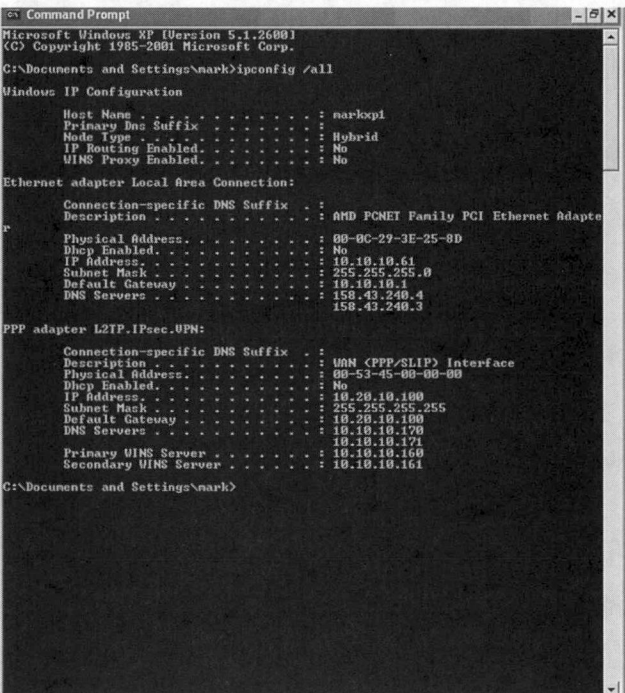

If you look down the output of the **ipconfig /all** command in Figure 8-8, you can see that the IP address 10.10.10.61 is applied to the Ethernet adapter (interface) and that the IP address 10.20.10.100 has been assigned to the PPP adapter (VPN tunnel interface) of the Windows XP remote access client workstation.

You might like to compare the IP address assigned to the VPN tunnel interface (10.20.10.100) with the IP address pool configured in Figure 8-7. The IP address is one of those in the pool, which is no accident, of course—the IP address is assigned to the remote access client during PPP (IPCP) negotiation with the Cisco VPN 3000 concentrator.

Step 2: Configure the Base Group

Settings that you specify in the base group can be inherited by other groups and users. You can configure settings such as tunneling protocols, DNS and WINS server addresses, IPsec SA, tunnel type, authentication server, and L2TP (PPP) authentication protocols under the base group.

Figure 8-9 depicts the configuration of DNS and WINS server addresses, as well as tunneling protocols under **Configuration > User Management > Base Group > General**.

Figure 8-9 *Configuration of DNS and WINS Servers as Well as Tunneling Protocols Under the Base Group*

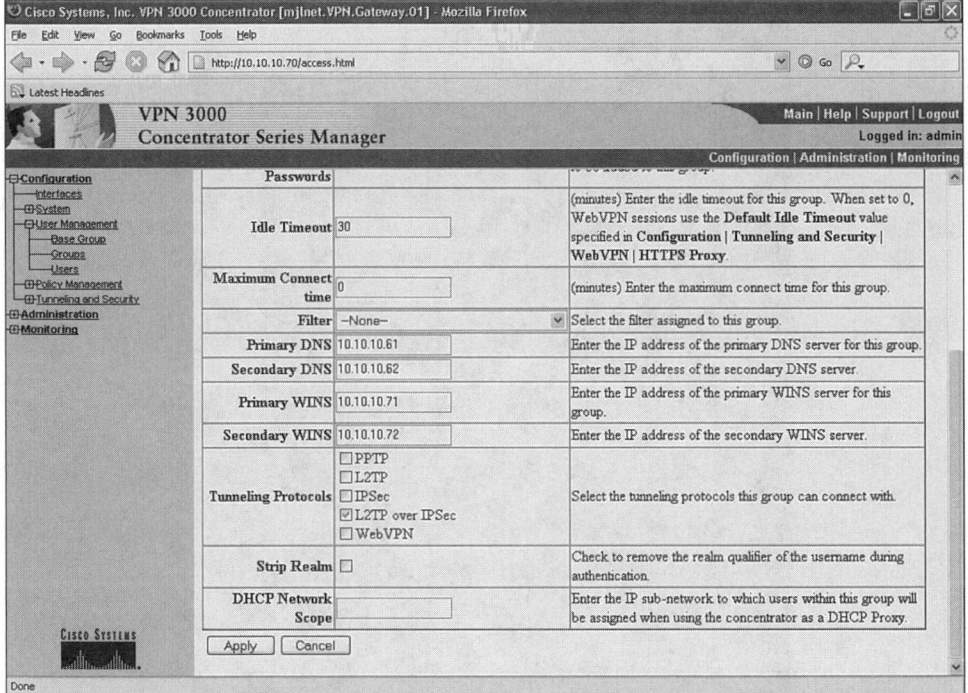

Primary/secondary DNS and WINS server addresses are set to 10.10.10.61/10.10.10.62 and 10.10.10.71/10.10.10.72, respectively, in Figure 8-9. If you look a little farther down the screen, you can see that L2TP over IPsec has been selected as a tunneling protocol.

In Figure 8-10, the IPsec SA, tunnel type, authentication server, and default PSK are configured under **Configuration > User Management > Base Group > IPSec**.

Starting at the top of the screen shown in Figure 8-10, the IPsec SA is selected as ESP-L2TP-TRANSPORT, the tunnel type is configured as Remote Access, and in this example, the authentication server is configured as Internal. The authentication server is used to authenticate the *users* of L2TP/IPsec remote access VPN client workstations during PPP authentication. Note that you might also have to enable L2TP (by checking the appropriate box) under **Configuration > Tunneling and Security**.

Figure 8-11 shows the configuration of a default PSK under **Configuration > User Management > Base Group > IPSec**.

Figure 8-10 *Configuration of IPsec SA, Tunnel Type, and Authentication Server Under the Base Group*

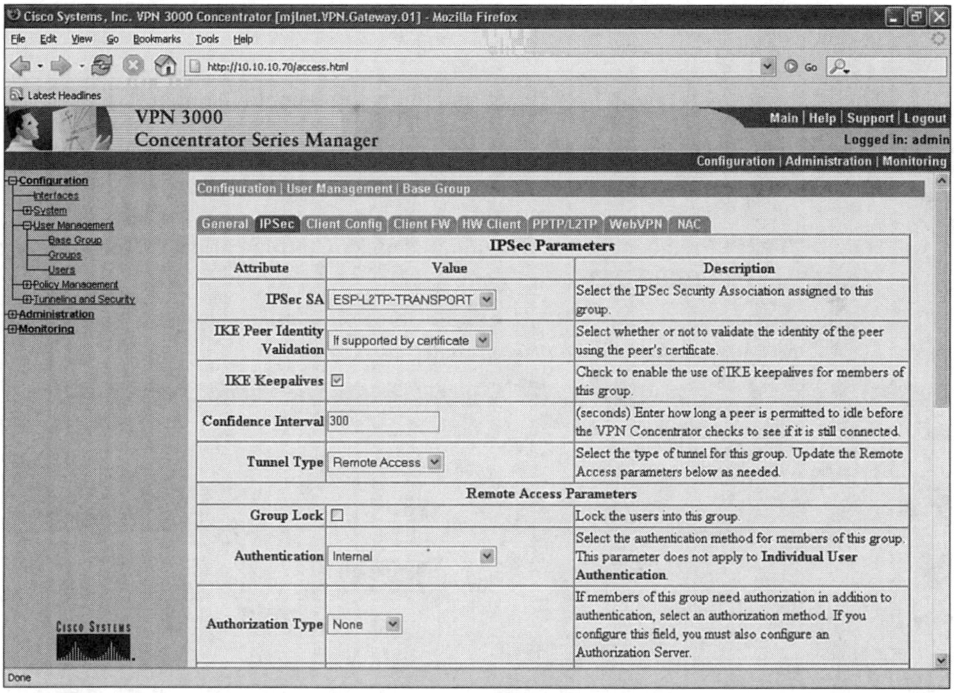

Figure 8-11 *Configuration of a Default PSK Under the Base Group*

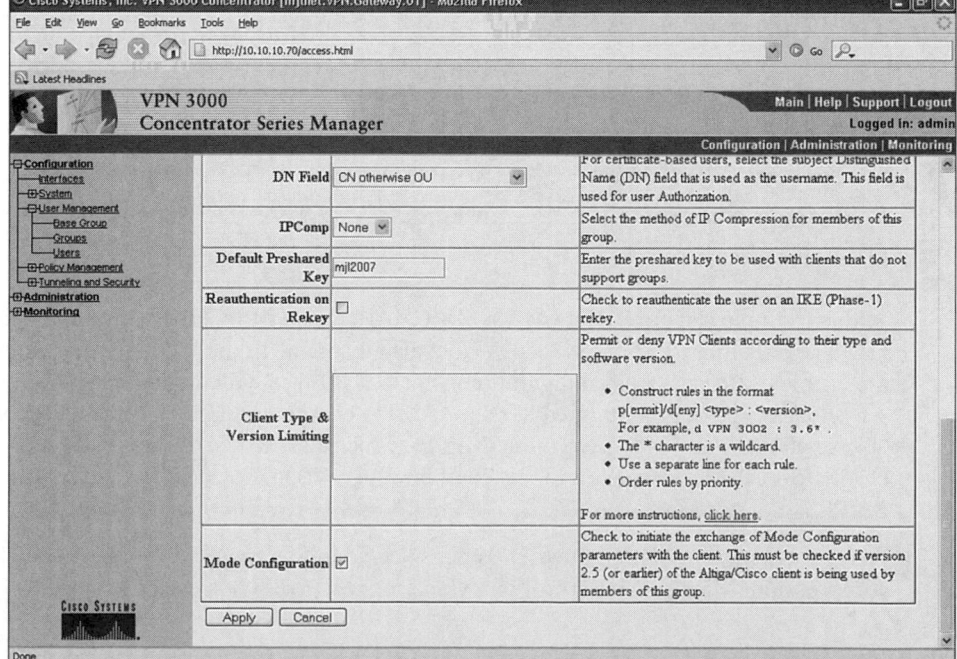

In Figure 8-11, the default PSK, mjl2007, is configured on the Cisco VPN concentrator.

NOTE   The PSK shown in Figure 8-11 is not secure. In a real deployment, a PSK should be a random (as possible) alphanumeric string.

Next, L2TP (PPP) authentication is configured under **Configuration > User Management > Base Group > PPTP/L2TP** (see Figure 8-12).

Figure 8-12 *L2TP (PPP) Authentication Is Configured Under the Base Group*

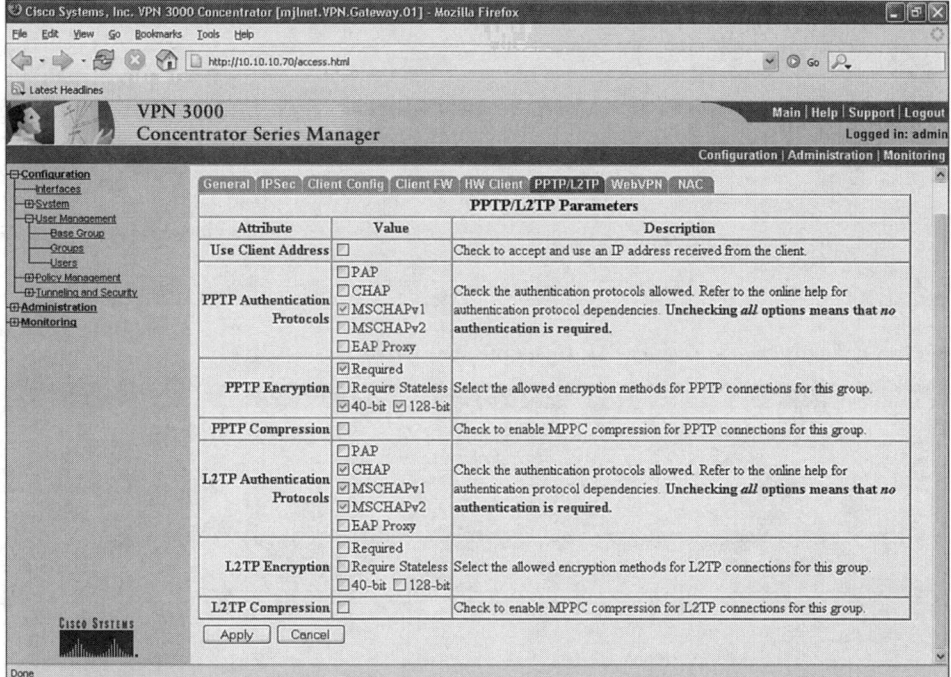

In this example (Figure 8-12), CHAP, MS-CHAPv1, and MS-CHAPv2 are configured as L2TP (PPP) authentication protocols. Note also that none of the L2TP encryption options are checked. Because this configuration is for L2TP/IPsec, you might be mystified as to why no encryption is configured here. In fact, the encryption options here correspond to Microsoft Point-to-Point Encryption (MPPE), which can be used to encrypt the PPP frames carried over the L2TP tunnel. In this case, however, IPsec protects the L2TP tunnel, so MPPE is not necessary.

Also, notice that L2TP compression is not selected in this example. If you select L2TP compression, Microsoft Point-to-Point Compression (MPPC) is used to compress PPP frames over the L2TP tunnel. Compression can be used to make efficient use of bandwidth but does incur additional memory and CPU overhead on the Cisco VPN concentrator. For this reason, it is usually only a good idea to configure compression if all remote access VPN client users use dialup connections.

Step 3: Configure L2TP/IPsec Remote Access Client User Accounts

Having configured the base group, the next step is to configure L2TP/IPsec remote access user accounts. Within user accounts, you can configure usernames and passwords. Figure 8-13 illustrates the configuration of a user account under **Configuration > User Management > Users**.

Figure 8-13 *Configuration of a User Account*

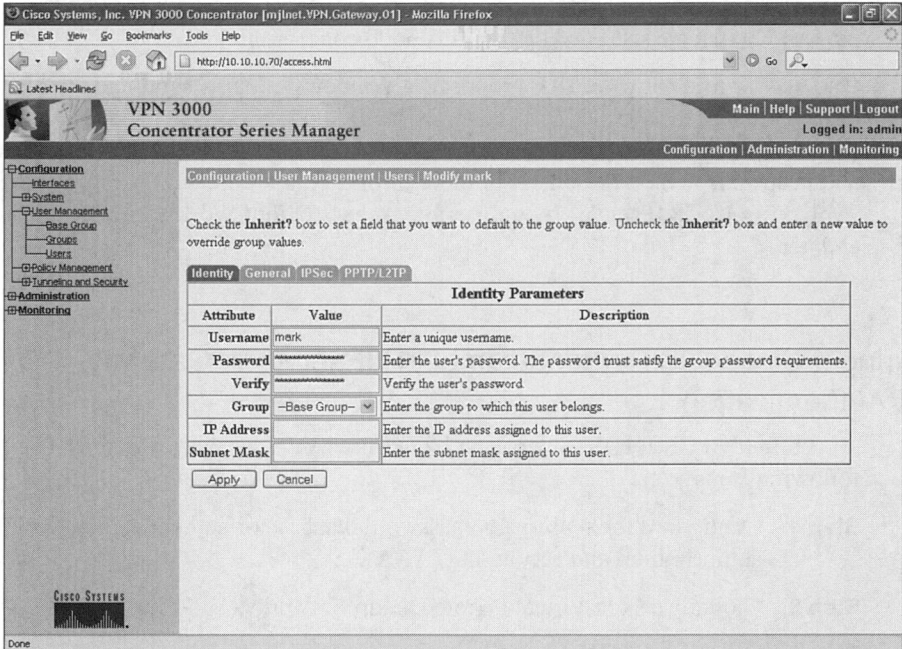

As shown in Figure 8-13, a user account with username mark is configured. A password is also configured. The username and password are used during PPP authentication. Notice that user mark is in the base group. Although not shown, other settings under the user's General, IPsec, PPTP/L2TP tabs of the user account include settings inherited from those settings configured under the base group (see Figures 8-9 through 8-12).

Step 4: Modify IPsec Parameters such as IKE and IPsec SA Proposals (Optional)

It is also possible to modify the IKE and IPsec SA proposals used with L2TP/IPsec by going to **Configuration > Policy Management > SAs**, selecting **ESP-L2TP-TRANSPORT**, and clicking **Modify** (see Figure 8-45 on page 758).

You can modify IKE phase 1 (main mode) proposals under the IKE Parameters heading (in particular, IKE Proposal) in the lower part of the screen and IKE phase 2 (quick mode) proposals under the IPSec Parameters heading (in particular, Authentication Algorithm and Encryption Algorithm) in the upper part of the screen.

The defaults should work fine with Windows clients, but you might want to choose stronger algorithms. The important point is that at least one of the main mode proposals that the remote access client sends during IKE phase 1 negotiation must match the IKE proposal that is specified on the VPN 3000 concentrator, and one of the quick mode proposals that the remote access client sends during IKE phase 2 negotiation must match the IPSec parameters that are specified on the VPN 3000 concentrator.

One way to find out what IKE proposals a Windows client is sending is to examine the oakley.log and look for MMOffer entries (main mode proposals) and QMOffer entries (quick mode proposals). If you are not sure, however, it is best to leave the parameters and proposals at their defaults. For more information on the oakley.log, see the section "Verifying L2TP/IPsec VPNs on Remote Access Client Workstations" later in this chapter.

Configuring a Cisco IOS Router as an L2TP/IPsec VPN Gateway for PSK Authentication

To configure a Cisco IOS router as an L2TP/IPsec VPN gateway, you must complete the following steps:

Step 1 Configure a local username/password database or authentication, authorization, and accounting (AAA).

Step 2 Globally enable Virtual Private Dialup Networks (VPDN).

Step 3 Configure VPDN groups.

Step 4 Configure virtual templates.

Step 5 Configure IP address pools and other IP options.

Step 6 Configure IPsec protection for L2TP.

Example 8-4 shows the configuration of a Cisco IOS router as an L2TP/IPsec remote access VPN gateway.

Example 8-4 *Configuration of a Cisco IOS Router as an L2TP/IPsec Remote Access VPN Gateway*

```
!
hostname mjlnet.VPN.Gateway.03 (line 1)
!
!
username mark@mjlnet.com password 0 mjlnet2006 (line 2)
username john@mjlnet.com password 0 mjlnet2007 (line 3)
!
vpdn enable (line 4)
!
vpdn-group 1 (line 5)
 accept-dialin (line 6)
 protocol l2tp (line 7)
 virtual-template 1 (line 8)
 l2tp security crypto-profile l2tpprof (line 9)
 no l2tp tunnel authentication (line 10)
!
!
async-bootp dns-server 10.10.10.61 (line 11)
async-bootp nbns-server 10.10.10.71 (line 12)
!
crypto isakmp policy 1 (line 13)
 authentication pre-share (line 14)
crypto isakmp key mjl2007 address 0.0.0.0 0.0.0.0 (line 15)
!
crypto ipsec transform-set l2tptrans esp-3des esp-md5-hmac (line 16)
 mode transport (line 17)
!
crypto map l2tpmap 10 ipsec-isakmp profile l2tpprof (line 18)
 set transform-set l2tptrans (line 19)
!
!
interface Loopback0 (line 20)
 ip address 10.30.10.1 255.255.255.0 (line 21)
!
interface FastEthernet0/0 (line 22)
 ip address 10.10.10.1 255.255.255.0 (line 23)
!
interface FastEthernet2/0 (line 24)
 ip address 10.40.10.1 255.255.255.0 (line 25)
 crypto map l2tpmap (line 26)
!
interface Virtual-Template1 (line 27)
 ip unnumbered Loopback0 (line 28)
 peer default ip address pool RA_VPN_pool (line 29)
 ppp authentication chap (line 30)
!
!
ip local pool RA_VPN_pool 10.20.10.1 10.20.10.100 (line 31)
!
```

Lines 2 and 3 show the configuration of a local username/password database using the **username** *username* **password** *password* command. These usernames and passwords are used for user authentication that takes place during PPP negotiation.

The **vpdn enable** command in line 4 is then used to globally enable VPDNs, including L2TP. After VPDNs have been globally enabled, the next step is to configure the VPDN group. A VPDN group is used to group L2TP configuration on the VPN gateway. The **vpdn-group** *name* command in line 5 is used to configure the (locally significant) name of a VPDN group.

In line 6, the **accept-dialin** command configures the VPN gateway to accept L2TP tunnel and session setup from remote access VPN clients.

The **protocol l2tp** command in line 7 is then used to configure the VPDN protocol as L2TP.

In line 8, the **virtual-template** *template-number* command is used to specify the virtual template from which virtual access interfaces will be copied (see lines 27 to 30). PPP connections (tunneled by L2TP) from remote access VPN clients are terminated on virtual access interfaces.

The **l2tp security crypto-profile** *profile-name* command (line 9) is used to enable IPsec protection for L2TP (L2TP/IPsec). The profile name specified using this command must match that configured using the **crypto map** *map-name sequence-number* **ipsec-isakmp profile** *profile-name* command in line 16.

In line 10, the **no l2tp tunnel authentication** command is used to ensure that authentication is not used for L2TP tunnel. L2TP tunnel authentication is unnecessary in this case because remote access VPN client machines are authenticated during IKE negotiation and the users are authenticated during PPP negotiation.

Lines 11 and 12 contain the **async-bootp dns-server** *address* and **async-bootp nbns-server** *address* commands. These commands configure DNS server and NetBIOS Name Server (WINS server) addresses, and these are supplied to remote access VPN clients in PPP (IPCP) negotiation.

Lines 13 to 14 show the configuration of the IKE policy. In this case, the policy consists of DES encryption, Diffie-Hellman group 1, a lifetime of 86,400 seconds, and PSK authentication (**authentication pre-share**). Because the encryption algorithm, Diffie-Hellman group, and lifetime are defaults, their configuration is not explicitly shown.

The **crypto isakmp key** *preshared-key* **address** *peer-address* mask command in line 15 is used to specify the PSK used to authenticate remote access VPN client machines with any IP address. Remote access VPN client machines can have any IP address because a wildcard address and mask are specified (0.0.0.0/0.0.0.0).

An IPsec transform set is configured in lines 16 and 17.

The **crypto ipsec transform-set** *transform-set-name transform1* [*transform2*] [*transform3*] [*transform4*] command in line 16 is used to configure a transform set called l2tptrans that specifies ESP-3DES encryption and ESP-MD5-HMAC authentication. If you have Windows remote access VPN clients, do not specify AH in the transform set; it is not supported with the Windows L2TP/IPsec client.

The **mode {tunnel | transport}** command in line 17 is used (in this case) to specify transport mode. If you have Windows remote access VPN clients, make sure that you specify transport mode as tunnel mode is not supported by the Windows L2TP/IPsec client.

In lines 18 and 19, a crypto map is created using the **crypto map** *map-name sequence-number* **ipsec-isakmp profile** *profile-name* command, and the **transform-set** created in lines 16 and 17 is specified using the **set transform-set** *transform-set-name* command.

The **profile** keyword in the **crypto map** *map-name sequence-number* **ipsec-isakmp profile** *profile-name* command is used to allow crypto maps to be created on demand from this template as remote access VPN clients connect to the VPN gateway.

Lines 20 to 26 show the configuration of loopback, inside, and outside interfaces. Note that crypto map created in lines 18 and 19 is applied to the outside interface (the interface on which remote access VPN clients will connect).

In lines 27 to 30, a virtual template interface is configured. This virtual template is referenced with the **virtual-template** command in line 8.

In line 28, the **ip unnumbered** *interface* command configures the virtual template to use the IP address configured on interface Loopback0.

The **peer default ip address pool** *pool-name* command (line 29) references a pool of IP addresses. IP addresses from this pool are supplied to remote access VPN clients during PPP (IPCP) negotiation.

In line 30, the **ppp authentication chap** configures the VPN gateway to authenticate remote access VPN clients using CHAP.

The **ip local pool** *pool-name* command in line 31 specifies an IP address pool. As previously mentioned, IP addresses from this pool are supplied to remote access clients (see also line 29).

The sample configuration shown in Example 8-4 includes the configuration of a local username/password database (lines 2 and 3) that is used for remote access user authentication. Although a local database works well for a small number of users, it does not scale well. It is common, therefore, to use an AAA server (often a RADIUS server) for user authentication.

To use RADIUS rather than a local username/password database, the commands in lines 2 and 3 (Example 8-4) can be replaced by the configuration contained in Example 8-5.

Example 8-5 shows the AAA configuration for a Cisco IOS VPN gateway.

Example 8-5 *Configuration for User Authentication Using a RADIUS Server*

```
aaa new-model
aaa authentication ppp default group radius
aaa authorization network default group radius
radius-server host 10.10.10.51 auth-port 1645 acct-port 1646 key cisco
```

The **aaa new-model** command enables AAA.

Next, the **aaa authentication ppp default group radius** command enables authentication for PPP using a RADIUS server using the default method list.

The **aaa authorization network default group radius** command configures authorization of network connections using a RADIUS server (using the default method list).

The **radius server host** command specifies the IP address/DNS name of the RADIUS server as well as the UDP ports used for authentication (**auth-port**) and accounting (**acct-port**) requests. This command is also can also be used to specify the key used to authenticate communications used between the VPN gateway and the RADIUS server.

It is also worth mentioning that you should make sure that user accounts on the RADIUS server specify the Service-Type (attribute type 6) as Framed, and the Framed-Protocol (attribute type 7) as PPP (configured, by default, under the group on a Cisco Secure ACS).

You can verify L2TP/IPsec remote access VPNs on a Cisco IOS router using a number of commands, including **show vpdn tunnel**, **show vpdn session**, and **show caller user**. These commands are discussed in detail later in this chapter.

Configuring Windows L2TP/IPsec Remote Access VPN Clients for PSK Authentication

After you have configured the VPN gateway, you can move on to configuring the L2TP/IPsec remote access VPN clients.

The configuration of a Windows XP L2TP/IPsec remote access client for PSK authentication begins with the following steps:

Step 1   Go to the Control Panel (via the Start menu).

Step 2   Click **Network and Internet Connections**.

Step 3   Click **Network Connections**.

Step 4   Click **Create a new connection**.

You will then be presented with the Welcome to the New Connection Wizard screen (see Figure 8-14).

Figure 8-14 *Welcome to the New Connection Wizard Screen*

Click **Next**, and you will see the New Connection Type screen shown in Figure 8-15.

Figure 8-15 *New Connection Type Screen*

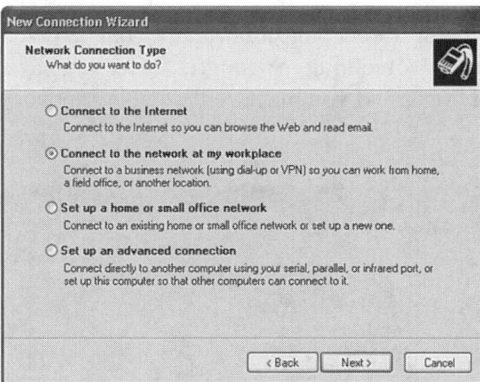

Choose **Connect to the network at my workplace** and click **Next**. You will now be
presented with the Network Connection screen (see Figure 8-16).

Figure 8-16 *Network Connection Screen*

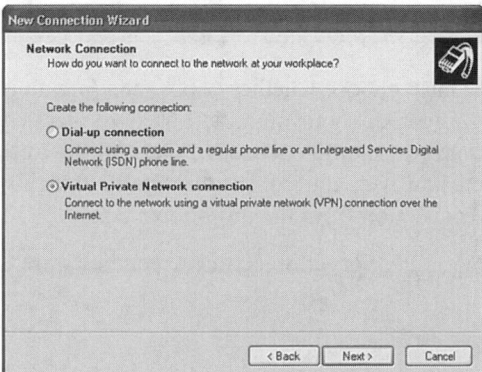

738 Chapter 8: Designing and Implementing L2TPv2 and L2TPv3 Remote Access VPNs

Choose **Virtual Private Network connection** and click **Next**. Now you will see the Connection Name screen in Figure 8-17.

Figure 8-17 *Connection Name Screen*

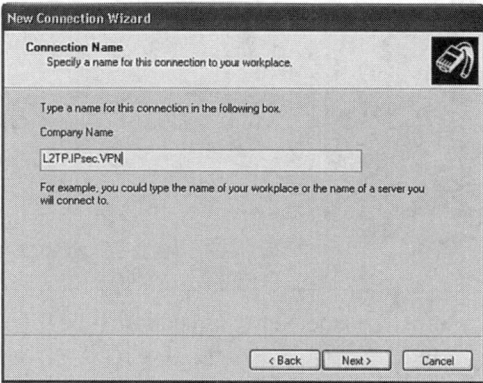

Type in a name for the VPN connection. It does not particularly matter what name you choose—just make it something meaningful. After you have typed a name for the connection, click **Next**, and you may see the Public Network screen in Figure 8-18.

Figure 8-18 *Public Network Screen*

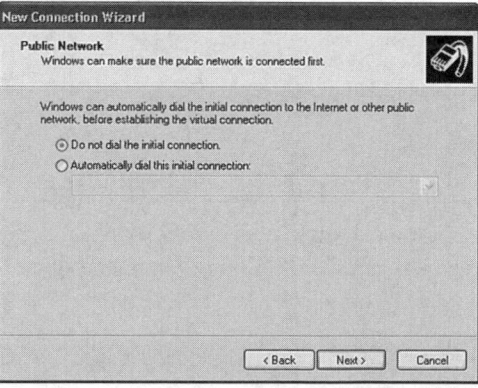

At this point, you must choose whether you want a (previously configured) dialup connection to be triggered when you initiate VPN connectivity. If you have a DSL or cable Internet connection, you should choose **Do not dial the initial connection**; if you have a dialup connection, however, choose **Automatically dial this initial connection** and then choose a dialup connection from the drop-down box.

Click **Next**, and the VPN Server Selection screen in Figure 8-19 will appear.

Figure 8-19 *VPN Server Selection Screen*

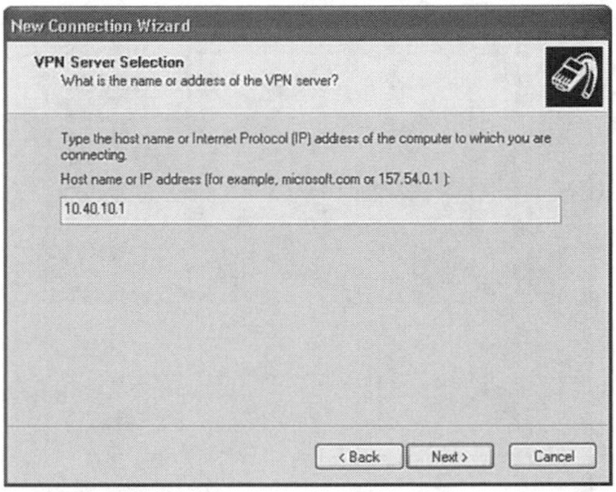

You can either type the IP address or the fully qualified domain name (FQDN) of the VPN gateway in the box. After you have done this, click **Next**.

Figure 8-20 shows the final screen, Completing the New Connection Wizard.

Figure 8-20 *Completing the New Connection Wizard Screen*

Click **Next**. You have now finished creating your VPN connection.

As you've been following the configuration of the Windows XP remote access VPN client, you might have noticed that one thing was missing—at no point did you specify the VPN protocols (L2TP over IPsec). And neither did you specify PSK or PPP authentication.

You will not be surprised to learn that the VPN connection that you have just created requires a little tweaking. Open the VPN connection you just created either by double-clicking the shortcut (if you created one) or by going to the Control Panel and clicking **Network And Internet Connections** and then clicking **Network Connections**. You will now see the dialog box in Figure 8-21.

Figure 8-21 *Connection Dialog Box*

Click **Properties**, and then the **Security** tab, choose **Advanced (custom settings)**, and click the **Settings** button. You will see the screen in Figure 8-22.

Figure 8-22 *Advanced Security Settings Screen*

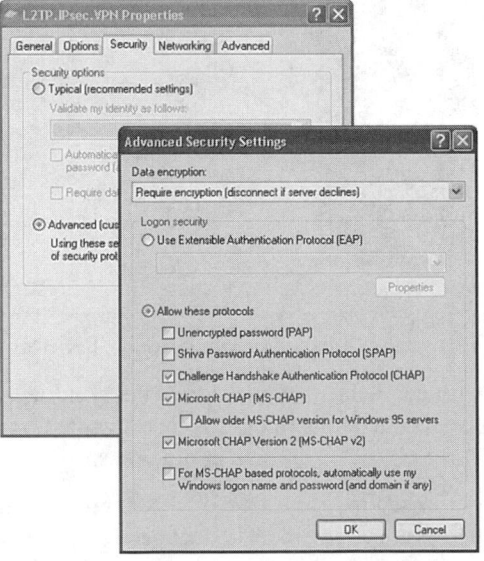

Click the **Data encryption** drop-down and choose **Require encryption (disconnect if server declines)**. It is important that you do not choose **No encryption allowed (server will disconnect if it requires encryption)**—if you specify this option, the remote access VPN client will *attempt* to negotiate null (RFC2410) IPsec encryption (meaning no encryption) during IKE phase 2! Do not worry too much, however, because any attempt by the remote access client to negotiate null encryption will fail, unless, that is, you specify the null encryption algorithm on the VPN gateway (almost always a bad idea!).

In the lower part of the dialog box, you can choose the appropriate PPP authentication protocols, one of which must match those configured on the VPN gateway (see Figure 8-12 and line 30 in Example 8-4).

Click **OK**, and you're now back to the Security tab. Now click the **IPSec Settings** button, and the IPSec dialog box will appear (see Figure 8-23).

Figure 8-23 *IPSec Settings Dialog Box*

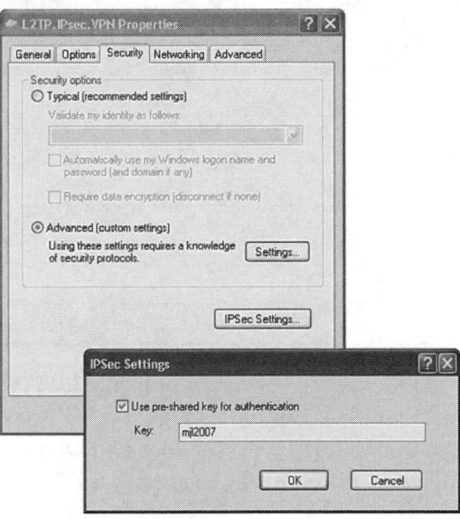

Check the **Use pre-shared key for authentication** and type same preshared key that you configured on the VPN gateway (see Figure 8-11 and line 14 in Example 8-4) into the box.

Click **OK**, followed by the **Networking** tab, and you will see the screen shown in Figure 8-24.

In the Type of VPN drop-down box, choose **L2TP IPSec VPN**.

Finally, click **OK**, and the configuration of your L2TP/IPsec remote access VPN client is complete.

Although not shown, you might also like to choose **Internet Protocol (TCP/IP)** (see Figure 8-24), click the **Properties** button, and in the General tab of the Advanced TCP/IP Settings ensure that the **Use default gateway on remote network** is checked. This ensures that the Windows XP client will use the VPN gateway as its default gateway when the VPN is connected, thus preventing split tunneling.

CAUTION Split tunneling is a situation in which a remote access client can directly access both the Internet and the VPN tunnel at the same time. This situation is a security risk because an attacker on the Internet might be able to gain control of the remote access client and then access the VPN tunnel.

Figure 8-24 *The Networking Tab*

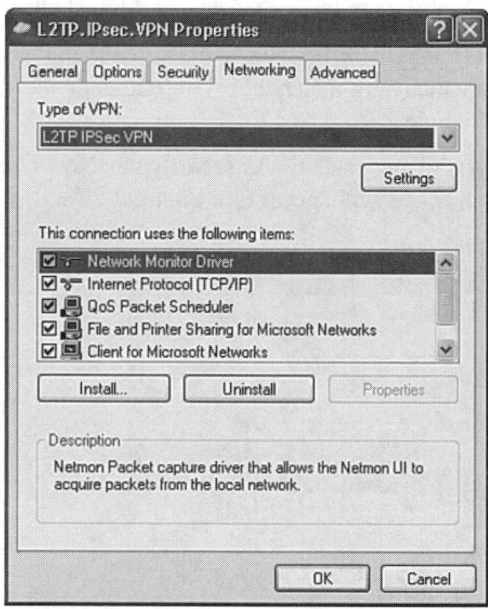

Configuration of Windows 2000 workstations for L2TP/IPsec is similar to that to that for Windows XP, in that you must create the VPN connection via the Make New Connection Wizard accessible from Network and Dial-up Connections in the Control Panel. However, there is no easy way to specify a PSK in Windows 2000—you have to do the following:

- Add a value called **ProhibitIpSec** to the registry. This disables the automatic creation of an IPsec policy for L2TP (the automatically created policy uses digital signature [digital certificate] IPsec authentication).

- Manually create an IPsec policy for L2TP with PSK authentication.

You can find detailed information on these tasks in Microsoft Knowledge Base article 240262. Just search for this article at http://www.microsoft.com.

NOTE   It is also possible to obtain L2TP/IPsec client software for Windows 98, Windows ME, and Windows NT 4.0 from the following URL:

http://www.microsoft.com/technet/prodtechnol/windows2000serv/support/vpnclientag.mspx

Other operating systems such as MacOS X include L2TP/IPsec remote access client software.

Implementing Digital Signature (Digital Certificate) Authentication with L2TP/IPsec Voluntary/Client-Initiated Tunnel Mode Remote Access VPNs

As already described, PSK is a relatively easy to configure method IPsec (IKE) authentication, but a more secure method of IPsec authentication using digital signatures (digital certificates). If you want to implement digital signature authentication, you must configure this on both the VPN gateway and the remote access VPN clients.

Configuring the L2TP/IPsec VPN Gateway for Digital Signature Authentication

This section examines the configuration of a Cisco VPN 3000 concentrator and a Cisco IOS router as an L2TP/IPsec VPN gateway for digital signature authentication.

Specifying Digital Signature Authentication on a Cisco VPN 3000 Concentrator

The configuration of a Cisco VPN 3000 concentrator consists of the following:

Step 1 Retrieve and install the CA's certificate.

Step 2 Enroll the VPN gateway with the CA and obtain a certificate.

Step 3 Configure an address pool (or other method of IP address assignment).

Step 4 Configure the base group.

Step 5 Configure a group for L2TP/IPsec remote access client users.

Step 6 Configure L2TP/IPsec remote access client *user* accounts.

Step 7 Modify IPsec parameters such as IKE and IPsec SA proposals (optional).

Notice that the configuration steps are almost identical to those necessary when configuring PSK authentication. The differences are described in Steps 1, 2, and 5. This section does not repeat Steps 3, 4, and 6—see the section "Configuring the L2TP/IPsec VPN Gateway for PSK Authentication" for more information on these steps. Steps 1, 2, and 5 are discussed further in the following three sections.

Step 1: Retrieve and Install the CA's Certificate   In Step 1, you must retrieve the CA's certificate and install it on the Cisco VPN 3000 concentrator.

NOTE   A Microsoft certificate server is used to illustrate example configurations in this chapter. This does not constitute a recommendation, and it should be noted that many other vendors produce similar products that can support the same functions.

Two methods of retrieving and installing the CA's certificate are as follows:

- Manually retrieving and installing the CA's certificate

- Using the Simple Certificate Enrollment Protocol (SCEP) to retrieve and install the CA's certificate

This chapter focuses on manual retrieval and installation; Chapter 9, "Designing and Deploying IPsec Remote Access and Teleworker VPNs," discusses retrieval using SCEP.

To retrieve the CA's certificate manually, navigate to the following URL (inserting either the IP address or the FQDN of the certificate server, as appropriate):

http://<*CA_ip_address_*or_*CA_FQDN*>/certsrv

Figure 8-25 shows the first page that you will see when retrieving the CA's certificate.

Figure 8-25 *Certificate Services Welcome Page*

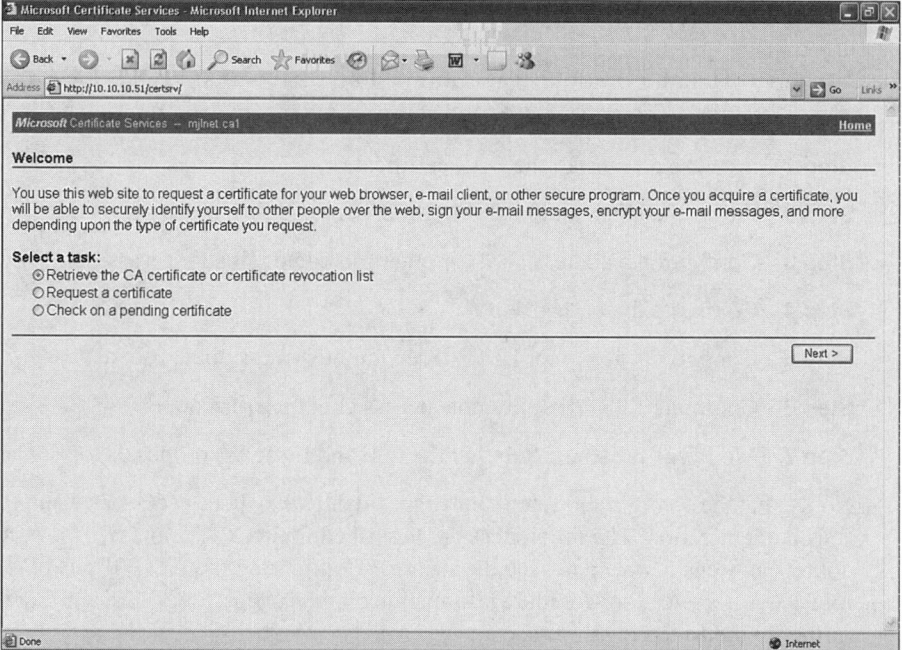

As shown in Figure 8-25, on the Welcome page, choose **Retrieve the CA certificate or certificate revocation list**, and then click **Next**.

You will then see the page shown in Figure 8-26.

On the Retrieve the CA certificate or certificate revocation list page, click the **Download CA certificate** link.

A dialog box titled Potential Scripting Violation followed by a dialog box titled Security Warning may appear—choose **Yes** in both, and save the CA's certificate to a convenient location on the local workstation.

Now go to **Administration > Certificate Management** on the Cisco VPN 3000 concentrator (see Figure 8-27). Notice that there is no existing certificate listed under the Certificate Authorities heading.

Figure 8-26 *Retrieve the CA Certificate or Certificate Revocation List Page*

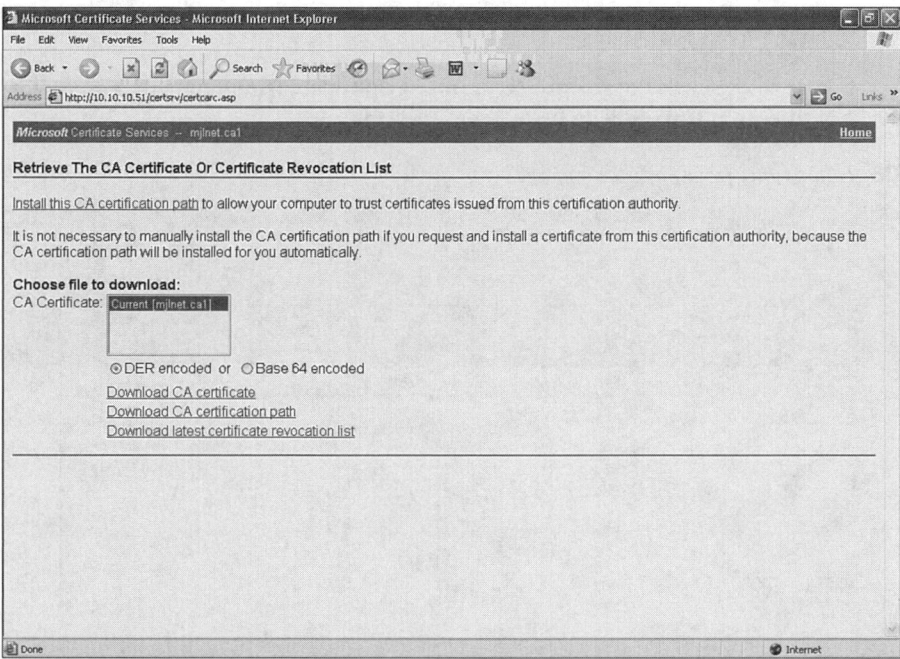

Figure 8-27 *Certificate Management Page*

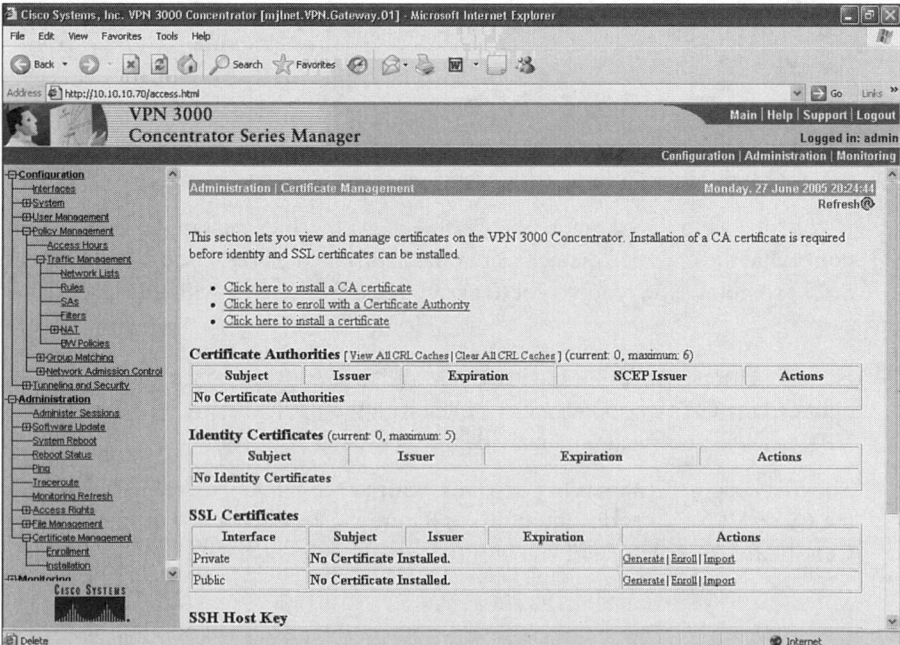

Choose the **Click here to install a CA certificate** link and on the following page choose **Upload File from Workstation** and browse to location that you saved the CA's certificate to on the local workstation.

Figure 8-28 shows the **Administration > Certificate Management > Install > CA Certificate > Upload File from Workstation** page.

Figure 8-28 *Upload File from Workstation Page*

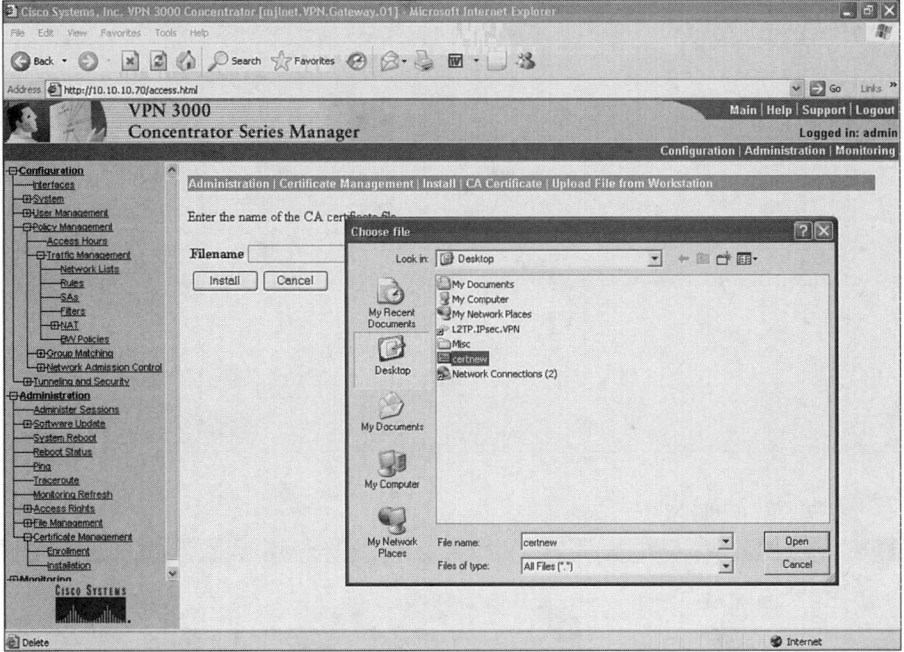

Select the CA's certificate and click the **Install** button. The CA's certificate is installed, and you will jump back to the Certificate Management page (see Figure 8-29).

If you take a close look under the Certificate Authorities heading in Figure 8-29, you will notice that the CA's certificate has now been installed on the Cisco VPN 3000 concentrator. So far so good. Now you've got to enroll the VPN gateway with the CA.

Step 2: Enroll the VPN Gateway with the CA and Obtain a Certificate   Having

obtained the CA's certificate and installed it on the VPN gateway, you are ready to enroll the VPN gateway itself and obtain an identity certificate for it.

The first task in this step is to go to the **Configuration > Certificate Management** page on the Cisco VPN 3000 concentrator (see Figure 8-29). Choose **Click here to enroll with a Certificate Authority**, and you will find yourself on the page shown in Figure 8-30.

Figure 8-29 *Certificate Management Page (the CA's Certificate Is Installed)*

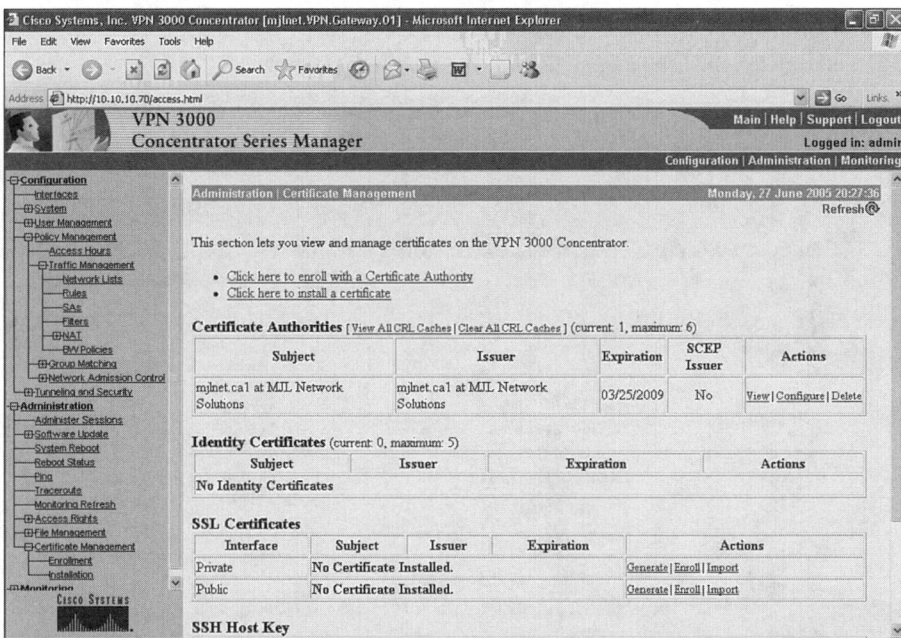

Figure 8-30 *Choosing an Enrollment Method*

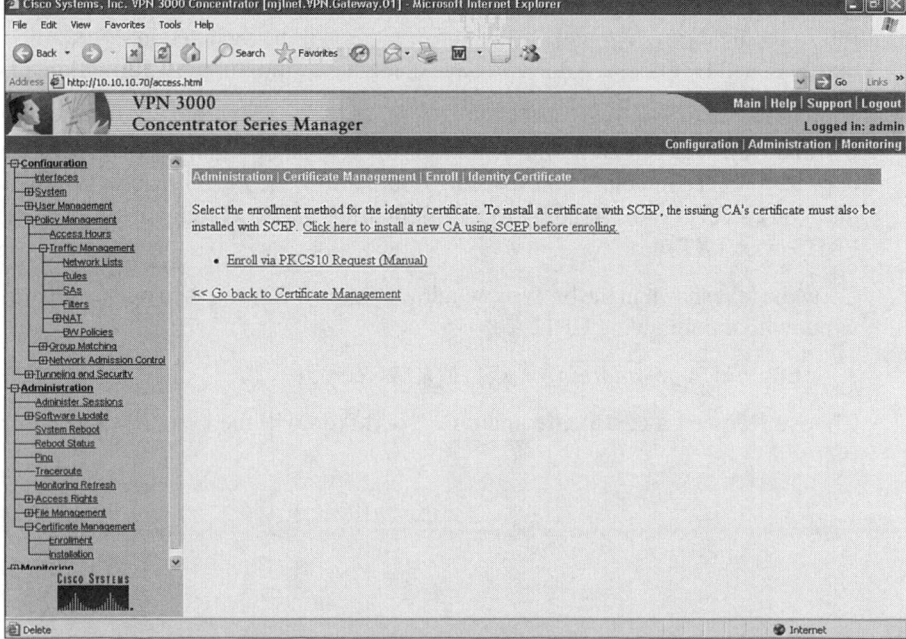

Choose **Enroll via PKCS10 Request (Manual)**, and the page in Figure 8-31 will appear.

Figure 8-31 *Entering Information to Be Included in the Certificate Request*

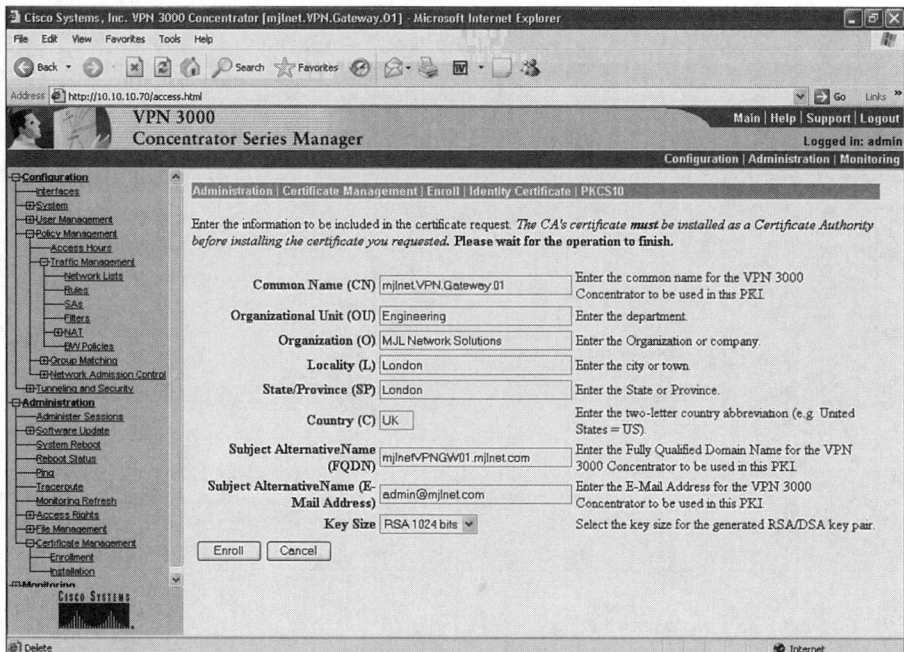

Fill in the fields appropriately—this information will be included in the X.509 certificate that is issued by the CA. After you have completed filling in the information, click the **Enroll** button; you will see a page similar to that shown in Figure 8-32.

If you do not see a screen similar to that shown in Figure 8-32, it might be because you have pop-ups blocked in your web browser—don't worry, the PKCS request is stored as a file that you can also view by going to **Configuration > File Management** (it is stored as a PKCSxxxx.TXT file).

Copy the text shown in the browser window (Figure 8-32) and then open a separate browser window to the following URL:

http://<*CA_ip_address_or_CA_FQDN*>/certsrv

Choose **Request a certificate** and click **Next**. You will then see the page shown in Figure 8-33.

Figure 8-32 *PKCS#10 Certificate Request*

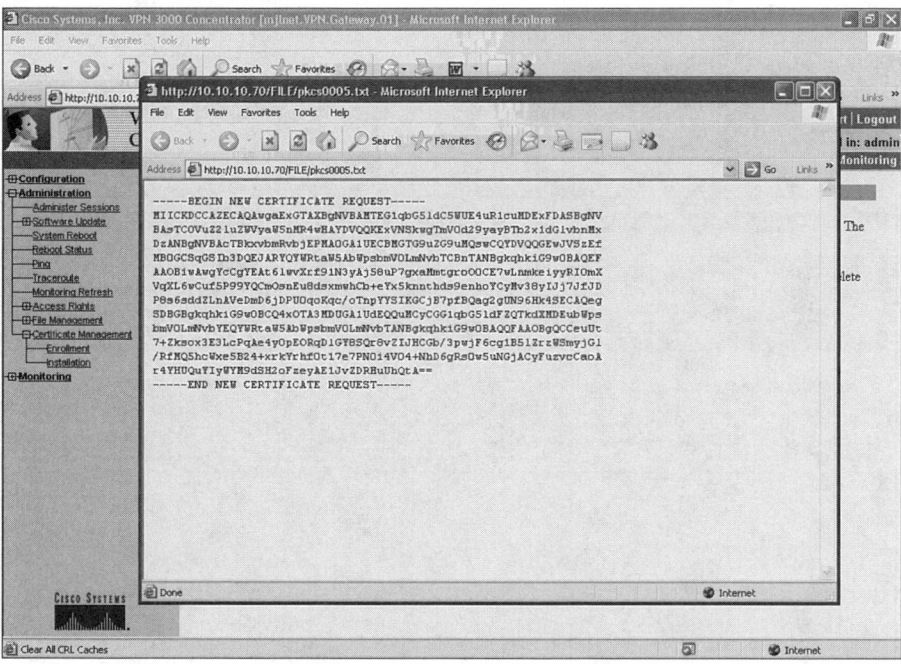

Figure 8-33 *Choose Request Type*

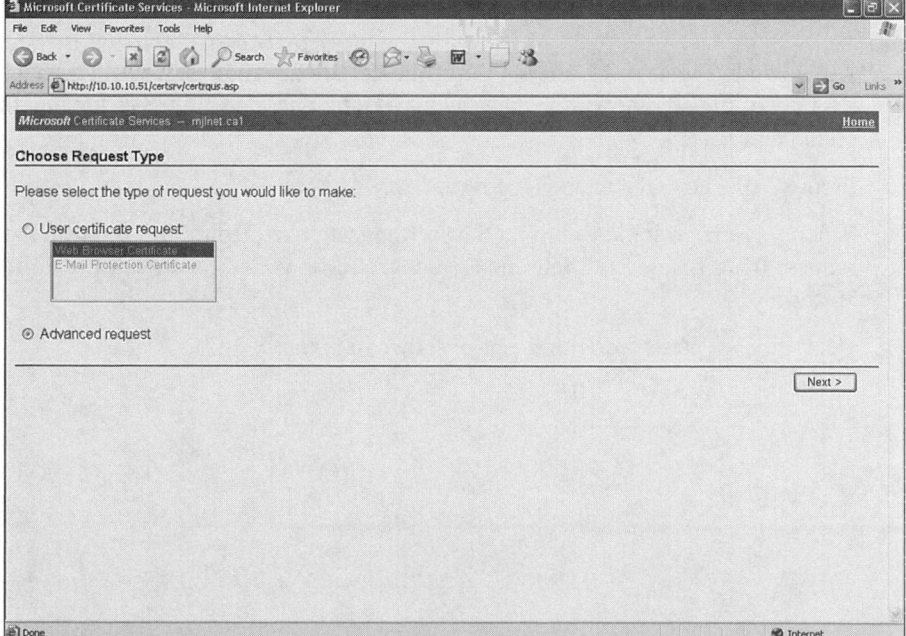

Now choose **Advanced request** and click **Next**, and you should see the screen in Figure 8-34.

Figure 8-34 *Advanced Certificate Requests*

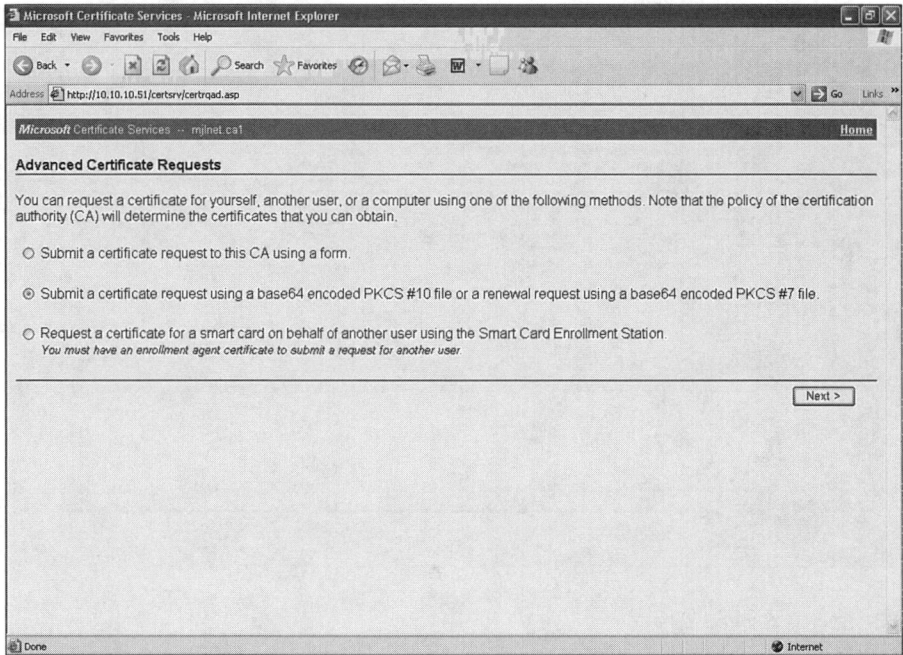

As shown in Figure 8-34, choose **Submit a certificate request using a base64 encoded PKCS#10 file or renewal request using base64 encoded PKCS#7 file** and then click **Next**.

Figure 8-35 shows the page that now appears.

When you arrive at the Submit a Saved Request page (Figure 8-35), paste the PKCS request from Figure 8-32 into the Saved Request box and then click the **Submit** button.

Next, you are presented with the page shown in Figure 8-36.

Figure 8-35 *Submit a Saved Request*

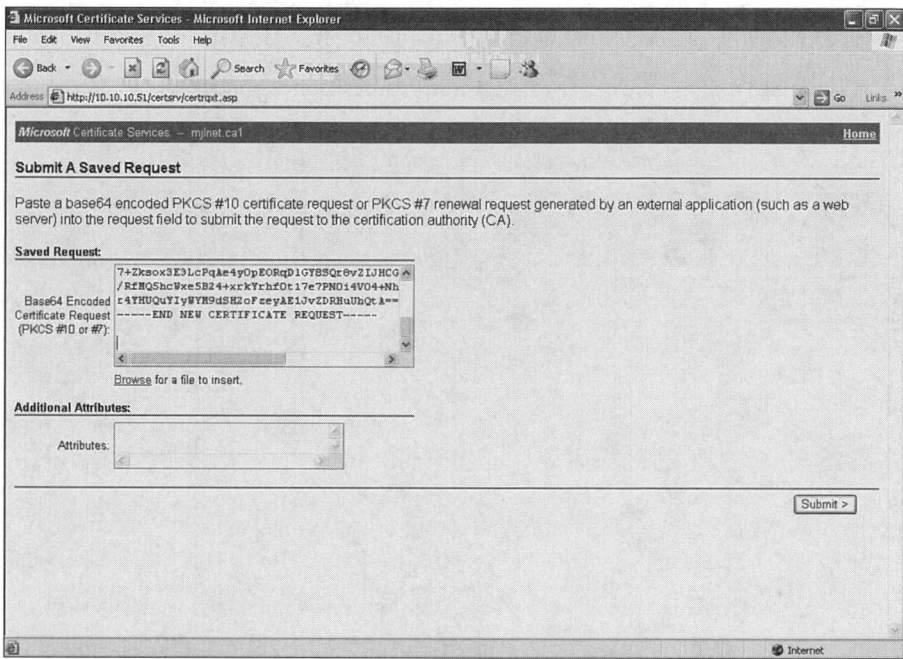

Figure 8-36 *Certificate Pending*

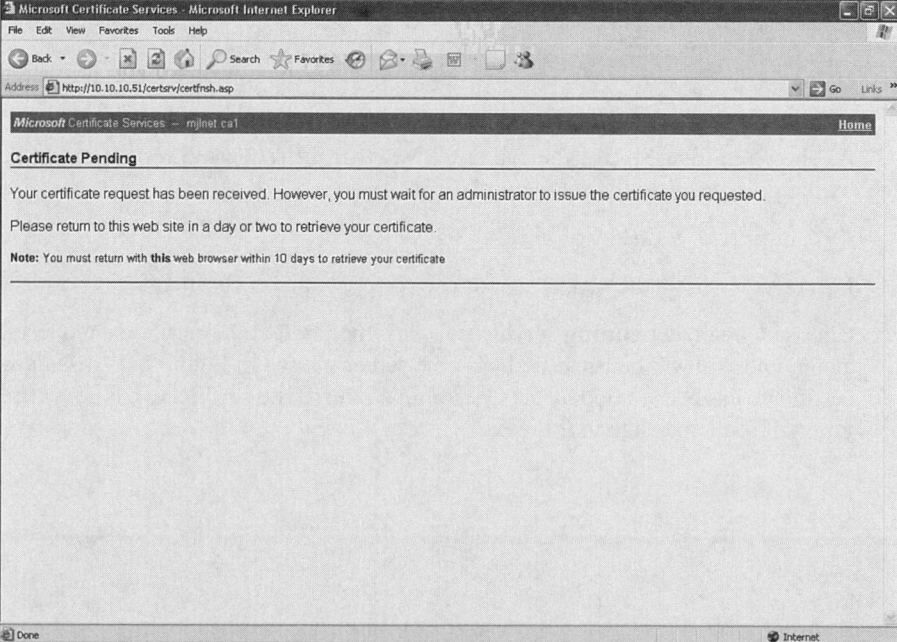

Your certificate request is now pending on the CA, and must be approved by the CA administrator before a certificate can be issued (assuming that the CA is not configured to automatically issues certificates [almost always a bad idea!]).

Figure 8-37 shows the approval and certificate issuance process on a Microsoft CA.

Figure 8-37 *Approval and Certificate Issuance on a Microsoft CA*

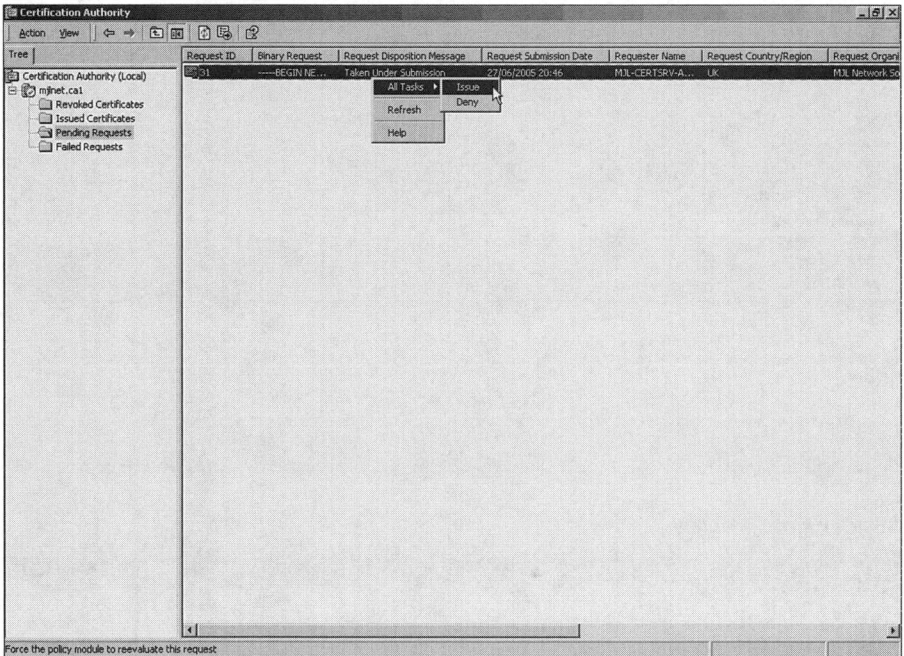

As shown in Figure 8-37, you can check whether the requested certificate has been issued by the going back to the following URL:

> http://*CA_ip_address_or_CA_FQDN*/certsrv

Figure 8-38 shows the procedure for checking whether a certificate has been issued.

Choose **Check on pending certificate**, click **Next**, select the certificate request, click **Next** again, and you will be presented with the screen shown in Figure 8-39, assuming that the certificate has been issued by the CA administrator. If the certificate has not yet been issued, you will see a message to this effect.

Figure 8-38 *Checking Whether a Certificate Has Been Issued*

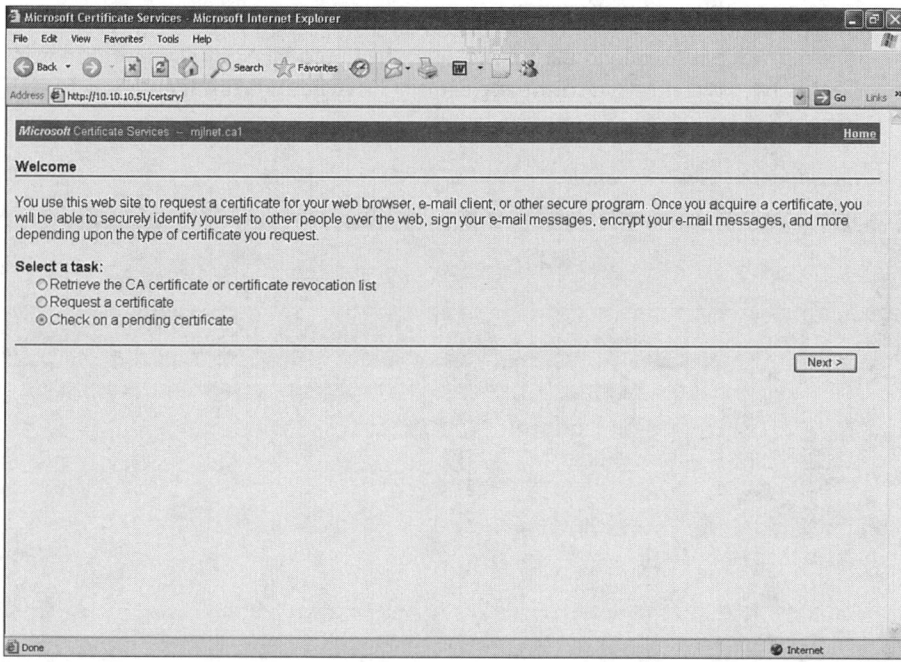

Figure 8-39 *Certificate Has Been Issued*

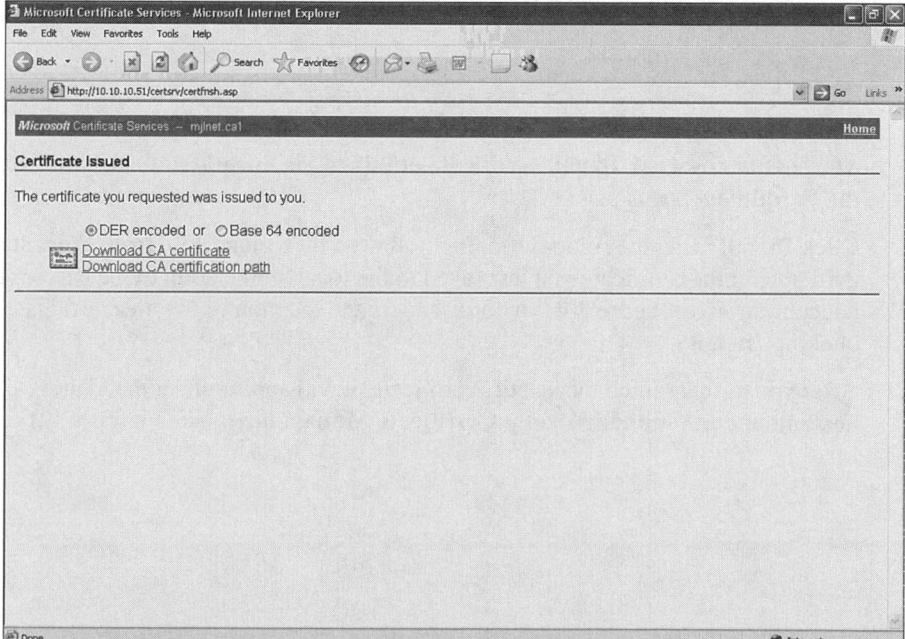

You should now click **Download CA certificate** and save the certificate to a convenient location on the local workstation.

The next step is to upload the certificate to the Cisco VPN 3000 concentrator. You can do this by navigating to **Administration > Certificate Management > Install** (see Figure 8-40).

Figure 8-40 *Installing the Certificate on the Cisco VPN 3000 Concentrator*

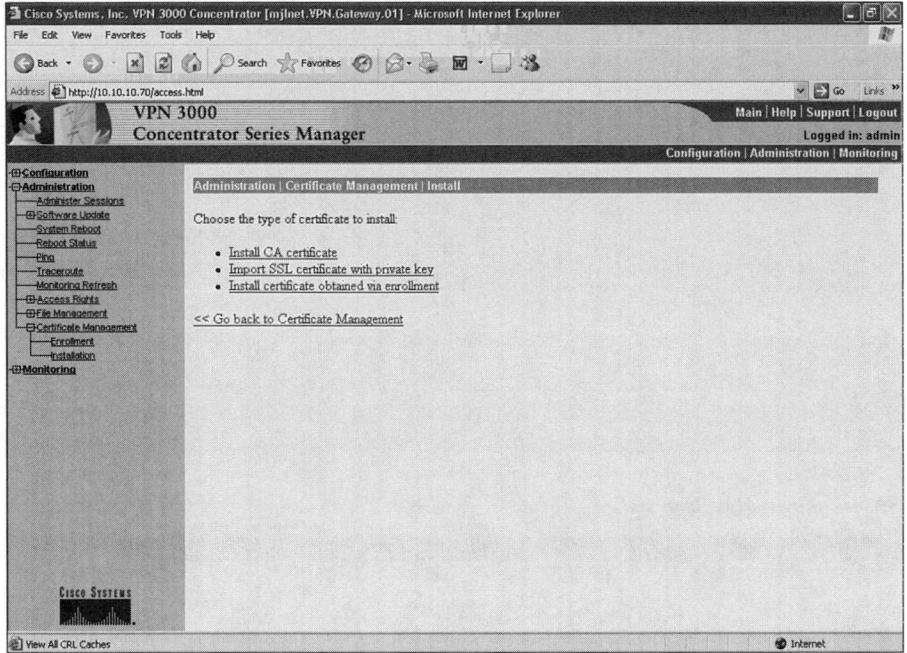

You should now click **Install certificate obtained via enrollment**, and you will come to the Enrollment Status page.

Click **Install** under the Actions heading, followed by **Upload File from Workstation**, and then upload the certificate you just saved to the local workstation to the Cisco VPN 3000 concentrator (see Figure 8-41) by browsing to the location of the file (certificate) and clicking **Install**.

After you have installed the identity certificate, it will appear under the Identity Certificates heading under **Administration > Certificate Management** (see Figure 8-42).

Figure 8-41 *Installing the Identity Certificate on the Cisco VPN 3000 Concentrator*

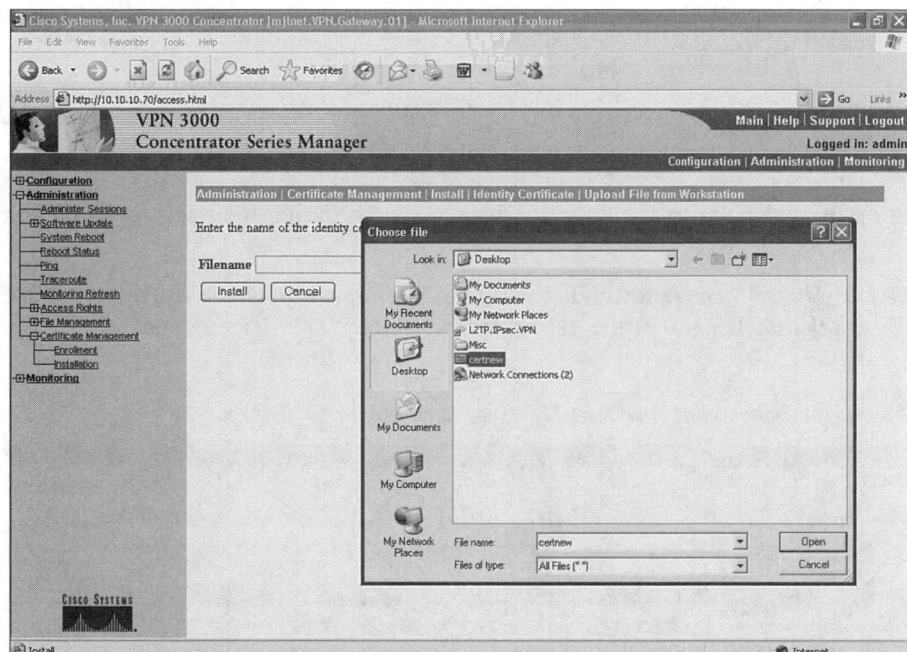

Figure 8-42 *Identity Certificate Has Been Installed*

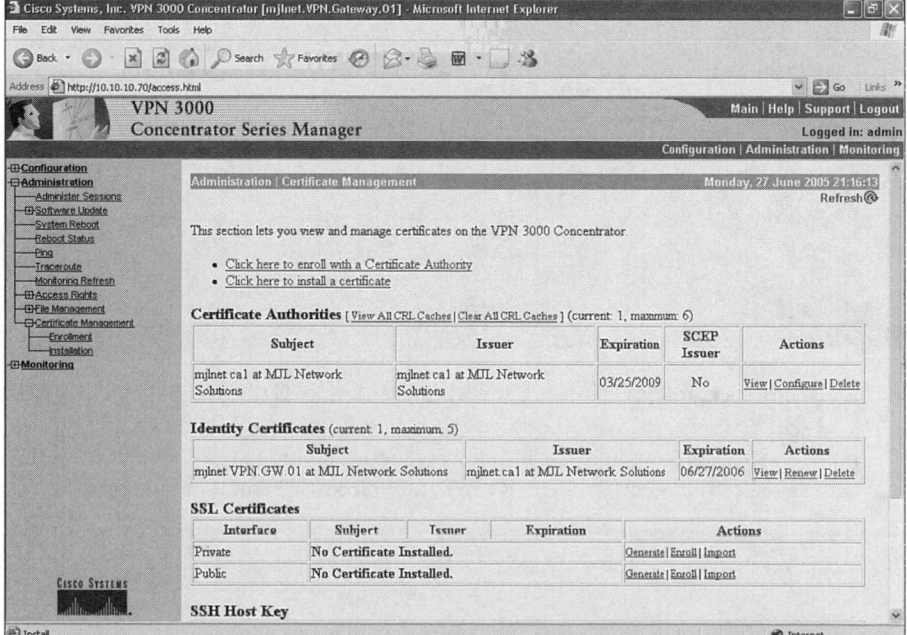

You have now obtained and installed both CA and identity certificates on the Cisco VPN 3000 concentrator, and you are ready to configure a group for L2TP/IPsec remote access client users.

Step 5: Configure a Group for L2TP/IPsec Remote Access Client Users

There is one important fact to remember when configuring a group with digital signature authentication—by default, the name of the group to which remote access clients belong must match the department name that you specify during enrolment for L2TP/IPsec remote access clients.

Figure 8-43 shows the configuration of a group whose name (Engineering in this case) matches that of the department to which L2TP/IPsec remote access clients belong.

Figure 8-43 *Configuration of a Group for L2TP/IPsec Remote Access Clients*

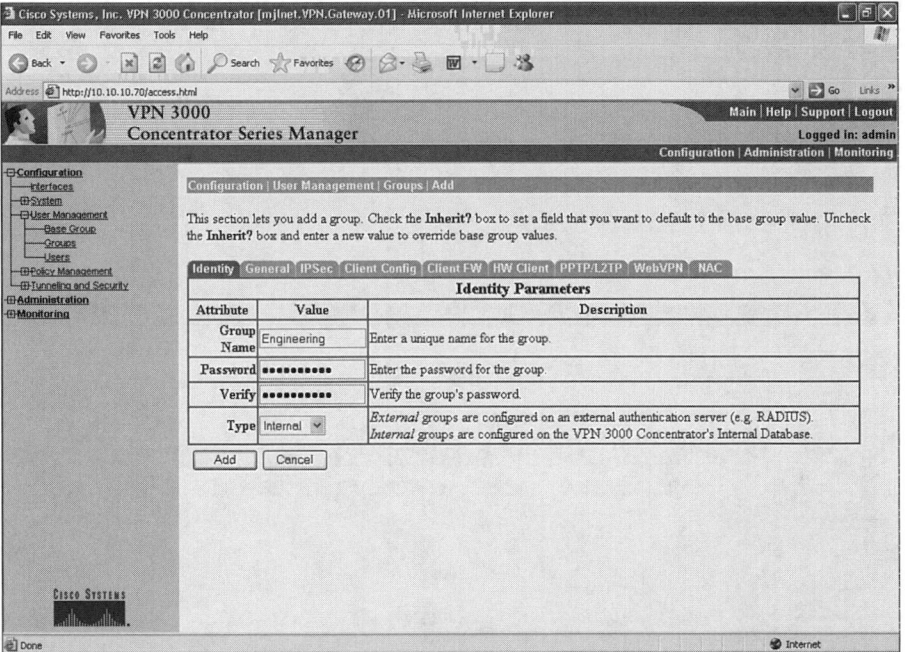

By going to **Configuration > User Management > Groups** and selecting **Add Group**, you will be presented with the screen shown in Figure 8-43. Then simply type in the group name (which as previously mentioned must correspond to the Department [OU] of remote access user clients certificates). Type in any password and then click **Add**.

After the group has been added, you can begin to create the account for the remote access users as described in the section "Configure L2TP/IPsec Remote Access Client User Accounts" earlier in this chapter but with the important difference that you should assign the users to the group that you have just created.

Figure 8-44 illustrates assignment of a remote access VPN user to a group called Engineering.

Figure 8-44 *Assignment of a Remote Access User to a Group Called Engineering*

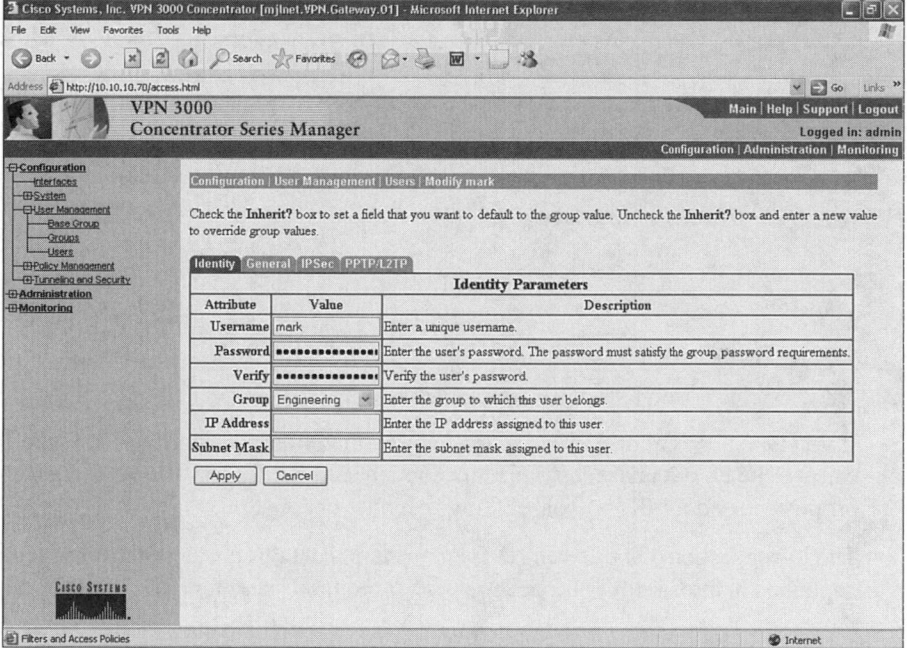

Step 7: Modify IPsec Parameters Such as IKE and IPsec SA Proposals

As discussed in the section "Configure the Base Group" earlier in this chapter, under **Configuration > User Management > Base Group**, IPSec tab, you should choose the IPSec SA called **ESP-L2TP-TRANSPORT** for use with L2TP/IPsec remote access VPNs.

You can examine and, if necessary, modify the parameters and algorithms associated with ESP-L2TP-TRANSPORT by going to **Configuration > Policy Management > Traffic Management > SAs** and then choosing **ESP-L2TP-TRANSPORT** and clicking **Modify**. Figure 8-45 shows the algorithms and parameters associated with ESP-L2TP-TRANSPORT.

Figure 8-45 *Modifying Algorithms and Parameters Associated with ESP-L2TP-TRANSPORT*

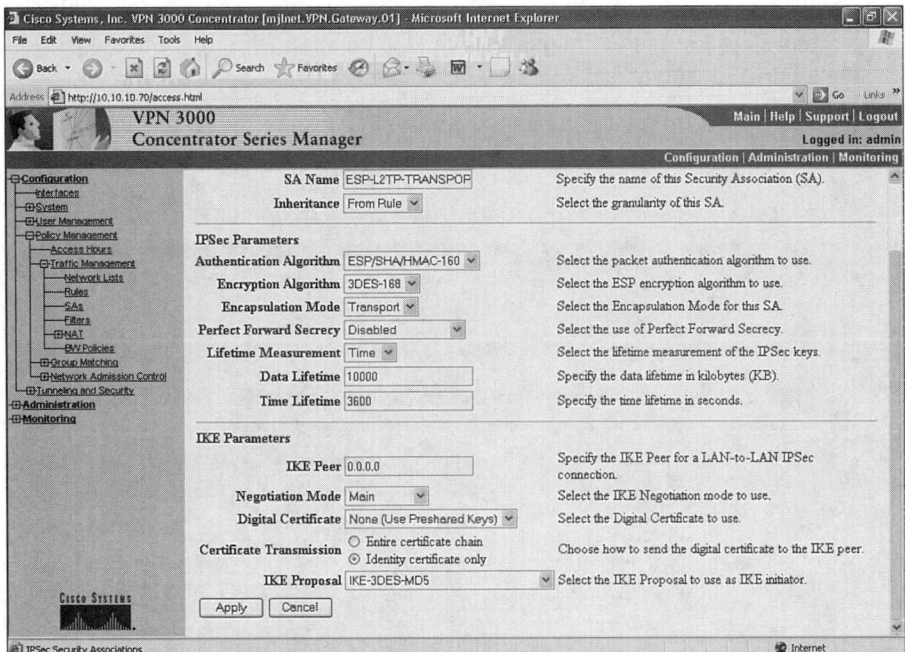

If you take a look at the IPSec Parameters section of the screen shown in Figure 8-45, you can see the algorithms and parameters contained in the Cisco VPN 3000 concentrator SA proposals used for IKEv1 phase 2 (quick mode) negotiation.

The lower section of the screen (IKE Parameters) contains the algorithms and parameters contained in the Cisco VPN concentrators SA proposals used for IKEv1 phase 1 negotiations.

The only parameter that it is usually necessary to modify when configuring digital signature authentication for L2TP/IPsec remote access VPNs is shown under the IKE Parameters section of the page in Figure 8-45. Specifically, you should choose the identity certificate that you have just obtained for the Cisco VPN 3000 concentrator in the Digital Certificate drop-down box (see the section "Step 2: Enroll the VPN Gateway with the CA and Obtain a Certificate").

After you have selected the identity certificate, click **Apply**, and you are done (as far as the VPN concentrator is concerned)—the Cisco VPN 3000 concentrator is now ready to terminate L2TP/IPsec remote access VPN tunnels from remote access users.

Implementing Digital Signature Authentication on a Cisco IOS VPN Gateway

The configuration of a Cisco IOS VPN gateway for digital signature is similar to that for PSK authentication. The difference is that you must, of course, configure IKE digital signature authentication and specify the **authentication rsa-sig** command rather than the **authentication pre-share** command (line 14 in Example 8-4), as well as remove the **crypto isakmp key** *preshared-key* **address** *peer-address* mask command in line 15 of Example 8-4.

See the section "IKE Digital Signature Authentication" in Chapter 6 on page 448 for detailed information about configuring digital signature authentication on a Cisco IOS router.

Configuring Windows L2TP/IPsec Remote Access Clients for Digital Signature (Digital Certificate) Authentication

The configuration of Windows XP/2000 L2TP/IPsec remote access clients for digital signature authentication is similar to that when using PSK authentication—the difference is, of course, that you must obtain the CA's certificate and then an identity certificate for the remote access client workstation.

The configuration of Windows XP/2000 L2TP/IPsec remote access clients consists of the following steps:

Step 1   Obtain and install the CA's certificate on the L2TP/IPsec remote access VPN client.

Step 2   Enroll and obtain an identity certificate for the remote access VPN client workstation.

Step 3   Create an L2TP/IPsec VPN connection using the Create a New Connection Wizard (accessible via the Control Panel).

Steps 1 and 2 are described in the following sections. Step 3 is actually the same as previously described in the section "Configuring Windows L2TP/IPsec Remote Access VPN Clients for PSK Authentication," but with the exception that you should *not* configure a PSK (the default method of authentication for L2TP/IPsec on Windows clients is digital signature authentication).

Step 1: Obtain and Install the CA's Certificate on the L2TP/IPsec Remote Access VPN Client

The process of obtaining the CA's certificate for a L2TP/IPsec remote access client workstation is similar to that described in the section "Step 1: Retrieve and Install the CA's Certificate" on page 743—the difference is that instead of clicking Download CA Certificate and temporarily saving the CA's certificate to a convenient location on the local workstation, and subsequently uploading the CA's certificate to the Cisco VPN 3000 concentrator, you must click the **Install this CA certificate path** in the upper-left corner of the Retrieve the CA Certificate or Certificate Revocation List page. When you click the **Install this CA certification path** link, the message shown in Figure 8-46 appears. Click **Yes**, and the CA's certificate will be installed.

Figure 8-46   *Obtain and Install the CA's Certificate*

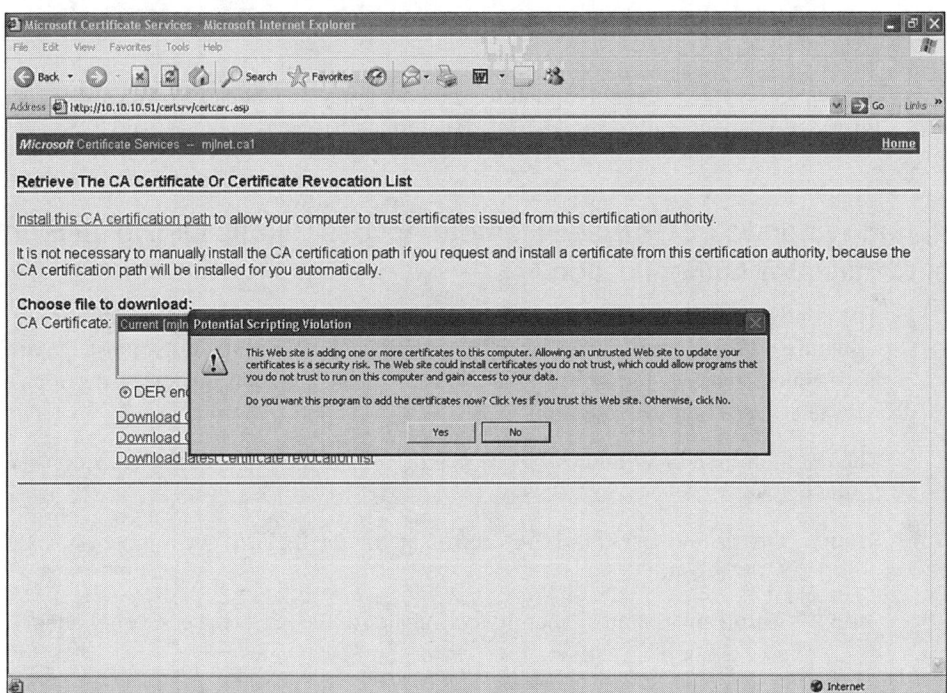

Step 2: Enroll and Obtain an Identity Certificate for the Remote Access VPN Client Workstation

After you have obtained and installed the CA's certificate, you can install the identity certificate on the L2TP/IPsec remote access VPN client workstation.

On the remote access VPN client workstation, navigate to the following URL:

http://*CA_ip_address_or_CA_FQDN*/certsrv

Choose **Request a certificate** and click **Next**. You will now see the page shown in Figure 8-47. Choose **Advanced request** and click **Next**. The page shown in Figure 8-48 will now appear.

Figure 8-47 *Choose Request Type Page*

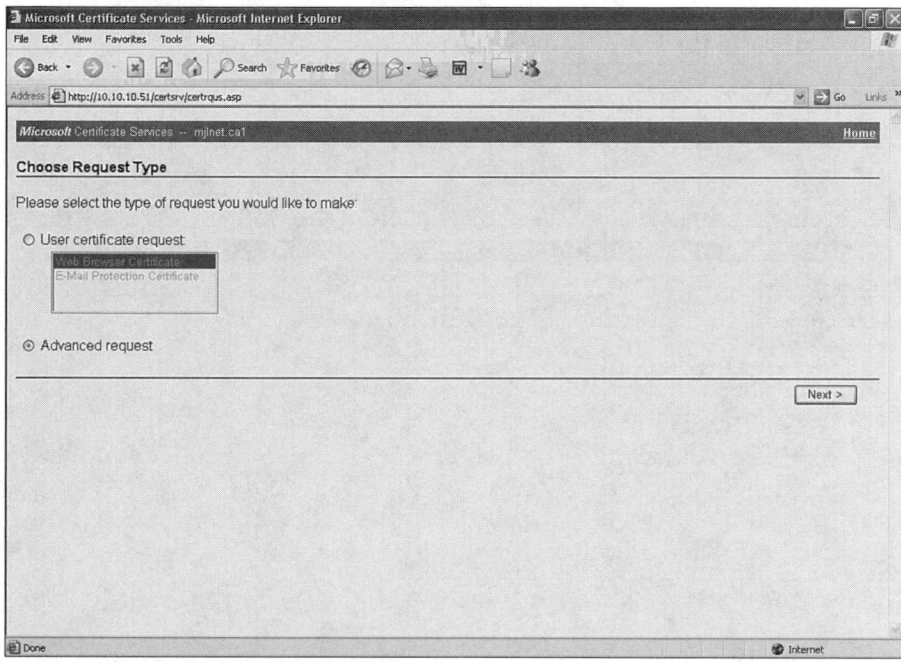

Figure 8-48 *Advanced Certificate Requests*

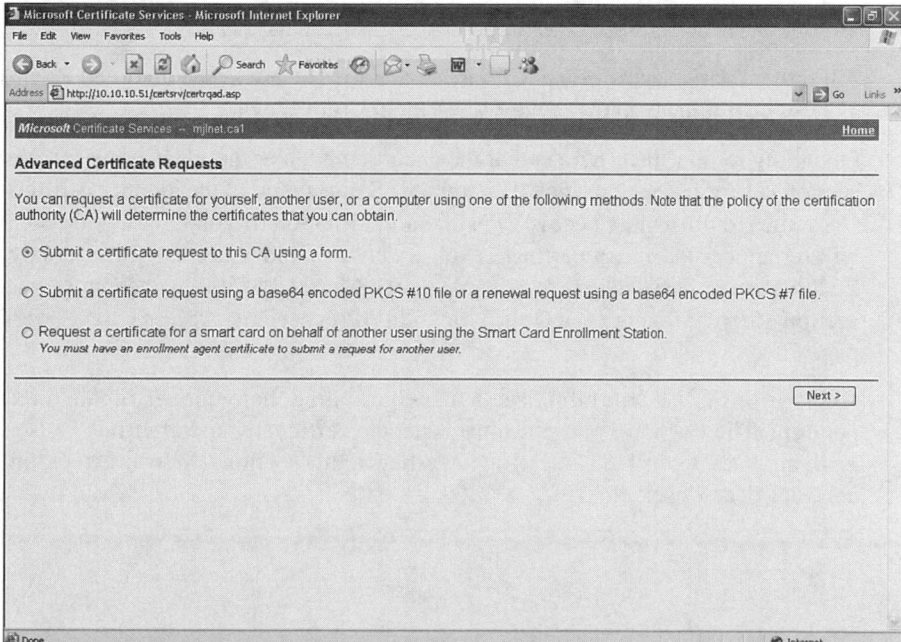

Choose **Submit a certificate request to this CA using a form** and then click **Next**. The form shown in Figure 8-49 will now appear.

Figure 8-49 *Advanced Certificate Request Form*

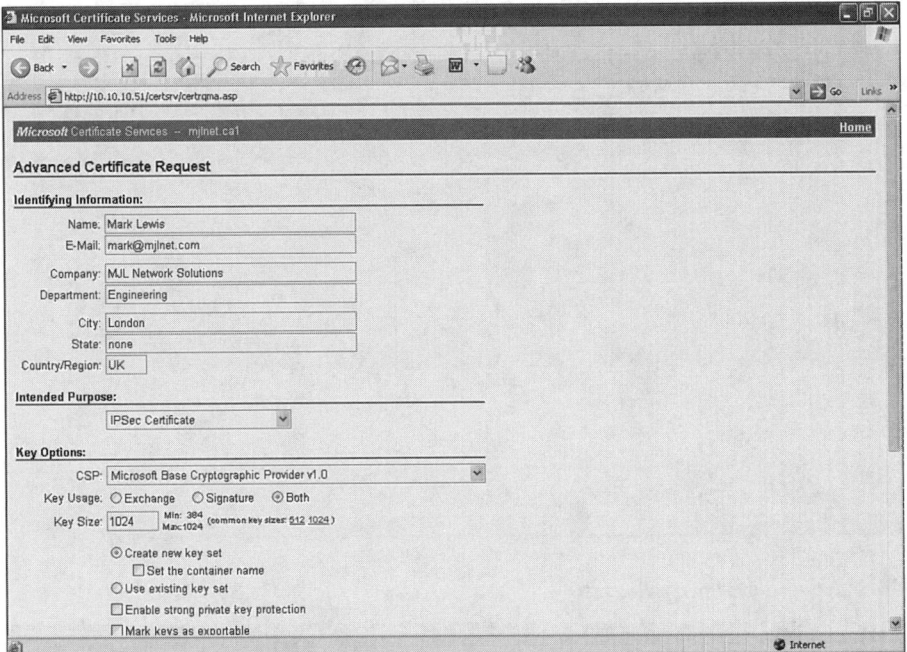

Fill in the form as appropriate. Choose **IPSec Certificate** as the Intended Purpose as well as **Use local machine store** under Key Options (not shown).

One thing to remember here is that the department under the Identifying Information section is later included as the OU within the Subject field of the identity certificate that the CA issues to the remote access VPN client workstation. If you have a good memory, you will remember that the department (Subject/OU) should match the group configured for L2TP/IPsec remote access VPN clients on the Cisco VPN 3000 concentrator (see the section "Step 5: Configure a Group for L2TP/IPsec Remote Access Client Users" on page 756).

Click **Submit**, and you might see a message stating that your certificate request is pending. The CA administrator must issue the certificate, and after he/she has, you can navigate back to the URL mentioned earlier in this section. Choose **Check on pending certificate** and click **Next**.

You will then be presented with a page on which you can select the certificate request in question. Choose the appropriate certificate request, click **Next**, and you will see a page indicating that the certificate has been issued, as shown in Figure 8-50.

Figure 8-50 *Certificate Issued*

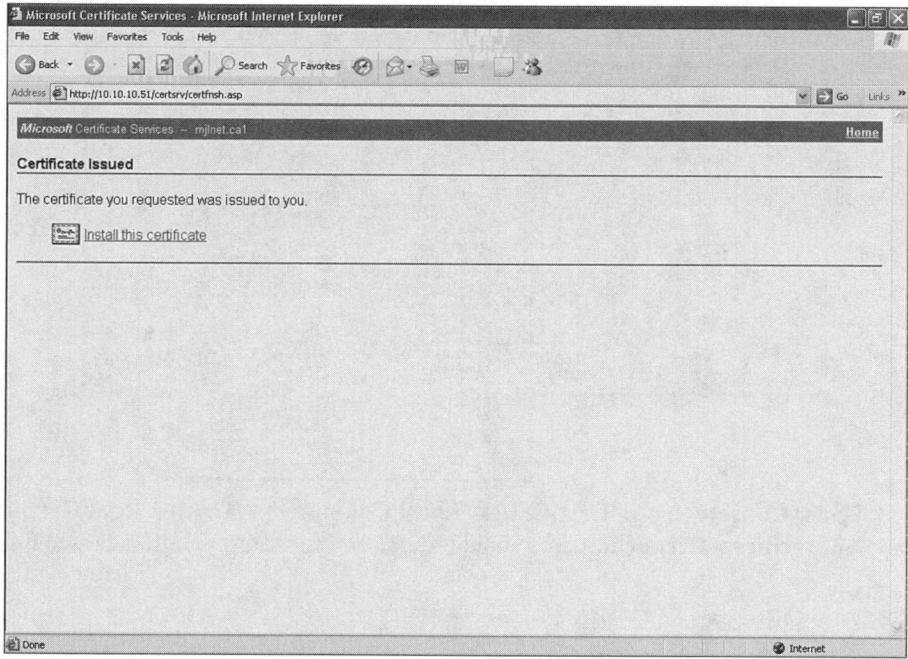

Now click **Install this certificate**. You should see a message indicating that the certificate has been successfully installed. You can verify the installation of both the CA and identity certificates on the L2TP/IPsec remote access VPN client workstation as follows:

Step 1   From the Start menu, choose **Run**, type **mmc**, and click **OK**.

Step 2   From the **File** menu, choose **Add/Remove Snap-in**.

Step 3   Click **Add**, choose **Certificates**, and click **Add**.

Step 4   Choose **Computer account** and click **Next**.

Step 5   Choose **Local computer: (the computer this console is running on)** and click **Finish**.

Step 6   Click **Close**, and then click **OK**.

If you look under **Console Root > Certificates (Local Computer) > Personal > Certificates** (on the left side of the MMC), you should be able to see the identity certificate that you have just obtained from the CA. Figure 8-51 illustrates the verification of the identity certificate.

Figure 8-51 *Verification of the Identity Certificate Using the MMC*

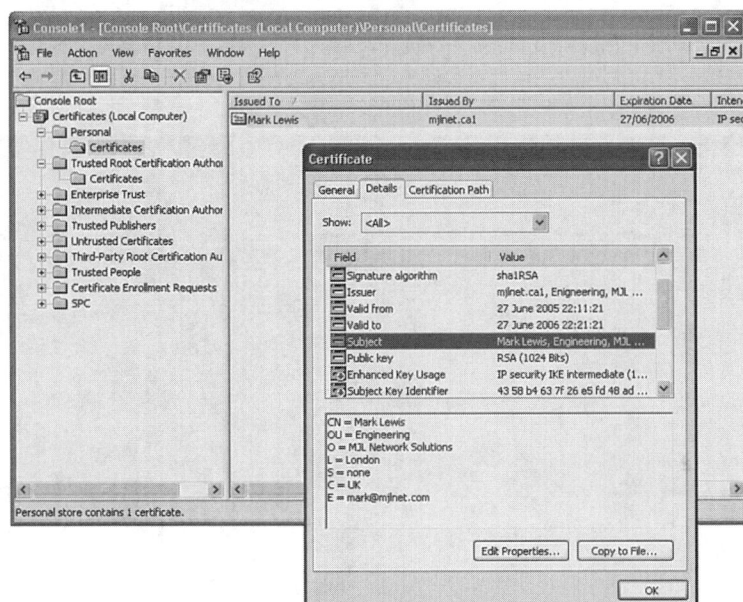

Under **Console Root > Certificates (Local Computer) > Trusted Root Certification Authorities > Certificates**, you should be able to see the CA's certificate (see Figure 8-52).

Figure 8-52 *Verification of the CA Certificate Using the MMC*

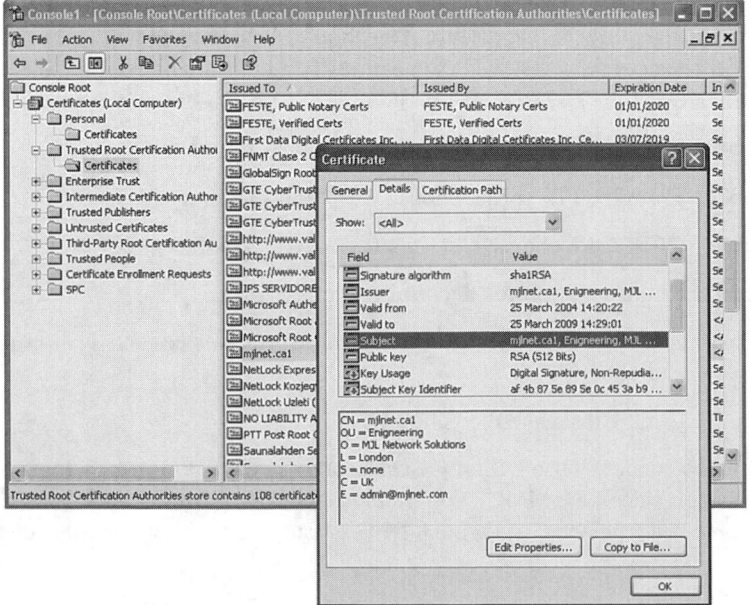

As shown in Figure 8-52, a certificate for CA mjlnet.ca1 is included in the Trusted Root Certification Authorities/Certificates folder. Note that if you cannot see the certificate here, you may find it in the Intermediate Certification Authorities/Certificates folder—if so, you can copy it to the Trusted Root Certification Authorities/Certificates folder.

Verifying L2TP/IPsec Voluntary Tunnel Mode Remote Access VPNs

You can verify L2TP/IPsec remote access VPN in a variety of ways, depending on the particular VPN gateway you are using and on the type of remote access client workstations you are using.

Verifying L2TP/IPsec VPNs on the VPN Gateway

If you are using a Cisco VPN 3000 concentrator, you can verify L2TP/IPsec tunnel setup using by going to **Monitoring > Filterable Event Log** and **Monitoring > Filterable Event Log > Live Event Log**.

Example 8-6 shows sample output shown in **Monitoring > Filterable Event Log** after L2TP/IPsec tunnel setup. If you want see these events in real time, you can view them by going to **Monitoring > Filterable Event Log > Live Event Log**.

Example 8-6 *Sample Output Shown in Monitoring > Filterable Event Log After L2TP/IPsec Tunnel Setup*

```
2 06/03/2005 19:59:37.290 SEV=4 IKE/119 RPT=1 192.168.1.1
Group [VPNC_Base_Group]
PHASE 1 COMPLETED (line 1)
3 06/03/2005 19:59:37.300 SEV=5 IKE/25 RPT=1 192.168.1.1
Group [VPNC_Base_Group]
Received remote Proxy Host data in ID Payload:
Address 192.168.1.1, Protocol 17, Port 1701
6 06/03/2005 19:59:37.300 SEV=5 IKE/24 RPT=1 192.168.1.1
Group [VPNC_Base_Group]
Received local Proxy Host data in ID Payload:
Address 10.40.10.1, Protocol 17, Port 0
9 06/03/2005 19:59:37.300 SEV=5 IKE/66 RPT=1 192.168.1.1
Group [VPNC_Base_Group]
IKE Remote Peer configured for SA: ESP-L2TP-TRANSPORT (line 2)
10 06/03/2005 19:59:37.310 SEV=4 IPSEC/7 RPT=1
IPSec ESP Tunnel Inb: invalid direction in security association
11 06/03/2005 19:59:37.310 SEV=4 IKE/49 RPT=1 192.168.1.1
Group [VPNC_Base_Group]
Security negotiation complete for User ()
Responder, Inbound SPI = 0x76a1bb8f, Outbound SPI = 0x69c78e2c
14 06/03/2005 19:59:37.330 SEV=4 IKE/120 RPT=1 192.168.1.1
Group [VPNC_Base_Group]
```

continues

Example 8-6 *Sample Output Shown in Monitoring > Filterable Event Log After L2TP/IPsec Tunnel Setup (Continued)*

```
PHASE 2 COMPLETED (msgid=9f3bf228) (line 3)
15 06/03/2005 19:59:37.540 SEV=4 L2TP/57 RPT=1 (line 4)
Tunnel to peer 192.168.1.1 established (line 5)
16 06/03/2005 19:59:37.550 SEV=4 L2TP/53 RPT=1 192.168.1.1 (line 6)
Session started on tunnel 192.168.1.1 (line 7)
17 06/03/2005 19:59:37.880 SEV=5 PPP/8 RPT=2 192.168.1.1 (line 8)
User [mark] (line 8)
Authenticated successfully with MSCHAP-V2 (line 10)
18 06/03/2005 19:59:39.700 SEV=5 PPP/49 RPT=2 192.168.1.1
User [mark]
IPCP assigned IP Address 10.20.10.101 (line 11)
19 06/03/2005 19:59:39.700 SEV=4 AUTH/22 RPT=2
User [mark] Group [Base Group] connected, Session Type: L2TP/IPSec (line 12)
```

In highlighted line 1, you can see the IKEv1 phase 1 has been successfully negotiated, and in highlighted line 2 that the remote peer is configured for the SA named ESP-L2TP-TRANSPORT.

Highlighted line 3 shows that IKEv1 phase 2 has been completed. IPsec negotiation finished, and the IPsec tunnel is up.

Highlighted lines 4 and 5 show that an L2TP tunnel has now been established, and in highlighted line 6 and 7, you can see that an L2TP session has been successfully set up.

PPP negotiation then starts, and in highlighted lines 8 to 10, you can see that user mark has been successfully authenticated using MS-CHAPv2.

Highlighted line 11 shows successful completion of IPCP negotiation. You can see that IP address 10.20.10.101 has been assigned to the remote access VPN client. This IP address will be applied to the remote access VPN client's VPN tunnel interface (PPP adapter).

Finally, highlighted line 12 confirms that user mark in group Base Group is connected via an L2TP/IPsec VPN tunnel.

You can also glean a variety of information regarding L2TP/IPsec VPN tunnels such as number of L2TP/IPsec sessions and detailed information on L2TP and IPsec negotiation and data transport by looking under the **Monitoring > Sessions and Monitoring > Statistics**.

If you are using a Cisco IOS L2TP/IPsec VPN gateway, you can obtain detailed information concerning L2TP/IPsec tunnel negotiation using the **debug crypto isakmp**, **debug vpdn l2x-events**, and **debug ppp negotiation** commands. The output of these commands was described earlier in this chapter, and so will not be reexamined here. As always, be careful when using **debug** commands in a production environment.

Other useful commands for verifying L2TP/IPsec on IOS VPN gateways *include* **show vpdn tunnel**, **show vpdn session**, **show interface virtual access**, **show caller user**, **show crypto isakmp sa**, and **show crypto ipsec sa**.

Example 8-7 shows sample output of the **show vpdn tunnel** command.

Example 8-7   **show vpdn tunnel** *Command Output*

```
mjlnet.VPN.Gateway.03#show vpdn tunnel
%No active L2F tunnels
L2TP Tunnel Information Total tunnels 1 sessions 1 (line 1)
LocID RemID Remote Name State Remote Address Port Sessions L2TP Class/
   VPDN Group
12726 3  markxp1  est 192.168.1.1  1701 1  1 (line 2)
%No active PPTP tunnels
mjlnet.VPN.Gateway.03#
```

Highlighted line 1 shows that 1 L2TP tunnel and 1 session have been negotiated. Then, in highlighted line 2, you can see information including the remote access client *computer name* (markxp1), the tunnel state (established [est]), the remote access client workstation's (Internet interface) IP address (192.168.1.1), and the VPDN group to which the tunnel corresponds (1).

Note that the computer name shown in Example 8-7 corresponds to that found by right-clicking **My Computer**, choosing **Properties**, and choosing the **Computer Name** tab on a Windows XP workstation.

Example 8-8 shows the output of the **show vpdn session** command.

Example 8-8   **show vpdn session** *Command Output*

```
mjlnet.VPN.Gateway.03#show vpdn session
%No active L2F tunnels
L2TP Session Information Total tunnels 1 sessions 1
LocID  RemID  TunID  Username, Intf/  State Last Chg Uniq ID
   Vcid, Circuit
3   1    12726  mark, Vi2.1   est 00:00:44 2
%No active PPTP tunnels
mjlnet.VPN.Gateway.03#
```

The highlighted line shows information including the remote access client's username (mark) and the virtual access interface on which the PPP connection is terminated (virtual access interface 2.1). The username shown in Example 8-8 corresponds to that entered in the Connection dialog box on Windows XP remote access clients (see Figure 8-21 on page 740).

If you want more detailed information on L2TP tunnels or sessions, just use the **show vpdn tunnel all** and **show vpdn session all** commands, respectively.

You can find out more information on parameters on the virtual access interfaces on which remote access clients' PPP connections are terminated using the **show interface virtual access** *number* command (see Example 8-9).

Example 8-9 **show interface virtual access** *Command Output*

```
mjlnet.VPN.Gateway.03#show interface virtual access 2.1
Virtual access2.1 is up, line protocol is up (line 1)
 Hardware is Virtual Access interface
 Interface is unnumbered. Using address of FastEthernet2/0 (10.40.10.1)
 MTU 1500 bytes, BW 10000 Kbit, DLY 100000 usec,
  reliability 255/255, txload 1/255, rxload 1/255
 Encapsulation PPP, LCP Open (line 2)
 Open: IPCP (line 3)
 PPPoVPDN vaccess, cloned from Virtual-Template1 (line 4)
 Vaccess status 0x0
 Protocol l2tp, tunnel id 12726, session id 3 (line 5)
 Keepalive set (10 sec)
  27 packets input, 2142 bytes
  18 packets output, 320 bytes
 Last clearing of "show interface" counters never
mjlnet.VPN.Gateway.03#
```

As you can see, the **show interface virtual access** command supplies a plethora of information regarding the virtual access interface. Highlighted line 1 shows that interface virtual access 2.1 is in an up/up state. Highlighted lines 2 to 5 show that the encapsulation type is PPP, that the LCP state is Open (LCP has been successfully negotiated), that IPCP is in an Open state (IPCP has been successfully negotiated), that the PPP connection is carried over a VPDN protocol, and finally that the specific VPDN protocol in this case is L2TP.

If your hunger for information is still not sated, you can also use the **show caller user** command to view remote access client user-specific information (see Example 8-10).

Example 8-10 **show caller user** *Command Output*

```
mjlnet.VPN.Gateway.03#show caller user mark
 User: mark, line Vi2.1, service PPPoVPDN
  Connected for 00:02:17, Idle for 00:02:05
 Timeouts: Limit  Remaining Timer Type
            -    -    -
 PPP: LCP Open, CHAP (<-), IPCP
 IP: Local 10.40.10.1, remote 10.20.10.1
 Counts: 34 packets input, 2254 bytes
    25 packets output, 432 bytes
mjlnet.VPN.Gateway.03#
```

The highlighted lines show that LCP and IPCP are both in an Open state and that CHAP was used to authenticate the remote access client *user* (rather than the workstation, which is authenticated during IKEv1 phase 1 using either PSKs or digital signatures).

You can see that IP address associated with the virtual access interface on the VPN gateway (10.40.10.1), and the IP address assigned to the remote access client during IPCP negotiation (10.20.10.1).

Verifying L2TP/IPsec VPNs on Remote Access Client Workstations

So, you now know how to verify L2TP/IPsec on the VPN gateway. But, you might also want to verify the connection on the (Windows XP) remote access VPN client workstation. In this case, you can use a variety of tools, including right-clicking the connection icon (on the right of the Windows XP taskbar) and viewing the connection status, as well as enabling Oakley (IKE) and PPP logging.

Figure 8-53 shows VPN connection status.

Figure 8-53 *VPN Connection Status*

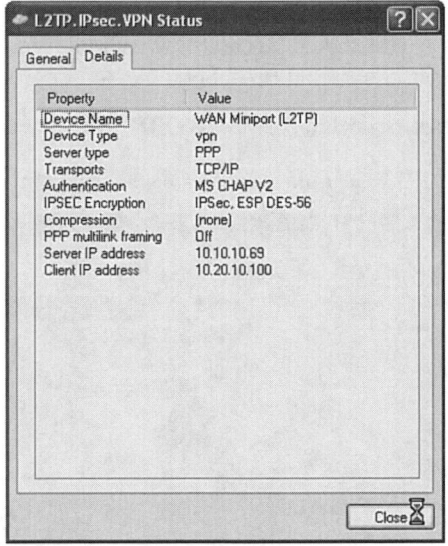

In Figure 8-53, you can see the following:

- The VPN protocol is L2TP.
- PPP is being tunneled over the L2TP tunnel.
- TCP/IP traffic is being transported over the PPP connection (IPCP has been negotiated).
- User (PPP) authentication was carried out using MS-CHAPv2.
- IPsec is being used to protect the L2TP tunnel (using ESP and 56-bit DES encryption).
- Neither compression nor Multilink PPP (MP) were negotiated.
- The VPN gateway and client (VPN tunnel interface [PPP adapter]) IP addresses are 10.10.10.69 and 10.20.10.100, respectively.

If you are unable to establish an L2TP/IPsec VPN tunnel between a remote access VPN client and a VPN gateway, you can examine logs or perform debugging on the VPN gateway (as previously discussed) and/or enable both PPP and Oakley (IKE) logging on the remote access VPN client.

If you want to enable Oakley logging on a Windows XP/2000 remote access VPN client, you need to perform the following steps:

Step 1 From the Start menu, choose **Run**, type **regedt32.exe**, and then click **OK**. You can now edit the registry.

Step 2 Create a key called **Oakley** under HKEY_LOCAL_MACHINE\System\ CurrentControlSet\Services\PolicyAgent.

Step 3 Create a DWORD value under HKEY_LOCAL_MACHINE\System\ CurrentControlSet\Services\PolicyAgent\Oakley called **EnableLogging** with a value of 1.

Note that, as always, you should be careful when modifying the registry; in extreme cases, a mistake can make the workstation unbootable.

Figure 8-54 illustrates the creation of the DWORD value called EnableLogging with a value of 1.

Figure 8-54 *Creation of the DWORD Value Called EnableLogging with a Value of 1*

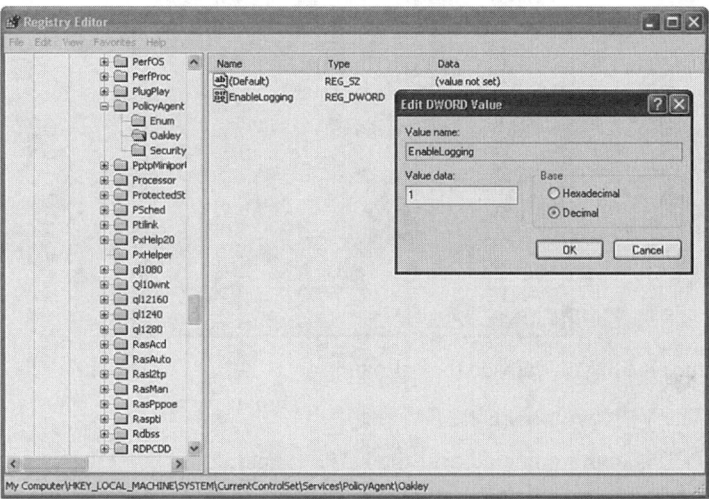

You can then find the log file itself (oakley.log) in systemroot\Debug folder. The systemroot is usually the Windows folder under the C: drive.

Example 8-11 shows sample (and selected) contents of the oakley.log after VPN tunnel setup.

Example 8-11 *Contents of the oakley.log After VPN Tunnel Setup*

```
6-10: 15:02:45:406:7d0 MM PolicyName: L2TP Main Mode Policy (line 1)
 6-10: 15:02:45:406:7d0 MMPolicy dwFlags 8 SoftSAExpireTime 28800
 6-10: 15:02:45:406:7d0 MMOffer[0] LifetimeSec 28800 QMLimit 0 DHGroup 268435457 (line 2)
 6-10: 15:02:45:406:7d0 MMOffer[0] Encrypt: Triple DES CBC Hash: SHA (line 3)
<output omitted>
6-10: 15:02:45:421:7d0 Auth[0]:RSA Sig E=admin@mjlnet.com, C=UK, S=none, (line 4)
L=London, O=MJL Network Solutions, OU=Engineering, CN=mjlnet.ca1 AuthFlags 0
```

Example 8-11 *Contents of the oakley.log After VPN Tunnel Setup (Continued)*

```
6-10: 15:02:45:421:7d0 QM PolicyName: L2TP Require Encryption Quick Mode Policy (line 5)
dwFlags 0
6-10: 15:02:45:421:7d0 QMOffer[0] LifetimeKBytes 250000 LifetimeSec 3600 (line 6)
6-10: 15:02:45:421:7d0 QMOffer[0] dwFlags 0 dwPFSGroup 0 (line 7)
6-10: 15:02:45:437:7d0 Algo[0] Operation: ESP Algo: Triple DES CBC HMAC: MD5 (line 8)
<output omitted>
6-10: 15:02:45:453:7d0 Sending: SA = 0x000E58D0 to 192.168.1.1:Type 2.500 (line 9)
6-10: 15:02:45:468:7d0 ISAKMP Header: (V1.0), len = 312 (line 10)
6-10: 15:02:45:468:7d0 I-COOKIE 0b9be0cf190d6514 (line 11)
6-10: 15:02:45:468:7d0 R-COOKIE 0000000000000000 (line 12)
6-10: 15:02:45:468:7d0 exchange: Oakley Main Mode (line 13)
6-10: 15:02:45:468:7d0 flags: 0 (line 14)
6-10: 15:02:45:468:7d0 next payload: SA (line 15)
6-10: 15:02:45:468:7d0 message ID: 00000000 (line 16)
6-10: 15:02:45:468:7d0 Ports S:f401 D:f401
6-10: 15:02:45:500:7d0 Activating InitiateEvent 000005C8
6-10: 15:02:45:609:7d0
<output omitted>
6-10: 15:02:45:609:7d0 Phase 1 SA accepted: transform=1 (line 17)
<output omitted>
6-10: 15:02:46:703:7d0 Phase 2 SA accepted: proposal=1 transform=1 (line 18)
<output omitted>
```

Highlighted line 1 shows that L2TP has triggered the creation of an IKEv1 phase 1 (main mode [MM]) policy.

Highlighted lines 2 and 3 show one of the main mode policy proposals, which specifies 3DES encryption and the SHA-1 hashing algorithm. By default, Windows XP offers 12 IKEv1 phase 1 (main mode) policy proposals to the VPN gateway—one of these proposals must be compatible with the VPN gateway's phase 1 policies for IKEv1 phase 1 negotiation to complete successfully.

Highlighted line 4 shows that RSA digital signature (digital certificate) authentication is being used. Highlighted lines 5 shows that L2TP has triggered the creation of an IKEv1 phase 2 (quick mode [QM]) policy.

In highlighted lines 6 to 8, you can see one of the quick mode policy proposals, which specifies ESP with 3DES encryption and MD5 authentication. Windows XP offers five quick mode policy proposals by default. For IKEv1 phase 2 (quick mode) negotiation to succeed, one of the five policy proposals must be compatible with those on the VPN gateway.

NOTE   The Windows L2TP/IPsec remote access client does not support either IPsec tunnel mode or Authentication Header (AH). So, don't bother configuring these on the VPN gateway.

Highlighted lines 9 to 16 show an ISAKMP packet sent by the Windows XP remote access VPN client during IKEv1 phase 1 (main mode) negotiation.

In highlighted lines 17 and 18, you can see that IKE phase 1 and phase 2 SA proposals have been accepted.

NOTE   For much more information on troubleshooting L2TP and L2TP/IPsec, refer to *Troubleshooting Virtual Private Networks* (Cisco Press).

If IKE negotiation looks good, it can be useful to enable PPP logging. You can do this by entering **netsh ras set tracing * enable** from a command prompt on a Windows XP workstation. This command creates a file called PPP.log (as well as a number of other useful RAS-related log files such as RASCHAP.log) under the systemroot\tracing folder.

Example 8-12 shows sample, selected output from the PPP.log.

Example 8-12 *Output from the PPP.log*

```
[880] 15:25:28:875: <PPP packet sent at 06/10/2005 14:25:28:875 (line 1)
[880] 15:25:28:875: <Protocol = LCP, Type = Configure-Req, Length = 0x17,
 Id = 0x0, (line 2)
 Port = 1
[880] 15:25:28:875: <C0 21 01 00 00 15 01 04 05 78 05 06 60 F6 38 A5
 |.!.......x..`.8.|
[880] 15:25:28:875: <07 02 08 02 0D 03 06 00 00 00 00 00 00 00 00 00
 |................|
<output omitted>
[880] 15:25:31:531: LCP Configured successfully (line 3)
<output omitted>
[880] 15:25:31:531: Authenticating phase started (line 4)
<output omitted>
[880] 15:25:31:531: >PPP packet received at 06/10/2005 14:25:31:531 (line 5)
[880] 15:25:31:531: >Protocol = CHAP, Type = Protocol specific, Length = 0x17,
 Id = 0x1, Port = 1 (line 6)
[880] 15:25:31:531: >C2 23 01 01 00 15 10 77 FA 0B 8F D8 31 E6 3B E1
 |.#.....w....1.;.|
[880] 15:25:31:531: >F5 19 2E 3F 59 6B 54 00 00 00 00 00 00 00 00 00
 |...?YkT.........|
<output omitted>
[880] 15:25:31:859: >PPP packet received at 06/10/2005 14:25:31:859 (line 7)
[880] 15:25:31:859: >Protocol = IPCP, Type = Configure-Req,
 Length = 0xc, Id = 0x0, Port = 1 (line 8)
[880] 15:25:31:859: >80 21 01 00 00 0A 03 06 C0 A8 01 01 00 00 00 00
 |.!..............|
<output omitted>
```

Highlighted lines 1 and 2 show that a PPP (specifically, an LCP Configure-Request) packet has been sent to the VPN gateway. LCP negotiation is underway.

In highlighted lines 3 and 4, you can see that LCP negotiation has successfully completed, and PPP authentication has begun.

Highlighted lines 5 and 6 show that a PPP CHAP packet has been sent to the VPN gateway. Much more information on the PPP authentication phase can be found in the RASCHAP.log file.

In highlighted lines 7 and 8, you can see that an IPCP Configure-Request packet has been received from the VPN gateway. IPCP negotiation is now in progress.

Configuring L2TP/IPsec Remote Access VPNs to Transit NAT Devices

If an L2TP/IPsec VPN device is present behind a NAT device, you might encounter problems establishing an L2TP/IPsec VPNs between remote access client workstations and a VPN gateway. This is because IPsec was not originally designed to operate in conjunction with Network Address Translation (NAT) devices.

NOTE   For much more information about the issues that you may encounter when configuring IPsec tunnels when there is a NAT device between the IPsec devices, see the section "Deploying IPsec VPNs with NAT/PAT" in Chapter 6.

As described in Chapter 6, there are various solutions when a NAT device is placed between IPsec peers, but the most popular solution is to enable NAT Traversal (NAT-T). Figure 8-55 shows how L2TP control- and data-plane packets are encapsulated when using NAT-T.

Figure 8-55 *L2TP Control- and Data-Plane Packet Encapsulation When Using NAT-T*

IP Header	UDP Header (NAT-T)	ESP Header	L2TP Control/Data Session Packet	ESP Trailer	Auth. Trailer

Configuring L2TP/IPsec Remote Access Clients to Support NAT-T

Windows XP Service Pack 2 includes support for NAT-T, but support for VPN gateways behind a NAT device does have to be enabled in the registry. Windows 2000 does not support NAT-T natively—you have to load update 818043 from the Windows update catalog at the following URL:

http://v4.windowsupdate.microsoft.com/catalog

Click **Find Microsoft Windows Updates** on the left, and then click **Advanced Search Options**. Now type **818043** in the Contain these words search box.

Note that the NAT-T update for Windows 2000 clients is designed only for a NAT traversal where a NAT device is in front of the client (not in front of the VPN gateway). To configure a Windows XP Service Pack 2 remote access VPN client to support NAT-T when a NAT device is in front of a VPN gateway, modify the registry as follows:

Step 1 From the Start menu, choose **Run**, type **regedt32.exe**, and click **OK**.

Step 2 Go to HKEY_LOCAL_MACHINE\SYSTEM\CurrentControlSet\ Services\IPSec.

Step 3 Create a new DWORD value called **AssumeUDPEncapsulation ContextOnSendRule**.

Step 4 Modify this new DWORD value, and change its value as appropriate:

— A value of 0 — VPN gateways behind NAT devices are not supported.

— A value of 1 — VPN gateways behind NAT devices are supported.

— A value of 2 — the client or VPN gateway can be behind NAT devices.

Step 5 Click **OK** and reboot the Windows XP remote access client.

As always when modifying the Windows registry, be careful; a mistake can, in extreme cases, render the workstation unbootable.

Figure 8-56 illustrates the addition of the DWORD value called AssumeUDP-EncapsulationContextOnSendRule and the modification of its value.

Figure 8-56 *Addition of the DWORD Value Called AssumeUDPEncapsulationContextOnSendRule and the Modification of Its Value*

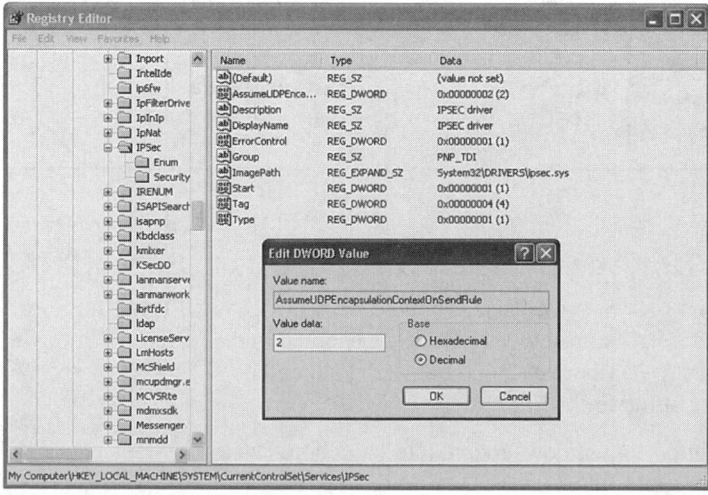

In Figure 8-56, the value of the DWORD value AssumeUDPEncapsulation-ContextOnSendRule is changed to 2.

Configuring the L2TP/IPsec VPN Gateway to Support NAT-T

The configuration of the L2TP/IPsec VPN gateway to support NAT-T is comparatively straightforward—routers running Cisco IOS Software Release 12.2(13)T support NAT-T by default (there is no need to explicitly configure it). On Cisco VPN 3000 concentrators, you do have to explicitly configure NAT-T, and this can be accomplished by going to **Configuration > System > Tunneling** and **Security > IPSec > NAT Transparency** and checking **IPSec over NAT-T** (see Figure 8-57).

Figure 8-57 *Enabling NAT-T on the Cisco VPN 3000 Concentrator*

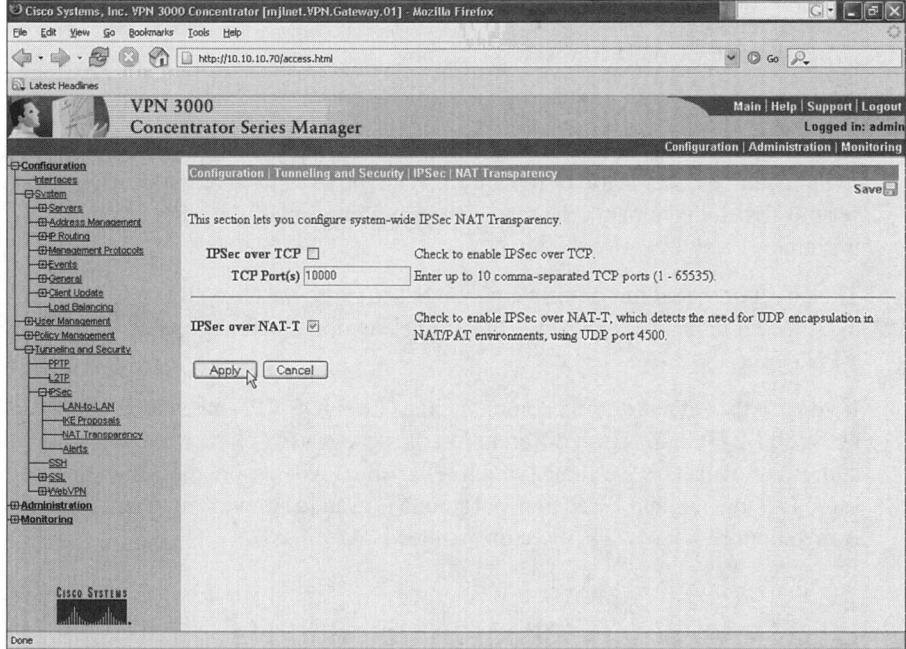

After you have checked the **IPSec over NAT-T** box, choose **Apply**, and NAT-T will be enabled.

After you have enabled NAT-T on the Windows remote access VPN clients and the VPN gateway, if they detect a NAT device, they will negotiate NAT-T, and this will allow L2TP/IPsec packets to successfully traverse the NAT device.

Ensuring That More Than One Windows L2TP/IPsec Remote Access Client Can Successfully Connect to a VPN Gateway from Behind the Same NAT Device (When Using NAT-T)

Cisco IOS Software Release 12.3(11)T4 introduced a new command (**set nat demux**) to ensure that more than one Windows remote access VPN client can connect to a VPN gateway when there is a NAT device in front of the Windows clients and the VPN gateway. Without configuring this command on the VPN gateway, clients might lose L2TP/IPsec connectivity to the VPN gateway.

Example 8-13 shows the configuration of the **set nat demux** command on a Cisco IOS VPN gateway.

Example 8-13 *Configuration of the* **set nat demux** *Command on a Cisco IOS VPN Gateway*

```
!
crypto map l2tpmap 10 ipsec-isakmp profile l2tpprof
 set nat demux
 set transform-set l2tptrans
!
```

As you can see, the **set nat demux** command is simply configured under the crypto map (which can be either static or dynamic). With the exception of the configuration of the **set nat demux** command, the rest of the configuration of the VPN gateway can remain the same.

The effect of the **set nat demux** command is to cause the Cisco IOS VPN gateway to assign a unique UDP port to each new L2TP tunnel/session that it negotiates with a remote access VPN client.

If you use the **set nat demux** command, the Cisco IOS VPN gateway is able to differentiate between L2TP traffic from different remote access VPN client even when the source IP address of packets is the same (which is the effect when more than one client is behind the same PAT device, and IPsec transport mode is used [as previously mentioned, tunnel mode is not supported for L2TP/IPsec on Windows machines]).

Deploying L2TP Voluntary/Client-Initiated VPNs on Cisco IOS Routers

When implementing a remote access VPN solution with L2TP, some of your telecommuters might require connectivity directly from their workstations, but some telecommuters might require connectivity from a router. In this case, you can deploy Cisco IOS L2TP client-initiated tunneling, as illustrated in Figure 8-58.

Figure 8-58 *Cisco IOS L2TP Client-Initiated Tunneling*

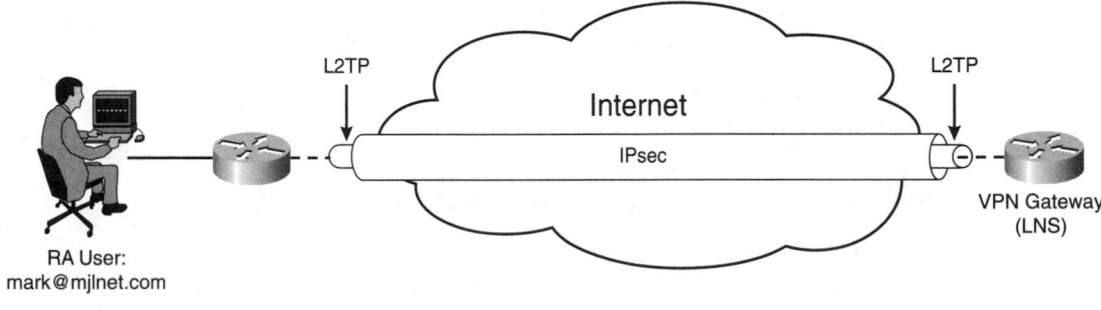

The fact that an L2TP tunnel is built from a telecommuter site router to a VPN head-end gateway makes no difference to basic L2TP tunnel setup and operation—it still works as illustrated in Figure 8-6 on page 717.

When deploying Cisco IOS L2TP client-initiated tunneling, you can choose between using L2TPv2 or L2TPv3. As previously described, the main advantage of L2TPv3 over L2TPv2 is that it can tunnel many different types of payload, whereas L2TPv2 is designed to tunnel only PPP. In this case, however, the payload is PPP, and the deployment model is basic LNS to LNS (L2TPv3)—otherwise known as LAC to LNS (L2TPv2)! So, L2TPv3 does not offer massive advantages over L2TPv2 in this type of deployment. The main advantage is the lower overhead (Cisco IOS L2TPv3 client-initiated tunneling uses an IP encapsulation [protocol 115] rather than a UDP/IP encapsulation).

Example 8-14 shows Cisco IOS L2TPv2 client-initiated configuration for a "client" Cisco IOS router.

Example 8-14 *Cisco IOS L2TPv2 Client-Initiated Configuration for a "Client" Cisco IOS Router*

```
!
hostname mjlnet.NewYork.01
!
l2tp-class client.init.class (line 1)
 authentication (line 2)
 password 7 02050D480809 (line 3)
!
pseudowire-class client.init.pw (line 4)
 encapsulation l2tpv2 (line 5)
 protocol l2tpv2 client.init.class (line 6)
 ip local interface Ethernet0 (line 7)
!
username mjlnet.London.Gateway.03 password 7 094F471A1A0A (line 8)
username mjlnet.NewYork.01 password 7 14141B180F0B (line 9)
!
```

continues

Example 8-14 *Cisco IOS L2TPv2 Client-Initiated Configuration for a "Client" Cisco IOS Router (Continued)*

```
interface Ethernet0
 ip address 10.2.1.1 255.255.255.0
 !
interface Virtual-PPP1 (line 10)
 ip unnumbered Ethernet0 (line 11)
 no cdp enable (line 12)
 ppp authentication chap (line 13)
 pseudowire 10.40.10.1 1001 pw-class client.init.pw (line 14)
 !
ip route 10.10.10.0 255.255.255.0 Virtual-PPP1 (line 15)
 !
```

A quick look at the configuration in Example 8-14 reveals that it is pretty similar to that for LAC-to-LAC pseudowires (see Chapter 2). In this case, however, the L2TP model used is LNS to LNS (because the PPP connection is terminated on both peers), and there are therefore one or two important differences in the configuration.

The **l2tp-class** *l2tp-class-name* in highlighted line 1 configures an L2TP class. This can be used to configure L2TP control-plane parameters, and in this case it is used to configure L2TP authentication—the **authentication** command (highlighted line 2) enables L2TP authentication, and the **password** *password* command (highlighted line 3) is used to specify the password used for L2TP authentication.

Highlighted lines 4 to 7 show the configuration of a pseudowire class. This is used to configure parameters such as data- and control-plane encapsulation types as well as source IP address.

In highlighted line 4, the **pseudowire-class** *pw-class-name* command is used to configure a pseudowire class called client.init.pw.

The **encapsulation** {**l2tpv2** | **l2tpv3** | [**manual**]} command (highlighted line 5) specifies the data-plane encapsulation, which in this case is L2TPv2.

The **protocol** {**l2tpv2** | **l2tpv3** | **none**} {*l2tp-class-name*} command (highlighted line 6) configures the control-plane protocol and links to an L2TP class. The control-plane protocol is configured as L2TPv2, and a link is specified to the L2TP class called client.init.class (configured in highlighted lines 1 to 3).

The **username** *username* **password** *password* commands in highlighted lines 7 and 8 are used to configure the usernames and passwords to be used for PPP authentication between the peer routers.

Highlighted lines 9 to 13 show the configuration of interface virtual-PPP 1. The PPP connection is terminated on this interface.

The **ip unnumbered** *interface-name* command (highlighted line 10) "borrows" the IP address configured on interface Ethernet 0 for use on interface virtual-PPP 1.

The **no cdp enable** command (highlighted line 11) is then used to disable CDP on the interface, and **ppp authentication chap** (highlighted line 12) is used to enable CHAP authentication.

In highlighted line 13, the **pseudowire** *peer-ip-address vc* **pw-class** *pw-class-name* command configures the remote endpoint of the L2TP tunnel (the VPN head-end gateway), as well as the pseudowire class name (configured in highlighted lines 4 to 7). The virtual circuit (VC) number specified using the **pseudowire** command is irrelevant to the configuration of L2TPv2 (specify any VC number you want!).

Finally, in highlighted line 14, the **ip route** command configures a route to a remote network at the VPN head-end gateway site via the virtual-PPP interface.

Example 8-15 shows the configuration of the VPN head-end gateway.

Example 8-15 *Configuration of the VPN Head-End Gateway*

```
!
hostname mjlnet.London.Gateway.03
!
username mjlnet.London.Gateway.03 password 7 094F471A1A0A (line 1)
username mjlnet.NewYork.01 password 7 14141B180F0B (line 2)
!
vpdn enable
!
vpdn-group 1
 accept-dialin
 protocol l2tp
 virtual-template 1
 terminate-from hostname mjlnet.NewYork.01
 l2tp tunnel password 0 cisco (line 3)
!
!
interface Loopback100
 ip address 10.30.10.1 255.255.255.0
!
!
interface FastEthernet2/0
 ip address 10.40.10.1 255.255.255.0
!
!
interface Virtual-Template1
 ip unnumbered Loopback100
 no peer default ip address (line 4)
 ppp authentication chap
!
```

If you compare the configuration shown in Example 8-15 to that shown in Example 8-4 on page 733, you will see that they are almost identical.

The only real differences are the fact that L2TP authentication is configured using the **l2tp tunnel password** *password* command (highlighted line 3), and no IP address is assigned to the remote access client (mjlnet.NewYork.01 in this case) because the **no peer default ip address** command is configured under the virtual template interface.

In fact, because PPP authentication is configured between the peers, you do not absolutely need L2TP authentication. And if you want to, you can dynamically assign IP addresses to the remote access clients using the **peer default ip address** command (highlighted line 4).

Highlighted lines 1 and 2 shows the username and passwords used for PPP authentication.

You can use a number of commands to verify L2TPv2 client-initiated tunneling on the head-end VPN gateway, including **show vpdn session**, **show vpdn tunnel**, and **show caller user**. Example 8-16 shows the output of the **show vpdn tunnel** command on mjlnet.London.Gateway.03.

Example 8-16 **show vpdn tunnel** *Command Output for mjlnet.London.Gateway.03*

```
mjlnet.London.Gateway.03#show vpdn tunnel
%No active L2F tunnels
L2TP Tunnel Information Total tunnels 1 sessions 1 (line 1)
LocID RemID Remote Name State Remote Address Port Sessions L2TP Class/
    VPDN Group
60057 1715 mjlnet.NewYor est 192.168.3.1  1701 1  1 (line 2)
%No active PPTP tunnels
mjlnet.VPN.Gateway.03#
```

Highlighted line 1 shows that 1 L2TP tunnel and 1 L2TP session have been established.

Highlighted line 2 shows information including the name of the remote peer (mjlnet.NewYork.01), the IP address of the remote peer (192.168.3.1), the tunnel (UDP) port (1701, L2TP).

Example 8-17 shows the output of the **show caller user** command on mjlnet.London.Gateway.03.

Example 8-17 **show caller user** *Command Output for mjlnet.London.Gateway.03*

```
mjlnet.VPN.Gateway.03#show caller user mjlnet.NewYork.01
 User: mjlnet.NewYork.01, line Vi2.1, service PPPoVPDN (line 1)
  Connected for 00:07:07, Idle for 00:07:05
 Timeouts: Limit  Remaining Timer Type
           -   -   -
 PPP: LCP Open, CHAP (<-->), IPCP (line 2)
 IP: Local 10.30.10.1, remote 10.2.1.1 (line 3)
 Counts: 85 packets input, 1348 bytes
    89 packets output, 1478 bytes
mjlnet.VPN.Gateway.03#
```

Highlighted line 1 shows the username (mljnet.NewYork.01), the interface on which the PPP connection is terminated (interface virtual access 2.1) and the service (PPP tunneled over a VPDN protocol [L2TP]).

In highlighted line 2, you can see that LCP is established (Open), that CHAP authentication takes places in both directions over the tunnel (look at the arrows—each peer authenticates the other), and that IPCP has been negotiated between the peers (IP is being transported).

Highlighted line 3 shows the local and remote IP addresses. These IP addresses are those applied to the virtual-PPP and virtual-template (virtual access) interfaces and are passed between the peers during IPCP negotiation.

So much for L2TPv2 client-initiated tunnel mode. How about L2TPv3 client-initiated tunnel mode? Example 8-18 shows sample configurations using L2TPv3.

Example 8-18 *Sample Configurations for Client-Initiated Tunneling with L2TPv3*

```
!
hostname mjlnet.NewYork.01
!
username mjlnet.London.Gateway.03 password 7 094F471A1A0A
username mjlnet.NewYork.01 password 7 14141B180F0B
!
l2tp-class client.init.class
authentication
 password 7 02050D480809
!
pseudowire-class client.init.pw
 encapsulation l2tpv3
 protocol l2tpv3 client.init.class
 ip local interface ethernet0
!
interface Virtual-PPP1
 ip unnumbered loopback1
 ppp authentication chap
 pseudowire 10.40.10.1 1000 pw-class client.init.pw
!
ip route 10.10.10.0 255.255.255.0 Virtual-PPP1

hostname mjlnet.London.Gateway.03
!
username mjlnet.London.Gateway.03 password 7 094F471A1A0A
username mjlnet.NewYork.01 password 7 14141B180F0B
!
l2tp-class client.init.class
authentication
 password 7 02050D480809
!
pseudowire-class client.init.pw
 encapsulation l2tpv3
 protocol l2tpv3 client.init.class
 ip local interface ethernet0
!
interface Virtual-PPP1
 ip unnumbered loopback100
 ppp authentication chap
 pseudowire 192.168.3.1 1000 pw-class client.init.pw
!
ip route 10.2.1.0 255.255.255.0 Virtual-PPP1
!
```

As you can see, the configuration of mjlnet.NewYork.01 greatly resembles that when using L2TPv2 (see Example 8-14). The key difference is that the **encapsulation** and **protocol** commands within the pseudowire class now specify L2TPv3 rather than L2TPv2.

The configuration of mjlnet.London.Gateway.03 is radically different when using L2TPv3 (compare with Example 8-15). The commands used are now the same as those used for the configuration of mjlnet.NewYork.01 — the only difference being the IP addresses used.

Designing and Implementing L2TP Compulsory/NAS-Initiated Tunnel Mode Remote Access VPNs

As discussed at the beginning of this chapter, there are two modes of operation with L2TP: voluntary/client-initiated tunnel mode and compulsory/NAS-initiated tunnel mode. Up to this point in the chapter, the focus has been on voluntary tunnel mode; this section examines compulsory tunnel mode.

Figure 8-59 depicts compulsory tunnel mode L2TP.

Figure 8-59 *Compulsory Tunnel Mode L2TP*

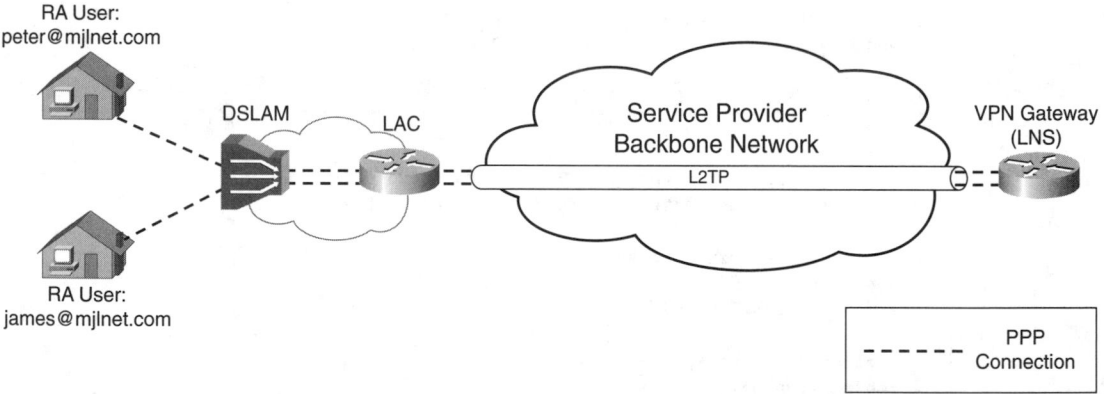

As shown in Figure 8-59, PPP connections (PPP over ATM [PPPoA] or PPP over Ethernet [PPPoE]) from users are transported via a DSL Access Multiplexor (DSLAM) and aggregation router over an L2TP tunnel to the a tunnel termination device (the VPN gateway). In Figure 8-59, the aggregation router functions as the LAC, and the tunnel termination device functions as the LNS. It is also possible that a DSLAM could function as a LAC.

Although Figure 8-59 shows the tunneling of PPP connections via a DSLAM and aggregation router (LAC) to an LNS, it does not really matter how PPP frames arrive at the LAC for tunneling to the LNS — they could arrive, for example, via analogue dialup lines, via ISDN lines, or they could as already discussed arrive via a DSLAM.

Figure 8-60 shows the operation of L2TP compulsory tunnel mode (when a remote access client initiates connectivity).

Figure 8-60 *Operation of L2TP Compulsory Tunnel Mode*

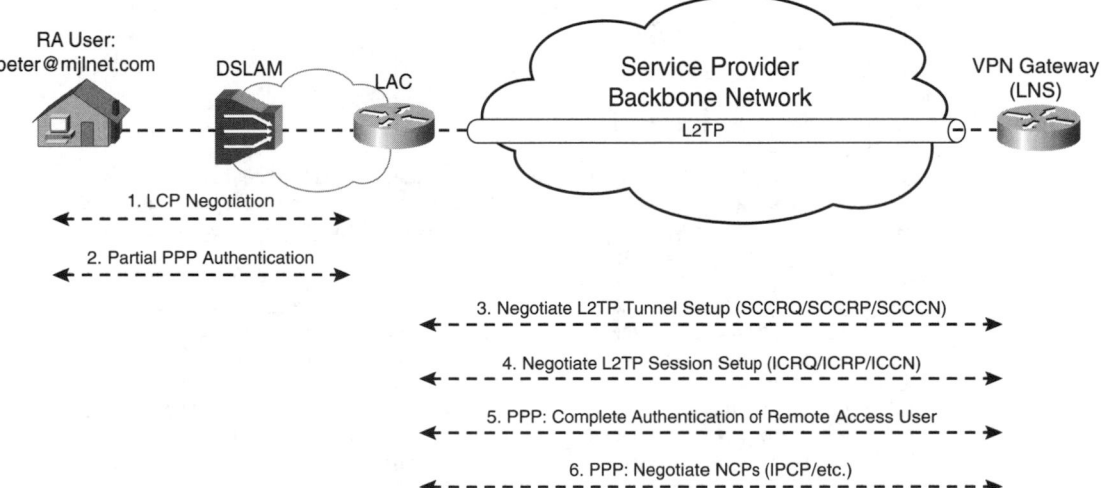

If you compare Figure 8-60 with Figure 8-6 on page 717, you can see that the operation of L2TP compulsory tunnel mode differs a little from the operation of L2TP voluntary tunnel mode.

As shown in Figure 8-60, when a remote access client connects to the LAC, the remote access client and the LAC negotiate LCP. In addition, *partial* PPP authentication is performed.

During partial PPP authentication, the LAC obtains the username of the remote access client and uses the username (or part of the username) to assign the PPP connection to the correct L2TP tunnel (there may be more than one).

At this point, if the L2TP tunnel has not already been established, the LAC will complete L2TP tunnel setup with the LNS. The LAC initiates L2TP tunnel setup by sending an SCCRQ message to the LNS (see Table 8-1 on page 716), the LNS replies with an SCCRP, and the LAC completes tunnel setup by sending an SCCCN.

After the L2TP tunnel has been established, the LAC and LNS will negotiate L2TP session setup. The LAC begins L2TP session establishment by sending an ICRP to the LNS. The LNS replies with an ICRP, and session setup is complete when the LAC sends an ICCN.

The LNS and the remote access client now complete PPP negotiation by completing PPP authentication and NCP negotiation. Note that it is also possible for the LNS to reinitiate LCP negotiation and authentication with the remote access client (rather than just completing the process).

L2TP Compulsory Tunnel Mode Setup: LAC Perspective

Example 8-19 shows L2TP compulsory tunnel mode setup from the LAC perspective.

Example 8-19 *L2TP Compulsory Tunnel Mode Setup from the LAC Perspective*

```
mjlnet.brux.lac#show debug
PPP:
 PPP protocol negotiation debugging is on
VPN:
 L2X protocol events debugging is on
mjlnet.brux.lac#
*Mar 1 00:19:07.236 UTC: BR0/0:1 PPP: Using dialer call direction
*Mar 1 00:19:07.236 UTC: BR0/0:1 PPP: Treating connection as a callin
*Mar 1 00:19:07.236 UTC: BR0/0:1 PPP: Phase is ESTABLISHING, Passive Open
 [0 sess, 0 load] (line 1)
*Mar 1 00:19:07.236 UTC: BR0/0:1 LCP: State is Listen (line 2)
*Mar 1 00:19:07.464 UTC: BR0/0:1 LCP: I CONFREQ [Listen] id 4 len 10
*Mar 1 00:19:07.464 UTC: BR0/0:1 LCP: MagicNumber 0x001DDF13 (0x0506001DDF13)
*Mar 1 00:19:07.464 UTC: BR0/0:1 LCP: O CONFREQ [Listen] id 4 len 15
*Mar 1 00:19:07.464 UTC: BR0/0:1 LCP: AuthProto CHAP (0x0305C22305)
*Mar 1 00:19:07.468 UTC: BR0/0:1 LCP: MagicNumber 0x0664DE58 (0x05060664DE58)
*Mar 1 00:19:07.468 UTC: BR0/0:1 LCP: O CONFACK [Listen] id 4 len 10
*Mar 1 00:19:07.468 UTC: BR0/0:1 LCP: MagicNumber 0x001DDF13 (0x0506001DDF13)
*Mar 1 00:19:07.480 UTC: BR0/0:1 LCP: I CONFACK [ACKsent] id 4 len 15
*Mar 1 00:19:07.480 UTC: BR0/0:1 LCP: AuthProto CHAP (0x0305C22305)
*Mar 1 00:19:07.480 UTC: BR0/0:1 LCP: MagicNumber 0x0664DE58 (0x05060664DE58)
*Mar 1 00:19:07.480 UTC: BR0/0:1 LCP: State is Open (line 3)
*Mar 1 00:19:07.480 UTC: BR0/0:1 PPP: Phase is AUTHENTICATING, by this end
 [0 sess, 0 load] (line 4)
*Mar 1 00:19:07.484 UTC: BR0/0:1 CHAP: O CHALLENGE id 4 len 32 from
 "mjlnet.brux.lac" (line 5)
*Mar 1 00:19:07.504 UTC: BR0/0:1 CHAP: I RESPONSE id 4 len 41 from
 "joebloggs@mjlnet.com" (line 6)
*Mar 1 00:19:07.504 UTC: BR0/0:1 PPP: Phase is FORWARDING [0 sess, 0 load]
*Mar 1 00:19:07.516 UTC: Tnl 58518 L2TP: SM State idle
*Mar 1 00:19:07.516 UTC: Tnl 58518 L2TP: O SCCRQ (line 7)
*Mar 1 00:19:07.520 UTC: Tnl 58518 L2TP: Tunnel state change from idle to
 wait-ctl-reply
*Mar 1 00:19:07.520 UTC: Tnl 58518 L2TP: SM State wait-ctl-reply
*Mar 1 00:19:07.573 UTC: Tnl 58518 L2TP: I SCCRP from mjlnet.london.lns (line 8)
*Mar 1 00:19:07.573 UTC: Tnl 58518 L2TP: Got a challenge from remote peer,
 mjlnet.london.lns
*Mar 1 00:19:07.573 UTC: Tnl 58518 L2TP: Got a response from remote peer,
 mjlnet.london.lns
*Mar 1 00:19:07.573 UTC: Tnl 58518 L2TP: Tunnel Authentication success
*Mar 1 00:19:07.573 UTC: Tnl 58518 L2TP: Tunnel state change from wait-ctl-reply to
 established
*Mar 1 00:19:07.573 UTC: Tnl 58518 L2TP: O SCCCN to
 mjlnet.london.lns tnlid 64727 (line 9)
*Mar 1 00:19:07.577 UTC: Tnl 58518 L2TP: SM State established
*Mar 1 00:19:07.581 UTC: Tnl/Cl 58518/3 L2TP: Session FS enabled
```

Example 8-19 *L2TP Compulsory Tunnel Mode Setup from the LAC Perspective (Continued)*

```
*Mar 1 00:19:07.581 UTC: Tnl/Cl 58518/3 L2TP: Session state change from idle to
wait-for-tunnel
*Mar 1 00:19:07.581 UTC: BR0/0:1 Tnl/Cl 58518/3 L2TP: Create session
*Mar 1 00:19:07.581 UTC: Tnl 58518 L2TP: SM State established
*Mar 1 00:19:07.585 UTC: BR0/0:1 Tnl/Cl 58518/3 L2TP: O ICRQ to
mjlnet.london.lns 64727/0 (line 10)
*Mar 1 00:19:07.585 UTC: BR0/0:1 Tnl/Cl 58518/3 L2TP: Session state change from
wait-for-tunnel to wait-reply
*Mar 1 00:19:07.613 UTC: BR0/0:1 Tnl/Cl 58518/3 L2TP: O ICCN to
mjlnet.london.lns 64727/3 (line 11)
*Mar 1 00:19:07.613 UTC: BR0/0:1 Tnl/Cl 58518/3 L2TP: Session state change from
wait-reply to established
mjlnet.brux.lac#
```

In highlighted lines 1 and 2, the PPP phase changes to ESTABLISHING, and LCP state changes to Listen. LCP negotiation is about to begin. The LCP state changes to Open in highlighted line 3—LCP negotiation has been completed. Next, in highlighted line 4, the PPP phase changes to AUTHENTICATING—(partial) PPP authentication is about to begin.

Highlighted line 5 and 6 show an outgoing CHAP challenge message (from the LAC to the remote access client) and an incoming CHAP Response message (from the remote access client to the LAC). You will notice, however, the absence of either a CHAP Success or Failure message—these messages are used to complete CHAP authentication. So, CHAP authentication is partial between the LAC and the remote access client.

The remote access client's username is included in the CHAP Response message shown in highlighted line 6, and this is used by the LAC to associate this PPP connection with an L2TP tunnel to the LNS, mjlnet.London.LNS.01.

Because there is no existing L2TP tunnel between the LAC (mjlnet.brux.lac) and the LNS (mjlnet.london.lns), the LAC begins L2TP tunnel establishment by sending an SCCRQ to the LNS (highlighted line 7).

The LNS then replies with an SCCRP in highlighted line 8. In highlighted line 9, the LAC responds with an SCCCN, and the tunnel is established. The LAC now begins L2TP session establishment by sending an ICRQ (see highlighted line 10). The LNS replies to the ICRQ with an ICRP (not shown in the **debug** output), and finally, the LAC finishes L2TP session setup by sending an ICCN to the LNS (highlighted line 11).

L2TP Compulsory Tunnel Mode Setup: LNS Perspective

Example 8-20 shows L2TP tunnel setup and PPP negotiation from the LNS perspective.

Example 8-20 *L2TP Compulsory Tunnel Mode Setup from the LNS Perspective*

```
mjlnet.london.lns#show debug
PPP:
 PPP protocol negotiation debugging is on
VPN:
 L2X protocol events debugging is on
mjlnet.london.lns#
*Jun 20 17:38:20.839 UTC: L2TP: I SCCRQ from mjlnet.brux.lac tnl 58518 (line 1)
*Jun 20 17:38:20.839 UTC: Tnl 64727 L2TP: Got a challenge in SCCRQ, mjlnet.brux.lac
*Jun 20 17:38:20.839 UTC: Tnl 64727 L2TP: Tunnel Authorization started for host
 mjlnet.brux.lac
*Jun 20 17:38:20.839 UTC: Tnl 64727 L2TP: New tunnel created for remote mjlnet.brux.lac,
 address 192.168.5.2
*Jun 20 17:38:20.839 UTC: L2X: Tunnel author reply found L2X info
*Jun 20 17:38:20.839 UTC: Tnl 64727 L2TP: O SCCRP to
 mjlnet.brux.lac tnlid 58518 (line 2)
*Jun 20 17:38:20.839 UTC: Tnl 64727 L2TP: Control channel retransmit delay
 set to 1 seconds
*Jun 20 17:38:20.843 UTC: Tnl 64727 L2TP: Tunnel state change from idle to
 wait-ctl-reply
*Jun 20 17:38:20.883 UTC: Tnl 64727 L2TP: I SCCCN from
 mjlnet.brux.lac tnl 58518 (line 3)
*Jun 20 17:38:20.883 UTC: Tnl 64727 L2TP: Got a Challenge Response in SCCCN from
 mjlnet.brux.lac
*Jun 20 17:38:20.883 UTC: Tnl 64727 L2TP: Tunnel Authentication success
*Jun 20 17:38:20.883 UTC: Tnl 64727 L2TP: Tunnel state change from
 wait-ctl-reply to established
*Jun 20 17:38:20.883 UTC: Tnl 64727 L2TP: SM State established
*Jun 20 17:38:20.899 UTC: Tnl 64727 L2TP: I ICRQ from
 mjlnet.brux.lac tnl 58518 (line 4)
*Jun 20 17:38:20.899 UTC: Tnl/Sn 64727/3 L2TP: Session state change from idle to
 wait-connect
*Jun 20 17:38:20.899 UTC: Tnl/Sn 64727/3 L2TP: Accepted ICRQ, new session created
*Jun 20 17:38:20.899 UTC: uid:2 Tnl/Sn 64727/3 L2TP: O ICRP to
 mjlnet.brux.lac 58518/3 (line 5)
*Jun 20 17:38:20.899 UTC: Tnl 64727 L2TP: Control channel retransmit delay set to
 1 seconds
*Jun 20 17:38:20.939 UTC: uid:2 Tnl/Sn 64727/3 L2TP: I ICCN from mjlnet.brux.lac
 tnl 58518, cl 3 (line 6)
*Jun 20 17:38:20.939 UTC: uid:2 Tnl/Sn 64727/3 L2TP: Session state change from
 wait-connect to wait-for-service-selection-iccn
*Jun 20 17:38:20.939 UTC: ppp2 PPP: Phase is ESTABLISHING (line 7)
*Jun 20 17:38:20.939 UTC: ppp2 LCP: I FORCED rcvd CONFACK len 11 (line 8)
*Jun 20 17:38:20.939 UTC: ppp2 LCP: AuthProto CHAP (0x0305C22305)
*Jun 20 17:38:20.939 UTC: ppp2 LCP: MagicNumber 0x0664DE58 (0x05060664DE58)
*Jun 20 17:38:20.939 UTC: ppp2 LCP: I FORCED sent CONFACK len 6 (line 9)
*Jun 20 17:38:20.939 UTC: ppp2 LCP: MagicNumber 0x001DDF13 (0x0506001DDF13)
*Jun 20 17:38:20.939 UTC: ppp2 PPP: Phase is FORWARDING, Attempting Forward
*Jun 20 17:38:20.939 UTC: ppp2 PPP: Phase is AUTHENTICATING, Unauthenticated User
```

Example 8-20 *L2TP Compulsory Tunnel Mode Setup from the LNS Perspective (Continued)*

```
*Jun 20 17:38:20.939 UTC: ppp2 PPP: Phase is FORWARDING, Attempting Forward
*Jun 20 17:38:20.943 UTC: Vi2.1 Tnl/Sn 64727/3 L2TP: Session state change from
wait-for-service-selection-iccn to established
*Jun 20 17:38:20.943 UTC: Vi2.1 PPP: Phase is AUTHENTICATING,
Authenticated User (line 10)
*Jun 20 17:38:20.943 UTC: Vi2.1 CHAP: O SUCCESS id 4 len 4 (line 11)
*Jun 20 17:38:20.943 UTC: Vi2.1 PPP: Phase is UP
*Jun 20 17:38:20.943 UTC: Vi2.1 PPP: Process pending ncp packets
*Jun 20 17:38:20.947 UTC: Vi2.1 IPCP: O CONFREQ [Closed] id 1 len 10 (line 12)
*Jun 20 17:38:20.947 UTC: Vi2.1 IPCP: Address 10.20.10.1 (0x03060A140A01)
*Jun 20 17:38:20.979 UTC: Vi2.1 IPCP: I CONFREQ [REQsent] id 3 len 10
*Jun 20 17:38:20.979 UTC: Vi2.1 IPCP: Address 0.0.0.0 (0x030600000000)
*Jun 20 17:38:20.979 UTC: Vi2.1 AAA/AUTHOR/IPCP: Start. Her address 0.0.0.0,
we want 0.0.0.0
*Jun 20 17:38:20.979 UTC: Vi2.1 AAA/AUTHOR/IPCP: Done. Her address 0.0.0.0,
we want 0.0.0.0
*Jun 20 17:38:20.979 UTC: Vi2.1 IPCP: Pool returned 10.30.10.50
*Jun 20 17:38:20.979 UTC: Vi2.1 IPCP: O CONFNAK [REQsent] id 3 len 10
*Jun 20 17:38:20.979 UTC: Vi2.1 IPCP: Address 10.30.10.50 (0x03060A1E0A32)
*Jun 20 17:38:20.987 UTC: Vi2.1 IPCP: I CONFACK [REQsent] id 1 len 10
*Jun 20 17:38:20.987 UTC: Vi2.1 IPCP: Address 10.20.10.1 (0x03060A140A01)
*Jun 20 17:38:21.003 UTC: Vi2.1 IPCP: I CONFREQ [ACKrcvd] id 4 len 10
*Jun 20 17:38:21.003 UTC: Vi2.1 IPCP: Address 10.30.10.50 (0x03060A1E0A32)
*Jun 20 17:38:21.003 UTC: Vi2.1 IPCP: O CONFACK [ACKrcvd] id 4 len 10
*Jun 20 17:38:21.003 UTC: Vi2.1 IPCP: Address 10.30.10.50 (0x03060A1E0A32)
*Jun 20 17:38:21.003 UTC: Vi2.1 IPCP: State is Open (line 13)
*Jun 20 17:38:21.007 UTC: Vi2.1 IPCP: Install route to 10.30.10.50
*Jun 20 17:38:21.007 UTC: Vi2.1 IPCP: Add link info for cef entry 10.30.10.50
mjlnet.london.lns#
```

Highlighted lines 1 to 3 show the exchange of SCCRQ, SCCRP, and SCCCN messages used to establish the L2TP tunnel between the LAC and the LNS.

In highlighted line 4 to 6, you can see the ICRQ, ICRP, and ICCN messages that set up the L2TP session.

Now that the L2TP session has been set up, the LNS can begin PPP negotiation with the remote access client (see highlighted line 7).

In highlighted line 8 and 9, the LNS processes LCP messages passed from the LAC during L2TP session setup (remember that the LAC negotiates LCP with the remote access client).

Highlighted line 10 shows that PPP authentication is about to begin, and in highlighted line 11, the LNS sends a CHAP Success message to the remote access client. The LAC also passed authentication information to the LAC during L2TP session setup, and so the LNS now only needs to send either a CHAP Success or Failure message to the remote access client depending on whether authentication was successful.

As soon as the LNS has authenticated the remote access client, it begins NCP (in this case IPCP) negotiation by sending an IPCP Configure-Request (CONFREQ, see highlighted line 12).

The IPCP state changes to Open in highlighted line 13, and IPCP negotiation is complete. The L2TP tunnel (and session) has been set up between the LAC and the LNS, and PPP negotiation has been completed between the LNS and the remote access client.

Configuring the LAC for Compulsory Tunnel Mode

The configuration of the LAC consists of the following steps:

Step 1   Configure access connectivity.

Step 2   Configure AAA (optional).

Step 3   Globally enable VPDNs.

Step 4   Configure the VPDN groups.

Example 8-21 shows a sample configuration of a LAC when using compulsory tunnel mode.

Example 8-21 *Sample Configuration of a LAC When Using Compulsory Tunnel Mode*

```
!
hostname mjlnet.brux.lac
!
vpdn enable (line 1)
vpdn search-order domain (line 2)
!
vpdn-group mjlnet.l2tp.vpn (line 3)
request-dialin (line 4)
protocol l2tp (line 5)
domain mjlnet.com (line 6)
initiate-to ip 192.168.5.1 (line 7)
l2tp tunnel password 7 045802150C2E (line 8)
!
!
interface FastEthernet0/0 (line 9)
ip address 192.168.3.1 255.255.255.0 (line 10)
!
controller E1 1/0 (line 11)
pri-group timeslots 1-31 (line 12)
!
interface Serial1/0:15 (line 13)
no ip address (line 14)
encapsulation ppp (line 15)
isdn switch-type primary-net5 (line 16)
isdn incoming-voice modem (line 17)
no peer default ip address (line 18)
ppp authentication chap (line 19)
!
interface Group-Async1 (line 20)
no ip address (line 21)
encapsulation ppp (line 22)
```

Example 8-21 *Sample Configuration of a LAC When Using Compulsory Tunnel Mode (Continued)*

```
async mode interactive (line 23)
no peer default ip address (line 24)
ppp authentication chap (line 25)
group-range 33 38 (line 26)
!
line 33 38 (line 27)
modem InOut (line 28)
modem autoconfigure type mica (line 29)
autoselect ppp (line 30)
!
```

The **vpdn enable** command in line 1 enable VPDNs (including L2TP) on the LAC.

The **vpdn search-order domain** command (line 2) then configures the LAC to attempt to associate the remote access clients' PPP connections to an L2TP tunnel using the domain name contained in the username of the remote access client (specified by the remote user using the syntax *username@domain_name*, and communicated to the LAC during PPP authentication).

The next step is to configure the VPDN group (Step 3). Line 3 shows the **vpdn-group** *name* command, which configures the VPDN group name. A VPDN group is used to collect together the configuration for a particular VPN/VPDN. It is worth noting that the VPDN group name is locally significant on the LAC.

The first command configured under the VPDN group is (in this case) **request-dialin** (line 4). This command is used to configure the LAC to initiate L2TP tunnel/session establishment with the LNS on reception of PPP connections from remote access clients.

Next is the **protocol l2tp** command is used to configure L2TP as the tunneling protocol (line 5).

In line 6, the **domain** *domain_name* command is used to match the domain name in the username of the remote access user (username@domain_name).

Line 7 contains the **initiate-to ip** *ip-address* command. This command configures the IP address of the LNS (the L2TP tunnel endpoint).

The **l2tp authentication password** *password* command (line 8) is used to configure the L2TP tunnel password, which is used by the LAC to authenticate the LNS and vice versa (during tunnel setup).

Lines 9 and 10 show the configuration of the interface that provides connectivity to the LNS (via intervening networks).

In this example, the access connectivity to remote access clients is provided via a Primary Rate ISDN line (clients connect over the PRI to digital MICA modems in the LAC).

Lines 11 and 12 show the configuration of the E1 controller. The **pri-groups timeslots** *timeslot-range* command in line 12 specifies timeslots 1 to 31.

Lines 13 to 19 show the ISDN D channel configuration.

The **encapsulation ppp** command (line 15) is used, unsurprisingly, to configure PPP encapsulation on the line.

Line 16 shows the **isdn switch-type** *switch-type*, used to configure the ISDN switch type.

The **isdn incoming-voice modem** command (line 17) configures the LAC to switch asynchronous calls received on the PRI to the internal MICA modems.

The **no peer default ip address** command (line 18) ensures that the LAC does not assign an IP address to any remote access clients whose calls are received on the PRI. This command makes sense because IP addresses are assigned (if at all) during IPCP negotiation, and IPCP is not negotiated between the remote access clients and the LAC (it is instead negotiated between the remote access clients and the LNS).

Line 19 contains the **ppp authentication chap** command. This command configures the LAC to use CHAP authentication with the remote access clients.

Lines 20 to 26 show the configuration of the asynchronous interfaces. These interfaces are configured together in a group (thus ensuring consistency).

The **encapsulation ppp** command (line 21) again configures PPP encapsulation.

Line 22 shows the **async mode interactive** command. This configures allows users to initiate interactive mode on the lines.

The **no peer default ip address** command (line 23) again ensures that the LAC does not assign IP addresses to the remote access clients.

The **group-range** *interface-range-start interface-range-finish* command in line 24 then applies the configuration under interface **Group-Async1** to the MICA modem lines.

In lines 25 to 28, you can see the configuration of the asynchronous lines.

The **modem InOut** command (line 26) ensures that the modems on the specified lines are able to both receive and make calls.

In line 27, the **modem autoconfigure type mica** command automatically configures the modems as type MICA.

Line 28 contains the **autoselect ppp** command ensures that the LAC can auto-detect PPP encapsulation on the modem lines.

Configuring Tunnel Definitions on a RADIUS Server

Although the configuration shown in Example 8-21 functions perfectly well, it is also common to store the VPDN/VPN configuration (configured under the VPDN group in Example 8-21) on a RADIUS server in the form of a *tunnel definition*.

There are two ways to configure tunnel definitions on a RADIUS server:

- Using IETF standard tunnel attributes. These attributes are described in RFC2868.
- Using Cisco AV pairs.

Table 8-2 shows the most relevant IETF standard tunnel attributes.

Table 8-2   *IETF Standard Tunnel Attributes*

Attribute Type	Attribute Name	Description
64	Tunnel-Type	This attribute is used to specify the tunnel protocol.
65	Tunnel-Medium-Type	This describes the medium used to transport the tunnel.
67	Tunnel-Server-Endpoint	This is the IP address of the tunnel endpoint (the LNS).
69	Tunnel-Password	This attribute specifies the password used for tunnel authentication.
82	Tunnel-Assignment-ID	Identifies the tunnel to which a session is assigned.

If you want to store tunnel configuration on a RADIUS server, you can remove the VPDN group configuration (**no vpdn-group** *name*) from the LAC and instead specify the commands shown in Example 8-22.

Example 8-22 *AAA Configuration on the LAC*

```
aaa new-model
aaa authentication ppp default group radius
aaa authorization network default group radius
radius-server host 10.100.10.51 auth-port 1645 acct-port 1646 key cisco
!
```

The **aaa new-model** command enables AAA on the LAC.

The **aaa authentication ppp default group radius** command is used to enable authentication for PPP using a RADIUS server (as specified using the default method list).

The **aaa authorization network default group radius** command configures the LAC to use a RADIUS server to authorize network connections. Again, the default method list is specified.

The **radius server host** command specifies the IP address or DNS name of the RADIUS server, the UDP ports used for authentication (**auth-port**) and accounting (**acct-port**) requests, and the key used to authenticate communications used between the LAC and the RADIUS server.

If you are using a Cisco Secure ACS, to get the tunnel definition to download correctly from the RADIUS server, you must complete the following steps:

Step 1   Configure a user account using the domain name as the username (for example, mjlnet.com).

Step 2   Configure the password for the user account as cisco. This password is hard-coded on Cisco routers.

Step 3   Configure a group, and within group settings configure the Service-Type attribute (attribute type 6) as outbound or dialout framed.

Step 4   Ensure that **No IP Assignment** is configured under the user or group settings.

Step 5   Configure IETF or Cisco AV-pair tunnel attributes under the group settings.

It is worth noting that the IETF or Cisco AV-pair tunnel attributes that will only appear in the group (or user) settings if they are enabled under Interface Configuration.

Figure 8-61 shows the configuration of IETF tunnel attributes on Cisco Secure ACS.

Figure 8-61   *Configuration of IETF Tunnel Attributes on Cisco Secure ACS*

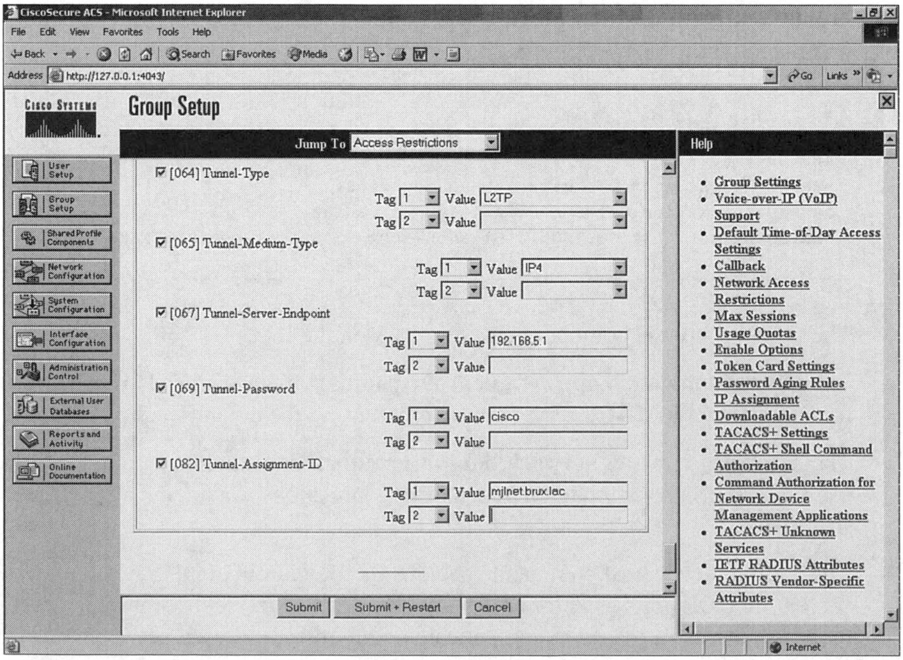

Example 8-23 shows the equivalent configuration of IETF tunnel attributes on a Merit RADIUS server.

Example 8-23 *Configuration of IETF Tunnel Attributes on a Merit RADIUS Server*

```
mjlnet.com Password="cisco" Service-Type=Outbound
Tunnel-Type = :1:L2TP
Tunnel-Medium-Type = :1:IP
Tunnel-Server-Endpoint = :1:192.168.5.1
Tunnel-Password = :1:"cisco"
Tunnel-Assignment-ID = :1:"mjlnet.brux.lac"
```

Figure 8-62 shows the configuration of Cisco AV-pairs on Cisco Secure ACS.

Figure 8-62 *Configuration of Cisco AV-Pairs Tunnel Attributes on Cisco Secure ACS*

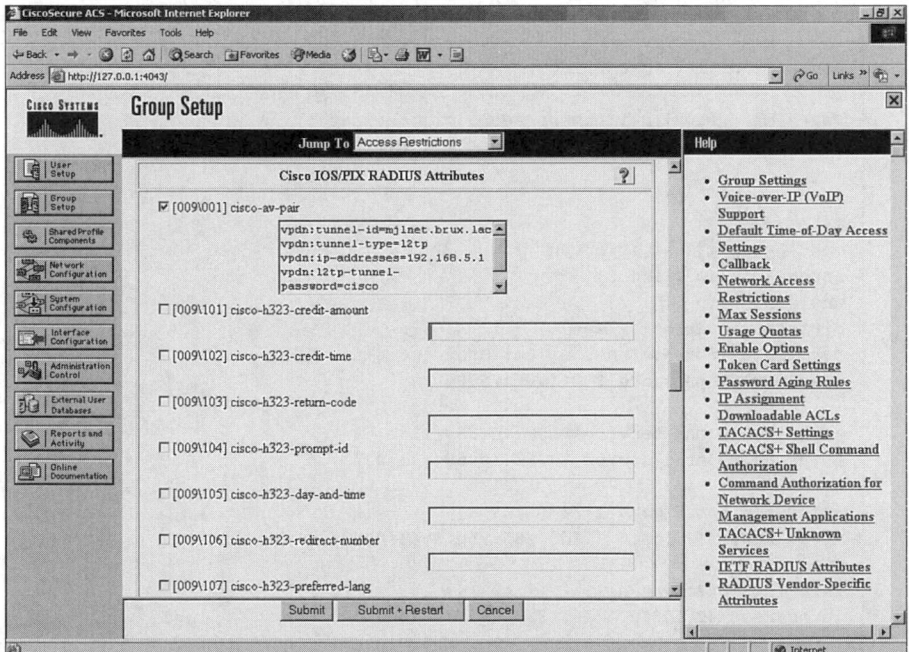

In Example 8-24, you can see the equivalent configuration of Cisco AV-pair tunnel attributes on a Merit RADIUS server.

Example 8-24 *Configuration of Cisco AV-Pair Tunnel Attributes on a Merit RADIUS Server*

```
mjlnet.com Password ="cisco" Service-Type=Outbound
cisco-avpair = "vpdn:tunnel-id=mjlnet.brux.lac"
cisco-avpair = "vpdn:tunnel-type=l2tp"
cisco-avpair = "vpdn:ip-addresses=192.168.5.1"
cisco-avpair = "vpdn:l2tp-tunnel-password=cisco"
```

Configuring the LNS for Compulsory Tunnel Mode

When you have finished configuring the LAC, you can move on to configuring the LNS.

Configuration of the LNS consists of the following steps:

Step 1   Globally enable VPDNS.

Step 2   Configure VPDN groups.

Step 3   Configure virtual templates.

Step 4   Configure IP address pools and other IP options.

Example 8-25 shows a sample configuration of an LNS when using compulsory tunnel mode.

Example 8-25 *Sample Configuration of an LNS When Using Compulsory Tunnel Mode*

```
!
hostname mjlnet.london.lac
!
username mark@mjlnet.com password cisco (line 1)
username john@mjlnet.com password disco (line 2)
!
vpdn enable
!
vpdn-group mjlnet.l2tp.vpn
accept-dialin (line 3)
protocol l2tp
virtual-template 1 (line 4)
terminate-from hostname mjlnet.brux.lac (line 5)
l2tp tunnel password 7 01100F175804
!
async-bootp dns-server 10.50.10.55 (line 6)
async-bootp nbns-server 10.50.10.56 (line 7)
!
interface FastEthernet1/0 (line 8)
ip address 192.168.5.1 255.255.255.0 (line 9)
!
interface FastEthernet1/1 (line 10)
ip address 10.50.10.1 255.255.255.0 (line 11)
!
interface Virtual-Template1 (line 12)
ip unnumbered FastEthernet1/1 (line 13)
peer default ip address pool RA.Client.Addrs (line 14)
ppp authentication chap (line 15)
!
ip local pool RA.Client.Addrs 10.60.1.1 10.60.1.100 (line 16)
!
```

Some of the commands configured on the LNS are the same as those configured on the LAC. These commands will not be reexamined here—see the descriptions of these commands earlier in this chapter for more information.

Lines 1 and 2 show the configuration of a local username/password database using the **username** *username* **password** *password* command. These usernames and passwords are used to authenticate remote access user during PPP negotiation.

The **accept-dialin** command (line 3) under the VPDN group is used to configure the LNS to accept L2TP tunnel and session setup initiated by the LAC. This command is the counterpart of the **request-dialin** command on the LAC.

Line 4 shows the **virtual-template** *template-number* command used to configure the virtual template from which virtual access interfaces will be cloned. These virtual access interfaces are used to terminate PPP connections that are tunneled from the remote access clients via the LAC to the LNS (one virtual access interface per PPP connection).

Next, the **terminate-from hostname** *hostname* command in line 5 is used to specify the hostname of the LAC from which L2TP tunnel and session setup will be accepted.

In lines 6 and 7, the **async-bootp dns-server** *address* and **async-bootp nbns-server** *address* commands are used to configure DNS server and NetBIOS Name Server (WINS server) addresses that are supplied to the remote access client during PPP (IPCP) negotiation.

Lines 8 and 9 show the configuration of the interface that provides connectivity (via intervening networks) to the LAC, and line 10 and 11 show the configuration an internal interface.

The virtual template interface is configured in lines 12 to 15. This is the virtual template referenced in the VPDN group using the **virtual-template** command (see line 4).

The **ip unnumbered** *interface* command (line 13) configures the virtual template to "borrow" the IP address from interface fast Ethernet 1/1.

Line 14 shows the **peer default ip address pool** *pool-name* command. This command is used to link to the pool of IP addresses from which an IP address will be assigned to the remote access clients during PPP (IPCP) negotiation.

The **ppp authentication chap** command (line 15) configures the LNS to use CHAP to authenticate remote access clients.

In line 16, the **ip local pool** *pool-name* command configures the IP address pool from which IP addresses are assigned to remote access clients. This is the pool referenced using the **peer default ip address pool** command in line 14.

The sample configuration shown in Example 8-25 includes the configuration of a local username/password database that is used for remote access user authentication. Although a local database works well for a small number of users, it does not scale well. It is common, therefore, to use a AAA server (often a RADIUS server) for user authentication.

If you want to use a RADIUS server for user authentication, you can remove any local username and passwords for remote access users from your LNS configuration and instead configure the commands shown in Example 8-26 on the LNS.

Example 8-26 *Configuration for User Authentication Using a RADIUS Server*

```
aaa new-model
aaa authentication ppp default group radius
aaa authorization network default group radius
radius-server host 10.50.10.31 auth-port 1645 acct-port 1646 key cisco
```

You will notice that these commands are the same as those configured on the LAC in Example 8-26 (the only difference is the IP address of the RADIUS server), and so they are not explained again here. See the explanation of these commands earlier in chapter for more information.

When configuring user accounts on the RADIUS server, make sure that the Service-Type (attribute type 6) is specified as Framed, and the Framed-Protocol (attribute type 7) is specified as PPP. These attributes can be configured under the group to which the user is assigned if you are using a Cisco Secure ACS.

It is also possible to store per-user interface configuration in the form of virtual profiles on a RADIUS. In this case, only the most generic configuration remains on the virtual template interface, and per-user (or per-group) configuration is configured on the RADIUS server.

Per-user interface configuration can be stored on the RADIUS server in the form **cisco-avpair = "lcp:interface-config="**.

Figure 8-63 shows the configuration of per-user (group) interface commands on a Cisco Secure ACS. These commands can be configured under group setup.

Figure 8-63 *Configuration of Per-User (Group) Interface Commands on a Cisco Secure ACS*

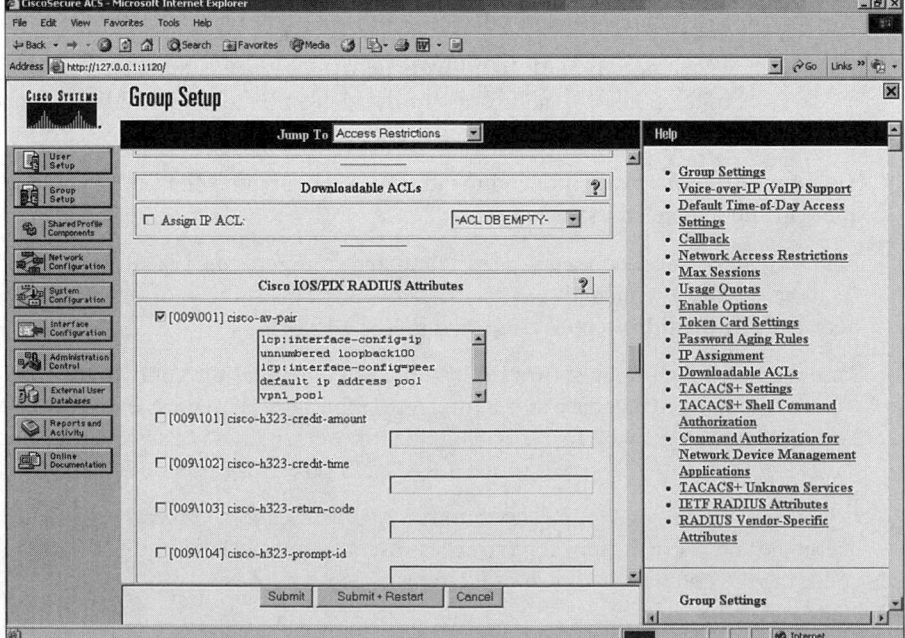

As you can see in Figure 8-63, the commands **ip unnumbered loopback100** and **peer default ip address pool vpn1_pool** are configured within the group setup. When a user that belongs to the group in question connects to the LNS, this configuration is downloaded and applied to the virtual access interface (in addition to any configuration configured on the virtual template).

Example 8-27 shows an equivalent configuration of per-user interface configuration on a Merit RADIUS server.

Example 8-27 *Configuration of Per-User Interface Configuration on a Merit RADIUS Server*

```
mark@mjlnet.com Password = "cisco" Service-Type = Framed-User
Framed-Protocol = PPP
cisco-avpair = "lcp:interface-config=ip unnumbered loopback100\npeer default ip
address pool vpn1_pool"
```

One thing to notice in Example 8-27 is **\n** in **lcp:interface-config=ip unnumbered loopback100\npeer default ip address pool vpn1_pool**. **\n** is simply used to indicate the beginning of a new command line.

Now, if per-user configuration is stored on the RADIUS server, you can remove the corresponding configuration on the LNS. This means that the **ip unnumbered** and **peer default ip address pool** commands can be removed from the configuration shown in Example 8-25 if the per-user interface configuration is stored on the RADIUS server as shown in Figure 8-61/Example 8-27. Example 8-28 shows the resulting virtual template interface configuration.

Example 8-28 *Resulting Virtual Template Interface Configuration When Storing Per-User Configuration on the RADIUS Server*

```
!
interface Virtual-Template1
 no ip address
 no ip redirects
 no ip proxy-arp
 no peer default ip address
 ppp authentication chap
!
```

The **debug vtemplate** (**cloning**) command can be used to examine the cloning of virtual access interfaces from the virtual template when remote access users connect to the LNS.

Example 8-29 shows the output of the **debug vtemplate cloning** command when using the per-user interface configuration on a RADIUS server. Note that only the relevant portion of the output is shown.

Example 8-29 debug vtemplate cloning *Command Output When Using Per-User Interface Configuration*

```
*Jun 23 18:16:31.915 UTC: %LINK-3-UPDOWN: Interface Virtual access2, changed state to
 Up (line 1)
*Jun 23 18:16:31.915 UTC: VT[Vi2]:Added new AAA cloneblk, now cloning from
 vtemplate/AAA (line 2)
*Jun 23 18:16:31.915 UTC: VT[Vi2]:Clone Vaccess from AAA (70 bytes) (line 3)
*Jun 23 18:16:31.915 UTC: VT[Vi2]:ip unnumbered loopback100 (line 4)
*Jun 23 18:16:31.915 UTC: VT[Vi2]:peer default ip address pool vpn1_pool (line 5)
*Jun 23 18:16:31.915 UTC: VT[Vi2]:end
*Jun 23 18:16:32.915 UTC: %LINEPROTO-5-UPDOWN: Line protocol on Interface
 Virtual access2, changed state to up (line 6)
mjlnet.london.lns#
```

Virtual access interface 2 changes state to Up in line 1. The remote access user has connected to the LNS.

Line 2 shows that the LNS is now cloning configuration from the virtual template and from the AAA (RADIUS) server.

In line 3, the LNS begins to clone per-user interface configuration that it has received from the RADIUS server.

The two per-user interface configuration commands configured on the RADIUS server are applied to the virtual access interface in lines 4 and 5.

Finally, in line 6, the line protocol on virtual access 2 changes state to up. The remote access user has completed PPP negotiation with the LNS.

To ensure that per-user interface configuration is downloaded from the RADIUS server and applied to the virtual access interface, only the configuration shown in Example 8-26 is required in newer versions of Cisco IOS Software. In older versions of Cisco IOS Software, the **virtual-profile aaa** command is also required.

Integrating L2TP Remote Access VPNs with MPLS VPNs

Another function of L2TP can be to provide remote access to MPLS Layer 3 VPNs (see Figure 8-64).

L2TP can be used in either compulsory or voluntary tunnel mode to provide remote access to MPLS Layer 3 VPNs. In this model, an MPLS Layer 3 VPN Provider Edge (PE) router also functions as an L2TP LNS.

Figure 8-64 *L2TP Can Be Used to Provide Remote Access to MPLS Layer 3 VPNs*

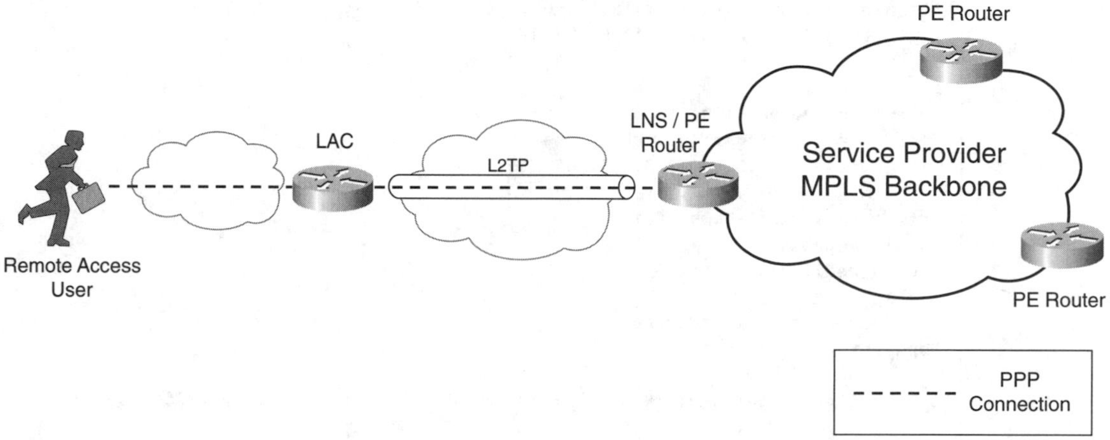

The key to configuring L2TP remote access for MPLS Layer 3 VPNs is to ensure that remote access users are assigned to the correct VPN routing and forwarding table (VRF). You can do this by configuring the **ip vrf forwarding** *vrf-name* command within the per-user (group) configuration that is downloaded from a RADIUS server.

Example 8-30 shows the relevant portion of the configuration on the LNS/PE router.

Example 8-30 *Relevant Configuration on the LNS/PE Router*

```
!
hostname mjlnet.london.lns.pe
!
aaa new-model
!
aaa authentication ppp default group radius
aaa authorization network default group radius
!
ip vrf mjlnet_VPN (line 1)
 rd 65535:100
 route-target export 65535:100
 route-target import 65535:100
!
vpdn enable
!
vpdn-group 1
 accept-dialin
 protocol l2tp
 virtual-template 1
```

continues

Example 8-30 *Relevant Configuration on the LNS/PE Router (Continued)*

```
 terminate-from hostname mjlnet.brux.lac
 l2tp tunnel password 7 01100F175804
!
!
interface Loopback100
 ip vrf forwarding mjlnet_VPN (line 2)
 ip address 172.16.1.1 255.255.255.255
!
interface Virtual-Template1
 no ip address
 no ip redirects
 no ip proxy-arp
 no peer default ip address
 ppp authentication chap
!
ip local pool vpn1_pool 10.90.10.1 10.90.10.100 group mjlnet_VPN (line 3)
!
!
!
radius-server host 10.10.10.51 auth-port 1645 acct-port 1646 key 7 121A0C041104
!
```

The **ip vrf** *vrf-name* command in highlighted line 1 is used to configure a VRF with the specified name.

In highlighted line 2, the **ip vrf forwarding** *vrf-name* command assigns an interface to the specified VRF.

In highlighted line 3, the familiar **ip local pool** command is used to configure an IP address pool. However, in this case, the **group** keyword is used to allow multiple pools (often one per VRF) to overlap.

Although not shown in Example 8-30, it is often a good idea to redistribute an aggregate route corresponding to the IP address pool for each VRF into Multiprotocol Border Gateway Protocol (MP-BGP). An alternative is to redistribute the individual host routes that are injected into the VRF when a remote access client connects to the LNS/PE router (using the **redistribute connected** command); if there are a large number of remote access clients, however, this is not a scalable solution.

For more information on the configuration of MPLS Layer 3 VPNs, see Chapter 4, "Designing MPLS Layer 3 Site-to-Site VPNs," and Chapter 5, "Advanced MPLS L3VPN Deployment Considerations."

Figure 8-65 shows the relevant configuration on a RADIUS server.

Figure 8-65 *Relevant Configuration on a RADIUS Server*

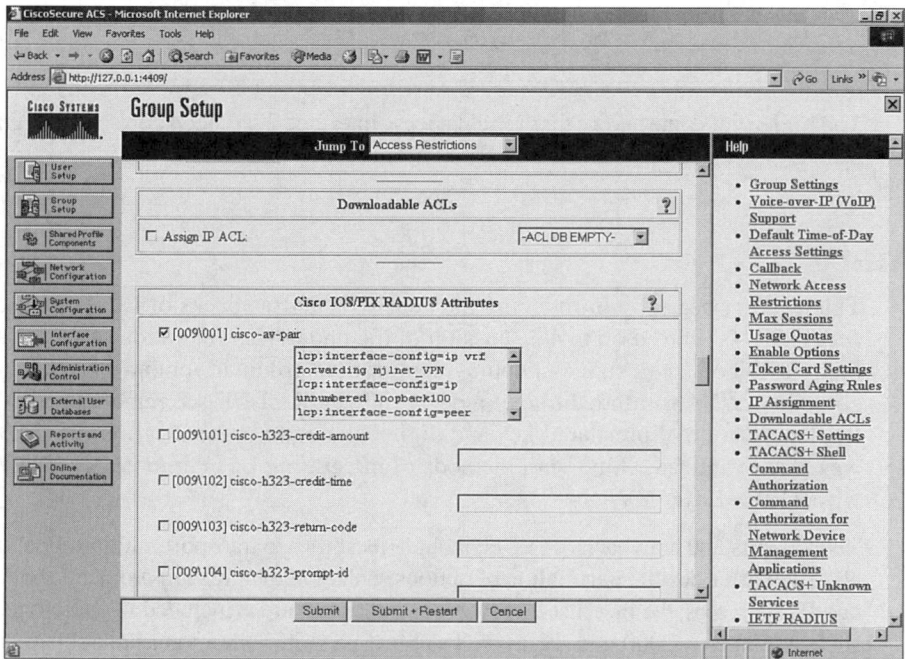

A comparison of the configuration shown in Figure 8-65 to that in Figure 8-61 reveals that the only difference is that the **lcp:interface-config=ip vrf forwarding mjlnet_VPN** command has been added. This command ensures that the virtual access interface that is created when a remote access client connects will be assigned to the mjlnet_VPN VRF—this corresponds to the VRF created in Example 8-30, highlighted line 1.

Example 8-31 shows an equivalent Merit RADIUS configuration.

Example 8-31 *Configuration of Per-User Interface Configuration on a Merit RADIUS Server*

```
mark@mjlnet.com Password = "cisco" Service-Type = Framed-User
Framed-Protocol = PPP
cisco-avpair = "lcp:interface-config=ip vrf forwarding mjlnet_VPN\nip unnumbered
   loopback100\npeer default ip address pool vpn1_pool"
```

You can use the **show ip vrf interfaces** *vrf-name* command to verify the correct assignment of a virtual access interface to a VRF, as demonstrated in Example 8-32.

Example 8-32 *Verifying the Correct Assignment of a Virtual Access Interface to a VRF*

```
mjlnet.london.lns.pe#show ip vrf interfaces mjlnet_VPN
Interface      IP-Address  VRF         Protocol
Loopback100    172.16.1.1  mjlnet_VPN       up
Virtual access2 172.16.1.1  mjlnet_VPN       up
mjlnet.london.lns.pe#
```

The highlighted line shows that virtual access interface 2 has been correctly assigned to the mjlnet_VPN VRF.

Summary

This chapter began by introducing the benefits and drawbacks of L2TP remote access VPNs, moved on to a discussion of the underlying operation of L2TP, and then described the design and deployment of both voluntary/client-initiated and compulsory/NAS-initiated tunnel mode L2TP and L2TP/IPsec remote access VPNs. Implementation of preshared key and digital signature authentication for L2TP/IPsec was also examined, along with methods of integrating L2TP remote access VPNs with MPLS Layer 3 VPNs.

The benefits and drawbacks of L2TP include its ability to transport multiprotocol traffic; its ability to offer flexible negotiation of options such as authentication protocols, compression, and IP addresses; the fact that L2TP/IPsec client software is included in operating systems such as Windows 2000 and XP, as well as MacOS X; its ability to back haul large numbers of PPP connections; the fact that L2TP remote access VPNs are completely IETF standards based; and the fact that L2TP/IPsec can potentially add a relatively large amount of overhead to encapsulated packets.

L2TP/IPsec voluntary/client-initiated tunnel mode remote access VPNs can be configured to use either preshared key or digital certificate (IKE) authentication. L2TP/IPsec remote access VPNs using preshared key authentication are less secure but relatively simple to deploy (depending on the remote access VPN client operating system), whereas L2TP/IPsec remote access VPNs using digital certificate authentication more secure but are relatively complex to deploy.

Compulsory/NAS-initiated tunnel mode L2TP remote access VPNs can be used to transport large number of PPP connections and can be scaled using tunnel definitions and per-user interface configuration stored on AAA servers.

Finally, L2TP can be integrated with MPLS Layer 3 VPNs and used to provide remote access by downloading per-user (group) configuration including (virtual access) interface to VRF assignment from a AAA server.

Review Questions

1 What are the two modes of operation for L2TP remote access VPNs?

2 What are some of the main advantages and disadvantages of L2TP VPNs?

3 How can security be configured for voluntary tunnel mode L2TP remote access VPNs?

4 What is the purpose of the **accept-dialin** command?

5 What is split tunneling, and why is it a potential security risk?

6 IPsec can be used to secure L2TP tunnels, and digital certificates can be used to authenticate IPsec peers. On the VPN 3000 concentrator, what are the two basic methods of enrolling and obtaining digital certificates from a CA?

7 When deploying Cisco IOS L2TP client-initiated tunneling (voluntary tunnel mode), what is the main advantage of L2TPv3 over L2TPv2?

8 How can you debug IKE negotiation packet by packet on a Windows 2000/XP client (examining packet detail)?

9 In compulsory tunnel mode, how is PPP authentication typically performed on the LAC?

10 What are the two methods of configuring tunnel definitions on a RADIUS server?

CHAPTER 9

Designing and Deploying IPsec Remote Access and Teleworker VPNs

IPsec remote access VPNs enable teleworkers and other remote access users to access resources at a central site and experience a similar level of functionality that they would experience if they were physically present at that central site.

Figure 9-1 illustrates IPsec remote access VPNs.

Figure 9-1   *IPsec Remote Access VPNs*

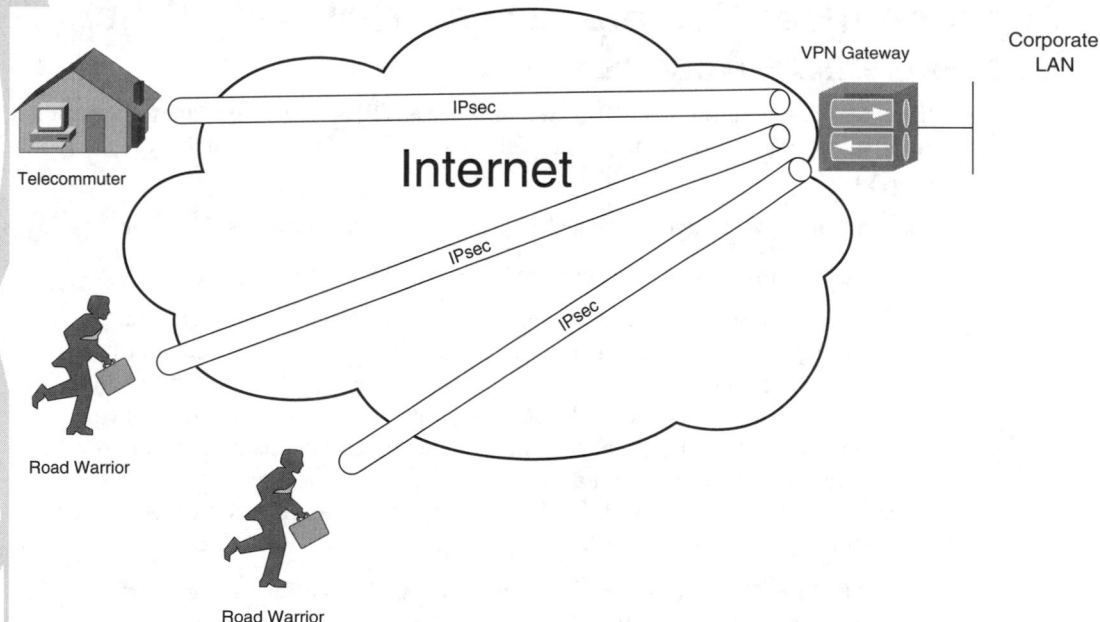

IPsec remote access VPNs can be deployed in two ways:

- **With software clients**—"Road warriors" and other remote access VPN users establish a VPN connection directly from their laptops, workstations, or other devices to the VPN gateway at the central site.

- **With hardware clients**—Telecommuters or users at a small remote site use a router or other hardware to establish a VPN connection to the VPN gateway at the central site. Telecommuter devices such as PCs make use of the VPN connection from the hardware client to access resources at the central site.

It is worth noting that an IPsec remote access VPN deployment can make use of both software and hardware clients to establish VPN connections, depending on the particular requirements of remote access users.

This chapter discusses the design and configuration of IPsec remote access VPNs using both software and hardware clients.

NOTE   If you do not already have a good understanding of the operation of IPsec, it may be a good idea to read Chapter 6, "Deploying Site-to-Site IPsec VPNs," prior to reading this chapter.

Comparing IPsec Remote Access VPNs with Other Types of Remote Access VPNs

Before deciding to implement IPsec remote access VPNs, it is important to understand their advantages and disadvantages, as well as how they compare to other types of remote access VPN.

Some of the main advantages and disadvantages of IPsec remote access VPNs are as follows:

- IPsec can provide strong security for remote access VPN traffic.

  The precise level of security offered by IPsec depends on a number of factors, *including* the type of Internet Key Exchange (IKE) phase 1 negotiation (main or aggressive mode), the type of IKE phase 1 authentication, the form of any preshared keys, the types and levels of security associated with any Public Key Infrastructure (PKI), the type of user authentication, the type (and key lengths) of encryption and hashing algorithms, whether Perfect Forward Secrecy (PFS) is used, and the duration of security association (SA) lifetimes.

  L2TP/IPsec (RFC 3193) and SSL remote access VPNs offer similar security to IPsec remote access VPNs.

- Extensions to IPsec that provide additional functionality such as IKE Extended Authentication (Xauth) and ISAKMP Configuration Method (Mode Config) are not industry standards, and therefore are not implemented on all operating systems or devices (this might cause some vendor interoperability issues).

  L2TP/IPsec remote access VPNs, on the other hand, rely on industry (IETF) standards.

Secure Sockets Layer (SSL) versions 2 and 3 are de facto standards, and Transport Layer Security (TLS) is an industry (IETF) standard.

- The Cisco VPN Client (which provides IPsec remote access VPN functionality) must be installed (and administered) on each remote access VPN client workstation.

  Operating systems such as Windows 2000, Windows XP, and MacOS X include an L2TP/IPsec remote access VPN client by default.

  Clientless SSL remote access VPNs do not require the installation of specific VPN client software.

- IPsec remote access VPNs, L2TP/IPsec remote access VPNs, and SSL remote access VPNs using the Cisco SSL VPN Client offer a similar level of functionality for remote users that they would experience if they were at their office or central site. Clientless SSL remote access VPNs, on the other hand, offer only a subset of this functionality.

- IPsec remote access VPNs provide IP unicast transport between VPN clients and gateways. L2TP/IPsec remote access VPNs, on the other hand, offer multiprotocol (IP, IPX, and so on) unicast and multicast transport between VPN clients and gateways.

- The Cisco VPN Client allows the integration of features such as enforcement of firewall type, antivirus software type and level, and OS service pack level on client operating systems, as well as the enforcement of split-tunneling (and split-DNS) policies. Additionally, Cisco VPN Client software can be auto-updated when remote access VPN users connect to a Cisco remote access VPN gateway such as the Cisco VPN 3000 concentrator or the Cisco ASA 5500.

Understanding IKE in an IPsec Remote Access VPN Environment

The purpose of IKE negotiation is to negotiate cryptographic parameters and algorithms, exchange keying material, and authenticate IPsec peer devices. When using IKE in an IPsec remote access VPN environment, however, a number of additional challenges must be addressed.

NOTE   This section specifically discusses some of the challenges when using IKEv1 in a remote access VPN environment. The new IKEv2 specification is designed to address many of these issues, and at the time of this writing, Cisco has stated that it will begin to integrate IKEv2 in its products in forthcoming software versions.

For more information on IKEv2, see Chapter 6.

The main issues and shortcomings relating to IKEv1 to address in an IPsec remote access VPN environment are as follows:

- Issues relating to user authentication
- Issues relating to negotiation of attributes such as IP addresses, DNS server addresses, and WINS servers addresses

The resolution of these challenges is discussed in the sections that follow. But, before examining these issues, it is worth taking a brief look at the IKE (ISAKMP) message format.

Figure 9-2 illustrates the overall IKE (ISAKMP) message format.

Figure 9-2 *Overall IKE (ISAKMP) Message Format*

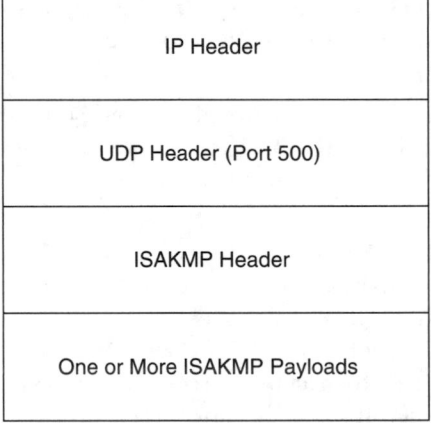

As shown in Figure 9-2, the overall ISAKMP message format consists of the following:

- An IP header
- An UDP header (port 500 [ISAKMP])
- An ISAKMP header
- One or more ISAKMP payloads

Figure 9-3 shows the ISAKMP header format.

Figure 9-3 *ISAKMP Header Format*

```
0 1 2 3 4 5 6 7 8 9 0 1 2 3 4 5 6 7 8 9 0 1 2 3 4 5 6 7 8 9 0 1
```

Initiator Cookie				
Responder Cookie				
Next Payload	MjVer	MnVer	Exchange Type	Flags
Message ID				
Length				

The ISAKMP header fields are as follows:

- **Initiator Cookie**—Cookie sent by the initiator of SA creation, notification, or deletion.

  Cookies can be used to verify the existence of an IPsec peer and act as identifiers (used in the course of IKE negotiation). Cookies can also help to prevent replay attacks (when an attacker resends ISAKMP messages).

  In a remote access VPN environment, the initiator is almost always the remote access VPN client.

- **Responder Cookie**—The cookie of the responder.

  The responder is typically the VPN gateway in a remote access VPN environment.

- **Next Payload**—This field indicates the type of the first payload.

  Each ISAKMP message contains one or more payloads. ISAKMP payloads contain information such as security attributes (for example, IKE policy information), key exchange information, identification information, certificates, vendor-specific feature information, and so on.

- **Major Version (MjVer) and Minor Version (MnVer)**—These two fields are used to indicate the IKE version.

- **Exchange Type**—This indicates the IKE exchange type. Exchange types include main mode, aggressive mode, and quick mode.

- **Flags**—There are three flags contained in this field:

  - **Encryption flag**—This flag indicates that the ISAKMP payloads following the header are encrypted.

  - **Commit flag**—This flag is used to ensure that encrypted messages are not received before SA establishment is complete.

  - **Authentication-only flag**—This flag indicates that this an informational message that is authenticated but not encrypted.

- **Message ID**—This field contains a unique, randomly generated ID that identifies an IKE phase 2 negotiation. During IKE phase 1, the Message ID is 0.

- **Length**—This field specifies the length of the ISAKMP message, including header and payloads.

As mentioned earlier, each ISAKMP message consists of the ISAKMP message header, together with one or more payloads. Each of these payloads is prefixed by a generic payload header (see Figure 9-4).

Figure 9-4 *ISAKMP Generic Payload Header Format*

	1	2	3
0 1 2 3 4 5 6 7 8	9 0 1 2 3 4 5	6 7 8 9 0 1 2 3 4 5	6 7 8 9 0 1
Next Payload	Reserved	Payload Length	

The fields in the ISAKMP generic payload header format are as follows:

- **Next Payload**—When an ISAKMP message contains more that one payload, these payloads are daisy-chained together, with the Next Payload field in the header of the preceding payload indicating the contents of the following payload. If there is no following payload, the Next Payload field contains a value of 0.

- **Reserved**—This field is unused, and must be set to 0.

- **Payload Length**—This field specifies the length of this payload (including its generic payload header).

Now that you have an understanding of the ISAKMP message format, it is time to take a look at issues relating to IKEv1 in a remote access VPN environment.

Resolving Issues Relating to User Authentication

IKEv1 phase 1 exchanges allow IPsec devices to authenticate each other but do not include any mechanism by which remote access VPN users may be authenticated.

The distinction between the authentication of a remote access VPN device (machine) and user is important because if only the device is authenticated, it would be possible for someone to steal a legitimate user's workstation and thereby gain access to the corporate network via the VPN. If the user of the device is also authenticated, someone who steals a legitimate user's workstation/laptop will not be able to automatically gain access to the corporate network (assuming, that is, that the legitimate user's authentication credentials are not stored on the workstation/laptop).

There are three main methods by which a VPN gateway may authenticate remote access VPN users:

- Extended Authentication with IKE (Xauth)
- Hybrid Authentication Mode for IKE ("Hybrid Authentication")
- IKE Challenge/Response for Authenticated Cryptographic Keys (CRACK)

These methods of remote access VPN user authentication are discussed in the following three sections.

Extended Authentication Within IKE (Xauth)

The Xauth mechanism provides a means for a VPN client user to authenticate him/herself to a VPN gateway. The precise type of authentication can vary—it could, for example, be a simple username/password authentication, challenge/response authentication, two-factor authentication, or a one-time password (OTP).

Xauth takes advantage of mechanisms and message types defined by the ISAKMP Configuration Method (described later in this chapter) and makes two minor modifications to IKEv1 phase 1 negotiation:

- Vendor ID payloads that indicate the specific version (Internet Draft) of Xauth being used are sent by the IPsec peers (this ensures consistent operation of Xauth).

- Authentication method IDs that specify the IKEv1 phase 1 authentication method, the fact that the Xauth is required after IKEv1 phase 1, and the IPsec peer that must be authenticated using Xauth (almost always the VPN client) are sent by IPsec peers.

Xauth takes place only after IKEv1 phase 1 negotiation has completed successfully (and optionally periodically thereafter). When Xauth has completed, IKEv1 phase 2 negotiation takes place.

Figure 9-5 depicts Xauth.

Figure 9-5   *Xauth*

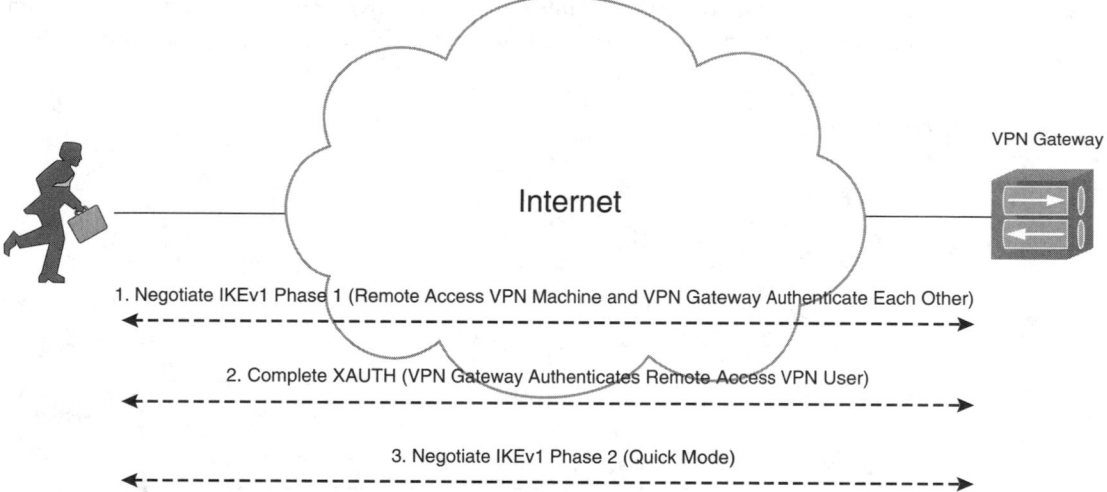

Xauth is supported on Cisco devices including Cisco VPN 3000 concentrators, Cisco 5500 Adaptive Security Appliances, Cisco IOS routers, PIX firewalls, as well as on the Cisco VPN Client.

It is worth noting that the SA created during IKE phase 1 protects Xauth. Xauth is vulnerable if a weak preshared key is used to authenticate IPsec peers during IKE phase 1 and, in particular, if aggressive mode is used during IKE phase 1. This is because unlike when using main mode, certain information is exchanged unencrypted when using aggressive mode, and this makes recovering a weak preshared key much easier than when using main mode.

Hybrid Authentication Mode for IKE

When using Hybrid Authentication mode for IKE (Hybrid Authentication), IKEv1 phase 1 is used to authenticate the VPN gateway only (using either RSA or DSA digital signature authentication). This is a modification to the regular IKEv1 phase 1, which is designed to authenticate both IPsec peers (both the VPN gateway and the VPN client). Both main mode and aggressive mode can be used for IKEv1 phase 1 exchange in conjunction with Hybrid Authentication.

At this point, it is important to note that although RSA or DSA digital signature authentication is used to authenticate the VPN gateway during IKEv1 phase 1, it is not necessary to deploy a full PKI. VPN gateways, but *not* VPN clients, need to enroll with CA servers and obtain identity certificates.

When IKEv1 phase 1 is complete, a Transaction exchange begins. This Transaction exchange consists of an ISAKMP Xauth exchange and serves to authenticate the VPN client.

So, the VPN gateway is authenticated during IKEv1 phase 1, and the VPN client is authenticated using ISAKMP Xauth immediately after IKEv1 phase 1 is complete. If Xauth is successful, IKEv1 phase 2 negotiation takes place. Figure 9-6 illustrates Hybrid Authentication.

Figure 9-6 *Hybrid Authentication*

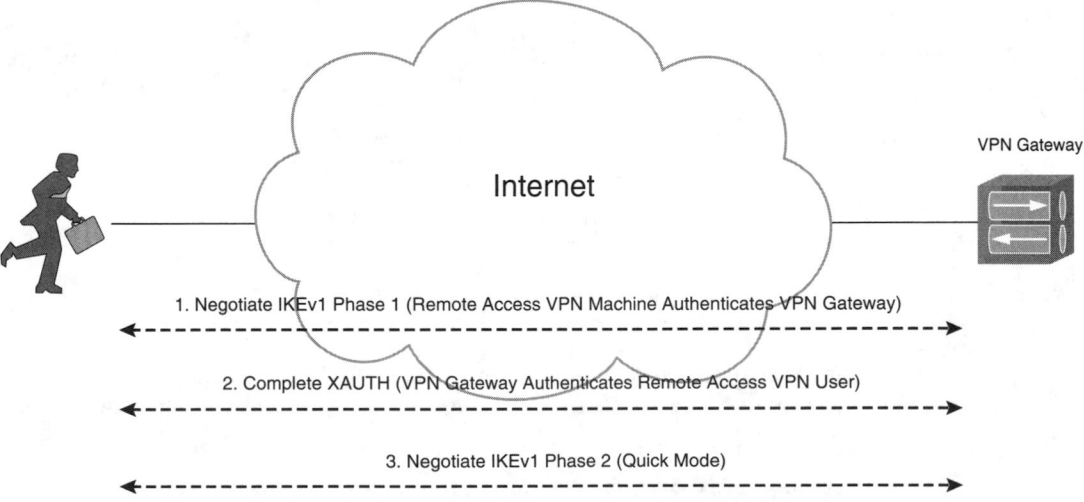

Cisco Hybrid Authentication is supported on the Cisco VPN 3000 concentrator and the Cisco VPN Client. It is not supported on Cisco IOS routers or ASA 5500s, but software releases for these platforms will add support for IKEv2.

Note that Hybrid Authentication as implemented on the Cisco VPN 3000 concentrator and Cisco VPN Client includes additional authentication using a group name and password.

Authentication using the group name and password is used simply to associate remote access VPN clients with the appropriate group on the Cisco VPN concentrator.

Hybrid Authentication is implemented on Cisco VPN 3000 concentrators to address the potential weakness of regular Xauth as described in the previous section. It is also implemented to address a shortcoming of group authentication using preshared keys, which is potentially insecure because of the fact that the preshared key is common to a number of clients and a VPN gateway (it is relatively widely known and therefore more insecure), and because a remote access VPN client is not sure that it is connecting to the real VPN gateway or another device masquerading as the real VPN gateway (because the preshared key is known by a number of other clients as well as the real VPN gateway).

IKE Challenge/Response for Authenticated Cryptographic Keys (CRACK)

IKE CRACK consists of a modified IKE phase 1 negotiation that includes user authentication (something not included in standard IKEv1 phase 1).

When using CRACK, one of the IPsec peers (the VPN client) authenticates using a secret key type user authentication method, and the other IPsec peer (the VPN gateway) authenticates uses public-key authentication (optionally involving digital certificates).

When IKEv1 phase 1 (including CRACK) has completed successfully, IKEv1 phase 2 negotiation continues as normal.

CRACK extends the IKE standard by defining a new IKE authentication method (IKE_ A_CRACK) as well as a new IKE payload (Challenge/Response payload [CHRE]). CRACK can operate in conjunction with IKEv1 phase 1 main mode and aggressive mode negotiation.

As with Hybrid Authentication, CRACK does not require the deployment of a full PKI.

Figure 9-7 illustrates CRACK.

Figure 9-7   *CRACK*

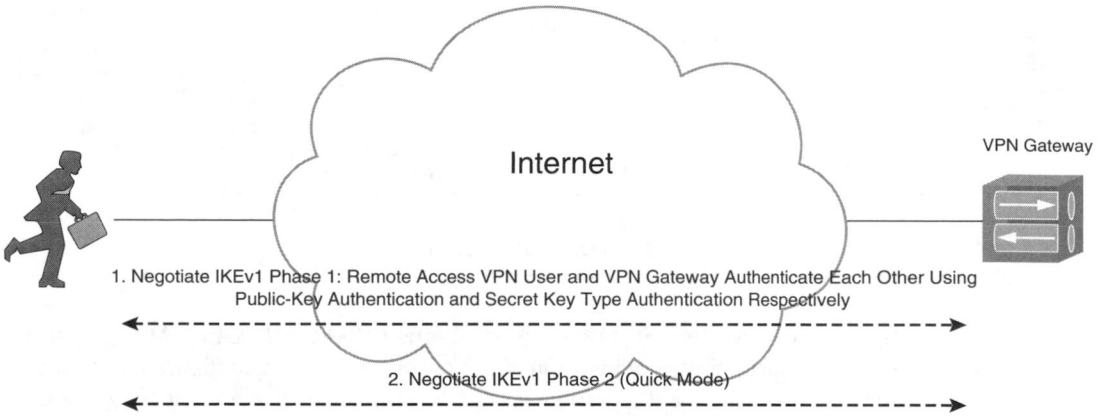

CRACK is supported only on the Cisco VPN 3000 concentrator beginning in software release 4.7 for use in conjunction with the VPN client on the Nokia 92xx Communicator series phones. At the time of this writing, CRACK is not supported on Cisco IOS routers, the ASA 5500, or by the Cisco VPN Client.

Resolving Issues Relating to Negotiation of Attributes Such as IP Addresses, DNS Server Addresses, and WINS Server Addresses

Because the basic IKEv1 specification cannot accomplish the assignment of configuration attributes such as IP addresses and DNS/WINS server addresses, ISAKMP Configuration Method (also known as *Mode Config*) was introduced. ISAKMP Configuration Method adds a new type of payload and a new type of ISAKMP message exchange. The new payload carries configuration attributes and is called the *Attribute payload*. The new type of exchange enables the assignment of configuration attributes and is called a *Transaction exchange*.

ISAKMP Configuration Method introduces two methods of configuration attribute assignment:

- **Request (ISAKMP_CFG_REQUEST) / Reply (ISAKMP_CFG_REPLY)**—This method involves the exchange of Request and Replay messages. The Request message is used to request or suggest a particular configuration attribute, and the Replay message is used to supply or confirm the requested attribute.

    Figure 9-8 illustrates the Request/Reply (pull) method of configuration attribute assignment.

Figure 9-8   *The Request/Reply (Pull) Method of Configuration Attribute Assignment*

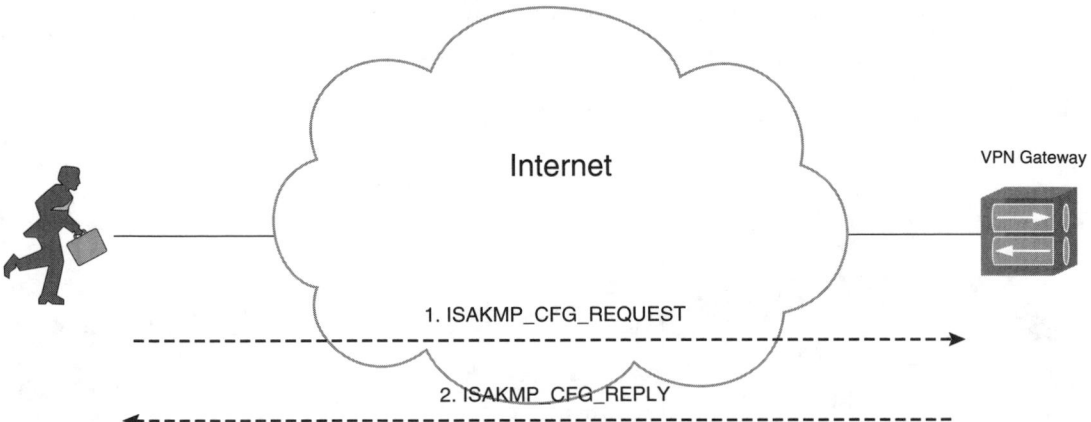

- **Set (ISAKMP_CFG_SET) / Acknowledgment (ISAKMP_CFG_ACK)**—When using this method of configuration attribute assignment, the configuration manager initiates the assignment of attributes, and the host acknowledges that assignment.

Figure 9-9 shows the Set/Acknowledgment (push) method of configuration attribute assignment.

Figure 9-9   *Set/Acknowledgment (Push) Method of Configuration Attribute Assignment*

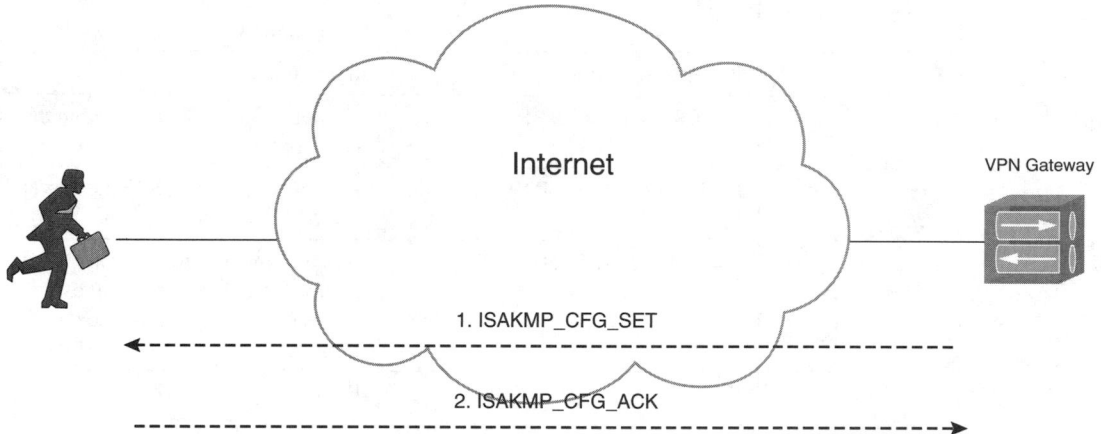

Table 9-1 shows common configuration attributes that can be assigned using ISAKMP Configuration Method.

Table 9-1   *Common Configuration Attributes That Can Be Assigned Using the ISAKMP Configuration Method*

Attribute Value	Attribute	Description
0	RESERVED	Unused
1	INTERNAL_IP4_ADDRESS	Specifies an address within the internal network
2	INTERNAL_IP4_NETMASK	Internal network's netmask
3	INTERNAL_IP4_DNS	Address of a DNS server within the network
4	INTERNAL_IP4_NBNS	Address of a NetBIOS Name Server (WINS) within the network
5	INTERNAL_ADDRESS_EXPIRY	Specifies the number of seconds that the host can use the internal IP address
6	INTERNAL_IP4_DHCP	Instructs the host to send any internal DHCP requests to the address contained within the attribute
7	APPLICATION_VERSION	Version or application information of the IPsec host

continues

Table 9-1 *Common Configuration Attributes That Can Be Assigned Using the ISAKMP Configuration Method (Continued)*

Attribute Value	Attribute	Description
8	INTERNAL_IP6_ADDRESS	Specifies an address within the internal network
9	INTERNAL_IP6_NETMASK	Internal network's netmask
10	INTERNAL_IP6_DNS	Address of a DNS server within the network
11	INTERNAL_IP6_NBNS	Address of a NetBIOS Name Server (WINS) within the network
12	INTERNAL_IP6_DHCP	Instructs the host to send any internal DHCP requests to the address contained within the attribute
13	INTERNAL_IP4_SUBNET	Protected subnetworks that this edge device protects
14	SUPPORTED_ATTRIBUTES	Attributes supported
15	INTERNAL_IP6_SUBNET	Protected subnetworks that this edge device protects
16-16383	Reserved for future use	Future use
16384-32767	Reserved for private use	Private use

Deploying IPsec Remote Access VPNs Using Preshared Key and Digital Signature Authentication

Now that you understand some of the challenges associated with the deployment of IPsec remote access VPNs, it is time move on to discussing their deployment.

The following sections discuss the configuration of IPsec remote access VPNs using preshared key and digital signature authentication.

Implementing IPsec Remote Access VPNs Using Preshared Key Authentication

The deployment of IPsec remote access VPNs using preshared keys is pretty simple. To configure an IPsec remote access VPN, you must configure both the IPsec VPN gateway and the IPsec remote access VPN clients. The configuration of the VPN gateway and the remote access VPN clients is described in the following two sections.

Configuring an IPsec Remote Access VPN Gateway for Preshared Key Authentication

This section describes the configuration of Cisco VPN 3000 concentrators, Cisco IOS routers, and the Cisco ASA 5500 IPsec VPN gateways.

Cisco VPN 3000 Concentrator as an IPsec Remote Access VPN Gateway Using Preshared Key Authentication

The following steps comprise the configuration of a Cisco VPN 3000 concentrator as an IPsec remote access VPN gateway:

Step 1   Specify an IP address pool or another form of IP address assignment.

Step 2   Configure a group for IPsec remote access VPN users.

Step 3   Configure user accounts for remote access VPN users.

Step 4   Optionally modify IPsec/IKE parameters.

If you have already read Chapter 8, "Designing and Implementing L2TPv2 and L2TPv3 Remote Access VPNs," the preceding steps will seem familiar. In fact, these *high-level* steps are the same as those described in Chapter 8. The detail is a little different, however.

Step 1: Specify an IP Address Pool or Other Form of IP Address Assignment   The Cisco VPN 3000 concentrator can assign IP addresses, together with other information such as DNS and WINS server addresses, to remote access VPN clients during ISAKMP Mode Config negotiation (assuming IKEv1 negotiation).

Note that IP addresses assigned by a VPN gateway (Cisco VPN 3000 concentrator) to IPsec remote access VPN clients are applied by the clients to their VPN tunnel interfaces (virtual adapters), not to their physical interfaces.

To configure a local IP address pool from which to assign addresses to IPsec remote access VPN clients, you need to go to **Configuration > System > Address Management > Pools** (see Figure 9-10).

In Figure 9-10, an address pool ranging from 10.30.20.1 to 10.30.20.150 and with mask 255.255.255.0 is configured. After you have configured the range, just click the **Add** button and the pool will be entered into the Cisco VPN 3000 concentrator's configuration.

Although the address pool is entered into the configuration file when you click the **Add** button, you also have to enable the pool by going to **Configuration > System > Address Management > Assignment** and check **Use Address Pools**, as shown in Figure 9-11.

Figure 9-10 *Configuration of a Local IP Address Pool*

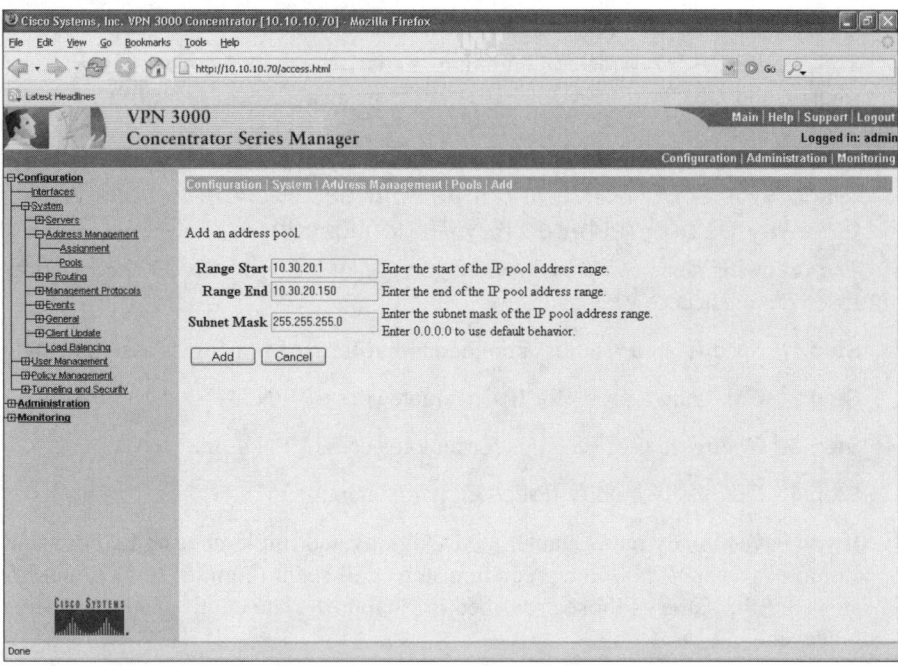

Figure 9-11 *Enabling Local Address Pool Assignment*

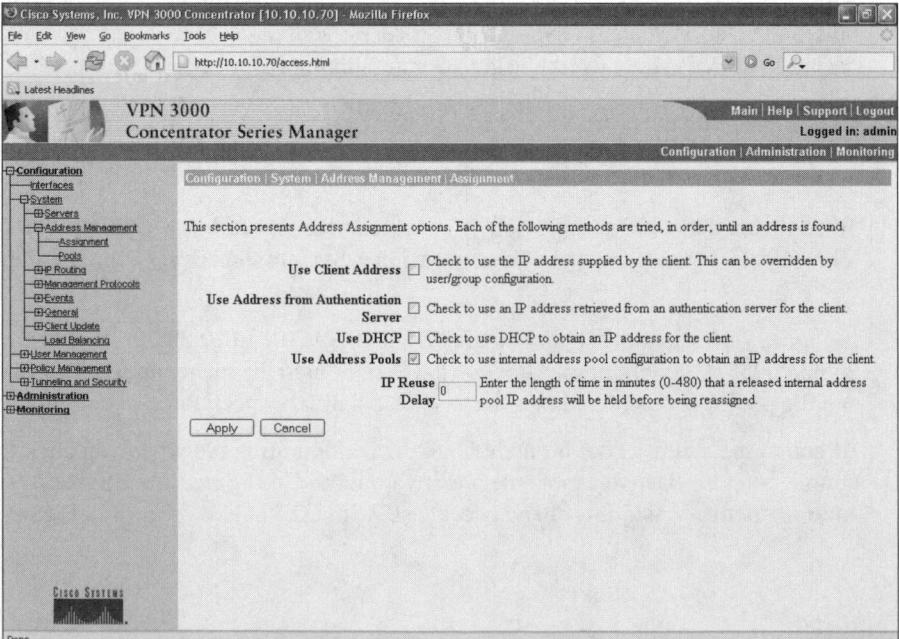

One look at the screen shown in Figure 9-11, and you will see that not only is it possible to assign IP addresses to IPsec remote access VPN clients from an address pool configured on the Cisco VPN 3000 concentrator, but it is also possible to allow clients to specify their own IP addresses, use an authentication server (such as RADIUS), or use DHCP.

When you have checked the **Use Address Pools** box as shown in Figure 9-11, click **Apply**. The Cisco VPN 3000 concentrator is now ready to assign IP addresses.

Step 2: Configure a Group for IPsec Remote Access VPN Users   Having
configured a method of IP address assignment, it is now time to configure a group for IPsec remote access VPN user. To do this, go to **Configuration > User Management > Groups**, click **Add Group**, and you will see the screen shown in Figure 9-12.

Figure 9-12   *Configuring a Group for IPsec Remote Access VPN Users (Identity Tab)*

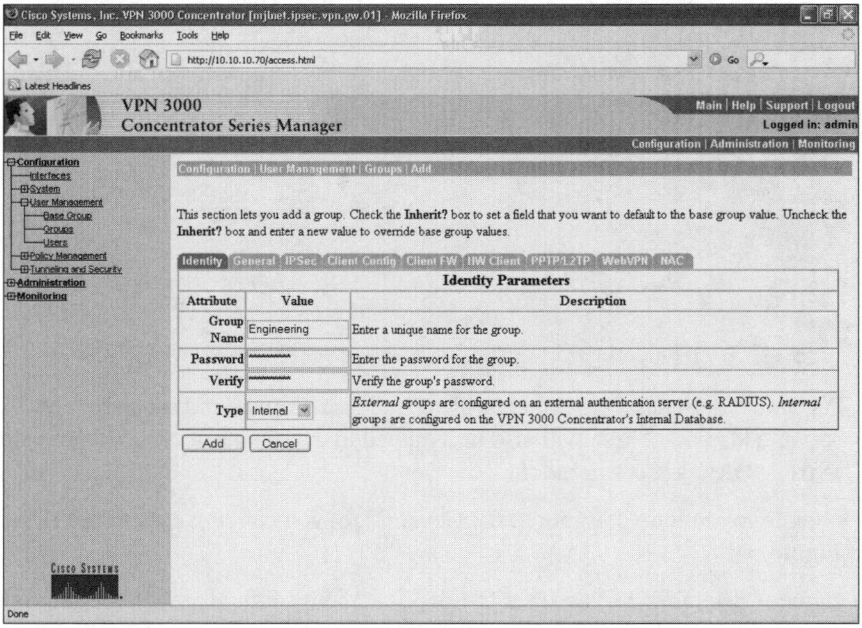

On the Identity tab, specify a group name and a password. This password is, in fact, the preshared key that is used for IKE phase 1 authentication of remote access VPN clients.

NOTE   Although there are no precise rules as to the best composition of preshared keys, to make preshared keys as secure as possible, it is a good idea to make them a random combination of numbers, upper- and lowercase characters, and punctuation characters. It is also a good idea to make preshared keys at least 10 characters long.

Note that the preshared keys shown in various figures and examples in this chapter are not secure and are used for illustrative purposes only.

Next, click the General tab, and ensure that **IPSec** is selected in the Tunneling Protocols section (see Figure 9-13).

Figure 9-13 *Configuring the General Tab*

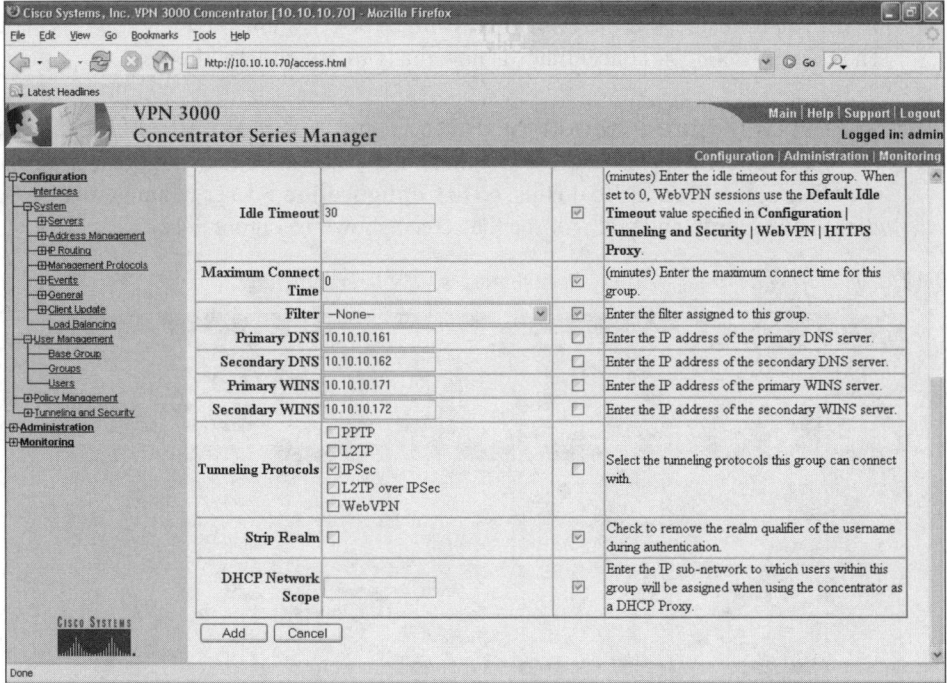

As shown in Figure 9-13, you can also configure primary and secondary DNS and WINS server addresses. These will also be assigned to the remote access VPN clients during ISAKMP Mode Configuration.

Now that you have configured the General tab, you can move on to the IPSec tab (see Figure 9-14).

In the IPSec tab, select an IPsec SA to protect user traffic that will be sent over the VPN tunnel between the remote access VPN clients and the Cisco VPN 3000 concentrator (this IPsec SA is negotiated during IKEv1 phase 2).

Also, ensure that you select the **Remote Access** tunnel type as well as the **Internal** authentication type (authentication via the locally configured username/password database).

Figure 9-14 *Configuring the IPSec Tab*

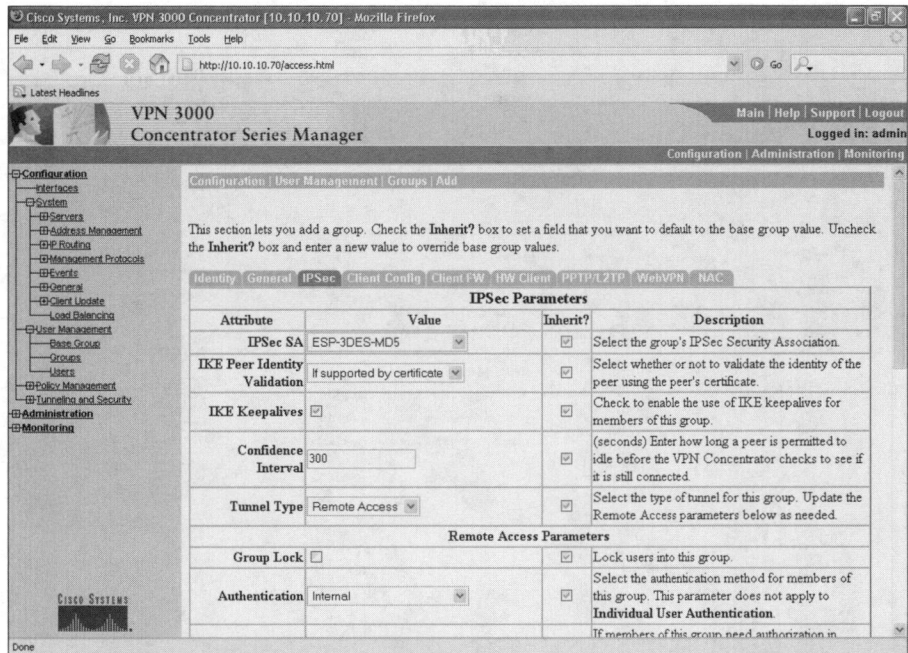

Step 3: Configure User Accounts for Remote Access VPN Users

Now that you have configured the group for IPsec remote access VPN users, you are ready to configure individual remote access VPN user accounts. You can do so by going to **Configuration > User Management > Users** and clicking the **Add** button. You then see the screen shown in Figure 9-15.

Type a username and password, and assign the user to the group that you have just configured for IPsec remote access VPN users by selecting the group from the drop-down box.

The password that you configure in the Identity tab is used to authenticate the user rather than the IPsec remote access VPN machine (which is authenticated by the group password [preshared key] during IKE negotiation). The user is authenticated using the Xauth mechanism during IKEv1 negotiation.

Finally, click the **Add** button, and the user is ready to go.

Note that is also possible to authenticate remote access VPN users using external authentication servers. This can be accomplished by specifying authentication servers under **Configuration > Systems > Servers > Authentication** and then configuring the appropriate authentication type in the IPSec tab for the appropriate group under **Configuration > User Management > Groups**.

Figure 9-15 *Configuring IPsec Remote Access VPN User Accounts (Identity Tab)*

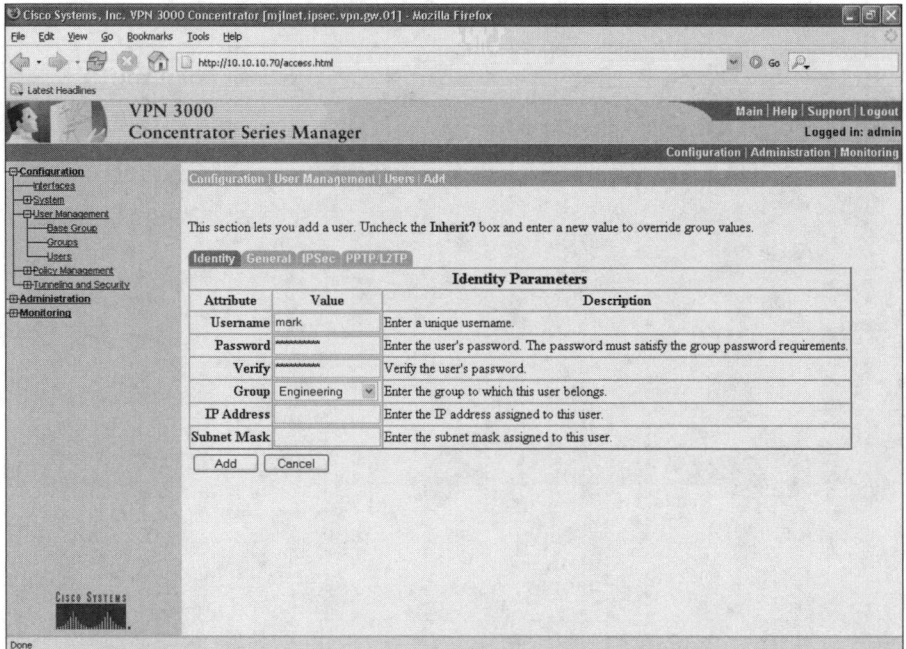

Step 4: Modify IPsec/IKE Parameters (Optional) A final task that you can

perform on the Cisco VPN 3000 concentrator is to modify the proposals (parameters) that
are negotiated using IKE (phase 1 and 2).

The IKE proposals specified on the Cisco VPN concentrator must match those used by the
IPsec remote access VPN clients. You can modify those used by the Cisco VPN 3000
concentrator by going to **Configuration > Policy Management > Traffic Management >
SAs**, selecting the IPsec SA that you specified under the group (see Figure 9-14 on
page 821), and clicking the **Modify** button.

It is useful just to run down each section of the screen (Figure 9-16). The top section of the
screen shows the SA name and the granularity of the SA.

The next section shows IKEv1 phase 2 parameters, including the authentication algorithm,
the encryption algorithm, the encapsulation mode, whether or not PFS is enabled, the
method by which the SAs lifetime is measured, and the data and time lifetimes.

The final section shows the IKE phase 1 parameters, including the IP address of the IKE
peer (only relevant for site-to-site VPN configurations), the method of IKEv1 phase 1
negotiation (aggressive or main mode), the digital certificate used for digital signature
authentication (if relevant), whether the Cisco VPN concentrator's identity certificate alone

or the complete certificate chain is supplied to the remote access VPN client during IKE phase 1 authentication, and the name of the IKE phase 1 proposal.

Figure 9-16 *Modifying IKE Proposals*

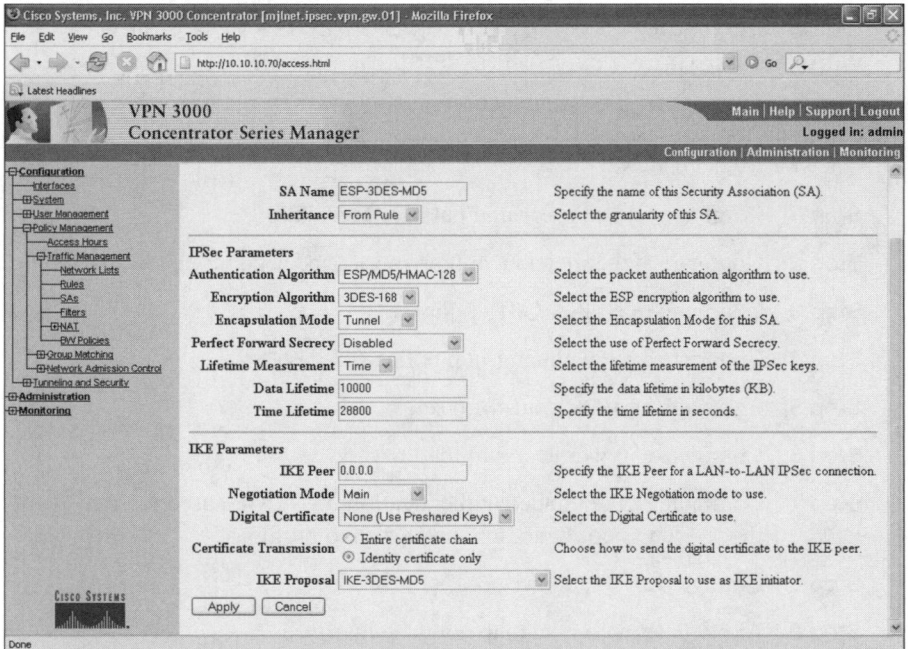

The specific algorithms associated with IKEv1 phase can be found by going to **Configuration > Tunneling and Security > IPSec > IKE Proposals**. You will see a number of active and inactive IKE phase 1 proposals.

Click the IKE phase 1 proposal specified under the **Configuration > Policy Management > Traffic Management > SAs** screen, and then click **Modify**. You will then see the specific algorithms and parameters associated with IKE proposal.

IKE proposals used by Cisco VPN Client are described in the administrator guide. See the following URL for those IKE phase 1 and phase 2 proposals supported by Cisco VPN Client version 4.6 (see Tables 8-3 and 8-4, respectively):

> http://www.cisco.com/en/US/products/sw/secursw/ps2308/products_administration_
> guide_chapter09186a00802d3ac3.html#wp1168133

URLs sometimes change, so if this URL does not work, search Cisco.com for the "VPN Client Administrator Guide" relating to the version of the Cisco VPN Client that you are using and then navigate to the section called "Troubleshooting and Programmer Notes."

You must make sure that at least one IKEv1 phase 1 and one phase 2 proposal on the Cisco VPN 3000 concentrator and the remote access VPN clients are compatible.

NOTE   For more information on specific IPsec/IKE parameters, see Chapter 6.

Cisco IOS Router as an IPsec Remote Access VPN Gateway with IKE Preshared Key Authentication

One alternative as an IPsec remote access VPN gateway is a Cisco IOS router. The configuration steps necessary to set up a Cisco IOS router as an IPsec remote access VPN gateway are as follows:

Step 1   Configure a local username/password database.

Step 2   Configure authentication, authorization, and accounting (AAA).

Step 3   Configure IKE (ISAKMP) policies.

Step 4   Configure a VPN client group policy profile.

Step 5   Configure an IPsec transform set.

Step 6   Configure a dynamic crypto map.

Step 7   Configure IKE extended authentication, ISAKMP authorization, client mode address configuration, and a crypto profile.

Step 8   Configure an IP address pool.

Step 9   Apply the crypto map to the outside interface.

Example 9-1 shows a sample configuration of a Cisco IOS IPsec remote access VPN gateway.

Example 9-1   *Sample Configuration of an IPsec Remote Access VPN Gateway*

```
!
hostname mjlnet.VPN.GW.01
!
username mark password 7 09414405170003405B5C52 (line 1)
username john password 7 05060C032F495A5B495540 (line 2)
!
aaa new-model (line 3)
aaa authentication login mjlLogin local (line 4)
aaa authorization network mjlAuth local (line 5)
!
crypto isakmp policy 10 (line 6)
hash md5 (line 7)
authentication pre-share (line 8)
group 2 (line 9)
!
crypto isakmp client configuration group mjlVPN (line 10)
key mjlnet2007 (line 11)
dns 10.10.10.161 (line 12)
wins 10.10.10.171 (line 13)
```

Example 9-1   *Sample Configuration of an IPsec Remote Access VPN Gateway (Continued)*

```
pool mjlPool (line 14)
!
crypto ipsec transform-set mjlTransform esp-des esp-md5-hmac (line 15)
!
crypto dynamic-map mjlDynmap 10 (line 16)
set transform-set mjlTransform (line 17)
!
crypto map mjlnetMap client authentication list mjlLogin (line 18)
crypto map mjlnetMap isakmp authorization list mjlAuth (line 19)
crypto map mjlnetMap client configuration address respond (line 20)
crypto map mjlnetMap 10 ipsec-isakmp dynamic mjlDynmap (line 21)
!
interface FastEthernet0/0
ip address 10.10.10.70 255.255.255.0 (line 22)
!
interface FastEthernet2/0
ip address 192.168.1.1 255.255.255.0 (line 23)
crypto map mjlnetMap (line 24)
!
!
ip local pool mjlPool 10.30.20.1 10.30.20.150 (line 25)
ip route 0.0.0.0 0.0.0.0 192.168.1.2 (line 26)
!
```

The **username** *username* **password** *password* command (lines 1 and 2) is used to configure a local database of username and passwords. These are used to authenticate remote access VPN *users* during Xauth.

Next is the **aaa new-model** command (line 3). This command is used to enable AAA on the IPsec remote access VPN gateway.

In line 4, the **aaa authentication login** *method-list-name* **local** command is used to configure a method list to be used for login authentication. The **local** keyword is used to specify the local username password database configured in lines 1 and 2. If you want to use a AAA server for user authentication, you can use the appropriate keyword such as **radius** to specify that (instead of using the **local** keyword).

The **aaa authorization network** *method-list-name* **local** command in line 5 is used to configure the VPN gateway to use local authorization for network connections (connections from remote access VPN clients). Again, it is possible to specify an external server to authorize remote access VPN clients.

If you do want to use AAA servers for user authentication/authorization, you can configure their IP addresses/host name and keys using commands such as **radius-server host**.

Lines 6 to 9 contain the IKE policy. The **crypto isakmp policy** *priority* command in line 6 is used to configure an IKE (ISAKMP) policy with the specified priority. In line 7, the **hash {sha | md5}** command is used to configure a hashing algorithm for the IKE policy. Next, the **authentication {rsa-sig | pre-share}** command (line 8 configures the method of authentication used in IKE phase 1, This method is used to authenticate the remote access VPN client's machine (rather than the user him/herself [users are authenticated using Xauth]).

The final command that makes up the IKE policy is **group {1 | 2}**. This configures the Diffie-Hellman group.

The VPN client group policy profile is configured next (see lines 10 to 14).

The **crypto isakmp client configuration group** {*group-name* | **default**} in line 10 is used to specify a policy profile that will be used to control remote access VPN client connectivity (IKE/ISAKMP Mode Config parameters and controls).

The **key** *preshared-key* command (line 11) is used to specify the IKE group preshared key.

The **wins** *server-ip-address* and **dns** *server-ip-address* commands in lines 12 and 13 are then used to specify the WINS and DNS server address to supply to remote access VPN clients during ISAKMP Mode Config exchange.

In line 14, the **pool** *pool-name* command links to a local IP address from which to assign addresses to the remote access VPN client during ISAKMP Configuration Mode exchange.

There are quite a number of other options that you can specify within the policy profile, including an access list number used to control split tunneling (**acl** *acl-number*), a list of backup VPN gateways for remote access VPN clients to use in the event that the main VPN gateway is down (**backup-gateway**), domain membership (**domain**), client firewall status (**firewall are-u-there**), and so on.

Lines 16 and 17 show the configuration of a dynamic crypto map. A dynamic crypto map is used to allow the VPN gateway to negotiate IPsec SAs with remote access VPN clients. Specifically, a dynamic crypto map is required when not all the parameters about an IPsec peer are known, and often the IP addresses of remote access VPN clients are not known.

The **crypto dynamic-map** *dynamic-map-name dynamic-seq-number* command (line 16) is used to create a dynamic crypto map entry.

Line 17 shows the **set transform-set** *transform-set-name1* [*transform-set-name2......
transform-set-name6*] command. This command links to the IPsec transform set created in highlighted line 15.

Lines 18 to 21 bring together the configuration for IKE Xauth, authorization, ISAKMP Mode Configuration (Mode Config), and a crypto profile.

The **crypto map** *map-name* **client authentication list** *method-list-name* command (line 18) is used to enable ISAKMP Xauth using the method list specified using the **aaa authentication login** *method-list-name* command in line 4.

In line 19, the **crypto map** *map-name* **isakmp authorization list** *method-list-name* command configures authorization for IKE (ISAKMP) and links to the method list configured by the **aaa authorization network** *method-list-name* command in line 5.

The **crypto map** *map-name* **client configuration address** {**initiate** | **respond**} command in line 20 configures the VPN gateway to either initiate IP address assignment with the remote access VPN clients or to accept IP address requests from remote access VPN clients.

Line 21 shows the **crypto map** *map-name seq-number* **ipsec-isakmp dynamic** *dynamic-map-name* command. This links to the dynamic crypto map created in lines 16 and 17 and is used to configure a crypto profile that is used to create dynamic crypto map as remote access VPN clients connect.

Inside and outside interface IP addresses are configured in lines 22 and 23. And in line 24, the crypto map is applied to the outside (external) interface using the **crypto map** *map-name* command. Notice that the crypto map name is that configured using the **crypto map** commands in lines 17 to 20.

In this example, IP addresses are assigned to remote access VPN clients from a local IP address pool. This pool is configured in line 25 using the **ip local pool** *pool-name start-address end-address* command. The IP address pool name is that which is specified using the **pool** command in line 14.

Finally, in line 26, the **ip route** command is used to configure a default route that provides reachability to the Internet (and remote access VPN clients).

Cisco ASA as an IPsec Remote Access VPN Gateway with IKE Preshared Key Authentication

A second alternative as an IPsec remote access VPN gateway is a Cisco ASA 5500. The configuration is similar to that for a Cisco IOS remote access VPN gateway:

Step 1   Configure a local username/password database.

Step 2   Configure an IP address pool.

Step 3   Configure IP route(s) for traffic received over IPsec VPN tunnels (optional).

Step 4   Configure default group policy attributes.

Step 5   Configure user group policy attributes.

Step 6   Configure IPsec transform set(s).

Step 7   Enable IKE (ISAKMP) on the outside interface.

Step 8   Configure IKE (ISAKMP) policies.

Step 9   Configure a dynamic crypto map.

Step 10 Configure a crypto map.

Step 11 Configure the tunnel group type.

Step 12 Configure tunnel group (general/IPsec) attributes.

Step 13 Apply the crypto map to the outside interface.

Example 9-2 shows a sample configuration of an IPsec remote access VPN using preshared key authentication on the Cisco ASA 5500.

Example 9-2 *Configuration of a Cisco ASA 5500 IPsec Remote Access VPN Gateway*

```
!
interface Ethernet0/0
 description Inside interface
 nameif Inside0/0
 security-level 100
 ip address 10.10.10.49 255.255.255.0
!
interface Ethernet0/1
 description Outside interface
 nameif Outside0/1
 security-level 0
 ip address 192.168.1.1 255.255.255.0
!
!
hostname mjlnet.VPN.GW.10
!
 ip local pool mjlPool 10.10.10.110-10.10.10.190 (line 1)
!
route outside 0.0.0.0 0.0.0.0 192.168.1.2 1
 route Inside0/0 0.0.0.0 0.0.0.0 10.10.10.1 tunneled (line 2)
!
 group-policy DfltGrpPolicy attributes (line 3)
   wins-server value 10.10.10.51 (line 4)
   dns-server value 10.10.10.52 (line 5)
   vpn-tunnel-protocol IPSec (line 6)
!
group-policy ipsec-users internal (line 7)
group-policy ipsec-users attributes (line 8)
   banner value Hello There! (line 9)
   default-domain value mjlnet.com (line 10)
!
username mark password 7EwWZdAmpPRnJfI1 encrypted (line 11)
username brian password lSVvOXM633DCBMur encrypted (line 12)
username arthur password a1uu0/TQulnjpblO encrypted (line 13)
username frank password 9Lq6Q3qF/2EfVCxY encrypted (line 14)
!
crypto ipsec transform-set mjlnet-trans esp-3des esp-sha-hmac (line 15)
!
 crypto dynamic-map mjlnet-dynamic 10 set transform-set mjlnet-trans (line 16)
 crypto map mjlnet-map 10 ipsec-isakmp dynamic mjlnet-dynamic (line 17)
 crypto map mjlnet-map interface Outside0/1 (line 18)
!
 isakmp enable Outside0/1 (line 19)
 isakmp policy 10 authentication pre-share (line 20)
 isakmp policy 10 encryption 3des (line 21)
 isakmp policy 10 hash sha (line 22)
 isakmp policy 10 group 2 (line 23)
 isakmp policy 10 lifetime 86400 (line 24)
!
 tunnel-group mjlnet-ipsec type ipsec-ra (line 25)
 tunnel-group mjlnet-ipsec general-attributes (line 26)
   address-pool mjlnet-addrs (line 27)
 tunnel-group mjlnet-ipsec ipsec-attributes (line 28)
   pre-shared-key * (line 29)
!
```

As previously discussed, IP addresses are assigned to remote access VPN clients during ISAKMP Configuration Mode (Mode Config) exchange. In this example, an IP address pool called mjlPool is configured using the **ip local pool** *poolname start-address end-address* [**mask** *mask*] (line 1), and it is from this pool that IP addresses are assigned to remote access VPN clients.

Next, in line 2, the **route** *interface-name ip-address netmask next-hop* [*metric* | **tunneled**] command is used to configure a default route, with the **tunneled** keyword specifying that this default route is used for traffic that is received over IPsec tunnels from remote access VPN clients. In this example, traffic received over the IPsec tunnels is routed via next hop 10.10.10.1 (a router reachable via inside interface Inside0/0).

As with the Cisco VPN 3000 concentrator, you can specify configuration attributes that apply to remote access VPN clients in a default group policy, in a user group policy, and in user policies on the Cisco ASA 5500. Attributes that are configured under the default group policy can be inherited by the group policy, and in turn, attributes configured under a group policy can be inherited by a user policy.

In line 3, the **group-policy** *name* **attributes** global configuration mode command is used to begin configuration of attributes that apply to the default policy (DfltGrpPolicy).

A wide variety of attributes can be configured, but in this case, the IP addresses of WINS and DNS servers addresses are configured (lines 4 and 5), and the IPsec is enabled as a VPN protocol type (line 6) under the default policy using the **wins-server value** {*ip_address*} [*ip_address*] | **none, dns-server** {**value** *ip_address* [*ip_address*] | **none**}, and **vpn-tunnel-protocol** {**webvpn** | **IPSec**} commands. The WINS and DNS server addresses are also advertised to remote access VPN clients during ISAKMP Configuration Mode exchange.

A user group called ipsec-users is then configured beginning with the **group-policy** *name* **internal** and **group-policy** *name* **attributes** global configuration mode commands in lines 7 and 8. The **group-policy** *name* **internal** command is used to specify that attributes for this group will be configured locally on the Cisco ASA 5500 (rather than on an external AAA server).

As with the default group, a wide variety of attributes can be configured under a user group. In this example, a login banner is configured using the **banner** {**value** *banner_string* | **none**} command (line 9), and a default domain name is configured using the **default-domain** {**value** *domain-name* | **none**} command (line 10).

Other attributes that can be configured under the default or user groups include a split-tunneling policy (**split-tunnel-network-list** / **split-tunnel-policy**), a list of backup VPN gateways (**backup-servers**), and a client firewall policy (**client-firewall**).

It is also possible to configure user policies with specific attributes (in addition to default group policy and user group policy attributes) using the **username** *username* **attributes** global configuration mode command. User policy attributes can be useful if, for example, you want to assign a particular IP address to a certain user rather than one from an address pool or other source.

A local username/password database for user authentication (Xauth) is configured next from lines 11 to 14 using the **username** *username* **password** *password* command. Passwords are encrypted by default by the Cisco ASA 5500, and so the **encrypted** keyword is added in the configuration file.

A local username/password database has limited scalability. A more scalable solution is to use a AAA server such as a RADIUS server. Example 9-3 shows configuration of a RADIUS server for remote access VPN user authentication.

Example 9-3 *Configuration of a RADIUS Server for Remote Access VPN User Authentication*

```
 !
 aaa-server radius_servers protocol radius
 aaa-server radius_servers host 10.10.10.51
  key cisco
 !
 tunnel-group mjlnet-ipsec general-attributes
 authentication-server-group radius_servers
 !
```

In Example 9-3, the **aaa-server** *server-tag* **protocol** *server-protocol* global configuration mode command is used to configure the AAA protocol as RADIUS.

The **aaa-server** *server-tag* [(*interface-name*)] **host** *server-ip* [*key*] [**timeout** *seconds*] command configures the RADIUS server's IP address, and the **key** *key* command configures the secret key used to authenticate communications between the RADIUS server and the Cisco ASA 5500 (as well as being used to encrypt passwords sent to the RADIUS server).

The **authentication-server-group** [(*interface name*)] *server group* [**LOCAL** | **NONE**] command is then used to reference the previously configured AAA server (using the *server_group* parameter) under the **tunnel-group general-attributes** configuration mode (more on this later). The **LOCAL** keyword can optionally be used to specify that the local username/password database should be used in the event that the RADIUS server is unreachable.

An IPsec transform set is configured next in Example 9-2, line 15 using the **crypto ipsec transform-set** *transform-set-name transform1* [*transform2*] command. In this example, an IPsec transform set called, **mjlnet-trans** is configured using ESP with 3DES encryption and SHA-1 as the hash algorithm.

In line 16, the **crypto dynamic-map** *dynamic-map-name dynamic-seq-num* **set transform-set** *transform-set-name1* [*... transform-set-name9*] command is used to configure a dynamic crypto map called mjlnet-dynamic. This dynamic crypto map references the transform set called mjlnet-trans that was configured in line 15.

The **crypto map** *map-name seq-num* **ipsec-isakmp dynamic** *dynamic-map-name* command (line 17) configures a crypto map called **mjlnet-map** that, in turn, links to the dynamic crypto map configured in line 16 (mjlnet-dynamic). This command allows the dynamic creation of crypto maps as remote access VPN clients connect to the Cisco ASA 5500.

Next, in line 18, the **crypto map** *map-name* **interface** *interface-name* command is used to apply the crypto map called mjlnet-map to the outside interface (Outside0/1).

The **isakmp policy** *priority* **authentication**, **isakmp policy** *priority* **encryption**, **isakmp policy** *priority* **hash**, **isakmp policy** *priority* **group**, and **isakmp policy** *priority* **lifetime** commands (lines 20 to 24) are used to configure an IKE (ISAKMP) policy with priority 10. This IKE policy specifies preshared key authentication (**pre-share**), 3DES encryption (**3des**), the SHA-1 hashing algorithm (**sha**), Diffie-Hellman group 2 (1024-bit), and a default IKE SA lifetime of 86,400 seconds.

The **isakmp enable** *interface-name* command in line 19 is then used to enable ISAKMP (IKE) on the outside interface (Outside0/1).

In line 25, the **tunnel-group** *name* **type** *type* global configuration mode command specifies that the tunnel group named mjlnet-ipsec will be used for IPsec remote access (**ipsec-ra**) VPNs. A tunnel group is used to manage certain parameters associated with remote access (or site-to-site) VPNs.

The **tunnel-group** *name* **general-attributes** command in line 26 begins the configuration of general parameters that are common for all tunneling protocols.

In the tunnel-group general attributes configuration mode, the **address-pool** [(*interface name*)] *address_pool1* [*...address_pool6*] command is used to specify that IP address pool configured in line 1 will be used to assign IP addresses to remote access VPN clients as they connect to the Cisco ASA 5500.

Note that it is also possible to assign IP addresses to remote access VPN clients using either DHCP or a AAA server. In this case, you can use the **vpn-addr-assign** [**aaa** | **dhcp** | **local**] global configuration mode command to specify the particular method of address assignment that you would like to use. If you specify DHCP as the method of address assignment, you'll also need to specify the DHCP server address using the **dhcp-server** *ip-address* command under tunnel group general attributes configuration mode (under **tunnel-group** *name* **general-attributes**). If you specify AAA as the method of address assignment, you'll need to configure the AAA protocol and AAA server IP address (and key) using the commands shown in Example 9-3.

Finally, the **tunnel-group** *name* **ipsec-attributes** command in line 28 begins the configuration of IPsec-specific attributes. In this case, a preshared key is configured under the tunnel-group ipsec-attributes configuration mode using the **pre-shared-key** *key* command (line 29). This preshared key is used to authenticate remote access client machines (rather than the users themselves) during IKE phase 1.

Before finishing this section, it is also worth mentioning the global configuration mode **sysopt connection permit-ipsec** and **crypto dynamic-map** *map-name seq-num* **set reverse route** commands. The **sysopt connection permit-ipsec** command is used to allow traffic received over IPsec tunnel from remote access VPN clients to pass through the Cisco ASA 5500 and it is enabled by default. The **crypto dynamic-map** *map-name seq-num* **set reverse-route** command can optionally be used to inject routes corresponding to (IPsec

SAs negotiated with) remote access clients into the routing table, and these routes can then be advertised to devices on the inside network.

Configuring the Cisco VPN Client for IKE Preshared Key Authentication

The configuration of the Cisco VPN Client for preshared key authentication is pretty simple. The following steps are required:

Step 1   From the Start menu (on Windows), start the VPN client.

Step 2   From the Connection Entries menu, choose **New**.

Step 3   In the Authentication tab, specify a connection entry name, description, and IP address or DNS name of the VPN gateway. Additionally, select **Group Authentication** and configure the group name and password.

Figure 9-17 shows the Authentication tab.

Figure 9-17   *Authentication Tab*

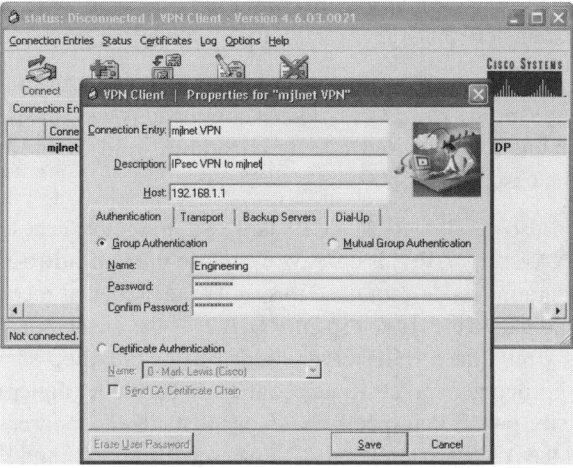

In Figure 9-17, a connection entry called mjlnet VPN is created (Connection Entry). This connection entry contains the configuration for an IPsec remote access VPN connection.

This connection entry configures a VPN connection to VPN gateway 192.168.1.1 (Host).

The group name associated with this entry is Engineering (Name), and must match the group name configured on the Cisco VPN 3000 concentrator (see Figure 9-12), Cisco IOS router (see line 9 in Example 9-1), or ASA 5500 (see Example 9-2).

The password specified is the preshared key and must match the group password/preshared key configured on the Cisco VPN 3000 concentrator, the Cisco IOS router, or Cisco ASA 5500.

Step 4   (Optional) If you are using a dial-up connection, in the Dial-Up tab, choose **Connect to Internet via dial-up** and select the appropriate entry from the drop-down menu.

Figure 9-18 shows the Dial-Up tab.

Figure 9-18 *Dial-Up Tab*

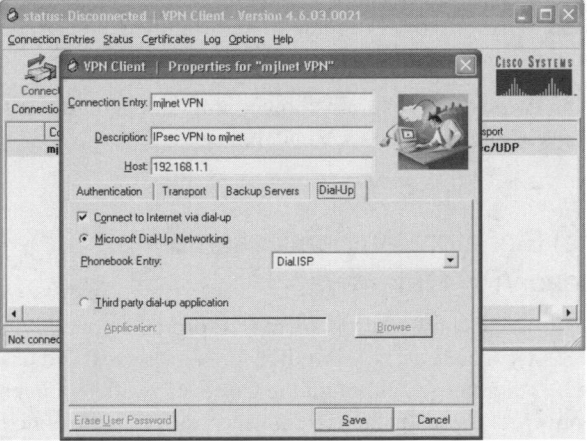

That's it! As you can see, it is simple to configure the Cisco VPN Client for preshared key authentication.

After you have configured the Cisco VPN Client, you are ready to connect to the VPN gateway, and you can do this by double-clicking the entry in the Connection Entries tab.

Designing and Deploying IPsec Remote Access VPNs Using Digital Signature Authentication

As already discussed in this book, one big problem with preshared keys is their scalability. If preshared keys are to be as secure as possible, each pair of IPsec peers needs a unique preshared key—group preshared keys are more vulnerable to compromise because the same key is used by a number of IPsec peers. Also, administrators will often choose easy-to-remember but less-secure preshared keys (see Chapter 6 for more information on preshared keys and their relative weakness).

So, if preshared key authentication is not as secure as you would like, what is? The answer is digital signature authentication (using digital certificates).

One challenge with digital signature authentication using digital certificates is the administration of those digital certificates. Specific challenges include the following:

- Enrolling and obtaining certificates for the VPN gateways as well as all of the remote access VPN clients
- Ensuring that time is accurately set on VPN gateways and remote access VPN clients

- Ensuring that new certificates are obtained before old ones expire
- Securing the PKI that is used to (among other things) store and issue certificates
- (Optionally) Ensuring that IPsec peers can check on the revocation status of certificates

So, just because digital signature authentication is more secure than preshared key authentication does not necessarily mean that it is a simple choice as to which type of authentication to use. If you do decide to use digital signature authentication, this section will tell you what you need to do to implement it in a remote access VPN environment.

The following two sections examine how to implement digital signature authentication on VPN gateways and remote access VPN clients.

Implementing Digital Signature Authentication on IPsec Remote Access VPN Gateways

This section describes how to implement IKE digital signature authentication on both Cisco VPN 3000 concentrators, Cisco IOS VPN gateways, and Cisco ASA 5500s—they all make a good VPN gateway, although the Cisco VPN 3000 concentrator and Cisco ASA 5500 are more specialized (as far as remote access VPNs are concerned) and therefore offer more functionality, and potentially better performance (although this depends on specific models used).

IKE Digital Signature Authentication on a Cisco VPN 3000 Concentrator

To implement IPsec remote access VPNs with digital signature authentication on a VPN gateway, you need to complete the following steps:

Step 1 Obtain the CA's certificate.

Step 2 Enroll the VPN gateway with the CA and obtain an identity certificate.

Step 3 Specify an IP address pool or another form of IP address assignment.

Step 4 Configure a group for IPsec remote access VPN users.

Step 5 Configure user accounts for remote access VPN users.

Step 6 Modify IPsec/IKE parameters.

Steps 2 to 5 are identical to those for preshared key authentication, and so will not be described again in this section.

As alluded to in the previous section, you should also ensure that the VPN gateway (and VPN clients) has accurate time—if it does not, this may cause authentication failures with remote access VPN clients.

Step 1: Obtain the CA's Certificate Using SCEP

Two methods you can use to obtain the CA's certificate are as follows:

- Manually, using a web browser (upload from workstation)
- Using the Simple Certificate Enrollment Protocol (SCEP)

The first method was outlined in the section "Step 1: Retrieving and Installing the Certificate Authority's (CA's) Certificate" in Chapter 8. The second method is described in this section.

This section describes how to obtain the CA's certificate using SCEP. Before starting, however, it is essential to ensure that your CA server supports enrollment via SCEP. If you are using a Microsoft CA, ensure that the administrator has installed the SCEP plug-in—this is an executable called cepsetup.exe, and it can be found on the Resource Kit CD and on the Microsoft website (http://www.microsoft.com).

To obtain the CA's certificate using SCEP, you should first go to the **Administration > Certificate Management** screen (see Figure 9-19).

Figure 9-19 *Certificate Management Screen*

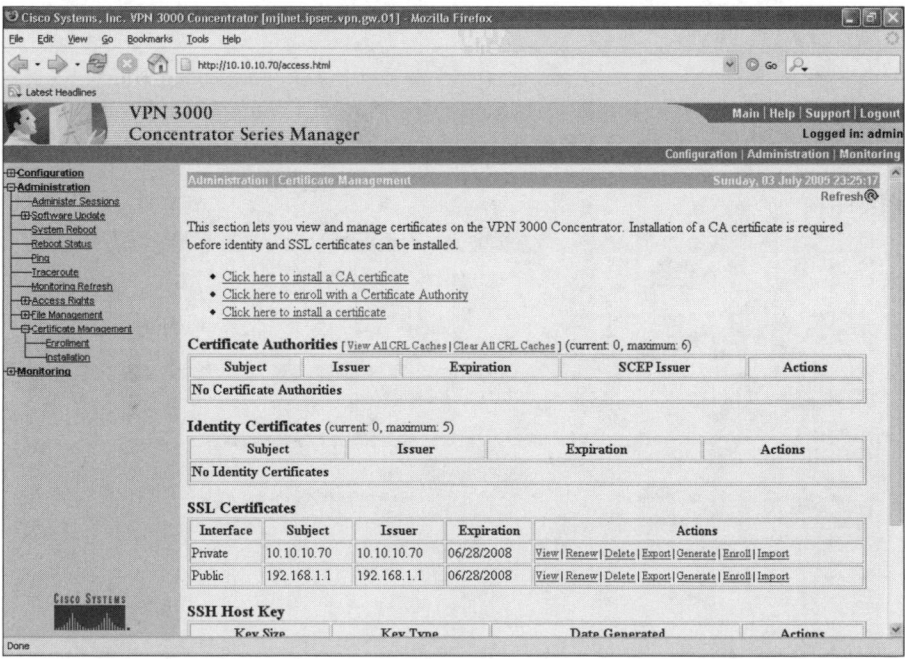

Click **Click here to install a CA certificate**, and you will see the page shown in Figure 9-20.

Figure 9-20 *CA Certificate Page*

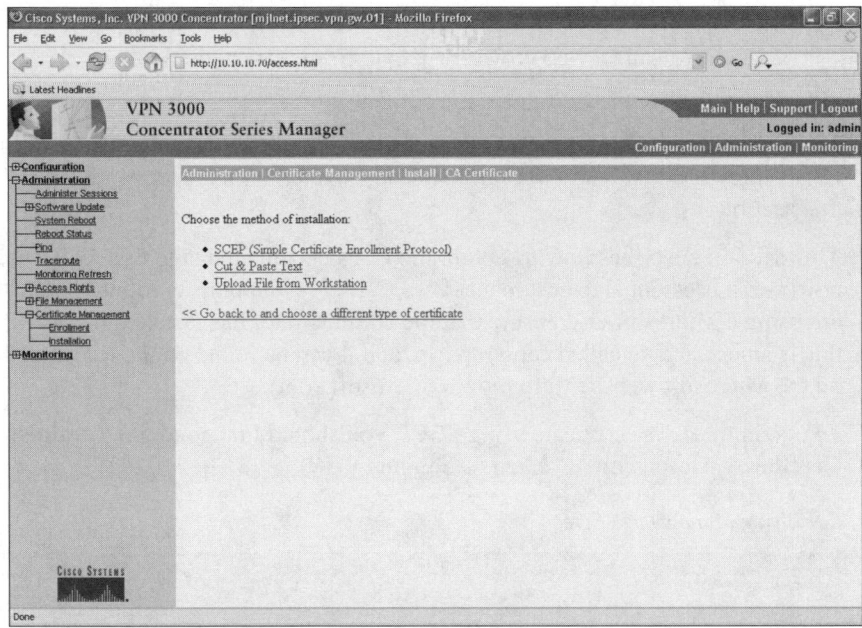

Next, click **SCEP (Simple Certificate Enrollment Protocol)**, and you will now be presented with the SCEP page (see Figure 9-21).

Figure 9-21 *SCEP Page*

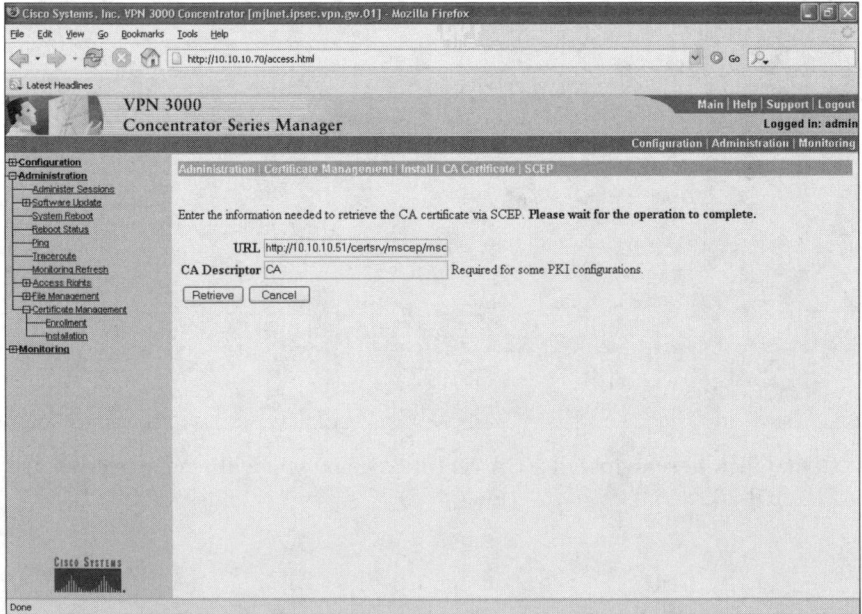

You must now type the URL and CA descriptor. If you are using a Microsoft CA server, the URL is in the form http://<*CA_server_name_or_ip_address*>/certsrv/mscep/mscep.dll.

Click the **Retrieve** button, and after a short wait, you should see the Certificate Management page again (see Figure 9-22).

Figure 9-22 *Certificate Management Page (Showing CA Certificate)*

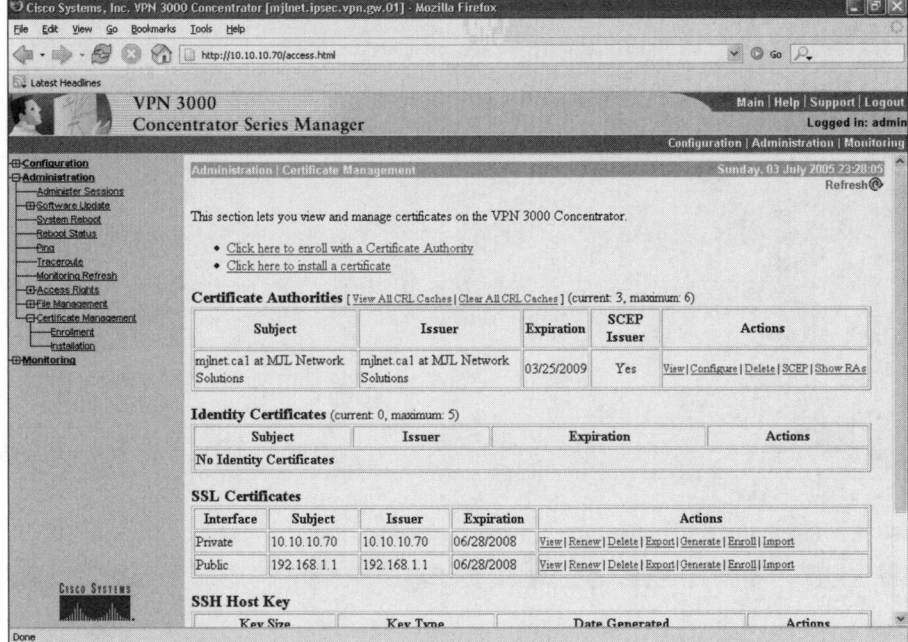

If you look under the Certificate Authorities heading in Figure 9-22, you can see that a CA certificate has now been installed.

Step 2: Enroll the VPN Gateway with the CA and Obtain an Identity Certificate Using SCEP
Now that the CA certificate is installed, you can enroll with the CA server and obtain an identity certificate for the Cisco VPN concentrator.

To enroll the Cisco VPN 3000 concentrator with the CA and obtain an identity certificate, click the **Click here to enroll with a Certificate Authority** link, and you will see the page shown in Figure 9-23.

You must now click the **Enroll via SCEP at** *CA_name* link.

You will then be asked to fill out the form shown in Figure 9-24. The information in this form is included in the certificate request sent to the CA.

Figure 9-23 *Identity Certificate Page*

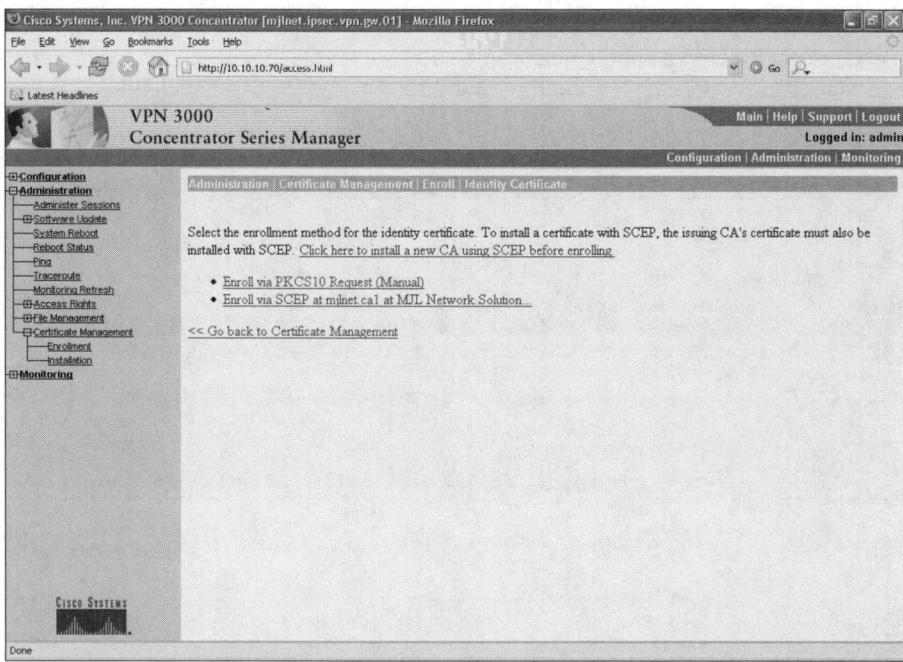

Figure 9-24 *Certificate Request Information*

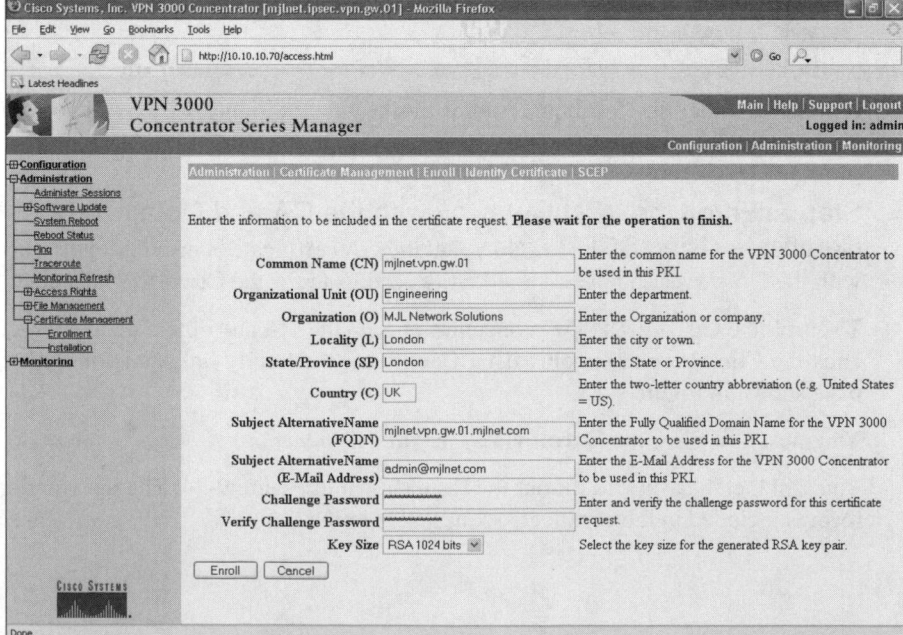

If you take a look at the lower part of the page shown in Figure 9-24, you can see boxes in which to enter a challenge password. This password is the SCEP challenge password—check with your CA server administrator to obtain this (if one exists).

After you have finished filling out the form, click **Enroll**, and the Cisco VPN 3000 concentrator will attempt to enroll and obtain an identity certificate.

Figure 9-25 shows the page that should appear when you enroll the Cisco VPN 3000 concentrator with the CA server.

Figure 9-25 *Identity Certificate Request Is Pending*

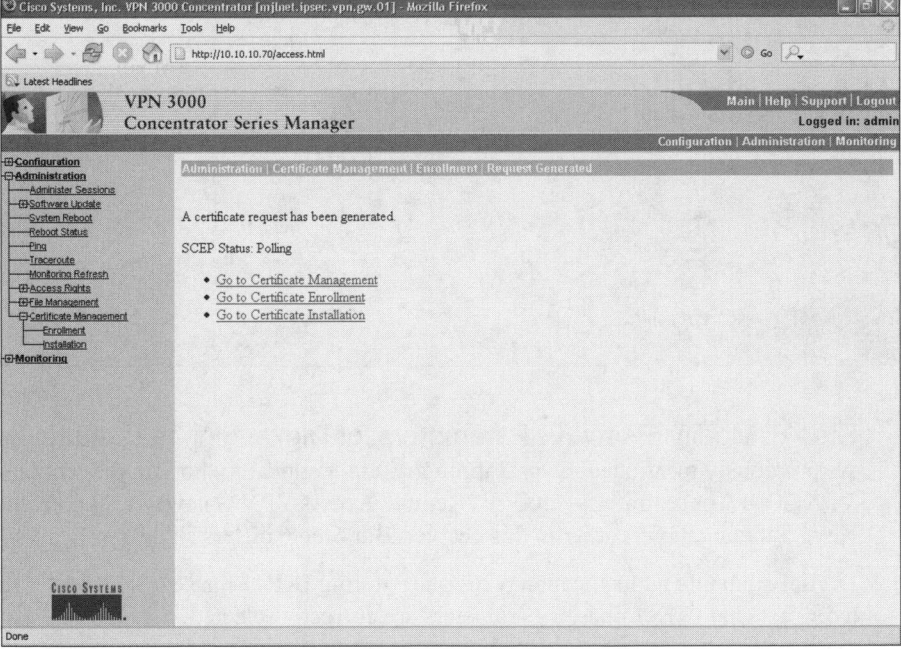

If you take a close look at the page shown in Figure 9-25, you can see that the SCEP status is Polling. This is an indication that the SCEP certificate request has been sent and is pending on the CA server (the Cisco VPN concentrator is polling the CA server). The CA administrator should now issue the certificate—see Figure 8-35 on page 751).

The Cisco VPN 3000 concentrator will continue to poll the CA server, and after the CA administrator has issued the identity certificate, it will appear in the Certificate Management page (see Figure 9-26).

If you take a look under the Identity Certificates heading in Figure 9-26, you can see that the CA server has issued the certificate to the Cisco VPN 3000 concentrator.

Figure 9-26 *Identity Certificate Has Been Issued*

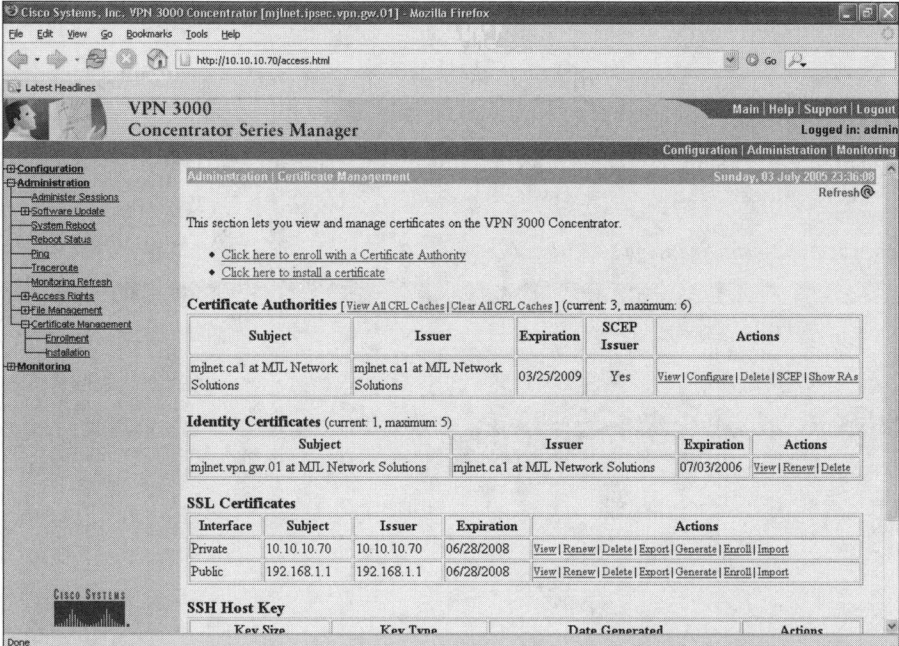

Step 6: Modify IPsec/IKE Parameters for Digital Signature Authentication

As previously mentioned, Steps 3 through 5 are identical to those in the section "Cisco VPN 3000 Concentrator as an IPsec Remote Access VPN Gateway Using Preshared Key Authentication" earlier in this chapter. But Step 6 differs slightly.

Digital signature authentication takes place during IKEv1 phase 1, so it is it is important to ensure that IKEv1 phase 1 parameters are correctly selected.

You can view and, if necessary, modify certain IKEv1 phase 1 parameters by going to **Configuration > Policy Management > Traffic Management > SAs**, selecting the IPsec SA that you specified in the group settings (Step 4), and clicking **Modify**.

The important part of the page shown in Figure 9-27 is the lower part (IKE Parameters)—this contains some of the parameters used during IKEv1 phase negotiation.

In the IKE Parameters section of the page, make sure that you select the identity certificate that you have just obtained for the Cisco VPN 3000 concentrator (Step 2) in the Digital Certificate drop-down box, and click **Apply**.

Additionally, it is important to ensure that the IKE proposal is configured to use digital signature authentication. You can do this by going to **Configuration > Tunneling and Security > IPSec > IKE Proposals**, selecting the IKE proposal, and clicking **Modify**. You will then see the page shown in Figure 9-28.

Figure 9-27 *Viewing and Modifying IKEv1 Phase 1 Parameters to Use the Appropriate Digital Certificate*

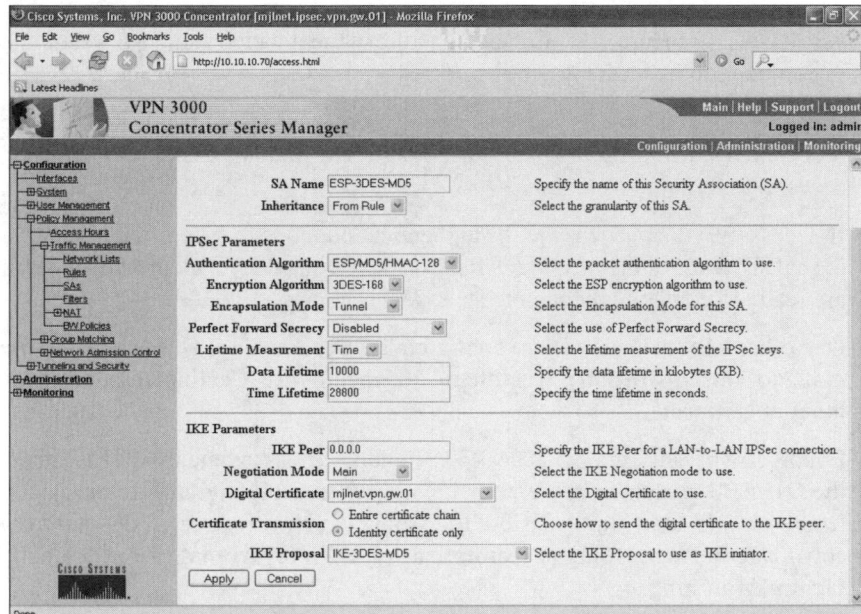

Figure 9-28 *Viewing and Modifying IKEv1 Phase 1 Parameters to Ensure That Digital Signature Authentication Is Used*

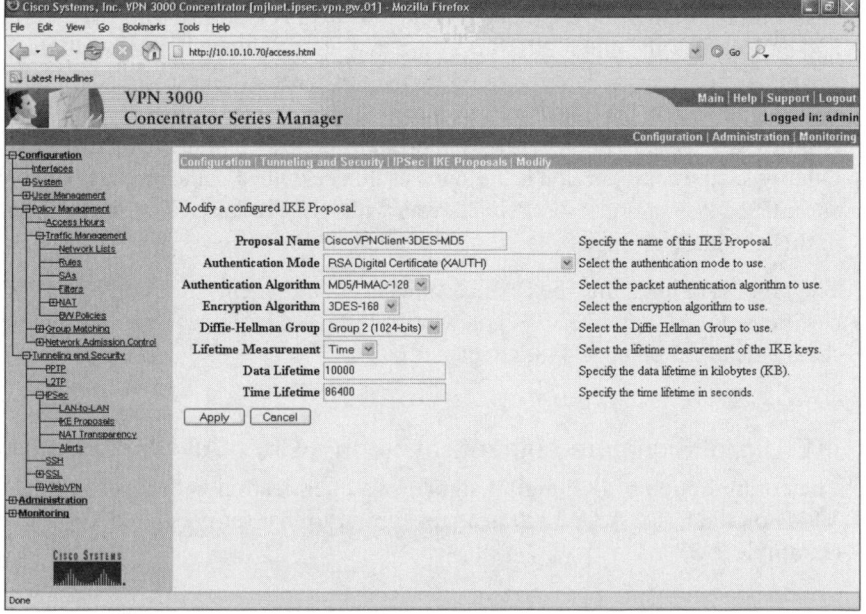

The relevant portion of the page shown in Figure 9-28 is the Authentication Mode drop-down box. This box is used to specify digital signature (either RSA or DSA) using digital certificates. In Figure 9-28, digital signature authentication using RSA digital certificates, in conjunction with IKE Xauth is selected.

Remember that digital signature authentication is used to authenticate the remote access VPN client *machine* during IKE phase 1, and IKE Xauth is used to authenticate the remote access VPN *user*.

If necessary, you must change the authentication mode to specify the appropriate type of digital signature authentication. After you have done that, click the **Apply** button, and you are ready to configure the remote access VPN clients.

One other important element to configure is CRL checking. This can be configured by going to **Administration > Certificate Management > Certificates** and clicking **CRL** on the root certificate.

Finally, by default, remote access VPN clients are associated with user groups using the OU field contained in their certificates when using digital signature authentication (more on this later). It is possible to associate clients to user groups based on other certificate fields by going to **Configuration > Policy Management > Certificate Group Matching**.

IKE Digital Signature Authentication on a Cisco IOS VPN Gateway

Configuring a Cisco IOS router as a VPN gateway with IKE digital signature authentication is similar to configuring a Cisco IOS router as a VPN gateway with IKE preshared key authentication—the major differences are that you must obtain the install the appropriate certificates (CA and identity), configure the **authentication rsa-sig** command in the IKE policy (rather than the **authentication pre-share** command), and also remove the **crypto isakmp key** *preshared-key* **address** *peer-address* mask command from the configuration. Otherwise, the configuration is the same as that described in the section "Cisco IOS Router as an IPsec Remote Access VPN Gateway with IKE Preshared Key Authentication" earlier in this chapter (see page 824).

The process of obtaining the CA's certificate, as well as enrolling and obtaining an identity certificate for a Cisco IOS VPN gateway, is described in the section "IKE Digital Signature Authentication" on page 448 in Chapter 6.

IKE Digital Signature Authentication on a Cisco ASA VPN Gateway

The configuration of IKE digital signature authentication with IPsec remote access VPNs on the Cisco ASA 5500 is again similar to that for preshared key authentication (Example 9-2).

When configuring digital signature authentication, you must first obtain the CA's certificate and then enroll and obtain an identity certificate for the Cisco ASA 5500. This can be achieved with SCEP using the following procedure:

- Set the time on the Cisco ASA 5500 manually using the global configuration mode **clock set** command, or using an NTP server with the global configuration mode **ntp server** *ip-address* command. You can also set the time zone using the **clock timezone** command.

- Configure the host name (if not already configured) and domain name using the global configuration mode **hostname** *name* and **domain-name** *name* commands.

- Generate RSA keys using the **crypto key generate rsa** global configuration mode command.

- Declare the CA using the global configuration mode **crypto ca trustpoint** *trustpoint-name* command, followed by (in crypto ca trustpoint configuration mode) the **enrollment url** *url* command to specify the URL to use for enrollment with the CA (**http://***CA_name_or_ip_address***/certsrv/mscep/mscep.dll** if you are using a Microsoft CA).

  The **crl optional** and **crl required** can also optionally be used to specify that CRL checking is either optional or required, respectively. Having specified the **crl optional** or **crl required** commands, the **crl configure** command can be used to configure parameters such as the protocol used to retrieve the CRL.

- Authenticate the CA using the **crypto ca authenticate** global configuration mode command.

- Enroll the Cisco ASA 5500 with the CA and obtain an identity certificate using the **crypto ca enroll** *trustpoint* global configuration mode command.

After you have obtained the CA's certificate and enrolled and obtained an identity certificate for the Cisco ASA 5500, you can then complete the configuration using the following steps:

- Specify the **ras-sig** parameter using the **isakmp policy** *priority* **authentication** command (rather than the **pre-share** parameter). Also, do not specify the **pre-shared-key** command under tunnel-group ipsec-attributes configuration mode.

- Configure VPN tunnel group parameters for digital signature authentication. Under the tunnel-group ipsec-attributes configuration mode (entered using the **tunnel-group** *name* **ipsec-attributes** global configuration mode command), specify that the identity of the remote access VPN clients should be validated using the **peer-id-validate cert** command, and configure the name of the previously configured trustpoint using the **trust-point** *trustpoint-name* command.

  It is worth noting that the VPN tunnel group name must, by default, match the OU field in the certificate supplied by the remote access VPN clients (during IKE phase 1 authentication).

If you want to associate remote access VPN clients to groups using other (DN) information in the remote access VPN clients' certificates, you can use the **crypto ca certificate map** command to specify the information that you want to match and the **tunnel-group-map** command to link to the group.

Deploying IKE Digital Signature Authentication on IPsec Remote Access VPN Clients

Okay, you are now halfway there. The VPN gateway is configured—now for the remote access VPN clients.

The configuration of a Cisco VPN Client for IKE digital signature authentication comprises the following steps:

Step 1   Obtain the CA's certificate.

Step 2   Enroll the Cisco VPN Client with the CA and obtain an identity certificate.

Step 3   Create a VPN connection entry and specify IKE digital signature authentication.

This section focuses on obtaining the CA's certificate and enrolling the Cisco VPN Client using SCEP, although it is also possible to perform these tasks manually.

Okay, without further ado, on to obtaining the CA's certificate and enrolling the Cisco VPN Client. The first thing you must do is start the Cisco VPN Client, and from the Certificates menu choose **Enroll**. The dialog box shown in Figure 9-29 should now appear.

Figure 9-29 *Certificate Enrollment Dialog Box*

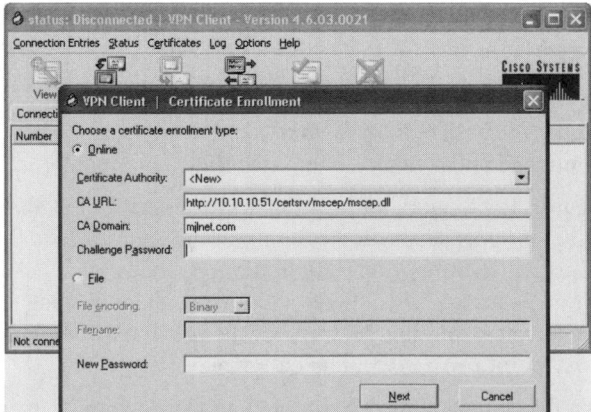

In the Certificate Enrollment dialog box shown in Figure 9-29, choose **Online**, and in the CA URL box type the CA's URL (for SCEP). If you are using a Microsoft CA server, this URL is in the format http://*CA_name_or_ip_address*/certsrv/mscep/mscep.dll.

Also, type the CA's domain in the CA Domain box, and if required type the SCEP challenge password in the Challenge Password box. Check with the CA server administrator to determine whether a password is required, and if so, what it is.

After you have done typed in the appropriate information, click **Next**, and you will see the dialog box shown in Figure 9-30.

Figure 9-30 *Enter Certificate Fields Dialog Box*

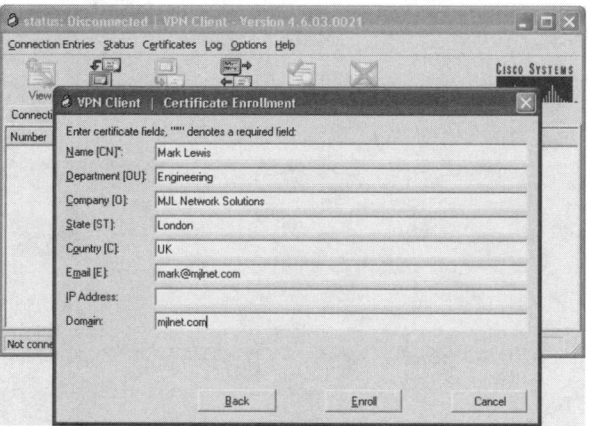

As indicated, you should now enter the information that will be included in the identity certificate request and, ultimately, the identity certificate itself. By default, the Department (OU) is used to map the user to a group, so make sure that the Department (OU) specified is the same as the group name that you have configured on the VPN gateway (see Figure 9-12 or Example 9-1 [highlighted line 9], as appropriate). As described earlier in this chapter, it is also possible to use other fields in the client identity certificate to map to the group on the VPN gateway.

Now click **Enroll**, and you will see the dialog box in Figure 9-31.

As shown in Figure 9-31, certificate enrollment is now pending.

The Cisco VPN Client should already have obtained the CA (and RA) certificates (to see these, select **Show CA/RA Certificates** from the Certificates menu) and has enrolled with the CA. But, the identity certificate has not yet been issued. The CA server administrator has to issue the identity certificate.

You can check the status of the identity certificate by right-clicking the identity certificate (request) and choosing **Retry Certificate Enrollment** (see Figure 9-32).

Figure 9-31 *Certificate Is Pending Dialog Box*

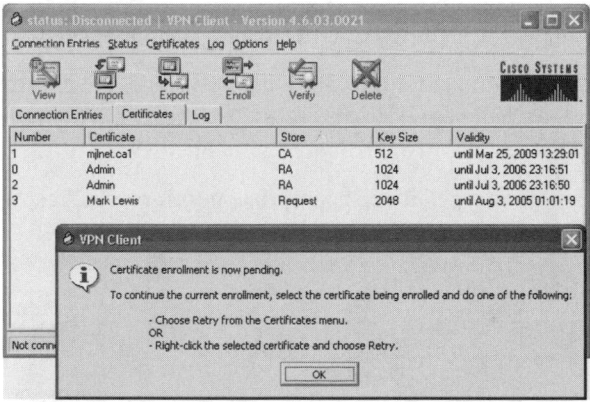

Figure 9-32 *Checking the Status of a Pending Identity Certificate*

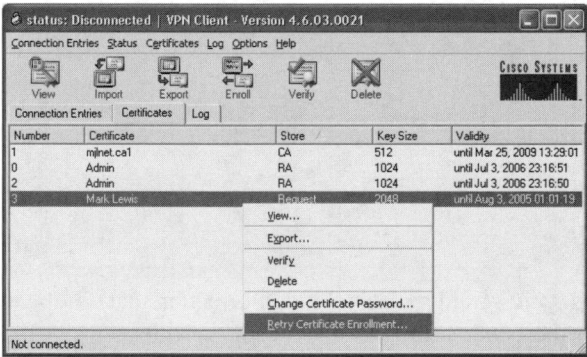

If the CA administrator has issued the identity certificate, you will now see the dialog box shown in Figure 9-33.

Figure 9-33 *Identity Certificate Has Been Issued*

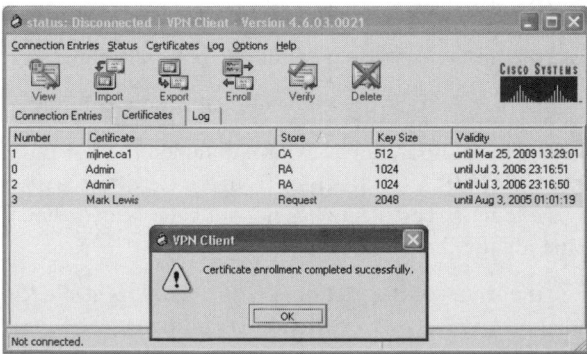

Click **OK**, and you are ready to configure the VPN connection entry using IKE digital signature authentication.

Creation of the VPN connection is exactly the same as that described in the section "Configuring a Cisco VPN Client for IKE Preshared Key Authentication," with the exception that you must choose **Certificate Authentication** rather than Group Authentication in the Authentication tab of the Cisco VPN Client (see Figure 9-34).

Figure 9-34 *Selecting Certificate Authentication in the Authentication Tab*

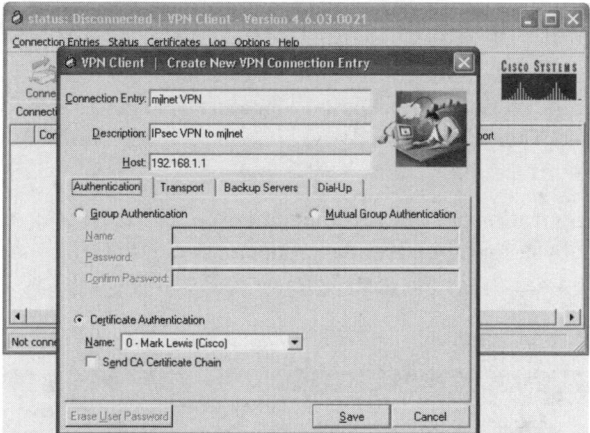

When you choose **Certificate Authentication** in the Authentication tab (Figure 9-34), you must also select the appropriate (certificate) name from the Name drop-down box.

And that is it—after you have finished configuring the VPN connection entry, you are ready to connect to the VPN gateway.

Implementing IPsec Remote Access VPNs Using Hybrid Authentication

As discussed at the beginning of the chapter, the problem with using group preshared key authentication with Xauth is that the Xauth exchange is protected by the IKEv1 SA that is set up using the group preshared key. This means that any member of the group (or an attacker that has obtained the inherently more insecure group preshared key) can impersonate the VPN gateway and obtain usernames and passwords used during Xauth or hijack an already established VPN connection.

So, how can you enhance the security of IPsec remote access VPNs? One option is to use digital signature authentication (using digital certificates). Another option is to use Hybrid Authentication.

Hybrid Authentication is a good option if you do not want to deploy a full PKI but want to enhance the security of your IPsec remote access VPN. The configuration of Hybrid Authentication on the Cisco VPN concentrator and the Cisco VPN Client is discussed in the following two sections.

NOTE   Hybrid Authentication is not supported on Cisco IOS routers or Cisco ASA 5500. However, IKEv2 (which addresses issues associated with IKEv1) will be supported on Cisco IOS routers and ASA 5500s.

Deploying Hybrid Authentication on the Cisco VPN 3000 Concentrator

To configure Hybrid Authentication on a Cisco VPN 3000 concentrator, follow the steps described in the section, "IKE Digital Signature Authentication on a Cisco VPN 3000 Concentrator." There are one or two *additional* considerations, however, and these are described in this section.

Under **Configuration > Policy Management > Traffic Management > SAs**, choose the IPsec SA that you configured for the group under the IPSec tab, and then click **Modify**, and you will see a screen similar to that shown in Figure 9-35.

Figure 9-35 *Modifying IPsec SA Parameters and Algorithms*

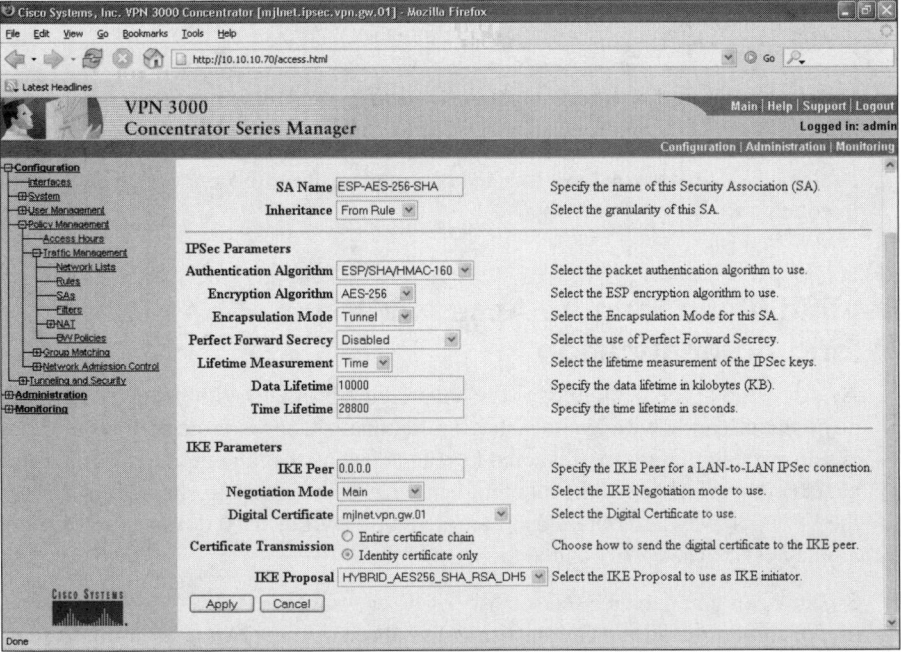

Under the section IKE Parameters at the bottom of the page, ensure that the Cisco VPN 3000 concentrator's identity certificate is selected in the Digital Certificate drop-down box and apply the configuration by clicking the **Apply** button.

Next, it is a good idea to go to **Configuration > Tunneling and Security > IPSec > IKE Proposals** and ensure that an IKE proposal that utilizes Hybrid Authentication (these include the word *Hybrid* in their names) is at the top of the Active Proposals column (see Figure 9-36).

Figure 9-36 *Active IKE Proposals*

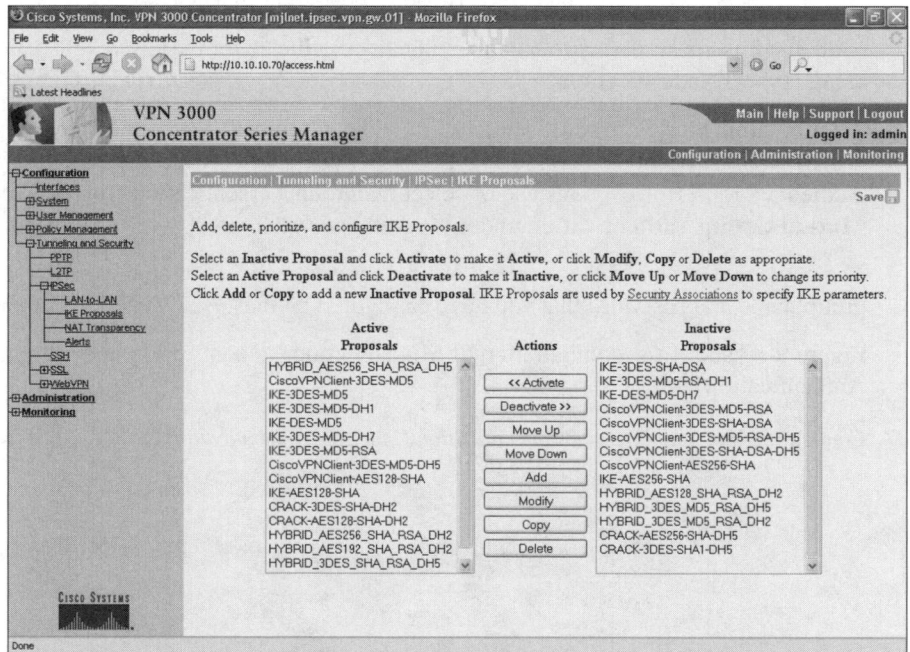

As shown in Figure 9-36, an IKE proposal that utilizes Hybrid Authentication is at the top of the Active Proposals list. You can ensure that your chosen IKE proposal is at the top of the list by selecting it and (repeatedly) clicking the **Move Up** button until it is at the top of the list.

Configuring Hybrid Authentication on Cisco VPN Clients

Now that the Cisco VPN 3000 concentrator is configured for Hybrid Authentication, you can move on to configuring the Cisco VPN Clients.

The configuration of the Cisco VPN Clients consists of the following steps:

Step 1 Obtain the CA's certificate.

Step 2 Configure a VPN connection entry and specify Mutual Group Authentication.

You can obtain the CA's certificate manually by importing it as a file. The procedure for importing a certificate can be found in the Cisco VPN Client user guide at the following

URL (select the appropriate client version and then navigate to the "Enrolling and Managing Certificates" section):

http://www.cisco.com/en/US/products/sw/secursw/ps2308/
products_user_guide_chapter09186a008031f1c5.html

Note that it is *not* necessary to obtain an identity certificate for the Cisco VPN Client when using Hybrid Authentication.

After obtaining the CA's certificate, you should configure a VPN connection entry as described in the section "Configuring a Cisco VPN Client For IKE Preshared Key Authentication." However, instead of selecting Group Authentication, you must choose **Mutual Group Authentication** under the Authentication tab.

The name and password that you enter under the Authentication tab must correspond the group name and password that you have configured on the Cisco VPN 3000 concentrator.

Figure 9-37 shows the configuration of Mutual Group Authentication under the Authentication tab.

Figure 9-37 *Configuration of Mutual Group Authentication Under the Authentication Tab*

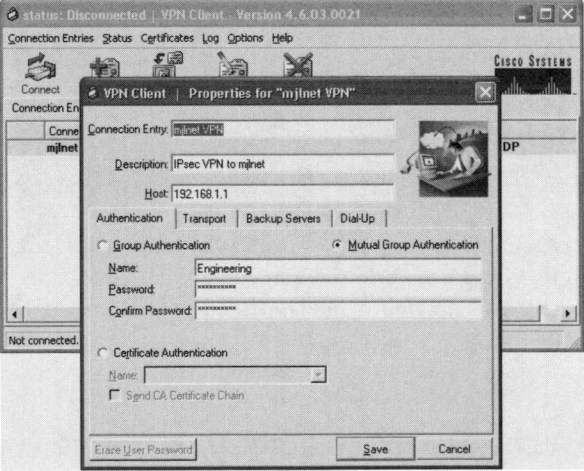

Verifying and Debugging IPsec Remote Access VPNs

You now know how to implement IPsec remote access VPNs, but how can you verify correct operation, and debug them if things go wrong?

Verifying IPsec Remote Access VPNs on Cisco VPN 3000 Concentrators

You can verify and debug IPsec remote access VPNs on the VPN gateway by going to **Monitoring > Filterable Event Log**. Example 9-4 shows a sample log when a Cisco VPN Client connects. Note that this log includes event classes IKE, IKEDBG, and IKEDECODE.

Example 9-4 *Sample Cisco VPN 3000 Concentrator Log When a Cisco VPN Client Connects*

```
1 07/04/2005 23:30:17.080 SEV=5 IKEDBG/64 RPT=6 172.16.1.1 (line 1)
IKE Peer included IKE fragmentation capability flags:
Main Mode:    True (line 2)
Aggressive Mode: False
3 07/04/2005 23:30:17.850 SEV=5 IKE/21 RPT=6 172.16.1.1
No Group found by matching IP Address of Cert peer 172.16.1.1
4 07/04/2005 23:30:17.850 SEV=5 CERT/101 RPT=6
Cert group matching feature is disabled
5 07/04/2005 23:30:17.970 SEV=5 IKE/79 RPT=6 172.16.1.1 (line 3)
Group [Engineering] (line 4)
Validation of certificate successful (line 5)
(CN=Mark Lewis, SN=6166B623000000000027) (line 6)
7 07/04/2005 23:30:27.750 SEV=4 IKE/52 RPT=4 172.16.1.1 (line 7)
Group [Engineering] User [mark] (line 8)
User (mark) authenticated. (line 9)
8 07/04/2005 23:30:28.580 SEV=5 IKE/184 RPT=4 172.16.1.1
Group [Engineering] User [mark]
Client Type: WinNT
Client Application Version: 4.6.03.0021
10 07/04/2005 23:30:28.690 SEV=4 IKE/119 RPT=3 172.16.1.1
Group [Engineering] User [mark]
PHASE 1 COMPLETED (line 10)
11 07/04/2005 23:30:28.700 SEV=4 AUTH/22 RPT=3 172.16.1.1
User [mark] Group [Engineering] connected, Session Type: IPSec
12 07/04/2005 23:30:28.710 SEV=5 IKE/25 RPT=3 172.16.1.1
Group [Engineering] User [mark]
Received remote Proxy Host data in ID Payload:
Address 10.30.20.1, Protocol 0, Port 0
15 07/04/2005 23:30:28.710 SEV=5 IKE/34 RPT=3 172.16.1.1
Group [Engineering] User [mark]
Received local IP Proxy Subnet data in ID Payload:
 Address 0.0.0.0, Mask 0.0.0.0, Protocol 0, Port 0
18 07/04/2005 23:30:28.710 SEV=5 IKE/66 RPT=3 172.16.1.1
Group [Engineering] User [mark]
IKE Remote Peer configured for SA: ESP-3DES-MD5 (line 11)
19 07/04/2005 23:30:28.720 SEV=5 IKE/75 RPT=3 172.16.1.1
Group [Engineering] User [mark]
Overriding Initiator's IPSec rekeying duration from 2147483 to 28800 seconds
21 07/04/2005 23:30:28.760 SEV=4 IKE/49 RPT=3 172.16.1.1
Group [Engineering] User [mark]
Security negotiation complete for User (mark)
Responder, Inbound SPI = 0x4c726a26, Outbound SPI = 0x8d8265a4
24 07/04/2005 23:30:28.770 SEV=4 IKE/120 RPT=3 172.16.1.1
Group [Engineering] User [mark]
PHASE 2 COMPLETED (msgid=225a047a) (line 12)
25 07/04/2005 23:30:28.770 SEV=4 NAC/27 RPT=3
NAC is disabled for peer - PUB_IP:172.16.1.1, PRV_IP:10.30.20.1
26 07/04/2005 23:30:47.310 SEV=5 IKE/50 RPT=2 172.16.1.1
Group [Engineering] User [mark]
Connection terminated for peer mark. (line 13)
Reason: Peer Terminate (line 14)
Remote Proxy 10.30.20.1, Local Proxy 0.0.0.0
```

continues

Example 9-4 *Sample Cisco VPN 3000 Concentrator Log When a Cisco VPN Client Connects (Continued)*

```
29 07/04/2005 23:30:47.320 SEV=5 IKE/194 RPT=6 172.16.1.1
Group [Engineering] User [mark]
Sending IKE Delete With Reason message: No Reason Provided.
31 07/04/2005 23:30:47.320 SEV=4 AUTH/28 RPT=3 172.16.1.1
User [mark] Group [Engineering] disconnected: (line 15)
 Session Type: IPSec (line 16)
 Duration: 0:00:18 (line 17)
 Bytes xmt: 256 (line 18)
 Bytes rcv: 584 (line 19)
 Reason: User Requested (line 20)
```

Lines 1 and 2 show that an IKEv1 phase 1 (main mode) message has been received from a remote access VPN client.

Lines 3 to 6 show that IKEv1 phase 1 (main mode) authentication has been successful and that remote access VPN client's certificate (OU field) has identified the user as belonging to the Engineering group.

IKE Xauth now succeeds. The user is identified as mark (lines 7 to 9).

IKEv1 phase 1 has been completed, as indicated in line 10.

Line 11 indicates the IPsec SA configured for user mark (the IPsec SA is, in this case, inherited from the group).

In line 12, you can see that IKEv1 phase 2 has been completed. The remote access VPN client is connected.

The remote access VPN client now terminates his connection (see lines 13 and 14).

Lines 15 to 20 show information related to the terminated remote access VPN client's connection. Specifically, they show that the VPN connection type was IPsec, the duration was 18 seconds, and the number of bytes transmitted (xmt) and received (rcv) to/from the remote access VPN client were 256 and 584 respectively.

You can also find information concerning IPsec remote access VPN connections by going to **Monitoring > Sessions** and **Monitoring > Statistics > IPSec**.

Verifying IPsec Remote Access VPNs on Cisco IOS VPN Gateways

You can use a number of **show** and **debug** commands to verify IPsec remote access VPNs, including **show crypto isakmp sa**, **show crypto ipsec sa**, and **debug crypto isakmp sa**.

Examples 9-5 to 9-8 shows the output of the **debug crypto isakmp sa** command, which shows IKE negotiation between a Cisco IOS VPN gateway and a remote access VPN client. Note that only the relevant output is shown.

As with all **debug** commands, you should be careful when using the **debug crypto isakmp sa** command because its use can severely disrupt the operation of a heavily loaded router.

Example 9-5 *IKE Phase 1 Is Negotiated*

```
mjlnet.VPN.GW.01#debug crypto isakmp
Crypto ISAKMP debugging is on
mjlnet.VPN.GW.01#
*Jul 16 13:09:13.827: ISAKMP (0:0): received packet from 172.16.1.1 dport 500 sport
 500 Global (N) NEW SA (line 1)
<output omitted>
*Jul 16 13:09:13.831: ISAKMP:(0:0:N/A:0): processing ID payload.
 message ID = 0 (line 2)
*Jul 16 13:09:13.831: ISAKMP (0:0): ID payload
        next-payload : 13
        type     : 11
        group id   : mjlVPN (line 3)
        protocol   : 17
        port     : 500
        length    : 14
*Jul 16 13:09:13.831: ISAKMP:(0:0:N/A:0):: peer matches *none* of the profiles
*Jul 16 13:09:13.831: ISAKMP:(0:0:N/A:0): processing vendor id payload
*Jul 16 13:09:13.831: ISAKMP:(0:0:N/A:0): vendor ID seems Unity/DPD but major 215
 mismatch
*Jul 16 13:09:13.831: ISAKMP:(0:0:N/A:0): vendor ID is XAUTH (line 4)
*Jul 16 13:09:13.831: ISAKMP:(0:0:N/A:0): processing vendor id payload
*Jul 16 13:09:13.831: ISAKMP:(0:0:N/A:0): vendor ID is DPD
*Jul 16 13:09:13.831: ISAKMP:(0:0:N/A:0): processing vendor id payload
*Jul 16 13:09:13.831: ISAKMP:(0:0:N/A:0): vendor ID seems Unity/DPD but major 123
 mismatch
*Jul 16 13:09:13.831: ISAKMP:(0:0:N/A:0): vendor ID is NAT-T v2
*Jul 16 13:09:13.831: ISAKMP:(0:0:N/A:0): processing vendor id payload
*Jul 16 13:09:13.831: ISAKMP:(0:0:N/A:0): vendor ID seems Unity/DPD but major 194
 mismatch
*Jul 16 13:09:13.831: ISAKMP:(0:0:N/A:0): processing vendor id payload
*Jul 16 13:09:13.831: ISAKMP:(0:0:N/A:0): vendor ID is Unity
*Jul 16 13:09:13.831: ISAKMP:(0:0:N/A:0): Authentication by xauth preshared
*Jul 16 13:09:13.831: ISAKMP:(0:0:N/A:0):Checking ISAKMP transform 1 against priority
 10 policy (line 5)
*Jul 16 13:09:13.831: ISAKMP:    encryption AES-CBC
*Jul 16 13:09:13.831: ISAKMP:    hash SHA
*Jul 16 13:09:13.831: ISAKMP:    default group 2
*Jul 16 13:09:13.831: ISAKMP:    auth XAUTHInitPreShared
*Jul 16 13:09:13.831: ISAKMP:    life type in seconds
*Jul 16 13:09:13.831: ISAKMP:    life duration (VPI) of 0x0 0x20 0xC4 0x9B
*Jul 16 13:09:13.831: ISAKMP:    keylength of 256
*Jul 16 13:09:13.831: ISAKMP:(0:0:N/A:0):Encryption algorithm offered does not match
 policy! (line 6)
<output omitted>
*Jul 16 13:09:13.839: ISAKMP:(0:0:N/A:0):Checking ISAKMP transform 13 against priority
 10 policy (line 7)
*Jul 16 13:09:13.839: ISAKMP:    encryption DES-CBC
*Jul 16 13:09:13.839: ISAKMP:    hash MD5
*Jul 16 13:09:13.839: ISAKMP:    default group 2
```

continues

Example 9-5 *IKE Phase 1 Is Negotiated (Continued)*

```
*Jul 16 13:09:13.839: ISAKMP:    auth XAUTHInitPreShared
*Jul 16 13:09:13.839: ISAKMP:    life type in seconds
*Jul 16 13:09:13.839: ISAKMP:    life duration (VPI) of 0x0 0x20 0xC4 0x9B
*Jul 16 13:09:13.839: ISAKMP:(0:0:N/A:0):atts are acceptable.
 Next payload is 3 (line 8)
<output omitted>
*Jul 16 13:09:13.979: ISAKMP:(0:1:SW:1):Old State = IKE_R_AM2 New State =
 IKE_P1_COMPLETE (line 9)
```

Line 1 shows that the Cisco IOS VPN gateway has received an ISAKMP packet from a remote access VPN client (172.16.1.1).

As shown in line 2, this packet contains an ID payload, and in line 3, you can see that the ID payload contains a group name. This group name must match one of those configured on the Cisco IOS VPN gateway.

The packet also contains a vendor ID that is used to specify Xauth (line 4).

Then, in line 5, the Cisco IOS VPN gateway begins to check ISAKMP transforms contained in the ISAKMP packet received from the remote access VPN client against its own locally configured IKE (ISAKMP) policies.

The algorithms and parameters associated with the first transform are shown below line 5.

In line 6, you can see that the encryption algorithm contained in the transform does not match the locally configured IKE policy.

The Cisco IOS VPN gateway then checks a further 11 transforms against its locally configured IKE policy, all of which do not, in one way or other, match, before getting to the thirteenth transform (line 7).

Line 8 shows that this transform is acceptable, and after the exchange of a further two messages (not shown), in line 9, you can see that IKE phase 1 (P1) is complete.

As shown in Example 9-6, IKE negotiation now continues with Xauth.

Example 9-6 *IKE Negotiation Continues with Xauth*

```
*Jul 16 13:09:13.979: ISAKMP:(0:1:SW:1):Need XAUTH
*Jul 16 13:09:13.979: ISAKMP: set new node -1863776210 to CONF_XAUTH
*Jul 16 13:09:13.979: ISAKMP/xauth: request attribute XAUTH_USER_NAME_V2 (line 1)
*Jul 16 13:09:13.979: ISAKMP/xauth: request attribute XAUTH_USER_PASSWORD_V2 (line 2)
*Jul 16 13:09:13.979: ISAKMP:(0:1:SW:1): initiating peer config to 172.16.1.1. ID = -
 1863776210
*Jul 16 13:09:13.979: ISAKMP:(0:1:SW:1): sending packet to 172.16.1.1 my_port 500
 peer_port 500 (R) CONF_XAUTH  (line 3)
*Jul 16 13:09:13.979: ISAKMP:(0:1:SW:1):Input = IKE_MESG_INTERNAL, IKE_PHASE1_COMPLETE
*Jul 16 13:09:13.979: ISAKMP:(0:1:SW:1):Old State = IKE_P1_COMPLETE New State =
 IKE_XAUTH_REQ_SENT
*Jul 16 13:09:18.083: ISAKMP (0:134217729): received packet from 172.16.1.1 dport 500
 sport 500 Global (R) CONF_XAUTH  (line 4)
```

Example 9-6 *IKE Negotiation Continues with Xauth (Continued)*

```
*Jul 16 13:09:18.083: ISAKMP:(0:1:SW:1):processing transaction payload from
 172.16.1.1. message ID = -1863776210
*Jul 16 13:09:18.083: ISAKMP: Config payload REPLY
*Jul 16 13:09:18.083: ISAKMP/xauth: reply attribute XAUTH_USER_NAME_V2 (line 5)
*Jul 16 13:09:18.083: ISAKMP/xauth: reply attribute XAUTH_USER_PASSWORD_V2 (line 6)
*Jul 16 13:09:18.083: ISAKMP:(0:1:SW:1):deleting node -1863776210 error FALSE reason
 "Done with xauth request/reply exchange"
*Jul 16 13:09:18.083: ISAKMP:(0:1:SW:1):Input = IKE_MESG_FROM_PEER, IKE_CFG_REPLY
*Jul 16 13:09:18.083: ISAKMP:(0:1:SW:1):Old State = IKE_XAUTH_REQ_SENT New State =
 IKE_XAUTH_AAA_CONT_LOGIN_AWAIT
<output omitted>
```

In lines 1 to 3, you can see that the Cisco IOS VPN gateway has sent an ISAKMP packet to the remote access VPN client requesting an Xauth username and password.

Lines 4 to 6 show that the remote access VPN client has replied with an Xauth username and password.

Xauth completes successfully, and in Example 9-7, IKE ISAKMP Configuration Method (Mode Config) exchange takes place.

Example 9-7 *ISAKMP Configuration Method Exchange Takes Place*

```
*Jul 16 13:09:18.287: ISAKMP (0:134217729): received packet from 172.16.1.1 dport 500
 sport 500 Global (R) QM_IDLE   (line 1)
*Jul 16 13:09:18.287: ISAKMP: set new node -1607912449 to QM_IDLE
*Jul 16 13:09:18.287: ISAKMP:(0:1:SW:1):processing transaction payload from
 172.16.1.1. message ID = -1607912449
*Jul 16 13:09:18.287: ISAKMP: Config payload REQUEST (line 2)
*Jul 16 13:09:18.287: ISAKMP:(0:1:SW:1):checking request:
*Jul 16 13:09:18.287: ISAKMP:   IP4_ADDRESS
*Jul 16 13:09:18.287: ISAKMP:   IP4_NETMASK
*Jul 16 13:09:18.287: ISAKMP:   IP4_DNS
*Jul 16 13:09:18.287: ISAKMP:   IP4_NBNS
*Jul 16 13:09:18.287: ISAKMP:   ADDRESS_EXPIRY
*Jul 16 13:09:18.287: ISAKMP:   UNKNOWN Unknown Attr: 0x7000
*Jul 16 13:09:18.287: ISAKMP:   MODECFG_SAVEPWD
*Jul 16 13:09:18.287: ISAKMP:   DEFAULT_DOMAIN
*Jul 16 13:09:18.287: ISAKMP:   SPLIT_INCLUDE
*Jul 16 13:09:18.287: ISAKMP:   SPLIT_DNS
*Jul 16 13:09:18.287: ISAKMP:   PFS
*Jul 16 13:09:18.287: ISAKMP:   UNKNOWN Unknown Attr: 0x700B
*Jul 16 13:09:18.287: ISAKMP:   BACKUP_SERVER
*Jul 16 13:09:18.287: ISAKMP:   APPLICATION_VERSION
*Jul 16 13:09:18.287: ISAKMP:   FW_RECORD
*Jul 16 13:09:18.287: ISAKMP:   UNKNOWN Unknown Attr: 0x700A
*Jul 16 13:09:18.287: ISAKMP:   UNKNOWN Unknown Attr: 0x7005
*Jul 16 13:09:18.287: ISAKMP/author: setting up the authorization request
*Jul 16 13:09:18.287: ISAKMP/author: Author request successfully sent to AAA
*Jul 16 13:09:18.287: ISAKMP:(0:1:SW:1):Input = IKE_MESG_FROM_PEER, IKE_CFG_REQUEST
*Jul 16 13:09:18.287: ISAKMP:(0:1:SW:1):Old State = IKE_P1_COMPLETE New State =
 IKE_CONFIG_AUTHOR_AAA_AWAIT
```

continues

Example 9-7 *ISAKMP Configuration Method Exchange Takes Place (Continued)*

```
*Jul 16 13:09:18.287: ISAKMP:(0:1:SW:1):attributes sent in message: (line 3)
*Jul 16 13:09:18.287:    Address: 0.2.0.0
*Jul 16 13:09:18.287: ISAKMP:(0:1:SW:1):allocating address 10.30.20.3
*Jul 16 13:09:18.287: ISAKMP: Sending private address: 10.30.20.3 (line 4)
*Jul 16 13:09:18.287: ISAKMP: Sending IP4_DNS server address: 10.10.10.161 (line 5)
*Jul 16 13:09:18.287: ISAKMP: Sending IP4_NBNS server address: 10.10.10.171 (line 6)
*Jul 16 13:09:18.287: ISAKMP: Sending ADDRESS_EXPIRY seconds left to use the address:
  86395
*Jul 16 13:09:18.287: ISAKMP (0/134217729): Unknown Attr: UNKNOWN (0x7000)
*Jul 16 13:09:18.287: ISAKMP: Sending save password reply value 0
*Jul 16 13:09:18.287: ISAKMP (0/134217729): Unknown Attr: UNKNOWN (0x700B)
*Jul 16 13:09:18.287: ISAKMP: Sending APPLICATION_VERSION string: Cisco IOS Software,
   7200 Software (C7200-A3JK9S-M), Version 12.3(8)T, RELEASE SOFTWARE (fc2)
   Technical Support: http://www.cisco.com/techsupport
   Copyright © 1986-2004 by Cisco Systems, Inc.
 Compiled Thu 13-May-04 21:20 by eaarmas
*Jul 16 13:09:18.291: ISAKMP (0/134217729): Unknown Attr: UNKNOWN (0x700A)
*Jul 16 13:09:18.291: ISAKMP (0/134217729): Unknown Attr: UNKNOWN (0x7005)
*Jul 16 13:09:18.291: ISAKMP:(0:1:SW:1): responding to peer config from 172.16.1.1.
   ID = -1607912449
*Jul 16 13:09:18.291: ISAKMP:(0:1:SW:1): sending packet to 172.16.1.1 my_port 500
   peer_port 500 (R) CONF_ADDR
<output omitted>
```

An ISAKMP packet is received from the remote access VPN client (line 1). This is an ISAKMP_CFG_REQUEST (see line 2).

Line 3 shows the Cisco IOS VPN gateway sending an ISAKMP_CFG_REPLY, which contains a number of attributes, including an IP address (line 4), a DNS server address (line 5), and a WINS server address (line 6).

IKE phase 2 (quick mode) now completes IKE negotiation (Example 9-8).

Example 9-8 *IKE Negotiation Now Completes with IKE Phase 2 (Quick Mode)*

```
*Jul 16 13:09:18.363: ISAKMP (0:134217729): received packet from 172.16.1.1 dport 500
  sport 500 Global (R) QM_IDLE  (line 1)
*Jul 16 13:09:18.363: ISAKMP: set new node -1293319992 to QM_IDLE
<output omitted>
*Jul 16 13:09:18.379: ISAKMP:(0:1:SW:1):Checking IPSec proposal 14 (line 2)
*Jul 16 13:09:18.379: ISAKMP: transform 1, ESP_DES
*Jul 16 13:09:18.379: ISAKMP:  attributes in transform:
*Jul 16 13:09:18.379: ISAKMP:   authenticator is HMAC-MD5
*Jul 16 13:09:18.379: ISAKMP:   encaps is 1 (Tunnel)
*Jul 16 13:09:18.379: ISAKMP:   SA life type in seconds
*Jul 16 13:09:18.379: ISAKMP:   SA life duration (VPI) of 0x0 0x20 0xC4 0x9B
*Jul 16 13:09:18.379: ISAKMP:(0:1:SW:1):atts are acceptable. (line 3)
<output omitted>
*Jul 16 13:09:18.635: %CRYPTO-5-SESSION_STATUS: Crypto tunnel is UP .
   Peer 172.16.1.1:500   Id: mjlVPN (line 4)
*Jul 16 13:09:18.691: ISAKMP:(0:1:SW:1):Old State = IKE_QM_R_QM2 New State =
  IKE_QM_PHASE2_COMPLETE (line 5)
```

An ISAKMP packet is received from the remote access VPN client in highlighted line 1—this packet is the first in the IKE phase 2 (quick mode [QM]) negotiation.

This packet contains a number of IPsec transforms, and these are checked against the IPsec transform configured locally on the Cisco IOS VPN gateway.

Line 2 shows the Cisco IOS VPN gateway checking the fourteenth proposal sent by the remote access VPN client against the locally configured IPsec transform, and line 3 shows that this proposal is acceptable. Note that the first 13 proposals sent by the remote access VPN client (not shown) were not acceptable.

In lines 4 and 5, you can see that IKE phase 2 (quick mode) is complete, and that the IPsec VPN (crypto) tunnel is up (active).

You can verify IKE SAs using the **show crypt isakmp sa** command (see Example 9-9).

Example 9-9 show crypto isakmp sa *Command Output*

```
mjlnet.VPN.GW.01#show crypto isakmp sa
dst          src         state       conn-id slot
192.168.1.1   172.16.1.1   QM_IDLE        1   0
mjlnet.VPN.GW.01#
```

The highlighted line in Example 9-9 shows the local and remote IP addresses (VPN tunnel endpoints) as well as the fact that IKE phase 2 (quick mode [QM]) has been negotiated and is now in an idle state.

As shown in Example 9-10, you can use the **show crypto ipsec sa** command to examine IPsec SAs negotiated between the local Cisco IOS VPN gateway and the remote access VPN client.

Example 9-10 show crypto ipsec sa *Command Output*

```
mjlnet.VPN.GW.01#show crypto ipsec sa
interface: FastEthernet2/0
  Crypto map tag: mjlnetMap, local addr. 192.168.1.1 (line 1)
  protected vrf:
  local ident (addr/mask/prot/port): (0.0.0.0/0.0.0.0/0/0)
  remote ident (addr/mask/prot/port): (10.2.2.3/255.255.255.255/0/0)
  current_peer: 172.16.1.1:500
   PERMIT, flags={}
  #pkts encaps: 0, #pkts encrypt: 0, #pkts digest: 0
  #pkts decaps: 40, #pkts decrypt: 40, #pkts verify: 40
  #pkts compressed: 0, #pkts decompressed: 0
  #pkts not compressed: 0, #pkts compr. failed: 0
  #pkts not decompressed: 0, #pkts decompress failed: 0
  #send errors 0, #recv errors 0
   local crypto endpt.: 192.168.1.1, remote crypto endpt.: 172.16.1.1 (line 2)
   path mtu 1500, media mtu 1500
   current outbound spi: 88FACC5D
   inbound esp sas: (line 3)
   spi: 0xA12E6583(2704172419)
    transform: esp-des esp-md5-hmac,
    in use settings ={Tunnel, }
```

continues

Example 9-10 **show crypto ipsec sa** *Command Output (Continued)*

```
            slot: 0, conn id: 2000, flow_id: 1, crypto map: mjlnetMap
            crypto engine type: Software, engine_id: 1
            sa timing: remaining key lifetime (k/sec): (4558818/3515)
            ike_cookies: 395D08CA 6998BFAF 4F693ECA 7505FBCC
            IV size: 8 bytes
            replay detection support: Y
         inbound ah sas:
         inbound pcp sas:
         outbound esp sas: (line 4)
         spi: 0x88FACC5D(2298137693)
           transform: esp-des esp-md5-hmac,
           in use settings ={Tunnel, }
           slot: 0, conn id: 2001, flow_id: 2, crypto map: mjlnetMap
           crypto engine type: Software, engine_id: 1
           sa timing: remaining key lifetime (k/sec): (4558833/3513)
           ike_cookies: 395D08CA 6998BFAF 4F693ECA 7505FBCC
           IV size: 8 bytes
           replay detection support: Y
         outbound ah sas:
         outbound pcp sas:
mjlnet.VPN.GW.01#
```

Highlighted line 1 shows that crypto map mjlnetMap is applied to interface FastEthernet 2/0.

In highlighted lines 2, you can see the local and remote VPN tunnel endpoints.

Then, below highlighted lines 3 and 4, you can see details of inbound and outbound (ESP) SAs negotiated with a remote access VPN client.

NOTE   For in-depth information about verifying and troubleshooting IPsec VPNs, see the book *Troubleshooting Virtual Private Networks* (Cisco Press).

Verifying IPsec Remote Access VPNs on the Cisco ASA

You can use a number of commands to verify IPsec remote access VPNs on the Cisco ASA 5500—two of the most useful are **show isakmp sa** and **show ipsec sa**.

Example 9-11 shows the output of the **show isakmp sa** command.

Example 9-11 **show isakmp sa** *Command Output*

```
mjlnet.VPN.GW.10# show isakmp sa

   Active SA: 1
   Rekey SA: 0 (A tunnel will report 1 Active and 1 Rekey SA during rekey)
   Total IKE SA: 1 (line 1)

1  IKE Peer: 192.168.1.147 (line 2)
   Type  : user      Role  : responder (line 3)
   Rekey : no        State : MM_ACTIVE (line 4)

mjlnet.VPN.GW.10#
```

Line 1 shows the total number of IKE (ISKAMP) SAs, which in this case is 1.

Lines 2 to 4 show information relating to the IKE SA. In particular, highlighted line 2 shows that the IKE peer (remote access VPN client) is 192.168.1.147, highlighted line 3 shows that the IKE role of the Cisco ASA 5500 in this case is responder (rather than initiator), and highlighted line 4 shows that the current state is MM_ACTIVE (IKE main mode has been negotiated).

Example 9-12 shows the output of the **show ipsec sa** command.

Example 9-12 **show ipsec sa** *Command Output*

```
mjlnet.VPN.GW.10# show ipsec sa

interface: Outside0/1 (line 1)
   Crypto map tag: mjlnet-dynamic, local addr: 192.168.1.149 (line 2)

     local ident (addr/mask/prot/port): (0.0.0.0/0.0.0.0/0/0)
     remote ident (addr/mask/prot/port):
(10.10.10.160/255.255.255.255/0/0)
     current_peer: 192.168.1.147 (line 3)
     dynamic allocated peer ip: 10.10.10.160 (line 4)

     #pkts encaps: 2081, #pkts encrypt: 2081, #pkts digest: 2081
     #pkts decaps: 1479, #pkts decrypt: 1479, #pkts verify: 1479
     #pkts compressed: 0, #pkts decompressed: 0
     #pkts not compressed: 2081, #pkts comp failed: 0, #pkts decomp
failed: 0
     #send errors: 0, #recv errors: 0

     local crypto endpt.: 192.168.1.149, remote crypto endpt.:
192.168.1.147
     path mtu 1500, ipsec overhead 60, media mtu 1500
     current outbound spi: A55CF4D3
   inbound esp sas: (line 5)
     spi: 0xEF2D9E27 (4012744231)
       transform: esp-3des esp-sha-hmac
       in use settings ={RA, Tunnel, }
       slot: 0, conn_id: 1, crypto-map: mjlnet-dynamic
       sa timing: remaining key lifetime (sec): 28496
       IV size: 8 bytes
       replay detection support: Y
   outbound esp sas: (line 6)
     spi: 0xA55CF4D3 (2774332627)
       transform: esp-3des esp-sha-hmac
       in use settings ={RA, Tunnel, }
       slot: 0, conn_id: 1, crypto-map: mjlnet-dynamic
       sa timing: remaining key lifetime (sec): 28496
       IV size: 8 bytes
       replay detection support: Y

mjlnet.VPN.GW.10#
```

Highlighted lines 1 and 2 show that a (dynamic) crypto map is applied to interface Outside0/1 and that the local address is 192.168.1.149.

In highlighted lines 3 and 4, you can see that the remote access VPN client's address is 192.168.1.147 and that it has been assigned the IP address 10.10.10.160 from the IP address pool (this is applied to the virtual adapter [VPN tunnel interface]).

You can also see details regarding inbound and outbound ESP SAs below lines 5 and 6.

Other useful commands include the following:

- **show crypto accelerator statistics**—This command displays information from the hardware crypto accelerator.

- **show isakmp stats**—This command displays IKE (ISAKMP) statistics including the number of active tunnels, packet statistics, and IKE phase 2 exchanges.

- **show ipsec stats**—This command displays IPsec statistics including the number active tunnels, the number of previous tunnels, packet/byte statistics, and statistics relating to authentication and encryption.

- **show crypto ca certificates**—This command displays certificates stored on the Cisco ASA 5500.

- **show crypto ca crls**—This command displays CRLs that have been cached by the Cisco ASA 5500.

- **show crypto key mypubkey**—This command displays key pairs.

- **debug crypto isakmp** [*level*]—This shows information relating to IKE (ISAKMP) negotiation. The *level* parameter can be a value from 1 to 255 (the default is 1), and it controls the amount of information displayed—a value of 127 displays a similar level of detail to that displayed by the **debug crypto isakmp** command on a Cisco IOS router.

- **debug crypto ipsec** [*level*]—This shows debug information relating to IPsec in general. The *level* parameter again controls the level of detail displayed.

Verifying IPsec Remote Access VPNs on Cisco VPN Clients

There are two main ways to verify a IPsec remote access VPN on a Cisco VPN Client:

- You can view VPN connection statistics.

- You can examine the log files.

You can view VPN connection statistics by going to the Status menu and choosing **Statistics**. You will then be presented with VPN connection information, as shown in Figure 9-38.

Figure 9-38 *Examining VPN Connection Statistics*

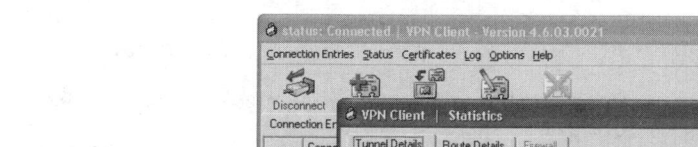

In Figure 9-38, the VPN connection statistics shown include the VPN client address (applied to the virtual adapter/VPN tunnel interface [supplied by the VPN gateway]), server address, entry name, connection duration, bytes sent and received, algorithms used for encryption and authentication, packets encrypted and decrypted, as well as the status of other transport options such as compression.

If you need more detailed information, you can enable logging by going to the Log menu and choosing **Enable**. You can then select the types and amount of logging information by choosing **Log Settings** from the Log menu.

Logging can be viewed by clicking the Log tab or navigating to <system_root> \Program Files\Cisco Systems\VPN Client\Logs and opening the text file that relates to a particular VPN connection attempt (the files are time and date stamped).

The (considerably edited/shortened) log file shown in Example 9-13 was produced by specifying a high level (3) of IKE logging in Log Settings.

Example 9-13 *Sample Cisco VPN Client Log*

```
Cisco Systems VPN Client Version 4.6.03.0021
Copyright © 1998-2005 Cisco Systems, Inc. All Rights Reserved.
Client Type(s): Windows, WinNT
Running on: 5.1.2600 Service Pack 2
Config file directory: C:\Program Files\Cisco Systems\VPN Client\
1    23:30:43.986 07/04/05 Sev=Info/6  IKE/0x6300003B
Attempting to establish a connection with 192.168.1.1.
2    23:30:45.699 07/04/05 Sev=Info/4  IKE/0x63000013
SENDING >>> ISAKMP OAK MM (SA, VID(Xauth), VID(dpd), VID(Nat-T), VID(Frag),
  VID(Unity)) to 192.168.1.1 (line 1)
3    23:30:45.869 07/04/05 Sev=Info/5  IKE/0x6300002F
Received ISAKMP packet: peer = 192.168.1.1
4    23:30:45.869 07/04/05 Sev=Info/4  IKE/0x63000014
RECEIVING <<< ISAKMP OAK MM (SA, VID(Frag)) from 192.168.1.1 (line 2)
<output omitted>
```

continues

Example 9-13 *Sample Cisco VPN Client Log (Continued)*

```
44   23:30:57.225 07/04/05 Sev=Info/5   IKE/0x63000010
MODE_CFG_REPLY: Attribute = INTERNAL_IPV4_ADDRESS: , value = 10.30.20.1 (line 3)
45   23:30:57.235 07/04/05 Sev=Info/5   IKE/0x63000010
MODE_CFG_REPLY: Attribute = INTERNAL_IPV4_NETMASK: , value = 255.255.255.0 (line 4)
46   23:30:57.235 07/04/05 Sev=Info/5   IKE/0x63000010
MODE_CFG_REPLY: Attribute = INTERNAL_IPV4_DNS(1): , value = 10.10.10.160 (line 5)
47   23:30:57.235 07/04/05 Sev=Info/5   IKE/0x63000010
MODE_CFG_REPLY: Attribute = INTERNAL_IPV4_DNS(2): , value = 10.10.10.161 (line 6)
<output omitted>

55   23:30:57.326 07/04/05 Sev=Info/4   IKE/0x63000013
SENDING >>> ISAKMP OAK QM *(HASH, SA, NON, ID, ID) to 192.168.1.1 (line 7)
56   23:30:57.356 07/04/05 Sev=Info/5   IKE/0x6300002F
Received ISAKMP packet: peer = 192.168.1.1
57   23:30:57.356 07/04/05 Sev=Info/4   IKE/0x63000014
RECEIVING <<< ISAKMP OAK INFO *(HASH, NOTIFY:STATUS_RESP_LIFETIME) from 192.168.1.1
   (line 8)
58   23:30:57.366 07/04/05 Sev=Info/5   IKE/0x63000045
RESPONDER-LIFETIME notify has value of 86400 seconds
59   23:30:57.376 07/04/05 Sev=Info/5   IKE/0x63000047
This SA has already been alive for 12 seconds, setting expiry to 86388 seconds from now
<output omitted>
```

Lines 1 and 2 show the exchange of the first two messages in IKEv1 phase 1 (main mode [MM]) negotiation. Main mode is made up of the exchange of six messages.

In lines 3 to 6, a number of ISAKMP Configuration Method (Mode Config [MODE CFG]) attributes are supplied by the VPN gateway to the Cisco VPN Client. The attributes shown include IPv4 address (to be applied to the virtual adapter/VPN tunnel interface), IPv4 network mask, and DNS server addresses.

Lines 7 and 8 show an exchange of messages during IKEv1 phase 2 (quick mode [QM]) negotiation. Quick mode consists of the exchange of 3 messages.

After quick mode has completed successfully, the VPN connection is active.

Configuring NAT Transparency for IPsec Remote Access VPNs

When there is a Network Address Translation / Port Address Translation (NAT/PAT) device between the Cisco VPN Client and the VPN gateway, there may be problems establishing IPsec remote access VPN connections (see Figure 9-39). Cisco VPN 3000 concentrators, IOS VPN gateways, Cisco ASA 5500s, and Cisco VPN Clients support a variety of methods of overcoming this issue.

NOTE   For more detailed information on issues with IPsec when there is a NAT/PAT device between IPsec peers, see the section "Deploying IPsec VPNs with NAT/PAT" in Chapter 6.

Figure 9-39 *NAT/PAT Devices May Prevent IPsec Remote Access VPN Connections from Being Established*

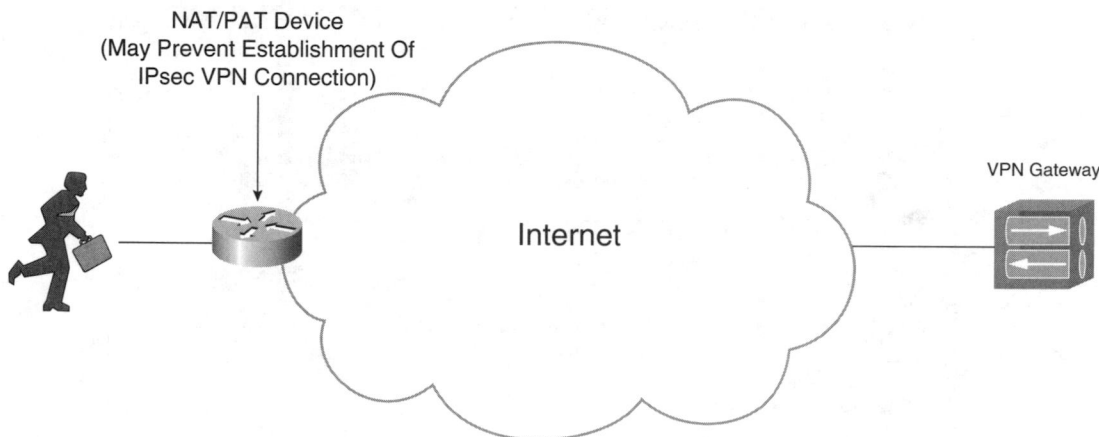

The sections that follow describe how you can overcome issues with NAT/PAT if your VPN gateway is a Cisco VPN 3000 concentrator, if your VPN gateway is a Cisco IOS router, or if your VPN gateway is a Cisco ASA 5500.

Overcoming Issues with NAT/PAT When Using Cisco VPN 3000 Concentrators

Cisco VPN concentrators provide a number of methods of overcoming issues with NAT/PAT. These methods each provide *NAT transparency* and can be summarized as follows:

- Configure NAT transparency for IPsec using TCP on an administrator-defined port (default 10000).

  It is worth noting that IPsec over TCP can, in certain circumstances, cause performance issues. So, this is not generally considered the preferred method of implementing NAT transparency.

- Configure NAT transparency for IPsec using UDP on an administrator-defined port (default 10000).

- Configure NAT transparency using IETF standard NAT Traversal (NAT-T). NAT-T uses UDP port 4500.

All three methods overcome issues with NAT/PAT devices by encapsulating IPsec packets in either TCP or UDP (NAT/PAT devices can typically much more easily handle TCP or UDP than ESP [AH does not work with NAT/PAT at all]).

The first two methods are not industry standards and will only work with Cisco VPN Clients. The third method is an IETF standard and so will work with both Cisco VPN Clients, and other VPN clients.

To configure NAT transparency, you need to go to **Configuration > Tunneling and Security > IPSec > NAT Transparency** (see Figure 9-40).

Figure 9-40 *Configuring NAT Transparency on Cisco VPN 3000 Concentrators*

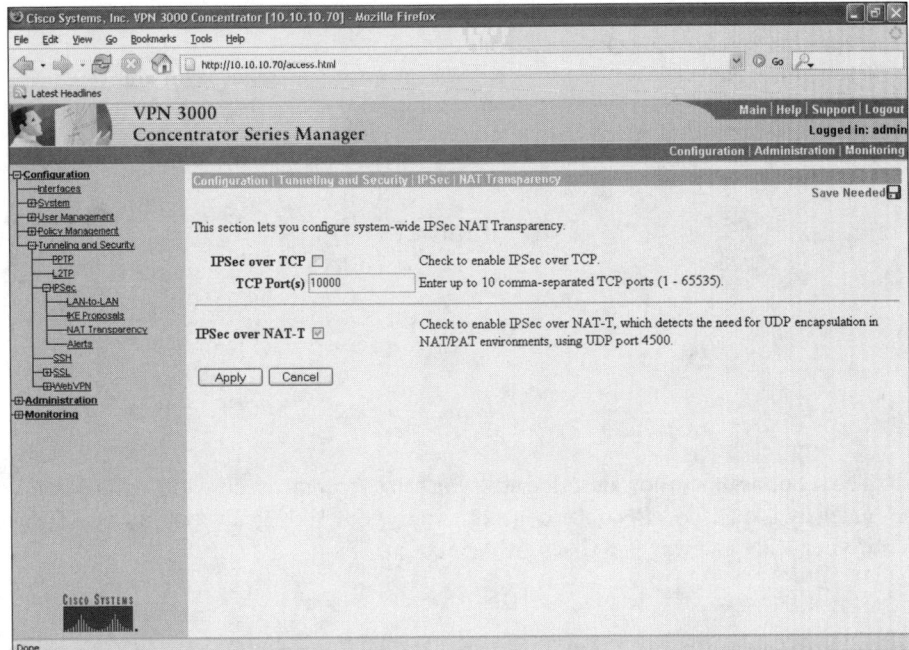

As you can see from looking at Figure 9-40, configuration is fairly straightforward:

- If you want to use NAT transparency for IPsec using TCP (IPsec over TCP), check the **IPSec over TCP** box (Figure 9-40), optionally modify the TCP port (the default is 10000), and click **Apply**.

- If you want to use NAT transparency for IPsec using UDP on an administrator-defined port, you must go to **Configuration > User Management > Groups**, select the appropriate group, click **Modify**, select the IPSec tab, check **IPSec through NAT**, and optionally specify a UDP port (the default is 10000). After you have done that, click **Apply**.

- If you want to use NAT transparency for IPsec using IETF standard NAT-T, check the **IPSec over NAT-T** box (Figure 9-40), and then click **Apply**.

Overcoming Issues with NAT/PAT When Using Cisco IOS VPN Gateways

Cisco IOS routers configured as VPN gateways support only one method of overcoming issues NAT/PAT—NAT-T.

NAT-T was introduced in Cisco IOS Release 12.2(13)T and it is enabled by default. So, no configuration is necessary as long as the VPN gateway is running Cisco IOS Software Release 12.2(13)T or later.

Overcoming Issues with NAT/PAT When Using the Cisco ASA 5500

The Cisco ASA 5500 supports all three methods of providing NAT transparency:

- To use IPsec over TCP, you can configure the **isakmp ipsec-over-tcp** [**port** *port1*… *port10*] global configuration mode command. This command can be used to specify up to 10 ports on which the Cisco ASA will accept IPsec over TCP connections, with the default port being 10000.

- IPsec over UDP can be configured using the **ipsec-udp enable** group policy configuration mode command. You can specify a particular port using the **ipsec-udp-port** *port* group policy configuration mode command (the default is 10000).

- You can configure the **isakmp nat-traversal** *natkeepalive* global configuration mode command to enable IETF NAT-T. The *natkeepalive* parameter can be used to specify the interval at which keepalives are sent (the default is every 20 seconds).

Configuring NAT/PAT Transparency on Cisco VPN Clients

Configuration of Cisco VPN Clients to support NAT/PAT transparency is simple. All that you need to do is click the Transport tab, check **Enable Transparent Tunneling**, and then select the appropriate method of NAT/PAT transparency (either IPsec over UDP or IPsec over TCP)—see Figure 9-41.

Figure 9-41   *Configuring Cisco VPN Clients to Support NAT/PAT Transparency*

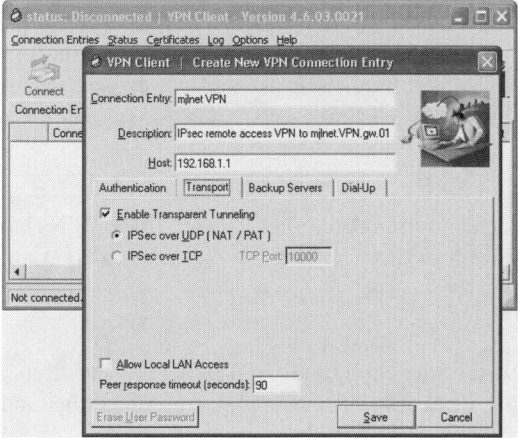

IPsec Remote Access/Telecommuter VPNs Using Easy VPN (EZVPN)

Up to this point, this chapter has focused on remote access VPNs where the client software is running on a PC or other workstation. But, there is often more than one device at telecommuters' sites that need to communicate over the VPN (PCs, IP phones, and so on). In this case, it may be more convenient or make more sense to deploy IPsec remote access

VPN between routers (hardware clients) at these telecommuter sites and the central site VPN gateway(s) (see Figure 9-42).

Figure 9-42 *Deploying an IPsec Remote Access VPN Between a Telecommuter Router (Hardware Client) and Central Site VPN Gateway(s)*

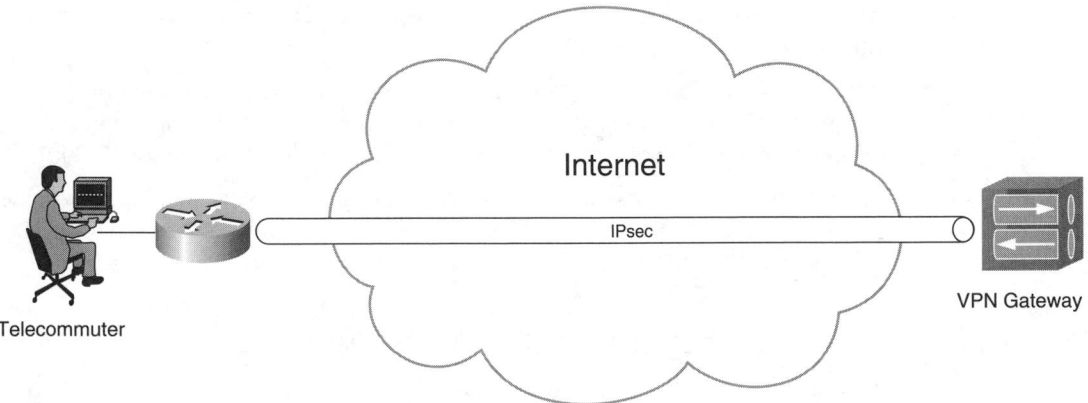

There are a number of ways to deploy the telecommuter solutions shown in Figure 9-42—you can deploy a standard point-to-point IPsec VPN solution; you can deploy a DMVPN solution; or you can deploy a point-to-point IPsec VPN solution using the EZVPN feature.

All of these solutions work well, but the EZVPN solution is especially applicable for this particular type of deployment scenario, and so this section focuses on this feature. One reason that the EZVPN solution is applicable is because it is based on the Cisco VPN Client software and is, as the name suggests, similarly easy to configure.

NOTE   For more information on standard point-to-point IPsec VPNs and DMVPN, see Chapters 6, "Deploying Site-to-Site IPsec VPNs," and 7, "Scaling and Optimizing IPsec VPNs."

There are two parts to the configuration of EZVPN—the client and the server. The client is the located at remote access VPN client/telecommuter site, and the server is the VPN gateway at the central site.

An EZVPN server can, for example, be a Cisco VPN concentrator, a Cisco IOS VPN gateway (router), or a Cisco ASA 5500. In fact, because the EZVPN client just mimics the operation of the Cisco VPN Client, you can use the configuration for the Cisco VPN concentrator and Cisco IOS VPN gateway described in the sections "Cisco VPN 3000 Concentrator as an IPsec Remote Access VPN Gateway Using Preshared Key Authentication," "Cisco IOS Router as an IPsec Remote Access VPN Gateway with IKE Preshared Key

Authentication," and "Cisco ASA as an IPsec Remote Access VPN Gateway with IKE Preshared Key Authentication," respectively.

Example 9-14 shows a sample configuration of a Cisco IOS EZVPN client.

Example 9-14 *Sample Configuration of a Cisco IOS EZVPN Client*

```
!
hostname mjlnet.EZVPN.Client
!
crypto ipsec client ezvpn mjlnet.VPN (line 1)
connect auto (line 2)
group Engineering key mjlnet2006 (line 3)
mode network-extension (line 4)
peer 192.168.1.1 (line 5)
!
interface FastEthernet0
ip address 10.10.20.1 255.255.255.0
ip nat inside (line 6)
crypto ipsec client ezvpn mjlnet.VPN inside (line 7)
!
interface Serial1
ip address 172.16.1.1 255.255.255.0
ip nat outside (line 8)
crypto ipsec client ezvpn mjlnet.VPN outside (line 9)
!
ip nat inside source list 150 interface Serial1 overload (line 10)
ip classless
ip route 0.0.0.0 0.0.0.0 172.16.1.2
!
access-list 150 deny  ip 10.10.20.0 0.0.255.255 10.10.10.0 0.0.255.255 (line 11)
access-list 150 permit ip 10.10.20.0 0.0.0.255 any (line 12)
!
```

Highlighted lines 1 to 5 are used to configure EZVPN client connection parameters.

The **crypto ipsec client ezvpn** *name* command (line 1) is used to enter Cisco Easy VPN remote configuration mode and create the VPN connection specified using the *name* parameter.

In line 2, the **connect** {**auto** | **manual**} command is used to configure the router to auto-initiate a VPN connection with the VPN gateway. The **manual** parameter causes the router to wait for manual intervention (the administrator typing the **crypto ipsec client ezvpn connect** *name* command at the privileged exec command prompt).

Next, the **group** *group-name* **key** *group-password* command (line 3) is used to configure the group name and password (the preshared key). These must be identical to the group name and password (preshared key) configured on your Cisco VPN concentrator, Cisco IOS VPN gateway, or Cisco ASA 5500.

The **mode** {**client** | **network-extension**} command (line 4) in this example configures the router inside interface as an extension of the central site network. That is, no NAT/PAT is performed on traffic that transits the VPN connection between the local router and the VPN gateway. The **client** parameter, on the other hand, ensures that all traffic transiting the VPN connection from the local inside interface to the VPN gateway is NAT'ed or PAT'ed. The choice or client or network-extension mode will often hinge on whether enterprise network address space is available for telecommuters, and/or whether telecommuter applications function well with NAT/PAT.

In line 5, the **peer** {**ip-address** | **hostname**} command is used to configure either the IP address or DNS name of the central site VPN gateway.

The **ip nat inside** command (line 6) is now used to specify the inside NAT interface, and the **crypto ipsec client ezvpn** *name* **inside** command (line 7) specifies the EZVPN inside interface (the local LAN interface, FastEthernet 0). The *name* parameter configured in the **crypto ipsec client ezvpn** *name* **inside** command corresponds to that specified using the **crypto ipsec client ezvpn** *name* command (line 1).

Lines 8 and 9 contain the **ip nat outside** and **crypto ipsec client ezvpn** *name* **outside** commands. It will probably be no surprise to learn that these commands configure the NAT outside interface and EZVPN outside interface respectively (interface serial 1). The *name* parameter in the **crypto ipsec client ezvpn** *name* **outside** command must again correspond to the *name* parameter specified using the **crypto ipsec client ezvpn** *name* command (line 1).

The **ip nat inside source list** *acl* **interface** *interface* **overload** command (line 10) is then used to link to an access list (150) that specifies the IP traffic that is PAT'ed/not PAT'ed (PAT is configured by the **overload** keyword) as well as the address to use for PAT (in this case, the IP address on interface serial 1).

In lines 11 and 12, you can see the access list specified in the **ip nat inside source list** *acl* **interface** *interface* **overload** command (150). The access list line shown in highlighted line 11 is used to specify that traffic that will *not* be PAT'ed (traffic going to/from the local LAN and central site LAN). And the access list line shown in line 12 specifies the traffic that will be PAT'ed (any other traffic from the local LAN).

That's it—pretty simple, isn't it?

One thing you may have noticed about the configuration shown in Example 9-14, however, is that at no point are IPsec or IKE parameters and algorithms specified. The reason for this is that, like the Cisco VPN Client, the EZVPN client does not require (or allow) the direct configuration of these parameters.

One other thing you might have noticed is that the configuration does not include the ISAKMP Xauth username or password. In fact, these can be entered at the command line during IKE negotiation with the VPN gateway.

During IKE negotiation with the VPN gateway, the EZVPN client (router) will display the following message:

```
EZVPN(mjlnet.VPN): Pending XAuth Request, Please enter the following command:
EZVPN: crypto ipsec client ezvpn xauth
```

At this point, you should enter the specified command (**crypto ipsec client ezvpn xauth** at the privileged exec prompt), and you will be prompted for your username and password, as follows:

```
Enter Username and Password.: mark
Password: : mjlnet2006
```

Enter the appropriate username and password, and, assuming IKE negotiation completes successfully, the VPN connection will be completed with the VPN gateway.

You can verify IPsec remote access VPNs on an EZVPN client by using the usual IPsec verification commands (**show crypto isakmp sa**, and so on) as well as by using the following:

- **show crypto ipsec ezvpn client**—This command output displays EZVPN client configuration.
- **debug crypto ipsec ezvpn client**—This command output displays EZVPN configuration and implementation information.

Integrating IPsec with MPLS VPNs

Some service providers might want to provide remote connectivity to MPLS VPNs using IPsec. Two common remote connectivity configurations using IPsec are as follows:

- IPsec remote access VPN connectivity into MPLS VPNs
- IPsec site-to-site VPN connectivity into an MPLS VPN

Figure 9-43 illustrates these types of connectivity.

Figure 9-43 *IPsec Remote Access and Site-to-Site VPN Connectivity into MPLS VPNs*

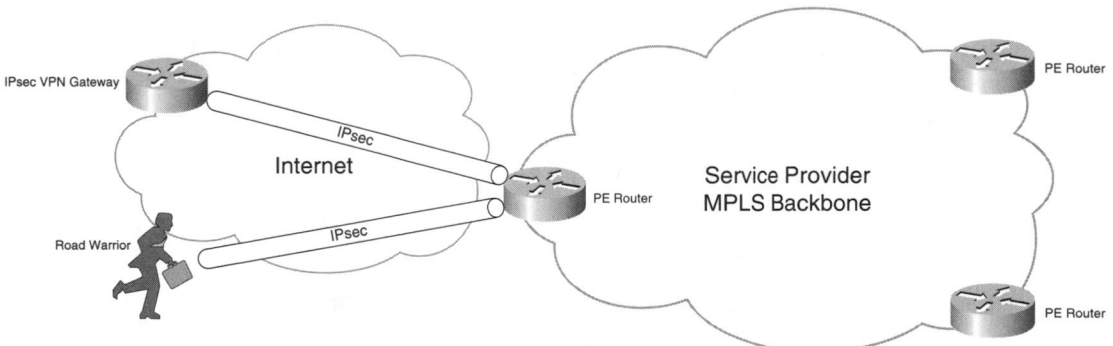

As shown in Figure 9-43, a remote access VPN users (a "road warrior") connects to an MPLS VPN over the Internet via a Provider Edge (PE) router. Similarly, an IPsec VPN gateway connects to an MPLS VPN over the Internet via PE router.

The integration of IPsec remote access and site-to-site connectivity to MPLS VPNs is discussed in the following two sections.

Providing IPsec Remote Access Connectivity to MPLS VPNs

Service providers can deploy IPsec remote access connectivity to MPLS VPNs. This allows road warriors and telecommuters to connect into their respective organizations' VPN across the Internet.

Figure 9-44 shows IPsec remote access VPN connectivity into MPLS VPNs.

Figure 9-44 *IPsec Remote Access VPN Connectivity into MPLS VPNs*

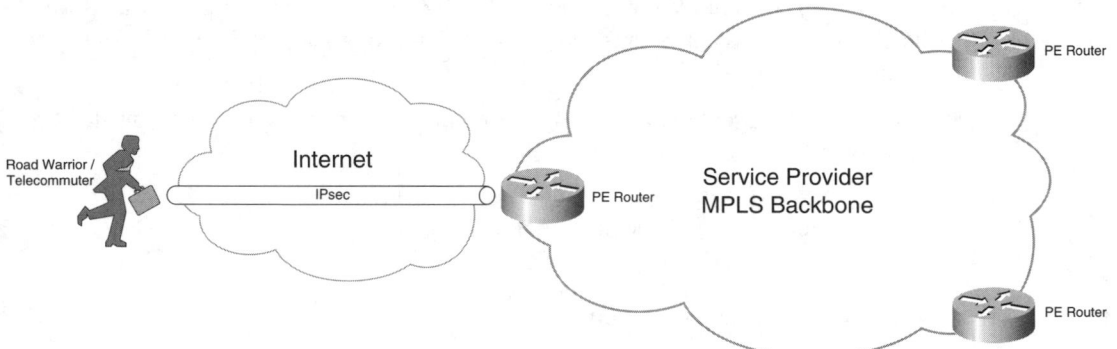

Example 9-15 shows the PE router configuration of IPsec remote access connectivity to MPLS VPNs. As you examine this configuration, you may want to compare it to a *standard* IPsec remote access VPN configuration for a Cisco IOS router. Many of the commands shown in Example 9-15 are identical to those in Example 9-1, and so they will not be explained again here.

Note that only the relevant configuration is shown in Example 9-15. For other MPLS PE router configuration, see Chapters 4, "Designing MPLS Layer 3 Site-to-Site VPNs," and 5, "Advanced MPLS L3VPN Deployment Considerations."

Example 9-15 *Configuration of IPsec Remote Access Connectivity to MPLS VPNs*

```
!
hostname London.PE
!
username mark password 0 mjlnet2006 (line 1)
username john password 0 mjlnet2007 (line 2)
!
aaa new-model (line 3)
!
aaa authentication login authen.mjlnet.remote local (line 4)
aaa authorization network authorize.mjlnet.remote local (line 5)
!
ip vrf mjlnet.VPN (line 6)
 rd 64512:100 (line 7)
 route-target export 64512:100 (line 8)
 route-target import 64512:100 (line 9)
!
ip cef
!
```

Example 9-15 *Configuration of IPsec Remote Access Connectivity to MPLS VPNs (Continued)*

```
crypto isakmp policy 10 (line 10)
 encr aes 256 (line 11)
 authentication pre-share (line 12)
 group 2 (line 13)
 !
crypto isakmp client configuration group mjlnet.eng (line 14)
 key mjlnet2006 (line 15)
 dns 10.10.10.161 (line 16)
 wins 10.10.10.171 (line 17)
 pool mjlnet.pool (line 18)
 !
crypto isakmp profile mjlnet.remote.prof (line 19)
  vrf mjlnet.VPN (line 20)
  match identity group mjlnet.eng (line 21)
  client authentication list authen.mjlnet.remote (line 22)
  isakmp authorization list authorize.mjlnet.remote (line 23)
  client configuration address initiate (line 24)
  client configuration address respond (line 25)
 !
crypto ipsec transform-set mjlnet.VPN.trans esp-aes 256 esp-sha-hmac (line 26)
 !
crypto dynamic-map mjlnet.map 10 (line 27)
 set transform-set mjlnet.VPN.trans (line 28)
 set isakmp-profile mjlnet.remote.prof (line 29)
 reverse-route (line 30)
 !
crypto map all.remote 10 ipsec-isakmp dynamic mjlnet.map (line 31)
 !
interface FastEthernet0/0
 ip address 172.31.1.1 255.255.0.0
 tag-switching ip (line 32)
 !
interface FastEthernet2/0
 ip address 192.168.1.1 255.255.255.0
 crypto map all.remote (line 33)
 !
ip local pool mjlnet.pool 10.30.20.1 10.30.20.100 group mjlnet.VPN (line 34)
 !
```

A local username/password database is configured in highlighted lines 1 and 2. This database is used for Xauth authentication of remote access VPN users.

Lines 3 to 5 contain the configuration of AAA. This configuration includes method lists for user login authentication (Xauth) and local authorization for network connections.

Local authentication is not a scalable solution, and so in order to specify a AAA server for user authentication and network connection authorization, configure the appropriate keyword (for example, **radius**) rather than the **local** keyword in the **aaa authentication** and **aaa authorization** commands.

Lines 6 to 9 include the configuration of an (inside) VRF to which remote access VPN users will connect. For more information on the configuration of VRFs, see the section "Deploying MPLS Layer 3 VPNs" in Chapter 4.

Lines 10 to 13 include the configuration of an IKE (ISAKMP) policy. For more information on these commands, see Chapter 6.

ISAKMP group parameters are configured in lines 14 to 18. The group name specified using the **crypto isakmp client configuration group** *name* command must be the same as that configured in the Name box in the Authentication tab of a connection entry on the Cisco VPN Client.

These ISAKMP parameters include configuration of a group preshared key (password), DNS server address, WINS server address, and link to an IP address pool (from which IP addresses are assigned to remote access VPN clients). The group preshared key must be the same as that configured in the Password box in the Authentication tab of a connection entry on the Cisco VPN Client and is used to authenticate the remote access VPN client machines during IKE phase 1. The other parameters are pushed to the remote access VPN clients using the ISAKMP Configuration Method (Mode Config) after IKE phase 1 has been completed.

Lines 19 to 25 show the configuration of an ISAKMP profile. The ISAKMP profile is used to group ISAKMP (IKE phase 1, Xauth, and ISAKMP Configuration Method) configuration that corresponds to a particular IVRF.

The **crypto isakmp profile** *profile-name* command (line 19) is used to specify the profile name and enter ISAKMP profile configuration mode.

The **vrf** *vrf-name* command in line 20 is used to link to a particular IVRF.

In line 21, the **match identity** {**group** *group-name* | **address** *address* [*mask*] [*fvrf*] | **host** *host-name* | **host domain** *domain-name* | **user** *user-fqdn* | **user domain** *domain-name*} command is used to specify the IKE identity that is passed to the remote access VPN clients during IKE phase 1. The identity specified in this example is the group name specified under the Authentication tab of a VPN connection entry on a Cisco VPN Client, and it links to the ISAKMP group parameters configured from lines 14 to 18.

The commands in lines 22 to 25 may be familiar from the configuration shown in Example 9-1 earlier in this chapter. The only difference is the command syntax — in Example 9-1, these commands are prefixed by the **crypto map** *map-name* syntax (for example, **client authentication list** *method-list-name* becomes **crypto map** *map-name* **client authentication list** *method-list-name* in Example 9-1).

The **client authentication list** *method-list-name* command in line 22 configures Xauth using the method list specified using the **aaa authentication login** *method-list-name* command in line 4.

The **isakmp authorization list** *method-list-name* command (line 23) specifies authorization for ISAKMP and links to the method list defined in the **aaa authorization network** *method-list-name* command in line 5.

In lines 24 and 25, the **client configuration address** {**initiate** I **respond**} commands configure the PE router to initiate IP address assignment with the remote access VPN clients and to accept IP address requests from remote access VPN clients.

NOTE   Note that the **initiate** keyword causes the PE router to use Set and Acknowledge ISAKMP Configuration Method messages to assign IP addresses, and the **respond** keyword causes the PE router to use Request and Reply ISAKMP Configuration Method messages to assign IP addresses. If you are not sure which to use with the particular type and version of remote access VPN clients that you use, just specify both, as shown in Example 9-15.

Line 26 contains the, by now familiar, **crypto ipsec transform-set** command. This is used to configure encryption, authentication, and compression algorithms and parameters negotiated during IKE phase 2.

Lines 27 to 30 show the configuration of a dynamic crypto map. This dynamic crypto map allows the VPN gateway to negotiate IPsec SAs with remote access VPN clients when not all the parameters about an IPsec peer are known (for example, often the IP addresses of remote access VPN clients are not known).

Line 28 contains the **set transform-set** *transform-set-name1* [*transform-set-name2...... transform-set-name6*] command. This command specifies the IPsec transform set created in line 25.

The **set isakmp-profile** *profile-name* command in line 29 links to the crypto profile created in lines 19 to 25.

In line 30, the **reverse-route** command configures the PE router to inject routes corresponding to IPsec SAs negotiated with remote access VPN clients.

The **crypto map** *map-name seq-number* **ipsec-isakmp dynamic** *dynamic-map-name* command in line 31 configures a crypto profile creates dynamic crypto maps as remote access VPN clients connect. This crypto profile links to the dynamic crypto map created in lines 26 to 29.

Line 32 shows the configuration of the **tag-switching ip** (**mpls ip**) command on an inside (MPLS backbone) interface.

In line 33, the **crypto map** *map-name* command is used to apply the crypto map created in line 31 to the outside interface (the interface that connects to the Internet and remote access VPN clients).

An IP address pool from which addresses are assigned via ISAKMP Configuration Method to remote access VPN clients is configured in line 34. This address pool is referenced by the **pool** command in line 18. The **group** *name* parameter configured using the IP local pool allows multiple IP address pools to overlap if necessary (IP address overlap between VPNs often occurs in an MPLS VPN architecture).

All the usual commands can be used to verify IPsec remote access VPN connectivity to MPLS VPNs. Example 9-16 shows the output of the **show crypto isakmp sa detail** command.

Example 9-16 *show crypto isakmp sa detail Command Output*

```
London.PE#show crypto isakmp sa detail
Codes: C - IKE configuration mode, D - Dead Peer Detection
    K - Keepalives, N - NAT-traversal
    X - IKE Extended Authentication
    psk - Preshared key, rsig - RSA signature
    renc - RSA encryption
C-id Local       Remote      I-VRF  Encr Hash Auth DH Lifetime Cap.
1    192.168.1.1   172.16.1.1   mjlnet.V aes sha    2 23:58:30 CX
     Connection-id:Engine-id = 1:1(software)
London.PE#
```

The highlighted line shows the local and remote IP addresses. The IVRF is also shown, along with the encryption, hash, Diffie-Hellman group, lifetime, and capabilities. The capabilities column shows that the local PE router and the remote access VPN client in question have negotiated ISAKMP Configuration Method (IKE Config Mode) and Xauth.

The **show crypto ipsec sa** command (Example 9-17) displays details of IPsec SAs negotiated with remote access VPN clients.

Example 9-17 *show crypto ipsec sa Command Output*

```
London.PE#show crypto ipsec sa
interface: FastEthernet2/0
  Crypto map tag: all.remote, local addr. 192.168.1.1 (line 1)
  protected vrf: mjlnet.VPN (line 2)
  local ident (addr/mask/prot/port): (0.0.0.0/0.0.0.0/0/0)
  remote ident (addr/mask/prot/port): (10.30.20.1/255.255.255.255/0/0)
  current_peer: 172.16.1.1:500
   PERMIT, flags={}
  #pkts encaps: 0, #pkts encrypt: 0, #pkts digest: 0
  #pkts decaps: 0, #pkts decrypt: 0, #pkts verify: 0
  #pkts compressed: 0, #pkts decompressed: 0
  #pkts not compressed: 0, #pkts compr. failed: 0
  #pkts not decompressed: 0, #pkts decompress failed: 0
  #send errors 0, #recv errors 0
   local crypto endpt.: 192.168.1.1, remote crypto endpt.: 172.16.1.1 (line 3)
   path mtu 1500, media mtu 1500
   current outbound spi: 60010B9
   inbound esp sas: (line 4)
   spi: 0xE9A560B(244995595)
```

Example 9-17 show crypto ipsec sa *Command Output (Continued)*

```
         transform: esp-256-aes esp-sha-hmac ,
         in use settings ={Tunnel, }
         slot: 0, conn id: 2000, flow_id: 1, crypto map: all.remote
         crypto engine type: Software, engine_id: 1
         sa timing: remaining key lifetime (k/sec): (4588787/3503)
         ike_cookies: 4A06F6D3 938DF69C BC6EA848 70932562
         IV size: 16 bytes
         replay detection support: Y
     inbound ah sas:
     inbound pcp sas:
     outbound esp sas: (line 5)
      spi: 0x60010B9(100667577)
         transform: esp-256-aes esp-sha-hmac ,
         in use settings ={Tunnel, }
         slot: 0, conn id: 2001, flow_id: 2, crypto map: all.remote
         crypto engine type: Software, engine_id: 1
         sa timing: remaining key lifetime (k/sec): (4588787/3502)
         ike_cookies: 4A06F6D3 938DF69C BC6EA848 70932562
         IV size: 16 bytes
         replay detection support: Y
     outbound ah sas:
     outbound pcp sas:
London.PE#
```

Highlighted lines 1, 2, and 3 show the crypto map name, IVRF (protected VRF) name, and local and remote IPsec tunnel endpoints.

The output below lines 4 and 5 shows the details of inbound and outbound IPsec SAs negotiated with a remote access VPN client, including encryption and authentication algorithms.

You can use the **show ip local pool** command to examine the IP address pool from which IP addresses assigned to remote access VPN clients (see Example 9-18). These IP addresses are assigned during ISAKMP Configuration Method negotiation.

Example 9-18 show ip local pool *Command Output*

```
London.PE#show ip local pool
  Pool            Begin       End        Free In use
  ** pool <mjlnet.pool> is in group <mjlnet.VPN> (line 1)
  mjlnet.pool       10.30.20.1   10.30.20.100    99     1 (line 2)
London.PE#
```

Highlighted lines 1 and 2 show the IP address pool name, associated group, pool start and end addresses, and allocation statistics. In this case, one IP address has been assigned to a remote access VPN client, and 99 addresses in the pool are free.

You can use the **ipconfig /all** command to examine IP parameters pushed to the remote access VPN client during ISAKMP Configuration Method negotiation (see Figure 9-45).

Figure 9-45 *IP Parameters Assigned to the Remote Access VPN Client (**ipconfig /all** Command Output)*

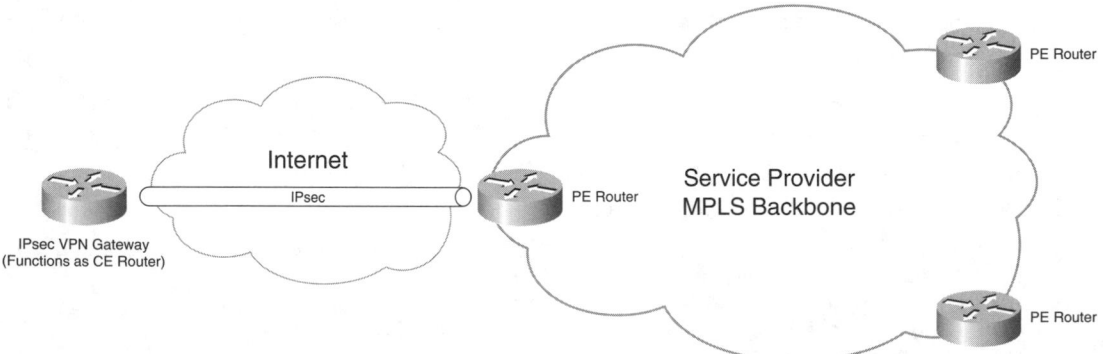

```
C:\WINDOWS\system32\cmd.exe                                    _ □ x

Ethernet adapter Local Area Connection 6:

        Connection-specific DNS Suffix  . :
        Description . . . . . . . . . . . : Cisco Systems VPN Adapter
        Physical Address. . . . . . . . . : 00-05-9A-3C-78-00
        Dhcp Enabled. . . . . . . . . . . : No
        IP Address. . . . . . . . . . . . : 10.30.20.1
        Subnet Mask . . . . . . . . . . . : 255.255.255.0
        Default Gateway . . . . . . . . . : 10.30.20.1
        DNS Servers . . . . . . . . . . . : 10.10.10.160
                                            10.10.10.161
        Primary WINS Server . . . . . . . : 10.10.10.170
        Secondary WINS Server . . . . . . : 10.10.10.171

C:\Documents and Settings\Mark>_
```

The output of the **ipconfig /all** command in the command window in Figure 9-45 shows that IP address 10.30.20.1 has been assigned to the remote access VPN client's virtual adapter (VPN tunnel interface). DNS and WINS server IP addresses have also been pushed to the remote access VPN client.

Integrating IPsec Site-to-Site VPNs with MPLS VPNs

It is also possible to implement IPsec site-to-site VPN connectivity into MPLS VPNs. This allows service providers to extend site-to-site customer VPNs across the Internet.

Figure 9-46 depicts the extension of customer site-to-site VPNs across the Internet.

Figure 9-46 *Extension of Customer Site-to-Site VPNs Across the Internet*

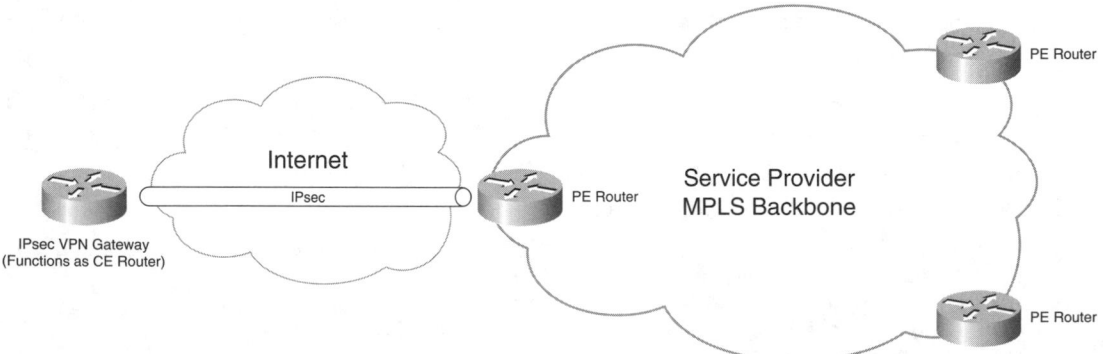

PE Router

Internet

IPsec

PE Router

Service Provider
MPLS Backbone

PE Router

IPsec VPN Gateway
(Functions as CE Router)

PE Router

Example 9-19 shows the configuration of site-to-site IPsec connectivity into MPLS VPNs.

Example 9-19 *Configuration of Site-to-Site IPsec Connectivity into MPLS VPNs*

```
!
hostname London.PE
!
!
ip vrf mjlnet.VPN
 rd 64512:100
```

Example 9-19 *Configuration of Site-to-Site IPsec Connectivity into MPLS VPNs (Continued)*

```
   route-target export 64512:100
   route-target import 64512:100
   !
   ip cef
   !
   crypto keyring mjlnet.key (line 1)
    pre-shared-key address 172.16.1.1 key mjlnet2007 (line 2)
   !
   crypto isakmp policy 10
    encr aes 256
    authentication pre-share
    group 2
   !
   crypto isakmp profile mjlnet.prof (line 3)
     vrf mjlnet.VPN (line 4)
     keyring mjlnet.key (line 5)
     match identity address 172.16.1.1 255.255.255.255 (line 6)
   !
   crypto ipsec transform-set mjlnet.trans esp-aes 256 esp-sha-hmac
   !
   crypto map mjlnet.map 10 ipsec-isakmp (line 7)
    set peer 172.16.1.1 (line 8)
    set transform-set mjlnet.trans (line 9)
    set isakmp-profile mjlnet.prof (line 10)
    match address 150 (line 11)
   !
   !
   interface FastEthernet0/0
    ip address 172.31.1.1 255.255.0.0
    tag-switching ip
   !
   interface FastEthernet2/0
    ip address 192.168.1.1 255.255.255.0
    crypto map mjlnet.map
   !
   !
   ip route vrf mjlnet.VPN 192.168.10.0 255.255.255.0 172.16.1.1 global (line 12)
   !
   access-list 150 permit ip 192.168.1.0 0.0.0.255 192.168.10.0 0.0.255.255 (line 13)
   !
```

Much of the configuration shown in Example 9-19 is the same as that contained in Example 9-15. The paragraphs that follow cover only the differences in the configurations. See the previous section for explanations of other commands.

Highlighted lines 1 and 2 show the configuration of a crypto keyring. This crypto keyring contains the configuration of a preshared key, which is then referenced from an ISAKMP profile.

The **crypto keyring** *keyring-name* command (line 1) is used specify the crypto keyring name and enter crypto keyring configuration mode.

In line 2, the **pre-shared-key** {**address** *address* [*mask*] | **hostname** *hostname*} **key** *preshared-key* command configures a preshared key and associates it with a particular remote IPsec peer's IP address or hostname.

Lines 3 to 6 shows the configuration of a crypto profile. The **keyring** *keyring-name* command (line 5) links to the crypto keyring configured in lines 1 and 2. Line 6 shows the configuration of the **match identity address** *ip-address mask* is used to specify the identity in the form of an IP address that is used to identify a remote IPsec peer.

Lines 7 through 11 show the configuration of a crypto map entry. The **set peer** *peer-ip-address* command in line 8 specifies the IP address of the remote IPsec peer. Then, in highlighted lines 9 and 10, the **set transform-set** *transform-set-name* and **set isakmp-profile** *profile-name* commands are used to reference the previously configured IPsec transform set (mjlnet.trans) and the ISAKMP profile configured in highlighted lines 3 to 6, respectively.

The **match address** *crypto-acl* command (line 11) references a crypto access list that is used to define traffic that is protected (and not protected) by IPsec.

In line 12, the **ip route vrf** *vrf-name ip-address mask next-hop* **global** command is used to configure a static route to the remote network via the remote IPsec peer, with the **global** keyword specifying that the remote IPsec peer is reachable via the global routing table.

Finally, the **access-list** command in line 13 is used to configure the crypto access list.

The **show crypto isakmp sa detail** command can again be used to examine IKE SA information (see Example 9-20).

Example 9-20 *Examining IKE SA Information Using the* **show crypto isakmp sa detail** *Command*

```
London.PE#show crypto isakmp sa detail
Codes: C - IKE configuration mode, D - Dead Peer Detection
    K - Keepalives, N - NAT-traversal
    X - IKE Extended Authentication
    psk - Preshared key, rsig - RSA signature
    renc - RSA encryption
C-id Local      Remote     I-VRF  Encr Hash Auth DH Lifetime Cap.
1   192.168.1.1  172.16.1.1   mjlnet.V aes sha psk 2 23:56:43
    Connection-id:Engine-id = 1:1(software)
London.PE#
```

The highlighted line shows information including the local and remote IPsec peer IP addresses, the IVRF name, the encryption and hashing algorithms, the method of authentication, and the lifetime.

If you compare the information shown in Example 9-20 with that shown in Example 9-16 on page 874, you can see that neither ISAKMP Configuration Method nor Xauth was negotiated with the remote IPsec peer. This is not surprising as ISAKMP Configuration Method and Xauth are used to assign configuration parameters and authenticate remote access VPN users but are not used in a site-to-site IPsec deployment.

As shown in Example 9-21, you can use the **show crypto ipsec sa** command to examine IPsec SA information.

Example 9-21 *Examining IPsec SA Information*

```
London.PE#show crypto ipsec sa
interface: FastEthernet2/0
  Crypto map tag: mjlnet.map, local addr. 192.168.1.1 (line 1)
  protected vrf: mjlnet.VPN (line 2)
  local ident (addr/mask/prot/port): (192.168.1.0/255.255.255.0/0/0)
  remote ident (addr/mask/prot/port): (192.168.10.0/255.255.0.0/0/0)
  current_peer: 172.16.1.1:500
   PERMIT, flags={origin_is_acl,}
  #pkts encaps: 0, #pkts encrypt: 0, #pkts digest: 0
  #pkts decaps: 0, #pkts decrypt: 0, #pkts verify: 0
  #pkts compressed: 0, #pkts decompressed: 0
  #pkts not compressed: 0, #pkts compr. failed: 0
  #pkts not decompressed: 0, #pkts decompress failed: 0
  #send errors 0, #recv errors 0
   local crypto endpt.: 192.168.1.1, remote crypto endpt.: 172.16.1.1 (line 3)
   path mtu 1500, media mtu 1500
   current outbound spi: 0
   inbound esp sas:
   inbound ah sas:
   inbound pcp sas:
   outbound esp sas:
   outbound ah sas:
   outbound pcp sas:
  protected vrf: mjlnet.VPN
  local ident (addr/mask/prot/port): (192.168.1.0/255.255.255.0/0/0)
  remote ident (addr/mask/prot/port): (192.168.10.0/255.255.255.0/0/0)
  current_peer: 172.16.1.1:500
   PERMIT, flags={}
  #pkts encaps: 4, #pkts encrypt: 4, #pkts digest: 4
  #pkts decaps: 4, #pkts decrypt: 4, #pkts verify: 4
  #pkts compressed: 0, #pkts decompressed: 0
  #pkts not compressed: 0, #pkts compr. failed: 0
  #pkts not decompressed: 0, #pkts decompress failed: 0
  #send errors 0, #recv errors 0
   local crypto endpt.: 192.168.1.1, remote crypto endpt.: 172.16.1.1
   path mtu 1500, media mtu 1500
   current outbound spi: 827BDE49
   inbound esp sas: (line 4)
   spi: 0x13FFD3E6(335533030)
    transform: esp-256-aes esp-sha-hmac ,
    in use settings ={Tunnel, }
    slot: 0, conn id: 2000, flow_id: 3, crypto map: mjlnet.map
    crypto engine type: Software, engine_id: 1
    sa timing: remaining key lifetime (k/sec): (4487540/3416)
    ike_cookies: B7CE1F4E 31452703 6862E8B8 AE2FFE24
    IV size: 16 bytes
    replay detection support: Y
   inbound ah sas:
   inbound pcp sas:
```

continues

Example 9-21 *Examining IPsec SA Information (Continued)*

```
  outbound esp sas: (line 5)
   spi: 0x827BDE49(2189155913)
    transform: esp-256-aes esp-sha-hmac ,
    in use settings ={Tunnel, }
    slot: 0, conn id: 2001, flow_id: 4, crypto map: mjlnet.map
    crypto engine type: Software, engine_id: 1
    sa timing: remaining key lifetime (k/sec): (4487541/3415)
    ike_cookies: B7CE1F4E 31452703 6862E8B8 AE2FFE24
    IV size: 16 bytes
    replay detection support: Y
   outbound ah sas:
   outbound pcp sas:
London.PE#
```

Highlighted lines 1 and 2 show the crypto map name and VRF name, respectively.

Line 3 shows local and remote IPsec peer addresses.

Below lines 4 and 5, you can see detailed information regarding inbound and outbound IPsec SAs negotiated with the remote IPsec peer.

High Availability: Enabling Redundancy for IPsec Remote Access VPNs

One of the most important considerations when designing and deploying IPsec remote access VPNs is high availability—that is, ensuring that IPsec remote access VPN users can still access corporate or organizational resources in the event of the failure of one or more VPN gateways or sites.

There are thee basic methods of provisioning high availability for IPsec remote access VPNs:

- Load balancing of IPsec remote access VPN connections over a number of VPN gateways at the same central site

- Failover between a number of VPN gateways at the same central site using the Virtual Router Redundancy Protocol (VRRP)

- The use of backup VPN gateways (servers) at geographically dispersed VPN gateways at a number of sites

These three different approaches to implementing high availability for IPsec remote access VPNs are discussed in the following three sections.

Load Balancing of IPsec Remote Access VPN Connections over a Number of VPN Gateways at the Same Central Site

It is possible to configure load balancing on either Cisco VPN 3000 concentrators or Cisco ASA 5520/5540s (the Cisco ASA 5510 does not support load balancing). The configuration of load balancing on the Cisco VPN 3000 concentrators and Cisco ASA 5500s is discussed in the following two sections.

Load Balancing on Cisco VPN 3000 Concentrators

When implementing load balancing of IPsec remote access VPN connections over a number of VPN gateways at the same central site, VPN connections are load balanced over a number of VPN gateways (called a *cluster*) based on the loading on those VPN gateways—this mechanism provides an active-active configuration. A single IP address represents the cluster as a whole.

When implementing load balancing, one of the VPN gateways functions as a cluster master and distributes connections among the cluster members based on load information that the secondary members (those VPN gateways that are not the master) report to it via keepalive messages.

Figure 9-47 illustrates load balancing of IPsec remote access VPN connections among VPN gateways in a cluster.

Figure 9-47 *Load Balancing of IPsec Remote Access VPN Connections Among VPN Gateways in a Cluster*

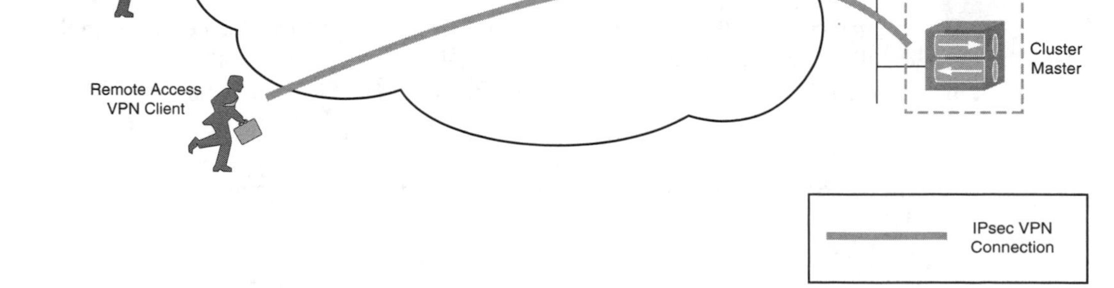

As shown in Figure 9-47, there is a master and two secondary gateways. IPsec remote access VPN connections are load balanced among the gateways, and load information is reported to the master via keepalive messages. The VPN gateways in the cluster must all share common IP subnets on public and private interfaces.

You might be wondering how VPN connection setup proceeds when using load balancing. During VPN connection setup, the Cisco VPN Client connects to the cluster IP address, the master responds by informing the client of the physical IP address of the least-loaded VPN gateway in the cluster, and finally, the client the connects to this VPN gateway.

NOTE   The type of load balancing described in this section can only be used if you are using Cisco VPN Client software (or Cisco hardware VPN clients). It will not function with other non-Cisco client software.

To configure load balancing on the Cisco VPN 3000 concentrator, you must do two things on *all* cluster members:

- Ensure that cluster members can communicate by reconfiguring VPN gateway public and private filters.

- Configure load-balancing parameters.

First, go to **Configuration > Interfaces**, choose (in turn) the Ethernet 1 (**Private**), ensure that the **1. Private (Default)** filter is selected in the Filter drop-down box on the General tab, and click **Apply**.

Next, under **Configuration > Interfaces**, choose the Ethernet 2 (**Public**) interface, ensure that the **2. Public (Default)** filter is selected in the Filter drop-down box on the General tab, and click **Apply**.

Go to **Configuration > Policy Management > Traffic Management > Filters** to configure public and private interface filters themselves (see Figure 9-48).

Choose **Public (Default)**, click **Assign Rules to Filter**, and you will be presented with the page shown in Figure 9-49.

Choose, in turn, **VCA In (forward/in)** and **VCA Out (forward/out)** in the Available Rules, and add them to the Current Rules in Filter by clicking **Add**. After both VCA In (forward/in) and VCA Out (forward/out) have been added to Current Rules in Filter, click **Done**.

NOTE   VCA is the virtual cluster agent, and is used to control load balancing among cluster members.

Now return to the **Configuration > Policy Management > Traffic Management > Filters** page, choose **Private (Default)**, click **Assign Rules to Filter**, and you will see a page almost identical to that in Figure 9-48 (the only difference being that the filter rules apply to the Private interface).

Figure 9-48 *Selecting and Configuring Public and Private Interface Filters*

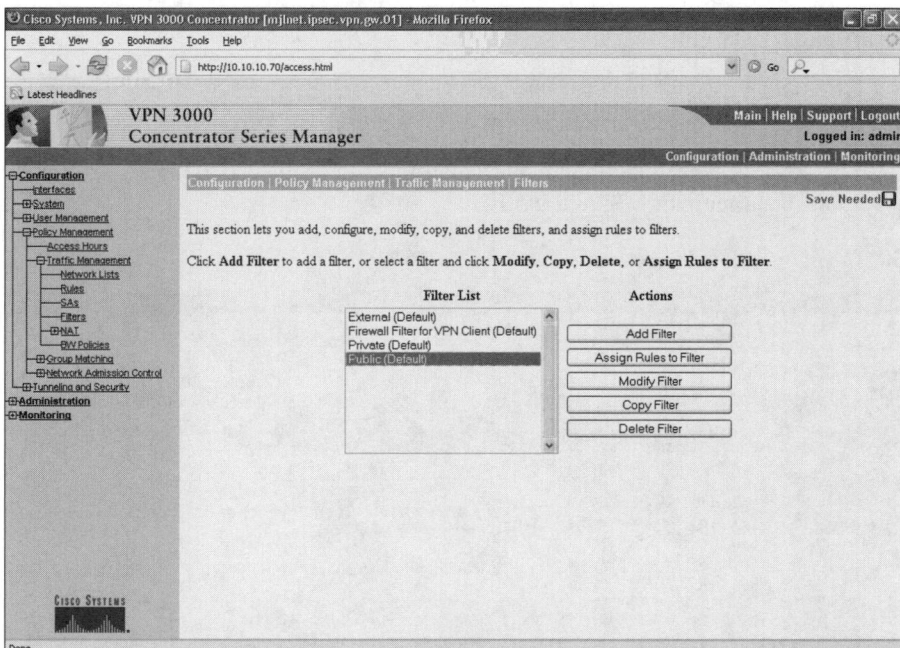

Figure 9-49 *Assigning Rules to Public and Private Interface Filters*

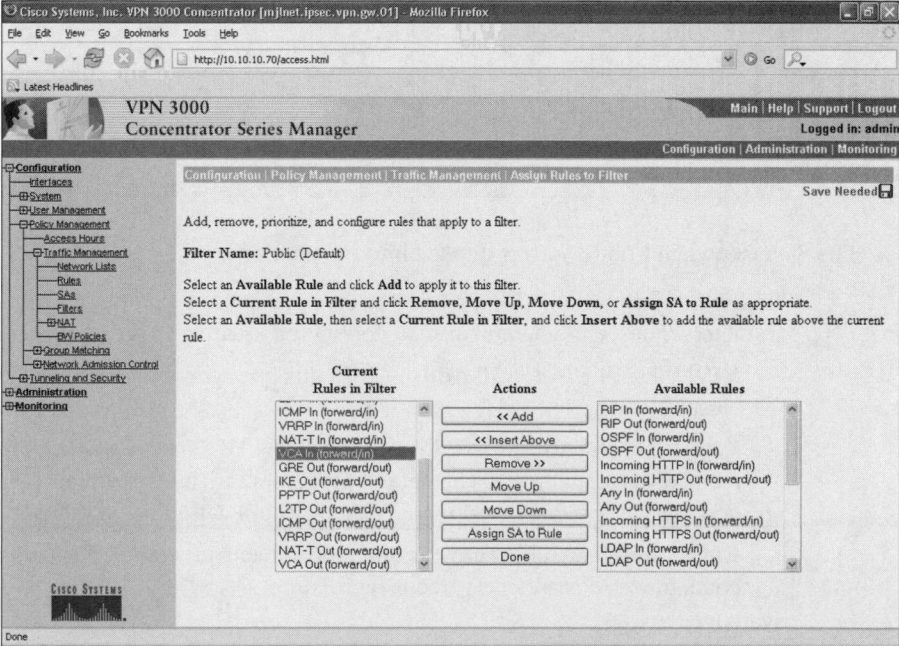

At this point, again select, in turn, **VCA In (forward/in)** and **VCA Out (forward/out)** in the Available Rules, add them to the Current Rules in Filter by clicking **Add**, and then click **Done**.

After you have configured Public and Private interface filters on all cluster members, cluster members will be able communicate on both public and private interfaces.

You are now ready to configure load balancing—to do this, go to **Configuration > System > Load Balancing** (see Figure 9-50).

Figure 9-50 *Configuring Load Balancing*

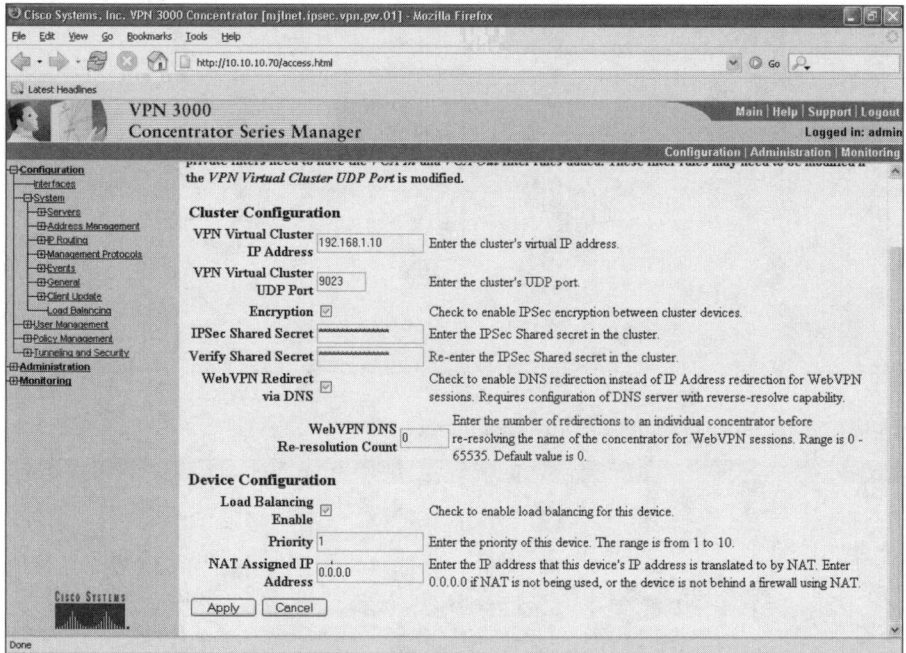

The page shown in Figure 9-50 is divided into two sections:

- **Cluster Configuration**—This section of the page is used to configure cluster-wide parameters. These parameters must be configured identically on all cluster members.

  — **VPN Virtual Cluster IP Address**—In this box, you must configure the cluster IP address.

  — **VPN Virtual Cluster UDP Port**—This is the UDP port on which cluster members communicate. The default port is 9023—it is only really necessary to change this if there is another application using this port.

  — **Encryption**—By checking this box, you can ensure that all intra-cluster communications are encrypted using IPsec.

— **IPSec Shared Secret**—When using IPsec to encrypt intra-cluster communications, preshared key authentication is used.

— **WebVPN Redirect via DNS / WebVPN DNS Re-resolution Count**— These two options are not covered in this chapter as they relate to SSL VPNs.

• **Device Configuration**—This section of the page is used to configure parameters that apply to this specific device.

— **Load Balancing Enable**—Check this to enable load balancing on this VPN gateway, and configure it as a member of the cluster.

— **Priority**—This priority is used to control the likelihood that this VPN gateway will become the cluster master.

The priority can be a value from 1 to 10. The higher the priority, the more likely that the VPN gateway will become the cluster master. It is a good idea to ensure that VPN gateways with greater capacities have higher priorities and are therefore more likely to becomes the cluster master (this is the default). The cluster master incurs additional overhead (compared to secondary devices).

The cluster master is selected according to which VPN gateway in the cluster is powered on first. If two or more VPN gateways are powered on at the same time, the VPN gateway with the highest priority becomes the cluster master. If two or more VPN gateways are powered on at the same time and have the same priority, the VPN gateway with the lowest physical IP address becomes the cluster master.

It is worth noting that the after a cluster master has been selected, all other VPN gateways in the cluster become secondary devices. If the cluster master fails, the secondary device with the highest priority becomes the new cluster master. If the priorities of the secondary devices are the same, the secondary device with the lowest physical IP address becomes the new cluster master.

— **NAT Assigned IP Address**—If the VPN gateways are located behind a NAT device on their public interface, the public IP address for this VPN gateway must be configured in this box. If there is no NAT device, this box should contain 0.0.0.0.

After you have configured all of the appropriate parameters, click the **Apply** button.

| **NOTE** | Remember that Cisco VPN Clients must be configured with the cluster IP address (or DNS name representing the IP address of the cluster) in the Host box of the VPN connection entry. |

You can verify the correct operation of the cluster by going to **Monitoring > Sessions > Load Balancing**.

Load Balancing on Cisco ASA 5500s

Load balancing with Cisco ASA 5500s works in exactly the same way as for Cisco VPN 3000 concentrators—a number of devices form a virtual cluster, and one of the devices performs the role of cluster master. Remote access VPN clients initially connect to the cluster master, which then redirects the connection to a member of the cluster.

NOTE   Load balancing on Cisco ASA 5500s is compatible with that on Cisco VPN 3000 concentrators.

Example 9-22 shows a sample configuration for load balancing on the Cisco ASA 5500.

Example 9-22 *Sample Configuration for Load Balancing on the Cisco ASA 5500*

```
!
vpn load-balancing
  priority 8
  interface lbpublic Outside0/1
  interface lbprivate Inside0/0
  cluster ip address 192.168.1.1
  cluster key mjlnet2008
  cluster encryption
  cluster port 9023
participate
!
```

The **vpn load-balancing** global configuration mode command is used to begin the configuration of load balancing (and enter load-balancing configuration mode).

Within load-balancing configuration mode, the **priority** *priority* command is used to help determine whether this Cisco ASA 5500 becomes the cluster master (the default priorities are 5 and 7 for the Cisco ASA 5520 and 5540, respectively).

Next, the **interface [lbprivate | lbpublic]** [*interface-name*] command is used to specify the names of the inside and outside interfaces used with load balancing.

The **cluster ip address** *ip-address* command is then used to configure the cluster virtual IP address.

The **cluster encryption** and **cluster key** *shared-key* commands are used to specify that load balancing information should be encrypted when exchanged between cluster members and to configure the key used to encrypt the information. The key used to encrypt load-balancing information must be the same on all cluster members.

The next command, **cluster port** *port*, configures the UDP port used for load balancing (the default is 9023).

When you are happy with the load-balancing configuration, you can use the **participate** command to cause the Cisco ASA 5500 to participate in the load-balancing cluster.

Note that ISAKMP must be enabled on all interfaces that are participating in load balancing (inside and outside) using the **isakmp enable** *interface-name* global configuration mode command.

Finally, if there is a NAT device in front of the Cisco ASA 5500s that form the cluster, you can use the **nat** *ip-address* load-balancing configuration mode command to configure the IP address to which the NAT device translates the IP address of the Cisco ASA 5500.

Failover Between a Number of VPN Gateways at the Same Central Site Using VRRP

A second method of implementing redundancy for VPN gateways at the same central site is to use VRRP.

When using VRRP, VPN gateways in a VRRP group operate in an active-standby configuration—there is a single VRRP master (a VPN gateway that is active when operational), and all other VPN gateways function as backups (they are in a standby state). When the master VPN gateway fails, one of the backups takes over traffic forwarding for VPN connections for the VRRP group.

Figure 9-51 shows redundancy of VPN gateways using VRRP.

Figure 9-51 *Redundancy of VPN Gateways Using VRRP*

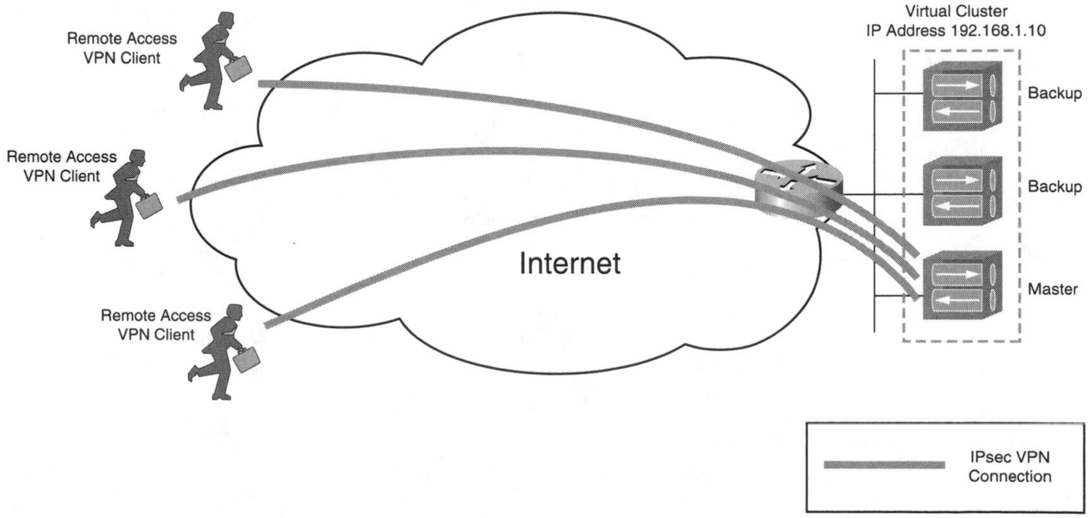

In Figure 9-51, you can see the when the VRRP master is active; it terminates VPN connections from IPsec remote access VPN clients. If the master fails, one of the backup VPN gateways takes over this role.

To implement VRRP redundancy, go to **Configuration > System > IP Routing > Redundancy** and configure the parameters shown in Figure 9-52.

Figure 9-52 *Implementing VRRP*

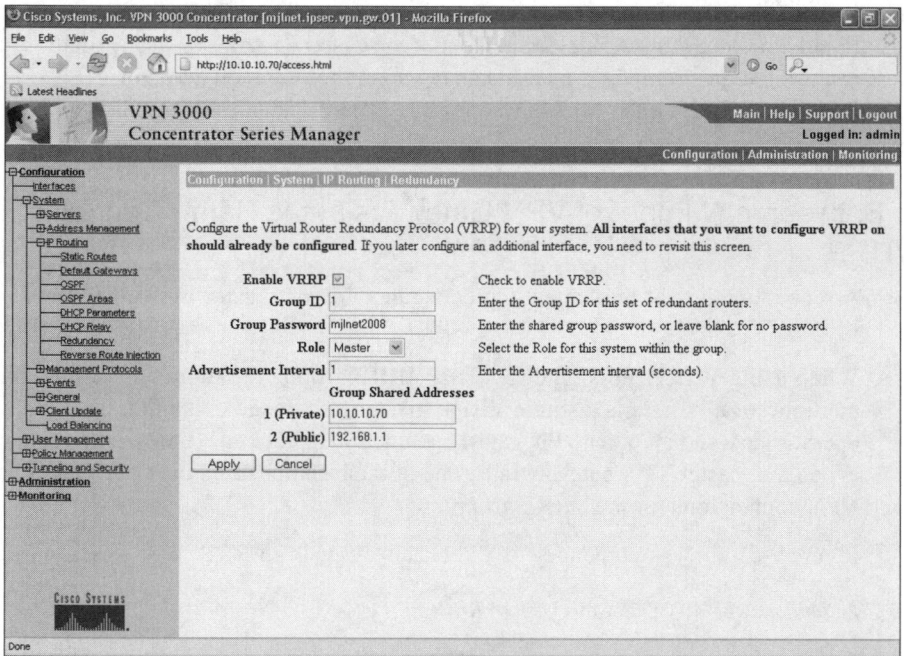

As you can see, there are a number of VRRP parameters and settings to configure:

- **Enable VRRP**—Check this to enable VRRP on each VPN gateway in the VRRP group.

- **Group ID**—This is an ID for the VRRP group, and can be a value from 1 to 255. This ID must be identical on all VPN gateways in the group.

- **Group Password**—If configured, this must be identical on all VPN gateways in the VRRP group.

- **Role**—One of the VPN gateways in the VRRP group must be configured as the master. Other VPN gateways in the group must be configured as backups (1–5). These roles can be selected from the drop-down box.

- **Advertisement Interval**—The number of seconds between VRRP advertisements. Configure this identically on all members of the group (or just leave it at the default of 1 second).

- **Group Shared Addresses**—These are the shared IP addresses for the VRRP group.

  - **1 (Private)**—This must be configured as the IP address of the master's private interface. Configure this identically on all VRRP group members.

  - **2 (Public)**—This must be configured as the IP address of the master's public interface. Again, configure this identically on all VRRP group members.

  VPN clients connect to this IP address (this IP address (or a DNS name corresponding to this IP address)—it is configured in the Host box in the VPN connection entry.

It is important to note that the configurations on all VRRP members must be configured identically with two exceptions:

- The VRRP role (as previously described)
- The *physical* interface IP addresses will be configured differently on each of the members of the VRRP group.

You can monitor the operation of VRRP on a Cisco VPN 3000 concentrator by going to **Monitoring > Statistics > VRRP**.

Using Backup VPN Gateways (Servers) at Geographically Dispersed VPN Gateways

The first two methods of deploying high availability for VPN gateways described in this section are based on a number of redundant VPN gateways at the same central site location. This section describes a method of implementing high availability by configuring a number of backup VPN gateways at geographically dispersed sites. These backup gateways allow IPsec remote access VPN clients to continue to access the corporate or organization's resources even when all the gateways at one or more sites have failed.

Figure 9-53 depicts the implementation of high availability using backup VPN gateways. As shown in Figure 9-53, if the VPN gateway at one site fails, the Cisco VPN Clients fail over to the VPN gateways at other sites.

The list of backup VPN gateways that Cisco VPN Clients use can be configured either locally on the clients or pushed to the client by a VPN gateway. Figure 9-54 shows the configuration of backup VPN gateways on a Cisco VPN Client.

Figure 9-53 *High Availability Using Backup VPN Gateways*

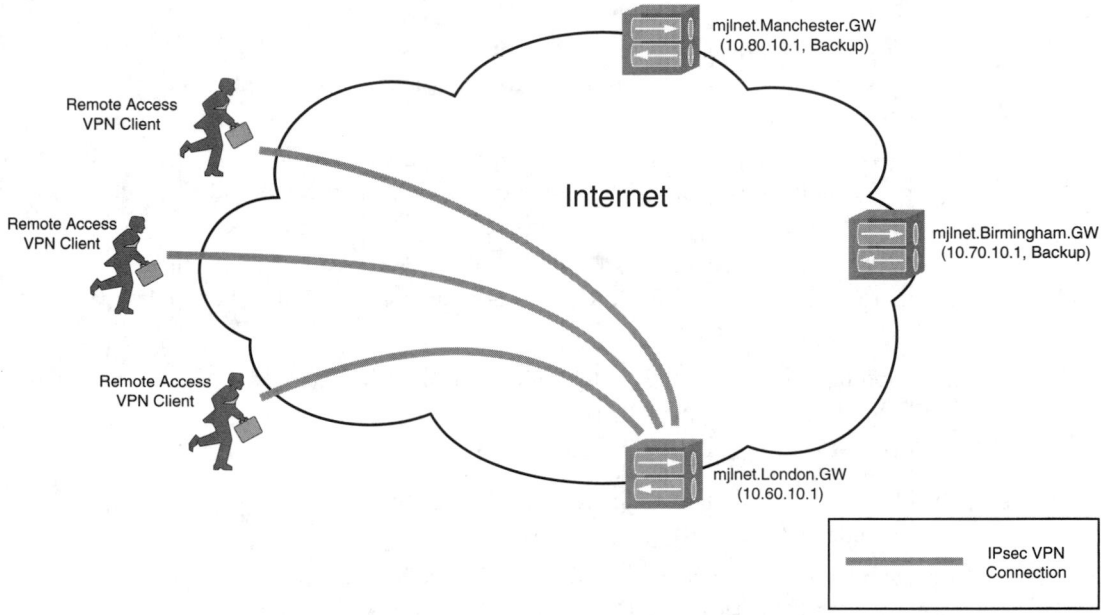

Figure 9-54 *Configuration of Backup VPN Gateways on a Cisco VPN Client*

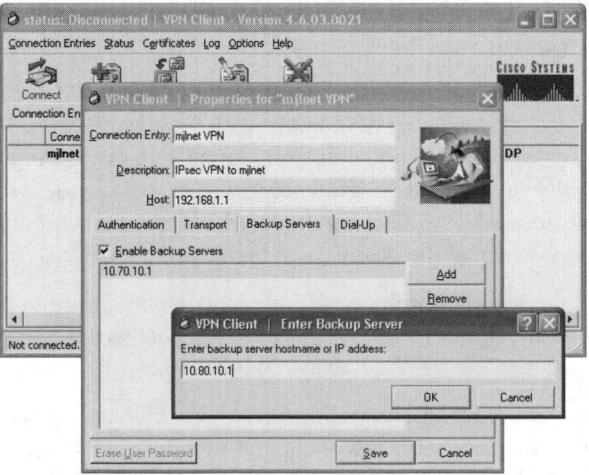

Backup VPN gateways can be configured under the Backup Servers tab of a VPN connection entry. The first step is to check the **Enable Backup Servers** box, and then add the backup VPN gateways to the backup list by clicking the **Add** button and specifying the IP address or host name (DNS name) of the gateway.

The order in which the Cisco VPN Client tries the backup VPN gateways depends on the order in which they are listed in the Backup Servers tab. You can change the order of the backup VPN gateways are listed by choosing a gateway in the list and either moving it up or down the list by clicking the up or down arrows.

Another way of implement backup VPN gateways is to configure them on the VPN gateway. As previously mentioned, the IP addresses or DNS names of these backup VPN gateways are pushed to the Cisco VPN Clients when they connect to the VPN gateway.

Figure 9-55 shows how backup VPN gateway IP addresses or DNS names are pushed to the Cisco VPN Clients when they connect to a VPN gateway.

Figure 9-55 *Backup VPN Gateway IP Addresses or DNS Names Are Pushed to Cisco VPN Clients*

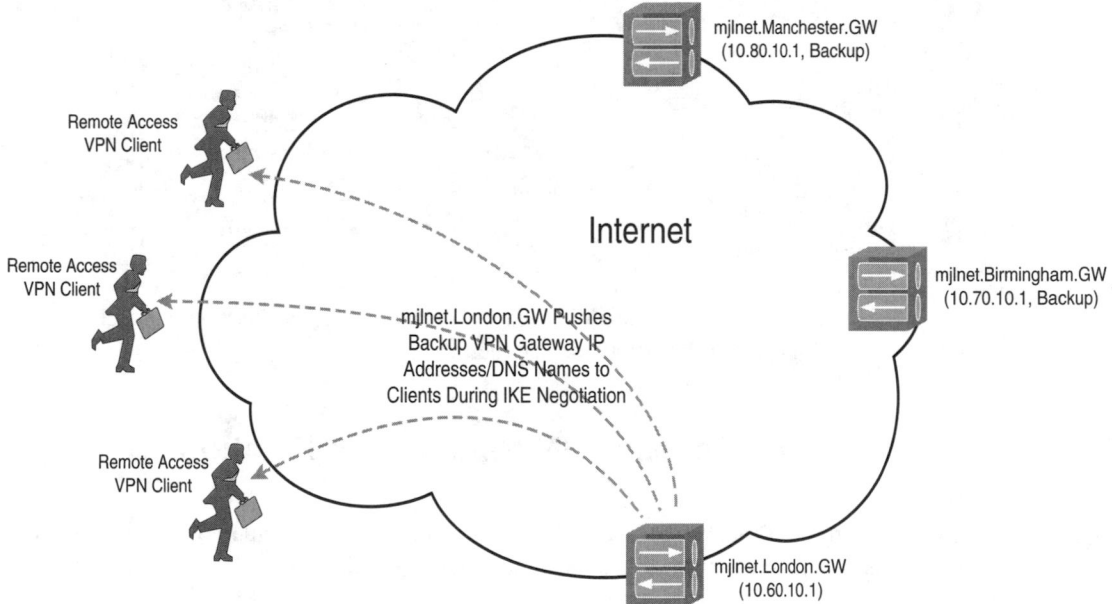

In Figure 9-55, mjlnet.London.GW pushes the IP addresses of mjlnet.Birmingham.GW (10.70.10.1) and mjlnet.Manchester.GW (10.80.10.1) to the Cisco VPN Client as it connects.

You can find the configuration of backup VPN gateways by going to **Configuration > User Management > Groups**, choosing a group, and clicking the **Client Config** tab.

Under the IPSec Backup Servers attribute, select **Use List Below** from the drop-down box, and then type up to 10 backup VPN gateway IP addresses or DNS names in the box (see Figure 9-56).

Figure 9-56 *Configuring Backup VPN Gateways Under the Group Settings*

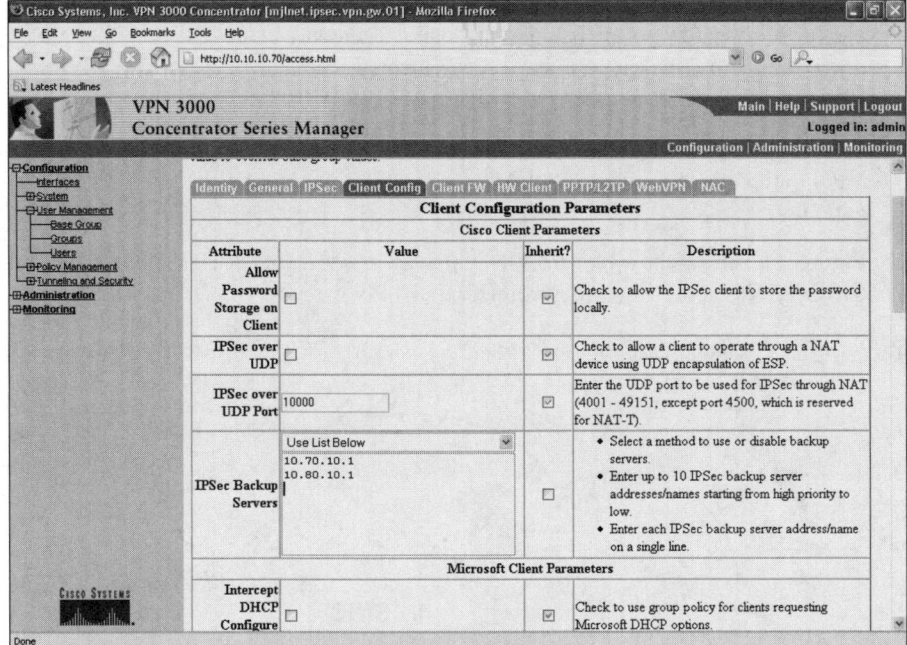

The order that you list the backup VPN gateway IP addresses or DNS names dictates the order in which the Cisco VPN Clients use them.

Placing IPsec Remote Access VPN Gateways in Relation to Firewalls

When designing IPsec remote access VPNs, it is important to decide how to place VPN gateways in relation to firewalls at the edge of the network.

There are two main ways to place VPN gateways in relation to firewalls:

- In parallel with the firewall(s)
- Behind the firewall(s)

Figure 9-57 depicts these methods of placing VPN gateways. Note that the dotted lines in Figure 9-57 represent connectivity options for the Private (inside) interface of the VPN gateway.

When VPN gateways are placed in parallel with a firewall, its public interface connects to an Internet router without any intermediate firewall. The inside interface can connect either to a firewall or directly to the corporate LAN (these connectivity options are labeled 1 and 2, respectively, in Figure 9-57).

Figure 9-57 *Placement of VPN Gateways*

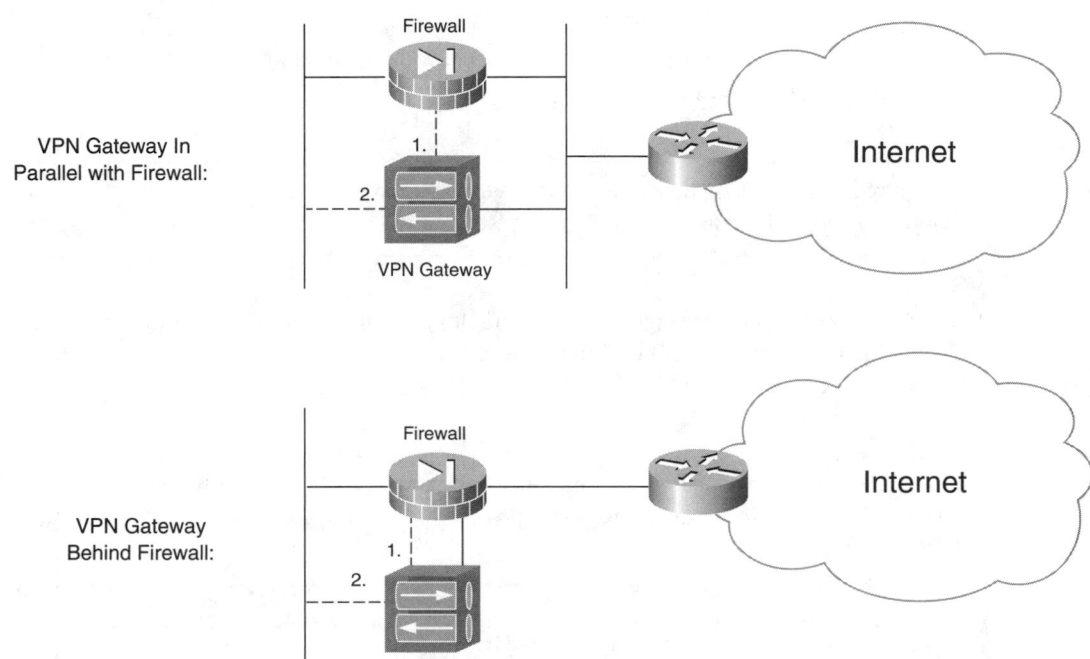

The advantage of connecting the inside interface to a firewall is that it can inspect traffic that has arrived inside the IPsec VPN tunnels from remote access VPN clients. This traffic can also be filtered on the Cisco VPN 3000 concentrator (or Cisco IOS VPN gateway/Cisco ASA 5500), but administrators might want to centralize the inspection of all traffic coming into the network from the Internet (including from the remote access VPN clients) on one firewall or cluster of firewalls.

If VPN gateways are placed behind a firewall, the firewall can inspect all traffic going to the public interface of the VPN gateway and allow only legitimate IPsec VPN traffic.

IPsec VPN traffic consists of the following:

- ISAKMP traffic (UDP port 500).
- ESP traffic (IP protocol 50).
- AH traffic (IP protocol 51). Note that the Cisco VPN 3000 concentrator does not support AH.
- IPsec traffic carried over UDP or TCP when traversing a NAT/PAT device. In this case, the form that IPsec traffic takes depends on how NAT-T is configured:
  - Industry standard NAT-T uses UDP port 4500.

— IPsec over a user-defined TCP port (10000, by default, on the Cisco VPN 3000 concentrator).

— IPsec over a user-defined UDP port (10000, by default, on the Cisco VPN 3000 concentrator).

NOTE   For more information on how IPsec traffic is transported when using NAT-T, see the section "Configuring NAT Transparency for IPsec Remote Access VPNs" earlier in this chapter.

The Cisco VPN 3000 concentrator has a default public interface filter (**Configuration > Policy Management > Traffic Management > Filters**) that you can easily modify to permit only IPsec VPN traffic.

NOTE   If some remote access users are using other VPN protocols to connect to the VPN gateway(s), do not forget to permit these protocols to access the public interface of the VPN gateway(s).

Also, some administrators may want to permit ICMP Echo/Echo Reply packets (ping) to the public interface of the VPN gateway(s) in order to allow diagnostics (remote access clients to test IP reachability to the VPN gateway[s]).

Again, the private interface can be connected either to a firewall or directly to the private LAN (labeled 1 and 2, respectively, in Figure 9-57). The primary consideration is again where administrators want to inspect traffic arriving over remote access VPN tunnels (on the VPN gateway or on a firewall).

In summary, it is a good idea to carefully consider exactly which traffic needs to be permitted/blocked to/on the public interface(s) of the VPN gateway(s). Then, decide where you want to permit or block this traffic (on a firewall connected to the public interface of the VPN gateway[s] or on the public interface of the VPN gateway[s]).

Similarly, consider which traffic should be allowed/denied into the corporate LAN from the remote access VPN clients (received over IPsec VPN tunnels), and then decide where to permit/block this traffic (on the VPN gateway[s] or on a firewall connected to the private interface of the VPN gateway[s]).

Considerations When Building Wireless IPsec VPNs

Although not something that follows the typical remote access VPN model, IPsec is also sometimes used to secure wireless LANs.

An IPsec remote access VPN model using one or more VPN gateways, and IPsec client software deployed on users workstations, laptops, or other mobile devices, can be used to address real (or imaginary) concerns with regard to the security of wireless LANs.

Figure 9-58 depicts the deployment of the IPsec remote access VPN model to secure a wireless LAN.

Figure 9-58 *Deployment of the IPsec Remote Access VPN Model to Secure a Wireless LAN*

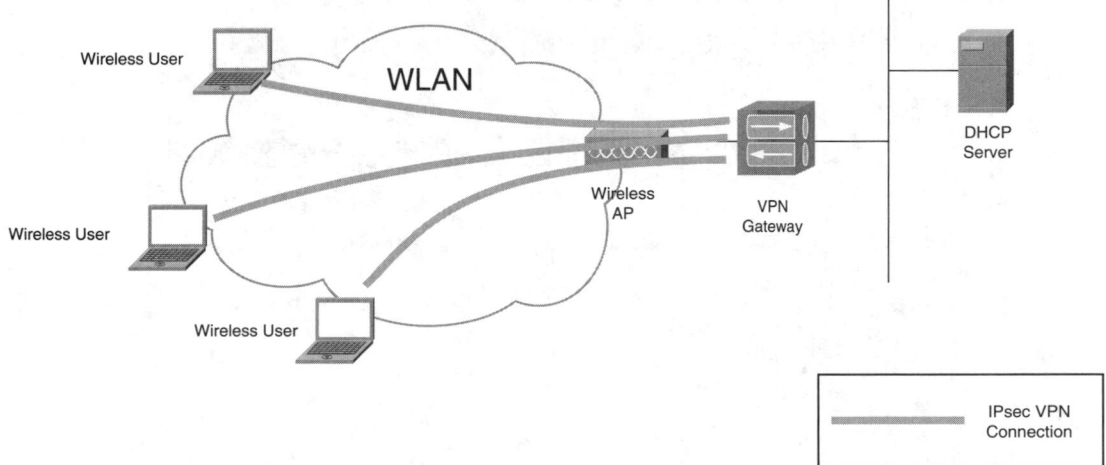

In Figure 9-58, user devices connect over an untrusted wireless LAN to a VPN gateway. User devices are authenticated during IKE phase 1, and users themselves are authenticated with Xauth. All user traffic is encrypted between the VPN gateway and user devices.

In this model, most, if not all, of the design and configuration considerations discussed already in this chapter apply when using IPsec in a wireless LAN environment. There are, however, one or two additional considerations for IPsec remote access VPNs in a wireless LANs:

- **Remote access VPN client auto-initiation**—To save users from having to manually connect to the VPN gateway, auto-initiation of VPN connections can be configured on the Cisco VPN Client.

- **DHCP relay**—Some people choose not to place a DHCP server on the outside interface of the VPN gateway because it could become the focus of a denial-of-service attack (users are unable to obtain IP addresses because the DHCP server is under attack). Instead, the VPN gateway can be configured to relay DHCP requests to DHCP server on the inside network (connected via the private interface of the VPN gateway).

You can configure the Cisco VPN Client to auto-initiate a VPN connection to a VPN gateway by modifying the vpnclient.ini file (contained in the system_root\Program Files\Cisco Systems\VPN Client directory).

TIP   It is a good idea to make a copy of the vpnclient.ini file and save it to a separate location
                 before modifying it.

Figure 9-59 shows a vpnclient.ini file modified to enable auto-initiation.

Figure 9-59   *vpnclient.ini File Modified to Enable Auto-Initiation*

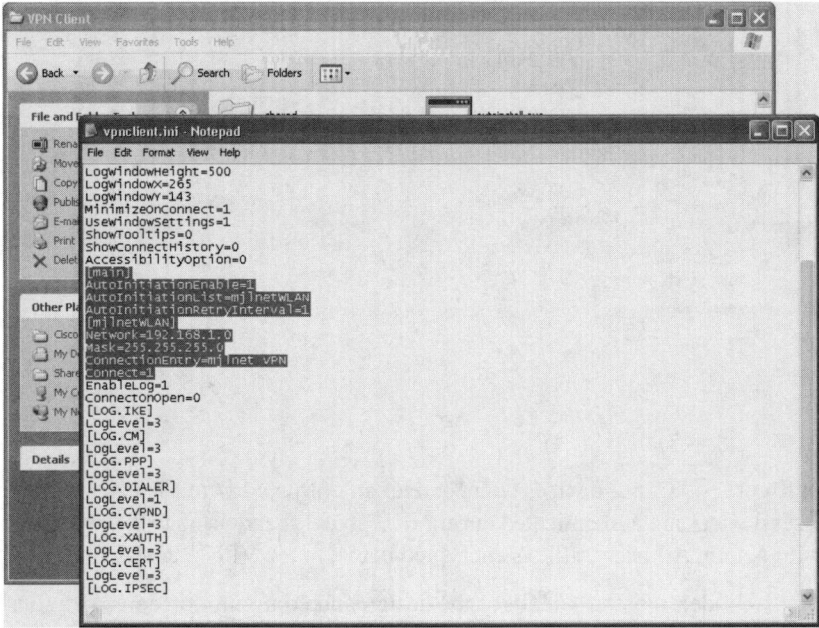

A number of keywords and a new section have been added to the vpnclient.ini file in
Figure 9-59:

- **AutoInitiationEnable=1** enables auto-initiation of VPN connections. A value of 0
  disables auto-initiation.

  This keyword and value add Automatic VPN Initiation to the options menu
  of the Cisco VPN Client, which allows automatic initiation to be enabled/
  disabled from the GUI allows modification of the interval at which the Cisco
  VPN Client attempts auto-initiation.

- **AutoInitiationList=** specifies a vpnclient.ini section name where details of the
  VPN connection(s) to auto-initiate can be found.

  If a user visits multiple sites where auto-initiation is required (multiple
  WLANs), links to sections where details of these VPN connections are found
  can be chained after the **AutoInitiationList=** keyword (these section names
  must be separated by a comma). Up to 64 sections can be specified.

For example, **AutoInitiationList=mjlnetWLAN,ciscoWLAN,blahWLAN**.

- **AutoInitiationRetryInterval=1** configures the auto-initiation interval to 1 minute (the default). This interval can range from 1 to 10 when the interval is in minutes, and 5 to 600 when the interval is in seconds.

  The interval type (minutes or seconds) can be modified using the **AutoInitiationRetryIntervalType=** keyword (the default is minutes).

- **[mjlnetWLAN]** delineates the beginning of the section where details of the VPN connection to auto-initiate are found (previously linked to using the **AutoInitiationList=** keyword).

  A number of keywords appear under the section header:

  — **Network=** specifies the network address which if detected causes the VPN connection in this section to be auto-initiated.

    If the local client receives an IP address from a DHCP server that falls within this network (or is manually configured with such as address) then it will auto-initiate the VPN connection in this section.

  — **Mask=** specifies the mask corresponding to the network configured using the **Network=** keyword.

  — **ConnectionEntry=** specifies the name of the VPN connection entry to auto-initiate.

    VPN connection entries are stored as .pcf files in the system_root\ Program Files\Cisco Systems\VPN Client\Profiles directory.

  — **Connect=1** causes auto-initiation of a VPN connection. A value of 0 stops auto-initiation and can be used in conjunction with the **Network=** and **Mask=** keywords to indicate an exception for auto-initiation.

    If you want to cause auto-initiation for network 192.168.0.0/16, with the exception of 192.168.1.0/24, you could create two sections, one specifying 192.168.1.0/24 with **Connect=0**, and one specifying 192.168.0.0/16 with **Connect=1**. By ordering the 192.168.1.0/24 section before the 192.168.0.0/16 section in the vpnclient.ini file, this would cause the desired auto-initiation (the sections are searched one by one in the order they appear in the [main] section of the vpnclient.ini file, in a manner similar to that used for an ACL).

To configure DHCP relay on the Cisco VPN 3000 concentrator, go to **Configuration > System > IP Routing > DHCP Relay** (see Figure 9-60).

Figure 9-60 *Enabling DHCP Relay*

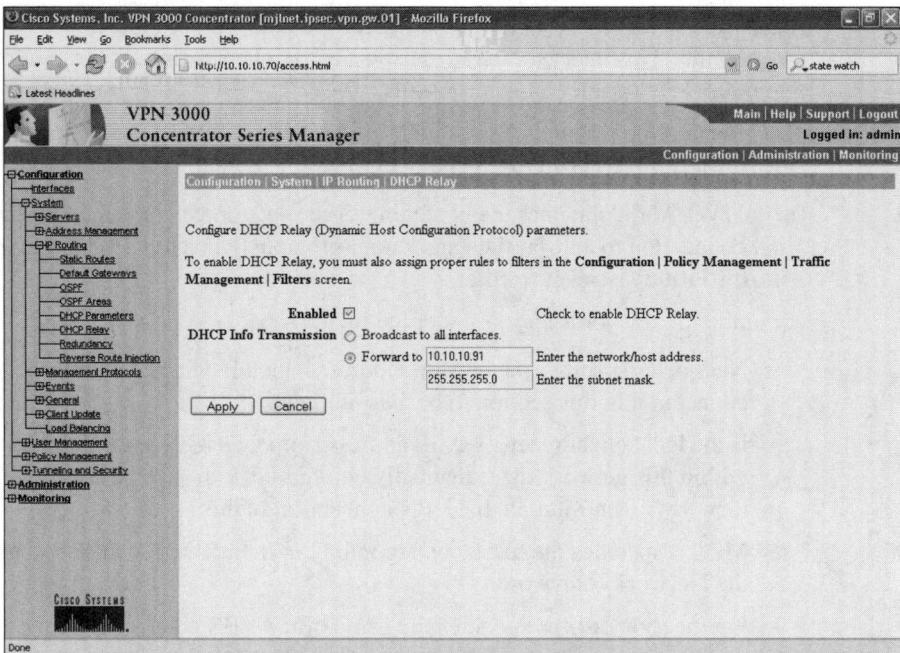

Check the **Enabled** box and specify the IP address and corresponding mask of the DHCP server in the Forward to boxes.

Also, make sure that DHCP is permitted by the filter on the Public interface. Verify this by going to **Configuration > Policy Management > Traffic Management > Filters**, choose the **Public (Default)** filter, click **Assign Rules to Filter**, and add the **DHCP In (forward/in)** and **DHCP Out (forward/out)** to Current Rules in Filter.

Allowing or Disallowing Split Tunneling for Remote Access VPN Clients

To maintain the security of a remote access VPN, it is necessary to control if and how split tunneling is permitted on VPN clients.

Split tunneling is when VPN clients are allowed to *directly* access other destinations such as the Internet at the same time as accessing corporate resources via a VPN connection, rather than having to access these other destinations over the VPN connection via an Internet gateway at the corporate site.

Split tunneling can be useful to optimize traffic flow, but is a potential security risk.

Figure 9-61 illustrates split tunneling.

Figure 9-61 *Split Tunneling*

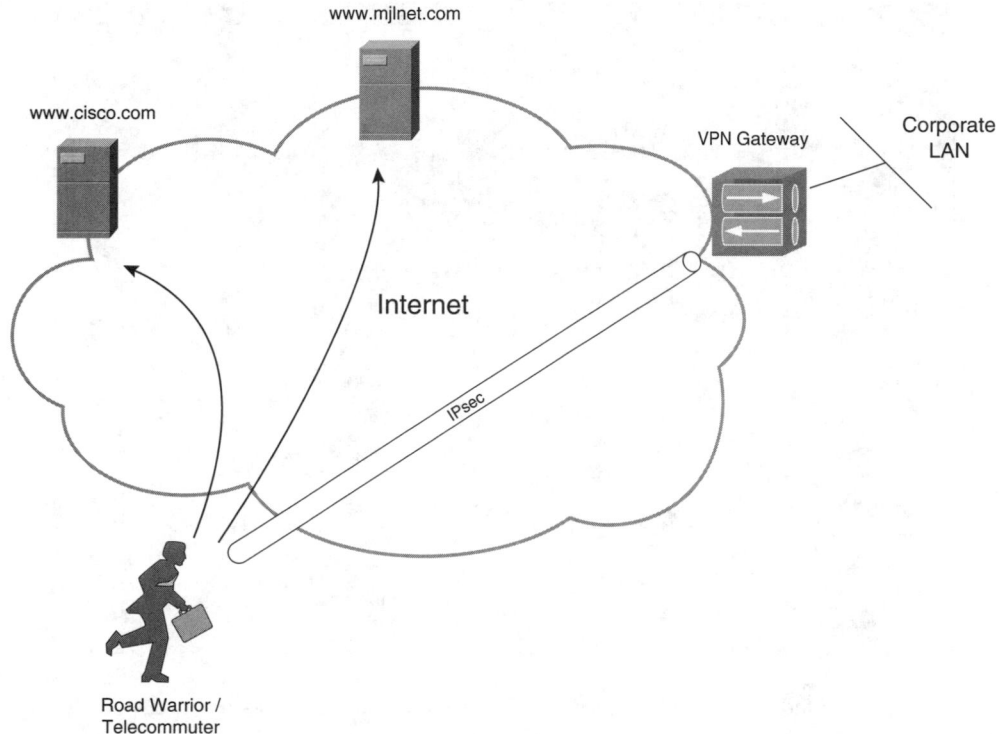

On the Cisco VPN concentrator, you can configure split tunneling under the Client Config tab of a group (see Figure 9-62). These settings are then pushed to Cisco VPN Clients as they connect to the Cisco VPN 3000 concentrator.

In the Split Tunneling Policy section, the Tunnel everything option ensures that all traffic is sent via the VPN tunnel (split tunneling is disabled). This is the default.

The Tunnel everything option is the most secure because it does not allow client workstations to send traffic to the Internet or other networks while at the same time connecting via a VPN to a corporate network. When split tunneling is enabled (not this option), on the other hand, clients can access other networks at the same time as connecting via a VPN, and this might open the corporate network up to attacks from individuals on the Internet (or elsewhere) who attack client workstations and access the corporate network via the VPN connection.

The second option is a limited form of split tunneling. This can be enabled by selecting **Tunneling everything**, checking the **Allow the networks in list to bypass the tunnel**, and then selecting **VPN Client Local LAN (Default)** from the Split Tunneling Network List drop-down box.

Figure 9-62 *Configuring Split Tunneling*

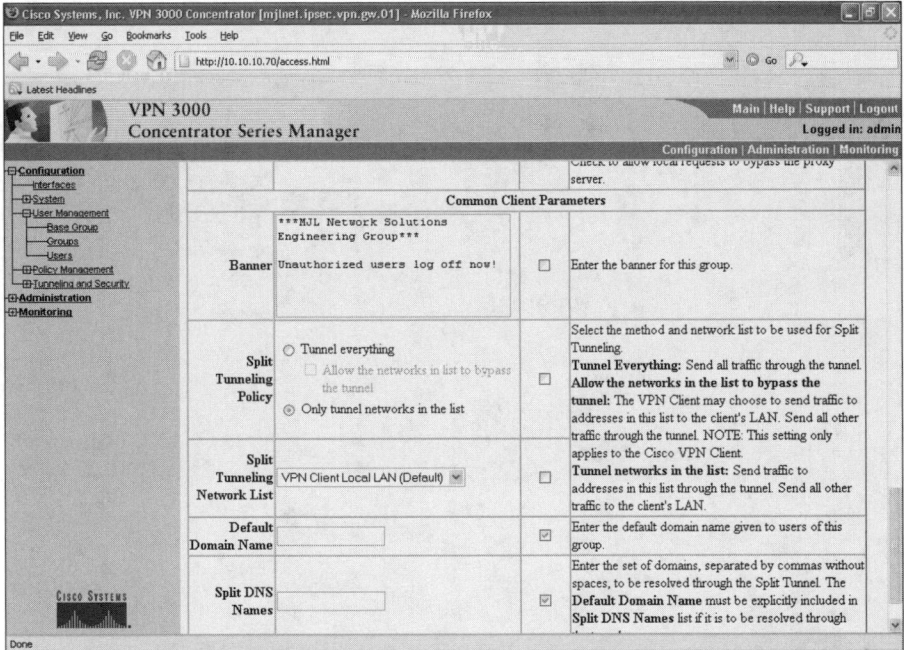

This limited form of split tunneling allows the clients to access resources on their local LANs (such as networked printers), but not other resources, such as those on the Internet, while connected to the Cisco VPN 3000 concentrator.

If you want to be more specific as to exactly which IP addresses can be accessed by the client, you can go to **Configuration > Policy Management > Traffic Management > Network Lists** and create a network list of resources that you would like clients in the group to be able to access (the network list in this case defines traffic that bypasses the VPN connection).

You can enable complete split tunneling allowing clients to access all other resources at the same time as connecting to the Cisco 3000 VPN concentrator by selecting **Only tunnel networks in the list**. In this case, you must configure a network list (**Configuration > Policy Management > Traffic Management > Network Lists**) and then select this network list in the Split Tunneling Network List drop-down box. In this case, the network list defines which traffic is sent over the VPN connection.

When configuring split tunneling (especially complete split tunneling), it is a good idea to enforce a firewall policy via the group Client FW tab. You can use a firewall policy to ensure that clients wanting to connect to the Cisco VPN 3000 concentrator are running certain types of firewall software. By enforcing a firewall policy, it becomes much more difficult for hackers on the Internet to gain access to the client to then access the corporate network via the VPN connection.

On the Cisco ASA 5500, you can control split tunneling for remote access VPN clients using the **split-tunnel-policy** {**tunnelall** | **tunnelspecified** | **excludespecified**} and **split-tunnel-network-list** {**value** *access-list name* | none} group policy configuration mode commands.

The **split-tunnel-policy** command is used to specify whether all traffic from remote access VPN clients should be tunneled to the Cisco ASA 5500 (**tunnelall**, the default), whether only traffic indicated in an access list should be tunneled (**tunnelspecified**), or whether all traffic *except* that indicated in an access list should be tunneled (**excludespecified**).

The **split-tunnel-network-list** command is used to reference the name of the access list that indicates what traffic should either be tunneled to the Cisco ASA (with **split-tunnel-policy tunnelspecified**) or indicates what traffic should not be tunneled to the Cisco ASA (with **split-tunnel-policy excludespecified**). The access list itself can be configured using the **access-list** global configuration mode command.

As previously mentioned, it is a good idea to configure a firewall policy for remote access VPN clients (the Cisco VPN Client) when split tunneling is allowed. You can configure a firewall policy using the **client-firewall** [**none** | **opt** | **req**] group policy configuration mode command on the Cisco ASA 5500. The **none** keyword specifies that a firewall is not required, the **opt** keyword specifies that a firewall is optional, and the **req** keyword specifies that a firewall is required.

A split tunneling policy can also be enforced on a Cisco IOS VPN gateway. You can find more information in the section "Cisco IOS Router as an IPsec Remote Access VPN Gateway with IKE Preshared Key Authentication" earlier in this chapter.

Summary

This chapter discussed the design and implementation of IPsec remote access VPNs and examined their strengths and weaknesses.

Strengths and weaknesses of IPsec remote access VPNs include strong security; the fact that remote users experience a similar level of functionality to that which they would experience if they were at their office or central site; the fact that functionality provided by mechanisms such as Xauth and Mode Config are not industry standards, which may cause some interoperability issues between different vendors' equipment; the fact that the Cisco VPN Client must be installed (and administered) on each client workstation; and the fact that the Cisco VPN Client includes features such as split tunneling/DNS, enforcement of firewall type, antivirus software type/level, and operating system service pack level on certain client workstation operating systems.

Issues relating to the fact that IKEv1 does not provide mechanisms for remote access VPN user authentication and the negotiation of certain attributes were described, and solutions such as Xauth and Mode Config were examined. Remote access VPN *devices* are authenticated during IKEv1 phase 1, whereas remote access VPN *users* are authenticated using mechanisms such as Xauth. Attributes such as IP addresses, DNS servers addresses, and WINS server addresses can be supplied to remote access VPN users using Mode Config during IKE negotiation.

This chapter also discussed in detail the implementation of IPsec remote access VPNs using preshared key, digital certificate, and Hybrid Authentication on devices such as the Cisco VPN 3000 concentrator, the Cisco ASA 5500, and Cisco IOS routers. IPsec remote access VPNs that use preshared key authentication are simple to configure but may not offer the strongest security, whereas IPsec remote access VPN that use digital signature authentication offer stronger security, but are more complex to deploy. IPsec remote access VPNs that use Hybrid Authentication address some of concerns relating to the strength of preshared key authentication but are not as complex to deploy as IPsec remote access VPNs that use digital signature authentication.

When implementing IPsec remote access VPNs, it is important to consider possible issues relating to NAT. These issues can be overcome by configuring NAT transparency mechanisms that involve Cisco proprietary TCP or UDP encapsulation of IPsec traffic, or, alternatively, IETF standard NAT-T.

Another important design and implementation consideration is high availability. High availability can be provided using load balancing of connections over a number of VPN gateways at a single site, failover of VPN gateways at a single site, and the configuration of backup VPN gateways (servers) at geographically dispersed sites.

Finally, the integration of IPsec VPNs with MPLS Layer 3 VPNs was described. IPsec VPNs can be used to extend the reach of MPLS Layer 3 VPNs to remote access users and sites that can connect to an MPLS Layer 3 VPN across the Internet.

Review Questions

1 What are some of the main benefits and drawbacks of IPsec remote access VPNs?

2 What are the two main types of issue with regard to IKEv1 an IPsec remote access VPN environment?

3 What are the three main methods by which a VPN gateway can authenticate remote access VPN users when using IKEv1?

4 What sort of functionality can Mode Config provide?

5 What information does the **debug crypto isakmp sa** command display?

6 What methods do the VPN 3000 concentrator and Cisco ASA 5500 provide to overcome issues with NAT/PAT and IPsec remote access VPNs?

7 When a hardware client (Cisco IOS router) is configured for EZVPN, how does a remote access user authenticate him/herself?

8 What are the three basic ways to configure high availability for IPsec remote access VPNs?

9 To allow IPsec remote access VPN connections through a firewall, which ports may have to be opened on the firewall?

10 What file can be modified to provide auto-initiation of Cisco VPN Client connections with wireless VPNs?

CHAPTER 10

Designing and Building SSL Remote Access VPNs (WebVPN)

Providing remote access VPN connectivity is a relatively new application for the Secure Sockets Layer (SSL). SSL was designed to secure TCP-based protocols and applications such as HTTP (HTTPS), FTP (FTPS), POP3 (POP3S), and SMTP (SMTPS).

SSL is built in to most, if not all, web browsers, and this fact allows the deployment of SSL remote access VPNs without the requirement to install specific client software on remote user workstations or devices—only a web browser is needed for basic (clientless) SSL remote access VPN connectivity.

Although clientless SSL remote access VPNs provide a basic level of access, more comprehensive access can be provided through the use of the Cisco SSL VPN Client. This software provides users with remote access VPN connectivity that is comparable to that provided by IPsec or Layer Two Tunneling Protocol (L2TP)/IPsec.

Figure 10-1 illustrates SSL remote access VPNs.

Figure 10-1 *SSL Remote Access VPNs*

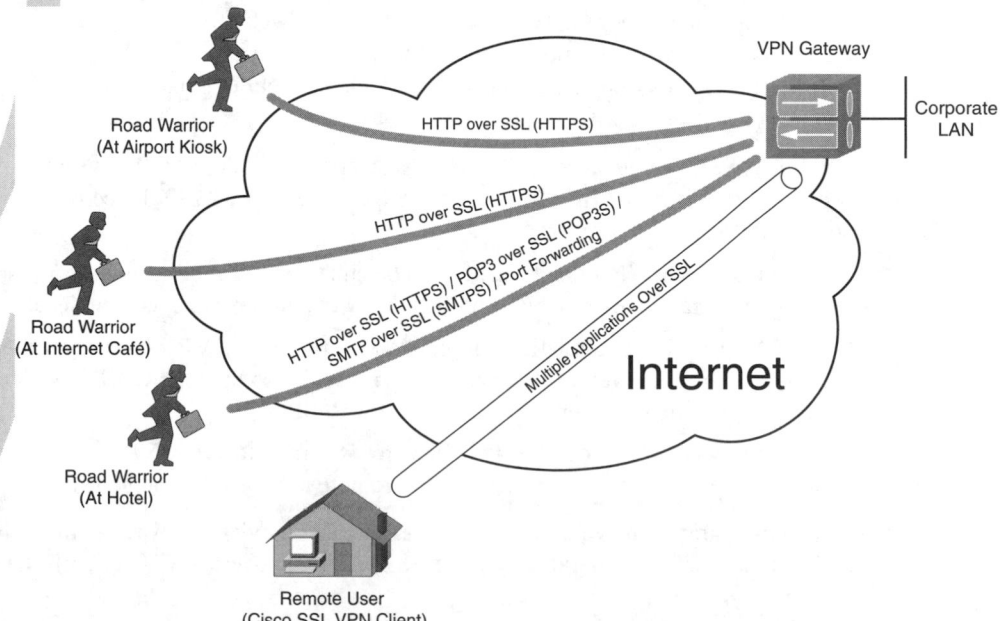

In Figure 10-1, remote access users at an Internet café, airport Internet kiosk, and a hotel access the corporate network using variously HTTPS, POP3S, SMTPS, and port forwarding (TCP-based application traffic redirected over SSL). A telecommuter accesses the corporate network using the Cisco SSL VPN Client.

In this chapter, you will learn how SSL remote access VPNs compare to other types of remote access VPN. You will also find out the characteristics of SSL remote access VPNs, as well as how to design and implement them to provide exactly the type and level of functionality required.

Finally, you will learn how to properly secure SSL remote access VPNs—a very important consideration, particularly when users may be accessing the corporate network from untrusted locations such as Internet cafés and airport kiosks.

Comparing SSL VPNs to Other Types of Remote Access VPNs

When deciding whether to implement SSL remote access VPNs, it is essential to understand how they compare to other types of remote access VPNs and what their advantages and disadvantages are.

Some of the main advantages and disadvantages of SSL remote access VPNs are as follows:

- SSL remote access VPNs are relatively simple to deploy because it is not necessary to install or administer a VPN client on remote user devices.

  It is only necessary for remote user devices to have a web browser to access the corporate network. Remote users can use a web browser to access corporate networks from a wide variety of locations, including Internet cafés and airport Internet kiosks.

- Clientless SSL remote access VPNs (those accessed using a web browser) provide a subset of the functionality provided by IPsec or L2TP/IPsec remote access VPNs.

- SSL remote access VPN functionality can be enhanced by configuring the VPN gateway to dynamically download an SSL VPN client to remote user devices.

- SSL VPNs can impose a relatively high CPU overhead on a VPN gateway if there are a large number of remote access users. This is due to the high CPU overhead incurred by public key operations associated with SSL.

  The relatively high CPU overhead imposed by SSL remote access VPNs can be ameliorated by careful selection of SSL remote access VPN gateways.

- Little configuration is required on firewalls and NAT devices to provide transit for SSL remote access VPN traffic because SSL is carried over (NAT-friendly) TCP.

Typically, TCP ports 443 (HTTPS) as well as (if e-mail proxy is configured) ports used for POP3 over SSL (POP3S), IMAP4 over SSL (IMAP4S), and SMTP over SSL (SMTPS) need to be opened for firewalls to ensure correct operation of SSL remote access VPNs.

- One major disadvantage of SSL remote access VPN has been that universal access that they offer can lead to vulnerabilities being introduced into a corporate network. This is due to the untrusted nature of locations/workstations from which users can connect (Internet cafés, kiosks, hotels, and so on).

Cisco addresses these concerns with the Cisco Secure Desktop.

Now that you understand the advantages and disadvantages of SSL VPNs, it is time to move on to their operation, design, and implementation.

Understanding the Operation of SSL Remote Access VPNs

Before getting into the design and implementation of SSL remote access VPNs, it is a very good idea to take a look at the underlying mechanisms that allow their operation. This section examines the protocols and mechanisms are used to enable SSL remote accessVPNs.

The Secure Sockets Layer (SSL) is a security protocol that is used to secure e-commerce, web transactions, and more recently, to provide remote access VPN connectivity.

SSL was invented by Netscape Communications, and there are a number of versions:

- **SSL version 1 (SSLv1)**—This version was not released by Netscape.
- **SSL version 2 (SSLv2)**—This version was released and is still supported by many web browsers, but it has a number of well-known weaknesses and deficiencies, including its vulnerability to downgrade attacks (an attacker can force the negotiation of a weak cipher suite [which is then subject to attack]); its vulnerability to truncation attacks (an attacker can cause either the server or the client to believe that data transfer has finished by simply forging a TCP FIN); the fact that SSLv2 relies on MD5 MACs and SHA-1 is not available for use; the fact that the same key is used for encryption and authentication (so breaking the key of one leads automatically to the breaking of the other); and the ability of an attacker to intercept and hijack a client's connection. So, SSLv2 is definitely not recommended.
- **SSL version 3 (SSLv3)**—This version addresses the weaknesses of SSLv2.
- **Transport Layer Security (TLS version 1.0, RFC 2246)**—This is an IETF standard that is based on but not compatible with SSLv3.

In this chapter, the term *SSL* is used as a generic term to describe SSLv3 and TLS.

SSL Overview: TCP, the Record Layer, and the Handshake Protocol

SSL sits on top of a reliable protocol, such as TCP. Application data can then be carried on top of SSL.

Figure 10-2 shows the overall SSL packet format.

Figure 10-2 *Overall SSL Packet Format*

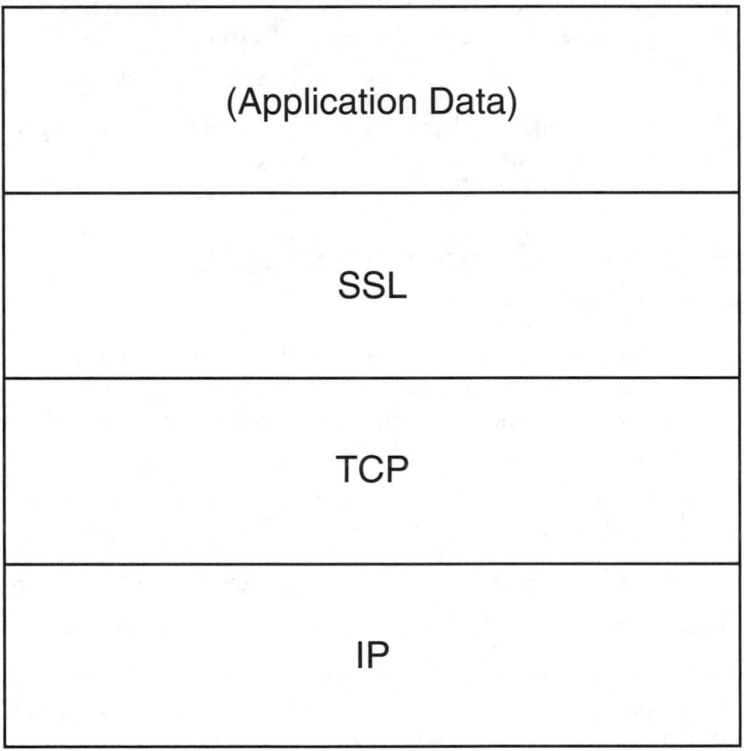

The SSL protocol itself consists of the record protocol plus the handshake protocol, the alert protocol, the change cipher spec protocol, and the application data protocol.

Figure 10-3 shows the relationship between the record protocol and the handshake, alert, change cipher spec, and application data protocols.

The Record layer (protocol) has a number of functions, including the following:

- **Fragmentation**—The record protocol fragments/reassembles data on transmission/ reception, if required.
- **Compression**—If negotiated between a client and server, the record protocol compresses/decompresses data.
- **Applies MAC**—The record protocol applies/verifies a MAC.
- **Encryption**—The record protocol encrypts/decrypts data.

Figure 10-3 *Relationship Between the Record Protocol and the Handshake, Alert, Change Cipher Spec, and Application Data Protocols*

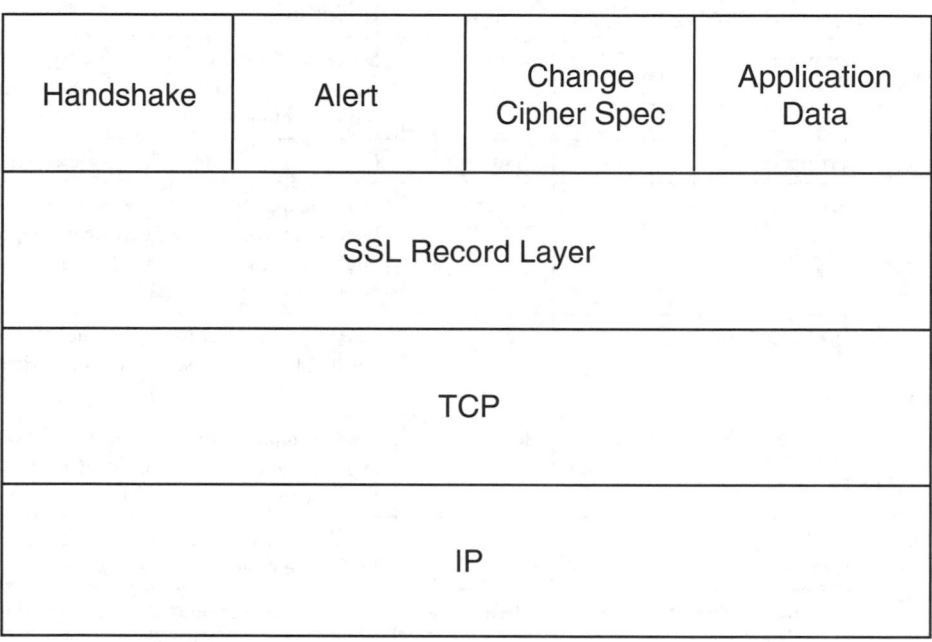

As shown in Figure 10-3, the handshake, alert, change cipher spec, and application data protocols sit on top of the Record layer. These protocols have the following functions:

- **Handshake protocol (type 22)**—This protocol consists of a number of messages exchanged between peers (the client and server) that allow those peers to negotiate SSL version, cryptographic algorithms, and parameters; optionally authenticate each other; and generate shared secret cryptographic keys using public key techniques.

    Table 10-1 summarizes SSLv3 and TLS handshake protocol messages.

Table 10-1 *Handshake Protocol Messages*

Handshake Protocol Message	Type	Sent By	Description
HelloRequest	0	Server	Notification that the client should begin negotiation again.
ClientHello	1	Client	Used to (re-)initiate an SSL connection. Specifies list of cryptographic algorithms/ parameters, plus optional compression method and random number.

continues

Table 10-1   *Handshake Protocol Messages (Continued)*

Handshake Protocol Message	Type	Sent By	Description
ServerHello	2	Server	Specifies chosen cryptographic algorithms/parameters and optional compression method. Includes random number.
Certificate	11	Client/server	Contains certificate or certificate chain.
ServerKeyExchange	12	Server	Used in ephemeral RSA or Diffie-Hellman handshake when server certificate message does not allow client to exchange premaster secret.
CertificateRequest	13	Server	Used by the server to request the client's certificate. Used when client authentication is required.
ServerHelloDone	14	Server	Used to indicate that the server will not send any more messages at this stage of the handshake.
CertificateVerify	15	Client	Used by the client to prove that it is the legitimate *owner* of its certificate.
ClientKeyExchange	16	Client	Used to send the premaster secret to the server.
Finished	20	Client/server	Ensures integrity of handshake exchange.

- **Alert protocol (type 21)**—This is used to signal error conditions. These error conditions include those that occur during an SSL handshake, when decrypting or integrity checking, or when closing a connection.

- **Change cipher spec protocol (type 20)**—This protocol (which consists of a single message type) is used by the client or server to signal that subsequent SSL messages will be protected using negotiated cryptographic algorithms, parameters, and keys.

- **Application data protocol (type 23)**—The application data protocol carries data from whichever application or applications are running over SSL. This data can include protocols such as HTTP, FTP, POP3, IMAP4, SMTP, as well as other higher-level protocol data.

Establishing an SSL Connection Between a Remote Access VPN User and an SSL VPN Gateway Using an RSA Handshake

As previously described, the function of SSL is to negotiate cryptographic algorithms, authenticate the server (VPN gateway) and optionally the remote access VPN client, and establish cryptographic keys.

The most common method of establishing an SSL connection between a remote access VPN client and a VPN gateway is using the Rivest, Shamir, and Addlemen (RSA) handshake with VPN gateway authentication. In this case, the remote access VPN client is not authenticated during the handshake, but may be authenticated using a separate mechanism after the SSL connection has been established.

Figure 10-4 illustrates the RSA handshake with VPN gateway only authentication.

Figure 10-4 *SSL RSA Handshake*

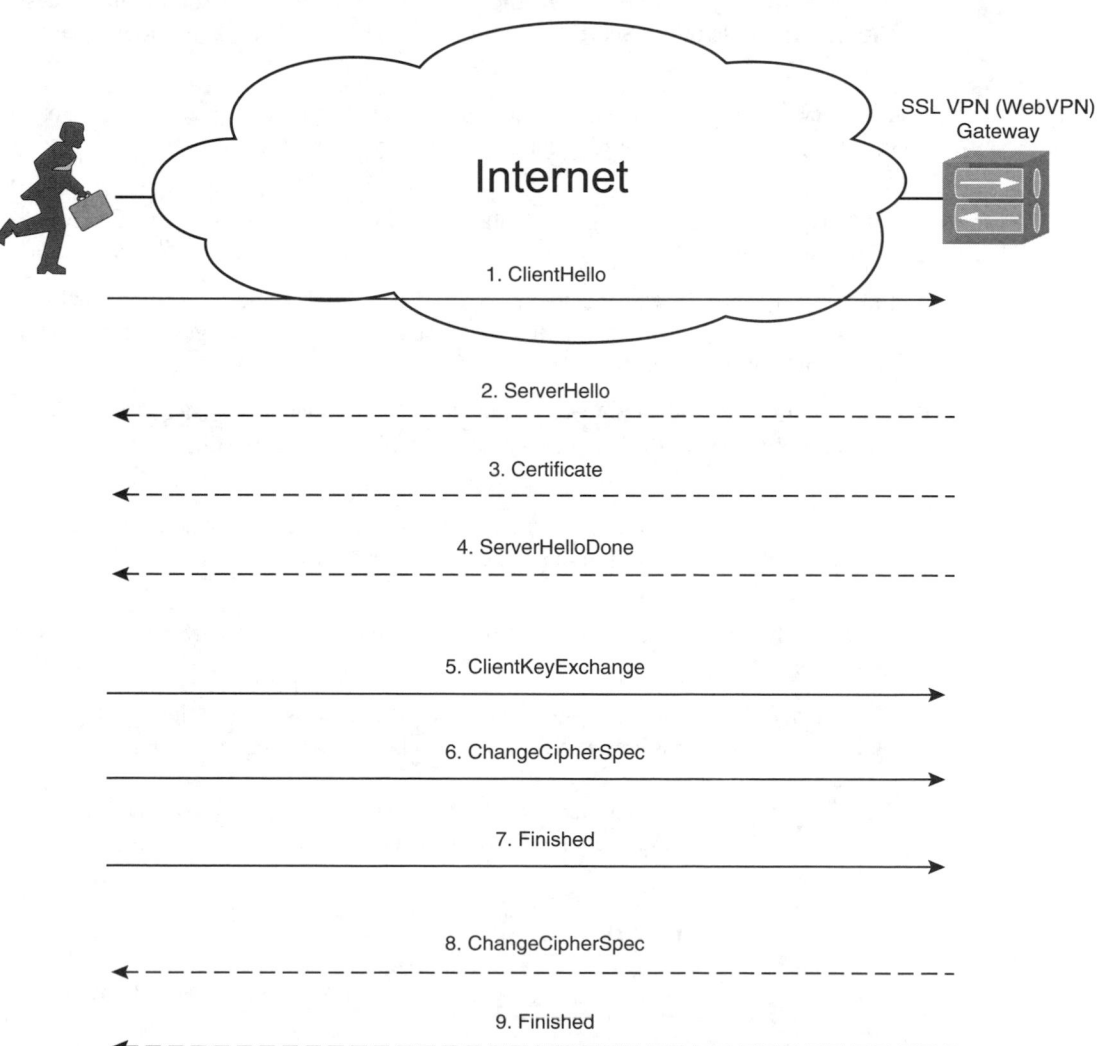

As shown in Figure 10-4, the RSA handshake with VPN gateway only authentication consists of the exchange of nine messages:

1 The first step in the RSA handshake is when the remote access client sends a ClientHello message to the VPN gateway (server). This message is used to propose a number of cryptographic parameters and algorithms (cipher suites), compression methods (if any), and well as being used to transmit a random number that is later used to generate cryptographic keys.

2 The VPN gateway now selects one of the cryptographic proposals (cipher suites), together with any compression method sent in the ClientHello and includes these chosen proposals in the ServerHello message that it sends to the remote access client.

   The ServerHello message also includes a random number generated by the VPN gateway, which is again used to later generate cryptographic keys.

3 Next, the VPN gateway's sends a Certificate message. This message contains the VPN gateway's certificate (including its public key) along with any other certificates in a certificate chain.

4 Immediately after the Certificate message is ServerHelloDone. The VPN gateway sends this message to signal that it will not send any more messages at this stage of the handshake sequence.

5 The remote access client now sends the ClientKeyExchange message. This message includes a key, called the pre_master_secret, which is encrypted using the VPN gateway's public key.

   The pre_master_secret, together with the random numbers sent in the ClientHello and ServerHello messages is used to generate the keys later used to encrypt and authenticate SSL traffic.

6 The ClientKeyExchange message is followed by the ChangeCipherSpec and Finished messages.

   The ChangeCipherSpec message signals that SSL messages from the client (starting with the Finished message) will from now on be protected using the negotiated cipher suite.
   The Finished message contains a hash of all the messages previously sent in the handshake—this ensures that an attacker has not modified any of the previous handshake messages.

7 The VPN gateway now completes the RSA handshake by sending its own ChangeCipherSpec and Finished messages.

Now that you know what happens in theory, it is time to take a look at an SSL connection in practice.

SSL Connection Establishment: ClientHello Message

Figure 10-5 shows a packet capture of an SSL ClientHello message.

Figure 10-5 *SSL ClientHello Message*

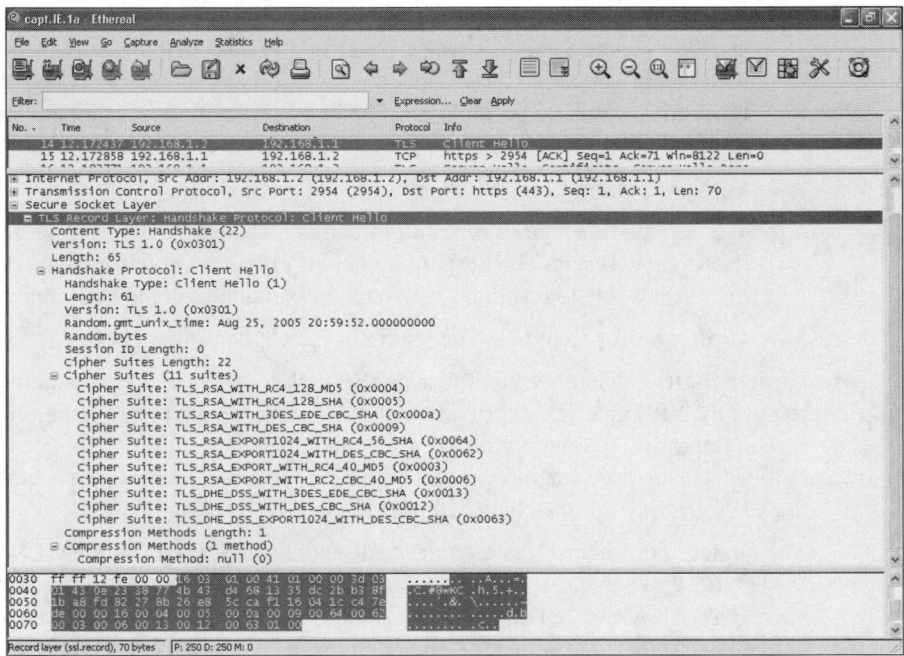

If you look at the highlighted line in the main portion of the screen shown in Figure 10-5, you can see the message is, in fact, a ClientHello message. Below the highlighted line there are a number of message fields that can be described as follows:

- Record layer header:

  — **Content Type**—This field specifies the record type, which in this case is Handshake (type 22).

  — **Version**—This defines the SSL version (major and minor versions). SSLv3 is 3.0 (0x0300), and TLS is 3.1 (0x0301).

  — **Length**—The length of the record. According to the specification, a record can be up to a maximum of 2^{14} bytes, although at least one browser type did erroneously send records of up to 2^{16-1} bytes.

- Handshake protocol header:

  — **Handshake Type**—The handshake protocol message type. Here, the message type is ClientHello (1).

  — **Length**—The length of the message.

  — **Version**—The highest version of the SSL protocol that the client supports.

— **Random number (Random.gmt_unix_time, plus Random.bytes)**—This is the previously described random number that is later used to generate cryptographic keys.

Notice that the random number is, in fact, made up of the number of seconds since midnight, January 1, 1970 (4 bytes in UNIX format), as well as a 28-byte randomly generated number. The UNIX time is included in the random number to ensure that the same random number is not chosen twice (this would be possible if all 32 bytes of the random number were randomly chosen!).

— **Session ID Length**—The length of the Session ID field.

The Session ID length is zero here, and this indicates that the Session ID field itself is not present. The Session ID field is only present in the ClientHello if the client wants to resume a previous SSL session with the VPN gateway.

— **Cipher Suites Length**—The length of the Cipher Suites list.

• **Cipher Suites**—There are a number of SSL cipher suites, including a number that require the VPN gateway to provide an RSA certificate, a number that are used for server authenticated (and optionally client authenticated) Diffie-Hellman, and a number that are used for anonymous Diffie-Hellman communications where neither the VPN gateway nor the client is authenticated.

The cipher suites themselves are fairly self-explanatory. For example, TLS_RSA_WITH_RC4_128_MD5 specifies RSA authentication with the RC4 stream cipher for encryption and Message Digest 5 (MD5) for integrity checking. One thing you might notice if you closely examine the cipher suites in Example 10-5 is the lack of any support for AES. This is due to the lack of any AES cipher suites in the base TLS v1.0 specification (RFC 2246 [SSLv3 includes no support for AES, by the way]). RFC 3268 describes support for AES cipher suites with TLS, and this support is integrated into the TLS v1.2 specification, which is under discussion in the IETF TLS working group at the time of this writing. It may be interesting to note that support for AES with HTTPS is added in Microsoft Vista (support is also included in Firefox).

— **Compression Methods Length**—The length of the Compression Methods field.

— **Compression Methods**—This specifies methods of compression that the client is willing to support. RFC2246 does not specify any compression methods because of intellectual property concerns, and so this client specifies NULL compression, meaning no compression.

Note that RFC3749 does specify the DEFLATE compression algorithm for use with SSL (DEFLATE itself is defined in RFC1951).

SSL Connection Establishment: ServerHello, Certificate, and ServerHelloDone Messages

The next messages in the SSL handshake sequence are ServerHello, Certificate, and ServerHelloDone. The VPN gateway sends these messages (see Figure 10-6).

Figure 10-6 *SSL server_hello, Certificate, and ServerHelloDone Messages*

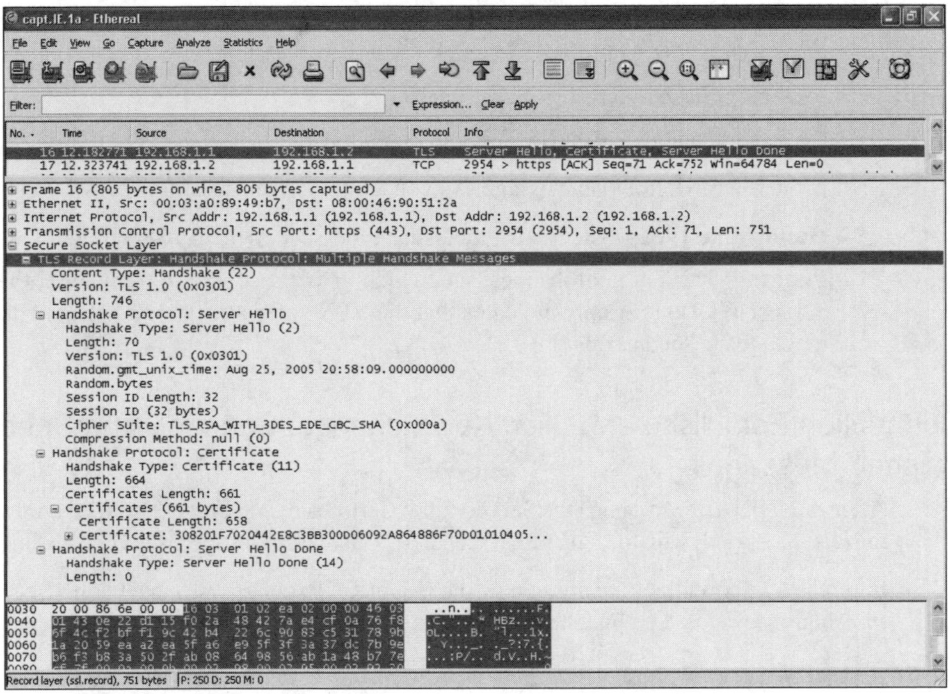

If you take a look in the main portion of Figure 10-6, you can see the common SSL record header (Content Type, Version, Length), followed by the ServerHello, Certificate, and ServerHelloDone messages.

The ServerHello message is similar to the ClientHello message, but there are one or two differences:

- The Handshake Type field now specifies that this message is a ServerHello (2).

- The Session ID Length field specifies a 32-byte length.

- The Session ID field specifies a Session ID that can be used to resume the session at a later stage if desired.

- The Cipher Suite field specifies the cipher suite chosen by the VPN gateway from those sent by the client in the ClientHello message.

Immediately after the ServerHello is the Certificate message. The Certificate message is relatively simple and consists of the following fields:

- **Handshake Type**—In this case, this field is used to specify that this is a certificate message (11).

- **Length**—The length of this message.

- **Certificates Length**—The length of the certificate(s) included in this message.

- **Certificates**—The certificate or certificates sent by the VPN gateway, including the following:
  - **Certificate Length**—The length of *this* certificate.
  - **Certificate**—The certificate itself.

  Note that a number of certificates can be included.

  Next is the ServerHelloDone message. As you can see, it consists of only two fields:

- **Handshake Type**—The type of handshake message, which is ServerHelloDone (14).
- **Length**—The length of the message, which in this case is zero (remember that ServerHelloDone simply indicates that the VPN gateway does not have any more messages to send at this stage).

SSL Connection Establishment: ClientKeyExchange, ChangeCipherSpec, and Finished Messages

After the VPN gateway sends the ServerHello, Certificate, and ServerHelloDone messages, the client responds with the ClientKeyExchange, ChangeCipherSpec, and Finished messages.

Figure 10-7 shows the transmission of the ClientKeyExchange, ChangeCipherSpec, and Finished messages. The Finished message is the first in the handshake to be encrypted.

Figure 10-7 *Transmission of the ClientKeyExchange, ChangeCipherSpec, and Finished Messages*

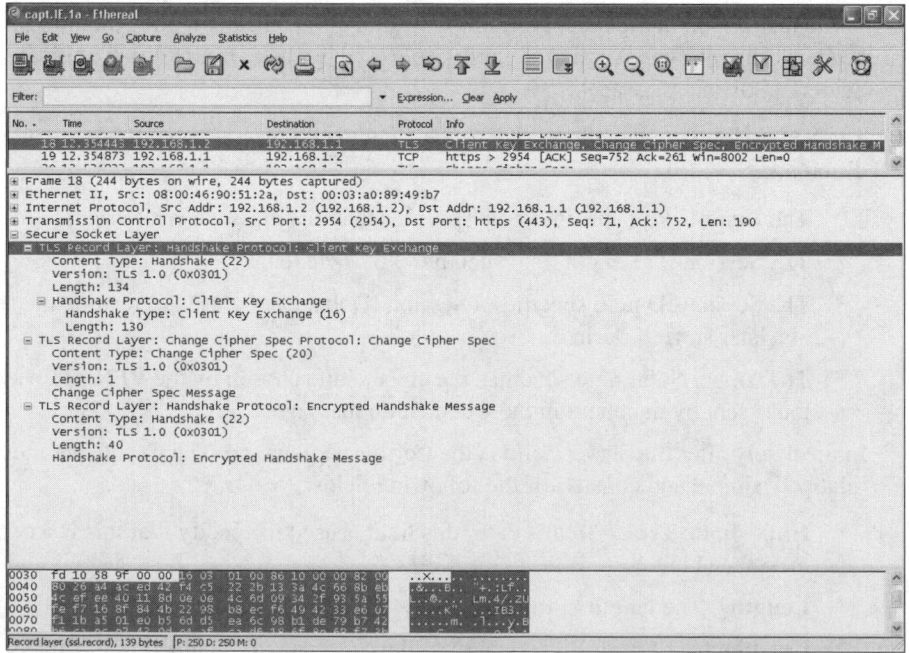

Figure 10-7 again shows the common Record layer header, followed by the ClientKeyExhange, ChangeCipherSpec, and Finished messages:

- The common Record layer header, including the following
  - **Content Type**—Specifies that this is a Handshake message (22).
  - **Version**—This is a TLS (SSL version 3.1) message.
  - **Length**—The length of this message is 134 bytes long.
- A ClientKeyExchange message, including the following
  - **Handshake Type**—This is a ClientKeyExchange message (16).
  - **Length**—This message is 130 bytes long.
- A ChangeCipherSpec message, including the following
  - **Content Type**—This is a ChangeCipherSpec message (20).
  - **Version**—This is a TLS message.
  - **Length**—The length of this message is 1 byte.
- An encrypted Finished message ("Encrypted Handshake Message").

The remote access client now completes the handshake by sending ChangeCipherSpec and Finished messages.

Figure 10-8 shows the ChangeCipherSpec message sent by the client.

Figure 10-8 *ChangeCipherSpec Message Sent by the Client*

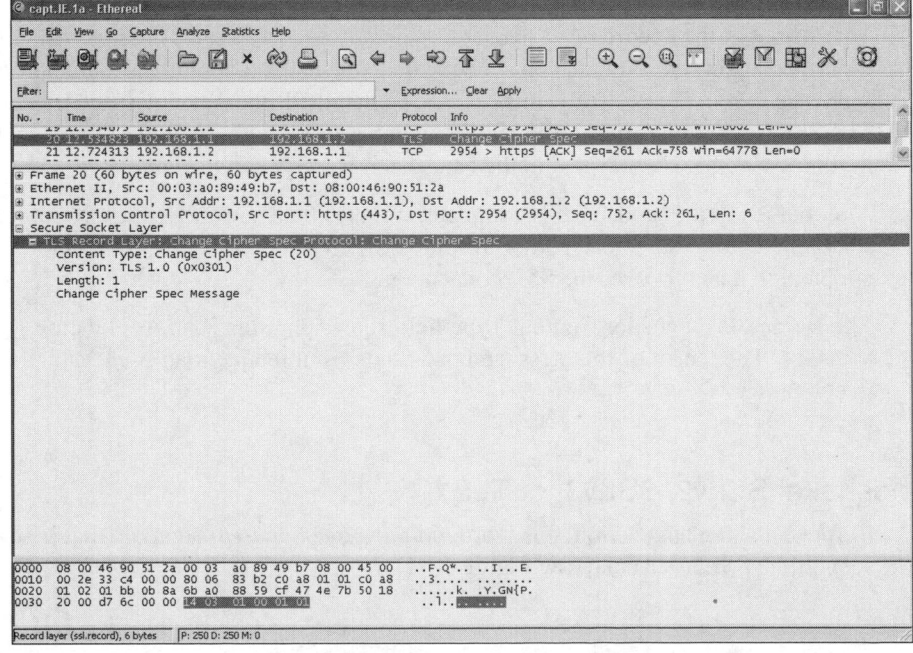

Figure 10-9 shows the Finished message sent by the client.

Figure 10-9 *Finished Message Sent by the Client*

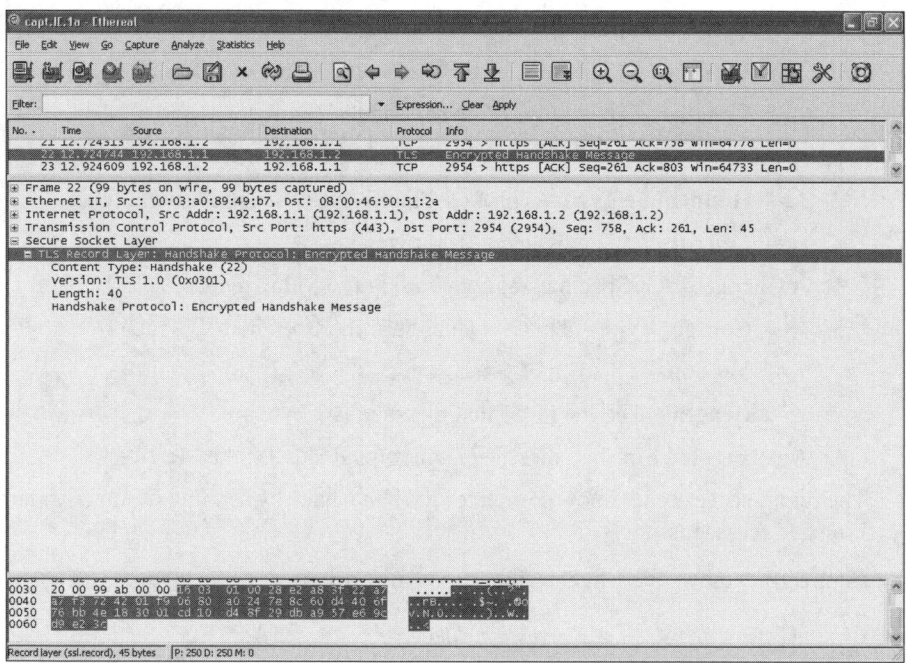

The format of the Record layer header has already been described, and so will not be described again here. Notice, however, the final line in the output in the main portion of the screen shown in Figure 10-9—this line shows that the Handshake message is encrypted. This should be no surprise, as you will remember that the Finished message is, in fact, the first message that is encrypted in the handshake.

And that is it—the handshake is complete, and the client and VPN gateway are ready to send application data to each other over the SSL connection. Figure 10-10 shows application data sent over the SSL connection.

The Record layer header Content Type field shows that this is an Application Data message. The length of the message is 264 bytes, but the payload is encrypted and so is not shown.

SSL Handshake: SSLv2, SSLv3, or TLS?

Before finishing this section, it is worth pointing one *apparent* anomaly that is sometimes seen in the SSL handshake (see Figure 10-11).

Figure 10-10 *Application Data Sent over the SSL Connection*

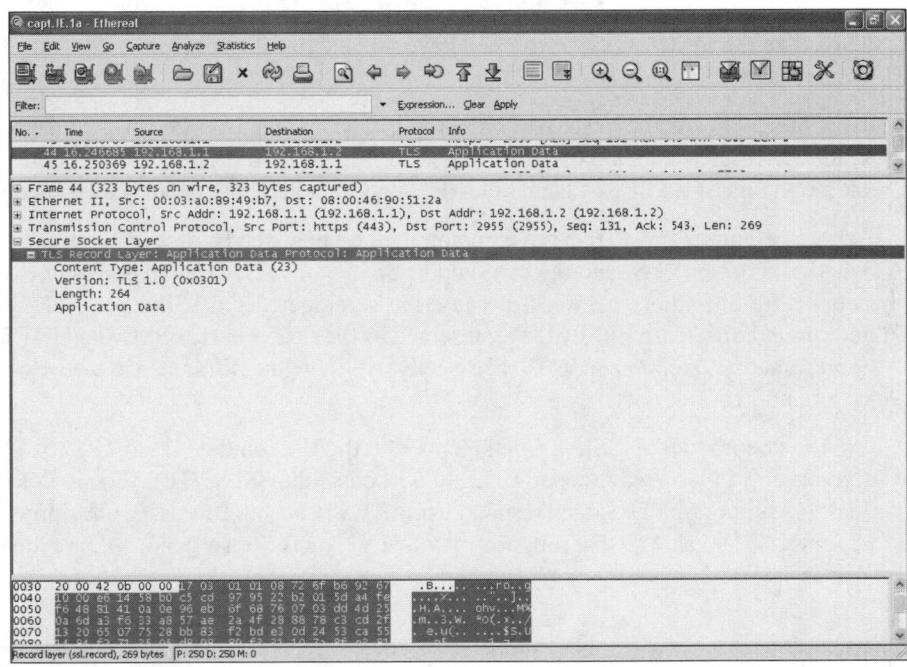

Figure 10-11 *SSL Handshake Anomaly*

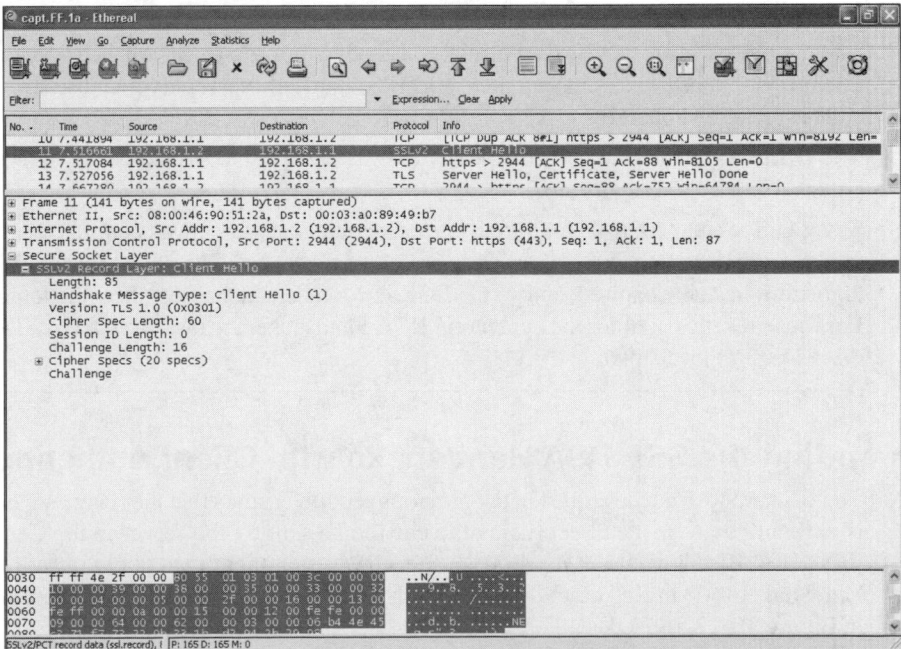

First, take a look at the upper portion of the screen capture. Look at the SSL messages; you will notice the familiar beginning of the RSA handshake (compare with Figure 10-4). If you are the observant type, you will have noticed one apparent anomaly—the TLS handshake begins with an SSLv2 ClientHello message!

Now take a look at the lower portion of the screen and you see the detail of the SSLv2 ClientHello. If you look closely at the fields of the Record header, you will notice that although this is an SSLv2 ClientHello, the Version field in the record header specifies TLS!

What is going on? Well, this is a common method that web browsers/clients use to check whether a server/VPN gateway can support SSLv3 or TLS. This method of checking support for SSLv3 or TLS works because the Version fields in SSLv2 and SSLv3/TLS are interpreted differently (SSLv2 is represented as 0x0002, whereas SSLv3 and TLS are represented as 0x0300 and 0x0301 respectively—note the difference in the way the high-order and low-order octets are used).

So, if a client sends an SSLv2 ClientHello with the Version field set to TLS (0x0301), and the server/VPN gateway supports TLS, it will parse the SSLv3/TLS version field and identify support for TLS, then respond using TLS handshake messages, as appropriate! A server/VPN gateway that supports only SSLv2, on the other hand, will not identify this as TLS.

NOTE   SSLv3 and TLS (RFC2246) also include a variation on the regular RSA handshake called an *ephemeral RSA*, as well as another type of handshake that takes advantage of the Digital Signature Standard (DSS) and Diffie-Hellman algorithms.

The ephemeral RSA handshake permits SSL connections to be established between export clients (which use weak cipher suites) and U.S. domestic servers (which use strong cipher suites) using a strong key.

The DSS/DH handshake, on the other hand, was designed to overcome any issues with patents on the RSA algorithm.

Since U.S. export controls for strong cryptographic software have been relaxed, the ephemeral RSA handshake has become much less relevant. The patent for the RSA algorithm has now expired, and so the DSS/DH handshake has also become less relevant. For these reasons, neither the ephemeral RSA handshake nor the DSS/DH handshake is discussed in this chapter.

Understanding the SSL RSA Handshake with Client Authentication

The RSA handshake described in the previous section ensures that the server/VPN gateway is authenticated by the client (using the certificate sent by the server in the Certificate message). But, how about if you want the server to authenticate client during the handshake, too? In this case, the SSL handshake with client authentication, illustrated in Figure 10-12, is used.

Figure 10-12 *SSL Handshake with Client Authentication*

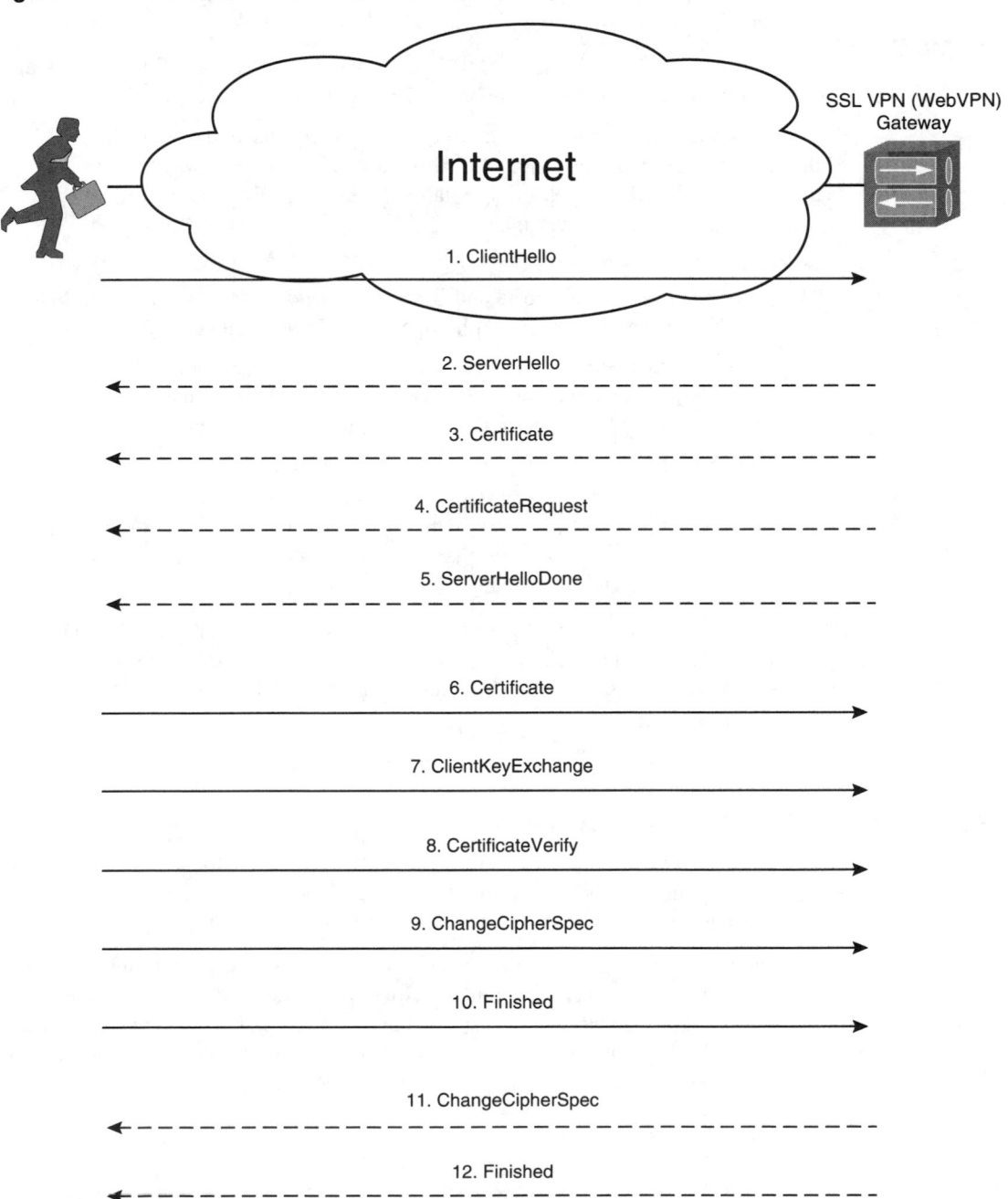

If you compare Figure 10-12 with Figure 10-4, you can see that the handshakes are very similar. There are one or two differences, however:

- In response to the ClientHello, the VPN gateway sends a CertificateRequest message in addition to the ServerHello, Certificate, and ServerHelloDone messages.

  As the name suggests, the CertificateRequest message is used to request that the client send its certificate (or certificate chain) to the VPN gateway as well as to specify which key types are acceptable (for example, RSA) and the CAs it will accept as issuers of certificates (the client's certificate must be issued by one of these).

- The client replies with Certificate and CertificateVerify messages in addition to the ClientKeyExchange, ChangeCipherSpec, and Finished messages.

  The Certificate message contains the client's certificate or certificate chain, and the CertificateVerify message is used by the client to prove that it possesses the private key corresponding to the public key contained in its certificate.

  The CertificateVerify message consists of a digital signature (using the private key corresponding to the public key in the certificate). Only the owner of the client's certificate should possess the private key, and so the client is able to prove that it really is the owner of the certificate sent in the certificate message.

So, the client authenticates the VPN gateway using the Certificate that the VPN gateway sends (this is the same as the regular RSA handshake with no client authentication), and the VPN gateway authenticates the client using the Certificate and CertificateVerify messages that the client sends.

Resuming an SSL Session

So far, this chapter has described SSL handshakes that allow the establishment of new SSL sessions. This section describes the resumption of a previous SSL session. Figure 10-13 shows the exchange of SSL messages necessary to resume a previous SSL session.

You might be wondering why you would want to resume an SSL session instead of just establishing a new one (as described in the previous two sections). The answer is that the public key operations that are necessary when establishing a new session are cryptographically expensive/processor intensive, whereas resuming a previous session does not require these expensive public key operations.

Figure 10-13 *Resuming an SSL Session*

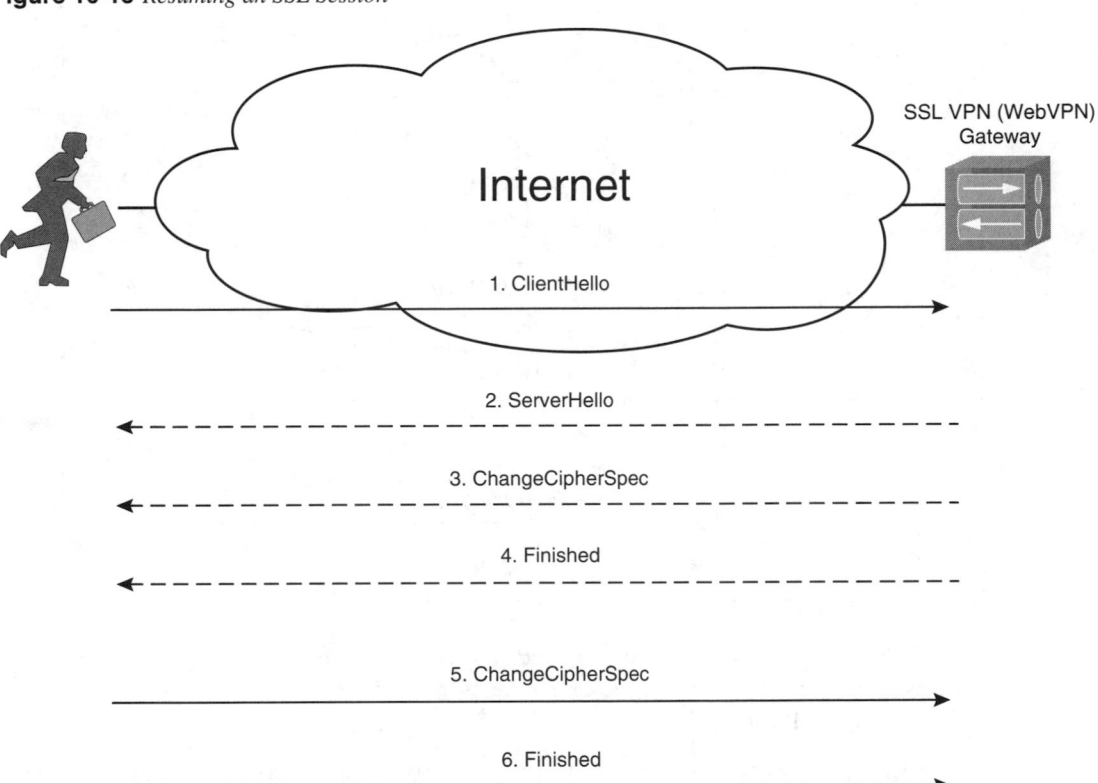

As you can see in Figure 10-13, to resume an SSL session, the follows happens:

1 The client sends a ClientHello message.

This message has the same format as that shown in Figure 10-5, with the difference that a Session ID field is included (the Session ID Length field is nonzero).

2 The Session ID in the ClientHello identifies a previous session, and the VPN gateway responds with a ServerHello confirming the resumption of that session, before changing to the previously negotiated cipher suite and ensuring the integrity of the handshake using the ChangeCipherSpec message and Finished messages, respectively.

3 The client now completes the resumption of the session by sending ChangeCipherSpec and Finished messages. After these messages have been sent, Application Data messages can begin to flow between the client and VPN gateway.

Closing an SSL Connection

The final action in an SSL connection is its closure. This is illustrated in Figure 10-14.

Figure 10-14 *SSL Connection Closure*

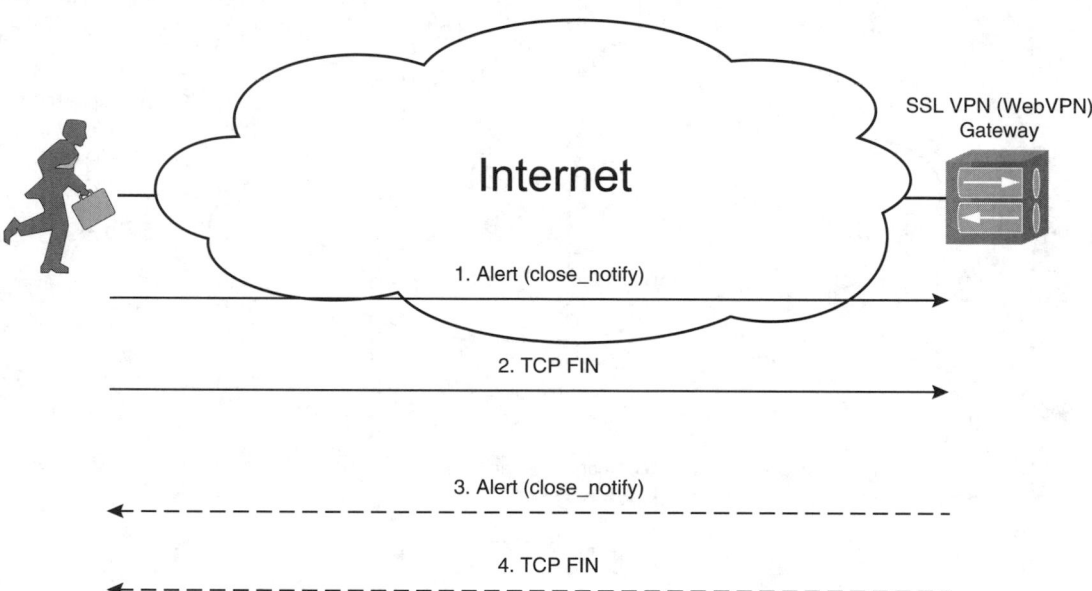

In Figure 10-14, the client initiates connection closure by sending a close_notify Alert message to the VPN gateway. The client then sends a TCP FIN message to terminate the underlying TCP connection.

The VPN gateway responds by sending its own close_notify Alert message, followed by a TCP FIN. The SSL connection is now closed.

Although Figure 10-14 shows the client initiating SSL connection closure, it is possible for either the client or the VPN gateway (server) to initiate connection closure.

Note that if a client or VPN gateway receives a TCP FIN before receiving a close_notify Alert, it marks the connection as being unresumable—this prevents truncation attacks, where an attacker inserts a TCP FIN into the traffic stream between the client and VPN gateway.

Using Clientless SSL Remote Access VPNs (WebVPN) on the Cisco VPN 3000 Concentrator

As discussed at the beginning of this chapter, one great advantage of SSL VPNs is that they do not *require* dedicated client software—the only software that is required is a standard web browser and e-mail software such as Microsoft Outlook Express, if e-mail functionality is required via POP3/IMAP4/SMTP.

This section examines how it is possible to provide file server access, website access, and TCP application access using clientless SSL remote access VPNs. Before enabling these types of access of SSL, however, it is necessary to complete basic SSL remote access VPN configuration tasks on the VPN 3000 concentrator.

Completing Basic SSL Remote Access VPN Access Configuration Tasks on the Cisco VPN 3000 Concentrator

Before you can enable SSL remote access VPN functionality such as file access or port forwarding, it is necessary to complete a number of basic configuration tasks:

Step 1 Enroll and obtain a (SSL) certificate for the VPN 3000 concentrator from a certificate authority (CA) (optional).

Step 2 Enable WebVPN for relevant user groups (or create a group specifically for WebVPN access).

Step 3 Specify acceptable versions of SSL and configure cryptographic algorithms associated with SSL cipher suites.

Step 4 Enable SSL on the VPN 3000 concentrator's public interface.

The sections that follow describe these steps in further detail. Before moving on to step 1, however, it is worth mentioning that on the Cisco VPN 3000 concentrator, WebVPN uses global DNS settings rather than those specified under a group. So, make sure that you specify global DNS settings under **Configuration > System > Servers > DNS**.

Step 1: Enroll and Obtain a (SSL) Certificate for the VPN 3000 Concentrator from a Certificate Authority (Optional)

As described earlier in this chapter, clients authenticate the VPN gateway during the RSA handshake using the VPN gateway's certificate (or certificate chain).

The certificate that the VPN gateway uses to identify itself is shown under the SSL Certificates heading (public interface) in **Administration > Certificate Management** (see Figure 10-15).

By default, the SSL certificate for the public interface is self-generated (it is not obtained from a CA). Although it is okay to use this certificate for testing, it is usually a good idea to enroll the VPN 3000 concentrator with a CA and obtain a certificate to use for the SSL handshake.

Obtain the CA's certificate, and then click **Enroll** under the Actions section under the SSL Certificates heading (public interface) to obtain a certificate for the SSL handshake. Obtaining the CA's certificate and enrolling with the CA can be achieved using the procedures described previously in Chapter 8, "Designing and Implementing L2TPv2 and L2TPv3 Remote Access VPNs," and Chapter 9, "Designing and Deploying IPsec Remote Access and Teleworker VPNs."

Figure 10-15 *SSL Certificate*

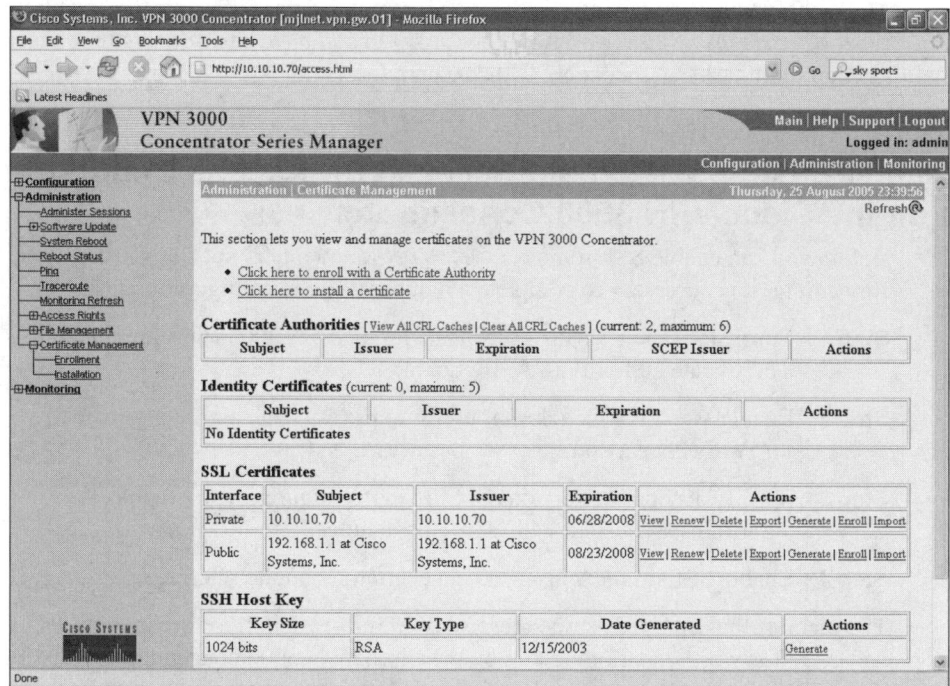

Note that during the SSL handshake, client web browsers will display a warning concerning the certificate(s) sent by the VPN gateway. Users can bypass this warning simply by clicking in the affirmative when asked whether the certificate should be accepted. If you do not want this warning to display, you can install the certificate of the CA with which the VPN gateway enrolled into the certificate store of the browser.

Step 2: Enable WebVPN for Relevant User Groups

The next step is for WebVPN to be enabled for relevant user groups. As shown in Figure 10-16, this is simply accomplished by going to **Configuration > User Management > Groups**, choosing the relevant group, clicking **Modify Group**, choosing the **General** tab, and checking the **WebVPN** box under Tunneling Protocols.

Step 3: Specify Acceptable Versions of SSL and Configure Cryptographic Algorithms Associated with SSL Cipher Suites (Optional)

Next, it is a good idea (although optional) to go to **Configuration > Tunneling and Security > SSL > Protocols**, and specify acceptable versions of SSL as well as cryptographic algorithms associated with SSL cipher suites (see Figure 10-17).

Figure 10-16 *Enabling WebVPN for Relevant User Groups*

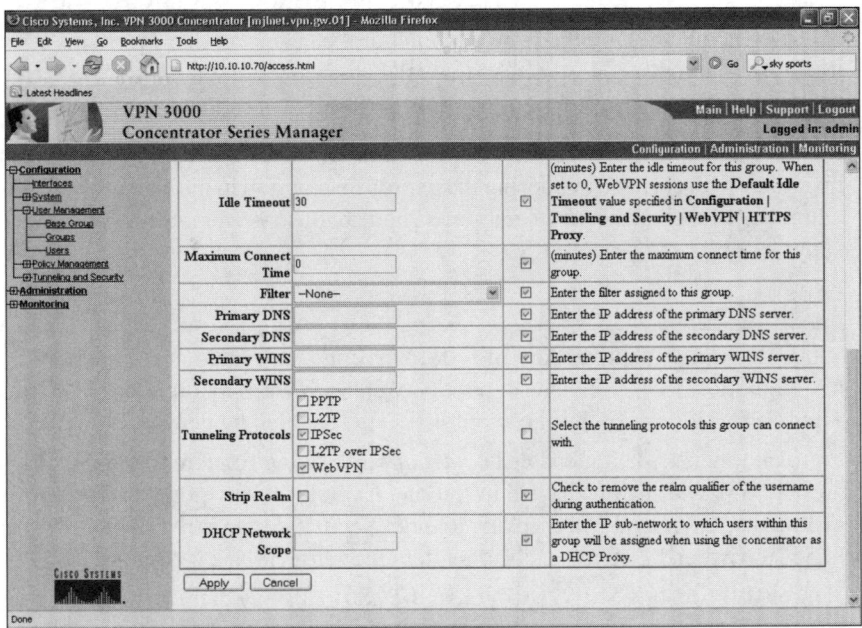

Figure 10-17 *Specifying Acceptable Versions of SSL, as Well as Cryptographic Algorithms Associated with SSL Cipher Suites*

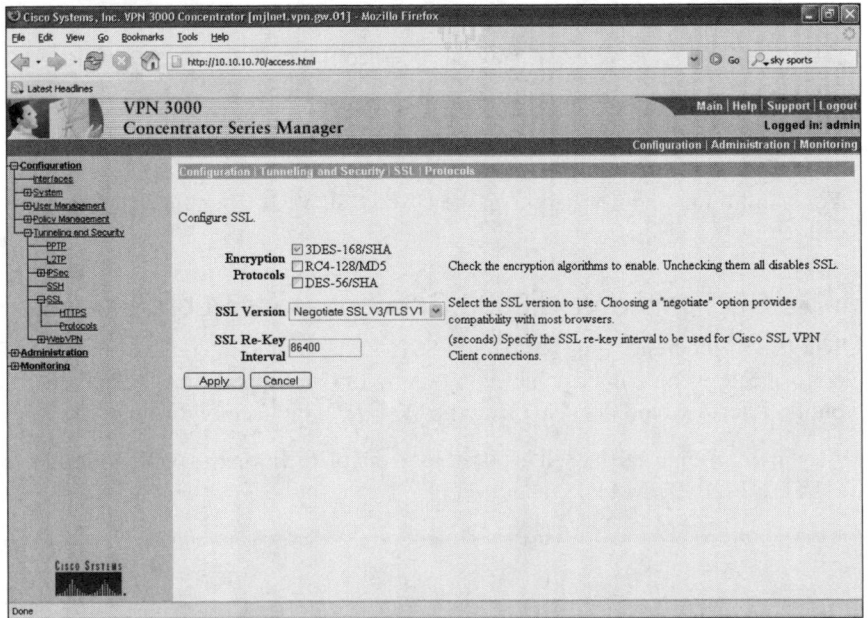

As you can see in Figure 10-17, the encryption (and hashing) algorithms associated with cipher suites that you can enable are 3DES-168/SHA, RC4-128/MD5, DES-56/SHA. By checking or unchecking these, an administrator can control the algorithms associated with the cipher suite that is accepted by the VPN gateway (and sent in the ServerHello message to the client). In Figure 10-17, only 3DES-168/SHA is enabled.

It is also possible to specify which versions of SSL that the VPN gateway will accept or negotiate with clients by choosing the appropriate option in the drop-down box. SSLv2 has a number of well-known vulnerabilities, and so, unsurprising, the VPN 3000 concentrator supports only SSLv3 and TLS.

NOTE When deciding which versions of SSL to accept or negotiate, it is important to note that although most recent versions of popular web browsers support both SSLv3 and TLS (and often SSLv2), some browsers do not have TLS enabled by default.

For example, TLS is not enabled *by default* in Internet Explorer 6.0 (SSLv2 and SSLv3 are). TLS (v1.0) can be enabled in Internet Explorer 6.0 by going to **Tools > Internet Options > Advanced** and checking it under **Security**. In Internet Explorer 7.0, on the other hand, SSLv3 and TLS are enabled by default, while SSLv2 is disabled.

Firefox 1.0 supports SSLv2, SSLv3, and TLS (v1.0) by default.

In summary, *if possible*, it is a good idea to establish which types of browser users will be connecting from. If this is not possible (if users will be connecting from Internet cafés, and so on), it is a good idea to accept or allow the negotiation of SSLv3 (and optionally TLS).

In Figure 10-17, the VPN gateway has been configured to negotiate either SSLv3 or TLS with clients.

Finally, it is possible to configure the interval at which the VPN gateway will rekey (establish new cryptographic keys) with workstation running the Cisco SSL VPN Client. You can find more information on the Cisco SSL VPN Client later in this chapter.

Step 4: Enable SSL on the VPN 3000 Concentrator's Public Interface

The last of the basic steps is enabling SSL on the public interface of the Cisco VPN 3000 concentrator. This can be achieved by going to **Configuration > Interfaces**, clicking the public interface, and then choosing the **WebVPN** tab (see Figure 10-18).

As shown in Figure 10-18, it is possible to enable SSL on the public interface by allowing HTTPS, POP3S, IMAP4S, and SMTPS.

Figure 10-18 *Enabling SSL on the Public Interface*

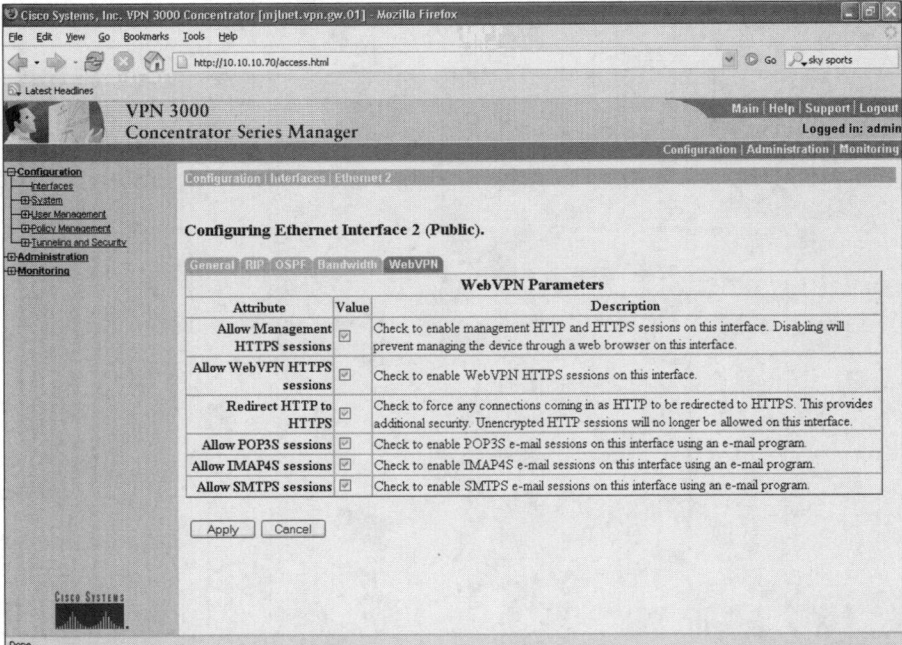

To enable SSL for basic features such as access to file and HTTP servers, as well as TCP application access via port forwarding, you must check the **Allow WebVPN HTTPS sessions** box.

If proxy e-mail access is also required, you must also check the **Allow POP3S sessions**, **Allow IMAP4S**, and **Allow SMTPS sessions** boxes as appropriate. POP3 and IMAP4 can be used for inbound e-mail access, and SMTP is used for outbound e-mail — you should check the boxes according to which protocols are used by your e-mail clients and servers.

Another useful option is Redirect HTTP to HTTPS. If this box is checked, the VPN concentrator will cause the browsers of remote access user who type **http://***ip_address_or_name_of_VPN_concentrator* to instead access the Cisco VPN 3000 concentrator using HTTPS (**https://***ip_address_or_name_of_VPN_concentrator*).

It is also a good idea to navigate to **Configuration > Tunneling and Security > SSL > HTTPS** and verify that HTTPS is enabled (the default), the TCP port used for HTTPS, and to enable client authentication if desired.

Figure 10-19 *Configuring Additional Basic SSL Options*

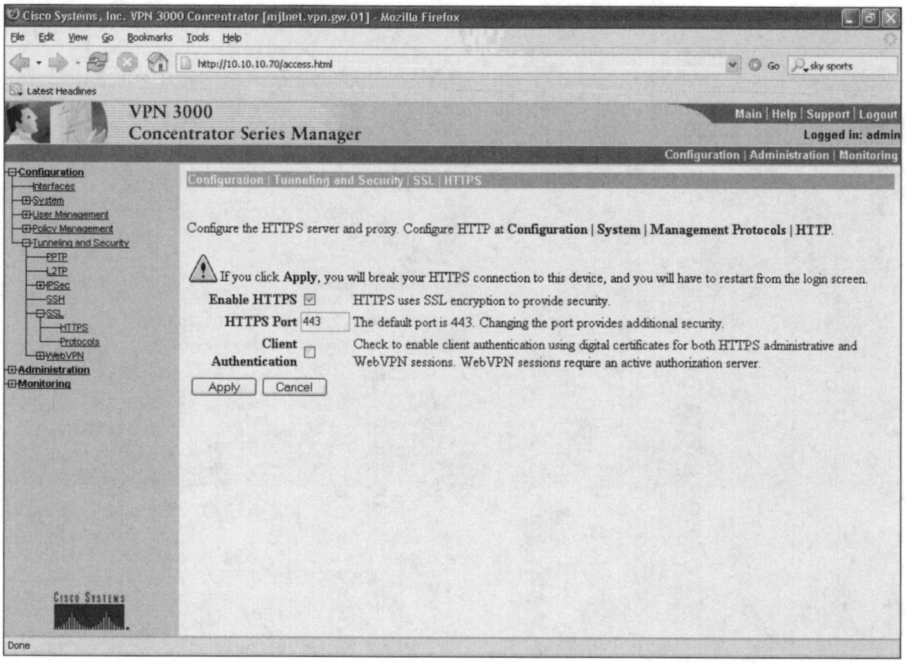

The HTTPS configuration options shown in Figure 10-19 are as follows:

- **Enable HTTPS**—This option, if checked, enables HTTP over SSL (the default).

- **HTTPS Port**—This is used to specify the TCP port used for HTTPS (default 443).

- **Client Authentication**—This option, if checked, configures client authentication with the RSA handshake.

  Note that when client authentication is enabled, the client must obtain the certificate of CA and also obtain an identity certificate.

  See the section, "Understanding the SSL RSA Handshake with Client Authentication" earlier in this chapter for more information on this topic.

Configuring File and Web Server Access via SSL Remote Access VPNs

One of the most basic levels of access that you can enable via an SSL remote access VPNs is file and/or web server access.

To enable file server access, it is necessary to complete the following tasks:

Step 1   Configure one or more NetBIOS name servers.

Step 2   Configure WebVPN file servers and shares.

Step 3   Enable file access for the WebVPN user group(s).

Step 1: Configure One or More NetBIOS Name Servers

You can accomplish configuration of a NetBIOS name server by going to **Configuration > System > Servers > NBNS** (see Figure 10-20).

Figure 10-20 *Configuring NBNS Addresses*

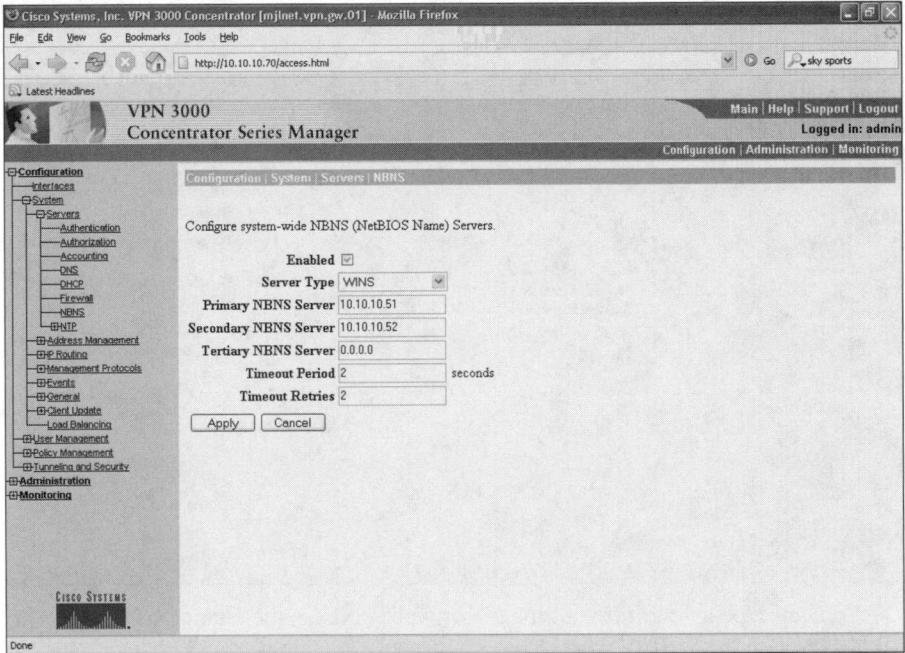

The first step is to enable NBNS by checking the **Enabled** box.

Next, you can choose **WINS** or **Master Browser** in the Server Type drop-down box.

The IP addresses of primary, secondary, and tertiary NBNS servers can then be configured in the appropriate boxes.

Finally, you can configure the timeout period in seconds, as well as the number of timeout retries. Unless you have a good reason, it is a good idea to leave these at their defaults (2 and 2).

Step 2: Configure WebVPN File Servers and Shares

To configure server names and shares for users to access, go to **Configuration > Tunneling and Security > WebVPN > Servers and URLs > Add**.

Figure 10-21 shows the configuration of file access for SSL remote access VPN users.

Figure 10-21 *Configuring File or Web Server Access*

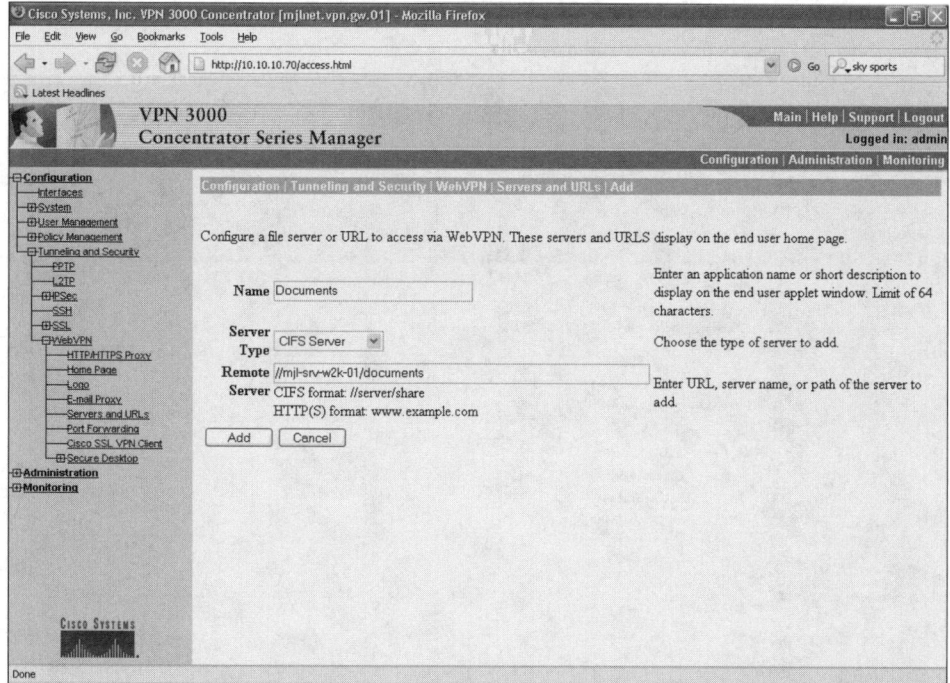

You can type a description of the file or web server in the Name box. This description appears on the WebVPN home page when SSL remote access VPN users successfully authenticate on the VPN 3000 concentrator.

In the Server Type drop-down box, you can choose the server type (either Common Internet File System [CIFS], HTTP, or HTTPS). CIFS is based on the Server Message Block (SMB) protocol and can be used to request file and print services from Windows or other servers.

You must then specify the name of the server or share in the Remote Server box. When using CIFS, you must specify the server name or share in the *//server/share* format.

When all the boxes have been completed, click the **Apply** box.

Step 3: Enable File and URL Access for the WebVPN User Group(s)

After server names and shares have been configured, the next step is to enable file access under the appropriate group or groups.

Under **Configuration > User Management > Groups**, choose the appropriate group, click **Modify Group**, click the **WebVPN** tab, and you will see the page shown in Figure 10-22.

Figure 10-22 *Enabling File and/or Web Server Access Under Group Settings*

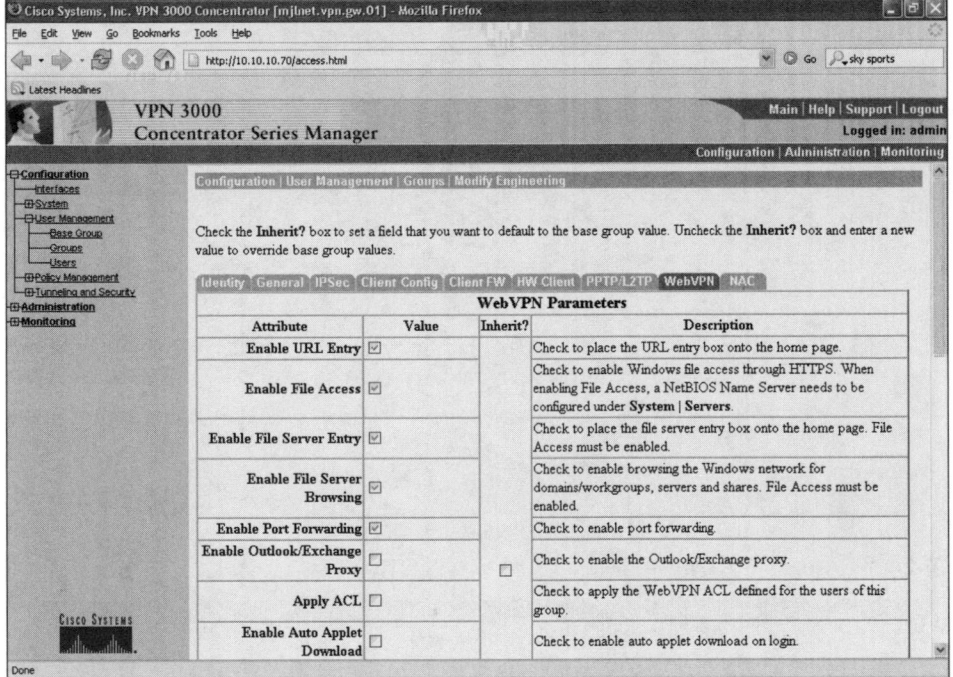

Check the **Enable File Access** box to enable (appropriately enough) file server access.

Checking the **Enable File Server Browsing** box allows users to browse files and folders on servers (server file and folder permissions permitting).

It may also be a good idea to check the **Enable File Server Entry** box to place server names or file paths on the home page of SSL remote access VPN users.

When a user connects to the VPN 3000 concentrator and authenticates, he/she will see the share listed in the home page (see Figure 10-23).

Figure 10-23 shows file shares, including in the one created in Figure 10-21. By clicking these links, the remote access VPN user will be able to access those resources (see Figure 10-24).

Figure 10-23 *Accessible File and Web Servers*

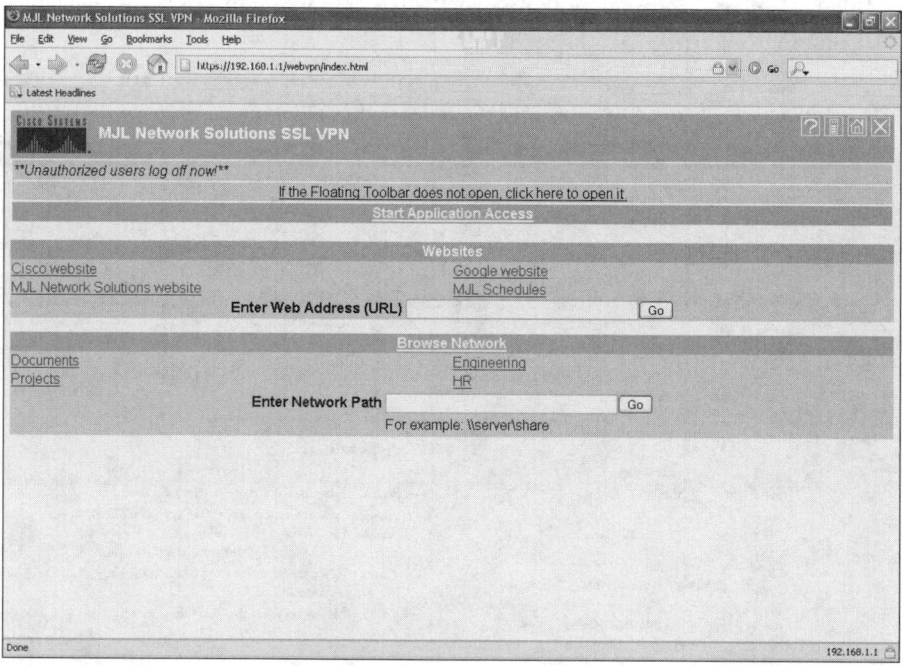

Figure 10-24 *Accessing Files on a File Server*

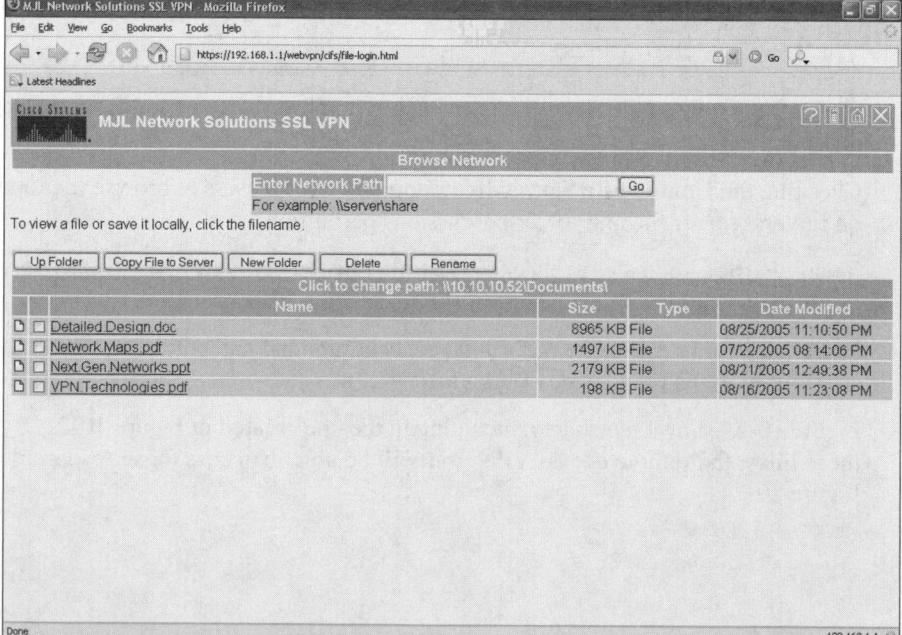

As shown in Figure 10-24, it is possible (file server and VPN 3000 concentrator configuration permitting) to browse files and folders, open, create, rename, and copy files to the server.

NOTE   The Java Runtime Environment (JRE) version 1.4 or later must be installed on client workstations for file access to function correctly.

It is also worth noting that it might be necessary to modify local policies on a Windows 2003 domain controller when configuring file access. Specifically, it might be necessary to open the Domain Controller Security Policy (found under Administrative Tools) and under **Local Policies > Security Options** disable the **Microsoft network server: Digitally sign communication (always)** policy (right-click and choose **Properties**).

Figure 10-25 shows modification of the Microsoft network server: Digitally sign communication (always) policy.

Figure 10-25 *Modifying Security Options on a Windows 2003 Domain Controller*

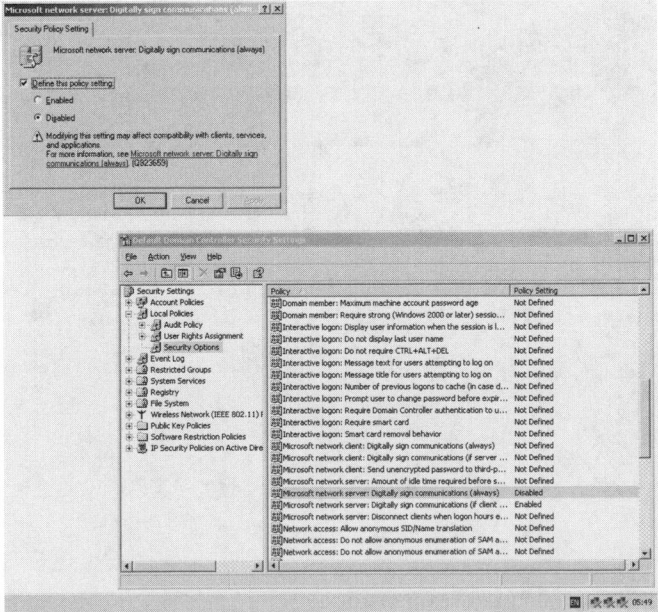

Configuration of URL access is similarly configured as follows:

Step 1 Configure HTTP/HTTPS proxy server addresses as required.

Step 2 Configure URLs under **Configuration > Tunneling and Security > WebVPN**, click **Servers and URLs** (see Figure 10-21), click **Add**, and then add a URL. The server type should be specified as HTTP or HTTPS as appropriate.

Step 3 Enable URL entries under **Configuration > User Management > Groups**, choose the appropriate group, click **Modify Group**, choose the **WebVPN** tab (see Figure 10-22), and check **Enable URL Entry**.

It is possible to control remote users' web access by configuring HTTP/HTTP proxy server addresses on the VPN 3000 concentrator. In this case, HTTP/HTTPS connections from remote users are forwarded from the VPN 3000 concentrator to the proxy server(s).

As shown in Figure 10-26, configuration of HTTP/HTTPS proxy servers is achieved under **Configuration > Tunneling and Security > WebVPN > HTTP/HTTPS Proxy**.

Figure 10-26 *Configuring HTTP/HTTPS Proxy*

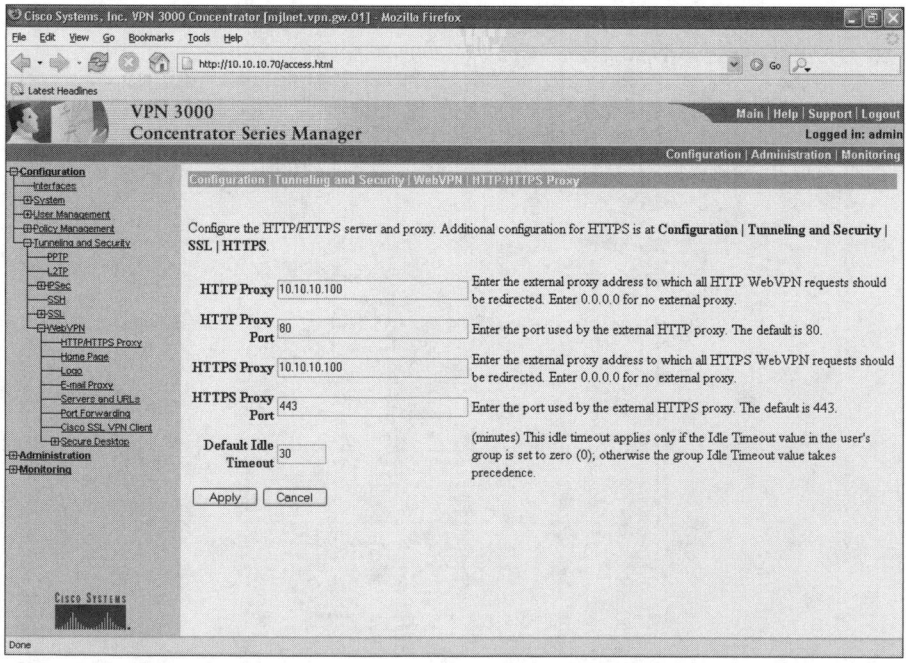

Configuration is fairly self-explanatory:

- **HTTP Proxy**—This is the IP address of the proxy server to which HTTP WebVPN requests are redirected by the VPN 3000 concentrator.

- **HTTP Proxy Port**—The TCP port used by the HTTP proxy server.

- **HTTPS Proxy**—The IP address of the proxy server to which HTTPS WebVPN requests are redirected.

- **HTTPS Proxy Port**—The TCP port used by the HTTPS proxy server.

- **Default Timeout**—The timeout, in minutes, for WebVPN sessions if one is not set in group settings.

Enabling TCP Applications over Clientless SSL Remote Access VPNs

Apart from file and web server access, another form of access via clientless SSL remote access VPNs is that for TCP-based applications. Remote access VPN users can access TCP-based applications via a VPN 3000 concentrator using a mechanism called *port forwarding*.

One of the most popular applications to enable using port forwarding is Windows Terminal Services, which allows remote access users to remotely access a desktop and applications that are installed on a Windows server, with screen bitmaps transported over the network between the remote users and the server. This method of server desktop and application hosting conforms to the *thin-client* model.

NOTE   To enable Citrix MetaFrame support with WebVPN, you must check the **Enable Citrix MetaFrame** box on the WebVPN tab under Groups.

Note that in this case, an SSL certificate with a fully qualified domain name (not an IP address as the common name) must be installed on the public interface on the VPN 3000 concentrator.

This section covers how to enable Windows Terminal Services for port forwarding over SSL. Other TCP-based applications can be similarly enabled.

Figure 10-27 illustrates the port-forwarding concept. In Figure 10-27, on the client, traffic sent to IP address 127.0.0.x, TCP port 3389 (Windows Terminal Services) is redirected over SSL to the VPN 3000 concentrator. The VPN 3000 concentrator then forwards this traffic to the application server. Return traffic from the server is then sent to the VPN 3000 concentrator, which then forwards it over SSL to the client.

Configuration of port forwarding is fairly straightforward. The first step is to enable port forwarding by checking the **Enable Port Forwarding** box under the user group, as illustrated in Figure 10-22 on page 933.

Figure 10-27 *The TCP Port-Forwarding Concept*

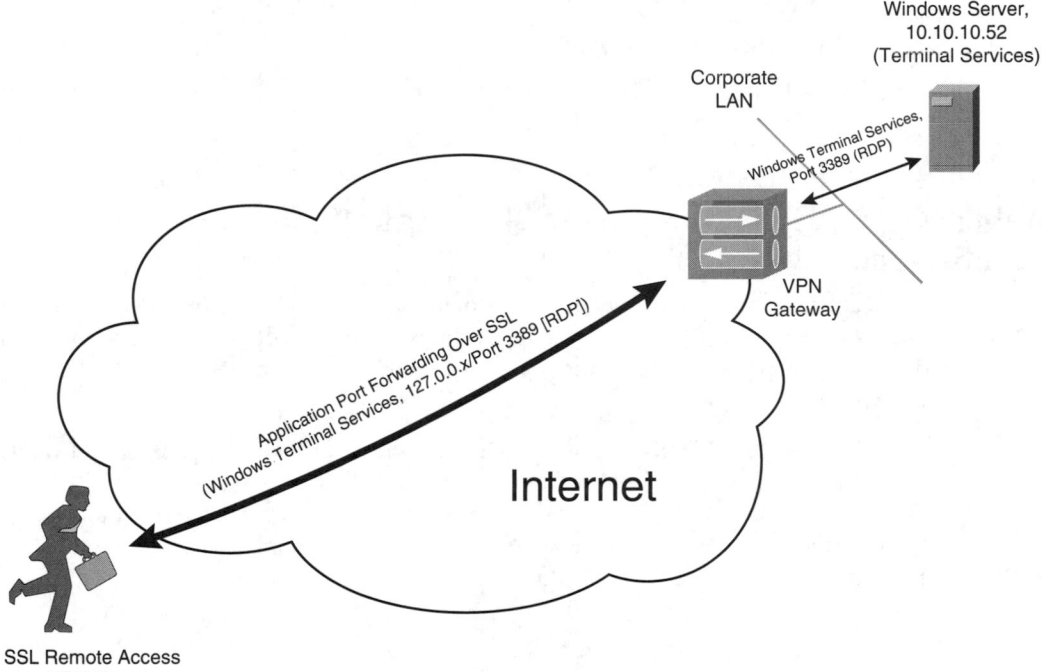

After port forwarding has been enabled for the user group, it is then simply a case of going to **Configuration > Tunneling and Security > WebVPN > Port Forwarding**, clicking **Add**, and specifying TCP port forwarding parameters (see Figure 10-28).

The various boxes shown in Figure 10-28 are fairly self-explanatory.

You can enter a description for the application in the Name box—this is displayed on the remote access VPN client when the user enables application access.

Next, the port that the client uses to connect to the application should be specified in the Local TCP Port box. This setting controls which TCP traffic will be redirected over SSL to the VPN 3000 concentrator by the remote client. In the example shown, traffic using TCP port 3389 (the default Windows Terminal Services port) will be redirected over SSL to the VPN 3000 concentrator.

The IP address or name of the application server must then be entered in the Remote Server box.

If the IP address of applications servers are specified then they are accessed from the user workstation by specifying the IP address 127.0.0.1.

If the names of application servers are specified, the hosts file on Windows user workstations are modified during WebVPN access, with the first application used for port forwarding being mapped to IP address 127.0.0.2, the second application being mapped to IP address 127.0.0.3, and so on.

Figure 10-28 *Configuring Port Forwarding*

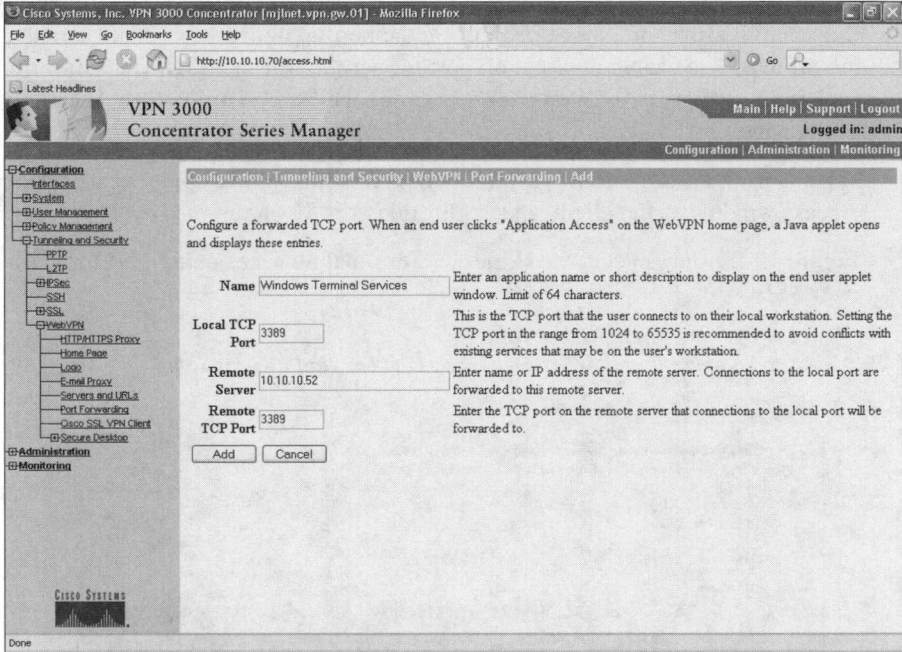

Finally, configure the TCP port that the application uses on the application server in the Remote TCP Port box. This TCP port will often be the same as that entered in the Local TCP Port box.

Click **Add**, and port forwarding will be ready for use for the particular application just configured.

For port forwarding to function, the Sun JRE must be installed on the clients, and this requires the person installing the software have administrative rights on that workstation. Because administrative rights are required for the installation of the JRE, it is unlikely that remote access users will be able to access applications using port forwarding from locations such as Internet cafés or airport Internet kiosks.

NOTE   JRE can be downloaded from the Sun website. At the time of this writing, the download location is as follows:

http://java.sun.com

Note that Microsoft Java cannot be used for port forwarding.

Also, make sure that either **Negotiate SSLv3** or **Negotiate SSLv3/TLS** is chosen under **Configuration > Tunneling and Security > SSL > Protocols**. If one of these two options is not chosen, port forwarding will not function.

Remote access VPN users must connect to the VPN 3000 concentrator and access their home page using their web browser. Users can then click the **Start Application Access** link on either the home page itself or on the pop-up dialog box (make sure that pop-ups are allowed!) to enable application port forwarding for the SSL connection. Take a look back at Figure 10-23 on page 934 to see the **Start Application Access** link on the home page.

When a user clicks the **Start Application Access** link, a Java applet opens the Application Access window on the client, and application port forwarding is enabled.

Figure 10-29 shows access to Windows Terminal Services using port forwarding over SSL.

Figure 10-29 *Access to Windows Terminal Services Using Port Forwarding over SSL*

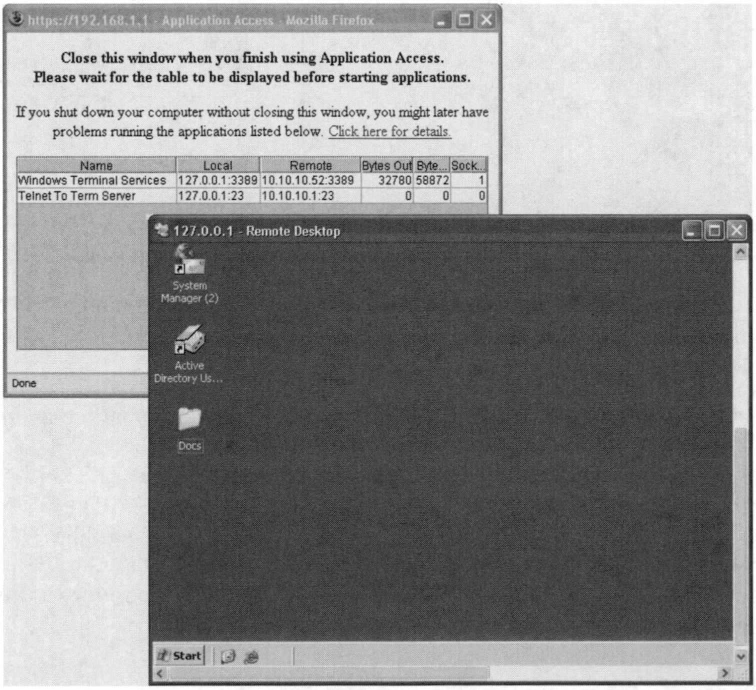

In the upper-left corner of the screen in Figure 10-29, you can see the Application Access window. As you can see, it lists the application names, associated local and remote TCP ports, remote application server IP addresses, the number of application data bytes sent (Bytes Out) and received (Bytes In), and the number of sockets open for particular applications. The application names, TCP ports, and remote application server IP addresses are, as previously described, configured under **Configuration > Tunneling and Security > WebVPN > Port Forwarding** (see Figure 10-22).

The main window in Figure 10-29 shows the remote desktop on the remote Windows Terminal Server accessed via the VPN 3000 concentrator.

One important detail in Figure 10-29 is the local IP address used to access the remote TCP application. Notice that the local IP address shown in the Application Access window (and in the upper-left corner of the main window) is 127.0.0.1. This is the IP address that is typed into the Computer box of the Remote Desktop Connection application used on Windows XP to access the Windows Terminal Server. Of course, 127.0.0.x is used to specify the local system, and this (TCP) traffic is then redirected over SSL to the VPN 3000 concentrator.

As previously mentioned, when using DNS names, the redirection of application traffic that port forwarding relies upon is achieved by the modification of the local system's Hosts file. The Hosts file is modified when application access is enabled (a copy of the original file is saved during application access, and restored later).

Figure 10-30 shows a modified Hosts file that enables application traffic redirection during application access.

Figure 10-30 *Modified Hosts File*

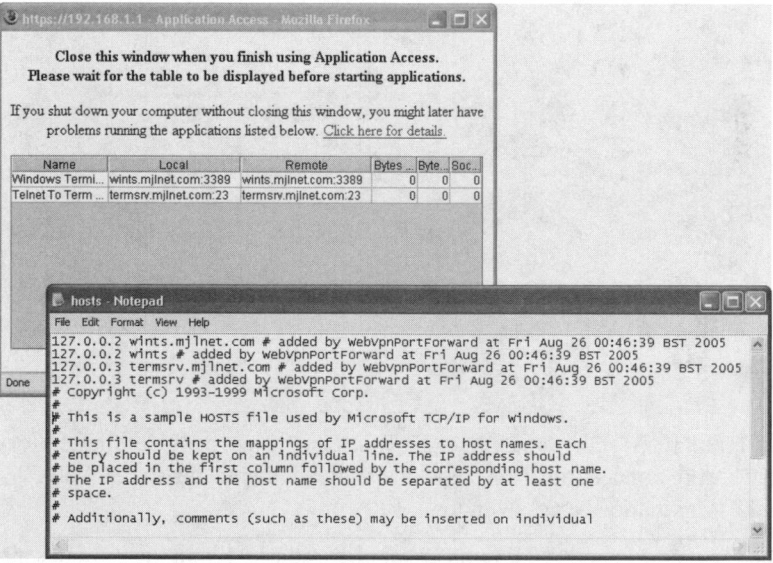

In Figure 10-30, the Hosts file has been modified to include four entries, two corresponding to port forwarding to wints.mjlnet.com/wints (127.0.0.2) and two corresponding to termsrv.mjlnet.com/termsrv (127.0.0.3).

When enabling an application for port forwarding over SSL, it is important to establish that the application is, in fact, TCP based, and if so, which TCP ports it uses. After this information has been confirmed and obtained, the application should be enabled for port forwarding in a similar manner to that for Windows Terminal Services described in this section.

If you want to enable a remote access VPN user to Telnet to a terminal server (router) via the VPN 3000 concentrator, for example, you first need to establish that the *application* is TCP based (it is, of course), and the TCP port(s) that it uses (port 23).

After these facts have been established, port forwarding for Telnet to the terminal server can be configured as shown in Figure 10-31.

Figure 10-31 *Configuring Port Forwarding for Telnet*

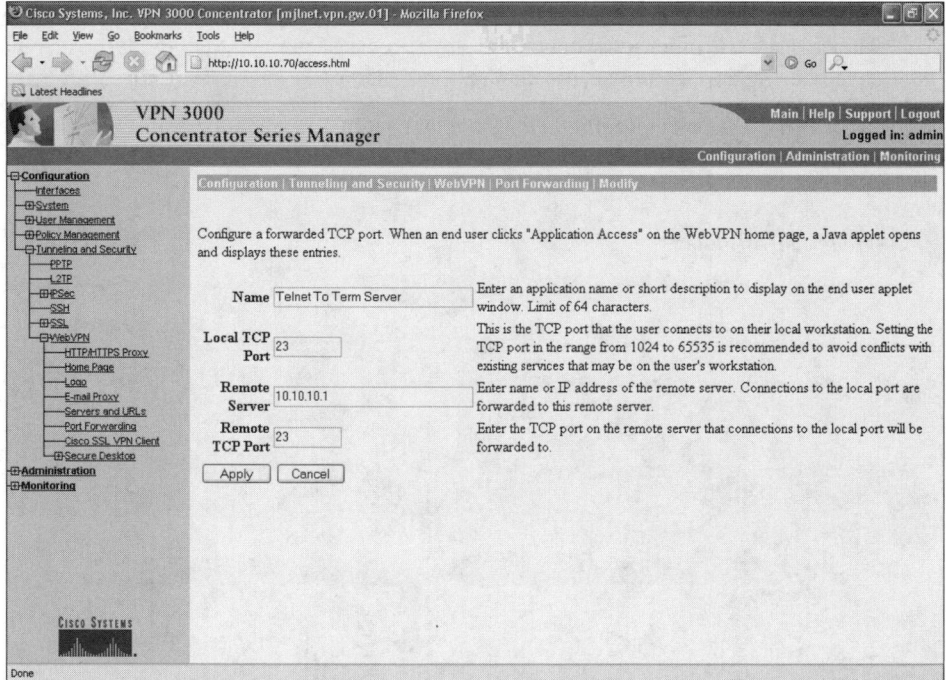

In Figure 10-31, the name Telnet To Term Server has been configured for the Telnet port forwarding connection. This name is, of course, displayed on the WebVPN home page and in the Application Access window.

The local and remote TCP ports are configured as 23, and the remote server (terminal server) IP address is configured as 10.10.10.1 (an internal IP address).

Figure 10-32 shows how Telnet to the terminal server functions on a remote access VPN client. As shown, the user Telnets to the local IP address (127.0.0.x) to connect to the remote terminal server. Telnet packets are then redirected over SSL to the VPN 3000 concentrator that then proxies the Telnet connection to the terminal server.

Figure 10-32 *Port Forwarding for Telnet on a Remote Access VPN Client*

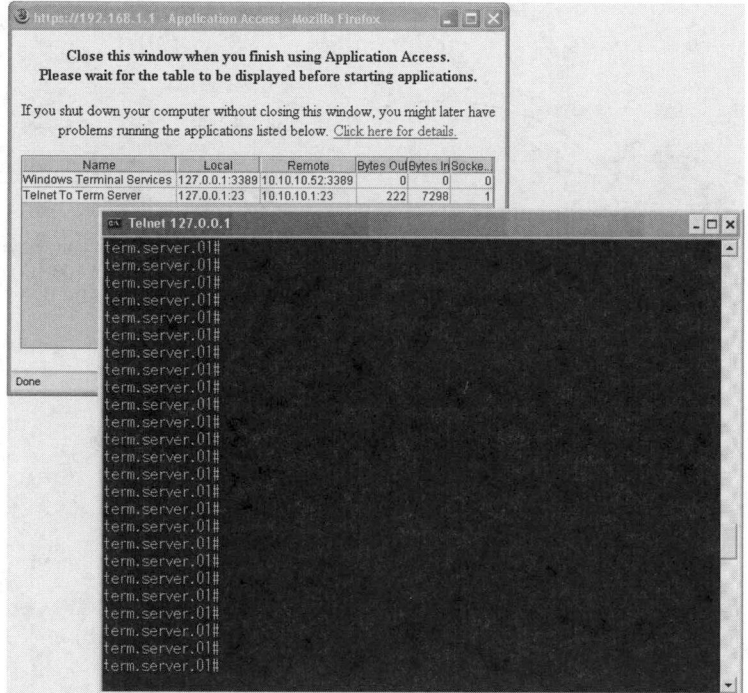

Configuring E-mail Proxy for SSL Remote Access VPN Users

E-mail proxy describes the process by which the VPN 3000 concentrator terminates POP3S (POP3 over SSL), IMAP4S (IMAP4 over SSL), and STMPS (SMTP over SSL) connections from remote access VPN clients and proxies those connections to internal e-mail servers.

Figure 10-33 depicts e-mail proxy for POP3S, IMAP4S, and SMTPS connections from remote access VPN clients.

In Figure 10-33, remote access VPN user Mark is using an e-mail client such as Outlook Express. His e-mail client is configured to connect to the VPN 3000 concentrator using POP3S (for incoming e-mail) and SMTPS for outgoing e-mail. The VPN 3000 concentrator proxies these connections to an internal e-mail server.

The configuration of e-mail proxy consists of enabling the appropriate e-mail protocols on the public interface and then configuring protocol port numbers, e-mail server IP addresses or names, and methods of authentication.

Enabling e-mail protocols (POP3S, IMAP4S, and SMTPS) on the public interface of the VPN 3000 concentrator by going to **Configuration > Interfaces**, choosing the public interface, and clicking the **WebVPN** tab. See Figure 10-18 on page 929 for information on the method of enabling e-mail protocols.

Figure 10-33 *E-Mail Proxy for POP3S, IMAP4S, and SMTPS Connections*

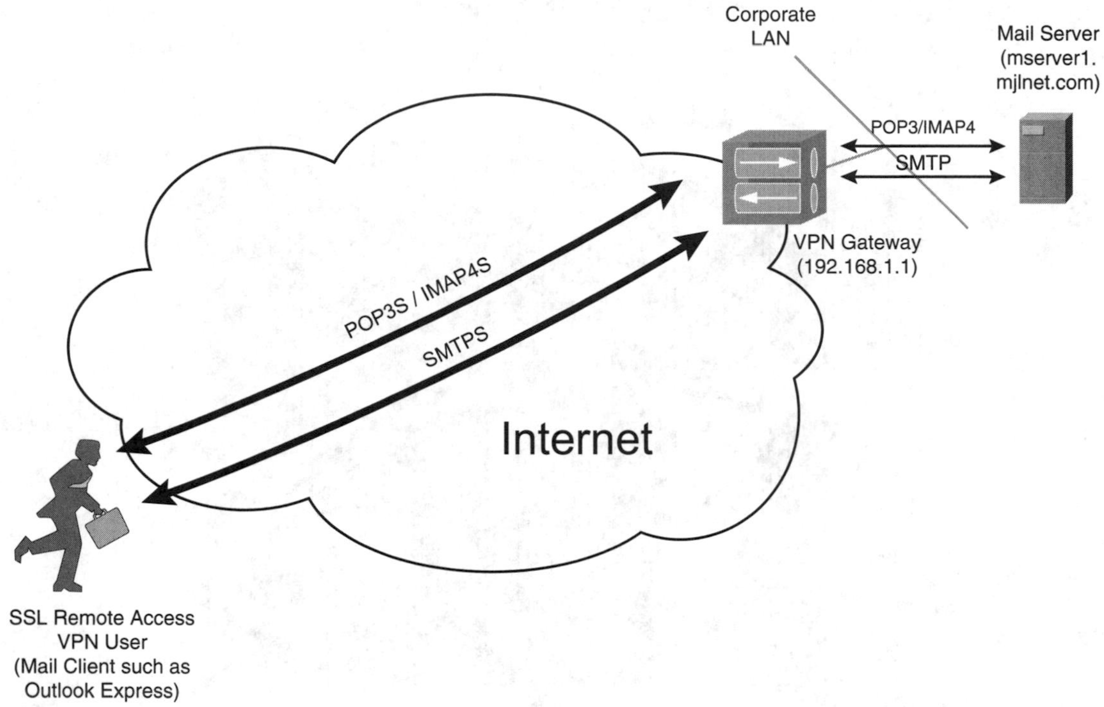

You can configure e-mail protocol port numbers, e-mail server IP addresses or names, and methods of authentication under **Configuration > Tunneling and Security > WebVPN > Email Proxy** (see Figure 10-34).

The first two parameters (VPN Name Delimiter and Service Delimiter) are, as their names suggest, used to delimit VPN and e-mail server usernames and passwords.

The VPN Name Delimiter is used to separate the VPN usernames/passwords and e-mail server usernames/passwords. This delimiter is used when configuring the e-mail client—in the box on the e-mail client where the username is entered, the username that the VPN 3000 concentrator uses to authenticate the user, as well as the username that the e-mail server uses to authenticate the user must be configured. These usernames are separated in the box using the delimiting character specified by the VPN Name Delimiter.

So, for example, if the username used to authenticate the user on the VPN 3000 concentrator is mark, the username used to authenticate the user on the e-mail server is markj, and the delimiting character specified on the VPN 3000 concentrator is :, then mark:markj should be entered into the username box on the e-mail client (more on this later).

Figure 10-34 *Configuring E-Mail Protocol Ports, Server Addresses or Names, and Methods of Authentication*

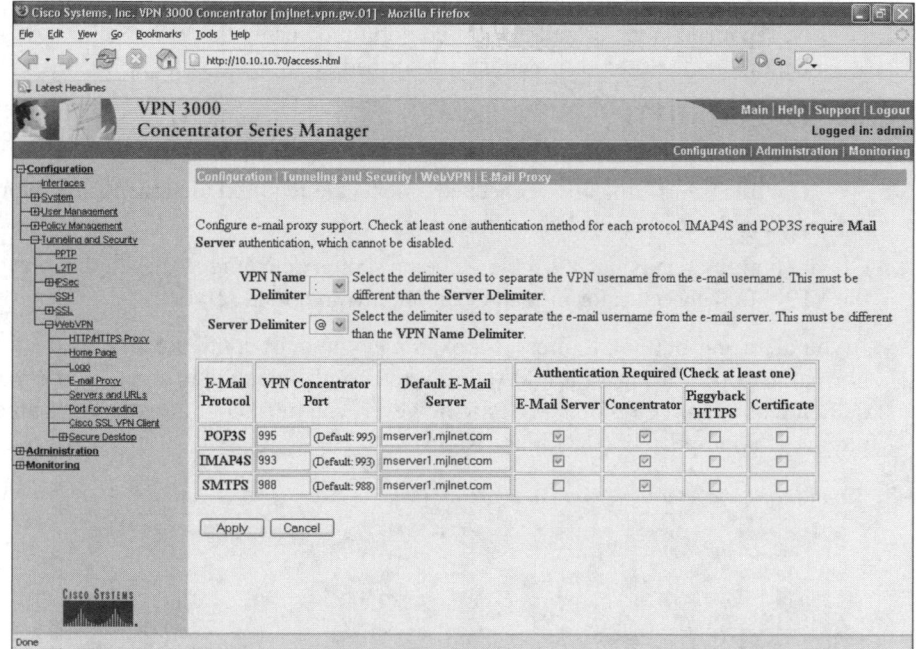

Similarly, the Service Delimiter is used to separate the e-mail server username from the e-mail server name itself. The default is @, which is often the delimiting character used on e-mail servers. If the delimiting character is different for your e-mail servers, the Service Delimiter should be modified using the drop-down box as appropriate.

Underneath the VPN Name Delimiter and Service Delimiter parameters are the settings for POP3S, IMAP4, and SMTPS ports, default e-mail server IP addresses or names, and methods of authentication.

The ports used for POP3S, IMAP4S, and SMTPS must match those specified on e-mail clients.

The *default* e-mail server IP addresses or DNS names should be entered into the appropriate boxes. Note that these are the mail servers to which e-mail traffic is sent when e-mail client do not explicitly specify e-mail servers.

As far as methods of authentication are concerned, it is possible to use one or more of the four different methods of authentication for POP3S, IMAP4S, and SMTPS:

- **Email Server**—If this box is checked then it indicates that the e-mail server(s) will authenticate POP3S, IMAP4S, and SMTPS. This box must be checked for POP3S and IMAP4S.

- **Concentrator**—This box must be checked if authentication of users on the VPN 3000 concentrator is also required.

In this case, the e-mail server and concentrator usernames passwords must be separated in the e-mail clients' configuration using the VPN Name Delimiter character, as previously described.

- **Piggyback HTTPS**—When this box is checked, a regular HTTPS (WebVPN) session must have already been established via a web browser with the VPN 3000 concentrator.

- **Certificate**—If this box is checked, clients are required to authenticate themselves during the RSA handshake using a certificate.

Client configuration is fairly simple—clients should be configured such that they point to the VPN 3000 concentrator instead of directly to an e-mail server.

If you are using Outlook Express, for example, you must configure an e-mail account as normal; if you are using VPN 3000 concentrator authentication in addition to e-mail server authentication for POP3S or IMAP4S, however, you must configure the username and password appropriately (see Figure 10-35).

Figure 10-35 *Configuring the Username and Password on Outlook Express When Using E-Mail Proxy*

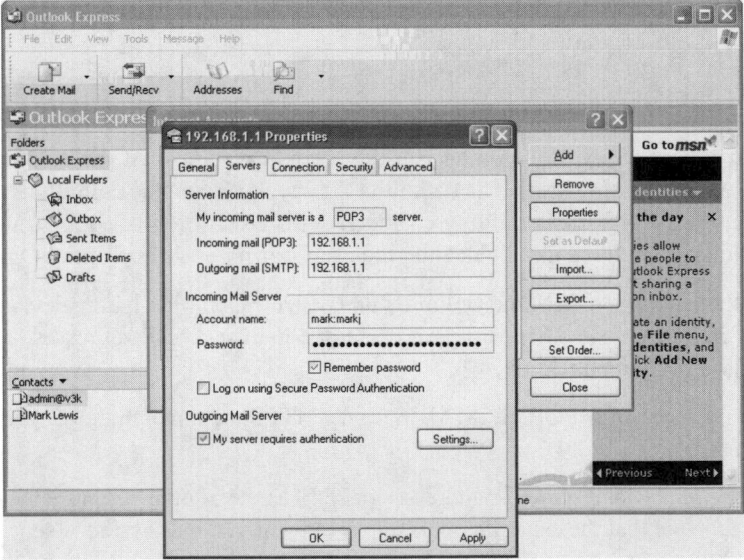

If you take a look under the "Incoming Mail Server" header in the Servers tab of the account properties, you will notice that the account name is mark:markj.

Because e-mail proxy via the VPN 3000 concentrator is being used, and Concentrator authentication is configured (see the Concentrator box in Figure 10-34), the VPN 3000 concentrator username (mark) is specified first, and the e-mail account name (markj) is specified next. The two usernames are separated using the VPN Name Delimiter (:) specified on the VPN 3000 concentrator (again, see Figure 10-34). If the usernames on both the VPN 3000 concentrator and the e-mail server are the same, it is only necessary to specify the username once (for example, mark).

Now, if the e-mail client in question wants to access e-mail on a mail server that is *not* the default (see configuration of Default E-Mail Server in Figure 10-34), the e-mail server name must be specified in this same box in this format:

(*e-mail_server_username*)[*Server Delimiter*](*e-mail_server_name*)

So, if the e-mail server is mserver2.mjlnet.com (not the default specified in Figure 10-34), the account name should be mark:markj@mserver2.mjlnet.com.

Next, the password on the Outlook Express account properties Server tab must be configured using a similar format—the VPN 3000 concentrator user password must be specified first, with the e-mail server account password configured second. The two must again be separated using the VPN Name Delimiter.

If the VPN 3000 concentrator is configured to authenticate users and the password user mark is hello, and the e-mail server password for user markj is hithere, the password specified in the Password box on the client must be hello:hithere.

One other important setting to notice on the Server tab is the My server requires authentication check box under Outgoing Mail Server heading. It may be necessary to check this box if you receive an error when attempting to connect to the e-mail server via the VPN 3000 concentrator.

Having configured authentication, the next step is to specify POP3S and SMTPS ports under the Advanced tab, as shown in Figure 10-36.

Figure 10-36 *Configuring SMTPS and POP3S Ports on Outlook Express When Using E-Mail Proxy*

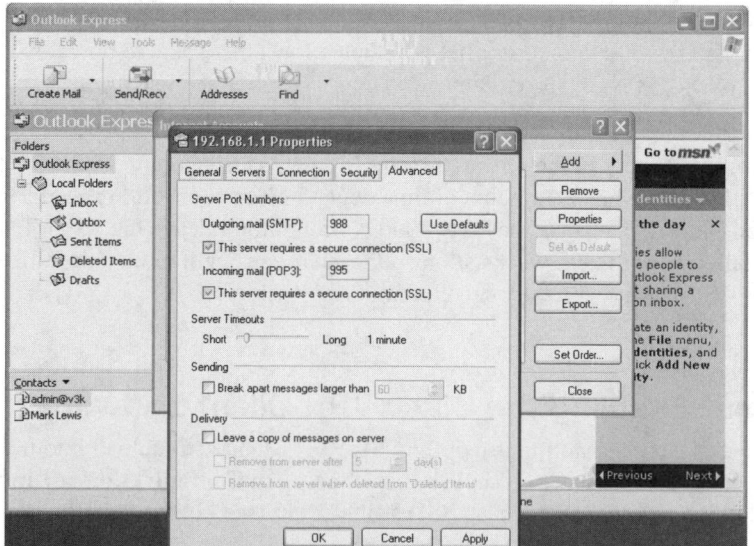

Under the Server Port Numbers heading you must check both of the **This server requires a secure connection (SSL)** boxes (for both SMTP and POP3).

Having checked the boxes, you must now specify the ports to use for each protocol. These ports *must* match those specified on the VPN 3000 concentrator. In Figure 10-36, for example, the SMTPS and POP3S ports are configured as 988 and 995, respectively—these match those specified on the VPN 3000 concentrator in Figure 10-34.

Implementing Full Network Access Using the Cisco SSL VPN Client

By this stage, you will know that the type of access offered by clientless SSL remote access VPNs is much more restricted than that offered by IPsec remote access VPNs. If you do want to offer more functionality via an SSL remote access VPN, you can use the Cisco SSL VPN Client.

The Cisco SSL VPN Client is loaded on the VPN 3000 concentrator and then dynamically downloaded from the VPN 3000 concentrator by remote access VPN users. The Cisco SSL VPN Client offers remote access connectivity comparable to that offered by IPsec remote access VPNs.

One advantage of the Cisco SSL VPN Client is that it does not have to be permanently installed on client workstations and does not require particular configuration or administration, unlike IPsec remote access VPN client software. The Cisco SSL VPN Client software package is also relatively small in size.

It is worth mentioning, however, that for the SSL VPN Client software to be downloaded and installed, the remote access user must have administrative privileges on the workstation. Cisco does, however, provide an install enabler utility (STCIE.EXE) that must itself be installed by an administrator but will then allow other users to download and install the Cisco SSL VPN Client on-demand.

When compared to IPsec remote access VPNs, the disadvantages of an SSL VPN Client include the fact that the client software is downloaded from the VPN 3000 concentrator, which takes a variable amount of time depending on connection speed. Having said that, it is possible to configure the VPN 3000 concentrator to leave the SSL VPN Client software installed on the client workstations rather than causing it to be uninstalled whenever the SSL VPN connection between is terminated (the default).

Installing and Enabling the Cisco VPN Client Software

The first step in enabling use of the SSL VPN Client is to upload it to the VPN 3000 concentrator. You can accomplish this by going to **Configuration > Tunneling and Security > WebVPN > Cisco SSL VPN Client** (see Figure 10-37).

Figure 10-37 *Installing the SSL Cisco VPN Client*

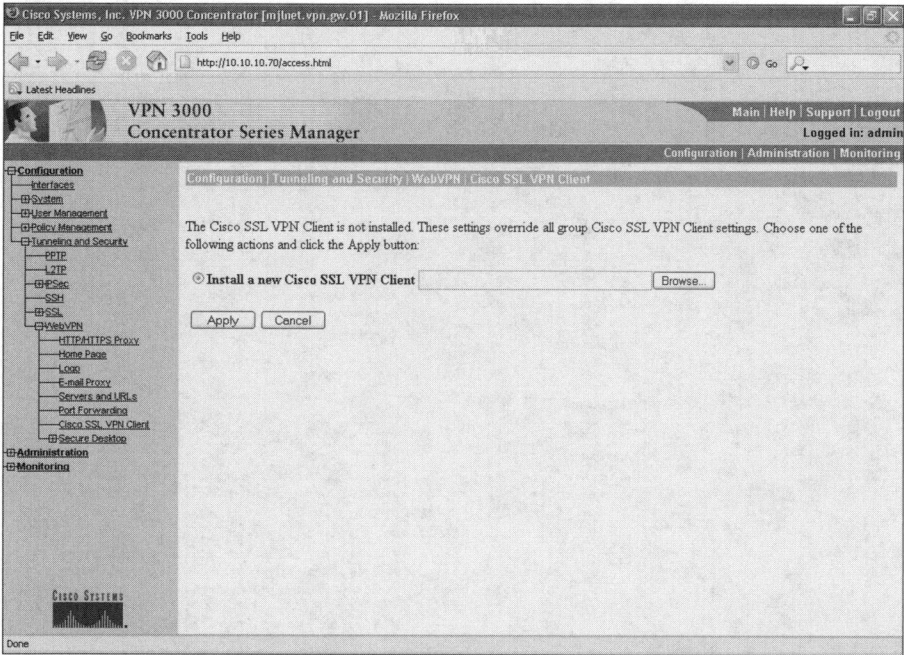

Choose **Install a new Cisco SSL VPN Client**, click the **Browse** button, browse to the location of the Cisco SSL VPN client software, and click **Apply** to install the software on the VPN 3000 concentrator.

After the client software is installed, the next step is to enable the use of the SSL VPN Client software for the appropriate user groups, as well as configure IP address pools (described in Chapters 8 and 9).

You can enable the user of the SSL VPN Client software by going to **Configuration > User Management > Groups**, choosing the appropriate group(s), clicking **Modify**, and clicking the **WebVPN** tab. The page shown in Figure 10-38 will then appear.

Checking the **Enable Cisco SSL VPN Client** box will, as it suggests, enable the use of the SSL VPN Client for the group.

It is also possible to require the use of the SSL VPN client by checking the **Require Cisco SSL VPN Client** box.

As discussed earlier in this section, the default behavior when using the SSL VPN Client is that the SSL VPN client software is removed when the client disconnects from the VPN 3000 concentrator. If the **Keep Cisco SSL VPN Client** box is checked, however, the client software remains on the client workstation even after disconnect. This clearly obviates the requirement to dynamically download the client software each time the client workstation connects to the VPN 3000 concentrator.

Figure 10-38 *Enabling the Use of the Cisco SSL VPN Client*

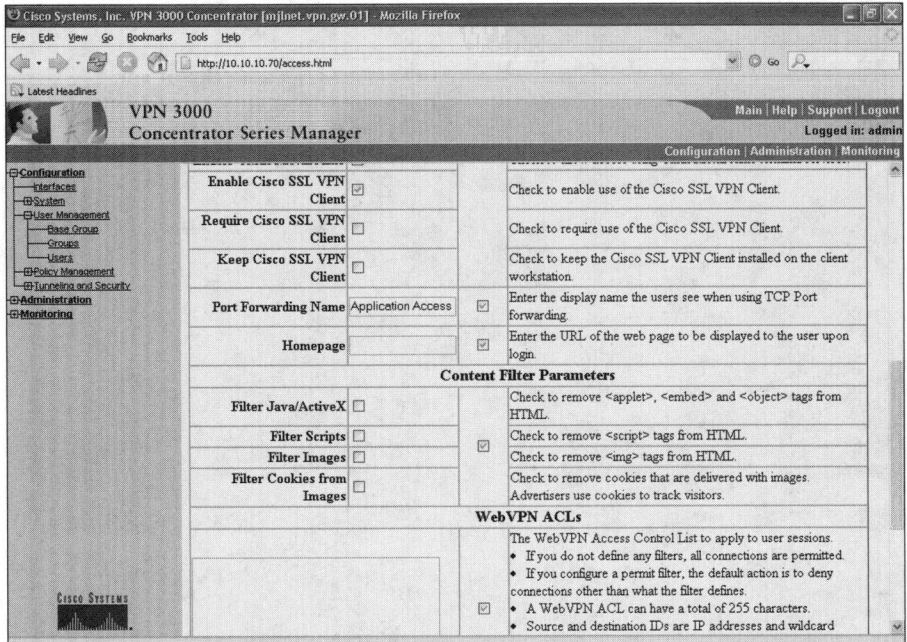

Understanding Remote Access Connectivity When Using the Cisco SSL VPN Client

When the Cisco SSL VPN Client is enabled for a particular user group, and when a user in that group connects to the VPN 3000 concentrator and logs in via the WebVPN login page, the Cisco VPN SSL Client will begin to download (assuming it is not installed already). After the SSL VPN client has downloaded, it extracts and installs (see Figure 10-39).

One thing to notice in Figure 10-39 is the text shown in the upper left (Click here to skip installation of the Cisco SSL VPN Client and proceed to the WebVPN Home page). This text does not appear if the Require Cisco SSL VPN Client box is checked in the WebVPN tab of group settings (see Figure 10-38).

After the SSL VPN Client software has been installed, a key symbol will appear on the right of the taskbar. Clicking the key will display information about the Cisco SSL VPN Client and SSL connection, as shown in Figure 10-40.

Figure 10-39 *Cisco SSL VPN Client Extracts and Installs*

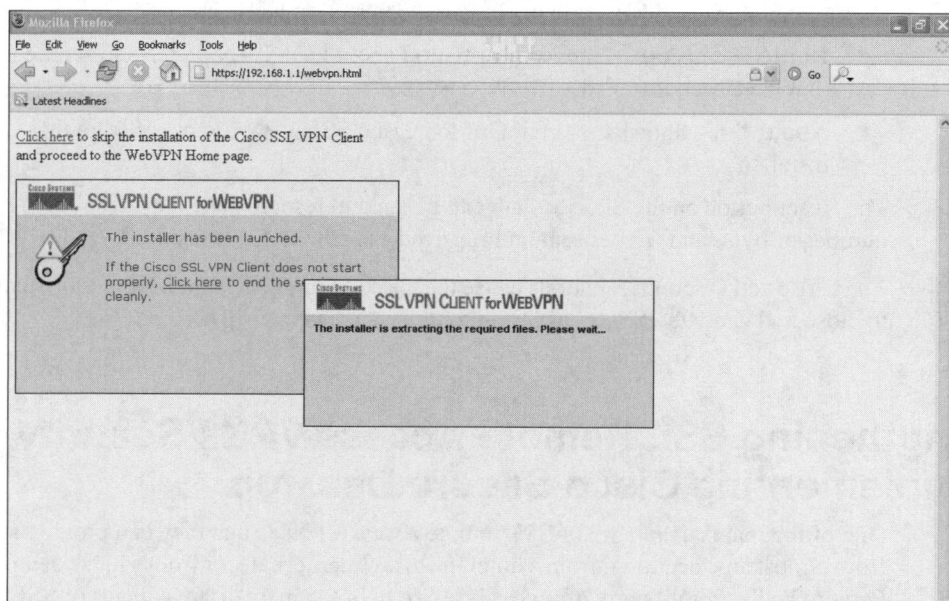

Figure 10-40 *Information About the Cisco SSL VPN Client Connection*

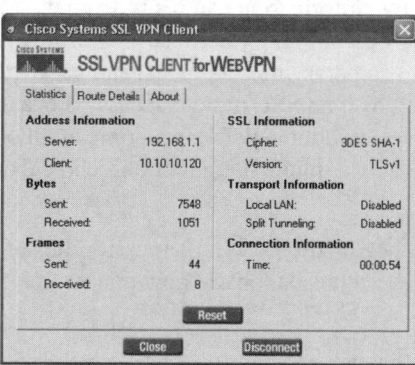

There are three tabs:

- **Statistics tab**—Displays information about the connection, including address information (the IP address of the VPN 3000 gateway and the IP address assigned by the VPN 3000 concentrator to the SSL VPN Client tunnel interface/adapter); the number of bytes and frames sent and received over the tunnel; the encryption and hashing algorithms used by the cipher suite negotiated by the client and VPN 3000 concentrator; whether the client is allowed to access its local LAN and whether split tunneling is enabled; and how long the connection has been up

- **Route Details tab**—Shows information about local LAN routes and secure routes that have been installed

- **About tab**—Shows the version of the Cisco SSL VPN Client software that is installed

The Reset button on the Statistics tab can be used to reset to zero statistics relating to the number of bytes and frames sent and received over the SSL connection.

The Close and Disconnect buttons cause the Cisco SSL VPN Client information dialog box to close and cause the SSL connection to terminate respectively.

Strengthening SSL Remote Access VPNs Security by Implementing Cisco Secure Desktop

One of the main advantages of SSL remote access VPNs is that they can provide access from almost any location—from a hotel, from an Internet café, or from a kiosk at an airport. Paradoxically, this ubiquity of access is also one of the main disadvantages of SSL remote access VPNs—these locations are often insecure, and a SSL remote access VPN implementation can, if you are not very careful, allow a hacker or cracker access to sensitive information including usernames, passwords, and data downloaded to the workstation from which a user is connecting.

This access to sensitive information can result from the installation of malware such as keystroke loggers as well as simply because web browser sessions leave traces such as caches, histories, temporary files, cookies, and password autocompletion. In addition, any data downloaded over an SSL remote access VPN and written to a hard disk is not effectively removed by its simple deletion—some or all of that data can be accessed fairly simply by someone with a minimal amount of technical expertise using readily available software tools.

So, having possibly horrified you with the possibilities of the compromise of SSL remote access VPNs, it is time to take a look at how the previously mentioned vulnerabilities can be addressed.

Cisco has software that helps to address these vulnerabilities called *Cisco Secure Desktop*. This software can be dynamically downloaded to client workstations upon initial connection via an ActiveX, Java, or .exe file.

The Cisco Secure Desktop suite can provide different levels of protection based on the location from which remote access users are connecting. In addition to the removal and overwrite of cache, histories, temporary files, and so on, the Secure Desktop suite can provide access based on the presence of antivirus software, firewall software, and operating systems and service packs.

Secure Desktop operates as follows:

1 A remote access VPN user connects to the VPN 3000 concentrator.

2 The Cisco Secure Desktop is dynamically downloaded from the concentrator to the user workstation, and the location of the workstation is assessed.

3 Depending on the location, a secure, virtual desktop is created; a cache cleaner is applied; and/or a VPN feature policy is applied on the user workstation. The secure desktop includes an encrypted *sandbox* or hard drive partition.

4 The user continues with his/her SSL remote access VPN session.

5 When the user logs out from the VPN 3000 concentrator, the secure desktop is eliminated, with all cache, history, temporary files, and user data (including e-mail attachments) being *overwritten* using the U.S. Department of Defense (DoD) method for secure data elimination.

Information elimination using overwrite ensures that data cannot be retrieved by another user at a later time.

Figure 10-41 illustrates the operation of Cisco Secure Desktop.

Figure 10-41 *Operation of Cisco Secure Desktop*

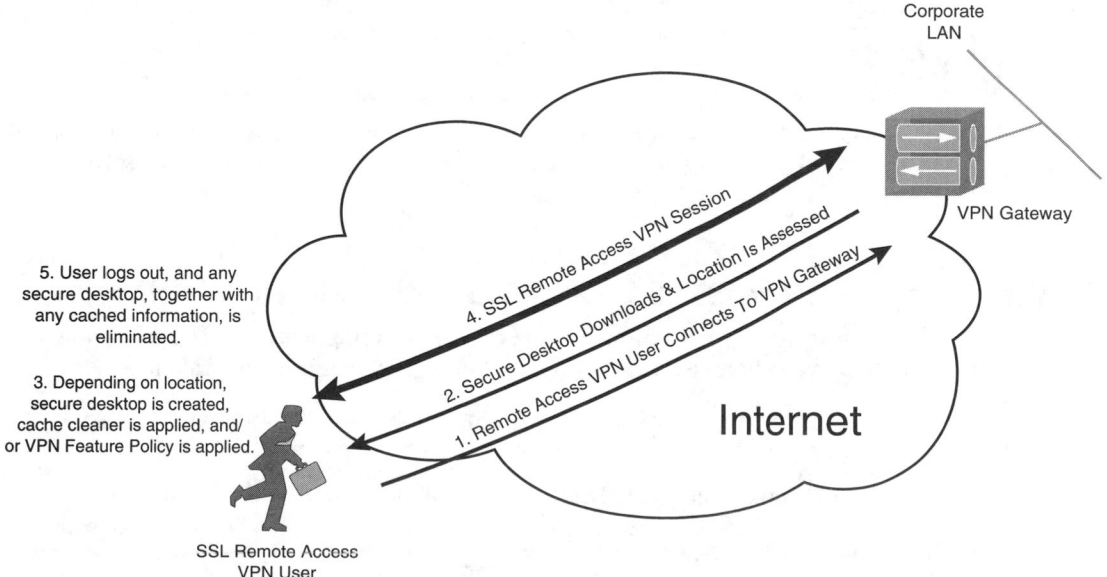

Installing the Cisco Secure Desktop

The first step in implementing the Cisco Secure Desktop is to install the software on the VPN 3000 concentrator. You can accomplish this by going to **Configuration > Tunneling and Security > WebVPN > Secure Desktop > Setup** (see Figure 10-42).

Figure 10-42 *Installing the Cisco Secure Desktop*

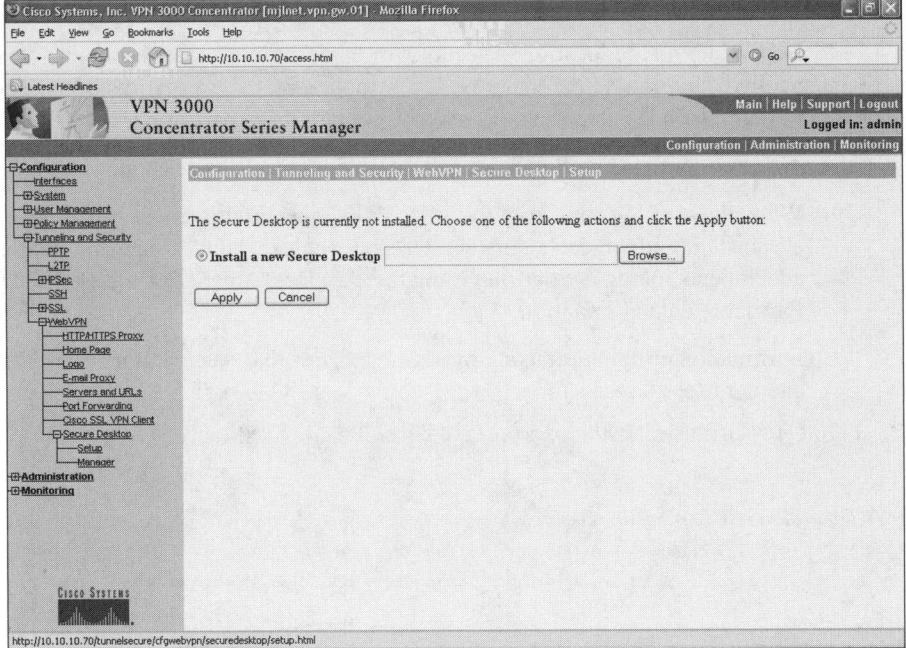

Choose **Install a new Secure Desktop**, browse to the location where the software is stored, and click **Apply**. If all is well and good, a page with a message stating that the software has been correctly uploaded will now display.

Configuring the Cisco Secure Desktop for Windows Clients

After the software has been installed, you can go to **Configuration > Tunneling and Security > WebVPN > Secure Desktop > Manager** to begin configuration.

As previously described, the Cisco Secure Desktop is location based. That is, the Cisco Secure Desktop applied depends on the location from which users connect.

Click the **Windows Location Settings** heading in the subtree on the left side of the Cisco Secure Desktop window. You will then see the Windows Location Settings page shown in Figure 10-43.

Figure 10-43 *Specifying Locations Within Cisco Secure Desktop*

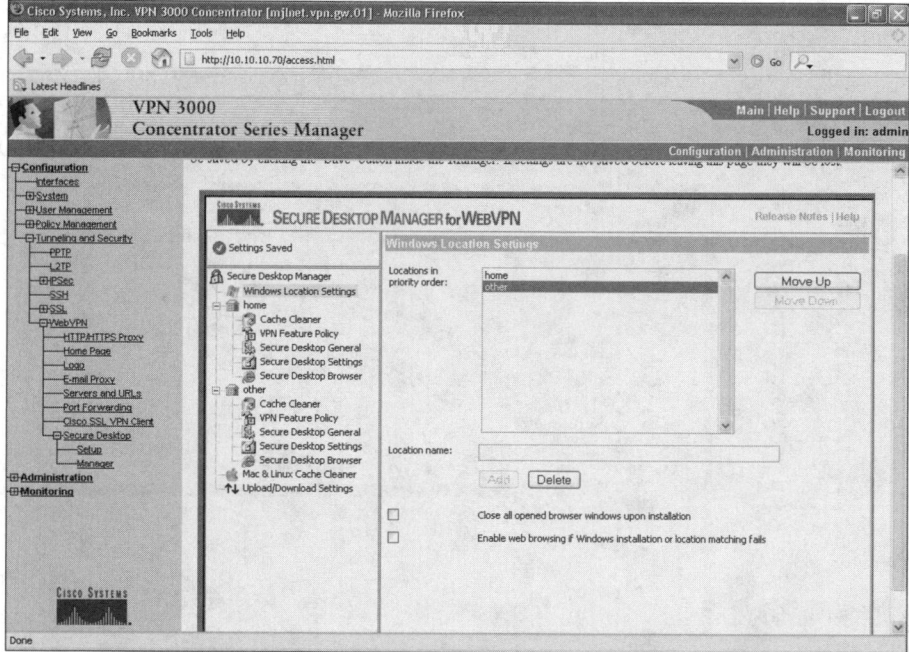

In the Location name box, you can specify the names of locations from which user can connect to the VPN 3000 concentrator and add them in turn by clicking the **Add** button. In Figure 10-43, two locations have been added, home and other.

When users connect to the VPN 3000 concentrator, they are matched against the configured locations *in the order that they are listed* in the Windows Location Settings window. So, it is important to list to locations in the correct order.

Configuration of the security setting associated with each location is achieved by clicking the location names in the left pane of the window.

You might be wondering how the VPN 3000 concentrator knows that, for example, a user is connecting from his home office and not some other location such as an Internet café or kiosk. Locations are identified by the Secure Desktop when it downloads to a user workstation depending on whether a certificate is installed on the machine, whether the machine NIC is assigned a certain IP address, or whether a machine has a certain registry setting or file.

Figure 10-44 shows the configuration of the identification criteria for a location (in this example, home).

Figure 10-44 *Configuration of the Identification Criteria for a Location*

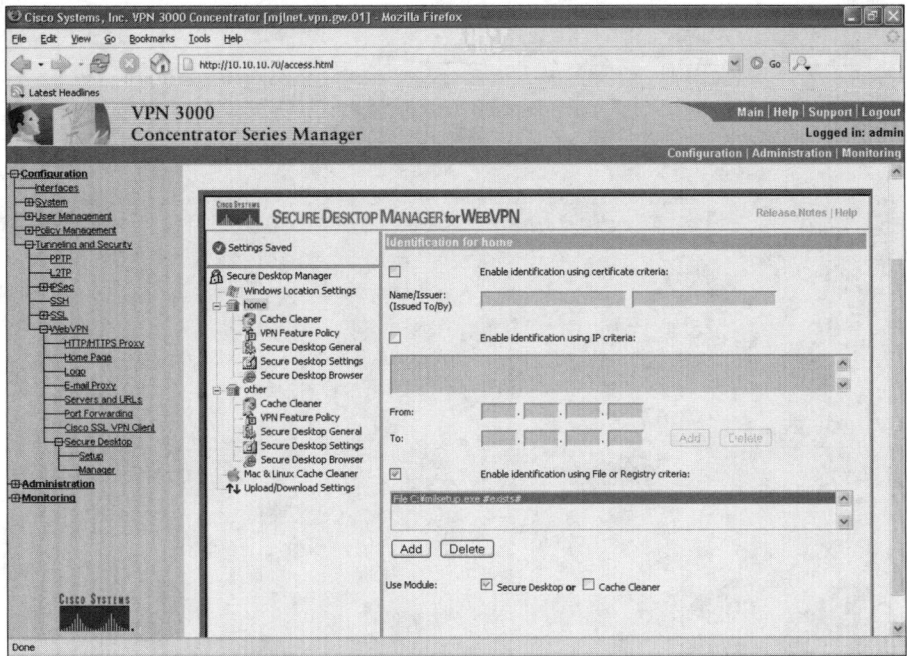

If you take a look at the Identification pane in Figure 10-44 (Identification for home), you will see that there are three options (check boxes):

- **Enable identification using certificate criteria**—By checking this box, it is possible to use the fields of a certificate installed on the user workstation to identify its location.

- **Enable identification using IP criteria**—Checking this box enables an administrator to specify a range of IP addresses. If a user workstation is assigned an IP address within this range, the workstation's location is identified on this basis.

- **Enable identification using File or Registry criteria**—This box, if checked, allows identification of a location based on a file or registry entry on a user workstation.

In Figure 10-44, the identification of the location home is based on the existence of a file called mjlsetup.exe on the user workstation.

In summary, when a user connects to the VPN 3000 concentrator, the Cisco Secure Desktop dynamically downloads, and the location of the workstation from which the user is connecting is assessed based on the configured criteria.

Having configured the location criteria, it is important to specify which Cisco Secure Desktop suite module or function will be applied on a user workstation according to its location. The modules and functions are as follows:

- **Cache Cleaner**—As the name suggests, this module deletes and disables information including browser caches, temporary files, and autocompletion information, including passwords.

- **VPN Feature Policy**—This module provides selective WebVPN access depending on the presence of components such as antivirus software, operating system type and service pack level, firewall software, and other Secure Desktop components.

- **Secure Desktop**—This module provides a secure, encrypted space (desktop) on Windows XP and Windows 2000. The user session is then created within this secure desktop.

The particular module that is used on a workstation at a particular location depends on the selection specified at the bottom of the Identification pane (see Figure 10-44).

It is possible to choose either Secure Desktop or Cache Cleaner for a particular location by checking the appropriate box next to Use Module. If you do not choose Secure Desktop or Cache Cleaner, the VPN Feature Policy is used for a location.

Configuring the Windows Cache Cleaner

The Cache Cleaner settings for a particular location can be configured by clicking **Cache Cleaner** in the subtree of that location on the left side of the Cisco Secure Desktop Manager.

Figure 10-45 shows the configuration settings for the Cache Cleaner.

Figure 10-45 *Configuration Settings for the Cache Cleaner*

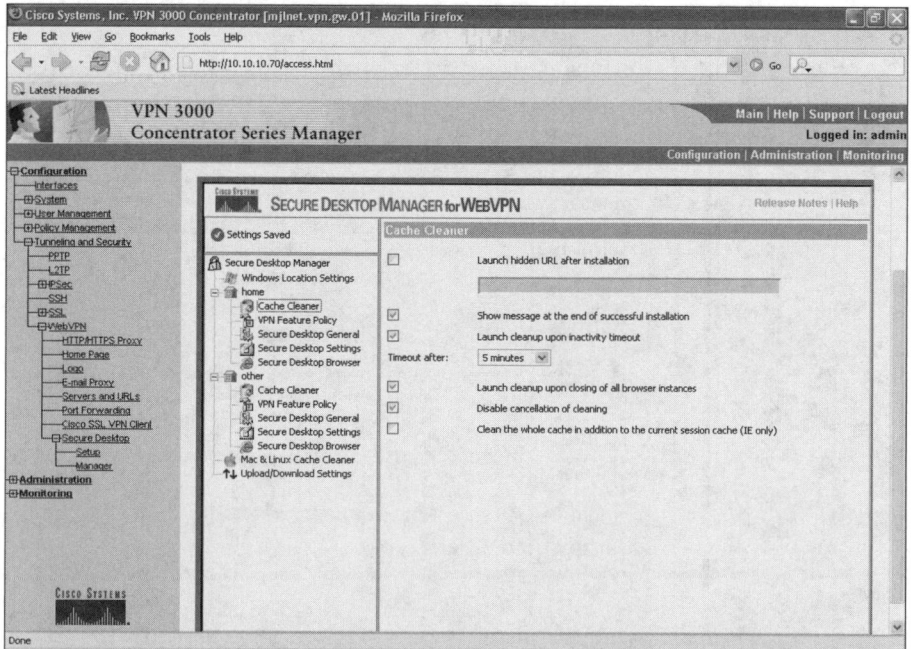

Specific settings for Cache Cleaner include the following:

- **Launch hidden URL after installation**—If this setting is checked, a URL can be entered which is launched after the installation of the Cache Cleaner.

- **Show message at the end of successful installation**—If this setting is checked, a message displays on the user workstation confirming the successful installation of the Cache Cleaner.

- **Launch cleanup upon inactivity timeout**—When this option is checked, the Cache Cleaner begins operation after a period of inactivity on the user workstation.

- **Launch cleanup upon closing of all browser instances**—This setting, if checked, causes the Cache Cleaner to begin operation when all browser windows are closed.

- **Disable cancellation of cleaning**—This prevents user cancellation of cache cleaning.

- **Clean the whole cache in addition to the current session cache (IE only)**—Checking this setting ensures that the Internet Explorer cache is cleaned when the Cache Cleaner starts.

Configuring VPN Feature Policy Settings

To configure VPN Feature Policy settings for a location, click the **VPN Feature Policy** on the subtree of the location; the screen shown in Figure 10-46 will appear.

Figure 10-46 *Configuring VPN Feature Policy Settings*

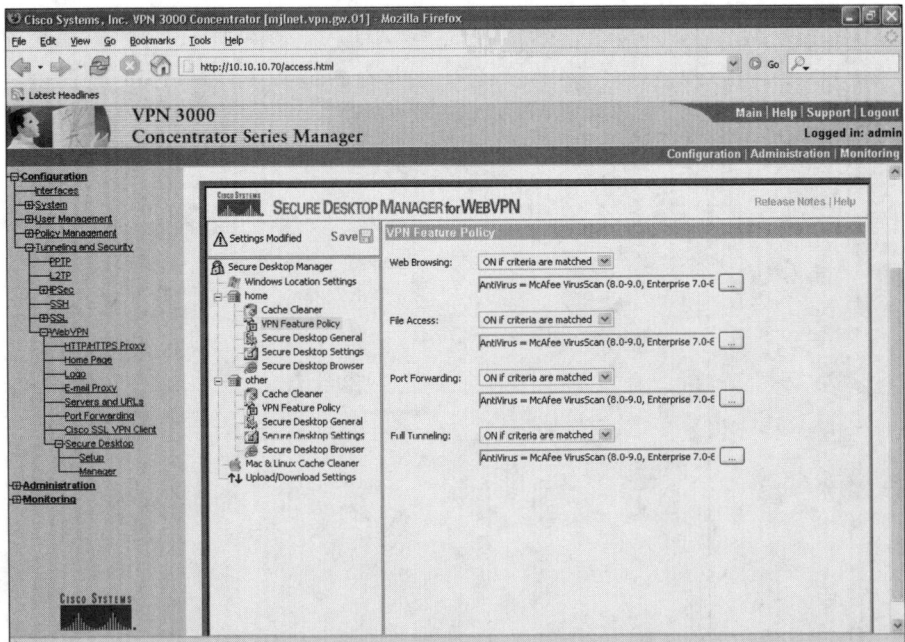

Settings for the VPN Feature Policy include Web Browsing, File Access, Port Forwarding, and Full Tunneling.

These settings (levels of access) can be enabled, enabled if certain conditions are fulfilled, or be disabled from a user workstation by choosing ON, ON if criteria are matched, or OFF, respectively, in the corresponding drop-down boxes.

If you choose the ON if criteria are matched option, the criteria that must be fulfilled for a particular level of access to be enabled can be specified by clicking on the ellipsis (. . .) button.

The criteria that can be matched include the presence of antivirus software, firewall software, operating system and service pack, and other Secure Desktop features on the user workstation.

Configuring Secure Desktop Options

When the Secure Desktop is specified for a particular location, you can configure the associated options by clicking **Secure Desktop General**, **Secure Desktop Settings**, and **Secure Desktop Browser** in location subtree.

Figure 10-47 shows the options associated with Secure Desktop General.

Figure 10-47 *Configuring Options Associated with Secure Desktop General*

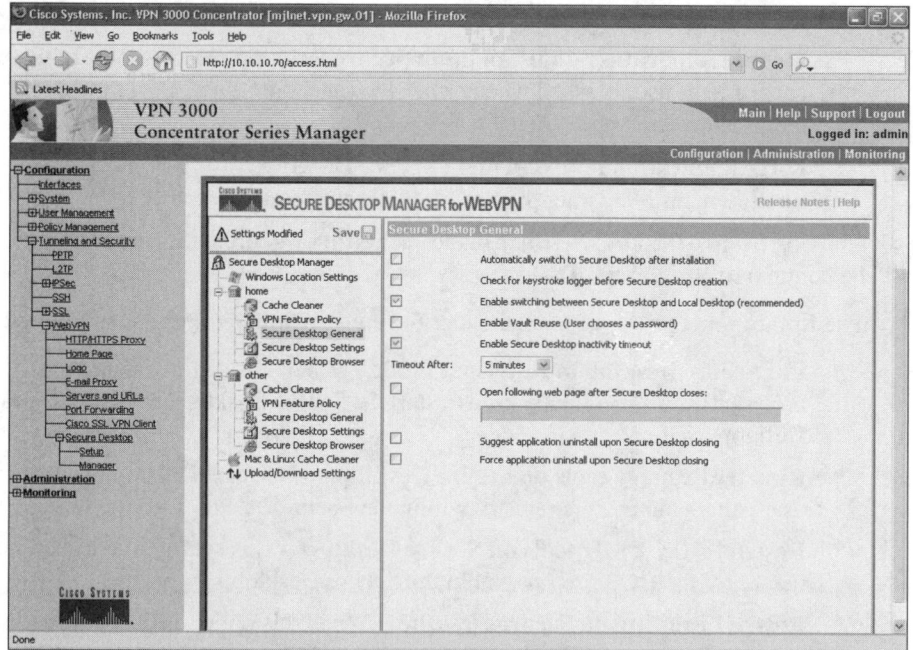

Secure Desktop General settings include the following:

- **Automatically switch to Secure Desktop after installation**—When checked, this setting causes the Secure Desktop to load immediately after installation.

- **Check for keystroke logger before Secure Desktop creation**—This setting, if checked, causes a check for a keystroke logger to run before the creation of the Secure Desktop on the user workstation.

  This setting only works if the user has administrator privileges on the workstation.

- **Enable switching between Secure Desktop and Local Desktop (recommended)**—If this option is checked, the user can switch between the secure desktop and the regular desktop on the workstation.

  It is a very good idea to check this option so that users can respond to any application prompts.

- **Enable Vault Reuse (User chooses a password)**—If checked, a Secure Desktop vault can be reused (and not overwritten between sessions).

  The user selects a password to allow access to this Secure Desktop.

- **Enable Secure Desktop inactivity timeout**—When checked, this option causes the Secure Desktop to automatically close after a period of inactivity.

- **Open following web page after Secure Desktop closes**—This setting, if checked, causes a URL to be opened after the Secure Desktop closes.

- **Suggest application uninstall upon Secure Desktop closes**—When this setting is checked, the user is asked whether he/she wants the Secure Desktop uninstalled after it closes.

- **Force application uninstall upon Secure Desktop closing**—The Secure Desktop is forcibly uninstalled after the Secure Desktop closes when checked.

Clicking **Secure Desktop Settings** in the subtree allows further Secure Desktop options to be configured (see Figure 10-48).

The further four options contained under Secure Desktop Settings are as follows:

- **Put Secure Desktop in restricted mode**—When this setting is checked, only the browser that was originally used to start the Secure Desktop can be used in the Secure Desktop itself.

- **Restrict Registry tools on Secure Desktop**—If checked, this option ensures that a user cannot modify the registry within the Secure Desktop.

- **Restrict DOS-CMD tools on Secure Desktop**—This setting, if checked, prevents the use of the DOS prompt within the Secure Desktop.

- **Restrict Printing on Secure Desktop**—When this option is checked, users cannot print from within the Secure Desktop.

Figure 10-48 *Configuring Secure Desktop Settings*

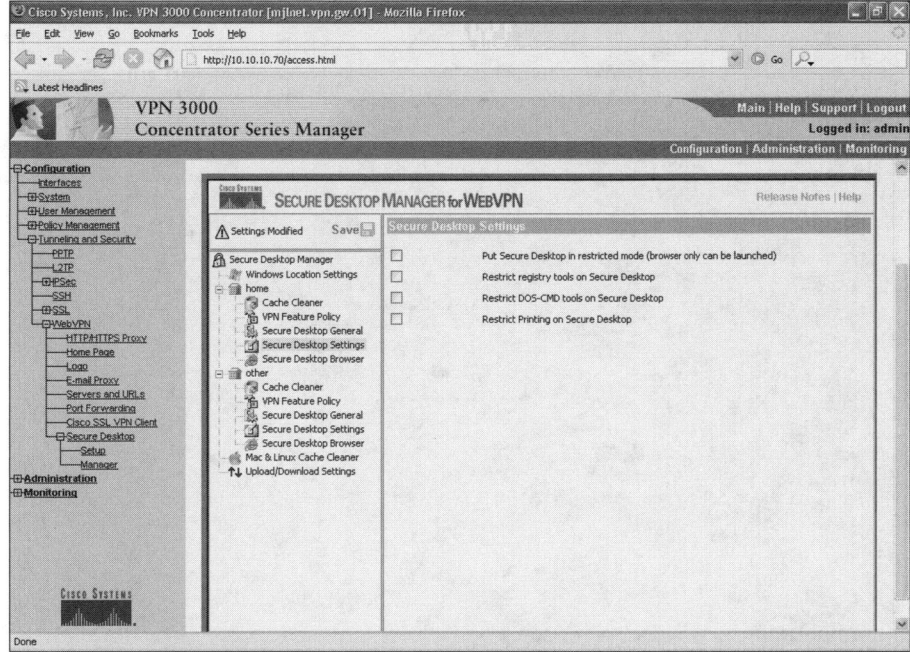

The options under Secure Desktop Settings can be chosen to ensure the highest level of security for the Secure Desktop.

Configuring Cache Cleaner Options for Mac and Linux Users

The Mac and Linux Cache Cleaner heading under the subtree in the Secure Desktop Manager allows the configuration of options associated with the Cache Cleaner for Mac and Linux users.

Figure 10-49 shows the configuration options for the Mac and Linux Cache Cleaner.

Mac and Linux Cache Cleaner options are as follows:

- **Launch cleanup upon global timeout**—When checked, this option causes the Cache Cleaner to run after a period of inactivity on the user workstation.

- **Let user reset timeout**—If this setting is checked, a user can reset the timeout time period.

- **Launch cleanup upon exiting of browser**—This option, if checked, causes the Cache Cleaner to start when all browser instances are closed.

- **Enable Cancel button of cleaning**—When this box is checked, users are able to cancel cache cleaning.

- **Enable web browsing if Mac or Linux installation fails**—This option ensures that web browsing is allowed if the installation of the Cache Cleaner fails.

Figure 10-49 *Configuration Options for the Mac and Linux Cache Cleaner*

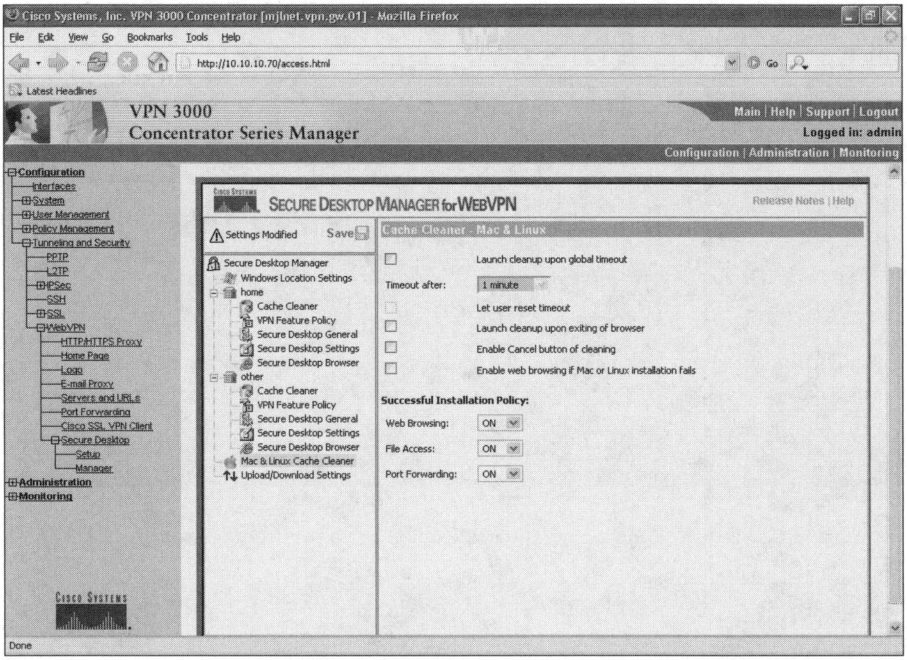

The Successful Installation Policy options allow the configuration of VPN Feature Policy settings for Mac and Linux users:

- **Web browsing**—If ON is chosen, web browsing is allowed from Mac and Linux workstations.

- **File Access**—Allow (ON) or disallow (OFF) file access.

- **Port Forwarding**—Allow or disallow port forwarding.

Note that VPN Feature Policy settings on Mac and Linux workstations do not depend on criteria such as the presence of antivirus software or access from a particular location (unlike Windows VPN Feature Policy settings).

NOTE   Having configured Cisco Secure Desktop, make sure that you save the configuration within the Cisco Secure Desktop—the configuration is independent of that for the VPN 3000 concentrator as a whole.

Enabling the Cisco Secure Desktop

After all the relevant settings have been configured within the Cisco Secure Desktop Manager, it is time to enable the Cisco Secure Desktop. You can accomplish this under **Configuration > Tunneling and Security > WebVPN > Secure Desktop > Setup** (Figure 10-50).

Figure 10-50 *Enabling the Secure Desktop*

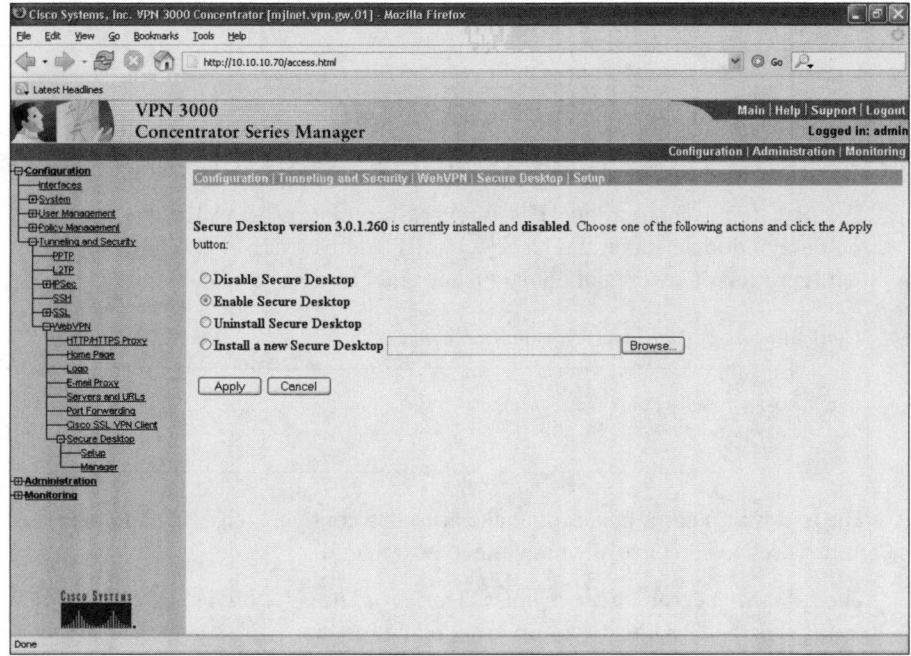

Choose **Enable Secure Desktop** and click **Apply**. The Secure Desktop is now enabled.

Enabling SSL VPNs (WebVPN) on Cisco IOS Devices

Enabling SSL VPNs on Cisco IOS Software is relatively straightforward and consists of eight basic steps:

Step 1   Configure domain name and name server addresses.

Step 2   Configure remote AAA for remote access user login authentication.

Step 3   Enroll with a CA and obtain an identity certificate.

Step 4   Enable WebVPN.

Step 5   Configure basic SSL parameters.

Step 6   Customize login and home pages (optional).

Step 7 Specify URLs.

Step 8 Configure port forwarding.

These steps are described in detail in the sections that follow.

Step 1: Configure Domain Name and Name Server Addresses

The first step in configuring a Cisco IOS SSL remote access VPN gateway is to configure the default domain name and name server IP addresses. Example 10-1 shows the configuration of the default domain name and name server IP address.

Example 10-1 *Configuration of the Default Domain Name and DNS Server IP Address*

```
!
ip domain name mjlnet.com
ip name-server 10.10.10.55
!
```

The **ip domain name** *name* command is used to configure the default domain name that the router uses to complete any unqualified host names.

The **ip name-server** *server-address1* [*server-address2…serveraddress6*] command configures the IP addresses of up to six name servers.

Step 2: Configure Remote AAA for Remote Access User Login Authentication

Example 10-2 shows the configuration of remote AAA for remote access user authentication.

Example 10-2 *Configuration of Remote AAA for Remote Access User Authentication*

```
!
aaa new-model (line 1)
!
!
aaa group server radius sslauth (line 2)
  server 10.10.10.51 auth-port 1645 acct-port 1646 (line 3)
!
aaa authentication login default group sslauth (line 4)
!
radius-server key mjlnetkey (line 5)
!
```

The **aaa new-model** command (line 1) enables authentication, authorization, and accounting.

The **aaa group server radius** *group-name* command in line 2 is then used to configure a group of RADIUS servers. In this case, the name of the group of servers is sslauth.

In line 3, the **server** *ip-address* [**auth-port** *port-number*] [**acct-port** *port-number*] command is then used to specify the IP addresses of RADIUS servers in the group, along with the ports used for authentication/authorization (**auth-port**) and accounting (**acct-port**). In this case, there is only one server in the group (10.10.10.51), and the ports used for AAA are the defaults (1645 and 1646).

The **aaa authentication login** [**default** | *method-list-name*] **group** *group-name* command (line 4) configures login authentication using the default method list and the (previously created) RADIUS server group called sslauth. Login authentication is required for SSL remote access VPN users.

Note that it is possible to configure local authentication for SSL remote access VPN users using the **aaa authentication login** [**default** | *method-list-name*] **local** command in conjunction with a local username/password database configured using the **username** *username* **password** *password* command.

In a practical sense, however, a local username/password database is much more difficult to administer than a local user database on a VPN 3000 concentrator—this is why RADIUS is recommended when configuring SSL remote access VPNs using Cisco IOS Software. RADIUS can also be used for WebVPN on the VPN 3000 concentrator.

Finally, the **radius-server key** {0 *string* | 7 *string* | *string*} command in line 5 configures the key that is used to authenticate communications between the router and the RADIUS server (as well as encrypting user passwords sent to the server).

Step 3: Enroll the IOS Router with a CA and Obtain an Identity Certificate

Enrolling the Cisco IOS router with a CA and obtaining an identity certificate consists of the following:

- Setting the time on the Cisco IOS router
- Configuring the router's host name and IP domain name
- Generating RSA keys on the router
- Declaring the CA
- Authenticating the CA
- Enrolling the router with the CA

These tasks are described in detail in the section "IKE Digital Signature Authentication," starting on page 448 in Chapter 6, "Deploying Site-to-Site IPsec VPNs."

Step 4: Enable WebVPN

As shown in Example 10-3, the **webvpn enable** global configuration mode command is used to enable SSL remote access VPNs (WebVPN).

Example 10-3   *Enabling SSL Remote Access VPNs (WebVPN)*

```
mjlnet.vpn.gw.02#conf t
Enter configuration commands, one per line.  End with CNTL/Z.
mjlnet.vpn.gw.02(config)#webvpn enable
mjlnet.vpn.gw.02(config)#exit
mjlnet.vpn.gw.02#
```

It is worth noting that if the Cisco IOS device is configured as a HTTP secure (HTTPS) server, it is necessary to add the **gateway-addr** *ip-address* parameter along with the **webvpn enable** command (**webvpn enable gateway-addr** *ip-address*). This parameter causes WebVPN to be only enabled on the (interface) IP address specified.

Step 5: Configure Basic SSL Parameters

Having enabled WebVPN, the next step is to configure basic SSL parameters, including cryptographic algorithms (and associated cipher suites), and specify the SSL trustpoint.

Example 10-4 shows the configuration of basic SSL parameters.

Example 10-4   *Configuration of Basic SSL Parameters*

```
!
webvpn
 ssl encryption 3des-sha1
 ssl trustpoint sslcert
!
```

The **webvpn** global configuration command is used to enter WebVPN configuration mode.

Next is the **ssl encryption** [**3des-sha1**] [**des-sha1**] [**rc4-md5**] command. This command specifies the encryption and hashing algorithms that the router will accept from the client as constituents of cipher suites.

So, when a client proposes a number of cipher suites in its ClientHello message, the router will accept one of those that uses the algorithms that you specify using the **ssl encryption** command. The accepted cipher suite is, as previously described, sent to the client in the ServerHello message—see the section, "Establishing an SSL Connection Between a Remote Access VPN User and an SSL VPN Gateway Using an RSA Handshake" earlier in this chapter for more information of the proposal and acceptance of cipher suites.

The **ssl trustpoint** *trustpoint-name* command specifies the PKI trustpoint, which in turn configures parameters (including the certificates, CRL configuration, and so on) that are used for authentication during the SSL RSA handshake. Make sure that the trustpoint name configured using the **ssl trustpoint-name** corresponds to that specified using the **crypto pki trustpoint** *name* command in Step 3.

Step 6: Customize Login and Home Pages (Optional)

As a final, optional, configuration step, it is also possible to customize the appearance of the WebVPN login and home pages using your own text and colors. Example 10-5 includes the commands that can be used to customize the text in login and home pages.

Example 10-5 *Commands Used to Customize the Login and Home Pages*

```
 !
webvpn
 title "TITLE.here"
 url-list "URL.List"
    heading "HEADING.here"
login-message "LOGIN.Message.here"
 !
```

The effect of the commands shown in Example 10-5 is best illustrated by examining Figures 10-51 and 10-52.

Figure 10-51 *Customizing Text in the WebVPN Login Page*

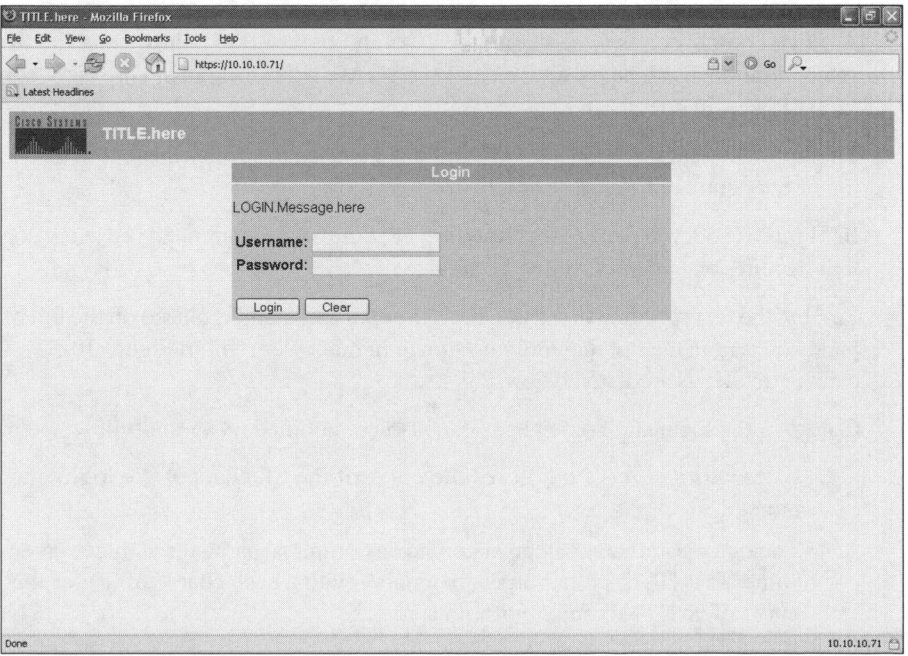

Figure 10-52 *Customizing Text in the WebVPN Home Page*

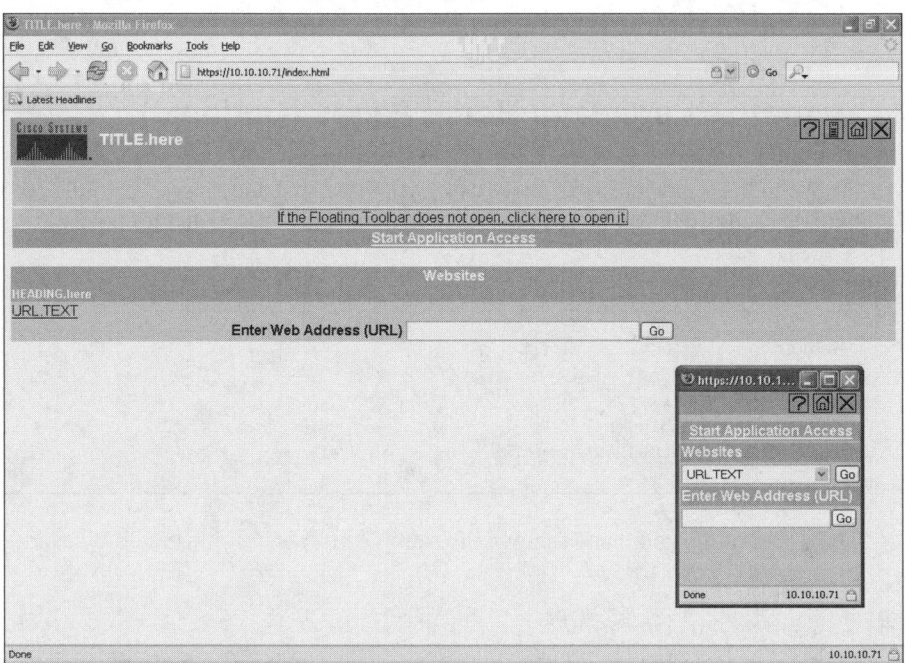

A quick comparison between Example 10-5 and Figure 10-51 shows that the **title** *title-string* command can be used to specify the HTML title string in the top right corner of the WebVPN login screen.

The **login-message** *message-string* command is used to specify the text in the login box in the upper centre of the login screen.

In Figure 10-52, you can see that **heading** *heading-string* command is used to configure the text heading on upper left of the home page.

Finally, the text specified in the **url-list** *list-name* command is placed on the left of the home page and within the floating toolbar (shown in the lower right in Figure 10-52). URLs that a user can access are listed below this text.

Colors in the login and home pages can also be modified using the following commands:

- **title-color** *color*—Configures the color of the title bars of the login and home pages.

    The *color* parameter can be specified as comma-separated red, blue, green values; as HTML color values, beginning with a hash character (#); or the name of an HTML color, with no spaces.

    For more information on HTML color values, do a search using your favorite Internet search engine—a huge number of sites describe these values.

- **text-color** [**black** | **white**]—This command is used to specify the color of the text in the title bars.

- **secondary-color** *color*—Use this command to specify the color of the secondary title bars of the login and home pages. The *color* parameter is specified in the same way as with the **title-color** command.

- **secondary-text-color** [**black** | **white**]—This specifies the color of the text in the secondary bars.

One final command that you can use to customize the appearance of the login and home pages is **logo** [**file** *filename* | **none**]. As you can probably guess, this command can be used to specify the logo image that is used (in place of the default Cisco logo in Figures 10-51 and 10-52). The image specified must be JPG, GIF, or PNG or a size less than 100k. The *filename* parameter is used to specify both the location and name of the image file.

Step 7: Specify URLs

The **url-text** *text* **url-value** *url* to configure the URLs that remote access users can access. The *text* parameter is used to specify the text that users can click to access the specified URL—the URL itself is specified with the *url* parameter. The text specified using this command displays under the text configured using the **url-list** command discussed in the previous section.

Example 10-6 shows some examples of the use of the **url-text** command.

Example 10-6 *Specifying URLs Using the url-text Command*

```
 !
 webvpn
  url-list "URL.List"
    url-text "URL.TEXT" url-value "http://www.mjlnet.com/engineering"
    url-text "URL.TEXT2" url-value "http://www.mjlnet.com/designs"
    url-text "URL.TEXT3" url-value "http://www.mjlnet.com/projects"
 !
```

Step 8: Configure Port Forwarding

It is also possible to configure port forwarding on a Cisco IOS router. To configure this feature, use the **port-forward** {**list** *list-name*} {**local-port** *port-number*} {**remote-server** *server-name-or-ip-address*} {**remote-port** *port-number*} command, as shown in Example 10-7.

Example 10-7 *Configuring Port Forwarding*

```
 !
 webvpn
  port-forward list terminal-services local-port 3389 remote-server 10.10.10.52
    remote-port 3389
 !
```

If you compare the **port-forward** command shown in Example 10-7 to the example of TCP port forwarding described in the section "Enabling TCP Applications over Clientless SSL Remote Access VPNs" earlier in this chapter (see page 937), you will see that the command syntax is fairly self-explanatory:

- The *list-name* parameter configures a name that identifies a TCP application and is displayed in the Application Access window on the client.
- The *local-port* parameter is used to specify TCP port of traffic on a client that is redirected over SSL to the Cisco IOS router
- The *server-name-or-ip-address* parameter specifies the DNS name or IP address of the TCP application server
- The *remote port* parameter specifies the TCP port of the application on the application server.

Example 10-7 shows the configuration of port forwarding for a Windows Terminal Server (10.10.10.52) using the default TCP port 3389.

Deploying SSL VPNs (WebVPN) on the ASA 5500

You should be getting the hang of this by now—you know all about SSL remote access VPNs including underlying operation, basic SSL parameters, customizing login and home pages, specifying URLs, port forwarding, e-mail proxy, and file access. So, this section is not going to bore you by reexamining these concepts in too much detail.

Configuring SSL VPNs (WebVPN) on the ASA is a very similar process to enabling SSL VPNs on the Cisco VPN 3000 concentrator or Cisco IOS router:

Step 1 Configure the HTTP server.

Step 2 Enable WebVPN on the outside interface.

Step 3 Configure the WebVPN group policy and attributes.

Step 4 Configure remote access user authentication.

Step 5 Specify URLs.

Step 6 Configure file access and browsing.

Step 7 Configure port forwarding.

Step 8 Specify an SSL trustpoint, SSL version, and SSL encryption algorithm (optional).

Step 9 Customize login and home pages (optional).

These steps are examined in the sections that follow.

Step 1: Configure the HTTP Server

The first step in configuring WebVPN is to enable the HTTP server on the ASA and optionally configure HTTP redirect using the **http server enable** and **http redirect** *interface* [*port*] commands in global configuration mode command (see Example 10-8).

Example 10-8 *Enabling the HTTP Server*

```
!
http server enable
http redirect Outside0/1 80
!
```

The **http redirect** command in Example 10-8 allows users that connect to the ASA on TCP port 80 (HTTP) on outside interface Outside0/1 to be redirected to port 443 (HTTPS).

Step 2: Enable WebVPN on the Outside Interface

Having enabled the HTTP server, the next step is to enable WebVPN on the outside interface using the **enable** *outside-interface-name* command in the WebVPN mode (see Example 10-9).

Example 10-9 *Enabling WebVPN on the Outside Interface*

```
!
webvpn
enable Outside0/1
!
```

In Example 10-9, the **webvpn** global configuration mode command is used to enter WebVPN mode.

The **enable** *interface-name* command then enables WebVPN on interface Outside0/1.

Step 3: Configure the WebVPN User Group Policy and Attributes

As described in Chapter 9, the ASA uses a similar policy-inheritance mechanism to the Cisco VPN 3000 concentrator—there is a user policy, a user group policy, and a default group policy. The user policy inherits setting from the group policy, which in turn inherits settings from the default policy.

The user group policy for WebVPN is configured as shown in Example 10-10.

Example 10-10 *Configuration of Group Policy for WebVPN*

```
!
group-policy webvpn.grp.policy internal
group-policy webvpn.grp.policy attributes
vpn-tunnel-protocol webvpn
webvpn
   <attributes configured here>
!
!
```

The **group-policy** *name* **internal** global configuration mode command is used to configure an internal user group policy with (in this case) the name **wevpn.grp.policy**.

The **group-policy** *name* **attributes** command then begins the configuration of attributes associated with the user group named web.grp.policy.

The **vpn-tunnel-protocol webvpn** specifies that this user group is restricted to WebVPN only (and does not include IPsec).

User group attributes relating to WebVPN are then configured under the **webvpn** command (more on this later).

Step 4: Configure Remote Access User Authentication

To authenticate remote access users during login, you can use either the local username/ password database or a AAA server.

Example 10-11 shows the configuration of a local username/password database.

Example 10-11 *Configuration of a Local Username/Password Database*

```
!
username pete password ueQDRVFmwEjd4hRT encrypted
username dave password IkTiDoEuVyjoxmBU encrypted
username john password hN7LzeyYjw12FSIU encrypted
username mark password 7EwWZdAmpPRnJfI1 encrypted
!
!
```

In Example 10-11, a local username and password database (consisting, in this case, of four users) is configured using the **username** *username* **password** *password* global configuration mode command. The ASA encrypts passwords by default, and so the **encrypted** keyword is added in the configuration file.

As previously described, a local username and password database is not scalable, and so is only suitable for small-scale deployments. For larger-scale deployments, users can be authenticated using RADIUS, TACACS+, NT domain, Kerberos, and SDI.

If you want to use an authentication server for user authentication, you can use the **aaa-server** *server-tag* **protocol** *server-protocol* and **aaa-server** *server-tag* [(*interface-name*)] **host** *server-ip* [*key*] [**timeout** *seconds*] commands.

The **aaa-server protocol** command is used to specify group AAA parameters and protocols associated with servers, and the **aaa-server host** command is used to configure parameters associated with a particular server (such as IP address and key).

Step 5: Specify URL Lists

The next step is to specify the URLs that the remote access users can access via links on his/her home page. As shown in Example 10-12, you can accomplish this by configuring a URL list.

Example 10-12 *Specifying URLs Using the url-list Command*

```
 !
 url-list URL.List "URL.TEXT" http://www.mjlnet.com/engineering
 url-list URL.List "URL.TEXT2" http://www.mjlnet.com/designs
 url-list URL.List "URL.TEXT3" http://www.mjlnet.com/projects
 !
```

The **url-list** *list-name displayname url* command configures the URLs that users can access. The *listname* parameter groups URLs together, and the *displayname* parameter configures the names that will be displayed, and users can click to access the specified URLs.

Having configured the URL list, you should now link to the list under the user group (WebVPN) attributes using the **url-list** {**value** *name* | **none**} command (see Example 10-13).

Example 10-13 *Linking to the URL List Under the User Group*

```
 !
 group-policy webvpn.grp.policy attributes
 webvpn
   functions url-entry (line 1)
   url-list value URL.List (line 2)
 !
```

The **url-list** {**value** *name* | **none**} command in highlighted line 2 links to the URL list configured in Example 10-13 (URL.List in this example).

If you want remote access users to also be able to manually enter URLs that they want to access via WebVPN (in addition to URLs accessible via the URL list), you can configure the **functions url-entry** command shown in highlighted line 1.

After the URL list is configured, you can then optionally configure an HTTP or HTTPS proxy server in WebVPN mode, as demonstrated in Example 10-14.

Example 10-14 *Configuring an HTTP/HTTPS Proxy Server*

```
 !
webvpn
 http-proxy 10.10.10.1 80
 https-proxy 10.10.10.1 443
 !
```

The **webvpn** global configuration mode command is used to enter WebVPN mode.

The **http-proxy** *ip-address* [*port*] and **https-proxy** *ip-address* [*port*] commands are then used to configure the IP addresses of HTTP and HTTPS proxy servers (10.10.10.1, in this case). Note that the default ports for HTTP and HTTPS are specified in this example (ports 80 and 443, respectively).

Step 6: Configure File Access, Entry, and Browsing

As shown in Example 10-15, to enable file access and file sharing, it is necessary to first configure one or more WINS servers/NetBIOS name servers (NBNS) using the **name-server** {*ip-address-or-hostname*} [**master**] [**timeout** *timeout*] [**retry** *retries*] command, and then to enable file access, entry, and browsing as appropriate using the **functions** command.

Example 10-15 *Configuring File Access, Entry, and Browsing*

```
 !
webvpn
nbns-server 10.10.10.51 master timeout 2 retry 2
nbns-server 10.10.10.52 timeout 2 retry 2
 !
group-policy webvpn.grp.policy attributes
 webvpn
  functions file-access file-entry file-browsing
 !
```

In this example, one master browser is configured (10.10.10.51, configured using the **master** keyword), with one other WINS server (10.10.10.52) in WebVPN mode. The **timeout** keyword can be used to specify the time before the ASA will resend a query, and the **retry** keyword can be used to specify the number of times to retry queries to WINS/NBNS servers respectively. In this case, the timeout and retry values are set to their defaults of 2 and 2.

The **functions file-access file-entry file-browsing** command is then used to enable file access, entry, and browsing under the group policy (webvpn.grp.policy in this example).

Step 7: Configure Port Forwarding

You can configure port forwarding using a list in global configuration mode, then referencing that list from the user group, and finally enabling port forwarding using the **functions** command (see Example 10-16).

Example 10-16 *Configuring Port Forwarding*

```
!
port-forward tcp.apps 1350 10.10.10.99 telnet (line 1)
!
group-policy webvpn.grp.policy attributes
webvpn
  functions port-forward (line 2)
  port-forward value tcp.apps (line 3)
  port-forward-name value Port-Forwarding (line 4)
!
```

The **port-forward** {*listname localport remoteserver remoteport description*} command in highlighted line 1 is used to configure the TCP applications that remote access users can access. The parameters used with the port-forward global configuration mode command are as follows:

- The *listname* parameter configures a name that identifies a set of TCP applications. In this case, the list of TCP applications is tcp.apps.

- The *localport* parameter is used to specify a TCP port of traffic on a client that is redirected over SSL to the ASA. In highlighted line 1, the **port-forward** command configures TCP traffic on port 1350 to be redirected from remote access clients over SSL to the ASA.

- The *remoteserver* parameter specifies the DNS name or IP address of the TCP application server to which the ASA will send TCP traffic forwarded by the remote access clients. In this example, the address of the TCP application server is 10.10.10.99. Note that you can specify DNS server addresses using the **dns name-server** *ip-address* global configuration mode command, and the interface on which to enable DNS lookup using the **dns domain-lookup** *interface-name* command.

- The *remote port* parameter specifies the TCP port of the application on the application server (TCP port 23 [Telnet], in this example).

The **port-forward** {**value** *listname* | **none**} in highlighted line 3 (under the user group attribute configuration) then references the port-forward list configured in highlighted line 1.

In highlighted line 4, the **port-forward-name** {**value** *listname* | **none**} configures the name that identifies TCP port forwarding on the WebVPN home page (the remote access users can click the name in the home page to launch port forwarding). In this case, the name is configured as Port-Forwarding.

Finally, the **functions port-forward** command in highlighted line 2 enables port forwarding on the ASA.

Step 8: Configure E-mail Proxy

Example 10-17 shows the configuration of e-mail proxy on the ASA.

Example 10-17 *Configuration of E-mail Proxy*

```
!
pop3s
 enable Outside0/1
 server 10.10.10.52
 default-group-policy webvpn.grp.policy
 authentication aaa
smtps
 enable Outside0/1
 server 10.10.10.52
 default-group-policy webvpn.grp.policy
!
```

In this Example 10-17, e-mail proxy for POP3S and SMTPS are specified.

The **pop3s** global configuration mode command commences the configuration of POP3S.

The **enable** *interface-name* command enables POP3S on the specified outside interface (in this case, Outside0/1). The **server** {*ip-address-or-hostname*} command is used to configure the IP address or host name of the default e-mail server to which POP3S traffic from remote access users' e-mail clients will be directed by the ASA (10.10.10.52 in this example).

The **default-group-policy** *group-policy* command is then used to specify the default user group, which in this case is webvpn.grp.policy.

Finally, the **authentication** {**aaa** | **certificate** | **piggyback**} command configures (in this example) the ASA to use a username and password for e-mail proxy authentication. Because no specific authentication server is configured in this particular example, the local username and password database is used for e-mail proxy authentication.

Alternative methods of e-mail proxy authentication to use are certificate authentication (**authentication certificate**) and piggyback authentication (**authentication piggyback**).

If certificate authentication is configured, the remote e-mail client must present a certificate for authentication (and the certificate must be issued by a CA trusted by the ASA [the CA's certificate must be installed on the ASA]). For more information on certificate authentication with the ASA, see Chapter 9.

Piggyback authentication requires the remote access user to already have established a standard WebVPN session with the ASA before connecting using his/her e-mail client.

The **smtps** command then begins the configuration of SMTPS on the ASA.

The **enable** *interface-name* command again enables SMTPS on the specified outside interface, the **server** {*ip-address-or-hostname*} command again specifies a default e-mail server IP address or host name, and the **default-group-policy** *group-policy* command again configures the default user group policy (webvpn.grp.policy).

In the case of SMTPS, mail host authentication (**authentication mailhost**) is available in addition to the other method of authentication. When mail host authentication is used, the remote e-mail client must present a username, password, and other information. Mail host authentication is used by default with POP3S (and IMAP4).

Depending on the specific types of e-mail client that remote users are using, you may also want to configure support for IMAP4S. Configuration is very similar to that for POP3S and SMTPS—you begin configuration with the **imap4s** global configuration mode command, enable IMAP4S on the outside interface (**interface** *interface-name*), specify a default e-mail server (**server** {*ip-address-or-hostname*}, and configure authentication (authentication {**aaa** | **certificate** | **piggyback**}).

Step 9: Specify an SSL Trustpoint, SSL Version, and SSL Encryption Algorithm (Optional)

The ASA can optionally be configured to specify an SSL trustpoint and to restrict the SSL client hellos that it accepts and the versions of SSL that it will negotiate and the cryptographic algorithms that the ASA will negotiate with the remote access client.

Specifying an SSL Trustpoint

By default the ASA uses a self-signed certificate during SSL negotiation, but it is also possible for the ASA to use a certificate obtained from a CA.

You can enroll the ASA with a CA and obtain an identity certificate using the method described in Chapter 9. After that has been accomplished, you can specify that the identity certificate obtained from the CA should be used for SSL negotiation using the **ssl trust-point** {*trustpoint* [*interface*]} command in global configuration mode.

The CA trustpoint configured using the **crypto ca trustpoint** should be referenced using the *trustpoint* parameter with the **ssl trust-point** command. If you want to limit the ASA to use only the certificate when negotiating SSL on a certain (outside) interface, you can specify that interface using the *interface* parameter.

Restricting Acceptable SSL Versions

It is also possible to specify the version of SSL that you want the ASA to use with remote access clients using the **ssl server-version** [**any** | **sslv3** | **tlsv1** | **sslv3-only** | **tlsv1-only**] global configuration mode command. By default, the ASA will accept SSLv2 client Hellos, and negotiate SSLv3 and TLSv1 (but not SSLv2). The various keywords used with the **ssl server-version** command have the following meanings:

- **any**—This keyword causes the ASA to accept SSLv2 client Hellos and negotiate either SSLv3 or TLS version 1 with the remote access clients.

- **sslv3**—This causes the ASA to accept SSLv2 client Hellos and negotiate to SSLv3.

- **tlsv1**—The ASA accepts SSL version 2 client Hellos and negotiates to TLSv1.

- **sslv3-only**—The ASA accepts SSLv3 client Hellos only and negotiates SSLv3 only.

- **tlsv1-only**—The ASA accepts TLSv1 client Hellos only and negotiates TLSv1 only.

Think carefully before changing the default (**any**) because port forwarding will only work if the ASA is configured to negotiate SSLv3 or SSLv3/TLSv1. It will not work if the ASA is configured to negotiate TLSv1, TLSv1 only, or SSLv3 only because Java download will not function.

Configuring the Cryptographic Algorithms That the ASA Will Negotiate with Remote Access Clients

Finally, it is also possible to configure the cryptographic algorithms that the ASA will negotiate with remote access clients using the **ssl encryption** global configuration mode command. At the time of this writing, the keywords (and cryptographic algorithms) that can be specified using this command are as follows:

- **3des-sha1**—This keyword configures the ASA to accept the 3DES and SHA-1 algorithms.

- **des-sha1**—This configures the ASA to accept the DES and SHA-1 algorithms.

- **rc4-md5**—This configures the ASA to accept the RC4 and MD5 algorithms.

By default, the ASA will accept all of these cryptographic algorithms (in the order specified above).

Step 10: Customize Login and Home Pages (Optional)

As with Cisco VPN 3000 concentrators and Cisco IOS routers, it is possible to customize the appearance of the WebVPN login and home pages on the ASA. This can be accomplished using the following commands (configured under WebVPN configuration mode [entered using the **webvpn** global configuration mode command]):

- **login-message** [*string*]—This command can be used configure a message that displays when a user logs in (the default is, "Please enter your username and password").

- **logo** {**file** *filename* | **none**}—This specifies a logo that is shown on the login and home pages. The default is the Cisco logo (the logo format can be JPG, PNG, or GIF, and must be less than 100k in size).

- **logout message** [*string*]—This can be used to specify a message that is shown when a remote access user logs out (the default is "Goodbye").

- **username-prompt** [*prompt*]—A string indicating input of a username on the login screen. The default is Login:.

- **password-prompt** [*string*]—The string indicating input of the password on the login screen, with the default being Password:.

- **title** [*string*]—This is a string that is shown as a title in the login page and as a title bar. The default is WebVPN Service.

- **title-color** {*color*}—The color of the title bars on the login page, home page, and file access page. The color can be specified as a comma separated RGB value, an HTML color value, or an HTML color name (the default is HTML value #999CC [lavender]).

- **text-color** [**black** | **white** | **auto**]—The color of the text in the text bars on the login page, home page, and file access page (the default is white).

- **secondary-color** {*color*}—The color of the secondary title bars on the login page, home page, and file access page. The default secondary color is lavender (HTML color value #CCCCFF).

- **secondary-text-color**—The color of the secondary text bars on the login page, home page, and file access page. The default is black.

Verifying SSL VPNs on the ASA

You can use a number of commands to verify the operation of WebVPN on the ASA 5500. One of the most useful is **show vpn-sessiondb** (see Example 10-18).

Example 10-18 show vpn-sessiondb webvpn *Command Output*

```
mjlnet.VPN.GW.10# show vpn-sessiondb webvpn

 Session Type: WebVPN (line 1)

 Username      : mark (line 2)
 Index         : 1                        IP Addr       : 172.16.34.145 (line 3)
 Protocol      : WebVPN                   Encryption    : 3DES (line 4)
 Bytes Tx      : 17529                    Bytes Rx      : 12469 (line 5)
 Client Type   : Mozilla/5.0 (Windows; U; Windows NT 5.1; en-GB; rv:1.7.12) Gecko (line 6)
 Group         : DfltGrpPolicy (line 7)
 Login Time    : 17:05:18 UTC Sat Nov 12 2005 (line 8)
 Duration      : 0h:01m:35s (line 9)
 Filter Name   :

mjlnet.VPN.GW.10#
```

Highlighted line 1 shows that the session type is WebVPN.

In highlighted lines 2 and 3, you can see the username and IP address of the remote access client.

Then, in highlighted line 4, you can see that the SSL session is using 3DES encryption.

Highlighted line 5 shows the number of bytes transmitted (Tx) and received (Rx), and highlighted line 6 shows information relating to the browser being used by the remote access client (Mozilla/5.0 [Firefox] in this case).

Highlighted line 7 shows that the group policy that has been applied is the default (DfltGrpPolicy).

In highlighted lines 8 and 9, you can see the time when the remote access user logged on and the duration of the session, respectively.

Summary

SSL remote access VPNs are a relatively new type of VPN (although the protocol itself is not new). They have a number of advantages and disadvantages when compared to other types of remote access VPN—no specific client software is required by remote access user (only a web browser is required); only limited functionality is offered by clientless SSL remote access VPNs (although more functionality can be achieved using the Cisco SSL VPN Client); little configuration is required on firewalls and NAT devices because HTTPS is typically permitted/SSL is carried over TCP; and SSL VPNs, if not correctly configured, can introduce vulnerabilities into a corporate network because of the untrusted locations from which they can allow access.

The operation of SSL remote access VPNs can include the basic RSA handshake, the RSA handshake with client authentication, resumption of an SSL session, and closing an SSL connection.

SSL remote access VPNs come in two basic forms: clientless SSL remote access VPNs, and SSL remote access VPNs using specific client software. Clientless SSL remote access VPNs can provide file and web server (URL) access, port forwarding, and e-mail proxy, whereas the Cisco SSL VPN Client provides access comparable to that provided by IPsec and L2TP/IPsec remote access VPNs.

As previously discussed, SSL remote access VPNs can potentially introduce vulnerabilities into a corporate network, but these can be addressed via the implementation of the Cisco Secure Desktop. The Cisco Secure Desktop has various modules, including Cache Cleaner, VPN Feature Policy, and the Secure Desktop itself, each of which can address different types/levels of potential vulnerability.

Review Questions

1 How many versions of SSL are there, and which can be implemented on Cisco equipment?

2 What are some of the main advantages and disadvantages of SSL remote access VPNs?

3 What type of protocol is SSL transported over?

4 What protocols does SSL consist of?

5 What are the functions of the record protocol?

6 What software is required on client workstations for port forwarding to function?

7 What types of applications can be used with port forwarding?

8 What is SSL VPN e-mail proxy?

9 How is the Cisco SSL VPN Client installed on remote access users' workstations?

10 How does the Cisco Secure Desktop assess the location of a remote access user's workstation?

Appendixes

VPLS and IPLS Layer 2 VPNs

Pseudowire technologies such as Layer Two Tunneling Protocol version 3 (L2TPv3) and Any Transport over MPLS (AToM) enable service providers to converge their existing legacy (ATM, Frame Relay, and leased line) and IP/Multiprotocol Label Switching (MPLS) networks; these technologies also enable them to offer point-to-point Ethernet services.

A Virtual Private LAN Service (VPLS) takes advantage of point-to-point pseudowire technologies to enable multipoint emulated Ethernet LAN services over a metropolitan-area network (MAN) or wide-area network (WAN). An IP-only Private LAN Service (IPLS) provides similar multipoint emulated Ethernet LAN service but for IP-only traffic.

This appendix discusses the operation of VPLS and IPLS.

Understanding VPLS

As previously mentioned, a VPLS is a multipoint emulated LAN service provisioned over a MAN or WAN. A VPLS is an Ethernet broadcast domain, and is fully capable of forwarding Ethernet traffic based on learned MAC addresses.

Figure A-1 illustrates a VPLS. This figure illustrates a single VPLS. As you can see, Provider Edge (PE) devices PE1, PE2, and PE3 are connected via pseudowires. The PE devices are also connected to Customer Edge (CE) devices CE1, CE2, and CE3. Customer traffic flows between CE devices CE1, CE2, and CE3.

The VPLS in Figure A-1 appears to the customer as a single broadcast domain, as shown in Figure A-2.

Figure A-1   *A VPLS*

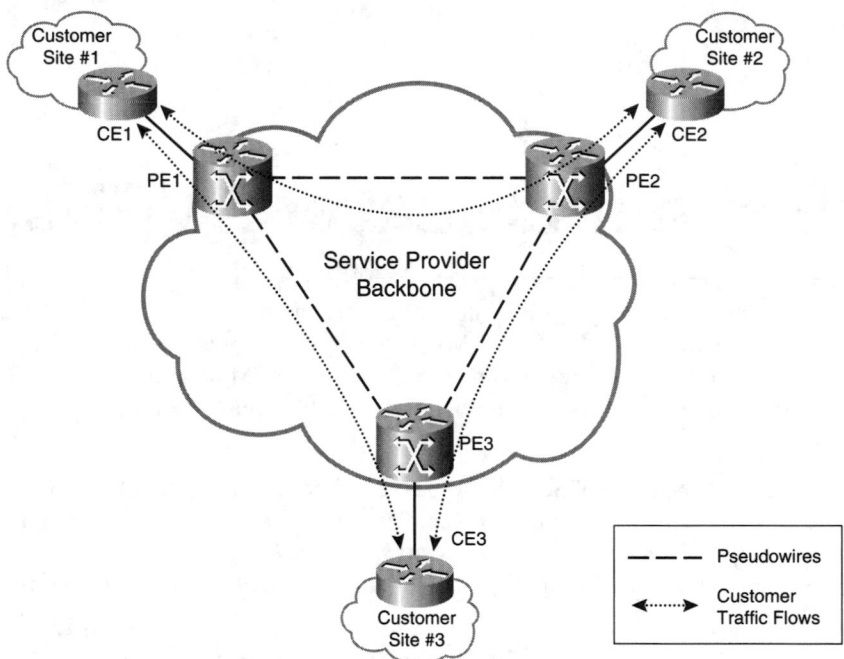

Figure A-2   *A VPLS Is a Single-Broadcast Domain*

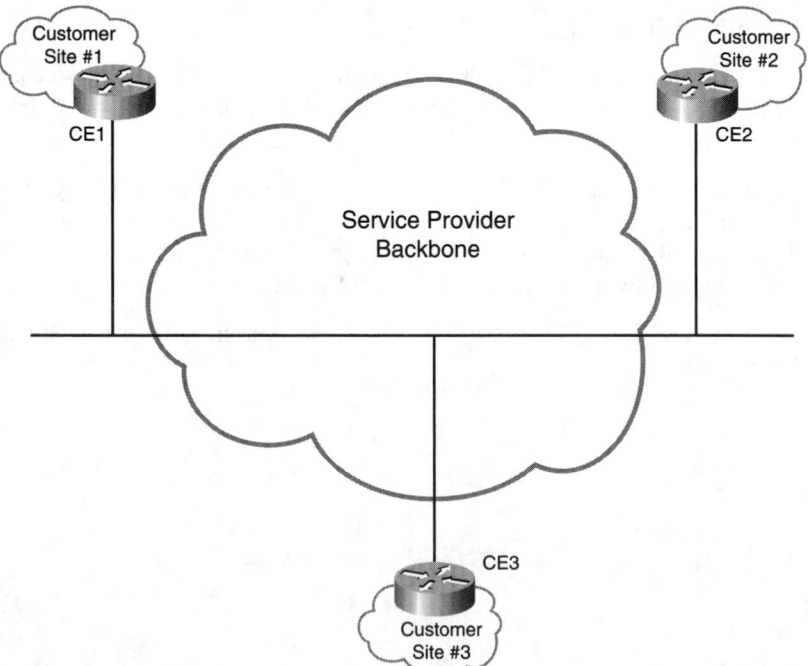

NOTE	Although a single VPLS is illustrated in Figure A-1, PE devices can support multiple separate VPLS (customer broadcast domains).

If a pair of PEs is in more than one VPLS, more than one pseudowire is required between that pair of PEs (one pseudowire per VPLS). In this case, the pseudowires can be carried over the same tunnel (either a tunnel Label Switched Path [LSP] or other tunnel type).

For more information on MPLS- and L2TPv3-based pseudowires, see Chapter 3, "Designing and Implementing AToM-Based Layer 2 VPNs (L2VPN)," and Chapter 2, "Designing and Deploying L2TPv3-Based Layer 2 VPNs (L2VPN)," respectively.

A VPLS can provide the following connectivity models:

- Connectivity between CE routers
- Connectivity between CE Ethernet switches

The VPLS in Figure A-1 provides connectivity between CE routers.

A VPLS provides the usual connectivity that would be expected in a LAN segment, including forwarding of unicast traffic, multicast traffic, and broadcast traffic.

Each PE device operates in a similar manner to an Ethernet switch and is capable of dynamically learning (and aging) MAC addresses and forwarding traffic based on those learned MAC addresses. Pseudowires between PE devices are treated as logical ports, and so a PE device will forward Ethernet traffic between attachment circuits (connected to CE routers/switches) and pseudowires (connected to other PE devices) in a similar manner to that which a regular Ethernet switch uses to forward traffic between ports.

NOTE	Forwarding of multicast traffic can be optimized in a VPLS by utilizing mechanisms such as Internet Group Multicast Protocol (IGMP) and Protocol Independent Multicast (PIM) snooping on PE devices.

Ensuring a Loop-Free Topology in a VPLS

The PEs in a VPLS can have a full mesh of pseudowires between themselves (see Figure A-1). As previously mentioned, these pseudowires function as logical ports as far as the learning of MAC addresses and forwarding of Ethernet traffic is concerned.

If a full mesh of pseudowires is maintained between PEs, the Spanning Tree Protocol (STP) is not required on the PEs. In this case, the PEs perform split-horizon forwarding—Ethernet traffic received on one pseudowire from one PE is not forwarded on another pseudowire to another PE.

Figure A-3 illustrates split-horizon forwarding in a VPLS.

Figure A-3 *Split-Horizon Forwarding in a VPLS*

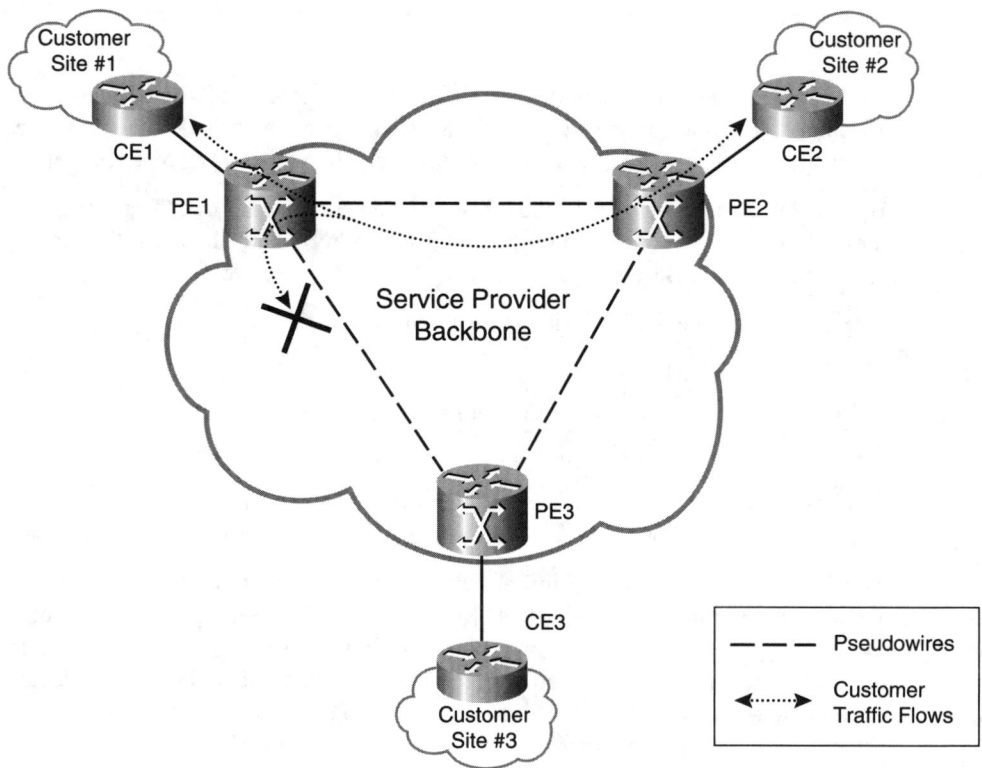

As you can see in Figure A-3, Ethernet traffic received by PE1 from PE2 is not then sent over the pseudowire to PE3.

Customers may still run STP to prevent loops if they maintain "backdoor" connections (connections not via the VPLS) between sites. In this case, Bridge Protocol Data Units (BPDU) are tunneled over the service provider network without being examined (and acted upon) by PE devices.

Figure A-4 illustrates a backdoor connection between customer sites and the corresponding STP configuration.

Figure A-4 *Backdoor Connection and Corresponding STP Configuration*

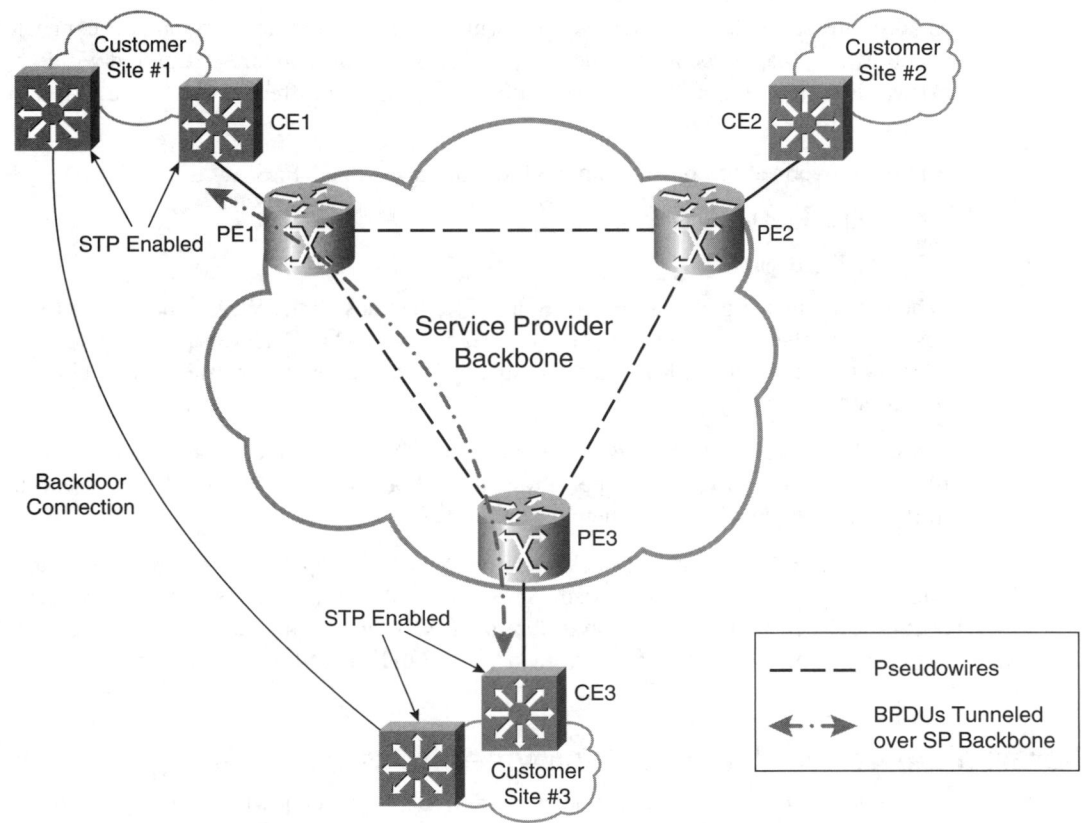

Frame Forwarding over a VPLS

Ethernet frames are sent over pseudowires between PEs in a VPLS as described in Chapter 3.

Although Figure A-1 shows CE devices connected to dedicated ports on PE devices, it is possible that more than one CE device (different customers) might be connected to a single physical port on a PE device. In this case, an identifier such as a VLAN tag may be used to separate traffic for different customer VPLSs on that port.

When a PE receives an Ethernet frame from a customer, any identifiers on Ethernet frames (such as a VLAN tag) used to identify a particular VPLS are removed before the frame is forwarded over a pseudowire to another PE. The egress PE may prepend an identifier back onto the frame before forwarding the frame.

If a PE receives an Ethernet frame from a customer with an identifier that does not identify a VPLS (for example, when VLAN tagging is used by a customer, and this tagging is not used by the PE device to distinguish between VPLSs), this identifier is not removed before the frame is forwarded over a pseudowire to another PE.

VPLS MAC Address Learning

MAC addresses are learned and associated with customer-connected ports and PE-connected pseudowires. Mappings of customer MAC addresses to pseudowires are stored within a Forwarding Information Base (FIB) on PEs. Mappings for different VPLSs are stored in separate FIBs.

There are two methods of MAC address learning used in a VPLS:

- Unqualified learning
- Qualified learning

When using unqualified learning, a single VPLS handles all the VLANs belonging to a customer. In this case, there must be no overlap between MAC addresses among customer VLANs (there is a single MAC address space). If an overlap occurs, traffic might be forwarded incorrectly.

Unqualified learning can be used when connectivity to a customer is on a nonmultiplexed port (there is only one customer per physical port), and the customer might be forwarding traffic for multiple VLANs on the physical port.

When using qualified learning, each customer VLAN is mapped to a separate VPLS and therefore is mapped to its own broadcast domain and MAC address space. If an overlap occurs between MAC addresses in different VLANs when using qualified learning, it will not affect traffic forwarding because each VPLS (and VLAN) has its own FIB.

Hierarchical VPLS (H-VPLS) Deployments

As previously discussed in this appendix, a full mesh of pseudowires can be provisioned between PEs in a VPLS. This means that the total number of pseudowires required per VPLS is $n(n - 1)/2$ (where n is the number of PE devices). The amount of signaling required to set up and maintain this number of pseudowires, as well as the amount of packet replication required, may impact the scalability of a VPLS deployment (as the number of PE devices and pseudowires grows).

To improve the scalability of VPLS deployments, a hierarchical architecture may be used (see Figure A-5). In Figure A-5, an additional level of hierarchy has been added to the basic VPLS architecture (compare to Figure A-1). The functionality of the PE device can now be divided between Network-facing PEs (N-PEs/PE-rs [routing- and bridging-capable PEs]) and User (customer)-facing PEs (U-PEs) or MTU-s (multitenant unit bridging-capable devices).

In a hierarchical VPLS architecture, a full mesh of pseudowires can be maintained between N-PEs/PE-rs, and connectivity between U-PEs/MTU-s is provided via either pseudowires or Q-in-Q (802.1Q in 802.1Q) encapsulation. Pseudowires between PE-rs and MTU-s terminate in virtual switch instances (VSI; called virtual forwarding instances [VFI] in Cisco terminology).

Figure A-5   *Hierarchical VPLS Architecture*

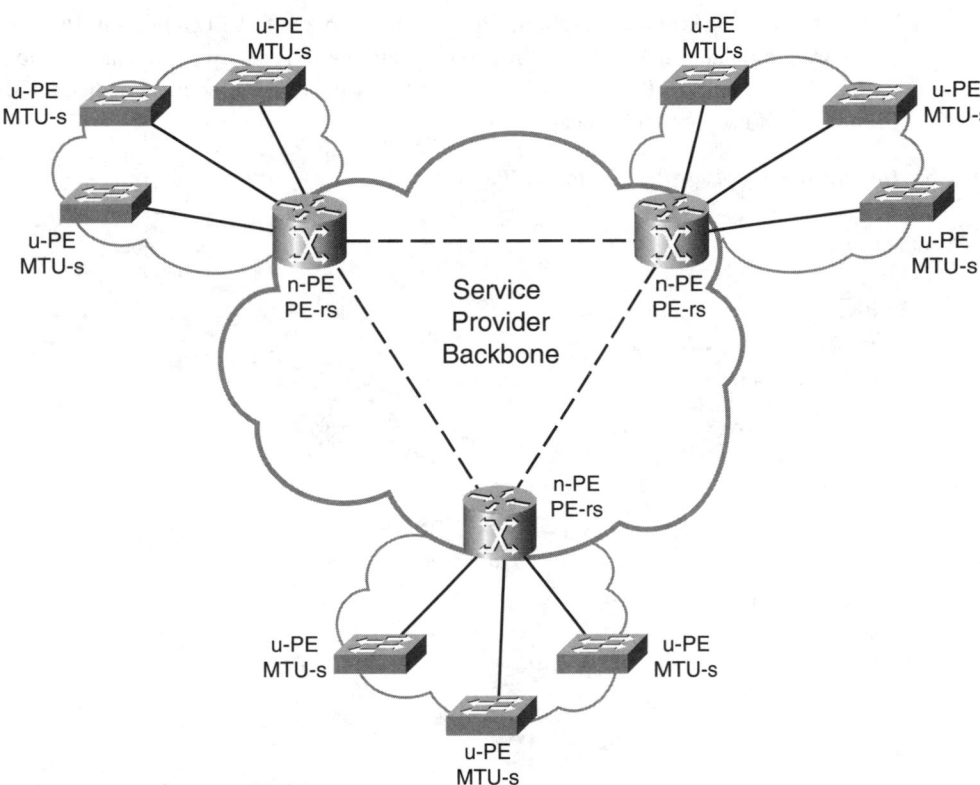

Understanding IPLS

VPLS is particularly applicable where multiprotocol multipoint Ethernet transport is required. If only multipoint IP connectivity is required between CE routers (rather than CE switches), IPLS might be an attractive option. IPLS provides IP-only emulated LAN connectivity across a MAN or WAN.

VPLS requires that PE devices have a MAC address learning capability, along with the associated mechanisms such as aging. Unfortunately, it might be difficult to add these capabilities in the data plane (the traffic-forwarding path) to some types of PE devices. In these circumstances, IPLS may be a good solution because instead of using the type of MAC address learning mechanisms inherent in Ethernet switches, in IPLS, MAC (and IP) address learning is accomplished via signaling between PE devices (in the control plane).

As the name suggests, an IPLS can only be used to transport IP and Address Resolution Protocol (ARP) traffic. Non-IP traffic received by PE devices on attachment circuits is dropped.

Unicast and Broadcast/Multicast Pseudowires in IPLS

Traffic forwarding is also different in IPLS when compared to VPLS. In each IPLS instance (a separate emulated LAN), a unidirectional pseudowire is set up for unicast traffic from each remote peer IPLS PE device to the local PE device for each locally attached CE device. Figure A-6 illustrates this concept.

Figure A-6 *Unidirectional Unicast Pseudowires in IPLS*

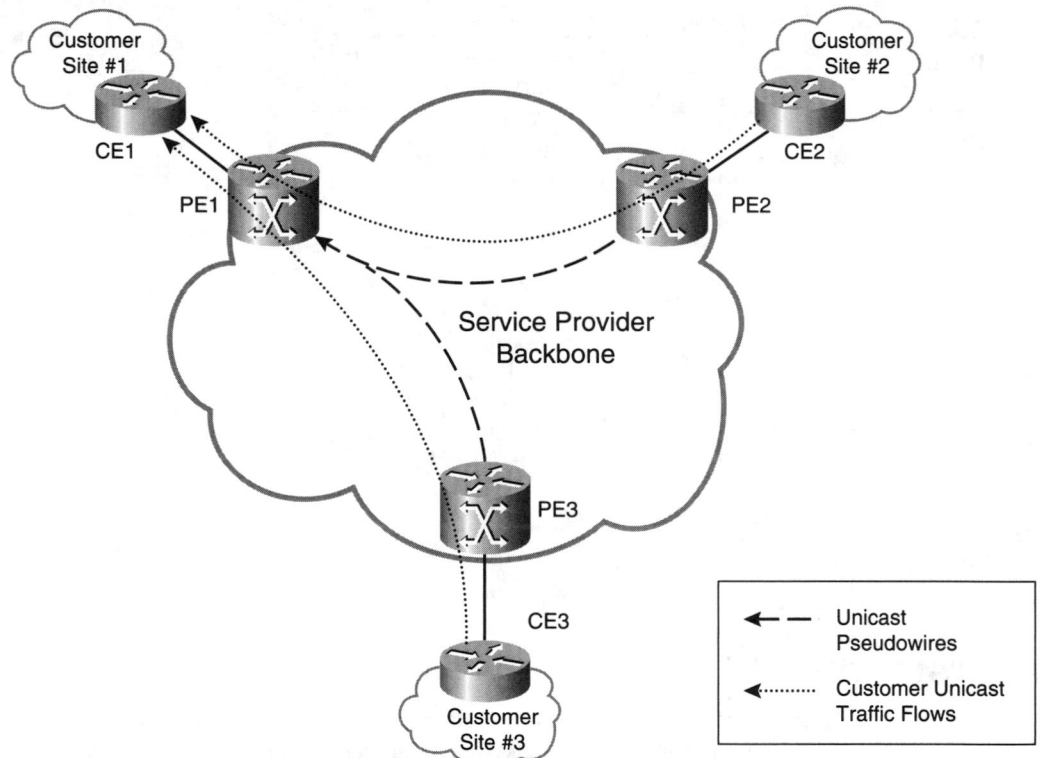

As shown in Figure A-6, there are three PE devices: PE1, PE2, and PE3. There are also three attached CE devices: CE1, CE2, and CE3. There is one IPLS instance in this example (one IP-only emulated LAN).

Unidirectional pseudowires are set up from PE2 and PE3 to PE1 to forward unicast traffic from CE devices directly attached to PE2 (CE2) and PE3 (CE3) to CE1.

Similarly, unidirectional pseudowires are set up from PE1 and PE3 to PE2 (not shown) to forward traffic from CE devices attached to those PE devices (CE1 and CE3) to CE2.

Unidirectional pseudowires are also established from PE1 and PE2 to PE3 to forward unicast traffic from CE devices attached to PE1 and PE2 to CE3.

The pseudowire type used for unicast pseudowires in IPLS is IP Layer 2 Transport (see Table 3-2 in Chapter 3).

Multicast and broadcast traffic is handled separately from unicast traffic in an IPLS instance. Separate broadcast/multicast pseudowires are set up from each PE device to every other PE device in an IPLS instance. These broadcast/multicast pseudowires are also unidirectional in nature and are used to forward IP broadcast and multicast traffic as well as ARP packets.

Figure A-7 illustrates the pseudowires used to forward broadcast/multicast traffic from CE2 and CE3 to CE1.

Figure A-7   *Broadcast/Multicast Pseudowires in IPLS*

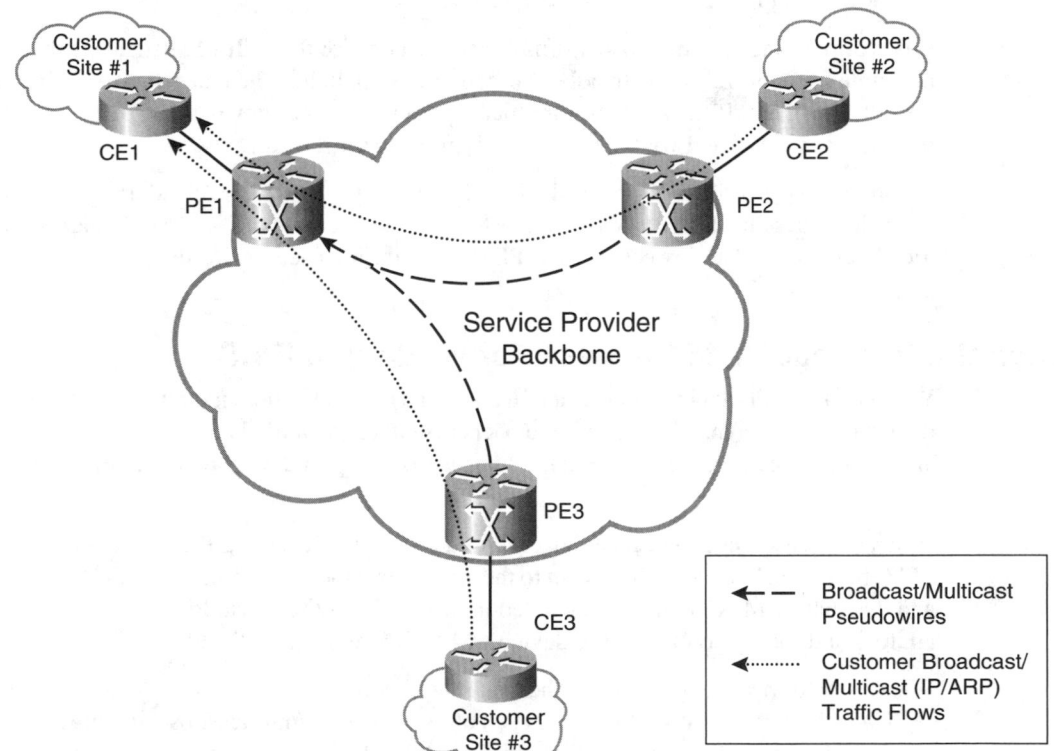

Although not shown in Figure A-7, separate unidirectional pseudowires are required to transport broadcast/multicast traffic from PE1 and PE3 to PE2 (per IPLS instance). Separate unidirectional pseudowires are also needed to transport broadcast/multicast traffic from PE1 and PE2 to PE3 (per IPLS instance).

The pseudowire type used for broadcast/multicast pseudowires in IPLS is Ethernet (see Table 3-2).

Both unicast and broadcast/multicast pseudowires are established and maintained using LDP. In fact, the setup and maintenance procedures are similar to that described in Chapter 3.

When setting up pseudowires for unicast traffic, a PE device can assign the same pseudowire (VC) label to each pseudowire that transports traffic to the same locally attached CE device, which in effect creates a multipoint-to-point pseudowire.

A PE device can also assign the same pseudowire (VC) label to each broadcast/multicast pseudowire in an IPLS instance. This again creates a multipoint-to-point pseudowire.

In summary, although there is a multipoint-to-point pseudowire for unicast traffic per CE device in an IPLS instance, there is only one multipoint-to-point broadcast/multicast pseudowire per PE device in an IPLS instance.

It is worth noting that the broadcast/multicast pseudowire for an IPLS instance is the principle pseudowire for the bundle of pseudowires, including the unicast pseudowires for the IPLS instance. If the broadcast/multicast pseudowire goes down, the unicast pseudowires associated with the same IPLS instance must be torn down.

As previously described, IPLS PE devices do not use the regular MAC address learning procedures described in IEEE 802.1D. Instead, PE advertises the IP and MAC addresses of locally connected CE devices to other PE devices during pseudowire setup.

Unicast and Broadcast/Multicast Forwarding in IPLS

When an IPLS PE device receives a unicast frame on an attachment circuit, the PE device does a lookup. If a match is found, the packet is either forwarded to another local attachment circuit or, minus its Ethernet header, over a pseudowire to a peer PE device as appropriate.

When a unicast packet is received over a pseudowire, the receiving PE device prepends a MAC header and forwards the packet to the appropriate local attachment circuit. The source and destination MAC addresses included in the header are the local PE device's MAC address and locally connected CE device's MAC address, respectively.

When a PE device receives an IP Ethernet broadcast/multicast on an attachment circuit, it replicates that broadcast/multicast on each of the broadcast/multicast pseudowires associated with the IPLS instance in question. A PE device that receives an IP broadcast/multicast over a pseudowire replicates this broadcast/multicast to each of the local attachment circuits that corresponds to the IPLS instance.

| NOTE | It is worth noting that although transport of customer traffic between PE devices is assumed to be via MPLS pseudowires in this appendix, it is also possible to use tunneling protocols such as Layer Two Tunneling Protocol version 3 (L2TPv3) or Generic Routing Encapsulation (GRE) to provide transport in IPLS. |

Like a VPLS instance, each IPLS instance is a separate broadcast domain. CE devices in an IPLS instance appear to be directly connected to each other.

PE devices discover the IP and MAC addresses of connected CE devices by snooping their transmissions of IP and ARP packets on the attachment circuits. After a CE device has been discovered on an attachment circuit, a PE device monitors its continued presence by periodically sending ARP requests. If the CE device fails to respond to a certain number of these requests, the PE device interprets this as a loss of connectivity with that CE device.

Summary: Comparing VPLS and IPLS

VPLS has one big advantage over IPLS: It provides multiprotocol, multipoint, emulated LAN transport, whereas IPLS provides IP-only multipoint emulated LAN transport.

IPLS, on the other hand, has a number of advantages over VPLS:

- Because unicast packets are transported over IP Layer 2 pseudowires, there is less packet overhead (packets are smaller) because unicast packets are transported over the unicast pseudowires between PE devices.

- There is less processing overhead for an IPLS PE device than there would be for a corresponding VPLS PE device. This is because an IPLS PE device performs a less-complex set of functions than a VPLS PE device.

- Unknown unicast frames (those unicast frames whose destination MAC address is unknown to a PE device) are not flooded in an IPLS as they would be in a VPLS.

- The risk of loops developing in an IPLS is much less than the risk of one developing in a VPLS because IPLS PE devices reject the advertisement of duplicate MAC addresses from peer PE devices.

Finally, it is worth noting that when CE devices are dual homed in IPLS, the connections must be to be to separate IPLS instances (on different IP subnets). Failover between connections can then be achieved using mechanisms such as those provided by dynamic routing protocols.

Answers to Review Questions

Chapter 1

1 What type of connectivity is provided by site-to-site and remote access VPNs?

Answer: Site-to-site VPNs provide connectivity between an organization or organizations' sites, whereas remote access VPNs provide access to a corporate network for remote users such as teleworkers or "road warriors."

2 What protocols and technologies are commonly used to enable site-to-site VPNs?

Answer: Protocols and technologies commonly used to enable site-to-site VPNs include MPLS, IPsec, L2TPv3, and GRE.

3 What protocols are commonly used to enable remote access VPNs?

Answer: Protocols commonly used to enable remote access VPNs include L2F, PPTP, L2TPv2/3, IPsec, and SSL.

4 What are the two main categories of provider-provisioned Layer 2 VPNs?

Answer: The two main categories of provider-provisioned L2VPNs are point-to-point L2VPNs (VPWS), and multipoint L2VPNs (VPLS and IPLS).

5 Name the two overall types of Layer 3 VPN.

Answer: The two overall types of L3VPN are PE-based VPNs and CE-based VPNs.

Chapter 2

1 What types of networks can L2TPv3-based L2VPNs be deployed over?

Answer: L2TPv3-based L2VPNs can be deployed over any IP-enabled network.

2 What are some of the main advantages of VPWS L2VPNs (including those that are L2TPv3 based)?

Answer: They allow service providers to consolidate legacy and IP infrastructures, decommission legacy infrastructure, and save both capex and opex; they allow enterprises to have complete control of routing, transport non-IP protocols, and can also help the migration from IPv4 to IPv6.

3 Name five types of Layer 2 protocols that L2TPv3 can tunnel over packet-switched networks.

Answer: Ethernet, ATM, Frame Relay, HDLC, and PPP.

4 Which L2TPv3 deployment model applies in a pseudowire configuration?

Answer: LAC-to-LAC deployment model.

5 What functions does the L2TPv3 control connection perform?

Answer: Setting up the control connection itself; dynamically establishing L2TPv3 sessions; providing a keepalive mechanism for the control connection and sessions; signaling circuit status changes; tearing down L2TP sessions; and tearing down the control connection itself.

6 If an LCCE wants to request that an L2TPv3 session be torn down, what type of control message does it send?

Answer: An LCCE sends a Call-Disconnect-Notify (CDN) message.

7 What are some drawbacks of the deployment of static L2TPv3 sessions?

Answer: Management of more than a small number is often impractical; PMTUD for L2TPv3 pseudowires is not supported.

8 What types of control connection authentication can be used with L2TPv3?

Answer: CHAP-like authentication and digest secret authentication.

9 Which Cisco IOS command enables you to bind attachment circuits to L2TPv3 pseudowires?

Answer: The **xconnect** command.

10 When an L2TPv3 pseudowire is used to transport PPP traffic, what part do the LACs take in PPP negotiation?

Answer: They take no part in PPP negotiation. PPP negotiation takes place between CE devices over the pseudowire.

Chapter 3

1 Which protocol is used for AToM pseudowire control-plane signaling?

Answer: LDP.

2 What are the three steps of AToM pseudowire setup between peer PE routers (assuming an LDP session has not yet been established between PE routers)?

Answer: LDP discovery, LDP session initialization (establishment), and LDP Label Mapping exchange (VC/PW label bindings exchange).

3 An AToM data-plane packet typically consists of which elements?

Answer: One or more tunnel labels, a PW/VC label, an optional control word, and a payload.

4 Can TDP be used to signal the tunnel LSP? Can TDP be used to signal AToM PW/VC labels?

Answers: Yes, it can be used to signal the tunnel LSP. No, it cannot be used to signal PW/VC labels; these must be signaled using LDP.

5 If an AToM HDLC pseudowire is used to transport Frame Relay (Frame Relay port mode), in what way do PE routers participate in LMI?

Answer: They do not participate at all in LMI.

6 How can Layer 2 traffic to be forwarded between attachment circuits on the same PE router?

Answer: Using local switching.

7 What is one method of configuring RVSP-TE signaled tunnel LSPs to transport AToM pseudowires between PE routers?

Answer: Tunnel selection.

8 When transporting ATM cells over an AToM cell relay pseudowire, how is it possible to transport more than one ATM cell per AToM data-plane packet?

Answer: By using ATM cell relay with cell packing.

9 How is it possible to connect dissimilar attachment circuit types over AToM pseudowires?

Answer: Using L2VPN interworking.

10 What are the two modes of L2VPN interworking?

Answer: Ethernet mode and IP mode.

Chapter 4

1 In an MPLS Layer 3 VPN, do CE routers exchange routing update directly with other CE routers or with connected PE routers?

Answer: CE routers exchange routes with connected PE routers.

2 How do PE routers store customer routing and forwarding information?

Answer: PE routers store customer routing and forwarding information in VPN routing and forwarding tables (VRF).

3   How is customer routing information exchanged between PE routers?

Answer: It is exchanged using MP-BGP.

4   In a simple MPLS Layer 3 VPN, with an MPLS-enabled backbone network where PE routers are not directly connected, how many labels are in the label stack of customer packets as they cross the backbone? What are the functions of those labels?

Answers: In a simple MPLS Layer 3 VPN, there are two labels in the label stack as customer packets cross the MPLS-enabled backbone. These labels are the IGP and VPN labels. The function of the IGP label is to transport packets between PE routers, and the function of the VPN label is to identify the correct VRF or outgoing interface on the egress PE router.

5   How can IGP labels be signaled in an MPLS network?

Answer: Using LDP, TDP, or RSVP-TE. TDP is a proprietary protocol, and its use is deprecated.

6   What is the function of the Route Distinguisher (RD)?

Answer: The function of the RD is to disambiguate overlapping IP address space.

7   What is the function of the Route Target (RT)?

Answer: The function of the RT is to control the import and export of customer routes into the appropriate VRFs.

8   Typically, which two IGPs are used in MPLS networks?

Answer: Typically, either OSPF or IS-IS is used in MPLS networks. The reason for this is that these are the only two IGPs that have the extensions necessary for MPLS traffic-engineering support.

9   Which attribute can be used to prevent routing loops when customer sites are multihomed to the service provider MPLS VPN backbone?

Answer: The Site of Origin (SoO) attribute can be used to prevent routing loops.

10   What are three common methods of provisioning Internet access for MPLS Layer 3 VPN customers?

Answer: Using a separate global interface on PE routers; using route leaking between VRFs and the global routing table on PE routers; and using a shared services VPN.

Chapter 5

1   In which type of MPLS Layer 3 VPN architecture does the backbone service provider offer an MPLS VPN service to customer service providers?

Answer: This type of architecture is known as carriers' carrier (CSC).

2 How are internal routes are advertised between CSC customer sites via the carriers' carrier backbone network?

Answer: Internal routes are advertised using any of the regular PE-CE routing protocols.

3 How are label bindings advertised between CSC PE and CE routers?

Answer: Label bindings are advertised using either LDP or BGP.

4 How are external routes advertised in a CSC architecture?

Answer: External routes are advertised directly between customer sites using BGP.

5 What type of MPLS Layer 3 VPN network architecture is required if a customer VPN has some of its sites connected to one autonomous system but other sites connected to other autonomous systems?

Answer: An inter-autonomous system MPLS VPN architecture is required in this case.

6 What are the three methods of provisioning an inter-autonomous system MPLS VPN architecture?

Answer: Using VRF-to-VRF connectivity at ASBRs; using the advertisement of labeled VPN-IPv4 (VPNv4) between ASBRs with MP-eBGP; and using the advertisement of labeled VPN-IPv4 (VPNv4) between route reflectors in different autonomous systems with multihop MP-eBGP.

7 Describe the label stack that is prepended to packets as they cross inter-autonomous system links in an inter-autonomous system MPLS VPN architecture when using VRF-to-VRF connectivity at ASBRs.

Answer: Packets are unlabeled in this case. The peer ASBRs regard each the other as a CE routers.

8 What is the effect of the **no bgp default route-target filter** command?

Answer: Usually, when a router receives VPN-IPv4 routes with route targets that do not match the import route targets configured within any of its VRFs, the router drops them. The **no bgp default route-target filter** command ensures that VPN-IPv4 routes are not dropped in this case.

9 What are the two common methods of supporting IP multicast transport between customer sites in an MPLS Layer 3 VPNs?

Answer: The two methods are point-to-point GRE tunnels and MVPNs.

10 What are the main advantages of using MVPN when compared to point-to-point GRE tunnels?

Answer: MVPN is much more scalable than a mesh of point-to-point GRE tunnels; MVPN does not require special configuration within the customer network.

Chapter 6

1 IPsec consists of what elements?

Answer: Cryptographic algorithms, security protocols, security associations, IPsec databases, and SA and key management techniques.

2 What services does IPsec provide to IP?

Answer: IPsec provides access control, connectionless integrity, data origin authentication, replay protection, data confidentiality, and limited traffic flow confidentiality.

3 What are the main characteristics of symmetric encryption algorithms?

Answer: The same key is required for encryption and decryption; the ciphertext is compact; symmetric encryption algorithms are fast and can be used for bulk encryption.

4 What are the two types of symmetric encryption algorithms?

Answer: Block ciphers and stream ciphers.

5 What are the characteristics of public key algorithms?

Answer: They are much slower than symmetric algorithms and are not suitable for bulk encryption; ciphertext produced by public key algorithms is not compact; public key algorithms do not have the same key distribution and management problems as symmetric algorithms; public key algorithms can be used for encryption, for digital signatures, and for symmetric key exchange.

6 What security services do AH and ESP provide?

Answer: AH provides connectionless integrity, data origin authentication, and optional replay protection. ESP provides connectionless integrity, data origin authentication, optional replay protection, data confidentiality, and limited traffic flow confidentiality.

7 What is an IPsec SA?

Answer: An IPsec SA defines how traffic for a particular traffic flow is protected by IPsec.

8 What is the function of IKE?

Answer: IKE allows IPsec peers to authenticate each other, generate keying material, and negotiate IPsec SAs.

9 What are some common considerations when selecting parameters for IPsec transform sets?

Answer: The type of user traffic to be protected; the specific type of protection; the length of time that user traffic must stay confidential; the volume of traffic that is to be encrypted; the type of VPN gateway hardware platforms; whether hardware crypto accelerators will be used; the version of Cisco IOS Software that IPsec VPN gateways will be running.

Chapter 7

1   Assuming that you are using IKE preshared key authentication, and that a unique preshared key is used between each pair of gateways, how many unique preshared keys are required for an IPsec VPN consisting of 10 gateways? How many (end-entity) certificates are required if IKE RSA digital signature authentication is used instead?

Answer: 45 unique preshared keys are required for an IPsec VPN consisting of 10 gateways. For the same number of gateways, 10 (end-entity) certificates are required.

2   What are two common ways to reduce the amount of configuration on gateways in an IPsec VPN?

Answer: TED and DMVPN. Wildcard preshared keys can also, to an extent, reduce the amount of configuration, although their use is not generally recommended.

3   What protocol does DMVPN rely on to provide direct spoke site-to-spoke site connectivity?

Answer: The Next Hop Resolution Protocol (NHRP).

4   What type of certificate is used for RSA digital signature authentication with IPsec?

Answer: The X.509 certificate is used.

5   What are two methods that a Cisco IOS router can use to check the revocation status of a certificate?

Answer: It can check the revocation status using a Certificate Revocation List (CRL) or it can use the Online Certificate Status Protocol (OCSP) to query an OCSP responder.

6   What are the three main ways to configure high availability in an (IOS) IPsec VPN?

Answer: The three main ways to configure high availability are to configure multiple IPsec peers (within a crypto) with IKE keepalives, use HSRP, or to use redundant GRE tunnels.

7   Why is fragmentation of IPsec packets undesirable?

Answer: It may cause IPsec packets to be dropped, and it will cause packet reassembly on a receiving IPsec gateway (which in turn causes high processor and memory overhead).

8   What ToS/DS value does an IPsec VPN gateway include in the outer header of an IPsec packet by default?

Answer: In transport mode, the ToS/DS value is preserved from the original user packet. In tunnel mode, the ToS/DS value is copied from the encapsulated user packet.

9   Why might packets associated with the same IPsec SA be dropped if they are subject to different QoS treatment in an intervening network between IPsec VPN gateways?

Answer: Packets might be dropped if QoS packet scheduling causes packet re-ordering, and this in turn causes some packets to fall outside (to the "left" of) the anti-replay window on the receiving IPsec VPN gateway.

10 What are some common ways to prevent fragmentation of IPsec packets?

Answer: Ensuring that end hosts send small user packets, fixing PMTUD, and using prefragmentation.

Chapter 8

1 What are the two modes of operation for L2TP remote access VPNs?

Answer: L2TP remote access VPNs can operate in either voluntary/client-initiated tunnel mode or compulsory/NAS-initiated tunnel mode.

2 What are some of the main advantages and disadvantages of L2TP VPNs?

Answer: L2TP can be used to transport multiprotocol traffic; PPP (tunneled over L2TP) offers flexible negotiation of user authentication protocols, compression, and assignment of IP addresses; Windows 2000, Windows XP, and MacOS X include a built-in L2TP/IPsec client; L2TP can be used to transport multicast traffic; L2TP allows service providers to back haul large numbers of remote access users' PPP connections across networks; L2TP's native security is relatively weak; L2TP/IPsec can add considerable overhead to encapsulated PPP packets.

3 How can security be configured for voluntary tunnel mode L2TP remote access VPNs?

Answer: L2TP with PPP user authentication (without IPsec protection) and L2TP over IPSec (L2TP/IPsec) with PPP user authentication.

4 What is the purpose of the **accept-dialin** command?

Answer: The **accept-dialin** command configures an L2TP VPN gateway to accept L2TP tunnel/session setup from remote access VPN clients/LACs.

5 What is split tunneling, and why is it a potential security risk?

Answer: Split tunneling is a situation in which a remote user can directly access both the Internet and the corporate network via a VPN tunnel at the same time. This situation can be a security risk because an attacker on the Internet may gain control of the remote user's workstation and thereby gain access to the corporate network over the VPN tunnel.

6 IPsec can be used to secure L2TP tunnels, and digital certificates can be used to authenticate IPsec peers. On the VPN 3000 concentrator, what are the two basic methods of enrolling and obtaining digital certificates from a CA?

Answer: It is possible to enroll and obtain digital certificates manually or using the Simple Certificate Enrollment Protocol (SCEP).

7 When deploying Cisco IOS L2TP client-initiated tunneling (voluntary tunnel mode), what is the main advantage of L2TPv3 over L2TPv2?

Answer: The main advantage is the lower overhead (assuming that L2TPv3 uses an IP encapsulation [protocol 115] rather than a UDP/IP encapsulation).

8 How can you debug IKE negotiation packet by packet on a Windows 2000/XP client (examining packet detail)?

Answer: You can enable Oakley logging on a Windows XP/2000 remote access VPN client.

9 In compulsory tunnel mode, how is PPP authentication typically performed on the LAC?

Answer: Partial PPP authentication is performed on the LAC. During partial PPP authentication, the LAC obtains the username of the remote access client and uses this username to assign the PPP connection to the appropriate L2TP tunnel.

10 What are the two methods of configuring tunnel definitions on a RADIUS server?

Answer: Using IETF standard (RFC2868) tunnel attributes and using Cisco attribute-value (AV) pairs.

Chapter 9

1 What are some of the main benefits and drawbacks of IPsec remote access VPNs?

Answer: IPsec can provide strong security for VPN traffic; IPsec extensions that provide additional functionality for remote access VPNs such as Xauth and Mode Config are not industry standards and are not implemented on all operating systems; the Cisco VPN Client must be installed on each client workstation; IPsec remote access VPNs offer a level of functionality similar to that users would experience if they were at their office or central site; the Cisco VPN Client includes features such as enforcement of firewall type, antivirus software type and level, and operating system service pack level on certain client workstation operating systems.

2 What are the two main types of issue with regard to IKEv1 an IPsec remote access VPN environment?

Answer: Issues relating to user authentication and issues relating to negotiation of parameters including IP addresses and DNS/WINS server addresses.

3 What are the three main methods by which a VPN gateway can authenticate remote access VPN users when using IKEv1?

Answer: Xauth, Hybrid Authentication, and CRACK.

4 What sort of functionality can Mode Config provide?

Answer: Assignment of configuration attributes such as IP addresses and DNS/WINS server addresses.

5 What information does the **debug crypto isakmp sa** command display?

Answer: It shows detailed information relating to IKE negotiation.

6 What methods do the VPN 3000 concentrator and Cisco ASA 5500 provide to overcome issues with NAT/PAT and IPsec remote access VPNs?

Answer: NAT transparency using TCP on an administrator-defined port; NAT transparency using UDP on an administrator-defined port; NAT transparency using IETF standard NAT Traversal (NAT-T, UDP port 4500).

7 When a hardware client (Cisco IOS router) is configured for EZVPN, how does a remote access user authenticate him/herself?

Answer: The router prompts the user for an Xauth username and password at the command line during IKE negotiation.

8 What are the three basic ways to configure high availability for IPsec remote access VPNs?

Answer: Load balancing of IPsec remote access VPN connections over two or more VPN gateways at the same site; failover between VPN gateways at the same site using VRRP; the configuration of geographically dispersed backup VPN gateways.

9 To allow IPsec remote access VPN connections through a firewall, which ports may have to be opened on the firewall?

Answer: UDP port 500 (ISAKMP), IP protocol 50 (ESP), IP protocol 51 (AH), administrator-defined UDP or TCP ports used for NAT transparency, UDP port 4500 (NAT-T).

10 What file can be modified to provide auto-initiation of Cisco VPN Client connections with wireless VPNs?

Answer: The Cisco VPN Client can be configured to auto-initiate a VPN connection to a VPN gateway by modifying the vpnclient.ini file.

Chapter 10

1 How many versions of SSL are there, and which can be implemented on Cisco equipment?

Answer: There are currently four different versions of SSL: SSLv1, SSLv2, SSLv3, and TLS 1.0 (TLS 1.1 is under development). SSLv3 and TLS can variously be configured on different types of Cisco equipment.

2 What are some of the main advantages and disadvantages of SSL remote access VPNs?

Answer: SSL remote access VPNs are relatively simple to deploy (only a web browser is necessary on client workstations for basic functionality); clientless SSL remote access VPNs (using a web browser) provide only a subset of the functionality provided by IPsec or L2TP/IPsec; functionality can be enhanced using the Cisco SSL VPN Client; SSL VPNs can impose a relatively high CPU overhead on a VPN gateway if there are a large number of remote access users; little or no configuration is required on firewalls to provide transit for SSL remote access VPN traffic; one major concern with SSL remote access VPNs is that the universal access they offer leads to vulnerabilities being introduced into a corporate network (some of these vulnerabilities can be addressed using the Cisco Secure Desktop).

3 What type of protocol is SSL transported over?

Answer: SSL is transported over a reliable protocol, which is almost always TCP.

4 What protocols does SSL consist of?

Answer: The record protocol, the handshake protocol, the alert protocol, the change cipher spec protocol, and the application data protocol.

5 What are the functions of the record protocol?

Answer: Fragmentation/reassembly, compression/decompression, application/ verification of a MAC, and encryption/decryption.

6 What software is required on client workstations for port forwarding to function?

Answer: The Sun Java Runtime Environment (JRE) must be installed on the clients for port forwarding to function.

7 What types of applications can be used with port forwarding?

Answer: TCP-based applications.

8 What is SSL VPN e-mail proxy?

Answer: SSL VPN e-mail proxy is the process by which an SSL VPN gateway terminates POP3S, IMAP4S, and STMPS connections from remote access VPN clients and proxies those connections to internal e-mail servers.

9 How is the Cisco SSL VPN Client installed on remote access users' workstations?

Answer: The Cisco SSL VPN client is dynamically downloaded from the VPN gateway.

10 How does the Cisco Secure Desktop assess the location of a remote access user's workstation?

Answer: The Cisco Secure Desktop assesses the location of a workstation based on the presence of a file or registry entry, fields in a certificate, or the assignment of an IP address in a certain range to the workstation's NIC.

Numerics

A

B

G

gateways

    authenticating CAs, 454-456

    backup VPN gateways, 889-892

    Cisco routers, 732-736

    Cisco VPN 3000 concentrators, configuring

        address pools, 725-727

        base groups, 727-731

        client user accounts, 731

        optional parameters, 732

    declaring CAs, 452-454

    defined, 409

    digital signature authentication

        described, 743-756

        groups, 756-759

        Windows, 759-765

    enrolling with CAs

        auto-enrolling, 459-460

        automating re-enrollment, 460-461

        described, 459-460

    firewalls, 892-894

    head end, 779

    host/domain names, configuring, 451

    IPsec VPNs

        described, 824-831

        DMVPN hub site gateways, configuring, 537-543

        DMVPN spoke site gateways, configuring, 543-545

        example configuration, 481, 485

        remote access, 892-894

    L2TP LNSs, 710

    L2TP/IPsec VPNs

        Cisco routers, 776-782

        NAT devices, 773-776

        verifying, 765-773

    PSK authentication, 736-742

    RSA keys, generating, 451-452

    setting time, 449-451

Generic Flow Control (GFC) field (UNI ATM cell header), 69

Generic Label TLV, 146

Generic Routing Encapsulation. *See* **GRE**

GFC (Generic Flow Control) field (UNI ATM cell header), 69

GRE (Generic Routing Encapsulation)

    AToM, 138

    overview, 8

    tunnels, 485-486

        crypto access lists, configuring, 489

        crypto maps, configuring/applying, 490

        example configuration, 490-495

        high availability, 628

        high availability, with DMVPN, 642-655

        high availability, with point-to-point tunnels, 628-639, 641-642

        IKE policies, configuring, 489

        interfaces, configuring, 486-487

        ip mtu command, configuring, 696-697

        ip tcp adjust-mss command, configuring, 697-699

        MPLS Layer 3 VPN multicast transport, 349-351

        routing protocol/static routes, configuring, 487-489

        spoke site gateway parameters, configuring, 543-545

        transform sets, configuring, 489

group command, 826, 867, 874

group-policy command, 829, 972

group-range command, 790

groups

    Diffie-Hellman, 463

    digital signature authentication, 756-758

    IPsec remote access, 819-820

H

handshake protocol, 908-910

hardware clients, 806

hash algorithms

    IKE, 463-464

    IPsec, 410-413

    MD5, 410

    shared keys, 413

hash command, 464, 825

Hashed Message Authentication Code (HMAC) algorithm, 413-414

HDLC traffic

    802.1 transport, 165-170

    described, 171

I

N

X - Z

Cisco Press

Learning is serious business.

Invest wisely.

CISCO SYSTEMS

Cisco Press

3 STEPS TO LEARNING

STEP 1

First-Step

STEP 2

Fundamentals

STEP 3

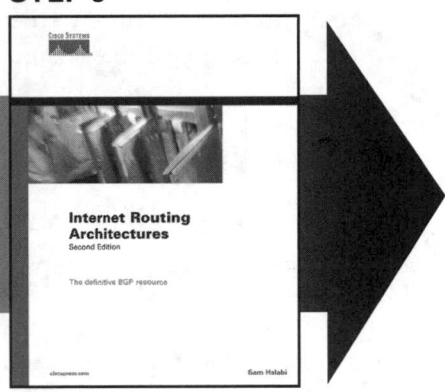

Networking Technology Guides

STEP 1 **First-Step**—Benefit from easy-to-grasp explanations. No experience required!

STEP 2 **Fundamentals**—Understand the purpose, application, and management of technology.

STEP 3 **Networking Technology Guides**—Gain the knowledge to master the challenge of the network.

NETWORK BUSINESS SERIES

The Network Business series helps professionals tackle the business issues surrounding the network. Whether you are a seasoned IT professional or a business manager with minimal technical expertise, this series will help you understand the business case for technologies.

Justify Your Network Investment.

Look for Cisco Press titles at your favorite bookseller today.

Visit **www.ciscopress.com/series** for details on each of these book series.

Learning is serious business. **Invest wisely.**

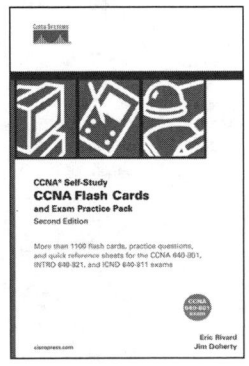

Cisco Press

Learning is serious business.

Invest wisely.

CISCO SYSTEMS

Cisco Press

SAVE UP TO 30%

Become a member and save at **ciscopress.com**!

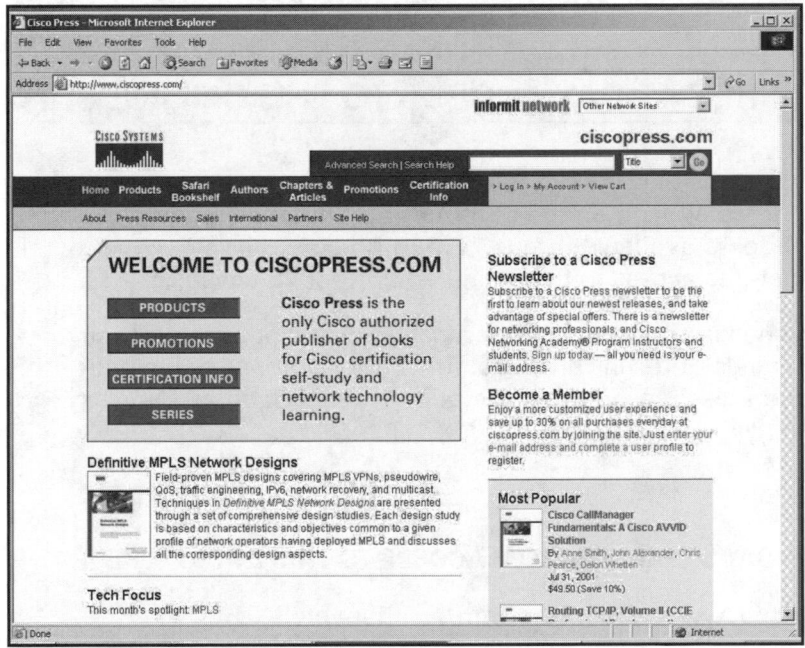

Complete a **user profile** at ciscopress.com today to become a member and benefit from **discounts up to 30% on every purchase** at ciscopress.com, as well as a more customized user experience. Your membership will also allow you access to the entire Informit network of sites.

Don't forget to subscribe to the monthly Cisco Press newsletter to be the first to learn about new releases and special promotions. You can also sign up to get your first **30 days FREE on Safari Bookshelf** and preview Cisco Press content. Safari Bookshelf lets you access Cisco Press books online and build your own customized, searchable electronic reference library.

Visit **www.ciscopress.com/register** to sign up and start saving today!

The profile information we collect is used in aggregate to provide us with better insight into your technology interests and to create a better user experience for you. You must be logged into ciscopress.com to receive your discount. Discount is on Cisco Press products only; shipping and handling are not included.

Learning is serious business.
Invest wisely.

THIS BOOK IS SAFARI ENABLED

INCLUDES FREE 45-DAY ACCESS TO THE ONLINE EDITION

The Safari® Enabled icon on the cover of your favorite technology book means the book is available through Safari Bookshelf. When you buy this book, you get free access to the online edition for 45 days.

Safari Bookshelf is an electronic reference library that lets you easily search thousands of technical books, find code samples, download chapters, and access technical information whenever and wherever you need it.

TO GAIN 45-DAY SAFARI ENABLED ACCESS TO THIS BOOK:

- Go to **http://www.ciscopress.com/safarienabled**
- Complete the brief registration form
- Enter the coupon code found in the front of this book before the "Contents at a Glance" page

If you have difficulty registering on Safari Bookshelf or accessing the online edition, please e-mail customer-service@safaribooksonline.com.